Thesaurus Linguae Graecae

Canon of Greek Authors and Works

´Thesaurus
Linguae Graecae
Canon of Greek Authors
and Works´

SECOND EDITION

Luci Berkowitz

Karl A. Squitier

with technical assistance from

William A. Johnson

New York   Oxford
Oxford University Press
1986

Oxford University Press

Oxford   New York   Toronto
Delhi   Bombay   Calcutta   Madras   Karachi
Petaling Jaya   Singapore   Hong Kong   Tokyo
Nairobi   Dar es Salaam   Cape Town
Melbourne   Auckland

and associated companies in

Beirut   Berlin   Ibadan   Nicosia

Published by Oxford University Press, Inc.,
200 Madison Avenue, New York, New York 10016

Oxford is a registered trademark of Oxford University Press

Library of Congress Cataloging-in-Publication Data

Berkowitz, Luci.
Thesaurus Linguae Graecae canon of Greek authors and works.

Rev. ed. of: Thesaurus Linguae Graecae canon of
Greek authors and works from Homer to A.D. 200. c1977.
Bibliography: p.
Includes index.
1. Greek literature—Bibliography.   2. Thesaurus
Linguae Graecae Project.   I. Squitier, Karl A.
II. Johnson, William A. (William Allen), 1956-
III. Berkowitz, Luci.   Thesaurus Linguae Graecae canon
of Greek authors and works from Homer to A.D. 200.
IV. Title.
Z7021.B47   1986   [PA3051]   016.88   85-25944

ISBN 0-19-503720-0

Printing (last digit):   9 8 7 6 5 4 3 2 1

Printed in the United States of America

CONTENTS

PREFACE

This volume sees the light of day at a juncture at which the Thesaurus Linguae Graecae (TLG), after more than thirteen years of operation, is nearing completion of its computer-based data bank of ancient Greek texts. The prefatory remarks which follow are meant to provide a brief summary of the TLG's history, objectives, and identity.

The latter part of the nineteenth century witnessed an ever-growing desire on the part of classicists for two comprehensive thesauri, one of Greek and one of Latin. To nineteenth-century classicists, the term *thesaurus* denoted a comprehensive lexicon citing and defining all (or essentially all) extant words of a language within a specific chronological framework.

The Thesaurus Linguae Latinae, focusing on approximately 9 million words of extant Latin text, was born in the last decade of the 1800s; work on a Thesaurus Linguae Graecae was to commence shortly thereafter. As it happened, human capability was not quite equal to scholarly ambition. By 1905, Hermann Diels, articulating a sentiment shared by most of his colleagues, declared that a TLG was simply an impossible dream. Diels's views on the subject can be found in the 1925 preface to the Liddell, Scott, and Jones Greek–English Lexicon:

> Any one who bears in mind the bulk of Greek literature, which is at least 10 times as great [as that of Latin], its dialectical variations, its incredible wealth of forms, the obstinate persistence of classical speech for thousands of years down to the fall of Constantinople, or, if you will, until the present day: who knows, moreover, that the editions of all the Greek classics are entirely unsuited for purposes of slipping, that for many important writers no critical editions whatever exist: and who considers the state of our collections and fragments and special Lexica, will see that at the present time all the bases upon which a Greek Thesaurus could be erected are lacking.
>
> But even if we were to assume that we possessed such editions and collections from Homer on down to Nonnus, or...down to Apostolius, and further that they had all been worked over, slipped, or excerpted by a gigantic staff of scholars, and that a great house had preserved and stored the thousands of boxes, whence would come the time, money, and power to sift these millions of slips and bring Νοῦς into this Chaos?

Sixty-seven years later, the Thesaurus Linguae Graecae was born. Its identity was determined by a conclave of American, Canadian, and European classicists convening at the University of California, Irvine, in late September of 1972. Diels's views were discussed and considered correct—correct, that is, in a 1905 context. But it was now time to reexamine and reconsider sixty-seven-year-old definitions.

The 1972 Thesaurus Linguae Graecae Planning Conference indeed resulted in new definitions and in the acceptance of new methodologies. A thesaurus created in the late twentieth century, it was felt, should take advantage of late-twentieth-century technology. Flexibility, rather than rigidity, should characterize the final product.

In essence, the conference members recommended that the Thesaurus Linguae Graecae should employ computer-assisted data entry rather than manual *Verzettelung* in the process of data collection; that word definition should be one of many pursuits, rather than the prinicipal pursuit, to be supported by such data collection; and that the TLG's product should be organic, i.e., readily adaptable to continuing progress in scholarship, rather than static and "frozen" as traditional books and lexica become at the moment of publication. Thus, they created a new definition of the term *thesaurus*: the Greek thesaurus would be not a lexicon, but a computer data bank.

Today, the Thesaurus Linguae Graecae is indeed a data bank of ancient Greek texts allowing for consultation by the broadest possible scholarly audience, and a body of information which, though compiled in the 1970s and 1980s, can readily be adapted to the state of the art of classical scholarship in the future. Ten years ago, computer-assisted research was virtually foreign to our field; a mere handful of classicists sought access to the TLG's resources. Five years later, their number had increased manifold. Today, TLG data-bank texts are being utilized for research and pedagogical purposes at more than a hundred institutions around the United States and abroad, and during the past two years alone more than another hundred individuals or institutions have availed themselves of data and information generated in their behalf by the TLG. This is not the place to enumerate the multiple uses to which TLG data-bank texts are being put. It seems reasonable to predict, however, that five years hence use of the TLG's resources will be commonplace within the field of classics.

By necessity, creation of the TLG data bank entailed consideration of a vast number of ancillary concerns. The 1972 TLG Planning Conference members, for instance, advised the project staff that, when completed, the data bank should reflect all ancient Greek authors and texts extant from the period between Homer and A.D. 600. They did not, however, specify precisely which authors and texts would be involved. By early 1977, the project had sufficiently firm control over the period from Homer to A.D. 200 to complete data entry of the materials falling within this span. Achieving this control necessitated literary-historical and bibliographical research conducted (initially at least) for in-house purposes only.

By early 1977, however, the TLG's activities were also sufficiently well known to occasion requests not only for TLG machine-readable texts (or data generated therefrom), but also for ancillary materials such as the TLG staff's compilation of the literary canon. Between March and August 1977, in an effort to meet requests for information residing in this canon, the project distributed numerous versions of the canon in computer-printout form. In doing so, the project was severely taxed in terms of both staff and financial resources. In December 1977, a more formal *Canon of Greek Authors and Texts between Homer and A.D. 200* was published by a specially created vehicle, TLG Publications, Inc. A total of 250 copies of the *Canon* were produced in December 1977; by April 1978, the *Canon* was out of print. Financial considerations argued against a second printing; furthermore, the TLG staff was now well on its way toward gaining control over the post–A.D. 200 period. TLG Publications, Inc., was placed in a state of dormancy; never meant to function as a publishing house in the first place, the Thesaurus Linguae Graecae could ill afford to let its progress be retarded by publishing tasks far better handled by others.

It was not until 1984 that publication of a second and expanded edition of the *Canon* was considered. Once again, it was decided that the product of TLG literary-historical and bibliographical research, though meant primarily to support only in-house activities (i.e., data-bank creation), should not be denied to the field at large. Furthermore, by early 1985, the number of requests for TLG data-bank texts had grown to a point at which ad hoc duplication and dissemination of the bibliographical documentation issued along with TLG text files had reached unmanageable proportions. This volume aims at affording access to the results of thousands of hours of scholarly labor on the part of the TLG's research staff to the broadest possible audience.

There are many who are owed a profound debt of gratitude; in fact, their number is so great as to render comprehensive acknowledgment impossible. It is only proper, however, that the following grateful acknowledgments be made in this preface.

Like every other aspect of the TLG's overall product, this *Canon* is the end result of a massive financial investment sustained by the wisdom and generosity of a large number of private, federal, and institutional TLG supporters. Particular mention must be made of Mr. James C. Gianulias, Dr. Marianne McDonald, the Andrew W. Mellon Foundation, the National Endowment for the Humanities, the David and Lucile Packard Foundation, and the University of California, Irvine.

Next, this printed volume reflects but a small segment of vastly larger amounts of data and information residing both in the TLG data bank and in the electronic version of the TLG *Canon* and constituting a substructure without which the TLG data bank would be unmanageable and unusable. Creation and maintenance of this substructure would have been impossible without complex computing facilities, highly sophisticated software, and other technological support which was not readily available in the general marketplace. Above all in this context, a debt of gratitude is owed to David

W. Packard, the creator of the Ibycus computer system which has been used by the Thesaurus Linguae Graecae since 1980. Without William A. Johnson, neither the electronic nor the printed *Canon* would exist today; his contributions to the design and implementation of both were invaluable.

Finally, though perhaps not readily visible, the labor of scores of TLG staff members who devoted their energies to the Thesaurus Linguae Graecae over the past thirteen years is also hidden in this volume. Their contributions are hereby gratefully acknowledged.

University of California, Irvine   Theodore F. Brunner, Director
October 1985   Thesaurus Linguae Graecae

INTRODUCTION

The *Thesaurus Linguae Graecae Canon of Greek Authors and Works* is an electronic register of the authors and literary works in the TLG data bank. As the data bank has grown, the *Canon* has kept its rapid pace. Originally developed as a form of necessary record keeping in order to exercise some measure of control over the massive amounts of text that were being converted to machine-readable form, the *Canon* has developed a character of its own, along with a utility that transcends the contents per se of the data bank.

Functions of the Canon

In a sense, the *Canon* is designed to function as an efficient electronic aid to the project staff who must confront nearly 2,900 authors and more than 8,000 individual pieces of extant writing. It must perform the work of an orderly guide to the authors and works selected for inclusion in the data bank, but it must also lend itself to daily maintenance, updating, and correction. For example, as previously unacknowledged authors receive attention from modern scholars in the form of text editions, these "new" authors are added to the *Canon* as candidates for a position in the TLG data bank. Accompanying the name of each author are various categories of information as they apply to individual authors, such as generic epithets which traditionally define the author's writings, geographical epithets which would identify the author's place of birth or place of domicile during the most active literary years, date by century (or centuries) in which the author flourished, patronymics, and professional titles. Furthermore, as new information pertaining to authors already ensconced in the data bank emerges, it is entered into the *Canon* as supplement or emendation.

As a bibliographical guide to the works of each author, the *Canon* identifies the text editions that have been recommended and endorsed for inclusion in the data bank by the American Philological Association's advisory committee on the Thesaurus Linguae Graecae.[1] It also accounts for the emergence of new, improved text editions which may replace older editions already in the data bank. In addition, the *Canon* performs the work of a calculator, tabulating a constantly growing word count, augmented each month by approximately 500,000 words of Greek text. In the process, the *Canon* is also expected to maintain a current record of the status of each text, that is, whether it has been converted to machine-readable form, verified, or corrected. This information assists users of TLG texts in determining what might be called the degree of doneness of a given text; the level of accuracy of a corrected text is expected to be higher than that of a verified text.[2]

---

[1] The name of this committee was changed in 1980 from APA TLG Advisory Committee to APA Committee on the Thesaurus Linguae Graecae.

[2] *Verification* involves the application of a number of programs and routines designed to

The electronic *Canon* is also expected to respond, promptly and efficiently, to questions requiring the vast amount of information stored in it. This *Canon* resides in an Ibycus computer system which offers, as one of its many virtues, a means for rapid retrieval of information regarding authors, bibliographical data, status of individual works, word counts, and prosopographical details. Quick retrieval of information is vital not only for the project staff on a daily basis but also for inquiring scholars in all parts of the world.

All of these expectations—cataloging, recording, counting, updating, responding quickly and accurately to queries—have been realized even as the *Canon* has continued to grow in size and complexity. In 1977, a first edition of the *Canon* was published; approximately 20,000,000 words resided in the data bank; 1,688 authors had been identified. By 1985, the first edition of the *Canon* was out of print (as well as out of date); nearly 57,000,000 words were housed in the data bank; the number of authors had grown to 2,884. As both the data bank and the *Canon* continue to grow, the number of scholars who consult the TLG grows as well. It seems appropriate at this time to produce a second, updated edition of the *Canon*.

Scope of the Canon

The scope of this edition extends beyond the original TLG cutoff date of A.D. 600, but with different degrees of completeness along the way. In fact and in practice, the year 600 does not lend itself to either reality or realization. Many authors who antedate 200 are recoverable only by consulting the texts of later quoters. Thus, although 600 remains a guideline for data capture, it has already been exceeded many times.

Inasmuch as the *Canon* is both a reflection of texts already deposited in the data bank and a projection of texts to be added to the data bank, its scope is somewhat broader than the actual contents of the data bank. In this edition of the *Canon*, the scope and status are defined differently for each chronological phase, as follows:

> *Phase I*. Homer to A.D. 200. Virtually all authors represented by text, whether in independent editions or in quoted form, are listed together with complete bibliographies for all works. With the exception of isolated fragments and certain difficult-to-capture authors,[3] Phase I may be considered essentially complete.

---

determine whether the printed text, originally submitted for data entry, has been successfully converted to machine-readable form. *Correction* requires the application of several sophisticated computer programs in order to detect errors which are then systematically corrected.

[3] For example, the various *Interpretes Veteris Testamenti*, such as Aquila, Symmachus, and Theodotion, whose Greek translations of the Hebrew Scriptures are physically interlocked with the Septuagint and with one another in Origen's *Hexapla* in such a way as to make data capture of their individual words a gargantuan effort with small returns.

Phase II. 200 to 400. Authors currently represented by text in the data bank are listed together with their bibliographies. Also listed are authors who may be represented in the data bank at this time only by pieces of text that belong to a larger generic collection. In several cases, the bibliography cited for such authors is incomplete and still in progress.[4] Nevertheless, Phase II is progressing well and nearing completion.

Phase III. Post-400. Authors currently represented by text in the data bank are listed together with a bibliography of the specific works that have been converted into machine-readable form. Although by no means systematically explored, this period is nonetheless already represented by 200 authors, some of them constituting important sources of quotations of earlier writers,[5] others associated with the corpus of medical writings,[6] and some of them occupying places in generic collections from which they are not easily extricated.[7] Thus, Phase III, although far from complete, is well under way.

Generally, the authors listed in the *Canon* are represented by some form of text, whether that text owes its provenance to codices, papyri, inscriptions, or quotations by later authors. There are, however, some authors who, in the consensus of scholars, are regrettably lost except for the testimonia provided by later authors. Although some have been subjected to the challenging (but sometimes dubious) task of reconstruction, or reconstitution, of their *ipsissima verba*, many others have been consigned to the roster of lost writers. Some of these lost writers have, in fact, been assigned a place in the *Canon*, although there has not been a consistent effort to include every lost author mentioned in the surviving testimonia. The only criterion that has been usefully operative in determining whether a lost author ought to be included has been the fact that the lost author occupies a place in a generic collection of fragments that either is or will be part of the data bank. A lost author may be represented by as little as a title (or a list of titles) or a descriptive word which

---

[4] For example, Theon of Alexandria, whose mathematical commentaries await data entry but whose three epigrams reside, along with the rest of the *Anthologia Graeca*, in the data bank.

[5] For example, Eustathius (A.D. 12), Photius (A.D. 9), Simplicius (A.D. 6), the *Suda* (A.D. 10).

[6] The Greek medical corpus, which accounts for nearly 5,400,000 words and some 411 authors, was added in toto under the auspices of a special grant from the National Endowment

for the Humanities during 1974 and 1975.

[7] For example, Theophanes Confessor (A.D. 8–9), whose two epigrams in the *Anthologia Graeca* qualify his listing among TLG authors, although the *Chronographia*, his major opus, has not been scheduled for data entry; or Michael Apostolius (A.D. 15), whose maxims constitute part of the *Corpus paroemiographorum Graecorum* but whose philosophical and theological writings have yet to be considered.

characterizes the literary genre to which the lost writings might have belonged. Entirely omitted from the *Canon*, however, is an author who is known to us only by way of an anecdote or a recollected or (ostensibly) reported conversation. Such an author remains lost, and it is the anecdotist whose text resides in the data bank.[8]

Use of the Canon

Altogether, there are 2,884 authors and 8,203 separate works in this *Canon*. Each author and work is identified with categories of information which may be useful to scholars interested in history, literary history, and prosopography as well as those simply wishing to know what editions have been deposited in the data bank. It should be emphasized, however, that the specific categories were devised initially to assist the project staff in quickly locating information about a given author or work. While certain kinds of information may give the appearance of esoterica,[9] the arrangement of the *Canon* should permit even the casual surveyor to locate easily only those items of particular interest.

The categories of information provided for each author or discrete work listed in this *Canon* are:

> TLG Author Number
> Author or Work Name
> Generic Epithet
> Date
> Geographical Epithet

The categories of information accompanying each work assigned to an author are:

> TLG Work Number
> Work Title
> Text Edition Selected for Data Entry
> Transmission
> Word Count or Word Estimate

TLG Author Number.   Each author in the *Canon* is assigned a permanent four-digit number meant to permit rapid identification in a computer environment. In the printed *Canon*, the author number is located in the extreme left-hand margin of the column. An exception is made in the case of authors whose text, if it exists, is to be located elsewhere in the *Canon*. For

---

[8] There are 679 lost works cited in this *Canon* and identifiable by the letters *NQ* (for *No Quotation*). For an explanation of codes used to identify the method of transmission of a given work, see pp. xxv–xxvii.

[9] For example, author number, work number, word estimate.

example, Alcinous, whose name has been transmitted to us as a scribal error for Albinus in all of the manuscripts,[10] is carried without an author number of his own,[11] but with an appropriate cross-reference, as follows:

ALCINOUS Phil.
  Cf. ALBINUS Phil. (0693).

This applies also to authors whose names tradition has subordinated to the names of works they are supposed to have authored, such as

ARCTINUS Epic.
  Cf. *AETHIOPIS* (0683)
  Cf. *ILIU PERSIS* (1445)
  Cf. *TITANOMACHIA* (1737)

as well as to works that once occupied an independent status but are now associated with authors, such as

ANAGRAPHE LINDIA
  Cf. TIMACHIDAS Hist. (1732)

and works which are commonly subsumed into other works, such as

VETUS TESTAMENTUM
  Cf. *SEPTUAGINTA* (0527)

The author number is also an abbreviated way of referring to authors. For example, it is simply easier and more efficient to cite according to the author number 1760 than to the author name Gaius Suetonius Tranquillus. Nevertheless, author numbers are more significant to those who interact directly with the computer than to those who consult the *Canon* simply for bibliographical data.[12]

Author or Work Name.   The order of the *Canon* is alphabetical according to authors' names or, where an author's name is not known, the commonly recognized name of an extant treatise, poem, or literary corpus. Authors' names are in boldface capital letters; names of literary works (in lieu of

---

[10] Cf. P. Louis, *Albinos. Épitomé* (Paris 1945) xii–xiii.

[11] In the electronic *Canon*, all entries are numbered, including those whose only function is to redirect the user to another entry. These are numbered with the prefix *X*. For example, ABERCIUS, who cross-refers to the entry *EPITAPHIUM ABERCII*, is numbered X001.

[12] The index of authors by author number on pp. 327–341 is meant to assist those who consult TLG machine-readable texts and require access to a reference system that quickly translates author numbers into author names.

authors' names) are in italic capitals, such as HIPPONAX, *HIPPIATRICA*, HIPPOCRATES et *CORPUS HIPPOCRATICUM, HYMNI HOMERICI*. Authors sharing the same name are further arranged according to the alphabetical priority of their commonly recognized generic epithets. For example, the three authors bearing the single name Eudoxus are arranged in the following order: EUDOXUS Astron., EUDOXUS Comic., EUDOXUS Hist.

In the case of authors with identical names and generic epithets, order is further determined by date. For example, the two authors known as ALEXANDER Rhet. are distinguished by the supposition that one seems to have flourished during the first century B.C. and the other during the second century A.D. The earlier author is listed first. When a date cannot even be conjectured, the author falls to the bottom of the order. Thus, the three authors listed as APOLLONIUS Hist. are arranged in the order of their surmised dates as follows: 3 B.C.?, 2 B.C., *Incertum*.

Authors who complicate matters with identical names, generic epithets, and dates are arranged in numerical order of their author numbers. The two writers of comedy who bear the name Apollodorus and who seem to have been contemporaries (even to the extent that they were sometimes confused with each other) are carried as follows: (0411) APOLLODORUS Comic. (4/3 B.C.: Carystius); (0413) APOLLODORUS Comic. (4/3 B.C.: Gelous).

With the exception of the PSEUDO-AUCTORES HELLENISTAE and PSEUDO-CALLISTHENES (which have been alphabetized in the appropriate spot under *P*), all *Pseudo-* authors are located in the alphabetical position dictated by the second element in the hyphenated name.

Authors whose names are recognized more readily in conjunction with some form of additional descriptive epithet (e.g., place of birth, place of literary activity, patronymic, nickname) are placed after authors of the same name who have only the generic epithet to determine their order. In the case of such complex names, order is determined by alphabetical sequence of the descriptive epithet. Thus, the four Gregorii are arranged as follows: GREGORIUS Paroemiogr., GREGORIUS NAZIANZENUS Theol., GREGORIUS NYSSENUS Theol., GREGORIUS THAUMATURGUS Scr. Eccl. Descriptive epithets are in boldface capitals if they have become an integral part of the author's identity: DIONYSIUS THRAX, but DIONYSIUS Sophista.

Sometimes an author who has managed to elude obscurity survives with praenomen, nomen, and cognomen intact. When this is the case, the author is in an alphabetical location determined by the author's most commonly recognized name. For example, Tiberius Claudius POLYBIUS will be found in the appropriate alphabetical order under *P*; Gaius SUETONIUS TRANQUILLUS will be located under the letter *S*.

Occasionally, an author's name is bracketed. Angle brackets < > indicate an author to whom a given work has been assigned, although that individual may not be the author of the work in question. Thus, the presumed author

<OSTANES Magus> may have no connection to the alchemical fragments assigned to him by Bidez and Cumont.[13] Similarly, <MYIA> Phil., purported to be the daughter of Pythagoras (6th c. B.C.), is also the presumed author of a letter on child care, which, despite its archaisms, seems to have been written no earlier than the third century B.C.[14]

Square brackets [ ] enclosing an author's name are intended to question the authenticity of the name, although even the existence of the author may be disputed. For instance, [BACIS] seems to have been the name not of an individual author, but of an entire class of inspired priests or prophets.[15] And [LINUS], despite the noble parentage the ancient poets have concocted for this much-bewailed name, may be nothing more than an eponym for a popular kind of threnody.[16]

In some instances, the author's identity may be referent to another author by means of the abbreviation *fiq* (*fortasse idem qui*). Thus, ADAEUS Epigr. is found with the notation *fiq Adaeus Rhet.*, and ATHENAEUS Epigr. is accompanied by *fiq Athenaeus Soph.* This kind of notation occurs 106 times, whenever there is reason to suggest that identities of two separately listed authors may be the same, although there is no conclusive evidence for merging them into one.

Occasionally, it is possible to suggest the name of an author for a work which has been transmitted to us without one. In such instances, the cautious formula *fort(asse) auctore* has been added: *AEGIMIUS* (fort. auctore Cercope vel Hesiodo).

In a few instances, the abbreviation *fort.* is used to suggest solutions to the missing pieces in a name. [ATH]ENODORUS might just as reasonably be conceived with other letters initiating the name, hence the notation fort. [Z]enodorus vel [M]enodorus.[17]

Generic Epithet.   The generic epithet attached to an author's name is intended to denote the literary genre that characterizes the bulk of the author's extant work.[18] For the most part, generic epithets are consistent with traditional usage in literary histories, biographical dictionaries, lexica, and

[13] Cf. J. Bidez and F. Cumont, *Les mages hellénisés*, vol. 1 (Paris 1938; repr. 1973) 173, 198–207.

[14] Cf. H. Thesleff, *An introduction to the Pythagorean writings of the Hellenistic period* (Åbo 1961) 90, 102, 115.

[15] E. Rohde, *Psyche*, vol. 2, 8th edn., trans. W. B. Hillis (New York 1966) 292–293, 314 (n. 58).

[16] Cf. H. J. Rose's article on Linus in *The Oxford classical dictionary (OCD)*, 2nd edn. (Oxford 1970) 611.

[17] Cf. B. Snell, *Tragicorum Graecorum fragmenta*, vol. 1 (Göttingen 1971) 309.

[18] Generic epithets are assigned only to the names of authors. The electronic version of the *Canon*, however, contains a provision for classification in generic terms of titles of literary works that stand in lieu of authors' names. Thus, a scholar requesting, for example, all citations of a word or word pattern in epic could expect to find citations not only from Homer, Hesiod, Apollonius Rhodius, Nicander, and so on, but also from the *Hymni Homerici*, *Titanomachia*, *Aegimius*, *Cypria*, and so on.

commentaries. The fifty-five generic epithets used are:

Alchem.	Epic.	Lexicogr.	Parodius	Poeta
Apol.	Epigr.	Lyr.	Paroemiogr.	Polyhist.
Astrol.	Epist.	Math.	Perieg.	Rhet.
Astron.	Geogr.	Mech.	Phil.	Scr. Eccl.
Attic.	Geom.	Med.	Philol.	Scr. Erot.
Biogr.	Gnom.	Mimogr.	Poet. Astrol.	Scr. Fab.
Bucol.	Gnost.	Mus.	Poet. Christ.	Scr. Rerum Nat.
Choliamb.	Gramm.	Myth.	Poet. Didac.	Soph.
Comic.	Hist.	Onir.	Poet. Ethic.	Tact.
Doxogr.	Iamb.	Orat.	Poet. Med.	Theol.
Eleg.	Int. Vet. Test.	Paradox.	Poet. Phil.	Trag.

Occasionally, two or even three epithets might be required to define an author, although there has been no attempt to reflect every possibility. For example, Aristotle would need at least ten different epithets if it were necessary to characterize him in terms of the entire Aristotelian corpus.[19] It is, however, quite in accordance with tradition to permit the single epithet *Phil.* to function, albeit imprecisely, in behalf of the entire corpus.

In the case of authors whose literary output cannot be conveniently classified with a traditional epithet, there has been no attempt to impose one artificially. Yet, where it has been possible to define the character of unconventional writing with a fairly simple description, the formula *Scriptor* has been applied: CHRYSIPPUS Scriptor Rei Coquinariae or SIMON Scriptor De Re Equestri. On the other hand, it has sometimes seemed useful to attach a generic epithet to a personality who is not usually enrolled in a *repertorium litterarum*. In such cases, an epithet enclosed in angle brackets is meant to suggest that the extant writing falls within the literary genre indicated, although the author in question was not primarily a writer in that genre, or even a writer, such as PRAXITELES <Epigr.>.

Since generic epithets do not always characterize accurately and precisely the contents of a writer's literary corpus, a caveat is in order here. Some epithets contain a hint of an intellectual or even religious persuasion rather than the distinctive literary qualities that might suggest a specific genre. For instance, the *gnostici* might be regarded more properly as *philosophi* or *theologi*, inasmuch as gnosticism implies an attitude rather than a style of writing. Similarly, the *philologi* and *polyhistores* occupy a special place in the history of literature because they seem almost to have made a profession of crossing literary barriers, and their works (mostly in fragmented form) reflect a wide range of generic writing. In addition, there are some thirty authors who are epithetized simply as *poetae*, without further concern for the specific kind of

---

[19] In alphabetical order, *astronomus, elegiacus, epistolographus, lyricus, mechanicus, onirocriti-* *cus, philosophus, physiognomonicus, rhetor, scriptor naturalium historiarum.*

poetry they wrote. This may be owing to the variety of meters they employed[20] or to the simple fact that certain remnants of poetry defy categorization.[21]

Date.　　The assignment of dates in the *Canon* is based on a need, realized early in the history of the TLG, to identify the authors and works surviving from the period between Homer and approximately A.D. 200, the first of the three (arbitrarily defined) periods which were to constitute the scope of the project. While neither the TLG staff nor the advisory committee imagined that the vexatious questions of chronology could be laid to rest by the assignment of dates, all agreed that dates could fulfill a useful, albeit limited, function. The scholar who might request a listing of all instances of the word ὕβρις in fifth century B.C. literature would have to either first provide the TLG with a list of the authors who should be searched or else rely upon the TLG's ability to provide such a list. The only way the TLG could identify fifth century B.C. authors who might have used the word ὕβρις would be to have recourse to an already established record of dates. Thus, dates—with all of the imperfections and speculativeness that they imply—became a fixture of the *Canon*, sometimes functioning as an organizing principle in responding to certain requests for information from the data bank.

Date information is located immediately beneath the author's name. Arabic numerals in cardinal form indicate the century of an author's *floruit*.[22] A dash between numerals indicates that the author's *floruit* spans the two centuries. Thus, the date given for Strabo Geogr. is 1 B.C.–A.D. 1, based upon the approximate dates of his sojourns in Rome (44–35 B.C., again ca. 31 B.C., and a third time in 7 B.C.), Egypt (25 until ca. 19 B.C.), and Amasia (ca. 7 B.C. until his death sometime after A.D. 21).[23]

When no firmer evidence can be adduced, a virgule between numerals is used to suggest the earliest and latest possible dates. Thus, the date given for Alciphron Rhet. et Soph. is A.D. 2/3, meaning that the earliest possible date for his letters (though purportedly written by Athenian fishermen, farmers, parasites, and courtesans of the fourth century B.C.) is the second century, and the latest is the third.[24]

---

[20] For example, Ion of Chios, whose poetry seems to have spanned the spectrum from tragedy to comedy, from lyric to elegiacs and epigrams. Cf. the article on Ion by A. W. Pickard-Cambridge and D. W. Lucas in the *OCD*, 549–550.

[21] For example, Cleomachus of Magnesia, who, if he were to be classified, might best be called κιναιδογράφος. Cf. Pauly-Wissowa 11, 677, #3; H. Lloyd-Jones and P. Parsons, *Supplementum Hellenisticum* (Berlin 1983) 162.

[22] The sources for dates in the *Canon* are the lexica (especially Liddell-Scott-Jones, *A*

Greek-English lexicon, Oxford 1968, repr. from the revised 9th edn. of 1940; and G. W. H. Lampe, *A patristic Greek lexicon*, Oxford 1961, repr. 1978), biographical dictionaries, encyclopedias, and literary histories, as well as modern publications that address specific chronological problems.

[23] Cf. E. H. Warmington on Strabo in the *OCD*, 1017.

[24] Cf. the lengthy discourse in A. R. Benner and F. H. Fobes, *Alciphron, Aelian, Philostratus: The letters* (London 1949; repr. 1962) 6–18. Benner and Fobes accept Reich's *termi-*

When only a *terminus ante quem* is discernible, or at least logically to be assumed, this is indicated by, for instance, *ante* A.D. 1 for a certain Demetrius Hist. whom Jacoby dates "vor Apion,"[25] on the grounds that the evidence from the *Suda* provides a reasonably solid date for Apion Gramm.[26] The word *ante*, however, is actually expected to encompass both antecedence and contemporaneity. Thus, Apollonius Med.—the one from Tarsus[27]—is datable only in relation to Galen (who can be dated with certainty to the second century), but whether he was Galen's contemporary or predecessor is indeterminable.

Similarly, a *terminus post quem* is indicated by the word *post* and the appropriate century, as for example Ariston Hist., whose date in the *Canon* is given as *post* 3 B.C.[28]

Question marks have been used for any date that is considered problematical, such as Democritus Epigr. (ante A.D. 3?), but also Aristocles Paradox. (3 B.C.?/A.D. 1). However, when it is simply impossible to suggest a date, the word *Incertum* may be found instead, as for example Zenodotus Trag.[29] *Incertum* is also noted for many of the letters which, though composed later, are sometimes attached to a well-known name, such as *Chilonis Epistula, Cratetis Epistulae, Euripidis Epistulae*.[30]

Geographical Epithet.   Except for certain authors whose names are usually combined with a descriptive word denoting a location,[31] geographical epithets are subordinated to an author's name and may be found on the next line following the date and separated from it by a colon.

Obviously, it is impossible to provide an appropriate geographical epithet for every author, although in some cases it is possible to suggest two or three places associated with an author's *floruit*. The inadequacy of geographical epithets lies in their failure to distinguish place of birth from place of literary activity or place of residence in an official or ecclesiastical capacity. For example, the geographical epithets Antiochenus and Constantinopolitanus in connection with Joannes Chrysostomus Scr. Eccl. do not tell us that the author studied law under Libanius and theology under Diodorus of Tarsus at Antioch or that he was appointed Bishop of Constantinople in 398.[32] Nor do the same two epithets in association with Libanius Rhet. et Soph. tell us that Libanius was born (314) and educated in Antioch, that he spent half a dozen

---

nus post quem of ca. 170 (p. 14), but insist that a *terminus ante quem* is "still to seek" (p. 18). Cf. also B. Baldwin, "The date of Alciphron," *Hermes* 110 (1982) 253–254, who dates the letters no later than the first decade of the third century.

[25] Cf. *FGrH* #643, vol. 3C, p. 188.

[26] Cf. *FGrH* #616, vol. 3C, pp. 122–123.

[27] Seven medical writers named simply Apollonius are listed. The one in question here is the seventh in order, bearing the TLG author number 0782.

[28] Jacoby dates him "frühestens s. III^a," *FGrH* #337, vol. 3B, p. 188.

[29] Cf. Snell, *TrGF*, vol. 1, pp. viii, 319, 325.

[30] Cf. Hercher, *Epist. Graec.*, pp. 193, 208–217, 275–279.

[31] For example, Apollonius Rhodius, Diodorus Siculus, Dionysius Thrax.

[32] Cf. F. L. Cross, *The Oxford dictionary of the Christian church* (London 1958; repr. 1966) 282–283.

years teaching rhetoric in Constantinople (340–346), and that he returned to Antioch where he assumed a chair of rhetoric (354) and spent the last three and a half decades of his life.[33]

An effort to be exhaustive in charting the life and activity of authors in terms of geographical epithets would be doomed to failure in most cases and altogether absurd in many others. What geographical epithets might be cited in connection with a writer as well traveled as, say, Herodotus? The result would be either too unwieldy to be useful for quick consultation or too abbreviated to convey the extent of his travels through the ancient world. In this *Canon*, the only geographical epithets retained for Herodotus are Halicarnassensis and Thurius. Halicarnassus was his birthplace, and Thurii was the panhellenic foundation he helped to colonize.[34]

As it is, geographical epithets can be useful for the purposes of the *Canon*, especially if they are used to distinguish authors of the same name, such as AESCHYLUS Trag. Atheniensis and AESCHYLUS Trag. Alexandrinus. But there has not been a systematic effort to include geographical epithets for all authors. Indeed, there is one generic group of authors, the *comici*, for whom the epithet *Atheniensis* might be applied without much additional investigation, but a systematic insertion of geographical epithets remains a target for more leisurely days in the future. In the meantime, those that do appear in this edition are the result of either a fairly firm tradition (including a firm tradition of uncertainty) or a need to distinguish one author from another. There are, however, many authors whose geographical connections we can only surmise. When this is the case, the geographical epithet is preceded by the word *fort(asse)*. For example, we know a great deal about the places Pausanias Perieg. visited because his *Graeciae descriptio* is a mine of information, but oddly enough we do not know for certain his place of birth. Hence, the most informative geographical epithet that can be attached to Pausanias is *fort. Lydius*.[35] Finally, there are many authors whose geographical connections we cannot possibly guess. When this is so, the space allotted for geographical epithets remains blank.

TLG Work Number.   Each work ascribed to an author bears a three-digit identification number. This number is located to the left of the work title. Generally, work numbers appear in numerical order, beginning with 001, although there are several lengthy bibliographies for which work numbers appear out of order.[36] The reason for this is that often a work was assigned

[33] Cf. R. Browning on Libanius in the *OCD*, 605–606; also A. F. Norman, *Libanius. Selected works* (London 1969) xxxix–xlv. In fact, some might argue that Atheniensis might be added to the list, inasmuch as Libanius spent four years (336–340) in Athens completing his education; cf. Norman, xxxix.

[34] Cf. W. W. How and J. Wells, *A commentary on Herodotus*, vol. 1 (Oxford 1912) 5–9, 16.

[35] But cf. J. G. Frazer, *Pausanias's description of Greece*, vol. 1 (Cambridge 1898) xix, who thinks that, on the basis of internal evidence, "there are good grounds for believing that he was a Lydian," and that it may even be reasonable to surmise that he was born and raised in the area of Mount Sipylus.

[36] For example, Aristotle, Galen, Gregory of

the next number in sequence when it was selected for data entry, even though its order in a meaningful bibliography may not be reflected by that work number. In fact, in the electronic *Canon* the sequence in a given bibliography is numerical, whereas in the printed *Canon* there has been some consideration for rearrangement of items in certain bibliographies that would otherwise be unwieldy.

In many instances, the work ascribed to an author may not warrant independent status. This is true of the many quotations (whether direct or indirect) or paraphrases (with at least a hint of *ipsissima verba*) that actually reside in the work of other authors, especially the compendious medical writers such as Galen, Oribasius, Paul of Aegina, and Aëtius, as well as those egregious collectors of quotations such as Athenaeus and Stobaeus. In the case of these works, the first of the three digits in the work number is replaced by an *x*, indicating that the work is not to be found in an independent text edition. For example, the works of Alexandrian medical scholar Erasistratus of Ceos (0690) do not survive except in the writings of others and are therefore regarded as quoted, or *x*, works. Thus, x01 is the work number for the fragments of Erasistratus that are quoted by Galen, x02 the fragments provided by Pseudo-Galen, and x03 the fragments cited by Oribasius.

Works that comprise part of a larger collection may or may not warrant consideration as separate works belonging to a given author. The epigrams in the *Anthologia Graeca*, for example, are regarded as though taken together they amount to independent works.[37] For instance, the thirty-eight epigrams, which in the *Anthologia Graeca* are attributed to Diogenes Laertius, bear Diogenes' author number 0004 and the work number 002. On the other hand, the sixteen epigrams, which in the *Anthologiae Graecae Appendix* are ascribed to Diogenes Laertius, bear the number 0004 x01. The reason for this discrepancy is that the *Appendix* (abbreviated *App. Anth.* in the *Canon*) does not lend itself so readily to analysis according to individual authors, but rather breaks naturally into classes of epigrams, such as *Epigrammata sepulcralia* (Book 2), *Epigrammata demonstrativa* (Book 3), *Epigrammata irrisoria* (Book 5). Other collections, such as *Iambi et elegi Graeci*[38] and the *Supplementum Hellenisticum*,[39] are easily broken into their constituent parts, that is to say into the individual authors represented therein. The *Appendix* defies such resolution.

Work Title.   The works assigned to each author are designated by their commonly recognized titles (in boldface letters), with a preference for the Latin, or sometimes Latinized, title. Where the title of a work either defies Latinization or is simply better known by its Greek counterpart, the Greek title is retained.

Nyssa, John Chrysostom, Plutarch, to name only a few.

[37] It is worth noting that the *Anthologia Graeca* is also given the status of "author"

with its own author number (7000).

[38] 2 vols., ed. M. L. West (Oxford 1971–1972).

[39] Ed. H. Lloyd-Jones and P. Parsons (Berlin 1983).

It is not always feasible and is sometimes not possible to assign a title to the remnants of an author's writings beyond the word *Fragmenta* or *Fragmentum*. While the seven surviving plays of Sophocles (0011), for example, are identified by their familiar Latin titles,[40] the thousand or so Sophoclean fragments, many of which can confidently be assigned to specific lost plays,[41] are called simply *Fragmenta*. This does not mean that the titles of the lost plays are ignored; on the contrary, titles are deposited in the data bank (and are retrievable) along with the text of the fragments they govern.

Occasionally, alternative titles of a work are included, especially if both titles seem to have been used interchangeably, as with Gregory of Nyssa (2017), where 063 is cited as **De spiritu sancto** *sive* **In pentecosten**.

In general, however, the titles of works are consistent with those found in lexica and biographical dictionaries, as well as the text editions themselves.

Text Edition Selected for Data Entry.   The text edition cited for each work in this *Canon* has been approved by the American Philological Association's Committee on the Thesaurus Linguae Graecae. The selection of a text is meant to indicate preference based on a number of considerations, including the scholarly superiority of that text over other editions but also its relative recency and its availability. Normally, then, each work is represented in the data bank by a single text edition. Occasionally, there is duplication of text material, especially if a particular work of an author constitutes part of a committee-approved edition but also occupies a place in a generic collection that defies subtraction of its parts. For example, Pfeiffer's two-volume edition of *Callimachus* includes the text of the author's epigrams.[42] These epigrams also comprise the *Anthologia Graeca* and cannot reasonably be extracted. As a result, the text of Callimachus' epigrams resides, in duplicate, in the data bank.[43]

Sometimes it is not possible to adopt a text that merits the approval of all scholars, such as Migne's *Patrologia Graeca*, which has been the only text available for many authors. As new editions emerge, the *MPG* text is superseded in the data bank. For example, when data entry of the works of John Chrysostom was begun in the late 1970s, the only available editions for the seven homilies *De laudibus sancti Pauli apostoli* were those of Savile (1612–1613) and Montfaucon (1862). The Montfaucon text (via *MPG* 50.473–514) was deposited in the data bank, but has subsequently been superseded by Piédagnel's new and incontestably superior edition.[44]

While one might question the rationale for depositing in the TLG data bank a text that is indisputably substandard, one might also acknowledge that

[40] *Trachiniae, Antigone, Ajax, Oedipus tyrannus, Electra, Philoctetes,* and *Oedipus Coloneus.*

[41] Cf. S. Radt, *Tragicorum Graecorum fragmenta,* vol. 4 (Göttingen 1977) 99–656.

[42] R. Pfeiffer, *Callimachus,* vol. 2 (Oxford 1953) 80–99.

[43] Cf. sub CALLIMACHUS (0533 003 and 004).

[44] *Jean Chrysostome. Panégyriques de S. Paul* (Paris 1982) 112–320. Cf. sub JOANNES CHRYSOSTOMUS (2062 486).

the alternative is to perpetuate a lacuna in the data bank which might not be filled by an acceptable edition for many years. For example, the editions in the *Corpus Medicorum Graecorum*, which were conceived as replacements for Kühn's edition of the Galenic corpus, do not seem to appear with the regularity that was once expected. Thus, while the TLG has adopted the available *CMG* and other more recent editions for Galen and Pseudo-Galen, more than half of the Galenic corpus still exists only by way of Kühn.[45] By necessity, then, it was a matter of either adopting (however reluctantly) the Kühn edition or accounting for less than half of the Galenic corpus in the data bank.

The bibliographical information cited for each text reflects the specific physical edition that is (or is to be) part of the TLG data bank. In many instances, the pagination for a given work might seem to be excessive, whereas inclusive pagination would seem to suffice.[46] The reason for the breakdown of pagination, as well as of fragments, is that the bibliography for each work accounts for precisely that text which resides in the data bank.[47]

Occasionally, a text was available at the time of data entry only in the form of a typescript. If the text subsequently appeared in published form, the bibliographical information cited includes the details associated with the published edition, as well as a note accounting for discrepancy in pagination which can be expected to occur between typescript and published text.[48]

If the bibliographical details for a given work are to be found in conjunction with another author, the formula *Cf.* (or *Cf. et*) plus the author's name and author or work number is used. For example, a work that had been traditionally carried as part of the Aristotelian bibliography is now assigned to Anaximenes of Lampsacus. All that remains of it in the bibliography to Aristotle (0086) is the following notation:

> x01 Rhetorica ad Alexandrum.
> Cf. ANAXIMENES Hist. et Rhet. (0547 001).

The complete details of the Fuhrmann edition are then carried under Anaximenes (0547) in connection with work 001.

The injunction *Cf. et*, usually found at the end of a bibliographical entry, directs the reader to additional works which ought properly to be considered along with the work in question. Sometimes, this injunction connects works

---

[45] Cf. sub GALENUS (0057) and Pseudo-GALENUS (0530).

[46] For example, sub EURIPIDES (0006 020), SOPHOCLES (0011 008), and many of the prolific *comici* in T. Kock's *Comicorum Atticorum fragmenta*, 3 vols. (Leipzig 1880–1888). However, pagination breakdown is not always given for texts that have not yet been added to the data bank.

[47] Obviously, pagination breakdown would be excessive for texts with facing translations, such as those in the Budé and Loeb series. Such texts are cited with inclusive pagination.

[48] For example, sub GALENUS (0057 032), where the bibliographical citation reflects De Lacy's edition of *De placitis Hippocratis et Platonis* in the *CMG* series.

that complement one another,[49] but at other times it may signal duplication of texts in the data bank under different names and different author and work numbers.[50] Sometimes also the notation *Cf. et* implies a question concerning attribution of a given work to a given author.[51] For the most part, however, the reason for the directive becomes apparent when the author's name at the end of that directive is consulted.

Generally, abbreviations are avoided in bibliographical citations unless they are used so extensively that the reader does not feel constantly compelled to consult the bibliographical code on pp. xxxiii–xxxvii. Abbreviations that appear regularly in lieu of detailed bibliographical citations include *AG, App. Anth., FGrH, FHG, MPG.* However, in the case of x-works, that is, works that are carried under another author and are accompanied by a note of cross-reference, abbreviations are used with high frequency to provide a shorthand reference to the precise locus in which the work in question is actually found. The abbreviation in such cases may be understood readily by following the cross-reference to the appropriate author and work where it is spelled out.

Transmission.   Each work is accompanied by a code or codes identifying the means by which that work has been transmitted to us. These codes, which appear in abbreviated form at the end of each bibliographical listing, are as follows: *Q*(uotation), *NQ* (No quotation), *Cod*(ex), *Pap*(yrus), *Epigr*(aph).

The abbreviation *Q* is used to identify both direct and indirect quotations. Direct quotations present no problems. In the case of indirect quotations, however, it has been necessary to confront the possibility that we may not be able to say with certainty that an accusative subject was originally a nominative in direct statement or that an infinitive accurately reflects its corresponding finite form. Often, it is simply not feasible (or justifiable) to attempt to separate *ipsissima verba* from surrounding testimonia, especially when the text in question is prose rather than poetry; in far too many cases, such a separation is at best artificial and at worst misleading for those who consult the data bank. Over the years, the TLG's efforts to isolate *ipsissima verba* have met with exasperation when the fine line between quoter and quoted is stretched so thin as to render a distinction meaningless if not altogether impossible to achieve. In the end, that line between indirect statement and

[49] For example, sub EURIPIDES (0006), works 023 (*Fragmenta Phaethontis*) and 032 (*Fragmenta Phaethontis incertae sedis*).

[50] For example, sub *SCOLIA ALPHABETICA* (0273), work 001, which is called simply *Fragmenta* (*P. Oxy.* 15.1795), is a duplication of the *ANONYMI AULODIA* (1836), work 001, which is now called *Anonymi aulodia* (*P. Oxy.* 15.1795) to reflect Young's edition, as well as a partial dupli-cation of *LYRICA ADESPOTA* (*CA*) (0230), work 001 (*Fragmenta lyrica*), specifically fr. 37 (*Aulodiae*, according to Powell).

[51] For example, sub ANONYMI HISTORICI (*FGrH*) (1139), work 019 raises the possibility of an author as it is listed, *Chronicon Olympicum* (fort. auctore Phlegonte), and actually directs the reader to consider also Publius Aelius PHLEGON (0585 002–003).

paraphrase is often so blurred that we are unfortunately but necessarily left with the pitfalls of conjecture, which is to say that educated guesses are sometimes granted the status of the *verba* of a quoted author.

To be sure, the designation *Q* is an imperfect way of suggesting that a work has been transmitted in the form of a direct statement or an indirect statement or even a paraphrase. Yet its usefulness perhaps is realized in relation to its counterpart, *NQ*.

One might argue that an author from whom we have no quotation, whether direct or indirect, is lost and therefore does not merit the status of an author in a canon designed as a record of the surviving works of authors. On the other hand, there are sometimes testimonia that yield the titles or suggest the content of otherwise lost works. *NQ* is used to designate titles or descriptions of lost works, from which not a single word, in either direct or oblique form, can be associated with the author supposed to have written the lost work.

Not so arguable are works that have been transmitted by means of the medieval manuscript tradition. If a text editor bases the edition of an author's work on one or more of the codices, the abbreviation *Cod* is assigned to that work, regardless of whether portions of the work are duplicated in and therefore verified by papyri.

The abbreviation *Pap* is used for a text that has been transmitted entirely through papyri. *Pap* may designate an author's literary works which, except for the papyri, would otherwise be lost to us;[52] *Pap* may also designate the *supplementa* to an existing literary corpus which owes its survival to another means of transmission.[53] *Pap* is not used, however, to designate a text that has been transmitted by the codices and for which the papyri simply represent confirmed or variant readings.

Similarly, the abbreviation *Epigr* designates a text that has been transmitted through epigraphical remains. It is not used for a text that has been transmitted through other means and for which the epigraphical evidence constitutes confirmed or variant readings.

Sometimes even the manner of transmission may be open to argument. For example, a fragment of Alexinus, who belonged to the Megarian school of philosophy,[54] survives in Philodemus' Περὶ ῥητορικῆς.[55] How should the means of transmission of the Alexinus fragment be designated—with *Q* because Philodemus is quoting Alexinus, or with *Pap* because the fragment, irrespective of the fact that it is quoted, is known to us through papyrus alone? It may not be an altogether satisfying solution to suggest, as does the transmission code for Alexinus' Fragmentum ap. Philodemum (2607 002), that Alexinus survives—if he survives—in papyrus, without consideration for Philodemus; the alternative, however, is hardly better. Fortunately, no such

---

[52] For example, Bacchylides, Hyperides, Menander, Philodemus.

[53] For example, Callimachus, Euripides, Nicander, Pindar.

[54] Cf. J. von Arnim's article on Alexinus in Pauly-Wissowa 1.1465–1466.

[55] The text, which is part of *P. Herc.* 1674, may be found in S. Sudhaus, *Philodemi volumina rhetorica*, vol. 1 (Leipzig 1892; repr. Amsterdam 1964) 79–80; also in von Arnim, "Ein Bruchstück des Alexinos," *Hermes* 28 (1893) 69.

problem arises in connection with the other work carried under Alexinus (2607 001). A *titulus* (παιὰν εἰς Κράτερον) is all that Athenaeus (*Deipn.* 15.696e) associates with Alexinus,[56] thus qualifying for the transmission code *NQ*.

A similar quandary exists sometimes in connection with fragments preserved in manuscripts.[57] Certain fragments are labeled *Cod* with a measure of confidence;[58] others are designated *Q*, but with less assurance, inasmuch as the fragments represent the reportage of other *astrologi*.[59]

Finally, it may be worth mentioning the relative frequency with which each of the transmission codes appears in the *Canon*. The following statistics represent the number of times each abbreviation is used:[60]

Q	3,670
Cod	3,299
Pap	1,054
NQ	679
Epigr	119

Word Count or Word Estimate.   Word counts and word estimates constitute information compiled by the TLG staff primarily for in-house purposes. It was felt, however, that the user of the printed *Canon* might occasionally find this type of statistical information interesting, perhaps even helpful. For this reason, word counts and word estimates, wherever available, have been included in the printed *Canon*.

Word estimates are determined by random statistical analysis prior to data entry. Word counts are generated electronically after the text has been converted to machine-readable form.

The definition of *word* may be subject to debate among classicists and linguists, but it is quite rigid to a computer. A word, as far as the TLG computer is concerned, is any aggregate of nonblanks which is separated by one or more blanks.[61] This purely technical definition is rendered even more irksome by the fact that nonblanks may not, even in the minds of the most generous scholars, be words of any conceivable sort, except to a computer. Nonblanks may be symbols peculiar to astrology, mathematics, music, or pharmacology, for which certain sequences of characters are required to represent the articulation of their meaning. Nonblanks may also be sigla of various sorts which are added to the text and are meant to indicate the format of the printed page. The result is that a word count for a given text will

---

[56] Cf. *Supplementum Hellenisticum*, 16.

[57] For example, the *Catalogus codicum astrologorum Graecorum*.

[58] For example, Vettius Valens (1764 004).

[59] For example, Vettius Valens (1764 003).

[60] A single work may owe its survival to more than one means of transmission. When this is the case, multiple codes are included.

[61] It should be emphasized that this definition was the result of an early decision on the part of the TLG staff. A computer, of course, can be programmed to recognize just about any definition of *word* and to interpret words accordingly.

usually be somewhat inflated.[62] In the final analysis, word counts are best regarded as relative rather than absolute figures, so that the size of the Galenic corpus (Galen, 2,608,974 words; Pseudo-Galen, 175,193 words) remains more than twice the size of the Aristotelian corpus (1,104,731 words).

All works that have been verified by the TLG correction staff are accompanied by word counts. In addition, many (although by no means all) works not yet in the data bank are accompanied by word estimates. These figures are located after the transmission code and separated from it by a colon. Numbers enclosed in square brackets [ ] represent word estimates; numbers without additional sigla signify computer-verified word counts. For example, the word count for Thucydides' *Historiae* (verified and corrected) is cited as Cod: 153,260. The word estimate for Herodian's *De prosodia catholica* (uncorrected) is given as Cod: [143,857].

Many entries in this *Canon*, although accompanied by fairly complete bibliographical information, contain no indication of a word estimate. Word estimates are added to the electronic *Canon* each month as specific works are prepared for data entry. Word counts replace word estimates when the works have been returned to the TLG premises and verified by the correction staff.

Sample Entry

The marked example presented here illustrates various categories of information discussed in detail on pages xiv–xxviii. Obviously, no single entry can exemplify all of the categories of information found in the *Canon*. The Sappho sample, however, is sufficiently representative to permit the user to recognize easily the major components of other *Canon* entries.

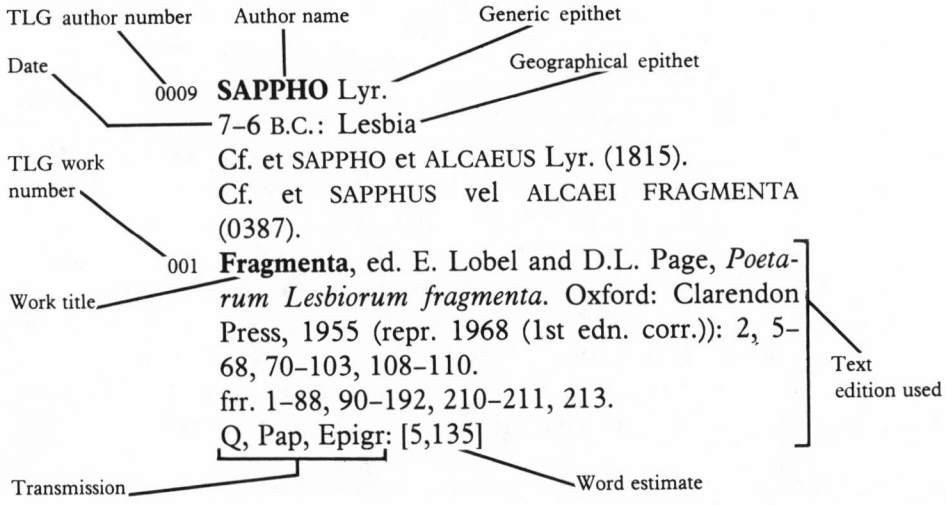

ACKNOWLEDGMENTS

Non omnia possumus omnes. From its very inception in 1972, the Thesaurus Linguae Graecae has had the benefit of a worldwide network of scholars on whom it has been possible to rely for expert guidance and assistance. These individuals have provided us with a special resource in the development and continual refinement of the *Canon*. Certain bibliographies, for example, have been adopted practically wholesale, with only minor adjustments in pagination or the addition of publishers' names. Others have been submitted to the scrutiny of impeccable authorities who have helped to hone what may initially have been tentative and unrefined. Still others have been recast to suit the purposes of an electronic repository designed to contain one version, and only one (if possible), of an edited work. To the many scholars who have loaned their expertise to this enterprise, a huge debt of gratitude is owed, along with apologies for any deviations that were not intended. We would hope that this *Canon* reflects, more often than it belies, their contributions.

The selection of appropriate texts for inclusion in the data bank has been the primary task of a panel of scholars appointed by the American Philological Association. The first chair of this committee was the late Professor Douglas C. C. Young (Paddison Professor of Greek, University of North Carolina). Following the death of Professor Young in the autumn of 1973, Lionel Pearson (Professor Emeritus, Stanford University) took the reins and held them until 1980. For brief periods in 1980 and 1981, the committee was chaired by Professor Glen W. Bowersock (Institute for Advanced Study, Princeton University) and the late Professor David Wiesen (University of Southern California). Thereafter and until 1984, Professor David C. Young (University of California, Santa Barbara) held the post. In early 1985, as the TLG moved closer to the literature of Byzantium, the chairship was passed to Professor Ihor Ševčenko (Harvard University). Those who have held membership on the committee during the past dozen years include Professors Hans-Dieter Betz (University of Chicago), Phillip De Lacy (Emeritus, University of Pennsylvania), Robert M. Grant (University of Chicago), Christian Habicht (Institute for Advanced Study, Princeton University), Albert Henrichs (Harvard University), Bernard M. W. Knox (Center for Hellenic Studies), Ludwig Koenen (University of Michigan), Miroslav Marcovich (University of Illinois), Bruce M. Metzger (Princeton Theological Seminary), Jon Mikalson (University of Virginia), John F. Oates (Duke University), David W. Packard (Ibycus), Robert Renehan (University of California, Santa Barbara), John M. Rist (University of Toronto), Catherine Rubincam (University of Toronto), L. G. Westerink (State University of New York, Buffalo), William H. Willis (Duke University), and corresponding member Winfried Buehler (Archiv für Lexicographie, Hamburg).

Some of the most prolific writers in the history of Greek literature are also the most difficult to pin down in terms of precisely what they wrote. In trying to sort out the tangles that seemed to grow along with the Greek corpus, we have had the expertise of others whom we regard as our collaborators.

The bibliographies to Galenus Med. and Pseudo-Galenus Med. were the work of a team led by Dr. Ronald F. Kotrc (formerly affiliated with the Division of Medical History, College of Physicians of Philadelphia), Professor Kenneth R. Walters (Wayne State University), and former TLG Assistant Director David C. Wilson (University of California, Irvine). Professors Phillip De Lacy and Hans Diller (Universität Kiel) contributed a number of important suggestions which were incorporated into the Galenic bibliographies.

The bibliography to Hippocrates Med. and the *Corpus Hippocraticum* was a collaborative effort between the TLG and the Projet Hippo, directed by Dr. Gilles Maloney at the Université Laval, Quebec.

For the bibliography to Hippolytus Scr. Eccl., we benefited from the vast knowledge of Miroslav Marcovich.

The bibliography to Joannes Chrysostomus was submitted to the careful inspection of Dr. Sever J. Voicu (Vatican Library). His thoughtful suggestions contributed to the development and organization of the works that survive under the name of our most voluminous author.

The bibliography to Philodemus Phil. has proven to be a peculiar thicket of thorns which we have invited many people to explore with us in the hope of seeing some light. Several former TLG staff members helped us to understand the sheer mass of text material Philodemus has generated, among them Renate Gordon, Peter Gimpel, and John Winieski. Many scholars in this country and in Europe supplied us with Philodemian bibliographies of their own, and their own became our own. We are especially grateful to Professor Phillip De Lacy; the Norwegian team of Professor Knut Kleve (University of Oslo), Kjell Gustafson (University of Oslo), and Jan Songstad (University of Bergen); Dr. Marcello Gigante (Centro Internazionale per lo Studio dei Papiri Ercolanesi, Naples), whose *Catalogo dei papiri Ercolanesi* provided us with the order of the treatises as well as the proper Greek titles; and Dr. Francesca Longo-Auricchio (Centro Internazionale per lo Studio dei Papiri Ercolanesi), who alerted us to the impending publication of newly edited fragments. Many scholars agreed to review the bibliography in its various stages; their suggestions for revision aided us in the selection of appropriate texts and in the rejection of materials that have since been superseded. For this difficult part of our bibliographical work, we benefited from the painstaking scrutiny of Professors Elizabeth Asmis (University of Chicago), David Sider (Queens College, CUNY), and especially Albert Henrichs (Harvard University), who challenged us to rethink the purpose and function of a TLG bibliography to Philodemus.

For the bibliography to Origenes Theol., we took advantage of the good will and the learned comments of the Reverend Professor Henry Chadwick (Regius Professor Emeritus of Divinity, Cambridge University).

The bibliography to Proclus Phil. owes its refinement to the detailed criticism and patient guidance extended to us by L. G. Westerink.

A number of the bibliographies, as well as the names of authors and titles of works, have benefited from our long-standing collaboration with the Spanish team associated with the Greek–Spanish Lexicon at the Instituto Antonio de Nebrija in Madrid. We have shared many of our difficulties and many of our solutions with Professor Francisco Rodriguez Adrados, Dr. Xavier López Facal, and Mr. Aníbal González.

A number of people have graciously read various portions of the *Canon* with a view toward correcting errors of commission and omission in typography. We owe our thanks to the following, some of whom were our students, others our colleagues: Cristina Calhoon, Charles Eberline, Carol Mitchell, Robin Pelzer, Sarolta Takacs, and John Winieski. Shirley Werner patiently assisted us whenever we confronted technical problems. Richard Whitaker did the page makeup and prepared the camera-ready copy on an Ibycus system.

Obviously, a work of this scope cannot be entirely free of faults, for which we ourselves acknowledge responsibility. It is our hope that scholars who detect errors might bring them to our attention.

BIBLIOGRAPHICAL ABBREVIATIONS

ACO   *Acta conciliorum oecumenicorum*, 3 vols., ed. E. Schwartz. Berlin: De Gruyter, 1924–1940 (repr. partim 1960–1965).

AG   *Anthologia Graeca*, 4 vols., 2nd edn., ed. H. Beckby. Munich: Heimeran, 1965–1968.

ALG   *Anthologia lyrica Graeca*, ed. E. Diehl. Leipzig: Teubner.

                      ALG^1: vols. 1–2 (1925).

                      ALG^2: vol. 1, fasc. 1–4, 2nd edn. (1936).

                      ALG^3: fasc. 1–3, 3rd edn. (1949–1952).

App. Anth.   *Epigrammatum anthologia Palatina cum Planudeis et appendice nova*, vol. 3, ed. E. Cougny. Paris: Didot, 1890.

CA   *Collectanea Alexandrina*, ed. J. U. Powell. Oxford: Clarendon Press, 1925 (repr. 1970).

CAF   *Comicorum Atticorum fragmenta*, 3 vols., ed. T. Kock. Leipzig: Teubner, 1880–1888.

CAG   *Commentaria in Aristotelem Graeca*, 23 vols. + 3 suppl. Berlin: Reimer, 1882–1909.

CGF   *Comicorum Graecorum fragmenta*, vol. 1.1, ed. G. Kaibel in *Poetarum Graecorum fragmenta*, vol. 6.1. Berlin: Weidman, 1899.

CGFPR   *Comicorum Graecorum fragmenta in papyris reperta*, ed. C. Austin. Berlin: De Gruyter, 1973.

CMG   *Corpus medicorum Graecorum*. Leipzig and Berlin: Teubner, 1908– ; Berlin: Akademie-Verlag, 1947– .

CPG   *Clavis patrum Graecorum*, 4 vols., ed. M. Geerard. Turnhout: Brepols, 1974–1983.

D-K   *Die Fragmente der Vorsokratiker*, 3 vols., 6th edn., ed. H. Diels and W. Kranz. Zürich: Weidmann, 1951–1952 (repr. 1966–1967).

Epist. Graec.   *Epistolographi Graeci*, ed. R. Hercher. Paris: Didot, 1873 (repr. Amsterdam: Hakkert, 1965).

FCG   *Fragmenta comicorum Graecorum*, 5 vols. in 7, ed. A. Meineke. Berlin: Reimer, 1839–1857 (repr. Berlin: De Gruyter, 1970).

FGrH   *Die Fragmente der griechischen Historiker*, 3 vols. in 15, ed. F. Jacoby. Leiden: Brill, 1926–1958 (repr. 1954–1960).

FHG   *Fragmenta historicorum Graecorum*, 5 vols., ed. K. Müller. Paris: Didot, 1841–1870.

Fonti I.2   *Fonti. Fascicolo ix. Discipline générale antique (iie–ixe s.),* vol. I.2 (*Les canons des synodes particuliers*), ed. P. Joannou. Rome: Tipografia Italo-Orientale "S. Nilo," 1962.

Fonti II   *Fonti. Fascicolo ix. Discipline générale antique (iie–ixe s.),* vol. II (*Les canons des pères grecs*), ed. P. Joannou. Rome: Tipografia Italo-Orientale "S. Nilo," 1963.

GCS   *Die griechischen christlichen Schriftsteller der ersten Jahrhunderte.* Berlin: Akademie-Verlag, 1897– .

GDRK   *Die griechischen Dichterfragmente der römischen Kaiserzeit*, vols. 1, 2nd edn. and 2, ed. E. Heitsch. Göttingen: Vandenhoeck & Ruprecht, 1963–1964.

GGM   *Geographi Graeci minores*, 2 vols. + *tabulae*, ed. K. Müller. Paris: Didot, 1855–1861 (repr. Hildesheim: Olms, 1965).

IEG   *Iambi et elegi Graeci*, 2 vols., ed. M. L. West. Oxford: Clarendon Press, 1971–1972.

K   *Claudii Galeni opera*, 20 vols. in 22, ed. C. G. Kühn. Leipzig: Knobloch, 1821–1833 (repr. Hildesheim: Olms, 1964–1965).

MPG   *Patrologiae cursus completus (series Graeca)*, 161 vols., ed. J.-P. Migne. Paris: Migne, 1857–1866.

PGM   *Papyri Graecae magicae. Die griechischen Zauberpapyri*, vols. 1–2, 2nd edn., ed. K. Preisendanz and A. Henrichs. Stuttgart: Teubner, 1973–1974.

PGR   *Paradoxographorum Graecorum reliquiae*, ed. A. Giannini. Milan: Istituto Editoriale Italiano, 1965.

PMG   *Poetae melici Graeci*, ed. D. Page. Oxford: Clarendon Press, 1962 (repr. 1967).

PsVTGr   *Pseudepigrapha veteris testamenti Graece* 3, ed. A.-M. Denis. Leiden: Brill, 1970.

Savile   Τοῦ ἐν ἁγίοις πατρὸς ἡμῶν ᾽Ιωάννου τοῦ Χρυσοστόμου τῶν εὑρισκομένων τόμος, 8 vols., ed. H. Savile. Eton: Norton, 1612–1613.

SH   *Supplementum Hellenisticum*, ed. H. Lloyd-Jones and P. Parsons. Berlin: De Gruyter, 1983.

SLG   *Supplementum lyricis Graecis*, ed. D. Page. Oxford: Clarendon Press, 1974.

ST   *Studi e Testi*. Vatican City: Biblioteca Apostolica Vaticana, 1900– .

Suppl. Com.   *Supplementum comicum*, ed. J. Demiańczuk. Krakau: Nakładem Akademii, 1912 (repr. Hildesheim: Olms, 1967).

TGF   *Tragicorum Graecorum fragmenta*, ed. A. Nauck. Leipzig: Teubner, 1889 (repr. with *Supplementum*, ed. B. Snell. Hildesheim: Olms, 1964).

TGL   *Thesaurus Graecae Linguae ab H. Stephano constructus*, 8 vols., ed. K. B. Haase, W. and L. Dindorf. Paris: Didot, 1831–1865.

Papyrological Abbreviations

The abbreviations listed below reflect only those volumes that are (or are to be) used, in part, as approved texts for data entry. Not included are the abbreviations that accompany (usually in parentheses) the title of a work or that, following the bibliographical information on a work, constitute a breakdown of fragments within that work.

P. Cair.

Greek papyri. Catalogue général des antiquités égyptiennes du Musée du Caire, ed. B. P. Grenfell and A. S. Hunt. Oxford: Oxford University Press, 1903.

P. Egerton

Fragments of an unknown gospel and other early Christian papyri, ed. H. I. Bell and T. C. Skeat. London: Trustees of the British Museum, 1935.

P. Flor.

Papiri greco-egizii. Papiri Florentini.

vol. 3: *Documenti e testi letterarii dell'età romana e bizantina*, ed. G. Vitelli. Milan: Hoepli, 1915.

P. Hamb.

Griechische Papyrusurkunden der Hamburger Staats- und Universitätsbibliothek.

vol. 2: *Griechische Papyri der Hamburger Staats- und Universitätsbibliothek mit einigen Stücken aus der Sammlung Hugo Ibscher*, ed B. Snell et al. [Veröffentlichungen aus der Hamburger Staats- und Universitätsbibliothek 4. Hamburg: Augustin, 1954].

P. Hibeh

The Hibeh papyri.

pt. 1, ed. B. P. Grenfell and A. S. Hunt. London: Egypt Exploration Fund, 1906.

P. Lit. Lond.

Catalogue of the literary papyri in the British Museum, ed. H. J. M. Milne. London: British Museum, 1927.

P. Oxy.

The Oxyrhynchus papyri. London: Egypt Exploration Fund.

vols. 1–6, ed. B. P. Grenfell and A. S. Hunt (1898–1908).

vols. 7–8, ed. Hunt (1910–1911).

vols. 10–11, ed. Grenfell and Hunt (1914–1915).

vol. 13, ed. Grenfell and Hunt (1919).

vol. 23, ed. E. Lobel (1956).

vol. 24, ed. Lobel, C. H. Roberts, E. G. Turner, and J. Barns (1957).

vol. 34, ed. L. Ingrams, P. Kingston, P. Parsons, and J. Rea (1968).

vol. 39, ed. Lobel (1972).

P. Petrie   *The Flinders Petrie papyri.*

pt. 1, ed. J. P. Mahaffy [*Royal Irish Academy, Cunningham memoirs* 8. Dublin 1891].

P. Rain.   *Corpus papyrorum Raineri archiducis Austriae.*

P. Rain. 1, vol. 1: *Griechische Texte I. Rechtsurkunden,* ed. C. Wessely. Vienna: Kaiserl. Königl. Hof- und Staatsdruckerei, 1895.

P. Rain. 3, vol. 6.1: *Griechische Texte III,* ed. H. Harrauer and S. M. E. van Lith. Vienna: Hollinek, 1978.

P. Ryl.   *Catalogue of the Greek and Latin papyri in the John Rylands Library at Manchester.* Manchester: Manchester University Press.

vol. 1, ed. A. S. Hunt (1911).

vol. 3, ed. C. H. Roberts (1938).

P. Schubart   *Griechische literarische Papyri,* ed. W. Schubart. Berlin: Akademie-Verlag, 1950.

PSI   *Papiri greci e latini (Pubblicazioni della Società Italiana per la ricerca dei papiri greci e latini in Egitto).*

vol. 13, ed. M. Norsa and V. Bartoletti. Florence: Ariani, 1949–1953.

CODES AND SIGLA

Category of Information	Siglum	Definition
TLG Author Number	4-digit number	This number is used to identify an author in the TLG data bank.
Author or Work Name	[ ]	Authenticity of the name, or even existence of the author, is questioned.
	< >	Author to whom a given work is attributed may not be the correct author.
	fiq + name	*Fortasse idem qui.* Author might be identified with the name indicated.
	Cf. + name	*Confer.* Extant works are carried under the name of a different author; bibliographical data may be found by consulting the name indicated.
	Cf. et + name	*Confer et.* Additional related information may be found by consulting the name indicated.
Generic Epithet	< >	Extant work falls within the literary genre indicated, although the author in question was not primarily a writer in the specified genre, or perhaps not primarily a writer.
Date	ante + century	Extant writing may be dated to the century indicated, or earlier.
	post + century	Extant writing may be dated to the century indicated, or later.
	/	Extant writing is dated to either of the two centuries indicated, *or* the two centuries define the earliest or latest range of dates.

Category of Information	Siglum	Definition
	–	Author's writings span the two centuries indicated.
Geographical Epithet	fort. + Latin proper adjective	*Fortasse.* Author might have lived in, or been associated with, the place indicated by the Latin proper adjective.
TLG Work Number	3-digit number	This number is used, in conjunction with 4-digit author number, to identify a work in the TLG data bank.
Work	[Sp.]	*Spurium.* Authenticity of the work is generally rejected.
	[Dub.]	*Dubium.* Authorship of the work is in doubt.
	Cf.	*Confer.* Bibliographical data for recommended text(s) may be found under the author or author and work indicated.
	Cf. et	*Confer et.* Attribution of extant writings may be questioned; additional bibliographical data may be found under the author or author and work indicated.
	Dup.	*Duplicat.* Text has been duplicated in data entry; bibliographical data may also be found under the author and work indicated.
Transmission	Q	*Quotation.* Work has been transmitted via quotation(s) from a later source.
	NQ	*No quotation.* Work does not survive; text cited may include testimonia or titles only.
	Cod	*Codex.* Work has been transmitted via manuscript(s).
	Pap	*Papyrus.* Work has been transmitted via papyri.

Category of Information	*Siglum*	*Definition*
	Epigr	*Epigraph*. Work has been transmitted via inscription(s).
Word Count or Word Estimate	[ ]	Number enclosed reflects an estimate only of the work(s) indicated; brackets are removed when word count is verified by computer.

1883 **ABARIS** Hist.
Incertum: Scythicus
001 **Testimonium**, FGrH #34: 1A:258.
NQ
002 **Fragmenta**, FGrH #34: 1A:*13–*14 addenda.
fr. 2: *P. Oxy.* 13.1611.
Q, Pap

1891 **ABAS** Hist.
ante A.D. 2
001 **Fragmenta**, FGrH #46: 1A:272.
Q

0754 **ABASCANTUS** Med.
ante A.D. 1: Lugdunensis
x01 **Fragmenta ap. Galenum.**
K13.71, 278; **14.**177.
Cf. GALENUS Med. (0057 076, 078).

ABERCIUS
A.D. 2: Hierapolitanus
Cf. EPITAPHIUM ABERCII (1353).

0115 *ABGARI EPISTULA*
A.D. 1
x01 **Fragmentum ap. Eusebium.**
HE 1.13.6–9.
Cf. EUSEBIUS Scr. Eccl. et Theol. (2018 002).

2473 **ABLABIUS** Hist.
A.D. 5/6?
001 **Testimonium**, FGrH #708: 3C:582.
NQ
002 **Fragmenta**, FGrH #708: 3C:582–583.
Q

4023 **ABLABIUS** Rhet.
A.D. 5
001 **Epigramma**, AG 9.762.
Q: 26

0116 **ABYDENUS** Hist.
A.D. 2?
001 **Fragmenta**, FGrH #685: 3C:399–403, 405–410.
Q

0755 **ACACIUS** Med.
ante A.D. 1
x01 **Fragmentum ap. Galenum.**
K13.79.
Cf. GALENUS Med. (0057 076).

2064 **ACACIUS** Theol.
A.D. 4: Caesariensis
Bibliography in progress
002 **Fragmenta in epistulam ad Romanos** (in catenis), ed. K. Staab, *Pauluskommentar aus der griechischen Kirche aus Katenenhandschriften gesammelt.* Münster: Aschendorff, 1933: 53–56.
Q

0101 **ACERATUS** Gramm.
A.D. 1
001 **Epigramma**, AG 7.138.
Q: 23

1832 **ACESANDER** Hist.
4?/2 B.C.
001 **Fragmenta**, FGrH #469: 3B:423–425.
Q
002 **Fragmentum** (*P. Oxy.* 32.2637), ed. H.J. Mette, "Die 'Kleinen' griechischen Historiker heute," *Lustrum* 21 (1978) 29–30.
fr. 6 bis.
Pap

1818 **ACESTODORUS** Hist.
3 B.C.: Megalopolitanus
x01 **Fragmentum.**
FGrH #334, fr. 22.
Cf. ISTER Hist. (1450 002).

1878 **ACESTORIDES** Hist.
Incertum
001 **Testimonia**, FGrH #28: 1A:212–213.
NQ

0309 **ACHAEUS** Trag.
5 B.C.
001 **Fragmenta**, ed. B. Snell, *Tragicorum Graecorum fragmenta*, vol. 1. Göttingen: Vandenhoeck & Ruprecht, 1971: 115–128.
frr. 1–5, 6–16, 17–38, 40–42, 43 (sub 24+43), 44, 47–56.
Q: [538]

0756 **ACHILLAS** Med.
1 B.C./A.D. 1
x01 **Fragmenta ap. Galenum.**
K13.90, 834.
Cf. GALENUS Med. (0057 076, 077).

2133 **ACHILLES TATIUS** Astron.
A.D. 3: fort. Alexandrinus
001 **Isagoga excerpta**, ed. E. Maass, *Commentariorum in Aratum reliquiae*, 2nd edn. Berlin: Weidmann, 1898 (repr. 1958): 27–75.
Cod
002 Γένος ᾿Αράτου καὶ βίος, ed. Maass, *op. cit.*, 76–79.
Cod
003 Περὶ ἐξηγήσεως, ed. Maass, *op. cit.*, 80–85.
Cod

0532 **ACHILLES TATIUS** Scr. Erot.
A.D. 2
001 **Leucippe et Clitophon**, ed. E. Vilborg, *Achilles Tatius. Leucippe and Clitophon.* Stockholm: Almqvist & Wiksell, 1955: 1–161.
Cod: 43,440

0757 **ACHOLIUS** Med.
ante A.D. 6

x01 **Fragmentum ap. Aëtium** (lib. 8).
CMG, vol. 8.2, p. 506.
Cf. AËTIUS Med. (0718 008).

2545 **Gaius ACILIUS** Phil. et Hist.
2 B.C.: Romanus
001 **Testimonia**, FGrH #813: 3C:883–884.
NQ
002 **Fragmenta**, FGrH #813: 3C:884–887.
Q

0300 **ACTA ALEXANDRINORUM**
A.D. 2/3
001 **Acta Alexandrinorum**, ed. H. Musurillo, *Acta Alexandrinorum*. Leipzig: Teubner, 1961: 1–72.
De senatu Alexandrinorum (*PSI* 1160): pp. 1–2.
Congressus cum Flacco (*P. Oxy.* 8.1089): pp. 2–5.
Sine titulo (*P. bibl. univ. Giss.* 46): pp. 6–10.
Acta Isidori (recensio A) (*P. Berol.* inv. 7118): pp. 11–13.
Acta Isidori (recensio B) (*P. Lond.* inv. 2785): pp. 14–16.
Acta Isidori (recensio C) (*P. Berol.* inv. 8877): pp. 16–17.
Acta Diogenis (*P. Oxy.* 20.2264): pp. 18–20.
Ingressus triumphalis Vespasiani (*P. Fuad* 8): p. 21.
Acta Hermiae (*P. Rendel Harris*): p. 22.
Acta Maximi (*P. Oxy.* 3.471 + *P. Schubart* 42): pp. 22–31.
Acta Hermaisci (*P. Oxy.* 10.1242): pp. 32–35.
Acta Pauli et Antonini (*P. Lond.* inv. 1 + *P. Louvre* 2376bis): pp. 36–43.
Acta Pauli et Antonini (recensio B Alexandrina brevior) (*P. Oxy.* 10.1242): pp. 44–45.
Acta Pauli et Antonini (textus C) (*P. Berol.* 8111): pp. 45–46.
Acta Athenodori (*P. Oxy.* 18.2177): pp. 47–50.
Acta Appiani (*P. Yale* inv. 1536 + *P. Oxy.* 1.33): pp. 51–56.
Fragmenta dubia vel incerta: pp. 56–72.
Pap: [6,886]

2949 **ACTA BARNABAE**
Incertum
001 **Acta Barnabae**, ed. M. Bonnet, *Acta apostolorum apocrypha*, vol. 2.2. Leipzig: Mendelssohn, 1903 (repr. Hildesheim: Olms, 1972): 292–302.
Cod

0304 **ACTA ET MARTYRIUM APOLLONII**
A.D. 2/4
001 **Acta et martyrium Apollonii**, ed. H. Musurillo, *The acts of the Christian martyrs*. Oxford: Clarendon Press, 1972: 90–104.
Cod: [1,944]

2012 **ACTA EUPLI**
post A.D. 4

001 **Acta Eupli**, ed. H. Musurillo, *The acts of the Christian martyrs*. Oxford: Clarendon Press, 1972: 310–312.
Cod: [490]

0317 **ACTA JOANNIS**
A.D. 2
001 **Acta Joannis**, ed. M. Bonnet, *Acta apostolorum apocrypha*, vol. 2.1. Leipzig: Mendelssohn, 1898 (repr. Hildesheim: Olms, 1972): 151–215.
Cod: [12,901]
002 **Acta Joannis** (recensio), ed. Bonnet, *op. cit.*, 152–160, 169, 171–179, 203–206, 209–210.
Cod: [2,577]

0384 **ACTA JUSTINI ET SEPTEM SODALIUM**
A.D. 2/3
001 **Acta Justini et septem sodalium** (recensio A), ed. H. Musurillo, *The acts of the Christian martyrs*. Oxford: Clarendon Press, 1972: 42–46.
Cod: [582]
002 **Acta Justini et septem sodalium** (recensio B), ed. Musurillo, *op. cit.*, 46–52.
Cod: [858]
003 **Acta Justini et septem sodalium** (recensio C), ed. Musurillo, *op. cit.*, 54–60.
Cod: [1,006]

0388 **ACTA PAULI**
A.D. 2
001 **Acta Pauli**, ed. W. Schubart and C. Schmidt, *Acta Pauli*. Glückstadt: Augustin, 1936: 22–72.
Pap: [3,661]
002 **Martyrium Pauli**, ed. R.A. Lipsius, *Acta apostolorum apocrypha*, vol. 1. Leipzig: Mendelssohn, 1891 (repr. Hildesheim: Olms, 1972): 104–117.
Cod: [1,295]
003 **Pauli et Corinthiorum epistulae** (*P. Bodmer* 10), ed. M. Testuz, *Papyrus Bodmer X–XII*. Geneva: Bibliotheca Bodmeriana, 1959: 30–44.
Pap: [133]
004 **Acta Pauli et Theclae**, ed. Lipsius, *op. cit.*, 235–271.
Cod: [3,805]
005 **Acta Pauli et Theclae** (partis finalis recensio ex codice G), ed. Lipsius, *op. cit.*, 271–272.
Cod: [789]

0389 **ACTA PETRI**
A.D. 2
001 **Martyrium Petri**, ed. L. Vouaux, *Les actes de Pierre*. Paris: Letouzey & Ané, 1922: 398–466.
Cod: [2,692]
002 **Fragmentum**, *P. Oxy.* 6.849.
Pap

2014 **ACTA PHILEAE**
post A.D. 4
Cf. et PHILEAE EPISTULA (2013).
001 **Acta Phileae** (*P. Bodmer* 20), ed. H. Musurillo,

The acts of the Christian martyrs. Oxford: Clarendon Press, 1972: 328–344.
Pap: [1,052]

2948 ACTA PHILIPPI
Incertum
001 **Acta Philippi**, ed. M. Bonnet, *Acta apostolorum apocrypha*, vol. 2.2. Leipzig: Mendelssohn, 1903 (repr. Hildesheim: Olms, 1972): 1–90.
Cod
002 **Acta Philippi** (recensio), ed. Bonnet, *op. cit.*, 41–90.
Cod
003 **Acta Philippi** (recensio), ed. Bonnet, *op. cit.*, 51–90.
Cod
004 **Acta Philippi** (epitome), ed. Bonnet, *op. cit.*, 91–98.
Cod

0391 ACTA SCILITANORUM MARTYRUM
A.D. 2–3
001 **Acta Scilitanorum martyrum**, ed. J.A. Robinson, *The passion of S. Perpetua* [*Texts and Studies* 1.2, appendix. Cambridge: Cambridge University Press, 1891 (repr. Nendeln, Liechtenstein: Kraus, 1967)]: 113–117.
Cod: [670]

2038 ACTA THOMAE
A.D. 3
001 **Acta Thomae**, ed. M. Bonnet, *Acta apostolorum apocrypha*, vol. 2.2. Leipzig: Mendelssohn, 1903 (repr. Hildesheim: Olms, 1972): 99–288.
Cod: [32,319]
004 **Acta Thomae** (recensio), ed. Bonnet, *op. cit.*, 108–109, 111–145, 251–258, 269–288.
Cod
005 **Actorum Thomae consummatio**, ed. Bonnet, *op. cit.*, 289–291.
Cod
002 **Carmen animae (De margarita)** (cod. Rom. vallicellanus B 35), ed. P.-H. Poirier, *L'hymne de la perle des actes de Thomas* [*Homo religiosus* 8. Louvain-La-Neuve: Université Catholique de Louvain, 1981]: 352–356.
Cod
003 **Carmen animae (De margarita)** (paraphrasis Nicetae), ed. Poirier, *op. cit.*, 366–369.
Cod
006 **Acta Thomae** (ex cod. Brit. Mus. add. 10,073), ed. M.R. James. *Apocrypha anecdota II* [*Texts and Studies* 5.1. Cambridge: Cambridge University Press, 1897 (repr. Nendeln, Liechtenstein: Kraus, 1967)]: 28–45.
Cod

2248 ACTA XANTHIPPAE ET POLYXENAE
A.D. 3
001 **Acta Xanthippae et Polyxenae**, ed. M.R. James, *Apocrypha anecdota* [*Texts and Studies*

2.3. Cambridge: Cambridge University Press, 1893 (repr. Nendeln, Liechtenstein: Kraus, 1967)]: 58–85.
Cod

0392 ACUSILAUS Hist.
5 B.C.: Argivus
001 **Testimonia**, FGrH #2: 1A:47–48.
NQ
002 **Fragmenta**, FGrH #2: 1A:49–58.
fr. 22: *P. Oxy.* 13.1611.
fr. 45 bis: *P. Giessen* 307.
Q, Pap
003 **Testimonia**, ed. H. Diels and W. Kranz, *Die Fragmente der Vorsokratiker*, vol. 1, 6th edn. Berlin: Weidmann, 1951 (repr. Dublin: 1966): 52–53.
test. 1–5.
NQ
004 **Fragmenta**, ed. Diels and Kranz, *op. cit.*, 53–60.
frr. 1–41.
Q

0102 ADAEUS Epigr.
fiq Adaeus Rhet.
A.D. 1: Macedo vel Mytilenensis
001 **Epigrammata**, AG **6**.228, 258; **7**.51, 238, 240, 305, 694; **9**.300, 303, 544; **10**.20.
Q: 344

2950 ADAMANTIUS Scr. Eccl.
A.D. 4
001 **De recta in deum fide**, ed. W.H. van de Sande Bakhuyzen, *Der Dialog des Adamantius περὶ τῆς εἰς θεὸν ὀρθῆς πίστεως* [*Die griechischen christlichen Schriftsteller* 4. Leipzig: Hinrichs, 1901]: 2–242.
Cod

0731 ADAMANTIUS JUDAEUS Med.
A.D. 4–5: Alexandrinus
001 **Physiognomonica**, ed. R. Foerster, *Scriptores physiognomonici Graeci et Latini*, vol. 1. Leipzig: Teubner, 1893: 297–426.
Cod: 8,223
002 **De ventis**, ed. V. Rose, *Anecdota Graeca et Graecolatina*, vol. 1. Berlin: Duemmler, 1864 (repr. Amsterdam: Hakkert, 1963): 29–48.
Cod: 5,753
003 **Physiognomonica** (epitome Matritensis), ed. Foerster, *op. cit.*, 320–347, 351–359, 386–424.
Cod
x01 **Fragmenta ap. Oribasium**.
CMG, vol. 6.3, pp. 50, 73, 74, 75, 76, 77.
Cf. ORIBASIUS Med. (0722 004).
x02 **Fragmenta ap. Aetium** (lib. 15).
Zervos, *Athena* 21, p. 23.
Cf. AËTIUS Med. (0718 015).

2433 ADDITAMENTA (FGrH)
Varia

001 Οἱ συντεταχότες τὰ Τρωικά, FGrH #48 bis: 1A:*19–*20.
fr. 1.
Q

002 **De Aeolia**, FGrH #301: 3B:4.
fr. 1.
Q

003 **De Argo**, FGrH #311: 3B:20–21.
test. 1–2, frr. 1–2.
Q

004 **Anonymi apud Pausaniam de Argo**, FGrH #314: 3B:22–25.
frr. 1–12.
Q

005 **De Arcadia**, FGrH #321: 3B:33–34.
frr. 1–3.
Q

006 **Anonymi apud Pausaniam de Arcadia**, FGrH #322: 3B:34–40.
frr. 1–37.
Q

007 **Testimonium de Arcadia** (ap. Plinium, *NH* 8.81), FGrH #320: 3B:33.
NQ

008 **De Chio**, FGrH #395: 3B:284, 757–758 addenda.
frr. 1–2, 3.
Q

010 **De Delo** (excerpta ex oratoribus Atticis) (testimonia et fragmenta), FGrH #401: 3B:293–297.
fr. c10 (Lycurgus): *P. Berol.*
Q, Pap

011 **De tabulis victorum Olympicorum** (testimonia et fragmenta), FGrH #416: 3B:309–314.
frr. 1–6.
fr. 6: *IG* 2².2326.
Q, Epigr

012 **De Euboea**, FGrH #427: 3B:323.
frr. 1–5.
Q

013 **De Ithaca**, FGrH #441: 3B:372.
fr. 1.
Q

014 **De Creta**, FGrH #468: 3B:404–423.
frr. 1–15.
fr. 15: *Inscr. Cret.* 3.
Q, Epigr

016 **De Magnesia**, FGrH #482: 3B:445–448.
frr. 1–5.
fr. 1: *Inscr. Magnesia* 46.
fr. 2: *Inscr. Magnesia* 16.
fr. 3: *Inscr. Magnesia* 17.
fr. 4: *Inscr. Magnesia* 20.
fr. 5: *Inscr. Magnesia* 215.
Epigr

017 **De Macedonia**, FGrH #483: 3B:448.
frr. 1–2.
fr. 1: *IG* 9.2.62.
fr. 2: *IG* 9.2.63.
Epigr

018 **De Megara**, FGrH #487: 3B:453–455.
frr. 1–13.
Q

019 **De Mileto**, FGrH #496: 3B:467–469.
frr. 1–9.

020 **De Naxo**, FGrH #501: 3B:475–478.
frr. 1–5.
Q

021 **De Rhodo**, FGrH #533: 3B:514–519.
frr. 1–11.
fr. 2 (auctore Demetrio Poliorcete): *P. Berol.* inv. 11632.
Q, Pap

022 **De Samo**, FGrH #545: 3B:527–530.
frr. 1–10.
Q

023 **De Samothrace**, FGrH #548: 3B:532–535.
frr. 1–6.
fr. 6: *Inscr. Priene* 69.
Q, Epigr

024 **De Sicyone**, FGrH #551: 3B:536–539.
frr. 1–3.
fr. 1b (= FGrH #105, fr. 2) (fort. auctore Aristotele vel Ephoro vel Menaechmo): *P. Oxy.* 11.1365.
Q, Pap

025 **De Siphno**, FGrH #553: 3B:539–540.
frr. 1–3.
Q

026 **De Sicilia et Magna Graecia**, FGrH #577: 3B:679–688.
frr. 1–17.
fr. 1, Siciliae historia (fort. epitome historiae Timaei vel argumentum Philisti): *P. Oxy.* 4.665.
fr. 2: *P. Oxy.* saeculi secundi.
Q, Cod, Pap

027 **De Sparta**, FGrH #596: 3B:719–729.
frr. 1–46.
Q

028 **De Troezene**, FGrH #607: 3B:739–740.
frr. 1–7.
Q

029 **De Aegypto**, FGrH #665: 3C:214–277.
frr. 1–208.
fr. 180 (Calendarium): *P. Hibeh* 1.27.
fr. 194d: *P. Oxy.* 15.1826.
Cf. et 2433 051.
Q, Pap

030 **De Aethiopia**, FGrH #673: 3C:284–337.
frr. 1–166.

031 **De Arabia**, FGrH #677: 3C:345–350.
frr. 1–8.
Cf. et 2433 052.
Q

032 **De Armenia**, FGrH #679: 3C:351–356.
frr. 1–4.
Q

033 **De Persia**, FGrH #696: 3C:534–547.
frr. 1–18, 20–35.
fr. 28: *P. Florent.* (= *PSI* 151).
Cf. et 2433 053.
Q, Pap

034 **De Epiro**, FGrH #704: 3C:561–565.
frr. 1–4, 6.
Q

035 **De Etruria**, FGrH #706: 3C:565–577.
frr. 1–38.
Q

036 **De India**, FGrH #721: 3C:657–666.
frr. 1–4a, 5a–21.
Q

037 **De Judaeis**, FGrH #737: 3C:701–713.
frr. 1–15, 17, 19–23.
Q

038 **De Caria**, FGrH #742: 3C:719–721.
frr. 1–9.
Q

039 **De Carthagine**, FGrH #744: 3C:722–727.
frr. 1–12.
Q

040 **De Cypro**, FGrH #758: 3C:737–741.
frr. 1–13.
fr. 11a: *PSI* 1221.
Q, Pap

041 **De Libya**, FGrH #764: 3C:745–750.
frr. 1–19.
Q

042 **De Lydia**, FGrH #768: 3C:759–760.
frr. 1–10.
fr. 3: *P. Oxy.* 15.1802.
Q

043 **De Macedonia**, FGrH #776: 3C:771.
frr. 1–2.
fr. 1: *P. Oxy.* 9.1176.
Q, Pap

044 **De Parthia**, FGrH #782: 3C:785–788.
frr. 2–6.
Q

045 **De Phoenicia**, FGrH #794: 3C:825–833.
frr. 1–19.
Q

046 **De Phrygia**, FGrH #800: 3C:836–839.
frr. 1–6a, 7–13.
Q

047 **De Roma et de Italia**, FGrH #840: 3C:908–927.
frr. 1–34, 36–42.
Q

048 **De Scythia**, FGrH #845: 3C:930–931.
frr. 1–5.
fr. 5: *P. Oxy.* 15.1802.
Q, Pap

049 **De Hispania**, FGrH #847: 3C:932–934.
frr. 1–3.
Q

050 **De Syria**, FGrH #855: 3C:942.
fr. 1.
Q

051 **De Aegypto** (*P. Oxy.* 37.2820), ed. H.J. Mette, "Die 'Kleinen' griechischen Historiker heute," *Lustrum* 21 (1978) 35–36.
fr. 209.
Cf. et 2433 029.
Pap

052 **De Arabia** (*P. Oxy.* 27.2466), ed. Mette, *op. cit.*, 36.
fr. 9.
Cf. et 2433 031.
Pap

053 **De Persia** (fort. auctore Choerilo Samio) (*P. Oxy.* 37.2814), ed. Mette, *op. cit.*, 37.
fr. 33/34 bis.
Cf. et 2433 033.
Pap

2648 *ADESPOTA PAPYRACEA* (SH)
Varia
001 **Hexametri**, ed. H. Lloyd-Jones and P. Parsons, *Supplementum Hellenisticum*. Berlin: De Gruyter, 1983: 399–406, 409, 411–417, 419–421, 424–432, 434–437, 439, 441–445, 447–450, 452–457.
frr. 900–935, 937–956.
Pap: 2,965
002 **Elegiae**, ed. Lloyd-Jones and Parsons, *op. cit.*, 458–459, 461–464, 466–471, 475–479.
frr. 957–970.
Pap: 856
003 **Epigrammata**, ed. Lloyd-Jones and Parsons, *op. cit.*, 482–489, 491, 493–499, 501, 503–505.
frr. 971–988.
Pap: 1,244
004 **Miscellanea**, ed. Lloyd-Jones and Parsons, *op. cit.*, 506–507, 509–516.
frr. 989–997.
Pap: 515

0665 **ADRIANUS** Hist.
post 4 B.C.
x01 **De historia Alexandri.**
FGrH #153, fr. 15.
Cf. ANONYMI HISTORICI (FGrH) (1139 007).

0666 **ADRIANUS** Rhet.
A.D. 2: Tyrius
001 **Declamatio**, ed. H. Hinck, *Polemonis declamationes quae exstant duae*. Leipzig: Teubner, 1873: 44–45.
Cod: [294]
x01 **Declamatio alia.**
Habrich, p. 73, fr. 101.
Cf. IAMBLICHUS Scr. Erot. (1441 001).

0668 *AEGIMIUS*
fort. auctore Cercope vel Hesiodo
6 B.C.?
001 **Aegimius** (fragmenta), ed. G. Kinkel, *Epicorum Graecorum fragmenta*. Leipzig: Teubner, 1877: 83–85.
frr. 3–5, 7–8.
Q: [81]

2700 **AELIANUS** Epigr.
post A.D. 2
x01 **Epigrammata demonstrativa.**
App. Anth. 3.111–113: Cf. EPIGRAMMATICI in *App. Anth.* (7052 003).

0545 **Claudius AELIANUS** Soph.
A.D. 2–3
001 **De natura animalium**, ed. R. Hercher, *Claudii Aeliani de natura animalium libri xvii, varia historia, epistolae, fragmenta*, vol. 1. Leipzig: Teubner, 1864 (repr. Graz: Akademische Druck- und Verlagsanstalt, 1971): 3–436.
Cod: [108,176]
002 **Variae historiae**, ed. Hercher, *op. cit.*, vol. 2 (1866; repr. 1971): 3–172.
Cod: [40,258]
003 **Epistulae rusticae**, ed. Hercher, *op. cit.*, 175–185.
Cod: [2,252]
004 **Fragmenta**, ed. Hercher, *op. cit.*, 189–283.
Q: [14,096]
005 **Titulus**, ed. A. Giannini, *Paradoxographorum Graecorum reliquiae*. Milan: Istituto Editoriale Italiano, 1965: 396.
NQ

0546 **AELIANUS** Tact.
A.D. 1–2
001 **Tactica**, ed. H. Koechly and W. Rüstow, *Asclepiodotos' Taktik. Aelianos' Theorie der Taktik* [*Griechische Kriegsschriftsteller*, vol. 2.1. Leipzig: Engelmann, 1855 (repr. Osnabrück: Biblio Verlag, 1969)]: 218–470.
Cod: [10,906]

2434 **AELIUS DIUS** Hist.
A.D. 2?
001 **Testimonia**, FGrH #629: 3C:179.
NQ
002 **Fragmentum**, FGrH #629: 3C:179.
Q

0674 **AELIUS PROMOTUS** Med.
A.D. 2: Alexandrinus
x01 **Fragmentum ap. Paulum.**
CMG, vol. 9.1, p. 314.
Cf. PAULUS Med. (0715 001).

0670 **AELIUS PUBLIUS JULIUS** <Epist.>
A.D. 2
x01 **Fragmentum ap. Eusebium.**
HE 5.19.3.
Cf. EUSEBIUS Scr. Eccl. et Theol. (2018 002).

2368 **AELURUS** Hist.
Incertum
001 **Titulus**, FGrH #528: 3B:505.
NQ

0103 **AEMILIANUS** Rhet.
A.D. 1: Nicaeanus
001 **Epigrammata**, AG 7.623; **9**.218, 756.
Q: 92

2378 **AENEAS** Hist.
Incertum
001 **Fragmentum**, FGrH #543: 3B:527.
Q

0753 **AENEAS** Med.
A.D. 1?
x01 **Fragmentum ap. Galenum.**
K12.589.
Cf. GALENUS Med. (0057 076).

4001 **AENEAS** Phil. et Rhet.
A.D. 6: Gazaeus
001 **Epistulae**, ed. L.M. Positano, *Enea di Gaza. Epistole*, 2nd edn. Naples: Libreria Scientifica Editrice, 1962: 39–53.
Cod
002 **Theophrastus**, ed. M.E. Colonna, *Enea di Gaza. Teofrasto*. Naples: Iodice, 1958: 1–68.
Cod

0058 **AENEAS** Tact.
4 B.C.: Stymphalicus
001 **Poliorcetica**, ed. A. Dain and A.-M. Bon, *Énée le tacticien. Poliorcétique*. Paris: Les Belles Lettres, 1967: 1–91.
Cod: [14,606]

2413 **AENESIDEMUS** Hist.
Incertum
001 **Fragmenta**, FGrH #600: 3B:731–732.
Q

0026 **AESCHINES** Orat.
4 B.C.: Atheniensis
001 **In Timarchum**, ed. V. Martin and G. de Budé, *Eschine. Discours*, vol. 1. Paris: Les Belles Lettres, 1927 (repr. 1962): 20–86.
Cod: 13,961
002 **De falsa legatione**, ed. Martin and de Budé, *op. cit.*, vol. 1, 110–169.
Cod: 12,758
003 **In Ctesiphontem**, ed. Martin and de Budé, *op. cit.*, vol. 2 (1928; repr. 1962): 25–117.
Cod: 19,171
004 **Epistulae** [Sp.], ed. Martin and de Budé, *op. cit.*, vol. 2, 123–143.
Cod: 4,392

0104 **AESCHINES** Rhet.
1 B.C.: Milesius
001 **Epigramma**, AG 6.330.
Q: 30

0673 **AESCHINES SOCRATICUS** Phil.
4 B.C.: Sphettius
001 **Fragmenta**, ed. H. Dittmar, *Aischines von Sphettos. Studien zur Literaturgeschichte der Sokratiker* [*Philologische Untersuchungen*, vol. 21. Berlin: Weidmann, 1912]: 266–281, 283–296.
Alcibiades (frr. 1–5, 7–9, 11).
Axiochus (frr. 12–14).
Aspasia (frr. 15–30, 32–33).
Callias (frr. 34–36).
Miltiades (frr. 37–38).
Rhinon (fr. 39).

Telauges (frr. 40–48).
Fragmenta sedis incertae (frr. 49–58).
Fragmentum dubium (fr. 59).
Q, Cod: [3,893]

002 **Alcibiades** (fragmenta), *P. Oxy.* 13.1608.
Pap

003 **Alcibiades** (fragmentum), *P. Lit. Lond.* 148.
Pap

x01 **Epistulae.**
Epist. Graec., pp. 618, 619–621, 625–626.
Cf. SOCRATICORUM EPISTULAE (0637 001).

2377 **AESCHRION** Epic.
4 B.C.: Mytilenensis

001 **Testimonium**, FGrH #118 bis: 3B:742 addenda.
NQ

002 **Fragmenta**, FGrH #118 bis: 3B:742 addenda.
Q

0679 **AESCHRION** Lyr.
fiq Aeschrion Mytilenensis
4 B.C.: Samius

001 **Epigramma**, AG 7.345.
Q: 62

002 **Fragmenta et tituli**, ed. H. Lloyd-Jones and P. Parsons, *Supplementum Hellenisticum*. Berlin: De Gruyter, 1983: 1–3.
frr. 1–10.
Q: [107]

2337 **AESCHYLUS** Hist.
ante A.D. 3: Alexandrinus

001 **Testimonium**, FGrH #488: 3B:456.
NQ

002 **Titulus**, ed. H. Lloyd-Jones and P. Parsons, *Supplementum Hellenisticum*. Berlin: De Gruyter, 1983: 4.
fr. 13.
NQ: [2]

0085 **AESCHYLUS** Trag.
6–5 B.C.: Atheniensis

001 **Supplices**, ed. G. Murray, *Aeschyli tragoediae*, 2nd edn. Oxford: Clarendon Press, 1955 (repr. 1960): 3–48.
Cod: 5,532

002 **Persae**, ed. Murray, *op. cit.*, 53–95.
Cod: 5,647

003 **Prometheus vinctus**, ed. Murray, *op. cit.*, 103–145.
Cod: 6,271

004 **Septem contra Thebas**, ed. Murray, *op. cit.*, 155–200.
Cod: 5,631

005 **Agamemnon**, ed. Murray, *op. cit.*, 207–274.
Cod: 8,754

006 **Choephoroe**, ed. Murray, *op. cit.*, 277–322.
Cod: 5,959

007 **Eumenides**, ed. Murray, *op. cit.*, 325–367.
Cod: 5,733

008 **Fragmenta**, ed. H.J. Mette, *Die Fragmente der*

Tragödien des Aischylos. Berlin: Akademie-Verlag, 1959: 1–255.
frr. 1–86, 88–106, 108–127, 128 (= 122), 129–134, 135 (= 116), 136 (= 408), 137–175, 176 (= 169), 177, 178 (= 116), 179 (= 169), 180–209, 210 (= 194–195), 211–271a, 273–323a, 325–380, 381 (= 150a–150f), 382–383, 384 (= 116), 385–436, 437 (= 430), 438, 440–458, 459a, 459d, 460–653, 653a (= 78), 654–655, 656 (= 647A/B), 657 (= 207), 658–689, 692–769.
Q, Pap: 41,448

009 **Fragmentum**, ed. M.L. West, *Iambi et elegi Graeci*, vol. 2. Oxford: Clarendon Press, 1972: 29.
fr. 2.
Q: 4

010 **Epigrammata**, AG 7.255; **10**.110.
Q: 44

x01 **Epigramma sepulcrale.**
App. Anth. 2.17: Cf. EPIGRAMMATICI in *App. Anth.* (7052 002).

0321 **AESCHYLUS** Trag.
3 B.C.?: Alexandrinus

001 **Fragmentum**, ed. B. Snell, *Tragicorum Graecorum fragmenta*, vol. 1. Göttingen: Vandenhoeck & Ruprecht, 1971: 312.
fr. 1.
Q: [15]

1980 **AESOPUS** Hist.
1 B.C.

001 **Testimonium**, FGrH #187a: 2B:918.
NQ

002 **Fragmenta**, FGrH #187a: 2B:918–919.
Q

0096 **AESOPUS** Scr. Fab. et ***AESOPICA***
6 B.C.
Cf. et VITA AESOPI (1765).

001 **Paroemiae**, ed. E.L. von Leutsch, *Corpus paroemiographorum Graecorum*, vol. 2. Göttingen: Vandenhoeck & Ruprecht, 1851 (repr. Hildesheim: Olms, 1958): 228–230.
Q: 109

002 **Fabulae**, ed. A. Hausrath and H. Hunger, *Corpus fabularum Aesopicarum*, vols. 1.1 & 1.2, 2nd edn. Leipzig: Teubner, 1.1:1970; 1.2:1959: **1.1**:1–210; **1.2**:1–116.
Cod: 46,077

003 **Fabulae tabulis ceratis Assendelftianis servatae**, ed. Hausrath and Hunger, *op. cit.*, vol. 1.2, 117–119.
Cod: 253

004 **Fabulae Dosithei**, ed. Hausrath and Hunger, *op. cit.*, vol. 1.2, 120–129.
Cod: 1,202

005 **Fabulae Libanii**, ed. Hausrath and Hunger, *op. cit.*, vol. 1.2, 130–132.
Cod: 505

006 **Fabulae Aphthonii rhetoris**, ed. Hausrath and

Hunger, *op. cit.*, vol. 1.2, 133–151.
Cod: 2,807

007 **Fabulae Themistii rhetoris**, ed. Hausrath and
Hunger, *op. cit.*, vol. 1.2, 152.
Q: 119

008 **Fabulae Theophylacti Simmocatti scholastici**,
ed. Hausrath and Hunger, *op. cit.*, vol. 1.2,
153–154.
Cod: 392

009 **Fabulae Syntipae philosophi**, ed. Hausrath and
Hunger, *op. cit.*, vol. 1.2, 155–183.
Cod: 4,839

010 **Fabulae rhetoris anonymi Brancatiani**, ed.
Hausrath and Hunger, *op. cit.*, vol. 1.2, 184–
185.
Cod: 290

011 **Fabula Nicephori**, ed. Hausrath and Hunger,
op. cit., vol. 1.2, 186.
Cod: 90

012 **Fabulae** (*P. Ryl.* 493), ed. Hausrath and Hunger, *op. cit.*, vol. 1.2, 187–189.
Pap: 332

013 **Fabulae ap. Dionem Chrysostomum**, ed.
Hausrath and Hunger, *op. cit.*, vol. 1.2, 189–
190.
Q: 331

014 **Epigramma**, AG 10.123.
Q: 47

015 **Fabulae** (dodecasyllabi), ed. E. Chambry, *Aesopi fabulae*. Paris: Les Belles Lettres, 1:1925;
2:1926: 1:43, 129, 134–135, 138, 151; 2:359,
371, 385, 397–400, 439–440, 467, 488, 510,
519, 532–533, 545–546, 564–565.
fab. 6, 59, 61, 63, 72, 220, 229, 238, 245–246,
269, 288, 301, 318, 326, 336, 346, 358–359.
Cod

016 **Proverbiorum sylloge quae inscribitur** Αἰσώ-
που κωμικαὶ κωμῳδίαι, ed. B.E. Perry, *Aesopica*,
vol. 1. Urbana: University of Illinois Press,
1952: 287–289.
Cod

0683 *AETHIOPIS*
fort. auctore Arctino Milesio
7–6 B.C.

001 **Fragmenta**, ed. G. Kinkel, *Epicorum Graecorum fragmenta*, vol. 1. Leipzig: Teubner, 1877:
34–35.
frr. 1, 3.
Q: [72]

0686 AETHLIUS Hist.
5–4 B.C.?: Samius
Cf. et SAMIORUM ANNALES (1657).

001 **Testimonium**, FGrH #536: 3B:521.
NQ

002 **Fragmenta**, FGrH #536: 3B:521–522.
Q

0528 AËTIUS Doxogr.
A.D. 1/2

001 **De placitis reliquiae** (Stobaei excerpta), ed. H.
Diels, *Doxographi Graeci*. Berlin: Reimer, 1879
(repr. De Gruyter, 1965): 275–289, 291–292,
297, 301–383, 386–389, 392–399, 401, 403–
411, 414–415, 417–430, 432–435, 438, 440,
442–443.
Q

002 **De placitis reliquiae** (Theodoreti et Nemesii
excerpta), ed. Diels, *op. cit.*, 284–289, 292,
307–308, 316, 321–327, 329–331, 341–344,
348–352, 355–357, 362, 386–394, 401–402,
404.
Q

x01 **De placitis reliquiae** (Pseudo-Plutarchi epi-
tome).
Mau, pp. 50–153.
Cf. Pseudo-PLUTARCHUS (0094 003).

0718 AËTIUS Med.
A.D. 6: Amidenus

001 **Iatricorum liber i**, ed. A. Olivieri, *Aëtii Amideni libri medicinales i–iv* [*Corpus medicorum
Graecorum*, vol. 8.1. Leipzig: Teubner, 1935]:
17–146.
Cod: 34,188

002 **Iatricorum liber ii**, ed. Olivieri, *CMG* 8.1, 152–
255.
Cod: 29,821

003 **Iatricorum liber iii**, ed. Olivieri, *CMG* 8.1,
260–355.
Cod: 27,696

004 **Iatricorum liber iv**, ed. Olivieri, *CMG* 8.1,
358–408.
Cod: 14,927

005 **Iatricorum liber v**, ed. A. Olivieri, *Aëtii Amideni libri medicinales v–viii* [*Corpus medicorum
Graecorum*, vol. 8.2. Berlin: Akademie-Verlag,
1950]: 6–119.
Cod: 33,099

006 **Iatricorum liber vi**, ed. Olivieri, *CMG* 8.2,
123–249.
Cod: 35,199

007 **Iatricorum liber vii**, ed. Olivieri, *CMG* 8.2,
253–399.
Cod: 38,757

008 **Iatricorum liber viii**, ed. Olivieri, *CMG* 8.2,
403–554.
Cod: 41,480

009 **Iatricorum liber ix**, ed. S. Zervos, "'Ἀετίου
Ἀμιδηνοῦ λόγος ἐνάτος," *Athena* 23 (1911)
273–390.
Cod: 35,935

011 **Iatricorum liber xi**, ed. C. Daremberg and C.É.
Ruelle, *Oeuvres de Rufus d'Éphèse*. Paris: Im-
primerie Nationale, 1879 (repr. Amsterdam:
Hakkert, 1963): 85–126, 568–581.
Cod: 19,195

012 **Iatricorum liber xii**, ed. G.A. Kostomiris,
Ἀετίου λόγος δωδέκατος. Paris: Klincksieck,
1892: 7–131.
Cod: 26,068

013 **Iatricorum liber xiii**, ed. S. Zervos, "᾿Αετίου ᾿Αμιδηνοῦ περὶ δακνόντων ζώων καὶ ἰοβόλων," *Athena* 18 (1906) 264–292.
capita 1–4, 6, 11–13, 15–24, 32, 34–37, 53–56, 58–59 solum.
Cod: 5,072

015 **Iatricorum liber xv**, ed. S. Zervos, "᾿Αετίου ᾿Αμιδηνοῦ λόγος δέκατος πέμπτος," *Athena* 21 (1909) 7–138.
Cod: 26,668

016 **Iatricorum liber xvi**, ed. S. Zervos, *Gynaekologie des Aëtios*. Leipzig: Fock, 1901: 1–172.
Cod: 40,406

Sextus Julius AFRICANUS Hist.
Cf. Sextus JULIUS AFRICANUS Hist. (2956).

0687 **AGACLYTUS** Hist.
ante 1 B.C.
001 **Fragmentum**, FGrH #411: 3B:303–304.
Q

2605 **AGAMESTOR** Eleg.
ante A.D. 1?: Pharsalius
001 **Fragmentum**, ed. H. Lloyd-Jones and P. Parsons, *Supplementum Hellenisticum*. Berlin: De Gruyter, 1983: 4.
fr. 14.
Q: [26]

0761 **AGAPETUS** Med.
ante A.D. 6
x01 **Fragmentum ap. Paulum**.
CMG, vol. 9.1, p. 312.
Cf. PAULUS Med. (0715 001).
x02 **Fragmentum ap. Alexandrum Trallianum**.
Puschmann, vol. 2, p. 529.
Cf. ALEXANDER Med. (0744 003).

0067 **AGATHARCHIDES** Geogr.
2 B.C.: Cnidius
001 **De mari Erythraeo** (excerpta), ed. K. Müller, *Geographi Graeci minores*, vol. 1. Paris: Didot, 1855 (repr. Hildesheim: Olms, 1965): 111–194.
Q: [12,393]
002 **Fragmenta**, ed. A. Giannini, *Paradoxographorum Graecorum reliquiae*. Milan: Istituto Editoriale Italiano, 1965: 144–145.
Q
003 **Testimonia**, FGrH #86: 2A:205–206.
NQ
004 **Fragmenta**, FGrH #86: 2A:206–222; 3B:741 addenda.
Q
005 **Fragmenta sedis incertae**, ed. Müller, *op. cit.*, 194–195.
Q

2192 **[AGATHARCHIDES]** Hist.
Incertum: Samius

001 **Fragmenta**, FGrH #284: 3A:162.
Q

0090 **AGATHEMERUS** Geogr.
post 1 B.C.
001 **Geographiae informatio**, ed. K. Müller, *Geographi Graeci minores*, vol. 2. Paris: Didot, 1861 (repr. Hildesheim: Olms, 1965): 471–487.
Cod: [2,079]

4024 **AGATHIAS Scholasticus** Hist. et Epigr.
A.D. 6: Myrinus, Constantinopolitanus
Bibliography in progress
001 **Historiae**, ed. R. Keydell, *Agathiae Myrinaei historiarum libri quinque*. Berlin: De Gruyter, 1967: 3–197.
Cod
002 **Epigrammata**, AG 1.34–36; 4.3; 5.216, 218, 220, 222, 237, 261, 263, 267, 269, 273, 276, 278, 280, 282, 285, 287, 289, 292, 294, 296–297, 299, 302; 6.32, 41, 59, 72, 74, 76, 79–80, 167; 7.204–205, 220, 551–552, 567–569, 572, 574, 578, 583, 589, 593, 596, 602, 612, 614; 9.152–155, 204, 442, 482, 619, 631, 641–644, 653, 662, 665, 677, 766–769; 10.14, 64, 66, 68–69; 11.57, 64, 350, 352, 354, 365, 372, 376, 379, 382; 16.36, 41, 59, 80, 109, 244, 331–332.
AG 5.241: Cf. PAULUS Silentiarius Poet. Christ. (4039 004).
AG 5.242: Cf. ERATOSTHENES Scholasticus Epigr. (4063 001).
AG 5.305; 6.87: Cf. ANONYMI EPIGRAMMATICI (0138 001).
AG 7.311: Cf. CALLIMACHUS Philol. (0533 004).
AG 9.344: Cf. Julius LEONIDAS Math. et Astrol. (1457 001).
AG 9.657: Cf. MARIANUS Epigr. (4073 001).
Q: 6,159
x01 **Epigramma demonstrativum** (auctore Agathia vel Pallada).
App. Anth. 3.145(?): Cf. EPIGRAMMATICI in *App. Anth.* (7052 003).
Cf. et PALLADAS Epigr. (2123 x01).

0675 **AGATHINUS** Med.
A.D. 1
x01 **Fragmenta ap. Galenum**.
K8.749–750, 935–938; 13.299, 830.
Cf. GALENUS Med. (0057 059, 060, 076, 077).
x02 **Fragmentum ap. Oribasium**.
CMG, vol. 6.1.2, p. 49.
Cf. ORIBASIUS Med. (0722 001).

0688 **AGATHOCLES** Hist.
5/4 B.C.: Cyzicenus, Babylonius
001 **Testimonia**, FGrH #472: 3B:430.
NQ
002 **Fragmenta**, FGrH #472: 3B:430–433.
Q
003 **Fragmentum**, ed. H.J. Mette, "Die 'Kleinen'

griechischen Historiker heute," *Lustrum* 21
(1978) 30.
fr. 7 bis.
Q

2534 **AGATHOCLES** Hist.
Incertum: Samius
001 **Titulus**, FGrH #799: 3C:836.
NQ

0762 **AGATHOCLES** Med.
A.D. 1?
x01 **Fragmentum ap. Galenum**.
K13.832.
Cf. GALENUS Med. (0057 077).

4086 **[AGATHODAEMON]** Alchem.
Incertum
001 **Fragmenta**, ed. M. Berthelot, *Collection des
anciens alchimistes grecs*. Paris: Steinheil, 1887
(repr. London: Holland Press, 1963): 115,
268–271.
Cod

1775 **Pseudo-AGATHON** Epigr.
Incertum
001 **Epigramma**, ed. E. Diehl, *Anthologia lyrica
Graeca*, fasc. 1, 3rd edn. Leipzig: Teubner,
1949: 134.
Q: [13]

2535 **AGATHON** Hist.
post 4 B.C.?
001 **Fragmentum**, FGrH #801: 3C:840.
Q

2566 **AGATHON** Hist.
Incertum: Samius
001 **Fragmenta**, FGrH #843: 3C:929.
Q

0318 **AGATHON** Trag.
5 B.C.
001 **Fragmenta**, ed. B. Snell, *Tragicorum Graecorum fragmenta*, vol. 1. Göttingen: Vandenhoeck & Ruprecht, 1971: 161–168.
frr. 1–2, 3, 4–9, 11–15, 16a, 18–32, 34.
Q: [346]

2606 **AGATHYLLUS** Eleg.
ante 1 B.C.?: Arcas
001 **Fragmentum**, ed. H. Lloyd-Jones and P. Parsons, *Supplementum Hellenisticum*. Berlin: De
Gruyter, 1983: 5.
fr. 15.
Q: [21]

2555 **AGESILAUS** Hist.
Incertum
001 **Fragmentum**, FGrH #828: 3C:900.
Q

0105 **AGIS** Epigr.
3–2 B.C.
001 **Epigramma**, AG 6.152.
Q: 28

0676 **AGLAÏS** Poet. Med.
4 B.C./A.D. 1: Byzantius
001 **Adversus suffusiones incipientes**, ed. U.C.
Bussemaker, *Poetae bucolici et didactici*. Paris:
Didot, 1862: 97–98.
Cod: 184
002 **Fragmentum**, ed. H. Lloyd-Jones and P. Parsons, *Supplementum Hellenisticum*. Berlin: De
Gruyter, 1983: 7–8.
fr. 18.
Cod: [184]

2345 **AGL(A)OSTHENES** Hist.
4–3 B.C.?
001 **Testimonia**, FGrH #499: 3B:470.
NQ
002 **Fragmenta**, FGrH #499: 3B:470–473.
Q

1776 *AGRAPHA*
Varia
Cf. et FRAGMENTA EVANGELIORUM INCER-
TORUM (1378).
001 **Agrapha**, ed. A. Resch, *Agrapha*, 2nd edn.
[*Texte und Untersuchungen* 30. Leipzig: Hinrichs, 1906]: 23–25, 29–32, 34–37, 39–40, 44–
45, 48–65, 67–72, 84–93, 96, 98–100, 102–
108, 110–122, 128–132, 136–137, 139, 141,
143, 146–147, 150, 152–153, 161–165, 167–
172, 174–185, 188–189, 192–195, 197–199,
204–205, 207–208, 210–211, 214.
Q, Cod, Pap
002 **Apocrypha**, ed. Resch, *op. cit.*, 215–216, 218–
219, 221–222, 224, 227–232, 241, 243, 248,
250, 252–262, 264–269, 271–289.
Q, Cod, Pap
003 **Logoi**, ed. Resch, *op. cit.*, 295–304, 306–310,
312–317, 320, 322–325, 327–334.
Q, Cod

0763 **Julius AGRIPPA** Med.
A.D. 2?
x01 **Fragmenta ap. Galenum**.
K13.185, 1030.
Cf. GALENUS Med. (0057 076, 077).

1835 **AGROETAS** Hist.
3/2 B.C.
001 **Fragmenta**, FGrH #762: 3C:743–744.
Q

0693 **ALBINUS** Phil.
vel Alcinous
A.D. 2: Smyrnaeus
001 **Epitome doctrinae Platonicae**, ed. P. Louis,

Albinos. Épitomé. Paris: Les Belles Lettres, 1945: 3–173.
Cod: 13,494

002 **Introductio in Platonem**, ed. K.F. Hermann, *Platonis dialogi secundum Thrasylli tetralogias dispositi*, vol. 6. Leipzig: Teubner, 1853: 147–151.
Cod

0400 **ALCAEUS** Comic.
4 B.C.

001 **Fragmenta**, ed. T. Kock, *Comicorum Atticorum fragmenta*, vol. 1. Leipzig: Teubner, 1880: 756–764.
frr. 1–3, 6–10, 12–15, 17–27, 29–34, 36, 38–39.
Q: 161

002 **Fragmenta**, ed. A. Meineke, *Fragmenta comicorum Graecorum*, vol. 2.2. Berlin: Reimer, 1840 (repr. De Gruyter, 1970): 824–832.
Q: 137

003 **Fragmentum**, ed. J. Demiańczuk, *Supplementum comicum*. Krakau: Nakładem Akademii, 1912 (repr. Hildesheim: Olms, 1967): 7.
fr. 1.
Q: 6

004 **Fragmentum**, ed. Meineke, *op. cit.*, vol. 5.1 (1857; repr. 1970): cxxi.
Q: [41]

0106 **ALCAEUS** Epigr.
3–2 B.C.: Messenius

001 **Epigrammata**, AG 5.10; 6.218; 7.1, 5, 55, 247, 412, 429, 495, 536; 9.518–519, 588; 11.12; 12.29–30, 64; 16.5, 7–8, 196, 226.
AG 6.187: Cf. ALPHEUS Epigr. (0108 001).
AG 7.89: Cf. CALLIMACHUS Philol. (0533 004).
AG 11.53: Cf. ANONYMI EPIGRAMMATICI (0138 001).
Q: 866

0383 **ALCAEUS** Lyr.
7–6 B.C.: Lesbius
Cf. et SAPPHO et ALCAEUS Lyr. (1815).
Cf. et SAPPHUS vel ALCAEI FRAGMENTA (0387).

001 **Fragmenta**, ed. E. Lobel and D.L. Page, *Poetarum Lesbiorum fragmenta*. Oxford: Clarendon Press, 1955 (repr. 1968 (1st edn. corr.)): 112–116, 118–176, 178–206, 208–286, 290.
frr. 1–424, 439.
Q, Pap: [10,649]

002 **Fragmentis addenda**, ed. Lobel and Page, *op. cit.*, 339.
frr. 128a, 304a.
Pap

003 **Fragmenta**, ed. D.L. Page, *Supplementum lyricis Graecis*. Oxford: Clarendon Press, 1974: 77–86.
frr. S262–S272.
Pap: [569]

0764 **ALCAMENES** Med.
ante A.D. 1: Abydenus

x01 **Fragmenta ap. Anonymum Londinensem.**
Iatrica 8.6–10.
Cf. ANONYMUS LONDINENSIS (0643 001).

2285 **ALCETAS** Hist.
3–2 B.C.?

001 **Fragmentum**, FGrH #405: 3B:300.
Q

0236 **ALCIBIADES** <Eleg.>
5 B.C.: Atheniensis

001 **Fragmentum**, ed. M.L. West, *Iambi et elegi Graeci*, vol. 2. Oxford: Clarendon Press, 1972: 29.
Q: [15]

x01 **Epigramma.**
App. Anth. 5.6b(?) addenda: Cf. EPIGRAMMATICI in *App. Anth.* (7052 008).

0610 **ALCIDAMAS** Rhet.
4 B.C.: Atheniensis

001 **Fragmenta**, ed. L. Radermacher, *Artium scriptores* [*Österreichische Akademie der Wissenschaften*, Philosoph.-hist. Kl., Sitzungsberichte, Bd. 227, Abh. 3. Vienna: Rohrer, 1951]: 135–147.
Περὶ τῶν τοὺς γραπτοὺς λόγους γραφόντων ἢ περὶ σοφιστῶν (fr. 15): pp. 135–141.
᾿Οδυσσεὺς κατὰ Παλαμήδους προδοσίας [Sp.] (fr. 16): pp. 141–147.
Cod: [4,008]

002 **Mouseion** (fragmentum), *P. Petrie* 1.25.
Pap

003 **Mouseion** (fragmentum), *P. Lit. Lond.* 191.
Pap

004 **Vita Homeri** (*P. Mich.* inv. 2754), ed. J.G. Winter, "A new fragment on the life of Homer," *Transactions and Proceedings of the American Philological Association* 56 (1925) 125–126.
Pap

1780 **ALCIMENES** Comic.
Incertum: Atheniensis

001 **Titulus**, ed. T. Kock, *Comicorum Atticorum fragmenta*, vol. 1. Leipzig: Teubner, 1880: 254.
NQ: 2

002 **Titulus**, ed. A. Meineke, *Fragmenta comicorum Graecorum*, vol. 1. Berlin: Reimer, 1839 (repr. De Gruyter, 1970): 101.
NQ

0765 **ALCIMION** Med.
A.D. 1
Cf. et ALCIMION vel NICOMACHUS Med. (0823).
Cf. et APOLLONIUS et ALCIMION Med. (0810).

x01 **Fragmenta ap. Galenum.**

K13.112, 493, 529, 835, 841, 973.
Cf. GALENUS Med. (0057 076–077).

0823 **ALCIMION vel NICOMACHUS** Med.
A.D. 1?
Cf. et ALCIMION Med. (0765).
x01 **Fragmentum ap. Galenum.**
K13.807.
Cf. GALENUS Med. (0057 077).

0695 **ALCIMUS** Hist.
4 B.C.: Siceliota
001 **Testimonium**, FGrH #560: 3B:570.
NQ
002 **Fragmenta**, FGrH #560: 3B:570–574.
fr. 7: *P. Rendel Harris* 59.
Q, Pap

ALCINOUS Phil.
Cf. ALBINUS Phil. (0693).

0640 **ALCIPHRON** Rhet. et Soph.
A.D. 2/3
001 **Epistulae**, ed. M.A. Schepers, *Alciphronis rhetoris epistularum libri iv*. Leipzig: Teubner, 1905 (repr. Stuttgart: 1969): 1–155.
Cod: [20,909]

0766 **ALCMAEON** Phil.
5 B.C.: Crotoniensis
001 **Testimonia**, ed. H. Diels and W. Kranz, *Die Fragmente der Vorsokratiker*, vol. 1, 6th edn. Berlin: Weidmann, 1951 (repr. Dublin: 1966): 210–214.
test. 1–18.
NQ
002 **Fragmenta**, ed. Diels and Kranz, *op. cit.*, 214–216.
frr. 1–5.
Q

0696 *ALCMAEONIS*
7 B.C.
001 **Fragmenta**, ed. G. Kinkel, *Epicorum Graecorum fragmenta*, vol. 1. Leipzig: Teubner, 1877: 76.
frr. 1–2.
Q: [38]

0291 **ALCMAN** Lyr.
7 B.C.: Lacedaemonius
001 **Fragmenta**, ed. D.L. Page, *Poetae melici Graeci*. Oxford: Clarendon Press, 1962 (repr. 1967 (1st edn. corr.)): 2–5, 10–38, 41–83, 85–87, 89–91.
frr. 1–10, 12–17, 19–20, 26–32, 34–43, 45–50, 53–60, 63–65, 68–70, 73–74, 77–98, 100–144, 146–159, 162, 168–171, 173–174, 177.
Q, Pap: [3,960]
002 **Fragmenta**, ed. D.L. Page, *Supplementum lyricis Graecis*. Oxford: Clarendon Press, 1974: 1–3.

frr. S1–S2: *P. Oxy.* 2737.
fr. S3: *P. Oxy.* 2801.
fr. S4: *P. Oxy.* 2812.
fr. S5: *P. Oxy.* 2802.
Pap: [113]

0401 **ALEXANDER** Comic.
1 B.C.
001 **Fragmenta**, ed. T. Kock, *Comicorum Atticorum fragmenta*, vol. 3. Leipzig: Teubner, 1888: 372–374.
frr. 1–6, 9 + titulus.
Q: 49
002 **Fragmenta**, ed. A. Meineke, *Fragmenta comicorum Graecorum*, vol. 4. Berlin: Reimer, 1841 (repr. De Gruyter, 1970): 553–555.
Q: 47

0107 **ALEXANDER** Epigr.
1 B.C.?: Magnes
001 **Epigramma**, AG 6.182.
Q: 50

2500 **ALEXANDER** Hist.
post 4 B.C.?: Chersonensis (Cariae)
001 **Testimonium**, FGrH #739: 3C:714.
NQ

1864 **ALEXANDER** Hist.
A.D. 1: Myndius
001 **Fragmenta**, FGrH #25: 1A:189.
Q
002 **Fragmenta**, ed. A. Giannini, *Paradoxographorum Graecorum reliquiae*. Milan: Istituto Editoriale Italiano, 1965: 164–166.
Q

0744 **ALEXANDER** Med.
A.D. 6: Trallianus
001 **Dedicatio ad Cosman**, ed. T. Puschmann, *Alexander von Tralles*, vol. 1. Vienna: Braumüller, 1878 (repr. Amsterdam: Hakkert, 1963): 289.
Cod: 148
002 **De febribus**, ed. Puschmann, *op. cit.*, vol. 1, 291–439.
Cod: 20,743
003 **Therapeutica**, ed. Puschmann, *op. cit.*, vols. 1 & 2 (1879; repr. 1963): 1:441–617; 2:3–585.
Cod: 103,803
004 **Epistula de lumbricis**, ed. Puschmann, *op. cit.*, vol. 2, 587–599.
Cod: 1,843
005 **De oculis libri tres**, ed. T. Puschmann, *Nachträge zu Alexander Trallianus*. Berlin: Calvary, 1887 (repr. Amsterdam: Hakkert, 1963): 134–178.
Cod: 6,028

0732 **ALEXANDER** Phil.
A.D. 2–3: Aphrodisiensis
001 **De mixtione**, ed. I. Bruns, *Alexandri Aphro-*

disiensis praeter commentaria scripta minora
[*Commentaria in Aristotelem Graeca*, suppl.
2.2. Berlin: Reimer, 1892]: 213-238.
Cod: 10,270

002 **Problemata** (lib. 1-2) [Sp.], ed. J.L. Ideler,
Physici et medici Graeci minores, vol. 1. Berlin:
Reimer, 1841 (repr. Amsterdam: Hakkert,
1963): 3-80.
Cf. et 0732 017.
Cod: 24,294

003 **De febribus** [Sp.], ed. Ideler, *op. cit.*, 81-106.
Cod: 8,357

004 **In Aristotelis metaphysica commentaria**, ed.
M. Hayduck, *Alexandri Aphrodisiensis in Aris-
totelis metaphysica commentaria* [*Commentaria
in Aristotelem Graeca* 1. Berlin: Reimer, 1891]:
1-837.
Lib. A, α, B, Γ, Δ: pp. 1-439.
Lib. E-N [Sp.]: pp. 440-837.
Cod: 343,472

005 **In Aristotelis analyticorum priorum librum
i commentarium**, ed. M. Wallies, *Alexandri
in Aristotelis analyticorum priorum librum i
commentarium* [*Commentaria in Aristotelem
Graeca* 2.1. Berlin: Reimer, 1883]: 1-418.
Cod: 162,312

006 **In Aristotelis topicorum libros octo commenta-
ria**, ed. M. Wallies, *Alexandri Aphrodisiensis in
Aristotelis topicorum libros octo commentaria*
[*Commentaria in Aristotelem Graeca* 2.2. Ber-
lin: Reimer, 1891]: 1-591.
Cod: 189,173

007 **In librum de sensu commentarium**, ed. P.
Wendland, *Alexandri in librum de sensu
commentarium* [*Commentaria in Aristotelem
Graeca* 3.1. Berlin: Reimer, 1901]: 1-173.
Cod: 51,593

008 **In Aristotelis metrologicorum libros commentaria**, ed. M. Hayduck, *Alexandri Aphrodisiensis in Aristotelis metrologicorum libros commentaria* [*Commentaria in Aristotelem Graeca*
3.2. Berlin: Reimer, 1899]: 1-227.
Cod: 86,005

009 **In Aristotelis sophisticos elenchos commentarius** [Sp.], ed. M. Wallies, *Alexandri quod fertur: in Aristotelis sophisticos elenchos commentarium* [*Commentaria in Aristotelem Graeca* 2.3.
Berlin: Reimer, 1898]: 1-198.
Cod: 73,417

010 **De anima**, ed. I. Bruns, *Alexandri Aphrodisiensis praeter commentaria scripta minora* [*Commentaria in Aristotelem Graeca*, suppl. 2.1. Berlin: Reimer, 1887]: 1-100.
Cod: 31,530

011 **De anima libri mantissa** (= **De anima liber
alter**) [Sp.], ed. Bruns, *CAG*, suppl. 2.1, 101-
186.
Cod: 36,520

012 Ἀπορίαι καὶ λύσεις [Sp.], ed. I. Bruns, *Alexandri Aphrodisiensis praeter commentaria scripta
minora* [*Commentaria in Aristotelem Graeca*,

suppl. 2.2. Berlin: Reimer, 1892]: 1-116.
Cod: 42,800

013 Ἠθικὰ προβλήματα [Sp.], ed. Bruns, *CAG*,
suppl. 2.2, 117-163.
Cod: 17,681

014 **De fato**, ed. Bruns, *CAG*, suppl. 2.2, 164-212.
Cod: 16,723

015 **In analytica posteriora commentariorum fragmenta**, ed. Wallies, *CAG* 2.1, xix-xxii.
Cod: 1,487

018 **In analytica posteriora commentariorum fragmenta**, ed. P. Moraux, *Le commentaire d'Alexandre d'Aphrodise aux seconds analytiques
d'Aristote* [*Peripatoi. Philologische-historische
Studien zum Aristotelismus* 13. Berlin: De
Gruyter, 1979].
Cod

016 **Fragmenta**, ed. P. Moraux, *Alexandre d'Aphrodise*. Paris: Droz, 1942: 207-212, 214, 216-
220.
Q: 1,401

017 **Problemata** (lib. 3-4) [Sp.], ed. H. Usener, *Al-
exandri Aphrodisiensis quae feruntur problema-
torum liber iii et iiii* [*Programm Gymnasium
Joachimsthal* (1859)]: 1-37.
Cf. et 0732 002.
Cod: 15,067

0697 **Cornelius ALEXANDER** Polyhist.
2-1 B.C.: Milesius
001 **Testimonia**, FGrH #273: 3A:96-97.
NQ
002 **Fragmenta**, FGrH #273: 3A:97-126.
Q

0698 **ALEXANDER** Rhet.
1 B.C.: Ephesius
001 **Fragmenta**, ed. A. Meineke, *Analecta Alexandrina*. Berlin: Enslin, 1843 (repr. Hildesheim:
Olms, 1964): 372-377.
Q: [256]
002 **Fragmenta et titulus**, ed. H. Lloyd-Jones and
P. Parsons, *Supplementum Hellenisticum*. Berlin: De Gruyter, 1983: 10, 12-15.
frr. 20-21, 25-34, 36-38.
Q: [250]

0594 **ALEXANDER** Rhet.
A.D. 2
001 Περὶ ῥητορικῶν ἀφορμῶν (fragmenta), ed. L.
Spengel, *Rhetores Graeci*, vol. 3. Leipzig:
Teubner, 1856 (repr. Frankfurt am Main: Mi-
nerva, 1966): 1-6.
Cod: [1,379]
002 **De figuris**, ed. Spengel, *op. cit.*, 9-40.
Cod: [7,226]

2951 **ALEXANDER** Scr. Eccl.
A.D. 3: Hierosolymitanus
x01 **Epistula ad Antionitas** (ap. Eusebium).
HE 7.2.3.
Cf. EUSEBIUS Scr. Eccl. (2018 002).

x02 **Epistula ad ecclesiam Antiochenam** (ap. Eusebium).
HE 7.2.5–8.
Cf. EUSEBIUS Scr. Eccl. (2018 002).

x03 **Epistula ad Origenem** (ap. Eusebium).
HE 6.14.8–9.
Cf. EUSEBIUS Scr. Eccl. (2018 002).

x04 **Epistula Alexandri et Theoctisti Caesariensis ad Pontianum Romanum** (ap. Eusebium).
HE 6.19.17–18.
Cf. EUSEBIUS Scr. Eccl. (2018 002).

2059 **ALEXANDER** Theol.
A.D. 4: Lycopolitanus

001 **Tractatus de placitis Manichaeorum**, ed. A. Brinckmann, *Alexandri Lycopolitani contra Manichaei opiniones disputatio*. Leipzig: Teubner, 1895: 3–40.
Cod

0216 **ALEXANDER** Trag. et Lyr.
4–3 B.C.: Aetolus

001 **Fragmenta**, ed. J.U. Powell, *Collectanea Alexandrina*. Oxford: Clarendon Press, 1925 (repr. 1970): 121–129.
frr. 1–9, 15, 18.
Q: [547]

002 **Epigrammata**, AG 7.534, 709; **16**.172.
AG 7.507: Cf. SIMONIDES Lyr. (0261 003).
Q: 99

003 **Fragmentum**, ed. B. Snell, *Tragicorum Graecorum fragmenta*, vol. 1. Göttingen: Vandenhoeck & Ruprecht, 1971: 279.
frr. 1–2.
Q

0767 **ALEXANDER** Philalethes Med.
A.D. 1: Laodicensis

x01 **Fragmenta ap. Galenum**.
K12.557, 580.
Cf. GALENUS Med. (0057 076).

x02 **Fragmentum ap. Pseudo-Galenum**.
K14.510.
Cf. Pseudo-GALENUS Med. (0530 029).

x03 **Fragmentum ap. Soranum**.
CMG, vol. 4, p. 122.
Cf. SORANUS Med. (0565 001).

0042 ***ALEXANDRI MAGNI EPISTULAE***
Incertum

001 **Epistulae**, ed. R. Hercher, *Epistolographi Graeci*. Paris: Didot, 1873 (repr. Amsterdam: Hakkert, 1965): 98–99.
Q: [422]

2556 **ALEXARCHUS** Hist.
Incertum

001 **Fragmentum**, FGrH #829: 3C:900.
Q

2607 **ALEXINUS** Phil.
4 B.C.?: Eleus

001 **Titulus**, ed. H. Lloyd-Jones and P. Parsons, *Supplementum Hellenisticum*. Berlin: De Gruyter, 1983: 16.
fr. 40.
NQ: [3]

002 **Fragmentum** (ap. Philodemum) (*P. Herc.* 1674, col. 44.23–45.30), ed. J. von Arnim, "Ein Bruchstück des Alexinos," *Hermes* 28 (1893) 69.
Pap

0699 **ALEXION** Gramm.
A.D. 1

001 **Fragmenta**, ed. R. Berndt, *De Charete, Chaeride, Alexione grammaticis eorumque reliquiis*, pt. 2. Königsberg: Hartung, 1906: 4–44.
Q: [4,573]

0402 **ALEXIS** Comic.
4–3 B.C.

001 **Fragmenta**, ed. T. Kock, *Comicorum Atticorum fragmenta*, vol. 2. Leipzig: Teubner, 1884: 297–329, 331–408.
frr. 1–7, 9–30, 32–49, 51–53, 55–66, 68–71, 73–102, 105–128, 130–135, 137–138, 140–150, 152–156, 158–165, 167–183, 185–198, 200–214, 216–299, 301–302, 305–329, 331–343, 345 + tituli.
Q: 7,345

002 **Fragmenta**, ed. A. Meineke, *Fragmenta comicorum Graecorum*, vol. 3. Berlin: Reimer, 1840 (repr. De Gruyter, 1970): 382–389, 391–423, 425–440, 442–462, 464–522, 524.
Q: 7,156

003 **Fragmentum**, ed. J. Demiańczuk, *Supplementum comicum*. Krakau: Nakładem Akademii, 1912 (repr. Hildesheim: Olms, 1967): 7.
fr. 1.
Q: 3

004 **Tituli**, ed. C. Austin, *Comicorum Graecorum fragmenta in papyris reperta*. Berlin: De Gruyter, 1973: 1.
NQ: 3

005 **Fragmenta**, ed. Kock, *op. cit.*, vol. 3 (1888): 744.
frr. 278b, 303b.
Q: 61

006 **Fragmenta**, ed. Meineke, *op. cit.*, vol. 5.1 (1857; repr. 1970): ccx, ccxviii.
Q: [14]

x01 **Aenigma**.
App. Anth. 7.11: Cf. EPIGRAMMATICI in *App. Anth.* (7052 007).

0707 **ALEXIS** Hist.
3/2 B.C.: Samius

001 **Fragmenta**, FGrH #539: 3B:522–523.
Q

0108 **ALPHEUS** Epigr.
A.D. 1: Mytilenensis

001 **Epigrammata**, AG **6**.187; 7.237; **9**.90, 95, 97,

100–101, 104, 110, 526; **12**.18; **16**.212.
Q: 434

2135 **ALYPIUS** Mus.
A.D. 3/4?
001 **Isagoge musica**, ed. K. Jan, *Musici scriptores Graeci*. Leipzig: Teubner, 1895 (repr. Hildesheim: Olms, 1962): 367–406.
Cod

0758 **AMARANTUS** Gramm.
A.D. 1/2: Alexandrinus
x01 **Fragmenta ap. Galenum**.
K**13**.84; **14**.208.
Cf. GALENUS Med. (0057 076, 078).

0043 *AMASIS EPISTULAE*
Incertum
001 **Epistulae**, ed. R. Hercher, *Epistolographi Graeci*. Paris: Didot, 1873 (repr. Amsterdam: Hakkert, 1965): 100.
Q: [201]

1777 **AMBROSIUS Rusticus** Med.
ante A.D. 1: Puteolanus
x01 **Fragmenta ap. Galenum**.
K**13**.309–310, 325–326; **14**.184.
Cf. GALENUS Med. (0057 076, 078).

2219 **AMELESAGORAS** Hist.
4–3 B.C.: Atheniensis
001 **Testimonia**, FGrH #330: 3B:162–163.
NQ
002 **Fragmenta**, FGrH #330: 3B:163–164.
Q

2004 *AMELII EPISTULA*
Incertum
001 **Epistula**, ed. R. Hercher, *Epistolographi Graeci*. Paris: Didot, 1873 (repr. Amsterdam: Hakkert, 1965): 101.
Q: [243]

1047 **AMERIAS** Gramm.
3 B.C.: Macedonius
001 **Fragmenta**, ed. O. Hoffmann, *Die Makedonen, ihre Sprache und ihr Volkstum*. Göttingen: Vandenhoeck & Ruprecht, 1906: 4–14.
Q

0403 **AMIPSIAS** Comic.
5–4 B.C.
001 **Fragmenta**, ed. T. Kock, *Comicorum Atticorum fragmenta*, vol. 1. Leipzig: Teubner, 1880: 670–678.
frr. 1–5, 7–10, 12–19, 21–26, 29–38.
Q: 250
002 **Fragmenta**, ed. A. Meineke, *Fragmenta comicorum Graecorum*, vol. 2.2. Berlin: Reimer, 1840 (repr. De Gruyter, 1970): 701–708, 710–711.
Q: 219
003 **Fragmentum**, ed. J. Demiańczuk, *Supplemen-*

tum comicum. Krakau: Nakładem Akademii, 1912 (repr. Hildesheim: Olms, 1967): 7.
fr. 1.
Q: 2
004 **Tituli**, ed. C. Austin, *Comicorum Graecorum fragmenta in papyris reperta*. Berlin: De Gruyter, 1973: 1.
fr. 1.
Pap: 4

0109 **AMMIANUS** Epigr.
A.D. 2
001 **Epigrammata**, AG **9**.573; **11**.13–16, 97–98, 102, 146–147, 150, 152, 156–157, 180–181, 188, 209, 221, 226–231, 413.
AG 11.95, 155: Cf. LUCILLIUS Epigr. (1468 001).
AG 11.268: Cf. ANONYMI EPIGRAMMATICI (0138 001).
AG 16.20: Cf. PALLADAS Epigr. (2123 001).
Q: 565

0110 **AMMONIDES** Epigr.
post 3 B.C.?
001 **Epigramma**, AG 11.201.
Q: 13

0289 **AMMONIUS** Epigr.
A.D. 5
001 **Fragmentum**, ed. E. Heitsch, *Die griechischen Dichterfragmente der römischen Kaiserzeit*, vol. 2. Göttingen: Vandenhoeck & Ruprecht, 1964: 48.
Q: [15]
002 **Epigramma**, AG 9.827.
Q: 21

0708 <**AMMONIUS**> Gramm.
fiq Ammonius Hist.
A.D. 1/2?
Cf. et AMMONIUS Hist. (2254).
Bibliography in progress
001 **De adfinium vocabulorum differentia**, ed. K. Nickau, *Ammonii qui dicitur liber de adfinium vocabulorum differentia*. Leipzig: Teubner, 1966: 1–136.
Cod: [18,255]
002 **De impropriis**, ed. Nickau, *op. cit.*, 138–153.
Cod: [1,926]
x01 **Supplementum glossarum**.
Nickau, pp. 156–159.
Cf. (H)EREN(N)IUS PHILO Hist. et Gramm. (1416 002).

2254 **AMMONIUS** Hist.
fiq Ammonius Gramm.
2 B.C.: fort. Alexandrinus
Cf. et <AMMONIUS> Gramm. (0708).
001 **Testimonia**, FGrH #350: 3B:212–213.
NQ
002 **Fragmenta**, FGrH #350: 3B:213–214.
Q

0709 **AMMONIUS** Hist.
2–1 B.C.?: Atheniensis
001 **Fragmenta**, FGrH #361: 3B:219–220.
Q

4016 **AMMONIUS** Phil.
A.D. 5
001 **In Porphyrii isagogen sive quinque voces**, ed.
A. Busse, *Ammonius in Porphyrii isagogen sive
quinque voces* [*Commentaria in Aristotelem
Graeca* 4.3. Berlin: Reimer, 1891]: 1–128.
Cod: [36,930]
002 **In Aristotelis categorias commentarius**, ed. A.
Busse, *Ammonius in Aristotelis categorias commentarius* [*Commentaria in Aristotelem Graeca*
4.4. Berlin: Reimer, 1895]: 1–106.
Cod: [30,586]
003 **In Aristotelis de interpretatione commentarius**, ed. A. Busse, *Ammonius in Aristotelis de
interpretatione commentarius* [*Commentaria in
Aristotelem Graeca* 4.5. Berlin: Reimer, 1897]:
1–272.
Cod: [103,844]
004 **In Aristotelis analyticorum priorum librum i
commentarium**, ed. M. Wallies, *Ammonii in
Aristotelis analyticorum priorum librum i commentarium* [*Commentaria in Aristotelem
Graeca* 4.6. Berlin: Reimer, 1899]: 1–36.
Cod: [15,501]
005 **In analytica priora** [Sp.], ed. Wallies, *op. cit.*,
37–76.
Cod: [20,984]

2724 **AMMONIUS** Scr. Eccl.
A.D. 5–6?: Alexandrinus
Bibliography in progress
003 **Fragmenta in Joannem** (in catenis), ed. J.
Reuss, *Johannes-Kommentare aus der griech-
ischen Kirche* [*Texte und Untersuchungen* 89.
Berlin: Akademie-Verlag, 1966]: 196–358.
Q

0768 **AMMONIUS Lithotomus** Med.
ante A.D. 1: Alexandrinus
x01 **Fragmentum ap. Oribasium.**
CMG, vol. 6.2.2, p. 188.
Cf. ORIBASIUS Med. (0722 003).
x02 **Fragmentum ap. Paulum.**
CMG, vol. 9.2, p. 339.
Cf. PAULUS Med. (0715 001).

2445 **AMOMETUS** Hist.
ante 4 B.C.
001 **Testimonium**, FGrH #645: 3C:190.
NQ
002 **Fragmenta**, FGrH #645: 3C:191.
Q

0710 *AMPHIARAI EXILIUM* (?)
ante 6 B.C.
001 **Fragmentum**, ed. J.U. Powell, *Collectanea*

Alexandrina. Oxford: Clarendon Press, 1925
(repr. 1970): 246.
Q: [22]

2699 **AMPHICRATES** Rhet.
ante A.D. 2: Atheniensis
x01 **Epigramma demonstrativum.**
App. Anth. 3.99: Cf. EPIGRAMMATICI in *App.
Anth.* (7052 003).

2112 **AMPHILOCHIUS** Scr. Eccl.
A.D. 4: Iconiensis
001 **In natalitia domini** (orat. 1), ed. C. Datema,
Amphilochii Iconiensis opera. Turnhout: Brepols, 1978: 5–9.
Cod: [1,580]
003 **In occursum domini** (orat. 2), ed. Datema, *op.
cit.*, 37–73.
Cod: [2,474]
004 **In Lazarum** (orat. 3), ed. Datema, *op. cit.*, 85–
92.
Cod: [1,380]
005 **In mulierem peccatricem** (orat. 4), ed. Datema,
op. cit., 107–126.
Cod: [4,245]
006 **In diem sabbati sancti** (orat. 5), ed. Datema,
op. cit., 133–136.
Cod: [860]
007 **In illud: Pater si possibile est** (orat. 6), ed.
Datema, *op. cit.*, 139–152.
Cod: [3,859]
008 **De recens baptizatis** (orat. 7), ed. Datema, *op.
cit.*, 155–162.
Cod: [1,702]
009 **In Zacchaeum** (orat. 8), ed. Datema, *op. cit.*,
165–171.
Cod: [2,420]
010 **In illud: Non potest filius a se facere** (orat. 9),
ed. Datema, *op. cit.*, 175–179.
Cod: [1,709]
011 **Contra haereticos**, ed. Datema, *op. cit.*, 185–
214.
Cod: [11,026]
015 **Epistula synodalis**, ed. Datema, *op. cit.*, 219–
221.
Cod: [816]
016 **Fragmenta**, ed. Datema, *op. cit.*, 227–239.
frr. 1–15.
Q, Cod: [2,967]
017 **Oratio in mesopentecosten** [Sp.], ed. Datema,
op. cit., 251–262.
Cod: [2,345]
018 **Fragmenta spuria**, ed. Datema, *op. cit.*, 263–
266.
frr. 1–5.
Q, Cod: [885]
002 **Iambi ad Seleucum**, ed. E. Oberg, *Amphilochii
Iconiensis iambi ad Seleucum* [*Patristische Texte
und Studien* 9. Berlin: De Gruyter, 1969]: 29–
40.
Cod: [1,954]
012 **Oratio in resurrectionem domini** (e cod. Vat.

gr. 1936), ed. S. Lilla, "La fonte inedita di un'
omelia greca sulla Pasqua," *Byzantion* 40
(1970) 68–73.
Cod: [773]

013 **Oratio in resurrectionem domini** (e cod. Vat.
gr. 2194), ed. S. Lilla, "Un omelia greca sulla
Pasqua," *Byzantion* 38 (1968) 282–284.
Cod: [713]

014 **Encomium sancti Basilii Magni**, ed. P.J. Alexander, *The iconoclastic council of St. Sophia
(815) and its definition (horos)* [*Dumbarton
Oaks Papers* 7. Cambridge, Mass.: Harvard
University Press, 1953]: 61.
fr. 22.
Cod: [163]

026 **Fragmenta**, ed. G. Ficker, *Amphilochiana.*
Leipzig: Barth, 1906: 4–5, 10–15.
frr. 1–3, 5–6.
Q: [618]

020 **Fragmenta ex tractatu in illud: *Dominus crea-
vit me*** (fr. 4), MPG 39: 101.
Q: [247]

021 **In Isaiam** (fr. 5) [Sp.], MPG 39: 101.
Q: [29]

022 **In illud: *Solvite templum hoc*** (fr. 9) [Sp.],
MPG 39: 105.
Q: [56]

019 **Expositio in illud: *De meo accipiet et annunti-
abit vobis*** (fr. 13) [Sp.], MPG 39: 109.
Q: [95]

023 **Fragmentum xvii** [Sp.], MPG 39: 116.
Q: [158]

027 **Fragmentum xix** (ap. Anastasium Sinaitam,
Viae dux) [Sp.], MPG 39: 117.
Q: [24]

024 **Fragmentum xx** [Sp.], MPG 39: 117.
Q: [20]

025 **Fragmentum xxi** [Sp.], MPG 39: 117.
Q: [34]

030 **Vita sancti Basilii Magni**, ed. F. Combefis, *SS.
patrum Amphilochii Iconiensis, Methodii Pata-
rensis et Andreae Cretensis opera omnia.* Paris,
1644: 155–225.
Cod

031 **Oratio in circumcisionem et in Basilium**, ed.
Combefis, *op. cit.*, 10–22.
Cod

2271 **AMPHION** Hist.
1 B.C./A.D. 2?: Thespiensis
001 **Fragmentum**, FGrH #387: 3B:264.
Q

0771 **AMPHION** Med.
ante A.D. 2
x01 **Fragmentum ap. Galenum.**
K13.736.
Cf. GALENUS Med. (0057 077).

0404 **AMPHIS** Comic.
4 B.C.
001 **Fragmenta**, ed. T. Kock, *Comicorum Atti-*

corum fragmenta, vol. 2. Leipzig: Teubner,
1884: 236–250.
frr. 1–23, 25–46, 49–51 + tituli.
Q: 821

002 **Fragmenta**, ed. A. Meineke, *Fragmenta comicorum Graecorum*, vol. 3. Berlin: Reimer, 1840
(repr. De Gruyter, 1970): 301–313, 315–319.
Q: 792

0711 **AMPHITHEUS (?)** Hist.
3/2 B.C.: Heracleota
001 **Fragmentum**, FGrH #431: 3B:327–328.
Q

2649 **AMYNTAS** Epigr.
2 B.C.?
001 **Fragmenta** (*P. Oxy.* 4.662), ed. H. Lloyd-Jones
and P. Parsons, *Supplementum Hellenisticum.*
Berlin: De Gruyter, 1983: 16–17.
frr. 42–44.
Pap

0712 **AMYNTAS** Hist.
4 B.C.
001 **Fragmenta**, FGrH #122: 2B:627–629.
Q: [113]

1951 **AMYNTIANUS** Hist.
A.D. 2
001 **Testimonium**, FGrH #150: 2B:818.
NQ
002 **Fragmenta**, FGrH #150: 2B:819.
Q

0770 **AMYTHAON** Med.
ante A.D. 1
x01 **Fragmenta ap. Galenum.**
K13.976, 983.
Cf. GALENUS Med. (0057 077).
x02 **Fragmentum ap. Oribasium.**
CMG, vol. 6.3, p. 83.
Cf. ORIBASIUS Med. (0722 004).
x03 **Fragmenta ap. Paulum.**
CMG, vol. **9.1**, p. 381; **9.2**, p. 355.
Cf. PAULUS Med. (0715 001).

0037 ***ANACHARSIDIS EPISTULAE***
Incertum
001 **Epistulae**, ed. R. Hercher, *Epistolographi
Graeci.* Paris: Didot, 1873 (repr. Amsterdam:
Hakkert, 1965): 102–105.
Cod: [1,388]

0237 **ANACREON** Lyr.
6 B.C.: Teius
001 **Fragmenta**, ed. M.L. West, *Iambi et elegi
Graeci*, vol. 2. Oxford: Clarendon Press, 1972:
30–34.
eleg. 1–5, iamb. 1–7.
Q: [129]
002 **Fragmenta**, ed. D.L. Page, *Poetae melici
Graeci.* Oxford: Clarendon Press, 1962 (repr.

1967 (1st edn. corr.)): 172–227, 232, 234.
frr. 1–4, 6–9, 11–98, 100, 102–116, 118, 120–
123, 125–126, 128–131, 133–136, 138–142,
156, 160.
Q, Pap: [1,782]

003 **Fragmenta**, ed. D.L. Page, *Supplementum lyricis Graecis*. Oxford: Clarendon Press, 1974:
103.
frr. S313–S314.
Q: [11]

004 **Epigrammata**, AG **6.**134–145, 346; **7.**160, 226,
263; **9.**715–716; **11.**47–48; **13.**4.
AG 16.388: Cf. JULIANUS <Epigr.> (4050
001).
Q: 412

x01 **Epigramma exhortatorium et supplicatorium.**
App. Anth. 4.9: Cf. EPIGRAMMATICI in *App.
Anth.* (7052 004).

0217 **ANACREON Junior** Eleg.
post 4 B.C.?

001 **Fragmentum**, ed. J.U. Powell, *Collectanea Alexandrina*. Oxford: Clarendon Press, 1925
(repr. 1970): 130.
Q: [8]

4150 *ANACREONTEA*
A.D. 1?/6

001 **Anacreontea**, ed. M.L. West, *Carmina Anacreontea*. Leipzig: Teubner, 1984: 1–49.
Q, Cod

ANAGRAPHE LINDIA
1 B.C.
Cf. TIMACHIDAS Hist. (1732).

0238 **ANANIUS** Iamb.
6 B.C.

001 **Fragmenta**, ed. M.L. West, *Iambi et elegi
Graeci*, vol. 2. Oxford: Clarendon Press, 1972:
34–36.
frr. 1–5.
Q: [140]

9005 **ANASTASIUS TRAULUS** Epigr.
Incertum

001 **Epigramma**, AG 15.28.
Q: 91

2577 **ANATOLIUS** Phil. et Math.
A.D. 3: Alexandrinus, Caesariensis

001 Περὶ δεκάδος καὶ τῶν ἐντὸς αὐτῆς ἀριθμῶν, ed.
J.L. Heiberg, *Anatolius. Sur les dix premiers
nombres*. Macon: Protat, 1901: 5–16.
Cod

002 **Fragmenta arithmetica** [Sp.], MPG 10: 232–
236.
Q

x01 **De paschate** (fragmenta).
Eusebius, HE 7.32.14–19.
Cf. EUSEBIUS Scr. Eccl. et Theol. (2018 002).

0713 **ANAXAGORAS** Phil.
6–5 B.C.: Clazomenius, Atheniensis

001 **Testimonia**, ed. H. Diels and W. Kranz, *Die
Fragmente der Vorsokratiker*, vol. 2, 6th edn.
Berlin: Weidmann, 1952 (repr. Dublin: 1966):
5–32.
test. 1–117.
NQ

002 **Fragmenta**, ed. Diels and Kranz, *op. cit.*, 32–
44.
frr. 1–24.
Q

2284 **ANAXANDRIDAS** Hist.
3–2 B.C.: Delphicus

001 **Testimonium**, FGrH #404: 3B:298.
NQ

002 **Fragmenta**, FGrH #404: 3B:298–300.
Q

0405 **ANAXANDRIDES** Comic.
4 B.C.

001 **Fragmenta**, ed. T. Kock, *Comicorum Atticorum fragmenta*, vol. 2. Leipzig: Teubner,
1884: 135–153, 155–164.
frr. 1–73, 75–81 + tituli.
Q: 1,585

002 **Fragmenta**, ed. A. Meineke, *Fragmenta comicorum Graecorum*, vol. 3. Berlin: Reimer, 1840
(repr. De Gruyter, 1970): 161–177, 179–185,
190–202.
Q: 1,556

003 **Fragmentum**, ed. J. Demiańczuk, *Supplementum comicum*. Krakau: Nakładem Akademii,
1912 (repr. Hildesheim: Olms, 1967): 7.
fr. 1.
Q: 2

004 **Fragmentum**, ed. C. Austin, *Comicorum Graecorum fragmenta in papyris reperta*. Berlin: De
Gruyter, 1973: 2.
fr. 2.
Pap: 7

x01 **Epigramma exhortatorium et supplicatorium.**
App. Anth. 4.1: Cf. EPIGRAMMATICI in *App.
Anth.* (7052 004).

0714 **ANAXARCHUS** Phil.
4 B.C.: Abderita

001 **Testimonia**, ed. H. Diels and W. Kranz, *Die
Fragmente der Vorsokratiker*, vol. 2, 6th edn.
Berlin: Weidmann, 1952 (repr. Dublin: 1966):
235–239.
test. 1–17.
NQ

002 **Fragmenta**, ed. Diels and Kranz, *op. cit.*, 239–
240.
frr. 1–2.
Q

2210 **ANAXICRATES** Hist.
ante 1 B.C.?

001 **Fragmenta**, FGrH #307: 3B:13–14.
Q

0406 **ANAXILAS** Comic.
4 B.C.
001 **Fragmenta**, ed. T. Kock, *Comicorum Atticorum fragmenta*, vol. 2. Leipzig: Teubner, 1884: 264–275.
frr. 1–5, 7–13, 15–25, 27–44 + titulus.
Q: 717
002 **Fragmenta**, ed. A. Meineke, *Fragmenta comicorum Graecorum*, vol. 3. Berlin: Reimer, 1840 (repr. De Gruyter, 1970): 341–348, 350–355.
Q: 676

0725 **ANAXIMANDER** Phil.
7–6 B.C.: Milesius
001 **Testimonia**, ed. H. Diels and W. Kranz, *Die Fragmente der Vorsokratiker*, vol. 1, 6th edn. Berlin: Weidmann, 1951 (repr. Dublin: 1966): 81–89.
test. 1–30.
NQ
002 **Fragmenta**, ed. Diels and Kranz, *op. cit.*, 89–90.
frr. 1–5.
Q

1120 **ANAXIMANDER Junior** Hist.
4 B.C.: Milesius
001 **Testimonia**, FGrH #9: 1A:159–160.
NQ
002 **Fragmenta**, FGrH #9: 1A:160.
Q

0547 **ANAXIMENES** Hist. et Rhet.
4 B.C.: Lampsacenus
001 **Ars rhetorica**, ed. M. Fuhrmann, *Anaximenis ars rhetorica*. Leipzig: Teubner, 1966: 1–97.
Cod: [19,375]
002 **Testimonia**, FGrH #72: 2A:112–116.
NQ
003 **Fragmenta**, FGrH #72: 2A:116–130.
Q
x01 **Fragmenta** (*P. Hibeh* 1.15).
FGrH #105, fr. 6.
Cf. ANONYMI HISTORICI (FGrH) (1139 004).

0617 **ANAXIMENES** Phil.
6 B.C.: Milesius
Cf. et ANAXIMENIS MILESII EPISTULAE (1121).
001 **Testimonia**, ed. H. Diels and W. Kranz, *Die Fragmente der Vorsokratiker*, vol. 1, 6th edn. Berlin: Weidmann, 1951 (repr. Dublin: 1966): 90–94.
test. 1–23.
NQ
002 **Fragmenta**, ed. Diels and Kranz, *op. cit.*, 95–96.
frr. 1–3.
Q

1121 **ANAXIMENIS MILESII EPISTULAE**
Incertum
001 **Epistulae**, ed. R. Hercher, *Epistolographi Graeci*. Paris: Didot, 1873 (repr. Amsterdam: Hakkert, 1965): 106.
Q: [168]

0833 **ANAXION** Trag.
Incertum: Mytilenensis
001 **Titulus**, ed. B. Snell, *Tragicorum Graecorum fragmenta*, vol. 1. Göttingen: Vandenhoeck & Ruprecht, 1971: 319.
NQ

0407 **ANAXIPPUS** Comic.
4–3 B.C.
001 **Fragmenta**, ed. T. Kock, *Comicorum Atticorum fragmenta*, vol. 3. Leipzig: Teubner, 1888: 296–301.
frr. 1–8.
Q: 433
002 **Fragmenta**, ed. A. Meineke, *Fragmenta comicorum Graecorum*, vol. 4. Berlin: Reimer, 1841 (repr. De Gruyter, 1970): 459–460, 463–466.
Q: 436

0027 **ANDOCIDES** Orat.
5–4 B.C.: Atheniensis
001 **De mysteriis**, ed. G. Dalmeyda, *Andocide. Discours*. Paris: Les Belles Lettres, 1930 (repr. 1966): 17–63.
Cod: 10,327
002 **De reditu suo**, ed. Dalmeyda, *op. cit.*, 69–77.
Cod: 2,010
003 **De pace**, ed. Dalmeyda, *op. cit.*, 87–100.
Cod: 2,772
004 **In Alcibiadem** [Sp.], ed. Dalmeyda, *op. cit.*, 113–127.
Cod: 2,855
005 **Fragmenta**, ed. Dalmeyda, *op. cit.*, 131–132.
frr. 1–2, 4, 7.
Q: 106

2393 **ANDREAS** Hist.
3/2 B.C.?: Panormitanus
001 **Fragmentum**, FGrH #571: 3B:668.
Q

0677 **ANDREAS** Med.
3 B.C.: fort. Carystius
x01 **Fragmenta ap. Galenum**.
K13.343, 735, 982; **14.**180.
Cf. GALENUS Med. (0057 076–078).
x02 **Fragmentum ap. Aetium** (lib. 6).
CMG, vol. 8.2, p. 197.
Cf. AËTIUS Med. (0718 006).
x03 **Fragmentum ap. Aetium** (lib. 9).
Zervos, *Athena* 23, p. 305.
Cf. AËTIUS Med. (0718 009).
x04 **Fragmentum ap. Soranum**.
CMG, vol. 4, p. 131.
Cf. SORANUS Med. (0565 001).

2715 **ANDREAS Libadinarius** Epigr.
Incertum
x01 **Epigramma exhortatorium et supplicatorium**.
App. Anth. 4.114: Cf. EPIGRAMMATICI in
App. Anth. (7052 004).

2346 **ANDRISCUS** Hist.
4–3 B.C.?
001 **Fragmenta**, FGrH #500: 3B:473–475.
Q

2507 **ANDROCLES** Hist.
4 B.C.?
001 **Fragmentum**, FGrH #751: 3C:734.
Q

2412 **ANDROETAS** Hist.
4/3 B.C.?: Tenedius
001 **Fragmentum**, FGrH #599: 3B:731.
Q

0280 **ANDROMACHUS** Poet. Med.
A.D. 1
001 **Fragmentum**, ed. E. Heitsch, *Die griechischen Dichterfragmente der römischen Kaiserzeit*, vol. 2. Göttingen: Vandenhoeck & Ruprecht, 1964: 8–15.
Q: [1,080]

0772 **ANDROMACHUS Minor** Med.
A.D. 1
x01 **Fragmenta ap. Galenum**.
K12.438; 13.441, 463; 14.42, 73, 106.
Cf. GALENUS Med. (0057 076–078).
x02 **Fragmentum ap. Oribasium**.
CMG, vol. 6.2.2, p. 217.
Cf. ORIBASIUS Med. (0722 003).
x03 **Fragmenta ap. Aetium** (lib. 8).
CMG, vol. 8.2, pp. 449, 466, 494, 516, 530.
Cf. AËTIUS Med. (0718 008).
x04 **Fragmentum ap. Aetium** (lib. 9).
Zervos, *Athena* 23, p. 292.
Cf. AËTIUS Med. (0718 009).
x05 **Fragmenta ap. Aetium** (lib. 15).
Zervos, *Athena* 21, pp. 39, 55.
Cf. AËTIUS Med. (0718 015).

2536 **ANDRON** Geogr.
4 B.C.: Teius
001 **Testimonium**, FGrH #802: 3C:840.
NQ
002 **Fragmenta**, FGrH #802: 3C:840–841.
Q

1123 **ANDRON** Hist.
4 B.C.?: Halicarnassensis
001 **Fragmenta**, FGrH #10: 1A:161–165, *9 addenda.
fr. 20: *P. Oxy.* 5.841.
Q

2172 **ANDRON** Hist.
2–1 B.C.?: Alexandrinus

001 **Fragmentum**, FGrH #246: 2B:1129.
Q

0678 **ANDRON** Med.
1 B.C.
x01 **Fragmentum ap. Galenum**.
K12.830.
Cf. GALENUS Med. (0057 076).
x02 **Fragmenta ap. Oribasium**.
CMG, vol. **6.2.2**, p. 218; **6.3**, p. 495.
Cf. ORIBASIUS Med. (0722 003, 005).

1122 **ANDRON** Paradox.
post 3 B.C.
001 **Fragmentum**, FGrH #360: 3B:218.
Q

0111 **ANDRONICUS** Epigr.
3 B.C.?
001 **Epigramma**, AG 7.181.
Q: 26

0773 **ANDRONICUS** Med.
ante A.D. 1
x01 **Fragmentum ap. Galenum**.
K13.114.
Cf. GALENUS Med. (0057 076).

1124 **ANDRONICUS RHODIUS** Phil.
1 B.C.: Rhodius
001 **De passionibus** (lib. 1) [Sp.], ed. X. Kreuttner, *Andronici qui fertur libelli περὶ παθῶν*, pt. 1 (De affectibus). Heidelberg: Winter, 1884: 11–21.
Cod: [999]
002 **De passionibus** (lib. 2) [Sp.], ed. K. Schuchhardt, *Andronici Rhodii qui fertur libelli περὶ παθῶν*, pt. 2 (De virtutibus et vitiis). Darmstadt: Winter, 1883: 19–31.
Cod: [2,391]
x01 **Ethicorum Nicomacheorum paraphrasis**.
Heylbut, pp. 1–233.
Cf. ANONYMA IN ETHICA NICOMACHEA COMMENTARIA (4033 003).

1778 **ANDROSTHENES** Perieg.
4 B.C.: Thasius
001 **Testimonia**, FGrH #711: 3C:592–593.
NQ
002 **Fragmenta**, FGrH #711: 3C:593–596.
Q

1125 **ANDROTION** Hist.
5–4 B.C.: Atheniensis
001 **Testimonia**, FGrH #324: 3B:60–62.
test. 4: *IG*² 2.61.
test. 5: *IG*² 2.216–217.
test. 7: *IG* 12.7, no. 5.
test. 12: *IG*² 2.212.
NQ
002 **Fragmenta**, FGrH #324: 3B:63–77.
Q

2703 **ANNA COMNENA** Hist.
A.D. 11–12: Constantinopolitana
Bibliography in progress
x01 **Epigrammata demonstrativa.**
App. Anth. 3.272, 416(?): Cf. EPIGRAMMATICI
in *App. Anth.* (7052 003).

1127 *ANONYMA DE MUSICA SCRIPTA BEL-*
LERMANNIANA
Varia
001 **Anonyma de musica scripta Bellermanniana,**
ed. D. Najock, *Anonyma de musica scripta*
Bellermanniana. Leipzig: Teubner, 1975: 1–33.
Cod: [4,931]

4026 *ANONYMA IN ARISTOTELIS ARTEM*
RHETORICAM COMMENTARIA
Varia
001 **In Aristotelis artem rhetoricam commenta-**
rium, ed. H. Rabe, *Anonymi et Stephani in*
artem rhetoricam commentaria [Commentaria
in Aristotelem Graeca 21.2. Berlin: Reimer,
1896]: 1–262.
Cod: [107,075]
002 **Fragmentum commentarii in Aristotelis rheto-**
rica, ed. Rabe, *op. cit.,* 323–329.
Cod: [2,244]
003 **Fragmentum paraphrasis in Aristotelis rhe-**
torica, ed. Rabe, *op. cit.,* 330–334.
Cod: [1,044]

4033 *ANONYMA IN ETHICA NICOMACHEA*
COMMENTARIA
Incertum
001 **In ethica Nicomachea ii–v commentaria,** ed.
G. Heylbut, *Eustratii et Michaelis et anonyma*
in ethica Nicomachea commentaria [Commenta-
ria in Aristotelem Graeca 20. Berlin: Reimer,
1892]: 122–255.
Cod: [53,937]
002 **In ethica Nicomachea vii commentaria,** ed.
Heylbut, *op. cit.,* 407–460.
Cod: [25,817]
003 **In ethica Nicomachea paraphrasis** (sub nomine
Heliodori), ed. G. Heylbut, *Heliodori in ethica*
Nicomachea paraphrasis [Commentaria in Aris-
totelem Graeca 19.2. Berlin: Reimer, 1889]: 1–
233.
Cod

1836 *ANONYMI AULODIA*
ante A.D. 1
001 **Anonymi aulodia** (*P. Oxy.* 15.1795), ed. D.
Young, *Theognis.* Leipzig: Teubner, 1971:
119–121.
Cf. et LYRICA ADESPOTA (CA) (0230 001).
Cf. et SCOLIA ALPHABETICA (0273 001).
Pap: [321]

1128 *ANONYMI COMMENTARIUS IN PLATO-*
NIS THEAETETUM
ante A.D. 2
001 **Commentarius in Platonis Theaetetum,** ed. H.

Diels and W. Schubart, *Anonymer Kommentar*
zu Platons Theaetet (Papyrus 9782). Berlin:
Weidmann, 1905: 3–51.
Pap: [12,334]

0227 *ANONYMI CURETUM HYMNUS*
4 B.C.
001 **Hymnus curetum,** ed. J.U. Powell, *Collectanea*
Alexandrina. Oxford: Clarendon Press, 1925
(repr. 1970): 160–161.
Epigr: [225]

1129 **ANONYMI DE BARBARISMO ET SOLOE-**
CISMO Gramm.
Varia
001 **De barbarismo et soloecismo,** ed. L.C. Valckenaer, *Ammonius.* Leipzig: Weigel, 1822: 176–
187.
Cod: [1,405]
002 **De barbarismo et soloecismo,** ed. A. Nauck,
Lexicon Vindobonense. St. Petersburg: Eggers,
1867 (repr. Hildesheim: Olms, 1965): 290–
293.
Cod: [348]

2584 *ANONYMI DE COMOEDIA*
A.D. 5?
001 **De comoedia,** ed. G. Kaibel, *Comicorum Grae-*
corum fragmenta, vol. 1.1 [*Poetarum Grae-*
corum fragmenta 6.1. Berlin: Weidmann,
1899]: 6–10.
Cod

0138 **ANONYMI EPIGRAMMATICI**
Varia
001 **Epigrammata,** AG 1.1–18, 21–22, 24–27, 29–
32, 37–50, 52–89, 91, 93–98, 100, 102–108,
110–121; **3.**1–19; **5.**2, 11, 26, 50–51, 65, 82–
84, 90–91, 95, 98–101, 135, 142, 168, 195b,
200–201, 205, 303–305, 310; **6.**6–8, 21, 23–24,
31, 37, 42, 44–45, 48–49, 51, 87, 169, 171–
172, 177, 194, 280, 283–284, 291, 341–344;
7.2b, 3, 5, 7, 10, 12, 23b, 28, 41–42, 44, 46–
48, 53, 56, 61–64, 82–84, 86, 90, 93–94, 119,
125, 128, 131–132, 134–135, 137, 139, 142–
144, 148, 151–152, 154–155, 157–158, 169,
179, 221, 224–225, 228, 257, 279, 298, 306,
309–311, 313, 319, 321–325, 327–340, 342–
343, 346–347, 350, 352, 356–361, 363, 416,
431, 449, 474, 482–483, 494, 507b, 543–544,
546, 558, 564, 570, 615–619, 621, 626, 667,
671–673, 676, 678, 689–691, 695, 699, 704,
714, 717, 723, 734, 737; **9.**15, 20–21, 31–32,
38, 47–49, 61, 65, 67–68, 74, 105, 108, 115,
115b, 116, 121–122, 124–127, 130–135, 137–
138, 141–142, 145–146, 148, 157–160, 162–
164, 177, 184–185, 187–191, 194–195, 198–
199, 207–213, 252, 317, 325, 328, 357–358,
362, 366, 371–376, 380–384, 386, 388/389,
392, 399, 431, 436, 448–449, 451–480, 483,
492–495, 498–501, 504–505, 510–512, 514–
515, 520–525, 527, 529–536, 538–540, 547,
553, 571, 574, 580–585, 589–596, 601, 606–

613, 615–618, 621–622, 632, 634–640, 646–
647, 655–656, 660, 666, 670–676, 678–680,
682–699, 701–705, 710, 713–714, 725–727,
729, 731, 733, 735–737, 741, 755, 759–761,
779–781, 783–786, 788–789, 799–807, 810–
822, 825–826; **10**.3, 9, 12, 30, 33, 39, 43, 106,
108–109, 111–112, 114–116, 118–119, 124b–
126; **11**.3, 8, 51–53, 56, 86, 108–109, 125–126,
145, 149, 151, 166, 193, 202–203, 220, 222,
244, 250, 260–262, 267–273, 282, 297–298,
316, 334–339, 342–345, 356, 358–360, 394,
411, 416–417, 420, 425–426, 442; **12**.17, 19,
39–40, 55, 61–62, 66–67, 69, 79, 87–90, 96,
99–100, 103–104, 107, 111–112, 115–116,
123–124, 130, 136, 140, 143, 145, 151–152,
155–156, 160; **13**.13, 15–17; **14**.2–62, 64–96,
100, 102–146, 149–150; **15**.1–8, 10–11, 18–19,
23, 39b, 41–50; **16**.4, 6, 9, 12, 15–19, 21–22,
27–29, 35, 42–48, 53–54, 56, 58, 62–67, 69–
74, 78, 83–86, 90–92, 96–102, 105–106, 112,
121–129, 135, 138, 140, 142, 145–146, 151,
156, 159, 162, 168–169, 174–175, 183, 185,
187, 189, 192, 202, 209, 217, 223–224, 227,
229, 246, 249–260, 262–266, 268–269, 271,
274, 279–281, 289, 292–295, 297–304, 309,
311–313, 318–322, 324, 326, 328–330, 335–
356, 358–378, 380–387, 387b–387c.
AG 9.137: Cf. et HADRIANUS Imperator (0195
001).
AG 9.388/389: Cf. et TRAJANUS Imperator
(1739 001).
Q: 30,623

7056 ANONYMI EPIGRAMMATICI (*App. Anth.*)
Varia
x01 **Epigrammata dedicatoria.**
App. Anth. 1.4–20, 22, 26–83, 85–91, 93–113,
118, 120–128, 130–133, 138–152, 154–158,
162–164, 166, 183, 197–198, 200–240, 243–
246, 249–256, 258–262, 265–298, 300–339,
341–372: Cf. EPIGRAMMATICI in *App. Anth.*
(7052 001).
x02 **Epigrammata sepulcralia.**
App. Anth. 2.1–3, 7–9, 11–16, 17–21, 27, 29,
31–45, 47–53, 121–123, 125–130, 132–133,
135–153, 155, 157–338, 340–379, 384–490,
492–495, 499–612, 614–624, 626–630, 632–
664, 666–746, 748–770: Cf. EPIGRAMMATICI
in *App. Anth.* (7052 002).
x03 **Epigrammata demonstrativa.**
App. Anth. 3.2–4, 15–16, 23–26, 30–32, 34,
36–42, 44–46, 49, 53–55, 57–58, 61, 69–70,
73–76, 83–84, 91–94, 100–103, 105, 107–110,
114–119, 121–122, 126–127, 130–131, 133–
144, 148–152, 162–165, 167–176, 178, 180–
213, 215–240, 242–253, 268–271, 277–283,
286–307, 311–410, 412–415, 417, 419–421:
Cf. EPIGRAMMATICI in *App. Anth.* (7052
003).
x04 **Epigrammata exhortatoria et supplicatoria.**
App. Anth. 4.10–11, 18–24, 27–29, 31–32, 37,
41–42, 44, 48–51, 54–73, 76, 78–88, 90–105,

108–110, 112–113, 121–140, 142–143: Cf. EPI-
GRAMMATICI in *App. Anth.* (7052 004).
x05 **Epigrammata irrisoria.**
App. Anth. 5.7–9, 11–12, 22–24, 26–28, 31–
33, 43–47, 50–57, 59–77: Cf. EPIGRAMMA-
TICI in *App. Anth.* (7052 005).
x06 **Oracula.**
App. Anth. 6.238–276, 299–301: Cf. EPI-
GRAMMATICI in *App. Anth.* (7052 006).
x07 **Aenigmata.**
App. Anth. 7.16–18, 21, 27–33, 46, 81: Cf.
EPIGRAMMATICI in *App. Anth.* (7052 007).

**2029 *ANONYMI GEOGRAPHIA IN SPHAERA
INTELLIGENDA***
post A.D. 2
001 **Anonymi summaria ratio geographiae in
sphaera intelligendae,** ed. K. Müller, *Geographi Graeci minores*, vol. 2. Paris: Didot, 1861
(repr. Hildesheim: Olms, 1965): 488–493.
Cod: [1,982]

**0092 *ANONYMI GEOGRAPHIAE EXPOSITIO
COMPENDIARIA***
Incertum
001 **Geographiae expositio compendiaria,** ed. K.
Müller, *Geographi Graeci minores*, vol. 2. Paris:
Didot, 1861 (repr. Hildesheim: Olms, 1965):
494–509.
Cod: [4,419]

0072 ANONYMI GRAMMATICI
Varia
001 **Supplementa artis Dionysianae vetusta,** ed. G.
Uhlig, *Grammatici Graeci*, vol. 1.1. Leipzig:
Teubner, 1883 (repr. Hildesheim: Olms,
1965): 105–132.
De prosodiis: pp. 105–114.
Definitio artis: pp. 115–117.
De pedibus et de metro heroico: pp. 117–124.
Tabula flexionum verbi τύπτω: pp. 125–132.
Cf. et DIONYSIUS THRAX Gramm. (0063 001).
Cod: 2,808
003 **Fragmentum grammaticum** (*P. Yale* 1.25 [inv.
446]) (fort. auctore Comano Naucratite), ed. A.
Wouters, *The grammatical papyri from Graeco-
Roman Egypt. Contributions to the study of the
'ars grammatica' in antiquity.* Brussels: Paleis
der Academiën, 1979: 49–52.
Pap
004 **Fragmentum grammaticum** (*P. Lit. Lond.* 182
= *P. Lond.* 126) (fort. auctore Tryphone Alexandrino), ed. Wouters, *op. cit.,* 67–73.
Pap
005 **Fragmentum grammaticum** (*P. Heid. Sieg-
mann* 197 [inv. 1893]), ed. Wouters, *op. cit.,*
127–129.
Pap
006 **Fragmentum grammaticum** (*PSI* sine numero
[inv. 505]), ed. Wouters, *op. cit.,* 136–137.
Pap

007 **Fragmentum grammaticum** (*P. Brooklyn* inv. 47.218.36), ed. Wouters, *op. cit.*, 139–140.
Pap

008 **Fragmentum grammaticum** (*P. Oslo* 2.13), ed. Wouters, *op. cit.*, 143–147.
Pap

009 **Fragmentum grammaticum** (*P. Iand.* 83a [inv. 664]), ed. Wouters, *op. cit.*, 158–159.
Pap

010 **Fragmentum grammaticum** (*P. Harr.* 59 [inv. 172b + 182h]), ed. Wouters, *op. cit.*, 166–169.
Pap

011 **Fragmentum grammaticum** (*P. Heid. Sieg-mann* 198 [inv. 201a]), ed. Wouters, *op. cit.*, 176–177.
Pap

012 **Fragmentum grammaticum** (*P. Iand.* 5.83 [inv. 555]), ed. Wouters, *op. cit.*, 185.
Pap

013 **Fragmentum grammaticum** (*P. Amh.* 2.21), ed. Wouters, *op. cit.*, 190–191.
Pap

014 **Fragmentum grammaticum** (*P. Ant.* 2.68), ed. Wouters, *op. cit.*, 199–201.
Pap

015 **Fragmentum grammaticum** (*PSI* 7.761), ed. Wouters, *op. cit.*, 205–206.
Pap

016 **Compendium catholicae Herodiani** (*P. Ant.* 2.67), ed. Wouters, *op. cit.*, 217–218.
Pap

017 **Commentarium in anonymi opus περὶ κλίσεως ὀνομάτων** (*P. Oxy.* 15.1801v), ed. Wouters, *op. cit.*, 226–228.
Pap

018 **Compendium Herodiani operis περὶ κλίσεως ὀνομάτων** (*P. Flor.* inv. 3005), ed. Wouters, *op. cit.*, 232–233.
Pap

019 **De participiis** (*P. Rain.* 1.19 [inv. 29772]), ed. Wouters, *op. cit.*, 238–239.
Pap

020 **Fragmentum grammaticum** (*PSI* 7.849), ed. Wouters, *op. cit.*, 255–258.
Pap

021 **Fragmentum grammaticum** (*P. Oxy.* 3.469), ed. Wouters, *op. cit.*, 264–265.
Pap

022 **Fragmentum grammaticum** (*P. Iand.* 1.5), ed. Wouters, *op. cit.*, 269–270.
Pap

023 **Περὶ Αἰολίδος** (?) (fragmentum) (*P. Bouriant* 8 [*P. Sorbonne* inv. 833]), ed. Wouters, *op. cit.*, 276–282.
Pap

x01 **Περὶ δυσκλίτων ῥημάτων** (*P. Rain.* 3.33A). Wouters, pp. 243–246.
Cf. HERACLIDES Gramm. (1408 002).

1139 **ANONYMI HISTORICI** (FGrH)
Varia

001 **Enchiridion** (*P. Ryl.* 22), FGrH #18: 1A:182–183.
fr. 1.
Pap

002 **Heraclis historia** (*Tabula Albana*) (*IG* 14.1293), FGrH #40: 1A:261–263.
fr. 1.
Epigr

003 **Anonymi ex historiis Polybii**, FGrH #83: 2A:189–191.
frr. 1–4.
Q

004 **Fragmenta historica**, FGrH #105: 2A:504–507.
frr. 1–8.
fr. 1: *P. Ryl.* 18.
fr. 2: Sicyonis historia (fort. auctore Aristotele vel Ephoro vel Menaechmo), *P. Oxy.* 11.1365.
fr. 3: Epitome historiae Herodoti (fort. auctore Theopompo Chio), *P. Oxy.* 6.857.
fr. 4: (fort. auctore Theopompo Chio), *P. Rain.*
fr. 5: *P. Berol.* inv. 13361.
fr. 6: (fort. auctore Theopompo Chio vel Anaximene Lampsaceno), *P. Hibeh* 1.15.
fr. 7: *P. Oxy.* 6.867.
fr. 8: *P. Oxy.* 7.1014.
Pap

005 **Alexandri historia** (*P. Oxy.* 15.1798), FGrH #148: 2B:816–818.
frr. 1–6, 44–45.
Cf. et 1139 039–040.
Pap

006 **Alexandri historia** (*Cod. Sabbaiticum* 29), FGrH #151: 2B:819–822.
fr. 1.
Cod

007 **De historia Alexandri**, FGrH #153: 2B:823–828.
frr. 1–15.
fr. 1: *P. Oxy.* 1.13.
fr. 7: *P. Freib.* 7–8.
fr. 8: *P. Oxy.* 2.216.
fr. 9: *P. Berol.* inv. 13044.
Q, Pap

008 **De historia diadochorum** (epitome Heidelbergensis), FGrH #155: 2B:835–837.
frr. 1–4.
Cod

009 **De Pyrrho**, FGrH #159: 2B:884.
test. 1.
NQ

010 **Belli Syrii tertii annales** (*P. Petrie* 2.45; 3.144), FGrH #160: 2B:885–887.
fr. 1.
Pap

011 **De Hannibale**, FGrH #180: 2B:907–909.
frr. 1–5.
Q

012 **De Marco Aurelio Antonino** (testimonium), FGrH #202: 2B:934.
test. 1.
NQ

013 **De bello Parthico**, FGrH #203: 2B:934–938.
frr. 1–9.
Q

014 **Anonymus Corinthius**, FGrH #204: 2B:938–939.
frr. 1–4.
Q

015 **Anonymus Milesius**, FGrH #205: 2B:939.
fr. 1.
Q

016 **Anonymus philosophus**, FGrH #206: 2B:940.
fr. 1.
Q

017 **Chronicon Romanum** (*IG* 14.1297), FGrH #252: 2B:1151–1152.
frr. A–B.
Epigr

018 **Chronicon Oxyrhynchi** (*P. Oxy.* 1.12), FGrH #255: 2B:1153–1156.
Pap

019 **Chronicon Olympicum** (fort. auctore Phlegonte), FGrH #257a: 2B:1194–1196.
frr. 1–11: *P. Oxy.* 17.2082.
Cf. et Publius Aelius PHLEGON (0585 002–003).
Pap

020 **Chronicon Archontum** (*P. Oxy.* 13.1613), FGrH #258: 2B:1197.
fr. 1.
Pap

021 **Εὐμολπιδῶν πάτρια** (testimonium), FGrH #355: 3B:217.
test. 1.
NQ

022 **Εὐπατριδῶν πάτρια** (fragmentum), FGrH #356: 3B:217.
fr. 1.
Q

023 **De sacris Atheniensibus**, FGrH #368: 3B:229–230.
frr. 1–8.
Q

024 **Anonymus periegeta** (*P. Hawara* 80/81), FGrH #369: 3B:230–231.
frr. 1–2.
fr. 1: *P. Hawara* 81.
fr. 2: *P. Hawara* 80.
Pap

025 **De finibus urbis**, FGrH #375: 3B:241.
fr. 1.
Q

026 **Victores Olympici** (fort. auctore Phlegonte vel Eratosthene) (*P. Oxy.* 2.222), FGrH #415: 3B:307–309.
frr. 1–2.
Cf. et 1139 041.
Pap

027 **Chronicon Pergamenum**, FGrH #506: 3B:483–484.
fr. 1: *O. Gr. Inscr. Sel.* 264.
Epigr

028 **Anagraphe Sicyonia**, FGrH #550: 3B:536.
frr. 1–2.
Q

029 **Anonymus de conditu Hermopolis**, FGrH #637: 3C:184–185.
fr. 1: *P. Strassburg* 481.
Pap

030 **Apophthegmata Romana**, FGrH #839: 3C: 905–908.
fr. 1.
Cod

031 **De agrimensore Syriae** (fort. auctore Xenophonte quodam), FGrH #849: 3C:935.
fr. 1.
Q

032 **Anonymi de imperatore Aureliano**, FGrH #213-215: 2B:944.
Q

033 **Anonymus exegeta**, FGrH #352: 3B:214–215.
fr. 1.
Q

034 **De Lesbo**, FGrH #479: 3B:443–444.
frr. 1–2.
Q

035 **De Nilo**, FGrH #647: 3C:199–203.
frr. 1–3.
Q, Cod

036 **Scriptores de Athenis**, FGrH #329: 3B:161–162.
frr. 1–8.
Q

037 **De Theramene** (*P. Mich.* 5982), ed. H.J. Mette, "Die 'Kleinen' griechischen Historiker heute," *Lustrum* 21 (1978) 11.
FGrH #64 bis.
Pap

038 **Philippica** (*P. Ryl.* 3.490), ed. Mette, *op. cit.*, 17–18.
FGrH #115 bis, fr. 1.
Pap

039 **Alexandri historia** (*P. Oxy.* 17.2081), ed. Mette, *op. cit.*, 19.
FGrH #148, fr. 55.
Cf. et 1139 005, 040.
Pap

040 **Alexandri historia** (*P. Hamb.* 652), ed. Mette, *op. cit.*, 19–20.
FGrH #148 bis.
Cf. et 1139 005, 039.
Pap

041 **Victores olympici** (*P. Oxy.* 23.2381), ed. Mette, *op. cit.*, 29.
FGrH #415, fr. 3.
Cf. et 1139 026.
Pap

x01 **Epistula cuidam Macedoniae regi** (fort. auctore Hieronymo Cardiano) (*P. Oxy.* 1.13).
FGrH #153, fr. 1.
Cf. ANONYMI HISTORICI (FGrH) (1139 007).

x02 **De Alexandri deificatione** (*P. Freib.* 7–8).
FGrH #153, fr. 7.
Cf. ANONYMI HISTORICI (FGrH) (1139 007).

x03 **Anonymus orator** (*P. Oxy.* 2.216).
FGrH #153, fr. 8.
Cf. ANONYMI HISTORICI (FGrH) (1139 007).

x04 **Alexandri Magni historia** (*P. Berol. inv.* 13044).
FGrH #153, fr. 9.
Cf. ANONYMI HISTORICI (FGrH) (1139 007).

0228 *ANONYMI HYMNUS IN DACTYLOS IDAEOS*
ante 4 B.C.

001 **Hymnus in Dactylos Idaeos** (*IG* 12.9.259), ed. J.U. Powell, *Collectanea Alexandrina*. Oxford: Clarendon Press, 1925 (repr. 1970): 171–172.
Epigr: [149]

4027 *ANONYMI IN ARISTOTELIS CATEGO-RIAS PARAPHRASIS*
A.D. 14?

001 **Paraphrasis categoriarum**, ed. M. Hayduck, *Anonymi in Aristotelis categorias paraphrasis* [*Commentaria in Aristotelem Graeca* 23.2. Berlin: Reimer, 1883]: 1–72.
Cod: [34,709]

9004 *ANONYMI IN LIBRUM ALTERUM ANA-LYTICORUM POSTERIORUM COMMEN-TARIUM*
Incertum

001 **Anonymi in analyticorum posteriorum librum alterum commentarium**, ed. M. Wallies, *Ioannis Philoponi in Aristotelis analytica posteriora commentaria cum anonymo in librum ii* [*Commentaria in Aristotelem Graeca* 13.3. Berlin: Reimer, 1909]: 547–603.
Cod: [19,749]

4032 *ANONYMI IN LIBRUM PRIMUM ANALY-TICORUM POSTERIORUM COMMENTA-RIUM*
A.D. 12?

001 **In primum librum analyticorum posteriorum commentarium**, ed. M. Hayduck, *Eustratii in analyticorum posteriorum librum secundum commentarium* [*Commentaria in Aristotelem Graeca* 21.1. Berlin: Reimer, 1907]: vii–xviii.
Cod: [5,487]

0642 *ANONYMI IN SOPHISTICOS ELENCHOS PARAPHRASIS*
A.D. 14

001 **In Aristotelis sophisticos elenchos paraphrasis**, ed. M. Hayduck, *Anonymi in Aristotelis sophisticos elenchos paraphrasis* [*Commentaria in Aristotelem Graeca* 23.4. Berlin: Reimer, 1884]: 1–68.
Cod: [31,808]

0721 **ANONYMI MEDICI**
Varia

001 Ὀνομασιῶν τῶν κατὰ ἄνθρωπον πρῶτον, ed.

C. Daremberg and C.É. Ruelle, *Oeuvres de Rufus d'Éphèse*. Paris: Imprimerie Nationale, 1879 (repr. Amsterdam: Hakkert, 1963): 233–236.
Cod: 1,449

002 Ὀνοματοποιία τῆς ἀνθρώπου φύσεως, ed. Daremberg and Ruelle, *op. cit.*, 599–600.
Cod: 579

003 Περὶ χροιᾶς τοῦ αἵματος τοῦ ἀπὸ φλεβοτομίας ἐκ τῆς ἰατρικῆς τῶν Περσῶν, ed. J.L. Ideler, *Physici et medici Graeci minores*, vol. 1. Berlin: Reimer, 1841 (repr. Amsterdam: Hakkert, 1963): 293.
Cod: 143

004 **De generatione et semine**, ed. Ideler, *op. cit.*, vol. 1, 294–296.
Cod: 831

005 **De corporis hominis natura**, ed. Ideler, *op. cit.*, vol. 1, 301–302.
Cod: 306

006 **De natura hominis**, ed. Ideler, *op. cit.*, vol. 1, 303–304.
Cod: 541

007 **Mensium adornatio**, ed. Ideler, *op. cit.*, vol. 1, 421–422.
Cod: 219

008 **De duodecim mensium natura**, ed. Ideler, *op. cit.*, vol. 1, 423–429.
Cod: 1,858

009 **De diaeta**, ed. Ideler, *op. cit.*, vol. 2 (1842; repr. 1963): 194–198.
Cod: 1,288

010 **De alimentis**, ed. Ideler, *op. cit.*, vol. 2, 257–281.
Cod: 6,229

011 Περὶ λυκανθρωπίας, ed. Ideler, *op. cit.*, vol. 2, 282.
Cod: 223

012 **De urinis secundum Syros**, ed. Ideler, *op. cit.*, vol. 2, 303–304.
Cod: 463

013 **De urinis secundum Persos**, ed. Ideler, *op. cit.*, vol. 2, 305–306.
Cod: 380

014 **Commentatio de urinis**, ed. Ideler, *op. cit.*, vol. 2, 307–316.
Cod: 2,762

015 **De pulsibus**, ed. Ideler, *op. cit.*, vol. 2, 317.
Cod: 115

016 **De urinis in febribus**, ed. Ideler, *op. cit.*, vol. 2, 323–327.
Cod: 1,435

017 **De cibis**, ed. F.Z. Ermerins, *Anecdota medica Graeca*. Leiden: Luchtmans, 1840 (repr. Amsterdam: Hakkert, 1963): 225–275.
Cod: 4,155

019 Διάγνωσις περὶ τῶν ἕξεων καὶ χρονίων νοσημάτων, ed. R. Fuchs, "Anecdota medica Graeca," *Rheinisches Museum* 49 (1894) 540–548.
Cod: 3,119

020 Περὶ τῆς τῶν πυρετῶν διαφορᾶς, ed. Darem-

berg and Ruelle, *op. cit.*, 601–610.
Cod: 4,571

021 Περὶ τροφῶν δυνάμεως, ed. A. Delatte, *Anec-dota Atheniensia et alia*, vol. 2. Paris: Droz, 1939: 467–479.
Cod: 3,246

022 **In aphorismos [Hippocratis]**, ed. H. Flashar, "Beiträge zur spätantiken Hippokratesdeu-tung," *Hermes* 90 (1962) 404–405.
Cod: 425

023 **Physiognomonica**, ed. R. Foerster, *Scriptores physiognomonici Graeci et Latini*, vol. 2. Leip-zig: Teubner, 1893: 225–232.
Cod: 1,224

024 Ὀνόματα τῶν ἰατρικῶν ἐργαλείων κατὰ στοι-χεῖα οἷς ἐν ταῖς χειρουργίαις χρώμεθα, ed. F.R. Dietz, *Severus Iatrosophista* [*Diss. med. Königs-berg* (1836)]: 46–48.
Cod: 105

025 **Fragmenta varia**, ed. R. Fuchs, "Anecdota medica Graeca," *Rheinisches Museum* 50 (1895) 577–581.
Cod: 670

026 Διάγνωσις περὶ τῶν ὀξέων καὶ χρονίων νοση-μάτων, ed. R. Fuchs, "Aus Themisons Werk über die acuten und chronischen Krankhei-ten," *Rheinisches Museum* 58 (1903) 69–114.
Cod: 10,594

x01 **Theriaca** (ap. Galenum).
K14.100–102.
Cf. GALENUS Med. (0057 078).

4037 **ANONYMI PARADOXOGRAPHI**
Varia

001 **De incredibilibus** (excerpta Vaticana), ed. N. Festa, *Palaephati περὶ ἀπίστων* [*Mythographi Graeci* 3.2. Leipzig: Teubner, 1902]: 88–99.
Cod: [1,536]

002 **Tractatus de mulieribus**, ed. A. Westermann, *Scriptores rerum mirabilium Graeci*. Braun-schweig: Westermann, 1839 (repr. Amsterdam: Hakkert, 1963): 213–218.
Cod: [1,028]

003 Τίνες οἶκοι ἀνάστατοι διὰ γυναῖκας ἐγένοντο, ed. Westermann, *op. cit.*, 218.
Cod: [73]

004 **De fratribus amicis**, ed. Westermann, *op. cit.*, 219.
Cod: [77]

005 **De amicis**, ed. Westermann, *op. cit.*, 219–220.
Cod: [71]

006 **De Cleobi et Bitone**, ed. Westermann, *op. cit.*, 220.
Cod: [20]

007 **De impiis**, ed. Westermann, *op. cit.*, 220–222.
Cod: [294]

008 **De transformationibus**, ed. Westermann, *op. cit.*, 222–223.
Cod: [254]

0598 **ANONYMI RHETORES**
Varia

001 Περὶ μεγαλοπρεπείας (*P. Oxy.* 3.410), ed. L. Radermacher, *Artium scriptores* [*Österreich-ische Akademie der Wissenschaften*, Philosoph.-hist. Kl., Sitzungsberichte, Bd. 227, Abh. 3. Vienna: Rohrer, 1951]: 231–232.
Pap: [389]

002 Περὶ τροπῶν, ed. L. Spengel, *Rhetores Graeci*, vol. 3. Leipzig: Teubner, 1856 (repr. Frankfurt am Main: Minerva, 1966): 227–229.
Cod: [428]

1130 **ANONYMI VALENTINIANI** Theol.
A.D. 2

001 **Fragmenta**, ed. W. Völker, *Quellen zur Ge-schichte der christlichen Gnosis*. Tübingen: Mohr, 1932: 60–63, 93–95.
Epistula cuiusdam Valentiniani: pp. 60–63.
Exegesis in Evangelium secundum Joannem: pp. 93–95.
Q

1131 **ANONYMUS AD AVIRCIUM MARCEL-LUM CONTRA CATAPHRYGAS**
A.D. 2–3

001 **Ad Avircium Marcellum contra Cataphrygas**, ed. M.J. Routh, *Reliquiae sacrae*, vol. 2, 2nd edn. Oxford: Oxford University Press, 1846 (repr. Hildesheim: Olms, 1974): 183–193.
Q: [1,323]

1132 **ANONYMUS ALEXANDRI** Phil.
4/3 B.C.

001 **Fragmenta**, ed. H. Thesleff, *The Pythagorean texts of the Hellenistic period*. Åbo: Åbo Aka-demi, 1965: 234–237.
Q: 960

ANONYMUS DE BLEMYOMACHIA
Cf. OLYMPIODORUS Hist. (2590 002).

2117 **ANONYMUS DE METRORUM RATIONE**
A.D. 3

001 **Fragmentum** (*P. Berol.* 9734r), ed. E. Heitsch, *Die griechischen Dichterfragmente der röm-ischen Kaiserzeit*, vol. 1, 2nd edn. Göttingen: Vandenhoeck & Ruprecht, 1963: 204.
Pap: [64]

1813 **ANONYMUS DE PLANTIS AEGYPTIIS**
ante A.D. 2

001 **Fragmentum** (*P. Oxy.* 15.1796), ed. Heitsch, *Die griechischen Dichterfragmente der röm-ischen Kaiserzeit*, vol. 1, 2nd edn. Göttingen: Vandenhoeck & Ruprecht, 1963: 203–204.
Pap: [142]

0282 **ANONYMUS DE VIRIBUS HERBARUM**
A.D. 3

001 **Carminis de viribus herbarum fragmentum**, ed. E. Heitsch, *Die griechischen Dichterfrag-mente der römischen Kaiserzeit*, vol. 2. Göttin-

gen: Vandenhoeck & Ruprecht, 1964: 23–38.
Cod: [1,434]

1133 **ANONYMUS DIODORI** Phil.
4 B.C.
001 **Fragmenta**, ed. H. Thesleff, *The Pythagorean texts of the Hellenistic period.* Åbo: Åbo Akademi, 1965: 229–234.
Q: 1,629

4005 **ANONYMUS Discipulus Isidori Milesii** Mech.
A.D. 6
001 **Euclidis elementorum qui fertur liber xv**, ed. E.S. Stamatis (post J.L. Heiberg), *Euclidis elementa*, vol. 5.1, 2nd edn. Leipzig: Teubner, 1977: 23–38.
Cf. et EUCLIDES Geom. (1799 001).
Cod: 2,816

1779 **ANONYMUS EPICUREUS** Phil.
ante A.D. 1
001 **Fragmenta** (*P. Herc.* 176), ed. A. Vogliano, *Epicuri et Epicureorum scripta in Herculanensibus papyris servata.* Berlin: Weidmann, 1928: 23–54.
frr. 1–5.
Pap: [3,770]
002 **Fragmenta** (ad *P. Herc.* 176 pertinentia), ed. Vogliano, *op. cit.*, 91–96.
frr. 4–34.
Pap
003 **Vita Philonidis** (*P. Herc.* 1044), ed. W. Crönert, "Der Epikureer Philonides," *Sitzungsberichte der königlich preussischen Akademie der Wissenschaften zu Berlin*, Jahrgang 1900. Berlin: Reimer, 1900: 942–959.
Pap
004 **Fragmenta** (*P. Oxy.* 2.215), ed. W. Schmid, "Chi è l'autore del Pap. 215?," *Miscellanea di studi alessandrini in memoriam di Augusto Rostagni.* Turin: Erasmo, 1963: 40–44.
Pap
x01 **Fragmenta** (*P. Herc.* 346).
Vogliano, pp. 77–89.
Cf. POLYSTRATUS Phil. (1629 002).

1134 **ANONYMUS IAMBLICHI** Phil.
5 B.C.?
001 **Fragmenta**, ed. H. Diels and W. Kranz, *Die Fragmente der Vorsokratiker*, vol. 2, 6th edn. Berlin: Weidmann, 1952 (repr. Dublin: 1966): 400–404.
frr. 1–7.
Q

ANONYMUS IN MONTANUM
Cf. ANONYMUS AD AVIRCIUM MARCELLUM CONTRA CATAPHRYGAS (1131).

9003 **ANONYMUS LEXICOGRAPHUS**
ante A.D. 12
001 **Fragmenta quattuor apud Eustathium**, ed. H.

Erbse, *Untersuchungen zu den attizistischen Lexika* [*Abhandlungen der deutschen Akademie der Wissenschaften zu Berlin*, Philosoph.-hist. Kl. Berlin: Akademie-Verlag, 1950]: 222.
Q: [66]

0643 **ANONYMUS LONDINENSIS** Med.
A.D. 1
001 **Iatrica** (fort. auctore Menone) (*P. Brit. Mus.* inv. 137), ed. H. Diels, *Anonymi Londinensis ex Aristotelis iatricis Menoniis et aliis medicis eclogae* [*Commentaria in Aristotelem Graeca*, suppl. 3.1. Berlin: Reimer, 1893]: 1–74.
Pap: [13,514]
002 **Fragmenta**, ed. Diels, *op. cit.*, 75–76.
Pap: [203]

0799 **ANONYMUS NAUCRATITES** Med.
ante A.D. 2
x01 **Fragmentum ap. Galenum**.
K12.764.
Cf. GALENUS Med. (0057 076).

1119 **ANONYMUS NEAPOLITANUS** Med.
fiq Gaius vel Lycus Neapolitanus
ante A.D. 2
Cf. et GAIUS Med. (0822).
Cf. et LYCUS Med. (0955).
x01 **Fragmenta ap. Galenum**.
K12.746, 751, 752, 755, 763, 986; 13.86, 87, 183, 825, 938, 976, 1020, 1030.
Cf. GALENUS Med. (0057 076, 077).

0800 **ANONYMUS OLYMPIONICES** Med.
ante A.D. 2
x01 **Fragmentum ap. Galenum**.
K12.753.
Cf. GALENUS Med. (0057 076).

ANONYMUS περὶ ἐρωτήσεως καὶ ἀποκρίσεως
Cf. ANONYMA IN ARISTOTELIS ARTEM RHETORICAM COMMENTARIA (4026 003).

1135 **ANONYMUS PHOTII** Phil.
3/2 B.C.
001 **Fragmenta**, ed. H. Thesleff, *The Pythagorean texts of the Hellenistic period.* Åbo: Åbo Akademi, 1965: 237–242.
Q: 2,008

1136 **ANONYMUS PRESBYTER** Scr. Eccl.
A.D. 2?
001 **Fragmentum**, ed. M.J. Routh, *Reliquiae sacrae*, vol. 1, 2nd edn. Oxford: Oxford University Press, 1846 (repr. Hildesheim: Olms, 1974): 385.
Q: [76]

1137 **ANONYMUS PYTHAGOREUS** Astrol.
Incertum
001 **De quaternionibus**, ed. S. Weinstock, *Codices Britannici* [*Catalogus codicum astrologorum*

Graecorum 9.1. Brussels: Academia, 1951]:
173–179.
Cod

ANONYMUS RHYTHMICUS
Cf. ARISTOXENUS Mus. (0088 005).

2002 **ANONYMUS SEGUERIANUS** Rhet.
A.D. 3
001 Τέχνη τοῦ πολιτικοῦ λόγου, ed. L. Spengel,
Rhetores Graeci, vol. 1. Leipzig: Teubner, 1853
(repr. Frankfurt am Main: Minerva, 1966):
427–460.
Cod

0705 **ANONYMUS SENEX** Med.
ante A.D. 6: Indus
x01 **Fragmentum ap. Aëtium** (lib. 11).
Daremberg-Ruelle, p. 571.
Cf. AËTIUS Med. (0718 011).

1086 **ANONYMUS THEBANUS** Med.
fiq Hierax Thebanus
ante A.D. 2
Cf. et HIERAX Med. (0930).
x01 **Fragmenta ap. Galenum**.
K12.489; **13**.739.
Cf. GALENUS Med. (0057 076–077).

ANONYMUS VATICANUS
Cf. PARADOXOGRAPHUS VATICANUS (0582).

0215 **ANTAGORAS** Epic.
3 B.C.: Rhodius
001 **Epigrammata**, ed. J.U. Powell, *Collectanea Alexandrina*. Oxford: Clarendon Press, 1925
(repr. 1970): 120–121.
frr. 1–3.
Q: [118]
002 **Epigrammata**, AG 7.103; **9**.147.
Q: 61
x01 **Epigramma demonstrativum**.
App. Anth. 3.60: Cf. EPIGRAMMATICI in *App.
Anth.* (7052 003).

2389 **ANTANDER** Hist.
4/3 B.C.?: Syracusanus
001 **Testimonia**, FGrH #565: 3B:580.
NQ

2322 **ANTENOR** Hist.
ante A.D. 2: Creticus
001 **Testimonia**, FGrH #463: 3B:400–401.
NQ
002 **Fragmenta**, FGrH #463: 3B:401.
fr. 3: *P. Oxy.* 15.1802.
Q, Pap

0775 **ANTHAEUS** Med.
ante A.D. 2
x01 **Fragmentum ap. Galenum**.
K12.764.
Cf. GALENUS Med. (0057 076).

7000 **ANTHOLOGIA GRAECA**
Varia
001 **Anthologia Graeca**, ed. H. Beckby, *Anthologia
Graeca*, 4 vols., 2nd edn. Munich: Heimeran,
1–2:1965; 3–4:1968: **1**:122–181, 186–210,
218–230, 240–252, 258–436, 444–652; **2**:14–
438, 448–568; **3**:12–468, 474–538, 546–764;
4:12–144, 150–168, 174–248, 258–300, 306–
512.
Cod: 139,201

0759 **ANTHUS** Med.
ante A.D. 6
x01 **Fragmentum ap. Aëtium** (lib. 12).
Kostomiris, p. 104.
Cf. AËTIUS Med. (0718 012).

1140 **ANTICLIDES** Hist.
3 B.C.: Atheniensis
001 **Testimonia**, FGrH #140: 2B:799.
NQ
002 **Fragmenta**, FGrH #140: **2B**:799–803; **3B**:743
addenda.
Q

1884 **ANTIDAMAS** Hist.
Incertum: Heracleopolitanus
001 **Fragmenta**, FGrH #152: 2B:822–823.
Q

0409 **ANTIDOTUS** Comic.
4 B.C.
001 **Fragmenta**, ed. T. Kock, *Comicorum Atticorum fragmenta*, vol. 2. Leipzig: Teubner,
1884: 410–411.
frr. 1–4.
Q: 70
002 **Fragmenta**, ed. A. Meineke, *Fragmenta comicorum Graecorum*, vol. 3. Berlin: Reimer, 1840
(repr. De Gruyter, 1970): 528–529.
Q: 72

1945 **ANTIGENES** Hist.
ante 3 B.C.
001 **Testimonium**, FGrH #141: 2B:804.
NQ
002 **Fragmenta**, FGrH #141: 2B:804.
Q
003 **Fragmentum**, ed. H.J. Mette, "Die 'Kleinen'
griechischen Historiker heute," *Lustrum* 21
(1978) 19.
fr. 3.
Q

0139 **ANTIGENES** Lyr.
5 B.C.
x01 **Epigramma**.
AG 13.28.
Cf. BACCHYLIDES Lyr. (0199 009).

0618 **ANTIGONI EPISTULA**
4/3 B.C.
001 **Epistula**, ed. R. Hercher, *Epistolographi Graeci*.

Paris: Didot, 1873 (repr. Amsterdam: Hakkert, 1965): 107.
Q: [105]

1142 **ANTIGONUS** Astrol.
A.D. 2: Nicaeanus
001 **Imperatoris Hadriani genitura**, ed. W. Kroll, *Codices Vindobonenses* [*Catalogus codicum astrologorum Graecorum* 6. Brussels: Lamertin, 1900]: 67–71.
Q

2547 **ANTIGONUS** Hist.
3 B.C.?
001 **Testimonia**, FGrH #816: 3C:892–893.
NQ
002 **Fragmenta**, FGrH #816: 3C:893.
Q

2521 **ANTIGONUS** Hist.
2 B.C.?: Macedo
001 **Fragmentum**, FGrH #775: 3C:770.
Q

0776 **ANTIGONUS** Med.
ante A.D. 2
x01 **Fragmenta ap. Galenum.**
K12.557–558.
Cf. GALENUS Med. (0057 076).

0568 **ANTIGONUS** Paradox.
3 B.C.: Carystius
001 **Historiarum mirabilium collectio**, ed. A. Giannini, *Paradoxographorum Graecorum reliquiae.* Milan: Istituto Editoriale Italiano, 1965: 32–106.
Cod: [6,710]
003 **Fragmenta**, ed. Giannini, *op. cit.*, 108–109.
frr. 3–6.
Q: [148]
004 **Fragmentum et titulus**, ed. H. Lloyd-Jones and P. Parsons, *Supplementum Hellenisticum.* Berlin: De Gruyter, 1983: 19–20.
frr. 47, 50.
Q: [15]
002 **Epigramma**, AG 9.406.
Q: 40
x01 **Fragmenta** (ap. Paradoxographum Vaticanum 11, 36).
Giannini, PGR, pp. 334, 340.
Cf. PARADOXOGRAPHUS VATICANUS (0582 001).

2173 **ANTILEON** Hist.
2–1 B.C.?
001 **Fragmenta**, FGrH #247: 2B:1130.
Q

0239 **ANTIMACHUS** Eleg. et Epic.
5/4 B.C.: Colophonius
001 **Fragmenta**, ed. M.L. West, *Iambi et elegi Graeci*, vol. 2. Oxford: Clarendon Press, 1972: 38, 40–43.

frr. 57, 66–67, 70, 72–73, 93, 99, 100, 102, 191–192.
Q, Pap: [114]
002 **Fragmenta**, ed. B. Wyss, *Antimachi Colophonii reliquiae.* Berlin: Weidmann, 1936: 1–7, 9–32, 36–50, 52–60, 68–72.
frr. 1–11, 15, 19–25, 27–28, 30, 32–37, 39–40, 42–50, 52–54, 57, 66–67, 70–74, 76–79, 82, 84–87, 89–91, 93–94, 96–97, 99–101, 105–123, 126, 149, 151–152, 154–159.
Q, Pap: [958]
003 **Epigramma**, AG 9.321.
Q: 41
004 **Fragmenta**, ed. H. Lloyd-Jones and P. Parsons, *Supplementum Hellenisticum.* Berlin: De Gruyter, 1983: 21–33.
frr. 52–79.
frr. 52–61: *P. Oxy.* 30.2518.
frr. 62–75: *P. Oxy.* 30.2516.
fr. 76: *P. Ant.* 120b.
Q, Pap: [376]

1141 **ANTIMACHUS** Epic.
8 B.C.: Teius
Cf. et EPIGONI (1351).
001 **Fragmentum** [Dub.], ed. J.U. Powell, *Collectanea Alexandrina.* Oxford: Clarendon Press, 1925 (repr. 1970): 247.
fr. 3.
Q: [14]
002 **Fragmentum**, ed. G. Kinkel, *Epicorum Graecorum fragmenta*, vol. 1. Leipzig: Teubner, 1877: 247.
fr. 1.
Q: [8]

0044 ***ANTIOCHI REGIS EPISTULAE***
Incertum
001 **Epistulae**, ed. R. Hercher, *Epistolographi Graeci.* Paris: Didot, 1873 (repr. Amsterdam: Hakkert, 1965): 108–109.
Q: [491]

1993 **ANTIOCHIANUS** Hist.
A.D. 2
001 **Fragmentum**, FGrH #207: 2B:940.
Q

1144 **ANTIOCHUS** Astrol.
1 B.C./A.D. 1: Atheniensis
001 **Fragmenta** (ex cod. Florentino 11), ed. A. Olivieri, *Codices Florentini* [*Catalogus codicum astrologorum Graecorum* 1. Brussels: Lamertin, 1898]: 108–113.
Cod
002 **Fragmenta** (ex cod. Neapolitano 19), ed. D. Bassi, F. Cumont, A. Martini and A. Olivieri, *Codices Italici* [*Catalogus codicum astrologorum Graecorum* 4. Brussels: Lamertin, 1903]: 154–155.
Cod
003 **Fragmenta** (ex cod. Monac. 7), ed. F. Boll, *Codices Germanici* [*Catalogus codicum astrolo-*

gorum Graecorum 7. Brussels: Lamertin, 1908]: 107–113, 114–116, 126–128.
Cod

004 **Fragmenta** (ex cod. Paris.), ed. P. Boudreaux, *Codices Parisini* [*Catalogus codicum astrologorum Graecorum* 8.3. Brussels: Lamertin, 1912]: 104–119.
Cod

005 **Fragmenta** (ex cod. Scorial. 24), ed. K.O. Zuretti, *Codices Hispanienses* [*Catalogus codicum astrologorum Graecorum* 11.2. Brussels: Lamertin, 1934]: 109–114.
Cod

0112 **ANTIOCHUS** Epigr.
A.D. 1–2

001 **Epigrammata**, AG 11.412, 422.
Q: 63

1145 **ANTIOCHUS** Hist.
5 B.C.: Syracusanus

001 **Testimonia**, FGrH #555: 3B:543.
NQ

002 **Fragmenta**, FGrH #555: 3B:543–551.
Q

1879 **ANTIOCHUS** Hist.
5 B.C.
Cf. et ANTIOCHUS-PHERECYDES Hist. (2221).

001 **Fragmenta**, FGrH #29: 1A:213–214.
Q

0778 **ANTIOCHUS** Med.
fiq Paccius Antiochus
A.D. 1?: Romanus
Cf. et PACCIUS ANTIOCHUS Med. (1013).

x01 **Fragmentum ap. Paulum**.
CMG, vol. 9.2, p. 286.
Cf. PAULUS Med. (0715 001).

x02 **Fragmentum ap. Aetium** (lib. 3).
CMG, vol. 8.1, p. 306.
Cf. AËTIUS Med. (0718 003).

1143 **ANTIOCHUS** Phil.
2–1 B.C.: Ascalonius

001 **Fragmenta**, ed. G. Luck, *Der akademiker Antiochus*. Bern: Haupt, 1953: 73, 75–82, 85–86, 88, 94.
frr. 1, 2, 7, 12, 13, 15, 18, 23, 31–33, 35–38, 54–55, 58, 65–66, 86.
Q, Pap: [1,263]

2503 **Publius Anteius ANTIOCHUS** Soph.
A.D. 2/3: Aegaeus

001 **Testimonia**, FGrH #747: 3C:731–732.
test. 2: *Inscr. Argos.*
NQ

002 **Titulus**, FGrH #747: 3C:732.
NQ

0777 **ANTIOCHUS Philometor** <Med.>
1 B.C.: Seleuciensis

x01 **Fragmentum ap. Galenum**.
K14.185.
Cf. GALENUS Med. (0057 078).

2221 **ANTIOCHUS-PHERECYDES** Hist.
5 B.C.: Atheniensis
Cf. et ANTIOCHUS Hist. (1879).
Cf. et PHERECYDES Hist. (1584).

001 **Testimonium**, FGrH #333: 3B:166.
NQ

002 **Fragmenta**, FGrH #333: 3B:166–168.
Q

0113 **ANTIPATER** Epigr.
2 B.C.: Sidonius

001 **Epigrammata**, AG **6**.10, 14–15, 46, 109, 111, 115, 118, 159–160, 174, 206, 219, 223, 276, 287; **7**.2, 6, 8, 14–15, 23, 26–27, 29–30, 34, 65, 75, 81, 146, 161, 164–165, 172, 209–210, 218, 232, 241, 246, 252, 303, 316, 353, 409, 413, 423–427, 464, 467, 493, 498, 711, 713, 743, 745, 748; **9**.58, 66, 76, 151, 323, 567, 603, 720–724, 728, 790; **10**.2; **12**.97; **16**.133, 167, 176, 178, 220, 296.
AG 6.47, 93; 7.625, 666; 9.93; 16.184: Cf. ANTIPATER Epigr. (0114 001).
AG 6.291; 9.729: Cf. ANONYMI EPIGRAMMATICI (0138 001).
AG 7.282: Cf. THEODORIDAS Epigr. (1715 001).
AG 7.470: Cf. MELEAGER Epigr. (1492 001).
AG 9.23, 143, 150; 16.131: Cf. ANTIPATER Epigr. (1865 001).
AG 9.25: Cf. LEONIDAS Epigr. (1458 001).
AG 9.45: Cf. STATYLLIUS FLACCUS Epigr. (1694 001).
AG 9.406: Cf. ANTIGONUS Paradox. (0568 002).
AG 9.569: Cf. EMPEDOCLES Poet. Phil. (1342 002).
Q: 3,744

x01 **Epigramma demonstrativum**.
App. Anth. 3.104: Cf. EPIGRAMMATICI in *App. Anth.* (7052 003).

1865 **ANTIPATER** Epigr.
fiq Antipater Sidonius vel Antipater Thessalonicensis
2/1 B.C.?: Sidonius vel Thessalonicensis
Cf. et ANTIPATER Sidonius Epigr. (0113).
Cf. et ANTIPATER Thessalonicensis Epigr. (0114).

001 **Epigrammata**, AG **9**.23, 143, 150; **16**.131.
Q: 207

0114 **ANTIPATER** Epigr.
1 B.C.: Thessalonicensis

001 **Epigrammata**, AG **5**.3, 30–31, 109; **6**.47, 93, 198, 208–209, 241, 249, 256, 335; **7**.18, 39, 136, 168, 185, 216, 236, 286–289, 367, 369, 390, 398, 402, 530–531, 625, 629, 637, 639–640, 666, 692, 705; **9**.3, 10, 26, 46, 59, 72, 77,

82, 92–93, 96, 112, 149, 186, 215, 231, 238, 241, 266, 268–269, 282, 297, 302, 305, 309, 407–408, 417–418, 420–421, 428, 517, 541, 550, 552, 557, 706, 752, 792; **10**.25; **11**.20, 23–24, 31, 37, 158, 219, 224, 327, 415; **16**.75, 143, 184, 197, 290, 305.
AG 7.138: Cf. ACERATUS Gramm. (0101 001).
AG 7.237; 9.101: Cf. ALPHEUS Epigr. (0108 001).
AG 7.409, 493: Cf. ANTIPATER Epigr. (0113 001).
AG 9.23, 143, 150: Cf. ANTIPATER Epigr. (1865 001).
AG 9.25, 107: Cf. LEONIDAS Epigr. (1458 001).
AG 9.45: Cf. STATYLLIUS FLACCUS Epigr. (1694 001).
AG 9.114: Cf. PARMENION Epigr. (1563 001).
AG 11.331: Cf. NICARCHUS II Epigr. (1532 001).
Q: 3,520

1910 **ANTIPATER** Hist.
4 B.C.: Magnes
001 **Testimonium**, FGrH #69: 2A:35–36.
NQ
002 **Fragmenta**, FGrH #69: 2A:36–37.
Q

1929 **ANTIPATER** Hist.
4 B.C.?: Macedo
001 **Testimonium**, FGrH #114: 2B:526.
NQ

2350 **ANTIPATER** Hist.
2 B.C./A.D. 1
001 **Testimonium**, FGrH #507: 3B:484.
NQ
002 **Fragmenta**, FGrH #507: 3B:484–485.
Q

1997 **ANTIPATER** Hist.
A.D. 2–3: Hierapolitanus
001 **Testimonia**, FGrH #211: 2B:942–943.
NQ

1898 **ANTIPATER** Hist.
Incertum: Acanthius
001 **Fragmenta**, FGrH #56: 1A:296–297.
Q

0779 **ANTIPATER** Med.
1 B.C.–A.D. 1
Cf. et ANTIPATER et CLEOPHANTUS Med. (0832).
x01 **Fragmenta ap. Galenum**.
K12.630; **13**.239, 292; **14**.160, 165–167.
Cf. GALENUS Med. (0057 076, 078).

1146 **ANTIPATER** Phil.
2 B.C.: Tarsensis
001 **Fragmenta**, ed. J. von Arnim, *Stoicorum vete-*

rum fragmenta, vol. 3. Leipzig: Teubner, 1903 (repr. Stuttgart: 1968): 244–258.
Q

0832 **ANTIPATER et CLEOPHANTUS** Med.
1 B.C./A.D. 1
Cf. et ANTIPATER Med. (0779).
Cf. et CLEOPHANTUS Med. (0821).
x01 **Fragmenta ap. Galenum**.
K14.108–109.
Cf. GALENUS Med. (0057 078).

0410 **ANTIPHANES** Comic.
4 B.C.
001 **Fragmenta**, ed. T. Kock, *Comicorum Atticorum fragmenta*, vol. 2. Leipzig: Teubner, 1884: 12–20, 22–33, 35–135.
frr. 1–21, 24–29, 31–40, 42–45, 47–50, 52–56, 58–62, 64–98, 100–110, 112–115, 117–169, 171–212, 214–302, 305–324, 327–332, 334 + tituli.
Q: 7,146
002 **Fragmenta**, ed. A. Meineke, *Fragmenta comicorum Graecorum*, vol. 3. Berlin: Reimer, 1840 (repr. De Gruyter, 1970): 3–13, 15–27, 29–30, 32–36, 39–41, 43–59, 61–64, 66–106, 108–112, 114–126, 128–157.
Q: 6,952
003 **Fragmenta**, ed. J. Demiańczuk, *Supplementum comicum*. Krakau: Nakładem Akademii, 1912 (repr. Hildesheim: Olms, 1967): 8.
frr. 1–2.
fr. 1: *P. Oxy.* 3.427.
Q, Pap: 13
004 **Fragmenta**, ed. C. Austin, *Comicorum Graecorum fragmenta in papyris reperta*. Berlin: De Gruyter, 1973: 2–4.
frr. 3, 9 + tituli.
Pap: 28
005 **Fragmenta**, ed. Meineke, *op. cit.*, vol. 5.1 (1857; repr. 1970): clxxiii.
Q: [23]
x01 **Aenigmata**.
App. Anth. 7.7–8: Cf. EPIGRAMMATICI in *App. Anth.* (7052 007).

0117 **ANTIPHANES** Epigr.
A.D. 1: Macedo vel Megalopolitanus
001 **Epigrammata**, AG **6**.88; **9**.84, 245, 256, 258, 409; **10**.100; **11**.168, 322, 348.
Q: 386

0780 **ANTIPHANES** Med.
2 B.C.: Delius
x01 **Fragmentum ap. Galenum**.
K12.877.
Cf. GALENUS Med. (0057 076).

2253 **ANTIPHANES Junior** Hist.
2 B.C.?
001 **Testimonium**, FGrH #349: 3B:211–212.
NQ

002 **Fragmenta**, FGrH #349: 3B:212.
Q

0118 **ANTIPHILUS** Epigr.
A.D. 1: Byzantius
001 **Epigrammata**, AG 5.111, 307–308; **6.**95, 97,
199, 250, 252, 257; **7.**141, 175–176, 375, 379,
399, 622, 630, 634–635, 641; **9.**13b–14, 29,
34–35, 71, 73, 86, 156, 178, 192, 222, 242,
263, 277, 294, 298, 306, 310, 404, 413, 415,
546, 549, 551; **10.**17; **11.**66; **16.**136, 147, 333–
334.
AG 5.308: Cf. et PHILODEMUS Phil. (1595
001).
AG 9.123: Cf. Julius LEONIDAS Math. et
Astrol. (1457 001).
AG 9.439: Cf. CRINAGORAS Epigr. (0154
001).
Q: 2,103

0028 **ANTIPHON** Orat.
5 B.C.: Atheniensis
001 **In novercam**, ed. L. Gernet, *Antiphon. Discours.* Paris: Les Belles Lettres, 1923 (repr.
1965): 38–46.
Cod: 1,807
002 **Tetralogia 1**, ed. Gernet, *op. cit.,* 53–67.
Cod: 2,580
003 **Tetralogia 2**, ed. Gernet, *op. cit.,* 72–84.
Cod: 2,228
004 **Tetralogia 3**, ed. Gernet, *op. cit.,* 88–100.
Cod: 2,010
005 **De caede Herodis**, ed. Gernet, *op. cit.,* 108–
136.
Cod: 6,508
006 **De choreuta**, ed. Gernet, *op. cit.,* 142–157.
Cod: 3,495
007 **Fragmenta**, ed. Gernet, *op. cit.,* 164–167.
frr. 1–6.
fr. 3.1: *P. Geneva.*
Q, Pap: 642

1147 **ANTIPHON** Soph.
5 B.C.: Atheniensis
001 **Fragmenta**, ed. L. Gernet, *Antiphon. Discours.*
Paris: Les Belles Lettres, 1923 (repr. 1965):
176–183.
frr. 1–6, Περὶ τῆς ἀληθείας: pp. 176–179.
frr. 7–9, Περὶ ὁμονοίας: p. 179.
frr. 10–23, Fragmenta incertae sedis: pp. 179–
183.
frr. 4–6: *P. Oxy.* 11.1364, fr. 1.
Q, Pap: [1,695]
002 **Testimonia**, ed. H. Diels and W. Kranz, *Die
Fragmente der Vorsokratiker,* vol. 2, 6th edn.
Berlin: Weidmann, 1952 (repr. Dublin: 1966):
334–337.
test. 1–9.
NQ
003 **Fragmenta**, ed. Diels and Kranz, *op. cit.,* 337–
370.
frr. 1–118.

fr. 44: *P. Oxy.* 11.1364 + 15.1797.
Q, Pap
004 **Fragmenta**, *P. Oxy.* 3.414.
Pap

0323 **ANTIPHON** Trag.
5–4 B.C.
001 **Fragmenta**, ed. B. Snell, *Tragicorum Graecorum fragmenta,* vol. 1. Göttingen: Vandenhoeck & Ruprecht, 1971: 195–196.
frr. 1a, 2, 4–6.
Q: [30]

2351 **ANTISTHENES** Hist.
3–2 B.C.: Rhodius
001 **Testimonia**, FGrH #508: 3B:485.
NQ
002 **Fragmenta**, FGrH #508: 3B:485–487.
Q

2435 **ANTISTHENES** Hist.
2 B.C./A.D. 1?
x01 **Fragmentum.**
FGrH #655: 3C:205.
Cf. DIONYSIUS Hist. (2446 001).

2313 **ANTISTHENES** Phil.
5–4 B.C.: Atheniensis
001 **Testimonia**, ed. H. Diels and W. Kranz, *Die
Fragmente der Vorsokratiker,* vol. 2, 6th edn.
Berlin: Weidmann, 1952 (repr. Dublin: 1966):
70.
test. 1–3.
NQ

0591 **ANTISTHENES** Rhet. et Phil.
5–4 B.C.: Atheniensis
Cf. et SOCRATICORUM EPISTULAE (0637).
001 **Declamationes**, ed. F. Caizzi, *Antisthenis fragmenta.* Milan: Istituto Editoriale Cisalpino,
1966: 24–28.
frr. 14–15.
Cod
002 **Fragmenta varia**, ed. Caizzi, *op. cit.,* 29–59.
frr. 16–24b, 25–26, 28–39a, 40a–101, 103–110,
111c–121.
Q

0119 **ANTISTIUS** <Epigr.>
fiq Antistius Vetus
A.D. 1
001 **Epigrammata**, AG 6.237; 7.366; 11.40; 16.243.
Q: 157

1149 ***ANTONINI PII IMPERATORIS EPIS-
TULA***
A.D. 2
001 **Epistula ad commune Asiae**, ed. J.C.T. Otto,
*Corpus apologetarum Christianorum saeculi se-
cundi,* vol. 1. Jena: Mauke, 1876 (repr. Wies-
baden: Sändig, 1969): 244–246.
Cod: [233]

0931 **ANTONINUS** Med.
ante A.D. 1 : Cous
x01 **Fragmenta ap. Galenum**.
K12.843–844; **14**.168–169.
Cf. GALENUS Med. (0057 076, 078).

0651 **ANTONINUS LIBERALIS** Myth.
A.D. 2?
001 **Metamorphoseon synagoge**, ed. I. Cazzaniga,
Antoninus Liberalis. Metamorphoseon synagoge.
Milan: Istituto Editoriale Cisalpino, 1962: 12–
77.
Cod: [10,378]

0120 **ANTONIUS** Epigr.
fiq Antonius Thallus
A.D. 1 : Argivus
Cf. et Antonius THALLUS Epigr. (1707).
001 **Epigramma**, AG 9.102.
AG 9.103: Cf. MUNDUS MUNATIUS Epigr.
(1519 001).
Q: 23

0850 **ANTONIUS** Med.
ante A.D. 1
x01 **Fragmenta ap. Galenum**.
K13.281–282.
Cf. GALENUS Med. (0057 076).

1148 **ANTONIUS DIOGENES** Scr. Erot.
A.D. 1/2
001 Τὰ ὑπὲρ Θούλην ἄπιστα (ap. Photium, *Bibl.*
cod. 166), ed. R. Hercher, *Erotici scriptores
Graeci*, vol. 1. Leipzig: Teubner, 1858: 233–
238.
Q: [2,295]
002 **Fragmentum** (*PSI* 1177), ed. F. Zimmermann,
*Griechische Roman-Papyri und verwandte
Texte*. Heidelberg: Bilabel, 1936: 85–89.
Pap

2478 **ANTONIUS JULIANUS** Hist.
A.D. 2
001 **Testimonium**, FGrH #735: 3C:700.
NQ

0669 **ANTONIUS MUSA** Med.
1 B.C./A.D. 1
Cf. et MUSA Med. (0808).
x01 **Fragmenta ap. Galenum**.
K12.636, 658, 737–738, 740, 741; **13**.57, 104,
108, 326.
Cf. GALENUS Med. (0057 076).
x02 **Fragmenta ap. Aëtium** (lib. 8).
CMG, vol. 8.2, pp. 491, 544.
Cf. AËTIUS Med. (0718 008).

0749 **ANTYLLUS** Med.
A.D. 2
Cf. et ANTYLLUS et HELIODORUS Med.
(0852).
Cf. et ANTYLLUS et POSIDONIUS Med.
(0853).

001 Ἐκ τοῦ περὶ κλυσμῶν ὅτι διὰ τρεῖς αἰτίας
παραλαμβάνονται, ed. F.R. Dietz, *Severus
Iatrosophista* [*Diss. med. Königsberg* (1836)]:
43–45.
Cod: 307
x01 **Fragmenta ap. Oribasium**.
CMG, vol. **6.1.1**, pp. 107, 146, 155, 157, 177,
183, 208, 210, 214, 215, 217, 219, 255, 262,
263; **6.1.2**, pp. 6, 11, 12, 14, 24, 44, 55, 61;
6.2.1, pp. 133, 161, 166, 168, 179, 237; **6.2.2**,
pp. 55, 58, 128; **6.3**, pp. 7, 13, 23, 51.
Cf. ORIBASIUS Med. (0722 001).
x02 **Fragmenta ap. Paulum**.
CMG, vol. 9.2, pp. 70, 347, 394, 397.
Cf. PAULUS Med. (0715 001).
x03 **Fragmenta ap. Aëtium** (lib. 3).
CMG, vol. 8.1, pp. 276, 277.
Cf. AËTIUS Med. (0718 003).
x04 **Fragmenta ap. Aëtium** (lib. 7).
CMG, vol. 8.2, p. 323.
Cf. AËTIUS Med. (0718 007).
x05 **Fragmenta ap. Aëtium** (lib. 9).
Athena 23 (1911) 374.
Cf. AËTIUS Med. (0718 009).

0852 **ANTYLLUS et HELIODORUS** Med.
A.D. 1/2
Cf. et ANTYLLUS Med. (0749).
Cf. et HELIODORUS Med. (0692).
x01 **Fragmenta ap. Oribasium**.
CMG, vol. **6.2.1**, pp. 118–120, 135–142; **6.2.2**,
p. 57.
Cf. ORIBASIUS Med. (0722 001).

0853 **ANTYLLUS et POSIDONIUS** Med.
A.D. 2/5
Cf. et ANTYLLUS Med. (0749).
x01 **Fragmentum ap. Aëtium** (lib. 3).
CMG, vol. 8.1, p. 309.
Cf. AËTIUS Med. (0718 003).

1126 **ANUBION** Poet. Astrol.
A.D. 1
001 **Fragmenta**, *P. Schubart* 15.
Pap
002 **Fragmenta** (ex cod. Veneto 7), ed. W. Kroll
and A. Olivieri, *Codices Veneti* [*Catalogus codicum astrologorum Graecorum* 2. Brussels:
Lamertin, 1900]: 202–212.
Cod
003 **Fragmenta** (ex cod. Paris. 2417), ed. W. Kroll
and A. Olivieri, *Codices Parisini* [*Catalogus
codicum astrologorum Graecorum* 8.1. Brussels:
Lamertin, 1929]: 147.
Cod

0121 **ANYTE** Epigr.
4 B.C. : Tegeates
001 **Epigrammata**, AG **6**.123, 153, 312; **7**.190, 202,
208, 215, 486, 490, 492, 538, 646, 649, 724;
9.144, 313–314, 745; **16**.228, 231, 291.
AG 6.82: Cf. PAULUS Silentiarius Poet. Christ.
(4039 004).

AG 7.189: Cf. ARISTODICUS Epigr. (0133 001).
AG 7.232: Cf. ANTIPATER Epigr. (0113 001).
AG 7.236: Cf. ANTIPATER Epigr. (0114 001).
AG 7.491: Cf. MNASALCES Epigr. (1513 001).
AG 16.229: Cf. ANONYMI EPIGRAMMATICI (0138 001).
Q: 580

1046 **APELLES** Gnost.
A.D. 2: Alexandrinus, Romanus
x01 **Fragmentum.**
Origenes, *In Genesim* (Baehrens, pp. 28–29).
Cf. ORIGENES Theol. (2042 022).

0858 **APELLES** Med.
1 B.C.–A.D. 1
x01 **Fragmentum ap. Galenum.**
K14.148.
Cf. GALENUS Med. (0057 078).

1150 **APHAREUS** Rhet.
4 B.C.: Atheniensis
001 **Epigramma**, ed. E. Diehl, *Anthologia lyrica Graeca*, fasc. 1, 3rd edn. Leipzig: Teubner, 1949: 114.
Q: [14]
002 **Tituli**, ed. B. Snell, *Tragicorum Graecorum fragmenta*, vol. 1. Göttingen: Vandenhoeck & Ruprecht, 1971: 239.
NQ

0783 **APHRODAS** Med.
ante A.D. 1
Cf. et APHRODAS et MOSCHION Med. (0866).
x01 **Fragmenta ap. Galenum.**
K12.695, 878; 13.94–95, 135–136, 551, 738, 1035; 14.111–112, 207–208.
Cf. GALENUS Med. (0057 076–078).

0866 **APHRODAS et MOSCHION** Med.
1 B.C./A.D. 1
Cf. et APHRODAS Med. (0783).
Cf. et MOSCHION ὁ διορθωτής Med. (0994).
x01 **Fragmentum ap. Galenum.**
K13.30.
Cf. GALENUS Med. (0057 076).

0760 **APHRODISEUS** Med.
ante A.D. 1
x01 **Fragmentum ap. Galenum.**
K13.1013.
Cf. GALENUS Med. (0057 077).

1151 **APHRODISIUS-EUPHEMIUS** Hist.
post 4 B.C.?: Thespiensis
001 **Fragmentum**, FGrH #386: 3B:263.
Q

0784 **APHTHONIUS** Soph.
ante A.D. 4: Romanus
x01 **Fragmentum ap. Oribasium.**

CMG, vol. 6.2.2, p. 246.
Cf. ORIBASIUS Med. (0722 003).

1152 **APION** Gramm.
A.D. 1: Alexandrinus, Oasites
001 **Testimonia**, FGrH #616: 3C:122–126.
NQ
002 **Fragmenta**, FGrH #616: 3C:126–144.
Q
003 **Fragmenta de glossis Homericis**, ed. A. Ludwich, "Über die homerischen Glossen Apions," *Philologus* **74** (1917) 209–247; **75** (1919) 95–103.
Q: [6,577]
004 **Fragmenta de glossis Homericis**, ed. S. Neitzel, *Die Fragmente des Grammatikers Dionysios Thrax* [*Sammlung griechischer und lateinischer Grammatiker* 3. Berlin: De Gruyter, 1977]: 213–218, 220–300.
Q

0769 **APION** Med.
ante A.D. 1
x01 **Fragmentum ap. Galenum.**
K13.856.
Cf. GALENUS Med. (0057 077).

1153 *APOCALYPSIS ADAM*
A.D. 1?
001 Νυχθήμερον, ed. J.A. Robinson, *Texts and Studies* 2.3. Cambridge: Cambridge University Press, 1893 (repr. Nendeln, Liechtenstein: Kraus, 1967): 139–144.
fort. auctore Apollonio (Tyanensi?) Math.
Cod: [502]

1154 *APOCALYPSIS BARUCH*
ante A.D. 3
001 **Apocalypsis Baruchi Graece** (iii Baruch), ed. J.C. Picard, *Apocalypsis Baruchi Graece* [*Pseudepigrapha veteris testamenti Graece* 2. Leiden: Brill, 1967]: 81–96.
Cod: [3,163]

1156 *APOCALYPSIS ELIAE*
ante A.D. 1
001 **Fragmenta**, ed. A.-M. Denis, *Fragmenta pseudepigraphorum quae supersunt Graeca* [*Pseudepigrapha veteris testamenti Graece* 3. Leiden: Brill, 1970]: 103–104.
Q: [104]

1157 *APOCALYPSIS ESDRAE*
2 B.C./A.D. 2
001 **Apocalypsis Esdrae**, ed. C. Tischendorf, *Apocalypses apocryphae*. Leipzig: Mendelssohn, 1866: 24–33.
Cod: [2,753]
002 **Apocalypsis Esdrae quarta**, ed. A.-M. Denis, *Fragmenta pseudepigraphorum quae supersunt Graeca* [*Pseudepigrapha veteris testamenti*

Graece 3. Leiden: Brill, 1970]: 130–132.
Q: [143]

1158 *APOCALYPSIS JOANNIS*
A.D. 2?

001 **Apocalypsis apocrypha Joannis**, ed. C. Tischendorf, *Apocalypses apocryphae.* Leipzig: Mendelssohn, 1866: 70–93.
Cod: [3,043]

002 **Apocalypsis apocrypha Joannis** (versio altera), ed. F. Nau, "Une deuxième apocalypse apocryphe grecque de saint Jean," *Revue Biblique* 23 (1914) 215–221.
Cod: [1,672]

003 **Apocalypsis apocrypha Joannis** (versio tertia), ed. A. Vassiliev, *Anecdota Graeco-Byzantina*, vol. 1. Moscow: Imperial University Press, 1893: 317–322.
Cod: [2,008]

APOCALYPSIS MOSIS
Cf. VITA ADAM et EVAE (1747).

1159 *APOCALYPSIS PETRI*
A.D. 2

001 **Apocalypsis Petri**, ed. E. Klostermann, *Apocrypha I: Reste des Petrusevangeliums, der Petrusapokalypse und des Kerygma Petri*, 2nd edn. [*Kleine Texte* 3. Bonn: Marcus & Weber, 1908]: 8–12.
Cod: [1,634]

002 **Kerygma Petri**, ed. Klostermann, *op. cit.*, 12–13.
Q

2243 *APOCALYPSIS SEDRACH*
Incertum

001 **Apocalypsis Sedrach**, ed. M.R. James, *Apocrypha anecdota* [*Texts and Studies* 2.3. Cambridge: Cambridge University Press, 1893 (repr. Nendeln, Liechtenstein: Kraus, 1967)]: 130–137.
Cod

1160 *APOCALYPSIS SOPHONIAE*
ante A.D. 2

001 **Fragmentum**, ed. A.-M. Denis, *Fragmenta pseudepigraphorum quae supersunt Graeca* [*Pseudepigrapha veteris testamenti Graece* 3. Leiden: Brill, 1970]: 129.
Q: [42]

1155 *APOCALYPSIS SYRIACA BARUCHI*
A.D. 1

001 **Fragmentum**, ed. A.-M. Denis, *Fragmenta pseudepigraphorum quae supersunt Graeca* [*Pseudepigrapha veteris testamenti Graece* 3. Leiden: Brill, 1970]: 118–120.
Pap: [182]

1161 *APOCRYPHON EZECHIEL*
Incertum

001 **Fragmenta**, ed. A.-M. Denis, *Fragmenta pseudepigraphorum quae supersunt Graeca* [*Pseudepigrapha veteris testamenti Graece* 3. Leiden: Brill, 1970]: 121–123, 125–127.
Q, Pap: [1,154]

1162 **APOLLAS** Hist.
vel Apellas
3 B.C.: Ponticus

001 **Fragmenta**, FGrH #266: 3A:74–75.
Q

2074 **APOLLINARIS** Theol.
A.D. 4: Laodicensis
Bibliography in progress

001 **Fides secundum partem**, ed. H. Lietzmann, *Apollinaris von Laodicea und seine Schule* [*Texte und Untersuchungen* 1. Tübingen: Mohr, 1904 (repr. Hildesheim: Olms, 1970)]: 167–185.
Cod

002 **De unione corporis et divinitatis in Christo**, ed. Lietzmann, *op. cit.*, 185–193.
Cod

003 **De fide et incarnatione contra adversarios**, ed. Lietzmann, *op. cit.*, 194–199.
Cod

004 **De unione** (fragmentum), ed. Lietzmann, *op. cit.*, 204.
fr. 2.
Q

005 **De incarnatione** (fragmenta), ed. Lietzmann, *op. cit.*, 204–207.
frr. 3–10.
Q

006 **Laudatio Mariae et de incarnatione**, ed. Lietzmann, *op. cit.*, 207–208.
frr. 11–12.
Q

007 **Demonstratio de divina incarnatione ad similitudinem hominis**, ed. Lietzmann, *op. cit.*, 208–232.
frr. 13–107.
Q

008 **In dei in carne manifestationem** (fragmenta), ed. Lietzmann, *op. cit.*, 232–233.
frr. 108–110.
Q

009 **Ad illos qui hominem a verbo assumptum fuisse dicebant** (fragmentum), ed. Lietzmann, *op. cit.*, 233.
fr. 111.
Q

010 **Syllogismi** (fragmenta), ed. Lietzmann, *op. cit.*, 233–235.
frr. 112–116.
Q

011 **Contra Diodorum ad Heraclium** (fragmenta), ed. Lietzmann, *op. cit.*, 235–237.
frr. 117–120.
Q

012 **Ad Diodorum** (fragmenta), ed. Lietzmann, *op. cit.*, 237–242.
frr. 121–146.
Q

013 **Recapitulatio**, ed. Lietzmann, *op. cit.*, 242–246.
Q, Cod

014 **Ad Flavianum** (fragmenta), ed. Lietzmann, *op. cit.*, 246–247.
frr. 147–148.
Q

015 **Ad Petrum** (fragmentum), ed. Lietzmann, *op. cit.*, 247.
fr. 149.
Q

016 **Ad Julianum** (fragmenta), ed. Lietzmann, *op. cit.*, 247–248.
frr. 150–152.
Q

017 **Sermones** (fragmenta), ed. Lietzmann, *op. cit.*, 248–249.
frr. 153–156.
Q

018 **Dialogi** (fragmentum), ed. Lietzmann, *op. cit.*, 249.
fr. 157.
Q

019 **Quod deus in carne Christus** (fragmentum), ed. Lietzmann, *op. cit.*, 249.
fr. 158.
Q

020 **Ad Jovianum**, ed. Lietzmann, *op. cit.*, 250–253.
Q

021 **Ad Serapionem** (fragmenta), ed. Lietzmann, *op. cit.*, 253–254.
frr. 159–161.
Q

022 **Ad Terentium** (fragmenta), ed. Lietzmann, *op. cit.*, 254–255.
frr. 162–163.
Q

023 **Ad episcopos Diocaesarienses**, ed. Lietzmann, *op. cit.*, 255–256.
Q

024 **Ad Dionysium 1**, ed. Lietzmann, *op. cit.*, 256–262.
Q

025 **Ad Dionysium 2** (fragmentum), ed. Lietzmann, *op. cit.*, 262.
fr. 164.
Q

026 **Tomus synodalis**, ed. Lietzmann, *op. cit.*, 262–263.
Q

027 **Fragmenta ex operibus incertis**, ed. Lietzmann, *op. cit.*, 269–270.
frr. 168–171.
Q

030 **Epistula de essentia dei** (epistula Sebastiani), ed. H. de Riedmatten, "La correspondance entre Basile de Césarée et Apollinaire de Laodicée," *Journal of Theological Studies*, n.s. 7 (1956) 208–210.
Q

031 **Fragmenta in proverbia**, ed. A. Mai, *Nova patrum bibliotheca*, vol. 7.2. Rome, 1854: 76–80.
Q

032 **Fragmenta in Ezechielem**, ed. Mai, *op. cit.*, 82–91.
Q

033 **Fragmenta in Isaiam**, ed. Mai, *op. cit.*, 128–130.
Q

034 **Fragmenta in Canticum**, *MPG* 87 bis: 1548–1549, 1552, 1553, 1556, 1581, 1584, 1608, 1662, 1697, 1704, 1708, 1721, 1724, 1749.
Q

035 **Fragmenta in Danielem**, ed. A. Mai, *Scriptorum veterum nova collectio*, vols. 1.2 & 1.3. Rome, 1.2:1825; 1.3:1837: **1.2**:161–221; **1.3**: 27–56.
Q

036 **Fragmenta in Lucam**, ed. Mai, *op. cit.*, vol. 1.1 (1825): 179–188.
Q

037 **Fragmenta in Matthaeum** (in catenis), ed. J. Reuss, *Matthäus-Kommentare aus der griechischen Kirche* [*Texte und Untersuchungen* 61. Berlin: Akademie-Verlag, 1957]: 2–54.
Q

038 **Fragmenta in Joannem** (in catenis), ed. J. Reuss, *Johannes-Kommentare aus der griechischen Kirche* [*Texte und Untersuchungen* 89. Berlin: Akademie-Verlag, 1966]: 3–64.
Q: [12,749]

039 **Fragmenta in epistulam ad Romanos** (in catenis), ed. K. Staab, *Pauluskommentar aus der griechischen Kirche aus Katenenhandschriften gesammelt*. Münster: Aschendorff, 1933: 57–82.
Q: [8,143]

041 **Fragmenta in Psalmos** (in catenis), ed. E. Mühlenberg, *Psalmenkommentare aus der Katenenüberlieferung*, vol. 1 [*Patristische Texte und Studien* 15. Berlin: De Gruyter, 1975]: 3–118.
Q: [23,432]

x01 **Epistula ad Basilium 1.**
Courtonne, vol. 3, pp. 222–224 (epist. 362).
Cf. BASILIUS Theol. (2040 004).

x02 **Epistula ad Basilium 2.**
Courtonne, vol. 3, pp. 225–226 (epist. 364).
Cf. BASILIUS Theol. (2040 004).

1163 **Claudius APOLLINARIUS** Apol.
vel Apollinaris
A.D. 2: Hierapolitanus

001 **Fragmenta**, ed. J.C.T. Otto, *Corpus apologetarum Christianorum saeculi secundi*, vol. 9. Jena: Mauke, 1872 (repr. Wiesbaden: Sändig, 1969): 486–487.
frr. 1–2: Ex apologia.

frr. 3–4: De pascha.
Q: [216]

1221 **APOLLINARIUS** Astrol.
A.D. 1–2?
001 **Fragmenta**, ed. C.É. Ruelle, *Codices Parisini*
[Catalogus codicum astrologorum Graecorum
8.2. Brussels: Lamertin, 1911]: 63, 132.
Q

0122 **APOLLINARIUS** Epigr.
A.D. 2
001 **Epigrammata**, AG 11.399, 421.
Q: 65

0785 **APOLLINARIUS** Med.
ante A.D. 4
x01 **Fragmentum ap. Oribasium**.
CMG, vol. 6.3, p. 98.
Cf. ORIBASIUS Med. (0722 004).

0411 **APOLLODORUS** Comic.
4/3 B.C.: Carystius
Cf. et APOLLODORUS Carystius vel APOLLO-
DORUS Gelous Comic. (0412).
001 **Fragmenta**, ed. T. Kock, *Comicorum Atti-*
corum fragmenta, vol. 3. Leipzig: Teubner,
1888: 280–288.
frr. 1–13, 23–27.
Q: 366
002 **Fragmenta**, ed. A. Meineke, *Fragmenta comi-*
corum Graecorum, vol. 4. Berlin: Reimer, 1841
(repr. De Gruyter, 1970): 440–442, 444–449.
Q: 354
003 **Fragmentum**, ed. J. Demiańczuk, *Supplemen-*
tum comicum. Krakau: Nakładem Akademii,
1912 (repr. Hildesheim: Olms, 1967): 9.
fr. 1.
Q: 8
004 **Fragmentum**, ed. C. Austin, *Comicorum Grae-*
corum fragmenta in papyris reperta. Berlin: De
Gruyter, 1973: 4.
fr. 10.
Pap: 68

0413 **APOLLODORUS** Comic.
4/3 B.C.: Gelous
Cf. et APOLLODORUS Carystius vel APOLLO-
DORUS Gelous Comic. (0412).
001 **Fragmenta**, ed. T. Kock, *Comicorum Atti-*
corum fragmenta, vol. 3. Leipzig: Teubner,
1888: 278–280.
frr. 1–5 + tituli.
Q: 65
002 **Fragmenta**, ed. A. Meineke, *Fragmenta comi-*
corum Graecorum, vol. 4. Berlin: Reimer, 1841
(repr. De Gruyter, 1970): 438–439.
Q: 56

0549 **APOLLODORUS** Gramm.
2 B.C.: Atheniensis

001 **Testimonia**, FGrH #244: **2B**:1022–1025; **3B**:
744 addenda.
test. 3: *IG* 2.953.
test. 4: *P. Oxy.* 10.1241.
test. 15 bis: *P. Tebt.*
NQ
002 **Fragmenta**, FGrH #244: **2B**:1025–1128; **3B**:
744 addenda.
fr. 89: *P. Oxy.* 15.1802.
fr. 302 ter: *P. Oxy.* 6.853.
Q
003 **Fragmenta**, ed. H.J. Mette, "Die 'Kleinen'
griechischen Historiker heute," *Lustrum* 21
(1978) 20–22.
frr. 217 bis, 257 bis, 280 bis, 354 bis.
fr. 354 bis: *P. Cologne* 5604.
Q, Pap

2537 **APOLLODORUS** Hist.
post 4 B.C.?
001 **Fragmentum**, FGrH #803: 3C:842.
Q

2295 **APOLLODORUS** Hist.
ante 2 B.C.: Erythraeus
001 **Fragmenta**, FGrH #422: 3B:318.
Q

1164 **APOLLODORUS** Hist.
1 B.C.: Artemita
001 **Fragmenta**, FGrH #779: 3C:773–776.
Q

0365 **APOLLODORUS** Lyr.
6 B.C.: fort. Atheniensis
001 **Fragmentum**, ed. D.L. Page, *Poetae melici*
Graeci. Oxford: Clarendon Press, 1962 (repr.
1967 (1st edn. corr.)): 364.
fr. 1.
Q: [10]

APOLLODORUS Math.
fiq Apollodorus Cyzicenus
ante A.D. 3
AG 7.119.
Cf. ANONYMI EPIGRAMMATICI (0138 001).

1165 **APOLLODORUS** Mech.
A.D. 1–2: Damascenus
001 **Poliorcetica**, ed. R. Schneider, *Griechische Po-*
liorketiker [Abhandlungen der königlichen Ge-
sellschaft der Wissenschaften zu Göttingen,
Philol.-hist. Kl., N.F. 10, no. 1. Berlin: Weidmann, 1908]: 8–50.
Cod: [6,265]

0786 **APOLLODORUS** Med.
3 B.C.: Alexandrinus
x01 **Fragmenta ap. Galenum**.
K14.181, 184.
Cf. GALENUS Med. (0057 078).

x02 **Fragmentum ap. Athenaeum.**
Deipnosophistae 15.681d.
Cf. ATHENAEUS Soph. (0008 001).

0548 **APOLLODORUS** Myth.
A.D. 1/2
001 **Bibliotheca**, ed. R. Wagner, *Apollodori biblio-theca* [*Mythographi Graeci* 1. Leipzig: Teubner, 1894]: 1–169.
Cod: 28,415

2319 **APOLLODORUS** Phil.
5 B.C.: Cyzicenus
001 **Testimonia**, ed. H. Diels and W. Kranz, *Die Fragmente der Vorsokratiker*, vol. 2, 6th edn. Berlin: Weidmann, 1952 (repr. Dublin: 1966): 246.
test. 1–3.
NQ

1166 **APOLLODORUS** Phil.
2 B.C.: Seleuciensis
001 **Fragmenta**, ed. J. von Arnim, *Stoicorum vete-rum fragmenta*, vol. 3. Leipzig: Teubner, 1903 (repr. Stuttgart: 1968): 259–261.
Q

0700 **APOLLODORUS** Trag.
4 B.C.: Tarsensis
001 **Tituli**, ed. B. Snell, *Tragicorum Graecorum fragmenta*, vol. 1. Göttingen: Vandenhoeck & Ruprecht, 1971: 209.
NQ

0412 **APOLLODORUS Carystius vel APOLLODO-RUS Gelous** Comic.
4/3 B.C.
Cf. et APOLLODORUS Carystius Comic. (0411).
Cf. et APOLLODORUS Gelous Comic. (0413).
001 **Fragmenta**, ed. T. Kock, *Comicorum Atti-corum fragmenta*, vol. 3. Leipzig: Teubner, 1888: 288–295.
frr. 1–23, 26.
Q: 441
002 **Fragmenta**, ed. Meineke, *Fragmenta comi-corum Graecorum*, vol. 4. Berlin: Reimer, 1841 (repr. De Gruyter, 1970): 450–457.
Q: 414

APOLLODOTUS Epigr.
AG 7.119.
Cf. ANONYMI EPIGRAMMATICI (0138 001).

0124 **APOLLONIDES** Epigr.
A.D. 1: Smyrnaeus
001 **Epigrammata**, AG **6**.105, 238–239; **7**.180, 233, 378, 389, 631, 642, 693, 702, 742; **9**.228, 243–244, 257, 264–265, 271, 280–281, 287, 296, 408, 422, 791; **10**.19; **11**.25; **16**.49–50, 235, 239.
Q: 1,146

0345 **APOLLONIDES** Trag.
fiq filius Ardonis
3/2 B.C.
001 **Fragmenta**, ed. B. Snell, *Tragicorum Grae-corum fragmenta*, vol. 1. Göttingen: Vanden-hoeck & Ruprecht, 1971: 308.
frr. 1–2.
Q: [45]

2451 **APOLLONIDES HORAPIUS** Hist.
ante A.D. 2
001 **Fragmenta**, FGrH #661: 3C:212–213.
Q

1167 **APOLLONIUS** Biogr.
A.D. 2?
001 **Vita Aeschinis**, ed. V. Martin and G. de Budé, *Eschine. Discours*, vol. 1. Paris: Les Belles Lettres, 1927 (repr. 1962): 4–6.
Cod: [864]

0394 **APOLLONIUS** Comic.
Incertum
001 **Fragmenta**, ed. C. Austin, *Comicorum Grae-corum fragmenta in papyris reperta*. Berlin: De Gruyter, 1973: 5.
frr. 11–12.
Pap: 13

0550 **APOLLONIUS** Geom.
3 B.C.: Pergaeus
001 **Conica**, ed. J.L. Heiberg, *Apollonii Pergaei quae Graece exstant*, vols. 1–2. Leipzig: Teub-ner, 1:1891; 2:1893 (repr. Stuttgart: 1974): **1**:2–450; **2**:2–96.
Cod: [62,043]
002 **Fragmenta**, ed. Heiberg, *op. cit.*, vol. 2, 101–139.
Q

1404 **APOLLONIUS** Gramm.
2/1 B.C.?
001 **Fragmenta**, ed. R. Berndt, *De Charete, Chae-ride, Alexione grammaticis eorumque reliquiis*, pt. 1. Königsberg: Hartung, 1902: 50–52.
frr. 1–4.
Q: [153]

1170 **APOLLONIUS** Hist.
3 B.C.?: Aphrodisiensis
001 **Testimonium**, FGrH #740: 3C:714.
NQ
002 **Fragmenta**, FGrH #740: 3C:715–717.
Q

1169 **APOLLONIUS** Hist.
2 B.C.: Atheniensis
001 **Testimonium**, FGrH #365: 3B:225.
test. 1: *IG² 2.3487*.
NQ
002 **Fragmenta**, FGrH #365: 3B:225–226.
Q

2283 **APOLLONIUS** Hist.
Incertum
001 **Fragmentum**, FGrH #403: 3B:298.
Q

APOLLONIUS Math.
fiq Apollonius Tyanensis
Cf. APOCALYPSIS ADAM (1153 001).

0680 **APOLLONIUS** Med.
3 B.C.: Memphiticus
Cf. et APOLLONIUS Med. (0741).
x01 **Fragmenta ap. Galenum.**
K8.759, 760–761; **14.**188.
Cf. GALENUS Med. (0057 059, 078).

0741 **APOLLONIUS** Med.
fiq Apollonius Memphiticus
3 B.C.?
Cf. et APOLLONIUS Med. (0680).
x01 **Fragmenta ap. Aëtium** (lib. 6–8).
CMG, vol. 8.2, pp. 223, 230, 238, 353, 375,
451.
Cf. AËTIUS Med. (0718 006–008).

0660 **APOLLONIUS** Med.
1 B.C.: Citiensis
Cf. et APOLLONIUS Med. (0739).
001 **In Hippocratis de articulis commentarius,** ed.
J. Kollesch and F. Kudlien, *Apollonios von
Kition. Kommentar zu Hippokrates über das
Einrenken der Gelenke [Corpus medicorum
Graecorum,* vol. 11.1.1. Berlin: Akademie-Ver-
lag, 1965]: 10–112.
Cod: 12,486

0739 **APOLLONIUS** Med.
fiq Apollonius Citiensis vel Apollonius Pergamenus
1 B.C./A.D. 1?
Cf. et APOLLONIUS Med. (0660).
Cf. et APOLLONIUS Med. (0792).
x01 **Fragmenta ap. Alexandrum Trallianum.**
Puschmann, vol. 1, pp. 559, 561.
Cf. ALEXANDER Med. (0744 003).

0789 **Claudius APOLLONIUS** Med.
A.D. 1
Cf. et APOLLONIUS Archistrator Med. (0747).
x01 **Fragmentum ap. Galenum.**
K14.171–172.
Cf. GALENUS Med. (0057 078).

0792 **APOLLONIUS** Med.
A.D. 1?: Pergamenus
Cf. et APOLLONIUS Med. (0739).
x01 **Fragmenta ap. Oribasium.**
CMG, vol. **6.1.1,** p. 218; **6.2.1,** p. 158; **6.3,** p.
12.
Cf. ORIBASIUS Med. (0722 001, 004).

0782 **APOLLONIUS** Med.
ante A.D. 2: Tarsensis
x01 **Fragmentum ap. Galenum.**
K13.843.
Cf. GALENUS Med. (0057 077).

0569 **APOLLONIUS** Paradox.
2 B.C.?
001 **Historiae mirabiles,** ed. A. Giannini, *Paradoxographorum Graecorum reliquiae.* Milan: Istituto
Editoriale Italiano, 1965: 120–142.
Cod: [2,425]

0619 **APOLLONIUS** Phil.
A.D. 1: Tyanensis
001 **Apotelesmata** [Sp.], ed. F. Nau, *Patrologia
Syriaca* 2 (1907): 1372–1391.
Cod
002 **De horis diei et noctis** (fragmenta e cod. Berol.
26) [Sp.], ed. F. Boll, *Codices Germanici [Cata-
logus codicum astrologorum Graecorum* 7. Brus-
sels: Lamertin, 1908]: 175–181.
Cod
x01 **Epistulae.**
Kayser, pp. 345–368.
Cf. Flavius PHILOSTRATUS Soph. (0638 002).
x02 **Fragmentum ap. Eusebium.**
Eusebius, *Praep. Ev.* 4.12.
Cf. EUSEBIUS Scr. Eccl. et Theol. (2018 001).
x03 Νυχθήμερον (fort. auctore Apollonio).
Robinson, pp. 139–144.
Cf. APOCALYPSIS ADAM (1153 001).

1171 **APOLLONIUS** Scr. Eccl.
A.D. 2–3: Ephesius
001 **Fragmenta ex libro adversus Cataphrygas seu
Montanistas,** ed. M.J. Routh, *Reliquiae sacrae,*
vol. 1, 2nd edn. Oxford: Oxford University
Press, 1846 (repr. Hildesheim: Olms, 1974):
467–472.
Q: [756]

1168 **APOLLONIUS** Soph.
A.D. 1–2
001 **Lexicon Homericum,** ed. I. Bekker, *Apollonii
Sophistae lexicon Homericum.* Berlin: Reimer,
1833 (repr. Hildesheim: Olms, 1967): 1–171.
Cod: [43,435]

0747 **APOLLONIUS Archistrator** Med.
fiq Claudius Apollonius
A.D. 1?
Cf. et Claudius APOLLONIUS Med. (0789).
x01 **Fragmentum ap. Galenum.**
K13.835.
Cf. GALENUS Med. (0057 077).

0082 **APOLLONIUS DYSCOLUS** Gramm.
A.D. 2: Alexandrinus
001 **De pronominibus,** ed. R. Schneider, *Grammatici Graeci,* vol. 2.1. Leipzig: Teubner, 1878

(repr. Hildesheim: Olms, 1965): 3–116.
Cod: [30,047]

002 **De adverbiis**, ed. Schneider, *op. cit.*, vol. 2.1, 119–210.
Cod: [25,633]

003 **De conjunctionibus**, ed. Schneider, *op. cit.*, vol. 2.1, 213–258.
Cod: [16,241]

004 **De constructione**, ed. G. Uhlig, *op. cit.*, vol. 2.2 (1910; repr. 1965): 1–497.
Cod: [68,339]

005 **Fragmenta librorum deperditorum**, ed. Schneider, *op. cit.*, vol. 2.3 (1910; repr. 1965): 1–140.
Q

0810 **APOLLONIUS et ALCIMION** Med.
A.D. 1
Cf. et ALCIMION Med. (0765).

x01 **Fragmentum ap. Galenum.**
K13.31.
Cf. GALENUS Med. (0057 076).

2491 **APOLLONIUS MOLO** Hist.
1 B.C.: Rhodius

001 **Testimonia**, FGrH #728: 3C:687–688.
NQ

002 **Fragmenta**, FGrH #728: 3C:688–689.
Q

0790 **APOLLONIUS MYS** Med.
1 B.C.: Alexandrinus

001 **Fragmentum**, *P. Oxy.* 2.234.
Pap

x01 **Fragmenta ap. Galenum.**
K12.475–478, 614–620, 633; 14.146.
Cf. GALENUS Med. (0057 076, 078).

x02 **Fragmenta ap. Philumenum.**
CMG, vol. 10.1.1, pp. 10, 24, 26, 30, 37.
Cf. PHILUMENUS Med. (0671 001).

x03 **Fragmentum ap. Athenaeum.**
Deipnosophistae 15.688e–689b.
Cf. ATHENAEUS Soph. (0008 001).

APOLLONIUS Opsis Med.
Cf. APOLLONIUS Organicus Med. (0817).
Cf. APOLLONIUS Ther Med. (0791).

0817 **APOLLONIUS Organicus** Med.
fiq Apollonius Opsis
1 B.C.?

x01 **Fragmentum ap. Galenum.**
K13.856.
Cf. GALENUS Med. (0057 077).

0001 **APOLLONIUS RHODIUS** Epic.
3 B.C.: Rhodius

001 **Argonautica**, ed. H. Fraenkel, *Apollonii Rhodii Argonautica*. Oxford: Clarendon Press, 1961 (repr. 1970 (1st edn. corr.)): 1–242.
Cod: 39,090

002 **Fragmenta**, ed. J.U. Powell, *Collectanea Alex-*

andrina. Oxford: Clarendon Press, 1925 (repr. 1970): 4–8.
frr. 1–2, 5, 7–10, 12–13.
Q: 243

004 **Tituli**, ed. Powell, *op. cit.*, 5–6.
frr. 4, 6.
NQ

003 **Epigramma**, AG 11.275.
Q: 16

0791 **APOLLONIUS Ther** Med.
fiq Apollonius Opsis
1 B.C.?

x01 **Fragmentum ap. Oribasium.**
CMG, vol. 6.2.1, p. 282.
Cf. ORIBASIUS Med. (0722 001).

0414 **APOLLOPHANES** Comic.
5–4 B.C.

001 **Fragmenta**, ed. T. Kock, *Comicorum Atticorum fragmenta*, vol. 1. Leipzig: Teubner, 1880: 797–799.
frr. 2–6, 8, 10 + tituli.
Q: 45

002 **Fragmenta**, ed. A. Meineke, *Fragmenta comicorum Graecorum*, vol. 2.2. Berlin: Reimer, 1840 (repr. De Gruyter, 1970): 879–881.
Q: 37

003 **Fragmentum**, ed. J. Demiańczuk, *Supplementum comicum*. Krakau: Nakładem Akademii, 1912 (repr. Hildesheim: Olms, 1967): 9.
fr. 1.
Q: 5

004 **Tituli**, ed. C. Austin, *Comicorum Graecorum fragmenta in papyris reperta*. Berlin: De Gruyter, 1973: 6.
fr. 13.
Pap: 4

0794 **APOLLOPHANES** Med.
3 B.C.: Seleuciensis

x01 **Fragmenta ap. Galenum.**
K13.220, 831, 979.
Cf. GALENUS Med. (0057 076–077).

x02 **Fragmentum ap. Oribasium.**
CMG, vol. 6.3, p. 87.
Cf. ORIBASIUS Med. (0722 004).

x03 **Fragmentum ap. Paulum.**
CMG, vol. 9.2, p. 373.
Cf. PAULUS Med. (0715 001).

x04 **Fragmentum ap. Alexandrum Trallianum.**
Puschmann, vol. 2, p. 387.
Cf. ALEXANDER Med. (0744 003).

2168 **APOLLOPHANES** Phil.
3 B.C.

001 **Fragmenta**, ed. J. von Arnim, *Stoicorum veterum fragmenta*, vol. 1. Leipzig: Teubner, 1905 (repr. Stuttgart: 1968): 90.
Q

9009 **Michael APOSTOLIUS** Paroemiogr.
A.D. 15: Constantinopolitanus, Creticus

001 **Collectio paroemiarum**, ed. E.L. von Leutsch, *Corpus paroemiographorum Graecorum*, vol. 2. Göttingen: Vandenhoeck & Ruprecht, 1851 (repr. Hildesheim: Olms, 1958): 233–744.
Cod: [56,540]

9007 *APPENDIX PROVERBIORUM*
Incertum
001 **Appendix proverbiorum**, ed. E.L. von Leutsch and F.G. Schneidewin, *Corpus paroemiographorum Graecorum*, vol. 1. Göttingen: Vandenhoeck & Ruprecht, 1839 (repr. Hildesheim: Olms, 1965): 379–467.
Cod: [8,284]

0551 **APPIANUS** Hist.
A.D. 1–2: Alexandrinus
001 **Prooemium**, ed. P. Viereck, A.G. Roos and E. Gabba, *Appiani historia Romana*, vol. 1. Leipzig: Teubner, 1939 (repr. 1962 (1st edn. corr.)): 1–12.
Cod: 2,396
002 **Basilica** (fragmenta), ed. Viereck, Roos, and Gabba, *op. cit.*, 12–20.
Q, Cod: 1,411
003 **Italica** (fragmenta), ed. Viereck, Roos, and Gabba, *op. cit.*, 20–27.
Q, Cod: 1,230
004 **Samnitica** (fragmenta), ed. Viereck, Roos, and Gabba, *op. cit.*, 27–43.
Q, Cod: 3,561
005 **Celtica** (fragmenta), ed. Viereck, Roos, and Gabba, *op. cit.*, 44–57.
Q, Cod: 2,321
006 **Sicelica** (fragmenta), ed. Viereck, Roos, and Gabba, *op. cit.*, 57–62.
Q, Cod: 1,019
007 **Iberica**, ed. Viereck, Roos, and Gabba, *op. cit.*, 62–140.
Cod: 16,514
008 **Annibaica**, ed. Viereck, Roos, and Gabba, *op. cit.*, 141–185.
Cod: 9,931
009 **Libyca**, ed. Viereck, Roos, and Gabba, *op. cit.*, 185–304.
Cod: 25,979
010 **Numidica** (fragmenta), ed. Viereck, Roos, and Gabba, *op. cit.*, 305–307.
Q, Cod: 407
011 **Macedonica** (fragmenta), ed. Viereck, Roos, and Gabba, *op. cit.*, 307–326.
Q, Cod: 3,852
012 **Illyrica**, ed. Viereck, Roos, and Gabba, *op. cit.*, 326–351.
Cod: 4,977
013 **Syriaca**, ed. Viereck, Roos, and Gabba, *op. cit.*, 352–418.
Cod: 14,027
014 **Mithridatica**, ed. Viereck, Roos, and Gabba, *op. cit.*, 418–531.
Cod: 24,766

015 **Fragmenta historiae Romanae**, ed. Viereck, Roos, and Gabba, *op. cit.*, 532–536.
frr. 2–24.
Q, Cod: 640
016 **Appiani ad Frontonem epistula**, ed. Viereck, Roos, and Gabba, *op. cit.*, 537–538.
Cod: 330
017 **Bellum civile**, ed. P. Viereck, *Appian's Roman history*, vols. 3–4 (ed. H. White). Cambridge, Mass.: Harvard University Press, 1913 (repr. 3:1964; 4:1961): **3**:2–566; **4**:2–616.
Cod: 120,226
018 **Testimonium**, FGrH #237: 2B:990.
NQ

2027 **APSINES** Rhet.
A.D. 3: Gadarensis
001 **Ars rhetorica**, ed. L. Spengel, *Rhetores Graeci*, vol. 1. Leipzig: Teubner, 1856 (repr. Frankfurt am Main: Minerva, 1966): 331–406.
Cod
002 Περὶ τῶν ἐσχηματισμένων προβλημάτων, ed. Spengel, *op. cit.*, 407–414.
Cod

1768 **AQUILA** Int. Vet. Test.
A.D. 2
001 **Fragmenta**, ed. J. Reider, *An index to Aquila* (rev. N. Turner). Leiden: Brill, 1966: passim.
Q

0795 **AQUILA SECUNDILLA** Med.
ante A.D. 1
x01 **Fragmentum ap. Galenum**.
K13.1031.
Cf. GALENUS Med. (0057 077).

4035 **ARABIUS** Epigr.
A.D. 6
001 **Epigrammata**, AG **9**.667; **16**.39, 144, 148–149, 225, 314.
Q: 199

0415 **ARAROS** Comic.
5–4 B.C.
001 **Fragmenta**, ed. T. Kock, *Comicorum Atticorum fragmenta*, vol. 2. Leipzig: Teubner, 1884: 215–219.
frr. 1–21.
Q: 115
002 **Fragmenta**, ed. A. Meineke, *Fragmenta comicorum Graecorum*, vol. 3. Berlin: Reimer, 1840 (repr. De Gruyter, 1970): 273–276.
Q: 93
003 **Tituli**, ed. C. Austin, *Comicorum Graecorum fragmenta in papyris reperta*. Berlin: De Gruyter, 1973: 6.
fr. 14.
Pap: 8
004 **Fragmentum**, ed. Kock, *op. cit.*, vol. 3 (1888): 738.
Q: [3]

0653 **ARATUS** Epic. et Astron.
4–3 B.C.: Soleus
001 **Phaenomena**, ed. J. Martin, *Arati phaenomena*.
Florence: La Nuova Italia Editrice, 1956: 3–154.
Cod: 7,867
002 **Fragmentum** (e cod. Vat. gr. 2130), ed. S.
Weinstock, *Codices Romani* [*Catalogus codicum astrologorum Graecorum* 5.4. Brussels: Academia, 1940]: 165–166.
Cf. et 0653 004.
Cod
004 **Fragmentum** (e cod. Matrit. 4616), ed. K.O.
Zuretti, *Codices Hispanienses* [*Catalogus codicum astrologorum Graecorum* 11.2. Brussels: Lamertin, 1934]: 133–134.
Cf. et 0653 002.
Cod
003 **Epigrammata**, AG 11.437; 12.129.
Q: 51
005 **Fragmenta et tituli**, ed. H. Lloyd-Jones and P.
Parsons, *Supplementum Hellenisticum*. Berlin: De Gruyter, 1983: 34–42.
frr. (+ titul.) 83–90, 92–120.
Q: [131]

2443 **ARATUS** Hist.
post 4 B.C.?: Cnidius
001 **Testimonium**, FGrH #642: 3C:188.
NQ

2162 **ARATUS** Hist.
3 B.C.: Sicyonius
001 **Testimonia**, FGrH #231: 2B:974–975.
NQ
002 **Fragmenta**, FGrH #231: 2B:975–978.
Q

2116 **ARCADIUS** Gramm.
A.D. 4?: Antiochenus
001 **De accentibus**, ed. M. Schmidt, Ἐπιτομὴ τῆς καθολικῆς προσῳδίας Ἡρωδιανοῦ. Jena: Mauke, 1860.
Q, Cod: [40,095]

0038 *ARCESILAI EPISTULA*
Incertum
Cf. et ARCESILAUS Phil. (1172).
001 **Epistula**, ed. R. Hercher, *Epistolographi Graeci*.
Paris: Didot, 1873 (repr. Amsterdam: Hakkert, 1965): 131.
Q: [97]

0520 **ARCESILAUS** Comic.
5 B.C.
001 **Fragmentum**, ed. J. Demiańczuk, *Supplementum comicum*. Krakau: Nakładem Akademii, 1912 (repr. Hildesheim: Olms, 1967): 10.
fr. 1.
Q: 11

1172 **ARCESILAUS** Phil.
vel Arcesilas
4–3 B.C.: Pitanaeus
Cf. et ARCESILAI EPISTULA (0038).
001 **Fragmenta**, ed. H. Lloyd-Jones and P. Parsons, *Supplementum Hellenisticum*. Berlin: De Gruyter, 1983: 42–43.
frr. 121–122.
Q: [69]
x01 **Epigrammata** (*App. Anth.*).
Epigramma sepulcrale: 2.382.
Epigramma demonstrativum: 3.56.
App. Anth. 2.382: Cf. EPIGRAMMATICI in *App. Anth.* (7052 002).
App. Anth. 3.56: Cf. EPIGRAMMATICI in *App. Anth.* (7052 003).

2608 **ARCHEBULUS** Poeta
3 B.C.: Thebaeus vel Theraeus
001 **Fragmentum**, ed. H. Lloyd-Jones and P. Parsons, *Supplementum Hellenisticum*. Berlin: De Gruyter, 1983: 44.
fr. 124.
Q: [5]

1173 **ARCHEDEMUS** Phil.
2 B.C.: Tarsensis
001 **Fragmenta**, ed. J. von Arnim, *Stoicorum veterum fragmenta*, vol. 3. Leipzig: Teubner, 1903 (repr. Stuttgart: 1968): 262–264.
Q

0416 **ARCHEDICUS** Comic.
4–3 B.C.
001 **Fragmenta**, ed. T. Kock, *Comicorum Atticorum fragmenta*, vol. 3. Leipzig: Teubner, 1888: 276–277.
frr. 1–3.
Q: 171
002 **Fragmenta**, ed. A. Meineke, *Fragmenta comicorum Graecorum*, vol. 4. Berlin: Reimer, 1841 (repr. De Gruyter, 1970): 435–437.
Q: 170

1935 **ARCHELAUS** Hist.
1 B.C.–A.D. 1: Cappadox
001 **Testimonia**, FGrH #123: 2B:629.
NQ
002 **Fragmenta**, FGrH #123: 2B:630–631.
fr. 6: *P. Oxy.* 2.218.
Q, Pap

0937 **ARCHELAUS** Med.
ante A.D. 1
x01 **Fragmentum ap. Galenum**.
K13.312.
Cf. GALENUS Med. (0057 076).

0570 **ARCHELAUS** Paradox.
3 B.C.: Aegyptius, Chersonesita
001 **Fragmenta**, ed. A. Giannini, *Paradoxographo-*

rum Graecorum reliquiae. Milan: Istituto Editoriale Italiano, 1965: 24–27.
Cod
002 **Epigramma,** AG 16.120.
Q: 33
003 **Fragmenta,** ed. H. Lloyd-Jones and P. Parsons, *Supplementum Hellenisticum.* Berlin: De Gruyter, 1983: 44–45.
frr. 125–129.
Q: [74]
x01 **Epigrammata demonstrativa.**
App. Anth. 3.50–52: Cf. EPIGRAMMATICI in *App. Anth.* (7052 003).

2303 **ARCHELAUS** Phil.
5 B.C.: Milesius, Atheniensis
001 **Testimonia,** ed. H. Diels and W. Kranz, *Die Fragmente der Vorsokratiker,* vol. 2, 6th edn. Berlin: Weidmann, 1952 (repr. Dublin: 1966): 44–47.
test. 1–18.
NQ
002 **Fragmenta,** ed. Diels and Kranz, *op. cit.,* 48.
frr. 1–2.
Q

1174 **ARCHEMACHUS** Hist.
3 B.C.?: Euboeus
001 **Fragmenta,** FGrH #424: 3B:319–322.
Q

1175 **ARCHESTRATUS** Parodius
4 B.C.: Gelensis vel Syracusanus
001 **Fragmenta,** ed. P. Brandt, *Corpusculum poesis epicae Graecae Ludibundae,* fasc. 1. Leipzig: Teubner, 1888: 140–170.
frr. 1–62.
Q: [2,617]
002 **Fragmenta et tituli,** ed. H. Lloyd-Jones and P. Parsons, *Supplementum Hellenisticum.* Berlin: De Gruyter, 1983: 46–74.
frr. (+ titul.) 132–133, 135–140, 142–192.
Q: [2,604]

1115 **ARCHESTRATUS** Trag.
4 B.C.
001 **Tituli,** ed. B. Snell, *Tragicorum Graecorum fragmenta,* vol. 1. Göttingen: Vandenhoeck & Ruprecht, 1971: 239.
NQ

0126 **Aulus Licinius ARCHIAS** Epigr.
1 B.C.: Antiochenus
001 **Epigrammata,** AG **5.**58–59, 98; **6.**16, 39, 179–181, 192, 195, 207; **7.**68, 140, 147, 165, 191, 213–214, 278, 696; **9.**19, 27, 64, 91, 111, 339, 343, 750; **10.**7–8, 10; **15.**51; **16.**94, 154, 179.
AG 6.194; 9.357: Cf. ANONYMI EPIGRAMMATICI (0138 001).
AG 7.164: Cf. ANTIPATER Epigr. (0113 001).
AG 9.345–348, 351, 354: Cf. Julius LEONIDAS

Math. et Astrol. (1457 001).
Q: 1,425
002 **Testimonium,** FGrH #186: 2B:918.
NQ

0796 **ARCHIBIUS** Med.
1 B.C.
x01 **Fragmentum ap. Galenum.**
K14.159–160.
Cf. GALENUS Med. (0057 078).

0661 **ARCHIGENES** Med.
A.D. 1–2: Apamensis
Cf. et ARCHIGENES et POSIDONIUS Med. (0869).
001 **Fragmenta,** ed. C. Brescia, *Frammenti medicinali di Archigene.* Naples: Libreria Scientifica, 1955: 9–24.
Περὶ φλεγμονῆς σπληνός: pp. 9–12.
Θεραπεία: pp. 12–14.
Περὶ τῶν ἑλμίνθων γενῶν καὶ πόσαι διαφοραί: pp. 14–20.
Περὶ λειεντερίας: pp. 20–24.
Q: 5,448
002 **Fragmenta inedita,** ed. G.L. Calabrò, "Frammenti inediti di Archigene," *Bollettino del comitato per la preparazione della edizione nazionale dei classici greci e latini* 9 (1961) 68–72.
Περὶ ἀποστήματος ἐν ἥπατι: pp. 68–69.
Θεραπεία ἡλκωμένου ἥπατος: pp. 69–70.
Περὶ καχεξίας: p. 71.
Κοινὴ δίαιτα πάντων τῶν ὑδρωπικῶν: p. 72.
Q: 1,753
x01 **Fragmenta ap. Galenum.**
K**12.**406–410, 432, 443–445, 460–462, 463, 468–469, 533–534, 537–541, 546, 550, 551, 572–573, 576–578, 582, 620–624, 644–646, 655–658, 661–662, 671–673, 675–677, 679–680, 681, 790–803, 807–814, 821–822, 846–847, 855–858, 859–864, 873–877, 954, 969, 972–974, 1000–1002; **13.**167–175, 217–219, 234–236, 254–256, 262–266, 331, 730–734.
Cf. GALENUS Med. (0057 076–077).
x02 **Fragmenta ap. Oribasium.**
CMG **6.1.1,** pp. 247, 250, 296; **6.2.1,** pp. 103, 146, 234, 236, 257; **6.2.2,** pp. 205, 299; **6.3,** pp. 104, 269.
Cf. ORIBASIUS Med. (0722 001, 003–004).
x03 **Fragmenta ap. Paulum.**
CMG **9.1,** pp. 117, 122, 222, 245, 326, 328, 333, 349, 356, 361, 367; **9.2,** pp. 17, 288.
Cf. PAULUS Med. (0715 001).
x04 **Fragmenta ap. Aëtium** (lib. 3).
CMG 8.1, pp. 341–343, 344, 351, 352–355.
Cf. AËTIUS Med. (0718 003).
x05 **Fragmentum ap. Aëtium** (lib. 8).
CMG 8.2, p. 475.
Cf. AËTIUS Med. (0718 008).
x06 **Fragmentum ap. Aëtium** (lib. 9).
Athena 23 (1911) 359–365.
Cf. AËTIUS Med. (0718 009).

x07 **Fragmenta ap. Philumenum.**
CMG 10.1.1, pp. 10, 17, 37, 40.
Cf. PHILUMENUS Med. (0671 001).

x08 **Fragmenta ap. Alexandrum Trallianum.**
Puschmann, vol. 1, pp. 557, 567.
Cf. ALEXANDER Med. (0744 003).

0869 **ARCHIGENES et POSIDONIUS** Med.
A.D. 1–2
Cf. et ARCHIGENES Med. (0661).

x01 **Fragmenta ap. Aëtium** (lib. 6).
CMG, vol. 8.2, pp. 128–141.
Cf. AËTIUS Med. (0718 006).

0232 **ARCHILOCHUS** Iamb. et Eleg.
7 B.C.: Parius

001 **Fragmenta,** ed. M.L. West, *Iambi et elegi Graeci,* vol. 1. Oxford: Clarendon Press, 1971: 1–60, 62, 65–96, 99–100, 102–104, 106–108.
frr. 1–6, 8–32, 34–38, 40–89, 91, 93a, 94–96, 98–166, 168–197, 200–203, 205–239, 242–246, 248–249, 251–258, 260, 262, 268, 276, 279, 282, 296–299, 306–307, 313, 322–331.
Q, Pap, Epigr: 3,394

002 **Fragmenta lyrica,** ed. D.L. Page, *Supplementum lyricis Graecis.* Oxford: Clarendon Press, 1974: 151–154.
fr. S478a–b.
Pap: 277

003 **Epigrammata,** AG **6**.133; 7.441.
Q: 24

x01 **Epigrammata** (*App. Anth.*).
Epigramma demonstrativum: 3.1.
Epigramma irrisorium: 5.1.
App. Anth. 3.1: Cf. EPIGRAMMATICI in *App. Anth.* (7052 003).
App. Anth. 5.1: Cf. EPIGRAMMATICI in *App. Anth.* (7052 005).

ARCHIMEDES Epigr.
AG 7.50.
Cf. ARCHIMELUS Epigr. (0131 001).

0552 **ARCHIMEDES** Geom.
3 B.C.: Syracusanus

001 **De sphaera et cylindro,** ed. C. Mugler, *Archimède,* vol. 1. Paris: Les Belles Lettres, 1970: 8–131.
Cod: [27,088]

002 **Dimensio circuli,** ed. Mugler, *op. cit.,* vol. 1, 138–143.
Cod: [1,174]

003 **De conoidibus et sphaeroidibus,** ed. Mugler, *op. cit.,* vol. 1, 152–252.
Cod: [23,983]

004 **De lineis spiralibus,** ed. Mugler, *op. cit.,* vol. 2 (1971): 8–74.
Cod: [15,089]

005 **De planorum aequilibriis,** ed. Mugler, *op. cit.,* vol. 2, 80–125.
Cod: [9,485]

006 **Arenarius,** ed. Mugler, *op. cit.,* vol. 2, 134–157.
Cod: [5,278]

007 **Quadratura parabolae,** ed. Mugler, *op. cit.,* vol. 2, 164–195.
Cod: [6,132]

008 **De corporibus fluitantibus,** ed. Mugler, vol. 3 (1971): 6–66.
Cod: [8,900]

009 **Stomachion,** ed. Mugler, *op. cit.,* vol. 3, 70–72.
Cod: [474]

010 **Ad Eratosthenem methodus,** ed. Mugler, *op. cit.,* vol. 3, 82–127.
Cod: [10,305]

011 **Liber assumptorum,** ed. Mugler, *op. cit.,* vol. 3, 134–164.
Cod: [3,869]

012 **Problema bovinum,** ed. Mugler, *op. cit.,* vol. 3, 170–173.
Problema: pp. 170–171.
Scholion: pp. 171–173.
Cod: [728]

013 **Fragmenta,** ed. J.L. Heiberg and E. Stamatis, *Archimedis opera omnia cum commentariis Eutocii,* vol. 2. Leipzig: Teubner, 1913 (repr. Stuttgart: 1972): 536–545, 547–554.
De polyedris (frr. 1–3): pp. 536–541.
De mensura circuli (frr. 4–5): p. 542.
Περὶ πλινθίδων καὶ κυλίνδρων (fr. 6): p. 542.
De superficiebus et corporibus irregularibus (frr. 7–8): pp. 543–544.
Appendix libri ii de sphaera et cylindro (fr. 9): p. 544.
Πρὸς Ζεύξιππον (fr. 10): p. 545.
Mechanica (frr. 11–15): pp. 545, 547–548.
Κατοπτρικά (frr. 17–21): pp. 549–551.
Περὶ σφαιροποιίας (fr. 22): pp. 551–554.
De anni magnitudine (fr. 23): p. 554.
Q: [2,906]

014 **Problema bovinum** [Dub.], ed. H. Lloyd-Jones and P. Parsons, *Supplementum Hellenisticum.* Berlin: De Gruyter, 1983: 77–78.
fr. 201.
Cf. et 0552 012.
Q: [273]

x01 **Problema.**
App. Anth. 7.5: Cf. EPIGRAMMATICI in *App. Anth.* (7052 007).

0131 **ARCHIMELUS** Epigr.
3 B.C.

001 **Epigramma,** AG 7.50.
Q: 37

002 **Fragmentum de Hieronis II navigio,** ed. H. Lloyd-Jones and P. Parsons, *Supplementum Hellenisticum.* Berlin: De Gruyter, 1983: 79.
fr. 202.
Q: [109]

x01 **Epigramma demonstrativum.**
App. Anth. 3.82: Cf. EPIGRAMMATICI in *App. Anth.* (7052 003).

2418 **ARCHINUS** Hist.
post 4 B.C.

001 **Fragmenta**, FGrH #604: 3B:738.
Q

0417 **ARCHIPPUS** Comic.
5 B.C.
001 **Fragmenta**, ed. T. Kock, *Comicorum Attico-rum fragmenta*, vol. 1. Leipzig: Teubner, 1880: 679–689.
frr. 1–19, 21–27, 29, 31–44, 46–54.
Q: 358
002 **Fragmenta**, ed. A. Meineke, *Fragmenta comico-rum Graecorum*, vol. 2.2. Berlin: Reimer, 1840 (repr. De Gruyter, 1970): 715–718, 720–728.
Q: 270
003 **Fragmenta**, ed. J. Demiańczuk, *Supplementum comicum*. Krakau: Nakładem Akademii, 1912 (repr. Hildesheim: Olms, 1967): 10–11.
frr. 1–7.
Q, Cod: 34
004 **Tituli**, ed. C. Austin, *Comicorum Graecorum fragmenta in papyris reperta*. Berlin: De Gruy-ter, 1973: 6.
fr. 15.
Pap: 6

2214 **ARCHITIMUS** Hist.
ante A.D. 2
001 **Fragmentum**, FGrH #315: 3B:25–26.
Q

1176 **ARCHYTAS** Epic.
3 B.C.: Amphissensis
001 **Fragmenta**, ed. J.U. Powell, *Collectanea Alex-andrina*. Oxford: Clarendon Press, 1925 (repr. 1970): 23.
frr. 1–4.
Q: [34]

0620 **ARCHYTAS** Phil.
4 B.C.: Tarentinus
001 **Testimonia**, ed. H. Diels and W. Kranz, *Die Fragmente der Vorsokratiker*, vol. 1, 6th edn. Berlin: Weidmann, 1951 (repr. Dublin: 1966): 421–431.
test. 1–26.
NQ
002 **Fragmenta**, ed. Diels and Kranz, *op. cit.*, 431–439.
frr. 1–9.
Q

1177 **Pseudo-ARCHYTAS** Phil.
Incertum
001 **Fragmenta**, ed. H. Thesleff, *The Pythagorean texts of the Hellenistic period*. Åbo: Åbo Aka-demi, 1965: 3–48.
Q: 13,025

ARCTINUS Epic.
7 B.C.?: Milesius
Cf. AETHIOPIS (0683).
Cf. ILIU PERSIS (1445).

Cf. TITANOMACHIA (1737).

1178 **<ARESAS>** Phil.
vel Aesara
3 B.C.
001 **Fragmentum**, ed. H. Thesleff, *The Pythagorean texts of the Hellenistic period*. Åbo: Åbo Aka-demi, 1965: 48–50.
Q: 527

2193 **[ARETADES]** Hist.
Incertum: Cnidius
001 **Fragmenta**, FGrH #285: 3A:162–163.
Q

0719 **ARETAEUS** Med.
A.D. 2
001 **De causis et signis acutorum morborum** (lib. 1), ed. K. Hude, *Aretaeus*, 2nd edn. [*Corpus medicorum Graecorum*, vol. 2. Berlin: Akade-mie-Verlag, 1958]: 3–35.
Cod: 9,752
002 **De causis et signis acutorum morborum** (lib. 2), ed. Hude, *op. cit.*, 36–90.
Cod: 17,621
003 **De curatione acutorum morborum libri duo**, ed. Hude, *op. cit.*, 91–143.
Cod: 16,676
004 **De curatione diuturnorum morborum libri duo**, ed. Hude, *op. cit.*, 144–170.
Cod: 8,255

2130 **ARETHAS** Scr. Eccl.
A.D. 9–10: Caesariensis (Cappadociae)
Bibliography in progress
001 **Epigrammata**, AG 15.32–34.
Q: 229
002 **Fragmenta in epistulam ad Romanos** (in cate-nis), ed. K. Staab, *Pauluskommentar aus der griechischen Kirche aus Katenenhandschriften gesammelt*. Münster: Aschendorff, 1933: 653–659.
Q: 1,698
003 **Fragmenta in epistulam i ad Corinthios** (in catenis), ed. Staab, *op. cit.*, 659–660.
Q: 173
004 **Fragmenta in epistulam ii ad Corinthios** (in catenis), ed. Staab, *op. cit.*, 660–661.
Q: 335
005 **Fragmenta in epistulam ii ad Thessalonicenses** (in catenis), ed. Staab, *op. cit.*, 661.
Q: 27
006 **Fragmenta in epistulam i ad Timotheum** (in catenis), ed. Staab, *op. cit.*, 661.
Q: 70
007 **Fragmenta in epistulam ad Hebraeos** (in cate-nis), ed. Staab, *op. cit.*, 661.
Q: 42

0132 **Marcus ARGENTARIUS** Rhet. et Epigr.
1 B.C.–A.D. 1
001 **Epigrammata**, AG 5.16, 32, 63, 89, 102, 104–

105, 110, 113, 116, 118, 127–128; **6**.201, 246,
248, 333; **7**.364, 374, 384, 395, 403; **9**.87, 161,
221, 229, 246, 270, 286, 554, 732; **10**.4, 18;
11.26, 28, 320; **16**.241.
AG 6.246: Cf. et PHILODEMUS Phil. (1595
001).
AG 9.733: Cf. ANONYMI EPIGRAMMATICI
(0138 001).
Q: 1,405

2215 **AR(I)AETHUS** Hist.
ante 2 B.C.?: Tegeates
001 **Fragmenta**, FGrH #316: 3B:26–30.
Q

1179 **<ARIMNESTUS>** Phil.
4–3 B.C.?
001 **Fragmentum**, ed. H. Thesleff, *The Pythagorean
texts of the Hellenistic period*. Åbo: Åbo Akademi, 1965: 51.
Q: 61

2658 **ARION** Lyr.
7 B.C.: Methymnaeus
x01 **Fragmentum**.
PMG, p. 507.
Cf. LYRICA ADESPOTA (PMG) (0297 001).
x02 **Epigramma dedicatorium**.
App. Anth. 1.3(?): Cf. EPIGRAMMATICI in
App. Anth. (7052 001).

0378 **ARIPHRON** Lyr.
4 B.C.: Sicyonius
001 **Fragmentum**, ed. D.L. Page, *Poetae melici
Graeci*. Oxford: Clarendon Press, 1962 (repr.
1967 (1st edn. corr.)): 422.
fr. 1.
Q: [66]
x01 **Epigramma exhortatorium et supplicatorium**.
App. Anth. 4.30: Cf. EPIGRAMMATICI in *App.
Anth.* (7052 004).

4000 **ARISTAENETUS** Epist.
A.D. 5
001 **Epistulae**, ed. O. Mazal, *Aristaeneti epistularum libri ii*. Stuttgart: Teubner, 1971: 1–100.
Cod

2519 **ARISTAENETUS** Hist.
post 4 B.C.?
001 **Fragmentum**, FGrH #771: 3C:766.
Q

2429 **ARISTAENETUS** Hist. et Rhet.
A.D. 2/3?: fort. Byzantius
001 **Testimonia**, FGrH #623: 3C:158.
NQ
002 **Fragmentum**, FGrH #623: 3C:158.
Q

1180 **<ARISTAEUS>** Phil.
3–2 B.C.?

001 **Fragmenta**, ed. H. Thesleff, *The Pythagorean
texts of the Hellenistic period*. Åbo: Åbo Akademi, 1965: 52–53.
Q: 322

0418 **ARISTAGORAS** Comic.
5 B.C.?
001 **Fragmenta**, ed. T. Kock, *Comicorum Atticorum fragmenta*, vol. 1. Leipzig: Teubner, 1880:
710–711.
frr. 1–7.
Q: 38
002 **Fragmenta**, ed. A. Meineke, *Fragmenta comicorum Graecorum*, vol. 2.2. Berlin: Reimer, 1840
(repr. De Gruyter, 1970): 761.
Q: 32

1190 **ARISTAGORAS** Hist.
4 B.C.: fort. Milesius
001 **Testimonia**, FGrH #608: 3C:2.
NQ
002 **Fragmenta**, FGrH #608: 3C:3–5.
Q

1181 **ARISTARCHUS** Astron.
4–3 B.C.: Samius
001 **De magnitudinibus et distantiis solis et lunae**,
ed. T. Heath, *Aristarchus of Samos, the ancient
Copernicus*. Oxford: Clarendon Press, 1913
(repr. 1966): 352–410.
Cod: [7,452]

2290 **ARISTARCHUS** Hist.
A.D. 1–2?: Eleus
001 **Fragmentum**, FGrH #412: 3B:304.
Q

0798 **ARISTARCHUS** Med.
ante A.D. 1: Tarsensis
x01 **Fragmentum ap. Galenum**.
K13.824–825.
Cf. GALENUS Med. (0057 077).

0871 **ARISTARCHUS** Med.
fiq Aristus Aristarchus
ante A.D. 2
Cf. et Aristus ARISTARCHUS Med. (0878).
x01 **Fragmentum ap. Galenum**.
K12.818.
Cf. GALENUS Med. (0057 076).

0878 **Aristus ARISTARCHUS** Med.
ante A.D. 2
x01 **Fragmentum ap. Galenum**.
K13.103–104.
Cf. GALENUS Med. (0057 076).
x02 **Fragmentum ap. Aëtium** (lib. 8).
CMG, vol. 8.2, p. 537.
Cf. AËTIUS Med. (0718 008).

1767 **ARISTARCHUS** Philol.
3–2 B.C.: Samothracenus

001 **Fragmenta**, ed. A. Ludwich, *Aristarchs Homerische Textkritik nach den Fragmenten des Didymos*, 2 vols. Leipzig: Teubner, 1:1884; 2:1885 (repr. Hildesheim: Olms, 1971): 1:175-631; 2:passim.
Q

002 **Fragmenta**, ed. K. Lehrs, *De Aristarchi studiis Homericis*. Leipzig: Hirzel, 1882 (repr. Hildesheim: Olms, 1964): passim.
Q

0306 **ARISTARCHUS** Trag.
5 B.C.: Tegeates
001 **Fragmenta**, ed. B. Snell, *Tragicorum Graecorum fragmenta*, vol. 1. Göttingen: Vandenhoeck & Ruprecht, 1971: 90-92.
frr. 1a-1b, 2-6.
fr. 1a: *P. Petrie* 2.49b.
Q, Pap: [115]

1183 *ARISTEAE EPISTULA*
3 B.C./A.D. 1
001 **Aristeae epistula ad Philocratem**, ed. A. Pelletier, *Lettre d'Aristée à Philocrate* [*Sources chrétiennes* 89. Paris: Cerf, 1962]: 100-240.
Cod: [13,187]

1182 **[ARISTEAS]** Epic.
6 B.C.: Proconnensis
001 **Fragmenta**, ed. G. Kinkel, *Epicorum Graecorum fragmenta*, vol. 1. Leipzig: Teubner, 1877: 245.
frr. 1-4.
Q: [77]

002 **Fragmenta**, ed. J.D.P. Bolton, *Aristeas of Proconnesus*. Oxford: Clarendon Press, 1962: 207-214.
Q

003 **Testimonia**, FGrH #35: 1A:259, *14-*15 addenda.
NQ

2488 **ARISTEAS** Hist.
2-1 B.C.: Judaeus
001 **Fragmentum**, FGrH #725: 3C:680.
Q

0305 **ARISTIAS** Trag.
5 B.C.
001 **Fragmenta**, ed. B. Snell, *Tragicorum Graecorum fragmenta*, vol. 1. Göttingen: Vandenhoeck & Ruprecht, 1971: 85-87.
frr. 1-8.
Q: [68]

1184 **ARISTIDES** Apol.
A.D. 2: Atheniensis
001 **Fragmenta** (*P. Oxy.* 15.1778), ed. C. Vona, *L'apologia di Aristide*. Rome: Facultas Theologica Pontificii Athenaei Lateranensis, 1950: 115.
Pap: [153]

002 **Fragmenta** (*P. Lond.* 2486), ed. Vona, *op. cit.*, 116-117.
Pap: [357]

003 **Fragmenta**, ed. Vona, *op. cit.*, 117-126.
Q: [3,050]

2342 **ARISTIDES** Hist.
2-1 B.C.
001 **Testimonia**, FGrH #495: 3B:466.
NQ

002 **Fragmentum**, FGrH #495: 3B:466.
Q

1185 **ARISTIDES** Hist.
ante A.D. 1
001 **Fragmenta**, FGrH #444: 3B:374-376.
Q

2194 **[ARISTIDES]** Hist.
Incertum: Milesius
001 **Fragmenta**, FGrH #286: 3A:163-168.
Q

0284 **Aelius ARISTIDES** Rhet.
A.D. 2: Mysius
001 Εἰς Δία, ed. W. Dindorf, *Aristides*, vol. 1. Leipzig: Reimer, 1829 (repr. Hildesheim: Olms, 1964): 1-11.
Cod: 2,065

002 Ἀθηνᾶ, ed. Dindorf, *op. cit.*, vol. 1, 12-28.
Cod: 2,314

003 Ἰσθμικὸς εἰς Ποσειδῶνα, ed. Dindorf, *op. cit.*, vol. 1, 29-46.
Cod: 3,493

004 Διόνυσος, ed. Dindorf, *op. cit.*, vol. 1, 47-52.
Cod: 789

005 Ἡρακλῆς, ed. Dindorf, *op. cit.*, vol. 1, 53-62.
Cod: 1,534

006 Λαλιὰ εἰς Ἀσκληπιόν, ed. Dindorf, *op. cit.*, vol. 1, 63-70.
Cod: 1,240

007 Ἀσκληπιάδαι, ed. Dindorf, *op. cit.*, vol. 1, 71-80.
Cod: 1,566

008 Εἰς τὸν Σάραπιν, ed. Dindorf, *op. cit.*, vol. 1, 81-97.
Cod: 2,669

009 Εἰς βασιλέα, ed. Dindorf, *op. cit.*, vol. 1, 98-112.
Cod: 2,982

010 Ἀπελλᾶ γενεθλιακός, ed. Dindorf, *op. cit.*, vol. 1, 113-125.
Cod: 2,142

011 Εἰς Ἐτεωνέα ἐπικήδειος, ed. Dindorf, *op. cit.*, vol. 1, 126-133.
Cod: 1,325

012 Ἐπὶ Ἀλεξάνδρῳ ἐπιτάφιος, ed. Dindorf, *op. cit.*, vol. 1, 134-149.
Cod: 2,802

013 Παναθηναϊκός, ed. Dindorf, *op. cit.*, vol. 1, 150-320.
Cod: 29,523

014 'Ρώμης ἐγκώμιον, ed. Dindorf, *op. cit.*, vol. 1, 321-370.
Cod: 8,680

015 Σμυρναϊκὸς πολιτικός, ed. Dindorf, *op. cit.*, vol. 1, 371-381.
Cod: 1,922

016 Πανηγυρικὸς ἐν Κυζίκῳ περὶ τοῦ ναοῦ, ed. Dindorf, *op. cit.*, vol. 1, 382-400.
Cod: 3,327

017 Εἰς τὸ Αἰγαῖον πέλαγος, ed. Dindorf, *op. cit.*, vol. 1, 401-407.
Cod: 1,203

018 Εἰς τὸ φρέαρ τοῦ 'Ασκληπιοῦ, ed. Dindorf, *op. cit.*, vol. 1, 408-414.
Cod: 1,287

019 'Ελευσίνιος, ed. Dindorf, *op. cit.*, vol. 1, 415-423.
Cod: 1,044

020 Μονῳδία ἐπὶ Σμύρνῃ, ed. Dindorf, *op. cit.*, vol. 1, 424-428.
Cod: 745

021 Παλινῳδία ἐπὶ Σμύρνῃ καὶ τῷ ταύτης ἀνοικισμῷ, ed. Dindorf, *op. cit.*, vol. 1, 429-438.
Cod: 1,734

022 Προσφωνητικὸς Σμυρναϊκός, ed. Dindorf, *op. cit.*, vol. 1, 439-444.
Cod: 1,137

023 'Ιερῶν λόγος α', ed. Dindorf, *op. cit.*, vol. 1, 445-464.
Cod: 5,331

024 'Ιερῶν λόγος β', ed. Dindorf, *op. cit.*, vol. 1, 465-487.
Cod: 5,858

025 'Ιερῶν λόγος γ', ed. Dindorf, *op. cit.*, vol. 1, 488-501.
Cod: 3,548

026 'Ιερῶν λόγος δ', ed. Dindorf, *op. cit.*, vol. 1, 502-533.
Cod: 8,137

027 'Ιερῶν λόγος ε', ed. Dindorf, *op. cit.*, vol. 1, 534-550.
Cod: 4,546

028 'Ιερῶν λόγος ς', ed. Dindorf, *op. cit.*, vol. 1, 551.
Cod: 132

029 Περὶ τοῦ πέμπειν βοήθειαν τοῖς ἐν Σικελίᾳ, ed. Dindorf, *op. cit.*, vol. 1, 552-570.
Cod: 3,906

030 Εἰς τὸ ἐναντίον, ed. Dindorf, *op. cit.*, vol. 1, 571-590.
Cod: 4,562

031 'Υπὲρ τῆς πρὸς Λακεδαιμονίους εἰρήνης, ed. Dindorf, *op. cit.*, vol. 1, 591-600.
Cod: 2,411

032 'Υπὲρ τῆς πρὸς 'Αθηναίους εἰρήνης, ed. Dindorf, *op. cit.*, vol. 1, 601-609.
Cod: 2,060

033 Λευκτρικὸς α' (ὑπὲρ Λακεδαιμονίων πρῶτος), ed. Dindorf, *op. cit.*, vol. 1, 611-641.
Cod: 5,903

034 Λευκτρικὸς β' (ὑπὲρ Θηβαίων πρῶτος), ed. Dindorf, *op. cit.*, 642-670.
Cod: 6,171

035 Λευκτρικὸς γ' (ὑπὲρ Λακεδαιμονίων δεύτερος), ed. Dindorf, *op. cit.*, vol. 1, 671-683.
Cod: 2,692

036 Λευκτρικὸς δ' (ὑπὲρ Θηβαίων δεύτερος), ed. Dindorf, *op. cit.*, vol. 1, 684-695.
Cod: 2,533

037 Λευκτρικὸς ε' (ὑπὲρ μηδετέροις βοηθεῖν), ed. Dindorf, *op. cit.*, vol. 1, 696-710.
Cod: 3,297

038 Συμμαχικὸς α', ed. Dindorf, *op. cit.*, vol. 1, 711-731.
Cod: 4,069

039 Συμμαχικὸς β' (πρὸς Θηβαίους περὶ τῆς συμμαχίας), ed. Dindorf, *op. cit.*, vol. 1, 732-750.
Cod: 4,275

040 Συμβουλευτικὸς περὶ τοῦ μὴ δεῖν κωμῳδεῖν, ed. Dindorf, *op. cit.*, vol. 1, 751-761.
Cod: 2,184

041 'Επιστολὴ περὶ Σμύρνης, ed. Dindorf, *op. cit.*, vol. 1, 762-767.
Cod: 1,230

042 Περὶ ὁμονοίας ταῖς πόλεσιν, ed. Dindorf, *op. cit.*, vol. 1, 768-796.
Cod: 6,621

043 'Ροδιακός, ed. Dindorf, *op. cit.*, vol. 1, 797-823.
Cod: 5,399

044 'Ροδίοις περὶ ὁμονοίας, ed. Dindorf, *op. cit.*, vol. 1, 824-844.
Cod: 4,467

045 Πρὸς Πλάτωνα περὶ ῥητορικῆς, ed. Dindorf, *op. cit.*, vol. 2 (1829; repr. 1964): 1-155.
Cod: 31,045

046 Πρὸς Πλάτωνα ὑπὲρ τῶν τεττάρων, ed. Dindorf, *op. cit.*, vol. 2, 156-414.
Cod: 54,081

047 Πρὸς Καπίτωνα, ed. Dindorf, *op. cit.*, vol. 2, 415-436.
Cod: 4,437

048 Αἰγύπτιος, ed. Dindorf, *op. cit.*, vol. 2, 437-490.
Cod: 11,116

049 Περὶ τοῦ παραφθέγματος, ed. Dindorf, *op. cit.*, vol. 2, 491-542.
Cod: 11,476

050 Κατὰ τῶν ἐξορχουμένων, ed. Dindorf, *op. cit.*, vol. 2, 543-570.
Cod: 4,201

051 Πρὸς τοὺς αἰτιωμένους ὅτι μὴ μελετῴη, ed. Dindorf, *op. cit.*, vol. 2, 571-583.
Cod: 2,319

052 Πρεσβευτικὸς πρὸς 'Αχιλλέα, ed. Dindorf, *op. cit.*, vol. 2, 584-608.
Cod: 3,542

053 Πρὸς Δημοσθένη περὶ ἀτελείας, ed. Dindorf, *op. cit.*, vol. 2, 609-641.
Cod: 9,257

054 Πρὸς Λεπτίνην ὑπὲρ ἀτελείας, ed. Dindorf, *op. cit.*, vol. 2, 651-706.
Cod: 11,262

055 Πανηγυρικὸς ἐπὶ τῷ ὕδατι ἐν Περγάμῳ, ed. Dindorf, *op. cit.*, vol. 2, 707-709.
Cod: 375

056 **Ars rhetorica** [Sp.], ed. L. Spengel, *Rhetores Graeci*, vol. 2. Leipzig: Teubner, 1854 (repr. Frankfurt am Main: Minerva, 1966): 459-554.
Cod: 23,686

057 **Fragmenta lyrica**, ed. E. Heitsch, *Die griechischen Dichterfragmente der römischen Kaiserzeit*, vol. 2. Göttingen: Vandenhoeck & Ruprecht, 1964: 41-42.
frr. 1-5.
Q: 52

x01 **Epigramma dedicatorium.**
App. Anth. 1.257: Cf. EPIGRAMMATICI in *App. Anth.* (7052 001).

x02 **Prolegomena in Aristidem.**
Cf. SOPATER Rhet. (2031 004).

2054 **ARISTIDES QUINTILIANUS** Mus.
A.D. 3

001 **De musica**, ed. R.P. Winnington-Ingram, *Aristidis Quintiliani de musica libri tres*. Leipzig: Teubner, 1963: 1-134.
Cod: [31,576]

2352 **ARISTION** Hist.
Incertum

001 **Titulus**, FGrH #509: 3B:487.
NQ

0801 **ARISTION** Med.
A.D. 1: Alexandrinus

x01 **Fragmentum ap. Oribasium.**
CMG, vol. 6.2.2, p. 35.
Cf. ORIBASIUS Med. (0722 001).

ARISTIPPI EPISTULAE
Epist. Graec., pp. 617-619, 622, 628-629.
Cf. SOCRATICORUM EPISTULAE (0637 001).

2513 **ARISTIPPUS** Hist.
4 B.C.: Cyrenaeus

001 **Testimonium**, FGrH #759: 3C:741.
NQ

2216 **ARISTIPPUS** Hist.
ante 2 B.C.

001 **Testimonium**, FGrH #317: 3B:30.
NQ
002 **Fragmenta**, FGrH #317: 3B:30-31.
Q

1187 **ARISTOBULUS** Hist.
4 B.C.: Cassandreus

001 **Testimonia**, FGrH #139: 2B:769.
NQ
002 **Fragmenta**, FGrH #139: **2B**:769-799; **3B**:743 addenda.
Q

2557 **ARISTOBULUS** Hist.
Incertum: Milesius

001 **Fragmentum**, FGrH #830: 3C:900.
Q

1186 **ARISTOBULUS Judaeus** Phil.
2 B.C.: Alexandrinus

001 **Fragmenta**, ed. A.-M. Denis, *Fragmenta pseudepigraphorum quae supersunt Graeca [Pseudepigrapha veteris testamenti Graece* 3. Leiden: Brill, 1970]: 217-228.
Q: [1,656]

2405 **ARISTOCLES** Hist.
ante 1 B.C.

001 **Titulus**, FGrH #586: 3B:701.
NQ

2302 **ARISTOCLES** Hist.
vel Aristoteles
ante A.D. 2

001 **Fragmenta**, FGrH #436: 3B:368-369.
Q

2453 **ARISTOCLES** Hist.
A.D. 2: Messenius

001 **Testimonium**, FGrH #664: 3C:214.
NQ

0802 **ARISTOCLES** Med.
ante A.D. 1

x01 **Fragmenta ap. Galenum.**
K12.936; 13.205, 977.
Cf. GALENUS Med. (0057 076-077).

1882 **ARISTOCLES** Myth.
1 B.C.?

001 **Testimonium**, FGrH #33: 1A:257.
NQ
002 **Fragmenta**, FGrH #33: 1A:257-258.
Q

0571 **ARISTOCLES** Paradox.
3 B.C.?/A.D. 1

001 **Testimonium**, ed. A. Giannini, *Paradoxographorum Graecorum reliquiae*. Milan: Istituto Editoriale Italiano, 1965: 390.
NQ
002 **Fragmenta**, ed. Giannini, *op. cit.*, 390-391.
frr. 1-3.
Q
003 **Fragmenta**, FGrH #831: 3C:901.
Q
004 **Fragmentum**, ed. H. Lloyd-Jones and P. Parsons, *Supplementum Hellenisticum*. Berlin: De Gruyter, 1983: 80-81.
fr. 206.
Q: [59]

x01 **Epigramma exhortatorium et supplicatorium.**
App. Anth. 4.45: Cf. EPIGRAMMATICI in *App. Anth.* (7052 004).

1188 **ARISTOCLES** Phil.
A.D. 2: Messanius

001 **Fragmenta**, ed. H. Heiland, *Aristoclis Messenii*

reliquiae. Giessen: Meyer, 1925: 23–42, 45–89.
Q: [9,590]

0803 **ARISTOCRATES** Gramm.
A.D. 1?
x01 **Fragmenta ap. Galenum.**
K12.878, 879.
Cf. GALENUS Med. (0057 076).

1189 **ARISTOCRATES** Hist.
1 B.C.–A.D. 1: Lacedaemonius
001 **Testimonium,** FGrH #591: 3B:705.
NQ
002 **Fragmenta,** FGrH #591: 3B:705–706.
Q

2659 **ARISTOCREON** Epigr.
3 B.C.
x01 **Epigramma dedicatorium.**
App. Anth. 1.129: Cf. EPIGRAMMATICI in
App. Anth. (7052 001).

2455 **ARISTOCREON** Hist.
3 B.C.?
001 **Testimonia,** FGrH #667: 3C:279.
NQ
002 **Fragmenta,** FGrH #667: 3C:279–280.
Q

2341 **ARISTOCRITUS** Hist.
3 B.C.?: fort. Milesius
001 **Testimonia,** FGrH #493: 3B:464.
NQ
002 **Fragmenta,** FGrH #493: 3B:464–465.
Q

2292 **ARISTODEMUS** Hist.
2 B.C.?: Eleus
001 **Fragmenta,** FGrH #414: 3B:306–307.
Q

2148 **ARISTODEMUS** Hist.
A.D. 4
001 **Fragmenta,** FGrH #104: 2A:493–503.
Q
002 **Fragmentum** (*P. Oxy.* 27.2469), ed. H.J.
Mette, "Die 'Kleinen' griechischen Historiker
heute," *Lustrum* 21 (1978) 15–16.
fr. 1b.
Pap

2269 **ARISTODEMUS** Hist. et Gramm.
2 B.C.: Thebanus, Alexandrinus
001 **Fragmenta,** FGrH #383: 3B:258–261.
Q

1875 **ARISTODEMUS** Myth. et Hist.
1 B.C.: Nyssensis
001 **Fragmenta,** FGrH #22: 1A:186.
Q

0133 **ARISTODICUS** Epigr.
3 B.C.: Rhodius

001 **Epigrammata,** AG 7.189, 473.
Q: 49

1885 **ARISTODICUS** Hist.
Incertum
001 **Fragmentum,** FGrH #36: 1A:259.
Q

1191 **<ARISTOMBROTUS>** Phil.
4 B.C.?
001 **Fragmentum,** ed. H. Thesleff, *The Pythagorean
texts of the Hellenistic period.* Åbo: Åbo Akademi, 1965: 53–54.
Q: 125

0419 **ARISTOMENES** Comic.
5–4 B.C.
001 **Fragmenta,** ed. T. Kock, *Comicorum Atticorum fragmenta,* vol. 1. Leipzig: Teubner, 1880:
690–693.
frr. 1–15 + tituli.
Q: 94
002 **Fragmenta,** ed. A. Meineke, *Fragmenta comicorum Graecorum,* vol. 2.2. Berlin: Reimer, 1840
(repr. De Gruyter, 1970): 730–734.
Q: 68
003 **Tituli,** ed. C. Austin, *Comicorum Graecorum
fragmenta in papyris reperta.* Berlin: De Gruyter, 1973: 7.
fr. 16.
Pap: 4

2261 **ARISTOMENES** Hist.
A.D. 2: Atheniensis
001 **Testimonium,** FGrH #364: 3B:225.
NQ
002 **Fragmenta,** FGrH #364: 3B:225.
Q

1992 **ARISTON** Apol.
A.D. 2: Pellaeus
001 **Fragmenta,** FGrH #201: 2B:933–934.
Q
002 **Disputatio Jasonis et Papisci** (fragmenta), ed.
J.C.T. Otto, *Corpus apologetarum Christianorum saeculi secundi,* vol. 9. Jena: Mauke, 1872
(repr. Wiesbaden: Sändig, 1969): 356–357.
Q

0134 **ARISTON** Epigr.
3/1 B.C.
001 **Epigrammata,** AG **6**.303, 306; **7**.457.
AG 9.77: Cf. ANTIPATER Epigr. (0114 001).
Q: 150

2223 **ARISTON** Hist.
post 3 B.C.
001 **Fragmentum,** FGrH #337: 3B:188.
Q

1192 **ARISTON** Phil.
3 B.C.: Ceus
001 **Fragmenta,** ed. F. Wehrli, *Lykon und Ariston*

von Keos [*Die Schule des Aristoteles*, vol. 6, 2nd edn. Basel: Schwabe, 1968]: 32–44.
Q

1193 **ARISTON** Phil.
3 B.C.: Chius
001 **Fragmenta**, ed. J. von Arnim, *Stoicorum veterum fragmenta*, vol. 1. Leipzig: Teubner, 1903 (repr. Stuttgart: 1968): 75–90.
Q
002 **Fragmenta**, ed. H. Lloyd-Jones and P. Parsons, *Supplementum Hellenisticum*. Berlin: De Gruyter, 1983: 80.
frr. 204–205.
Q: [14]
x01 **Epigramma demonstrativum.**
App. Anth. 3.62(?): Cf. EPIGRAMMATICI in *App. Anth.* (7052 003).

2587 **ARISTON** Phil.
3/2 B.C.: Cous
001 **Fragmenta rhetorica**, ed. F. Wehrli, *Hieronymus von Rhodos. Kritolaus und seine Schüler* [*Die Schule des Aristoteles*, vol. 10, 2nd edn. Basel: Schwabe, 1969]: 79–80. frr. 2–4.
Q, Pap

2447 **ARISTON** Phil.
1 B.C.: Alexandrinus
001 **Testimonium**, FGrH #649: 3C:203–204.
NQ
002 **Fragmenta**, ed. I. Mariotti, *Aristone d'Alessandria*. Bologna: Patron, 1966: 11–19.
Q

1194 **ARISTONICUS** Gramm.
1 B.C.–A.D. 1: Alexandrinus
001 **De signis Odysseae**, ed. O. Carnuth, *Aristonici περὶ σημείων Ὀδυσσείας reliquiae emendatiores*. Leipzig: Hirzel, 1869: 3–164.
Q
002 **De signis Iliadis**, ed. L. Friedländer, *Aristonici περὶ σημείων Ἰλιάδος reliquiae emendatiores*. Göttingen: Dieterich, 1853 (repr. Amsterdam: Hakkert, 1965): 39–350.
Q
003 **Testimonia**, FGrH #53 & #633: **1A**:295; **3C**:182.
NQ
004 **Fragmentum**, FGrH #633: 3C:182.
Q

1899 **ARISTONICUS** Hist.
ante A.D. 2: Tarentinus
001 **Fragmenta**, FGrH #57: 1A:297.
Q

0204 **ARISTONOUS** Lyr.
3 B.C.: Corinthius
001 **Paean in Apollinem**, ed. J.U. Powell, *Collectanea Alexandrina*. Oxford: Clarendon Press, 1925 (repr. 1970): 162–164.
Epigr: [187]

002 **Hymnus in Vestam**, ed. Powell, *op. cit.*, 164–165.
Epigr: [73]

0420 **ARISTONYMUS** Comic.
5–4 B.C.
001 **Fragmenta**, ed. T. Kock, *Comicorum Atticorum fragmenta*, vol. 1. Leipzig: Teubner, 1880: 668–669.
frr. 1–3, 5–9.
Q: 40
002 **Fragmenta**, ed. A. Meineke, *Fragmenta comicorum Graecorum*, vol. 2.2. Berlin: Reimer, 1840 (repr. De Gruyter, 1970): 698–699.
Q: 26

1195 **ARISTONYMUS** Gnom.
Incertum
x01 **Fragmenta ap. Stobaeum.**
Anth. **III**.1.96, 97; 4.105; 10.49, 50, 51; 13.41; 14.9; 21.7; 23.7; 38.36; **IV**.31d.111; 33.29; 35.33; 40.19a; 42.14; 46.21, 22, 23.
Cf. Joannes STOBAEUS (2037 001).

2353 **ARISTONYMUS** Hist.
Incertum
001 **Titulus**, FGrH #510: 3B:487.
NQ

0019 **ARISTOPHANES** Comic.
5–4 B.C.: Atheniensis
001 **Acharnenses**, ed. V. Coulon and M. van Daele, *Aristophane*, vol. 1. Paris: Les Belles Lettres, 1923 (repr. 1967 (1st edn. corr.)): 12–66.
Cod: 7,818
002 **Equites**, ed. Coulon and van Daele, *op. cit.*, vol. 1, 80–141.
Cod: 9,764
003 **Nubes**, ed. K.J. Dover, *Aristophanes. Clouds*. Oxford: Clarendon Press, 1968 (repr. 1970): 7–88.
Cod: 10,463
004 **Vespae**, ed. D.M. MacDowell, *Aristophanes. Wasps*. Oxford: Clarendon Press, 1971: 48–122.
Cod: 10,560
005 **Pax**, ed. Coulon and van Daele, *op. cit.*, vol. 2 (1924; repr. 1969 (1st edn. corr.)): 99–156.
Cod: 8,796
006 **Aves**, ed. Coulon and van Daele, *op. cit.*, vol. 3 (1928; repr. 1967 (1st edn. corr.)): 23–108.
Cod: 11,612
007 **Lysistrata**, ed. Coulon and van Daele, *op. cit.*, vol. 3, 119–177.
Cod: 8,853
008 **Thesmophoriazusae**, ed. Coulon and van Daele, *op. cit.*, vol. 4 (1928; repr. 1967 (1st edn. corr.)): 17–71.
Cod: 7,977
009 **Ranae**, ed. Coulon and van Daele, *op. cit.*, vol. 4, 85–157.
Cod: 10,108

010 **Ecclesiazusae**, ed. R.G. Ussher, *Aristophanes. Ecclesiazusae*. Oxford: Clarendon Press, 1973: 5–69.
Cod: 8,444

011 **Plutus**, ed. Coulon and van Daele, *op. cit.*, vol. 5 (1930; repr. 1963 (1st edn. corr.)): 89–147.
Cod: 8,864

012 **Fragmenta**, ed. J.M. Edmonds, *The fragments of Attic comedy*, vol. 1. Leiden: Brill, 1957: 572–580, 584–676, 680–766, 782–788.
frr. 1–11, 18–31, 41–55a, 63–84, 100–111, 125–142, 149–154, 155a–161, 163–168, 184–192, 198–228, 244a–258, 266–274, 278–283, 286–288, 294–307, 318–335, 345–351, 356–367, 376–380, 387–395, 400–405, 407–417, 430–437, 442, 451–455, 461–467, 471–483, 488–507, 528–531, 534–536, 542–552, 558–561, 566–569, 579–640, 642–660, 662–664, 668–670, 672–699, 897–900b, 901b–904a, 912–914.
Q, Pap: 5,054

013 **Fragmenta**, ed. T. Kock, *Comicorum Atticorum fragmenta*, vol. 1. Leipzig: Teubner, 1880: 392–439, 441–474, 477–536, 538–562, 564–599.
frr. 1–11, 14–69, 71–85, 87–89, 91–98, 100–111, 117–159, 161–164, 166–167, 171–198, 200–208, 210–228, 234–259, 262–273, 275–283, 285–288, 292–307, 310–338, 340–349, 352–366, 368–395, 397–430, 432–437, 440–467, 469–507, 509–522, 524–537, 541–543, 545–552, 558–563, 566–569, 575–578, 580–640, 642, 644–699, 708–724, 726–915, 920–951, 959.
Q: 5,050

014 **Fragmenta**, ed. A. Meineke, *Fragmenta comicorum Graecorum*, vol. 2.2. Berlin: Reimer, 1840 (repr. De Gruyter, 1970): 940, 944–949, 953–959, 961–966, 972, 974–977, 979–983, 985–991, 994–1002, 1004–1005, 1007–1011, 1014–1016, 1018–1020, 1026–1031, 1033, 1037–1044, 1047–1063, 1065–1066, 1068, 1070–1074, 1076–1079, 1082–1086, 1088, 1092–1094, 1096, 1098–1101, 1103–1111, 1113, 1118–1124, 1126–1144, 1146–1154, 1158–1161, 1163–1165, 1167–1173, 1175–1201.
Q: 4,294

015 **Fragmenta**, ed. J. Demiańczuk, *Supplementum comicum*. Krakau: Nakładem Akademii, 1912 (repr. Hildesheim: Olms, 1967): 11–27.
frr. 1–60.
Q, Pap: 322

016 **Fragmenta**, ed. C. Austin, *Comicorum Graecorum fragmenta in papyris reperta*. Berlin: De Gruyter, 1973: 7–32.
frr. 17–18, 56–66 + tituli.
Pap: 1,379

017 **Fragmenta**, ed. Kock, *op. cit.*, vol. 3 (1888): 724–726.
frr. 344b, 644b, 645b, 676b, 692b, 739b, 899b, 900b, 901b, 902b.
Q: 73

018 **Fragmenta**, ed. Meineke, *op. cit.*, vol. 5.1 (1857; repr. 1970): cxxxiii, cxxxix–cxli, cxlvii, cliii–cliv, clviii.
Q: [100]

x01 **Oracula ficta**.
App. Anth. 6.277–290.
Cf. EPIGRAMMATICI in *App. Anth.* (7052 006).

0644 **ARISTOPHANES** Gramm.
3–2 B.C.: Byzantius

001 **Historiae animalium epitome**, ed. S.P. Lambros, *Excerptorum Constantini de natura animalium libri duo Aristophanis historiae animalium epitome* [*Commentaria in Aristotelem Graeca*, suppl. 1.1. Berlin: Reimer, 1885]: 1–154.
Cod: [41,589]

002 **Nomina aetatum** (fragmentum Parisinum), ed. A. Nauck, *Aristophanis Byzantii grammatici Alexandrini fragmenta*, 2nd edn. Halle: Lippert & Schmid, 1848 (repr. Hildesheim: Olms, 1963): 79–81.
Cod: [371]

003 **Fragmenta**, ed. Nauck, *op. cit.*, 87–88, 99–102, 104, 111–112, 128–131, 133, 137–138, 143, 146, 149, 151–152, 159, 163–173, 175, 178–179, 181–184, 186–189, 191, 193–197, 200–207, 210–229, 231–234.
frr. 1–101.
Q, Cod: [6,117]

004 **Paroemiae** (fragmenta), ed. Nauck, *op. cit.*, 236–241.
frr. 1–13.
Q: [488]

005 **Commentaria in Callimachi pinaces** (fragmenta), ed. Nauck, *op. cit.*, 247, 249–251.
frr. 1, 3–8.
Q: [395]

006 **Ceteri Aristophanis libri** (fragmenta), ed. Nauck, *op. cit.*, 264, 271, 273–277, 279–282.
frr. 1–7.
Q: [640]

007 **Argumenta fabularum Aristophani tributa** (fragmenta), ed. Nauck, *op. cit.*, 256–263.
frr. 1–11.
Q: [872]

008 **Testimonia**, FGrH #347: 3B:209–210.
NQ

009 **Fragmenta**, FGrH #347: 3B:210.
Q

010 **De suspectis apud veteres verbis** (fragmenta), ed. E. Miller, *Mélanges de littérature grecque*. Paris: Imprimerie Impériale, 1868 (repr. Amsterdam: Hakkert, 1965): 427–428.
Q

011 **Nomina aetatum** (fragmenta), ed. Miller, *op. cit.*, 428–434.
Q

x01 **Epigrammata demonstrativa**.
App. Anth. 3.85–90: Cf. EPIGRAMMATICI in *App. Anth.* (7052 003).

1196 **ARISTOPHANES** Hist.
4 B.C.: Boeotus
001 **Testimonia**, FGrH #379: 3B:247.
NQ
002 **Fragmenta**, FGrH #379: 3B:247-249.
Q
003 **Fragmentum** (*P. Oxy.* 27.2463), ed. H.J. Mette, "Die 'Kleinen' griechischen Historiker heute," *Lustrum* 21 (1978) 27.
fr. 2 bis.
Pap

0421 **ARISTOPHON** Comic.
4 B.C.
001 **Fragmenta**, ed. T. Kock, *Comicorum Atticorum fragmenta*, vol. 2. Leipzig: Teubner, 1884: 276-281.
frr. 1-15.
Q: 463
002 **Fragmenta**, ed. A. Meineke, *Fragmenta comicorum Graecorum*, vol. 3. Berlin: Reimer, 1840 (repr. De Gruyter, 1970): 356-364.
Q: 460

2296 **ARISTOTELES** Hist.
4 B.C.?: Chalcidensis
001 **Testimonium**, FGrH #423: 3B:319.
NQ
002 **Fragmenta**, FGrH #423: 3B:319.
Q

0086 **ARISTOTELES** Phil. et *CORPUS ARISTOTELICUM*
4 B.C.: Stagirites, Pellaeus, Atheniensis
001 **Analytica priora et posteriora**, ed. W.D. Ross, *Aristotelis analytica priora et posteriora*. Oxford: Clarendon Press, 1964 (repr. 1968): 3-183 (24a10-31b38, 71a1-100b17).
Cod: 61,800
002 **De anima**, ed. W.D. Ross, *Aristotle. De anima*. Oxford: Clarendon Press, 1961 (repr. 1967): 402a1-435b25.
Cod: 21,477
052 **De anima** (codicis E fragmenta recensionis a vulgata diversae), ed. Ross, *De anima*, appendix 1 (412a3-424b18).
fr. 1: 412a3-412a12.
fr. 2: 414b13-416a9.
fr. 3: 421a5-422a24.
fr. 4: 423b8-424b18.
Cod: 2,466
053 **De anima** (codicis P lectiones quae valde a lectionibus ceterorum codicum distant), ed. Ross, *De anima*, appendix 2 (412b10-423b8).
fr. 1: 412b10-412b23a.
fr. 2: 413a3-414a15.
fr. 3: 420b5-420b10.
fr. 4: 421a1-421a6.
fr. 5: 422b32-423b8.
Cod: 1,450
003 Ἀθηναίων πολιτεία, ed. H. Oppermann, *Aristotelis Ἀθηναίων πολιτεία*. Leipzig: Teubner,

1928 (repr. Stuttgart: 1968): 1-98.
Pap: 16,828
004 **De audibilibus**, ed. I. Bekker, *Aristotelis opera*, vol. 2. Berlin: Reimer, 1831 (repr. De Gruyter, 1960): 800a1-804b39.
Cod: 3,612
005 **De caelo**, ed. P. Moraux, *Aristote. Du ciel*. Paris: Les Belles Lettres, 1965: 1-154 (268a1-313b22).
Cod: 30,719
006 **Categoriae**, ed. L. Minio-Paluello, *Aristotelis categoriae et liber de interpretatione*. Oxford: Clarendon Press, 1949 (repr. 1966): 3-45 (1a1-15b32).
Cod: 10,537
007 **De coloribus**, ed. Bekker, *op. cit.*, 791a1-799b20.
Cod: 5,193
008 **De divinatione per somnum**, ed. W.D. Ross, *Aristotle. Parva naturalia*. Oxford: Clarendon Press, 1955 (repr. 1970): 462b12-464b18a.
Cod: 1,260
011 **Epistulae**, ed. R. Hercher, *Epistolographi Graeci*. Paris: Didot, 1873 (repr. Amsterdam: Hakkert, 1965): 172-174.
Cod: 832
009 **Ethica Eudemia**, ed. F. Susemihl, [*Aristotelis ethica Eudemia*]. Leipzig: Teubner, 1884 (repr. Amsterdam: Hakkert, 1967): 1-123 (1214a1-1249b25).
Cod: 27,112
010 **Ethica Nicomachea**, ed. I. Bywater, *Aristotelis ethica Nicomachea*. Oxford: Clarendon Press, 1894 (repr. 1962): 1-224 (1094a1-1181b23).
Cod: 58,040
012 **De generatione animalium**, ed. H.J. Drossaart Lulofs, *Aristotelis de generatione animalium*. Oxford: Clarendon Press, 1965 (repr. 1972): 1-204 (715a1-789b20).
Cod: 52,022
013 **De generatione et corruptione**, ed. C. Mugler, *Aristote. De la génération et de la corruption*. Paris: Les Belles Lettres, 1966: 1-74 (314a1-338b19).
Cod: 16,849
014 **Historia animalium**, ed. P. Louis, *Aristote. Histoire des animaux*, vols. 1-3. Paris: Les Belles Lettres, 1:1964; 2:1968; 3:1969: 1:1-157; 2:1-155; 3:1-145, 156-175.
Lib. 1-4 (486a5-538b23): vol. 1.
Lib. 5-7 (538b28-588a12): vol. 2.
Lib. 8-10 (588a16-633b8, 633b12-638b36): vol. 3.
Cod: 97,577
015 **De incessu animalium**, ed. W. Jaeger, *Aristotelis de animalium motione et de animalium incessu. Ps.-Aristotelis de spiritu libellus*. Leipzig: Teubner, 1913: 21-47 (704a4-714b23).
Cod: 6,592
016 **De insomniis**, ed. Ross, *Parva naturalia*, 458a33-462b11.
Cod: 2,511

017 **De interpretatione**, ed. Minio-Paluello, *op. cit.*, 49–72 (16a1–24b9).
Cod: 6,201

018 **De juventute et senectute + De vita et morte**, ed. Ross, *Parva naturalia*, 467b10–470b5.
Cf. et 0086 037 (De respiratione).
Cod: 1,911

019 **De lineis insecabilibus**, ed. Bekker, *op. cit.*, 968a1–972b33.
Cod: 3,035

020 **De longitudine et brevitate vitae**, ed. Ross, *Parva naturalia*, 464b19–467b9.
Cod: 1,842

022 **Magna moralia**, ed. F. Susemihl, *Aristotle*, vol. 18 (ed. G.C. Armstrong). Cambridge, Mass.: Harvard University Press, 1935 (repr. 1969): 446–684 (1181a23–1213b30).
Cod: 24,131

023 **Mechanica**, ed. Bekker, *op. cit.*, 847a11–858b31.
Cod: 8,621

024 **De memoria et reminiscentia**, ed. Ross, *Parva naturalia*, 449b4–453b11.
Cod: 2,589

025 **Metaphysica**, ed. W.D. Ross, *Aristotle's metaphysics*, 2 vols. Oxford: Clarendon Press, 1924 (repr. 1970 [of 1953 corr. edn.]): 1:980a21–1028a6; 2:1028a10–1093b29.
Cod: 80,635

026 **Meteorologica**, ed. F.H. Fobes, *Aristotelis meteorologicorum libri quattuor*. Cambridge, Mass.: Harvard University Press, 1919 (repr. Hildesheim: Olms, 1967): 338a20–390b22.
Cod: 34,820

027 **Mirabilium auscultationes**, ed. Bekker, *op. cit.*, 830a5–847b10.
Cod: 9,483

021 **De motu animalium**, ed. Jaeger, *op. cit.*, 3–18 (698a1–704b2).
Cod: 4,253

028 **De mundo**, ed. W.L. Lorimer, *Aristotelis qui fertur libellus de mundo*. Paris: Les Belles Lettres, 1933: 47–103 (391a1–401b29).
Cod: 6,738

029 **Oeconomica**, ed. B.A. van Groningen and A. Wartelle, *Aristote. Économique*. Paris: Les Belles Lettres, 1968: 1–35 (1343a1–1353b27).
Cod: 6,491

030 **De partibus animalium**, ed. P. Louis, *Aristote. Les parties des animaux*. Paris: Les Belles Lettres, 1956: 1–166 (639a1–697b30).
Cod: 39,595

031 **Physica**, ed. W.D. Ross, *Aristotelis physica*. Oxford: Clarendon Press, 1950 (repr. 1966 (1st edn. corr.)): 184a10–267b26.
Cod: 57,057

054 **Physicorum libri octavi textus alter** (post 267b26), ed. Ross, *op. cit.*, 241b24–248b28.
Cod: 2,484

032 **Physiognomonica**, ed. Bekker, *op. cit.*, 805a1–814b8.
Cod: 6,014

034 **Poetica**, ed. R. Kassel, *Aristotelis de arte poetica*

liber. Oxford: Clarendon Press, 1965 (repr. 1968 [of 1966 corr. edn.]): 3–49 (1447a8–1462b19).
Cod: 10,549

035 **Politica**, ed. W.D. Ross, *Aristotelis politica*. Oxford: Clarendon Press, 1957 (repr. 1964): 1–269 (1252a1–1342b34).
Cod: 67,723

036 **Problemata**, ed. Bekker, *op. cit.*, 859a1–967b27.
Cod: 76,106

033 **Protrepticus**, ed. I. Düring, *Aristotle's protrepticus*. Stockholm: Almqvist & Wiksell, 1961: 46–92.
Q, Pap: 6,196

037 **De respiratione**, ed. Ross, *Parva naturalia*, 470b6–480b30.
Cf. et 0086 018 (De juventute et senectute + De vita et morte).
Cod: 6,275

038 **Rhetorica**, ed. W.D. Ross, *Aristotelis ars rhetorica*. Oxford: Clarendon Press, 1959 (repr. 1964): 1–191 (1354a1–1420a8).
Cod: 44,373

041 **De sensu et sensibilibus**, ed. Ross, *Parva naturalia*, 436a1–480b30.
Cod: 8,130

042 **De somno et vigilia**, ed. Ross, *op. cit.*, 453b11–458a32.
Cod: 3,099

040 **De sophisticis elenchis**, ed. W.D. Ross, *Aristotelis topica et sophistici elenchi*. Oxford: Clarendon Press, 1958 (repr. 1970 (1st edn. corr.)): 190–251 (164a20–184b8).
Cod: 14,649

043 **De spiritu**, ed. Jaeger, *op. cit.*, 51–64 (481a1–486b4).
Cod: 3,577

044 **Topica**, ed. Ross, *Aristotelis topica et sophistici elenchi*, 1–189 (100a18–164b19).
Cod: 45,655

046 **De ventorum situ et nominibus**, ed. Bekker, *op. cit.*, 973a1–973b25.
Cod: 452

045 **De virtutibus et vitiis**, ed. Bekker, *op. cit.*, 1249a26–1251b37.
Cod: 1,554

047 **De Xenophane, de Zenone, de Gorgia**, ed. Bekker, *op. cit.*, 974a1–980b21.
De Xenophane: 974a1–977a11.
De Zenone: 977a13–979a9.
De Gorgia: 979a11–980b21.
Cod: 4,984

048 **Divisiones Aristoteleae**, ed. H. Mutschmann, *Divisiones quae vulgo dicuntur Aristoteleae*. Leipzig: Teubner, 1906: 1–66.
Q, Cod: 10,005

049 **Fragmenta**, ed. M.L. West, *Iambi et elegi Graeci*, vol. 2. Oxford: Clarendon Press, 1972: 44–45.
frr. 672–673.
Q: 53

050 **Fragmentum**, ed. D.L. Page, *Poetae melici*

Graeci. Oxford: Clarendon Press, 1962 (repr. 1967 (1st edn. corr.)): 444.
fr. 1.
Q: 94

051 **Fragmenta varia**, ed. V. Rose, *Aristotelis qui ferebantur librorum fragmenta*. Leipzig: Teubner, 1886 (repr. Stuttgart: 1967): 23–425.
Dialogi (testimonia + frr. 1–111): pp. 23–104.
Logica (testimonia + frr. 112–124): pp. 105–114.
Rhetorica et poetica (testimonia + frr. 125–179): pp. 114–137.
Ethica (frr. 180–184): pp. 137–147.
Philosophica (frr. 185–208): pp. 148–167.
Physica (testimonia + frr. 209–278): pp. 167–214.
Zoica (testimonia + frr. 279–380): pp. 215–257.
Historica (testimonia + frr. 381–644): pp. 258–407.
Orationes et epistulae (testimonia + frr. 645–670): pp. 407–421.
Carmina (frr. 671–675): pp. 421–423.
Dubia (frr. 676–680): pp. 424–425.
Q: 88,480

055 **Testimonia**, FGrH #646: 3C:192–193.
NQ

056 **Fragmenta**, FGrH #646: 3C:194–199.
Q

x01 **Rhetorica ad Alexandrum**.
Cf. ANAXIMENES Hist. et Rhet. (0547 001).

x02 **Sicyonis historia** (*P. Oxy.* 11.1365).
FGrH #551, fr. 1b (= FGrH #105, fr. 2).
Cf. ADDITAMENTA (FGrH) (2433 024).
Cf. ANONYMI HISTORICI (FGrH) (1139 004).

x03 **Epigramma**.
AG 7.145.
Cf. ASCLEPIADES Epigr. (0137 001).

x04 **Epigrammata** (*App. Anth.*).
Epigrammata sepulcralia: 2.54–120(?).
Epigrammata demonstrativa: 3.47–48(?).
App. Anth. 2.54–120(?): Cf. EPIGRAMMATICI in *App. Anth.* (7052 002).
App. Anth. 3.47–48(?): Cf. EPIGRAMMATICI in *App. Anth.* (7052 003).

2562 **ARISTOTHEUS** Hist.
2 B.C.: Troezenius

001 **Testimonium**, FGrH #835: 3C:903.
NQ

0241 **ARISTOXENUS** <Comic.>
7/6 B.C.: Selinuntius

002 **Fragmentum**, ed. M.L. West, *Iambi et elegi Graeci*, vol. 2. Oxford: Clarendon Press, 1972: 45.
Q: [8]

003 **Fragmentum**, ed. G. Kaibel, *Comicorum Graecorum fragmenta*, vol. 1.1 [*Poetarum Graecorum fragmenta*, vol. 6.1. Berlin: Weidmann, 1899]: 87.
Q: 9

0806 **ARISTOXENUS** Med.
1 B.C.–A.D. 1

x01 **Fragmenta ap. Galenum**.
K8.734, 746–747.
Cf. GALENUS Med. (0057 059).

0088 **ARISTOXENUS** Mus.
4 B.C.: Tarentinus

001 **Elementa harmonica**, ed. R. da Rios, *Aristoxeni elementa harmonica*. Rome: Polygraphica, 1954: 5–92.
Cod: 14,789

002 **Elementa rhythmica**, ed. G.B. Pighi, *Aristoxeni rhythmica*. Bologna: Patron, 1959: 15–16.
Q: [393]

003 **Pselli prolambanomena**, ed. Pighi, *op. cit.*, 17–26.
Q, Cod: [2,707]

004 **Fragmenta Parisina** (e cod. bibl. imp. Par. 3027), ed. Pighi, *op. cit.*, 27–28.
Cod: [496]

005 **Fragmenta** (*P. Oxy.* 1.9), ed. Pighi, *op. cit.*, 29–32.
Pap: [562]

006 **Fragmenta**, ed. F. Wehrli, *Aristoxenos* [*Die Schule des Aristoteles*, vol. 2, 2nd edn. Basel: Schwabe, 1967]: 10–41.
Q: [6,875]

1946 **ARISTUS** Hist.
3 B.C.: Salaminius (Cypri)

001 **Testimonia**, FGrH #143: 2B:812.
NQ

002 **Fragmenta**, FGrH #143: 2B:812–813.
Q

2668 **ARIUS** Epic.
Incertum

x01 **Epigramma dedicatorium**.
App. Anth. 1.192: Cf. EPIGRAMMATICI in *App. Anth.* (7052 001).

0947 **Lecanius ARIUS** Med.
A.D. 1: Tarsensis

x01 **Fragmenta ap. Galenum**.
K12.829; 13.247–248, 840.
Cf. GALENUS Med. (0057 076–077).

0529 **ARIUS DIDYMUS** Doxogr.
1 B.C.

001 **Physica** (fragmenta), ed. H. Diels, *Doxographi Graeci*. Berlin: Reimer, 1879 (repr. De Gruyter, 1965): 447–472.
Q: [8,026]

0360 **ARMENIDAS** Hist.
5 B.C.

001 **Fragmenta**, FGrH #378: 3B:245–247.
Q

0807 **ARRHABIANUS** Med.
ante A.D. 2

x01 **Fragmentum ap. Galenum**.
K13.83–84.
Cf. GALENUS Med. (0057 076).

1798 **ARRIANUS** Astron.
2 B.C.
x01 **Fragmentum ap. Stobaeum**.
Anth. I.28.2.
Cf. Joannes STOBAEUS (2037 001).

2650 **ARRIANUS** Epic.
2 B.C.
001 **Fragmentum et tituli**, ed. H. Lloyd-Jones and
P. Parsons, *Supplementum Hellenisticum*. Berlin: De Gruyter, 1983: 81–82.
frr. (+ titul.) 207–211.
Q: [23]

2669 **ARRIANUS** Epigr.
Incertum
x01 **Epigramma dedicatorium**.
App. Anth. 1.193: Cf. EPIGRAMMATICI in
App. Anth. (7052 001).

0074 **Flavius ARRIANUS** Hist. et Phil.
A.D. 1–2: Bithynius
001 **Alexandri anabasis**, ed. A.G. Roos and G.
Wirth, *Flavii Arriani quae exstant omnia*, vol.
1. Leipzig: Teubner, 1967 (1st edn. corr.): 1–
390.
Cod: [80,682]
002 **Historia Indica**, ed. Roos and Wirth, *op. cit.*,
vol. 2 (1968 (1st edn. corr.)): 1–73.
Cod: [14,426]
003 **Cynegeticus**, ed. Roos and Wirth, *op. cit.*, vol.
2, 74–102.
Cod: [5,868]
004 **Periplus ponti Euxini**, ed. Roos and Wirth, *op.
cit.*, vol. 2, 103–128.
Cod: [4,506]
005 **Tactica**, ed. Roos and Wirth, *op. cit.*, vol. 2,
129–176.
Cod: [9,457]
006 **Acies contra Alanos**, ed. Roos and Wirth, *op.
cit.*, vol. 2, 177–185.
Cod: [1,334]
007 **Fragmenta de rebus physicis**, ed. Roos and
Wirth, *op. cit.*, vol. 2, 186–195.
Q: [1,609]
008 **Epistula ad Lucium Gellium**, ed. Roos and
Wirth, *op. cit.*, vol. 2, 196.
Cod: [201]
009 **Bithynicorum fragmenta**, ed. Roos and Wirth,
op. cit., vol. 2, 198–223.
Q: [1,772]
010 **Parthicorum fragmenta**, ed. Roos and Wirth,
op. cit., vol. 2, 224–252.
Cf. et 0074 015.
Q: [2,550]
011 **Historia successorum Alexandri** (fragmenta ap.
Photium, *Bibl*. cod. 92), ed. Roos and Wirth,

op. cit., vol. 2, 253–286.
Cf. et 0074 016.
Q: [3,924]
012 **Fragmentum ex historia Alanica** (?), ed. Roos
and Wirth, *op. cit.*, vol. 2, 286.
Q: [60]
013 **Fragmenta incerta** (utrum e Parthicis an ex
historia successorum Alexandri desumpta sint),
ed. Roos and Wirth, *op. cit.*, vol. 2, 287–290.
Q: [384]
014 **Fragmentum** (*PSI* 1284), ed. Roos and Wirth,
op. cit., vol. 2, 323–324.
Pap: [182]
015 **Parthicorum fragmenta** (ap. Joannem Lydum
et Syncellum), ed. Roos and Wirth, *op. cit.*, vol.
2, 224–226.
Cf. et 0074 010.
Q
016 **Historia successorum Alexandri** (fragmenta ap.
Photium, *Bibl*. cod. 82), ed. Roos and Wirth,
op. cit., vol. 2, 253–258.
Cf. et 0074 011.
Q
017 **Testimonia**, FGrH #156: 2B:837–840.
NQ
018 **Fragmenta**, FGrH #156: 2B:840–883.
Q, Cod
x01 **Dissertationes ab Arriano digestae**.
Schenkl, pp. 7–454.
Cf. EPICTETUS Phil. (0557 001).
x02 **Dissertationum Epicteti sive ab Arriano
sive ab aliis digestarum fragmenta**.
Schenkl, pp. 455–460, 462–475.
Cf. EPICTETUS Phil. (0557 003).
x03 **Periplus maris Erythraei**.
GGM, vol. 1, pp. 257–305.
Cf. PERIPLUS MARIS ERYTHRAEI (0071).
x04 **Periplus ponti Euxini**.
GGM, vol. 1, pp. 402–423.
Cf. PERIPLUS PONTI EUXINI (0075).

9018 **ARSENIUS** Paroemiogr.
A.D. 15–16: Monembasiensis
001 **Apophthegmata**, ed. E.L. von Leutsch, *Corpus
paroemiographorum Graecorum*, vol. 2. Göttingen: Vandenhoeck & Ruprecht, 1851 (repr.
Hildesheim: Olms, 1958): 240–744.
Cod: [24,229]

2489 **ARTAPANUS** Hist.
ante 2 B.C.
001 **Fragmenta**, FGrH #726: 3C:680–686.
Q

2463 **ARTAVASDES** Hist.
1 B.C.: Armenius
001 **Testimonium**, FGrH #678: 3C:350.
NQ

0045 ***ARTAXERXIS EPISTULAE***
Incertum
001 **Epistulae**, ed. R. Hercher, *Epistolographi*

Graeci. Paris: Didot, 1873 (repr. Amsterdam: Hakkert, 1965): 175–176.
Q: [654]

2651 **ARTEMIDORUS** Eleg.
ante 2 B.C.
001 **Tituli**, ed. H. Lloyd-Jones and P. Parsons, *Supplementum Hellenisticum.* Berlin: De Gruyter, 1983: 82.
frr. 213–214.
NQ: [4]

0080 **ARTEMIDORUS** Geogr.
2 B.C.: Ephesius
002 **Fragmentum**, FGrH #438: 3B:371.
Q
x01 **Geographia.**
GGM, vol. 1, pp. 574–576.
Cf. MARCIANUS Geogr. (4003 003).

0135 **ARTEMIDORUS** Gramm.
1 B.C.: Tarsensis
002 **Epigramma**, AG 9.205.
Q: 16
x01 **Fragmenta ap. Athenaeum.**
Deipnosophistae 4.182d; 14.663d–e.
Cf. ATHENAEUS Soph. (0008 001).

2472 **ARTEMIDORUS** Hist.
ante A.D. 1?: Ascalonius
001 **Testimonium**, FGrH #698: 3C:552.
NQ

0553 **ARTEMIDORUS** Onir.
A.D. 2: Daldianus
001 **Onirocriticon**, ed. R.A. Pack, *Artemidori Daldiani onirocriticon libri v.* Leipzig: Teubner, 1963: 1–324.
Cod: [66,978]

0809 **ARTEMIDORUS CAPITO** Med.
A.D. 2
x01 **Fragmentum ap. Galenum.**
K15.22 in CMG, vol. 5.9.1, p. 13.
Cf. GALENUS Med. (0057 085).

0136 **ARTEMON** Epigr.
3 B.C.: Atheniensis
001 **Epigrammata**, AG 12.55, 124.
Q: 88

1197 **ARTEMON** Gramm.
fiq Artemon Pergamenus Hist.
2/1 B.C.?: Cassandrensis
001 **Fragmenta**, FHG 4: 342–343.
frr. 9–14.
Q

2307 **ARTEMON** Hist.
4 B.C.?: Clazomeneus
001 **Fragmenta**, FGrH #443: 3B:374.
Q

2392 **ARTEMON** Hist.
2 B.C.: Pergamenus
001 **Testimonia**, FGrH #569: 3B:661–662.
NQ
002 **Fragmenta**, FGrH #569: 3B:662–663.
Q

ASCENSIO ISAIAE
Cf. MARTYRIUM ET ASCENSIO ISAIAE (1483).

0137 **ASCLEPIADES** Epigr.
3 B.C.: Samius
001 **Epigrammata**, AG 5.7, 64, 85, 145, 150, 153, 158, 161–162, 164, 167, 169, 181, 185, 189, 194, 202–203, 207, 209–210; 6.308; 7.11, 145, 217, 284, 500; 9.63–64, 752; 12.36, 46, 50, 75, 77, 105, 135, 153, 161–163, 166; 13.23; 16.68, 120.
AG 7.12; 12.17: Cf. ANONYMI EPIGRAMMATICI (0138 001).
AG 13.29: Cf. NICAENETUS Epic. (0218 002).
Q: 1,533
002 **Fragmenta**, ed. H. Lloyd-Jones and P. Parsons, *Supplementum Hellenisticum.* Berlin: De Gruyter, 1983: 83–84.
frr. 215–217, 219.
Q: [17]
x01 **Epigrammata dedicatoria.**
App. Anth. 1.167–176: Cf. EPIGRAMMATICI in *App. Anth.* (7052 001).

2224 **ASCLEPIADES** Gramm.
3–2 B.C.?: Nicaeanus, Alexandrinus
001 **Testimonia**, FGrH #339: 3B:195–196.
NQ
002 **Fragmenta**, FGrH #339: 3B:196.
Q

1955 **ASCLEPIADES** Hist.
4–3 B.C.
001 **Fragmentum**, FGrH 157: 2B:883.
Q

1198 **ASCLEPIADES** Hist.
3 B.C.?: Cyprius
001 **Fragmentum**, FGrH #752: 3C:735.
Q

2430 **ASCLEPIADES** Hist.
A.D. 5: Aegyptius
001 **Testimonium**, FGrH #624: 3C:158–159.
NQ
002 **Fragmenta**, FGrH #624: 3C:159–160.
Q

1199 **ASCLEPIADES** Hist. et Gramm.
1 B.C.: Myrleanus
001 **Testimonia**, FGrH #697: 3C:548.
NQ
002 **Fragmenta**, FGrH #697: 3C:548–551.
Q

2423 **ASCLEPIADES** Hist. et Gramm.
   1 B.C.–A.D. 1?: Mendesicus
001 **Fragmenta**, FGrH #617: 3C:144–145.
   Q

0811 **ASCLEPIADES** Med.
   1 B.C.: Bithynius
x01 **Fragmenta ap. Galenum**.
   K3.446–467 in Helmreich, vol. 1, pp. 340–341.
   Cf. GALENUS Med. (0057 017).
x02 **Fragmentum ap. Galenum**.
   K8.757.
   Cf. GALENUS Med. (0057 059).
x03 **Praecepta salubria**.
   Bussemaker, pp. 132–134.
   Cf. PRAECEPTA SALUBRIA (0663 001).

1200 **ASCLEPIADES** Myth.
   4 B.C.: Tragilensis
001 **Testimonia**, FGrH #12: 1A:166.
   NQ
002 **Fragmenta**, FGrH #12: 1A:166–176.
   Q

0681 **ASCLEPIADES Pharmacion** Med.
   vel Asclepiades Junior
   A.D. 1
x01 **Fragmenta ap. Galenum**.
   K12.378–1007; **13**.1–361, 442–1058; **14**.1–209.
   Cf. GALENUS Med. (0057 076–078).
x02 **Fragmenta ap. Aëtium** (lib. 5–8).
   CMG, vol. 8.2, pp. 68, 155, 156, 201, 370, 371,
   391, 449, 496, 513, 530.
   Cf. AËTIUS Med. (0718 005–008).
x03 **Fragmenta ap. Aëtium** (lib. 9).
   Zervos, *Athena* 23, pp. 283, 288, 295, 335.
   Cf. AËTIUS Med. (0718 009).
x04 **Fragmenta ap. Aëtium** (lib. 12).
   Kostomiris, pp. 22, 26, 61, 62, 103, 105.
   Cf. AËTIUS Med. (0718 012).
x05 **Fragmentum ap. Aëtium** (lib. 13).
   Zervos, *Athena* 18, p. 279.
   Cf. AËTIUS Med. (0718 013).
x06 **Fragmenta ap. Aëtium** (lib. 15).
   Zervos, *Athena* 21, pp. 58, 67, 91.
   Cf. AËTIUS Med. (0718 015).
x07 **Fragmenta ap. Aëtium** (lib. 16).
   Zervos, *Gynaekologie des Aëtios*, pp. 57, 141,
   156.
   Cf. AËTIUS Med. (0718 016).
x08 **Fragmentum ap. Hippiatrica**.
   Oder & Hoppe, vol. 2, p. 211.
   Cf. HIPPIATRICA (0738 006).

0556 **ASCLEPIODOTUS** Tact.
   1 B.C.
001 **Tactica**, ed. C.H. Oldfather and W.A. Oldfather, *Aeneas Tacticus, Asclepiodotus, Onasander*. Cambridge, Mass.: Harvard University
   Press, 1923 (repr. 1962): 244–332.
   Cod: [7,007]

0812 **ASCLEPIUS** Med.
   A.D. 1?
   Cf. et ASCLEPIUS et MACHAON Med. (0879).
x01 **Fragmentum ap. Galenum**.
   K13.841.
   Cf. GALENUS Med. (0057 077).
x02 **Fragmentum ap. Paulum**.
   CMG, vol. 9.2, p. 326.
   Cf. PAULUS Med. (0715 001).

4018 **ASCLEPIUS** Phil.
   A.D. 6: Trallianus
001 **In Aristotelis metaphysicorum libros A–Z
   commentaria**, ed. M. Hayduck, *Asclepii in
   Aristotelis metaphysicorum libros A–Z commentaria* [*Commentaria in Aristotelem Graeca* 6.2.
   Berlin: Reimer, 1888]: 1–452.
   Cod: [192,961]
002 **Commentaria in Nicomachi Geraseni Pythagorei introductionem arithmeticam**, ed. L. Ta-
   rán, *Asclepius of Tralles. Commentary to Nicomachus' introduction to arithmetic* [*Transactions of the American Philosophical Society*,
   N.S. 59.4. Philadelphia: American Philosophical Society, 1969]: 24–72.
   Cod

0879 **ASCLEPIUS et MACHAON** Med.
   A.D. 1?
   Cf. et ASCLEPIUS Med. (0812).
x01 **Fragmentum ap. Galenum**.
   K12.774.
   Cf. GALENUS Med. (0057 076).

2122 **Gaius ASINIUS QUADRATUS** Hist.
   A.D. 3?
001 **Epigramma**, AG 7.312.
   Q: 27
002 **Testimonia**, FGrH #97: 2A:447–448.
   NQ
003 **Fragmenta**, FGrH #97: 2A:448–451.
   Q

0242 **ASIUS** Epic. et Eleg.
   6 B.C.?: Samius
001 **Fragmentum**, ed. M.L. West, *Iambi et elegi
   Graeci*, vol. 2. Oxford: Clarendon Press, 1972:
   46.
   Q: [22]
002 **Fragmenta**, ed. G. Kinkel, *Epicorum Graecorum fragmenta*, vol. 1. Leipzig: Teubner,
   1877: 203, 205–206.
   frr. 1–2, 8, 10, 13.
   Q: [88]
x01 **Epigramma irrisorium**.
   App. Anth. 5.2: Cf. EPIGRAMMATICI in *App.
   Anth.* (7052 005).

2609 **ASOPODORUS** Iamb.
   Incertum: Phliasius
001 **Tituli**, ed. H. Lloyd-Jones and P. Parsons,

Supplementum Hellenisticum. Berlin: De Gruyter, 1983: 84.
frr. 222–223.
NQ: [6]

2711 **ASPASIA** <Epigr.>
5 B.C.: Milesia
x01 **Epigrammata** (*App. Anth.*).
Epigramma exhortatorium et supplicatorium: 4.17.
Epigramma irrisorium: 5.6.
App. Anth. 4.17(?): Cf. EPIGRAMMATICI in *App. Anth.* (7052 004).
App. Anth. 5.6(?): Cf. EPIGRAMMATICI in *App. Anth.* (7052 005).

2529 **ASPASIUS** Hist.
A.D. 2: Byblius
001 **Testimonium**, FGrH #792: 3C:825.
NQ
002 **Titulus**, FGrH #792: 3C:825.
NQ

2530 **ASPASIUS** Hist.
Incertum: Tyrius
001 **Testimonium**, FGrH #793: 3C:825.
NQ
002 **Tituli**, FGrH #793: 3C:825.
NQ

0813 **ASPASIUS** Med.
ante A.D. 1
x01 **Fragmentum ap. Galenum**.
K13.302.
Cf. GALENUS Med. (0057 076).

0615 **ASPASIUS** Phil.
A.D. 2
001 **In ethica Nichomachea commentaria**, ed. G. Heylbut, *Aspasii in ethica Nicomachea quae supersunt commentaria* [*Commentaria in Aristotelem Graeca* 19.1. Berlin: Reimer, 1889]: 1–186.
Cod: [78,618]

1201 ***ASSUMPTIO MOSIS***
A.D. 1
001 **Fragmenta**, ed. A.-M. Denis, *Fragmenta pseudepigraphorum quae supersunt Graeca* [*Pseudepigrapha veteris testamenti Graece* 3. Leiden: Brill, 1970]: 63–67.
Q: [274]

0814 **ASTERIUS** Med.
ante A.D. 6
x01 **Fragmentum ap. Aëtium** (lib. 7).
CMG, vol. 8.2, p. 398.
Cf. AËTIUS Med. (0718 007).

2060 **ASTERIUS** Scr. Eccl.
A.D. 4–5: Amasenus
001 **Homiliae 1–14**, ed. C. Datema, *Asterius of*

Amasea. Homilies i–xiv. Leiden: Brill, 1970: 7–15, 17–24, 27–37, 39–43, 45–52, 59–64, 71–78, 85–106, 115, 117, 119, 121, 123, 125, 127, 135–146, 153–155, 165–173, 183–194, 205–219.
Cod: [45,196]
002 **Homilia 9** (ex Symeone Metaphraste), ed. Datema, *op. cit.*, 116, 118, 120, 122, 124, 126.
Cod: [1,806]
003 **Homiliae 15–16**, ed. A. Bretz, *Studien und Texte zu Asterios von Amaseia* [*Texte und Untersuchungen* 40.1 (1914)]: 107–121.
Cod
004 **Homilia in bonum Samaritanum**, MPG 104: 204–208.
Q
005 **Homilia in Zacchaeum**, MPG 104: 209.
Q
006 **Homilia in servum centurionis**, MPG 104: 213–216.
Q
007 **Homilia in Jairum et in mulierem sanguinis profluvio labentem**, MPG 104: 221–224.
Q

2061 **ASTERIUS Sophista** Scr. Eccl.
A.D. 4: Antiochenus
001 **Commentarii in Psalmos** (homiliae 31), ed. M. Richard, *Asterii sophistae commentariorum in Psalmos quae supersunt* [*Symbolae Osloenses*, fasc. suppl. 16. Oslo: Brøgger, 1956]: 3–245.
Cod
002 **Fragmenta in Psalmos** (in catenis), ed. Richard, *op. cit.*, 249–273.
Q
003 **Syntagmation** (fragmenta), ed. G. Bardy, *Recherches sur saint Lucien d'Antioche et son école.* Paris: Beauchesne, 1936: 341–348.
Q
004 **Epistula**, ed. Bardy, *op. cit.*, 348–354.
Q

2642 **<ASTRAMPSYCHUS Magus>** Onir.
ante 4 B.C.
001 **Onirocrita**, ed. N. Rigalt, *Artemidorus.* Paris, 1603.
Cod
002 **Oracula**, ed. R. Hercher, *Astrampsychi oraculorum decades ciii* [*Programm Gymnasium Joachimsthal* (1863)]: 1–48.
Cod
003 **Sortes**, ed. G.M. Browne, *The papyri of the Sortes Astrampsychi.* Meisenheim am Glan: Hain, 1974: 18–20, 32–35, 44–51.
P. Oxy. 12.1477: pp. 18–20.
P. Oxy. 38.2832: pp. 32–35.
P. Oxy. 38.2833: pp. 44–51.
Pap
x01 Φιλτροκατάδεσμος (*P. Brit. Mus.* 122).
PGM, vol. 2, pp. 45–50.
Cf. MAGICA (5002 001).

0325 **ASTYDAMAS Junior** Trag.
4 B.C.

001 **Fragmenta**, ed. B. Snell, *Tragicorum Grae-corum fragmenta*, vol. 1. Göttingen: Vanden-hoeck & Ruprecht, 1971: 200–207.
frr. 1c, 1h–1i, 2, 2a, 3–4, 5, 6–9.
fr. 1h: *P. Hibeh* 2.174.
fr. 1i: *P. Amherst* 2.10.
fr. 2a: *P. Strassb.* W.G. 304.2.
Q, Pap: [451]

x01 **Epigramma demonstrativum.**
App. Anth. 3.43: Cf. EPIGRAMMATICI in *App. Anth.* (7052 003).

1202 **<ATHAMAS>** Phil.
3 B.C.?

001 **Fragmentum**, ed. H. Thesleff, *The Pythagorean texts of the Hellenistic period.* Åbo: Åbo Aka-demi, 1965: 54.
Q: 63

2035 **ATHANASIUS** Theol.
A.D. 4: Alexandrinus

001 **Contra gentes**, ed. R.W. Thomson, *Athanasius. Contra gentes and de incarnatione.* Oxford: Clarendon Press, 1971: 2–132.
Cod: [19,490]

002 **De incarnatione verbi**, ed. C. Kannengiesser, *Sur l'incarnation du Verbe* [*Sources chrétiennes* 199. Paris: Cerf, 1973]: 258–468.
Cod: [19,929]

003 **De decretis Nicaenae synodi**, ed. H.G. Opitz, *Athanasius Werke*, vol. 2.1. Berlin: De Gruyter, 1940: 1–45.
Epistula Eusebii Caesariensis ad ecclesiam suam: pp. 28–31.
Depositio Arii: p. 31.
Epistula Alexandri Alexandrini: pp. 31–35.
Epistula synodi Nicaenae ad ecclesiam Alexan-driae: pp. 35–36.
Symbolum Nicaenum: pp. 36–37.
Epistula Constantini imperatoris ad ecclesiam Alexandriae: p. 37.
Epistula Constantini imperatoris ad episcopos et populos: pp. 37–38.
Epistula Constantini imperatoris ad Arium et socios: pp. 38–43.
Epistula Constantini imperatoris ad ecclesiam Nicomediae: pp. 43–45.
Epistula Constantini imperatoris ad Theodo-tum Laodicensem: p. 45.
Cod: [21,711]

004 **De sententia Dionysii**, ed. Opitz, *op. cit.*, 46–67.
Cod: [7,825]

005 **Apologia contra Arianos** (*sive* **Apologia se-cunda**), ed. Opitz, *op. cit.*, 87–168.
Epistula synodi Alexandriae: pp. 89–101.
Epistula Julii episcopi Romae: pp. 102–113.
Epistula synodi Sardicensis ad Alexandrinos: pp. 115–118.

Epistula synodalis synodi Sardicensis: pp. 119–132.
Epistula Constantii imperatoris ad Athanasium: p. 132.
Epistula secunda Constantii imperatoris: pp. 132–133.
Epistula tertia Constantii imperatoris: p. 133.
Epistula Julii episcopi Romae ad Alexandrinos: pp. 133–134.
Epistula Constantii imperatoris ad episcopos et presbyteros catholicae ecclesiae: p. 135.
Epistula secunda Constantii imperatoris ad po-pulos catholicae ecclesiae: pp. 135–136.
Epistula Constantii imperatoris de abolendis quae contra Athanasium acta fuerant: p. 136.
Epistula synodi Hierosolymitanae: pp. 136–137.
Epistula Ursacii et Valentis ad Julium papam: p. 138.
Epistula Ursacii et Valentis ad Athanasium: p. 138.
Pars epistulae Constantini: p. 140.
Epistula Constantini imperatoris ad populum Alexandriae: pp. 141–142.
Epistula Ischyrae ad Athanasium: pp. 143–144.
Epistula Alexandri Thessalonicensis ad Atha-nasium: p. 145.
Pinnes presbyter ad fratrem Joannem: pp. 145–146.
Constantinus imperator ad Athanasium: pp. 146–147.
Arsenius episcopus ad Athanasium: pp. 147–148.
Constantinus ad Joannem: p. 148.
Breviarium a Meletio datum Alexandro epis-copo: pp. 149–151.
Presbyteri et diaconi ecclesiae Alexandrinae ad synodum Tyriam: pp. 152–153.
Presbyteri et diaconi qui in Mareote sunt ad synodum Tyriam: pp. 153–155.
Presbyteri et diaconi qui in Mareote ad Phila-grium praefectum: pp. 155–156.
Episcopi Aegyptii ad episcopos Tyri congrega-tos: pp. 156–157.
Epistula prima episcopi Aegyptii ad Flavium Dionysium comitem: pp. 158–159.
Epistula secunda episcopi Aegyptii ad Flavium Dionysium comitem: pp. 159–160.
Alexander Thessalonicensis ad Dionysium: pp. 160–161.
Dionysius comes ad Eusebianos: p. 161.
Epistula synodi Hierosolymitanae: pp. 162–163.
Flavius Himerius ad exactorem Mareotae: p. 164.
Constantinus imperator ad episcopos qui Ty-rum convenere: pp. 164–165.
Constantinus imperator ad ecclesiam Alexan-drinam: p. 166.
Cod: [28,149]

006 **Epistula encyclica**, ed. Opitz, *op. cit.*, 169–177.
Cod: [2,971]

007 **Epistula ad Serapionem de morte Arii**, ed.
Opitz, *op. cit.*, 178–180.
Cod: [1,009]

008 **Epistula ad monachos**, ed. Opitz, *op. cit.*, 181–182.
Cod: [679]

009 **Historia Arianorum**, ed. Opitz, *op. cit.*, 183–230.
Epistula Constantii imperatoris Nestorio praefecto: p. 195.
Constantius imperator ad Athanasium: p. 196.
Hosius Constantio imperatori: pp. 207–209.
Contestatio secunda: pp. 228–230.
Cod: [19,789]

010 **De synodis Arimini in Italia et Seleuciae in Isauria**, ed. Opitz, *op. cit.*, 231–278.
Fidei formula synodi Sirmiensis: pp. 235–236.
Epistula synodi Ariminensis: pp. 237–238.
Decretum synodi Ariminensis (fragmentum): pp. 238–239.
Blasphemiae Arii: pp. 242–243.
Arius ad Alexandrum: pp. 243–244.
Epistula synodi Hierosolymitanae: pp. 247–248.
Epistula synodi Antiochenae ad Julium episcopum Romae: pp. 248–249.
Formula altera: pp. 249–250.
Formula tertia Theophronii Tyanensis: p. 250.
Formula quarta: p. 251.
Ἔκθεσις μακρόστιχος: pp. 251–254.
Ἔκθεσις Sirmiensis (anno 351): pp. 254–256.
Ἔκθεσις Sirmiensis (anno 357): pp. 256–257.
Ἔκθεσις Seleuciensis: pp. 257–258.
Ἔκθεσις Constantinopolitana: pp. 258–259.
Constantius imperator ad episcopos qui Ariminium convenere: pp. 277–278.
Episcopi ad imperatorem: p. 278.
Cod: [21,261]

011 **Apologia ad Constantium imperatorem**, ed. J.-M. Szymusiak, *Athanase d'Alexandrie. Apologie à l'empereur Constance. Apologie pour sa fuite* [Sources chrétiennes 56. Paris: Cerf, 1958]: 88–132.
Epistula Constantii imperatoris ad Alexandrinos: pp. 122–124.
Epistula Constantii imperatoris ad Aizanam et Sazanam: pp. 125–126.
Cod: [8,641]

012 **Apologia de fuga sua**, ed. Szymusiak, *op. cit.*, 133–167.
Cod: [6,117]

013 **Epistula ad Amun**, FONTI II: 63–71.
Cod: [1,017]

014 **Epistulae festales** (epistula xxxix in collectione canonum), FONTI II: 71–76.
Cod: [647]

015 **Epistula ad Rufinianum**, FONTI II: 76–80.
Cod: [524]

016 **De non participando divinis mysteriis sine discrimine** [Sp.], FONTI II: 82–84.
Cod: [267]

017 **In illud: *Profecti in pagum invenietis pullum***

alligatum [Sp.], ed. H. Nordberg, *Athanasiana I* [Commentationes humanarum litterarum 30.2. Helsinki: Centraltryckeriet, 1962]: 1–19.
Cod: [2,932]

018 **Homilia in illud: *Ite in castellum*** [Sp.], ed. Nordberg, *op. cit.*, 20–28.
Cod: [2,179]

019 **Homilia in illud: *Euntem autem illo*** [Sp.], ed. Nordberg, *op. cit.*, 29–41.
Cod: [2,834]

020 **Sermo in ramos palmarum** [Sp.], ed. Nordberg, *op. cit.*, 42–45.
Cod: [762]

021 **Homilia de jejunio et de passione Christi** [Sp.], ed. Nordberg, *op. cit.*, 46–48.
Cod: [628]

023 **Sermo major de fide** [Sp.], ed. E. Schwartz, "Der s.g. sermo maior de fide des Athanasius," *Sitzungsberichte der bayerischen Akademie der Wissenschaften*, Philosoph.-philol. und hist. Kl. 6 (1925) 5–37.
Cod

024 **Quaestio 136 e quaestionibus ad Antiochum ducem** (e cod. Paris. 635) [Sp.], ed. W. Dindorf, *Athanasii Alexandrini praecepta ad Antiochum.* Leipzig: Weigel, 1857: vii–ix.
Cf. et 2035 077.
Cod: [353]

025 **Quaestio 136 e quaestionibus ad Antiochum ducem** (e cod. Guelferbytano-Gudiano 51) [Sp.], ed. Dindorf, *op. cit.*, vii–ix.
Cf. et 2035 077.
Cod: [323]

026 **Doctrina ad Antiochum ducem** [Sp.], ed. Dindorf, *op. cit.*, 3–39.
Cod: [9,597]

027 **De sancta trinitate** (dialogi 2 & 4) [Sp.], ed. C. Bizer, *Studien zu pseudathanasianischen Dialogen der Orthodoxos und Aëtios* [Diss. Bonn (1970)]: 80–126, 307–334.
Cf. et 2035 109.
Cod: [9,098]

028 **Epistula ad imperatorem Jovianum** [Sp.], ed. Bizer, *op. cit.*, 299–301.
Cod: [208]

029 **De virginitate** [Sp.], ed. E.F. von der Goltz, Λόγος σωτηρίας πρὸς τὴν παρθένον [Texte und Untersuchungen N.F. 14. Leipzig: Hinrichs, 1905]: 35–60.
Cod: [6,083]

030 **Commentarius de templo Athenarum** [Sp.], ed. A. Delatte, "Le déclin de la légende des vii sages et les prophéties théosophiques," *Musée Belge* 27 (1923) 107–111.
Cod: [919]

031 **Sermo major** (collatio cod. Laurentiani gr. 4.23) [Sp.], ed. Nordberg, *op. cit.*, 57–71.
Cod

032 **Commentarius de templo Athenarum** (cod. Bodleianus Roe 5) [Sp.], ed. A. von Premerstein, "Ein pseudo-athanasianischer Traktat mit apokryphen Philosophensprüchen im Co-

dex Bodleianus Roe 5," Εἰς μνήμην Σπυρίδωνος Λάμπρου. Athens: Hestia, 1935: 183–186.
Cod: [636]

033 **Epistula ad Liberium** [Sp.], ed. M. Tetz, "Zur Theologie des Markell von Ankyra III," *Zeitschrift für Kirchengeschichte* 83 (1972) 152.
Cod: [401]

034 **Dialogus Athanasii et Zacchaei** [Sp.], ed. F.C. Conybeare, *The dialogues of Athanasius and Zacchaeus and of Timothy and Aquila.* Oxford: Clarendon Press, 1898: 1–63.
Cod: [10,181]

035 **De morbo et valetudine** (fragmenta), ed. F. Diekamp, *Analecta patristica* [*Orientalia Christiana analecta* 117. Rome: Pont. Institutum Orientalium Studiorum, 1938 (repr. 1962)]: 5–8.
Cod: [1,116]

036 **Oratio in resurrectionem et in recens baptizatos** [Sp.], ed. M. Aubineau, "Une homélie pascale attribuée à S. Athanase d'Alexandrie dans le Sinaiticus gr. 492," *Zetesis* (Festschrift E. de Strycker). Antwerp: De Nederlandsche Boekhandel, 1973: 670–674.
Cod: [824]

037 **De fallacia diaboli** (= **Homilia in diabolum**) [Sp.], ed. R.P. Casey, "An early homily on the devil ascribed to Athanasius of Alexandria," *Journal of Theological Studies* 36 (1935) 4–10.
Cod: [2,849]

038 **Sermo exhortatorius** [Sp.], ed. F. Nau, "Notes sur diverses homélies pseudépigraphiques, sur les oeuvres attribuées à Eusèbe d'Alexandrie et sur un nouveau manuscrit de la chaîne *contra Severianos,*" *Revue de l'Orient chrétien* 13 (1908) 418–420.
Cod: [568]

039 **In illud:** *Omnia mihi tradita sunt,* MPG 25: 208–220.
Cod

040 **Epistula ad Dracontium,** MPG 25: 524–533.
Cod

041 **Epistula ad episcopos Aegypti et Libyae,** MPG 25: 537–593.
Epistula = Fragmentum contra Macedonianos (MPG 26.1313b–1313c) (2035 054).
Cf. et 2035 054.
Cod

042 **Orationes tres contra Arianos,** MPG 26: 12–468.
Cod: 79,416

043 **Epistulae quattuor ad Serapionem,** MPG 26: 529–648b.

044 **In illud:** *Qui dixerit verbum in filium,* MPG 26: 648c–676.
Cod

045 **Tomus ad Antiochenos,** MPG 26: 796–809.
Cod

046 **Petitiones Arianorum,** MPG 26: 820–824.
Cod

047 **Vita Antonii,** MPG 26: 835–976b.
Cod

049 **Epistula ad Afros episcopos,** MPG 26: 1029–1048.
Cod

050 **Epistula ad Adelphium,** MPG 26: 1072–1084.
Cod

051 **Epistula ad Maximum,** MPG 26: 1085–1089.
Cod

052 **Epistula ad Joannem et Antiochum presbyteros,** MPG 26: 1165–1168b.
Cod

053 **Epistula ad Palladium,** MPG 26: 1168b–1169.
Cod

054 **Fragmenta varia,** MPG 26: 1224, 1233–1249, 1252–1260, 1293b–1296c, 1313b–1313c, 1320–1325.
Contra Valentinum: col. 1224.
De exemplo ex natura hominis allato: coll. 1233–1237c.
Fragmenta sermonis majoris de fide (ex Theodoreti eraniste): coll. 1237d–1240c.
Fragmentum de incarnatione contra Apollinarium: col. 1244d.
Fragmentum orationis quartae contra Arianos et fragmentum epistulae ad Adelphium: col. 1245a–b.
Fragmentum ex Joanne Damasceno de duabus in Christo voluntatibus: col. 1249a.
Fragmentum de mortuis in domino ex Joannis Damasceni oratione de defunctis: col. 1249a.
Fragmentum quod vocatur εἰς τοὺς κοιμηθέντας παναρμονίῳ λόγῳ ex Joannis Damasceni oratione de defunctis: col. 1249b.
Fragmentum ex interpretatione in Matthaeum: coll. 1252–1253a.
In illud: Laudate dominum de terra, dracones et omnes abyssi: col. 1256b–c.
Fragmentum e sermone contra haereses: coll. 1256d–1257a.
Fragmentum e cod. Vaticano 392: col. 1257c.
Fragmentum epistulae dogmaticae ad Antiochenos: col. 1260a.
Fragmentum historicum primum: col. 1293b.
Fragmentum historicum alterum: coll. 1293c–1296b.
Fragmentum contra Macedonianos: col. 1313b–c: Cf. et 2035 041 (MPG 25.560–561).
Fragmentum de amuletis: col. 1320a–b.
Fragmenta quaedam alia, coll. 1320b–1325d.
Q, Cod

055 **Epistula ad monachos,** MPG 26: 1185–1188.
Cf. et 2035 120.
Cod

056 **Sermo de patientia** [Sp.], MPG 26: 1297–1309.
Cod

057 **Scholia in Actus** (fort. ex libris *Contra Novatianos*), MPG 26: 1316–1317.
Q

058 **De azymis** [Sp.], MPG 26: 1328–1332.
Cod

059 Epistula ad Marcellinum de interpretatione Psalmorum, MPG 27: 12–45.
Cod

060 Argumentum in Psalmos [Sp.], MPG 27: 56–60.
Cod

061 Expositiones in Psalmos, MPG 27: 60–545, 548–589.
Cod

062 Scholia in cantica canticorum, MPG 27: 1348–1349.
Q

063 Homilia in Canticum canticorum [Sp.], MPG 27: 1349–1361.
Cod

064 Testimonia e scriptura (de communi essentia patris et filii et spiritus sancti) [Sp.], MPG 28: 29–80.
Cod

065 Epistula catholica [Sp.], MPG 28: 81–84.
Cod

066 Refutatio hypocriseos Meletii et Eusebii [Sp.], MPG 28: 85–88.
Cod

067 Contra Sabellianos [Sp.], MPG 28: 96–121.
Cod

068 De sabbatis et circumcisione [Sp.], MPG 28: 133–141.
Cod

069 Homilia de semente [Sp.], MPG 28: 144–168.
Cod

070 Homilia de passione et cruce domini [Sp.], MPG 28: 185–249.
Cf. et 2035 125.
Cod

071 Synopsis scripturae sacrae [Sp.], MPG 28: 284–437.
Cod

072 Disputatio contra Arium [Sp.], MPG 28: 440–501.
Cod

073 Sermo contra omnes haereses [Sp.], MPG 28: 501–524.
Cod

074 Historia de Melchisedech [Sp.], MPG 28: 525–529.
Cod

075 Liber de definitionibus [Sp.], MPG 28: 533–553.
Cod

076 Sermo ad Antiochum ducem [Sp.], MPG 28: 589–597.
Cod

077 Quaestiones ad Antiochum ducem [Sp.], MPG 28: 597–700.
Cf. et 2035 024, 025, 111.
Cod

078 Quaestiones in evangelia [Sp.], MPG 28: 700–708.
Q

079 Fragmentum sermonis de imaginibus [Sp.], MPG 28: 709.
Cod

080 Quaestiones in scripturam sacram [Sp.], MPG 28: 712–773.
Cod

081 Quaestiones aliae [Sp.], MPG 28: 773–796.
Cod

082 Narratio de cruce seu imagine Berytensi [Sp.], MPG 28: 797–812.
Recensio e codd. Colbert.: col. 797–805.
Recensio e cod. Pal. vet.: col. 805–812.

083 Sermo contra Latinos [Sp.], MPG 28: 824–832.
Cod

084 Vitae monasticae institutio [Sp.], MPG 28: 845–849.
Cod

085 Epistulae ad Castorem [Sp.], MPG 28: 849–905.
Cod

086 In nativitatem praecursoris [Sp.], MPG 28: 905–913.
Cod

087 Sermo in annuntiationem deiparae [Sp.], MPG 28: 917–940.
Cod

088 Sermo de descriptione deiparae [Sp.], MPG 28: 944–957.
Cod

089 Sermo in nativitatem Christi [Sp.], MPG 28: 960–972.
Cod

090 Homilia in occursum domini [Sp.], MPG 28: 973–1000.
Cod

091 In caecum a nativitate [Sp.], MPG 28: 1001–1024.
Cod

092 Homilia in feriam v et in proditionem Judae [Sp.], MPG 28: 1048–1053.
Cod

093 Homilia in passionem domini et in parasceve [Sp.], MPG 28: 1053–1061.
Cod

094 Homilia in sanctos patres et prophetas [Sp.], MPG 28: 1061–1073.
Cod

095 Homilia in sanctum pascha [Sp.], MPG 28: 1073–1081.
Cod

096 Homilia in sanctum pascha et in recens illuminatos [Sp.], MPG 28: 1081–1092.
Cod

097 Homilia in assumptionem domini [Sp.], MPG 28: 1092–1100.
Cod

098 Homilia in sanctum Andream [Sp.], MPG 28: 1101–1108.
Cod

109 De sancta trinitate (dialogi 1, 3, 5) [Sp.], MPG

28: 1116–1173a, 1201c–1249b, 1265c–1285b.
Cf. et 2035 027.
Cod

099 **Dialogi duo contra Macedonianos** [Sp.], MPG 28: 1292–1337.
Cod

100 **Syntagma ad quendam politicum** [Sp.], MPG 28: 1396–1408.
Cod

101 **Sermo pro iis qui saeculo renuntiarunt** [Sp.], MPG 28: 1409–1420.
Cod

102 **Doctrina ad monachos** [Sp.], MPG 28: 1421–1425.
Cod

103 **De corpore et anima** [Sp.], MPG 28: 1432–1433.
Cod

104 **Vita sanctae Syncleticae** [Sp.], MPG 28: 1488–1557.
Cod: 14,641

105 **Epistula ad episcopum Persarum** [Sp.], MPG 28: 1565–1568.
Cod

106 **Symbolum "quicumque"** [Sp.], MPG 28: 1581–1592.
Cod

107 **De trinitate** [Sp.], MPG 28: 1604–1605.
Cod

108 **Recensio definitionum** (ap. Anastasium Sinaitam) [Sp.], MPG 89: 52–88.
Q

110 **Epistula ad Epictetum**, ed. G. Ludwig, *Athanasii epistula ad Epictetum* [*Diss. Jena* (1911)]: 3–18.
Cod

111 **Quaestio cxii ad Antiochum ducem in collectione canonum**, FONTI II: 80–82.
Cf. et 2035 077.
Cod

112 **Epistula prima ad Orsisium**, ed. F. Halkin, *Sancti Pachomii vitae Graecae* [*Subsidia hagiographica* 19. Brussels: Société des Bollandistes, 1932]: 91.
Q

113 **Epistula altera ad Orsisium**, ed. Halkin, *op. cit.*, 95–96.
Q

114 **Narratio Athanasii** (ap. epistulam Ammonis), ed. Halkin, *op. cit.*, 119–120.
Q

115 **Scholia in Job**, MPG 27: 1344–1348.
Cf. et 2035 116.
Cod

116 **Scholia in Job** (e cod. Vat. Pii II), ed. J.B. Pitra, *Analecta sacra et classica spicilegio Solesmensi* 5. Paris: Roger & Chernowitz, 1888: 21–26.
Cf. et 2035 115.
Q

117 **Oratio quarta contra Arianos** [Sp.], ed. A. Steg-

mann, *Die pseudoathanasianische 'IVte Rede gegen die Arianer' als 'κατὰ Ἀρειανῶν λόγος' ein Apollinarisgut.* Rottenburg: Bader, 1917: 43–87.
Cod

118 **Syntagma ad monachos** (Cod. Vossianus gr. in fol. n. 46) [Sp.], ed. P. Batiffol, *Studia patristica. Études d'ancienne littérature chrétienne*, fasc. 2. Paris: Leroux, 1890: 121–128.
Cf. et 2035 127.
Cod

119 **Epistula ad Jovianum**, MPG 26: 813–820.
Cod

120 **Epistula ad monachos**, ed. G. de Jerphanion, "La vraie teneur d'un texte de saint Athanase rétablie par l'épigraphie: l'epistula ad monachos," *Recherches de science religieuse* 20 (1930). Textus post 540.
Cf. et 2035 055.
Epigr

121 **Epistula ad Epiphanium** (fragmentum ap. *Chronicon paschale*), MPG 26: 1257–1260.
Q

122 **Homilia in illud:** *Nunc anima mea turbata est* (fragmenta), MPG 26: 1240–1244.
Q

123 **Epistula ad Eupsychium** (fragmenta), MPG 26: 1245–1248.
Q

124 **De incarnatione contra Apollinarium libri ii** [Sp.], MPG 26: 1093–1165.
Cod

125 **Homilia de passione et cruce domini** (additamenta), MPG 28: 249.
Cf. et 2035 070.
Cod

126 **Didascalia cccxviii patrum Nicaenorum** [Sp.], MPG 28: 1637–1644.
Cod

127 **Syntagma ad monachos** (Cod. Vaticanus gr. 733) [Sp.], ed. Batiffol, *op. cit.*, 121–128.
Cf. et 2035 118.
Cod

x01 **Epistulae festales** (ap. Cosmam Indicopleustem).
Topographia Christiana 10.3–13.
Cf. COSMAS INDICOPLEUSTES (4061 002).

x02 **Epistula exhortatoria ad virgines** (ap. Theodoretum Cyrrhensem).
HE 2.14.13 (GCS 44.127–128).
Cf. THEODORETUS Scr. Eccl. et Theol. (4089 003).

x03 **Fragmentum de fide** (in *Doctrina patrum*).
Diekamp, p. 11, fr. 4.
Cf. DOCTRINA PATRUM (7051 001).

x04 **Subscriptio Paulini Antiocheni**.
Tomus ad Antiochenos (MPG 26.809).
Cf. 2035 045.

x05 **Expositio fidei**.
Athanasiana I, pp. 49–56.
Cf. MARCELLUS Theol. (2041 004).

x06 **Interpretatio in symbolum** [Sp.].
ACO 1.1.7, p. 66.
Cf. CONCILIA OECUMENICA (ACO) (5000 001).

2207 **ATHANIDAS** Hist.
3 B.C.?
001 **Fragmentum**, FGrH #303: 3B:5–6.
Q

2387 **ATHANIS** Hist.
vel Athanas
4 B.C.: Syracusanus
001 **Testimonia**, FGrH #562: 3B:576.
NQ
002 **Fragmenta**, FGrH #562: 3B:576–577.
Q

2379 **ATHENACON** Hist.
4 B.C.?
001 **Testimonium**, FGrH #546: 3B:530.
NQ
002 **Fragmenta**, FGrH #546: 3B:531–532.
Q

0141 **ATHENAEUS** Epigr.
fiq Athenaeus Soph.
A.D. 2–3?
Cf. et ATHENAEUS Soph. (0008).
002 **Epigramma**, AG 9.496.
Q: 41
003 **Fragmenta**, ed. H. Lloyd-Jones and P. Parsons, *Supplementum Hellenisticum*. Berlin: De Gruyter, 1983: 85.
frr. 225–226.
Q: [79]
x01 **Epigramma exhortatorium et supplicatorium.**
App. Anth. 4.43: Cf. EPIGRAMMATICI in *App. Anth.* (7052 004).

ATHENAEUS Geogr.
Cf. HERACLIDES Criticus Perieg. (1405 001).

2465 **ATHENAEUS** Hist.
1 B.C.?
001 **Fragmentum**, FGrH #681: 3C:398.
Q

1204 **ATHENAEUS** Mech.
1 B.C.?
001 **De machinis**, ed. R. Schneider, *Griechische Poliorketiker*, vol. 1 [*Abhandlungen der königlichen Gesellschaft der Wissenschaften zu Göttingen*, Philol.-hist. Kl., N.F. 12, no. 5. Berlin: Weidmann, 1912]: 8–36.
Cod: [3,862]

0682 **ATHENAEUS** Med.
A.D. 1: Attalensis
x01 **Fragmenta ap. Galenum.**
K8.757; **13.296.**

Cf. GALENUS Med. (0057 059, 076).
x02 **Fragmentum ap. Pseudo-Galenum.**
K19.356.
Cf. Pseudo-GALENUS Med. (0530 041).
x03 **Fragmenta ap. Oribasium.**
CMG, vol. **6.1.1**, pp. 7, 11, 12; **6.1.2**, pp. 8, 12; **6.2.2**, pp. 99, 105, 106, 112, 115, 138, 146.
Cf. ORIBASIUS Med. (0722 001–002).
x04 **Fragmentum ap. Aëtium** (lib. 3).
CMG, vol. 8.1, p. 332.
Cf. AËTIUS Med. (0718 003).

0008 **ATHENAEUS** Soph.
fiq Athenaeus Epigr.
A.D. 2–3: Naucratites
Cf. et ATHENAEUS Epigr. (0141).
001 **Deipnosophistae**, ed. G. Kaibel, *Athenaei Naucratitae deipnosophistarum libri xv*, 3 vols. Leipzig: Teubner, 1–2:1887; 3:1890 (repr. Stuttgart: 1–2:1965; 3:1966): **1**:1–491; **2**:1–498; **3**:1–560.
Cod: 288,521
003 **Deipnosophistae** (epitome), ed. S.P. Peppink, *Athenaei dipnosophistarum epitome*, vols. 2.1-2.2. Leiden: Brill, 2.1:1937; 2.2:1939: **2.1**:3–174; **2.2**:3–162.
Cod
002 **Fragmentum**, FGrH #166: 2B:891–892.
Q

1205 **ATHENAGORAS** Apol.
A.D. 2: Atheniensis
001 **Legatio**, ed. W.R. Schoedel, *Athenagoras. Legatio and de resurrectione*. Oxford: Clarendon Press, 1972: 2–86.
Cod: 11,646
002 **De resurrectione**, ed. Schoedel, *op. cit.*, 88–148.
Cod: 9,134

0422 **ATHENIO** Comic.
3 B.C.
001 **Fragmentum**, ed. T. Kock, *Comicorum Atticorum fragmenta*, vol. 3. Leipzig: Teubner, 1888: 369–370.
fr. 1.
Q: 281
002 **Fragmentum**, ed. A. Meineke, *Fragmenta comicorum Graecorum*, vol. 4. Berlin: Reimer, 1841 (repr. De Gruyter, 1970): 557–558.
Q: 284

ATHENODORUS Epigr.
AG 7.494.
Cf. ANONYMI EPIGRAMMATICI (0138 001).

1206 **ATHENODORUS** Phil.
1 B.C.: Tarsensis
001 **Testimonia**, FGrH #746: 3C:729.
NQ
002 **Fragmenta**, FGrH #746: 3C:729–731.
Q

0621 **[ATH]ENODORUS** Trag.
fort. [Z]enodorus vel [M]enodorus
2 B.C.
001 **Titulus**, ed. B. Snell, *Tragicorum Graecorum
fragmenta*, vol. 1. Göttingen: Vandenhoeck &
Ruprecht, 1971: 309.
NQ

0815 **ATIMETRUS** Med.
ante A.D. 2
x01 **Fragmentum ap. Galenum**.
K12.771.
Cf. GALENUS Med. (0057 076).

1212 ***ATRIDARUM REDITUS***
post 7 B.C.
Cf. et NOSTOI (1541).
001 **Fragmentum**, ed. J.U. Powell, *Collectanea Alexandrina*. Oxford: Clarendon Press, 1925
(repr. 1970): 246.
Q: [10]

1207 **ATTALUS** Math. et Astron.
2 B.C.: Rhodius
001 **Fragmenta Aratea**, ed. E. Maass, *Commentariorum in Aratum reliquiae*. Berlin: Weidmann,
1898 (repr. 1958): 3–24.
frr. 1–28.
Q: [5,749]

1982 **Titus Pomponius ATTICUS** Hist.
2–1 B.C.: Romanus
001 **Testimonia**, FGrH #189: 2B:923.
NQ

1208 **ATTICUS** Phil.
A.D. 2
001 **Fragmenta**, ed. J. Baudry, *Atticos. Fragments
de son oeuvre*. Paris: Les Belles Lettres, 1931:
1–33.
frr. 2, 4–9, 12–13.
Q: [5,789]

2505 **Cnaeus AUFIDIUS** Hist.
2–1 B.C.: Romanus
001 **Testimonium**, FGrH #814: 3C:887.
NQ
002 **Fragmentum**, FGrH #814: 3C:887.
Q

1782 **AUGEAS** Comic.
fiq Augias vel Agias
Incertum: Atheniensis
001 **Fragmentum**, ed. A. Meineke, *Fragmenta
comicorum Graecorum*, vol. 1. Berlin: Reimer,
1839 (repr. De Gruyter, 1970): 416.
Q
002 **Tituli**, ed. Meineke, *op. cit.*, 416.
NQ

2727 **AULICALAMUS** Epigr.

fiq Theodorus Aulicalamus
A.D. 12?
x01 **Aenigmata**.
App. Anth. 7.79–80: Cf. EPIGRAMMATICI in
App. Anth. (7052 007).

2643 **Decimus Magnus AUSONIUS** Gramm. et
Rhet.
A.D. 4: Burdigalensis
001 **Epistulae**, ed. R. Peiper, *Decimi Magni Ausonii
Burdigalensis opuscula*. Leipzig: Teubner, 1886
(repr. Stuttgart: 1976): 232–236.
Cod
002 **Epigrammata**, ed. Peiper, *op. cit.*, 316, 318,
330–331, 333.
Cod
x01 **Epigrammata** (*App. Anth.*).
Epigrammata demonstrativa: 3.153–156.
Epigrammata irrisoria: 5.48–49.
App. Anth. 3.153–156: Cf. EPIGRAMMATICI
in *App. Anth.* (7052 003).
App. Anth. 5.48–49: Cf. EPIGRAMMATICI in
App. Anth. (7052 005).

2205 **AUTESION** Hist.
3–2 B.C.?
001 **Fragmenta**, FGrH #298: 3B:1.
Q
002 **Fragmenta**, ed. H.J. Mette, "Die 'Kleinen'
griechischen Historiker heute," *Lustrum* 21
(1978) 25.
fr. 2a–b.
fr. 2a: *P. Oxy.* 26.2442.
Q, Pap

2175 **<AUTOCHARIS>** Hist.
Incertum
001 **Fragmentum**, FGrH #249: 2B:1130.
Q

1209 **AUTOCLIDES** Hist.
3 B.C.?
001 **Fragmenta**, FGrH #353: 3B:215–216.
fr. 6: *P. Oxy.* 15.1802.
Q, Pap

0423 **AUTOCRATES** Comic.
5–4 B.C.
001 **Fragmenta**, ed. T. Kock, *Comicorum Atticorum fragmenta*, vol. 1. Leipzig: Teubner, 1880:
806.
frr. 1, 3.
Q: 39
002 **Fragmenta**, ed. A. Meineke, *Fragmenta comicorum Graecorum*, vol. 2.2. Berlin: Reimer, 1840
(repr. De Gruyter, 1970): 891–892.
Q: 42
003 **Titulus**, ed. C. Austin, *Comicorum Graecorum
fragmenta in papyris reperta*. Berlin: De Gruyter, 1973: 33.
fr. 67.
Pap: 3

2204 **AUTOCRATES** Hist.
3–2 B.C.?
001 **Fragmenta**, FGrH #297: 3B:1.
Q

1210 **AUTOLYCUS** Astron.
4 B.C.: Pitanaeus
001 **De sphaera quae movetur**, ed. J. Mogenet,
Autolycus de Pitane. Louvain: Université de
Louvain, 1950: 195–213.
Cod: [4,622]
002 **De ortibus et occasibus**, ed. Mogenet, *op. cit.*,
214–258.
Cod: [10,795]

0140 **AUTOMEDON** Epigr.
A.D. 1: Cyzicenus
001 **Epigrammata**, AG 5.129; 7.534; 10.23; 11.29,
46, 50, 319, 324–326, 346, 361; 12.34.
Q: 565

0424 **AXIONICUS** Comic.
4 B.C.
001 **Fragmenta**, ed. T. Kock, *Comicorum Atticorum fragmenta*, vol. 2. Leipzig: Teubner, 1884:
411–416.
frr. 1–10.
Q: 316
002 **Fragmenta**, ed. A. Meineke, *Fragmenta comicorum Graecorum*, vol. 3. Berlin: Reimer, 1840
(repr. De Gruyter, 1970): 530–536.
Q: 289
003 **Fragmentum**, ed. Meineke, *op. cit.*, vol. 5.1
(1857; repr. 1970): ccxviii.
Q: [19]

AXIOPISTUS Poet. Ethic.
CGFPR, p. 79 (fr. 86).
Cf. EPICHARMUS Comic. et PSEUDEPI-
CHARMEA (0521 005).

0774 **AXIORIUS** Med.
ante A.D. 2
x01 **Fragmentum ap. Galenum**.
K12.841.
Cf. GALENUS Med. (0057 076).

0818 **AZANITES** Med.
1 B.C.?
x01 **Fragmentum ap. Galenum**.
K13.784.
Cf. GALENUS Med. (0057 077).
x02 **Fragmentum ap. Paulum**.
CMG, vol. 9.2, p. 376.
Cf. PAULUS Med. (0715 001).

0614 **Valerius BABRIUS** Scr. Fab.
A.D. 2
001 **Mythiambi Aesopici**, ed. B.E. Perry, *Babrius
and Phaedrus*. Cambridge, Mass.: Harvard
University Press, 1965: 2–186.
Cod: [11,079]

0819 **BACCHIUS** Med.
3–2 B.C.: Tanagraeus
x01 **Fragmentum ap. Galenum**.
K13.987.
Cf. GALENUS Med. (0057 077).
x02 **Fragmentum ap. Pseudo-Galenum**.
K19.408.
Cf. Pseudo-GALENUS Med. (0530 041).

2136 **BACCHIUS GERON** Mus.
A.D. 3–4
001 **Isagoge artis musicae**, ed. K. Jan, *Musici scrip-
tores Graeci*. Leipzig: Teubner, 1895 (repr.
Hildesheim: Olms, 1962): 292–316.
Cod

0199 **BACCHYLIDES** Lyr.
5 B.C.: Ceus
001 **Epinicia**, ed. H. Maehler (post B. Snell),
Bacchylidis carmina cum fragmentis, 10th edn.
Leipzig: Teubner, 1970: 1–51.
Pap: 3,797
002 **Dithyrambi**, ed. Maehler, *op. cit.*, 52–56, 59–
67, 69–72.
Pap: 1,267
003 **Dithyramborum vel epinicorum fragmenta**, ed.
Maehler, *op. cit.*, 72–81.
Pap: 451
004 **Fragmenta**, ed. Maehler, *op. cit.*, 82–87, 89–
109, 111.
Q, Pap: 1,257
005 **Fragmenta dubia**, ed. Maehler, *op. cit.*, 111–
120.
Q, Pap: 480
006 **Epigrammata**, ed. Maehler, *op. cit.*, 121.
Q: 46
007 **Scholia ad Bacchylidis carmina**, ed. Maehler,
op. cit., 122–127.
Pap: 229
008 **Scholia ad dithyrambos**, ed. Maehler, *op. cit.*,
128–129.
Scholia ad dithyrambos e papyro B, col. 1: *P.
Oxy.* 23.2368.
Pap: 129
009 **Epigrammata**, AG 6.53, 313; 13.28.
Q: 126

0142 **[BACIS]**
5 B.C.: Eleus
001 **Epigrammata**, AG 14.97–99.
Q: 88

1932 **BAETO** Hist.
post 4 B.C.
001 **Testimonia**, FGrH #119: 2B:622.
NQ
002 **Fragmenta**, FGrH #119: 2B:623–626.
Q

1211 **BALAGRUS** Hist.
2 B.C.

001 **Testimonium**, FGrH #773: 3C:767.
NQ
002 **Fragmenta**, FGrH #773: 3C:767.
Q

1213 **Julia BALBILLA** Lyr.
A.D. 2
001 **Epigrammata**, ed. G. Kaibel, *Epigrammata Graeca ex lapidibus conlecta*. Berlin: Reimer, 1878: 414–417.
frr. 988–992.
Epigr: [423]
x01 **Epigrammata dedicatoria**.
App. Anth. 1.177–180, 181(?): Cf. EPIGRAMMATICI in *App. Anth.* (7052 001).

1215 **BALBILLUS** Astrol.
vel Barbillus
A.D. 1: Ephesius
001 **Fragmenta**, ed. W. Kroll and A. Olivieri, *Codices Parisini* [*Catalogus codicum astrologorum Graecorum* 8.3. Brussels: Lamertin, 1912]: 103–104.
Cod: [550]
002 **Fragmenta**, ed. P. Boudreaux, *Codices Parisini* [*Catalogus codicum astrologorum Graecorum* 8.4. Brussels: Lamertin, 1921]: 233–238.
Cod

0820 **BAPHULLUS vel HERAS** Med.
ante A.D. 1
Cf. et HERAS Med. (0917).
x01 **Fragmentum ap. Galenum**.
K14.173.
Cf. GALENUS Med. (0057 078).

4051 **Joannes BARBUCALLUS** Gramm.
A.D. 6: Berytensis
001 **Epigrammata**, AG **6**.55; **7**.555–555b; **9**.425–427, 628–629; **16**.38, 218–219, 327.
Q: 291

1214 **BARDESANES** Gnost.
A.D. 2–3: Edessenus
001 **Fragmenta**, FGrH #719: 3C:643–656.
Q

1216 *BARNABAE EPISTULA*
A.D. 1/2
001 **Barnabae epistula**, ed. R.A. Kraft, *Épître de Barnabé* [*Sources chrétiennes* 172. Paris: Cerf, 1971]: 72–218.
Cod: [6,771]

1217 **BASILIDES** Gnost.
A.D. 2
001 **Fragmenta**, ed. W. Völker, *Quellen zur Geschichte der christlichen Gnosis*. Tübingen: Mohr, 1932: 40–41.
Q

2398 **BASILIDES** Phil.
Incertum

001 **Fragmentum**, ed. J. von Arnim, *Stoicorum veterum fragmenta*, vol. 3. Leipzig: Teubner, 1903 (repr. Stuttgart: 1968): 268.
Q

1218 **BASILIS** Hist.
3/2 B.C.
001 **Testimonia**, FGrH #718: 3C:642.
NQ
002 **Fragmenta**, FGrH #718: 3C:642.
Q

2084 **BASILIUS** Scr. Eccl.
A.D. 4: Ancyranus
001 **De virginitate**, MPG 30: 669–809.
Cod
x01 **Epistula synodica**.
Epiphanius, *Haer*. 73.
Cf. EPIPHANIUS Scr. Eccl. (2021 002).
x02 **Basilii ac Georgii Laodiceni et sociorum professio**.
Epiphanius, *Haer*. 73.
Cf. EPIPHANIUS Scr. Eccl. (2021 002).

2040 **BASILIUS** Theol.
A.D. 4: Caesariensis (Cappadociae)
001 **Homiliae in hexaemeron**, ed. S. Giet, *Basile de Césarée. Homélies sur l'hexaéméron*, 2nd edn. [*Sources chrétiennes* 26 bis. Paris: Cerf, 1968]: 86–522.
Cod: [35,917]
002 **De legendis gentilium libris**, ed. F. Boulenger, *Saint Basile. Aux jeunes gens sur la manière de tirer profit des lettres Helléniques*. Paris: Les Belles Lettres, 1935 (repr. 1965): 41–61.
Cod: [4,771]
003 **De spiritu sancto**, ed. B. Pruche, *Basile de Césarée. Sur le Saint-Esprit*, 2nd edn. [*Sources chrétiennes* 17 bis. Paris: Cerf, 1968]: 250–530.
Cod: [26,524]
004 **Epistulae**, ed. Y. Courtonne, *Saint Basile. Lettres*, 3 vols. Paris: Les Belles Lettres, 1:1957; 2:1961; 3:1966: 1:3–219; 2:1–218; 3:1–229.
Cod: [138,464]
005 **Epistulae tres**, ed. S.Y. Rudberg, *Études sur la tradition manuscrite de saint Basile*. Lund: Håkan Ohlssons Boktryckeri, 1953: 156–168, 195–200, 205–207.
Cod: [3,402]
006 **Homilia in illud: Attende tibi ipsi**, ed. S.Y. Rudberg, *L'homélie de Basile de Césarée sur le mot 'observe-toi toi-même'*. Stockholm: Almqvist & Wiksell, 1962: 23–37.
Cod: [3,795]
007 **Homilia in illud: Destruam horrea mea**, ed. Y. Courtonne, *Saint Basile. Homélies sur la richesse*. Paris: Didot, 1935: 15–37.
Cod: [3,213]
008 **Homilia in divites**, ed. Courtonne, *Homélies*, 39–71.
Cod: [4,673]
009 **Enarratio in prophetam Isaiam** [Dub.], ed. P.

Trevisan, *San Basilio. Commento al profeta Isaia*, 2 vols. Turin: Societa Editrice Internazionale, 1939: 1:3–397; 2:3–575.
Cod: [98,369]

010 **Expositio fidei Nicaenae** [Sp.], ed. G.L. Hahn, *Bibliothek der Symbole und Glaubensregeln der alten Kirche*, 3rd edn. Breslau: Morgenstern, 1897: 308–310.
Cod: [398]

011 **Homilia in aquas** [Sp.], ed. S. Costanza, *Ps.-Basilii εἰς τὰ ὕδατα καὶ εἰς τὸ ἅγιον βάπτισμα*. Messina: Peloritana Editrice, 1967: 39–44.
Cod: [949]

012 **Homilia de virginitate** [Sp.], ed. D. Amand and M.C. Moons, "Une curieuse homélie grecque inédite sur la virginité adressée aux pères de famille," *Revue Bénédictine* 63 (1953) 35–69.
Cod: [3,284]

013 **De spiritu**, ed. P. Henry, *Études plotiniennes I. Les états du texte de Plotin*. Paris: Brouwer, 1938: 185–196.
Cod: [954]

018 **Homiliae super Psalmos**, MPG 29: 209–494.
Cod: [53,149]

019 **Adversus Eunomium** (libri 5), MPG 29: 497–669, 672–768.
Lib. 1–3: col. 497–669.
Lib. 4–5 [Sp.]: col. 672–768.
Cod: [47,462]

020 **De jejunio** (homilia 1), MPG 31: 164–184.
Cod: [3,502]

021 **De jejunio** (homilia 2), MPG 31: 185–197.
Cod: [2,392]

022 **Homilia de gratiarum actione**, MPG 31: 217–237.
Cod: [3,361]

023 **Homilia in martyrem Julittam**, MPG 31: 237–261.
Cod: [4,340]

024 **Homilia dicta tempore famis et siccitatis**, MPG 31: 304–328.
Cod: [4,346]

025 **Quod deus non est auctor malorum**, MPG 31: 329–353.
Cod: [4,655]

026 **Homilia adversus eos qui irascuntur**, MPG 31: 353–372.
Cod: [3,386]

027 **Homilia de invidia**, MPG 31: 372–385.
Cod: [2,739]

028 **Homilia in principium proverbiorum**, MPG 31: 385–424.
Cod: [6,706]

029 **Homilia exhortatoria ad sanctum baptisma**, MPG 31: 424–444.
Cod: [3,883]

030 **In ebriosos**, MPG 31: 444–464.
Cod: [3,304]

031 **De fide**, MPG 31: 464–472.
Cod: [1,401]

032 **In illud:** *In principio erat verbum*, MPG 31: 472–481.
Cod: [2,011]

033 **In Barlaam martyrem** [Sp.], MPG 31: 484–489.
Cod: [1,023]

034 **In Gordium martyrem**, MPG 31: 489–508.
Cod: [3,207]

035 **In quadraginta martyres Sebastenses**, MPG 31: 508–525.
Cod: [2,836]

036 **De humilitate**, MPG 31: 525–540.
Cod: [2,627]

037 **Quod rebus mundanis adhaerendum non sit**, MPG 31: 540–564.
Cod: [4,749]

038 **In Mamantem martyrem**, MPG 31: 589–600.
Cod: [1,867]

039 **Contra Sabellianos et Arium et Anomoeos**, MPG 31: 600–617.
Cod: [3,490]

040 **Sermo 10 (praevia institutio ascetica)** [Dub.], MPG 31: 620–625.
Cod: [1,072]

041 **Sermo 11 (sermo asceticus et exhortatio de renuntiatione mundi)** [Dub.], MPG 31: 625–648.
Cod: [3,832]

042 **Sermo 12 (de ascetica disciplina)** [Dub.], MPG 31: 648–652.
Cod: [737]

043 **Prologus 7 (de judicio dei)**, MPG 31: 653–676.
Cod: [4,331]

044 **Sermo 13 (sermo asceticus)** [Dub.], MPG 31: 869–881.
Cod: [2,162]

045 **Prologus 8 (de fide)**, MPG 31: 676–692.
Cod: [2,829]

046 **Prologus 5 (sermo asceticus)** [Dub.], MPG 31: 881–888.
Cod: [1,480]

047 **Prologus 4 (prooemium in asceticum magnum)**, MPG 31: 889–901.
Cod: [2,072]

048 **Asceticon magnum** *sive* **Quaestiones** (regulae fusius tractatae), MPG 31: 901–1052.
Cod: [24,734]

049 **Prologus 3 (prooemium in regulas brevius tractatas)**, MPG 31: 1080.
Cod: [216]

050 **Asceticon magnum** *sive* **Quaestiones** (regulae brevius tractatae), MPG 31: 1052–1305.
Cod: [39,028]

051 **Regulae morales**, MPG 31: 692–869.
Cod: [30,761]

052 **De baptismo libri duo** [Dub.], MPG 31: 1513–1628.
Cod: [22,040]

053 **In Psalmum 28** (homilia 2) [Sp.], MPG 30: 72–81.
Cod: [1,854]

054 **Homilia in Psalmum 37** [Sp.], MPG 30: 81–104.
Cod: [4,172]

055 **Homilia in Psalmum 115** [Dub.], MPG 30: 104–116.
Cod: [2,181]

056 **Homilia in Psalmum 132** [Sp.], MPG 30: 116–117.
Cod: [457]

057 **Homilia de spiritu sancto** [Sp.], MPG 31: 1429–1437.
Cod: [1,791]

058 **Homilia dicta in Lacisis** [Dub.], MPG 31: 1437–1457.
Cod: [3,608]

059 **In sanctam Christi generationem** [Dub.], MPG 31: 1457–1476.
Cod: [3,138]

060 **Homilia de paenitentia** [Dub.], MPG 31: 1476–1488.
Cod: [2,540]

061 **Adversus eos qui per calumniam dicunt dici a nobis tres deos** [Dub.], MPG 31: 1488–1496.
Cod: [1,586]

062 **Homilia in illud:** *Ne dederis somnum oculis tuis* [Sp.], MPG 31: 1497–1508.
Cod: [1,888]

063 **De jejunio** (homilia 3) [Sp.], MPG 31: 1508–1509.
Cod: [555]

064 **Orationes** *sive* **Exorcismi** [Sp.], MPG 31: 1677–1684.
Cod: [1,364]

065 **Poenae in monachos delinquentes** (epitimia 24) [Sp.], MPG 31: 1305–1308.
Cod: [360]

066 **Epitimia in canonicas** (epitimia 25) [Sp.], MPG 31: 1313–1316.
Cod: [311]

067 **Epitimia** (epitimia 26) [Sp.], MPG 31: 1308–1313.
Cod: [909]

068 **Consolatoria ad aegrotum** [Sp.], MPG 31: 1713–1722.
Cod: [1,446]

069 **Homilia de misericordia et judicio** [Sp.], MPG 31: 1705–1714.
Cod: [1,367]

070 **Sermo ob sacerdotum instructionem** (recensio brevior) [Sp.], MPG 31: 1685–1688.
Cod: [374]

071 **Liturgia** (recensio brevior vetusta), MPG 31: 1629–1656.
Cod: [5,425]

072 **Sermo de contubernalibus** [Sp.], MPG 30: 812–828.
Cod: [3,221]

073 **Oratio pro inimicis et amicis** [Sp.], MPG 31: 1685.
Cod: [248]

074 **Constitutiones asceticae** [Dub.], MPG 31: 1320–1428.
Cod: [18,882]

075 **Sermones de moribus a Symeone Metaphrasta collecti**, MPG 32: 1116–1381.
Cod: [51,574]

076 **Sermo ob sacerdotum instructionem** (recensio fusior) [Sp.], FONTI II: 187–191.
Cod

077 **Liturgia** (recensio longior Byzantina) [Sp.], ed. F.E. Brightman, *Liturgies eastern and western*, vol. 1. Oxford: Clarendon Press, 1896: 309–345.
Cod

078 **Prologus 6** (prooemium ad *Hypotyposin*), ed. J. Gribomont, *Histoire du texte des ascétiques de S. Basile* [*Bibliothèque du Muséon* 32. Louvain: Université de Louvain, 1953]: 279–282.
Cod

079 **Sermo 14 (De fide)** [Sp.], ed. Gribomont, *op. cit.*, 314–316.
Cod

080 **Sermo 15 (De vita monastica)** (excerptum) [Sp.], ed. Gribomont, *op. cit.*, 317–319.
Cod

081 **Sermo 16 (De calumnia)** [Sp.], ed. Gribomont, *op. cit.*, 320.
Cod

082 **Canon 96 (De haereticis)** (fragmentum), FONTI II: 63–71.
Cod

083 **Scholia in Job** (in catenis, typus II), ed. P. Young, *Catena Graecorum patrum in beatum Iob, collectore Niceta Heraclea metropolita, Graece nunc primum edita et Latine versa.* London, 1637.
Q

084 **Scholion in Danielem** (in catenis), ed. A. Mai, *Scriptorum veterum nova collectio*, vol. 1.2. Rome, 1825.
Q

085 **Scholia in Matthaeum** (in catenis, typus A: catena integra), ed. J.A. Cramer, *Catenae Graecorum patrum in Novum Testamentum*, vol. 1. Oxford: Oxford University Press, 1840.
Q

086 **Scholia in Matthaeum** (in catenis, typus C: Nicetae catena), ed. B. Corderius, *Symbolarum in Matthaeum tomus alter, quo continetur catena patrum Graecorum triginta collectore Niceta episcopo Serrarum.* Toulouse, 1647.
Q

087 **Scholia in Matthaeum** (in catenis, typus D), ed. P. Possinus, *Symbolarum in Matthaeum tomus prior exhibens catenam Graecorum patrum unius et viginti.* Toulouse, 1648.
Q

088 **Scholia in Lucam** (in catenis, typus F: Nicetae catena), ed. Mai, *op. cit.*, vol. 9 (1837).
Q

089 **Scholia in Joannem** (in catenis, typus A: catena integra), ed. Cramer, *op. cit.*, vol. 2 (1844).
Q

090 **Scholia in Joannem** (in catenis, typus F), ed. B. Corderius, *Catena patrum Graecorum in S. Johannem.* Antwerp, 1630.
Q

091 **Scholia in Actus** (catena Andreae), ed. Cramer, *op. cit.*, vol. 3 (1838).
Q

092 **Scholia in Pauli epistulas** (in catenis, typus

Vaticanus), ed. Cramer, *op. cit.*, vols. 4 (1844) & 5 (1841).

Q

093 **Scholia in Pauli epistulas** (in catenis, typus Monacensis), ed. Cramer, *op. cit.*, vol. 4 (1844).

Q

094 **Scholia in Pauli epistulas** (in catenis, typus Parisinus), ed. Cramer, *op. cit.*, vols. 6 (1842) & 7 (1843).

Q

095 **Scholia in Pauli epistulas** (catena Nicetae), ed. Cramer, *op. cit.*, vol. 7 (1843).

Q

096 **Scholia in epistulas catholicas** (catena Andreae), ed. Cramer, *op. cit.*, vol. 8 (1844).

Q

x01 **Aenigma.**
App. Anth. 7.24: Cf. EPIGRAMMATICI in *App. Anth.* (7052 007).

2726 **BASILIUS Megalomytes** Epigr.
Incertum

x01 **Aenigmata.**
App. Anth. 7.47-78: Cf. EPIGRAMMATICI in *App. Anth.* (7052 007).

0941 **Julius BASSUS** Med.
fiq Tullius Bassus
1 B.C.-A.D. 1

x01 **Fragmenta ap. Galenum.**
K13.60, 278, 280-281, 1017-1018, 1033.
Cf. GALENUS Med. (0057 076-077).

x02 **Fragmentum ap. Oribasium.**
CMG, vol. 6.3, p. 98.
Cf. ORIBASIUS Med. (0722 004).

x03 **Fragmentum ap. Aëtium** (lib. 7).
CMG, vol. 8.2, p. 355.
Cf. AËTIUS Med. (0718 007).

x04 **Fragmentum ap. Aëtium** (lib. 12).
Kostomiris, p. 103.
Cf. AËTIUS Med. (0718 012).

0781 **Pomponius BASSUS** <Med.>
A.D. 1/2?

x01 **Fragmentum ap. Galenum.**
K12.781-782.
Cf. GALENUS Med. (0057 076).

0425 **BATO** Comic.
3 B.C.

001 **Fragmenta,** ed. T. Kock, *Comicorum Atticorum fragmenta,* vol. 3. Leipzig: Teubner, 1888: 326-329.
frr. 1-5, 7.
Q: 366

002 **Fragmenta,** ed. A. Meineke, *Fragmenta comicorum Graecorum,* vol. 4. Berlin: Reimer, 1841 (repr. De Gruyter, 1970): 499-504.
Q: 369

1219 **BATO** Hist. et Rhet.
2 B.C.: Sinopensis

001 **Testimonia,** FGrH #268: 3A:77.
NQ

002 **Fragmenta,** FGrH #268: 3A:77-79.
Q

1220 *BATRACHOMYOMACHIA*
2/1 B.C.

001 **Batrachomyomachia,** ed. T.W. Allen, *Homeri opera,* vol. 5. Oxford: Clarendon Press, 1912 (repr. 1969): 168-183.
Cod: 1,888

002 **Batrachomyomachia** (prosodia Byzantina), ed. Allen, *op. cit.,* 170, 172-173, 176, 178-182.
Cod: 288

2152 **BEMARCHIUS** Hist.
A.D. 4: Caesariensis (Cappadociae)

001 **Testimonia,** FGrH #220: 2B:950.
NQ

1222 **BEROS(S)US** Hist.
3 B.C.: Babylonius

001 **Testimonia,** FGrH #680: 3C:364-367.
NQ

002 **Fragmenta,** FGrH #680: 3C:367-397.
Q

0144 <**BESANTINUS**> Epigr.
A.D. 2

001 **Epigrammata,** AG 9.118; 15.25.
AG 9.119: Cf. PALLADAS Epigr. (2123 001).
AG 15.27: Cf. SIMIAS Gramm. (0211 002).
Q: 134

0145 **BIANOR** Epigr.
1 B.C.-A.D. 1: Bithynius

001 **Epigrammata,** AG 7.49, 387-388, 396, 644, 671; 9.223, 227, 259, 272-273, 278, 295, 308, 423, 548; 10.22, 101; 11.248, 364; 16.276.
AG 9.252: Cf. ANONYMI EPIGRAMMATICI (0138 001).
Q: 763

1223 **BIAS** <Phil.>
6 B.C.: Prienaeus
Cf. et <SEPTEM SAPIENTES> (1667).

001 **Fragmentum,** ed. T. Bergk, *Poetae lyrici Graeci,* vol. 3, 4th edn. Leipzig: Teubner, 1882: 199.
Q: [20]

002 **Testimonium,** FGrH #439: 3B:371.
NQ

0036 **BION** Bucol.
2 B.C.: Smyrnaeus

001 **Epitaphius Adonis,** ed. A.S.F. Gow, *Bucolici Graeci.* Oxford: Clarendon Press, 1952 (repr. 1969): 153-157.
Cod: [756]

002 **Epithalamium Achillis et Deidameiae** [Sp.], ed. Gow, *op. cit.,* 157-158.
Cod: [240]

003 **Fragmenta**, ed. Gow, *op. cit.*, 159–165.
Q: [890]

1871 **BION** Hist.
4 B.C.: Proconnensis
001 **Testimonia**, FGrH #14, #332: 1A:177; 3B:165.
NQ
002 **Fragmenta**, FGrH #14, #332: 1A:177; 3B:166.
Q

1225 **BION** Hist.
3 B.C.?: Soleus
001 **Testimonia**, FGrH #668: 3B:280.
NQ
002 **Fragmenta**, FGrH #668: 3B:280–282.
Q

1224 **BION** Phil.
3 B.C.: Borysthenius
001 **Fragmenta**, ed. J.F. Kindstrand, *Bion of Borysthenes.* Uppsala: Uppsala University Press, 1976: 113–130.
Q, Pap
002 **Fragmenta**, ed. H. Lloyd-Jones and P. Parsons, *Supplementum Hellenisticum.* Berlin: De Gruyter, 1983: 86.
frr. 227–228.
Q: [30]

2153 **BION** Phil. et Math.
4 B.C.: Abderita
001 **Testimonia**, ed. H. Diels and W. Kranz, *Die Fragmente der Vorsokratiker*, vol. 2, 6th edn. Berlin: Weidmann, 1952 (repr. Dublin: 1966): 251.
test. 1–2.
NQ

1919 **BION** Rhet.
2/1 B.C.?
001 **Testimonium**, FGrH #89: 2A:324.
NQ
002 **Fragmentum**, FGrH #89: 2A:324.
Q

1792 **BIOTTUS** Comic.
post 2 B.C.
001 **Tituli**, ed. T. Kock, *Comicorum Atticorum fragmenta*, vol. 3. Leipzig: Teubner, 1888: 366.
NQ: 3

0348 **BIOTUS** Trag.
fiq Biottus Comic.
2 B.C.?
001 **Fragmentum**, ed. B. Snell, *Tragicorum Graecorum fragmenta*, vol. 1. Göttingen: Vandenhoeck & Ruprecht, 1971: 319.
fr. 1.
Q: [15]

1226 **BITON** Mech.
3/2 B.C.

001 Κατασκευαὶ πολεμικῶν ὀργάνων καὶ καταπαλτικῶν, ed. A. Rehm and E. Schramm, *Bitons Bau von Belagerungsmaschinen und Geschützen* [*Abhandlungen der bayerischen Akademie der Wissenschaften*, Philosoph.-hist. Abt., N.F. 2. Munich: Oldenbourg, 1929]: 9–28.
Cod: [2,589]

1227 **BLAESUS** Comic.
2/1 B.C.?: Capreensis
001 **Fragmentum**, ed. G. Kaibel, *Comicorum Graecorum fragmenta*, vol. 1.1 [*Poetarum Graecorum fragmenta*, vol. 6.1. Berlin: Weidmann, 1899]: 191.
fr. 2 + tituli.
Q: 9

0787 **BLASTUS** Med.
vel Blostus
ante A.D. 1
x01 **Fragmenta ap. Galenum.**
K13.17, 19, 20.
Cf. GALENUS Med. (0057 076).

1228 **[BOEO]** Epic.
fiq [Boeus]
4 B.C.?
Cf. et [BOEUS] Epic. (1229).
001 **Fragmenta**, ed. J.U. Powell, *Collectanea Alexandrina.* Oxford: Clarendon Press, 1925 (repr. 1970): 24.
frr. 1–2.
Q: [25]

0146 **BOETHUS** Epigr.
1 B.C.–A.D. 1: Tarsensis
001 **Epigramma**, AG 9.248.
Q: 41
002 **Titulus**, ed. H. Lloyd-Jones and P. Parsons, *Supplementum Hellenisticum.* Berlin: De Gruyter, 1983: 87.
fr. 232.
NQ: [3]

1986 **BOETHUS** Hist.
1 B.C.: Tarsensis
001 **Testimonium**, FGrH #194: 2B:928.
NQ

2397 **BOETHUS** Phil.
1 B.C.: Sidonius
001 **Fragmenta**, ed. J. von Arnim, *Stoicorum veterum fragmenta*, vol. 3. Leipzig: Teubner, 1903 (repr. Stuttgart: 1968): 265–267.
Q

1229 **[BOEUS]** Epic.
fiq [Boeo]
4 B.C.?
Cf. et [BOEO] Epic. (1228).
001 **Fragmentum**, ed. J.U. Powell, *Collectanea Al-*

exandrina. Oxford: Clarendon Press, 1925 (repr. 1970): 24–25.
Q: [82]

2230 **BOÏDAS** Phil.
5 B.C.
001 **Testimonium,** ed. H. Diels and W. Kranz, *Die Fragmente der Vorsokratiker,* vol. 2, 6th edn. Berlin: Weidmann, 1952 (repr. Dublin: 1966): 376.
NQ

2610 **BOISCUS** Iamb.
ante A.D. 4: Cyzicenus
001 **Fragmentum,** ed. H. Lloyd-Jones and P. Parsons, *Supplementum Hellenisticum.* Berlin: De Gruyter, 1983: 87.
fr. 233.
Q: [13]
x01 **Epigramma dedicatorium.**
App. Anth. 1.92: Cf. EPIGRAMMATICI in *App. Anth.* (7052 001).

1306 **BOLUS** Phil.
3 B.C.: Mendesicus
001 Περὶ συμπαθειῶν καὶ ἀντιπαθειῶν, ed. W. Gemoll, *Nepualii fragmentum περὶ τῶν κατὰ ἀντιπάθειαν καὶ συμπάθειαν et Democriti περὶ συμπαθειῶν καὶ ἀντιπαθειῶν* [*Städtisches Realprogymnasium zu Striegau* (1884)]: 3–6.
Cod
002 **Physica et mystica,** ed. M. Berthelot, *Collection des anciens alchimistes grecs.* Paris: Steinheil, 1887 (repr. London: Holland Press, 1963): 41–53.
Cod
003 **Ad Leucippem,** ed. Berthelot, *op. cit.,* 53–56.
Cod
004 **Testimonia,** FGrH #263: 3A:8–9.
NQ
005 **Fragmenta,** FGrH #263: 3A:9–10.
Q
006 **Testimonium,** ed. H. Diels and W. Kranz, *Die Fragmente der Vorsokratiker,* vol. 2, 6th edn. Berlin: Weidmann, 1952 (repr. Dublin: 1966): 251.
NQ
007 **Fragmenta,** ed. Diels and Kranz, *op. cit.,* 207–224.
Q
008 **Fragmentum,** ed. A. Giannini, *Paradoxographorum Graecorum reliquiae.* Milan: Istituto Editoriale Italiano, 1965: 377.
Q

1900 **BOTRYAS** Hist.
ante A.D. 2: Myndius
001 **Fragmentum,** FGrH #58: 1A:297.
Q

1230 <**BROTINUS**> Phil.
vel Brontinus

3/2 B.C.: Metapontinus
001 **Fragmentum,** ed. H. Thesleff, *The Pythagorean texts of the Hellenistic period.* Åbo: Åbo Akademi, 1965: 55.
Q: 121
002 **Testimonia,** ed. H. Diels and W. Kranz, *Die Fragmente der Vorsokratiker,* vol. 1, 6th edn. Berlin: Weidmann, 1951 (repr. Dublin: 1966): 106–107.
NQ

1803 *BRUTI EPISTULAE*
post 1 B.C.
Cf. et MITHRIDATIS EPISTULA (0039).
001 **Epistulae,** ed. R. Hercher, *Epistolographi Graeci.* Paris: Didot, 1873 (repr. Amsterdam: Hakkert, 1965): 178–191.
Cod: [3,973]

1231 <**BRYSON**> Phil.
3 B.C.?
001 **Fragmentum,** ed. H. Thesleff, *The Pythagorean texts of the Hellenistic period.* Åbo: Åbo Akademi, 1965: 56–57.
Q: 220

1559 *BUCOLICUM*
ante A.D. 3
001 **Fragmentum bucolicum: Pan et Echo** (*P. Vindob.* 29801), ed. E. Heitsch, *Die griechischen Dichterfragmente der römischen Kaiserzeit,* vol. 1, 2nd edn. Göttingen: Vandenhoeck & Ruprecht, 1963: 56–58.
Pap: [305]

1032 **BUPHANTUS** Med.
ante A.D. 6
x01 **Fragmentum ap. Alexandrum Trallianum.** Puschmann, vol. 2, p. 577.
Cf. ALEXANDER Med. (0744 003).

2611 **BUTAS** Eleg.
1 B.C.: Romanus
001 **Fragmentum,** ed. H. Lloyd-Jones and P. Parsons, *Supplementum Hellenisticum.* Berlin: De Gruyter, 1983: 88.
fr. 234.
Q: [12]

1232 <**BUTHERUS**> Phil.
4 B.C.?: Cyzicenus
001 **Fragmentum,** ed. H. Thesleff, *The Pythagorean texts of the Hellenistic period.* Åbo: Åbo Akademi, 1965: 59.
Q: 164

2448 **BUTORIDAS** Hist.
2 B.C./A.D. 1?
x01 **Fragmentum.**
FGrH #654: 3C:205.
Cf. DIONYSIUS Hist. (2446 001).

2338 **CADMUS** Hist.
6/5 B.C.: Milesius
001 **Testimonia**, FGrH #489: 3B:456–457.
NQ
002 **Fragmentum**, FGrH #489: 3B:457.
Q

2222 **CADMUS Junior** Hist.
Incertum: Milesius
001 **Testimonium**, FGrH #335: 3B:187.
NQ

2612 **CAECALUS (?)** Epic.
ante A.D. 2: Argivus
001 **Titulus**, ed. H. Lloyd-Jones and P. Parsons, *Supplementum Hellenisticum*. Berlin: De Gruyter, 1983: 89.
fr. 237.
NQ: [1]

2664 **CAECILIA** Epigr.
A.D. 2: Trebulana
x01 **Epigrammata dedicatoria**.
App. Anth. 1.184–185: Cf. EPIGRAMMATICI in *App. Anth.* (7052 001).

1233 **CAECILIUS** Rhet.
A.D. 2: Calactinus
001 **Fragmenta**, ed. E. Ofenloch, *Caecilii Calactini fragmenta*. Leipzig: Teubner, 1907 (repr. Stuttgart: 1967): 2–205.
Q: [409]
002 **Testimonia**, FGrH #183: 2B:911.
NQ
003 **Fragmenta**, FGrH #183: 2B:911–912.
Q

1234 **Pseudo-CAECILIUS** Rhet.
Incertum
001 **Apophthegmata Romana**, ed. E. Ofenloch, *Caecilii Calactini fragmenta*. Leipzig: Teubner, 1907 (repr. Stuttgart: 1967): 206–210.
Cod

2484 **CAEMARON** Hist.
Incertum
001 **Fragmentum**, FGrH #720: 3C:656–657.
Q

0040 *CALANI EPISTULA*
Incertum
001 **Epistula**, ed. R. Hercher, *Epistolographi Graeci*. Paris: Didot, 1873 (repr. Amsterdam: Hakkert, 1965): 192.
Q: [97]

0147 **CALLEAS** Epigr.
vel Callias
Incertum: Argivus
001 **Epigramma**, AG 11.232.
Q: 29

CALLENIUS Epigr.
AG 9.46.
Cf. ANTIPATER Epigr. (0114 001).

0426 **CALLIAS** Comic.
5 B.C.
001 **Fragmenta**, ed. T. Kock, *Comicorum Atticorum fragmenta*, vol. 1. Leipzig: Teubner, 1880: 693–699.
frr. 1, 3–8, 10–13, 16–30 + tituli.
Q: 142
002 **Fragmenta**, ed. A. Meineke, *Fragmenta comicorum Graecorum*, vol. 2.2. Berlin: Reimer, 1840 (repr. De Gruyter, 1970): 735–741.
Q: 104
003 **Fragmenta**, ed. J. Demiańczuk, *Supplementum comicum*. Krakau: Nakładem Akademii, 1912 (repr. Hildesheim: Olms, 1967): 27–28.
frr. 1–3.
Q: 32
004 **Titulus**, ed. C. Austin, *Comicorum Graecorum fragmenta in papyris reperta*. Berlin: De Gruyter, 1973: 33.
NQ: 2
005 **Fragmenta**, ed. Meineke, *op. cit.*, vol. 5.1 (1857; repr. 1970): cxiii.
Q: [17]

1235 **CALLIAS** Hist.
4–3 B.C.: Syracusanus
001 **Testimonia**, FGrH #564: 3B:577–578.
NQ
002 **Fragmenta**, FGrH #564: 3B:578–580.
Q

1238 **CALLICRATES** Astrol.
Incertum
001 **Fragmenta**, ed. W. Kroll and A. Olivieri, *Codices Parisini* [*Catalogus codicum astrologorum Graecorum* 8.3. Brussels: Lamertin, 1912]: 102–103.
Q: [121]

1783 **CALLICRATES** Comic.
Incertum
001 **Titulus**, ed. T. Kock, *Comicorum Atticorum fragmenta*, vol. 2. Leipzig: Teubner, 1884: 416.
NQ: 2
002 **Titulus**, ed. A. Meineke, *Fragmenta comicorum Graecorum*, vol. 1. Berlin: Reimer, 1839 (repr. De Gruyter, 1970): 418.
NQ

1940 **CALLICRATES** Hist.
A.D. 3–4?: Tyrius
001 **Fragmentum**, FGrH #213: 2B:944-945.
Q

1236 **CALLICRATES-MENECLES** Perieg.
2/1 B.C.

001 **Fragmenta**, FGrH #370: 3B:231–233.
Q

1237 **<CALLICRATIDAS>** Phil.
3 B.C.?
001 **Fragmenta**, ed. H. Thesleff, *The Pythagorean texts of the Hellenistic period*. Åbo: Åbo Akademi, 1965: 103–107.
Q: 1,272

0148 **CALLICTER** Epigr.
vel Cillactor
A.D. 1/2
001 **Epigrammata**, AG 5.29, 45; 11.2, 5–6, 118–122, 333.
AG 5.31: Cf. ANTIPATER Epigr. (0114 001).
Q: 197

0533 **CALLIMACHUS** Philol.
4–3 B.C.: Cyrenaeus
001 **Fragmenta**, ed. R. Pfeiffer, *Callimachus*, vol. 1. Oxford: Clarendon Press, 1949: 1–2, 4–6, 8–10, 12, 14–16, 18, 20–30, 32–37, 39, 41–46, 48–58, 60–104, 106–109, 111–112, 114, 116, 118, 120, 122, 124–159, 161–162, 164, 166–226, 229–272, 274–306, 308–327, 330–338, 354–399, 401–402, 406–429, 431–437, 440–452, 454, 456, 458–486, 489–492, 495.
Aetia (frr. 1–7, 10–12, 15, 17–28, 30, 32–33, 37, 41, 43–46, 48–49, 51, 55, 57–59, 61, 63–70, 72–87, 90–98, 100–106, 108, 110, 112–184, 186).
Iambi (frr. 191–216, 218–225).
Lyrica (frr. 226–229).
Hecala (frr. 230–236, 238–248, 251, 253–263, 265–289, 291–295, 298–305, 309–315, 317–348, 350–351, 353–377).
Carmina epica et elegiaca minora (frr. 378–380, 383–392).
Epigrammatum fragmenta (frr. 393–395, 398–401).
Fragmenta grammatica (fr. 407).
Fragmenta incertae sedis (frr. 467–472, 474–477, 480–500, 502, 504–512, 514–520, 522–536, 538–540, 544, 546–557, 560–562, 567, 571–575, 586–588, 590–593, 597, 599, 601–608, 610–613, 617–621, 623, 625–631, 633–639, 644–648, 650–652, 654–659, 668–677, 680–683, 686–691, 694–695, 700–701, 705, 713–716, 719, 721, 724–725).
Fragmenta incerti auctoris (frr. 726–732, 734–740, 742–776, 778–782, 784–788, 799–803, 805–807, 813–814).
Q, Pap: 12,521
002 **Hymni**, ed. Pfeiffer, *op. cit.*, vol. 2 (1953): 1–40.
Hymn. 1, In Jovem: pp. 1–5.
Hymn. 2, In Apollinem: pp. 5–9.
Hymn. 3, In Dianam: pp. 9–18.
Hymn. 4, In Delum: pp. 18–29.
Hymn. 5, In lavacrum Palladis: pp. 30–34.

Hymn. 6, In Cererem: pp. 35–40.
Cod: 7,443
003 **Epigrammata**, ed. Pfeiffer, *op. cit.*, vol. 2, 80–99.
Epigr. 1–63.
Q: 1,984
004 **Epigrammata**, AG 5.6, 23, 146; **6.**121, 146–150, 301, 310–311, 347, 351; 7.80, 89, 170, 271–272, 277, 317–318, 344b, 415, 447, 451, 453–454, 458–460, 471, 517–525, 725, 728; 9.336, 507, 565–566; 11.362; 12.43, 51, 71, 73, 102, 118, 134, 139, 148–150, 230; 13.7, 9–10, 24–25.
AG 7.320: Cf. HEGESIPPUS Epigr. (1396 001).
AG 7.729: Cf. TYMNES Epigr. (1744 001).
AG 9.67: Cf. ANONYMI EPIGRAMMATICI (0138 001).
Q: 2,066
005 **Fragmenta et titulus**, ed. H. Lloyd-Jones and P. Parsons, *Supplementum Hellenisticum*. Berlin: De Gruyter, 1983: 89–90, 92–98, 101–110, 117–119, 122–127, 131–132, 134–143.
frr. (+ titul.) 238–255, 257–265, 267–268, 271–276, 280–283, 285–298, 300–308.
Pap: 2,611
x01 **Epigrammata** (*App. Anth.*).
Epigramma dedicatorium: 1.114.
Epigrammata demonstrativa: 3.63–66.
Epigrammata irrisoria: 5.19; Addenda 5.19b.
App. Anth. 1.114: Cf. EPIGRAMMATICI in *App. Anth.* (7052 001).
App. Anth. 3.63–66: Cf. EPIGRAMMATICI in *App. Anth.* (7052 003).
App. Anth. 5.19: Cf. EPIGRAMMATICI in *App. Anth.* (7052 005).
App. Anth. 5.19b: Cf. EPIGRAMMATICI in *App. Anth.* (7052 008).
x02 **Fragmentum papyraceum** (fort. auctore Callimacho).
SH, p. 511, fr. 992.
Cf. ADESPOTA PAPYRACEA (SH) (2648 004).

2613 **CALLIMACHUS Junior** Epic.
3 B.C.: Cyrenaeus
001 **Titulus**, ed. H. Lloyd-Jones and P. Parsons, *Supplementum Hellenisticum*. Berlin: De Gruyter, 1983: 144.
fr. 309.
NQ: [2]

1996 **CALLIMORPHUS** Med.
A.D. 2
001 **Fragmenta**, FGrH #210: 2B:941–942.
Q

0824 **CALLINICUS** Med.
ante A.D. 1
x01 **Fragmentum ap. Galenum**.
K13.984.
Cf. GALENUS Med. (0057 077).

2189 **CALLINICUS** Soph.
A.D. 3: Petraeus
001 **Testimonia**, FGrH #281: 3A:159–160.
NQ
002 **Fragmenta**, FGrH #281: 3A:160–161.
Q, Cod
003 Εἰς τὰ πάτρια ʿΡώμης, ed. H. Hinck, *Polemonis declamationes quae exstant duae*. Leipzig: Teubner, 1873: 43–44.
Cod

0243 **CALLINUS** Eleg.
7 B.C.: Ephesius
001 **Fragmenta**, ed. M.L. West, *Iambi et elegi Graeci*, vol. 2. Oxford: Clarendon Press, 1972: 47–49.
frr. 1–2a, 4–5a.
Q: [186]

2218 **CALLIPHON et DEMOCEDES** Med. et Phil.
6 B.C.: Cnidius, Crotoniensis
001 **Testimonia**, ed. H. Diels and W. Kranz, *Die Fragmente der Vorsokratiker*, vol. 1, 6th edn. Berlin: Weidmann, 1951 (repr. Dublin: 1966): 110–112.
test. 1–3.
NQ

0427 <**CALLIPPUS**> Comic.
Incertum: Atheniensis
001 **Fragmenta**, ed. T. Kock, *Comicorum Atticorum fragmenta*, vol. 3. Leipzig: Teubner, 1888: 378–379.
frr. 1–2.
Q: 18
002 **Fragmentum**, ed. A. Meineke, *Fragmenta comicorum Graecorum*, vol. 4. Berlin: Reimer, 1841 (repr. De Gruyter, 1970): 561.
Q: 16

2270 **CALLIPPUS** Hist.
ante A.D. 2: Corinthius
001 **Fragmenta**, FGrH #385: 3B:263.
Q

0534 **CALLISTHENES** Hist.
4 B.C.: Olynthius
001 **Testimonia**, FGrH #124: **2B**:631–639; **3B**:743
addenda.
test. 23: *Inscr. Delphi*.
test. 33 bis: *P. Zenon* 60.
NQ
002 **Fragmenta**, FGrH #124: **2B**:639–657; **3B**:743
addenda.
fr. 55: *P. Oxy*. 2.222.
Q, Pap
003 **Testimonium et fragmentum**, ed. H.J. Mette, "Die 'Kleinen' griechischen Historiker heute," *Lustrum* 21 (1978) 18–19.
test. 37: *P. Mich*. 1316.
fr. 32 bis.
Q, Pap

2199 **[CALLISTHENES]** Hist.
Incertum: Sybarita
001 **Fragmenta**, FGrH #291: 3A:175.
Q

2155 **CALLISTION** Hist.
A.D. 4
001 **Testimonia**, FGrH #223: 2B:951.
NQ
002 **Fragmentum**, FGrH #223: 2B:951.
Q

2252 **CALLISTRATUS** Gramm.
2 B.C.: Alexandrinus
001 **Fragmenta**, FGrH #348: 3B:210–211.
Q

1239 **Domitius CALLISTRATUS** Hist.
1 B.C.?
001 **Fragmenta**, FGrH #433: 3B:334–336.
Q

4091 **CALLISTRATUS** Soph.
A.D. 4
001 **Statuarum descriptiones**, ed. K. Schenkl and A. Reisch, *Philostrati minoris imagines et Callistrati descriptiones*. Leipzig: Teubner, 1902: 45–72.
Cod

1845 **CALLISTRATUS** Trag.
Incertum
001 **Tituli**, ed. B. Snell, *Tragicorum Graecorum fragmenta*, vol. 1. Göttingen: Vandenhoeck & Ruprecht, 1971: 155.
NQ

1240 **CALLIXENUS** Hist.
2 B.C.: Rhodius
001 **Testimonia**, FGrH #627: 3C:161.
NQ
002 **Fragmenta**, FGrH #627: 3C:161–178.
Q

2504 **CANDIDUS** Hist.
A.D. 5: Isauricus
001 **Testimonium**, FGrH #748: 3C:732.
NQ
002 **Fragmenta**, FHG 4: 135–137.
Q

0942 **CANDIDUS** <Med.>
ante A.D. 2
x01 **Fragmentum ap. Galenum**.
K13.926.
Cf. GALENUS Med. (0057 077).
x02 **Fragmentum ap. Aëtium** (lib. 7).
CMG, vol. 8.2, p. 393.
Cf. AËTIUS Med. (0718 007).

1242 *CANON LIBRORUM*
A.D. 2

001 **Canon librorum**, ed. J.P. Audet, "A Hebrew-Aramaic list of books of the Old Testament in Greek transcription," *Journal of Theological Studies*, n.s. 1 (1950) 138.
Cod

0428 **CANTHARUS** Comic.
5 B.C.
001 **Fragmenta**, ed. T. Kock, *Comicorum Atticorum fragmenta*, vol. 1. Leipzig: Teubner, 1880: 764–766.
frr. 1–8, 10 + tituli.
Q: 37
002 **Fragmenta**, ed. A. Meineke, *Fragmenta comicorum Graecorum*, vol. 2.2. Berlin: Reimer, 1840 (repr. De Gruyter, 1970): 835–836.
Q: 30
003 **Fragmenta**, ed. J. Demiańczuk, *Supplementum comicum*. Krakau: Nakładem Akademii, 1912 (repr. Hildesheim: Olms, 1967): 28–29.
frr. 1–3.
Q: 12
004 **Titulus**, ed. C. Austin, *Comicorum Graecorum fragmenta in papyris reperta*. Berlin: De Gruyter, 1973: 33.
NQ: 2

2138 *CANTICUM EURIPIDIS*
ante 3 B.C.
001 **Ex Orestis stasimo i** (*P. Vindob.* 2315), ed. K. Jan, *Musici scriptores Graeci*. Leipzig: Teubner, 1895 (repr. Hildesheim: Olms, 1962): 430.
Cf. et EURIPIDES Trag. (0006 016).
Pap

0276 *CANTUS LUGUBRIS*
ante A.D. 2
001 **Fragmentum** (*P. Brit. Mus.* 2103), ed. E. Heitsch, *Die griechischen Dichterfragmente der römischen Kaiserzeit*, vol. 1, 2nd edn. Göttingen: Vandenhoeck & Ruprecht, 1963: 43–44.
Pap: [122]

0149 **CAPITO** Epigr.
Incertum
001 **Epigramma**, AG 5.67.
Q: 14

2506 **CAPITO** Hist.
A.D. 5/6?: Lycius
001 **Testimonium**, FGrH #750: 3C:733.
NQ
002 **Fragmenta**, FGrH #750: 3C:733–734.
Q

CARCINUS Epic.
Incertum: Naupactous
Cf. CARMEN NAUPACTIUM (1241).

0310 **CARCINUS** Trag.
5 B.C.
001 **Fragmentum**, ed. B. Snell, *Tragicorum Graeco-*

rum fragmenta, vol. 1. Göttingen: Vandenhoeck & Ruprecht, 1971: 131.
fr. 2.
Q: [5]

0327 **CARCINUS Junior** Trag.
4 B.C.
001 **Fragmenta**, ed. B. Snell, *Tragicorum Graecorum fragmenta*, vol. 1. Göttingen: Vandenhoeck & Ruprecht, 1971: 211–215.
frr. 1a, 1c–1d, 2–10.
Q: [231]

0286 *CARMEN ASTROLOGICUM*
A.D. 4?
001 **Fragmentum**, ed. E. Heitsch, *Die griechischen Dichterfragmente der römischen Kaiserzeit*, vol. 2. Göttingen: Vandenhoeck & Ruprecht, 1964: 43–44.
Q: [102]

CARMEN AUREUM
Cf. <PYTHAGORAS> Phil. (0632 001).

1241 *CARMEN NAUPACTIUM*
fort. auctore Carcino Naupactoo
Incertum
001 **Fragmenta**, ed. G. Kinkel, *Epicorum Graecorum fragmenta*, vol. 1. Leipzig: Teubner, 1877: 198–200.
frr. 1–2, 7–8.
Q: [60]

0295 *CARMINA POPULARIA* (PMG)
Varia
001 **Fragmenta**, ed. D.L. Page, *Poetae melici Graeci*. Oxford: Clarendon Press, 1962 (repr. 1967 (1st edn. corr.)): 450–470.
frr. 1–12, 14–17, 19–37.
Q, Pap: [633]

0296 *CARMINA CONVIVIALIA* (PMG)
Varia
001 **Fragmenta**, ed. D.L. Page, *Poetae melici Graeci*. Oxford: Clarendon Press, 1962 (repr. 1967 (1st edn. corr.)): 472–482.
frr. 1–31, 33–34.
Q, Pap: [679]

0362 *CARMINA DELPHIS INVENTA*
A.D. 1–2
001 **Carmina Delphis inventa**, ed. K. Jan, *Musici scriptores Graeci*. Leipzig: Teubner, 1895 (repr. Hildesheim: Olms, 1962): 434–448.
Epigr

1244 **CARNEISCUS** Phil.
3/2 B.C.
001 **Fragmenta**, ed. W. Crönert, *Kolotes und Menedemos*. Leipzig: Avenarius, 1906 (repr. Amsterdam: Hakkert, 1965): 69–71.
Pap

0150 **CARPHYLLIDES** Epigr.
3 B.C.
001 **Epigrammata**, AG 7.260; **9**.52.
Q: 87

1245 **CARYSTIUS** Hist.
2 B.C.: Pergamenus
001 **Fragmenta**, FHG 4: 356–359.
frr. 1–19.
Q

1822 **Julius CASSIANUS** Gnost.
A.D. 2
x01 **Fragmentum ap. Clementem Alexandrinum.**
Stromata 3.13.92.
Cf. CLEMENS ALEXANDRINUS Theol. (0555 004).

1806 **CASSIUS** Med.
fiq Cassius Dionysius Uticensis
1 B.C.
x01 **Fragmentum ap. Hippiatrica.**
Oder & Hoppe, vol. 1, pp. 41–42.
Cf. HIPPIATRICA (0738 001).

0733 **CASSIUS** Med.
A.D. 2–3
001 **Quaestiones medicae et problemata physica,**
ed. J.L. Ideler, *Physici et medici Graeci minores*, vol. 1. Berlin: Reimer, 1841 (repr. Amsterdam: Hakkert, 1963): 144–167.
Cod: 7,174

CASSIUS DIO Hist.
Cf. DIO CASSIUS Hist. (0385).

1246 **CASTOR** Rhet.
1 B.C.: Rhodius
001 **Testimonia**, FGrH #250: 2B:1130–1131.
NQ
002 **Fragmenta**, FGrH #250: 2B:1132–1133, 1135, 1137, 1143–1145.
Q

0382 **CASTORION** Lyr.
4 B.C.: Soleus
001 **Fragmentum**, ed. D.L. Page, *Poetae melici Graeci*. Oxford: Clarendon Press, 1962 (repr. 1967 (1st edn. corr.)): 447.
fr. 1.
Q: [11]
002 **Fragmenta**, ed. H. Lloyd-Jones and P. Parsons, *Supplementum Hellenisticum*. Berlin: De Gruyter, 1983: 144–145.
frr. 310, 312.
Q: [39]

0826 **CASTUS** Med.
A.D. 1?
x01 **Fragmenta ap. Galenum.**
K13.739, 1037.
Cf. GALENUS Med. (0057 077).

2661 **CATILIUS** Epigr.
post A.D. 1
x01 **Epigrammata dedicatoria.**
App. Anth. 1.159–161: Cf. EPIGRAMMATICI in *App. Anth.* (7052 001).

2672 **CATULLINUS** Epigr.
Incertum
x01 **Epigramma dedicatorium.**
App. Anth. 1.196: Cf. EPIGRAMMATICI in *App. Anth.* (7052 001).

2666 **CATULUS** Epigr.
Incertum
x01 **Epigramma dedicatorium.**
App. Anth. 1.189: Cf. EPIGRAMMATICI in *App. Anth.* (7052 001).

1887 **CAUCALUS** Rhet.
4 B.C.: Chius
001 **Fragmenta**, FGrH #38: 1A:259–260.
Q

1247 **<CEBES>** Phil.
A.D. 1
001 **Cebetis tabula**, ed. C. Praechter, *Cebetis tabula*. Leipzig: Teubner, 1893: 1–34.
Cod: [4,838]

2662 **CELSUS** Epigr.
3 B.C.
x01 **Epigramma dedicatorium.**
App. Anth. 1.165: Cf. EPIGRAMMATICI in *App. Anth.* (7052 001).

1248 **CELSUS** Phil.
A.D. 2
001 **Ἀληθὴς λόγος**, ed. R. Bader, *Der Ἀληθὴς λόγος des Kelsos* [*Tübinger Beiträge zur Altertumswissenschaft* 33. Stuttgart: Kohlhammer, 1940]: 39–216.
Cod: [25,219]

1249 **CEPHALION** Hist. et Rhet.
A.D. 2
001 **Testimonia**, FGrH #93: 2A:436–437.
NQ
002 **Fragmenta**, FGrH #93: 2A:438–445.
Q

0429 **CEPHISODORUS** Comic.
5–4 B.C.
001 **Fragmenta**, ed. T. Kock, *Comicorum Atticorum fragmenta*, vol. 1. Leipzig: Teubner, 1880: 800–802.
frr. 1, 3–4, 7–9, 11–12 + titulus.
Q: 90
002 **Fragmenta**, ed. A. Meineke, *Fragmenta comicorum Graecorum*, vol. 2.2. Berlin: Reimer, 1840 (repr. De Gruyter, 1970): 883–886.
Q: 90

1927 **CEPHISODORUS** Hist.
4 B.C.: Atheniensis vel Thebanus
001 **Fragmenta**, FGrH #112: 2B:524.
Q

0827 **CEPHISOPHON** Med.
ante A.D. 4
x01 **Fragmentum ap. Oribasium.**
CMG, vol. 6.2.1, p. 215.
Cf. ORIBASIUS Med. (0722 003).

1250 **CERCIDAS** Iamb.
3 B.C.: Megalopolitanus
Cf. et CHOLIAMBICA ADESPOTA (ALG)
(1797).
001 **Fragmenta**, ed. J.U. Powell, *Collectanea Alexandrina*. Oxford: Clarendon Press, 1925 (repr.
1970): 202–218.
frr. 1–18.
fr. 17: *P. Lond.* 2.155.
fr. 18: *P. Heidelb.* inv. 310.
Q, Pap: [1,291]

CERCOPS Epic.
6 B.C.?: Milesius
Cf. AEGIMIUS (0668).

2286 **CERCOPS** Phil.
6 B.C.: Milesius
001 **Testimonium**, ed. H. Diels and W. Kranz, *Die
Fragmente der Vorsokratiker*, vol. 1, 6th edn.
Berlin: Weidmann, 1951 (repr. Dublin: 1966):
105–106.
NQ

0151 **CEREALIUS** Epigr.
A.D. 1/2?
001 **Epigrammata**, AG 11.129, 144.
Q: 71

1252 *CERTAMEN HOMERI ET HESIODI*
3 B.C./A.D. 2
Cf. et VITAE HOMERI (1805).
001 **Certamen Homeri et Hesiodi** (*P. Petrie* 25),
ed. T.W. Allen, *Homeri opera*, vol. 5. Oxford:
Clarendon Press, 1912 (repr. 1969): 225.
Pap: 198
002 **Certamen Homeri et Hesiodi**, ed. Allen, *op.
cit.*, 225–238.
Cod: 2,449

0152 **CHAEREMON** Epigr.
3 B.C.
001 **Epigrammata**, AG 7.469, 720–721.
Q: 53

2424 **CHAEREMON** Hist. et Phil.
A.D. 1: Alexandrinus
001 **Testimonia**, FGrH #618: 3C:145–146.
NQ
002 **Fragmenta**, FGrH #618: 3C:146–153.
Q

0328 **CHAEREMON** Trag.
4 B.C.
001 **Fragmenta**, ed. B. Snell, *Tragicorum Graecorum fragmenta*, vol. 1. Göttingen: Vandenhoeck & Ruprecht, 1971: 216–226.
frr. 1, 2–3, 5–9, 10–12, 13–14, 14b, 15–33, 35–
39, 41.
fr. 14b: *P. Hibeh* 2.224.
Q, Pap: [516]

1795 **CHAERION** Comic.
Incertum
001 **Titulus**, ed. T. Kock, *Comicorum Atticorum
fragmenta*, vol. 3. Leipzig: Teubner, 1888: 366.
NQ: 3

1253 **CHAERIS** Gramm.
2 B.C.
001 **Fragmenta**, ed. R. Berndt, *De Charete, Chaeride, Alexione grammaticis eorumque reliquiis*,
pt. 1. Königsberg: Hartung, 1902: 31–46.
Q

1251 **CHAMAELEON** Phil.
4–3 B.C.: Heracleota
001 **Fragmenta**, ed. F. Wehrli, *Phainias von Eresos.
Chamaileon. Praxiphanes* [*Die Schule des Aristoteles*, vol. 9, 2nd edn. Basel: Schwabe, 1969]:
49–63.
Q
002 **Fragmenta**, ed. H.J. Mette, "Die 'Kleinen'
griechischen Historiker heute," *Lustrum* 21
(1978) 41.
frr. 28 bis, 32c.
fr. 28 bis: *P. Oxy.* 29.2506.
fr. 32c: *P. Oxy.* 26.2451.
Pap

1254 **CHARAX** Hist.
A.D. 2?: Pergamenus
001 **Testimonia**, FGrH #103: 2A:482–483.
NQ
002 **Fragmenta**, FGrH #103: **2A:**483–493; **3B:**741–
742 addenda.
Q

1256 **CHARES** Gnom.
4/3 B.C.
001 **Sententiae**, ed. S. Jaekel, *Menandri sententiae*.
Leipzig: Teubner, 1964: 26–30.
fr. 1: *P. Heidelb.* inv. 434.
Q, Pap: 211
002 **Sententiae**, ed. D. Young (post E. Diehl),
Theognis. Leipzig: Teubner, 1971: 113–118.
fr. 2: *P. Heidelb.* inv. 434.
Q, Pap: [236]

1850 **CHARES** Gramm.
1 B.C.: Alexandrinus
001 **Fragmenta**, ed. R. Berndt, *De Charete, Chaeride, Alexione grammaticis eorumque reliquiis*,

pt. 1. Königsberg: Hartung, 1902: 18–22.
frr. 1–5.
Q

1255 **CHARES** Hist.
4 B.C.: Mytilenensis
001 **Testimonia**, FGrH #125: 2B:657–658.
NQ
002 **Fragmenta**, FGrH #125: 2B:658–665.
Q

2263 **CHARICLES** Hist.
ante A.D. 3
001 **Fragmentum**, FGrH #367: 3B:229.
Q

0788 **CHARICLES** Med.
A.D. 1
x01 **Fragmenta ap. Galenum**.
K13.94, 109, 282, 329.
Cf. GALENUS Med. (0057 076).

0430 **CHARICLIDES** Comic.
Incertum
001 **Fragmentum**, ed. T. Kock, *Comicorum Attico-rum fragmenta*, vol. 3. Leipzig: Teubner, 1888: 393–394.
fr. 1.
Q: 10
002 **Fragmentum**, ed. A. Meineke, *Fragmenta comicorum Graecorum*, vol. 4. Berlin: Reimer, 1841 (repr. De Gruyter, 1970): 556.
Q: 9

1257 **CHARINUS** Choliamb.
1 B.C.?
001 **Fragmentum**, ed. A.D. Knox, *Herodes, Cercidas, and the Greek choliambic poets*. Cambridge, Mass.: Harvard University Press, 1929 (repr. 1967): 274.
Q: [19]
002 **Fragmentum**, ed. H. Lloyd-Jones and P. Parsons, *Supplementum Hellenisticum*. Berlin: De Gruyter, 1983: 146.
fr. 313.
Q: [19]

0828 **CHARITON** Med.
ante A.D. 1
x01 **Fragmentum ap. Galenum**.
K14.180.
Cf. GALENUS Med. (0057 078).

0554 **CHARITON** Scr. Erot.
A.D. 2?: Aphrodisiensis
001 **De Chaerea et Callirhoe**, ed. W.E. Blake, *Charitonis Aphrodisiensis de Chaerea et Callirhoe amatoriarum narrationum libri octo*. Oxford: Clarendon Press, 1938: 1–127.
Cod: 35,523

0829 **CHARIXENES** Med.
A.D. 1
x01 **Fragmenta ap. Galenum**.
K12.635, 638, 685; 13.48, 49, 50, 82–83, 102, 108–109.
Cf. GALENUS Med. (0057 076).
x02 **Fragmentum ap. Aëtium** (lib. 8).
CMG, vol. 8.2, p. 492.
Cf. AËTIUS Med. (0718 008).

1258 **CHARON** Hist.
5 B.C.: Lampsacenus
001 **Testimonia**, FGrH #262 & #687b: 3A:1–2; 3C:414–415.
NQ
002 **Fragmenta**, FGrH #262 & #687b: 3A:2–8; 3C:415–416.
Q

2421 **CHARON** Hist.
post 4 B.C.?: Naucratites
001 **Testimonium**, FGrH #612: 3C:120.
NQ

1259 **<CHARONDAS>** <Phil.>
4/2 B.C.: Cataneus
001 **Fragmentum**, ed. H. Thesleff, *The Pythagorean texts of the Hellenistic period*. Åbo: Åbo Akademi, 1965: 60–63.
Q: 870

1260 **CHERSIAS** Epic.
6 B.C.
001 **Fragmentum**, ed. G. Kinkel, *Epicorum Graecorum fragmenta*, vol. 1. Leipzig: Teubner, 1877: 207.
Q: [13]
x01 **Epigramma**.
AG 7.54: Cf. MNASALCES Epigr. (1513 001).

2209 **CHERSIPHRON-METAGENES** Hist.
6 B.C.?
001 **Testimonium**, FGrH #420: 3B:316.
NQ

1261 **CHILON** <Phil.>
6 B.C.
Cf. et CHILONIS EPISTULA (0386).
Cf. et <SEPTEM SAPIENTES> (1667).
001 **Fragmentum**, ed. T. Bergk, *Poetae lyrici Graeci*, vol. 3. Leipzig: Teubner, 1882: 199.
Q

0386 *CHILONIS EPISTULA*
Incertum
Cf. et CHILON <Phil.> (1261).
001 **Epistula**, ed. R. Hercher, *Epistolographi Graeci*. Paris: Didot, 1873 (repr. Amsterdam: Hakkert, 1965): 193.
Q: [35]

0041 **CHION** <Epist.>
4 B.C.: Heracleensis
001 **Epistulae**, ed. R. Hercher, *Epistolographi Graeci*. Paris: Didot, 1873 (repr. Amsterdam: Hakkert, 1965): 194–206.
Cod: [4,907]

0431 **CHIONIDES** Comic.
5 B.C.
001 **Fragmenta**, ed. T. Kock, *Comicorum Atticorum fragmenta*, vol. 1. Leipzig: Teubner, 1880: 4–6.
frr. 1–6, 8 + tituli.
Q: 68
002 **Fragmenta**, ed. A. Meineke, *Fragmenta comicorum Graecorum*, vol. 2.1. Berlin: Reimer, 1839 (repr. De Gruyter, 1970): 5–7.
Q: 57
003 **Fragmentum**, ed. Meineke, *op. cit.*, vol. 5.1 (1857; repr. 1970): 14.
Q: [5]

2689 **CHIRISOPHUS** Epigr.
A.D. 2
x01 **Epigramma sepulcrale.**
App. Anth. 2.631: Cf. EPIGRAMMATICI in *App. Anth.* (7052 002).

1263 **CHOERILUS** Epic.
5 B.C.: Samius
001 **Fragmentum** (*P. Oxy.* 11.1399), ed. J.U. Powell, *Collectanea Alexandrina*. Oxford: Clarendon Press, 1925 (repr. 1970): 250.
Pap: [4]
002 **Fragmenta**, ed. G. Kinkel, *Epicorum Graecorum fragmenta*, vol. 1. Leipzig: Teubner, 1877: 266–271.
frr. 1–4, 6–10.
Q: [166]
003 **Fragmenta et tituli**, ed. H. Lloyd-Jones and P. Parsons, *Supplementum Hellenisticum*. Berlin: De Gruyter, 1983: 146–151.
frr. 314, 316–320, 322–324.
fr. 314: *P. Oxy.* 11.1399.
Q, Pap: [155]
004 **Fragmenta dubia** (fort. auctore Choerilo Iasense), ed. Lloyd-Jones and Parsons, *op. cit.*, 152.
frr. 329–330.
Q: [24]
x01 **Epigrammata.**
AG 7.325; 16.27: Cf. ANONYMI EPIGRAMMATICI (0138 001).
x02 **De Persia** (fort. auctore Choerilo Samio) (*P. Oxy.* 37.2814).
Cf. ADDITAMENTA (FGrH) (2433 053).

1262 **CHOERILUS** Epic.
4 B.C.: Iasensis
001 **Fragmentum**, ed. G. Kinkel, *Epicorum Graeco-*

rum fragmenta, vol. 1. Leipzig: Teubner, 1877: 309.
Q: [56]
002 **Fragmentum et titulus**, ed. H. Lloyd-Jones and P. Parsons, *Supplementum Hellenisticum*. Berlin: De Gruyter, 1983: 154–155.
frr. 334–335.
Cf. et CHOERILUS Samius Epic. (1263 004).
Q: [56]
x01 **Epigramma sepulcrale.**
App. Anth. 2.130(?): Cf. EPIGRAMMATICI in *App. Anth.* (7052 002).

0302 **CHOERILUS** Trag.
5 B.C.: Atheniensis
001 **Fragmenta**, ed. B. Snell, *Tragicorum Graecorum fragmenta*, vol. 1. Göttingen: Vandenhoeck & Ruprecht, 1971: 67–68.
frr. 1–3.
Q: [35]

4093 **Georgius CHOEROBOSCUS** Gramm.
A.D. 6/7: Constantinopolitanus
Bibliography in progress
001 **Prolegomena et scholia in Theodosii Alexandrini canones isagogicos de flexione nominum**, ed. A. Hilgard, *Grammatici Graeci*, vol. 4.1. Leipzig: Teubner, 1894 (repr. Hildesheim: Olms, 1965): 103–417.
Cod: [238,259]
002 **Prolegomena et scholia in Theodosii Alexandrini canones isagogicos de flexione verborum**, ed. Hilgard, *op. cit.*, vol. 4.2 (1894; repr. 1965): 1–371.
Cod

1797 *CHOLIAMBICA ADESPOTA* (ALG)
3 B.C.?
001 **Anonymus in turpilucrum** (fort. auctore Cercida), ed. E. Diehl, *Anthologia lyrica Graeca*, fasc. 3, 3rd edn. Leipzig: Teubner, 1952: 131–136.
Cf. et CERCIDAS Iamb. (1250 001).
Pap: [509]
002 **Fragmenta choliambica**, ed. Diehl, *op. cit.*, 139–140.
Q: [61]

CHOLIAMBICA ADESPOTA (CA)
CA, p. 190.
Cf. LYRICA ADESPOTA (CA) (0230 001).

1267 *CHRISTI EPISTULA*
Incertum
x01 **Fragmentum ap. Eusebium.**
HE 1.13.10.
Cf. EUSEBIUS Scr. Eccl. et Theol. (2018 002).

2119 **CHRISTODORUS** Epic.
A.D. 5–6: Coptites
001 **Fragmenta**, ed. E. Heitsch, *Die griechischen*

Dichterfragmente der römischen Kaiserzeit, vol.
2. Göttingen: Vandenhoeck & Ruprecht, 1964:
48.
frr. 1–2.
Q: [20]
002 **Epigrammata**, AG **2**; 7.697–698.
Q: 2,719
003 **Testimonium**, FGrH #283: 3A:161.
NQ
004 **Fragmentum**, FGrH #283: 3A:161.
Q

2195 **[CHRYSERMUS]** Hist.
Incertum: Corinthius
001 **Fragmenta**, FGrH #287: 3A:168–170.
Q

0830 **CHRYSERMUS** Med.
1 B.C.
x01 **Fragmenta ap. Galenum.**
K8.741; 13.243.
Cf. GALENUS Med. (0057, 059, 076).

1922 **CHRYSERUS** Hist.
A.D. 2
001 **Testimonium**, FGrH #96: 2A:446.
NQ
002 **Fragmentum**, FGrH #96: 2A:447.
Q

2559 **CHRYSIPPUS** Hist.
Incertum
001 **Fragmentum**, FGrH #832: 3C:901–902.
Q

0831 **CHRYSIPPUS** Med.
4 B.C.: fort. Cnidius
x01 **Fragmentum ap. Rufum.**
Daremberg-Ruelle, pp. 6–7.
Cf. RUFUS Med. (0564 001).

1264 **CHRYSIPPUS** Phil.
3 B.C.: Soleus
001 **Fragmenta logica et physica**, ed. J. von Arnim,
Stoicorum veterum fragmenta, vol. 2. Leipzig:
Teubner, 1903 (repr. Stuttgart: 1968): 1–348.
Q, Pap: [138,742]
002 **Fragmenta moralia**, ed. von Arnim, *op. cit.*,
vol. 3 (1903; repr. 1968): 3–191.
Q, Pap
003 **Fragmenta quae ad explicationem carminum
Homericorum pertinent**, ed. von Arnim, *op.
cit.*, vol. 3, 192–193.
Q
004 **Fragmenta ad singulos libros relata**, ed. von
Arnim, *op. cit.*, vol. 3, 194–205.
Q
005 **Fragmenta poetica**, ed. H. Lloyd-Jones and P.
Parsons, *Supplementum Hellenisticum*. Berlin:
De Gruyter, 1983: 158.
frr. 336–338.
Q: [53]

006 **Fragmenta** (*P. Herc.* 307), ed. L. Marrone,
"Nuove letture nel P. Herc. 307 (questioni
logiche di Crisippo)," *Cronache Ercolanesi* 12
(1982) 15–18.
Pap
x01 **Epigramma sepulcrale.**
App. Anth. 2.131?: Cf. EPIGRAMMATICI in
App. Anth. (7052 002).

1265 **CHRYSIPPUS Scriptor Rei Coquinariae**
A.D. 1: Tyanensis
x01 **Fragmentum ap. Athenaeum.**
Deipnosophistae 14.647c–648a.
Cf. ATHENAEUS Soph. (0008 001).

9008 **Macarius CHRYSOCEPHALUS** Paroemiogr.
A.D. 14: Philadelphius
001 **Paroemiae**, ed. E.L. von Leutsch, *Corpus
paroemiographorum Graecorum*, vol. 2. Göttingen: Vandenhoeck & Ruprecht, 1851 (repr.
Hildesheim: Olms, 1958): 135–227.
Cod: [8,251]

2165 **Marcus Tullius CICERO** Orat.
2–1 B.C.: Arpinius
001 **Testimonia**, FGrH #235 & #648: **2B**:987;
3C:203.
NQ
002 **Fragmenta**, FGrH #235: 2B:987–988.
Q

CINAETHON Epic.
7 B.C.?: Lacedaemonius
Cf. ILIAS PARVA (1444).
Cf. OEDIPODEA (1547).

2543 **Lucius CINCIUS ALIMENTUS** Hist.
3 B.C.: Romanus
001 **Testimonia**, FGrH #810: 3C:876–877.
NQ
002 **Fragmenta**, FGrH #810: 3C:877–880.
Q

2417 **CINEAS** Rhet.
4/3 B.C.?: Thessalius
001 **Testimonia**, FGrH #603: 3B:736–737.
NQ
002 **Fragmenta**, FGrH #603: 3B:737.
Q

0375 **CINESIAS** Lyr.
5–4 B.C.: Atheniensis
001 **Fragmentum**, ed. D.L. Page, *Poetae melici
Graeci*. Oxford: Clarendon Press, 1962 (repr.
1967 (1st edn. corr.)): 398.
fr. 2.
Q: [3]
002 **Titulus**, ed. Page, *op. cit.*, 398.
NQ

4057 **CLAUDIANUS** Epigr.
A.D. 5

001 **Epigrammata,** AG 1.19–20.
Q: 92

002 **Testimonia,** FGrH #282: 3A:161.
NQ

4056 **Claudius CLAUDIANUS** Poeta
A.D. 4–5: Alexandrinus
Bibliography in progress
001 **Epigrammata,** AG 5.86; 9.139–140, 753–754.
Q: 109

1268 **CLAUDIUS** Hist.
A.D. 1?: Iolaus
001 **Fragmenta,** FGrH #788: 3C:800–801.
Q

1971 **CLAUDIUS EUSTHENIUS** Hist.
A.D. 4?
001 **Fragmentum,** FGrH #218: 2B:948.
Q

2184 **Tiberius CLAUDIUS Nero Germanicus** Hist.
1 B.C.–A.D. 1
001 **Testimonia,** FGrH #276: 3A:155–156.
NQ
002 **Fragmenta,** FGrH #276: 3A:156–157.
Q

0332 **CLEAENETUS** Trag.
4 B.C.
001 **Fragmenta,** ed. B. Snell, *Tragicorum Graecorum fragmenta,* vol. 1. Göttingen: Vandenhoeck & Ruprecht, 1971: 251.
frr. 1–2.
Q: [21]

1269 **CLEANTHES** Phil.
4–3 B.C.: Assius
001 **Fragmenta,** ed. J.U. Powell, *Collectanea Alexandrina.* Oxford: Clarendon Press, 1925 (repr. 1970): 227–231.
frr. 1–10.
Q: [491]
002 **Testimonia et fragmenta,** ed. J. von Arnim, *Stoicorum veterum fragmenta,* vol. 1. Leipzig: Teubner, 1903 (repr. Stuttgart: 1968): 103–137.
Q
x01 **Epigrammata exhortatoria et supplicatoria.**
App. Anth. 4.34–35: Cf. EPIGRAMMATICI in *App. Anth.* (7052 004).

0432 **CLEARCHUS** Comic.
4 B.C.
001 **Fragmenta,** ed. T. Kock, *Comicorum Atticorum fragmenta,* vol. 2. Leipzig: Teubner, 1884: 408–410.
frr. 1–5.
Q: 104
002 **Fragmenta,** ed. A. Meineke, *Fragmenta comicorum Graecorum,* vol. 4. Berlin: Reimer, 1841

(repr. De Gruyter, 1970): 562–564.
Q: 106

2730 **CLEARCHUS** Epigr.
Incertum
x01 **Aenigma.**
App. Anth. 7.15: Cf. EPIGRAMMATICI in *App. Anth.* (7052 007).

1270 **CLEARCHUS** Phil.
4–3 B.C.: Soleus
001 **Fragmenta,** ed. F. Wehrli, *Klearchos* [*Die Schule des Aristoteles,* vol. 3, 2nd edn. Basel: Schwabe, 1969]: 9–40.
Q

2147 **CLEMENS** Hist.
Incertum
001 **Testimonium,** FGrH #102: 2A:482.
NQ

0834 **Flavius CLEMENS** <Med.>
A.D. 1?
x01 **Fragmentum ap. Galenum.**
K13.1026.
Cf. GALENUS Med. (0057 077).

0555 **CLEMENS ALEXANDRINUS** Theol.
A.D. 2–3: Alexandrinus
001 **Protrepticus,** ed. C. Mondésert, *Clément d'Alexandrie. Le protreptique,* 2nd edn. [*Sources chrétiennes* 2. Paris: Cerf, 1949]: 52–193.
Cod: 23,716
002 **Paedagogus,** ed. H.-I. Marrou, M. Harl, C. Mondésert and C. Matray, *Clement d'Alexandrie. Le pédagogue,* 3 vols. [*Sources chrétiennes* 70, 108, 158. Paris: Cerf, 1:1960; 2:1965; 3:1970]: **1:**108–294; **2:**10–242; **3:**12–190.
Cod: 57,864
003 **Hymnus Christi servatoris,** ed. C. Mondésert and C. Matray, *Clément d'Alexandrie. Le pédagogue,* vol. 3 [*Sources chrétiennes* 158. Paris: Cerf, 1970]: 192–202.
Cod: 150
004 **Stromata,** ed. O. Stählin, L. Früchtel and U. Treu, *Clemens Alexandrinus,* vols. 2, 3rd edn. & 3, 2nd edn. [*Die griechischen christlichen Schriftsteller* 52(15), 17. Berlin: Akademie-Verlag, 2:1960; 3:1970]: **2:**3–518; **3:**3–102.
Cod: 166,077
005 **Eclogae propheticae,** ed. Stählin, Früchtel and Treu, *op. cit.,* vol. 3, 137–155.
Cod: 5,098
006 **Quis dives salvetur,** ed. Stählin, Früchtel, and Treu, *op. cit.,* vol. 3, 159–191.
Cod: 9,411
007 **Excerpta ex Theodoto,** ed. F. Sagnard, *Clément d'Alexandrie. Extraits de Théodote,* 2nd edn. [*Sources chrétiennes* 23. Paris: Cerf, 1948 (repr. 1970)]: 52–212.
Cod: 7,691
008 **Fragmenta,** ed. Stählin, Früchtel and Treu, *op.*

cit., vol. 3, 195–202, 216–230.
Q, Cod

1271 **CLEMENS ROMANUS** Theol. et *CLEMEN-TINA*
A.D. 1: Romanus
001 **Epistula i ad Corinthios**, ed. A. Jaubert, *Clément de Rome. Épître aux Corinthiens [Sources chrétiennes* 167. Paris: Cerf, 1971]: 98–204.
Cod: 10,302
002 **Epistula ii ad Corinthios** [Sp.], ed. K. Bihlmeyer and W. Schneemelcher (post F.X. Funk), *Die apostolischen Väter,* 3rd edn. Tübingen: Mohr, 1970: 71–81.
Cod: 3,161
003 **Epistula Petri ad Jacobum** [Sp.], ed. B. Rehm, J. Irmscher and F. Paschke, *Die Pseudoklementinen I. Homilien,* 2nd edn. [*Die griechischen christlichen Schriftsteller* 42. Berlin: Akademie-Verlag, 1969]: 1–2.
Cod: 512
004 **Contestatio** [Sp.], ed. Rehm, Irmscher, and Paschke, *op. cit.,* 2–4.
Cod: 677
005 **Epistula Clementis ad Jacobum** [Sp.], ed. Rehm, Irmscher, and Paschke, *op. cit.,* 5–22.
Cod: 2,563
006 **Homiliae** [Sp.], ed. Rehm, Irmscher, and Paschke, *op. cit.,* 23–281.
Cod: 72,715
007 **Recognitiones** [Sp.], ed. B. Rehm and F. Paschke, *Die Pseudoklementinen II. Rekognitionen [Die griechischen christlichen Schriftsteller* 51. Berlin: Akademie-Verlag, 1965]: 64, 116, 152, 225–226, 234–237, 242–244, 267, 268, 330–334, 342–344.
Q: 1,687
008 **Recognitiones** (ex Eusebio) [Sp.], ed. Rehm and Paschke, *op. cit.,* 270, 272, 274, 276, 278, 280, 282, 284, 286, 288, 290, 292, 294, 296, 298, 300, 302, 304, 306, 308, 310, 312, 314, 316.
Q: 1,795
009 **Recognitiones** (e Pseudo-Caesario) [Sp.], ed. Rehm and Paschke, *op. cit.,* 271, 273, 275, 277, 279, 281, 283, 287, 289, 291, 293, 295, 297, 299, 301, 303, 307, 309.
Q: 1,239
010 **Epistulae de virginitate** [Sp.], ed. F.X. Funk and F. Diekamp, *Patres apostolici,* vol. 2, 3rd edn. Tübingen: Laupp, 1913: 1–45.
Q: 2,254
011 **Epitome prior** [Sp.], ed. A.R.M. Dressel, *Clementinorum epitomae duae,* 2nd edn. Leipzig: Hinrichs, 1873: 2–118.
Cod: 25,983
012 **Epitome altera** [Sp.], ed. Dressel, *op. cit.,* 122–232.
Cod: 26,605

0622 *CLEOBULI EPISTULA*
Incertum

Cf. et CLEOBULUS Scriptor Aenigmatum (1274).
001 **Epistula**, ed. R. Hercher, *Epistolographi Graeci.* Paris: Didot, 1873 (repr. Amsterdam: Hakkert, 1965): 207.
Q: [37]

0244 **[CLEOBULINA]** <Eleg.>
6 B.C.: Lindia
001 **Fragmenta**, ed. M.L. West, *Iambi et elegi Graeci,* vol. 2. Oxford: Clarendon Press, 1972: 50–51.
frr. 1–3.
Q: [41]
x01 **Epigramma.**
AG 14.101: Cf. CLEOBULUS Lyr. et Epigr. (1274 002).
x02 **Epigramma exhortatorium et supplicatorium.**
App. Anth. 4.8: Cf. EPIGRAMMATICI in *App. Anth.* (7052 004).

1274 **CLEOBULUS** Lyr. et Epigr.
7–6 B.C.: Lindius
Cf. et CLEOBULI EPISTULA (0622).
Cf. et [CLEOBULINA] <Eleg.> (0244).
Cf. et <SEPTEM SAPIENTES> (1667).
001 **Fragmenta lyrica**, ed. T. Bergk, *Poetae lyrici Graeci,* vol. 3, 4th edn. Leipzig: Teubner, 1882: 201–202.
frr. 1–2.
Q: [52]
002 **Epigrammata**, AG 7.153; **14.101.**
Q: 65

0835 **CLEOBULUS** Med.
ante A.D. 2
x01 **Fragmentum ap. Galenum.**
K13.854.
Cf. GALENUS Med. (0057 077).

2490 **CLEODEMUS-MALCHUS** Hist.
vel Cleodemus
vel Malchus
ante 2 B.C.
001 **Fragmentum**, FGrH #727: 3C:686–687.
Q

2614 **CLEOMACHUS** Poeta
ante A.D. 2: Magnes
001 **Fragmenta**, ed. H. Lloyd-Jones and P. Parsons, *Supplementum Hellenisticum.* Berlin: De Gruyter, 1983: 162.
frr. 341–342.
Q: [12]

1272 **CLEOMEDES** Astron.
A.D. 2
001 **De motu circulari corporum caelestium**, ed. H. Ziegler, *Cleomedis de motu circulari corporum caelestium libri duo.* Leipzig: Teubner, 1891: 2–228.
Cod: 24,880

2411 **CLEOMENES III** Hist.
3 B.C.: Lacedaemonius
001 **Fragmentum**, FGrH #598: 3B:730–731.
Q

0900 **CLEOMENES** Lyr.
5 B.C.: Rheginus
001 **Titulus**, ed. D.L. Page, *Poetae melici Graeci*.
Oxford: Clarendon Press, 1962 (repr. 1967 (1st
edn. corr.)): 442.
NQ

1273 **CLEON** Eleg.
4 B.C.: Siculus vel Curiensis
001 **Fragmentum**, ed. E. Diehl, *Anthologia lyrica
Graeca*, fasc. 1, 3rd edn. Leipzig: Teubner,
1949: 128.
Q: [11]
002 **Fragmenta et titulus**, ed. H. Lloyd-Jones and
P. Parsons, *Supplementum Hellenisticum*. Berlin: De Gruyter, 1983: 159–161.
frr. 339–340.
fr. 339a: *P. Mich.* inv. 1316.
Q, Pap: [174]

0836 **CLEON** Med.
1 B.C.?
x01 **Fragmenta ap. Oribasium**.
CMG, vol. 6.3, pp. 102, 104.
Cf. ORIBASIUS Med. (0722 004).
x02 **Fragmentum ap. Paulum**.
CMG, vol. 9.2, p. 342.
Cf. PAULUS Med. (0715 001).
x03 **Fragmentum ap. Aëtium** (lib. 7).
CMG, vol. 8.2, p. 375.
Cf. AËTIUS Med. (0718 007).

0837 **CLEONIACUS** Med.
vel Cloniacus
ante A.D. 2
x01 **Fragmentum ap. Galenum**.
K13.987–988.
Cf. GALENUS Med. (0057 077).

0361 **CLEONIDES** Mus.
A.D. 2
001 **Introductio harmonica**, ed. H. Menge, *Euclidis
opera omnia*, vol. 8. Leipzig: Teubner, 1916:
186–222.
Cod: 3,791

0684 **CLEOPATRA VII PHILOPATOR** <Med.>
1 B.C.
x01 **Fragmenta ap. Galenum**.
K12.403–405, 432–434, 492–493.
Cf. GALENUS Med. (0057 076).
x02 **Fragmentum ap. Pseudo-Galenum**.
K19.767–771, ed. Hultsch, vol. 1, pp. 233–236.
Cf. Pseudo-GALENUS Med. (0530 022).
x03 **Fragmentum ap. Aëtium** (lib. 8).
CMG, vol. 8.2, p. 408.
Cf. AËTIUS Med. (0718 008).

0821 **CLEOPHANTUS** Med.
1 B.C.
Cf. et ANTIPATER et CLEOPHANTUS Med.
(0832).
x01 **Fragmenta ap. Galenum**.
K13.262, 310, 985.
GALENUS Med. (0057 076–077).
x02 **Fragmenta ap. Soranum**.
CMG, vol. 4, pp. 129–130.
SORANUS Med. (0565 001).

1087 **CLEOPHON** Trag.
4 B.C.: Atheniensis
001 **Tituli**, ed. B. Snell, *Tragicorum Graecorum
fragmenta*, vol. 1. Göttingen: Vandenhoeck &
Ruprecht, 1971: 247.
NQ

1275 **CLEOSTRATUS** Poet. Phil.
6 B.C.: Tenedius
001 **Testimonia**, ed. H. Diels and W. Kranz, *Die
Fragmente der Vorsokratiker*, vol. 1, 6th edn.
Berlin: Weidmann, 1951 (repr. Dublin: 1966):
41.
test. 1–4.
NQ
002 **Fragmenta**, ed. Diels and Kranz, *op. cit.*, 41–
42.
fr. 1–4.
Q

1276 **CLIDEMUS** Hist.
vel Clitodemus
4 B.C.: Atheniensis
001 **Testimonia**, FGrH #323: 3B:51.
NQ
002 **Fragmenta**, FGrH #323: 3B:51–60, 757 addenda.
Q

2305 **CLIDEMUS** Phil.
4 B.C.?
001 **Testimonia**, ed. H. Diels and W. Kranz, *Die
Fragmente der Vorsokratiker*, vol. 2, 6th edn.
Berlin: Weidmann, 1952 (repr. Dublin: 1966):
50.
test. 1–6.
NQ

2441 **CLINIAS** Hist.
3 B.C.?
001 **Testimonium**, FGrH #819: 3C:894.
NQ

1277 **<CLINIAS>** Phil.
4 B.C.: Tarentinus
001 **Fragmenta**, ed. H. Thesleff, *The Pythagorean
texts of the Hellenistic period*. Åbo: Åbo Akademi, 1965: 108.
Q: 280
002 **Testimonia**, ed. H. Diels and W. Kranz, *Die
Fragmente der Vorsokratiker*, vol. 1, 6th edn.
Berlin: Weidmann, 1951 (repr. Dublin: 1966):
443–444.

test. 1–6: auctores alii nominantur Prorus et
Amyclas.
NQ

1278 **CLITARCHUS** Gnom.
Incertum
001 **Sententiae**, ed. H. Chadwick, *The sentences of*
Sextus. Cambridge: Cambridge University
Press, 1959: 76–83.
Cod: [1,206]

1279 **CLITARCHUS** Hist.
4 B.C.: Alexandrinus
001 **Testimonia**, FGrH #137: 2B:741–743.
NQ
002 **Fragmenta**, FGrH #137: 2B:743–752.
fr. 32: *P. Oxy.* 2.218.
Q, Pap

1280 **CLITOMACHUS** Phil.
2 B.C.
x01 **Fragmenta ap. Stobaeum.**
Anth. III.7.55; **IV.**34.67; 41.29.
Cf. Joannes STOBAEUS (2037 001).

2190 **[CLITONYMUS]** Hist.
Incertum
001 **Fragmenta**, FGrH #292: 3A:176.
Q

1281 **[CLITOPHON]** Hist.
Incertum: Rhodius
001 **Fragmenta**, FGrH #293: 3A:176–177.
Q

1282 **CLYTUS** Hist.
4 B.C.: Milesius
001 **Fragmenta**, FGrH #490: 3B:457–458.
Q

0838 **CODAMUS vel NICOMEDES Rex Bithyniae**
<Med.>
ante A.D. 2
x01 **Fragmentum ap. Galenum.**
K13.929.
Cf. GALENUS Med. (0057 077).

0839 **CODIUS TUCUS** Med.
ante 1 B.C.?
x01 **Fragmentum ap. Galenum.**
K14.147.
Cf. GALENUS Med. (0057 078).

4081 **COLLUTHUS** Epic.
A.D. 5: Lycopolitanus
001 **Raptio Helenae**, ed. A.W. Mair, *Oppian, Collu-*
thus, Tryphiodorus. Cambridge, Mass.: Harvard
University Press, 1928 (repr. 1963): 542–570.
Cod: [2,346]

1283 **COLOTES** Phil.
4–3 B.C.: Lampsacenus

001 **Fragmenta**, ed. W. Crönert, *Kolotes und Mene-*
demos. Leipzig: Avenarius, 1906 (repr. Amsterdam: Hakkert, 1965): 5–7, 163–170.
Pap

1841 **COMANUS** Gramm.
2 B.C.: Naucratites
001 **Fragmenta**, ed. A.R. Dyck, *The fragments of*
Comanus of Naucratis. Berlin: De Gruyter, In
press.
Q, Pap
x01 **Fragmentum grammaticum** (*P. Yale* 1.25
[inv.446]).
Wouters, pp. 49–52.
Cf. ANONYMI GRAMMATICI (0072 003).

1284 **COMARCHUS** Hist.
3 B.C.?
001 **Fragmentum**, FGrH #410: 3B:303.
Q

4058 **COMETAS Chartularius** Epigr.
fiq Cometas Grammaticus
fiq Cometas Scholasticus
A.D. 6?
Cf. et COMETAS Grammaticus Epigr. (4059).
Cf. et COMETAS Scholasticus Epigr. (4060).
001 **Epigrammata**, AG 5.265; 9.586.
Q: 78

4059 **COMETAS Grammaticus** Epigr.
fiq Cometas Chartularius
fiq Cometas Scholasticus
A.D. 9
Cf. et COMETAS Chartularius Epigr. (4058).
Cf. et COMETAS Scholasticus Epigr. (4060).
001 **Epigrammata**, AG 15.36–38, 40.
Q: 463

4060 **COMETAS Scholasticus** Epigr.
fiq Cometas Chartularius
fiq Cometas Grammaticus
A.D. 9
Cf. et COMETAS Chartularius Epigr. (4058).
Cf. et COMETAS Grammaticus Epigr. (4059).
001 **Epigramma**, AG 9.597.
Q: 54

0408 *COMICA ADESPOTA* (CAF)
Varia
001 **Fragmenta incertorum poetarum**, ed. T. Kock,
Comicorum Atticorum fragmenta, vol. 3. Leipzig: Teubner, 1888: 397–418, 420–425, 428–
462, 464–547, 553–632, 635–641.
frr. 1–6, 8–23, 25–26, 29–42, 44–57, 61–62,
70–75, 77–102, 104–110, 114–187, 189–298,
310–311, 314–336, 338–621, 625–634, 636–
781, 783–793, 823–824, 827–1059, 1066–
1211, 1213–1220, 1222–1250, 1253–1327,
1329–1331, 1345–1382.
fr. 104: *P. Didot.*
Q, Pap: 7,586

002 **Fragmenta**, ed. Kock, *op. cit.*, 754–755.
frr. 352a, 570b–c, 675b, 698b, 743b, 1300b.
Q: 42

0662 *COMICA ADESPOTA* (CGFPR)
Varia
001 **Adespota Doriensium comoediae**, ed. C. Austin, *Comicorum Graecorum fragmenta in papyris reperta*. Berlin: De Gruyter, 1973: 219–220.
frr. 223–224.
Pap: 191
002 **Adespota veteris comoediae**, ed. Austin, *op. cit.*, 221–238.
frr. 225–238.
Pap: 1,439
003 **Adespota novae comoediae**, ed. Austin, *op. cit.*, 240–243, 245, 247–251, 253–275, 277–313.
frr. 239–242, 244–286.
Pap: 6,353
004 **Excerpta, florilegia et sententiae**, ed. Austin, *op. cit.*, 314–333.
frr. 289–319.
Pap: 1,390
005 **Argumenta metrica**, ed. Austin, *op. cit.*, 337.
fr. 339.
Pap: 162
006 **Argumenta comica**, ed. Austin, *op. cit.*, 338–339.
frr. 340–341.
Pap: 125
007 **Λέξεις κωμικαί**, ed. Austin, *op. cit.*, 339–343.
frr. 342–343.
Pap: 372
008 **Κωμῳδούμενοι**, ed. Austin, *op. cit.*, 344.
fr. 344.
Pap: 27
009 **Dubia**, ed. Austin, *op. cit.*, 345–368.
frr. 345–368.
Pap: 1,719

0602 *COMICA ADESPOTA* (FCG)
Varia
001 **Fragmenta comicorum anonymorum**, ed. A. Meineke, *Fragmenta comicorum Graecorum*, vol. 4. Berlin: Reimer, 1841 (repr. De Gruyter, 1970): 599–616, 618–630, 638, 645–655, 657–664, 667–679, 683–700.
frr. 1–13, 15–19b, 20b–27b, 27d–29, 31–42, 43b, 47–55, 57–63, 65–67, 71–73a, 74–75, 76b–79, 83–84, 89, 92–94, 95b–98, 100–101, 103, 132, 164, 167, 172, 174–175, 179, 182–188, 194–200, 202–206, 209, 216, 219–220, 222, 228, 235–236, 239–242, 245, 247–248, 253, 264, 280–282, 284–295a, 296a–307, 309b–311, 322, 326–327, 329–336, 339–341, 343a–372, 374–377, 379–383.
Q: 2,160
002 **Fragmenta**, ed. Meineke, *op. cit.*, vol. 5.1 (1857; repr. 1970): cccliii, ccclix–ccclxii, ccclxiv–ccclxvi, ccclxviii, ccclxx, ccclxxiv, ccclxxvi, 118, 122–123.
Q: [100]

0659 *COMICA ADESPOTA* (Suppl. Com.)
Varia
001 **Adespota veteris comoediae**, ed. J. Demiańczuk, *Supplementum comicum*. Krakau: Nakładem Akademii, 1912 (repr. Hildesheim: Olms, 1967): 89–95.
frr. 1–12b.
fr. 4: *P. Amherst* 2.13.
fr. 5: *P. Oxy.* 2.212.
fr. 12: *P. Oxy.* 1.12.
fr. 12a: *P. Oxy.* 9.1176 (fr. 39, col. 16, vv. 6 sqq.).
fr. 12b: *P. Oxy.* 9.1176 (col. 4, vv. 1–15).
Q, Pap: 345
002 **Adespota novae comoediae**, ed. Demiańczuk, *op. cit.*, 95–114.
frr. 13–26.
fr. 14: *P. Argent.* 53.
fr. 15: *P. Berol.* inv. 9941.
fr. 16: *P. Hibeh* 1.5.
frr. 17–20: *P. Sorbonne* inv. 72.
fr. 21: *P. Hibeh* 1.6.
frr. 22–23: *P. Sorbonne* inv. 72.
fr. 24: *P. Oxy.* 1.10.
fr. 25: *P. Oxy.* 1.11.
fr. 25a: *P. Oxy.* 9.1176 (col. 5, vv. 12 sqq.).
fr. 26: *P. Flinders Petrie* 4.1.
Q, Pap: 2,193
003 **Fragmenta incertae comoediae**, ed. Demiańczuk, *op. cit.*, 114–121.
frr. 27–53.
fr. 39: *P. Oxy.* 4.677.
fr. 40: *P. Oxy.* 6.863.
Q, Pap: 209
004 **Adespota dubia**, ed. Demiańczuk, *op. cit.*, 121–122.
frr. 54–59.
Q, Pap: 33
005 **Fragmentum incerti poetae Dorici**, ed. Demiańczuk, *op. cit.*, 126.
fr. 1: *P. Oxy.* 9.1176 (col. 17, vv. 10–13).
Pap: 8

5000 *CONCILIA OECUMENICA* (ACO)
Varia
001 **Concilium universale Ephesenum anno 431**, ed. E. Schwartz, *Acta conciliorum oecumenicorum*, vol. 1.1.1–1.1.7. Berlin: De Gruyter, 1.1.1 (1927; repr. 1965); 1.1.2–1.1.3 (1927); 1.1.4 (1928); 1.1.5 (1927); 1.1.6 (1928; repr. 1960); 1.1.7 (1929; repr. 1962): **1.1.1**:3–121; **1.1.2**:3–104; **1.1.3**:3–101; **1.1.4**:3–67; **1.1.5**:3–136; **1.1.6**:3–162; **1.1.7**:3–167, 171–174.
Cod
002 **Concilium universale Ephesenum anno 431**, ed. Schwartz, *op. cit.*, vol. 1.5.1 (1924–1925; repr. 1963): 219–231.
Cod
003 **Concilium universale Chalcedonense anno 451**, ed. Schwartz, *op. cit.*, vol. 2.1.1–2.1.3. Berlin: De Gruyter, 2.1.1–2.1.2 (1933; repr. 1962); 2.1.3 (1935; repr. 1965): **2.1.1**:3–32,

35–52, 55–196; **2.1.2**:3–42, 45–65, 69–163; **2.1.3**:3–136.
Cod

004 **Synodus Constantinopolitana et Hierosolymi-tana anno 536**, ed. Schwartz, *op. cit.*, vol. 3 (1940; repr. 1965): 3–214, 217–231.
Cod

1285 **CONON** Hist.
1 B.C.–A.D. 1
001 **Testimonia**, FGrH #26: 1A:190, *12 addenda.
NQ
002 **Fragmenta**, FGrH #26: 1A:190–211.
Q

9014 **CONSTANTINUS** <Epigr.>
A.D. 9–10: Rhodius
Bibliography in progress
001 **Epigrammata**, AG 15.15–17.
Q: 127

9015 **CONSTANTINUS** Gramm.
A.D. 9–10: Sicelius
Bibliography in progress
001 **Epigramma**, AG 15.13.
Q: 31

0840 **CONSTANTINUS** Med.
ante A.D. 6
x01 **Fragmentum ap. Paulum.**
CMG, vol. 9.2, p. 327.
Cf. PAULUS Med. (0715 001).
x02 **Fragmentum ap. Aëtium** (lib. 6).
CMG, vol. 8.2, p. 197.
Cf. AËTIUS Med. (0718 006).

9013 **CONSTANTINUS CEPHALAS** <Epigr.>
A.D. 9–10
001 **Epigramma**, AG 5.1.
Q: 16

0271 *CONVENTUS AVIUM*
ante A.D. 2/3
001 **Fragmentum** (*P. Cairo* inv. 67860), ed. E. Heitsch, *Die griechischen Dichterfragmente der römischen Kaiserzeit*, vol. 1, 2nd edn. Göttingen: Vandenhoeck & Ruprecht, 1963: 34.
Pap: [35]

0294 **CORINNA** Lyr.
5/3 B.C.?: Tanagraea
001 **Fragmenta**, ed. D.L. Page, *Poetae melici Graeci*. Oxford: Clarendon Press, 1962 (repr. 1967 (1st edn. corr.)): 326–331, 333–339, 341–357.
frr. 1–2, 4–11, 13–14, 16, 21–28, 31–32, 34, 36–41.
Q, Pap: [2,028]

0841 **CORNELIUS** Med.
ante A.D. 2

x01 **Fragmentum ap. Galenum.**
K13.292.
Cf. GALENUS Med. (0057 076).

1842 **CORNELIUS** Scr. Eccl.
A.D. 3: Romanus
x01 **Epistula ad Fabianum Antiochenum** (fragmenta).
Eusebius, HE 6.43.5–43.20.
Cf. EUSEBIUS Scr. Eccl. et Theol. (2018 002).

0153 **CORNELIUS LONG(IN)US** Epigr.
A.D. 1?
001 **Epigrammata**, AG **6**.191; **16**.117.
Q: 86

0654 **Lucius Annaeus CORNUTUS** Phil.
A.D. 1
001 **Ars rhetorica**, ed. C. Hammer (post L. Spengel), *Rhetores Graeci*, vol. 1. Leipzig: Teubner, 1894: 352–398.
Cod: 9,200
002 **De natura deorum**, ed. C. Lang, *Cornuti theologiae Graecae compendium*. Leipzig: Teubner, 1881: 1–76.
Cod: 12,578

1286 *CORPUS HERMETICUM*
A.D. 2?/4
001 **Poimandres**, ed. A.D. Nock and A.-J. Festugière, *Corpus Hermeticum*, vol. 1. Paris: Les Belles Lettres, 1946 (repr. 1972): 7–19.
Cod: [2,229]
002 **Dialogus** (sine titulo), ed. Nock and Festugière, *op. cit.*, vol. 1, 32–39.
Cod: [1,301]
003 **Hieros logos**, ed. Nock and Festugière, *op. cit.*, vol. 1, 44–46.
Cod: [341]
004 Πρὸς Τὰτ ὁ κρατὴρ ἢ μονάς, ed. Nock and Festugière, *op. cit.*, vol. 1, 49–53.
Cod: [899]
005 Πρὸς Τὰτ υἱὸν ὅτι ἀφανὴς θεὸς φανερώτατός ἐστιν, ed. Nock and Festugière, *op. cit.*, vol. 1, 60–65.
Cod: [1,096]
006 Ὅτι ἐν μόνῳ τῷ θεῷ τὸ ἀγαθόν ἐστιν, ἀλλαχόθι δὲ οὐδαμοῦ, ed. Nock and Festugière, *op. cit.*, vol. 1, 72–76.
Cod: [764]
007 Ὅτι μέγιστον κακὸν ἐν ἀνθρώποις ἡ περὶ τοῦ θεοῦ ἀγνωσία, ed. Nock and Festugière, *op. cit.*, vol. 1, 81–82.
Cod: [242]
008 Ὅτι οὐδὲν τῶν ὄντων ἀπόλλυται, ἀλλὰ τὰς μεταβολὰς ἀπωλείας καὶ θανάτους πλανώμενοι λέγουσιν, ed. Nock and Festugière, *op. cit.*, vol. 1, 87–89.
Cod: [471]
009 Περὶ νοήσεως καὶ αἰσθήσεως. [ὅτι ἐν μόνῳ τῷ θεῷ τὸ καλὸν καὶ ἀγαθόν ἐστιν, ἀλλαχόθι δὲ

οὐδαμοῦ], ed. Nock and Festugière, *op. cit.*, vol. 1, 96–100.
Cod: [984]

010 Κλείς, ed. Nock and Festugière, *op. cit.*, vol. 1, 113–126.
Cod: [2,415]

011 Νοῦς πρὸς ʽΕρμῆν, ed. Nock and Festugière, *op. cit.*, vol. 1, 147–157.
Cod: [2,217]

012 Περὶ νοῦ κοινοῦ πρὸς Τάτ, ed. Nock and Festugière, *op. cit.*, vol. 1, 174–183.
Cod: [2,065]

013 Πρὸς τὸν υἱὸν Τὰτ ἐν ὄρει λόγος ἀπόκρυφος, περὶ παλιγγενεσίας καὶ σιγῆς ἐπαγγελίας, ed. Nock and Festugière, *op. cit.*, vol. 2 (1946; repr. 1973): 200–209.
Cod: [1,798]

014 ᾿Ασκληπιῷ εὖ φρονεῖν, ed. Nock and Festugière, *op. cit.*, vol. 2, 222–226.
Cod: [819]

016 ῞Οροι ᾿Ασκληπιοῦ πρὸς ῎Αμμωνα βασιλέα, ed. Nock and Festugière, *op. cit.*, vol. 2, 231–238.
Cod: [1,294]

017 **Dialogus** (sine titulo), ed. Nock and Festugière, *op. cit.*, vol. 2, 244.
Cod: [129]

018 Περὶ τῆς ὑπὸ τοῦ πάθους τοῦ σώματος ἐμποδιζομένης ψυχῆς, ed. Nock and Festugière, *op. cit.*, vol. 2, 248–255.
Cod: [1,322]

019 **Asciepius** (verba Graeca solum), ed. Nock and Festugière, *op. cit.*, vol. 2, 304, 305, 308, 312, 313, 315, 316, 317, 318, 319, 349, 350, 351.
Q: [39]

020 **Fragmenta**, ed. Nock and Festugière, *op. cit.*, vol. 3 & 4 (1954; repr. 1972): **3**:2–8, 13–14, 17–18, 21–27, 30–31, 34–39, 44, 47–48, 51–58, 61, 64–67, 72–73, 76–77, 80–83, 86–87, 90–91; **4**:1–22, 52–58, 68–72, 80–88, 97–99.
Q: [16,232]

021 **Fragmenta varia** (verba Graeca solum), ed. Nock and Festugière, *op. cit.*, vol. 4, 105, 106, 110, 111, 113, 114, 126, 128, 129–135, 137–143.
frr. 3a, 4a–b, 10, 11a, 12a, 14–15, 23–36.
Q: [936]

022 ᾿Εκ τοῦ ὕμνου πρὸς τὸν παντοκράτορα (fragmentum), ed. Nock and Festugière, *op. cit.*, vol. 4, 147.
Q: [109]

x01 **Epigrammata** (*App. Anth.*).
Epigramma demonstrativum: *App. Anth.* 3.147.
Epigramma exhortatorium et supplicatorium: *App. Anth.* 4.47.
App. Anth. 3.147(?): Cf. EPIGRAMMATICI in *App. Anth.* (7052 003).
App. Anth. 4.47(?): Cf. EPIGRAMMATICI in *App. Anth.* (7052 004).
App. Anth. 3.147: Cf. et THEON Math. (2033 x03).

x02 **De deo** (*P. Berol.* inv. 17027)
Stahlschmidt, pp. 162–165.
Cf. PHILO JUDAEUS Phil. (0018 041).

4061 **COSMAS INDICOPLEUSTES** Geogr.
A.D. 6: Alexandrinus
Bibliography in progress
001 **Epigramma**, AG 16.114.
Q: 16
002 **Topographia Christiana**, ed. W. Wolska-Conus, *Cosmas Indicopleustès. Topographie chrétienne*, 3 vols. [*Sources chrétiennes* 141, 159, 197. Paris: Cerf, 1:1968; 2:1970; 3:1973]: **1**:255–569: **2**:13–373; **3**:13–381.
Cod

1287 **CRANTOR** Phil.
4–3 B.C.: Soleus
001 **Fragmenta**, ed. F.W.A. Mullach, *Fragmenta philosophorum Graecorum*, vol. 3. Paris: Didot, 1881 (repr. Aalen: Scientia, 1968): 139–152.
Q
002 **Fragmenta et titulus**, ed. H. Lloyd-Jones and P. Parsons, *Supplementum Hellenisticum*. Berlin: De Gruyter, 1983: 163.
frr. 344–346.
Q: [35]

1288 **CRATERUS** Hist.
4–3 B.C.: Macedo
001 **Testimonia**, FGrH #342: 3B:199.
NQ
002 **Fragmenta**, FGrH #342: 3B:199–205.
Q

0842 **CRATERUS** Med.
1 B.C.
x01 **Fragmentum ap. Galenum**.
K13.96.
Cf. GALENUS Med. (0057 076).

0433 **CRATES** Comic.
5 B.C.: Atheniensis
001 **Fragmenta**, ed. T. Kock, *Comicorum Atticorum fragmenta*, vol. 1. Leipzig: Teubner, 1880: 130–144.
frr. 1–17, 19–24, 26–37, 39–51, 53–56 + tituli.
Q: 444
002 **Fragmenta**, ed. A. Meineke, *Fragmenta comicorum Graecorum*, vol. 2.1. Berlin: Reimer, 1839 (repr. De Gruyter, 1970): 233–249.
Q: 402
003 **Fragmenta**, ed. J. Demiańczuk, *Supplementum comicum*. Krakau: Nakładem Akademii, 1912 (repr. Hildesheim: Olms, 1967): 29–30.
frr. 1–6.
Q: 33
004 **Fragmentum**, ed. C. Austin, *Comicorum Graecorum fragmenta in papyris reperta*. Berlin: De Gruyter, 1973: 34.
fr. 68.
Pap: 32

005 **Fragmenta**, ed. Meineke, *op. cit.*, vol. 5.1
(1857; repr. 1970): xlix.
Q: [24]

1290 **CRATES** Gramm.
2 B.C.: Mallotes
001 **Epigramma**, AG 1.218.
Q: 27
002 **Sphairopoiia**, ed. H.J. Mette, *Sphairopoiia.*
Munich: Beck, 1936: 113–298.
Q

1289 **CRATES** Hist.
1 B.C.: Atheniensis
001 **Fragmenta**, FGrH #362: 3B:220–224.
Q

0336 **CRATES** Poet. Phil.
4–3 B.C.: Thebanus
Cf. et CRATETIS EPISTULAE (0623).
001 **Fragmentum**, ed. B. Snell, *Tragicorum Graecorum fragmenta*, vol. 1. Göttingen: Vandenhoeck & Ruprecht, 1971: 259.
Q: [22]
002 **Fragmenta**, ed. E. Diehl, *Anthologia lyrica
Graeca*, fasc. 1, 3rd edn. Leipzig: Teubner,
1949: 120–126.
frr. 1–21.
Q: [438]
003 **Epigrammata**, AG 7.326; **9**.497; **10**.104.
AG 9.359: Cf. POSIDIPPUS Epigr. (1632 001).
AG 9.359: Cf. PLATO Comic. (0497 001).
Q: 62
004 **Fragmenta et titulus**, ed. H. Lloyd-Jones and
P. Parsons, *Supplementum Hellenisticum*. Ber-
lin: De Gruyter, 1983: 164–172.
frr. 347–349, 351–368.
Q: [469]
x01 **Epigrammata** (*App. Anth.*).
Epigramma exhortatorium et supplicatorium:
4.33.
Epigrammata irrisoria: 5.13, 13b.
App. Anth. 4.33: Cf. EPIGRAMMATICI in *App.
Anth.* (7052 004).
App. Anth. 5.13, 13b: Cf. EPIGRAMMATICI in
App. Anth. (7052 005).

0623 *CRATETIS EPISTULAE*
Incertum
Cf. et CRATES Poet. Phil. (0336).
001 **Epistulae**, ed. R. Hercher, *Epistolographi
Graeci*. Paris: Didot, 1873 (repr. Amsterdam:
Hakkert, 1965): 208–217.
Cod: [3,110]

0657 **CRATEUAS** Med.
2–1 B.C.
001 **Fragmenta**, ed. M. Wellmann, *Pedanii Dioscuridis Anazarbei de materia medica libri quinque*, vol. 3. Berlin: Weidmann, 1914 (repr.
1958): 144–146.
Cod: 508

0434 **CRATINUS** Comic.
5 B.C.
001 **Fragmenta**, ed. T. Kock, *Comicorum Atticorum fragmenta*, vol. 1. Leipzig: Teubner,
1880: 11–17, 19–21, 23–30, 32–43, 45, 47–
109, 113–130.
frr. 1–10, 15–17, 21–30, 36–58, 65–66, 69–74,
76–82, 85–87, 90–98, 100, 107–116, 120–129,
131–132, 135–148, 152–154, 157–170, 172,
175, 177–179, 181–199, 205–209, 211, 213–
214, 218–222, 224–225, 227–229, 231–241,
244–246, 249–260, 264–265, 268–269, 271–
307, 309–325, 327, 342–343, 346–347, 352–
353, 355–361, 365–367, 369–462 + tituli.
Q: 2,424
002 **Fragmenta**, ed. A. Meineke, *Fragmenta comicorum Graecorum*, vol. 2.1. Berlin: Reimer,
1839 (repr. De Gruyter, 1970): 15–20, 22, 26–
27, 29–31, 33–44, 46–49, 51, 53, 56–57, 60–
64, 67–69, 72–75, 77, 80, 82, 84–90, 92–105,
107–111, 113, 116–119, 122–127, 129–130,
132–133, 135–137, 141–142, 144–157, 161–
167, 172, 174, 176–179, 181–187, 189, 192,
194–195, 198, 202, 206, 210–212, 215, 217–
218, 221–222, 225–226, 230–232.
Q: 2,175
003 **Fragmenta**, ed. J. Demiańczuk, *Supplementum
comicum*. Krakau: Nakładem Akademii, 1912
(repr. Hildesheim: Olms, 1967): 30–31, 33–39.
frr. 1–29.
Q: 151
004 **Fragmenta**, ed. C. Austin, *Comicorum Graecorum fragmenta in papyris reperta*. Berlin: De
Gruyter, 1973: 34–40, 42–49.
frr. 69–76 + tituli.
Pap: 988
005 **Fragmenta**, ed. Kock, *op. cit.*, vol. 3 (1888):
713.
frr. 389b, 459b.
Q: 7
006 **Fragmenta**, ed. Meineke, *op. cit.*, vol. 5.1
(1857; repr. 1970): xlviii.
Q: [50]

0435 **CRATINUS Junior** Comic.
4 B.C.
001 **Fragmenta**, ed. T. Kock, *Comicorum Atticorum fragmenta*, vol. 2. Leipzig: Teubner,
1884: 289–293.
frr. 1–2, 4–5, 7–14 + titulus.
Q: 207
002 **Fragmenta**, ed. A. Meineke, *Fragmenta comicorum Graecorum*, vol. 3. Berlin: Reimer, 1840
(repr. De Gruyter, 1970): 374–379.
Q: 205

1907 **CRATIPPUS** Hist.
1 B.C.?: Atheniensis
Cf. et HELLENICA (0558).
001 **Testimonia**, FGrH #64: 2A:13–14.
NQ

002 **Fragmenta**, FGrH #64: 2A:14–15.
Q

0843 **CRATIPPUS** Med.
1 B.C.
x01 **Fragmenta ap. Galenum.**
K12.959; **14**.170.
Cf. GALENUS Med. (0057 076, 078).

2291 **CRATYLUS** Phil.
5–4 B.C.: Atheniensis
001 **Testimonia**, ed. H. Diels and W. Kranz, *Die
Fragmente der Vorsokratiker*, vol. 2, 6th edn.
Berlin: Weidmann, 1952 (repr. Dublin: 1966):
69–70.
test. 1–5.
NQ

2508 **CREON** Hist.
4 B.C.?
001 **Fragmentum**, FGrH #753: 3C:735–736.
Q

CREOPHYLUS Epic.
Incertum: Samius vel Chius
Cf. OECHALIAE HALOSIS (1546).

1291 **CREOPHYLUS** Hist.
5–4 B.C.?: Ephesius
001 **Fragmenta**, FGrH #417: 3B:314–315.
fr. 2: *Inscr. Priene* 37.
Q, Epigr

1994 **CREPEREIUS CALPURNIANUS** Hist.
A.D. 2: Pompeiopolitanus
001 **Fragmenta**, FGrH #208: 2B:940–941.
Q

0154 **CRINAGORAS** Epigr.
1 B.C./A.D. 1: Mytilenensis
001 **Epigrammata**, AG 5.108, 119; **6**.100, 161, 227,
229, 232, 242, 244, 253, 261, 345, 350; **7**.371,
376, 380, 401, 628, 633, 636, 638, 643, 645,
741; **9**.81, 224, 234–235, 239, 276, 283–284,
291, 419, 429–430, 439, 513, 516, 542, 545,
555, 559–560, 562; **10**.24; **11**.42; **16**.40, 61,
199, 273.
AG 7.744: Cf. DIOGENES LAERTIUS Biogr.
(0004 002).
AG 9.65: Cf. ANONYMI EPIGRAMMATICI
(0138 001).
Q: 1,899

1293 **CRINIS** Phil.
2 B.C.
001 **Fragmenta**, ed. J. von Arnim, *Stoicorum
veterum fragmenta*, vol. 3. Leipzig: Teubner,
1903 (repr. Stuttgart: 1968): 268–269.
Q

0844 **CRISPUS** Med.
A.D. 1

x01 **Fragmenta ap. Galenum.**
K**12**.831; **13**.67, 841, 984.
Cf. GALENUS Med. (0057 076–077).

0319 **CRITIAS** Phil., Trag. et Eleg.
5 B.C.: Atheniensis
001 **Fragmenta**, ed. B. Snell, *Tragicorum Graecorum fragmenta*, vol. 1. Göttingen: Vandenhoeck & Ruprecht, 1971: 172–184.
frr. 1–14, 16–19, 21–25.
frr. 5, 7–9: *P. Oxy.* 17.2078.
Q, Pap: [989]
002 **Fragmenta**, ed. M.L. West, *Iambi et elegi
Graeci*, vol. 2. Oxford: Clarendon Press, 1972:
52–56.
frr. B2, 4–9.
Q: [375]
003 **Testimonia**, ed. H. Diels and W. Kranz, *Die
Fragmente der Vorsokratiker*, vol. 2, 6th edn.
Berlin: Weidmann, 1952 (repr. Dublin: 1966):
371–375.
test. 1–23.
NQ
004 **Fragmenta**, ed. Diels and Kranz, *op. cit.*, 375–
399.
frr. 1–75.
Q

0436 **CRITO** Comic.
2 B.C.
001 **Fragmenta**, ed. T. Kock, *Comicorum Atticorum fragmenta*, vol. 3. Leipzig: Teubner,
1888: 354.
frr. 1–3 + titulus.
Q: 55
002 **Fragmenta**, ed. A. Meineke, *Fragmenta comicorum Graecorum*, vol. 4. Berlin: Reimer, 1841
(repr. De Gruyter, 1970): 537–538.
Q: 55

1867 **CRITO** Hist.
fiq Titus Statilius Crito Med.
A.D. 1–2: Pieriota
Cf. et Titus Statilius CRITO Med. (0685).
001 **Testimonia**, FGrH #200, #277: **2B**:931;
3A:157; **3B**:743–744 addenda.
NQ
002 **Fragmenta**, FGrH #200: 2B:931–932.
Q

0685 **Titus Statilius CRITO** Med.
fiq Crito Pieriota Hist.
A.D. 1–2
Cf. et CRITO et HERODOTUS Med. (0882).
Cf. et CRITO Hist. (1867).
x01 **Fragmenta ap. Galenum.**
K**12**.401–402, 435–439, 453–454, 458, 483–
492, 587–588, 659–660, 817, 825–826, 827–
829, 830–831, 880–881, 933–935, 953–954,
987–988, 991–992; **13**.35–37, 38–39, 257–258,
515–516, 708–716, 786–796, 797–798, 800–
801, 863–864, 869–870, 877–880, 883–884,

903–905, 1040–1041; **14**.103–105.
Cf. GALENUS Med. (0057 076–078).
x02 **Fragmentum ap. Oribasium.**
CMG, vol. 6.3, p. 73.
Cf. ORIBASIUS Med. (0722 004).
x03 **Fragmenta ap. Paulum.**
CMG, vol. **9.1**, pp. 130, 328; **9.2**, p. 326.
Cf. PAULUS Med. (0715 001).
x04 **Fragmentum ap. Aëtium** (lib. 4).
CMG, vol. 8.1, p. 369.
Cf. AËTIUS Med. (0718 004).
x05 **Fragmenta ap. Aëtium** (lib. 6, 8).
CMG, vol. 8.2, pp. 201, 405, 419.
Cf. AËTIUS Med. (0718 006, 008).
x06 **Fragmentum ap. Aëtium** (lib. 15).
Zervos, *Athena* 21, pp. 103–105.
Cf. AËTIUS Med. (0718 015).

1292 **CRITO** Phil.
3 B.C.: Argivus
001 **Fragmentum**, ed. H. Thesleff, *The Pythagorean
texts of the Hellenistic period*. Åbo: Åbo Akademi, 1965: 109.
Q: 145

0882 **CRITO et HERODOTUS** Med.
A.D. 1–2
Cf. et Titus Statilius CRITO Med. (0685).
Cf. et HERODOTUS Med. (0926).
x01 **Fragmentum ap. Aëtium** (lib. 15).
Zervos, *Athena* 21, p. 61.
Cf. AËTIUS Med. (0718 015).

1295 **CRITODEMUS** Astrol.
3 B.C.
001 **Fragmenta**, ed. W. Kroll, *Codices Romani* [*Catalogus codicum astrologorum Graecorum* 5.2.
Brussels: Lamertin, 1906]: 52–53, 113, 120–
121.
Q
002 **Fragmenta**, ed. F. Cumont, *Codices Parisini*
[*Catalogus codicum astrologorum Graecorum*
8.1. Brussels: Lamertin, 1929]: 257–261.
Q
003 **Fragmenta**, ed. P. Boudreaux, *Codices Parisini*
[*Catalogus codicum astrologorum Graecorum*
8.3. Brussels: Lamertin, 1912]: 102.
Q
x01 **Fragmenta ap. Vettium Valentem.**
Kroll, pp. 142–144.
Cf. VETTIUS VALENS Astrol. (1764 001).

2552 **CRITOLAUS** Hist.
ante 1 B.C.
001 **Fragmenta**, FGrH #823: 3C:896–897.
Q

1294 **CRITOLAUS** Phil.
2 B.C.
001 **Fragmenta**, ed. F. Wehrli, *Hieronymos von
Rhodos. Kritolaos und seine Schüler* [*Die Schule

des Aristoteles, vol. 10, 2nd edn. Basel:
Schwabe, 1969]: 51–58.
Q

0437 **CROBYLUS** Comic.
4 B.C.
001 **Fragmenta**, ed. T. Kock, *Comicorum Atticorum fragmenta*, vol. 3. Leipzig: Teubner,
1888: 379–382.
frr. 1–10.
Q: 159
002 **Fragmenta**, ed. A. Meineke, *Fragmenta comicorum Graecorum*, vol. 4. Berlin: Reimer, 1841
(repr. De Gruyter, 1970): 565–569.
Q: 161

0845 **CTESIAS** Hist. et Med.
5–4 B.C.: Cnidius
001 **Testimonia**, FGrH #688: 3C:416–420.
NQ
002 **Fragmenta**, FGrH #688: 3C:420–517.
fr. 8b: *P. Oxy.* 22.2330.
Q, Pap
003 **Fragmentum** (*P. Oxy.* 24.2389), ed. H.J.
Mette, "Die 'Kleinen' griechischen Historiker
heute," *Lustrum* 21 (1978) 36.
fr. 66 bis.
Pap

2201 **[CTESIPHON]** Hist.
Incertum
001 **Fragmenta**, FGrH #294: 3A:177–178.
Q

0846 **CTESIPHON** Med.
1 B.C.
x01 **Fragmenta ap. Galenum.**
K13.927, 936.
Cf. GALENUS Med. (0057 077).

2567 **CTESIPPUS** Hist.
Incertum
001 **Fragmentum**, FGrH #844: 3C:929–930.
Q

0368 **CYDIAS** Lyr.
6/5 B.C.: Hermioneus
001 **Fragmentum**, ed. D.L. Page, *Poetae melici
Graeci*. Oxford: Clarendon Press, 1962 (repr.
1967 (1st edn. corr.)): 370.
fr. 1.
Q: [10]

0156 **CYLLENIUS** Epigr.
A.D. 1
001 **Epigrammata**, AG 9.4, 33.
AG 9.35: Cf. ANTIPHILUS Epigr. (0118 001).
AG 9.46: Cf. ANTIPATER Epigr. (0114 001).
Q: 53

2154 **CYLLENIUS** Hist.
A.D. 4

001 **Testimonium**, FGrH #222: 2B:950–951.
NQ

1296 *CYPRIA*
fort. auctore Hegesia vel Stasino
7–6 B.C.?
001 **Fragmenta**, ed. T.W. Allen, *Homeri opera*, vol.
5. Oxford: Clarendon Press, 1912 (repr. 1969):
118–120, 122–125.
frr. 1, 4–7, 11, 13, 16, 23–25.
Q

1482 *CYRANIDES*
fort. auctoribus Cyrano et Harpocratione
ante A.D. 1/2
Cf. et HARPOCRATIONIS EPISTULA (0691).
001 **Cyranides**, ed. D. Kaimakis, *Die Kyraniden*.
Meisenheim am Glan: Hain, 1976: 14–310.
Cod

0157 **CYRILLUS** Epigr.
1 B.C./A.D. 1
001 **Epigramma**, AG 9.369.
Q: 16

2110 **CYRILLUS** Scr. Eccl.
A.D. 4: Hierosolymitanus
001 **Procatechesis**, ed. W.C. Reischl and J. Rupp,
*Cyrilli Hierosolymorum archiepiscopi opera
quae supersunt omnia*, vol. 1. Munich: Lentner,
1848 (repr. Hildesheim: Olms, 1967): 1–26.
Cod: [2,700]
002 **Mystagogiae 1–5** [Sp.], ed. A. Piédagnel and P.
Paris, *Cyrille de Jérusalem. Catéchèses mystago-
giques* [*Sources chrétiennes* 126. Paris: Cerf,
1966]: 82–174.
Cod: [5,718]
003 **Catecheses ad illuminandos 1–18**, ed. Reischl
and Rupp, *op. cit.*, vols. 1 & 2 (1860; repr.
1967): 1:28–320; 2:2–342.
Cod: [76,611]
004 **Additamentum ad catechesis illuminandorum
sextae decimae caput tertium**, ed. Reischl and
Rupp, *op. cit.*, vol. 2, 248–249.
Cod: [328]
005 **Tituli catechesium**, ed. Reischl and Rupp, *op.
cit.*, vol. 2, 396–398.
Cod: [607]
006 **Homilia in paralyticum juxta piscinam jacen-
tem**, ed. Reischl and Rupp, *op. cit.*, vol. 2,
405–426.
Cod: [2,673]
007 **Homilia in occursum domini** [Sp.], ed. Reischl
and Rupp, *op. cit.*, vol. 2, 444–456.
Cod: [1,988]
008 **Homilia aquae in vinum conversae** (fragmenta)
[Sp.], ed. F. Diekamp, *Doctrina patrum de incarnatione verbi*. Münster: Aschendorff, 1907:
92–93.
Q: [164]
009 **Homilia in illud:** *Ego vado ad patrem meum*
(fragmenta) [Sp.], ed. F. Diekamp, *Analecta pa-

tristica* [*Orientalia Christiana analecta* 117.
Rome: Pont. Institutum Orientalium Studiorum, 1938 (repr. 1962)]: 10.
Q: [83]
010 **Suppositarum Cyrilli et Julii pontificis epistularum compendium** [Sp.], MPG 33: 1208–
1209.
Cod: [375]
011 **Catechesis ad illuminandos 2** (exemplar alterum), MPG 33: 409–424.
Cod: [2,776]
012 **Catechesis ad illuminandos 2** (ex cod. Paris.
409), ed. J.B. Pitra, *Iuris ecclesiastici Graecorum historia et monumenta*, vol. 2. Rome:
Congregatio de Propaganda Fide, 1868: 291–
292.
Cod
013 **Epistula ad Constantium imperatorem**, ed. E.
Bihain, "L'épître de Cyrille de Jérusalem à
Constance sur la vision de la Croix," *Byzantion*
43 (1973) 286–291.
Cod

4090 **CYRILLUS** Theol.
A.D. 4–5: Alexandrinus
001 **Commentarius in xii prophetas minores**, ed.
P.E. Pusey, *Sancti patris nostri Cyrilli archiepiscopi Alexandrini in xii prophetas*, 2 vols.
Oxford: Clarendon Press, 1868 (repr. Brussels:
Culture et Civilisation, 1965): 1:1–740; 2:1–
626.
Cod: [325,108]
002 **Commentarii in Joannem**, ed. P.E. Pusey,
*Sancti patris nostri Cyrilli archiepiscopi Alexan-
drini in D. Joannis evangelium*, 3 vols. Oxford:
Clarendon Press, 1872 (repr. Brussels: Culture
et Civilisation, 1965): 1:1–728; 2:1–737; 3:1–
171.
Cf. et 4090 031.
Cod: [407,019]
003 **Fragmenta in sancti Pauli epistulam ad Romanos**, ed. Pusey, *In Joannis evangelium*, vol. 3,
173–248.
Cod: [16,920]
004 **Fragmenta in sancti Pauli epistulam i ad
Corinthios**, ed. Pusey, *In Joannis evangelium*,
vol. 3, 249–318.
Cod: [14,350]
005 **Fragmenta in sancti Pauli epistulam ii ad
Corinthios**, ed. Pusey, *In Joannis evangelium*,
vol. 3, 320–360.
Cod: [8,210]
006 **Fragmenta in sancti Pauli epistulam ad Hebraeos**, ed. Pusey, *In Joannis evangelium*, vol.
3, 362–423.
Cod: [11,750]
008 **Fragmenta homiliae de uno filio**, ed. Pusey, *In
Joannis evangelium*, vol. 3, 452–454.
fr. 1.
Q: [676]
009 **Fragmenta homiliae quod unus est Christus**,

ed. Pusey, *In Joannis evangelium*, vol. 3, 455–458.
fr. 2.
Q: [952]

010 **Quod homo non deiferus** (homilia diversa 20) (fragmenta), ed. Pusey, *In Joannis evangelium*, vol. 3, 459–460.
fr. 3.
Q: [383]

011 **Sermo ad Alexandrinos** (fragmentum), ed. Pusey, *In Joannis evangelium*, vol. 3, 460–461.
fr. 4.
Q: [250]

012 **Homiliarum incertarum fragmenta**, ed. Pusey, *In Joannis evangelium*, vol. 3, 461–468, 470–475.
frr. 5–11, 13–15.
Q: [3,031]

013 **Fragmenta homiliae de die novissima**, ed. Pusey, *In Joannis evangelium*, vol. 3, 469.
fr. 12.
Q: [186]

014 **Fragmenta ex libro contra Diodorum Tarsensem**, ed. Pusey, *In Joannis evangelium*, vol. 3, 492–497.
Cod: [837]

015 **Fragmenta ex libro ii contra Theodorum Mopsuestenum**, ed. Pusey, *In Joannis evangelium*, vol. 3, 511–513.
Cod: [364]

016 **Fragmenta ex libro iii contra Theodorum Mopsuestenum**, ed. Pusey, *In Joannis evangelium*, vol. 3, 525–526.
Cod: [169]

017 **Sermo prosphoneticus ad Alexandrinos de fide** (homilia diversa 21) (fragmenta), ed. Pusey, *In Joannis evangelium*, vol. 3, 538–541.
Cod: [344]

018 **Adversus eos qui negant offerendum esse pro defunctis**, ed. Pusey, *In Joannis evangelium*, vol. 3, 541–544.
Q: [380]

019 **Quaestio ad Cyrillum** (e tractatu de dogmatum solutione), ed. Pusey, *In Joannis evangelium*, vol. 3, 547–548.
Cod: [560]

020 **Solutiones** (e tractatu de dogmatum solutione), ed. Pusey, *In Joannis evangelium*, vol. 3, 549–566.
Cod: [3,551]

021 **Responsiones ad Tiberium diaconum sociosque suos**, ed. Pusey, *In Joannis evangelium*, vol. 3, 577–602.
Cod: [5,144]

022 **Ad Calosyrium** (epistula 83), ed. Pusey, *In Joannis evangelium*, vol. 3, 603–607.
Cod: [890]

023 **De sancta trinitate dialogi i–vii**, ed. G.M. de Durand, *Cyrille d'Alexandrie. Dialogues sur la Trinité*, 3 vols. [*Sources chrétiennes* 231, 237, 246. Paris: Cerf, 1:1976; 2:1977; 3:1978]:

1:126–354; 2:10–384; 3:10–226.
Cod: [104,966]

026 **De incarnatione unigeniti**, ed. G.M. de Durand, *Cyrille d'Alexandrie. Deux dialogues christologiques* [*Sources chrétiennes* 97. Paris: Cerf, 1964]: 188–300.
Cod: [27,348]

027 **Quod unus sit Christus**, ed. de Durand, *SC* 97, 302–514.
Cod: [27,606]

029 **Commentarii in Matthaeum** (scholia in catenis), ed. J. Reuss, *Matthäus-Kommentare aus der griechischen Kirche* [*Texte und Untersuchungen* 61. Berlin: Akademie-Verlag, 1957]: 153–269.
Cf. et 4090 174.
Q: [30,509]

030 **Commentarii in Lucam**, ed. J. Sickenberger, *Fragmente der Homilien des Cyrill von Alexandrien zum Lukasevangelium* [*Texte und Untersuchungen* 34. Leipzig: Hinrichs, 1909]: 76–107.
Q: [7,938]

031 **Commentarii in Joannem** (additamenta), ed. J. Reuss, *Johannes-Kommentare aus der griechischen Kirche* [*Texte und Untersuchungen* 89. Berlin: Akademie-Verlag, 1966]: 188–195.
Cf. et 4090 002.
Q: [1,896]

095 **Fragmenta in Acta apostolorum et in epistolas catholicas**, MPG 74: 757–773, 1008–1024.
Q: [3,534]

096 **De adoratione et cultu in spiritu et veritate**, MPG 68: 132–1125.
Cod: [399,186]

097 **Glaphyra in Pentateuchum**, MPG 69: 9–677.
Cod: [130,550]

098 **Fragmenta duo in Numeros**, MPG 69: 641.
Q: [109]

099 **Fragmenta in libros Regum**, MPG 69: 680–697.
Q: [3,618]

100 **Expositio in Psalmos**, MPG 69: 717–1273.
Cod: [114,972]

101 **Fragmentum in Proverbia**, MPG 69: 1277.
Q: [63]

102 **Fragmenta in Canticum canticorum**, MPG 69: 1277–1293.
Q: [3,618]

103 **Commentarius in Isaiam prophetam**, MPG 70: 9–1449.
Cod: [289,440]

104 **Fragmenta in Jeremiam**, MPG 70: 1452–1457.
Q: [460]

105 **Fragmentum in librum Baruch**, MPG 70: 1457.
Q: [101]

106 **Fragmenta in Ezechielem**, MPG 70: 1457–1460.
Q: [564]

107 **Fragmenta in Danielem**, MPG 70: 1461.
Q: [164]

108 **Commentarii in Lucam** (scholia in catenis), MPG 72: 476–949.
Q: [97,686]

109 **Thesaurus de sancta consubstantiali trinitate,** MPG 75: 9–656.
Cf. et 4090 130.
Cod: [129,640]

110 **Dialogus cum Nestorio** [Sp.], MPG 76: 249–256.
Cod: [1,206]

111 **Contra Julianum imperatorem,** MPG 76: 504–1057.
Cf. et 4090 175.
Cod: [137,060]

112 **De synagogae defectu** (fragmentum) [Sp.], MPG 76: 1421–1424.
Q: [288]

114 **Ad Xystum episcopum Romae** (epistula 53) (fragmentum), MPG 77: 285–288.
Q: [62]

115 **Ad Optimum episcopum** (epistula 80), MPG 77: 365–372.
Q: [1,206]

116 **Commentarii in Lucam** (homilia 51) (= **In transfigurationem** [homilia diversa 9]), MPG 77: 1009–1016.
Cod: [1,407]

117 **Encomium in sanctam Mariam deiparam** (homilia diversa 11), MPG 77: 1029–1040.
Cod: [1,932]

118 **Commentarii in Lucam** (homilia 3 et 4) (= **In occursum domini** [homilia diversa 12]), MPG 77: 1040–1049.
Cod: [2,010]

119 **De exitu animi** (homilia diversa 14), MPG 77: 1072–1089.
Cod: [4,148]

120 **In parabolam vineae** (homilia diversa 17), MPG 77: 1096–1100.
Cod: [735]

121 **Fragmenta de translatione reliquiarum martyrum Cyri et Joannis** (homilia diversa 18), MPG 77: 1100–1105.
Cod: [965]

122 **Sermo de obitu sanctorum trium puerorum** (fragmenta) [Sp.], MPG 77: 1117.
Cod: [226]

123 **De sancta trinitate** [Sp.], MPG 77: 1120–1173.
Cod: [11,055]

124 **Collectio dictorum Veteris Testamenti** [Sp.], MPG 77: 1176–1289.
Cod: [23,316]

125 **Expositio in Psalmos** (prooemium), ed. G. Mercati, *Osservazioni a Proemi del Salterio di Origene, Ippolito, Eusebio, Cirillo Alessandrino e altri, con frammenti inediti* [Studi e Testi 142. Vatican City: Biblioteca Apostolica Vaticana, 1948]: 140–144.
Cod: [1,299]

126 **Fragmentum in Psalmum 1.5,** ed. G. Mercati, *Alla ricerca dei nomi degli "altri" traduttori nelle Omilie sui Salmi di S. Giovanni Crisostomo e variazioni su alcune catene del Salterio* [Studi e Testi 158. Vatican City: Biblioteca Apostolica Vaticana, 1952]: 186.
Cod: [100]

127 **Fragmentum in Psalmum 2.7,** ed. Mercati, *ST* 142, p. 144.
Cod: [271]

129 **Fragmentum in sancti Pauli epistulam i ad Corinthios,** ed. M. Richard, "Le florilège du Cod. Vatopédi 236 sur le corruptible et l'incorruptible," *Muséon* 86 (1973) 262.
fr. 21.
Cod: [103]

130 **Thesaurus de sancta et consubstantiali trinitate** (additamenta), ed. J.B. Pitra, *Analecta sacra et classica spicilegio Solesmensi parata,* vol. 5.1. Paris: Roger & Chernowitz, 1888: 38–41.
Cf. et 4090 109.
Cod: [1,616]

135 **Solutiones** (fragmentum e tractatu de dogmatum solutione), ed. G. Mercati, *Un nuovo frammento del "de dogmatum solutione" di S. Cirillo Alessandrino* in *Varia sacra* [Studi e Testi 11. Rome: Tipografia Vaticana, 1903]: 85–86.
Cod

139 **Contra Julianum imperatorem** (fragmentum apud Aretham Caesariensem), ed. K.J. Neumann, "Ein neues Bruchstück aus Kaiser Julians Büchern gegen die Christen," *Theologische Literatur Zeitung* 24 (1899) 298–304.
Q

140 **Contra Julianum imperatorem** (fragmentum e libro xiv apud Joannem Thessalonicensem), ed. A. Brinkmann, "Klassische Reminiscenzen," *Rheinisches Museum* 60 (1905) 632.
Q

141 **Contra Julianum imperatorem** (Cyrillus Plotinum citans), ed. P. Henry, *Les états du texte de Plotin.* Paris: Brouwer, 1938: 71–74, 125–140, 170.
Q

142 **Contra Julianum imperatorem** (Cyrillus Hermen Trismegistum citans), ed. A.D. Nock and A.J. Festugière, *Corpus Hermeticum,* vol. 4. Paris: Cerf, 1954: 126–142.
frr. 23–35.
Q

144 **Contra Julianum imperatorem** (fragmenta), ed. F. Diekamp, *Analecta patristica* [Orientalia Christiana analecta 117. Rome: Pont. Institutum Orientalium Studiorum, 1938 (repr. 1962)]: 228–229.
Q

146 **De incarnatione dei verbi** (homilia diversa 15), ed. E. Schwartz, *Codex Vaticanus gr. 1431, eine antichalkedonische Sammlung aus der Zeit Kaiser Zenos* [Abhandlungen der bayerischen Akademie der Wissenschaften, Philosoph.-philol.

und hist. Kl., Bd. 32, Abh. 6. Munich: Oldenbourg, 1927]: 13–15.

Cod

147 **Contra eunuchos** (homilia diversa 19), ed. C. de Boor and P. Wirth, *Georgii monachi chronica*, vol. 2. Leipzig: Teubner, 1904 (repr. Stuttgart: 1978): 651–654.

Q

148 **Oratio in ascensionem domini**, ed. C. Datema, "Une homélie inédite sur l'ascension," *Byzantion* 44 (1974) 126–137.

Cod: [3,233]

149 **Homilia habita in ecclesia Cyrini** (fragmentum), ed. M. Richard, "Le florilège du cod. Vatopédi 236 sur le corruptible et l'incorruptible," *Muséon* 86 (1973) 262.

fr. 27.

Cod: [90]

150 **Ad Rufum Thessalonicensem** (epistula 42), ed. Schwartz, *op. cit.*, 19.

Cod: [195]

151 **Ad Rufum Thessalonicensem** (epistula 43), ed. Schwartz, *op. cit.*, 19–20.

Cod: [288]

152 **Ad Gennadium presbyterum et archimandritam** (epistula 56), ed. Schwartz, *op. cit.*, 17.

Cod: [195]

154 **Commonitorium ad Maximum diaconum Antiochenum** (epistula 57), ed. Schwartz, *op. cit.*, 21.

Cod: [171]

156 **Ad Maximum diaconum Antiochenum** (epistula 58), ed. Schwartz, *op. cit.*, 20–21.

Cod: [288]

157 **Ad Joannem Antiochenum** (epistula 62), ed. Schwartz, *op. cit.*, 15.

Cod: [148]

158 **Ad Acacium Melitenum** (epistula 69), ed. Schwartz, *op. cit.*, 15–16.

Cod: [429]

159 **Ad Lamponem presbyterum Alexandrinum** (epistula 70), ed. Schwartz, *op. cit.*, 16–17.

Cod: [265]

160 **Ad Proclum Constantinopolitanum** (epistula 72), ed. Schwartz, *op. cit.*, 17–19.

Cod: [663]

161 **Ad Atticum Constantinopolitanum** (epistula 76), ed. Schwartz, *op. cit.*, 25–28.

Cod: [1,407]

162 **Epistula canonica ad Domnum** (epistula 78), FONTI II: 276–281.

Q: [600]

163 **Ad episcopos qui sunt in Libya et Pentapoli** (epistula 79), FONTI II: 281–284.

Q: [309]

164 **Ad Amphilochium episcopum Sidae** (epistula 82), ed. Schwartz, *op. cit.*, 20.

Cod: [187]

165 **Ad Carthaginiense concilium** (epistula 85), FONTI I.2: 422–424.

Q: [187]

166 **Epistula ad Theodosium imperatorem** (frag-

menta), ed. M. Richard, "Deux lettres perdues de Cyrille d'Alexandrie," *Opera minora* 2. Turnhout: Brepols, 1977: 274–275.

Q

167 **Epistula ad Photium presbyterum** (fragmentum), ed. Richard, *Opera minora* 2, 275.

Cod: [24]

168 **Epistula ad monachos Constantinopolitanos** (fragmentum), ed. Schwartz, *op. cit.*, 34.

Cod: [25]

170 **Fragmentum incertum papyraceum** (*P. Johnson*), ed. J.W. Barns, "Literary texts from the Fayum," *Classical Quarterly* 43 (1949) 5–8.

Pap: [230]

171 **Fragmenta in Job** (in catenis, typus II), ed. P. Young, *Catena Graecorum patrum in beatum Iob, collectore Niceta Heraclea metropolita, Graece nunc primum edita et Latine versa*, 2nd edn. Venice, 1792.

Q

172 **Commentarii in Lucam** (scholia in catenis), ed. J. Reuss, *Matthäus-Kommentare aus der griechischen Kirche* [*Texte und Untersuchungen* 61. Berlin: Akademie-Verlag, 1957]: 153–269 (passim et in apparatu).

Cf. 4090 029 (textus in scholiis in Matthaeum).

Q

174 **Commentarii in Matthaeum** (fragmenta e cod. Vat. gr. 1431), ed. Schwartz, *op. cit.*, 42–45.

Cf. et 4090 029.

Cod

175 **Contra Julianum imperatorem** (fragmenta), MPG 76: 1057–1064.

Cf. et 4090 111.

Q

x01 **Ad monachos Aegypti** (epistula 1).

ACO 1.1.1, pp. 10–23.

Cf. CONCILIA OECUMENICA (ACO) (5000 001).

x02 **Ad Nestorium** (epistula 2).

ACO 1.1.1, pp. 23–25.

Cf. CONCILIA OECUMENICA (ACO) (5000 001).

x04 **Ad Nestorium** (epistula 4).

ACO 1.1.1, pp. 25–28 (= ACO 2.1.1, pp. 104–106).

Cf. CONCILIA OECUMENICA (ACO) (5000 001, 003).

x05 **Ad Nestorium** (una cum synodo Alexandrina) (epistula 17).

ACO 1.1.1, pp. 33–42.

Cf. CONCILIA OECUMENICA (ACO) (5000 001).

x06 **Oratio ad Theodosium imperatorem de recta fide**.

ACO 1.1.1, pp. 42–72.

Cf. CONCILIA OECUMENICA (ACO) (5000 001).

x07 **Ad Joannem Antiochenum** (epistula 13).

ACO 1.1.1, pp. 92–93.

Cf. CONCILIA OECUMENICA (ACO) (5000 001).

x08 **Ad Juvenalem Hierosolymitanum** (epistula 16).
ACO 1.1.1, pp. 96-98.
Cf. CONCILIA OECUMENICA (ACO) (5000 001).

x09 **Ad Acacium Beroeensem** (epistula 14).
ACO 1.1.1, pp. 98-99.
Cf. CONCILIA OECUMENICA (ACO) (5000 001).

x10 **Ad quendam Nestorii studiosum** (epistula 9).
ACO 1.1.1, p. 108.
Cf. CONCILIA OECUMENICA (ACO) (5000 001).

x11 **Ad vituperatores** (epistula 8).
ACO 1.1.1, p. 109.
Cf. CONCILIA OECUMENICA (ACO) (5000 001).

x12 **Ad apocrisiarios Constantinopoli constitutos** (epistula 10).
ACO 1.1.1, pp. 110-112.
Cf. CONCILIA OECUMENICA (ACO) (5000 001).

x13 **Ad clerum populumque Constantinopolitanum** (una cum synodo Alexandrina) (epistula 18).
ACO 1.1.1, pp. 113-114.
Cf. CONCILIA OECUMENICA (ACO) (5000 001).

x14 **Ad clerum populumque Alexandrinum** (epistula 20).
ACO 1.1.1, p. 116.
Cf. CONCILIA OECUMENICA (ACO) (5000 001).

x15 **Ad clerum populumque Alexandrinum** (epistula 21).
ACO 1.1.1, p. 117.
Cf. CONCILIA OECUMENICA (ACO) (5000 001).

x16 **Ad clerum populumque Alexandrinum** (epistula 24).
ACO 1.1.1, pp. 117-118.
Cf. CONCILIA OECUMENICA (ACO) (5000 001).

x17 **Ad clerum populumque Alexandrinum** (epistula 25).
ACO 1.1.1, pp. 118-119.
Cf. CONCILIA OECUMENICA (ACO) (5000 001).

x18 **Ad Comarium et Potamonem episcopos et Dalmatium archimandritam et Timotheum et Eulogium presbyteros** (epistula 23).
ACO 1.1.2, pp. 66-68.
Cf. CONCILIA OECUMENICA (ACO) (5000 001).

x19 **Ad patres monachorum** (epistula 26).
ACO 1.1.2, pp. 69-70.
Cf. CONCILIA OECUMENICA (ACO) (5000 001).

x20 **Ephesi dicta deposito Nestorio** (homilia diversa 5).
ACO 1.1.2, pp. 92-94.

Cf. CONCILIA OECUMENICA (ACO) (5000 001).

x21 **Ephesi habita in basilica sancti Joannis evangelistae** (homilia diversa 2).
ACO 1.1.2, pp. 94-96.
Cf. CONCILIA OECUMENICA (ACO) (5000 001).

x22 **Ephesi habita, valde pulchra** (homilia diversa 1).
ACO 1.1.2, pp. 96-98.
Cf. CONCILIA OECUMENICA (ACO) (5000 001).

x23 **Ephesi dicta in Joannem Antiochenum** (homilia diversa 6).
ACO 1.1.2, pp. 98-100.
Cf. CONCILIA OECUMENICA (ACO) (5000 001).

x24 **Ephesi dicta priusquam a comite comprehenderetur** (homilia diversa 7).
ACO 1.1.2, pp. 100-102.
Cf. CONCILIA OECUMENICA (ACO) (5000 001).

x25 **De Maria deipara in Nestorium** (homilia diversa 4).
ACO 1.1.2, pp. 102-104.
Cf. CONCILIA OECUMENICA (ACO) (5000 001).

x26 **Libellus Cyrilli et Memnonis Ephesini ad concilium Ephesinum.**
ACO 1.1.3, pp. 16-17.
Cf. CONCILIA OECUMENICA (ACO) (5000 001).

x27 **Ad clerum populumque Constantinopolitanum** (epistula 27).
ACO 1.1.3, pp. 45-46.
Cf. CONCILIA OECUMENICA (ACO) (5000 001).

x28 **Ad Theopemptum, Potamonem et Danielem episcopos** (epistula 28).
ACO 1.1.3, pp. 50-51.
Cf. CONCILIA OECUMENICA (ACO) (5000 001).

x29 **Ad Maximianum Constantinopolitanum** (epistula 31).
ACO 1.1.3, p. 72.
Cf. CONCILIA OECUMENICA (ACO) (5000 001).

x30 **Apologeticus ad Theodosium imperatorem.**
ACO 1.1.3, pp. 75-90.
Cf. CONCILIA OECUMENICA (ACO) (5000 001).

x31 **Ad Valerianum episcopum Iconii** (epistula 50).
ACO 1.1.3, pp. 90-101.
Cf. CONCILIA OECUMENICA (ACO) (5000 001).

x32 **De Paulo Emeseno** (homilia diversa 3).
ACO 1.1.4, pp. 14-15.
Cf. CONCILIA OECUMENICA (ACO) (5000 001).

x33 **Ad Joannem Antiochenum** (de pace) (epistula 39).

ACO 1.1.4, pp. 15–20 (= ACO 2.1.1, pp. 107–111).
Cf. CONCILIA OECUMENICA (ACO) (5000 001, 003).

x34 **Ad Acacium Melitenum** (epistula 40).
ACO 1.1.4, pp. 20–31.
Cf. CONCILIA OECUMENICA (ACO) (5000 001).

x35 **Ad Dynatum episcopum Nicopolis** (epistula 48).
ACO 1.1.4, pp. 31–32.
Cf. CONCILIA OECUMENICA (ACO) (5000 001).

x36 **Ad Maximianum Constantinopolitanum** (epistula 49).
ACO 1.1.4, p. 34.
Cf. CONCILIA OECUMENICA (ACO) (5000 001).

x37 **Commonitorium ad Eulogium presbyterum.**
ACO 1.1.4, pp. 35–37.
Cf. CONCILIA OECUMENICA (ACO) (5000 001).

x38 **Ad Joannem Antiochenum et synodum Antiochenum** (epistula 67).
ACO 1.1.4, pp. 37–39.
Cf. CONCILIA OECUMENICA (ACO) (5000 001).

x39 **Ad Acacium episcopum Scythopolis** (epistula 41).
ACO 1.1.4, pp. 40–48.
Cf. CONCILIA OECUMENICA (ACO) (5000 001).

x40 **Ad Anastasium, Alexandrum, Martinianum, Joannem, Paregorium presbyteros et Maximum diaconum ceterosque monachos orientales** (epistula 55).
ACO 1.1.4, pp. 49–61.
Cf. CONCILIA OECUMENICA (ACO) (5000 001).

x41 **Expositio et interrogatio de incarnatione verbi dei filii patris** [Sp.].
ACO 1.1.5, pp. 3–6.
Cf. CONCILIA OECUMENICA (ACO) (5000 001).

x42 **Ad Caelestinum papam** (epistula 11).
ACO 1.1.5, pp. 10–12.
Cf. CONCILIA OECUMENICA (ACO) (5000 001).

x43 **Ad monachos Constantinopolitanos** (una cum synodo Alexandrina) (epistula 19).
ACO 1.1.5, pp. 12–13.
Cf. CONCILIA OECUMENICA (ACO) (5000 001).

x44 **Explanatio xii capitulorum.**
ACO 1.1.5, pp. 15–25.
Cf. CONCILIA OECUMENICA (ACO) (5000 001).

x45 **Oratio ad Pulcheriam et Eudociam augustas de fide.**
ACO 1.1.5, pp. 26–61.
Cf. CONCILIA OECUMENICA (ACO) (5000 001).

x46 **Oratio ad Arcadiam et Marinam augustas de fide.**
ACO 1.1.5, pp. 62–118.
Cf. CONCILIA OECUMENICA (ACO) (5000 001).

x47 **Libri v contra Nestorium.**
ACO 1.1.6, pp. 13–106.
Cf. CONCILIA OECUMENICA (ACO) (5000 001).

x48 **Ad Euoptium episcopum Ptolemaidis** (epistula 84).
ACO 1.1.6, pp. 110–111.
Cf. CONCILIA OECUMENICA (ACO) (5000 001).

x49 **Apologia xii anathematismorum contra Theodoretum.**
ACO 1.1.6, pp. 111–146.
Cf. CONCILIA OECUMENICA (ACO) (5000 001).

x50 **Ad Successum episcopum Diocaesareae** (epistula 45).
ACO 1.1.6, pp. 151–157.
Cf. CONCILIA OECUMENICA (ACO) (5000 001).

x51 **Ad Successum episcopum Diocaesareae** (epistula 46).
ACO 1.1.6, pp. 157–162.
Cf. CONCILIA OECUMENICA (ACO) (5000 001).

x52 **Contra eos qui Theotocon nolunt confiteri** [Dub.].
ACO 1.1.7, pp. 19–32.
Cf. CONCILIA OECUMENICA (ACO) (5000 001).

x53 **Apologia xii capitulorum contra orientales.**
ACO 1.1.7, pp. 33–65.
Cf. CONCILIA OECUMENICA (ACO) (5000 001).

x76 **Epistula ad Juvenalem et ceteros concilii legatos Constantinopolim missos** (epistula 32).
ACO 1.1.7, p. 137.
Cf. CONCILIA OECUMENICA (ACO) (5000 001).

x54 **Epistula ad Acacium Beroeensem.**
ACO 1.1.7, pp. 140–142.
Cf. CONCILIA OECUMENICA (ACO) (5000 001).

x77 **Epistula ad Acacium Beroeensem** (epistula 33).
ACO 1.1.7, pp. 147–150.
Cf. CONCILIA OECUMENICA (ACO) (5000 001).

x55 **Epistula ad Joannem Antiochenum.**
ACO 1.1.7, p. 153.
Cf. CONCILIA OECUMENICA (ACO) (5000 001).

x56 **Epistula ad Joannem Antiochenum.**
ACO 1.1.7, pp. 153–154.
Cf. CONCILIA OECUMENICA (ACO) (5000 001).

x57 **Ad Theognostum et Charmosynum presbyteros et Leontium diaconum** (epistula 37).
ACO 1.1.7, p. 154.

Cf. CONCILIA OECUMENICA (ACO) (5000 001).

x58 **Epistula ad Maximianum Constantinopolitanum.**
ACO 1.1.7, pp. 162–163.
Cf. CONCILIA OECUMENICA (ACO) (5000 001).

x59 **Ad Eusebium presbyterum Antiochenum** (epistula 54).
ACO 1.1.7, pp. 164–165.
Cf. CONCILIA OECUMENICA (ACO) (5000 001).

x60 **Commonitorium ad Posidonium diaconum** (epistula 11a).
ACO 1.1.7, pp. 171–172.
Cf. CONCILIA OECUMENICA (ACO) (5000 001).

x61 **De concordia ecclesiarum** (homilia 16) (fragmentum).
ACO 1.1.7, p. 173.
Cf. CONCILIA OECUMENICA (ACO) (5000 001).

x62 **Scholia de incarnatione unigeniti** (fragmenta).
ACO 1.5.1, pp. 219–231.
Cf. CONCILIA OECUMENICA (ACO) (5000 002).
Cf. et 4090 x69.

x63 **Ad Domnum episcopum Antiochiae** (epistula 77).
ACO 2.1.3, pp. 66–67.
Cf. CONCILIA OECUMENICA (ACO) (5000 003).

x64 **Ad monachos in Phua constitutos** (epistula 81).
ACO 3, pp. 201–202.
Cf. CONCILIA OECUMENICA (ACO) (5000 004).

x65 **Fragmentum in Psalmum 5.8** (in *Doctrina patrum*).
Diekamp, pp. 186–187 (fr. 21).
Cf. DOCTRINA PATRUM (7051 001).

x70 **Liber contra Synousiastas** (fragmenta Graeca).
Hespel, pp. 138–150, frr. 76–90.
Cf. FLORILEGIUM CYRILLIANUM (4147 001).

x72 **Contra Julianum imperatorem** (fragmenta e libris ii, viii, xii, xiii, xiv).
Hespel, pp. 185–187, frr. 176–180.
Cf. FLORILEGIUM CYRILLIANUM (4147 001).

x73 **Tractatus de inhumanatione.**
Hespel, p. 137, fr. 73.
Cf. FLORILEGIUM CYRILLIANUM (4147 001).

x75 **Sermo prosphoneticus ad Alexandrinos de fide** (homilia diversa 21) (fragmenta) (in *Doctrina patrum*).
Diekamp, pp. 17–18 (frr. 22–24), 21 (fr. 34), 66 (fr. 4).
Cf. DOCTRINA PATRUM (7051 001).

x76 **Epistula ad Juvenalem et ceteros concilii legatos Constantinopolim missos** (epistula 32).
ACO 1.1.7, p. 137.
Cf. CONCILIA OECUMENICA (ACO) (5000 001).

4055 **Flavius CYRUS** Epic.
A.D. 5: Panopolitanus
001 **Epigrammata**, AG 1.99; 7.557; 9.136, 623, 808–809; 15.9.
AG 9.813: Cf. ANONYMI EPIGRAMMATICI (0138 001).
Q: 270
002 **Homilia in nativitatem** (ap. Theophanem Confessorem), ed. T.C. Gregory, "The remarkable Christmas homily of Kyros Panopolites," *Greek, Roman and Byzantine Studies* 16 (1975) 318.
Q

0847 **CYRUS** Med.
ante A.D. 6: Edessenus
x01 **Fragmentum ap. Aëtium** (lib. 6).
CMG, vol. 8.2, p. 237.
Cf. AËTIUS Med. (0718 006).

1908 **DAIMACHUS** Hist.
4 B.C.: Plataeeus
Cf. et HELLENICA (0558).
001 **Testimonia**, FGrH #65: 2A:15.
NQ
002 **Fragmenta**, FGrH #65: 2A:15–17.
Q

2482 **DAIMACHUS** Hist.
vel Deimachus
post 3 B.C.: Plataeeus
001 **Testimonia**, FGrH #716: 3C:639.
NQ
002 **Fragmenta**, FGrH #716: 3C:640–641.
Q

2454 **DALION** Hist.
4/3 B.C.?
001 **Testimonia**, FGrH #666: 3C:277–278.
NQ
002 **Fragmenta**, FGrH #666: 3C:278–279.
Q

0158 **DAMAGETUS** Epigr.
3 B.C.: Achaeus
001 **Epigrammata**, AG 6.277; 7.9, 231, 355, 432, 438, 497, 540–541, 735; 16.1, 95.
Q: 417

DAMASCIUS Med.
Cf. THEOPHILUS Protospatharius, DAMASCIUS et STEPHANUS ATHENIENSIS Med. (0728).

4066 **DAMASCIUS** Phil.
A.D. 5/6: Damascenus
Bibliography in progress
001 **Epigramma**, AG 7.553.
Q: 16
002 **Vita Isidori**, ed. C. Zintzen, *Vitae Isidori reliquiae*. Hildesheim: Olms, 1967: 2–319.
Q, Cod

003 **De principiis**, ed. C.É. Ruelle, *Damascii successoris dubitationes et solutiones*, vols. 1 & 2. Paris: Klincksieck, 1:1889; 2:1899 (repr. Brussels: Culture et Civilisation, 1964): 1:1-324; 2:1-4.
Cod

004 **In Parmenidem**, ed. Ruelle, *op. cit.*, vol. 2, 5-322.
Cod

005 **In Phaedonem** (versio 1), ed. L.G. Westerink, *The Greek commentaries on Plato's Phaedo*, vol. 2 (Damascius). Amsterdam: North-Holland, 1977: 27-285.
Cf. et 4066 008.
Cod

008 **In Phaedonem** (versio 2), ed. L.G. Westerink, *The Greek commentaries on Plato's Phaedo*, vol. 2 (Damascius). Amsterdam: North-Holland, 1977: 289-371.
Cf. et 4066 005.
Cod

006 **In Philebum**, ed. L.G. Westerink, *Lectures on the Philebus*. Amsterdam: North-Holland, 1959: 3-121.
Cod

x01 **Paradoxa**.
Photius, *Bibliotheca* 130.
Cf. PHOTIUS (4040 001).

x02 Περὶ ἀριθμοῦ καὶ τόπου καὶ χρόνου.
Simplicius, *Physica* 183v45.
Cf. SIMPLICIUS Phil. (4013 004).

1868 **DAMASTES** Hist.
5 B.C.: Sigeus

001 **Testimonia**, FGrH #5: 1A:152-153.
NQ

002 **Fragmenta**, FGrH #5: 1A:153-156, *8 addenda.
fr. 4 bis: *P. Oxy.* 13.1611.
Q, Pap

2627 **DAMIANUS Scriptor De Opticis**
A.D. 4: fort. Larissaeus

001 **Optica**, ed. R. Schöne, *Damianos Schrift über Optik*. Berlin: Reichsdruckerei, 1897: 2-22.
Cod

2655 **<DAMIGERON Magus>**
Incertum

001 **De lapidibus**, ed. V. Rose, "Damigeron de lapidibus," *Hermes* 9 (1875) 481-490.
Q

002 **De lapidibus** (Cod. V et A), ed. J. Mesk, "Ein unedierter Tractat περὶ λίθων," *Wiener Studien* (1898) 318-321.
Cod

1297 **DAMIPPUS** Phil.
3 B.C.

001 **Fragmenta**, ed. H. Thesleff, *The Pythagorean texts of the Hellenistic period*. Åbo: Åbo Akademi, 1965: 68-69.
Q: 520

4067 **DAMOCHARIS** Gramm.
A.D. 6: Cous

001 **Epigrammata**, AG **6**.63; **7**.206; **9**.633; **16**.310.
Q: 174

0848 **Servilius DAMOCRATES** Poet. Med.
A.D. 1

x01 **Fragmenta ap. Galenum**.
K**12**.889-892; **13**.40-42, 220-227, 350-353, 455-457, 821-823, 915-923, 940-945, 988-990, 996-1005, 1047-1058; **14**.90-99, 115-135, 191-201.
Cf. GALENUS Med. (0057 076-078).

2493 **DAMOCRITUS** Hist.
1 B.C.-A.D. 1?

001 **Fragmentum**, FGrH #730: 3C:691.
Q

2273 **DAMON** Hist.
ante A.D. 3

001 **Fragmentum**, FGrH #389: 3B:266.
Q

2232 **DAMON** Mus.
5 B.C.: Atheniensis

001 **Testimonia**, ed. H. Diels and W. Kranz, *Die Fragmente der Vorsokratiker*, vol. 1, 6th edn. Berlin: Weidmann, 1951 (repr. Dublin: 1966): 381-382.
test. 1-8.
NQ

002 **Fragmenta**, ed. Diels and Kranz, *op. cit.*, 382-384.
frr. 1-10.
Q

2244 **DAMON et PHINTIAS** Phil.
4 B.C.: Syracusanus

001 **Testimonium**, ed. H. Diels and W. Kranz, *Die Fragmente der Vorsokratiker*, vol. 1, 6th edn. Berlin: Weidmann, 1951 (repr. Dublin: 1966): 444.
NQ

0849 **Claudius DAMONICUS** Med.
ante A.D. 1

x01 **Fragmenta ap. Galenum**.
K**12**.637; **13**.740.
Cf. GALENUS Med. (0057 076-077).

0438 **DAMOXENUS** Comic.
4/3 B.C.

001 **Fragmenta**, ed. T. Kock, *Comicorum Atticorum fragmenta*, vol. 3. Leipzig: Teubner, 1888: 348-351, 353.
frr. 1-3.
Q: 555

002 **Fragmenta**, ed. A. Meineke, *Fragmenta comicorum Graecorum*, vol. 4. Berlin: Reimer, 1841 (repr. De Gruyter, 1970): 529-532, 536.
Q: 554

0364 *DANAIS*
Incertum

001 **Danais**, ed. G. Kinkel, *Epicorum Graecorum fragmenta*, vol. 1. Leipzig: Teubner, 1877: 78.
fr. 1.
Q: [12]

2615 **DAPHITAS** Gramm. vel Soph.
3 B.C.: Telmessensis
001 **Fragmentum**, ed. H. Lloyd-Jones and P. Parsons, *Supplementum Hellenisticum*. Berlin: De Gruyter, 1983: 173.
fr. 370.
Q: [9]
x01 **Epigramma irrisorium**.
App. Anth. 5.20: Cf. EPIGRAMMATICI in *App. Anth.* (7052 005).

1894 **DARES** Hist.
Incertum: Phrygius
001 **Testimonia**, FGrH #51: 1A:294.
NQ

0851 **DARIUS** Med.
ante A.D. 1
x01 **Fragmenta ap. Galenum**.
K13.69, 832.
Cf. GALENUS Med. (0057 076–077).

4021 **DAVID** Phil.
A.D. 6
001 **Prolegomena philosophiae**, ed. A. Busse, *Davidis prolegomena et in Porphyrii isagogen commentarium* [*Commentaria in Aristotelem Graeca* 18.2. Berlin: Reimer, 1904]: 1–79.
Cod: [32,133]
002 **In Porphyrii isagogen commentarium**, ed. Busse, *op. cit.*, 80–219.
Cod: [49,650]
x01 **In Aristotelis categorias commentaria**.
CAG 18.1, pp. 107–255.
Cf. ELIAS Phil. (4020 002).

0272 *DE ARBORIBUS AVIBUSQUE FABULAE*
ante A.D. 2/3
001 **Fragmenta** (*P. Heidelb.* 222), ed. E. Heitsch, *Die griechischen Dichterfragmente der römischen Kaiserzeit*, vol. 1, 2nd edn. Göttingen: Vandenhoeck & Ruprecht, 1963: 34–38.
frr. 1–5.
Pap: [329]

2326 **DEI(L)OCHUS** Hist.
vel Deiochus
5–4 B.C.?: Cyzicenus, Proconnensis
001 **Testimonia**, FGrH #471: 3B:427.
NQ
002 **Fragmenta**, FGrH #471: 3B:427–429.
Q
003 **Fragmentum**, ed. H.J. Mette, "Die 'Kleinen' griechischen Historiker heute," *Lustrum* 21 (1978) 30.
fr. 11.
Q

0877 **DELETIUS** Med.
ante A.D. 2
x01 **Fragmentum ap. Galenum**.
K13.300.
Cf. GALENUS Med. (0057 076).

1989 **Quintus DELLIUS** Hist.
1 B.C.
001 **Fragmenta**, FGrH #197: 2B:929.
Q

0535 **DEMADES** Orat. et Rhet.
4 B.C.: Atheniensis
001 **Fragmenta**, ed. V. de Falco, *Demade oratore. Testimonianze e frammenti*, 2nd edn. Naples: Libreria Scientifica Editrice, 1955: 19–54, 60–68, 83–87.
fr. 9: *P. Oxy.* 2.226.
Q, Cod, Pap: [3,382]
002 **Testimonium**, FGrH #227: 2B:955.
NQ
003 **Fragmentum**, FGrH #227: 2B:955.
Q

1812 **DEMARATUS** Hist.
3–2 B.C.
001 **Fragmenta**, FGrH #42: 1A:264–265.
Q

2616 **DEMARETA** Poeta
ante A.D. 2
001 **Titulus**, ed. H. Lloyd-Jones and P. Parsons, *Supplementum Hellenisticum*. Berlin: De Gruyter, 1983: 174.
fr. 372.
NQ: [1]

2347 **DEMEAS** Hist.
4–3 B.C.?: Parius
001 **Fragmentum**, FGrH #502: 3B:479–481.
fr. 1: *IG* 12.5, no. 445.
Epigr

1298 *DEMETRII PHALEREI EPISTULA*
Incertum
Cf. et DEMETRIUS Phil. et Hist. (0624).
001 **Epistula**, ed. R. Hercher, *Epistolographi Graeci*. Paris: Didot, 1873 (repr. Amsterdam: Hakkert, 1965): 218.
Q: 179

DEMETRIUS I Poliorcetes Hist.
4 B.C.: Macedo
Cf. ADDITAMENTA (FGrH) (2433 021).

0439 **DEMETRIUS** Comic.
5/4 B.C.
001 **Fragmenta**, ed. T. Kock, *Comicorum Atticorum fragmenta*, vol. 1. Leipzig: Teubner, 1888: 795–796.
frr. 1–2, 4–5.
Q: 70
002 **Fragmenta**, ed. A. Meineke, *Fragmenta comi-*

corum Graecorum, vol. 2.2. Berlin: Reimer, 1840 (repr. De Gruyter, 1970): 876–878.
Q: 71

003 **Tituli**, ed. C. Austin, *Comicorum Graecorum fragmenta in papyris reperta*. Berlin: De Gruyter, 1973: 50.
fr. 77.
Pap: 5

0159 **DEMETRIUS** Epigr.
2 B.C.: Bithynius
001 **Epigramma**, AG 9.730.
AG 9.731: Cf. ANONYMI EPIGRAMMATICI (0138 001).
AG 9.732: Cf. Marcus ARGENTARIUS Epigr. (0132 001).
Q: 18

DEMETRIUS Epigr.
3 B.C.?: Halicarnassensis
AG 13.29.
Cf. NICAENETUS Epic. (0218).

1756 **DEMETRIUS** Gramm.
3–2 B.C.: Scepsius
001 **Fragmenta**, ed. R. Gaede, *Demetrii Scepsii quae supersunt* [*Diss. Greifswald* (1880)]: 17–36, 38–52, 54–59.
frr. 1–75.
Q: [5,590]

2208 **DEMETRIUS** Hist.
4 B.C.: fort. Argivus
001 **Testimonium**, FGrH #304: 3B:7.
NQ
002 **Fragmentum**, FGrH #304: 3B:7.
Q

1957 **DEMETRIUS** Hist.
3 B.C.: Byzantius
001 **Testimonium**, FGrH #162: 2B:889.
NQ

2485 **DEMETRIUS** Hist.
3 B.C.
001 **Fragmenta**, FGrH #722: 3C:666–671.
Q

2381 **DEMETRIUS** Hist.
3 B.C.?: Seriphius
001 **Fragmentum**, FGrH #549: 3B:535.
Q

1917 **DEMETRIUS** Hist.
3–2 B.C.: Callatianus
001 **Testimonia**, FGrH #85: 2A:202–203.
NQ
002 **Fragmenta**, FGrH #85: 2A:203–204.
Q

2522 **DEMETRIUS** Hist.
2 B.C.?

001 **Fragmentum**, FGrH #777: 3C:772.
Q

1299 **DEMETRIUS** Hist.
fiq Demetrius Judaeus Alexandrinus
ante A.D. 1
001 **Testimonium**, FGrH #643: 3C:188.
NQ
002 **Fragmenta**, FGrH #643: 3C:189.
Q

1901 **DEMETRIUS** Hist.
ante A.D. 2: Iliensis
001 **Fragmenta**, FGrH #59: 1A:298.
Q

1995 **DEMETRIUS** Hist.
A.D. 2: Sagalassensis
001 **Fragmentum**, FGrH #209: 2B:941.
Q

2511 **DEMETRIUS** Hist.
Incertum: Salaminius
001 **Fragmentum**, FGrH #756: 3C:736–737.
Q

2541 **DEMETRIUS** Hist.
Incertum: Odessius
001 **Testimonium**, FGrH #808: 3C:844.
NQ

2572 **DEMETRIUS** Hist.
Incertum
001 **Fragmenta**, FGrH #852: 3C:936.
Q

0624 **DEMETRIUS** Phil. et Hist.
4–3 B.C.: Phalereus
Cf. et DEMETRII PHALEREI EPISTULA (1298).
001 **Fragmenta**, ed. F. Wehrli, *Demetrios von Phaleron* [*Die Schule des Aristoteles*, vol. 4, 2nd edn. Basel: Schwabe, 1968]: 21–44.
Q
002 **Testimonia**, FGrH #228: 2B:956–960.
NQ
003 **Fragmenta**, FGrH #228: **2B**:960–973; **3B**:744 addenda.
Q

x01 **Septem sapientium apophthegmata**.
D-K vol. 1, pp. 63–66.
Cf. <SEPTEM SAPIENTES> (1667 002–003).
x02 **Formae epistolicae**.
Weichert, pp. 1–12.
Cf. DEMETRIUS Rhet. (1302 001–002).
x03 **De elocutione**.
Radermacher, pp. 3–62.
Cf. <DEMETRIUS> Rhet. (0613 001).

1301 **DEMETRIUS** Poet. Phil.
A.D. 1: Troezenius
001 **Fragmentum**, ed. H. Diels, *Poetarum philosophorum fragmenta, Poetarum Graecorum frag-*

menta 3.1. Berlin: Weidmann, 1901: 224.
fr. 1.
Q

002 **Fragmenta et titulus**, ed. H. Lloyd-Jones and P. Parsons, *Supplementum Hellenisticum*. Berlin: De Gruyter, 1983: 174–175.
frr. 374, 376.
Q: [15]

2617 **DEMETRIUS** Poeta
ante A.D. 3
001 **Fragmentum**, ed. H. Lloyd-Jones and P. Parsons, *Supplementum Hellenisticum*. Berlin: De Gruyter, 1983: 174.
fr. 373.
Q: [18]

1302 **DEMETRIUS** Rhet.
2/1 B.C.
001 **Formae epistolicae**, ed. V. Weichert, *Demetrii et Libanii qui feruntur τύποι ἐπιστολικοί et ἐπιστολιμαῖοι χαρακτῆρες*. Leipzig: Teubner, 1910: 1–12.
Cod: [1,903]
002 **Formae epistolicae** (duo exempla spuria), ed. Weichert, *op. cit.*, 12.
Cod: [178]

0613 **<DEMETRIUS>** Rhet.
1 B.C./A.D. 1?
001 **De elocutione**, ed. L. Radermacher, *Demetrii Phalerei qui dicitur de elocutione libellus*. Leipzig: Teubner, 1901 (repr. Stuttgart: 1967): 3–62.
Cod: [16,862]

1849 **DEMETRIUS** Trag.
Incertum
001 **Titulus** (+ dramatis personae), ed. B. Snell, *Tragicorum Graecorum fragmenta*, vol. 1. Göttingen: Vandenhoeck & Ruprecht, 1971: 189.
NQ

0958 **DEMETRIUS IXION** Gramm.
2 B.C.: Alexandrinus, Pergamenus
001 **Fragmenta**, ed. T. Staesche, *De Demetrio Ixione grammatico* [*Diss. Halle* (1883)]: 41–44, 46–47, 50–59.
Q

DEMETRIUS Judaeus Hist.
ante A.D. 1: Alexandrinus
Cf. DEMETRIUS Hist. (1299).

0440 **DEMETRIUS** Junior Comic.
4/3 B.C.
001 **Fragmentum**, ed. T. Kock, *Comicorum Atticorum fragmenta*, vol. 3. Leipzig: Teubner, 1888: 357–358.
fr. 1.
Q: 73
002 **Fragmentum**, ed. A. Meineke, *Fragmenta*

comicorum Graecorum, vol. 4. Berlin: Reimer, 1841 (repr. De Gruyter, 1970): 539.
Q: 52

1300 **DEMETRIUS LACON** Phil.
2 B.C.
001 **Fragmenta** (*P. Herc.* 124, 188, 1006, 1013, 1014, 1055, 1061, 1113, 1258, 1429, 1642, 1647, 1696, 1786), ed. V. de Falco, *L'Epicureo Demetrio Lacone*. Naples: Cimmaruta, 1923: 25–60, 62–65, 69–82, 85–101, 103–107.
Pap
002 **Περὶ ποιημάτων** (*P. Herc.* 188 + 1014), ed. C. Romeo, "Nuove letture nei libri 'sulla poesia' di Demetrio Lacone," *Cronache Ercolanesi* 8 (1978) 105–107, 111–123.
Pap
003 **Fragmenta philosophica** (*P. Herc.* 1013), ed. C. Romeo, "Demetrio Lacone sulla grandezza del sole," *Cronache Ercolanesi* 9 (1979) 17–20.
Pap
004 **Fragmenta incerti operis** (*P. Herc.* 1012 + 1786), ed. E. Puglia, "Nuove letture nei P. Herc. 1012 e 1786 (Demetrii Laconis opera incerta)," *Cronache Ercolanesi* 10 (1980) 28–49, 51–52.
Pap
005 **Περὶ ποιημάτων** (*P. Herc.* 1014), ed. C. Romeo, "Demetrio Lacone interprete di Alceo," *Cronache Ercolanesi* 12 (1982) 35, 36, 38, 40, 41.
Pap
006 **Fragmenta incerti operis** (*P. Herc.* 1055), ed. E. Renna, "Nuove letture nel P. Herc. 1055 (libro incerto di Demetrio Lacone)," *Cronache Ercolanesi* 12 (1982) 46–49.
Pap

0160 **DEMIURGUS** Epigr.
1 B.C.
001 **Epigramma**, AG 7.52.
Q: 12

1303 **DEMOCHARES** Rhet.
4–3 B.C.: Atheniensis
001 **Testimonia**, FGrH #75: 2A:133–134.
NQ
002 **Fragmenta**, FGrH #75: 2A:134–136.
Q

0161 **DEMOCRITUS** Epigr.
ante A.D. 3?
001 **Epigramma**, AG 16.180.
Q: 35

1305 **DEMOCRITUS** Hist.
3 B.C.: Ephesius
001 **Testimonium**, FGrH #267: 3A:76.
NQ
002 **Fragmenta**, FGrH #267: 3A:76.
Q

1304 **DEMOCRITUS** Phil.
5–4 B.C.: Abderita
Cf. et BOLUS Phil. (1306).
001 **Testimonia**, ed. H. Diels and W. Kranz, *Die
Fragmente der Vorsokratiker*, vol. 2, 6th edn.
Berlin: Weidmann, 1952 (repr. Dublin: 1966):
81–129.
test. 1–170.
NQ
002 **Fragmenta**, ed. Diels and Kranz, *op. cit.*, 130–
207.
frr. 1–298a.
Q
x01 **Epigramma**.
AG 9.360: Cf. METRODORUS Gramm. (4077
001).

Pseudo-DEMOCRITUS Phil.
Incertum
Cf. BOLUS Phil. (1306).

2299 **DEMODAMAS** Hist.
4–3 B.C.: Halicarnassensis, Milesius
001 **Testimonia**, FGrH #428: 3B:324.
NQ
002 **Fragmenta**, FGrH #428: 3B:324–325.
Q

0245 **DEMODOCUS** Eleg.
6 B.C.?: Lerius
001 **Fragmenta**, ed. M.L. West, *Iambi et elegi
Graeci*, vol. 2. Oxford: Clarendon Press, 1972:
56–58.
frr. 1–6.
Q: [117]
002 **Epigrammata**, AG 11.235–238.
Q: 89

2308 **DEMOGNETUS** Hist.
ante A.D. 2
001 **Fragmentum**, FGrH #445: 3B:376.
Q

1307 **DEMON** Hist.
4–3 B.C.: fort. Atheniensis
001 **Testimonium**, FGrH #327: 3B:87.
NQ
002 **Fragmenta**, FGrH #327: 3B:87–96.
Q

2969 **DEMONAX** Phil.
A.D. 2.: Cyprius
001 **Fragmenta**, ed. F.W.A. Mullach, *Fragmenta
philosophorum Graecorum*, vol. 2. Paris: Didot,
1867 (repr. Aalen: Scientia, 1968): 351–357.
Q

0349 **DEMONAX** <Trag.>
Incertum
001 **Fragmenta**, ed. B. Snell, *Tragicorum Grae-

corum fragmenta, vol. 1. Göttingen: Vandenhoeck & Ruprecht, 1971: 320.
frr. 1–3.
Q: [18]

0441 **DEMONICUS** Comic.
5/4 B.C.?
001 **Fragmentum**, ed. T. Kock, *Comicorum Atticorum fragmenta*, vol. 3. Leipzig: Teubner,
1888: 375.
fr. 1.
Q: 27
002 **Fragmentum**, ed. A. Meineke, *Fragmenta
comicorum Graecorum*, vol. 4. Berlin: Reimer,
1841 (repr. De Gruyter, 1970): 570.
Q: 28

DEMOPHILUS Gnom.
Cf. SENTENTIAE PYTHAGOREORUM (1759
001).

1308 **DEMOSTHENES** Epic.
2 B.C.?: Bithynius
001 **Fragmenta**, ed. J.U. Powell, *Collectanea Alexandrina*. Oxford: Clarendon Press, 1925 (repr.
1970): 25–27.
frr. 4, 6, 7, 14.
Q: [63]
002 **Fragmenta**, FGrH #699: 3C:552–554.
Q

1819 **Pseudo-DEMOSTHENES** Epigr.
Incertum
001 **Epigramma**, ed. E. Diehl, *Anthologia lyrica
Graeca*, fasc. 1, 3rd edn. Leipzig: Teubner,
1949: 135.
Q: [13]

0014 **DEMOSTHENES** Orat.
4 B.C.: Atheniensis
001 **Olynthiaca 1**, ed. S.H. Butcher, *Demosthenis
orationes*, vol. 1. Oxford: Clarendon Press,
1903 (repr. 1966): [9–17].
Cod: 1,858
002 **Olynthiaca 2**, ed. Butcher, *op. cit.*, vol. 1, [18–
27].
Cod: 2,085
003 **Olynthiaca 3**, ed. Butcher, *op. cit.*, vol. 1, [28–
39].
Cod: 2,407
004 **Philippica 1**, ed. Butcher, *op. cit.*, vol. 1, [40–
55].
Cod: 3,338
005 **De pace**, ed. Butcher, *op. cit.*, vol. 1, [57–63].
Cod: 1,488
006 **Philippica 2**, ed Butcher, *op. cit.*, vol. 1, [65–
74].
Cod: 2,039
007 **De Halonneso**, ed. Butcher, *op. cit.*, vol. 1,
[76–88].
Cod: 2,494

008 **De Chersoneso**, ed. Butcher, *op. cit.*, vol. 1, [90–109].
Cod: 4,291

009 **Philippica 3**, ed. Butcher, *op. cit.*, vol. 1, [110–130].
Cod: 4,396

010 **Philippica 4** [Sp.], ed. Butcher, *op. cit.*, vol. 1, [131–151].
Cod: 4,535

011 **In epistulam Philippi** [Sp.], ed. Butcher, *op. cit.*, vol. 1, [152–158].
Cod: 1,324

012 **[Philippi] epistula**, ed. Butcher, *op. cit.*, vol. 1, [158–165].
Cod: 1,456

013 Περὶ συντάξεως [Sp.], ed. Butcher, *op. cit.*, vol. 1, [166–177].
Cod: 2,370

014 Περὶ τῶν συμμοριῶν, ed. Butcher, *op. cit.*, vol. 1, [178–189].
Cod: 2,640

015 **De Rhodiorum libertate**, ed. Butcher, *op. cit.*, vol. 1, [190–201].
Cod: 2,248

016 **Pro Megalopolitanis**, ed. Butcher, *op. cit.*, vol. 1, [202–210].
Cod: 1,900

017 Περὶ τῶν πρὸς ᾿Αλέξανδρον συνθηκῶν [Sp.], ed. Butcher, *op. cit.*, vol. 1, [211–220].
Cod: 1,831

018 **De corona**, ed. Butcher, *op. cit.*, vol. 1, [225–332].
Cod: 22,893

019 **De falsa legatione**, ed. Butcher, *op. cit.*, vol. 1, [341–451].
Cod: 23,576

020 **Adversus Leptinem**, ed. Butcher, *op. cit.*, vol. 2.1 (1907; repr. 1966): [457–508].
Cod: 11,543

021 **In Midiam**, ed. Butcher, *op. cit.*, vol. 2.1, [514–587].
Cod: 16,013

022 **Adversus Androtionem**, ed. Butcher, *op. cit.*, vol. 2.1, [593–618].
Cod: 5,728

023 **In Aristocratem**, ed. Butcher, *op. cit.*, vol. 2.1, [621–693].
Cod: 15,704

024 **In Timocratem**, ed. Butcher, *op. cit.*, vol. 2.1, [700–767].
Cod: 14,896

025 **In Aristogitonem 1**, ed. Butcher, *op. cit.*, vol. 2.1, [770–800].
Cod: 6,828

026 **In Aristogitonem 2**, ed. Butcher, *op. cit.*, vol. 2.1, [800–808].
Cod: 1,718

027 **In Aphobum 1**, ed. W. Rennie, *op. cit.*, vol. 2.2 (1921; repr. 1966): [813–835].
Cod: 4,687

028 **In Aphobum 2**, ed. Rennie, *op. cit.*, vol. 2.2, [835–843].
Cod: 1,548

029 **Contra Aphobum**, ed. Rennie, *op. cit.*, vol. 2.2, [844–862].
Cod: 4,006

030 **Contra Onetorem 1**, ed. Rennie, *op. cit.*, vol. 2.2, [864–875].
Cod: 2,407

031 **Contra Onetorem 2**, ed. Rennie, *op. cit.*, vol. 2.2, [876–880].
Cod: 966

032 **Contra Zenothemin**, ed. Rennie, *op. cit.*, vol. 2.2, [882–891].
Cod: 1,956

033 **Contra Apatourium** [Sp.], ed. Rennie, *op. cit.*, vol. 2.2, [892–904].
Cod: 2,596

034 **Contra Phormionem**, ed. Rennie, *op. cit.*, vol. 2.2, [907–922].
Cod: 3,350

035 **Contra Lacritum** [Sp.], ed. Rennie, *op. cit.*, vol. 2.2, [923–943].
Cod: 3,727

036 **Pro Phormione**, ed. Rennie, *op. cit.*, vol. 2.2, [944–963].
Cod: 4,049

037 **Contra Pantaenetum**, ed. Rennie, *op. cit.*, vol. 2.2, [966–984].
Cod: 3,860

038 **Contra Nausimachum et Xenopeithea**, ed. Rennie, *op. cit.*, vol. 2.2, [984–993].
Cod: 1,900

039 **Contra Boeotum 1**, ed. Rennie, *op. cit.*, vol. 2.2, [994–1007].
Cod: 2,802

040 **Contra Boeotum 2** [Sp.], ed. Rennie, *op. cit.*, vol. 2.2, [1008–1026].
Cod: 3,987

041 **Contra Spudiam**, ed. Rennie, *op. cit.*, vol. 3 (1931; repr. 1960): [1028–1037].
Cod: 2,017

042 **Contra Phaenippum** [Sp.], ed. Rennie, *op. cit.*, vol. 3, [1038–1049].
Cod: 2,285

043 **Contra Macartatum** [Sp.], ed. Rennie, *op. cit.*, vol. 3, [1050–1079].
Cod: 6,416

044 **Contra Leocharem** [Sp.], ed. Rennie, *op. cit.*, vol. 3, [1081–1100].
Cod: 4,319

045 **In Stephanum 1**, ed. Rennie, *op. cit.*, vol. 3, [1101–1128].
Cod: 5,850

046 **In Stephanum 2** [Sp.], ed. Rennie, *op. cit.*, vol. 3, [1129–1137].
Cod: 1,900

047 **In Evergum et Mnesibulum** [Sp.], ed. Rennie, *op. cit.*, vol. 3, [1139–1164].
Cod: 5,495

048 **In Olympiodorum** [Sp.], ed. Rennie, *op. cit.*, vol. 3, [1167–1183].
Cod: 3,592

049 **Contra Timotheum** [Sp.], ed. Rennie, *op. cit.*, vol. 3, [1184–1205].
Cod: 4,414

050 **Contra Polyclem** [Sp.], ed. Rennie, *op. cit.*, vol. 3, [1206–1227].
Cod: 4,732

051 **De corona trierarchiae**, ed. Rennie, *op. cit.*, vol. 3, [1228–1234].
Cod: 1,382

052 **Contra Callippum** [Sp.], ed. Rennie, *op. cit.*, vol. 3, [1235–1245].
Cod: 2,168

053 **Contra Nicostratum**, ed. Rennie, *op. cit.*, vol. 3, [1246–1255].
Cod: 2,063

054 **In Cononem**, ed. Rennie, *op. cit.*, vol. 3, [1256–1271].
Cod: 3,259

055 **Contra Calliclem**, ed. Rennie, *op. cit.*, vol. 3, [1272–1281].
Cod: 2,166

056 **In Dionysodorum** [Sp.], ed. Rennie, *op. cit.*, vol. 3, [1282–1298].
Cod: 3,392

057 **Contra Eubulidem**, ed. Rennie, *op. cit.*, vol. 3, [1299–1320].
Cod: 4,729

058 **In Theocrinem** [Sp.], ed. Rennie, *op. cit.*, vol. 3, [1322–1344].
Cod: 4,795

059 **In Neaeram** [Sp.], ed. Rennie, *op. cit.*, vol. 3, [1345–1388].
Cod: 9,415

060 **Epitaphius**, ed. Rennie, *op. cit.*, vol. 3, [1388–1400].
Cod: 2,594

061 **Eroticus** [Sp.], ed. Rennie, *op. cit.*, vol. 3, [1400–1418].
Cod: 3,735

062 **Exordia**, ed. Rennie, *op. cit.*, vol. 3, [1418–1462].
Cod: 9,755

063 **Epistulae**, ed. Rennie, *op. cit.*, vol. 3, [1462–1492].
Cod: 6,225

064 **Fragmenta**, ed. J. Baiter and H. Sauppe, *Oratores Attici*. Zürich: Hoehr, 1850 (repr. Hildesheim: Olms, 1967): 251–257.
frr. 1–13.
Q: 2,527

DEMOSTHENES Ophthalmicus Med.
Cf. DEMOSTHENES Philalethes Med. (0689).

0689 **DEMOSTHENES Philalethes** Med.
A.D. 1
x01 **Fragmentum ap. Galenum**.
K12.843.

Cf. GALENUS Med. (0057 076).

x02 **Fragmenta ap. Oribasium**.
CMG, vol. 6.3, pp. 100, 104, 264.
Cf. ORIBASIUS Med. (0722 004).

x03 **Fragmenta ap. Aëtium** (lib. 7).
CMG, vol. 8.2, pp. 265, 283, 300, 306, 308, 322, 324, 325, 329, 373, 389.
Cf. AËTIUS Med. (0718 007).

2281 **DEMOTELES** Hist.
4–3 B.C.: Andrius
001 **Testimonium**, FGrH #400: 3B:293.
test. 1: *IG* 11.4, no. 544.
NQ

2196 **[DERCYLLUS]** Hist.
Incertum
001 **Fragmenta**, FGrH #288: 3A:170–172.
Q

DERCYLUS Hist.
Cf. (H)AGIAS-DERCYLUS Hist. (1387).

0442 **DEXICRATES** Comic.
4/3 B.C.?
001 **Fragmentum**, ed. T. Kock, *Comicorum Atticorum fragmenta*, vol. 3. Leipzig: Teubner, 1888: 374.
fr. 1.
Q: 17
002 **Fragmentum**, ed. A. Meineke, *Fragmenta comicorum Graecorum*, vol. 4. Berlin: Reimer, 1841 (repr. De Gruyter, 1970): 571.
Q: 17

2141 **DEXIPPUS** Hist.
A.D. 3: Atheniensis
001 **Testimonia**, FGrH #100: 2A:452–454.
test. 4: *IG* 3.716.
NQ
002 **Fragmenta**, FGrH #100: 2A:454–480.
Q

2036 **DEXIPPUS** Phil.
A.D. 4
001 **In Aristotelis categorias commentarium**, ed. A. Busse, *Dexippi in Aristotelis categorias commentarium* [*Commentaria in Aristotelem Graeca* 4.2. Berlin: Reimer, 1888]: 1–71.
Cod: [24,452]

0371 **DIAGORAS** Lyr.
5 B.C.: Melius
001 **Fragmenta**, ed. D.L. Page, *Poetae melici Graeci*. Oxford: Clarendon Press, 1962 (repr. 1967 (1st edn. corr.)): 382.
fr. 1.
Q: [26]
002 **Testimonia et fragmenta**, ed. M. Winiarczyk, *Diagorae Melii et Theodori Cyrenaei reliquiae*.

Leipzig: Teubner, 1981: 1–29.
Q, Pap

0854 **DIAGORAS** Med.
3 B.C.: Cyprius
x01 **Fragmentum ap. Oribasium.**
CMG, vol. 6.3, p. 106.
Cf. ORIBASIUS Med. (0722 004).
x02 **Fragmentum ap. Aëtium** (lib. 7).
CMG, vol. 8.2, p. 375.
Cf. AËTIUS Med. (0718 007).

1309 *DIALEXEIS* (Δισσοὶ λόγοι)
5/4 B.C.
001 **Fragmenta**, ed. H. Diels and W. Kranz, *Die Fragmente der Vorsokratiker*, vol. 2, 6th edn. Berlin: Weidmann, 1952 (repr. Dublin: 1966): 405–416.
frr. 1–9.
Cod

0066 **DICAEARCHUS** Phil.
4 B.C.: Messanius
001 **Fragmenta**, ed. F. Wehrli, *Dikaiarchos [Die Schule des Aristoteles*, vol. 1, 2nd edn. Basel: Schwabe, 1967]: 13–37.
Q: [319]
x01 Περὶ τῶν ἐν τῇ Ἑλλάδι πόλεων.
GGM, vol. 1, pp. 97–110.
Cf. HERACLIDES Criticus Perieg. (1405 001).

0322 **DICAEOGENES** Trag.
4 B.C.
001 **Fragmenta**, ed. B. Snell, *Tragicorum Graecorum fragmenta*, vol. 1. Göttingen: Vandenhoeck & Ruprecht, 1971: 192.
frr. 1b, 2, 4–5.
Q: [51]

1310 **DICTYS** Hist.
A.D. 2/3: Cretensis
001 **Ephemeridos belli Troiani libri** (*P. Tebt.* 268), ed. W. Eisenhut, *Dictyis Cretensis ephemeridos belli Troiani libri*. Leipzig: Teubner, 1958: 134–139.
Pap: [634]
002 **Testimonia**, FGrH #49: 1A:273–275.
NQ
003 **Fragmenta**, FGrH #49: 1A:275–284.
fr. 7a: *P. Tebt.* 268.
Q, Pap

1311 *DIDACHE XII APOSTOLORUM*
A.D. 2
001 Διδαχαὶ τῶν ἀποστολῶν, ed. J.P. Audet, *La Didachè. Instructions des Apôtres*. Paris: Lecoffre, 1958: 226–242.
Cod: [2,208]

2618 **DIDYMARCHUS** Poeta
4 B.C.?

001 **Titulus**, ed. H. Lloyd-Jones and P. Parsons, *Supplementum Hellenisticum*. Berlin: De Gruyter, 1983: 175.
fr. 378a.
NQ: [4]

1312 **DIDYMUS** Gramm.
1 B.C.: Alexandrinus
001 **Fragmentum**, FGrH #340: 3B:196–197.
Q
002 **Fragmenta**, ed. M. Schmidt, *Didymi Chalcenteri grammatici Alexandrini fragmenta quae supersunt omnia*. Leipzig: Teubner, 1854 (repr. Amsterdam: Hakkert, 1964): 19–261, 299–405.
Q
003 **In Demosthenem** (*P. Berol.* 9780), ed. L. Pearson and S. Stephens, *Didymi in Demosthenem commenta*. Stuttgart: Teubner, 1983: 1–54.
Pap
004 **De dubiis apud Platonem lectionibus** [Sp.], ed. E. Miller, "Opuscles divers," *Lexica Graeca minora* (ed. K. Latte & H. Erbse). Hildesheim: Olms, 1965: 245–252.
Q
x01 **Mensurae marmorum ac lignorum.**
Hultsch, pp. 238–244.
Cf. DIDYMUS Scriptor De Mensuris (0357 001).

0855 **DIDYMUS** Med.
A.D. 4/5: Alexandrinus
x01 **Fragmentum ap. Aëtium** (lib. 6).
CMG, vol. 8.2, p. 155.
Cf. AËTIUS Med. (0718 006).
x02 **Fragmentum ap. Aëtium** (lib. 9).
Zervos, *Athena* 23, p. 389.
Cf. AËTIUS Med. (0718 009).

0357 **DIDYMUS Scriptor De Mensuris**
1 B.C.: Alexandrinus
001 **Mensurae marmorum ac lignorum**, ed. F. Hultsch, *Heronis Alexandrini geometricorum et stereometricorum reliquiae*. Berlin: Weidmann, 1864: 238–244.
Cod

2102 **DIDYMUS CAECUS** Scr. Eccl.
A.D. 4: Alexandrinus
001 **Commentarii in Job** (1–4), ed. A. Henrichs, *Didymos der Blinde. Kommentar zu Hiob*, pt. 1 [*Papyrologische Texte und Abhandlungen* 1. Bonn: Habelt, 1968]: 24–308.
Pap: [20,682]
002 **Commentarii in Job** (5.1–6.29), ed. A. Henrichs, *Didymos der Blinde. Kommentar zu Hiob*, pt. 2 [*Papyrologische Texte und Abhandlungen* 2. Bonn: Habelt, 1968]: 14–194.
Pap: [13,161]
003 **Commentarii in Job** (7.20c–11), ed. U. Hagedorn, D. Hagedorn and L. Koenen, *Didymos der Blinde. Kommentar zu Hiob*, pt. 3 [*Papyro-*

logische Texte und Abhandlungen 3. Bonn: Habelt, 1968]: 2–220.
Pap: [17,164]

004 **Commentarii in Job** (12–16.2), ed. U. Hagedorn, D. Hagedorn and L. Koenen, *Didymos der Blinde. Kommentar zu Hiob*, pt. 4 [*Papyrologische Texte und Abhandlungen* 22. Bonn: Habelt, in press].
Pap

005 **Commentarii in Ecclesiasten** (5–6), ed. J. Kramer, *Didymos der Blinde. Kommentar zum Ecclesiastes*, pt. 3 [*Papyrologische Texte und Abhandlungen* 13. Bonn: Habelt, 1970]: 2–86.
Pap: [10,537]

006 **Commentarii in Ecclesiasten** (7–8.8), ed. J. Kramer and B. Krebber, *Didymos der Blinde. Kommentar zum Ecclesiastes*, pt. 4 [*Papyrologische Texte und Abhandlungen* 16. Bonn: Habelt, 1972]: 2–154.
Pap: [16,484]

007 **Commentarii in Ecclesiasten** (11–12), ed. G. Binder and L. Liesenborghs, *Didymos der Blinde. Kommentar zum Ecclesiastes*, pt. 6 [*Papyrologische Texte und Abhandlungen* 9. Bonn: Habelt, 1969]: 2–244.
Pap: [16,562]

008 **De trinitate** (lib. 1) [Sp.], ed. J. Hönscheid, *Didymus der Blinde. De trinitate, Buch 1* [*Beiträge zur klassischen Philologie* 44. Meisenheim am Glan: Hain, 1975]: 14–238.
Cf. et 2102 009, 042, 043.
Cod: [24,664]

009 **De trinitate** (lib. 2.1–7) [Sp.], ed. I. Seiler, *Didymus der Blinde. De trinitate, Buch 2, Kapitel 1–7* [*Beiträge zur klassischen Philologie* 52. Meisenheim am Glan: Hain, 1975]: 2–246.
Cf. et 2102 008, 042, 043.
Cod: [23,768]

010 **Commentarii in Zacchariam**, ed. L. Doutreleau, *Didyme l'Aveugle sur Zacharie*, 3 vols. [*Sources chrétiennes* 83, 84, 85. Paris: Cerf, 1962]: **83**:190–412; **84**:426–788; **85**:802–1086.
Cod, Pap: [94,787]

011 **Commentarii in Ecclesiasten** (1.1–8), ed. G. Binde and L. Liesenborghs, *Didymos der Blinde. Kommentar zum Ecclesiastes*, pt. 1 [*Papyrologische Texte und Abhandlungen* 25. Bonn: Habelt, 1979]: 2–240.
Pap

012 **Contra Manichaeos**, MPG 39: 1085–1109.
Cod

013 **Commentarii in Octateuchum et Reges** (fragmenta in catenis), MPG 39: 1112–1116.
Q

014 **Commentarii in Job** (scholia in catenis), MPG 39: 1120–1153.
Q

015 **Fragmenta in Jeremiam** (in catenis), ed. M. Ghisler, *In Ieremiam prophetam commentarii*, 2 vols. Lyon: Durand, 1623: **1**:39a; **2**:704, 754.
Q

016 **Commentarii in Psalmos 20–21**, ed. L. Doutre-

leau, A. Gesché and M. Gronewald, *Didymos der Blinde. Psalmenkommentar*, pt. 1 [*Papyrologische Texte und Abhandlungen* 7. Bonn: Habelt, 1969]: 2–228.
Pap

017 **Commentarii in Psalmos 22–26.10**, ed. M. Gronewald, *Didymos der Blinde. Psalmenkommentar*, pt. 2 [*Papyrologische Texte und Abhandlungen* 4. Bonn: Habelt, 1968]: 2–246.
Pap

018 **Commentarii in Psalmos 29–34**, ed. M. Gronewald, *Didymos der Blinde. Psalmenkommentar*, pt. 3 [*Papyrologische Texte und Abhandlungen* 8. Bonn: Habelt, 1969]: 2–414.
Pap

019 **Commentarii in Psalmos 35–39**, ed. M. Gronewald, *Didymos der Blinde. Psalmenkommentar*, pt. 4 [*Papyrologische Texte und Abhandlungen* 6. Bonn: Habelt, 1969]: 2–314.
Pap

020 **Commentarii in Psalmos 40–44.4**, ed. M. Gronewald, *Didymos der Blinde. Psalmenkommentar*, pt. 5 [*Papyrologische Texte und Abhandlungen* 12. Bonn: Habelt, 1970]: 2–244.
Pap

021 **Fragmenta in Psalmos** (e commentario altero), ed. E. Mühlenberg, *Psalmenkommentare aus der Katenenüberlieferung*, 2 vols. [*Patristische Texte und Studien* 15 & 16. Berlin: De Gruyter, 1:1975; 2:1977]: **1**:121–375; **2**:3–367.
Q

022 **Fragmenta in Proverbia**, MPG 39: 1621–1645.
Q

023 **Fragmentum in Canticum canticorum** (in catenis), ed. J. Meurs, *Eusebii, Polychronii, Pselli in Canticum canticorum expositiones Graece*. Leiden: Meurs, 1617: 19.
Q

025 **Fragmenta in Joannem** (in catenis), ed. J. Reuss, *Johannes-Kommentare aus der griechischen Kirche* [*Texte und Untersuchungen* 89. Berlin: Akademie-Verlag, 1966]: 177–186.
Q

026 **Fragmenta in epistulam ad Romanos** (in catenis), ed. K. Staab, *Pauluskommentar aus der griechischen Kirche aus Katenenhandschriften gesammelt*. Münster: Aschendorff, 1933: 1–6.
Q

027 **Fragmenta in epistulam i ad Corinthios** (in catenis), ed. Staab, *op. cit.*, 6–14.
Q

028 **Fragmenta in epistulam ii ad Corinthios** (in catenis), ed. Staab, *op. cit.*, 14–44.
Q

046 **Fragmenta in epistulam ad Hebraeos** (in catenis), ed. Staab, *op. cit.*, 44–45.
Q

029 **Fragmenta in Acta** (in catenis), ed. J.A. Cramer, *Catenae Graecorum patrum in Novum Testamentum*, vol. 3. Oxford: Oxford University Press, 1838: 21, 25, 34, 38, 40, 46, 48, 52, 65, 66, 69, 74, 79, 90, 94, 100, 112, 116, 119,

121, 128, 132, 139, 146, 147, 152, 153, 157,
166, 167, 168, 175, 187, 189, 191, 198, 215,
216, 230, 251, 269, 291, 295, 299, 304, 307,
309, 312, 317, 320, 331, 333, 335, 337, 341,
347, 367, 378, 394, 413.
Q

030 **In epistulas catholicas brevis enarratio** (fragmenta in catenis), ed. F. Zoepfl, *Didymi Alexandrini in epistulas canonicas brevis enarratio* [*Neutestamentliche Abhandlungen* 4.1. Münster: Aschendorff, 1914]: 1–4, 6–15, 17–25, 27–52, 57–63, 66–69, 73–91, 95–96.
Q

031 **Fragmentum in Osee** (ap. Joannem Damascenum, *Sacra parallela*), MPG 95: 1381.
Q

032 **Ad philosophum** (ap. Joannem Damascenum, *Sacra parallela*), MPG 39: 1109.
Q

033 **De incorporeo** (ap. Joannem Damascenum, *Sacra parallela*), MPG 39: 1109.
Q

034 **Fragmentum in Lot et David** (ap. Joannem Damascenum, *Sacra parallela*), MPG 96: 141.
Q

035 **Fragmenta** (ap. Maximum Confessorem, *Loci communes* [Sp.]), MPG 91: 725, 813, 822, 944, 948, 965, 968.
Q

036 **Fragmenta** (ap. Joannem Damascenum, *Sacra parallela*), MPG 95:1097, 1473, 1548, 1560; 96:61, 101, 236, 360, 537.
Q

037 **Fragmenta** (ap. Antonium Melissam, *Loci communes*), MPG 136: 824, 892, 933, 952–953, 1084.
Q

038 **Fragmenta** (ap. Joannem Damascenum, *Sacra parallela*), MPG 95:1080, 1085, 1097, 1256, 1312, 1353, 1396, 1416; 96:73, 89, 101, 141, 220, 236, 248, 274, 320–321, 324, 325, 340, 344, 348, 372–373, 397, 421, 436.
Q

040 **Dialexis Montanistae et orthodoxi** [Sp.], ed. G. Ficker, "Widerlegung eines Montanisten," *Zeitschrift für Kirchengeschichte* 26 (1905) 449–458.
Cod

041 **In Genesim**, ed. P. Nautin and L. Doutreleau, *Didyme l'Aveugle. Sur la Genèse*, vols. 1–2 [*Sources chrétiennes* 233, 244. Paris: Cerf, 1:1976; 2:1978]: 1:32–332; 2:8–238.
Pap

042 **De trinitate** (lib. 2.8–27) [Sp.], MPG 39: 600–769.
Cf. et 2102 008, 009, 043.
Cod

043 **De trinitate** (lib. 3) [Sp.], MPG 39: 773–992.
Cf. et 2102 008, 009, 042.
Cod

045 **Fragmenta in Isaiam** (ap. Joannem Damasce-

num, *Sacra parallela*, MPG **95**:1093, 1169; **96**:525.
Q

x01 Συμβουλὴ ἠθική (fragmentum ap. Socratem). Socrates, HE 4.23.
Cf. SOCRATES Scr. Eccl. (2057 001).

x02 **De dogmatibus et contra Arianos** [Sp.] (ap. Basilium, *Adversus Eunomium* 4–5 [Sp.]). MPG 29.672–768.
Cf. BASILIUS Theol. (2040 019).

1809 **Claudius DIDYMUS Junior** Gramm.
A.D. 1
001 **Fragmentum** [Dub.], ed. M. Schmidt, *Didymi Chalcenteri grammatici Alexandrini fragmenta quae supersunt omnia*. Leipzig: Teubner, 1854 (repr. Amsterdam: Hakkert, 1964): 349.
Q

0856 **DIEUCHES** Med.
3 B.C.
001 **Fragmentum**, ed. H. Lloyd-Jones and P. Parsons, *Supplementum Hellenisticum*. Berlin: De Gruyter, 1983: 176.
fr. 379.
Q: [8]
x01 **Fragmenta ap. Oribasium**.
CMG **6.1.1**, pp. 101, 102, 292; **6.3**, p. 167.
Cf. ORIBASIUS Med. (0722 001, 004).

1313 **DIEUCHIDAS** Hist.
4 B.C.: Megareus
001 **Testimonium**, FGrH #485: 3B:449.
NQ
002 **Fragmenta**, FGrH #485: 3B:449–451.
Q

2324 **DINARCHUS** Hist.
ante 4 B.C.
001 **Testimonium**, FGrH #465: 3B:402.
NQ

2280 **DINARCHUS** Hist.
4 B.C.?: Delius
001 **Testimonium**, FGrH #399: 3B:292.
NQ
002 **Fragmenta**, FGrH #399: 3B:293.
Q

0029 **DINARCHUS** Orat.
4–3 B.C.: Corinthius, Atheniensis
004 **In Demosthenem**, ed. N.C. Conomis, *Dinarchi orationes cum fragmentis*. Leipzig: Teubner, 1975: 11–54.
Cod: 7,775
005 **In Aristogitonem**, ed. Conomis, *op. cit.*, 54–64.
Cod: 1,831
006 **In Philoclem**, ed. Conomis, *op. cit.*, 65–72.
Cod: 1,430
007 **Fragmenta**, ed. Conomis, *op. cit.*, 73–145.
frr. 1–97.
Q, Pap: 8,491

008 **Fragmenta incertae sedis**, ed. Conomis, *op. cit.*, 145–151.
frr. 3–42.
Q: 935

1314 **DINIAS** Hist.
3 B.C.: Argivus
001 **Testimonium**, FGrH #306: 3B:10.
NQ
002 **Fragmenta**, FGrH #306: 3B:10–13.
Q
003 **Fragmentum**, ed. H.J. Mette, "Die 'Kleinen' griechischen Historiker heute," *Lustrum* 21 (1978) 26.
fr. 3 bis.
Q

1315 **DINOLOCHUS** Comic.
5 B.C.
001 **Fragmentum**, ed. G. Kaibel, *Comicorum Graecorum fragmenta*, vol. 1.1 [*Poetarum Graecorum fragmenta*, vol. 6.1. Berlin: Weidmann, 1899]: 149–150.
fr. 4 + tituli.
Cod: 11
002 **Tituli**, ed. C. Austin, *Comicorum Graecorum fragmenta in papyris reperta*. Berlin: De Gruyter, 1973: 50–51.
fr. 78.
Pap: 23

1316 **DINON** Hist.
4 B.C.
001 **Testimonia**, FGrH #690: 3C:522.
NQ
002 **Fragmenta**, FGrH #690: 3C:522–531.
fr. 29: *P. Oxy.* 15.1802.
Q, Pap

0385 **DIO CASSIUS** Hist.
A.D. 2–3: Nicaeensis
001 **Historiae Romanae**, ed. U.P. Boissevain, *Cassii Dionis Cocceiani historiarum Romanarum quae supersunt*, 3 vols. Berlin: Weidmann, 1:1895; 2:1898; 3:1901 (repr. 1955): 1:1–4, 6–20, 23, 25–27, 30–38, 40–49, 51–65, 69–70, 76–81, 83–88, 90–133, 135, 137–139, 141–149, 153–155, 157–161, 163, 165–168, 172, 174–185, 187, 190–199, 201–204, 206–208, 210–217, 219–224, 227–229, 234, 237–241, 243–245, 251, 253–267, 269–278, 280, 286–288, 290, 292, 295–302, 309–311, 313–314, 318, 321–355, 360–466, 468–539; 2:1–412, 414–441, 443–476, 479–487, 490–492, 494–496, 498–540, 542–544, 546–556, 559–575, 596–615, 617–649, 660, 664–689; 3:1–161, 164–279, 282–476.
Q, Cod: [96,350]
002 **Historiae Romanae** (versio 1 in volumine 1), ed. Boissevain, *op. cit.*, vol. 1, 1–37, 39–95, 97–98, 100–108, 110, 113–191, 194–320, 345.
Q: [56,649]
003 **Historiae Romanae** (versio 1 in volumine 2),

ed. Boissevain, *op. cit.*, vol. 2, 647–648, 660.
Q: [128]
004 **Historiae Romanae** (versio 1 in volumine 3), ed. Boissevain, *op. cit.*, vol. 3, 7–8, 10, 12, 17–21, 27, 51–52, 85–86, 89–99, 103, 105–106, 108–110, 113, 116, 122–123, 154–156, 169–170, 177, 189, 193–195, 214–215, 245, 247–249, 253, 256, 262–265, 267–268, 270–271, 284, 292, 298, 303, 310, 315, 319, 322, 324, 345–346, 367, 375–377, 381–382, 384–385, 390–391, 470.
Q: [6,470]
005 **Historiae Romanae** (versio 2 in volumine 1), ed. Boissevain, *op. cit.*, vol. 1, 1–8, 13–14, 28–29, 51–52, 55–57, 72, 74–75, 87–89, 160, 170, 183, 189, 219–220, 223, 232–233, 235, 251–252, 275, 293, 307–308.
Q: [1,960]
006 **Historiae Romanae** (versio 2 in volumine 2), ed. Boissevain, *op. cit.*, vol. 2, 647–649, 660.
Q: [371]
007 **Historiae Romanae** (versio 2 in volumine 3), ed. Boissevain, *op. cit.*, vol. 3, 19, 27, 51, 86–90, 92, 96–99, 177, 270–271, 390–391.
Q: [669]
008 **Historiae Romanae** (versio 3 in volumine 1), ed. Boissevain, *op. cit.*, vol. 1, 72–74.
Q: [97]
009 **Reliquiae incertae sedis**, ed. Boissevain, *op. cit.*, vol. 1, 356–358.
Q: [473]
010 **Historiae Romanae** (Xiphilini epitome), ed. Boissevain, *op. cit.*, vol. 3, 479–730.
Cod: [122,342]
011 **Historiae Romanae** (Petri Patricii excerpta Vaticana sive Maiana), ed. Boissevain, *op. cit.*, vol. 3, 731–749.
Q: [3,697]
012 **Historiae Romanae** (excerpta Planudea), ed. Boissevain, *op. cit.*, vol. 3, 749–750.
Q: [282]
013 **Historiae Romanae** (Joannis Antiocheni excerpta e Dione derivata), ed. Boissevain, *op. cit.*, vol. 3, 750–762.
Q: [4,959]
014 **Historiae Romanae** (excerpta Salmasiana), ed. Boissevain, *op. cit.*, vol. 3, 763–766.
Q: [1,799]
015 **Historiae Romanae** (excerpta Constantiniana cum Dionis verbis composita), ed. Boissevain, *op. cit.*, vol. 3, 767–775.
Q: [2,024]
016 **Historiae Romanae** (e Photii *Bibliotheca* cod. 71), ed. Boissevain, *op. cit.*, vol. 3, 775–776.
Q: [284]
017 **Testimonia**, FGrH #707: 3C:577–578.
NQ
018 **Fragmenta**, FGrH #707: 3C:578–582.
Q

0612 **DIO CHRYSOSTOMUS** Soph.
A.D. 1–2: Prusensis
Cf. et DIONIS EPISTULAE (1327).

001 **Orationes**, ed. J. von Arnim, *Dionis Prusaensis quem vocant Chrysostomum quae exstant omnia*, vols. 1–2, 2nd edn. Berlin: Weidmann, 1:1893; 2:1896 (repr. 1962): 1:1–338; 2:1–306.
De regno 1 (orat. 1): vol. 1, pp. 1–16.
De regno 2 (orat. 2): vol. 1, pp. 16–33.
De regno 3 (orat. 3): vol. 1, pp. 34–56.
De regno 4 (orat. 4): vol. 1, pp. 56–79.
Libycus mythos (orat. 5): vol. 1, pp. 79–83.
De tyrannide (orat. 6): vol. 1, pp. 83–95.
De virtute (orat. 8): vol. 1, pp. 95–102.
Isthmiaca (orat. 9): vol. 1, pp. 103–107.
De servis (orat. 10): vol. 1, pp. 107–115.
Trojana (orat. 11): vol. 1, pp. 115–154.
De dei cognitione (orat. 12): vol. 1, pp. 155–179.
De exilio (orat. 13): vol. 1, pp. 179–189.
Venator (orat. 7): vol. 1, pp. 189–219.
Rhodiaca (orat. 31): vol. 1, pp. 219–266.
Ad Alexandrinos (orat. 32): vol. 1, pp. 267–297.
Tarsica prior (orat. 33): vol. 1, pp. 297–316.
Tarsica altera (orat. 34): vol. 1, pp. 316–331.
Celaenis Phrygiae (orat. 35): vol. 1, pp. 331–338.
Borysthenitica (orat. 36): vol. 2, pp. 1–16.
Corinthiaca (orat. 37): vol. 2, pp. 17–29.
Ad Nicomedienses (orat. 38): vol. 2, pp. 29–43.
Ad Nicaeenses (orat. 39): vol. 2, pp. 43–46.
De concordia cum Apamensibus (orat. 40): vol. 2, pp. 46–57.
Ad Apamenses (orat. 41): vol. 2, pp. 57–61.
Dialexis (orat. 42): vol. 2, pp. 61–63.
Politica (orat. 43): vol. 2, pp. 63–66.
Gratitudo (orat. 44): vol. 2, pp. 67–70.
Defensio (orat. 45): vol. 2, pp. 70–76.
De tumultu (orat. 46): vol. 2, pp. 76–80.
Contio (orat. 47): vol. 2, pp. 80–87.
In contione (orat. 48): vol. 2, pp. 87–93.
Recusatio magistratus (orat. 49): vol. 2, pp. 93–97.
De administratione (orat. 50): vol. 2, pp. 98–101.
Ad Diodorum (orat. 51): vol. 2, pp. 101–104.
De Philoctetae arcu (orat. 52): vol. 2, pp. 104–109.
De Homero (orat. 53): vol. 2, pp. 109–113.
De Socrate (orat. 54): vol. 2, pp. 113–114.
De Homero et Socrate (orat. 55): vol. 2, pp. 114–120.
De regno (orat. 56): vol. 2, pp. 121–125.
Nestor (orat. 57): vol. 2, pp. 125–129.
Achilles (orat. 58): vol. 2, pp. 129–131.
Philoctetes (orat. 59): vol. 2, pp. 131–134.
Nessus (orat. 60): vol. 2, pp. 134–137.
Chryseis (orat. 61): vol. 2, pp. 137–142.
De regno et tyrannide (orat. 62): vol. 2, pp. 142–144.
De fortuna 1 (orat. 63) [Sp.]: vol. 2, pp. 145–147.
De fortuna 2 (orat. 64) [Sp.]: vol. 2, pp. 147–155.

De fortuna 3 (orat. 65) [Sp.]: vol. 2, pp. 156–160.
De gloria 1 (orat. 66): vol. 2, pp. 160–169.
De gloria 2 (orat. 67): vol. 2, pp. 169–171.
De gloria 3 (orat. 68): vol. 2, pp. 171–174.
De virtute (orat. 69): vol. 2, pp. 174–177.
De philosophia (orat. 70): vol. 2, pp. 177–180.
De philosopho (orat. 71): vol. 2, pp. 181–184.
De habitu (orat. 72): vol. 2, pp. 184–189.
De fide (orat. 73): vol. 2, pp. 189–192.
De diffidentia (orat. 74): vol. 2, pp. 192–201.
De lege (orat. 75): vol. 2, pp. 202–204.
De consuetudine (orat. 76): vol. 2, pp. 205–206.
De invidia (orat. 77/78): vol. 2, pp. 206–219.
De divitiis (orat. 79): vol. 2, pp. 220–222.
De libertate (orat. 80): vol. 2, pp. 222–226.
De servitute et libertate 1 (orat. 14): vol. 2, pp. 227–232.
De servitute et libertate 2 (orat. 15): vol. 2, pp. 232–241.
De aegritudine (orat. 16): vol. 2, pp. 241–244.
De avaritia (orat. 17): vol. 2, pp. 244–250.
De dicendi exercitatione (orat. 18): vol. 2, pp. 250–257.
De audiendi affectione (orat. 19): vol. 2, pp. 257–258.
De secessu (orat. 20): vol. 2, pp. 259–266.
De pulchritudine (orat. 21): vol. 2, pp. 266–271.
De pace et bello (orat. 22): vol. 2, pp. 271–273.
De quod felix sit sapiens (orat. 23): vol. 2, pp. 273–276.
De felicitate (orat. 24): vol. 2, pp. 276–277.
De genio (orat. 25): vol. 2, pp. 278–281.
De consultatione (orat. 26): vol. 2, pp. 281–283.
De compotatione (orat. 27): vol. 2, pp. 283–285.
Melancomas 1 (orat. 29): vol. 2, pp. 286–291.
Melancomas 2 (orat. 28): vol. 2, pp. 292–294.
Charidemus (orat. 30): vol. 2, pp. 295–306.
Cod: [196,034]

002 **Encomium comae**, ed. von Arnim, *op. cit.*, vol. 2, 307–308.
Cod: [436]

003 **Fragmenta**, ed. von Arnim, *op. cit.*, vol. 2, 309–310.
Q: [274]

0443 **DIOCLES** Comic.
5 B.C.

001 **Fragmenta**, ed. T. Kock, *Comicorum Atticorum fragmenta*, vol. 1. Leipzig: Teubner, 1880: 766–769.
frr. 1–14, 16–18 + tituli.
Q: 99

002 **Fragmenta**, ed. A. Meineke, *Fragmenta comicorum Graecorum*, vol. 2.2. Berlin: Reimer, 1840 (repr. De Gruyter, 1970): 838–841.
Q: 87

003 **Fragmentum**, ed. J. Demiańczuk, *Supplementum comicum*. Krakau: Nakładem Akademii,

1912 (repr. Hildesheim: Olms, 1967): 39.
fr. 1.
Q: 2

004 **Fragmenta**, ed. C. Austin, *Comicorum Grae-*
corum fragmenta in papyris reperta. Berlin: De
Gruyter, 1973: 51.
frr. 79–80.
Pap: 6

DIOCLES Gramm.
1 B.C.–A.D. 1
Cf. TYRANNION Junior Gramm. (1611).

2549 **DIOCLES** Hist.
3 B.C.: Peparethius
001 **Testimonia**, FGrH #820: 3C:894–895.
NQ
002 **Titulus**, FGrH #820: 3C:895.
NQ

2470 **DIOCLES** Hist.
3 B.C.?
001 **Fragmenta**, FGrH #693: 3C:532–533.
Q

2206 **DIOCLES** Hist.
Incertum: Rhodius
001 **Fragmentum**, FGrH #302: 3B:5.
Q

1317 **DIOCLES** Math.
3/1 B.C.?
001 **Fragmenta de speculis causticis**, ed. J.L. Heiberg, *Archimedis opera omnia*, vol. 3. Leipzig:
Teubner, 1915 (repr. Stuttgart: 1972): 66–70,
160–176.
Q

0664 **DIOCLES** Med.
4 B.C.: Carystius
001 **Fragmentum**, *P. Ryl.* 1.39.
Pap
x01 **Fragmenta ap. Galenum**.
K6.455, 511–512, 544 in CMG, vol. **5.4.2**, pp.
202–203, 235, 255; K8.185–187; **9**.863;
11.472–474; 12.785, 880; 18.1.7, 519.
Cf. GALENUS Med. (0057 037, 065, 075–076,
092, 095).
x02 **Fragmenta ap. Oribasium**.
CMG, vol. **6.1.1**, pp. 99, 121, 144, 268, 292;
6.2.1, pp. 133, 276; **6.2.2**, pp. 141, 212; **6.3**, p.
166.
Cf. ORIBASIUS Med. (0722 001–004).
x03 **Fragmentum ap. Paulum**.
CMG, vol. 9.1, pp. 68–72.
Cf. PAULUS Med. (0715 001).
x04 **Fragmentum ap. Apollonium**.
CMG, vol. 11.1.1, p. 46.
Cf. APOLLONIUS Med. (0660 001).
x05 **Fragmentum ap. Pseudo-Dioscoridem**.
Sprengel, p. 47.
Cf. Pseudo-DIOSCORIDES Med. (1118 002).
x06 **Fragmentum ap. Erotianum**.

Nachmanson, p. 92.
Cf. EROTIANUS Med. (0716 001).
x07 **Fragmenta ap. Aëtium**.
Placita 5.14.3, 29.2.
Cf. AËTIUS Doxogr. (0528 001).
x08 **Fragmenta ap. Athenaeum**.
Deipnosophistae 2.53d, 61c, 68d; 3.110b;
7.305b, 316c; 15.681b.
Cf. ATHENAEUS Soph. (0008 001).

0884 **DIOCLES** Med.
ante A.D. 2: Chalcedonius
x01 **Fragmentum ap. Galenum**.
K13.87.
Cf. GALENUS Med. (0057 076).

0162 **Julius DIOCLES** Rhet.
A.D. 1: Carystius
001 **Epigrammata**, AG **6**.186; **7**.393; **9**.109; **12**.35.
Q: 163

0444 **DIODORUS** Comic.
3 B.C.: Sinopensis
001 **Fragmenta**, ed. T. Kock, *Comicorum Atti-*
corum fragmenta, vol. 2. Leipzig: Teubner,
1884: 420–422.
frr. 1–3 + tituli.
Q: 310
002 **Fragmenta**, ed. A. Meineke, *Fragmenta comi-*
corum Graecorum, vol. 3. Berlin: Reimer, 1840
(repr. De Gruyter, 1970): 543–546.
Q: 308

2652 **DIODORUS** Eleg.
ante 1 B.C.: Elaita
001 **Titulus**, ed. H. Lloyd-Jones and P. Parsons,
Supplementum Hellenisticum. Berlin: De Gruyter, 1983: 177.
fr. 381.
NQ: [1]

0163 **DIODORUS** Epigr.
fiq Diodorus Sardianus Rhet. vel Diodorus
Tarsensis Gramm. vel Diodorus Zonas Sardianus Rhet.
1 B.C./A.D. 1
Cf. et DIODORUS Sardianus Rhet. (0165).
Cf. et DIODORUS Tarsensis Gramm. (0166).
Cf. et DIODORUS ZONAS Sardianus Rhet.
(0164).
001 **Epigrammata**, AG 5.122; 7.38, 40, 74, 370,
624, 632.
Q: 214

0166 **DIODORUS** Gramm.
1 B.C.: Tarsensis
Cf. et DIODORUS Epigr. (0163).
001 **Epigrammata**, AG **6**.348(?); 7.235, 700–701.
Q: 145

2315 **DIODORUS** Hist.
ante 3 B.C.?

001 **Fragmentum**, FGrH #452: 3B:381.
Q

060 **DIODORUS SICULUS** Hist.
1 B.C.: Siculus
001 **Bibliotheca historica** (lib. 1–20), ed. F. Vogel
and K.T. Fischer (post I. Bekker & L. Dindorf), *Diodori bibliotheca historica*, 5 vols., 3rd
edn. Leipzig: Teubner, 1:1888; 2:1890; 3:1893;
4–5:1906 (repr. Stuttgart: 1964): 1:1–533; 2:1–
461; 3:1–497; 4:1–426; 5:1–336.
Cod: 419,932
003 **Bibliotheca historica** (lib. 21–40), ed. F.R. Walton, *Diodorus of Sicily*, vols. 11–12. Cambridge, Mass.: Harvard University Press,
11:1957 (repr. 1968); 12:1967: 11:2–456; 12:2–
294.
Cod: 65,583
002 **Fragmenta sedis incertae**, ed. Walton, *op. cit.*,
vol. 12, 296–302.
frr. 1–14.
Q: 539

265 **DIODORUS** Perieg.
4–3 B.C.
001 **Fragmenta**, FGrH #372: 3B:233–239.
Q

681 **DIODORUS** Phil.
4 B.C.: Aspendius
001 **Fragmentum**, ed. F.W.A. Mullach, *Fragmenta
philosophorum Graecorum*, vol. 2. Paris: Didot,
1867 (repr. Aalen: Scientia, 1968): 112.
Q

383 **DIODORUS** Phil.
2 B.C.: Tyrius
001 **Fragmentum**, ed. F. Wehrli, *Hieronymus von
Rhodos. Kritolaus und seine Schüler* [*Die Schule
des Aristoteles*, vol. 10, 2nd edn. Basel:
Schwabe, 1969]: 88. fr. 4h.
Q

165 **DIODORUS** Rhet.
fiq Diodorus Sardianus Junior
1 B.C.: Sardianus
Cf. et DIODORUS Epigr. (0163).
001 **Epigrammata**, AG 6.243(?), 245(?); 9.60, 219,
405, 776.
Q: 200
002 **Titulus**, ed. H. Lloyd-Jones and P. Parsons,
Supplementum Hellenisticum. Berlin: De Gruyter, 1983: 178.
fr. 384.
NQ: [4]

318 **DIODORUS** Rhet.
Incertum
001 **Fragmentum de viris duobus**, ed. H. Hinck,
Polemonis declamationes quae exstant duae.
Leipzig: Teubner, 1873: 51–55.
Cod: [752]

4134 **DIODORUS** Scr. Eccl.
A.D. 4: Tarsensis
Bibliography in progress
005 **Fragmenta in epistulam ad Romanos** (in catenis), ed. K. Staab, *Pauluskommentar aus der
griechischen Kirche aus Katenenhandschriften
gesammelt*. Münster: Aschendorff, 1933: 83–
112.
Q

0857 **DIODORUS CRONUS** Med.
1 B.C.: Iasensis
x01 **Fragmenta ap. Galenum**.
K12.834; 13.248, 361, 857.
Cf. GALENUS Med. (0057 076–077).

0164 **DIODORUS ZONAS** Rhet.
1 B.C.: Sardianus
Cf. et DIODORUS Epigr. (0163).
001 **Epigrammata**, AG 6.22, 98, 106; 7.365, 404,
627(?); 9.226, 312, 556; 11.43.
AG 6.42: Cf. ANONYMI EPIGRAMMATICI
(0138 001).
AG 6.256: Cf. ANTIPATER Epigr. (0114 001).
Q: 374

2128 **DIOGENES** Epigr.
A.D. 6: Amisenus
001 **Epigramma**, AG 7.613.
Q: 41

2348 **DIOGENES** Hist.
post 4 B.C.?: Sicyonius
001 **Testimonium**, FGrH #503: 3B:481.
NQ

2469 **DIOGENES** Hist.
3 B.C.?
001 **Fragmentum**, FGrH #692: 3C:532.
Q

2328 **DIOGENES** Hist.
vel Diogenianus
A.D. 4–5?: Cyzicenus
001 **Testimonium**, FGrH #474: 3B:433.
NQ
002 **Fragmenta**, FGrH #474: 3B:433–434.
Q

0859 **DIOGENES** Med.
1 B.C.–A.D. 1
x01 **Fragmenta ap. Galenum**.
K12.686; 13.313.
Cf. GALENUS Med. (0057 076).
x02 **Fragmenta ap. Aëtium** (lib. 2–3).
CMG, vol. 8.1, pp. 166, 301.
Cf. AËTIUS Med. (0718 002–003).

1319 **DIOGENES** Phil.
5 B.C.: Apolloniates
001 **Testimonia**, ed. H. Diels and W. Kranz, *Die
Fragmente der Vorsokratiker*, vol. 2, 6th edn.

Berlin: Weidmann, 1952 (repr. Dublin: 1966):
51–58.
test. 1–33.
NQ

002 **Fragmenta**, ed. Diels and Kranz, *op. cit.*, 59–66.
frr. 1–10.
Q

2314 **DIOGENES** Phil.
5 B.C.: Smyrnaeus
001 **Testimonia**, ed. H. Diels and W. Kranz, *Die Fragmente der Vorsokratiker*, vol. 2, 6th edn. Berlin: Weidmann, 1952 (repr. Dublin: 1966): 235.
test. 1–2.
NQ

1320 **DIOGENES** Phil.
2 B.C.: Babylonius
001 **Fragmenta**, ed. J. von Arnim, *Stoicorum veterum fragmenta*, vol. 3. Leipzig: Teubner, 1903 (repr. Stuttgart: 1968): 210–243.
Q

1321 **DIOGENES** Phil.
A.D. 2: Oenoandensis
008 **Fragmenta**, ed. C.W. Chilton, *Diogenis Oenoandensis fragmenta*. Leipzig: Teubner, 1967: 1–93.
Epigr: [7,903]
001 **Fragmenta** (NF 1–4), ed. M.F. Smith, "Fragments of Diogenes of Oenoanda discovered and rediscovered," *American Journal of Archaeology* 74.1 (1970) 57, 59, 61–62.
Epigr: [339]
002 **Fragmenta** (NF 5–11, 14–16, HK 68), ed. M.F. Smith, "New fragments of Diogenes of Oenoanda," *American Journal of Archaeology* 75.4 (1971) 359–360, 366–367, 370, 372–374, 376, 382–383, 385–388.
Epigr: [1,203]
003 **Fragmenta** (NF 17–18), ed. M.F. Smith, "Two new fragments of Diogenes of Oenoanda," *Journal of Hellenic Studies* 92 (1972) 149–150, 154.
Epigr: [180]
004 **Fragmenta** (NF 19–31), ed. M.F. Smith, *Thirteen new fragments of Diogenes of Oenoanda* [*Österreichische Akademie der Wissenschaften*, Philosoph.-hist. Kl., Denkschriften, Bd. 117. Vienna: Österreichische Akademie der Wissenschaften, 1974]: 13, 17–18, 21–22, 26, 29, 33, 38–40, 42–44.
Epigr: [560]
005 **Fragmenta** (NF 12–13), ed. Smith, *op. cit.*, 45–46.
Epigr: [108]
006 **Fragmenta** (NF 32–38), ed. M. Smith, "Seven new fragments of Diogenes of Oenoanda," *Hermathena* 118 (1974) 113–114, 117, 120, 124, 126, 128.
Epigr: [145]

007 **Fragmenta** (NF 39–51), ed. M.F. Smith, "More new fragments of Diogenes of Oenoanda," *Cahiers de Philologie* 1 (1976) 286–288, 295–296, 298, 301–303, 306–311, 313.
Epigr: [697]
009 **Fragmenta** (NF 52–106), ed. M.F. Smith, "Fifty-five new fragments of Diogenes of Oenoanda," *Anatolian studies* 28 (1978) 46–90.
Epigr
010 **Fragmenta** (NF 107–114), ed. M.F. Smith, "Eight new fragments of Diogenes of Oenoanda," *Anatolian studies* 29 (1979) 71–85.
Epigr

0334 **DIOGENES** Phil. et Trag.
4 B.C.: Sinopensis
Cf. et DIOGENIS SINOPENSIS EPISTULAE (1325).
001 **Fragmenta**, ed. B. Snell, *Tragicorum Graecorum fragmenta*, vol. 1. Göttingen: Vandenhoeck & Ruprecht, 1971: 256–258.
frr. 1h, 2–7.
Q: [191]
x01 **Epigramma**.
AG 7.66: Cf. HONESTUS Epigr. (1440 001).

0320 **DIOGENES** Trag.
5 B.C.: Atheniensis
001 **Fragmentum**, ed. B. Snell, *Tragicorum Graecorum fragmenta*, vol. 1. Göttingen: Vandenhoeck & Ruprecht, 1971: 185.
fr. 1.
Q: [59]

0004 **DIOGENES LAERTIUS** Biogr.
A.D. 3: Laertius
001 **Vitae philosophorum**, ed. H.S. Long, *Diogenis Laertii vitae philosophorum*, 2 vols. Oxford: Clarendon Press, 1964 (repr. 1966): 1:1–246; 2:247–565.
Cod: 114,802
002 **Epigrammata**, AG 7.57, 85, 87–88, 91–92, 95–98, 101–102, 104–116, 118, 121–124, 126–127, 129–130, 133, 620, 706, 744.
AG 7.89: Cf. CALLIMACHUS Philol. (0533 004).
Q: 1,120
x01 **Epigrammata** (*App. Anth.*).
Epigrammata sepulcralia: 2.380–381.
Epigrammata demonstrativa: 3.128–129.
Epigramma exhortatorium et supplicatorium: 4.46.
Epigrammata irrisoria: 5.34–42.
Problemata: 7.19–20.
App. Anth. 2.380–381: Cf. EPIGRAMMATICI in *App. Anth.* (7052 002).
App. Anth. 3.128–129: Cf. EPIGRAMMATICI in *App. Anth.* (7052 003).
App. Anth. 4.46: Cf. EPIGRAMMATICI in *App. Anth.* (7052 004).
App. Anth. 5.34–42: Cf. EPIGRAMMATICI in *App. Anth.* (7052 005).

App. Anth. 7.19-20: Cf. EPIGRAMMATICI in
App. Anth. (7052 007).

0097 <DIOGENIANUS> Paroemiogr.
A.D. 2: Heracleensis
001 **Paroemiae**, ed. E.L. von Leutsch and F.G.
Schneidewin, *Corpus paroemiographorum
Graecorum*, vol. 1. Göttingen: Vandenhoeck &
Ruprecht, 1839 (repr. Hildesheim: Olms,
1965): 177-320.
Cod: [11,515]
002 **Paroemiae** (litterarum ordine), ed. E.L. von
Leutsch, *Corpus paroemiographorum Grae-
corum*, vol. 2. Göttingen: Vandenhoeck &
Ruprecht, 1851 (repr. Hildesheim: Olms,
1958): 1-52.
Cod: [5,132]

1322 **DIOGENIANUS** Phil.
A.D. 2
001 **Fragmenta**, ed. A. Gercke, "Chrysippea,"
Jahrbücher für classische Philologie, suppl. 14
(1885) 748-755.
frr. 1-4.
Q: [2,663]

1325 *DIOGENIS SINOPENSIS EPISTULAE*
Incertum
Cf. et DIOGENES Phil. et Trag. (0334).
001 **Epistulae**, ed. R. Hercher, *Epistolographi
Graeci*. Paris: Didot, 1873 (repr. Amsterdam:
Hakkert, 1965): 235-258.
Q: [9,169]

1952 **DIOGNETUS** Hist.
post 4 B.C.: fort. Erythraeus
001 **Testimonia**, FGrH #120: 2B:626.
NQ
002 **Fragmentum**, FGrH #120: 2B:626.
Q

0860 **DIOMEDES** Med.
ante A.D. 2
x01 **Fragmenta ap. Galenum**.
K12.759, 771.
Cf. GALENUS Med. (0057 076).

0861 **DION** Med.
ante A.D. 1
x01 **Fragmentum ap. Oribasium**.
CMG, vol. 6.3, p. 103.
Cf. ORIBASIUS Med. (0722 004).

1327 *DIONIS EPISTULAE*
Incertum
Cf. et DIO CHRYSOSTOMUS Soph. (0612).
001 **Epistulae**, ed. R. Hercher, *Epistolographi
Graeci*. Paris: Didot, 1873 (repr. Amsterdam:
Hakkert, 1965): 259.
Cod: [275]

0330 **DIONYSIUS I** <Trag.>
4 B.C.: Syracusanus

001 **Fragmenta**, ed. B. Snell, *Tragicorum Graecorum fragmenta*, vol. 1. Göttingen: Vandenhoeck & Ruprecht, 1971: 242-246.
frr. 1-2, 3-12.
Q: [191]
002 **Testimonium**, FGrH #557: 3B:568.
NQ

0247 **DIONYSIUS II** <Eleg.>
4 B.C.: Syracusanus
001 **Fragmenta**, ed. M.L. West, *Iambi et elegi
Graeci*, vol. 2. Oxford: Clarendon Press, 1972:
60-61.
frr. 1-2.
Q: [16]

1323 **Aelius DIONYSIUS** Attic.
A.D. 2: Halicarnassensis
001 'Αττικὰ ὀνόματα, ed. H. Erbse, *Untersuchungen zu den attizistischen Lexika* [*Abhandlungen der deutschen Akademie der Wissenschaften zu Berlin*, Philosoph.-hist. Kl. Berlin:
Akademie-Verlag, 1950]: 95-151.
Q: [16,733]

0445 **DIONYSIUS** Comic.
5/4 B.C.: Sinopensis
001 **Fragmenta**, ed. T. Kock, *Comicorum Atticorum fragmenta*, vol. 2. Leipzig: Teubner,
1884: 423-428.
frr. 1-11.
Q: 597
002 **Fragmenta**, ed. A. Meineke, *Fragmenta comicorum Graecorum*, vol. 3. Berlin: Reimer, 1840
(repr. De Gruyter, 1970): 547-549, 551-555.
Q: 554
003 **Fragmentum**, ed. Meineke, *op. cit.*, vol. 5.1
(1857; repr. 1970): ccxxi.
Q: [6]

0246 **DIONYSIUS** Eleg.
5 B.C.: Chalcus
001 **Fragmenta**, ed. M.L. West, *Iambi et elegi
Graeci*, vol. 2. Oxford: Clarendon Press, 1972:
58-60.
frr. 1-6.
Q: [165]

1326 **DIONYSIUS** Epic.
fiq Dionysius Perieg. vel Dionysius Samius
Hist.
ante A.D. 3
Cf. et DIONYSIUS Perieg. (0084).
Cf. et DIONYSIUS Samius Hist. (1331).
001 **Fragmenta**, ed. E. Heitsch, *Die griechischen
Dichterfragmente der römischen Kaiserzeit*, vol.
1, 2nd edn. Göttingen: Vandenhoeck & Ruprecht, 1963: 61-77.
frr. 1-28.
Q, Pap: [1,434]

2619 **DIONYSIUS** Epic.
Incertum: Corinthius

001 **Tituli**, ed. H. Lloyd-Jones and P. Parsons, *Supplementum Hellenisticum*. Berlin: De Gruyter, 1983: 178.
frr. 387–388.
NQ: [4]

0169 **DIONYSIUS** Epigr.
3 B.C.?: Cyzicenus
001 **Epigramma**, AG 7.78.
AG 7.462: Cf. DIONYSIUS Epigr. (0170 001).
Q: 40

0170 **DIONYSIUS** Epigr.
3 B.C.?: Rhodius
001 **Epigrammata**, AG 7.462(?), 716.
AG 7.51: Cf. ADAEUS Epigr. (0102 001).
AG 7.717: Cf. ANONYMI EPIGRAMMATICI (0138 001).
Q: 50

0168 **DIONYSIUS** Epigr.
fiq Dionysius Sophista
A.D. 2?: Andrius
Cf. et DIONYSIUS Sophista <Epigr.> (0171).
001 **Epigramma**, AG 7.533.
Q: 20

0167 **DIONYSIUS** Epigr.
Incertum
001 **Epigrammata**, AG 6.3; 12.108.
AG 9.523: Cf. ANONYMI EPIGRAMMATICI (0138 001).
Q: 53

0083 **DIONYSIUS** Geogr.
A.D. 2: Byzantius
001 **Per Bosporum navigatio**, ed. K. Müller, *Geographi Graeci minores*, vol. 2. Paris: Didot, 1861 (repr. Hildesheim: Olms, 1965): 1–2.
Cod: [219]
002 **Titulus**, ed. H. Lloyd-Jones and P. Parsons, *Supplementum Hellenisticum*. Berlin: De Gruyter, 1983: 178.
fr. 386.
NQ: [2]

0069 **DIONYSIUS** Geogr.
A.D. 2?
001 **Descriptio Graeciae**, ed. K. Müller, *Geographi Graeci minores*, vol. 1. Paris: Didot, 1855 (repr. Hildesheim: Olms, 1965): 238–243.
Q: [941]

2466 **DIONYSIUS** Hist.
5 B.C.: Milesius
001 **Testimonia**, FGrH #687: 3C:410–411.
NQ
002 **Fragmenta**, FGrH #687: 3C:411.
Q

2257 **DIONYSIUS** Hist.
5–4 B.C.

001 **Testimonium**, FGrH #357: 3B:217.
NQ

1328 **DIONYSIUS** Hist.
4 B.C.?: Chalcidensis
001 **Fragmenta**, FHG 4: 393–396.
Q

1324 **DIONYSIUS** Hist.
4–3 B.C.?: Argivus
001 **Fragmentum**, FGrH #308: 3B:14.
Q

2538 **DIONYSIUS** Hist.
post 4 B.C.?: Olbianus
001 **Fragmentum**, FGrH #804: 3C:842.
Q

2483 **DIONYSIUS** Hist.
3 B.C.
001 **Testimonia**, FGrH #717: 3C:641.
NQ
002 **Fragmentum**, FGrH #717: 3C:641–642.
Q

1331 **DIONYSIUS** Hist.
3/2 B.C.?: Samius
Cf. et DIONYSIUS Epic. (1326).
001 **Testimonia**, FGrH #15: 1A:178.
NQ
002 **Fragmenta**, FGrH #15: 1A:178–180.
Q

1881 **DIONYSIUS** Hist.
2 B.C.: Scytobrachion
001 **Testimonia**, FGrH #32: 1A:228.
NQ
002 **Fragmenta**, FGrH #32: 1A:228–257.
Q
003 **Fragmentum** (*P. Mich.* 1316), ed. H.J. Mette, "Die 'Kleinen' griechischen Historiker heute," *Lustrum* 21 (1978) 8.
fr. 14 bis.
Pap

2446 **DIONYSIUS** Hist.
2 B.C./A.D. 1?
001 **Fragmentum**, FGrH #653: 3C:205.
Q

2354 **DIONYSIUS** Hist.
Incertum: Rhodius
001 **Testimonium**, FGrH #511: 3B:488.
NQ

2390 **DIONYSIUS** Hist.
Incertum: Siculus
001 **Fragmentum**, FGrH #567: 3B:659.
Q

0793 **DIONYSIUS** Med.
3/1 B.C.: Aegaeus

x01 **Fragmenta.**
Photius, *Bibliotheca* 211.
Cf. PHOTIUS Scr. Eccl. (4040 001).

865 **DIONYSIUS** Med.
A.D. 2?: Samius
x01 **Fragmentum ap. Galenum.**
K13.745–746.
Cf. GALENUS Med. (0057 077).

864 **DIONYSIUS** Med.
ante A.D. 4: fort. Hierapolitanus
x01 **Fragmentum ap. Oribasium.**
CMG, vol. 6.2.2, p. 281.
Cf. ORIBASIUS Med. (0722 003).

084 **DIONYSIUS** Perieg.
A.D. 2
Cf. et DIONYSIUS Epic. (1326).
001 **Orbis descriptio,** ed. K. Müller, *Geographi Graeci minores,* vol. 2. Paris: Didot, 1861 (repr. Hildesheim: Olms, 1965): 104–176.
Cod: [7,757]
002 **Lithiaca vel lithica** (fragmenta), ed. Müller, *op. cit.,* xxvi.
Q
003 **Ixeuticon** *sive* **De aucupio,** ed. A. Garzya, *Dionysii ixeuticon seu de aucupio libri tres in epitomen metro solutam redacti.* Leipzig: Teubner, 1963: 1–49.
Cod

185 **DIONYSIUS** Phil.
3 B.C.: Heracleota
001 **Fragmenta,** ed. J. von Arnim, *Stoicorum veterum fragmenta,* vol. 1. Leipzig: Teubner, 1905 (repr. Stuttgart: 1968): 93–96.
Q

683 **DIONYSIUS** Poeta
A.D. 2: Magnes
x01 **Epigramma sepulcrale.**
App. Anth. 2.339: Cf. EPIGRAMMATICI in *App. Anth.* (7052 002).

329 **DIONYSIUS** Scr. Eccl.
A.D. 2: Corinthius
001 **Fragmenta,** ed. M.J. Routh, *Reliquiae sacrae,* vol. 1, 2nd edn. Oxford: Oxford University Press, 1846 (repr. Hildesheim: Olms, 1974): 179–183.
Epistula ad Romanos: pp. 179–181.
De reliquis septem epistulis: pp. 181–183.
Q: [675]

952 **DIONYSIUS** Scr. Eccl.
A.D. 3: Alexandrinus
001 **Epistulae,** ed. C.L. Feltoe, *The letters and other remains of Dionysius of Alexandria.* Cambridge: Cambridge University Press, 1904: 5–21, 23–36, 38–40, 44–46, 49–64, 66–91, 94–105.
Ad Fabium Antiochenum: pp. 5–21.

Ad Germanum: pp. 23–36.
Ad Novatianum: pp. 38–39.
Ad Cornelium: p. 40.
Ad Stephanum Romanum: pp. 44–46.
Ad Xystum (Sixtum II) Romanum: pp. 49–52, 56–59.
Ad Philemonem presbyterum Romanum: pp. 52–55.
Ad Dionysium Romanum: pp. 55–56.
Ad Colonem (vel Cononem): pp. 60–62.
De paenitentia (fragmenta duo): pp. 62–64.
Ad Dometium et Didymum: pp. 66–69.
Ad Hermammonem: pp. 70–78.
Ad Alexandrinos: pp. 80–84.
Ad Hieracem: pp. 85–89.
Ex epistula secunda: p. 90.
Ex epistula quarta festali: p. 91.
Ad Basilidem: pp. 94–105.
Q
002 **Fragmenta,** ed. Feltoe, *op. cit.,* 108–126, 131–164, 182–208, 210–229, 231–260.
De promissionibus: pp. 108–126.
De natura (adversus Epicureos): pp. 131–164.
Refutatio et apologia: pp. 182–198.
In Origenem [Dub.]: pp. 199–200.
In Job [Dub.]: pp. 201–208.
In Ecclesiasten [Dub.]: pp. 210–227.
In Canticum canticorum [Dub.]: pp. 228–229.
In Lucam [Sp.]: pp. 231–250.
In Acta apostolorum: p. 251.
In epistulam ad Romanos: p. 251.
In epistulam Jacobi [Dub.]: pp. 252–253.
In Apocalypsem [Dub.]: p. 253.
Ad Aphrodisium: pp. 254–256.
De gymnasio: p. 256.
De matrimonio: p. 257.
Fragmenta varia [Dub.]: pp. 257–260.
Q
003 **Ad Heuresium et Pasicriten** (fragmentum), ed. W.A. Bienert, "Neue Fragmente des Dionysius und des Petrus von Alexandrien aus Cod. Vatop. 236," Κληρονομία 5 (1973) 309.
Cod
004 **Commentarii in Ecclesiasten** (fragmenta duo), ed. Bienert, *op. cit.,* 310.
Cf. et 2952 002.
Cod
005 **Epistula ad Theodosium monachum,** MPG 78: 205–208.
Cod
006 **Epistula ad Ursenuphium lectorem,** MPG 78: 901–904.
Cod
007 **Epistula ad Paulum Samosatenum,** ed. E. Schwartz, "Eine fingierte Korrespondenz mit Paulus dem Samosatener," *Sitzungsberichte der bayerischen Akademie der Wissenschaften,* Philosoph.-philol. und hist. Kl., Heft 3 (1927) 3–9.
Cod
x01 **Quaestiones et responsiones.**

Feltoe, pp. 259-260.
Cf. 2952 002.

2953 **DIONYSIUS** Scr. Eccl.
A.D. 3: Romanus
001 **Epistula ad Dionysium Alexandrinum**, ed.
C.L. Feltoe, *The letters and other remains of
Dionysius of Alexandria*. Cambridge: Cam-
bridge University Press, 1904: 176-182.
Q

0350 **<DIONYSIUS>** Trag. vel Comic.
Incertum: Scymnaeus
001 **Fragmentum**, ed. B. Snell, *Tragicorum Graecorum fragmenta*, vol. 1. Göttingen: Vandenhoeck & Ruprecht, 1971: 320.
fr. 1.
Q: [8]

0862 **DIONYSIUS CYRTUS** Med.
ante A.D. 1
x01 **Fragmentum ap. Galenum**.
K13.928.
Cf. GALENUS Med. (0057 077).

0863 **DIONYSIUS Empiricus** Med.
1 B.C.: fort. Milesius
x01 **Fragmenta ap. Galenum**.
K12.741-742, 760, 835.
Cf. GALENUS Med. (0057 076).

0081 **DIONYSIUS HALICARNASSENSIS** Rhet. et
Hist.
1 B.C.: Halicarnassensis
Cf. et DIONYSIUS Sophista <Epigr.> (0171).
001 **Antiquitates Romanae**, ed. K. Jacoby, *Dionysii
Halicarnasei antiquitatum Romanarum quae
supersunt*, 4 vols. Leipzig: Teubner, 1:1885;
2:1888; 3:1891; 4:1905 (repr. Stuttgart: 1967):
1:1-403; 2:1-408; 3:1-400; 4:1-336.
Cod: 295,473
002 **De antiquis oratoribus**, ed. H. Usener and L.
Radermacher, *Dionysii Halicarnasei quae exstant*, vol. 5. Leipzig: Teubner, 1899 (repr.
Stuttgart: 1965): 3-7.
Cod: 914
003 **De Lysia**, ed. Usener and Radermacher, *op.
cit.*, vol. 5, 8-53.
Cod: 8,007
004 **De Isocrate**, ed. Usener and Radermacher, *op.
cit.*, vol. 5, 54-92.
Cod: 6,645
005 **De Isaeo**, ed. Usener and Radermacher, *op.
cit.*, vol. 5, 93-124.
Cod: 5,459
006 **De Demosthenis dictione**, ed. Usener and Radermacher, *op. cit.*, vol. 5, 127-252.
Cod: 22,970
007 **Libri secundi de antiquis oratoribus reliquiae**,
ed. Usener and Radermacher, *op. cit.*, vol. 5,
253-254.
Q: 248

008 **Ad Ammaeum**, ed. Usener and Radermacher,
op. cit., vol. 5, 257-279.
Cod: 3,620
009 **De Dinarcho**, ed. Usener and Radermacher,
op. cit., vol. 5, 297-321.
Cod: 4,438
010 **De Thucydide**, ed. Usener and Radermacher,
op. cit., vol. 5, 325-418.
Cod: 17,529
011 **De Thucydidis idiomatibus** (epistula ad Ammaeum), ed. Usener and Radermacher, *op. cit.*,
vol. 5, 421-438.
Cod: 2,720
012 **De compositione verborum**, ed. Usener and
Radermacher, *op. cit.*, vol. 6 (1929; repr. 1965):
3-143.
Cod: 21,690
013 **De compositione verborum** (epitome), ed.
Usener and Radermacher, *op. cit.*, vol. 6, 145-
194.
Cod: 9,985
014 **De imitatione** (fragmenta), ed. Usener and
Radermacher, *op. cit.*, vol. 6, 197, 200, 202-
216.
frr. 1-3, 6-6a, 9-10.
Q: 2,178
015 **Epistula ad Pompeium Geminum**, ed. Usener
and Radermacher, *op. cit.*, vol. 6, 221-248.
Cod: 4,569
016 **Ars rhetorica** [Sp.], ed. Usener and Radermacher, *op. cit.*, vol. 6, 255-292, 295-387.
Cod: 23,725
017 **Testimonium**, FGrH #251: 2B:1146.
NQ
018 **Fragmenta**, FGrH #251: 2B:1146-1151.
Q

2620 **DIONYSIUS IAMBUS** Gramm. et Poeta
3 B.C.
001 **Fragmentum**, ed. H. Lloyd-Jones and P. Parsons, *Supplementum Hellenisticum*. Berlin: De
Gruyter, 1983: 179.
fr. 389.
Q: [5]
x01 **Fragmentum de dialectis** (ap. Athenaeum).
Deipnosophistae 7.284b.
Cf. ATHENAEUS Soph. (0008 001).

0171 **DIONYSIUS Sophista** <Epigr.>
fiq Dionysius Halicarnassensis Rhet. et Hist.
A.D. 2?
Cf. et DIONYSIUS Epigr. (0168).
Cf. et DIONYSIUS HALICARNASSENSIS Rhet.
et Hist. (0081).
001 **Epigrammata**, AG 5.81; 11.182.
AG 5.82-83: Cf. ANONYMI EPIGRAMMATICI
(0138 001).
AG 10.38: Cf. TIMON Phil. (1735 002).
AG 12.60: Cf. MELEAGER Epigr. (1492 001).
AG 15.35: Cf. THEOPHANES Confessor Hist.
(4046 002).
Q: 33

0063 **DIONYSIUS THRAX** Gramm.
2 B.C.: Alexandrinus

001 **Ars grammatica**, ed. G. Uhlig, *Grammatici Graeci*, vol. 1.1. Leipzig: Teubner, 1883 (repr. Hildesheim: Olms, 1965): 5–100.
Cf. et ANONYMI GRAMMATICI (0072 001).
Cod: 3,536

002 **Testimonium**, FGrH #512: 3B:488.
NQ

003 **Fragmentum**, FGrH #512: 3B:488.
Q

004 **Fragmenta**, ed. K. Linke, *Die Fragmente des Grammatikers Dionysios Thrax* [*Sammlung griechischer und lateinischer Grammatiker 3.* Berlin: De Gruyter, 1977]: 13–33.
Q, Pap

1909 **DIONYSODORUS** Hist.
4 B.C.?: Boeotus

001 **Testimonium**, FGrH #68: 2A:35.
NQ

002 **Fragmentum**, FGrH #68: 2A:35.
Q

2574 **DIONYSOPHANES** Hist.
ante A.D. 3

001 **Fragmenta**, FGrH #856: 3C:943.
Q

0172 **DIOPHANES** Epigr.
1 B.C.: Myrinus

001 **Epigramma**, AG 5.309.
Q: 12

0395 **DIOPHANTUS** Comic.
Incertum

001 **Fragmentum**, ed. T. Kock, *Comicorum Atticorum fragmenta*, vol. 3. Leipzig: Teubner, 1888: 375.
fr. 1.
Q: 5

002 **Fragmenta**, ed. A. Meineke, *Fragmenta comicorum Graecorum*, vol. 1. Berlin: Reimer, 1839 (repr. De Gruyter, 1970): 492.
Q

2712 **DIOPHANTUS** Epigr.
Incertum: Atheniensis

x01 **Epigramma exhortatorium et supplicatorium.**
App. Anth. 4.52: Cf. EPIGRAMMATICI in *App. Anth.* (7052 004).

2539 **DIOPHANTUS** Hist.
3 B.C.?

001 **Testimonium**, FGrH #805: 3C:842.
NQ

002 **Fragmenta**, FGrH #805: 3C:842–843.
Q

2039 **DIOPHANTUS** Math.
A.D. 3: Alexandrinus

001 **Arithmeticorum libri sex**, ed. P. Tannery, *Dio-phanti Alexandrini opera omnia*, vol. 1. Leipzig: Teubner, 1893 (repr. Stuttgart: 1974): 2–448.
Cod: [49,331]

002 **De polygonis numeris**, ed. Tannery, *op. cit.*, vol. 1, 450–480.
Cod: [3,661]

003 **Fragmentum** (Cod. Paris. suppl. gr. 387, fol. 181r) [Sp.], ed. Tannery, *op. cit.*, vol. 2 (1895; repr. 1974): 3.
Cod: [94]

004 **Fragmentum** (Cod. Paris. 453) [Sp.], ed. Tannery, *op. cit.*, vol. 2, 3–15.
Cod: [2,644]

005 **Fragmentum** (Cod. Paris. gr. 2448) [Sp.], ed. Tannery, *op. cit.*, vol. 2, 15–31.
Cod: [3,349]

x01 **Problema.**
App. Anth. 7.3(?): Cf. EPIGRAMMATICI in *App. Anth.* (7052 007).

0867 **DIOPHANTUS** Med.
ante A.D. 1: Lycius

x01 **Fragmenta ap. Galenum.**
K12.845; 13.281, 507, 805.
Cf. GALENUS Med. (0057 076–078).

2621 **DIOPHILUS vel DIOPHILA** Poeta
4–3 B.C.?

001 **Fragmentum**, ed. H. Lloyd-Jones and P. Parsons, *Supplementum Hellenisticum*. Berlin: De Gruyter, 1983: 179–180.
fr. 391: *P. Oxy.* 20.2258c, fr. 1.
Pap: [53]

0173 **DIOSCORIDES** Epigr.
3 B.C.: Alexandrinus

001 **Epigrammata**, AG 5.52–56, 138, 193; 6.126, 220, 290; 7.31, 37, 76, 162, 166–167, 178, 229, 351, 407, 410–411, 430, 434, 450, 456, 484–485, 707–708; 9.340, 568, 734; 11.195, 363; 12.14, 37, 42, 169–171.
AG 7.287: Cf. ANTIPATER Epigr. (0114 001).
Q: 1,692

0656 **DIOSCORIDES PEDANIUS** Med.
A.D. 1: Anazarbensis
Cf. et Pseudo-DIOSCORIDES Med. (1118).

001 **De materia medica**, ed. M. Wellman, *Pedanii Dioscuridis Anazarbei de materia medica libri quinque*, 3 vols. Berlin: Weidmann, 1:1907; 2:1906; 3:1914 (repr. 1958): 1:1–255, 2:1–339, 3:1–108.
Cod: [97,423]

002 **Euporista vel de simplicibus medicinis**, ed. Wellmann, *op. cit.*, vol. 3, 151–317.
Cod: [32,379]

1118 **Pseudo-DIOSCORIDES** Med.
post A.D. 1
Cf. et DIOSCORIDES PEDANIUS Med. (0656).

001 **De venenis eorumque praecautione et medica-**

tione (= **Alexipharmaca**), ed. K. Sprengel, *Pedanii Dioscoridis Anazarbei*, vol. 2 [*Medicorum Graecorum opera quae exstant* (ed. C.G. Kühn), vol. 26.2. Leipzig: Knobloch, 1830]: 1–41.
Cod: 5,291

002 **De iis, quae virus ejaculantur, animalibus libellus, in quo et de rabioso cane** (= **Theriaca**), ed. Sprengel, *op. cit.*, 42–91.
Cod: 6,474

003 **De lapidibus**, ed. C.É. Ruelle, *Les lapidaires de l'antiquité et du Moyen Age*, vol. 2.1. Paris: Leroux, 1898: 179–183.
Cod: 1,092

0870 **DIOSCORIDES Phacas** Med.
1 B.C.: Alexandrinus
x01 **Fragmentum ap. Paulum.**
CMG, vol. 9.1, p. 345.
Cf. PAULUS Med. (0715 001).

2121 **DIOSCORUS** Epic.
A.D. 6: Thebanus (Aegypti)
001 **Fragmenta**, ed. E. Heitsch, *Die griechischen Dichterfragmente der römischen Kaiserzeit*, vol. 1, 2nd edn. Göttingen: Vandenhoeck & Ruprecht, 1963: 128–152.
fr. 1, Encomium Justini II (*P. Cairo Cat.* 2.67183): pp. 128–129.
fr. 2, Encomium Johannis (*P. Cairo Cat.* 1.67055v): pp. 129–130.
fr. 3, Encomium Johannis (*P. Berol.* 10580 + *P. Cairo Cat.* 3.67317): pp. 130–133.
fr. 4, Encomium Athanasii (*P. Cairo Cat.* 1.67097v B C): pp. 133–134.
fr. 5, Encomium Callinici (*P. Cairo Cat.* 3.67315v): pp. 134–136.
fr. 6, Encomium (*P. Cairo Cat.* 2.67177): pp. 136–137.
fr. 7, Encomium (*P. Cairo Cat.* 3.67316v): pp. 137–138.
fr. 8, Encomium (*P. Walters Art Gallery*, Baltimore, inv. 517): p. 138.
fr. 9, Encomium (*P. Cairo Cat.* 1.67097 E): pp. 138–139.
fr. 10, Encomium (*P. Cairo Cat.* 2.67131v): pp. 139–140.
fr. 11, Encomium (*P. Cairo Cat.* 3.67279v): pp. 140–141.
fr. 12, Encomium Romani domini (*P. Brit. Mus.* 1552 + *P. Rain.* 2070): pp. 141–142.
fr. 13, Encomium Constantini dioecetae (*P. Cairo Cat.* 1.67120v): pp. 142–143.
fr. 14, Encomium Dorothei comitis (*P. Cairo Cat.* 1.67120v): p. 143.
fr. 15, Encomium Constantini (*P. Cairo Cat.* 1.67120v): pp. 143–144.
fr. 16, Εἰς τὴν τύχην τῆς γενεθλίας (*P. Cairo Cat.* 1.67120v): p. 144.
fr. 17, Encomium Colluthi comitis (*P. Cairo Cat.* 1.67120v): pp. 144–145.

fr. 18, Encomium Johannis jurisconsulti (*P. Brit. Mus.* 1728 + 1745v): p. 145.
fr. 19, Encomium Hypatii excubitoris praefecti (*P. Cairo Cat.* 2.67185v A): pp. 145–146.
fr. 20, Encomium Pauli cancellarii (*P. Cairo Cat.* 2.67185v B): p. 146.
fr. 21, Epithalamium Callinici comitis (*P. Cairo Cat.* 2.67179 A): pp. 146–147.
fr. 22, Epithalamium (*P. Brit. Mus.* 1733 + *P. Cairo Cat.* 2.67181 et 67180): pp. 147–148.
fr. 23, Epithalamium acrostichum (*P. Cairo Cat.* 3.67318): pp. 148–149.
fr. 24, Epithalamium (*P. Brit. Mus.* 1728 + 1745v): pp. 149–150.
fr. 25, Epithalamium (*P. Brit. Mus.* 1745v): p. 150.
fr. 26, Achilles de Polyxena (*P. Cairo Cat.* 3.67316v): p. 151.
fr. 27, Apollo de Hyacintho et Daphne (*P. Cairo Cat.* 2.67188v): p. 151.
fr. 28, Symposiaca (*P. Cairo Cat.* 1.67097v F): pp. 151–152.
Pap: [3,811]

0868 **DIOSCORUS** Med.
ante A.D. 2
x01 **Fragmentum ap. Galenum.**
K13.204–205.
Cf. GALENUS Med. (0057 076).

2409 **DIOSCURIDES** Hist.
vel Dioscorides
fiq Dioscurides Isocratis discipulus vel Dioscorides compositor constitutionis Laconicae vel Dioscurides Tarsensis Gramm.
4/1 B.C.?
001 **Testimonia**, FGrH #594: 3B:707.
test. 3: *Inscr. Cret. Cnossus* 12.
NQ
002 **Fragmenta**, FGrH #594: 3B:707–713.
frr. 9–11 (auctore Dioscoride Alexandrino).
Cf. et DIOSCORIDES Epigr. (0173 001).
Q
003 **Fragmentum**, ed. H.J. Mette, "Die 'Kleinen' griechischen Historiker heute," *Lustrum* 21 (1978) 32.
fr. 3 bis.
Q

1333 **DIOTIMUS** Epic.
fiq Diotimus Adramyttenus
3 B.C.?
Cf. et DIOTIMUS Epigr. (0174).
001 **Fragmentum**, ed. G. Kinkel, *Epicorum Graecorum fragmenta*, vol. 1. Leipzig: Teubner, 1877: 213–214.
fr. 2.
Q: [21]

0175 **DIOTIMUS** Epigr.
4 B.C.: Atheniensis

001 **Epigrammata,** AG 7.261(?), 420.
Q: 74

0174 **DIOTIMUS** Epigr.
fiq Diotimus Epic.
3 B.C.: Adramyttenus
Cf. et DIOTIMUS Epic. (1333).
001 **Epigrammata,** AG **6.**267, 358; **7.**173, 227(?),
475(?), 733(?); **12.**36; **16.**158(?).
AG 7.261: Cf. DIOTIMUS Epigr. (0175 001).
Q: 297
002 **Fragmentum et titulus,** ed. H. Lloyd-Jones and
P. Parsons, *Supplementum Hellenisticum.* Berlin: De Gruyter, 1983: 181–182.
frr. 393–394.
Cf. et DIOTIMUS Epic. (1333 001).
Q: [21]

0176 **DIOTIMUS** Epigr.
1 B.C.: Milesius
001 **Epigrammata,** AG **5.**106; **9.**391.
AG 16.158: Cf. DIOTIMUS Epigr. (0174 001).
Q: 83

2340 **DIOTIMUS** Phil.
4 B.C.?: Tyrius
001 **Testimonia,** ed. H. Diels and W. Kranz, *Die
Fragmente der Vorsokratiker,* vol. 2, 6th edn.
Berlin: Weidmann, 1952 (repr. Dublin: 1966):
250.
test. 1–4.
NQ

1332 **<DIOTOGENES>** Phil.
4 B.C./A.D. 2
001 **Fragmenta,** ed. H. Thesleff, *The Pythagorean
texts of the Hellenistic period.* Åbo: Åbo Akademi, 1965: 71–77.
Q: 1,667

0446 **DIOXIPPUS** Comic.
4 B.C.?
001 **Fragmenta,** ed. T. Kock, *Comicorum Atticorum fragmenta,* vol. 3. Leipzig: Teubner,
1888: 358–360, 753.
frr. 1–5 + titulus.
Q: 72
002 **Fragmenta,** ed. A. Meineke, *Fragmenta comicorum Graecorum,* vol. 4. Berlin: Reimer, 1841
(repr. De Gruyter, 1970): 541–543.
Q: 75

2316 **DIOXIPPUS** Hist.
Incertum: Corinthius
001 **Fragmentum,** FGrH #454: 3B:382–383.
Q

0447 **DIPHILUS** Comic.
4–3 B.C.: Sinopensis
001 **Fragmenta,** ed. T. Kock, *Comicorum Atticorum fragmenta,* vol. 2. Leipzig: Teubner,
1884: 541–580.

frr. 1–8, 12–14, 16–24, 26–27, 29–36, 38, 40–
46, 48–49, 51–69, 71–84, 86–123, 126–136 +
tituli.
Q: 2,297
002 **Fragmenta,** ed. A. Meineke, *Fragmenta comicorum Graecorum,* vol. 4. Berlin: Reimer, 1841
(repr. De Gruyter, 1970): 375–381, 383–395,
397–428.
Q: 2,213
003 **Fragmenta,** ed. J. Demiańczuk, *Supplementum
comicum.* Krakau: Nakładem Akademii, 1912
(repr. Hildesheim: Olms, 1967): 40.
frr. 1–2.
Q: 3
004 **Fragmenta** (*P. Louvre* inv. no. 7733v), ed. F.
Lasserre, "L'élégie de l'huître," *Quaderni urbi-
nati di cultura classica* 19 (1975) 145–176.
Pap

0248 **DIPHILUS** Epic.
Incertum
001 **Fragmentum,** ed. M.L. West, *Iambi et elegi
Graeci,* vol. 2. Oxford: Clarendon Press, 1972:
61.
Q: [15]

0177 **DIPHILUS** Epigr.
4 B.C.: Atheniensis
001 **Epigramma,** AG 11.439.
Q: 10

0872 **DIPHILUS** Med.
3 B.C.: Siphnius
x01 **Fragmenta ap. Athenaeum.**
Deipnosophistae 2.51a–b, 61d–e, 64b; 8.357a–
358c.
Cf. ATHENAEUS Soph. (0008 001).

0279 *DISCIPULORUM CANTIUNCULA*
ante A.D. 4
001 **Fragmentum** (*P. Med.*), ed. E. Heitsch, *Die
griechischen Dichterfragmente der römischen
Kaiserzeit,* vol. 1, 2nd edn. Göttingen: Vandenhoeck & Ruprecht, 1963: 46–47.
Pap: [47]

1330 **DIUS** Hist.
2 B.C.?
001 **Testimonium,** FGrH #785: 3C:797.
NQ
002 **Fragmentum,** FGrH #785: 3C:798.
Q

1334 **DIUS** Phil.
Incertum
001 **Fragmenta,** ed. H. Thesleff, *The Pythagorean
texts of the Hellenistic period.* Åbo: Åbo Akademi, 1965: 70–71.
Q: 286

1911 **DIYLLUS** Hist.
4–3 B.C.: Atheniensis

001 **Testimonia,** FGrH #73: 2A:130–131.
NQ
002 **Fragmenta,** FGrH #73: 2A:131–132.
Q

7051 *DOCTRINA PATRUM*
A.D. 7–8
001 **Doctrina patrum,** ed. F. Diekamp, *Doctrina patrum de incarnatione verbi.* Münster: Aschendorff, 1907: 1–337.
Cod

0873 **DOMITIUS NIGRINUS** Med.
ante A.D. 2
x01 **Fragmentum ap. Galenum.**
K13.1021.
Cf. GALENUS Med. (0057 077).

2622 **DORIEUS** Poeta
ante A.D. 2
001 **Epigramma,** ed. H. Lloyd-Jones and P. Parsons, *Supplementum Hellenisticum.* Berlin: De Gruyter, 1983: 182.
fr. 396.
Q: [53]
x01 **Epigramma demonstrativum.**
App. Anth. 3.95: Cf. EPIGRAMMATICI in *App. Anth.* (7052 003).

1335 **DORION Scriptor Rerum Naturalium**
1 B.C.
x01 **Fragmenta ap. Athenaeum.**
Deipnosophistae 7.287c, 300f, 319d, 330a.
Cf. ATHENAEUS Soph. (0008 001).

1337 **DOROTHEUS** Astrol.
1 B.C.–A.D. 1: Sidonius
001 **Fragmenta Graeca,** ed. D. Pingree, *Dorothei Sidonii carmen astrologicum.* Leipzig: Teubner, 1976: 323–330, 332–427.
Q, Cod: [29,395]
002 **Fragmenta e Hephaestionis** ᾽Αποτελεσματικῶν libris hausta, ed. Pingree, *op. cit.,* 427–434.
Q: [1,463]
003 **Fragmenta alia antiqua,** ed. Pingree, *op. cit.,* 435–437.
Q, Cod: [421]

1336 **DOROTHEUS** Hist.
ante A.D. 1: Atheniensis
001 **Testimonium,** FGrH #145: 2B:813.
NQ
002 **Fragmenta,** FGrH #145: 2B:813–814.
Q

2197 **[DOROTHEUS]** Hist.
Incertum: Chaldaeus
001 **Fragmenta,** FGrH #289: 3A:172–173.
Q

0874 **DOROTHEUS** Med.
ante A.D. 1: Heliopolitanus
x01 **Fragmenta ap. Galenum.**

K14.183, 187.
Cf. GALENUS Med. (0057 078).

1338 **DOSIADAS** Hist.
4–3 B.C.?: fort. Cydonius
001 **Testimonium,** FGrH #458: 3B:394.
NQ
002 **Fragmenta,** FGrH #458: 3B:394–396.
Q

0208 **DOSIADAS** Lyr.
3/2 B.C.: Creticus
001 Βωμός, ed. J.U. Powell, *Collectanea Alexandrina.* Oxford: Clarendon Press, 1925 (repr. 1970): 175.
Q: [74]
002 **Epigramma,** AG 15.26.
AG 15.27: Cf. SIMIAS Gramm. (0211 002).
Q: 72

1896 **DOSITHEUS** Hist.
ante A.D. 2
001 **Fragmenta,** FGrH #54: 1A:295–296.
Q

2198 **[DOSITHEUS]** Hist.
Incertum
001 **Fragmenta,** FGrH #290: 3A:173–175.
Q

0875 **DOSITHEUS** Med.
ante A.D. 6
x01 **Fragmentum ap. Paulum.**
CMG, vol. 9.2, p. 308.
Cf. PAULUS Med. (0715 001).
x02 **Fragmentum ap. Aëtium** (lib. 8).
CMG, vol. 8.2, p. 530.
Cf. AËTIUS Med. (0718 008).

2249 **DRACO** Hist.
2 B.C.: Atheniensis
001 **Fragmentum,** FGrH #344: 3B:208.
Q

0448 **DROMO** Comic.
4 B.C.
001 **Fragmenta,** ed. T. Kock, *Comicorum Atticorum fragmenta,* vol. 2. Leipzig: Teubner, 1884: 419.
frr. 1–2.
Q: 47
002 **Fragmenta,** ed. A. Meineke, *Fragmenta comicorum Graecorum,* vol. 3. Berlin: Reimer, 1840 (repr. De Gruyter, 1970): 541.
Q: 47

0178 **DURIS** Epigr.
4 B.C.: Eleaticus
001 **Epigramma,** AG 9.424.
Q: 52

1339 **DURIS** Hist.
4–3 B.C.: Samius

001 **Testimonia**, FGrH #76: 2A:136–138.
NQ

002 **Fragmenta**, FGrH #76: 2A:138–158.
fr. 25: *Inscr. Priene* 37.
Q, Cod, Epigr

003 **Fragmenta**, ed. H.J. Mette, "Die 'Kleinen'
griechischen Historiker heute," *Lustrum* 21
(1978) 13–15.
fr. 15 bis: *P. Oxy.* 24.2399.
fr. 18b: *P. Oxy.* 32.2637.
Pap

1340 **<ECCELUS>** Phil.
3/2 B.C.

001 **Fragmentum**, ed. H. Thesleff, *The Pythagorean
texts of the Hellenistic period.* Åbo: Åbo Akademi, 1965: 77–78.
Q: 193

2242 **ECHECRATES** Phil.
5–4 B.C.

001 **Testimonia**, ed. H. Diels and W. Kranz, *Die
Fragmente der Vorsokratiker*, vol. 1, 6th edn.
Berlin: Weidmann, 1951 (repr. Dublin: 1966):
443.
test. 1–4: auctores alii nominantur Diocles,
Polymnastus, Phanto et Arion.
NQ

0249 **ECHEMBROTUS** Lyr. et Eleg.
6 B.C.: Arcas

001 **Fragmentum**, ed. M.L. West, *Iambi et elegi
Graeci*, vol. 2. Oxford: Clarendon Press, 1972:
62.
Q: [20]

2320 **ECHEMENES** Hist.
ante A.D. 3: fort. Creticus

001 **Fragmenta**, FGrH #459: 3B:396–397.
Q

2289 **ECHEPHYLIDAS** Hist.
4–3 B.C.?

001 **Fragmenta**, FGrH #409: 3B:302.
Q

002 **Fragmenta**, ed. H.J. Mette, "Die 'Kleinen'
griechischen Historiker heute," *Lustrum* 21
(1978) 28.
frr. 4a–b, 5a–b.
Q

0449 **ECPHANTIDES** Comic.
5 B.C.

001 **Fragmenta**, ed. T. Kock, *Comicorum Atticorum fragmenta*, vol. 1. Leipzig: Teubner,
1880: 9–10.
frr. 1, 3, 5.
Q: 17

002 **Fragmenta**, ed. A. Meineke, *Fragmenta comicorum Graecorum*, vol. 2.1. Berlin: Reimer,
1839 (repr. De Gruyter, 1970): 12–13.
Q: 17

003 **Titulus**, ed. C. Austin, *Comicorum Graecorum

fragmenta in papyris reperta. Berlin: De Gruyter, 1973: 52.
NQ: 2

1341 **<ECPHANTUS>** Phil.
3 B.C.: Syracusanus vel Crotoniensis

001 **Fragmenta** [Sp.], ed. H. Thesleff, *The Pytha-
gorean texts of the Hellenistic period.* Åbo: Åbo
Akademi, 1965: 79–84.
Q: 1,468

002 **Testimonia**, ed. H. Diels and W. Kranz, *Die
Fragmente der Vorsokratiker*, vol. 1, 6th edn.
Berlin: Weidmann, 1951 (repr. Dublin: 1966):
442.
NQ

2156 **ELEAZAR** Hist.
A.D. 4

001 **Testimonium**, FGrH #224: 2B:951.
NQ

ELEAZARI EPISTULA
Cf. PTOLEMAEI II PHILADELPHI ET ELEA-
ZARI EPISTULAE (0050).

0231 ***ELEGIACA ADESPOTA*** (CA)
Varia

001 **Fragmenta**, ed. J.U. Powell, *Collectanea Alex-
andrina.* Oxford: Clarendon Press, 1925 (repr.
1970): 130–131.
Aurea aetas (*P. Oxy.* 1.14) (fr. 1): p. 130.
De Galatis (*P. Hamburgensis*) (fr. 2): p. 131.
Pap: [188]

0234 ***ELEGIACA ADESPOTA*** (IEG)
Varia

001 **Fragmenta**, ed. M.L. West, *Iambi et elegi
Graeci*, vol. 2. Oxford: Clarendon Press, 1972:
1–15.
frr. 1–8, 10–12, 14–17, 19–62.
Q, Pap: [859]

1897 **ELEUSIS** Hist.
3 B.C.

001 **Fragmentum**, FGrH #55: 1A:296.
Q

4020 **ELIAS** Phil.
A.D. 6

001 **In Porphyrii isagogen**, ed. A. Busse, *Eliae in
Porphyrii isagogen et Aristotelis categorias commentaria* [*Commentaria in Aristotelem Graeca*
18.1. Berlin: Reimer, 1900]: 1–104.
Cod: [37,439]

002 **Eliae (olim Davidis) in Aristotelis categorias
commentarium**, ed. Busse, *op. cit.*, 107–255.
Cod: [61,369]

1342 **EMPEDOCLES** Poet. Phil.
5 B.C.: Agrigentinus

002 **Epigramma**, AG 9.569.
AG 7.508: Cf. SIMONIDES Lyr. (0261 003).
Q: 56

003 **Testimonia**, ed. H. Diels and W. Kranz, *Die Fragmente der Vorsokratiker*, vol. 1, 6th edn. Berlin: Weidmann, 1951 (repr. Dublin: 1966): 276–307.
test. 1–98.
NQ

004 **Fragmenta**, ed. Diels and Kranz, *op. cit.*, 308–374.
frr. 1–161.
Q

x01 **Epigramma irrisorium**.
App. Anth. 5.4: Cf. EPIGRAMMATICI in *App. Anth.* (7052 005).

1984 **EMPYLUS** Hist.
1 B.C.: Rhodius
001 **Testimonia**, FGrH #191: 2B:926.
NQ

0290 *ENCOMIUM DUCIS THEBAIDOS*
ante A.D. 5?
001 **Fragmentum** (*P. Berol.* 9799), ed. E. Heitsch, *Die griechischen Dichterfragmente der römischen Kaiserzeit*, vol. 2. Göttingen: Vandenhoeck & Ruprecht, 1964: 50–51.
Pap: [197]

2685 **ENNOEUS** Poeta
A.D. 3/4
x01 **Epigramma sepulcrale**.
App. Anth. 2.491(?): Cf. EPIGRAMMATICI in *App. Anth.* (7052 002).

0356 **EPAPHRODITUS** Gramm.
A.D. 1: Chaeronensis, Romanus
001 **Fragmenta**, ed. E. Lünzner, *Epaphroditi grammatici quae supersunt* [*Diss. Bonn* (1866)]: 21–49.
Q

1343 **EPARCHIDES** Hist.
3 B.C.?: fort. Oeneius
001 **Fragmenta**, FGrH #437: 3B:369–370.
Q

2436 *EPHEMERIDES*
4 B.C.
001 **Ephemerides Alexandri** (fort. auctore Eumene Cardiano) (testimonia), FGrH #117: 2B:618.
NQ

002 **Ephemerides Alexandri** (fort. auctore Eumene Cardiano) (fragmenta), FGrH #117: 2B:618–622.
Q

0450 **EPHIPPUS** Comic.
4 B.C.
001 **Fragmenta**, ed. T. Kock, *Comicorum Atticorum fragmenta*, vol. 2. Leipzig: Teubner, 1884: 250–264.
frr. 1–29.
Q: 780

002 **Fragmenta**, ed. A. Meineke, *Fragmenta comicorum Graecorum*, vol. 3. Berlin: Reimer, 1840 (repr. De Gruyter, 1970): 322–323, 325–330, 332, 334–340.
Q: 747

003 **Fragmentum**, ed. Meineke, *op. cit.*, vol. 5.1 (1857; repr. 1970): cxcvi.
Q: [12]

1936 **EPHIPPUS** Hist.
post 4 B.C.: Olynthius
001 **Testimonia**, FGrH #126: 2B:665.
NQ

002 **Fragmenta**, FGrH #126: 2B:665–667.
Q

0536 **EPHORUS** Hist.
4 B.C.: Cumaeus
001 **Fragmenta**, *P. Lit. Lond.* 114.
Pap

002 **Testimonia**, FGrH #70: 2A:37–43.
NQ

003 **Fragmenta**, FGrH #70: 2A:43–109.
fr. 191: *P. Oxy.* 13.1610.
Q, Pap

004 **Fragmenta**, ed. H.J. Mette, "Die 'Kleinen' griechischen Historiker heute," *Lustrum* 21 (1978) 13.
frr. 120b1–120b2.
Q

x01 **Sicyonis historia** (*P. Oxy.* 11.1365).
FGrH #551, fr. 1b (= FGrH #105, fr. 2).
Cf. ADDITAMENTA (FGrH) (2433 024).
Cf. ANONYMI HISTORICI (FGrH) (1139 004).

1998 **EPHORUS Junior** Hist.
A.D. 3: Cumaeus
001 **Testimonium**, FGrH #212: 2B:943.
NQ

1346 **EPHRAEM** Scr. Eccl.
A.D. 4?: Chersonensis
001 **De miraculo Clementis Romani**, MPG 2: 633–646.
Cod

1344 *EPICA ADESPOTA* (CA)
Varia
001 **Epica adespota**, ed. J.U. Powell, *Collectanea Alexandrina*. Oxford: Clarendon Press, 1925 (repr. 1970): 71–87.
Actaeonis epyllium (?) (fr. 1): pp. 71–72.
Epyllium Diomedis (fr. 2): pp. 72–75.
Telephi epyllium (?) (*P. Oxy.* 2.214) (fr. 3): pp. 76–77.
Epyllium incerti argumenti (*P. Oxy.* 15.1794) (fr. 4): pp. 78–79.
Sine titulo (*P. Oxy.* 2.221, col. 9.1–9.3) (fr. 5): p. 79.
Sine titulo (*P. Oxy.* 3.422) (fr. 6): p. 80.
Hymnus in Junonem (*P. Oxy.* 4.670) (fr. 7): pp. 80–81.

Heraclea (?) (*P. Halensis* 1.182) (fr. 8): p. 81.
Hymnorum Ptolemaicorum fragmenta in Arsi-
noen-Aphroditen (?) (*P. Chicaginiensis*) (fr. 9):
pp. 82–87.
Q, Pap: [1,849]

1816 *EPICA ADESPOTA* (GDRK)
A.D. 1–7
001 **Lusus verborum**, ed. E. Heitsch, *Die griechischen Dichterfragmente der römischen Kaiserzeit*, vol. 1, 2nd edn. Göttingen: Vandenhoeck
& Ruprecht, 1963: 51.
Q: [8]

002 **Laudes Theonis gymnasiarchi** (*P. Oxy.*
7.1015), ed. Heitsch, *op. cit.*, 55.
Pap: [147]

003 **Fragmentum epicum** (*P. Brit. Mus.* 1181), ed.
Heitsch, *op. cit.*, 59–60.
Pap: [225]

004 **Exercitatio ethopoeiaca** (*P. Ryl.* 3.487), ed.
Heitsch, *op. cit.*, 78–79.
Pap: [147]

005 **Fragmentum epicum historicum** (*P. Argent.*
480), ed. Heitsch, *op. cit.*, 79–81.
Pap: [262]

006 **Mercurius mundi et Hermupolis magnae con-
ditor** (*P. Strassburg* 481), ed. Heitsch, *op. cit.*,
82–85.
Pap: [399]

007 **Epithalamium** (*P. Ryl.* 1.17), ed. Heitsch, *op.
cit.*, 85.
Pap: [42]

008 **Exercitationes ethopoeiacae** (collectio C.
Graves), ed. Heitsch, *op. cit.*, 86–88.
Pap: [227]

009 **Encomium iambicum** (*P. Vindob.* gr. 29788b),
ed. Heitsch, *op. cit.*, 88–90.
Pap: [282]

010 Λόγος ἐπιβατήριος (*P. Vindob.* gr. 29788a), ed.
Heitsch, *op. cit.*, 90–91.
Pap: [173]

011 **Laudatio professoris Smyrnaei in universitate
Beryti docentis** (*P. Berol.* 10559 A et B), ed.
Heitsch, *op. cit.*, 94–97.
Pap: [563]

012 **Laudatio professoris in universitate Beryti docentis** (*P. Berol.* 10558), ed. Heitsch, *op. cit.*,
98–99.
Pap: [159]

013 **Fragmentum epicum historicum** (*P. Berol.*
5003), ed. Heitsch, *op. cit.*, 99–103.
Pap: [499]

014 **Encomium** (*PSI* 149), ed. Heitsch, *op. cit.*,
103–104.
Pap: [84]

015 **Encomium Heraclii ducis** (*PSI* 253), ed.
Heitsch, *op. cit.*, 104–108.
Pap: [457]

016 **Encomium ducis Romani** (*P. Flor.* 2.114), ed.
Heitsch, *op. cit.*, 120–124.
Pap: [512]

017 **Polyxena et Achilles** (*P. Flor.* 390), ed.
Heitsch, *op. cit.*, 124–125.
Pap: [91]

018 **Exercitatio ethopoeiaca** (Tab. lignea Caironen-
sis), ed. Heitsch, *op. cit.*, 125.
Pap: [49]

019 **Carmen in Nilum crescentem** (*PSI* 845), ed.
Heitsch, *op. cit.*, 126.
Pap: [93]

020 **In Thebas** (*P. Berol.* 5226v), ed. Heitsch, *op.
cit.*, 127.
Pap: [18]

021 **Fragmentum** (sine titulo) (*P. Berol.* 5227r), ed.
Heitsch, *op. cit.*, 127.
Pap: [9]

1345 *EPICA INCERTA* (CA)
Varia
001 **Fragmenta**, ed. J.U. Powell, *Collectanea Alexandrina*. Oxford: Clarendon Press, 1925 (repr.
1970): 89–90.
frr. 1–7.
Q: [28]

002 **Fragmentum**, ed. Powell, *op. cit.*, 251.
Pap: [32]

0521 **EPICHARMUS** Comic. et *PSEUDEPICHAR-
MEA*
5 B.C.: Syracusanus
001 **Fragmenta Epicharmi**, ed. G. Kaibel, *Comicorum Graecorum fragmenta*, vol. 1.1 [*Poetarum Graecorum fragmenta*, vol. 6.1. Berlin:
Weidmann, 1899]: 91–126, 128–132.
frr. 1, 5–7, 9–11, 19, 21, 23–25, 29–31, 33–35,
37–39, 42–51, 53–72, 76, 78–85, 87–91, 99–
102, 107, 109–111, 113–118, 123–125, 127–
128, 130–134, 136–137, 139–140, 146–155,
157–161, 164–166, 168–173, 179–180, 182,
185, 188–189, 207, 216–219, 221, 228–229,
232–233, 235, 238–239.
Q: 1,971

002 **Fragmenta Pseudepicharmea**, ed. Kaibel, *op.
cit.*, 135–146.
frr. 239, 245–247, 249–250, 252–258, 261–
290, 296–298.
Q: 573

003 **Fragmenta**, ed. J. Demiańczuk, *Supplementum
comicum*. Krakau: Nakładem Akademii, 1912
(repr. Hildesheim: Olms, 1967): 123–125.
frr. 1–6.
fr. 2: *P. Hibeh* 1.1.
fr. 3: *P. Berol.* 9772.
Q, Pap: 282

004 **Fragmenta Epicharmi**, ed. C. Austin, *Comicorum Graecorum fragmenta in papyris reperta*.
Berlin: De Gruyter, 1973: 52–78.
frr. 81–85a.
Pap: 2,682

005 **Fragmenta Pseudepicharmea**, ed. Austin, *op.
cit.*, 79–83.
frr. 86–91.
Pap: 447

006 **Fragmentum Epicharmi**, ed. Kaibel, *op. cit.*,
vii.
fr. 100a.
Q: 12

007 **Testimonia**, ed. H. Diels and W. Kranz, *Die
Fragmente der Vorsokratiker*, vol. 1, 6th edn.
Berlin: Weidmann, 1951 (repr. Dublin: 1966):
190–193.
NQ

008 **Fragmenta**, ed. Diels and Kranz, *op. cit.*, 195–
210.
frr. 1–65.
Q

x01 **Epigramma exhortatorium et supplicatorium**.
App. Anth. 4.6(?): Cf. EPIGRAMMATICI in
App. Anth. (7052 004).

0451 **EPICRATES** Comic.
4 B.C.

001 **Fragmenta**, ed. T. Kock, *Comicorum Atticorum fragmenta*, vol. 2. Leipzig: Teubner,
1884: 282–288.
frr. 1–12 + tituli.
Q: 539

002 **Fragmenta**, ed. A. Meineke, *Fragmenta comicorum Graecorum*, vol. 3. Berlin: Reimer, 1840
(repr. De Gruyter, 1970): 365–372.
Q: 492

0557 **EPICTETUS** Phil.
A.D. 1–2: Hierapolitanus, Romanus

001 **Dissertationes ab Arriano digestae**, ed. H.
Schenkl, *Epicteti dissertationes ab Arriano digestae*. Leipzig: Teubner, 1916 (repr. Stuttgart:
1965): 7–454.
Cod: 78,609

002 **Enchiridion**, ed. Schenkl, *op. cit.*, 5*–38*.
Cod: 5,154

003 **Dissertationum Epictetearum sive ab Arriano
sive ab aliis digestarum fragmenta**, ed.
Schenkl, *op. cit.*, 455–460, 462–475.
Q: 1,994

004 **Gnomologium Epicteteum** (e Stobaei libris 1–
2), ed. Schenkl, *op. cit.*, 476–477.
Q: 286

005 **Gnomologium Epicteteum** (e Stobaei libris 3–
4), ed. Schenkl, *op. cit.*, 478–492.
Q: 1,921

006 **Arriani epistula ad Lucium Gellium**, ed.
Schenkl, *op. cit.*, 5–6.
Cod: 200

x01 **Epigramma**.
AG 7.676.
Cf. ANONYMI EPIGRAMMATICI (0138 001).

x02 **Sententiae** (Moschionis).
Schenkl, pp. 493–494, frr. 1–25.
Cf. <MOSCHION> Gnom. (0575 001).

x03 **Hypothecae** (Moschionis).
Schenkl, pp. 495–496, frr. 1–18.
Cf. <MOSCHION> Gnom. (0575 002).

0537 **EPICURUS** Phil.
4–3 B.C.: Samius, Atheniensis

001 **Ratae sententiae**, ed. G. Arrighetti. Turin:
Einaudi, 1960: 121–137.
Cod: [1,401]

002 **Gnomologium Vaticanum Epicureum**, ed.
Arrighetti, *op. cit.*, 141–157.
Cod: [1,174]

003 **Deperditorum librorum reliquiae**, ed. Arrighetti, *op. cit.*, 161–379.
Q, Pap: [10,638]

004 **Epistularum fragmenta**, ed. Arrighetti, *op. cit.*,
383–437.
Q, Pap: [1,989]

005 **Incertae sedis fragmenta**, ed. Arrighetti, *op.
cit.*, 441–443.
Q, Pap: [58]

006 **Epistula ad Herodotum**, ed. P. von der
Muehll, *Epicuri epistulae tres et ratae sententiae
a Laertio Diogene servatae*. Leipzig: Teubner,
1922 (repr. Stuttgart: 1966): 3–27.
Cod: [4,678]

007 **Epistula ad Pythoclem**, ed. von der Muehll, *op.
cit.*, 27–43.
Cod: [3,130]

008 **Epistula ad Menoeceum**, ed. von der Muehll,
op. cit., 44–50.
Cod: [1,375]

009 **Incerti operis fragmenta** (*P. Herc.* 1639), ed.
W. Crönert, "Neues über Epikur und einige
herkulanensische Rollen," *Rheinisches Museum*
56 (1901) 610–611.
Pap

0880 **EPIDAURUS** Med.
ante A.D. 2

x01 **Fragmentum ap. Galenum**.
K13.985.
Cf. GALENUS Med. (0057 077).

0452 **EPIGENES** Comic.
4 B.C.

001 **Fragmenta**, ed. T. Kock, *Comicorum Atticorum fragmenta*, vol. 2. Leipzig: Teubner,
1884: 416–419.
frr. 1–8 + tituli.
Q: 120

002 **Fragmenta**, ed. A. Meineke, *Fragmenta comicorum Graecorum*, vol. 3. Berlin: Reimer, 1840
(repr. De Gruyter, 1970): 537–540.
Q: 115

1351 *EPIGONI*
fort. auctore Antimacho Teio
post 7 B.C.
Cf. et ANTIMACHUS Epic. (1141).

001 **Fragmentum**, ed. T.W. Allen, *Homeri opera*,
vol. 5. Oxford: Clarendon Press, 1912 (repr.
1969): 115.
fr. 1.
Q

0179 **EPIGONUS** Epigr.
1 B.C.?: Thessalonicensis
001 **Epigramma**, AG 9.261.
AG 9.260: Cf. SECUNDUS Epigr. (0274 001).
AG 9.406: Cf. ANTIGONUS Paradox. (0568 002).
Q: 27

0881 **EPIGONUS** Med.
A.D. 1
Cf. et EPIGONUS vel HERMON Med. (0922).
x01 **Fragmenta ap. Galenum**.
K13.492–493, 775.
Cf. GALENUS Med. (0057 077).

0922 **EPIGONUS vel HERMON** Med.
A.D. 1?
Cf. et EPIGONUS Med. (0881).
x01 **Fragmentum ap. Aëtium** (lib. 15).
Zervos, *Athena* 21, p. 39.
Cf. AËTIUS Med. (0718 015).

7052 **EPIGRAMMATICI in** *App. Anth.*
Varia
001 **Epigrammata dedicatoria**, ed. E. Cougny, *Epigrammatum anthologia Palatina cum Planudeis et appendice nova*, vol. 3. Paris: Didot, 1890: 1–60.
Epigr. 1.1–372.
Q, Epigr
002 **Epigrammata sepulcralia**, ed. Cougny, *op. cit.*, 94–224.
Epigr. 2.1–775.
Q, Epigr
003 **Epigrammata demonstrativa**, ed. Cougny, *op. cit.*, 287–359.
Epigr. 3.1–422.
Q, Epigr
004 **Epigrammata exhortatoria et supplicatoria**, ed. Cougny, *op. cit.*, 390–426.
Epigr. 4.1–143.
Q, Epigr
005 **Epigrammata irrisoria**, ed. Cougny, *op. cit.*, 442–457.
Epigr. 5.1–82.
Q, Epigr
006 **Oracula**, ed. Cougny, *op. cit.*, 464–533.
Epigr. 6.1–323.
Q, Epigr
007 **Problemata et aenigmata**, ed. Cougny, *op. cit.*, 563–578.
Epigr. 7.1–81.
Q, Epigr
008 **Addenda**, ed. Cougny, *op. cit.*, 587–602.
Epigr. **1.**10b–c, 67b, 86b, 101b, 126b, 128b, 174b, 224b–c, 242b, 249b, 253b, 266b–c, 287b, 292b, 300b, 319b, 329b, 331b, 347b; **2.**53b–c, 121b, 131b, 173b–c, 181b, 182b, 198b–e, 242b, 247b, 254b, 255b–c, 257b–c, 320b, 361b, 367b, 371b, 372b–c, 379b, 424b, 447b, 462b, 539b, 641b–c, 671b–d, 680b, 704b, 705b, 712b;

3.66b, 81b, 103b, 115b–c, 138b, 256b–f; **4.**62b; **5.**6b, 13b, 19b; **6.**24b, 30b, 104b, 107; **7.**10b.
Q, Epigr

EPILOGUS MOSQUENSIS
Cf. MARTYRIUM POLYCARPI (1484 001).

0453 **EPILYCUS** Comic.
5/4 B.C.?
001 **Fragmenta**, ed. T. Kock, *Comicorum Atticorum fragmenta*, vol. 1. Leipzig: Teubner, 1880: 803–804.
frr. 1–3, 5–8.
Q: 37
002 **Fragmenta**, ed. A. Meineke, *Fragmenta comicorum Graecorum*, vol. 2.2. Berlin: Reimer, 1840 (repr. De Gruyter, 1970): 887, 889.
Q: 26
003 **Fragmentum**, ed. J. Demiańczuk, *Supplementum comicum*. Krakau: Nakładem Akademii, 1912 (repr. Hildesheim: Olms, 1967): 40.
fr. 1.
Q: 10

1347 **EPIMENIDES** Phil.
6–5 B.C.: Creticus
001 **Testimonia**, FGrH #457: 3B:384–389.
NQ
002 **Fragmenta**, FGrH #457: 3B:390–394.
Q
003 **Testimonia**, ed. H. Diels and W. Kranz, *Die Fragmente der Vorsokratiker*, vol. 1, 6th edn. Berlin: Weidmann, 1951 (repr. Dublin: 1966): 27–31.
NQ
004 **Fragmenta**, ed. Diels and Kranz, *op. cit.*, 31–37.
Q
005 **Fragmentum** (*P. Oxy.* 26.2442), ed. H.J. Mette, "Die 'Kleinen' griechischen Historiker heute," *Lustrum* 21 (1978) 29.
fr. 2 bis.
Pap

0454 **EPINICUS** Comic.
3/2 B.C.
001 **Fragmenta**, ed. T. Kock, *Comicorum Atticorum fragmenta*, vol. 3. Leipzig: Teubner, 1888: 330–331.
frr. 1–2.
Q: 142
002 **Fragmenta**, ed. A. Meineke, *Fragmenta comicorum Graecorum*, vol. 4. Berlin: Reimer, 1841 (repr. De Gruyter, 1970): 505–506.
Q: 135

1348 **EPIPHANES** Gnost.
A.D. 2
001 **De justitia** (fragmenta), ed. W. Völker, *Quellen zur Geschichte der christlichen Gnosis*. Tübin-

gen: Mohr, 1932: 34–35.
Q

2021 **EPIPHANIUS** Scr. Eccl.
A.D. 4: Constantiensis (Cypri)
001 **Ancoratus**, ed. K. Holl, *Epiphanius, Band 1: Ancoratus und Panarion* [*Die griechischen christlichen Schriftsteller* 25. Leipzig: Hinrichs, 1915]: 1–149.
Cod: 39,802
002 **Panarion** (= **Adversus haereses**), ed. K. Holl, *Epiphanius, Bände 1–3: Ancoratus und Panarion* [*Die griechischen christlichen Schriftsteller* 25, 31, 37. Leipzig: Hinrichs, 1:1915; 2:1922; 3:1933]: 1:153–161, 169–233, 238–464; 2:5–210, 215–523; 3:2–229, 232–414, 416–526.
Epistula ab Acacio et Paulo: vol. 1, pp. 153–154.
Rescriptum ad Acacium et Paulum: vol. 1, pp. 155–161.
Haereses 1–33: vol. 1, pp. 169–233, 238–464.
Haereses 34–64: vol. 2, pp. 5–210, 215–523.
Haereses 65–80: vol. 3, pp. 2–229, 232–414, 416–496.
De fide: vol. 3, pp. 496–526.
Cod: 351,979
003 **Anacephalaeosis** [Sp.], ed. Holl, *op. cit.*, 1:162–168, 234–237; 2:1–4, 211–214; 3:1–2, 230–232, 415.
Cod: 4,529
004 **De xii gemmis**, ed. C.É. Ruelle, *Les lapidaires de l'antiquité et du Moyen Age*, vol. 2.1. Paris: Leroux, 1898: 193–199.
Cod: [2,133]
005 **De xii gemmis** (fragmenta ap. Anastasium Sinaitam), MPG 89: 588–589.
Q: [604]
006 **De xii gemmis** (fragmenta alia ap. Anastasium Sinaitam), MPG 89: 596–597.
Q: [217]
007 **Epistula ad Eusebium, Marcellum, Vivianum, Carpum et ad Aegyptios** (fragmentum), ed. K. Holl, *Gesammelte Aufsätze zur Kirchengeschichte*, vol. 2. Tübingen: Mohr, 1928 (repr. Darmstadt: Wissenschaftliche Buchgesellschaft, 1964): 204–207.
Cod: [891]
008 **Tractatus contra eos qui imagines faciunt** (fragmenta), ed. Holl, *Gesammelte Aufsätze zur Kirchengeschichte*, 356–359.
Q: [412]
009 **Epistula ad Theodosium imperatorem** (fragmenta), ed. Holl, *Gesammelte Aufsätze zur Kirchengeschichte*, 360–362.
Q: [459]
010 **Testamentum ad cives** (fragmenta), ed. Holl, *Gesammelte Aufsätze zur Kirchengeschichte*, 363.
Q: [109]
011 **Epistula ad Joannem Hierosolymitanum** (fragmentum), ed. P. Maas, "Die ikonoklastischen Episode in dem Brief des Epiphanios an Jo-

hannes," *Byzantinische Zeitschrift* 30 (1929–1930) 281–283.
Q: [307]
012 **Homilia in festo palmarum** [Sp.], MPG 43: 428–437.
Cod: [2,113]
013 **Homilia in divini corporis sepulturam** [Sp.], MPG 43: 440–464.
Cod: [5,353]
014 **Homilia in Christi resurrectionem** (inc. Ὁ τῆς δικαιοσύνης) [Sp.], MPG 43: 465–477.
Cod: [2,688]
015 **Homilia in assumptionem Christi** [Sp.], MPG 43: 477–485.
Cod: [1,539]
016 **Homilia in laudes Mariae deiparae** [Sp.], MPG 43: 485–501.
Cod: [3,330]
017 **Homilia in festo palmarum** (fragmentum) [Sp.], MPG 43: 501–505.
Cod: [796]
018 **Tractatus de numerorum mysteriis** [Sp.], MPG 43: 507–517.
Cod: [1,745]
019 **Fragmenta precationis et exorcismi** [Sp.], MPG 43: 537–538.
Cod: [61]
020 **Enumeratio lxxii prophetarum et prophetissarum** [Sp.], ed. T. Schermann, *Prophetarum vitae fabulosae*. Leipzig: Teubner, 1907: 1–3.
Dup. VITAE PROPHETARUM (1750 001).
Cod: [301]
021 **De prophetarum vita et obitu** (recensio prior) [Sp.], ed. Schermann, *op. cit.*, 4–25.
Dup. VITAE PROPHETARUM (1750 002).
Cod: [3,867]
022 **De prophetarum vita et obitu** (recensio altera) [Sp.], ed. Schermann, *op. cit.*, 55–67.
Dup. VITAE PROPHETARUM (1750 004).
Cod: [2,633]
023 **Index apostolorum** [Sp.], ed. Schermann, *op. cit.*, 107–117.
Dup. VITAE PROPHETARUM (1750 007).
Cod: [1,327]
024 **Index discipulorum** [Sp.], ed. Schermann, *op. cit.*, 118–126.
Dup. VITAE PROPHETARUM (1750 008).
Cod: [1,280]
025 **Nomina apostolorum** [Sp.], ed. T. Schermann, *Propheten und Apostellegenden* [*Texte und Untersuchungen* 31.3. Leipzig: Hinrichs, 1907]: 232.
Cod: [182]
026 **Testimonia ex divinis et sacris scripturis** (= **De divina inhumanatione**) [Sp.], ed. R.V. Hotchkiss, *A Pseudo-Epiphanius testimony book*. Missoula, Montana: Scholars Press, 1974: 8–76.
Cod: [6,848]
027 **Notitiae episcopatum** [Sp.], ed. H. Gelzer, *Texte der Notitiae Episcopatuum* [*Abhandlungen der philosophisch-philologischen Classe*

der königlich bayerischen Akademie der Wissen-schaften 21.3. Munich: Franz, 1901]: 534–542.
Cod: [1,563]

028 **Apophthegmata** (ap. *Apophthegmata patrum*) [Sp.], MPG 65: 161–168.
Q: [773]

029 **De fide** (fragmentum) [Sp.], ed. F. Diekamp, *Doctrina patrum de incarnatione verbi.* Münster: Aschendorff, 1907: 299.
Q: [66]

030 **De trinitate** (fragmentum) [Sp.], ed. Diekamp, *op. cit.*, 317.
Q: [40]

031 **Liturgia praesanctificatorum**, ed. D.N. Morai-tes, Ἡ λειτουργία τῶν προηγιασμένων. Thes-salonica: University of Thessalonica, 1955: 53–77.
Cod

032 **Anaphora Graeca** (fragmenta) [Sp.], ed. G. Garitte, "Un opuscule grec traduit de l'armé-nien sur l'addition d'eau au vin eucharistique," *Muséon* 73 (1960) 298–299.
Cod: [304]

033 **De mensuribus et ponderibus**, ed. E. Mout-soulas, "Τὸ 'Περὶ μέτρων καὶ σταθμῶν' ἔργον 'Επιφανίου τοῦ Σαλαμῖνος," Θεολογία 44 (1973) 157–198.
Cod: [9,406]

035 **De mensuribus et ponderibus** (excerptum Graecum 1), ed. P. de Lagarde, *Symmicta* I. Göttingen: Dieterich, 1877: 211–223.
Cod

036 **De mensuribus et ponderibus** (excerptum Graecum 2), ed. de Lagarde, *op. cit.*, 223–225.
Cod: [648]

037 **De mensuribus et ponderibus** (excerptum Graecum 3), ed. I. Sakkelion, Πατμιακὴ βιβλιοθήκη. Athens: Papageorgios, 1890: 131–133.
Q: [884]

038 **De mensuribus et ponderibus** (excerptum Graecum 4), ed. F. Hultsch, *Metrologicorum scriptorum reliquiae*, vol. 1. Leipzig: Teubner, 1864: 259–276.
Q, Cod: [3,002]

039 **De mensuribus et ponderibus** (ap. Cosmam) (excerptum Graecum 6), ed. W. Wolska-Conus, *Cosmas Indicopleustès. Topographie chrétienne*, vol. 3 [*Sources chrétiennes* 197. Paris: Cerf, 1973]: 283–285.
Q: [198]

040 **De mensuribus et ponderibus** (ap. *Chronicon paschale*) (excerptum Graecum 7), MPG 92: 617, 644, 652.
Q: [50]

041 **De mensuribus et ponderibus** (ap. Joannem Damascenum) (excerptum Graecum 8), ed. B. Kotter, *Die Schriften des Johannes von Damas-kos* [*Patristische Texte und Studien* 12. Berlin: De Gruyter, 1973]: 210–211.
Q: [309]

042 **Homilia in Christi resurrectionem** (inc. Νῦν τὸ

πένθος) [Sp.], ed. P. Nautin, *Le dossier d'Hippolyte et de Méliton* [*Patristica* 1. Paris: Cerf, 1953]: 155–159.
Cod: [737]

043 **Appendices ad indices apostolorum discipu-lorumque**, ed. Schermann, *Prophetarum vitae fabulosae*, 126–131.
Dup. VITAE PROPHETARUM (1750 009).
Cod: [626]

x01 **Epistula ad Arabos.**
Panarion 78.2–25.
Cf. 2021 002.

x02 **Physiologus.**
Cf. PHYSIOLOGUS GRAECUS (2654 001–003).

1349 *EPISTULA A MARTYRIBUS LUGDUNEN-SIBUS*
A.D. 2

001 **Fragmentum epistulae a martyribus Lugdu-nensibus**, ed. M.J. Routh, *Reliquiae sacrae*, vol. 1, 2nd edn. Oxford: Oxford University Press, 1846 (repr. Hildesheim: Olms, 1974): 287.
Q: [77]

1350 *EPISTULA AD DIOGNETUM*
A.D. 2

001 **Epistula ad Diognetum**, ed. H.-I. Marrou, *A Diognète*, 2nd edn. [*Sources chrétiennes* 33 bis. Paris: Cerf, 1965]: 52–84.
Cod: [2,624]

1352 *EPISTULA ECCLESIARUM APUD LUG-DUNUM ET VIENNAM*
A.D. 2

001 **Epistula ecclesiarum apud Lugdunum et Vi-ennam**, ed. H. Musurillo, *The acts of the Chris-tian martyrs.* Oxford: Clarendon Press, 1972: 62–84.
Cod: [3,968]

0589 *EPISTULAE PRIVATAE*
3–1 B.C.

001 **Epistulae**, ed. S. Witkowsky, *Epistulae privatae Graecae quae in papyris aetatis Lagidarum ser-vantur*, 2nd edn. Leipzig: Teubner, 1911: 4–137.
Pap

1353 *EPITAPHIUM ABERCII*
A.D. 2

001 **Epitaphium**, ed. J. Quasten, *Monumenta eucha-ristica et liturgica vetustissima*, vol. 1.1 [*Flori-legium patristicum tam veteris quam medii aevi auctores complectens*, vol. 7.1. Bonn: Hanstein, 1935]: 22, 24.
Epigr: [152]

2954 *EPITAPHIUM FLAVIAE*
A.D. 2

001 **Epitaphium Flaviae**, ed. E. Curtius and A. Kirchhoff, *Corpus inscriptionum Graecarum* 4.

Berlin: Reimer, 1877 (repr. Hildesheim: Olms, 1977): 594 (no. 9595a).
Epigr

1570 *EPITAPHIUM PECTORII*
A.D. 2/3
001 **Epitaphium**, ed. J. Quasten, *Monumenta eucharistica et liturgica vetustissima*, vol. 1 [*Florilegium patristicum tam veteris quam medii aevi auctores complectens* 7.1. Bonn: Hanstein, 1935]: 24, 26.
Epigr: [65]

2139 *EPITAPHIUM SICILI*
Incertum
001 **Sicili epitaphium**, ed. K. Jan, *Musici scriptores Graeci*. Leipzig: Teubner, 1895 (repr. Hildesheim: Olms, 1962): 452.
Epigr

0690 **ERASISTRATUS** Med.
3 B.C.: Ceus
x01 **Fragmenta ap. Galenum.**
K5.123, 125 in CMG, vol. **5.4.1.1**, pp. 80–82; K5.880 in *Script. Min.*, vol. **3**, p. 86; K**8**.14, 311–313, 317–318, 321; **11**.148–149, 155–156, 158, 160–161, 175–177, 196, 220–221, 225, 228, 230–231, 235–240, 246; **18**.1.6–7.
Cf. GALENUS Med. (0057 030, 033, 057, 068, 069, 092).
x02 **Fragmentum ap. Pseudo-Galenum.**
K1.184.
Cf. Pseudo-GALENUS Med. (0530 043).
x03 **Fragmenta ap. Oribasium.**
CMG, vol. 6.3, pp. 101, 167.
Cf. ORIBASIUS Med. (0722 004).
x04 **Fragmenta ap. Paulum.**
CMG, vol. 9.2, pp. 21, 346.
Cf. PAULUS Med. (0715 001).
x05 **Fragmentum ap. Aëtium** (lib. 7).
CMG, vol. 8.2, p. 265.
Cf. AËTIUS Med. (0718 007).
x06 **Fragmenta ap. Aëtium.**
Placita 5.29.1, 30.3.
Cf. AËTIUS Doxogr. (0528 001).
x07 **Fragmentum ap. Athenaeum.**
Deipnosophistae 7.324a.
Cf. ATHENAEUS Soph. (0008 001).

2502 **ERATOSTHENES** Hist.
2 B.C.–A.D. 1: Cyrenaeus
001 **Testimonium**, FGrH #745: 3C:728.
NQ
002 **Fragmenta**, FGrH #745: 3C:728.
Q

0222 **ERATOSTHENES** Philol. et *ERATOSTHENICA*
3–2 B.C.: Cyrenaeus
001 **Catasterismi**, ed. A. Olivieri, *Pseudo-Eratosthenis catasterismi* [*Mythographi Graeci* 3.1. Leip-

zig: Teubner, 1897]: 1–52.
Cod: [7,915]
002 **Geographica**, ed. H. Berger, *Die geographischen Fragmente des Eratosthenes*. Leipzig: Teubner, 1880 (repr. Amsterdam: Meridian, 1964): 1–382 (passim).
Q
003 **Mercurius**, ed. G. Bernhardy, *Eratosthenica*. Berlin: Reimer, 1822 (repr. Osnabrück: Biblio Verlag, 1968): 110–167 (passim).
Q
004 **De mathematicis disciplinis**, ed. Bernhardy, *op. cit.*, 168–174 (passim).
Q
005 **De cubi duplicatione**, ed. Bernhardy, *op. cit.*, 175–185 (passim).
Q
006 **Opera philosophica**, ed. Bernhardy, *op. cit.*, 186–202 (passim).
Q
007 **De antiqua comoedia**, ed. Bernhardy, *op. cit.*, 203–237 (passim).
Q
008 **De chronographiis**, ed. Bernhardy, *op. cit.*, 238–262 (passim).
Q
009 **Fragmenta**, ed. J.U. Powell, *Collectanea Alexandrina*. Oxford: Clarendon Press, 1925 (repr. 1970): 59–68.
frr. 4, 6–12, 15–19, 22–27, 29–33, 35–37.
Q: [472]
010 **Fragmentum Eratosthenicum**, ed. Powell, *op. cit.*, 252.
Q: [6]
011 **Testimonia**, FGrH #241: 2B:1010–1012.
test. 7: *P. Oxy.* 10.1241.
NQ
012 **Fragmenta historica**, FGrH #241: 2B:1012–1021.
fr. 8: *P. Oxy.* 3.409.
Q, Pap
013 **Fragmenta**, ed. H. Lloyd-Jones and P. Parsons, *Supplementum Hellenisticum*. Berlin: De Gruyter, 1983: 183–186.
frr. 397–399.
fr. 397: *P. Oxy.* 42.3000.
Q, Pap: [90]
x01 **Victores Olympici** (fort. auctore Phlegonte vel Eratosthene).
FGrH #415.
Cf. ANONYMI HISTORICI (FGrH) (1139 026).
x02 **Fragmentum papyraceum** (fort. auctore Eratosthene).
SH, p. 424, fr. 922.
Cf. ADESPOTA PAPYRACEA (SH) (2648 001).

4063 **ERATOSTHENES Scholasticus** Epigr.
A.D. 6
001 **Epigrammata**, AG **5**.242, 277; **6**.77–78; **9**.444.
AG 5.243: Cf. MACEDONIUS II Epigr. (4064 001).

AG 5.244, 246: Cf. PAULUS Silentiarius Poet. Christ. (4039 004).
AG 7.601: Cf. JULIANUS <Epigr.> (4050 001).
Q: 156

x01 **Epigrammata** (*App. Anth.*).
Epigramma dedicatorium: 1.119.
Epigramma demonstrativum: 3.68.
Epigramma exhortatorium et supplicatorium: 4.38.
App. Anth. 1.119: Cf. EPIGRAMMATICI in *App. Anth.* (7052 001).
App. Anth. 3.68: Cf. EPIGRAMMATICI in *App. Anth.* (7052 003).
App. Anth. 4.38: Cf. EPIGRAMMATICI in *App. Anth.* (7052 004).

EREN(N)IUS PHILO Hist. et Gramm.
Cf. (H)EREN(N)IUS PHILO His. et Gramm. (1416).

2149 **ERETES** Hist.
vel Aretes vel Crates
3 B.C.?
001 **Fragmenta**, FGrH #242: 2B:1021.
Q

1354 **ERGIAS** Hist.
4 B.C.?: Rhodius
001 **Fragmenta**, FGrH #513: 3B:488–489.
Q

1355 **ERINNA** Lyr.
4 B.C.: Telia
001 **Fragmenta**, ed. E. Diehl, *Anthologia lyrica Graeca*, vol. 1.4, 2nd edn. Leipzig: Teubner, 1936: 207–213.
frr. 1–5.
Q, Pap: [694]
002 **Epigrammata**, AG **6**.352; 7.710, 712.
Q: 139
003 **Fragmenta et titulus**, ed. H. Lloyd-Jones and P. Parsons, *Supplementum Hellenisticum*. Berlin: De Gruyter, 1983: 186–189, 192–193.
frr. (+ titul.) 400–402, 404.
Q, Pap: [222]

0455 **ERIPHUS** Comic.
4 B.C.
001 **Fragmenta**, ed. T. Kock, *Comicorum Atticorum fragmenta*, vol. 2. Leipzig: Teubner, 1884: 428–430.
frr. 1–7.
Q: 203
002 **Fragmenta**, ed. A. Meineke, *Fragmenta comicorum Graecorum*, vol. 3. Berlin: Reimer, 1840 (repr. De Gruyter, 1970): 556–559.
Q: 199

0716 **EROTIANUS** Gramm. et Med.
A.D. 1
001 **Vocum Hippocraticarum collectio**, ed. E.

Nachmanson, *Erotiani vocum Hippocraticarum collectio cum fragmentis*. Göteborg: Eranos, 1918: 3–96.
Cod: 12,089
002 **Fragmenta**, ed. Nachmanson, *op. cit.*, 99–122.
Q: 2,489

5003 *EROTICA ADESPOTA*
Varia
001 **Sesonchosis** (*P. Oxy.* 15.1826), ed. F. Zimmermann, *Griechische Roman-Papyri und verwandte Texte*. Heidelberg: Bilabel, 1936: 36–40.
Pap
002 **De Chione** (Codex Thebanus deperditus), ed. Zimmermann, *op. cit.*, 41–46.
Cod
003 **Calligone** (*PSI* 981 = *P. Cairo* 47992), ed. Zimmermann, *op. cit.*, 47–50.
Pap
004 **Dionysius** (*PSI* 151), ed. Zimmermann, *op. cit.*, 50–52.
Pap
005 **Metiochus et Parthenope** (*P. Berol.* inv. 7927 + 9588), ed. Zimmermann, *op. cit.*, 53–61.
Pap
006 **Metiochus et Parthenope** (?) (*P. Oxy.* 3.435 = *P. Yale* inv. 45), ed. Zimmermann, *op. cit.*, 62.
Pap
007 **Fragmenta** (*P. Berol.* inv. 10535), ed. Zimmermann, *op. cit.*, 64–68.
Pap
008 **Herpyllis** (*P. Dublin* inv. C3), ed. Zimmermann, *op. cit.*, 68–78.
Pap
009 **Antheia** (?) (*PSI* 726), ed. Zimmermann, *op. cit.*, 79–84.
Pap
010 **Olenius** (*PSI* 725), ed. Zimmermann, *op. cit.*, 90–92.
Pap
011 **Fragmenta** (*P. Brit. Mus.* 2037D = *P. Lit. Lond.* 245), ed. Zimmermann, *op. cit.*, 93.
Pap
012 **Fragmenta** (*P. Brit. Mus.* inv. 1847A = *P. Lit. Lond.* 194), ed. Zimmermann, *op. cit.*, 94–98.
Pap

2312 **ERXIAS** Hist.
ante 2 B.C.?
001 **Fragmentum**, FGrH #449: 3B:377.
Q

0180 **ERYCIUS** Epigr.
fiq Erycius Poeta
1 B.C.: Cyzicenus
Cf. et ERYCIUS Poeta (2653).
001 **Epigrammata**, AG **6**.96, 234, 255; 7.36, 174, 230, 368, 377, 397; **9**.233, 237, 558, 824; **16**.242.
Q: 571

2653 **ERYCIUS** Poeta
fiq Erycius Cyzicenus
1 B.C.?
Cf. et ERYCIUS Epigr. (0180).
001 **Fragmentum**, ed. H. Lloyd-Jones and P. Parsons, *Supplementum Hellenisticum*. Berlin: De Gruyter, 1983: 193.
fr. 407.
Q: [4]

1356 ***ESDRAS V/VI***
A.D. 2/3
001 **Fragmenta**, *P. Oxy*. 7.1010.
Pap

0885 **Pseudo-ESDRAS**
ante A.D. 7
x01 **Fragmentum ap. Paulum**.
CMG, vol. 9.2, p. 303.
Cf. PAULUS Med. (0715 001).

0181 **ETRUSCUS** Epigr.
1 B.C.?
001 **Epigramma**, AG 7.381.
Q: 41

2372 **EUAGON** Hist.
5 B.C.: Samius
001 **Testimonia**, FGrH #535: 3B:520.
NQ
002 **Fragmenta**, FGrH #535: 3B:520–521.
Q

2425 **EUAGORAS** Hist.
A.D. 1/3?: Lindius
001 **Testimonium**, FGrH #619: 3C:153.
NQ

2293 **EUALCES** Hist.
ante 3 B.C.: Ephesius
001 **Fragmentum**, FGrH #418: 3B:316.
Q

0456 **EUANGELUS** Comic.
post 4 B.C.
001 **Fragmentum**, ed. T. Kock, *Comicorum Atticorum fragmenta*, vol. 3. Leipzig: Teubner, 1888: 376.
fr. 1.
Q: 88
002 **Fragmenta**, ed. A. Meineke, *Fragmenta comicorum Graecorum*, vol. 4. Berlin: Reimer, 1841 (repr. De Gruyter, 1970): 572.
Q: 90

0886 **EUANGELUS** Med.
ante A.D. 1
x01 **Fragmentum ap. Galenum**.
K13.806.
Cf. GALENUS Med. (0057 077).

2623 **EUANTHES** Epic.
ante A.D. 2

001 **Titulus**, ed. H. Lloyd-Jones and P. Parsons, *Supplementum Hellenisticum*. Berlin: De Gruyter, 1983: 194.
fr. 409.
NQ: [3]

1096 **EUARETUS** Trag.
4 B.C.
001 **Tituli**, ed. B. Snell, *Tragicorum Graecorum fragmenta*, vol. 1. Göttingen: Vandenhoeck & Ruprecht, 1971: 251.
frr. 1–2.
NQ

1800 **EUBOEUS** Parodius
5–4 B.C.: Parius
001 **Fragmenta**, ed. P. Brandt, *Corpusculum poesis epicae Graecae Ludibundae*, fasc. 1. Leipzig: Teubner, 1888: 52.
frr. 1–2.
Q: [17]
002 **Fragmenta et titulus**, ed. H. Lloyd-Jones and P. Parsons, *Supplementum Hellenisticum*. Berlin: De Gruyter, 1983: 194.
frr. (+ titul.) 410–412.
Q: [18]

0457 **EUBULIDES** Comic.
4 B.C.?
001 **Fragmentum**, ed. T. Kock, *Comicorum Atticorum fragmenta*, vol. 2. Leipzig: Teubner, 1884: 431.
fr. 1.
Q: 13
002 **Fragmentum**, ed. A. Meineke, *Fragmenta comicorum Graecorum*, vol. 3. Berlin: Reimer, 1840 (repr. De Gruyter, 1970): 559.
Q: 13

0458 **EUBULUS** Comic.
4 B.C.
001 **Fragmenta**, ed. T. Kock, *Comicorum Atticorum fragmenta*, vol. 2. Leipzig: Teubner, 1884: 164–214.
frr. 1–4, 6–21, 23–32, 34–39, 41–57, 60–122, 124–131, 133–134, 136–151 + tituli.
Q: 2,745
002 **Fragmenta**, ed. A. Meineke, *Fragmenta comicorum Graecorum*, vol. 3. Berlin: Reimer, 1840 (repr. De Gruyter, 1970): 203–205, 207–232, 234–255, 257–271.
Q: 2,584
003 **Fragmenta**, ed. J. Demiańczuk, *Supplementum comicum*. Krakau: Nakładem Akademii, 1912 (repr. Hildesheim: Olms, 1967): 40–41.
frr. 1–2.
Q: 20
004 **Titulus**, ed. C. Austin, *Comicorum Graecorum fragmenta in papyris reperta*. Berlin: De Gruyter, 1973: 83.
NQ: 2

005 **Fragmentum**, ed. Kock, *op. cit.*, vol. 3 (1888): 738.
fr. 145b.
Q: 2

006 **Fragmentum**, ed. Meineke, *op. cit.*, vol. 5.1 (1857; repr. 1970): clxxxvi.
Q: [10]

x01 **Aenigmata.**
App. Anth. 7.9–10: Cf. EPIGRAMMATICI in *App. Anth.* (7052 007).
App. Anth. 7.10b addenda: Cf. EPIGRAMMATICI in *App. Anth.* (7052 008).

0887 **EUBULUS** Med.
ante A.D. 1

x01 **Fragmenta ap. Galenum.**
K13.297, 911.
Cf. GALENUS Med. (0057 076–077).

0250 **EUCLIDES** Comic. vel Iamb.
ante 5 B.C.: fort. Atheniensis

001 **Fragmenta**, ed. M.L. West, *Iambi et elegi Graeci*, vol. 2. Oxford: Clarendon Press, 1972: 63.
frr. 1–2.
Q: [15]

1799 **EUCLIDES** Geom.
3 B.C.: Alexandrinus

001 **Elementa**, ed. E.S. Stamatis (post J.L. Heiberg), *Euclidis elementa*, vols. 1–4, 2nd edn. Leipzig: Teubner, 1:1969; 2:1970; 3:1972; 4:1973: 1:1–179; 2:1–227; 3:1–210; 4:1–186.
Lib. 1–4: vol. 1, pp. 1–179.
Lib. 5–9: vol. 2, pp. 1–227.
Lib. 10: vol. 3, pp. 1–210.
Lib. 11–13: vol. 4, pp. 1–186.
Lib. 14: Cf. HYPSICLES Math. et Astron. (0717 001).
Lib. 15: Cf. ANONYMUS Discipulus Isidori Milesii Mech. (4005 001).
Cod: 155,536

002 **Elementa** (demonstrationes alterae, lib. 1–3), ed. Stamatis (post Heiberg), *op. cit.*, vol. 1, 181–186.
Cod: 895

003 **Elementa** (demonstrationes alterae, lib. 5–9), ed. Stamatis (post Heiberg), *op. cit.*, vol. 2, 229–237, 239.
Cod: 1,698

004 **Elementa** (demonstrationes alterae, lib. 10), ed. Stamatis (post Heiberg), *op. cit.*, vol. 3, 211–234.
Cod: 4,197

005 **Elementa** (demonstrationes alterae, lib. 11–13), ed. Stamatis (post Heiberg), *op. cit.*, vol. 4, 187–206.
Cod: 4,166

006 **Elementa** (recensio altera, lib. 11.36–12.17), ed. Stamatis (post Heiberg), *op. cit.*, vol. 4, 207–238.
Cod: 10,354

007 **Data**, ed. H. Menge, *Euclidis opera omnia*, vol. 6. Leipzig: Teubner, 1896: 2–186.
Cod: 19,815

008 **Data** (demonstrationes alterae), ed. Menge, *op. cit.*, vol. 6, 190–230.
Cod: 4,363

009 **Optica**, ed. J.L. Heiberg, *Euclidis opera omnia*, vol. 7. Leipzig: Teubner, 1895: 2–120.
Cod: 11,435

010 **Opticorum recensio Theonis**, ed. Heiberg, *op. cit.*, vol. 7, 144–246.
Cod

011 **Catoptrica**, ed. Heiberg, *op. cit.*, vol. 7, 286–342.
Cod: 5,436

012 **Phaenomena**, ed. Menge, *op. cit.*, vol. 8 (1916): 2–104.
Cod: 8,344

013 **Phaenomena** (recensio b), ed. Menge, *op. cit.*, vol. 8, 44–82, 86–102, 106–112.
Cod: 5,284

014 **Phaenomena** (demonstrationes alterae recensionis b), ed. Menge, *op. cit.*, vol. 8, 114–132.
Cod: 2,411

015 **Sectio canonis** [Sp.], ed. Menge, *op. cit.*, vol. 8, 158–180.
Cod: 2,502

016 **Fragmenta**, ed. Heiberg, *op. cit.*, vol. 8, 227, 236–284.
Q, Cod: [12,220]

017 **Epigramma**, ed. Heiberg, *op. cit.*, vol. 8, 286.
Q: [48]

x01 **Problema.**
App. Anth. 7.2: Cf. EPIGRAMMATICI in *App. Anth.* (7052 007).

x02 **Scholia in opticorum recensionem Theonis.**
Heiberg, pp. 251–284.
Cf. SCHOLIA (4101 003).

x03 **Introductio harmonica.**
Menge, pp. 186–222.
Cf. CLEONIDES Mus. (0361 001).

2356 **EUCRATES** Hist.
ante A.D. 3

001 **Fragmenta**, FGrH #514: 3B:490.
Q

2343 **EUDEMUS** Hist.
5 B.C.?: Naxius vel Parius

001 **Testimonia**, FGrH #497: 3B:469.
NQ

2365 **EUDEMUS** Hist.
4 B.C.?

001 **Titulus**, FGrH #524: 3B:503.
NQ

0735 **EUDEMUS** Med.
3 B.C.: Alexandrinus

001 **Fragmenta**, *P. Ryl.* 1.21.
Pap

1357 **EUDEMUS** Phil.
4 B.C.: Rhodius
001 **Fragmenta**, ed. F. Wehrli, *Eudemos von Rhodos* [*Die Schule des Aristoteles*, vol. 8, 2nd edn. Basel: Schwabe, 1969]: 11–72.
Q

0888 **EUDEMUS** Poet. Med.
A.D. 1
001 **Fragmentum**, ed. H. Lloyd-Jones and P. Parsons, *Supplementum Hellenisticum*. Berlin: De Gruyter, 1983: 195.
fr. 412a.
Q: [103]
x01 **Fragmenta ap. Galenum**.
K14.185, 201.
Cf. GALENUS Med. (0057 078).

1376 **EUDEMUS** Rhet.
A.D. 2?: fort. Argivus
001 Περὶ λέξεων ῥητορικῶν (excerpta), ed. B. Niese, "Excerpta ex Eudemi codice Parisino n. 2635," *Philologus*, suppl. 15 (1922) 145–160.
Cod: [2,333]

0903 **EUDEMUS Senior** Med.
ante A.D. 2
x01 **Fragmentum ap. Galenum**.
K13.291.
Cf. GALENUS Med. (0057 076).

1847 **EUDORUS** Hist.
1 B.C.: Alexandrinus
x01 **Testimonium**
FGrH #650: 3C:203–204.
Cf. ARISTON Phil. (2447 001).

1358 **EUDOXUS** Astron.
4 B.C.: Cnidius
001 **Fragmenta**, ed. F. Lasserre, *Die Fragmente des Eudoxos von Knidos*. Berlin: De Gruyter, 1966: 39–127.
frr. 2–11, 13–20, 22–30, 32–43, 45, 47–48, 50–54, 56–57, 59, 62–130, 132–133, 137, 139, 141–143, 147a–173b, 174b, 176–192a, 193a–313, 315–326, 328–339, 341, 344a–363, 365–368, 370–374.
Q, Pap: [17,590]
002 **Fragmenta** [Sp.], ed. F. Boll, *Codices Germanici* [*Catalogus codicum astrologorum Graecorum* 7. Brussels: Lamertin, 1908]: 183–187.
Cod: [1,922]
003 **Ars astronomica** [Sp.] (*P. Par.* 1), ed. F. Blass, *Eudoxi ars astronomica qualis in charta Aegyptiaca superest* [*Programm Kiel* (1887)]: 12–25.
Pap

0399 **EUDOXUS** Comic.
4–3 B.C.?
001 **Fragmenta**, ed. A. Kock, *Comicorum Atticorum fragmenta*, vol. 3. Leipzig: Teubner, 1888: 332.
frr. 1–2.
Q: 6

002 **Tituli**, ed. A. Meineke, *Fragmenta comicorum Graecorum*, vol. 4. Berlin: Reimer, 1841 (repr. De Gruyter, 1970): 508.
NQ: 3

1915 **EUDOXUS** Hist.
3 B.C.: Rhodius
001 **Testimonia**, FGrH #79: 2A:159.
NQ
002 **Fragmenta**, FGrH #79: 2A:159–160.
Q

2399 **EUDROMUS** Phil.
Incertum
001 **Fragmenta**, ed. J. von Arnim, *Stoicorum veterum fragmenta*, vol. 3. Leipzig: Teubner, 1903 (repr. Stuttgart: 1968): 268.
Q

0251 **EUENUS** Eleg.
5–4 B.C.: Parius
001 **Fragmenta**, ed. M.L. West, *Iambi et elegi Graeci*, vol. 2. Oxford: Clarendon Press, 1972: 64–67.
frr. 1–9a.
Q: [166]
x01 **Epigrammata exhortatoria et supplicatoria**.
App. Anth. 4.13–15: Cf. EPIGRAMMATICI in *App. Anth.* (7052 004).

0183 **EUENUS** Epigr.
1 B.C.?: Atheniensis
001 **Epigramma**, AG 9.602.
Q: 51

0182 **EUENUS** Gramm.
1 B.C.?: Ascalonius
001 **Epigrammata**, AG **9**.62, 75, 122, 251, 717–718; **11**.49; **12**.172; **16**.165–166.
Q: 256

0184 **EUGENES** Epigr.
post 3 B.C.
001 **Epigramma**, AG 16.308.
Q: 43

0891 **EUGENIUS** Med.
A.D. 1–2
x01 **Fragmentum ap. Galenum**.
K13.114.
Cf. GALENUS Med. (0057 076).

0892 **EUGERASIA** Med.
ante A.D. 2
x01 **Fragmentum ap. Galenum**.
K13.244.
Cf. GALENUS Med. (0057 076).

1905 **EUHEMERUS Scriptor De Sacra Historia**
4–3 B.C.: Messenius
001 **Testimonia**, FGrH #63: 1A:300–302.
NQ

002 **Fragmenta**, FGrH #63: 1A:302–313, *20 addenda.
Q

1972 **EUMACHUS** Hist.
3–2 B.C.: Neapolitanus
001 **Fragmenta**, FGrH #178: 2B:906.
Q

1361 **EUMEDES** Comic.
post 4 B.C.?
001 **Titulus**, ed. T. Kock, *Comicorum Atticorum fragmenta*, vol. 3. Leipzig: Teubner, 1888: 377.
NQ: 2

0298 **EUMELUS** Epic.
8 B.C.?: Corinthius
Cf. et TITANOMACHIA (1737).
001 **Fragmentum**, ed. D.L. Page, *Poetae melici Graeci*. Oxford: Clarendon Press, 1962 (repr. 1967 (1st edn. corr.)): 361.
fr. 1.
Q: [14]
002 **Fragmenta**, ed. G. Kinkel, *Epicorum Graecorum fragmenta*, vol. 1. Leipzig: Teubner, 1877: 188, 191, 193, 195.
frr. 2, 9, 11, 13, 16.
Q: [130]
003 **Testimonia**, FGrH #451: 3B:378.
NQ
004 **Corinthiaca** (fragmenta), FGrH #451: 3B:378–381.
Q

1913 **EUMELUS** Hist.
3 B.C.?
001 **Fragmenta**, FGrH #77: 2A:158.
Q

EUMENES Hist.
4 B.C.: Cardianus
Cf. EPHEMERIDES (2436 001–002).

0890 **EUMERUS** Med.
ante A.D. 2
x01 **Fragmenta ap. Galenum**.
K12.774, 777, 778, 788.
Cf. GALENUS Med. (0057 076).

2723 **EUMETIS** Epigr.
ante A.D. 2
x01 **Aenigma**.
App. Anth. 7.6(?): Cf. EPIGRAMMATICI in *App. Anth.* (7052 007).

2050 **EUNAPIUS** Hist. et Soph.
A.D. 4–5: Sardianus
001 **Vitae sophistarum**, ed. J. Giangrande, *Eunapii vitae sophistarum*. Rome: Polygraphica, 1956: 1–101.
Cod: [22,283]
002 **Fragmenta historica**, ed. L. Dindorf, *Historici*

Graeci minores, vol. 1. Leipzig: Teubner, 1870: 205–274.
Q: [16,189]

0459 **EUNICUS** Comic.
5 B.C.
001 **Fragmentum**, ed. T. Kock, *Comicorum Atticorum fragmenta*, vol. 1. Leipzig: Teubner, 1880: 781.
fr. 1 + titulus.
Q: 9
002 **Fragmentum**, ed. A. Meineke, *Fragmenta comicorum Graecorum*, vol. 2.2. Berlin: Reimer, 1840 (repr. De Gruyter, 1970): 856.
Q: 8

EUNOMIANUS Epigr.
AG 9.193.
Cf. PHILOSTORGIUS Scr. Eccl. (2058 006).

0893 **EUNOMUS** Med.
A.D. 1
x01 **Fragmentum ap. Galenum**.
K13.851.
Cf. GALENUS Med. (0057 077).

0185 **EUODUS** Epigr.
A.D. 2/3
001 **Epigrammata**, AG 16.116, 155.
Q: 22

0396 **EUPHANES** Comic.
4 B.C.
001 **Fragmentum**, ed. T. Kock, *Comicorum Atticorum fragmenta*, vol. 2. Leipzig: Teubner, 1884: 296–297.
fr. 1.
Q: 12

1912 **EUPHANTUS** Hist.
4–3 B.C.: Olynthius
001 **Testimonia**, FGrH #74: 2A:132.
test. 3: *P. Herc.* 1112.
NQ
002 **Fragmenta**, FGrH #74: 2A:132–133.
Q

0221 **EUPHORION** Epic.
3 B.C.: Chalcidensis
001 **Fragmenta**, ed. J.U. Powell, *Collectanea Alexandrina*. Oxford: Clarendon Press, 1925 (repr. 1970): 29–34, 36–47, 49–56, 58.
frr. 2–5, 8–14, 16–17, 21, 23–25, 30, 33–35, 38, 40–44, 46–48, 50–54, 57–61, 63–66, 73–75, 77–96, 98, 103–104, 107–108, 110–114, 118–125, 127–141, 145, 149–154, 158–162, 175–176.
Q: [1,199]
002 **Fragmenta**, ed. H. Lloyd-Jones and P. Parsons, *Supplementum Hellenisticum*. Berlin: De Gruyter, 1983: 196–199, 205–207, 210–218, 221–233.
frr. 413–454.

frr. 413–416: *PSI* 1390.
frr. 418–421: *P. Oxy.* 19.2219.
frr. 422–427: *P. Oxy.* 19.2220.
fr. 428: *P. Oxy.* 30.2525.
fr. 429: *P. Berol.* 13873.
frr. 430–431: *P. Oxy.* 17.2085.
fr. 432: *P. Oxy.* 30.2528.
frr. 433–452: *P. Oxy.* 30.2526.
fr. 453: *P. Berol.* 9780.
fr. 454: *P. Oxy.* 30.2527.
Q, Pap: [2,200]
003 **Fragmenta prosaica**, ed. B.A. van Groningen, *Euphorion*. Amsterdam: Hakkert, 1977: 226–248.
Q: [1,096]
004 **Epigrammata**, AG **6.279; 7.651.**
Q: 63

0894 EUPHRANOR Med.
A.D. 1
x01 **Fragmentum ap. Galenum.**
K13.525.
Cf. GALENUS Med. (0057 077).

0460 EUPHRO Comic.
3 B.C.
001 **Fragmenta**, ed. T. Kock, *Comicorum Atticorum fragmenta*, vol. 3. Leipzig: Teubner, 1888: 317–324.
frr. 1–12.
Q: 576
002 **Fragmenta**, ed. A. Meineke, *Fragmenta comicorum Graecorum*, vol. 4. Berlin: Reimer, 1841 (repr. De Gruyter, 1970): 486–487, 489–495.
Q: 582

0210 EUPHRONIUS Lyr.
3 B.C.: Chersonesites
001 **Priapeia**, ed. J.U. Powell, *Collectanea Alexandrina*. Oxford: Clarendon Press, 1925 (repr. 1970): 176.
Q: [29]

2129 EUPITHIUS Epigr.
A.D. 3: Atheniensis
001 **Epigramma**, AG 9.206.
Q: 27

2486 EUPOLEMUS Hist.
2 B.C.: Judaeus
001 **Testimonia**, FGrH #723: 3C:671–672.
NQ
002 **Fragmenta**, FGrH #723: 3C:672–678.
Q

2487 Pseudo-EUPOLEMUS Hist.
2 B.C.?
001 **Fragmenta**, FGrH #724: 3C:678–679.
Q

0461 EUPOLIS Comic.
5 B.C.

001 **Fragmenta**, ed. T. Kock, *Comicorum Atticorum fragmenta*, vol. 1. Leipzig: Teubner, 1880: 258–270, 272–355, 357–369.
frr. 1–16, 18–32, 34–38, 42–52, 58, 60–79, 86, 88–121, 128–134, 138–141, 143–144, 146–163, 168–177, 179–188, 190–192, 198–236, 242–248, 250–259, 261–272, 275–293, 295–362, 372, 374–453, 455–459.
Q: 2,936
002 **Fragmenta**, ed. A. Meineke, *Fragmenta comicorum Graecorum*, vol. 2.1. Berlin: Reimer, 1839 (repr. De Gruyter, 1970): 426, 428–433, 435, 437–438, 440–444, 447–453, 455–458, 460–461, 463–475, 477, 479–482, 484–486, 488–495, 497–502, 505–521, 523–526, 528–543, 546–568, 577.
p. 447, fr. 1: lines 3–4 supplied from vol. 5.1, p. lxx.
p. 520: fr. 35 supplied from vol. 5.1, p. lxxxii.
Q: 2,840
003 **Fragmenta**, ed. J. Demiańczuk, *Supplementum comicum*. Krakau: Nakładem Akademii, 1912 (repr. Hildesheim: Olms, 1967): 41–53.
frr. 1–27.
fr. 7–12: *P. Cairo* inv. 43227.
Q, Pap: 668
004 **Fragmenta**, ed. C. Austin, *Comicorum Graecorum fragmenta in papyris reperta*. Berlin: De Gruyter, 1973: 83–119.
frr. 92–100.
Pap: 2,808
005 **Fragmenta**, ed. Meineke, *op. cit.*, vol. 5.1 (1857; repr. 1970): lxviii, lxxviii–lxxix, xc–xci.
Q: [43]
006 **Fragmentum**, ed. A. Guida, "Frammenti inediti di Eupoli, Teleclide, Teognide, Giuliano e Imerio da un nuovo codice del Lexicon Vindobonense," *Prometheus* 5 (1979) 201.
Q

0006 EURIPIDES Trag.
5 B.C.: Atheniensis
Cf. et EURIPIDIS EPISTULAE (1367).
001 **Cyclops**, ed. G. Murray, *Euripidis fabulae*, vol. 1. Oxford: Clarendon Press, 1902 (repr. 1966).
Cod: 4,469
002 **Alcestis**, ed. Murray, *op. cit.*, vol. 1.
Cod: 7,089
003 **Medea**, ed. Murray, *op. cit.*, vol. 1.
Cod: 8,394
004 **Heraclidae**, ed. Murray, *op. cit.*, vol. 1.
Cod: 6,643
005 **Hippolytus**, ed. Murray, *op. cit.*, vol. 1.
Cod: 8,647
006 **Andromacha**, ed. Murray, *op. cit.*, vol. 1.
Cod: 7,763
007 **Hecuba**, ed. Murray, *op. cit.*, vol. 1.
Cod: 7,676
008 **Supplices**, ed. Murray, *op. cit.*, vol. 2, 3rd edn. (1913; repr. 1966).
Cod: 7,548

009 **Hercules**, ed. Murray, *op. cit.*, vol. 2.
Cod: 8,468

010 **Ion**, ed. Murray, *op. cit.*, vol. 2.
Cod: 10,100

011 **Troiades**, ed. Murray, *op. cit.*, vol. 2.
Cod: 7,633

012 **Electra**, ed. Murray, *op. cit.*, vol. 2.
Cod: 8,263

013 **Iphigenia Taurica**, ed. Murray, *op. cit.*, vol. 2.
Cod: 9,025

014 **Helena**, ed. Murray, *op. cit.*, vol. 3 (1902; repr. 1966).
Cod: 10,581

015 **Phoenissae**, ed. Murray, *op. cit.*, vol. 3.
Cod: 10,477

016 **Orestes**, ed. Murray, *op. cit.*, vol. 3.
Cf. et CANTICUM EURIPIDIS (2138 001).
Cod: 10,753

017 **Bacchae**, ed. Murray, *op. cit.*, vol. 3.
Cod: 8,207

018 **Iphigenia Aulidensis**, ed. Murray, *op. cit.*, vol. 3.
Cod: 10,044

019 **Rhesus**, ed. Murray, *op. cit.*, vol. 3.
Cod: 5,799

020 **Fragmenta**, ed. A. Nauck, *Tragicorum Graecorum fragmenta*. Leipzig: Teubner, 1889 (repr. Hildesheim: Olms, 1964): 363–378, 380–410, 412–419, 421–427, 429–468, 470–496, 498–513, 515–516, 518–578, 580–599, 601–609, 611–612, 616–623, 625–667, 670–716.
frr. 1–38, 40–63, 65–177, 179–181, 183–224, 226–369, 371–426, 428–478, 480–484, 486–487, 489–495, 497–513, 515–567, 569–588, 590–740, 742–779, 781–819, 821–837, 839–850, 852–859, 861–880, 882–890, 892–924, 926–941, 943–953, 955–1003, 1005–1015, 1017–1020, 1023–1092, 1095–1115, 1117, 1123–1127, 1129–1132 + tituli.
Q, Cod, Pap: [20,058]

021 **Fragmenta papyracea**, ed. C. Austin, *Nova fragmenta Euripidea in papyris reperta*. Berlin: De Gruyter, 1968: 12–21, 23–40, 42–48, 50–58, 60–65, 67–87.
frr. 1–156 + tituli.
Q, Pap: [5,206]

022 **Epinicium in Alcibiadem** (fragmenta), ed. D.L. Page, *Poetae melici Graeci*. Oxford: Clarendon Press, 1962 (repr. 1967 (1st edn. corr.)): 391.
frr. 1–2.
Q: [39]

023 **Fragmenta Phaethontis**, ed. J. Diggle, *Euripides. Phaethon*. Cambridge: Cambridge University Press, 1970: 55–69.
Cf. et 0006 032.
Q, Cod, Pap: [1,409]

032 **Fragmenta Phaethontis incertae sedis**, ed. Diggle, *op. cit.*, 70–71.
frr. 3, 5, 6.
Cf. et 0006 023.
Q

024 **Fragmenta Antiopes**, ed. J. Kambitsis, *L'Antiope d'Euripide*. Athens: Hourzamanis, 1972: 1–19, 130, 134.
frr. 1–48, 910N, 911N.
Q, Pap: [1,515]

025 **Fragmenta Alexandri**, ed. B. Snell, *Euripides Alexandros und andere Strassburger Papyri mit Fragmenten griechischer Dichter* [*Hermes Einzelschriften* 5 (1937)]: 5–21.
frr. 2–7, 9*, 11*, 13–14*, 16, 18, 23, 25*, 26–29, 30*–31*, 32–41, 43–44, 45*, 46–58, 60, 62–68.
Pap: [1,630]

026 **Fragmenta Hypsipyles**, ed. G.W. Bond, *Euripides. Hypsipyle*. Oxford: Clarendon Press, 1963: 23–52, 157.
p. 23: fr. 752N
pp. 23-24: fr. 61+82
p. 24: frr. 70+96, 764N
p. 25: frr. I.i, 2
pp. 25-27: fr. I.ii
pp. 27-28: fr. I.iii
pp. 28-30: fr. I.iv
p. 30: fr. 4
pp. 30-32: fr. I.v
p. 32: frr. 753N, 6, 7
p. 33: fr. 8/9
pp. 33-34: fr. 10
p. 34: frr. 12+14, 11
pp. 34-35: fr. 754N
p. 35: fr. 32
pp. 35-36: fr. 20/21
p. 36: fr. 34/35
pp. 36-37: fr. 18
p. 37: frr. 19, 31+38, 33
p. 38: frr. 36, 23, 24, 758N, 760N
p. 39: frr. 27, 28
pp. 39-44: frr. 22 et 60
p. 44: fr. 63
pp. 44-45: fr. 57
pp. 45-46: fr. 58
p. 46: frr. 59, 81
pp. 46-48: fr. 64
p. 48: fr. ap. Lydum
p. 49: frr. 62, 76, 66
p. 50: frr. 72, 73, 74
p. 51: frr. 755N, 756N, 761N, 762N, 763N, 765N, 766N, 767N
p. 52: frr. 769N, fragmenta dubia (a= 856N; b= *P. Petrie* 2.49d)
p. 157: addendum (= *P. Hamb.* 118b)
Pap: [3,086]

027 **Fragmenta Phrixei**, *P. Oxy.* 34.2685.
Pap: [170]

028 **Fragmenta fabulae incertae**, ed. Snell, *Hermes Einzelschriften* 5, 79–82.
Pap: [401]

029 **Fragmenta**, ed. D.L. Page, *Select papyri*, vol. 3 [*Literary papyri*]. London: Heinemann, 1941 (repr. 1970): 54–70, 74–76, 82–108, 112–118, 122–134, 154–158.

frr. 8–18, 26–28 + tituli.
Pap: [5,451]
030 **Fragmenta Oenei**, ed. J. von Arnim, *Supplementum Euripideum*. Bonn: Marcus & Weber, 1913: 38, 39–40.
Pap: [86]
031 **Epigrammata**, AG 10.107, 107b.
Q: 28
033 **Fragmenta**, ed. B. Snell, *Tragicorum Graecorum fragmenta. Supplementum*. Hildesheim: Olms, 1964: 3–20.
frr. 11a–c, 13a, *42a, **42b, *42c, 73a, 78a, 87a, **114a, **124.4, **125a(?), 155a, **164a, 179, 182a, 184.1, 185.4–5, *264a, 265a, 282a, 308.1, *312a, 330a, **330b, *360a, 369a–b, 379a, 386a, 397a, **426a, 447a, 472a, 477a, 539a, 554a, 556, 617a, 645a, 646a, 660a, 665a, 674a, 681a, *683a, 705a, 708a, 741a, 751a, **790a, 799a, 813a, 838a, 845a, 860, 882a, *889a, 898a, 908a, *908b, 913, 920a, 921.3, 925a–b, 926a, 929a, *941a, 942a, 944a, 954a, 955a–i, 989a, 1007a–f, 1007g(?), 1009a, 1024, 1043a, 1087, 1097a, 1098a, 1100a, 1110a, 1128a–b.
Q, Pap
x01 **Epigrammata** (*App. Anth.*).
Epigrammata sepulcralia: 2.22–25.
Epigrammata demonstrativa: 3.27–28.
App. Anth. 2.22–25: Cf. EPIGRAMMATICI in *App. Anth.* (7052 002).
App. Anth. 3.27–28: Cf. EPIGRAMMATICI in *App. Anth.* (7052 003).

1840 **EURIPIDES II** Trag.
5 B.C.
001 **Tituli**, ed. B. Snell, *Tragicorum Graecorum fragmenta*, vol. 1. Göttingen: Vandenhoeck & Ruprecht, 1971: 94.
NQ

1367 *EURIPIDIS EPISTULAE*
Incertum
Cf. et EURIPIDES Trag. (0006).
001 **Epistulae**, ed. R. Hercher, *Epistolographi Graeci*. Paris: Didot, 1873 (repr. Amsterdam: Hakkert, 1965): 275–279.
Cod: [1,865]

1360 <**EURYPHAMUS**> Phil.
vel Euryphemos
3 B.C.: Metapontinus
001 **Fragmentum**, ed. H. Thesleff, *The Pythagorean texts of the Hellenistic period*. Åbo: Åbo Akademi, 1965: 85–87.
Q: 728

0895 **EURYPHON** Med.
5 B.C.: Cnidius
x01 **Fragmenta ap. Galenum**.
K17.1.886, 888 in CMG, vol. 5.10.2.2, pp. 54, 55.
Cf. GALENUS Med. (0057 091).

x02 **Fragmentum ap. Anonymum Londinensem**.
Iatrica 4.31–40.
Cf. ANONYMUS LONDINENSIS (0643 001).

1363 **EURYTUS** Lyr.
Incertum: Lacedaemonius
001 **Fragmentum**, ed. T. Bergk, *Poetae lyrici Graeci*, vol. 3. Leipzig: Teubner, 1882: 639.
Q: [2]

1362 <**EURYTUS**> Phil.
vel Eurysus
3 B.C.: fort. Crotoniensis
001 **Fragmentum**, ed. H. Thesleff, *The Pythagorean texts of the Hellenistic period*. Åbo: Åbo Akademi, 1965: 88.
Q: 164
002 **Testimonia**, ed. H. Diels and W. Kranz, *Die Fragmente der Vorsokratiker*, vol. 1, 6th edn. Berlin: Weidmann, 1951 (repr. Dublin: 1966): 419–420.
NQ

0896 **EUSCHEMUS** Med.
ante A.D. 2
x01 **Fragmentum ap. Galenum**.
K13.287.
Cf. GALENUS Med. (0057 076).

2146 **EUSEBIUS** Hist.
A.D. 3
001 **Testimonium**, FGrH #101: 2A:480.
NQ
002 **Fragmenta**, FGrH #101: 2A:480–482.
Q

2640 **EUSEBIUS** Phil.
A.D. 4: Myndius
001 **Fragmenta**, ed. F.W.A. Mullach, *Fragmenta philosophorum Graecorum*, vol. 3. Paris: Didot, 1881 (repr. Aalen: Scientia, 1968): 7–19.
Q

4124 **EUSEBIUS** Scr. Eccl.
A.D. 4: Emesenus
Bibliography in progress
007 **Fragmenta in epistulam ad Romanos** (in catenis), ed. K. Staab, *Pauluskommentar aus der griechischen Kirche aus Katenenhandschriften gesammelt*. Münster: Aschendorff, 1933: 46.
Q
008 **Fragmenta in epistulam ad Galatas** (in catenis), ed. Staab, *op. cit.*, 46–52.
Q
009 **Fragmenta in epistulam i ad Corinthios** (in catenis), ed. Staab, *op. cit.*, 52.
Q

2018 **EUSEBIUS** Scr. Eccl. et Theol.
A.D. 4: Caesariensis
001 **Praeparatio evangelica**, ed. K. Mras, *Eusebius Werke, Band 8: Die Praeparatio evangelica [Die*

griechischen christlichen Schriftsteller 43.1 &
43.2. Berlin: Akademie-Verlag, 43.1:1954;
43.2:1956]: **43.1**:5–613; **43.2**:5–426.
Cod: [254,268]

002 **Historia ecclesiastica**, ed. G. Bardy, *Eusèbe de Césarée. Histoire ecclésiastique*, 3 vols. [*Sources chrétiennes* 31, 41, 55. Paris: Cerf, 1:1952; 2:1955; 3:1958 (repr. 3:1967)]: **1**:3–215; **2**:4–231; **3**:3–120.
Cod: [101,114]

003 **De martyribus Palaestinae** (recensio brevior), ed. Bardy, *op. cit.*, vol. 3, 121–174.
Cod: [7,967]

004 **De martyribus Palaestinae** (recensio prolixior), ed. Bardy, *op. cit.*, vol. 3, 128–138, 140–142, 153–167.
Cod: [4,748]

005 **Demonstratio evangelica**, ed. I.A. Heikel, *Eusebius Werke, Band 6: Die Demonstratio evangelica* [*Die griechischen christlichen Schriftsteller* 23. Leipzig: Hinrichs, 1913]: 1–492.
Cod: [169,267]

006 **Demonstratio evangelica** (fragmenta libri xv), ed. Heikel, *GCS* 23, 493–496.
Cod: [997]

007 **Contra Marcellum**, ed. E. Klostermann and G.C. Hansen, *Eusebius Werke, Band 4: Gegen Marcell. Über die kirchliche Theologie. Die Fragmente Marcells* [*Die griechischen christlichen Schriftsteller* 14, 2nd edn. Berlin: Akademie-Verlag, 1972]: 1–58.
Cod: [19,335]

008 **Epistula ad Flacillum**, ed. Klostermann and Hansen, *op. cit.*, 60.
Cod: [197]

009 **De ecclesiastica theologia**, ed. Klostermann and Hansen, *op. cit.*, 61–182.
Cod: [44,813]

010 **De theophania** (fragmenta), ed. H. Gressmann, *Eusebius Werke, Band 3.2: Die Theophanie* [*Die griechischen christlichen Schriftsteller* 11.2. Leipzig: Hinrichs, 1904]: 3*–35*.
Cod: [9,413]

011 **Onomasticon**, ed. E. Klostermann, *Eusebius Werke, Band 3.1: Das Onomastikon* [*Die griechischen christlichen Schriftsteller* 11.1. Leipzig: Hinrichs, 1904]: 2–176.
Cod: [19,433]

012 **In cantica canticorum interpretatio**, ed. J. Pitra, *Analecta sacra spicilegio Solesmensi parata*, vol. 3. Venice: St. Lazarus Monastery, 1883: 530–537.
Cod: [1,663]

013 **Epistula ad Carpianum ad canones evangeliorum praemissa**, ed. E. Nestle, *Novum Testamentum Graece*, 25th edn. London: United Bible Societies, 1963 (repr. 1971): 32*–33*.
Cod: [392]

014 **Epistula ad Caesarienses**, ed. H.G. Opitz, *Athanasius Werke*, vol. 2.1. Berlin: De Gruyter, 1935: 28–31.
Q: [1,298]

015 **Epistula ad Alexandrum Alexandrinum**, ed. Opitz, *op. cit.*, vol. 3.1 (1934): 14–15.
Q: [269]

016 **Epistula ad Euphrationem**, ed. Opitz, *op. cit.*, vol. 3.1, 4–6.
Q: [315]

017 **Contra Hieroclem**, ed. C.L. Kayser, *Flavii Philostrati opera*, vol. 1. Leipzig: Teubner, 1870 (repr. Hildesheim: Olms, 1964): 369–413.
Cod: [10,825]

018 **De mensuris et ponderibus** (fragmenta), ed. F. Hultsch, *Metrologicorum scriptorum reliquiae*, vol. 1. Leipzig: Teubner, 1864 (repr. Stuttgart: 1971): 276–278.
Cod: [389]

019 **Commentarius in Isaiam**, ed. J. Ziegler, *Eusebius Werke, Band 9: Der Jesajakommentar* [*Die griechischen christlichen Schriftsteller*. Berlin: Akademie-Verlag, 1975]: 3–411.
Cod: [172,950]

020 **Vita Constantini**, ed. F. Winkelmann, *Eusebius Werke, Band 1.1: Über das Leben des Kaisers Konstantin* [*Die griechischen christlichen Schriftsteller*. Berlin: Akademie-Verlag, 1975]: 3–151.
Cod: [42,255]

021 **Oratio ad coetum sanctorum**, ed. I.A. Heikel, *Eusebius Werke, Band 1: Über das Leben Constantins. Constantins Rede an die heilige Versammlung. Tricennatsrede an Constantin* [*Die griechischen christlichen Schriftsteller* 7. Leipzig: Hinrichs, 1902]: 151–192.
Cod: [12,535]

022 **De laudibus Constantini**, ed. Heikel, *GCS* 7, 195–259.
Cod: [21,116]

023 **Generalis elementaria introductio** (= **Eclogae propheticae**), ed. T. Gaisford, *Eusebii Pamphili episcopi Caesariensis eclogae propheticae*. Oxford: Oxford University Press, 1842: 1–236.
Cod: [54,919]

024 **Generalis elementaria introductio** (fragmenta), ed. K. Holl, *Fragmente vornicänischer Kirchenväter aus den Sacra Parallela* [*Texte und Untersuchungen* 20. Leipzig: Hinrichs, 1899]: 121, 213–214.
Q: [265]

025 **Antiquorum martyriorum collectio** (fragmenta), MPG 20: 1520–1533.
Cod: [3,058]

026 **Passio sanctorum decem martyrum Aegyptiorum** (fragmenta), MPG 20: 1533–1536.
Cod: [442]

027 **Epistula ad Constantiam Augustam**, MPG 20: 1545–1549.
Q: [829]

028 **Quaestiones evangelicae ad Stephanum**, MPG 22: 880–936.
Cod: [11,844]

029 **Quaestiones evangelicae ad Marinum**, MPG 22: 937–957.
Cod: [3,943]

030 **Supplementa ad quaestiones ad Stephanum,** MPG 22: 957–976.
Q: [3,603]
031 **Supplementa ad quaestiones ad Marinum,** MPG 22: 984–1005.
Q: [5,224]
032 **Supplementa minora ad quaestiones ad Marinum,** MPG 22: 1008–1016.
Q: [1,463]
033 **De vitis prophetarum** (fragmenta), MPG 22: 1261–1272.
Cod: [1,724]
034 **Commentaria in Psalmos:** MPG 23:66–1396; 24:9–76.
Cod: [312,746]
035 **Fragmenta in proverbia,** MPG 24: 76–78.
Q: [95]
036 **Fragmenta in Danielem,** MPG 24: 525–528.
Q: [556]
037 **Fragmenta in Lucam,** MPG 24: 529–605.
Q: [16,378]
038 **Fragmenta in Hebraeos,** MPG 24: 605.
Q: [81]
039 **De solemnitate paschali,** MPG 24: 693–706.
Q: [2,554]
040 **Chronicon,** ed. A. Schöne, *Eusebi chronicorum canonum quae supersunt,* 2 vols. Berlin: Weidmann, 1:1875; 2:1866 (repr. 1967): **1:**2–286; **2:**4–190.
Cod

2717 **EUSTATHIUS** Epigr.
A.D. 11: Iconiensis
x01 **Epigramma exhortatorium et supplicatorium.**
App. Anth. 4.116: Cf. EPIGRAMMATICI in *App. Anth.* (7052 004).

4083 **EUSTATHIUS** Scr. Eccl.
A.D. 12: Thessalonicensis
Bibliography in progress
001 **Commentarii ad Homeri Iliadem** (lib. A–P), ed. M. van der Valk, *Eustathii archiepiscopi Thessalonicensis commentarii ad Homeri Iliadem pertinentes,* vols. 1–3. Leiden: Brill, 1:1971; 2:1976; 3:1979: **1:**1–802; **2:**1–838; **3:**1–944.
Cod: 820,814
002 **Commentarii ad Homeri Iliadem** (lib. Σ–Ω), ed. G. Stallbaum, *Eustathii archiepiscopi Thessalonicensis commentarii ad Homeri Iliadem,* vol. 4. Leipzig: Weigel, 1830 (repr. Hildesheim: Olms, 1970): 47–386.
Cod
003 **Commentarii ad Homeri Odysseam,** ed. G. Stallbaum, *Eustathii archiepiscopi Thessalonicensis commentarii ad Homeri Odysseam,* 2 vols. in 1. Leipzig: Weigel, 1:1825; 2:1826 (repr. Hildesheim: Olms, 1970): **1:**1–443; **2:**1–334.
Cod

2499 **EUSTOCHIUS** Soph.
A.D. 4: Cappadox

001 **Testimonium,** FGrH #738: 3C:713–714.
NQ
002 **Fragmentum,** FGrH #738: 3C:714.
Q

4031 **EUSTRATIUS** Phil.
A.D. 11–12: Nicaeensis
001 **In analyticorum posteriorum librum secundum commentarium,** ed. M. Hayduck, *Eustratii in analyticorum posteriorum librum secundum commentarium* [*Commentaria in Aristotelem Graeca* 21.1. Berlin: Reimer, 1907]: 1–270.
Cod: [116,861]
002 **In ethica Nicomachea i commentaria,** ed. G. Heylbut, *Eustratii et Michaelis et anonyma in ethica Nicomachea commentaria* [*Commentaria in Aristotelem Graeca* 20. Berlin: Reimer, 1892]: 1–121.
Cod: [49,910]
003 **In ethica Nicomachea vi commentaria,** ed. Heylbut, *op. cit.,* 256–406.
Cod: [66,335]

0752 **EUTECNIUS** Soph.
A.D. 3/10
001 **Paraphrasis in Nicandri theriaca,** ed. I. Gualandri, *Eutecnii paraphrasis in Nicandri theriaca.* Milan: Istituto Editoriale Cisalpino, 1968: 21–70.
Cod: 12,849

0462 **EUTHYCLES** Comic.
5/4 B.C.?
001 **Fragmenta,** ed. T. Kock, *Comicorum Atticorum fragmenta,* vol. 1. Leipzig: Teubner, 1880: 805.
frr. 1–4.
Q: 23
002 **Fragmenta,** ed. A. Meineke, *Fragmenta comicorum Graecorum,* vol. 2.2. Berlin: Reimer, 1840 (repr. De Gruyter, 1970): 890.
Q: 19

0897 **EUTHYDEMUS** Med.
2 B.C.: Atheniensis
001 **Fragmentum,** ed. H. Lloyd-Jones and P. Parsons, *Supplementum Hellenisticum.* Berlin: De Gruyter, 1983: 233–234.
fr. 455.
Q: [60]
x01 **Fragmentum ap. Athenaeum.**
Deipnosophistae 7.315f.
Cf. ATHENAEUS Soph. (0008 001).

2170 **EUTHYMENES** Hist.
2 B.C.?
001 **Fragmentum,** FGrH #243: 2B:1021–1022.
Q

4072 **EUTOCIUS** Math.
A.D. 5–6: Ascalonius
001 **Commentarii in libros de sphaera et cylindro,**

ed. J.L. Heiberg and E. Stamatis, *Archimedis opera omnia cum commentariis Eutocii*, vol. 3. Leipzig: Teubner, 1915 (repr. Stuttgart: 1972): 2–224.

Cod

002 **Commentarius in dimensionem circuli**, ed. Heiberg and Stamatis, *op. cit.*, 228–260.

Cod

003 **Commentarius in libros de planorum aequilibriis**, ed. Heiberg and Stamatis, *op. cit.*, 264–318.

Cod

004 **Commentaria in conica**, ed. J.L. Heiberg, *Apollonii Pergaei quae Graece exstant*, vol. 2. Leipzig: Teubner, 1893 (repr. Stuttgart: 1974): 168–360.

Cod

4068 **EUTOLMIUS** Epigr.
A.D. 4

001 **Epigrammata**, AG **6.**86; 7.608, 611; **9.**587.
Q: 81

0898 **EUTONIUS** Med.
ante A.D. 4

x01 **Fragmentum ap. Oribasium.**
CMG, vol. 6.3, p. 93.
Cf. ORIBASIUS Med. (0722 004).

2236 **EUTROPIUS** Hist.
A.D. 4

001 **Breviarium ab urbe condita** (Paeanii translatio), ed. S.P. Lambros, "Παιανίου μετάφρασις εἰς τὴν τοῦ Εὐτροπίου ῾Ρωμαϊκὴν ἱστορίαν," Νέος ῾Ελληνομνήμων 9 (1912) 9–113.
Cod: [29,004]

2158 **EUTYCHIANUS** Hist.
A.D. 4: Cappadox

001 **Fragmentum**, FGrH #226: 2B:954.
Q

0899 **EUTYCHIANUS** Med.
ante A.D. 4

x01 **Fragmentum ap. Oribasium.**
CMG, vol. 6.2.2, p. 272.
Cf. ORIBASIUS Med. (0722 005).

4110 **EVAGRIUS** Scr. Eccl.
A.D. 4: Ponticus
Bibliography in progress

001 **Practicus**, ed. A. Guillamont and C. Guillamont, *Évagre le Pontique. Traité pratique ou le moine*, vol. 2 [*Sources chrétiennes* 171. Paris: Cerf, 1971]: 482–712.
Q

010 **Sententiae ad monachos**, ed. H. Gressmann, *Nonnenspiegel und Mönchsspiegel des Euagrios Pontikos* [*Texte und Untersuchungen* 39.4. Leipzig: Hinrichs, 1913]: 152–165.
Q

011 **Ad virginem**, ed. Gressmann, *op. cit.*, 146–151.
Q

1364 *EVANGELIUM AEGYPTIUM*
A.D. 2

001 **Evangelium Aegyptium**, ed. E. Klostermann, *Apocrypha II. Evangelien*, 2nd edn. [*Kleine Texte* 8. Bonn: Marcus & Weber, 1910]: 12–13.
Cod: [210]

x01 **Fragmenta.**
P. Oxy. 2.210; 4.655.
Cf. FRAGMENTA EVANGELIORUM INCERTORUM (1378 004).

EVANGELIUM APOCRYPHUM SECUNDUM MATTHIAM
Cf. MATTHIAE TRADITIONES (1560).

1366 *EVANGELIUM BARTHOLOMAEI*
A.D. 3

001 **Evangelium Bartholomaei**, ed. N. Bonwetsch, "Die apokryphen Fragen des Bartholomäus," *Nachrichten von der Gesellschaft der Wissenschaften zu Göttingen*, Philol.-hist. Kl (1897) 9–29.
Cod: [4,167]

002 **Fragmenta evangelii Bartholomaei**, ed. A. Wilmart and E. Tisserant, "Fragments grecs et latins de l'Évangile de Barthélemy," *Revue Biblique* 10 (1913) 185–190, 321–333.
Cod: [2,573]

1368 *EVANGELIUM EBIONITUM*
A.D. 2/3
Cf. et EVANGELIUM SECUNDUM HEBRAEOS (1374).

001 **Evangelium Ebionitum**, ed. E. Klostermann, *Apocrypha II. Evangelien*, 2nd edn. [*Kleine Texte* 8. Bonn: Marcus & Weber, 1910]: 9–12.
Q: [538]

1372 *EVANGELIUM EVAE*
ante A.D. 4

001 **Evangelium Evae**, ed. E. Klostermann, *Apocrypha II. Evangelien*, 2nd edn. [*Kleine Texte* 8. Bonn: Marcus & Weber, 1910]: 15.
Q: [141]

1369 *EVANGELIUM MARIAE*
ante A.D. 3?

001 **Evangelium Mariae**, ed. E. Preuschen, *Antilegomena*, 2nd edn. Gieszen: Töpelmann, 1905: 82–83.
Q: [173]

002 **Fragmentum**, *P. Ryl.* 3.463.
Pap

1370 *EVANGELIUM NAASSENUM*
A.D. 1/2?

001 **Sermo Naassenorum** (fragmenta), ed. W. Völker, *Quellen zur Geschichte der christlichen Gnosis*. Tübingen: Mohr, 1932: 11–25.
Q

1371 *EVANGELIUM PETRI*
A.D. 2

001 **Evangelium Petri**, ed. M.G. Mara, *Évangile de Pierre*. [*Sources chrétiennes* 201. Paris: Cerf, 1973]: 40–66.
Cod

1373 *EVANGELIUM PHILIPPI*
A.D. 2/3?
001 **Evangelium Philippi**, ed. E. Klostermann, *Apocrypha II. Evangelien*, 2nd edn. [*Kleine Texte* 8. Bonn: Marcus & Weber, 1910]: 15.
Q: [104]

1374 *EVANGELIUM SECUNDUM HEBRAEOS*
A.D. 1/2
Cf. et EVANGELIUM EBIONITUM (1368).
001 **Evangelium secundum Hebraeos**, ed. E. Klostermann, *Apocrypha II. Evangelien*, 2nd edn. [*Kleine Texte* 8. Bonn: Marcus & Weber, 1910]: 5–9.
frr. 5–6, 9–10, 15–16, 22, 27.
Q: [313]

1375 *EVANGELIUM THOMAE*
A.D. 2?
001 **Evangelium Thomae**, ed. E. Klostermann, *Apocrypha II. Evangelien*, 2nd edn. [*Kleine Texte* 8. Bonn: Marcus & Weber, 1910]: 13.
Q: [101]
x01 **Evangelium Thomae** (fragmenta).
P. Oxy. 1.1; 4.654, 655.
Cf. FRAGMENTA EVANGELIORUM INCERTORUM (1378 004).

0343 **EZECHIEL** Trag.
2 B.C.
001 'Εξαγωγή, ed. B. Snell, *Tragicorum Graecorum fragmenta*, vol. 1. Göttingen: Vandenhoeck & Ruprecht, 1971: 288–301.
Q: [1,744]

1968 **FABIUS CERYLLIANUS** Hist.
A.D. 3–4?
001 **Fragmentum**, FGrH #217: 2B:947.
Q

2542 **Quintus FABIUS PICTOR** Hist.
3 B.C.: Romanus
001 **Testimonia**, FGrH #809: 3C:845–848.
NQ
002 **Fragmenta**, FGrH #809: 3C:849–876.
Q

1377 **FAVORINUS** Phil.
A.D. 2: Arelatensis
001 **Fragmenta**, ed. E. Mensching, *Favorin von Arelate*, vol. 1 [*Texte und Kommentare. Eine altertumswissenschaftliche Reihe*, vol. 3. Berlin: De Gruyter, 1963]: 65–67, 69, 71, 73–75, 77, 80–81, 84, 88–89, 91–92, 94, 97–101, 103, 110, 114–116, 118–122, 124–127, 130–131, 133, 138–142, 144–147, 150–154.
frr. 1–21: Memorabilia.

frr. 22–51a: Omnigena historia.
frr. 51–66: Memorabilia vel Omnigena historia.
fr. 67: Epitome (Omnigena historia?).
Q: [2,658]
002 **De fuga** (*P. Vat. Gr.* 11), ed. M. Norsa and G. Vitelli, *Il papiro Vaticano greco 11* [*Studi e Testi* 53. Vatican City: Biblioteca Apostolica Vaticana, 1931]: 17–32.
Pap: [8,647]
003 **Fragmenta**, ed. A. Barigazzi, *Favorino di Arelate. Opere*. Florence: Monnier, 1966: 139–551.
Q, Pap

0901 **FLAVIANUS** Med.
ante A.D. 2: Cretensis
x01 **Fragmentum ap. Galenum**.
K13.72.
Cf. GALENUS Med. (0057 076).

0902 **FLAVIUS** Med.
ante A.D. 2
x01 **Fragmentum ap. Galenum**.
K13.294.
Cf. GALENUS Med. (0057 076).

4148 *FLORILEGIUM ANTICHALCEDONIUM*
A.D. 5
001 **Florilegium** (Cod. Vat. gr. 1431), ed. E. Schwartz, *Codex Vaticanus gr. 1431, eine antichalkedonische Sammlung aus der Zeit Kaiser Zenos* [*Abhandlungen der bayerischen Akademie der Wissenschaften*, Philosoph.-philol. und hist. Kl., Bd. 32, Abh. 6. Munich: Oldenbourg, 1927]: 13–62.
Cod

4147 *FLORILEGIUM CYRILLIANUM*
post A.D. 6
001 **Florilegium Cyrillianum**, ed. R. Hespel, *Le florilège cyrillien réfuté par Sévère d'Antioche* [*Bibliothèque du Muséon* 37. Louvain: Université de Louvain, 1955]: 103–208.
frr. 1–230.
Cod

2646 *FRAGMENTA ADESPOTA* (SH)
Varia
001 **Frustula adespota ex auctoribus**, ed. H. Lloyd-Jones and P. Parsons, *Supplementum Hellenisticum*. Berlin: De Gruyter, 1983: 517–561, 863.
frr. 1000–1185, 1134a.
Q: [900]

1817 *FRAGMENTA ANONYMA* (PsVTGr)
Varia
001 **Fragmenta**, ed. A.-M. Denis, *Fragmenta pseudepigraphorum quae supersunt Graeca* [*Pseudepigrapha veteris testamenti Graece* 3. Leiden: Brill, 1970]: 229–238.
Q, Pap: [1,877]

1378 *FRAGMENTA EVANGELIORUM INCER-*
TORUM
ante A.D. 3
Cf. et AGRAPHA (1776).
001 **Fragmenta**, *P. Cairo* 10735.
Pap
002 **Fragmenta**, *P. Egerton* 2.
Pap
003 **Fragmentum** (*P. Rain.*), ed. G. Bickell, "Das nichtkanonische Evangelienfragment," *Mittheilungen aus der Sammlung der Papyrus Erzherzog Rainer* 1 (Vienna, 1887): 54.
Pap
004 **Fragmenta**, *P. Oxy.* 1.1; 2.210; 4.654, 655; 5.840; 10.1224.
Pap

1379 *FRAGMENTUM ALCHEMICUM*
ante A.D. 2
001 **Fragmentum**, *P. Oxy.* 3.467.
Pap

2287 *FRAGMENTUM STOICUM*
Incertum
001 **Fragmentum**, ed. J. von Arnim, *Stoicorum veterum fragmenta*, vol. 1. Leipzig: Teubner, 1905 (repr. Stuttgart: 1968): 142.
Q

1381 *FRAGMENTUM SYNODICAE EPISTULAE CONCILII CAESARIENSIS*
A.D. 2
001 **Fragmentum epistulae**, ed. M.J. Routh, *Reliquiae sacrae*, vol. 2, 2nd edn. Oxford: Oxford University Press, 1846 (repr. Hildesheim: Olms, 1974): 3.
Q: [80]

1382 *FRAGMENTUM TELIAMBICUM*
ante A.D. 3
001 **Fragmentum teliambicum** (*P. Oxy.* 1.15), ed. D. Young (post E. Diehl), *Theognis*. Leipzig: Teubner, 1971: 122.
Pap: [78]

0186 **Marcus Cornelius FRONTO** Rhet.
A.D. 2: Numidianus
001 **Ad Marcum Caesarem et invicem** (lib. 1), ed. M.P.J. van den Hout, *M. Cornelii Frontonis epistulae*. Leiden: Brill, 1954 (repr. New York: Arno, 1975): 16–17, 20–23.
Herodi Attico (epist. 8): pp. 16–17.
Matri Caesaris (epist. 10): pp. 20–23.
Cod: [877]
002 **Ad Marcum Caesarem et invicem** (lib. 2), ed. van den Hout, *op. cit.*, 32–33.
Matri Caesaris (epist. 12).
Cod: [297]
003 **Ad amicos** (lib. 1), ed. van den Hout, *op. cit.*, 165.
Apollonidae (epist. 2).
Cod: [71]

004 **Additamentum epistularum variarum acephalum**, ed. van den Hout, *op. cit.*, 228–239.
Appiano (epist. 5): pp. 228–233.
Epistula acephala (epist. 8): pp. 234–239.
Cod: [2,279]
005 **Epigrammata**, AG 12.174, 233.
Q: 56
x01 **Epigramma demonstrativum**.
App. Anth. 3.125: Cf. EPIGRAMMATICI in *App. Anth.* (7052 003).

4069 **GABRIELIUS** Epigr.
A.D. 6: Constantinopolitanus
001 **Epigramma**, AG 16.208.
Q: 14

0188 **GAETULICUS I** Epigr.
A.D. 1
001 **Epigrammata**, AG 5.17; 6.154, 190, 331; 7.71, 244, 245(?), 275, 354.
Q: 332

0187 **GAETULICUS II** Epigr.
A.D. 1
001 **Epigramma**, AG 11.409.
Q: 37

0822 **GAIUS** Med.
ante A.D. 1: Neapolitanus
Cf. et ANONYMUS NEAPOLITANUS Med. (1119).
Cf. et GAIUS Med. (0904).
x01 **Fragmentum ap. Galenum**.
K13.830.
Cf. GALENUS Med. (0057 077).

0904 **GAIUS** Med.
fiq Gaius Neapolitanus
ante A.D. 2
Cf. et GAIUS Med. (0822).
x01 **Fragmentum ap. Galenum**.
K12.771.
Cf. GALENUS Med. (0057 076).

0572 **GAIUS** Scr. Eccl.
vel Caius
A.D. 3: Romanus
001 **Fragmenta**, ed. M.J. Routh, *Reliquiae sacrae*, vol. 2, 2nd edn. Oxford: Oxford University Press, 1846 (repr. Hildesheim: Olms, 1974): 127–134.
Q: [1,074]

0057 **GALENUS** Med.
A.D. 2: Pergamenus
006 **De constitutione artis medicae ad Patrophilum**, ed. C.G. Kühn, *Claudii Galeni opera omnia*, vol. 1. Leipzig: Knobloch, 1821 (repr. Hildesheim: Olms, 1964): 224–304.
Cod: 12,396
007 **Ars medica**, ed. Kühn, *op. cit.*, vol. 1, 305–412.
Cod: 16,776

011 **De anatomicis administrationibus libri ix**, ed. Kühn, *op. cit.*, vol. 2 (1821; repr. 1964): 215–731.
Cod: 81,247

012 **De ossibus ad tirones**, ed. Kühn, *op. cit.*, vol. 2, 732–778.
Cod: 7,165

013 **De venarum arteriarumque dissectione**, ed. Kühn, *op. cit.*, vol. 2, 779–830.
Cod: 7,824

014 **De nervorum dissectione**, ed. Kühn, *op. cit.*, vol. 2, 831–856.
Cod: 3,736

018 **De motu musculorum libri ii**, ed. Kühn, *op. cit.*, vol. 4 (1822; repr. 1964): 367–464.
Cod: 15,264

114 **De causis respirationis**, ed. Kühn, *op. cit.*, vol. 4, 465–469.
Cod: 706

021 **De semine libri ii**, ed. Kühn, *op. cit.*, vol. 4, 512–651.
Cod: 21,557

022 **De foetuum formatione libellus**, ed. Kühn, *op. cit.*, vol. 4, 652–702.
Cod: 8,011

084 **De substantia facultatum naturalium fragmentum** (= **De propriis placitis fragmentum**), ed. Kühn, *op. cit.*, vol. 4, 757–766.
Cf. et 0057 026.
Cod: 1,424

031 **De usu pulsuum**, ed. Kühn, *op. cit.*, vol. 5 (1823; repr. 1965): 149–180.
Cod: 4,655

040 **De dignotione ex insomniis**, ed. Kühn, *op. cit.*, vol. 6 (repr. 1823; repr. 1965): 832–835.
Cod: 527

041 **De morborum differentiis**, ed. Kühn, *op. cit.*, vol. 6, 836–880.
Cod: 6,905

042 **De causis morborum liber**, ed. Kühn, *op. cit.*, vol. 7 (1824; repr. 1965): 1–41.
Cod: 6,336

043 **De symptomatum differentiis liber**, ed. Kühn, *op. cit.*, vol. 7, 42–84.
Cod: 6,857

044 **De symptomatum causis libri iii**, ed. Kühn, *op. cit.*, vol. 7, 85–272.
Cod: 30,535

045 **De differentiis febrium libri ii**, ed. Kühn, *op. cit.*, vol. 7, 273–405.
Cod: 21,703

048 **De typis liber**, ed. Kühn, *op. cit.*, vol. 7, 463–474.
Cod: 1,651

049 **Adversos eos qui de typis scripserunt vel de circuitibus**, ed. Kühn, *op. cit.*, vol. 7, 475–512.
Cod: 5,801

050 **De plenitudine liber**, ed. Kühn, *op. cit.*, vol. 7, 513–583.
Cod: 11,502

051 **De tremore, palpitatione, convulsione et rigore liber**, ed. Kühn, *op. cit.*, vol. 7, 584–642.
Cod: 9,451

053 **De marcore liber**, ed. Kühn, *op. cit.*, vol. 7, 666–704.
Cod: 6,018

055 **De inaequali intemperie liber**, ed. Kühn, *op. cit.*, vol. 7, 733–752.
Cod: 3,278

056 **De difficultate respirationis libri iii**, ed. Kühn, *op. cit.*, vol. 7, 753–960.
Cod: 33,093

057 **De locis affectis libri vi**, ed. Kühn, *op. cit.*, vol. 8 (1824; repr. 1965): 1–452.
Cod: 72,559

058 **De pulsibus libellus ad tirones**, ed. Kühn, *op. cit.*, vol. 8, 453–492.
Cod: 6,221

059 **De differentia pulsuum libri iv**, ed. Kühn, *op. cit.*, vol. 8, 493–765.
Cod: 44,391

060 **De dignoscendis pulsibus libri iv**, ed. Kühn, *op. cit.*, vol. 8, 766–961.
Cod: 32,375

061 **De causis pulsuum libri iv**, ed. Kühn, *op. cit.*, vol. 9 (1825; repr. 1965): 1–204.
Cod: 33,321

062 **De praesagitione ex pulsibus libri iv**, ed. Kühn, *op. cit.*, vol. 9, 205–430.
Cod: 37,699

063 **Synopsis librorum suorum de pulsibus**, ed. Kühn, *op. cit.*, vol. 9, 431–533.
Cod: 16,348

065 **De diebus decretoriis libri iii**, ed. Kühn, *op. cit.*, vol. 9, 769–941.
Cod: 28,286

066 **De methodo medendi libri xiv**, ed. Kühn, *op. cit.*, vol. 10 (1825; repr. 1965): 1–1021.
Cod: 163,139

067 **Ad Glauconem de medendi methodo libri ii**, ed. Kühn, *op. cit.*, vol. 11 (1826; repr. 1965): 1–146.
Cod: 23,690

068 **De venae sectione adversus Erasistratum**, ed. Kühn, *op. cit.*, vol. 11, 147–186.
Cod: 6,173

069 **De venae sectione adversus Erasistrateos Romae degentes**, ed. Kühn, *op. cit.*, vol. 11, 187–249.
Cod: 9,371

070 **De curandi ratione per venae sectionem**, ed. Kühn, *op. cit.*, vol. 11, 250–316.
Cod: 10,398

071 **De hirundinibus, revulsione, cucurbitula, incisione et scarificatione**, ed. Kühn, *op. cit.*, vol. 11, 317–322.
Cod: 726

075 **De simplicium medicamentorum temperamentis ac facultatibus libri xi**, ed. Kühn, *op. cit.*, vols. 11 & 12 (1826; repr. 1965): 11:379–892; 12:1–377.
Cod: 139,244

076 **De compositione medicamentorum secundum locos libri x**, ed. Kühn, *op. cit.*, vols. 12 & 13 (1827; repr. 1965): 12:378–1007; 13:1–361.
Cod: 150,524

077 De compositione medicamentorum per genera libri vii, ed. Kühn, *op. cit.*, vol. 13, 362–1058.
Cod: 109,210

078 De antidotis libri ii, ed. Kühn, *op. cit.*, vol. 14 (1827; repr. 1965): 1–209.
Cod: 28,945

079 De theriaca ad Pisonem, ed. Kühn, *op. cit.*, vol. 14, 210–294.
Cod: 13,556

083 De praenotione ad Posthumum (Epigenem), ed. Kühn, *op. cit.*, vol. 14, 599–673.
Cod: 11,530

092 In Hippocratis aphorismos commentarii vii, ed. Kühn, *op. cit.*, vols. 17.2 & 18.1 (1829; repr. 1965): **17.2**:345–887; **18.1**:1–195.
Cod: 102,970

095 In Hippocratis librum de articulis et Galeni in eum commentarii iv, ed. Kühn, *op. cit.*, vol. 18.1, 300–345, 423–767.
Cod: 55,499

096 De humero iis modis prolapso quos Hippocrates non vidit, ed. Kühn, *op. cit.*, vol. 18.1, 346–422.
Cod: 10,593

100 In Hippocratis librum de fracturis commentarii iii, ed. Kühn, *op. cit.*, vol. 18.2 (1830; repr. 1965): 318–628.
Cod: 44,698

101 In Hippocratis librum de officina medici commentarii iii, ed. Kühn, *op. cit.*, vol. 18.2, 629–925.
Cod: 43,376

102 De musculorum dissectione ad tirones, ed. Kühn, *op. cit.*, vol. 18.2, 926–1026.
Cod: 15,368

106 Linguarum seu dictionum exoletarum Hippocratis explicatio, ed. Kühn, *op. cit.*, vol. 19 (1830; repr. 1965): 62–157.
Cod: 9,956

002 De optima doctrina, ed. J. Marquardt, *Claudii Galeni Pergameni scripta minora*, vol. 1. Leipzig: Teubner, 1884 (repr. Amsterdam: Hakkert, 1967): 82–92.
Cod: 1,916

103 De consuetudinibus, ed. J. Marquardt, I. Müller and G. Helmreich, *Claudii Galeni Pergameni scripta minora*, vol. 2. Leipzig: Teubner, 1891 (repr. Amsterdam: Hakkert, 1967): 9–31.
Cod: 4,180

027 Quod animi mores corporis temperamenta sequantur, ed. Marquardt, Müller, and Helmreich, *op. cit.*, 32–79.
Cod: 8,840

105 De ordine librorum suorum ad Eugenianum, ed. Marquardt, Müller, and Helmreich, *op. cit.*, 80–90.
Cod: 2,051

104 De libris propriis liber, ed. Marquardt, Müller, and Helmreich, *op. cit.*, 91–124.
Cod: 6,514

004 De sectis ad eos qui introducuntur, ed. Marquardt, Müller and Helmreich, *op. cit.*, vol. 3

(1893; repr. 1967): 1–32.
Cod: 6,494

033 Thrasybulus sive utrum medicinae sit an gymnasticae hygieine, ed. Marquardt, Müller, and Helmreich, *op. cit.*, vol. 3, 33–100.
Cod: 14,352

010 De naturalibus facultatibus, ed. Marquardt, Müller, and Helmreich, *op. cit.*, vol. 3, 101–257.
Cod: 33,104

017 De usu partium, ed. G. Helmreich, *Galeni de usu partium libri xvii*. Leipzig: Teubner, 1:1907; 2:1909 (repr. Amsterdam: Hakkert, 1968): **1**:1–496; **2**:1–451.
Cod: 202,076

009 De temperamentis libri iii, ed. G. Helmreich, *Galeni de temperamentis libri iii*. Leipzig: Teubner, 1904 (repr. Stuttgart: 1969): 1–115.
Cod: 28,600

054 De tumoribus praeter naturam, ed. J. Reedy, *Galen. De tumoribus praeter naturam* [*Diss. University of Michigan* (1968)]: 1–28.
Cod: 4,313

064 De crisibus libri iii, ed. B. Alexanderson, *Galenos. Περὶ κρίσεων* [*Studia Graeca et Latina Gothoburgensia* 23. Göteborg: Elanders, 1967]: 69–212.
Cod: 34,406

016 De uteri dissectione, ed. D. Nickel, *Galeni de uteri dissectione* [*Corpus medicorum Graecorum*, vol. 5.2.1. Berlin: Akademie-Verlag, 1971]: 34–58.
Cod: 3,295

028 De propriorum animi cuiuslibet affectuum dignotione et curatione, ed. W. de Boer, *Galeni de propriorum animi cuiuslibet affectuum dignotione et curatione* [*Corpus medicorum Graecorum*, vol. 5.4.1.1. Leipzig: Teubner, 1937]: 3–37.
Cod: 8,605

029 De animi cuiuslibet peccatorum dignotione et curatione (= De animi cuiuslibet peccatorum dignotione et medela), ed. W. de Boer, *Galeni de animi cuiuslibet peccatorum dignotione et curatione* [*Corpus medicorum Graecorum*, vol. 5.4.1.1. Leipzig: Teubner, 1937]: 41–68.
Cod: 6,706

030 De atra bile, ed. W. de Boer, *Galeni de atra bile libellus* [*Corpus medicorum Graecorum*, vol. 5.4.1.1. Leipzig: Teubner, 1937]: 71–93.
Cod: 6,484

032 De placitis Hippocratis et Platonis, ed. P. De Lacy, *Galen. On the doctrines of Hippocrates and Plato* [*Corpus medicorum Graecorum*, vol. 5.4.1.2, pts. 1–2. Berlin: Akademie-Verlag, 1978]: **1**:65–358; **2**:360–608.
N.B.: Text in the TLG data bank is based upon the editor's 1975 typescript.
Cod: 98,570

036 De sanitate tuenda libri vi, ed. K. Koch, *Galeni de sanitate tuenda libri vi* [*Corpus medicorum Graecorum*, vol. 5.4.2. Leipzig: Teubner, 1923]: 3–198.
Cod: 69,757

037 **De alimentorum facultatibus libri iii**, ed. G. Helmreich, *Galeni de alimentorum facultatibus libri iii* [*Corpus medicorum Graecorum*, vol. 5.4.2. Leipzig: Teubner, 1923]: 201–386.
Cod: 46,318

038 **De rebus boni malique suci**, ed. G. Helmreich, *Galeni de rebus boni malique suci libellus* [*Corpus medicorum Graecorum*, vol. 5.4.2. Leipzig: Teubner, 1923]: 389–429.
Cod: 10,678

019 **De victu attenuante**, ed. K. Kalbfleisch, *Galeni de victu attenuante* [*Corpus medicorum Graecorum*, vol. 5.4.2. Leipzig: Teubner, 1923]: 433–451.
Cod: 6,663

039 **De ptisana**, ed. O. Hartlich, *Galeni qui fertur de ptisana libellus* [*Corpus medicorum Graecorum*, vol. 5.4.2. Leipzig: Teubner, 1923]: 455–463.
Cod: 2,301

085 **In Hippocratis de natura hominis librum commentarii iii**, ed. J. Mewaldt, *Galeni in Hippocratis de natura hominis commentaria tria* [*Corpus medicorum Graecorum*, vol. 5.9.1. Leipzig: Teubner, 1914]: 3–88.
Cod: 25,350

086 **In Hippocratis vel Polybi opus de salubri victus ratione privatorum commentarius** (= Galeni in Hippocratis de natura hominis commentarius tertius), ed. Mewaldt, *op. cit.*, 89–113.
Cod: 6,764

087 **In Hippocratis de victu acutorum commentaria iv**, ed. G. Helmreich, *Galeni in Hippocratis de victu acutorum commentaria iv* [*Corpus medicorum Graecorum*, vol. 5.9.1. Leipzig: Teubner, 1914]: 117–366.
Cod: 69,473

088 **In Hippocratis prorrheticum i commentaria iii**, ed. H. Diels, *Galeni in Hippocratis prorrheticum i commentaria iii* [*Corpus medicorum Graecorum*, vol. 5.9.2. Leipzig: Teubner, 1915]: 3–178.
Cod: 47,475

052 **De comate secundum Hippocratem liber**, ed. J. Mewaldt, *Galeni de comate secundum Hippocratem liber* [*Corpus medicorum Graecorum*, vol. 5.9.2. Leipzig: Teubner, 1915]: 181–187.
Cod: 1,820

099 **In Hippocratis prognosticum commentaria iii**, ed. J. Heeg, *Galeni in Hippocratis prognosticum commentaria iii* [*Corpus medicorum Graecorum*, vol. 5.9.2. Leipzig: Teubner, 1915]: 197–378.
Cod: 43,712

089 **In Hippocratis librum primum epidemiarum commentarii iii**, ed. E. Wenkebach, *Galeni in Hippocratis epidemiarum librum i commentaria iii* [*Corpus medicorum Graecorum*, vol. 5.10.1. Leipzig: Teubner, 1934]: 6–151.
Cod: 40,571

090 **In Hippocratis librum iii epidemiarum commentarii iii**, ed. E. Wenkebach, *Galeni in*

Hippocratis epidemiarum librum iii commentaria iii [*Corpus medicorum Graecorum*, vol. 5.10.2.1. Leipzig: Teubner, 1936]: 1–187.
Cod: 42,912

091 **In Hippocratis librum vi epidemiarum commentarii vi**, ed. E. Wenkebach, *Galeni in Hippocratis sextum librum epidemiarum commentaria i–vi* [*Corpus medicorum Graecorum*, vol. 5.10.2.2. Leipzig: Teubner, 1940]: 3–351.
Cod: 79,741

115 **Quomodo morborum simulantes sint deprehendendi**, ed. K. Deichgräber and F. Kudlien, *Galens Kommentare zu den Epidemien des Hippokrates* [*Corpus medicorum Graecorum*, vol. 5.10.2.4. Berlin: Akademie-Verlag, 1960]: 113–116.
Cod: 871

093 **Adversus Lycum libellus**, ed. E. Wenkebach, *Galeni adversus Lycum et adversus Iulianum libelli* [*Corpus medicorum Graecorum*, vol. 5.10.3. Berlin: Akademie-Verlag, 1951]: 3–29.
Cod: 7,717

094 **Adversus ea quae a Juliano in Hippocratis aphorismos enuntiata sunt libellus**, ed. Wenkebach, *Adversus Lycum*, 33–70.
Cod: 7,971

035 **De venereis** (ap. Oribasium), ed. J. Raeder, *Oribasii collectionum medicarum reliquiae* [*Corpus medicorum Graecorum*, vol. 6.1.1. Leipzig: Teubner, 1928]: 187–189.
Q: 416

073 **Quos quibus catharticis medicamentis et quando purgare oporteat** (ap. Oribasium), ed. Raeder, *op. cit.*, 221–227.
Q: 2,043

121 **De melancholia** (ap. Aëtium), ed. A. Olivieri, *Aëtii Amideni libri medicinales v–viii* [*Corpus medicorum Graecorum*, vol. 8.2. Berlin: Akademie-Verlag, 1950]: 143–146.
Q: 1,077

005 **In Platonis Timaeum commentarii fragmenta**, ed. H.O. Schröder, *Galeni in Platonis Timaeum commentarii fragmenta* [*Corpus medicorum Graecorum*, *supplementum*, vol. 1. Leipzig: Teubner, 1934]: 9–26.
Cod: 5,359

015 **De instrumento odoratus**, ed. J. Kollesch, *Galeni de instrumento odoratus* [*Corpus medicorum Graecorum*, *supplementum*, vol. 5. Berlin: Akademie-Verlag, 1964]: 30–64.
Cod: 4,585

001 **Adhortatio ad artes addiscendas**, ed. E. Wenkebach, "Galens Protreptikosfragment," *Quellen und Studien zur Geschichte der Naturwissenschaften und Medizin* 4.3 (1935) 90–120.
Cod: 5,224

003 **Quod optimus medicus sit quoque philosophus**, ed. E. Wenkebach, "Der hippokratische Arzt als das Ideal Galens," *Quellen und Studien zur Geschichte der Naturwissenschaften und Medizin* 3.4 (1933) 170–175.
Cod: 1,438

008 **De elementis ex Hippocrate libri ii**, ed. G. Helmreich, *Galeni de elementis ex Hippocrate libri ii*. Erlangen: Deichert, 1878: 1–69.
Cod: 13,951

020 **De utilitate respirationis liber**, ed. R. Noll, *Galeni περὶ χρείας ἀναπνοῆς libellus* [*Diss. Marburg* (1915)]: 1–33.
Cod: 6,350

023 **An in arteriis natura sanguis contineatur**, ed. F. Albrecht, *Galeni an in arteriis natura sanguis contineatur* [*Diss. Marburg* (1911)]: 1–21.
Cod: 4,884

024 **De optima corporis nostri constitutione**, ed. G. Helmreich, *Galenus de optima corporis constitutione. Idem de bono habitu* [*Programm Gymnasium Hof, 1900–1901* (1901)]: 7–16.
Cod: 1,820

025 **De bono habitu liber**, ed. Helmreich, *Programm Hof*, 16–20.
Cod: 837

026 **De propriis placitis fragmenta inedita**, ed. G. Helmreich, "Galeni περὶ τῶν ἑαυτῷ δοκούντων fragmenta inedita," *Philologus* 52 (1894) 432–434.
Cf. et 0057 084.
Cod: 1,049

034 **De parvae pilae exercitio**, ed. E. Wenkebach, "Galenos von Pergamon: Allgemeine Ertüchtigung durch Ballspiel. Eine sporthygienische Schrift aus dem zweiten Jahrhundert n. Chr.," *Sudhoffs Archiv für Geschichte der Medizin und der Naturwissenschaften* 31 (1938) 258–272.
Cod: 1,791

046 **De morborum temporibus liber**, ed. I. Wille, *Die Schrift Galens Περὶ τῶν ἐν ταῖς νόσοις καιρῶν und ihre Überlieferung*, pt. 2 [*Diss. Kiel* (1960)]: 1–70.
Cod: 5,673

047 **De totius morbi temporibus liber**, ed. Wille, *op. cit.*, 70–114.
Cod: 3,777

072 **De purgantium medicamentorum facultate**, ed. J. Ehlert, *Galeni de purgantium medicamentorum facultate* [*Diss. Göttingen* (1959)]: 1–21.
Cod: 3,132

074 **Pro puero epileptico consilium**, ed. W. Keil, *Galeni puero epileptico consilium* [*Diss. Göttingen* (1959)]: 1–23.
Cod: 3,327

080 **De septimestri partu**, ed. H. Schöne, "Galenos' Schrift über die Siebenmonatskinder," *Quellen und Studien zur Geschichte der Naturwissenschaften und Medizin* 3.4 (1933) 127–130.
Cod: 1,351

081 **Institutio logica**, ed. K. Kalbfleisch, *Galeni institutio logica*. Leipzig: Teubner, 1896: 3–49.
Cod: 8,730

082 **De sophismatis seu captionibus penes dictionem**, ed. K. Gabler, *Galeni libellus de captioni-bus quae per dictionem fiunt* [*Diss. Rostock* (1903)]: 1–16.
Cod: 2,585

107 **De experientia medica**, ed. R. Walzer, *Galen on medical experience*. London: Oxford University Press, 1944: 93–96, 113–114.
Cod: 1,021

111 **Quod qualitates incorporeae sint**, ed. J. Westenberger, *Galeni qui fertur de qualitatibus incorporeis libellus* [*Diss. Marburg* (1906)]: 1–19.
Cod: 3,371

0530 **Pseudo-GALENUS** Med.
post A.D. 2

043 **De optima secta ad Thrasybulum liber**, ed. C.G. Kühn, *Claudii Galeni opera omnia*, vol. 1. Leipzig: Knobloch, 1821 (repr. Hildesheim: Olms, 1964): 106–223.
Cod: 18,213

032 **De theriaca ad Pamphilianum**, ed. Kühn, *op. cit.*, vol. 14 (1827; repr. 1965): 295–310.
Cod: 2,240

029 **De remediis parabilibus libri iii**, ed. Kühn, *op. cit.*, vol. 14, 311–581.
Cod: 36,890

012 **Introductio seu medicus**, ed. Kühn, *op. cit.*, vol. 14, 674–797.
Cod: 19,693

005 **De fasciis liber**, ed. Kühn, *op. cit.*, vol. 18.1 (1829; repr. 1965): 768–827.
Cod: 8,609

041 **Definitiones medicae**, ed. Kühn, *op. cit.*, vol. 19 (1830; repr. 1965): 346–462.
Cod: 15,715

009 **De humoribus liber**, ed. Kühn, *op. cit.*, vol. 19, 485–496.
Cod: 1,746

023 **Praesagitio omnino vera expertaque**, ed. Kühn, *op. cit.*, vol. 19, 512–518.
Cod: 913

036 **De venae sectione**, ed. Kühn, *op. cit.*, vol. 19, 519–528.
Cod: 1,315

024 **Prognostica de decubitu ex mathematica scientia**, ed. Kühn, *op. cit.*, vol. 19, 529–573.
Cod: 6,880

033 **De urinis**, ed. Kühn, *op. cit.*, vol. 19, 574–601.
Cod: 3,983

034 **De urinis compendium**, ed. Kühn, *op. cit.*, vol. 19, 602–608.
Cod: 976

035 **De urinis ex Hippocrate, Galeno et aliis quibusdam**, ed. Kühn, *op. cit.*, vol. 19, 609–628.
Cod: 3,096

026 **De pulsibus ad Antonium disciplinae studiosum ac philosophum**, ed. Kühn, *op. cit.*, vol. 19, 629–642.
Cod: 2,120

045 **De affectuum renibus insidentium dignotione et curatione liber adscriptitius**, ed. Kühn, *op. cit.*, vol. 19, 643–698.
Cod: 8,517

031 **De succedaneis liber**, ed. Kühn, *op. cit.*, vol. 19, 721–747.
Cod: 2,218

037 **De victus ratione in morbis acutis ex Hippocratis sententia liber**, ed. J. Westenberger, *Galeni de diaeta Hippocratis in morbis acutis* [*Corpus medicorum Graecorum*, vol. 5.9.1. Leipzig: Teubner, 1914]: 369–392.
Cod: 5,711

020 **De partibus philosophiae**, ed. R. Kotrc, Γαλήνου τοῦ ἰατροῦ περὶ εἴδων φιλοσοφίας [*Corpus medicorum Graecorum* (in press)]: 6–14.
N.B.: Text in the TLG data bank is based upon the editor's 1975 typescript.
Cod: 2,244

001 **De causa affectionum**, ed. G. Helmreich, *Handschriftliche Studien zu Galen* [*Programm Gymnasium Ansbach* (1911)]: 5–19.
Cod: 3,408

002 **An animal sit quod est in utero**, ed. H. Wagner, *Galeni qui fertur libellus* Εἰ ζῷον τὸ κατὰ γαστρός [*Diss. Marburg* (1914)]: 1–18.
Cod: 3,827

003 **Λέξεις βοτανῶν**, ed. A. Delatte, *Anecdota Atheniensia et alia*, vol. 2. Paris: Droz, 1939: 358–393.
Cod: 1,452

006 **Ad Gaurum quomodo animetur fetus**, ed. K. Kalbfleisch, *Die neuplatonische, fälschlich dem Galen zugeschriebene Schrift* Πρὸς Γαῦρον περὶ τοῦ πῶς ἐμψυχοῦνται τὰ ἔμβρυα [*Abhandlungen der königlichen Akademie der Wissenschaften zu Berlin*, Philol.-hist. Kl. Berlin: Reimer, 1895]: 33–62.
Cod: 9,944

022 **De ponderibus et mensuris**, ed. F. Hultsch, *Metrologicorum scriptorum reliquiae*, vol. 1. Leipzig, Stuttgart: Teubner (repr. 1971): 218–244.
Cod: 3,942

042 **De historia philosophica**, ed. H. Diels, *Doxographi Graeci*. Berlin: Reimer, 1879 (repr. De Gruyter, 1965): 597–648.
Cod: 11,550

2452 **GALITAS** (?) Hist.
3 B.C.?
001 **Testimonium**, FGrH #818: 3C:894.
NQ

0189 **C. Cornelius GALLUS** <Epigr.>
1 B.C.
001 **Epigramma**, AG 16.89.
Q: 38

0797 **GALLUS** Med.
fiq Aelius Gallus
1 B.C.?
Cf. et Aelius GALLUS Med. (0905).
x01 **Fragmenta ap. Galenum**.
K12.784; **13**.77, 138, 202–203, 310, 472–473, 556, 838.

Cf. GALENUS Med. (0057 076–077).

0905 **Aelius GALLUS** Med.
1 B.C.
Cf. et GALLUS Med. (0797).
Cf. et Marcus GALLUS Med. (0804).
x01 **Fragmenta ap. Galenum**.
K**12**.625–626, 738; **14**.114, 158–159, 161–162, 170–171.
Cf. GALENUS Med. (0057 076, 078).

0804 **Marcus GALLUS** Med.
fiq Aelius Gallus
1 B.C.?
Cf. et Aelius GALLUS Med. (0905).
x01 **Fragmentum ap. Galenum**.
K13.179–180.
Cf. GALENUS Med. (0057 076).

2137 **GAUDENTIUS** Phil. et Mus.
A.D. 2/6
001 **Harmonica introductio**, ed. K. Jan, *Musici scriptores Graeci*. Leipzig: Teubner, 1895 (repr. Hildesheim: Olms, 1962): 327–355.
Cod

0190 **GAURADAS** Epigr.
Incertum
001 **Epigramma**, AG 16.152.
Q: 50

2663 **GEMELLUS** Epigr.
A.D. 2
x01 **Epigramma dedicatorium**.
App. Anth. 1.182: Cf. EPIGRAMMATICI in *App. Anth.* (7052 001).

0906 **GEMELLUS** Med.
ante A.D. 2
x01 **Fragmentum ap. Galenum**.
K13.299.
Cf. GALENUS Med. (0057 076).

1383 **GEMINUS** Astron.
1 B.C.
001 **Elementa astronomiae**, ed. G. Aujac, *Géminos. Introduction aux phénomènes*. Paris: Les Belles Lettres, 1975: 1–98.
Cod: [20,572]
002 **Calendarium** [Sp.?], ed. Aujac, *op. cit.*, 98–108.
Cod: [1,821]
003 **De Posidonii meteorologicis** (epitome ap. Simplicium), ed. Aujac, *op. cit.*, 111–113.
Q
004 **Περὶ τῆς τῶν μαθημάτων τάξεως** (vel θεωρίας), ed. Aujac, *op. cit.*, 114–117.
Q
005 **Fragmenta optica** [Dub.], ed. R. Schöne, *Damianos Schrift über Optik*. Berlin: Reichsdruckerei, 1897: 22–30.
Q

GEMINUS Epigr.
Cf. TULLIUS GEMINUS Epigr. (1742).

0907 **GENNADIUS** Med.
ante A.D. 2
x01 **Fragmentum ap. Galenum.**
K12.760.
Cf. GALENUS Med. (0057 076).

2762 **GENNADIUS** Scr. Eccl.
A.D. 5: Constantinopolitanus
Bibliography in progress
004 **Fragmenta in epistulam ad Romanos** (in catenis), ed. K. Staab, *Pauluskommentar aus der griechischen Kirche aus Katenenhandschriften gesammelt.* Münster: Aschendorff, 1933: 352–418.
Q
005 **Fragmenta in epistulam i ad Corinthios** (in catenis), ed. Staab, *op. cit.*, 418–419.
Q
006 **Fragmentum in epistulam ii ad Corinthios** (in catenis), ed. Staab, *op. cit.*, 419.
Q
007 **Fragmenta in epistulam ad Galatas** (in catenis), ed. Staab, *op. cit.*, 419–420.
Q
008 **Fragmentum in epistulam ii ad Thessalonicenses** (in catenis), ed. Staab, *op. cit.*, 420.
Q
009 **Fragmenta in epistulam ad Hebraeos** (in catenis), ed. Staab, *op. cit.*, 420–422.
Q

GENETHLIUS Soph.
A.D. 3: Petraeus
Cf. MENANDER Rhet. (2586 001).

2030 *GEOGRAPHICA ADESPOTA* (GGM)
Incertum
001 **Fragmenta**, ed. K. Müller, *Geographi Graeci minores*, vol. 2. Paris: Didot, 1861 (repr. Hildesheim: Olms, 1965): 509–511.
Cod: [210]

4087 **Joannes GEOMETRES** Poeta
A.D. 10–11: Constantinopolitanus
Bibliography in progress
x01 **Epigrammata demonstrativa.**
App. Anth. 3.241, 284: Cf. EPIGRAMMATICI in *App. Anth.* (7052 003).

4080 *GEOPONICA*
A.D. 10
001 **Geoponica**, ed. H. Beckh, *Geoponica*. Leipzig: Teubner, 1895: 1–529.
Cod: [81,995]

2690 **GEORGIUS** <Epigr.>
A.D. 12: Corcyraeus
x01 **Epigramma sepulcrale.**

App. Anth. 2.747: Cf. EPIGRAMMATICI in *App. Anth.* (7052 002).

2701 **GEORGIUS PISIDES** Poeta
A.D. 7: Pisides, Constantinopolitanus
Bibliography in progress
x01 **Epigrammata.**
AG 1.120, 121: Cf. ANONYMI EPIGRAMMATICI (0138 001).
x02 **Epigramma demonstrativum.**
App. Anth. 3.254: Cf. EPIGRAMMATICI in *App. Anth.* (7052 003).

0191 **Tiberius Drusus Nero GERMANICUS CAESAR** <Epigr.>
1 B.C.–A.D. 1
001 **Epigrammata**, AG 9.17–18, 387(?).
AG 7.73: Cf. TULLIUS GEMINUS Epigr. (1742 001).
AG 9.387: Cf. et HADRIANUS Imperator (0195 001).
Q: 124

4070 **GERMANUS** Epigr.
A.D. 4
001 **Epigramma**, AG 14.148.
Q: 48

0908 **GLAUCIAS** Med.
2 B.C.: Tarentinus
x01 **Fragmentum ap. Galenum.**
K13.835.
Cf. GALENUS Med. (0057 077).
x02 **Fragmentum ap. Oribasium.**
CMG, vol. 6.2.1, p. 283.
Cf. ORIBASIUS Med. (0722 001).

2191 **GLAUCIPPUS** Hist.
Incertum
001 **Fragmentum**, FGrH #363: 3B:224.
Q

0192 **GLAUCUS** Epigr.
Incertum: Atheniensis
001 **Epigrammata**, AG **9**.774–775; **16**.111.
Q: 82

0193 **GLAUCUS** Epigr.
Incertum: Nicopolitanus
001 **Epigrammata**, AG 7.285; **9**.341; **12**.44.
Q: 105

2460 **GLAUCUS** Hist.
2 B.C./A.D. 3
001 **Fragmenta**, FGrH #674: 3C:338–339.
Q

1385 **GLAUCUS** Hist.
ante A.D. 3
001 **Fragmentum**, FGrH #806: 3C:843.
fr. 1: *P. Oxy.* 15.1802.
Pap

0194 **GLYCON** Epigr.
Incertum
001 **Epigramma**, AG 10.124.
AG 10.124b–126: Cf. ANONYMI EPIGRAMMA-
TICI (0138 001).
Q: 17

0911 **GLYTUS** Med.
ante A.D. 1?
x01 **Fragmentum ap. Galenum.**
K13.1036–1037.
Cf. GALENUS Med. (0057 077).

2945 *GNOMOLOGIUM VATICANUM*
A.D. 14
001 **Gnomologium Vaticanum**, ed. L. Sternbach,
*Gnomologium Vaticanum e codice Vaticano
Graeco 743 [Texte und Kommentare 2* (repr.
Berlin: De Gruyter, 1963)]: 4–204.
Cod

2255 **GORGIAS** Hist.
A.D. 1–2?: Atheniensis
001 **Testimonium**, FGrH #351: 3B:214.
NQ
002 **Fragmenta**, FGrH #351: 3B:214.
Q

0593 **GORGIAS** Rhet. et Soph.
5–4 B.C.: Leontinus
001 **Testimonium**, FGrH #407: 3B:301.
NQ
002 **Testimonia**, ed. H. Diels and W. Kranz, *Die
Fragmente der Vorsokratiker*, vol. 2, 6th edn.
Berlin: Weidmann, 1952 (repr. Dublin: 1966):
271–279.
test. 1–35.
NQ
003 **Fragmenta**, ed. Diels and Kranz, *op. cit.*, 279–
306.
frr. 1–31.
Q

2357 **GORGON** Hist.
2 B.C.?: fort. Rhodius
001 **Fragmenta**, FGrH #515: 3B:490–491.
Q

2369 **GORGOSTHENES** Hist.
5 B.C.: Rhodius
001 **Testimonium**, FGrH #529: 3B:505.
NQ

1872 **GORGUS** Epigr.
ante 2 B.C.: Colophonius
001 **Testimonium**, FGrH #17: 1A:182.
test. 1: *Inscr. Athen. Mitt.* 11.428.
NQ

0964 **Chrysantus GRATIANUS** Med.
ante A.D. 2
x01 **Fragmentum ap. Galenum.**

K12.631–632.
Cf. GALENUS Med. (0057 076).

9006 **GREGORIUS** Paroemiogr.
A.D. 13: Cyprius
001 **Paroemiae**, ed. E.L. von Leutsch and F.G.
Schneidewin, *Corpus paroemiographorum
Graecorum*, vol. 1. Göttingen: Vandenhoeck &
Ruprecht, 1839 (repr. Hildesheim: Olms,
1965): 349–378.
Cod: [2,816]
002 **Paroemiae** (e codice Leidense), ed. von
Leutsch, *op. cit.*, vol. 2 (1851; repr. 1958): 53–
92.
Cod: [3,559]
003 **Paroemiae** (e codice Mosquense), ed. von
Leutsch, *op. cit.*, vol. 2, 93–130.
Cod: [4,392]
004 **Paroemiae** (e codice Vaticano), ed. von
Leutsch, *op. cit.*, vol. 2, 131–134.
Cod: [716]

2022 **GREGORIUS NAZIANZENUS** Theol.
A.D. 4: Nazianzenus
Bibliography in progress
001 **Epistulae**, ed. P. Gallay, *Saint Grégoire de
Nazianze. Lettres*, 2 vols. Paris: Les Belles
Lettres, 1:1964; 2:1967: 1:1–118; 2:1–148.
Epist. 1–100: vol. 1.
Epist. 103–201, 203–249: vol. 2.
Cod: [41,717]
002 **Epistulae theologicae**, ed. P. Gallay, *Grégoire
de Nazianze. Lettres théologiques [Sources chré-
tiennes 208.* Paris: Cerf, 1974]: 36–94.
Epist. 101: pp. 36–68.
Epist. 102: pp. 70–84.
Epist. 202: pp. 86–94.
Cod: [4,385]
003 **Christus patiens** [Dub.], ed. A. Tuilier, *Grégoire de Nazianze. La passion du Christ
[Sources chrétiennes 149.* Paris: Cerf, 1969]:
124–338.
Cod: 16,043
004 **De vita sua**, ed. C. Jungck, *Gregor von Nazianz. De vita sua.* Heidelberg: Winter, 1974:
54–148.
Cod: [11,890]
005 **Funebris in laudem Caesarii fratris oratio**
(orat. 7), ed. F. Boulenger, *Grégoire de Nazianze. Discours funèbres en l'honneur de son
frère Césaire et de Basile de Césarée.* Paris:
Picard, 1908: 2–56.
Cod: [5,446]
006 **Funebris oratio in laudem Basilii Magni Cae-
sareae in Cappadocia episcopi** (orat. 43), ed.
Boulenger, *op. cit.*, 58–230.
Cod: [17,688]
007 **Adversus Eunomianos** (orat. 27), ed. J. Barbel,
*Gregor von Nazianz. Die fünf theologischen
Reden.* Düsseldorf: Patmos-Verlag, 1963: 38–
60.
Cod: [2,208]

008 **De theologia** (orat. 28), ed. Barbel, *op. cit.*, 62–126.
Cod: [7,828]

009 **De filio** (orat. 29), ed. Barbel, *op. cit.*, 128–168.
Cod: [5,175]

010 **De filio** (orat. 30), ed. Barbel, *op. cit.*, 170–216.
Cod: [5,239]

011 **De spiritu sancto** (orat. 31), ed. Barbel, *op. cit.*, 218–276.
Cod: [6,630]

012 **Comparatio vitarum** (= Carmen morale 8), ed. H.M. Werhahn, *Gregorii Nazianzeni σύγκρισις βίων* [*Klassisch-philologische Studien* 15. Wiesbaden: Harrassowitz, 1953]: 22–29.
Cod: [1,559]

013 **De testamentis et adventu Christi** (= Carmen dogmaticum 9, additamentum inter vv. 18 et 19), ed. B. Wyss, *Phyllobolia für Peter von der Mühll*. Basel: Schwabe, 1946: 161–163.
Cf. et 2022 059.
Cod: [424]

014 **Alphabeticum paraeneticum 1** (e cod. Patm. 33), ed. J. Sakkelion, Πατμιακή βιβλιοθήκη. Athens: Papageorgiu, 1890: 18–19.
Cod: [145]

015 **In sanctum Pascha et in tarditatem** (orat. 1), MPG 35: 396–401.
Cod: [852]

016 **Apologetica** (orat. 2), MPG 35: 408–513.
Cod: [14,988]

017 **Ad eos qui ipsum acciverant nec occurrerant** (orat. 3), MPG 35: 517–525.
Cod: [1,043]

018 **Contra Julianum imperatorem 1** (orat. 4), MPG 35: 532–664.
Cod: [18,917]

019 **Contra Julianum imperatorem 2** (orat. 5), MPG 35: 664–720.
Cod: [7,900]

020 **De pace 1** (orat. 6), MPG 35: 721–752.
Cod: [4,832]

021 **In laudem sororis Gorgoniae** (orat. 8), MPG 35: 789–817.
Cod: [4,490]

022 **Apologeticus ad patrem** (orat. 9), MPG 35: 820–825.
Cod: [1,210]

023 **In seipsum ad patrem et Basilium magnum** (orat. 10), MPG 35: 828–832.
Cod: [802]

024 **Ad Gregorium Nyssenum** (orat. 11), MPG 35: 832–841.
Cod: [1,618]

025 **Ad patrem** (orat. 12), MPG 35: 844–849.
Cod: [1,231]

026 **In consecratione Eulalii Doarensium episcopi** (orat. 13), MPG 35: 852–856.
Cod: [647]

027 **De pauperum amore** (orat. 14), MPG 35: 857–909.
Cod: [8,574]

028 **In Machabaeorum laudem** (orat. 15), MPG 35: 912–933.
Cod: [3,246]

029 **In patrem tacentem** (orat. 16), MPG 35: 933–964.
Cod: [4,722]

030 **Ad cives Nazianzenos** (orat. 17), MPG 35: 964–981.
Cod: [2,654]

031 **Funebris in patrem** (orat. 18), MPG 35: 985–1044.
Cod: [9,593]

032 **Ad Julianum tributorum exaequatorem** (orat. 19), MPG 35: 1044–1064.
Cod: [3,297]

033 **De dogmate et constitutione episcoporum** (orat. 20), MPG 35: 1065–1080.
Cod: [2,475]

034 **In laudem Athanasii** (orat. 21), MPG 35: 1081–1128.
Cod: [7,325]

035 **De pace 2** (orat. 22), MPG 35: 1132–1152.
Cod: [3,553]

036 **De pace 3** (orat. 23), MPG 35: 1152–1168.
Cod: [2,706]

037 **In laudem Cypriani** (orat. 24), MPG 35: 1169–1193.
Cod: [3,784]

038 **In laudem Heronis philosophi** (orat. 25), MPG 35: 1197–1225.
Cod: [4,414]

039 **In seipsum, cum rure rediisset, post ea quae a Maximo perpetrata fuerant** (orat. 26), MPG 35: 1228–1252.
Cod: [4,101]

040 **De moderatione in disputando** (orat. 32), MPG 36: 173–212.
Cod: [6,635]

041 **Contra Arianos et de seipso** (orat. 33), MPG 36: 213–237.
Cod: [3,438]

042 **In Aegyptiorum adventum** (orat. 34), MPG 36: 241–256.
Cod: [2,413]

043 **De martyribus et adversus Arianos** (orat. 35) [Sp.], MPG 36: 257–261.
Cod: [1,066]

044 **De seipso et ad eos qui ipsum cathedram Constantinopolitanam affectare dicebant** (orat. 36), MPG 36: 265–279.
Cod: [2,630]

045 **In dictum evangelii: Cum consummasset Jesus hos sermones** (orat. 37), MPG 36: 281–308.
Cod: [4,392]

046 **In theophania** (orat. 38), MPG 36: 312–333.
Cod: [3,556]

047 **In sancta lumina** (orat. 39), MPG 36: 336–360.
Cod: [4,025]

048 **In sanctum baptisma** (orat. 40), MPG 36: 360–425.
Cod: [10,918]

049 **In pentecosten** (orat. 41), MPG 36: 428–452.
Cod: [3,784]

050 **Supremum vale** (orat. 42), MPG 36: 457–492.
Cod: [5,803]

051 **In novam Dominicam** (orat. 44), MPG 36: 608–621.
Cod: [2,229]

052 **In sancta Pascha** (orat. 45), MPG 36: 624–664.
Cod: [6,832]

053 **Significatio in Ezechielem** [Sp.], MPG 36: 665–669.
Cod: [534]

054 **Fragmentum ex oratione contra astronomos** [Sp.], MPG 36: 675–678.
Cod: [924]

055 **Liturgia sancti Gregorii** [Sp.], MPG 36: 700–733.
Cod: [5,878]

056 ʼΑλάτιον σκευασθὲν ὑπὸ τῆς ἐνεργείας τοιᾶσδε, ed. J.L. Ideler, *Physici et medici Graeci minores*, vol. 1. Berlin: Reimer, 1841 (repr. Amsterdam: Hakkert, 1963): 297–298.
Cod: 91

058 **Testamentum**, ed. J.B. Pitra, *Iuris ecclesiastici Graecorum historia et monumenta*, vol. 2. Rome: Congregatio de Propaganda Fide, 1868: 155-159.
Cod

059 **Carmina dogmatica**, *MPG* 37: 397-522.
De patre (carm. 1): coll. 397-401.
De filio (carm. 2): coll. 401-408.
De spiritu sancto (carm. 3): coll. 408-415.
De mundo (carm. 4): coll. 415-425.
De providentia (carm. 5): coll. 424-429.
De eodem argumento (carm. 6): coll. 430-438.
De substantiis mente praeditis (carm. 7): coll. 438-446.
De anima (carm. 8): coll. 446-456.
De testamentis et adventu Christi (carm. 9): coll. 456-464.
De incarnatione adversus Apollinarium (carm. 10): coll. 464-470.
De Christi incarnatione (carm. 11): coll. 470-471.
De veris scripturae libris (carm. 12): coll. 472-474.
Patriarchae filii Jacob (carm. 13): col. 475.
Plagae Aegypti (carm. 14): coll. 475-476.
Moysis decalogus (carm. 15): coll. 476-477.
Eliae et Elisaei miracula (carm. 16): coll. 477-479.
Epigramma in templum Eliae quod Χηρεῖον appellabatur (carm. 17): coll. 479-480.
De Christi genealogia (carm. 18): coll. 480-487.
Discipuli Christi duodecim (carm. 19): col. 488.
Miracula Christi secundum Matthaeum (carm. 20): coll. 488-491.
Miracula Christi secundum Marcum (carm. 21): coll. 491-492.

Miracula Christi secundum Lucam (carm. 22): coll. 492-494.
Miracula Christi secundum Joannem (carm. 23): col. 494.
Parabolae Christi et aenigmata secundum Matthaeum (carm. 24): coll. 495-496.
Parabolae Christi secundum Marcum (carm. 25): coll. 496-497.
Parabolae Christi secundum Lucam (carm. 26): coll. 497-498.
Parabolae Christi secundum omnes evangelistas (carm. 27): coll. 498-506.
Tempestas a Christo sedata (carm. 28): coll. 506-507.
Hymnus ad deum (carm. 29) [Sp.]: coll. 507-508.
Hymnus alius ad deum (carm. 30): coll. 508-510.
Hymnus alius (carm. 31) [Dub.]: coll. 510-511.
Hymnus vespertinus (carm. 32) [Dub.]: coll. 511-514.
Actio gratiarum (carm. 33) [Dub.]: col. 514.
Alia gratiarum actio (carm. 34) [Dub.]: coll. 515-517.
Precatio ante scripturae lectionem (carm. 35) [Dub.]: coll. 517-518.
Precatio ante iter suscipiendum (carm. 36): coll. 518-520.
Alia de prospero itinere precatio (carm. 37) [Dub.]: coll. 520-521.
Alia precatio (carm. 38) [Dub.]: coll. 521-522.
Carm. 9: Cf. et 2022 013.
Cod

060 **Carmina moralia**, *MPG* 37: 521-968.
In laudem virginitatis (carm. 1): coll. 521-578.
Praecepta ad virgines (carm. 2): coll. 578-632.
Exhortatio ad virgines (carm. 3) [Dub.]: coll. 632-640.
Ad virginem (carm. 4): coll. 640-642.
Ad monachos in monasterio degentes (carm. 5): coll. 642-643.
De pudicitia (carm. 6): coll. 643-648.
De castitate (carm. 7): coll. 648-649.
Comparatio vitarum (carm. 8): coll. 649-667.
De virtute (carm. 9): coll. 667-680.
De virtute (carm. 10): coll. 680-752.
Dialogus cum mundo (carm. 11): coll. 752-753.
De naturae humanae fragilitate (carm. 12): coll. 753-754.
De eodem argumento (carm. 13): coll. 754-755.
De humana natura (carm. 14): coll. 755-765.
De exterioris hominis vilitate (carm. 15): coll. 766-778.
De vitae itineribus (carm. 16): coll. 778-781.
Variorum vitae generum beatitudines (carm. 17): coll. 781-786.
De vita humana (carm. 18) [Sp.]: coll. 786-787.
De eodem argumento (carm. 19) [Sp.]: coll. 787-788.

De desiderio (carm. 20) [Sp.]: col. 788.

De morte carorum (carm. 21) [Sp.]: col. 789.

De falsis amicis (carm. 22): col. 789.

De eodem argumento (carm. 23) [Sp.]: col. 790.

Dialogus adversus eos qui frequenter jurant (carm. 24): coll. 790-813.

Adversus iram (carm. 25): coll. 813-851.

In nobilem male moratum (carm. 26): coll. 851-854.

De eodem argumento (carm. 27): coll. 854-856.

Adversus opum amantes (carm. 28): coll. 856-884.

Adversus mulieres se nimis ornantes (carm. 29): coll. 884-908.

Versus iambici acrostichi (carm. 30): coll. 908-910.

Distichae sententiae (carm. 31): coll. 910-915.

Aliae generis eiusdem sententiae (carm. 32) [Sp.]: coll. 916-927.

Tetrastichae sententiae (carm. 33): coll. 927-945.

Definitiones minus exactae (carm. 34): coll. 945-964.

De philosophica paupertate (carm. 35): col. 965.

De eodem argumento (carm. 36): coll. 965-966.

De patientia (carm. 37): col. 966.

De eodem argumento (carm. 38): col. 967.

De fortuna et providentia (carm. 39) [Sp.]: coll. 967-968.

De rerum humanarum vanitate (carm. 40) [Sp.]: col. 968.

Carm. 8: Cf. et 2022 012.

Cod

061 **Carmina de se ipso**, *MPG* 37: 969-1029, 1166-1452.

Carm. 1-10: coll. 969-1029.

Carm. 12-99: coll. 1166-1452.

Carm. 99 est dubium.

Carm. 11 (De vita sua): Cf. 2022 004.

Cod

062 **Carmina quae spectant ad alios**, *MPG* 37: 1451-1577.

Ad Hellenium pro monachis exhortatorium (carm. 1): coll. 1451-1477.

Ad Julianum (carm. 2): coll. 1477-1480.

Ad Vitalianum (carm. 3): coll. 1480-1505.

Nicobuli filii ad patrem (carm. 4): coll. 1505-1521.

Nicobuli patris ad filium (carm. 5): coll. 1521-1542.

Ad Olympiadem (carm. 6): coll. 1542-1550.

Ad Nemesium (carm. 7): coll. 1551-1577.

Carm. 8 (Ad Seleucum): Cf. AMPHILOCHIUS Scr. Eccl. (2112 002).

Cod

063 **Epitaphia**, *MPG* 38: 11-82.

Epitaph. 1-3, 6-78, 80-128 etiam exstant in *Anthologia Graeca* (lib. 8).

Epitaph. 129 spurium est.

Cod

064 **Epigrammata**, *MPG* 38: 81-130.

Epigr. 26-29, 47-94 etiam exstant in *Anthologia Graeca* (lib. 8).

Epigr. 30 spurium est.

Cod

065 **Alphabeticum A** [Sp.], ed. C. Müller, "Handschriftliches zu Ignatius Diaconus," *Byzantinische Zeitschrift* 3 (1894) 521.

Cod

057 **Epigrammata**, AG 1.51, 92(?); 8.1-254.

Q: 6,776

x01 **Epigramma demonstrativum**.

App. Anth. 3.161: Cf. EPIGRAMMATICI in *App. Anth.* (7052 003).

x02 **Metaphrasis in Ecclesiasten** [Sp.].

MPG 10.998-1017.

Cf. GREGORIUS THAUMATURGUS Scr. Eccl. (2063 006).

x03 **Alphabeticum paraeneticum 2** (e cod. Vind. philos. gr. 165 N).

FCG 4.356-357.

Cf. MENANDER Comic. (0541 047).

2017 **GREGORIUS NYSSENUS** Theol.

A.D. 4: Nyssenus

030 **Contra Eunomium**, ed. W. Jaeger, *Gregorii Nysseni opera*, vols. 1.1 & 2.2. Leiden: Brill, 1960: **1.1**:3-409; **2.2**:3-311.

Cod: 172,463

031 **Refutatio confessionis Eunomii**, ed. Jaeger, *op. cit.*, vol. 2.2, 312-410.

Cod: [23,755]

001 **Ad Eustathium de sancta trinitate**, ed. F. Mueller, *op. cit.*, vol. 3.1 (1958): 3-16.

Cod: [2,803]

002 **Ad Graecos ex communibus notionibus**, ed. Mueller, *op. cit.*, vol. 3.1, 19-33.

Cod: [3,146]

003 **Ad Ablabium quod non sint tres dei**, ed. Mueller, *op. cit.*, vol. 3.1, 37-57.

Cod: [4,126]

004 **Ad Simplicium de fide**, ed. Mueller, *op. cit.*, vol. 3.1, 61-67.

Cod: [1,614]

005 **Adversus Arium et Sabellium de patre et filio**, ed. Mueller, *op. cit.*, vol. 3.1, 71-85.

Cod: [4,079]

006 **Adversus Macedonianos de spiritu sancto**, ed. Mueller, *op. cit.*, vol. 3.1, 89-115.

Cod: [7,774]

007 **Ad Theophilum adversus Apolinaristas**, ed. Mueller, *op. cit.*, vol. 3.1, 119-128.

Cod: [1,737]

008 **Antirrheticus adversus Apolinarium**, ed. Mueller, *op. cit.*, vol. 3.1, 131-233.

Cod: [27,790]

027 **In inscriptiones Psalmorum**, ed. J. McDonough, *op. cit.*, vol. 5 (1962): 24-175.

Cod: [36,400]

028 **In sextum Psalmum**, ed. McDonough, *op. cit.*, vol. 5, 187-193.
Cod: [1,590]

029 **In Ecclesiasten homiliae**, ed. P. Alexander, *op. cit.*, vol. 5, 277-442.
Cod: [31,453]

032 **In Canticum canticorum commentarius**, ed. H. Langerbeck, *op. cit.*, vol. 6 (1960): 3-469.
Cod: [80,433]

024 **De instituto Christiano**, ed. Jaeger, *op. cit.*, vol. 8.1 (1963): 40-89.
Cod: [9,163]

025 **De professione Christiana**, ed. Jaeger, *op. cit.*, vol. 8.1, 129-142.
Cod: [2,564]

026 **De perfectione**, ed. Jaeger, *op. cit.*, vol. 8.1, 173-214.
Cod: [7,861]

033 **Epistulae**, ed. G. Pasquali, *op. cit.*, vol. 8.2, 2nd edn. (1959): 3-95.
Cod: [19,407]

009 **De mortuis oratio**, ed. G. Heil, *op. cit.*, vol. 9.1 (1967): 28-68.
Cod: [9,405]

010 **De beneficentia** (*vulgo* **De pauperibus amandis i**), ed. A. van Heck, *op. cit.*, vol. 9.1, 1967: 93-108.
Cod: [3,200]

011 **In illud: Quatenus uni ex his fecistis mihi fecistis** (*vulgo* **De pauperibus amandis ii**), ed. van Heck, *op. cit.*, vol. 9.1, 111-127.
Cod: [3,792]

012 **Contra usurarios oratio**, ed. E. Gebhardt, *op. cit.*, vol. 9.1, 195-207.
Cod: [2,930]

013 **Contra fornicarios oratio**, ed. Gebhardt, *op. cit.*, vol. 9.1, 211-217.
Cod: [1,296]

014 **In diem luminum** (*vulgo* **In baptismum Christi oratio**), ed. Gebhardt, *op. cit.*, vol. 9.1, 221-242.
Cod: [4,596]

015 **In sanctum Pascha** (*vulgo* **In Christi resurrectionem oratio iii**), ed. Gebhardt, *op. cit.*, vol. 9.1, 245-270.
Cod: [5,730]

016 **De tridui inter mortem et resurrectionem domini nostri Jesu Christi spatio** (*vulgo* **In Christi resurrectionem oratio i**), ed. Gebhardt, *op. cit.*, vol. 9.1, 273-306.
Cod: [6,310]

017 **In sanctum et salutare Pascha** (*vulgo* **In Christi resurrectionem oratio iv**), ed. Gebhardt, *op. cit.*, vol. 9.1, 309-311.
Cod: [639]

018 **In luciferam sanctam domini resurrectionem** (*vulgo* **In Christi resurrectionem oratio v**), ed. Gebhardt, *op. cit.*, vol. 9.1, 315-319.
Cod: [1,068]

019 **In ascensionem Christi oratio**, ed. Gebhardt, *op. cit.*, vol. 9.1, 323-327.
Cod: [986]

020 **De deitate adversus Evagrium** (*vulgo* **In suam ordinationem oratio**), ed. Gebhardt, *op. cit.*, vol. 9.1, 331-341.
Cod: [2,099]

021 **Oratio funebris in Meletium episcopum**, ed. A. Spira, *op. cit.*, vol. 9.1, 441-457.
Cod: [2,493]

022 **Oratio consolatoria in Pulcheriam**, ed. Spira, *op. cit.*, vol. 9.1, 461-472.
Cod: [2,859]

023 **Oratio funebris in Flacillam imperatricem**, ed. Spira, *op. cit.*, vol. 9.1, 475-490.
Cod: [3,036]

034 **De creatione hominis sermo primus**, ed. H. Hörner, *op. cit.*, suppl. (1972): 2-40.
Cod: 4,622

035 **De creatione hominis sermo alter**, ed. Hörner, *op. cit.*, suppl., 41-72.
Cod: 4,211

036 **De paradiso**, ed. Hörner, *op. cit.*, suppl., 75-84.
Cod: 1,675

037 **De creatione hominis sermo primus** (recensio C), ed. Hörner, *op. cit.*, suppl., 2a-39a, 40.
Cod: 5,775

038 **De creatione hominis sermo alter** (recensio C), ed. Hörner, *op. cit.*, suppl., 41a-72a.
Cod: 4,683

039 **De paradiso** (recensio ΛF), ed. Hörner, *op. cit.*, suppl., 75a-84a.
Cod: 1,927

040 **Encomium in sanctum Stephanum protomartyrem**, ed. O. Lendle, *Gregorius Nyssenus. Encomium in sanctum Stephanum protomartyrem.* Leiden: Brill, 1968: 4-44.
Cod: 3,925

041 **Vita sanctae Macrinae**, ed. P. Maraval, *Grégoire de Nysse. Vie de sainte Macrine* [*Sources chrétiennes* 178. Paris: Cerf, 1971]: 136-266.
Cod: 9,131

042 **De vita Mosis**, ed. J. Daniélou, *Grégoire de Nysse. La vie de Moïse*, 3rd edn. [*Sources chrétiennes* 1 ter. Paris: Cerf, 1968]: 44-326.
Cod: 30,573

043 **De virginitate**, ed. M. Aubineau, *Grégoire de Nysse. Traité de la virginité* [*Sources chrétiennes* 119. Paris: Cerf, 1966]: 246-560.
Cod: 20,454

044 **De virginitate** (recensio altera), ed. Aubineau, *op. cit.*, 258-260, 508, 514-516, 546-548.
Cod: 634

045 **Contra fatum**, ed. J. McDonough, *The treatise of Gregory of Nyssa contra fatum* [*Diss. Harvard* (1952)]: 1-37.
Cod: [6,842]

046 **Oratio catechetica magna**, ed. J. Srawley, *The catechetical oration of Gregory of Nyssa.* Cambridge: Cambridge University Press, 1903 (repr. 1956): 1-164.
Cod: [21,011]

047 **De oratione dominica orationes v**, ed. F. Oehler, *Gregor's Bischof's von Nyssa Abhandlung von der Erschaffung des Menschen und*

fünf Reden auf das Gebet. Leipzig: Engelmann, 1859: 202–314.
Cod: [16,491]

048 **In Basilium fratrem**, ed. J. Stein, *Encomium of Saint Gregory Bishop of Nyssa on his brother Saint Basil.* Washington, D.C.: The Catholic University of America, 1928: 2–60.
Cod: [6,403]

049 **Oratio in diem natalem Christi**, ed. F. Mann, *Die Weihnachtspredigt Gregors von Nyssa Überlieferungsgeschichte und Text* [*Diss. Münster* (1975)]: 263–292.
Cod: [4,936]

050 **De pythonissa ad Theodosium episcopum**, ed. E. Klostermann, *Origenes Eustathius von Antiochien und Gregor von Nyssa über die Hexe von Endor.* Bonn: Marcus & Weber, 1912: 63–68.
Cod: [1,530]

051 **In annuntiationem** [Sp.], ed. D. Montagna, "La lode alla theotokos nei testi greci dei secoli iv-vii," *Marianum* 24 (1962) 536–539.
Cod: [1,881]

052 **Inventio imaginis in Camulianis** [Sp.], ed. E. Dobschütz, *Christusbilder. Untersuchungen zur christlichen Legende* [*Texte und Untersuchungen* 18. Leipzig: Hinrichs, 1899]: 12**–18**.
Cod: [874]

053 **Orationes viii de beatitudinibus**, MPG 44: 1193–1301.
Cod: [23,120]

054 **In illud: Tunc et ipse filius**, MPG 44: 1304–1325.
Cod: [5,411]

055 **Ad imaginem dei et ad similitudinem** [Sp.], MPG 44: 1328–1345.
Cod: [4,144]

056 **Dialogus de anima et resurrectione**, MPG 46: 12–160.
Cod: [24,476]

057 **De infantibus praemature abreptis**, MPG 46: 161–192.
Cod: [6,626]

058 **Testimonia adversus Judaeos** [Sp.], MPG 46: 193–233.
Cod: [6,777]

059 **Adversus eos qui castigationes aegre ferunt**, MPG 46: 308–316.
Cod: [1,984]

060 **De iis qui baptismum differunt**, MPG 46: 416–432.
Cod: [3,117]

061 **Decem syllogismi contra Manichaeos** [Sp.], MPG 46: 541.
Cod: [240]

062 **De deitate filii et spiritus sancti**, MPG 46: 553–576.
Cod: [4,760]

063 **De spiritu sancto** *sive* **In pentecosten**, MPG 46: 696–701.
Cod: [1,287]

064 **Encomium in sanctum Stephanum protomar-**

tyrem ii, MPG 46: 721–736.
Cod: [2,471]

065 **De sancto Theodoro**, MPG 46: 736–748.
Cod: [2,524]

066 **Encomium in xl martyres**, MPG 46: 749–772.
Cod: [4,816]

067 **Encomium in xl martyres ii**, MPG 46: 773–788.
Cod: [3,009]

068 **In sanctum Ephraim**, MPG 46: 820–849.
Cod: [6,429]

069 **De vita Gregorii Thaumaturgi**, MPG 46: 893–957.
Cod: [13,958]

070 **Epistula xxvi ad Evagrium monachum** [Sp.], MPG 46: 1101–1108.
Cod: [1,135]

071 **Sermo in illud: Hic est filius meus dilectus** (ap. Joannem Damascenum) (fragmenta), MPG 46: 1109–1112.
Cod: [218]

072 **Sermo in Mariam et Joseph** (fragmentum), MPG 46: 1112.
Cod: [109]

073 **De occursu domini**, MPG 46: 1152–1181.
Cod: [6,108]

074 **Tractatus ad Xenodorum** (fragmentum), ed. F. Diekamp, *Analecta patristica* [*Orientalia Christiana analecta* 117. Rome: Pont. Institutum Orientalium Studiorum, 1938 (repr. 1962)]: 14–15.
Cod: [120]

075 **Sermo in sanctum Romanum** (fragmentum), MPG 96: 476–477.
Cod: [66]

076 **Epistula canonica ad Letoium**, MPG 45: 221–236.
Cod: [3,137]

077 **Liber de cognitione dei** (= Θεογνωσία) (fragmenta), MPG 130: 28–29, 257–276, 312–317.
Cod: [5,104]

x01 **Ad Petrum fratrem de differentia essentiae hypostaseos.**
Basilius, *Epist.* 38.
Cf. BASILIUS Theol. (2040 004).

x02 **De anima** [Sp.].
Nemesius, *De natura hominis*, cap. 2–3.
Cf. NEMESIUS Theol. (0743 001).

2063 **GREGORIUS THAUMATURGUS** Scr. Eccl.
A.D. 3: Neocaesariensis

001 **In Originem oratio panegyrica**, ed. H. Crouzel, *Grégoire le Thaumaturge. Remerciement à Origène suivi de la lettre d'Origène à Grégoire* [*Sources chrétiennes* 148. Paris, Cerf, 1969]: 94–182.
Cod

005 **Epistula canonica**, FONTI II: 19–30.
Cod

006 **Metaphrasis in Ecclesiasten Salamonis**, MPG 10: 988–1017.
Cod

008 **Ad Tatianum de anima per capita disputatio**

[Sp.], MPG 10: 1137–1145.
Cod

009 **In annuntiationem sanctae virginis Mariae** (homiliae 1–3) [Sp.], MPG 10: 1145–1169.
Cod

010 **Sermo in omnes sanctos** [Sp.], MPG 10: 1197–1204.
Cod

013 **Fragmentum in evangelium Matthaei** (6.22–23), MPG 10: 1189.
Q

016 **Fragmentum in Job** (in catenis), ed. J.B. Pitra, *Analecta sacra spicilegio Solesmensi parata*, vol. 3. Venice: St. Lazarus Monastery, 1883: 589–591.
Cod

017 **Exorcismus**, ed. A. Strittmatter, "Ein griechisches Exorzismusbüchlein. Ms. car. C 143b der Zentralbibliothek in Zürich," *Orientalia Christiana* 26.2. Rome, 1932: 129–137.
Cod

018 **Precatio**, ed. Strittmatter, *op. cit.*, 141–143.
Cod

020 **De deitate et tribus personis**, ed. C.P. Caspari, "Nogle nye kirkehistoriske Anecdota II. Et Gregorius Thaumaturgus tillagt Fragment," *Theologisk Tidsskrift for den evangelisk-lutherske Kirche i Norge*, ser. 2, vol. 8 (1882) 53–59.
Q

021 **Sententiae** (ap. Antonium Melissam), ed. V. Ryssel, *Gregorius Thaumaturgus. Sein Leben und seine Schriften*. Leipzig: Fernau, 1880: 52–53.
frr. 1–6.
Q

022 Εἰς τὸ οὐδὲν εἴδωλον ἐν κόσμῳ (fragmentum), ed. K. Holl, *Fragmente vornicänischer Kirchenväter aus den Sacra parallela herausgegeben* [*Texte und Untersuchungen* 20. Leipzig: Hinrichs, 1899]: 159.
fr. 405.
Q

025 **Fragmenta in Jeremiam** (in catenis), ed. Pitra, *op. cit.*, 591–595.
Q

026 **Fragmentum in Matthaeum** (in catenis, typus C), ed. B. Corderius, *Symbolarum in Matthaeum tomus alter, quo continetur catena patrum Graecorum triginta collectore Niceta episcopo Serrarum*. Toulouse, 1647.
Q

028 **De fide capitula duodecim**, ed. L. Casson and E.L. Hettich, *Excavations at Nessana, vol. 2: literary papyri*. Princeton: Princeton University Press, 1950: 155–158.
Cf. et 2063 x02.
Pap

x01 **Fragmentum** (in *Doctrina patrum*). Diekamp, p. 251.
Cf. DOCTRINA PATRUM (7051 001).

x02 **De fide capitula duodecim** (= **Liber de dei verbi incarnatione**).

ACO 1.1.6, pp. 146–151.
Cf. CONCILIA OECUMENICA (ACO) (5000 001).
Cf. et 2063 028.

x03 **Confessio fidei**.
ACO 3, p. 3.
Cf. CONCILIA OECUMENICA (ACO) (5000 004).

2118 *GRYLLUS*
ante A.D. 3

001 **Fragmentum** (*P. Oxy.* 22.2331), ed. E. Heitsch, *Die griechischen Dichterfragmente der römischen Kaiserzeit*, vol. 2. Göttingen: Vandenhoeck & Ruprecht, 1964: 48–49.
Pap: [87]

1758 **HABRON** Gramm.
A.D. 1: Phrygius, Rhodius

001 **Fragmenta**, ed. R. Berndt, "Die Fragmente des Grammatikers Habron," *Philologische Wochenschrift* 35 (1915) coll. 1452–1455, 1483.
frr. 1–21.
Q

2259 **HABRON** Hist.
2 B.C.?: Atheniensis

001 **Testimonium**, FGrH #359: 3B:218.
NQ

HADRIANUS Rhet.
A.D. 2: Tyrius
Cf. ADRIANUS Rhet. (0666).

0195 **HADRIANUS Imperator** <Epigr.>
A.D. 1–2

001 **Epigrammata**, AG 6.332; 7.674; 9.137, 387(?), 402.
AG 9.17, 387: Cf. (et) Tiberius Drusus Nero GERMANICUS CAESAR <Epigr.> (0191 001).
AG 9.137: Cf. et ANONYMI GRAMMATICI (0072 002).
Q: 163

x01 **Epigrammata dedicatoria**.
App. Anth. 1.241–242: Cf. EPIGRAMMATICI in *App. Anth.* (7052 001).

2358 **HAGELOCHUS** Hist.
post 3 B.C.

001 **Titulus**, FGrH #516: 3B:491
NQ

2359 **HAGESTRATUS** Hist.
post 3 B.C.

001 **Titulus**, FGrH #517: 3B:491.
NQ

1387 **(H)AGIAS-DERCYLUS** Hist.
4 B.C.

001 **Testimonia**, FGrH #305: 3B:7.
NQ

002 **Fragmenta**, FGrH #305: 3B:7–10, 757 addenda.
Q

0909 HALIEUS Med.
ante A.D. 1
x01 **Fragmenta ap. Galenum.**
K13.645, 785–786, 802, 1025–1026, 1032.
Cf. GALENUS Med. (0057 077).

1974 HANNIBAL Hist.
3–2 B.C.
001 **Testimonium**, FGrH #181: 2B:909.
NQ

HANNO Rex Carthaginiensium <Geogr.>
Cf. PERIPLUS HANNONIS (0064).

1388 HARMODIUS Hist.
3 B.C.?: Lepreates
001 **Fragmenta**, FGrH #319: 3B:32–33.
Q

0720 HARMODIUS Trag.
1 B.C.: Tarsensis
001 **Titulus**, ed. B. Snell, *Tragicorum Graecorum fragmenta*, vol. 1. Göttingen: Vandenhoeck & Ruprecht, 1971: 309.
NQ

0912 HARPALUS Med.
ante A.D. 1
x01 **Fragmenta ap. Galenum.**
K13.928–929; 14.167.
Cf. GALENUS Med. (0057 077–078).

0914 HARPOCRAS Med.
A.D. 1–2: Alexandrinus
x01 **Fragmenta ap. Galenum.**
K12.631, 943; 13.729, 838, 840–841, 978.
Cf. GALENUS Med. (0057 076–077).

1389 HARPOCRATION Gramm.
A.D. 1/2?: Alexandrinus
001 **Lexicon in decem oratores Atticos**, ed. W. Dindorf, *Harpocrationis lexicon in decem oratores Atticos*, vol. 1. Oxford: Oxford University Press, 1853 (repr. Groningen: Bouma, 1969): 1–310.
Cod: 40,215

0913 HARPOCRATION Med.
ante A.D. 1?
x01 **Fragmentum ap. Galenum.**
K12.629.
Cf. GALENUS Med. (0057 076).

0691 *HARPOCRATIONIS EPISTULA*
fort. auctore Harpocratione Alexandrino
A.D. 4?
Cf. et CYRANIDES (1482).
001 **Epistula**, ed. C. Graux, "Lettre inédite

d'Harpocration à un empereur," *Revue philologique* 2 (1878) 70–77.
Cod: [1,026]

0196 HECATAEUS Epigr.
3 B.C.: Thasius
001 **Epigramma**, AG 7.167.
Q: 42

0538 HECATAEUS Hist.
6–5 B.C.: Milesius
001 **Testimonia**, FGrH #1: 1A:1–7, *1 addenda.
NQ
002 **Fragmenta**, FGrH #1: 1A:7–47, *1–*4 addenda.
Q
003 **Fragmenta**, ed. H.J. Mette, "Die 'Kleinen' griechischen Historiker heute," *Lustrum* 21 (1978) 6.
fr. 145 bis a–b.
Q

1390 HECATAEUS Hist.
4–3 B.C.: Abderita
001 **Testimonia**, FGrH #264: 3A:11–12.
NQ
002 **Fragmenta**, FGrH #264: 3A:12–64.
Q
003 **Testimonia**, ed. H. Diels and W. Kranz, *Die Fragmente der Vorsokratiker*, vol. 2, 6th edn. Berlin: Weidmann, 1952 (repr. Dublin: 1966): 240–241.
test. 1–6.
NQ
004 **Fragmenta**, ed. Diels and Kranz, *op. cit.*, 241–245.
frr. 1–17.
Q

0197 HEDYLE Epigr.
4–3 B.C.
001 **Fragmentum**, ed. H. Lloyd-Jones and P. Parsons, *Supplementum Hellenisticum*. Berlin: De Gruyter, 1983: 234.
fr. 456.
Q: [32]

0198 HEDYLUS Epigr.
3 B.C.: Atheniensis vel Samius
001 **Epigrammata**, AG 5.161, 199; 6.292; 11.123, 414.
Q: 156
002 **Fragmentum et titulus**, ed. H. Lloyd-Jones and P. Parsons, *Supplementum Hellenisticum*. Berlin: De Gruyter, 1983: 235.
frr. 458–459.
Q: [40]
x01 **Epigrammata** (*App. Anth.*).
Epigramma dedicatorium: 1.115.
Epigramma sepulcrale: 2.134.
Epigramma demonstrativum: 3.67.

Epigrammata exhortatoria et supplicatoria: 4.25–26.

Epigrammata irrisoria: 5.16–18.

App. Anth. 1.115: Cf. EPIGRAMMATICI in *App. Anth.* (7052 001).

App. Anth. 2.134: Cf. EPIGRAMMATICI in *App. Anth.* (7052 002).

App. Anth. 3.67: Cf. EPIGRAMMATICI in *App. Anth.* (7052 003).

App. Anth. 4.25–26: Cf. EPIGRAMMATICI in *App. Anth.* (7052 004).

App. Anth. 5.16–18: Cf. EPIGRAMMATICI in *App. Anth.* (7052 005).

1391 **HEGEMON** Epigr.
fiq Hegemon Hist.
3 B.C.
Cf. et HEGEMON Hist. (1925).

001 **Epigramma**, AG 7.436.
Q: 25

002 **Titulus**, ed. H. Lloyd-Jones and P. Parsons, *Supplementum Hellenisticum*. Berlin: De Gruyter, 1983: 236.
fr. 462.
NQ: [1]

1925 **HEGEMON** Hist.
fiq Hegemon Epigr.
3/2 B.C.: Alexandrinus (Troadis)
Cf. et HEGEMON Epigr. (1391).

001 **Testimonium**, FGrH #110: 2B:523.
NQ

002 **Fragmentum**, FGrH #110: 2B:523–524.
Q

0463 **HEGEMON** Parodius
5 B.C.: Thasius

001 **Fragmentum**, ed. T. Kock, *Comicorum Atticorum fragmenta*, vol. 1. Leipzig: Teubner, 1880: 700.
fr. 1.
Q: 14

002 **Fragmentum**, ed. A. Meineke, *Fragmenta comicorum Graecorum*, vol. 2.2. Berlin: Reimer, 1840 (repr. De Gruyter, 1970): 743.
Q: 14

003 **Fragmentum**, ed. P. Brandt, *Corpusculum poesis epicae Graecae Ludibundae*, fasc. 1. Leipzig: Teubner, 1888: 42–44.
Q: [151]

1392 **HEGESANDER** Hist.
3 B.C.: Delphicus

001 **Fragmenta**, FHG 4: 412–422.
Q

1393 **HEGESIANAX** Epic. et Astron.
2 B.C.: Alexandrinus (Troadis)

001 **Fragmenta**, ed. J.U. Powell, *Collectanea Alexandrina*. Oxford: Clarendon Press, 1925 (repr. 1970): 8–9.
frr. 1–2.
Q: [36]

002 **Testimonia**, FGrH #45: 1A:268–270, *19 addenda.
NQ

003 **Fragmenta**, FGrH #45: 1A:270–272.
Q

004 **Fragmenta et titulus**, ed. H. Lloyd-Jones and P. Parsons, *Supplementum Hellenisticum*. Berlin: De Gruyter, 1983: 237–238.
frr. (+ titul.) 465–467.
Q: [35]

HEGESIAS Epic.
Cf. CYPRIA (1296).

1394 **HEGESIAS** Hist.
3 B.C.: Magnes

001 **Testimonia**, FGrH #142: 2B:804–806.
NQ

002 **Fragmenta**, FGrH #142: 2B:806–811.
Q, Cod

1395 **HEGESINUS** Epic.
ante A.D. 2

001 **Fragmentum**, ed. G. Kinkel, *Epicorum Graecorum fragmenta*, vol. 1. Leipzig: Teubner, 1877: 208.
Q: [28]

002 **Testimonia**, FGrH #331: 3B:165.
NQ

003 **Fragmentum**, FGrH #331: 3B:165.
Q

0464 **HEGESIPPUS** Comic.
3 B.C.

001 **Fragmenta**, ed. T. Kock, *Comicorum Atticorum fragmenta*, vol. 3. Leipzig: Teubner, 1888: 312–314.
frr. 1–3.
Q: 238

002 **Fragmenta**, ed. A. Meineke, *Fragmenta comicorum Graecorum*, vol. 4. Berlin: Reimer, 1841 (repr. De Gruyter, 1970): 479–481.
Q: 234

1396 **HEGESIPPUS** Epigr.
3 B.C.

001 **Epigrammata**, AG **6**.124, 178, 266; **7**.276, 320, 446, 545; **13**.12.
Q: 234

1397 **HEGESIPPUS** Hist.
4 B.C.?: Mecybernaeus

001 **Testimonia**, FGrH #391: 3B:273.
NQ

002 **Fragmenta**, FGrH #391: 3B:273–275.
Q

1398 **HEGESIPPUS** Scr. Eccl.
A.D. 2: Palaestinus

001 **Fragmenta** (ex incerto libro), ed. M.J. Routh, *Reliquiae sacrae*, vol. 1, 2nd edn. Oxford: Oxford University Press, 1846 (repr. Hildesheim:

Olms, 1974): 207–219.
Q: [1,796]

1831 HEGETOR Med.
2 B.C.
x01 **Fragmentum ap. Apollonium.**
CMG, vol. 11.1.1, pp. 78–80.
Cf. APOLLONIUS Med. (0660 001).

2420 HEGIAS Hist.
post 4 B.C.?: Troezenius
001 **Fragmentum,** FGrH #606: 3B:739.
Q

0692 HELIODORUS Med.
A.D. 1
Cf. et ANTYLLUS et HELIODORUS Med. (0852).
x01 **Fragmenta ap. Oribasium.**
CMG, vol. **6.2.1,** pp. 120–125, 164–165, 166, 168, 176, 216–227, 232–234, 236, 239–240, 258–260, 273–275, 279–281; **6.2.2,** pp. 4–12, 13–43, 57, 60–69.
Cf. ORIBASIUS Med. (0722 001).
x02 **Fragmentum ap. Paulum.**
CMG, vol. 9.1, p. 371.
Cf. PAULUS Med. (0715 001).

1400 HELIODORUS Perieg.
2 B.C.?: Atheniensis
001 **Testimonia,** FGrH #373: 3B:239.
NQ
002 **Fragmenta,** FGrH #373: 3B:239–241.
Q

0658 HELIODORUS Scr. Erot.
A.D. 3?
001 **Aethiopica,** ed. R.M. Rattenbury, T.W. Lumb and J. Maillon, *Héliodore. Les Éthiopiques (Théagène et Chariclée),* 3 vols., 2nd edn. Paris: Les Belles Lettres, 1960: **1:**2–124; **2:**2–164; **3:**2–126.
Cod: 80,126
002 **Epigrammata,** AG 9.485, 490.
Q: 84

0750 HELIODORUS Trag.
ante 1 B.C.: Atheniensis
001 **Italica theamata,** ed. A. Meineke, *Commentationum miscellanearum fasciculus primus.* Halle, 1822: 36–37.
Q: 105
002 **Fragmenta,** ed. H. Lloyd-Jones and P. Parsons, *Supplementum Hellenisticum.* Berlin: De Gruyter, 1983: 240–242.
frr. 471–474.
Q: [173]

1401 HELLADIUS Epigr.
A.D. 1–2
001 **Epigramma,** AG 11.423.
Q: 13

2438 HELLADIUS Hist.
A.D. 4: Antinoupolitanus
001 **Testimonium,** FGrH #635: 3C:183.
NQ

0539 HELLANICUS Hist.
5 B.C.: Lesbius
001 **Testimonia,** FGrH #4, #323a, #687a: **1A:**104–107; **3B:**40–41: **3C:**412.
NQ
002 **Fragmenta,** FGrH #4, #323a, #601a, #608a, #645a, #687a: **1A:**107–152, *6–*8 addenda; **3B:**41–50, 732–733; **3C:**1–2, 190, 412–414.
fr. 124b: *PSI* 1173.
fr. 189: *P. Oxy.* 10.1241.
fr. 201 bis: *P. Giessen* 307v.
Q, Pap
003 **Fragmentum** (*P. Oxy.* 26.2442), ed. H.J. Mette, "Die 'Kleinen' griechischen Historiker heute," *Lustrum* 21 (1978) 7.
fr. 133 bis.
Pap

0558 *HELLENICA*
fort. auctore Cratippo vel Daimacho
4 B.C.?
Cf. et CRATIPPUS Hist. (1907).
Cf. et DAIMACHUS Hist. (2482).
001 **Fragmenta Florentina** (*PSI* 1304), ed. V. Bartoletti, *Hellenica Oxyrhynchia.* Leipzig: Teubner, 1959: 1–5.
Pap: 747
002 **Fragmenta Londinensia** (*P. Oxy.* 5.842), ed. Bartoletti, *op. cit.,* 6–37.
Pap: 5,348
003 **Fragmenta Londinensia incertae sedis** (*P. Oxy.* 5.842), ed. Bartoletti, *op. cit.,* 37–41.
Pap: 611
004 **Fragmenta** (*P. Oxy.* 5.842), FGrH #66: **2A:**17–35.
Pap
005 **Fragmentum** (*P. Cairo* inv. 26/6/27/1–35), ed. H.J. Mette, "Die 'Kleinen' griechischen Historiker heute," *Lustrum* 21 (1978) 12.
Pap

0465 HENIOCHUS Comic.
4 B.C.: Atheniensis
001 **Fragmenta,** ed. T. Kock, *Comicorum Atticorum fragmenta,* vol. 2. Leipzig: Teubner, 1884: 431–434.
frr. 1–5 + tituli.
Q: 245
002 **Fragmenta,** ed. A. Meineke, *Fragmenta comicorum Graecorum,* vol. 3. Berlin: Reimer, 1840 (repr. De Gruyter, 1970): 560–563.
Q: 240

2043 HEPHAESTION Astrol.
A.D. 4: Thebanus
001 **Apotelesmatica,** ed. D. Pingree, *Hephaestionis Thebani apotelesmaticorum libri tres,* vol. 1.

Leipzig: Teubner, 1973: 1–333.
Q, Cod: [74,994]

002 **Apotelesmatica** (epitomae quattuor), ed. Pingree, *op. cit.*, vol. 2 (1974): 1–350.
Cod: [87,858]

003 **Excerptum** (Cod. Paris. graec. 2506), ed. Pingree, *op. cit.*, vol. 2, VI–VII.
Cod: [414]

004 **Excerptum** (Cod. Marcian. graec. 334), ed. Pingree, *op. cit.*, vol. 2, X–XI.
Cod: [480]

005 **Excerptum** (Cod. Vat. graec. 1056), ed. Pingree, *op. cit.*, vol. 2, XXI–XXII.
Cod: [224]

1402 **HEPHAESTION** Gramm.
A.D. 2

001 **Enchiridion de metris**, ed. M. Consbruch, *Hephaestionis enchiridion cum commentariis veteribus.* Leipzig: Teubner, 1906 (repr. Stuttgart: 1971): 1–58.
Cod: [7,856]

002 **Introductio metrica**, ed. Consbruch, *op. cit.*, 58–62.
Cod: [651]

003 **De poematis**, ed. Consbruch, *op. cit.*, 62–73.
Cod: [1,650]

004 **De signis**, ed. Consbruch, *op. cit.*, 73–76.
Cod: [580]

005 **Fragmenta Hephaestionea**, ed. Consbruch, *op. cit.*, 76–78.
frr. 1–5.
Cod: [327]

0883 **HERACLAS** Med.
A.D. 1–2

x01 **Fragmentum ap. Oribasium.**
CMG, vol. 6.2.1, pp. 262–268.
Cf. ORIBASIUS Med. (0722 001).

1403 **HERACLEON** Gnost.
A.D. 2

001 **Fragmenta**, ed. W. Völker, *Quellen zur Geschichte der christlichen Gnosis.* Tübingen: Mohr, 1932: 63–86.
Q

0567 **HERACLEON** Gramm.
A.D. 1: Ephesius

001 **Fragmenta**, ed. R. Berndt, *Die Fragmente des Homererklärers Herakleon* [*Programm Gymnasium Insterburg* (1914)]: 18–24.
Q

0466 **HERACLIDES** Comic.
4 B.C.
Cf. et <HERACLITUS> Comic. (1784).

001 **Fragmentum**, ed. T. Kock, *Comicorum Atticorum fragmenta*, vol. 2. Leipzig: Teubner, 1884: 435.
fr. 1.
Q: 29

002 **Fragmentum**, ed. A. Meineke, *Fragmenta comicorum Graecorum*, vol. 3. Berlin: Reimer, 1840 (repr. De Gruyter, 1970): 565.
Q: 27

1410 **HERACLIDES** Epigr.
1 B.C.–A.D. 1: Sinopensis

001 **Epigrammata**, AG 7.281, 392.
AG 7.465: Cf. HERACLITUS Epigr. (1415 001).
Q: 63

1408 **HERACLIDES** Gramm.
A.D. 1–2: Milesius

001 **Fragmenta**, ed. L. Cohn, *De Heraclide Milesio grammatico.* Berlin: Calvary, 1884: 37–64, 66–79, 81–91, 93–107.
Περὶ καθολικῆς προσῳδίας (frr. 1–15): pp. 37–44.
Περὶ δυσκλίτων ῥημάτων (frr. 16–55): pp. 45–64, 66–79, 81–91, 93–102.
Fragmenta sedis incertae (frr. 56–60): pp. 103–106.
Fragmenta dubia (frr. 61–62): pp. 106–107.
Q: [14,878]

002 Περὶ δυσκλίτων ῥημάτων (fragmentum) (*P. Rain.* 3.33A = *P. Vindob.* gr. 29815A), ed. A. Wouters, *The grammatical papyri from Graeco-Roman Egypt. Contributions to the study of the 'ars grammatica' in antiquity.* Brussels: Paleis der Academiën, 1979: 243–246.
Pap

1406 **HERACLIDES** Hist.
4 B.C.: Cumaeus

001 **Testimonium**, FGrH #689: 3C:517.
NQ

002 **Fragmenta**, FGrH #689: 3C:517–522.
Q

1979 **HERACLIDES** Hist.
1 B.C.?: Magnes

001 **Testimonium**, FGrH #187: 2B:918.
NQ

0694 **HERACLIDES** Med.
1 B.C.: Tarentinus
Cf. et HERACLIDES Med. (1033).

x01 **Fragmenta ap. Galenum.**
K12.402–403, 435, 454–455, 583–584, 639–640, 691–693, 730, 741, 785, 835, 847–848, 867, 957; **13**.33, 328, 507–508, 717–728, 811–812, 826, 854, 857; **14**.186–187.
Cf. GALENUS Med. (0057 076–078).

x02 **Fragmentum ap. Aëtium** (lib. 6).
CMG, vol. 8.2, p. 230.
Cf. AËTIUS Med. (0718 006).

x03 **Fragmenta ap. Athenaeum.**
Deipnosophistae 2.64a, 64e; 3.120b.
Cf. ATHENAEUS Soph. (0008 001).

x04 **Fragmenta ap. Hippiatrica.**
Oder & Hoppe, vol. 2, pp. 194, 199.
Cf. HIPPIATRICA (0738 006).

0916 **HERACLIDES** Med.
1 B.C.–A.D. 1: Erythraeus
Cf. et HERACLIDES Med. (1033).
x01 **Fragmentum ap. Paulum.**
CMG, vol. 9.2, p. 371.
Cf. PAULUS Med. (0715 001).

1033 **HERACLIDES** Med.
fiq Heraclides Tarentinus vel Heraclides Erythraeus
1 B.C./A.D. 1?
Cf. et HERACLIDES Med. (0694).
Cf. et HERACLIDES Med. (0916).
x01 **Fragmentum ap. Alexandrum Trallianum.**
Puschmann, vol. 2, p. 527.
Cf. ALEXANDER Med. (0744 003).

0915 **HERACLIDES** Med.
ante A.D. 1: Ephesius
x01 **Fragmentum ap. Oribasium.**
CMG, vol. 6.2.2, p. 278.
Cf. ORIBASIUS Med. (0722 003).

1844 **HERA[CLIDES]** Trag.
Incertum
001 **Titulus**, ed. B. Snell, *Tragicorum Graecorum
fragmenta*, vol. 1. Göttingen: Vandenhoeck &
Ruprecht, 1971: 155.
NQ

1405 **HERACLIDES Criticus** Perieg.
3–2 B.C.
001 **Descriptio Graeciae**, ed. K. Müller, *Geographi
Graeci minores*, vol. 1. Paris: Didot, 1855 (repr.
Hildesheim: Olms, 1965): 97–110.
Cod: [2,816]

1407 **HERACLIDES LEMBUS** Hist.
2 B.C.: Alexandrinus
001 **Excerpta politiarum**, ed. M.R. Dilts, *Heraclidis
Lembi excerpta politiarum* [*Greek, Roman and
Byzantine monographs* 5. Durham: Duke University Press, 1971]: 14–40.
Cod: [4,498]
002 **Fragmenta**, FHG 3: 167–171.
Q
003 **Hermippi** περὶ νομοθετῶν (epitome), *P. Oxy.*
11.1367.
Pap

1409 **HERACLIDES PONTICUS** Phil.
4 B.C.: Heracleensis
001 **Fragmenta**, ed. F. Wehrli, *Herakleides Pontikos
[Die Schule des Aristoteles*, vol. 7, 2nd edn.
Basel: Schwabe, 1969]: 13–54.
Q, Pap

0283 **HERACLIDES PONTICUS Junior** Gramm.
A.D. 1: Ponticus
Cf. et HERACLIDES LEMBUS Hist. (1407).
001 **Fragmenta**, ed. E. Heitsch, *Die griechischen
Dichterfragmente der römischen Kaiserzeit*, vol.

2. Göttingen: Vandenhoeck & Ruprecht, 1964:
41.
frr. 1–2.
Q: [19]
002 **Fragmenta et titulus**, ed. H. Lloyd-Jones and
P. Parsons, *Supplementum Hellenisticum*. Berlin: De Gruyter, 1983: 242–244.
frr. (+ titul.) 475, 480–481.
Q: [10]

1411 ***HERACLITI EPHESII EPISTULAE***
Incertum
Cf. et HERACLITUS Phil. (0626).
Cf. et Pseudo-HERACLITI EPISTULAE (1412).
001 **Epistulae**, ed. R. Hercher, *Epistolographi
Graeci*. Paris: Didot, 1873 (repr. Amsterdam:
Hakkert, 1965): 280–283, 285–288.
Cod: [1,966]

1412 ***Pseudo-HERACLITI EPISTULAE***
Incertum
Cf. et HERACLITUS Phil. (0626).
Cf. et HERACLITI EPHESII EPISTULAE (1411).
001 **Epistulae**, ed. A.-M. Denis, *Fragmenta pseud-
epigraphorum quae supersunt Graeca [Pseudepi-
grapha veteris testamenti Graece* 3. Leiden:
Brill, 1970]: 157–160.
Cod: [1,287]

1784 **<HERACLITUS>** Comic.
fiq Heraclides
4 B.C.
Cf. et HERACLIDES Comic. (0466).
001 **Titulus**, ed. T. Kock, *Comicorum Atticorum
fragmenta*, vol. 2. Leipzig: Teubner, 1884: 435.
NQ: 2
002 **Titulus**, ed. A. Meineke, *Fragmenta comicorum
Graecorum*, vol. 1. Berlin: Reimer, 1839 (repr.
De Gruyter, 1970): 422.
NQ

1415 **HERACLITUS** Epigr.
3 B.C.: Halicarnassensis
001 **Epigramma**, AG 7.465.
Q: 50

HERACLITUS Epigr.
fiq Heraclitus Ephesius Phil.
AG 9.359, 524.
Cf. POSIDIPPUS Epigr. (1632 001).
Cf. PLATO Comic. (0497 005).
Cf. ANONYMI EPIGRAMMATICI (0138 001).

1962 **HERACLITUS** Hist.
3 B.C.: Lesbius
001 **Testimonia**, FGrH #167: 2B:893.
NQ

1413 **HERACLITUS** Paradox.
post 4 B.C.?
001 **De incredibilibus**, ed. N. Festa, *Palaephati
περὶ ἀπίστων [Mythographi Graeci* 3.2. Leip-

zig: Teubner, 1902]: 73–87.
Cod: [1,825]

0626 **HERACLITUS** Phil.
6–5 B.C.: Ephesius
Cf. et HERACLITI EPHESII EPISTULAE (1411).
Cf. et Pseudo-HERACLITI EPISTULAE (1412).

001 **Testimonia**, ed. H. Diels and W. Kranz, *Die Fragmente der Vorsokratiker*, vol. 1, 6th edn. Berlin: Weidmann, 1951 (repr. Dublin: 1966): 139–149.
test. 1–23.
NQ

002 **Fragmenta**, ed. Diels and Kranz, *op. cit.*, 150–182.
frr. 1–139.
Q

1414 **HERACLITUS** Phil.
A.D. 1?

001 **Allegoriae** (= **Quaestiones Homericae**), ed. F. Buffière, *Héraclite. Allégories d'Homère*. Paris: Les Belles Lettres, 1962: 1–88.
Cod: [14,290]

2671 **HERACLIUS** Epigr.
Incertum

x01 **Epigramma dedicatorium.**
App. Anth. 1.195: Cf. EPIGRAMMATICI in *App. Anth.* (7052 001).

0917 **HERAS** Med.
1 B.C./A.D. 1: Cappadox
Cf. et BAPHULLUS vel HERAS Med. (0820).

x01 **Fragmenta ap. Galenum.**
K12.398–400, 439, 593, 610–614, 819, 929, 941–942; 13.297–298, 338, 422–423, 431–432, 511–513, 544–549, 557–560, 747, 765–768, 774–775, 815–816, 914–915, 986, 1045–1046; 14.201.
Cf. GALENUS Med. (0057 076–078).

x02 **Fragmentum ap. Paulum.**
CMG, vol. 9.2, p. 318.
Cf. PAULUS Med. (0715 001).

x03 **Fragmentum ap. Aëtium** (lib. 12).
Kostomiris, p. 106.
Cf. AËTIUS Med. (0718 012).

x04 **Fragmenta ap. Aëtium** (lib. 15).
Zervos, *Athena* 21, pp. 53, 67, 136.
Cf. AËTIUS Med. (0718 015).

2336 **HEREAS** Hist.
vel Heragoras
4–3 B.C.?: Megareus

001 **Fragmenta**, FGrH #486: 3B:451–452.
Q

1416 **(H)EREN(N)IUS PHILO** Hist. et Gramm.
A.D. 1–2: Byblius
Cf. et <AMMONIUS> Gramm. (0708).
Cf. et PHILO <Epigr.> (1593).

002 **Supplementum glossarum**, ed. K. Nickau, *Ammonii qui dicitur liber de adfinium vocabulorum differentia*. Leipzig: Teubner, 1966: 156–159.
Cod: [688]

001 **De diversis verborum significationibus** (e cod. Paris. suppl. gr. 1238), ed. V. Palmieri, *Herennius Philo. De diversis verborum significationibus*. Naples, 1983: 125–239.
Cod

003 **De propria dictione** (epitome) (e cod. Venet. Marciano gr. 512), ed. Palmieri, *op. cit.*, 247–252.
Cod

004 **De aetatum cognitione** (epitome) (e cod. Ambrosiano C 22 et cod. Berol. Phill.), ed. Palmieri, *op. cit.*, 255.
Cod

005 **Testimonia**, FGrH #790: 3C:802–803.
NQ

006 **Fragmenta**, FGrH #790: 3C:803–824.
Q

2169 **HERILLUS** Phil.
3 B.C.: Carthaginiensis

001 **Fragmenta**, ed. J. von Arnim, *Stoicorum veterum fragmenta*, vol. 1. Leipzig: Teubner, 1905 (repr. Stuttgart: 1968): 91–93.
Q

2426 **HERMAEUS** Hist.
A.D. 1?

001 **Fragmenta**, FGrH #620: 3C:153–154.
Q

1417 **HERMAGORAS** Rhet.
1 B.C.–A.D. 1

001 **Fragmenta**, ed. D. Matthes, *Hermagorae Temnitae testimonia et fragmenta*. Leipzig: Teubner, 1962: 56–59.
Q

1380 **HERMAGORAS Minor** Rhet.
A.D. 1/2

001 **Fragmenta**, ed. D. Matthes, *Hermagorae Temnitae testimonia et fragmenta*. Leipzig: Teubner, 1962: 59–65.
Q

1418 **HERMAPION** Hist.
A.D. 1?

001 **Fragmenta**, FGrH #658: 3C:206–208.
Q

1439 **HERMARCHUS** Phil.
3 B.C.: Mytilenensis

001 **Fragmenta**, ed. K. Krohn, *Der Epikureer Hermarchos* [*Diss. Berlin* (1921)].
Q, Pap

0974 **HERMAS** Med.
ante A.D. 2

x01 **Fragmentum ap. Philumenum.**
CMG, vol. 10.1.1, p. 13.
Cf. PHILUMENUS Med. (0671 001).

1419 **HERMAS** Scr. Eccl.
A.D. 2
001 **Pastor,** ed. M. Whittaker, *Die apostolischen Väter I. Der Hirt des Hermas* [*Die griechischen christlichen Schriftsteller* 48, 2nd edn. Berlin: Akademie-Verlag, 1967]: 1–98.
Cod: [29,983]
002 **Fragmenta ap. Antiochum,** ed. Whittaker, *op. cit.,* 101, 103.
Q: [273]
003 **Fragmenta** (*P. Oxy.* 3.404), ed. Whittaker, *op. cit.,* 109, 111.
Pap: [113]
004 **Fragmentum in F** (cod. Paris. gr. 1143), ed. Whittaker, *op. cit.,* 118.
Cod: [146]
005 **Fragmentum** (*P. Berol.* 5104), ed. K. Treu, "Ein neuer Hermas-Papyrus," *Vigiliae Christianae* 24 (1970) 34–39.
Pap

2437 **HERMATELES** Hist.
A.D. 2?
001 **Testimonium,** FGrH #657: 3C:205–206.
NQ

[HERMES TRISMEGISTUS]
Cf. CORPUS HERMETICUM (1286).

0213 **HERMESIANAX** Eleg.
4–3 B.C.: Colophonius
001 **Fragmenta,** ed. J.U. Powell, *Collectanea Alexandrina.* Oxford: Clarendon Press, 1925 (repr. 1970): 96, 98–100.
frr. 1, 7.
Q: [599]
002 **Testimonia,** FGrH #691: 3C:531–532.
NQ
003 **Fragmenta,** FGrH #691: 3C:532.
Q

2532 **HERMESIANAX** Hist.
Incertum: Cyprius
001 **Fragmenta,** FGrH #797: 3C:835–836.
Q

2384 **HERMIAS** Hist.
4 B.C.?: Methymnaeus
001 **Testimonium,** FGrH #558: 3B:568.
NQ
002 **Fragmentum,** FGrH #558: 3B:568.
Q

2440 **HERMIAS** Hist.
A.D. 4/5: Hermupolitanus
001 **Testimonium,** FGrH #638: 3C:185.
NQ

1420 **HERMIAS** Iamb.
3 B.C.?: Curiensis
Cf. et HERMIAS Poeta (2624).
001 **Fragmentum,** ed. J.U. Powell, *Collectanea Alexandrina.* Oxford: Clarendon Press, 1925 (repr. 1970): 237.
Q: [27]

0919 **HERMIAS** Med.
ante A.D. 2
x01 **Fragmentum ap. Galenum.**
K12.754.
Cf. GALENUS Med. (0057 076).

0531 **HERMIAS** Phil.
A.D. 2/6
001 **Irrisio gentilium philosophorum,** ed. H. Diels, *Doxographi Graeci.* Berlin: Reimer, 1879 (repr. De Gruyter, 1965): 651–656.
Cod: [650]

2317 **HERMIAS** Phil.
A.D. 5: Alexandrinus
001 **In Platonis Phaedrum scholia,** ed. P. Couvreur, *Hermeias von Alexandrien. In Platonis Phaedrum scholia.* Paris: Bouillon, 1901 (repr. Hildesheim: Olms, 1971): 1–266.
Cod

2624 **HERMIAS** Poeta
fiq Hermias Curiensis
3 B.C.?
Cf. et HERMIAS Iamb. (1420).
001 **Fragmentum,** ed. H. Lloyd-Jones and P. Parsons, *Supplementum Hellenisticum.* Berlin: De Gruyter, 1983: 244.
fr. 484.
Q: [6]

1796 **HERMINUS** Phil.
A.D. 2
001 **Fragmenta,** ed. H. Schmidt, *De Hermino peripatetico* [*Diss. Marburg* (1907)].
Q

0252 **HERMIPPUS** Comic.
5 B.C.: Atheniensis
001 **Fragmenta,** ed. T. Kock, *Comicorum Atticorum fragmenta,* vol. 1. Leipzig: Teubner, 1880: 224–243, 245–253.
frr. 1–6, 8, 10–32, 34–63, 66–68, 70–71, 75–97.
Q: 941
002 **Fragmenta,** ed. A. Meineke, *Fragmenta comicorum Graecorum,* vol. 2.1. Berlin: Reimer, 1839 (repr. De Gruyter, 1970): 379–395, 397–408, 410–417.
Q: 890
003 **Fragmenta,** ed. J. Demiańczuk, *Supplementum comicum.* Krakau: Nakładem Akademii (repr. Hildesheim: Olms, 1967): 53.
frr. 1–3.
Q: 10

004 **Fragmenta**, ed. M.L. West, *Iambi et elegi Graeci*, vol. 2. Oxford: Clarendon Press, 1972: 68–69.
frr. 2–6.
Q: [55]

005 **Fragmentum** (*P. Oxy.* 13.1611), ed. C. Austin, *Comicorum Graecorum fragmenta in papyris reperta*. Berlin: De Gruyter, 1973: 120.
fr. 101 + titulus.
Pap: 11

1421 **HERMIPPUS** Gramm. et Hist.
fiq Hermippus Astronomus
3 B.C.: Smyrnaeus

001 **Fragmenta**, ed. F. Wehrli, *Hermippos der Kallimacheer* [*Die Schule des Aristoteles*, suppl. 1. Basel: Schwabe, 1974]: 11–41.
Q, Pap

002 **Fragmentum astrologicum**, ed. W. Kroll, *Codices Romani* [*Catalogus codicum astrologorum Graecorum* 5.2. Brussels: Lamertin, 1906]: 71.
Q

003 **Titulus**, ed. H. Lloyd-Jones and P. Parsons, *Supplementum Hellenisticum*. Berlin: De Gruyter, 1983: 245.
fr. 485.
NQ: [2]

0207 **HERMOCLES** Lyr.
4–3 B.C.: Cyzicenus

001 **Ithyphalli**, ed. J.U. Powell, *Collectanea Alexandrina*. Oxford: Clarendon Press, 1925 (repr. 1970): 173–174.
Q: [185]

1422 **HERMOCREON** Epigr.
Incertum

001 **Epigrammata**, AG **9**.327; **16**.11.
Q: 48

1423 **HERMODORUS** Epigr.
Incertum

001 **Epigramma**, AG 16.170.
AG 9.77: Cf. ANTIPATER Thessalonicensis Epigr. (0114 001).
Q: 28

1424 **HERMOGENES** Hist.
post 4 B.C.?

001 **Fragmenta**, FGrH #795: 3C:833–834.
Q

2143 **HERMOGENES** Hist.
3-2 B.C.: fort. Prienaeus

001 **Testimonia**, FGrH #481: 3B:445.
NQ

0921 **HERMOGENES** Med.
A.D. 2: Smyrnaeus

001 **Testimonium**, FGrH #579: 3B:690.

test. 1: *Inscr. Smyrna* (CIG 331).
NQ

x01 **Fragmentum ap. Oribasium**.
CMG, vol. 6.2.2, p. 287.
Cf. ORIBASIUS Med. (0722 003).

0592 **HERMOGENES** Rhet.
A.D. 2–3: Tarsensis

001 **Progymnasmata**, ed. H. Rabe, *Hermogenis opera*. Leipzig: Teubner, 1913 (repr. Stuttgart: 1969): 1–27.
Cod: 4,088

002 **De statibus**, ed. Rabe, *op. cit.*, 28–92.
Cod: 10,906

003 **De inventione**, ed. Rabe, *op. cit.*, 93–212.
Cod: 21,237

004 **Περὶ ἰδεῶν λόγου**, ed. Rabe, *op. cit.*, 213–413.
Cod: 41,547

005 **Περὶ μεθόδου δεινότητος**, ed. Rabe, *op. cit.*, 414–456.
Cod: 6,753

006 **Testimonia**, FGrH #851: 3C:936.
NQ

007 **Titulus**, FGrH #851: 3C:936.
NQ

x01 **Scholia ad Hermogenis status seu artem rhetoricam**.
Cf. SOPATER Rhet. (2031 002).
Cf. SYRIANI, SOPATRI ET MARCELLINI SCHOLIA AD HERMOGENIS STATUS (2047 001).
Cf. SCHOLIA (4101 004).

0240 **HERMOLOCHUS** Lyr.
4 B.C.?

001 **Fragmentum**, ed. D.L. Page, *Poetae melici Graeci*. Oxford: Clarendon Press, 1962 (repr. 1967 (1st edn. corr.)): 447.
fr. 1.
Q: [39]

HERMON Med.
Cf. EPIGONUS vel HERMON Med. (0922).

1425 **HERMONAX** Epic.
vel Hermon
4 B.C./A.D. 2: Delius

001 **Fragmenta**, ed. J.U. Powell, *Collectanea Alexandrina*. Oxford: Clarendon Press, 1925 (repr. 1970): 251–252.
frr. 1–2.
Q: [63]

0923 **HERMOPHILUS** Med.
ante A.D. 2

x01 **Fragmentum ap. Galenum**.
K12.781.
Cf. GALENUS Med. (0057 076).

x02 **Fragmentum ap. Aëtium** (lib. 7).
CMG, vol. 8.2, p. 388.
Cf. AËTIUS Med. (0718 007).

0650 **HERODAS** Mimogr.
vel Herondas
3 B.C.
001 **Mimiambi**, ed. I.C. Cunningham, *Herodas.
Mimiambi*. Oxford: Clarendon Press, 1971: 27–
56.
Q, Pap: 5,009

2166 **HERODES I** Hist.
1 B.C.: Palaestinus
001 **Fragmentum**, FGrH #236: 2B:988–990.
Q

1426 **<HERODES ATTICUS>** Soph.
A.D. 2: Atheniensis, Romanus
001 Περὶ πολιτείας, ed. U. Albini, *[Erode Attico]*.
Περὶ πολιτείας. Florence: Le Monnier, 1968:
29–35.
Cod: [2,053]

0015 **HERODIANUS** Hist.
A.D. 2–3: Syrus
001 **Ab excessu divi Marci**, ed. K. Stavenhagen,
Herodiani ab excessu divi Marci libri octo. Leipzig: Teubner, 1922 (repr. Stuttgart: 1967): 1–
223.
Cod: 48,888

0087 **Aelius HERODIANUS et Pseudo-HERODIA-
NUS** Gramm. et Rhet.
A.D. 2: Alexandrinus, Romanus
001 **De prosodia catholica**, ed. A. Lentz, *Grammatici Graeci*, vol. 3.1. Leipzig: Teubner, 1867
(repr. Hildesheim: Olms, 1965): 3–547.
Cod: [155,994]
002 **De enclisi** (epitome ap. Arcadium), ed. Lentz,
op. cit., vol. 3.1, 551–564.
Q: [3,155]
003 Περὶ κυρίων καὶ ἐπιθέτων καὶ προσηγορικῶν
μονόβιβλον, ed. Lentz, *op. cit.*, vol. 3.2 (1870;
repr. 1965): 1–6.
Q: [2,106]
004 Περὶ διχρόνων, ed. Lentz, *op. cit.*, vol. 3.2, 7–
20.
Cod: [4,339]
005 Περὶ πνευμάτων, ed. Lentz, *op. cit.*, vol. 3.2,
20.
Q: [80]
006 Περὶ Ἀττικῆς προσῳδίας, ed. Lentz, *op. cit.*,
vol. 3.2, 20–21.
Q: [167]
007 Περὶ Ἰλιακῆς προσῳδίας, ed. Lentz, *op. cit.*,
vol. 3.2, 22–128.
Cod: [43,383]
008 Περὶ Ὀδυσσειακῆς προσῳδίας, ed. Lentz, *op.
cit.*, vol. 3.2, 129–165.
Cod: [10,434]
009 Περὶ παθῶν, ed. Lentz, *op. cit.*, vol. 3.2, 166–
389.
Περὶ παθῶν: pp. 166–388.
Ἐκ τῶν Ἡρωδιανοῦ ὑπομνημάτων τῶν περὶ

παθῶν Διδύμου: p. 389.
Q: [43,935]
010 Περὶ συντάξεως τῶν στοιχείων, ed. Lentz, *op.
cit.*, vol. 3.2, 390–406.
Q: [6,585]
011 Περὶ ὀρθογραφίας, ed. Lentz, *op. cit.*, vol. 3.2,
407–611.
Q: [58,179]
012 Περὶ ὀνομάτων, ed. Lentz, *op. cit.*, vol. 3.2,
612–633.
Q: [8,735]
013 Περὶ κλίσεως ὀνομάτων, ed. Lentz, *op. cit.*, vol.
3.2, 634–777.
Q: [59,213]
014 Εἰς τὸ περὶ γενῶν Ἀπολλωνίου ὑπόμνημα, ed.
Lentz, *op. cit.*, vol. 3.2, 777.
Q: [62]
015 Μονόβιβλον περὶ τοῦ ὕδωρ, ed. Lentz, *op. cit.*,
vol. 3.2, 777.
Q: [94]
016 Περὶ τοῦ ζώς, ed. Lentz, *op. cit.*, vol. 3.2, 778.
Q: [109]
017 Περὶ συζυγιῶν, ed. Lentz, *op. cit.*, vol. 3.2, 779.
Q: [83]
018 Μονόβιβλον περὶ τοῦ μὴ πάντα τὰ ῥήματα
κλίνεσθαι εἰς πάντας τοὺς χρόνους, ed. Lentz,
op. cit., vol. 3.2, 779–784.
Q: [1,703]
019 Περὶ μετοχῶν, ed. Lentz, *op. cit.*, vol. 3.2, 784–
785.
Q: [178]
020 Μονόβιβλον περὶ τοῦ ἦν, ed. Lentz, *op. cit.*,
vol. 3.2, 785–786.
Q: [120]
021 Περὶ ῥημάτων, ed. Lentz, *op. cit.*, vol. 3.2, 787–
824.
Q: [17,127]
022 Περὶ τῶν εἰς μι, ed. Lentz, *op. cit.*, vol. 3.2,
825–844.
Q: [10,419]
023 Περὶ ἀντωνυμιῶν, ed. Lentz, *op. cit.*, vol. 3.2,
845–846.
Q: [517]
024 Περὶ ἐπιρρημάτων, ed. Lentz, *op. cit.*, vol. 3.2,
846.
Q: [70]
025 Περὶ σχημάτων, e. Lentz, *op. cit.*, vol. 3.2,
847–849.
Q: [768]
026 Περὶ παρωνύμων, ed. Lentz, *op. cit.*, vol. 3.2,
849–897.
Q: [16,708]
027 Περὶ ῥηματικῶν ὀνομάτων, ed. Lentz, *op. cit.*,
vol. 3.2, 897–903.
Q: [2,421]
028 Περὶ μονοσυλλάβων, ed. Lentz, *op. cit.*, vol.
3.2, 903–904.
Q: [266]
029 Περὶ γάμου καὶ συμβιώσεως, ed. Lentz, *op. cit.*,
vol. 3.2, 904.
Q: [75]

030 Συμπόσιον, ed. Lentz, *op. cit.*, vol. 3.2, 904–906.
Q: [666]

031 Προτάσεις, ed. Lentz, *op. cit.*, vol. 3.2, 907.
Q: [132]

032 Εἰς τὴν Ἀπολλωνίου εἰσαγωγήν, ed. Lentz, *op. cit.*, vol. 3.2, 907.
Q: [61]

033 Περὶ μονήρους λέξεως, ed. Lentz, *op. cit.*, vol. 3.2, 908–952.
Cod: [12,049]

034 Περὶ παθῶν (supplementum), ed. Lentz, *op. cit.*, vol. 3.2, 167–388.
Q: [16,667]

035 **De figuris**, ed. L. Spengel, *Rhetores Graeci*, vol. 3. Leipzig: Teubner, 1856 (repr. Frankfurt am Main: Minerva, 1966): 83–104.
Cod: [4,078]

036 **Partitiones**, ed. J.F. Boissonade, *Herodiani partitiones*. London, 1819 (repr. Amsterdam: Hakkert, 1963): 1–282.
Cod: [33,279]

037 **Philetaerus**, ed. A. Dain, *Le "Philétaeros" attribué à Hérodien*. Paris: Les Belles Lettres, 1954: 41–72.
Cod: [5,243]

038 Περὶ τῶν ζητουμένων κατὰ πάσης κλίσεως ὀνόματος (e cod. Paris. suppl. gr. 1238), ed. Dain, *op. cit.*, 73–74.
Cf. et 0087 047.
Cod: [311]

039 **Fragmenta**, ed. Dain, *op. cit.*, 75–82.
Cod: [1,791]

040 **De versibus**, ed. W. Studemund, "Der Pseudo-Herodianische Tractat über die εἴδη des Hexameters," *Jahrbücher für classische Philologie* 95 (1867) 618–619.
Cod: [270]

041 **Schematismi Homerici**, ed. P. Egenolff, "Zu Herodianos technikos," *Jahrbücher für classische Philologie* 149 (1894) 338–345.
Cod: [2,724]

042 Περὶ ἀριθμῶν (ap. Stephanum), TGL 8.345 appendix.
Q

043 Περὶ αὐθυποτάκτων καὶ ἀνυποτάκτων, ed. I. Bekker, *Anecdota Graeca*, vol. 3. Berlin: Reimer, 1821 (repr. Graz: Akademische Druck- und Verlagsanstalt, 1965): 1086–1088.
Cod: [837]

044 Περὶ σολοικισμοῦ καὶ βαρβαρισμοῦ, ed. A. Nauck, *Lexicon Vindobonense*. St. Petersburg: Eggers, 1867 (repr. Hildesheim: Olms, 1965): 294–312.
Cod: [2,834]

045 Περὶ παραγωγῶν γενικῶν ἀπὸ διαλέκτων, ed. J.A. Cramer, *Anecdota Graeca e codd. manuscriptis bibliothecarum Oxoniensium*, vol. 3. Oxford: Oxford University Press, 1836 (repr. Amsterdam: Hakkert, 1963): 228–236.
Cod: [2,689]

046 Ζητούμενα τῶν μερῶν τοῦ λόγου, ed. J. Pier-

son and G.A. Koch, *Moeridis Atticistae lexicon Atticum*. Leipzig: Lauffer, 1830 (repr. Hildesheim: Olms, 1969): 412–437.
Cod: [1,586]

047 Περὶ τῶν ζητουμένων κατὰ πάσης κλίσεως ὀνόματος (e cod. Barocciano 76), ed. Cramer, *op. cit.*, 246–255.
Cf. et 0087 038.
Cod: [2,583]

048 Περὶ κλίσεως ῥημάτων, ed. Cramer, *op. cit.*, 256–262.
Cod: [1,572]

049 Περὶ λέξεως τῶν στίχων, ed. F. de Furia, *Appendix ad Draconem Stratonicensem*. Leipzig: Weigel, 1814: 88.
Cod: [233]

050 Παρεκβολαὶ τοῦ μεγάλου ῥήματος, ed. J. La Roche, Παρεκβολαὶ τοῦ μεγάλου ῥήματος ἐκ τῶν Ἡρωδιανοῦ [*Programm Akad. Gymn. Vienna* (1863)]: 4–37.
Cod

052 Ἀπορίαι καὶ λύσεις, ed. A. Manuzio, *Thesaurus. Cornucopiae et horti Adonidis*. Venice: Aldus, 1496.
Cod

x01 **De impropriis**.
Cf. <AMMONIUS> (0708 002).

2625 **HERODICUS** Gramm.
2 B.C.: Babylonius

001 **Fragmenta**, ed. H. Lloyd-Jones and P. Parsons, *Supplementum Hellenisticum*. Berlin: De Gruyter, 1983: 247–248.
frr. 494–495.
Q: [126]

x01 **Epigramma irrisorium**.
App. Anth. 5.25: Cf. EPIGRAMMATICI in *App. Anth.* (7052 005).

1427 **HERODORUS** Hist.
5–4 B.C.: Heracleota

001 **Testimonia**, FGrH #31: 1A:215.
NQ

002 **Fragmenta**, FGrH #31: 1A:215–228, *12–*13 addenda.
Q

0016 **HERODOTUS** Hist.
5 B.C.: Halicarnassensis, Thurius

001 **Historiae**, ed. Ph.-E. Legrand, *Hérodote. Histoires*, 9 vols. Paris: Les Belles Lettres, 1:1932 (repr. 1970); 2:1930 (repr. 1963); 3:1939 (repr. 1967); 4 (3rd edn.):1960; 5:1946 (repr. 1968); 6:1948 (repr. 1963); 7:1951 (repr. 1963); 8:1953 (repr. 1964); 9:1954 (repr. 1968): 1:13–204; 2.65–194; 3:37–185; 4:47–201; 5:18–147; 6:7–128; 7:24–235; 8:9–161; 9:9–109.
Cod: 189,489

0926 **HERODOTUS** Med.
A.D. 1–2
Cf. et CRITO et HERODOTUS Med. (0882).

Cf. et HERODOTUS et PHILUMENUS Med. (0910).

x01 **Fragmentum ap. Galenum.**
K13.801.
Cf. GALENUS Med. (0057 077).

x02 **Fragmenta ap. Oribasium.**
CMG, vol. **6.1.1**, pp. 144–146, 147–151, 175–177, 182, 209, 217, 253, 254, 261; **6.1.2**, pp. 46, 53–55, 59–61, 75–78; **6.2.2**, p. 284; **6.3**, pp. 204–206.
Cf. ORIBASIUS Med. (0722 001, 003, 004).

x03 **Fragmentum ap. Aëtium** (lib. 4).
CMG, vol. 8.1, p. 389.
Cf. AËTIUS Med. (0718 004).

x04 **Fragmenta ap. Aëtium** (lib. 5).
CMG, vol. 8.2, pp. 98, 107–111.
Cf. AËTIUS Med. (0718 005).

x05 **Fragmenta ap. Aëtium** (lib. 9).
Zervos, *Athena* 23, pp. 276–279, 299, 366–368.
Cf. AËTIUS Med. (0718 009).

x06 **Fragmentum ap. Aëtium** (lib. 15).
Zervos, *Athena* 21, p. 61.
Cf. AËTIUS Med. (0718 015).

0910 **HERODOTUS et PHILUMENUS** Med.
A.D. 2?
Cf. et HERODOTUS Med. (0926).
Cf. et PHILUMENUS Med. (0671).

x01 **Fragmentum ap. Aëtium** (lib. 5).
CMG, vol. 8.2, p. 97.
Cf. AËTIUS Med. (0718 005).

Pseudo-HERODOTUS
Cf. VITAE HOMERI (1805 001).

0559 **HERON** Mech.
A.D. 1?: Alexandrinus

001 **Pneumatica**, ed. W. Schmidt, *Heronis Alexandrini opera quae supersunt omnia*, vol. 1. Leipzig: Teubner, 1899: 2–332.
Cod: [23,010]

002 **De automatis**, ed. Schmidt, *op. cit.*, vol. 1, 338–452.
Cod: [9,383]

003 **Fragmenta de horoscopiis**, ed. Schmidt, *op. cit.*, vol. 1, 456, 506.
Q: [300]

004 **Mechanicorum fragmenta**, ed. L. Nix and W. Schmidt, *op. cit.*, vol. 2.1 (1900): 256–298.
Q: [3,285]

005 **Catoptrica**, ed. Nix and Schmidt, *op. cit.*, vol. 2.1, 368–372.
Q: [501]

006 **Metrica**, ed. H. Schöne, *op. cit.*, vol. 3 (1903): 2–184.
Cod: [21,228]

007 **Dioptra**, ed. Schöne, *op. cit.*, vol. 3, 188–314.
Cod: [13,349]

008 **Definitiones**, ed. J.L. Heiberg, *op. cit.*, vol. 4 (1903): 2–168.
Cod: [14,985]

009 **Geometrica**, ed. Heiberg, *op. cit.*, vol. 4, 172–448.
Cod: [34,662]

010 **Stereometrica**, ed. Heiberg, *op. cit.*, vol. 5 (1914): 2–162.
Cod: [18,555]

011 **De mensuris**, ed. Heiberg, *op. cit.*, vol. 5, 164–218.
Cod: [5,246]

012 **Belopoeica**, ed. H. Diels and E. Schramm, *Herons Belopoiika* [*Abhandlungen der königlich preussischen Akademie der Wissenschaften*, Philosoph.-hist. Kl. 2. Berlin: Reimer, 1918]: 5–55.
Cod: 5,667

013 Χειροβαλλίστρας κατασκευὴ καὶ συμμετρία, ed. V. Prou, *La chirobaliste d'Héron d'Alexandrie* [*Notices et extraits des manuscrits de la Bibliothèque Nationale* 26.2. Paris: Imprimerie Nationale, 1877]: 116–149.
Cod: 1,168

014 **Fragmenta Heroniana**, ed. F. Hultsch, *Metrologicorum scriptores reliquiae*, vol. 1. Leipzig: Teubner, 1864 (repr. Stuttgart: 1971): 180–197, 202–205.
Cod: [2,788]

015 **Geodaesia** [Sp.], ed. Heiberg, *op. cit.*, vol. 5, LXX–XCIII.
Cod: [5,166]

016 **Liber geeponicus** [Sp.], ed. F. Hultsch, *Heronis Alexandrini geometricorum et stereometricorum reliquiae*. Berlin: Weidmann, 1864: 208–234.
Cod: [6,100]

0927 **HERON** Med.
ante A.D. 1

x01 **Fragmentum ap. Galenum.**
K12.745.
Cf. GALENUS Med. (0057 076).

2419 **HEROPHANES** Hist.
post 1 B.C.: Troezenius

001 **Fragmentum**, FGrH #605: 3B:739.
Q

0928 **HEROPHILUS** Med.
4–3 B.C.: Chalcedonius
Cf. et TROPHILUS <Paradox.> (0588).

x01 **Fragmenta ap. Galenum.**
K2.570–571, 895, in CMG, vol. 2.1, p. 42; K4.596–597; 8.592, 956, 959; 12.843; 13.308.
Cf. GALENUS Med. (0057 011, 016, 021, 059, 060, 076).

x02 **Fragmentum ap. Oribasium.**
CMG, vol. 6.2.1, p. 36.
Cf. ORIBASIUS Med. (0722 001).

x03 **Fragmentum ap. Anonymum Londinensem.**
Iatrica 21.22.
Cf. ANONYMUS LONDINENSIS (0643 001).

x04 **Fragmentum ap. Soranum.**
CMG, vol. 4, pp. 130–131.
Cf. SORANUS Med. (0565 001).

2311 **HEROPYTHUS** Hist.
  5–4 B.C.: fort. Colophonius
  001 **Fragmenta**, FGrH #448: 3B:377.
  Q

2516 **HESIANAX** Hist.
  Incertum
  001 **Fragmentum**, FGrH #763: 3C:745.
  Q

0020 **HESIODUS** Epic.
  8/7 B.C.?: Ascraeus
  Cf. et AEGIMIUS (0668).
  Cf. et VITAE HESIODI PARTICULA (1749).
  001 **Theogonia**, ed. M.L. West, *Hesiod. Theogony*.
  Oxford: Clarendon Press, 1966: 111–149.
  Cod: 6,969
  002 **Opera et dies**, ed. F. Solmsen, *Hesiodi opera*.
  Oxford: Clarendon Press, 1970: 49–85.
  Cod: 5,900
  003 **Scutum**, ed. Solmsen, *op. cit.*, 88–107.
  Cod: 3,336
  004 **Fragmenta**, ed. R. Merkelbach and M.L. West,
  Fragmenta Hesiodea. Oxford: Clarendon Press,
  1967: 3–78, 80–117, 119–127, 129–137, 139–
  141, 144, 147, 149–156, 158, 160–169, 171–
  172, 176–178, 181–186, 188–190.
  frr. 1, 5, 7–14, 16–17a, 21–23a, 25–27, 29–31,
  33–37, 40–41, 43a, 44–49, 51, 54a, 55–62, 64–
  67, 69–70, 73, 75–77, 79–86, 88–124, 128–
  129, 132–137, 141, 143–146, 150–151, 154,
  156, 158–159, 161, 165, 167, 169–181, 185–
  188, 190, 193, 195–201, 203–206, 209, 211,
  212b, 215, 217, 221, 227–229, 231, 233–236,
  239–240, 242–245, 248–249, 251–253, 257,
  259b, 264, 266a, 266c, 268–276, 278, 280–281,
  283, 286, 288–291, 293–294, 296, 298, 301–
  310, 313–324, 328–333, 335–339, 343, 357,
  361–363, 372–373, 380–381, 384, 386, 388,
  392–393, 403, 405–406, 412.
  Q, Pap: 11,210
  005 **Testimonia**, ed. H. Diels and W. Kranz, *Die
  Fragmente der Vorsokratiker*, vol. 1, 6th edn.
  Berlin: Weidmann, 1951 (repr. Dublin: 1966):
  38.
  NQ
  006 **Fragmenta astronomica**, ed. Diels and Kranz,
  op. cit., 38–40.
  Q
  007 **Fragmenta**, ed. R. Merkelbach and M.L. West,
  Hesiodi opera (ed. F. Solmsen), 2nd edn. Oxford: Clarendon Press, 1983: 227–232.
  Q, Pap
  x01 **Problema**.
  App. Anth. 7.1: Cf. EPIGRAMMATICI in *App.
  Anth.* (7052 007).

1428 **HESTIAEUS** Hist.
  ante A.D. 1
  001 **Fragmenta**, FGrH #786: 3C:799.
  Q

4085 **HESYCHIUS** Lexicogr.
  A.D. 5: Alexandrinus
  001 **Epistula ad Eulogium**, ed. K. Latte, *Hesychii
  Alexandrini lexicon*, vol. 1. Copenhagen:
  Munksgaard, 1953: 1–2.
  Cod: [623]
  002 **Lexicon (A–O)**, ed. Latte, *op. cit.*, vols. 1 & 2
  (1966): 1:3–492; 2:1–806.
  Cod: [248,055]
  003 **Lexicon (Π–Ω)**, ed. M. Schmidt, *Hesychii Alexandrini lexicon*, vols. 3–4. Halle, 3:1861;
  4:1862 (repr. Amsterdam: Hakkert, 1965):
  3:251–439; 4:1–336.
  Cod: [70,280]

2274 **HESYCHIUS Illustrius** Hist.
  A.D. 6: Milesius
  001 **Fragmentum**, FGrH #390: 3B:266–272.
  Cod
  006 **Fragmenta**, FHG 4: 145–177.
  Q, Cod

0929 **HICESIUS** Med.
  1 B.C.
  x01 **Fragmentum ap. Galenum**.
  K13.788.
  Cf. GALENUS Med. (0057 077).
  x02 **Fragmentum ap. Paulum**.
  CMG, vol. 9.2, p. 359.
  Cf. PAULUS Med. (0715 001).
  x03 **Fragmentum ap. Aëtium** (lib. 15).
  Zervos, *Athena* 21, p. 58.
  Cf. AËTIUS Med. (0718 015).
  x04 **Fragmentum ap. Athenaeum**.
  Deipnosophistae 15.681c, 689c.
  Cf. ATHENAEUS Soph. (0008 001).

2240 **HICETAS** Phil.
  5 B.C.: Syracusanus
  001 **Testimonia**, ed. H. Diels and W. Kranz, *Die
  Fragmente der Vorsokratiker*, vol. 1, 6th edn.
  Berlin: Weidmann, 1951 (repr. Dublin: 1966):
  441–442.
  test. 1–2.
  NQ

0930 **HIERAX** Med.
  ante A.D. 2: Thebanus
  Cf. et ANONYMUS THEBANUS Med. (1086).
  x01 **Fragmenta ap. Galenum**.
  K12.775–776; 13.829.
  Cf. GALENUS Med. (0057 076–077).

2370 **HIEROBOLUS** Hist.
  4 B.C.: Rhodius
  001 **Testimonium**, FGrH #530: 3B:505.
  NQ

2408 **HIEROCLES** Hist.
  A.D. 3?
  001 **Fragmenta**, FHG 4: 430.
  Q

1429 **HIEROCLES** Phil.
A.D. 2
001 'Ηθικὴ Στοιχείωσις, ed. J. von Arnim, *Hierokles. Ethische Elementarlehre (Papyrus 9780)* [*Berliner Klassikertexte* 4. Berlin: Weidmann, 1906]: 7–47.
Pap: [4,078]
002 **Fragmenta ethica ap. Stobaeum**, ed. von Arnim, *op. cit.*, 48–63.
Q: [5,800]
003 **Fragmenta ap. Suidam**, ed. von Arnim, *op. cit.*, 64.
Q: [116]

2404 **HIEROCLES et PHILAGRIUS Scriptores Facetiarum**
A.D. 4?
001 **Facetiae**, ed. A. Thierfelder, *Philogelos der Lachfreund von Hierokles und Philagrios*. Munich: Heimeran, 1968: 28–126.
Cod

2571 **HIEROCLES Platonicus** Phil.
A.D. 5
001 **In aureum carmen**, ed. F.G. Köhler, *Hieroclis in aureum Pythagoreorum carmen commentarius*. Stuttgart: Teubner, 1974: 5–122.
Cod
x01 **De providentia et fato.**
Photius, *Bibliotheca* 214, 251.
Cf. PHOTIUS Scr. Eccl. (4040 001).

2360 **HIERON** Hist.
Incertum
001 **Titulus**, FGrH #518: 3B:491.
NQ

1953 **HIERONYMUS** Hist.
3 B.C.: Cardianus
001 **Testimonia**, FGrH #154: 2B:829–830.
NQ
002 **Fragmenta**, FGrH #154: 2B:830–835.
Q
x01 **Epistula cuidam Macedoniae regi.**
FGrH #153, fr. 1.
Cf. ANONYMI HISTORICI (FGrH) (1139 007).

2526 **HIERONYMUS** Hist.
ante A.D. 1: Aegyptius
001 **Fragmenta**, FGrH #787: 3C:799–800.
Q

1430 **HIERONYMUS** Phil.
3 B.C.: Rhodius
001 **Fragmenta**, ed. F. Wehrli, *Hieronymos von Rhodos. Kritolaos und seine Schüler* [*Die Schule des Aristoteles*, vol. 10, 2nd edn. Basel: Schwabe, 1969]: 13–23.
Q

0745 **HIEROPHILUS** Soph. et Phil.
A.D. 4/6?

001 **De nutriendi methodo**, ed. J.L. Ideler, *Physici et medici Graeci minores*, vol. 1. Berlin: Reimer, 1841 (repr. Amsterdam: Hakkert, 1963): 409–417.
Cod: 2,248
002 Πῶς ὀφείλει διαιτᾶσθαι ἄνθρωπος ἐφ' ἑκάστῳ μηνί, ed. A. Delatte, *Anecdota Atheniensia et alia*, vol. 2. Paris: Droz, 1939: 546–566.
Cod: 2,141

2051 **HIMERIUS** Soph.
A.D. 4: Prusensis, Atheniensis
001 **Declamationes et orationes**, ed. A. Colonna, *Himerii declamationes et orationes cum deperditarum fragmentis*. Rome: Polygraphica, 1951: 13–248.
Declamatio Hyperidis pro Demosthene (orat. 1): pp. 13–16.
Declamatio Demosthenis pro Aeschine (orat. 2): pp. 16–21.
Declamatio contra Epicurum (orat. 3): pp. 22–28.
Declamatio contra divitem (orat. 4): pp. 29–36.
Declamatio Themistoclis contra Persarum regem (orat. 5): pp. 37–47.
Polemarchica (orat. 6): pp. 48–63.
Areopagitica (orat. 7): pp. 63–64.
Lamentatio in filium Rufinum defunctum (orat. 8): pp. 64–73.
Epithalamia in Severum (orat. 9): pp. 74–86.
Diogenes sive in abitum amici (orat. 10): pp. 87–92.
Ad amicos cum ipse abiret Corinthum (orat. 11): p. 92.
In Flaviani discessum (orat. 12): pp. 93–99.
In Pisonis domus advenas (orat. 13): pp. 100–101.
In Aegyptium advenam (orat. 14): pp. 101–102.
In discessum amici (orat. 15): pp. 102–103.
Extemporalis ob tumultum in schola coortum (orat. 16): pp. 103–104.
In adventum Cypriorum civium (orat. 17): pp. 105–106.
In civem Cappadocem auditorem (orat. 18): pp. 106–107.
Quia pulchra sint rara (orat. 19): pp. 107–109.
In Musonium proconsulem (orat. 20): pp. 109–110.
In Severum advenam (orat. 21): pp. 110–111.
Declamatio (orat. 22): p. 111.
In Ursacium comitem (orat. 23): pp. 112–115.
In Severum amicum (orat. 24): pp. 115–118.
In Scylacium Graeciae proconsulem (orat. 25): pp. 119–123.
In advenas Ephesios et Mysos (orat. 26): pp. 123–125.
In discipulos e patria sua advectos (orat. 27): pp. 125–127.
In Athenaeum comitem (orat. 28): pp. 128–130.
In privatum Romanum (orat. 29): pp. 131–132.

Ad familiares postquam ipse Corintho reverterat (orat. 30): pp. 133–134.

Hortativa in Ampelium (orat. 31): pp. 135–139.

In Anatolium praefectum praetorii (orat. 32): pp. 139–142.

In Phoebum Alexandri proconsulis filium (orat. 33): pp. 142–143.

In Arcadium comitem et medicum (orat. 34): pp. 144–145.

In accessum discipulorum (orat. 35): pp. 146–148.

In abitum Flaviani (orat. 36): pp. 149–152.

Epithalamia in Panathenaeum (orat. 37): p. 153.

Declamatio in Cerbonium proconsulem (orat. 38): pp. 154–158.

Declamatio in Julianum et Musonium (orat. 39): pp. 159–165.

Oratio Philippis habita (orat. 40): pp. 165–168.

In urbem Constantinopolim (orat. 41): pp. 168–176.

In Sallustium praesidem (orat. 42): pp. 176–177.

In Flavianum proconsulem (orat. 43): pp. 178–179.

In diem natalem amici (orat. 44): pp. 179–182.

Declamatio in sanitatem amici reciperatam (orat. 45): pp. 183–184.

In insidiatores et in Basilium proconsulem (orat. 46): pp. 185–189.

Altera in Basilium proconsulem (orat. 47): pp. 189–195.

In Hermogenem Graeciae proconsulem (orat. 48): pp. 196–212.

In Plotianum proconsulem (orat. 49) (titulus solum): p. 213.

In Ampelium proconsulem (orat. 50) (titulus solum): p. 213.

In Praetextatum Graeciae proconsulem et in familiares (orat. 51) (titulus solum): p. 213.

In Julianum imperatorem (orat. 52) (titulus solum): p. 214.

Declamatio habita Nicomediae (orat. 53) (titulus solum): p. 214.

In advenas (orat. 54): pp. 214–217.

In advenam (orat. 55) (titulus solum): p. 217.

In Zenonem familiarem (orat. 56) (titulus solum): p. 217.

In Aphobium advenam (orat. 57) (titulus solum): p. 218.

In quendam discipulum factum propter Neptuni oraculum (orat. 58) (titulus solum): p. 218.

In cives ex Ionia peregrinos (orat. 59): pp. 218–220.

In hospites Iones (orat. 60): pp. 220–222.

In auditores (orat. 61): pp. 222–223.

In honorem amici Constantinopolitani (orat. 62): pp. 224–227.

Oratio habita postquam ipse a patria reverterat (orat. 63): pp. 227–229.

Oratio extemporalis in auditorium suum (orat. 64): pp. 230–232.

Contra eos qui segniter orationes audiebant (orat. 65): pp. 232–233.

In discipulos qui contumaces videbantur (orat. 66): pp. 234–237.

In Quintiani asseclas qui tumultuose audiebant (orat. 67) (titulus solum): p. 237.

Ad persequendam in dicendo varietatem (orat. 68): pp. 238–242.

Oratio habita postquam ipse a volnere sanatus erat (orat. 69): pp. 242–245.

Oratio habita postquam ipse Corintho reverterat (orat. 70) (titulus solum): p. 245.

In stilum et in discipulos (orat. 71) (titulus solum): p. 246.

In Lacedaemonum urbem (orat. 72) (titulus solum): p. 246.

Quia minime deceat auditiones esse publicas (orat. 73) (titulus solum): p. 246.

Quia semper exercitationibus vacandum sit (orat. 74): pp. 247–248.

Declamatio Corinthi habita (orat. 75) (titulus solum): p. 248.

Cod: [43,295]

002 **Fragmenta ex incertis orationibus**, ed. Colonna, *op. cit.*, 249–253.

Q: [386]

003 **Fragmenta** (*P. Oslo* inv. 1478), ed. S. Eitrem and L. Amundsen, "Fragments from the speeches of Himerios, P. Oslo inv. no. 1478," *Classica et mediaevalia* 17 (1956) 29–30.

frr. e–f.

Pap: [105]

004 **Fragmenta**, ed. A. Guida, "Frammenti inediti di Eupoli, Teleclide, Teognide, Giuliano e Imerio da un nuovo codice del Lexicon Vindobonense," *Prometheus* 5 (1979) 210, 212, 213.

Q

2501 **HIPPAGORAS** Hist.

3 B.C.?

001 **Fragmentum**, FGrH #743: 3C:722.

Q

1431 **HIPPARCHUS** Astron. et Geogr.

2 B.C.: Nicaeensis

001 **Fragmenta** [Sp.?], ed. S. Weinstock, *Codices Britannici* [*Catalogus codicum astrologorum Graecorum* 9.1. Brussels: Academia, 1951]: 189–190.

Cod

002 **Fragmenta geographica**, ed. D.R. Dicks, *The geographical fragments of Hipparchus*. London: Athlone Press, 1960: 48–102.

Q

003 **In Arati et Eudoxi phaenomena commentariorum libri iii**, ed. C. Manitius, *Hipparchi in Arati et Eudoxi phaenomena commentariorum libri iii*. Leipzig: Teubner, 1894: 2–280.

Cod

0468 **HIPPARCHUS** Comic.

3 B.C.?

001 **Fragmenta**, ed. T. Kock, *Comicorum Attico-*

rum fragmenta, vol. 3. Leipzig: Teubner, 1888: 272–274.
frr. 1–3, 5.
Q: 91

002 **Fragmenta**, ed. A. Meineke, *Fragmenta comicorum Graecorum*, vol. 4. Berlin: Reimer, 1841 (repr. De Gruyter, 1970): 431–432.
Q: 89

2626 **HIPPARCHUS** Epic.
ante A.D. 2

001 **Fragmenta**, ed. H. Lloyd-Jones and P. Parsons, *Supplementum Hellenisticum*. Berlin: De Gruyter, 1983: 249.
frr. 496–497.
Q: [27]

1433 **HIPPARCHUS** <Epigr.>
6 B.C.: Atheniensis

001 **Fragmenta**, ed. E. Diehl, *Anthologia lyrica Graeca*, fasc. 1, 3rd edn. Leipzig: Teubner, 1949: 75.
frr. 1–2.
Q, Epigr: [13]

1432 <**HIPPARCHUS**> Phil.
3 B.C.

001 **Fragmentum**, ed. H. Thesleff, *The Pythagorean texts of the Hellenistic period*. Åbo: Åbo Akademi, 1965: 89–91.
Q: 616

2406 **HIPPASUS** Hist.
ante 1 B.C.: Lacon

001 **Testimonium**, FGrH #589: 3B:703.
NQ

002 **Fragmentum**, FGrH #589: 3B:704.
Q

2260 **HIPPASUS** Phil.
6 B.C.: Metapontinus

001 **Testimonia**, ed. H. Diels and W. Kranz, *Die Fragmente der Vorsokratiker*, vol. 1, 6th edn. Berlin: Weidmann, 1951 (repr. Dublin: 1966): 107–110.
test. 1–15.
NQ

002 **Tituli**, ed. H. Thesleff, *The Pythagorean texts of the Hellenistic period*. Åbo: Åbo Akademi, 1965: 93.
NQ

1435 **HIPPIAS** Hist.
post 4 B.C.?: Erythraeus

001 **Fragmentum**, FGrH #421: 3B:317–318.
Q

1434 **HIPPIAS** Soph.
5 B.C.: Eleus

001 **Testimonia**, FGrH #6: 1A:156.
NQ

002 **Fragmenta**, FGrH #6: 1A:156–158.
Q

003 **Testimonia**, ed. H. Diels and W. Kranz, *Die Fragmente der Vorsokratiker*, vol. 2, 6th edn. Berlin: Weidmann, 1952 (repr. Dublin: 1966): 326–330.
frr. 1–16.
NQ

004 **Fragmenta**, ed. Diels and Kranz, *op. cit.*, 330–333.
frr. 1–21.
Q

x01 **Epigramma sepulcrale**.
App. Anth. 2.26(?): Cf. EPIGRAMMATICI in *App. Anth.* (7052 002).

0738 *HIPPIATRICA*
A.D. 9

001 **Hippiatrica Berolinensia**, ed. E. Oder and K. Hoppe, *Corpus hippiatricorum Graecorum*, vol. 1. Leipzig: Teubner, 1924 (repr. Stuttgart: 1971): 1–439.
Cod: 84,234

002 **Appendices ad hippiatrica Berolinensia**, ed. Oder and Hoppe, *op. cit.*, vol. 1, 440–450.
Cod: 2,382

003 **Hippiatrica Parisina**, ed. Oder and Hoppe, *op. cit.*, vol. 2 (1927; repr. 1971): 29–114.
Cod: 16,855

004 **Fragmenta Anatolii**, ed. Oder and Hoppe, *op. cit.*, vol. 2, 115–121.
Cod: 1,039

005 **Fragmenta Timothei Gazaei**, ed. Oder and Hoppe, *op. cit.*, vol. 2, 121–124.
Cod: 512

006 **Hippiatrica Cantabrigiensia**, ed. Oder and Hoppe, *op. cit.*, vol. 2, 125–252.
Cod: 26,259

007 **Additamenta Londinensia ad hippiatrica Cantabrigiensia**, ed. Oder and Hoppe, *op. cit.*, vol. 2, 253–271.
Cod: 4,214

008 **Excerpta Lugdunensia**, ed. Oder and Hoppe, *op. cit.*, vol. 2, 272–313.
Cod: 11,612

009 **Fragmenta Anatolii de equis**, ed. Oder and Hoppe, *op. cit.*, vol. 2, 325–330.
Cod: 1,482

010 **Fragmenta Anatolii de bubus**, ed. Oder and Hoppe, *op. cit.*, vol. 2, 330–336.
Cod: 1,896

2235 **HIPPOCRATES** Math.
5 B.C.: Chius

001 **Testimonia**, ed. H. Diels and W. Kranz, *Die Fragmente der Vorsokratiker*, vol. 1, 6th edn. Berlin: Weidmann, 1951 (repr. Dublin: 1966): 395–397.
test. 1–6.
NQ

0627 **HIPPOCRATES** Med. et *CORPUS HIPPO-CRATICUM*
5–4 B.C.: Cous

001 **De prisca medicina**, ed. É. Littré, *Oeuvres*

complètes d'Hippocrate, vol. 1. Paris: Baillière, 1839 (repr. Amsterdam: Hakkert, 1973): 570–636.
Cod: 5,705

002 **De aëre aquis et locis**, ed. Littré, *op. cit.*, vol. 2 (1840; repr. 1961): 12–92.
Cod: 7,685

003 **Prognosticon**, ed. Littré, *op. cit.*, vol. 2, 110–190.
Cod: 5,363

004 **De diaeta in morbis acutis**, ed. Littré, *op. cit.*, vol. 2, 224–376.
Cod: 6,381

005 **De diaeta acutorum** [Sp.], ed. Littré, *op. cit.*, vol. 2, 394–528.
Cod: 5,569

006 **De morbis popularibus**, ed. Littré, *op. cit.*, vols. 2; 3 (1841; repr. 1961); 5 (1846; repr. 1962): 2:598–716; 3:24–148; 5:72–138, 144–196, 204–258, 266–356, 364–468.
Lib. 1: vol. 2, pp. 598–716.
Lib. 2: vol. 5, pp. 72–138.
Lib. 3: vol. 3, pp. 24–148.
Lib. 4: vol. 5, pp. 144–196.
Lib. 5: vol. 5, pp. 204–258.
Lib. 6: vol. 5, pp. 266–356.
Lib. 7: vol. 5, pp. 364–468.
Cod: 43,404

007 **De capitis vulneribus**, ed. Littré, *op. cit.*, vol. 3, 182–260.
Cod: 5,130

008 **De officina medici**, ed. Littré, *op. cit.*, vol. 3, 272–336.
Cod: 2,221

009 **De fracturis**, ed. Littré, *op. cit.*, vol. 3, 412–562.
Cod: 11,593

010 **De articulis**, ed. Littré, *op. cit.*, vol. 4 (1844; repr. 1962): 78–326.
Cod: 21,905

011 **Vectiarius**, ed. Littré, *op. cit.*, vol. 4, 340–394.
Cod: 5,091

012 **Aphorismi**, ed. Littré, *op. cit.*, vol. 4, 458–608.
Cod: 7,374

013 **Jusjurandum**, ed. Littré, *op. cit.*, vol. 4, 628–632.
Cf. et 0627 057.
Cod: 262

014 **Lex**, ed. Littré, *op. cit.*, vol. 4, 638–642.
Cod: 335

015 **De humoribus**, ed. Littré, *op. cit.*, vol. 5, 476–502.
Cod: 2,330

016 **Prorrheticon**, ed. Littré, *op. cit.*, vols. 5 & 9 (1861; repr. 1962): 5:510–572; 9:6–74.
Cod: 10,563

017 **Coa praesagia**, ed. Littré, *op. cit.*, vol. 5, 588–732.
Cod: 13,170

018 **De arte**, ed. Littré, *op. cit.*, vol. 6 (1849; repr. 1962): 2–26.
Cod: 2,801

019 **De natura hominis**, ed. Littré, *op. cit.*, vol. 6, 32–68.
Cod: 4,017

020 **De diaeta salubri**, ed. Littré, *op. cit.*, vol. 6, 72–86.
Cod: 1,509

021 **De flatibus**, ed. Littré, *op. cit.*, vol. 6, 90–114.
Cod: 2,923

022 **De humidorum usu**, ed. Littré, *op. cit.*, vol. 6, 118–136.
Cod: 1,532

023 **De morbis i–iii**, ed. Littré, *op. cit.*, vols. 6 & 7 (1851; repr. 1962): 6:140–204; 7:8–114, 118–160.
Cf. et 0627 024.
Cod: 26,143

024 **De semine, de natura pueri, de morbis iv**, ed. Littré, *op. cit.*, vol. 7, 470–614.
Cf. et 0627 023.
Cod: 19,474

025 **De affectionibus**, ed. Littré, *op. cit.*, vol. 6, 208–270.
Cod: 7,640

026 **De locis in homine**, ed. Littré, *op. cit.*, vol. 6, 276–348.
Cod: 8,723

027 **De morbo sacro**, ed. Littré, *op. cit.*, vol. 6, 352–396.
Cod: 4,876

028 **De ulceribus**, ed. Littré, *op. cit.*, vol. 6, 400–432.
Cod: 3,434

029 **De haemorrhoidibus**, ed. Littré, *op. cit.*, vol. 6, 436–444.
Cod: 928

030 **De fistulis**, ed. Littré, *op. cit.*, vol. 6, 448–460.
Cod: 1,603

031 **De diaeta i–iv**, ed. Littré, *op. cit.*, vol. 6, 466–662.
Cod: 20,472

032 **De affectionibus interioribus**, ed. Littré, *op. cit.*, vol. 7, 166–302.
Cod: 16,553

033 **De natura muliebri**, ed. Littré, *op. cit.*, vol. 7, 312–430.
Cod: 12,199

034 **De septimestri partu**, ed. Littré, *op. cit.*, vol. 7, 436–452.
Cod: 1,722

035 **De octimestri partu**, ed. Littré, *op. cit.*, vol. 7, 452–460.
Cod: 804

036 **De mulierum affectibus i–iii**, ed. Littré, *op. cit.*, vol. 8 (1853; repr. 1962): 10–462.
Lib. 1: pp. 10–232.
Lib. 2: pp. 234–406.
Lib. 3 (= De sterilibus): pp. 408–462.
Cod: 50,007

037 **De virginum morbis**, ed. Littré, *op. cit.*, vol. 8, 466–470.
Cod: 472

038 **De superfetatione**, ed. Littré, *op. cit.*, vol. 8, 476–508.
Cod: 3,485

039 **De exsectione foetus**, ed. Littré, *op. cit.*, vol. 8, 512–518.
Cod: 495

040 **De anatome**, ed. Littré, *op. cit.*, vol. 8, 538–540.
Cod: 260

041 **De dentitione**, ed. Littré, *op. cit.*, vol. 8, 544–548.
Cod: 403

042 **De glandulis**, ed. Littré, *op. cit.*, vol. 8, 556–574.
Cod: 1,810

043 **De carnibus**, ed. Littré, *op. cit.*, vol. 8, 584–614.
Cod: 3,467

045 **De corde**, ed. Littré, *op. cit.*, vol. 9, 80–92.
Cod: 1,062

046 **De alimento**, ed. Littré, *op. cit.*, vol. 9, 98–120.
Cod: 1,339

047 **De visu**, ed. Littré, *op. cit.*, vol. 9, 152–160.
Cod: 806

048 **De ossium natura**, ed. Littré, *op. cit.*, vol. 9, 168–196.
Cod: 3,411

049 **De medico**, ed. Littré, *op. cit.*, vol. 9, 204–220.
Cod: 1,552

050 **De decente habitu**, ed. Littré, *op. cit.*, vol. 9, 226–244.
Cod: 1,558

051 **Praeceptiones**, ed. Littré, *op. cit.*, vol. 9, 250–272.
Cod: 1,384

052 **De judicationibus**, ed. Littré, *op. cit.*, vol. 9, 276–294.
Cod: 2,025

053 **De diebus judicatoriis**, ed. Littré, *op. cit.*, vol. 9, 298–306.
Cod: 1,316

055 **Epistulae**, ed. Littré, *op. cit.*, vol. 9, 312–428.
Cod: 12,141

044 **De septimanis** (= **De hebdomadibus**), ed. W.H. Roscher, *Die hippokratische Schrift von der Siebenzahl* [*Studien zur Geschichte und Kultur des Altertums* 6. Paderborn: Schöningh, 1913 (repr. New York: Johnson Reprint, 1967)]: 1–10, 20–23, 29–31, 36–37, 42–43, 45, 48–50, 68–69, 72–73, 74–79.
Cod: 2,162

054 **De purgantibus** (= **De remediis**), ed. H. Schöne, "Hippokrates. Περὶ φαρμάκων," *Rheinisches Museum* 73 (1924) 440–443.
Cod: 504

056 **De septimestri partu** [Sp.], ed. H. Grensemann, *Hippokrates. Über Achtmonatskinder. Über das Siebenmonatskind* [*Corpus medicorum Graecorum*, vol. 1.2.1. Berlin: Akademie-Verlag, 1968]: 122–124.
Cod: 414

057 **Jusjurandum 2**, ed. J.L. Heiberg, *Hippocratis opera* [*Corpus medicorum Graecorum*, vol. 1.1. Leipzig: Teubner, 1927]: 5–6.
Cf. et 0627 013.
Cf. et JUSJURANDUM MEDICUM (0740 001).
Cod

0751 **Pseudo-HIPPOCRATES** Med.
post 5 B.C.

001 **Epistula ad Ptolemaeum regem**, ed. J.F. Boissonade, *Anecdota Graeca*, vol. 3. Paris: Imprimerie Nationale, 1831 (repr. Hildesheim: Olms, 1962): 422–428.
Cod: 796

002 **Epistula ad Ptolemaeum regem de hominis fabrica**, ed. F.Z. Ermerins, *Anecdota medica Graeca*. Leiden: Luchtmans, 1840 (repr. Amsterdam: Hakkert, 1963): 279–297.
Cod: 1,495

003 Περὶ διαφόρων καὶ παντοίων τροφῶν, ed. A. Delatte, *Anecdota Atheniensia et alia*, vol. 2. Paris: Droz, 1939: 479–482.
Cod: 651

004 Περὶ διαφορᾶς τροφῶν πρὸς Πτολεμαῖον, ed. Delatte, *op. cit.*, 483–499.
Cod: 2,746

005 Ἑρμηνεία περὶ ἐνεργῶν λίθων, ed. C.É. Ruelle, *Les lapidaires de l'antiquité et du Moyen Age*, vol. 2.1. Paris: Leroux, 1898: 185–190.
Cod: 1,640

2698 **HIPPODAMAS** Epigr.
Incertum: Salaminius

x01 **Epigramma demonstrativum.**
App. Anth. 3.17: Cf. EPIGRAMMATICI in *App. Anth.* (7052 003).

1436 **<HIPPODAMUS>** Phil.
3 B.C.: Milesius

001 **Fragmenta** [Sp.], ed. H. Thesleff, *The Pythagorean texts of the Hellenistic period*. Åbo: Åbo Akademi, 1965: 94–102.
Q: 2,658

002 **Testimonia**, ed. H. Diels and W. Kranz, *Die Fragmente der Vorsokratiker*, vol. 1, 6th edn. Berlin: Weidmann, 1951 (repr. Dublin: 1966): 389–391.
test. 1–5: auctor alter nominatur Phaleas.
NQ

2115 **HIPPOLYTUS** Scr. Eccl.
A.D. 3: Romanus

001 **Refutatio omnium haeresium** (= **Philosophumena**), ed. P. Wendland, *Hippolytus Werke*, vol. 3 [*Die griechischen christlichen Schriftsteller* 26. Leipzig: Hinrichs, 1916]: 1–293.
Cod: [59,335]

002 **Contra haeresin Noeti**, ed. R. Butterworth, *Hippolytus of Rome. Contra Noetum*. London: Heythrop College (University of London), 1977: 43–93.
Cod

003 **De Antichristo**, ed. H. Achelis, *Hippolyt's kleinere exegetische und homiletische Schriften* [*Die griechischen christlichen Schriftsteller* 1.2. Leipzig: Hinrichs, 1897]: 1–47.
Cod

004 **Fragmenta in Genesim**, ed. Achelis, *op. cit.*, 51–53, 55–71.
frr. 1–6, 8–52.
Cf. et 2115 005.
Cf. et 2115 038.
Cod

005 **Fragmenta in Genesim** [Sp.], ed. Achelis, *op. cit.*, 72–81.
frr.53–81.
Cf. et 2115 004.
Cf. et 2115 033.
Q, Cod

006 **De benedictione Balaam** (fragmentum ex Leontio), ed. Achelis, *op. cit.*, 82.
Cf. et 2115 046.
Cod

007 **In canticum Mosis**, ed. Achelis, *op. cit.*, 83–84.
frr. 1–3.
Q

008 **Ex interpretatione Ruth**, ed. Achelis, *op. cit.*, 120.
Cod

009 **In Helcanam et Annam**, ed. Achelis, *op. cit.*, 121–122.
frr. 1–4.
Q

010 **Fragmentum de engastrimytho** [Sp.], ed. Achelis, *op. cit.*, 123.
Cod

011 **Fragmenta in Psalmos**, ed. Achelis, *op. cit.*, 130, 146–147, 153.
frr. 1, 18–20, 37.
Q

012 **Fragmenta in Psalmos** [Sp.], ed. Achelis, *op. cit.*, 131–145, 147–153.
frr. 2–17, 21–36, 38.
Cf. et 2115 052.
Q, Cod

013 **Fragmenta in Proverbia**, ed. Achelis, *op. cit.*, 157–167, 176–178.
frr. 1–29, 54.
Cf. et 2115 044.
Cf. et 2115 045.
Cf. et 2115 053.
Q, Cod

014 **Fragmenta in Proverbia** [Dub.], ed. Achelis, *op. cit.*, 168.
30–31.
Q

015 **Fragmenta in Proverbia** [Sp.], ed. Achelis, *op. cit.*, 169–175.
frr. 32–53.
Q

016 **In Ecclesiasten** (fragmentum e cod. Vat. 1694), ed. Achelis, *op. cit.*, 179.
Cod

017 **Fragmentum in Ecclesiasten** [Sp.], ed. Achelis, *op. cit.*, 179.
Q

018 **In principium Isaiae**, ed. Achelis, *op. cit.*, 180.
Q

019 **Fragmentum in Ezechielem**, MPG 10: 632–633.
Q: [140]

020 **Fragmentum in Matthaeum 6.11** [Sp.], ed. Achelis, *op. cit.*, 208.
Q

021 **Fragmentum de distributione talantorum** (Matth. 25.24), ed. Achelis, *op. cit.*, 209.
Q

022 **De duobus latronibus** (Joh. 19.33–34), ed. Achelis, *op. cit.*, 211.
Q

023 **In evangelium Joannis et de resurrectione Lazari** [Dub.], ed. Achelis, *op. cit.*, 215–220, 224–227.
Q

024 **Fragmenta epistulae ad reginam (Mammeam?)**, ed. Achelis, *op. cit.*, 253.
frr. 7–8.
Cf. et 2115 048.
Q

025 **Fragmentum de resurrectione et incorruptione**, ed. Achelis, *op. cit.*, 254.
Q

026 **De theophania** [Dub.], ed. Achelis, *op. cit.*, 257–263.
Q

027 **De sancta pascha**, ed. Achelis, *op. cit.*, 267–271.
frr. 1–3, 5, 7.
Q

028 **Narratio de virgine Corinthiaca** [Dub.], ed. Achelis, *op. cit.*, 275–277.
Cod

029 **De consummatione mundi** [Sp.], ed. Achelis, *op. cit.*, 289–309.
Cod

030 **Commentarium in Danielem**, ed. M. Lefèvre, *Hippolyte. Commentaire sur Daniel* [*Sources chrétiennes* 14. Paris: Cerf, 1947]: 70–386.
Cf. et 2115 032.
Cf. et 2115 035.
Q, Cod

031 **In Canticum canticorum**, ed. G.N. Bonwetsch and H. Achelis, *Hippolytus Werke*, vol. 1 [*Die griechischen christlichen Schriftsteller* 1.1. Leipzig: Hinrichs, 1897]: 343.
Cf. et 2115 049.
Q

032 **Commentarium in Danielem 1.18**, ed. M. Richard, "Les difficultés d'une édition du commentaire de S. Hippolyte sur Daniel," *Revue d'histoire des textes* 2 (1972) 5–7.
Cf. et 2115 030.
Cf. et 2115 035.
Cod

033 **De benedictionibus Isaaci et Jacobi,** ed. M. Brière, L. Mariès and B.-C. Mercier, *Patrologia Orientalis* 27 (1954): 2–114.
Cf. et 2115 005.
Cod

034 **De benedictione Mosis** (fragmenta), ed. Brière, Mariès, and Mercier, *op. cit.*, ix.
Q

035 **Fragmenta in Danielem 1.18.3,** ed. M. Richard, "Le chapitre sur l'église du commentaire sur Daniel de Saint-Hippolyte," *Revue d'histoire des textes* 3 (1973) 16.
Cf. et 2115 030.
Cf. et 2115 032.
Cod

036 **Chronicon,** ed. R. Helm (post A. Bauer), *Hippolytus Werke,* vol. 4, 2nd edn. [*Die griechischen christlichen Schriftsteller* 46. Berlin: Akademie-Verlag, 1955]: 6–69, 128–134.
Q, Cod

037 **Chronicon** (fragmentum), *P. Oxy.* 6.870.
Pap

038 **Fragmentum in Genesim 4.23** (cod. Ath. bibl. nat. 2492), ed. M. Richard, "Un fragment inédit de S. Hippolyte sur Genèse 4.23," *Serta Turyniana: Studies in Greek literature and palaeography in honor of Alexander Turyn.* Urbana: University of Illinois Press, 1974: 396–397.
Cf. et 2115 004.
Cod

039 **Demonstratio adversus Judaeos** [Sp.], ed. E. Schwartz, "Zwei Predigten Hippolyts," *Sitzungsberichte der bayerischen Akademie der Wissenschaften,* Philosoph.-hist. Kl., Heft 3. Munich, 1936: 19–23.
Cod

042 **De universo,** ed. K. Holl, *Fragmente vornicänischer Kirchenväter aus den Sacra Parallela* [*Texte und Untersuchungen* 20. Leipzig: Hinrichs, 1899]: 137–143.
Cf. et 2115 043, 058, x05.
Q

043 **De universo** (fragmenta), ed. W.J. Malley, "Four unedited fragments of the 'De universo' of the Pseudo-Josephus found in the Chronicon of George Hamartolus (Coislin 305)," *Journal of Theological Studies,* n.s. 16 (1965) 15–16.
Cf. et 2115 042, 058, x05.
Q

044 **Fragmenta in Proverbia** (e cod. Coislin 193), ed. M. Richard, "Les fragments du commentaire de S. Hippolyte sur les proverbes de Salomon," *Muséon* 79 (1966) 75–94.
frr. 1–48, 52–79.
Cf. et 2115 013.
Cod

045 **Fragmenta in Proverbia** (e Pseudo-Anastasio Sinaite), ed. Richard, *Muséon* 79, 82–94.
frr. 37–61, 65, 67–72, 74–76.

Cf. et 2115 013.
Q

046 **De benedictione Balaam** (fragmenta ap. Irenaeum), ed. W.W. Harvey, *Sancti Irenaei episcopi Lugdunensis libri quinque adversus haereses,* vol. 2. Cambridge: Cambridge University Press, 1857: 486, 489–491, 509.
frr. 15, 20–27.
Cf. et 2115 006.
Q

047 **Fragmentum e traditione apostolica** [Sp.], ed. M. Richard, "Quelques nouveaux fragments des pères anténicéens et nicéens," *Symbolae Osloenses* 38 (1963) 79.
Cod

048 **Fragmentum epistulae ad Mammeam,** ed. Richard, *SO* 38, 79–80.
Cf. et 2115 024.
Cod

049 **In Canticum canticorum** (paraphrasis), ed. M. Richard, "Une paraphrase grecque résumée du commentaire d'Hippolyte sur le cantique des cantiques," *Muséon* 77 (1964) 140–154.
Cf. et 2115 031.
Cod

050 **Fragmenta varia** [Dub.], ed. Harvey, *op. cit.,* 497–498.
frr. 33–34.
Q

051 **Fragmentum in Helcanam et Annam,** ed. P. Nautin, *Le dossier d'Hippolyte et de Méliton* [*Patristica* 1. Paris: Cerf, 1953]: 34.
Q

052 **Fragmenta in Psalmos,** ed. Nautin, *op. cit.,* 167–183.
Cf. et 2115 011.
Q

053 **Fragmenta in Proverbia,** ed. M. Richard, "Les fragments du commentaire de S. Hippolyte sur les proverbes de Salomon," *Muséon* 78 (1965) 263–289.
Cf. et 2115 013.
Q

054 **Canones Hippolyti** (fragmenta) [Sp.], ed. H. Achelis, *Die ältesten Quellen des orientalischen Kirchenrechtes. Erstes Buch: die Canones Hippolyti* [*Texte und Untersuchungen* 6. Leipzig: Hinrichs, 1891]: passim.
Cod: [45]

055 **Traditio apostolica** [Sp.], ed. B. Botte, *Hippolyte de Rome. La tradition apostolique d'après les anciennes versions,* 2nd edn. [*Sources chrétiennes* 11 bis. Paris: Cerf, 1968]: 42–46, 66, 96, 112.
Oratio consecrationis episcopi: pp. 42–46.
De lectore: p. 66.
De jejunio: p. 96.
De fructibus quos oportet offerre episcopo: p. 112.
Cod

056 **Contra Beronem et Heliconem** [Sp.], ed. F. Diekamp, *Doctrina patrum de incarnatione*

verbi. Münster: Aschendorff, 1907: 321–326.

057 **Canon paschalis**, ed. M. Guarducci, *Epigrafia greca IV. Epigrafi sacre pagane e cristiani*. Rome: Istituto Poligrafico, 1978: 542–543.
Epigr

058 **De universo** (fragmenta), ed. P.A. de Lagarde, *Hippolyti Romani quae feruntur omnia graece*. Leipzig: Teubner, 1858 (repr. Osnabrück: Zeller, 1966): 124.
fr. 17.
Cf. et 2115 042, 043, x05.
Q

059 **Syntagma** (fragmentum), MPG 10: 868–869.
Q

x01 **Contra Artemonem** (*sive* **Parvus labyrinthus**) [Dub.].
Eusebius, HE 5.28.
Cf. EUSEBIUS Scr. Eccl. et Theol. (2018 002).

x02 **De xii apostolis** [Sp.].
Schermann, pp. 164–167.
Cf. VITAE PROPHETARUM (1750 012).

x03 **De lxx apostolis** [Sp.].
Schermann, pp. 167–170.
Cf. VITAE PROPHETARUM (1750 012).

x04 **Adversus Graecos**.
Cf. De universo (2115 042, 043, 058, x05).

x05 **De universo** (fragmenta).
Photius, *Bibliotheca* 48.
Cf. PHOTIUS Scr. Eccl. (4040 001).
Cf. et 2115 042, 043, 058.

1437 **HIPPON** Phil.
5 B.C.: Rheginus

001 **Testimonia**, ed. H. Diels and W. Kranz, *Die Fragmente der Vorsokratiker*, vol. 1, 6th edn. Berlin: Weidmann, 1951 (repr. Dublin: 1966): 385–387.
test. 1–19.
NQ

002 **Fragmenta**, ed. Diels and Kranz, *op. cit.*, 387–389.
frr. 1–4.
Q

x01 **Epigramma sepulcrale** [Sp.].
App. Anth. 2.340: Cf. EPIGRAMMATICI in *App. Anth.* (7052 002).

0233 **HIPPONAX** Iamb.
6 B.C.: Ephesius

001 **Fragmenta**, ed. M.L. West, *Iambi et elegi Graeci*, vol. 1. Oxford: Clarendon Press, 1971: 110–152, 156–160, 162–171.
frr. 1–10, 12–17, 19–30, 32, 34–44, 47–54, 56–125, 127–129a, 132, 135–135b, 144–145, 147, 148b, 151a, 154–155b, 158, 161, 165b, 166–167, 172, 175–177, 182.
Q, Pap: [2,295]

2391 **HIPPOSTRATUS** Hist.
3 B.C.?

001 **Testimonia**, FGrH #568: 3B:659.
NQ

002 **Fragmenta**, FGrH #568: 3B:660–661.
Q

0351 **[HIPPOTHOON]** Trag.
vel Hippothous
Incertum

001 **Fragmenta**, ed. B. Snell, *Tragicorum Graecorum fragmenta*, vol. 1. Göttingen: Vandenhoeck & Ruprecht, 1971: 321–322.
frr. 1–6.
Q: [81]

1438 **HIPPYS** Hist.
5 B.C.?: Rheginus

001 **Testimonium**, FGrH #554: 3B:540–541.
NQ

002 **Fragmenta**, FGrH #554: 3B:541–543.
Q

1386 ***HISTORIA ALEXANDRI MAGNI***
post 4 B.C.
Cf. et ANONYMI HISTORICI in FGrH (1139 007).

001 **Recensio** α, ed. W. Kroll, *Historia Alexandri Magni*, vol. 1. Berlin: Weidmann, 1926: 1–146.
Cod: 31,522

002 **Recensio** β, ed. L. Bergson, *Der griechische Alexanderroman. Rezension β*. Stockholm: Almqvist & Wiksell, 1965: 1–192.
Cod: 27,729

010 **Recensio** β (ex cod. Leidense Vulc. 93), ed. Bergson, *op. cit.*, 193–204.
Cod: 2,718

011 **Recensio** β (ex cod. Paris. gr. 1685 et cod. Messinense 62), ed. Bergson, *op. cit.*, 205–207.
Cod: 587

003 **Recensio** γ (lib. 1), ed. U. von Lauenstein, *Der griechische Alexanderroman. Rezension γ. Buch I* [*Beiträge zur klassischen Philologie* 4. Meisenheim am Glan: Hain, 1962]: 2–150.
Cod: 16,408

004 **Recensio** γ (lib. 2), ed. H. Engelmann, *Der griechische Alexanderroman. Rezension γ. Buch II* [*Beiträge zur klassischen Philologie* 12. Meisenheim am Glan: Hain, 1963]: 152–328.
Cod: 18,492

005 **Recensio** γ (lib. 3), ed. F. Parthe, *Der griechische Alexanderroman. Rezension γ. Buch III* [*Beiträge zur klassischen Philologie* 33. Meisenheim am Glan: Hain, 1969]: 330–462.
Cod: 11,555

006 **Recensio** ε, ed. J. Trumpf, *Anonymi Byzantini vita Alexandri regis Macedonum*. Stuttgart: Teubner, 1974: 1–178.
Cod: 24,971

007 **Recensio** λ (lib. 3), ed. H. van Thiel, *Die Rezension λ des Pseudo-Kallisthenes*. Bonn: Habelt, 1959: 37–65.
Cod: 6,366

008 **Recensio** λ (Pseudo-Methodius, redactio 1), ed. van Thiel, *op. cit.*, 72, 74.
Cod: [445]

009 **Recensio** λ (Pseudo-Methodius, redactio 2), ed. van Thiel, *op. cit.*, 73, 75.
Cod: [368]

2744 *HISTORIA MONACHORUM IN AEGYPTO*
fort. auctore monacho Hierosolymitano
Incertum

001 **Historia monachorum in Aegypto**, ed. A.J. Festugière, *Historia monachorum in Aegypto*. Brussels: Société des Bollandistes, 1971: 4–138.
Cod: [21,596]

4065 **Manuel HOLOBOLUS** Polyhist.
fiq Maximus
A.D. 13
Bibliography in progress

x01 **Epigrammata** (*App. Anth.*).
Epigramma demonstrativum: 3.214.
Epigramma exhortatorium et supplicatorium: 4.89.
App. Anth. 3.214: Cf. EPIGRAMMATICI in *App. Anth.* (7052 003).
App. Anth. 4.89: Cf. EPIGRAMMATICI in *App. Anth.* (7052 004).

0012 **HOMERUS** Epic.
8 B.C.
Cf. et VERSUS HEROICI (1802).

001 **Ilias**, ed. T.W. Allen, *Homeri Ilias*, vols. 2–3. Oxford: Clarendon Press, 1931: 2:1–356; 3:1–370.
Cod: 115,477

002 **Odyssea**, ed. P. von der Muehll, *Homeri Odyssea*. Basel: Helbing & Lichtenhahn, 1962: 1–456.
Cod: 87,765

003 **Epigrammata**, AG 7.153; 14.147.
AG 10.32: Cf. PALLADAS Epigr. (2123 001).
Q: 59

x01 **Epigramma dedicatorium**.
App. Anth. 1.2(?): Cf. EPIGRAMMATICI in *App. Anth.* (7052 001).

0253 **[HOMERUS]** <Epic.>
7/6 B.C.: fort. Colophonius

001 **Margites** (fragmenta), ed. M.L. West, *Iambi et elegi Graeci*, vol. 2. Oxford: Clarendon Press, 1972: 72–73, 75–76.
frr. 1–3, 4b, 7.
Q, Pap: [130]

1440 **HONESTUS** Epigr.
A.D. 1: Byzantius vel Corinthius

001 **Epigrammata**, AG 5.20; 7.66, 274; 9.216, 225, 230, 250, 292; 11.32, 45.
Q: 312

x01 **Epigrammata dedicatoria**.
App. Anth. 1.134–137: Cf. EPIGRAMMATICI in *App. Anth.* (7052 001).

2052 **HORAPOLLO** Gramm.
A.D. 4/5?: Nilous

001 **Hieroglyphica**, ed. F. Sbordone, *Hori Apollinis hieroglyphica*. Naples: Loffredo, 1940: 1–216.
Cod: [9,553]

002 **Testimonia**, FGrH #630: 3C:180.
NQ

HYBRIAS Lyr.
PMG, p. 478.
Cf. CARMINA CONVIVIALIA (PMG) (0296 001).

0932 **HYBRISTUS** Med.
ante 3 B.C.: Oxyrhynchites

x01 **Fragmentum ap. Galenum**.
K14.188.
Cf. GALENUS Med. (0057 078).

0933 **HYGIENUS** Med.
A.D. 1/2

x01 **Fragmenta ap. Galenum**.
K12.488, 788; 13.353, 512, 747.
Cf. GALENUS Med. (0057 076–077).

0742 *HYMNI ANONYMI*
Varia

001 **Naassenorum carmina**, ed. E. Heitsch, *Die griechischen Dichterfragmente der römischen Kaiserzeit*, vol. 1, 2nd edn. Göttingen: Vandenhoeck & Ruprecht, 1963: 155–157.
fr. 1, sine titulo: pp. 155–156.
fr. 2, In Attinem: pp. 156–157.
fr. 3, In Attinem: p. 157.
Q: [225]

002 **Christianorum carmina**, ed. Heitsch, *op. cit.*, vol. 1, 157–164.
fr. 1, In Christum salvatorem: pp. 157–159.
fr. 2, In trinitatem (*P. Oxy.* 15.1786): p. 160.
fr. 3, In Christum (*P. Berol. Mus.* 8299): p. 161.
fr. 4, De moribus Christianorum (*P. Amh.* 1, 23–28): pp. 161–164.
Q, Pap: [522]

003 **Carminis de mundi creatione exordium**, ed. Heitsch, *op. cit.*, vol. 1, 164–165.
Pap: [55]

004 **Hymnus in Jovem**, ed. Heitsch, *op. cit.*, vol. 1, 165.
Q: [30]

005 **Hymnus in Isim** (*PSI* 844), ed. Heitsch, *op. cit.*, vol. 1, 165–166.
Pap: [97]

006 **Hymnus in Sarapidem** (*P. Schubart* 12), ed. Heitsch, *op. cit.*, vol. 1, 166.
Pap: [58]

007 **Aretalogia Sarapidis** (*P. Berol.* 10525), ed. Heitsch, *op. cit.*, vol. 1, 167–168.
Pap: [153]

008 **Hymnus in Apollinem**, ed. Heitsch, *op. cit.*, vol. 1, 168.
Q: [47]

009 **Paean in Apollinem** (*P. Berol.* 68670v), ed. Heitsch, *op. cit.*, vol. 1, 169–170.
Pap: [51]

010 **Hymnus in Asclepium**, ed. Heitsch, *op. cit.*,
vol. 1, 171.
Q: [66]

011 **Hymnus in Hecatam**, ed. Heitsch, *op. cit.*, vol.
1, 171.
Q: [50]

012 **Hymnus in Fortunam** (*P. Berol. Mus.* 9734v),
ed. Heitsch, *op. cit.*, vol. 1, 172.
Pap: [63]

013 **Hymnus in Dionysum** (*P. Ross. Georg.* 1.11),
ed. Heitsch, *op. cit.*, vol. 1, 173–175.
Pap: [433]

014 **Carmen mystarum** (*P. Argent.* 1313), ed.
Heitsch, *op. cit.*, vol. 1, 175–176.
Pap: [74]

015 **Descensus ad inferos** (*P. Brit. Mus.* 1192), ed.
Heitsch, *op. cit.*, vol. 1, 177–179.
Pap: [259]

016 **Hymni e papyris magicis collecti**, ed. Heitsch,
op. cit., vol. 1, 180–199.
fr. 1, In Pantocratorem (*P. Gr. Lugd. Bat.*
1.384, col. 7–8): p. 180.
fr. 2, In Pana (=Pantocratorem) (*P. Louvre*
2391, col. 17): p. 180.
fr. 3, In Solem (*P. Paris. Bibl. Nat.* suppl. gr.
574, fol. 11v): p. 181.
fr. 4, In Solem (*P. Paris. Bibl. Nat.* suppl. gr.
574 + *P. Brit.* Mus. gr. 122 + *P. Berol.* 5025 A
et B): pp. 181–183.
fr. 5, In Solem (*P. Louvre* 2391, col. 8 et 9):
pp. 183–184.
fr. 6, In Typhona (*P. Paris. Bibl. Nat.* suppl.
gr. 574, fol. 4r): p. 185.
fr. 7, In Typhona (*P. Paris. Bibl. Nat.* suppl.
gr. 574, fol. 4v–5r): p. 186.
fr. 8, In Mercurium (*P. Argent.* gr. 1179v): pp.
186–187.
fr. 9, In Lunam (*P. Paris. Bibl. Nat.* suppl. gr.
574, fol. 25v–26v): pp. 187–191.
fr. 10, In Lunam (*P. Paris Bibl. Nat.* suppl. gr.
574, fol. 30v–31v): pp. 191–193.
fr. 11, In Lunam (*P. Paris. Bibl. Nat.* suppl. gr.
574, fol. 28r–29v): pp. 193–195.
fr. 12, In Dianam (=Lunam) (*P. Paris. Bibl.
Nat.* suppl. gr. 574, fol. 28): pp. 195–196.
fr. 13, In Hecatam (*P. Paris. Bibl. Nat.* suppl.
gr. 574, fol. 30): pp. 197–198.
fr. 14, In Venerem (*P. Paris. Bibl. Nat.* suppl.
gr. 574, fol. 32r): pp. 198–199.
Cod, Pap: [2,883]

017 **Hymnus in omnes deos**, ed. Heitsch, *op. cit.*,
vol. 2 (1964): 43.
fr. S3.
Q: [70]

018 **Hymnus in Apollinem**, ed. Heitsch, *op. cit.*,
vol. 2, 44.
fr. S5.
Q: [33]

019 **Hymnus in Isim**, ed. F.H. von Gärtringen,
*Inscriptiones insularum Maris Aegaei praeter
Delum* [*Inscriptiones Graecae*, vol. 12.5. Berlin:

Reimer, 1909]: 214–217.
no. 739.
Epigr

020 **Φῶς ἱλαρόν**, ed. W. Christ and M. Paranikas,
Anthologia Graeca carminum Christianorum.
Leipzig: Teubner, 1871 (repr. Hildesheim:
Olms, 1963): 40.
Cod

0013 ***HYMNI HOMERICI***
8–6 B.C.
Cf. et VERSUS HEROICI (1802).

001 **Fragmenta hymni in Bacchum**, ed. T.W. Allen, W.R. Halliday and E.E. Sikes, *The Ho-
meric hymns*, 2nd edn. Oxford: Clarendon
Press, 1936: 1–2.
Q, Cod: 149

002 **In Cererem**, ed. Allen, Halliday, and Sikes, *op.
cit.*, 2–20.
Cod: 3,401

003 **In Apollinem**, ed. Allen, Halliday, and Sikes,
op. cit., 20–42.
Cod: 3,842

004 **In Mercurium**, ed. Allen, Halliday, and Sikes,
op. cit., 42–64.
Cod: 4,030

005 **In Venerem**, ed. Allen, Halliday, and Sikes, *op.
cit.*, 64–75.
Cod: 2,067

006 **In Venerem**, ed. Allen, Halliday, and Sikes, *op.
cit.*, 75.
Cod: 135

007 **In Bacchum**, ed. Allen, Halliday, and Sikes, *op.
cit.*, 76–78.
Cod: 429

008 **In Martem**, ed. Allen, Halliday, and Sikes, *op.
cit.*, 78.
Cod: 104

009 **In Dianam**, ed. Allen, Halliday, and Sikes, *op.
cit.*, 79.
Cod: 60

010 **In Venerem**, ed. Allen, Halliday, and Sikes, *op.
cit.*, 79.
Cod: 42

011 **In Minervam**, ed. Allen, Halliday, and Sikes,
op. cit., 79.
Cod: 38

012 **In Junonem**, ed. Allen, Halliday, and Sikes, *op.
cit.*, 80.
Cod: 30

013 **In Cererem**, ed. Allen, Halliday, and Sikes, *op.
cit.*, 80.
Cod: 22

014 **In matrem deorum**, ed. Allen, Halliday, and
Sikes, *op. cit.*, 80.
Cod: 50

015 **In Herculem**, ed. Allen, Halliday, and Sikes,
op. cit., 81.
Cod: 64

016 **In Aesculapium**, ed. Allen, Halliday, and
Sikes, *op. cit.*, 81.
Cod: 35

017 **In Dioscuros**, ed. Allen, Halliday, and Sikes, *op. cit.*, 81–82.
Cod: 30

018 **In Mercurium**, ed. Allen, Halliday, and Sikes, *op. cit.*, 82.
Cod: 77

019 **In Pana**, ed. Allen, Halliday, and Sikes, *op. cit.*, 82–84.
Cod: 342

020 **In Volcanum**, ed. Allen, Halliday, and Sikes, *op. cit.*, 84.
Cod: 54

021 **In Apollinem**, ed. Allen, Halliday, and Sikes, *op. cit.*, 85.
Cod: 40

022 **In Neptunum**, ed. Allen, Halliday, and Sikes, *op. cit.*, 85.
Cod: 45

023 **In Jovem**, ed. Allen, Halliday, and Sikes, *op. cit.*, 85.
Cod: 25

024 **In Vestam**, ed. Allen, Halliday, and Sikes, *op. cit.*, 85–86.
Cod: 36

025 **In Musas et Apollinem**, ed. Allen, Halliday, and Sikes, *op. cit.*, 86.
Cod: 55

026 **In Bacchum**, ed. Allen, Halliday, and Sikes, *op. cit.*, 86.
Cod: 93

027 **In Dianam**, ed. Allen, Halliday, and Sikes, *op. cit.*, 87.
Cod: 133

028 **In Minervam**, ed. Allen, Halliday, and Sikes, *op. cit.*, 87–88.
Cod: 114

029 **In Vestam**, ed. Allen, Halliday, and Sikes, *op. cit.*, 88–89.
Cod: 100

030 **In Tellurem matrem omnium**, ed. Allen, Halliday, and Sikes, *op. cit.*, 89.
Cod: 137

031 **In Solem**, ed. Allen, Halliday, and Sikes, *op. cit.*, 89–90.
Cod: 128

032 **In Lunam**, ed. Allen, Halliday, and Sikes, *op. cit.*, 90–91.
Cod: 126

033 **In Dioscuros**, ed. Allen, Halliday, and Sikes, *op. cit.*, 91–92.
Cod: 119

034 **Εἰς ξένους**, ed. Allen, Halliday, and Sikes, *op. cit.*, 92.
Cod: 31

0030 **HYPERIDES** Orat.
4 B.C.: Atheniensis

001 **In Demosthenem**, ed. C. Jensen, *Hyperidis orationes sex.* Leipzig: Teubner, 1917 (repr. Stuttgart: 1963): 2–24.
Pap: 2,695

002 **Pro Lycophrone**, ed. Jensen, *op. cit.*, 25–37.
Pap: 1,725

003 **Pro Euxenippo**, ed. Jensen, *op. cit.*, 38–56.
Pap: 3,121

004 **In Philippidem**, ed. Jensen, *op. cit.*, 57–68.
Pap: 1,210

005 **In Athenogenem**, ed. Jensen, *op. cit.*, 69–89.
Pap: 2,585

006 **Epitaphius**, ed. Jensen, *op. cit.*, 90–114.
Pap: 2,346

007 **Fragmenta**, ed. Jensen, *op. cit.*, 115–154.
frr. 1–43, 45–179, 181–212, 219–276.
Q: 6,681

2277 **HYPERMENES** Hist.
ante A.D. 2

001 **Fragmentum**, FGrH #394: 3B:284.
Q

2396 **HYPEROCHUS** Hist.
post 3 B.C.: Cumaeus

001 **Fragmenta**, FGrH #576: 3B:678–679.
Q

002 **Titulus**, ed. H. Lloyd-Jones and P. Parsons, *Supplementum Hellenisticum.* Berlin: De Gruyter, 1983: 249.
titul. 498.
NQ: [1]

0717 **HYPSICLES** Math. et Astron.
2 B.C.: Alexandrinus

001 **Hypsiclis liber sive elementorum liber xiv qui fertur**, ed. E.S. Stamatis (post J.L. Heiberg), *Euclidis elementa*, vol. 5.1, 2nd edn. Leipzig: Teubner, 1977: 1–22.
Cf. et EUCLIDES Geom. (1799 001).
Cod: 3,840

002 **Anaphoricus**, ed. V. de Falco and M. Krause, *Hypsikles. Die Aufgangszeiten der Gestirne [Abhandlungen der Akademie der Wissenschaften in Göttingen,* Philol.-hist. Kl., ser. 3, no. 62. Göttingen: Vandenhoeck & Ruprecht, 1966]: 34–40.
Cod: 1,864

1983 **HYPSICRATES** Hist.
1 B.C.–A.D. 1: Amisenus

001 **Testimonium**, FGrH #190: 2B:923.
NQ

002 **Fragmenta**, FGrH #190: **2B**:923–926; **3B**:743 addenda.
fr. 12: *P. Oxy.* 18.2192.
Q, Pap

1821 *IAMBICA ADESPOTA* (ALG)
Varia

001 **Fragmenta iambica adespota**, ed. E. Diehl, *Anthologia lyrica Graeca*, fasc. 3, 3rd edn. Leipzig: Teubner, 1952: 73–79.
frr. 1–16b, 18–33.
Q: [269]

002 **Anonymorum iambica**, ed. Diehl, *op. cit.*, 68–72.
frr. 1–2.
Pap: [242]

0235 *IAMBICA ADESPOTA* (IEG)
Varia
001 **Fragmenta**, ed. M.L. West, *Iambi et elegi Graeci*, vol. 2. Oxford: Clarendon Press, 1972: 16–28.
frr. 1–42, 49–61.
Q, Pap: [487]

2140 **IAMBLICHUS** Alchem.
post A.D. 3
001 **Fragmenta**, ed. M. Berthelot, *Collection des anciens alchimistes grecs*. Paris: Steinheil, 1887 (repr. London: Holland Press, 1963): 285–289.
Cod

2023 **IAMBLICHUS** Phil.
A.D. 3–4: Chalcidensis
001 **De vita Pythagorica**, ed. U. Klein (post L. Deubner), *Iamblichi de vita Pythagorica liber*. Leipzig: Teubner, 1937 (repr. Stuttgart: 1975): 1–147.
Cod: 30,873
002 **Protrepticus**, ed. H. Pistelli, *Iamblichi protrepticus ad fidem codicis Florentini*. Leipzig: Teubner, 1888 (repr. Stuttgart: 1967): 3–126.
Cod: 26,867
003 **De communi mathematica scientia**, ed. U. Klein (post N. Festa), *Iamblichi de communi mathematica scientia liber*. Leipzig: Teubner, 1891 (repr. Stuttgart: 1975): 3–99.
Cod: 20,536
004 **In Nicomachi arithmeticam introductionem**, ed. U. Klein (post H. Pistelli), *Iamblichi in Nicomachi arithmeticam introductionem liber*. Leipzig: Teubner, 1894 (repr. Stuttgart: 1975): 3–125.
Cod: 27,506
005 **Theologoumena arithmeticae**, ed. V. de Falco, *[Iamblichi] theologoumena arithmeticae*. Leipzig: Teubner, 1922: 1–87.
Cod: 17,194
006 **De mysteriis**, ed. E. des Places, *Jamblique. Les mystères d'Égypte*. Paris: Les Belles Lettres, 1966: 38–215.
Cod: 42,940
007 **Fragmenta exegetica**, ed. B.D. Larsen, *Jamblique de Chalcis. Exégète et philosophe. Appendice: testimonia et fragmenta exegetica*. Aarhus: Universitetsforlaget, 1972: 9–130.
Q
008 **In Platonis dialogos commentariorum fragmenta**, ed. J.M. Dillon, *Iamblichi Chalcidensis in Platonis dialogos commentariorum fragmenta*. Leiden: Brill, 1973: 72–224.
Q
009 **Sententiae**, ed. D.J. O'Meara, "New fragments

of Iamblichus' collection of Pythagorean doctrines," *American Journal of Philology* 102 (1981) 26–40.
Q

1441 **IAMBLICHUS** Scr. Erot.
A.D. 2
001 **Babyloniaca**, ed. E. Habrich, *Iamblichi Babyloniacorum reliquiae*. Leipzig: Teubner, 1960: 5–79.
Fragmenta (frr. 1–89): pp. 5–69.
Fragmenta incertae sedis (frr. 90–100): pp. 70–72.
Fragmenta dubia (frr. 101–126): pp. 73–79.
Q, Cod: [3,372]

0293 **IBYCUS** Lyr.
6 B.C.: Rheginus
001 **Fragmenta**, ed. D.L. Page, *Poetae melici Graeci*. Oxford: Clarendon Press, 1962 (repr. 1967 (1st edn. corr.)): 144–150, 152–162, 164–167.
frr. 1–2, 4–7, 12, 17, 21–22, 25, 29–40, 48–49, 51–53, 56–57.
Q, Pap: [792]
002 **Fragmenta**, ed. D.L. Page, *Supplementum lyricis Graecis*. Oxford: Clarendon Press, 1974: 44–73.
frr. S151–S165: *P. Oxy.* 1790 + 2081.
frr. S166–S219: *P. Oxy.* 2735.
frr. S220–S257: *P. Oxy.* 2637.
fr. S258: ex Herodiano, *De prosodia catholica*.
Q, Pap: [2,315]

2226 **ICCUS** Phil.
6 B.C.: Tarentinus
001 **Testimonia**, ed. H. Diels and W. Kranz, *Die Fragmente der Vorsokratiker*, vol. 1, 6th edn. Berlin: Weidmann, 1951 (repr. Dublin: 1966): 216–217.
test. 1–3.
NQ

0935 **ICODOTUS** Med.
ante A.D. 2
x01 **Fragmentum ap. Galenum**.
K13.311–312.
Cf. GALENUS Med. (0057 076).

2628 **IDAEUS** Epic.
Incertum: Rhodius
001 **Titulus**, ed. H. Lloyd-Jones and P. Parsons, *Supplementum Hellenisticum*. Berlin: De Gruyter, 1983: 250.
fr. 502.
NQ: [1]

2304 **IDAEUS** Phil.
5 B.C.: Himeraeus
001 **Testimonium**, ed. H. Diels and W. Kranz, *Die Fragmente der Vorsokratiker*, vol. 2, 6th edn.

Berlin: Weidmann, 1952 (repr. Dublin: 1966): 51.
NQ

0936 **IDIUS** Med.
ante A.D. 2
x01 **Fragmentum ap. Galenum.**
K13.297.
Cf. GALENUS Med. (0057 076).

1442 **IDOMENEUS** Hist.
4-3 B.C.: Lampsacenus
001 **Testimonia,** FGrH #338: 3B:189.
NQ
002 **Fragmenta,** FGrH #338: 3B:190-195.
Q
003 **Fragmenta,** ed. A. Angeli, "I frammenti di Idomeno di Lampsaco," *Cronache Ercolanesi* 11 (1981) 64-72.
frr. 16, 18, 30-31, 35: *P. Herc.* 1418.
frr. 20, 29, 32-34: *P. Herc.* 176.
fr. 21: *P. Herc.* 1471.
Q, Pap

2380 **IDOMENEUS** Hist.
Incertum
001 **Testimonium,** FGrH #547: 3B:532.
NQ

0012 **IGNATIUS** Biogr.
A.D. 8-9
001 **Epigrammata,** AG 15.29-31, 39.
Q: 124

0011 **IGNATIUS** Epigr.
A.D. 9
001 **Epigramma,** AG 1.109.
Q: 25

443 **IGNATIUS** Scr. Eccl.
A.D. 1-2: Antiochenus
001 **Epistulae,** ed. P.T. Camelot, *Ignace d'Antioche. Polycarpe de Smyrne. Lettres. Martyre de Polycarpe,* 4th edn. [*Sources chrétiennes* 10. Paris: Cerf, 1969]: 56-154.
Cod: [8,076]
002 **Epistulae spuriae,** ed. F.X. Funk and F. Diekamp, *Patres apostolici,* vol. 2, 3rd edn. Tübingen: Laupp, 1913: 88-268.
Cod: [20,304]
003 **Fragmenta spuria,** MPG **95**:1208c, 1548d, 1564d; **96**:81a, 264d, 429a, 429b.
Q

444 *ILIAS PARVA*
fort. auctore Cinaethone Lacedaemonio vel Lesche Mytilenensi
7/6 B.C.?
001 **Fragmenta,** ed. T.W. Allen, *Homeri opera,* vol. 5. Oxford: Clarendon Press, 1912 (repr. 1969): 129-133, 135.

frr. 1-2, 4-6, 10-12, 19.
Q

1445 *ILIU PERSIS*
fort. auctore Arctino Milesio vel Lesche Mytilenensi
7/6 B.C.?
001 **Fragmenta,** ed. T.W. Allen, *Homeri opera,* vol. 5. Oxford: Clarendon Press, 1912 (repr. 1969): 138-140.
frr. 1, 3, 5-6.
Q

2731 **IOMEDES** Epigr.
A.D. 2/3
x01 **Epigramma sepulcrale.**
App. Anth. 2.665: Cf. EPIGRAMMATICI in *App. Anth.* (7052 002).

1446 **ION** Eleg.
5 B.C.: Samius
001 **Fragmentum,** ed. E. Diehl, *Anthologia lyrica Graeca,* fasc. 1, 3rd edn. Leipzig: Teubner, 1949: 87.
Epigr: [28]
002 **Epigramma,** AG 7.43.
AG 7.44: Cf. ANONYMI EPIGRAMMATICI (0138 001).
Q: 26

0308 **ION** Poeta et Phil.
5 B.C.: Chius
001 **Fragmenta,** ed. B. Snell, *Tragicorum Graecorum fragmenta,* vol. 1. Göttingen: Vandenhoeck & Ruprecht, 1971: 96-114.
frr. 1-29, 31-43, 43b-43c, 44-68.
Q: [652]
002 **Fragmenta,** ed. M.L. West, *Iambi et elegi Graeci,* vol. 2. Oxford: Clarendon Press, 1972: 78-80.
frr. 26-30, 32.
Q: [247]
003 **Fragmenta,** ed. D.L. Page, *Poetae melici Graeci.* Oxford: Clarendon Press, 1962 (repr. 1967 (1st edn. corr.)): 384-386.
frr. 5-7.
Q: [53]
004 **Fragmentum,** ed. D.L. Page, *Supplementum lyricis Graecis.* Oxford: Clarendon Press, 1974: 105.
fr. S316.
Pap: [4]
005 **Tituli,** ed. Page, *Poetae melici Graeci,* 383-384.
NQ
006 **Testimonia,** FGrH #392: 3B:276-278.
NQ
007 **Fragmenta,** FGrH #392: 3B:278-283.
Q
008 **Testimonia,** ed. H. Diels and W. Kranz, *Die Fragmente der Vorsokratiker,* vol. 1, 6th edn.

Berlin: Weidmann, 1951 (repr. Dublin: 1966): 377–378.
test. 1–7.
NQ

009 **Fragmenta**, ed. Diels and Kranz, *op. cit.*, 379–381.
frr. 1–5.
Q

0311 **IOPHON** Trag.
5 B.C.
001 **Fragmenta**, ed. B. Snell, *Tragicorum Graecorum fragmenta*, vol. 1. Göttingen: Vandenhoeck & Ruprecht, 1971: 134–135.
frr. 1, 2.
Q: [33]

4071 **IRENAEUS** Epigr.
A.D. 6
001 **Epigrammata**, AG 5.249, 251, 253.
Q: 103

1447 **IRENAEUS** Scr. Eccl.
A.D. 2: Lugdunensis
001 **Adversus haereses** (libri 1–2), ed. W.W. Harvey, *Sancti Irenaei episcopi Lugdunensis libri quinque adversus haereses*, vol. 1. Cambridge: Cambridge University Press, 1857: 1–188, 192–198, 204–207, 209–212, 214–216, 220–230, 232–233, 241–242, 331, 345, 347, 351–352, 360, 362, 370, 374–375, 380.
Q: 22,657
002 **Adversus haereses** (liber 3), ed. A. Rousseau and L. Doutreleau, *Irénée de Lyon. Contre les hérésies, livre 3*, vol. 2 [*Sources chrétiennes* 211. Paris: Cerf, 1974]: 22–24, 28, 32–44, 50, 84–86, 106–108, 128, 160–170, 176–178, 182–184, 190–192, 196–198, 206–208, 214–216, 246–248, 320, 336–338, 348–350, 364–374, 378, 398–406, 414, 428–430, 434–436.
Q: 3,064
007 **Adversus haereses** (liber 4), ed. A. Rousseau, B. Hemmerdinger, L. Doutreleau and C. Mercier, *Irénée de Lyon. Contre les hérésies, livre 4*, vol. 2 [*Sources chrétiennes* 100. Paris: Cerf, 1965]: 418–420, 432–434, 440, 446, 472, 610–612, 628, 634, 640–642, 672, 712–714, 726, 788, 790, 810, 816–818, 830, 910–912, 920–930, 940–956, 968–970, 974, 978–982.
Q: 2,436
008 **Adversus haereses** (liber 5), ed. A. Rousseau, L. Doutreleau and C. Mercier, *Irénée de Lyon. Contre les hérésies, livre 5*, vol. 2 [*Sources chrétiennes* 153. Paris: Cerf, 1969]: 14–16, 20–24, 32–48, 50, 52, 54, 62, 64, 66, 68, 70, 74, 98, 114, 116, 118, 120, 140, 142, 144, 146, 148, 150, 166–168, 172–174, 216–222, 232–234, 300–304, 334–336, 342–380, 384, 394, 416, 452–458.
Q: 4,581
004 **Adversus haereses 3.9** (*P. Oxy.* 3.405), ed. Rousseau and Doutreleau, *Irénée de Lyon.*

Contre les hérésies, livre 3, vol. 2, 104, 107–108.
Pap: 139
003 **Adversus haereses 5.3–13** (*P. Jena*), ed. Rousseau, Doutreleau and Mercier, *Irénée de Lyon. Contre les hérésies, livre 5*, vol. 2, 49, 51, 53, 55, 56, 60, 63, 65, 67, 69, 71, 76, 78–96, 99–100, 103–115, 117, 119–126, 141, 143, 145, 147, 149, 152–164.
Pap: 2,274
005 **Fragmenta deperditorum operum**, ed. Harvey, *op. cit.*, vol. 2 (1857): 470–511.
frr. 33–34.
Q, Cod: 3,763
006 **Fragmentum**, ed. A. de Santos Otero, "Dos capitulos ineditos del original griego de Ireneo de Lyon (*Adversus haereses II:50–51*) en el codice Vadopedi 236," *Emerita* 41 (1973) 486–488.
Cod

0017 **ISAEUS** Orat.
5–4 B.C.: Atheniensis
fort. Chalcidicus
001 **De Cleonymo**, ed. P. Roussel, *Isée. Discours*, 2nd edn. Paris: Les Belles Lettres, 1960: 20–32.
Cod: 2,698
002 **De Menecle**, ed. Roussel, *op. cit.*, 36–48.
Cod: 2,737
003 **De Pyrrho**, ed. Roussel, *op. cit.*, 52–71.
Cod: 4,535
004 **De Nicostrato**, ed. Roussel, *op. cit.*, 74–81.
Cod: 1,818
005 **De Dicaeogene**, ed. Roussel, *op. cit.*, 88–102.
Cod: 3,059
006 **De Philoctemone**, ed. Roussel, *op. cit.*, 108–124.
Cod: 3,727
007 **De Apollodoro**, ed. Roussel, *op. cit.*, 129–140.
Cod: 2,715
008 **De Cirone**, ed. Roussel, *op. cit.*, 144–158.
Cod: 3,110
009 **De Astyphilo**, ed. Roussel, *op. cit.*, 162–173.
Cod: 2,334
010 **De Aristarcho**, ed. Roussel, *op. cit.*, 179–186.
Cod: 1,808
011 **De Hagnia**, ed. Roussel, *op. cit.*, 190–205.
Cod: 3,580
012 **Pro Euphileto**, ed. Roussel, *op. cit.*, 211–215.
Cod: 853
013 **Fragmenta**, ed. Roussel, *op. cit.*, 220–230.
Q: 975

1449 **ISIDORUS** Epigr.
1 B.C.?: Aegeates
001 **Epigrammata**, AG 7.156, 280, 293, 532; 9.94.
Q: 182

4052 **ISIDORUS** Epigr.
A.D. 6: Bolbythiotus

001 **Epigrammata**, AG **6**.58; **9**.11.
Q: 70

‹070 **ISIDORUS** Geogr.
1 B.C.–A.D. 1: Characenus
001 **Testimonia**, FGrH #781: 3C:777–778.
Q
002 **Fragmenta**, FGrH #781: 3C:778–785.
Q, Cod

‹448 **ISIDORUS** Gnost.
A.D. 2
001 **Fragmenta**, ed. W. Völker, *Quellen zur Ge-schichte der christlichen Gnosis*. Tübingen: Mohr, 1932: 41–43.
Q

‹938 **ISIDORUS** Med.
ante A.D. 2: Antiochenus
x01 **Fragmenta ap. Galenum**.
K13.250, 295–296, 341, 833, 834–835, 885, 908.
Cf. GALENUS Med. (0057 076–077).

‹939 **ISIDORUS** Med.
ante A.D. 2: Memphiticus
x01 **Fragmentum ap. Aëtium** (lib. 7).
CMG, vol. 8.2, p. 387.
Cf. AËTIUS Med. (0718 007).

‹359 **ISIDORUS Scriptor Hymnorum**
ante 1 B.C.: Aegyptius
001 **Hymni in Isim**, ed. V.F. Vanderlip, *The four Greek hymns of Isidorus and the cult of Isis* [*American studies in papyrology* 12. Toronto: Hakkert, 1972]: 17–18, 34–35, 49–50, 63–64.
Epigr

‹352 **ISIDORUS** Trag.
Incertum
001 **Fragmenta**, ed. B. Snell, *Tragicorum Graecorum fragmenta*, vol. 1. Göttingen: Vandenhoeck & Ruprecht, 1971: 323.
frr. 1–2.
Q: [33]

1083 **ISIGONUS** Paradox.
3 B.C./A.D. 1: Nicaeensis
001 **Fragmenta**, ed. A. Giannini, *Paradoxographorum Graecorum reliquiae*. Milan: Istituto Editoriale Italiano, 1965: 147–148.
Q

‹0010 **ISOCRATES** Orat.
5–4 B.C.: Atheniensis
001 **In Euthynum** (orat. 21), ed. G. Mathieu and É. Brémond, *Isocrate. Discours*, vol. 1. Paris: Les Belles Lettres, 1929 (repr. 1963): 7–11.
Cod: 1,138
002 **In Callimachum** (orat. 18), ed. Mathieu and Brémond, *op. cit.*, vol. 1, 19–34.
Cod: 3,698

003 **In Lochitem** (orat. 20), ed. Mathieu and Brémond, *op. cit.*, vol. 1, 39–44.
Cod: 1,151
004 **De bigis** (orat. 16), ed. Mathieu and Brémond, *op. cit.*, vol. 1, 51–64.
Cod: 3,017
005 **Trapeziticus** (orat. 17), ed. Mathieu and Brémond, *op. cit.*, vol. 1, 71–87.
Cod: 3,476
006 **Aegineticus** (orat. 19), ed. Mathieu and Brémond, *op. cit.*, vol. 1, 93–106.
Cod: 3,036
007 **Ad Demonicum** (orat. 1), ed. Mathieu and Brémond, *op. cit.*, vol. 1, 122–135.
Cod: 3,000
008 **In sophistas** (orat. 13), ed. Mathieu and Brémond, *op. cit.*, vol. 1, 144–150.
Cod: 1,382
009 **Helenae encomium** (orat. 10), ed. Mathieu and Brémond, *op. cit.*, vol. 1, 163–179.
Cod: 3,893
010 **Busiris** (orat. 11), ed. Mathieu and Brémond, *op. cit.*, vol. 1, 188–200.
Cod: 2,833
011 **Panegyricus** (orat. 4), ed. Mathieu and Brémond, *op. cit.*, vol. 2 (1938; repr. 1967 (1st edn. rev. et corr.)): 15–64.
Cod: 11,249
012 **Plataicus** (orat. 14), ed. Mathieu and Brémond, *op. cit.*, vol. 2, 74–88.
Cod: 3,353
013 **Ad Nicoclem** (orat. 2), ed. Mathieu and Brémond, *op. cit.*, vol. 2, 97–111.
Cod: 3,119
014 **Nicocles** (orat. 3), ed. Mathieu and Brémond, *op. cit.*, vol. 2, 120–137.
Cod: 3,908
015 **Evagoras** (orat. 9), ed. Mathieu and Brémond, *op. cit.*, vol. 2, 146–168.
Cod: 4,820
016 **Archidamus** (orat. 6), ed. Mathieu and Brémond, *op. cit.*, vol. 2, 175–205.
Cod: 6,412
017 **De pace** (orat. 8), ed. Mathieu, *op. cit.*, vol. 3 (1942; repr. 1966): 12–51.
Cod: 8,278
018 **Areopagiticus** (orat. 7), ed. Mathieu, *op. cit.*, vol. 3, 63–84.
Cod: 4,743
019 **Antidosis** (orat. 15), ed. Mathieu, *op. cit.*, vol. 3, 103–181.
Cod: 18,731
020 **Philippus** (orat. 5), ed. Mathieu and Brémond, *op. cit.*, vol. 4 (1962): 19–60.
Cod: 9,031
021 **Panathenaicus** (orat. 12), ed. Mathieu and Brémond, *op. cit.*, vol. 4, 87–159.
Cod: 16,409
022 **Ad Dionysium** (epist. 1), ed. Mathieu and Brémond, *op. cit.*, vol. 4, 185–187.
Cod: 633

023 **Ad filios Jasonis** (epist. 6), ed. Mathieu and Brémond, *op. cit.*, vol. 4, 188–192.
Cod: 920

024 **Ad Archidamum** (epist. 9), ed. Mathieu and Brémond, *op. cit.*, vol. 4, 193–198.
Cod: 1,179

025 **Ad reges Mytilenaeos** (epist. 8), ed. Mathieu and Brémond, *op. cit.*, vol. 4, 199–202.
Cod: 683

026 **Ad Timotheum** (epist. 7), ed. Mathieu and Brémond, *op. cit.*, vol. 4, 203–206.
Cod: 805

027 **Ad Philippum** (epist. 2), ed. Mathieu and Brémond, *op. cit.*, vol. 4, 207–213.
Cod: 1,321

028 **Ad Alexandrum** (epist. 5), ed. Mathieu and Brémond, *op. cit.*, vol. 4, 214–215.
Cod: 296

029 **Ad Antipatrum** (epist. 4), ed. Mathieu and Brémond, *op. cit.*, vol. 4, 216–220.
Cod: 860

030 **Ad Philippum** (epist. 3), ed. Mathieu and Brémond, *op. cit.*, vol. 4, 221–223.
Cod: 432

031 **Fragmenta**, ed. Mathieu and Brémond, *op. cit.*, vol. 4, 229–232, 234–239.
frr. 1–2, 4–6, 8–41.
Q: 1,408

1450 **ISTER** Hist.
vel Istrus
3 B.C.: Cyrenaeus
001 **Testimonia**, FGrH #334: 3B:168.
NQ
002 **Fragmenta**, FGrH #334: 3B:169–186.
Q, Cod
003 **Fragmentum** (*P. Oxy.* 26.2442), ed. H.J. Mette, "Die 'Kleinen' griechischen Historiker heute," *Lustrum* 21 (1978) 27.
fr. 41 bis.
Pap

0201 **ISYLLUS** Lyr.
3 B.C.: Epidaurius
001 **Fragmenta** (*IG* 4.950), ed. J.U. Powell, *Collectanea Alexandrina.* Oxford: Clarendon Press, 1925 (repr. 1970): 132–135.
Epigr: [564]

0934 **JACOBUS Psychrestus** Med.
A.D. 5: Alexandrinus
x01 **Fragmentum ap. Aëtium** (lib. 12).
Kostomiris, p. 92.
Cf. AËTIUS Med. (0718 012).
x02 **Fragmentum ap. Alexandrum Trallianum.**
Puschmann, vol. 2, pp. 161–163, 565, 571.
Cf. ALEXANDER Med. (0744 003).

2183 **JASON** Hist.
ante 2 B.C.?: Nyssenus
Cf. et JASON Hist. (2309).
001 **Fragmentum**, FGrH #632: 3C:182.
Q

2309 **JASON** Hist.
fiq Jason Nyssenus
ante 2 B.C.?
Cf. et JASON Hist. (2183).
001 **Titulus**, FGrH #446: 3B:376.
NQ

1975 **JASON** Hist.
2 B.C.: Cyrenaeus
001 **Testimonium**, FGrH #182: 2B:910.
NQ

2575 **JASON** Hist.
Incertum: Byzantius
001 **Fragmentum**, FGrH #12c: 1A:*10 addenda.
Q

1921 **JASON** Hist. et Gramm.
A.D. 2: Argivus
001 **Testimonium**, FGrH #94: 2A:445–446.
NQ

2498 **JOANNES I** Hist.
2 B.C.: Hyrcanus
001 **Testimonium**, FGrH #736: 3C:700.
NQ

0727 **JOANNES** Med.
A.D. 7: Alexandrinus
001 **Commentarii in Hippocratis librum de natura pueri**, ed. F.R. Dietz, *Scholia in Hippocratem et Galenum*, vol. 2. Königsberg: Borntraeger, 1834 (repr. Amsterdam: Hakkert, 1966): 205–235.
Cod: 8,605

2062 **JOANNES CHRYSOSTOMUS** Scr. Eccl.
A.D. 4–5: Antiochenus, Constantinopolitanus
001 **Ad Theodorum lapsum** (lib. 2) (= **Epistula ad Theodorum monachum**), ed. J. Dumortier, *Jean Chrysostome. A Théodore* [*Sources chrétiennes* 117. Paris: Cerf, 1966]: 46–78.
Cod: [3,145]
002 **Ad Theodorum lapsum** (lib. 1), ed. Dumortier, *op. cit.*, 80–218.
Cod: [14,778]
003 **Adversus oppugnatores vitae monasticae** (lib. 1–3), MPG 47: 319–386.
Cod: [32,287]
004 **Ad Demetrium de compunctione** (lib. 1), MPG 47: 393–410.
Cod: [7,971]
005 **Ad Stelechium de compunctione** (lib. 2), MPG 47: 411–422.
Cod: [5,758]
006 **Ad Stagirium a daemone vexatum** (lib. 1–3), MPG 47: 423–494.
Cod: [33,093]
007 **Contra eos qui subintroductas habent virgines**, ed. J. Dumortier, *Saint Jean Chrysostome. Les cohabitations suspectes.* Paris: Les Belles Lettres, 1955: 44–94.
Cod: [9,281]

008 **Quod regulares feminae viris cohabitare non debeant**, ed. Dumortier, *Les cohabitations suspectes*, 95–137.
Cod: [8,659]

009 **De virginitate**, ed. H. Musurillo and B. Grillet, *Jean Chrysostome. La virginité* [*Sources chrétiennes* 125. Paris: Cerf, 1966]: 92–394.
Cod: [32,488]

010 **Ad viduam juniorem**, ed. G.H. Ettinger and B. Grillet, *Jean Chrysostome. A une jeune veuve. Sur le mariage unique* [*Sources chrétiennes* 138. Paris: Cerf, 1968]: 112–159.
Cod: [4,799]

011 **De non iterando conjugio**, ed. Ettinger and Grillet, *op. cit.*, 160–201.
Cod: [4,368]

085 **De sacerdotio** (lib. 1–6), ed. A.-M. Malingrey, *Jean Chrysostome. Sur le sacerdoce* [*Sources chrétiennes* 272. Paris: Cerf, 1980]: 60–362.
De sacerdotio (lib. 7): Cf. 2062 119.
Cod: [31,648]

496 **Sermo cum presbyter fuit ordinatus**, ed. Malingrey, *op. cit.*, 388–418.
Cod

012 **De incomprehensibili dei natura** (homiliae 1–5), ed. A.-M. Malingrey, *Jean Chrysostome. Sur l'incompréhensibilité de Dieu* [*Sources chrétiennes* 28 bis. Paris: Cerf, 1970]: 92–322.
Cod: [21,417]

014 **De beato Philogonio**, MPG 48: 747–756.
Cod: [3,540]

015 **De consubstantiali**, MPG 48: 755–768.
Cod: [5,660]

016 **De petitione matris filiorum Zebedaei**, MPG 48: 767–778.
Cod: [4,197]

017 **In quatriduanum Lazarum**, MPG 48: 779–784.
Cod: [1,989]

018 **De Christi precibus**, MPG 48: 783–796.
Cod: [4,951]

019 **Contra Anomoeos** (homilia 11), MPG 48: 795–802.
Cod: [2,925]

020 **De Christi divinitate**, MPG 48: 801–812.
Cod: [4,260]

372 **Contra Judaeos et gentiles quod Christus sit deus**, ed. N.G. McKendrick, *Quod Christus sit Deus* [*Diss. Fordham* (1966)].

021 **Adversus Judaeos** (orationes 1–8), MPG 48: 843–942.
Cod: [46,317]

022 **In Kalendas**, MPG 48: 953–962.
Cod: [4,224]

023 **De Lazaro** (conciones 1–7), MPG 48: 963–1054.
Cod: [40,398]

024 **Ad populum Antiochenum** (homiliae 1–21), MPG 49: 15–222.
Cod: [99,130]

025 **Ad illuminandos catecheses 1–2** (series prima et secunda), MPG 49: 223–240.
Cod: [8,622]

026 **De diabolo tentatore** (homiliae 1–3), MPG 49: 241–276.
Cod: [13,490]

027 **De paenitentia** (homiliae 1–9), MPG 49: 277–350.
Homiliae 5, 7–9 sunt spuriae.
Cod: [32,309]

028 **In diem natalem**, MPG 49: 351–362.
Cod: [5,008]

029 **De baptismo Christi**, MPG 49: 363–372.
Cod: [3,769]

030 **De proditione Judae** (homiliae 1–2), MPG 49: 373–392.
Cod: [9,155]

031 **De coemeterio et de cruce**, MPG 49: 393–398.
Cod: [2,364]

032 **De cruce et latrone** (homilia 1), MPG 49: 399–408.
Cod: [3,775]

033 **De cruce et latrone** (homilia 2), MPG 49: 407–418.
Cod: [4,842]

034 **De resurrectione mortuorum**, MPG 50: 417ter–432.
Cod: [6,593]

035 **De resurrectione domini nostri Jesu Christi**, MPG 50: 433–442.
Cod: [3,687]

036 **In ascensionem domini nostri Jesu Christi**, MPG 50: 441–452.
Cod: [4,147]

037 **De sancta pentecoste** (homiliae 1–2), MPG 50: 453–470.
Cod: [7,521]

486 **De laudibus sancti Pauli apostoli** (homiliae 1–7), ed. A. Piédagnel, *Jean Chrysostome. Panégyriques de S. Paul* [*Sources chrétiennes* 300. Paris: Cerf, 1982]: 112–320.
Cod

039 **De sancto Meletio Antiocheno**, MPG 50: 515–520.
Cod: [2,229]

040 **In sanctum Lucianum martyrem**, MPG 50: 519–526.
Cod: [2,151]

041 **De sancto hieromartyre Babyla**, MPG 50: 527–534.
Cod: [2,176]

373 **De Babyla contra Julianum et gentiles**, ed. M. Schatkin, *Critical edition of, and introduction to, St. John Chrysostom's "De sancto Babyla, contra Iulianum et gentiles"* [*Diss. Fordham* (1967)]: 1–106.
Cod

042 **In Juventinum et Maximum martyres**, MPG 50: 571–578.
Cod: [2,284]

043 **De sancta Pelagia virgine et martyre**, MPG 50: 579–584.
Cod: [2,575]

044 **In sanctum Ignatium martyrem**, MPG 50: 587–596.
Cod: [4,140]

045 **In sanctum Eustathium Antiochenum**, MPG 50: 597–606.
Cod: [3,250]

046 **In sanctum Romanum**, MPG 50: 605–612.
Cod: [2,754]

047 **De Maccabeis** (homiliae 1–3), MPG 50: 617–628.
Cod: [4,560]

048 **De sanctis Bernice et Prosdoce**, MPG 50: 629–640.
Cod: [5,359]

049 **In quatriduanum Lazarum**, MPG 50: 641–644.
Cod: [1,326]

050 **De sanctis martyribus**, MPG 50: 645–654.
Cod: [3,225]

051 **Non esse ad gratiam concionandum**, MPG 50: 653–662.
Cod: [4,001]

052 **Homilia in martyres**, MPG 50: 661–666.
Cod: [1,232]

053 **In sanctum Julianum martyrem**, MPG 50: 665–676.
Cod: [4,066]

054 **In sanctum Barlaam martyrem**, MPG 50: 675–682.
Cod: [2,891]

055 **De sancto Droside martyre**, MPG 50: 683–694.
Cod: [4,429]

056 **In martyres Aegyptios**, MPG 50: 693–698.
Cod: [1,783]

057 **De sancto hieromartyre Phoca**, MPG 50: 699–706.
Cod: [3,035]

058 **De sanctis martyribus**, MPG 50: 705–712.
Cod: [2,472]

059 **De terrae motu**, MPG 50: 713–716.
Cod: [1,470]

060 **De fato et providentia** (orationes 1–6), MPG 50: 749–774.
Cod: [11,499]

061 **De decem millium talentorum debitore**, MPG 51: 17*–30.
Cod: [5,946]

062 **In illud:** *Pater, si possibile est, transeat*, MPG 51: 31–40.
Cod: [4,261]

063 **In paralyticum demissum per tectum**, MPG 51: 47–64.
Cod: [6,777]

064 **In principium Actorum** (homiliae 1–4), MPG 51: 65–112.
Cod: [20,383]

065 **De mutatione nominum** (homiliae 1–4), MPG 51: 113–156.
Cod: [19,043]

066 **De gloria in tribulationibus**, MPG 51: 155–164.
Cod: [3,931]

067 **In illud:** *Diligentibus deum omnia cooperantur in bonum*, MPG 51: 165–172.
Cod: [2,803]

068 **In illud:** *Si esurierit inimicus*, MPG 51: 171–186.
Cod: [6,442]

069 **In illud:** *Salutate Priscillam et Aquilam* (sermones 1–2), MPG 51: 187–208.
Cod: [9,110]

070 **In illud:** *Propter fornicationes uxorem*, MPG 51: 207–218.
Cod: [4,385]

071 **De libello repudii**, MPG 51: 217–226.
Cod: [3,482]

072 **Quales ducendae sint uxores**, MPG 51: 225–242.
Cod: [7,883]

073 **In dictum Pauli:** *Nolo vos ignorare*, MPG 51: 241–252.
Cod: [5,076]

074 **In dictum Pauli:** *Oportet haereses esse*, MPG 51: 251–260.
Cod: [3,690]

075 **De eleemosyna**, MPG 51: 261–272.
Cod: [4,931]

076 **In illud:** *Habentes eundem spiritum* (homiliae 1–3), MPG 51: 271–302.
Cod: [13,410]

077 **In illud:** *Utinam sustineretis modicum*, MPG 51: 301–310.
Cod: [3,941]

078 **De profectu evangelii**, MPG 51: 311–320.
Cod: [4,512]

079 **In illud:** *Vidua eligatur*, MPG 51: 321–338.
Cod: [7,161]

080 **In Heliam et viduam**, MPG 51: 337–348.
Cod: [4,132]

081 **De futurae vitae deliciis**, MPG 51: 347–354.
Cod: [2,529]

082 **Peccata fratrum non evulganda**, MPG 51: 353–364.
Cod: [4,610]

083 **Non esse desperandum**, MPG 51: 363–372.
Cod: [3,062]

084 **In illud:** *In faciem ei restiti*, MPG 51: 371–388.
Cod: [7,511]

089 **In Eutropium**, MPG 52: 391–396.
Cod: [2,169]

090 **Cum Saturninus et Aurelianus**, MPG 52: 413–420.
Cod: [2,137]

374 **De regressu**, ed. A. Wenger, "L'homélie de saint Jean Chrysostome 'à son retour d'Asie'," *Revue des études byzantines* 19 (1961) 114–122.
Cod

091 **Sermo antequam iret in exsilium**, MPG 52: 427*–432.
Cod: [1,936]

092 **Sermo cum iret in exsilium**, MPG 52: 435*–438.
Cod: [868]

375 **Post reditum a priore exsilio** (sermo 1), ed. B. de Montfaucon, *Sancti patris nostri Ioannis Chrysostomi opera omnia*, vol. 3. Paris: Guerin, 1721: 424.
Cod

093 **Post reditum a priore exsilio** (sermo 2), MPG 52: 443–448.
Cod: [2,014]

086 **Quod nemo laeditur nisi a se ipso**, ed. A.-M. Malingrey, *Lettre d'exil à Olympias et à tous les fidèles* [*Sources chrétiennes* 103. Paris: Cerf, 1964]: 56–144.
Cod: [8,618]

087 **Ad eos qui scandalizati sunt**, ed. A.-M. Malingrey, *Jean Chrysostome. Sur la providence de Dieu* [*Sources chrétiennes* 79. Paris: Cerf, 1961]: 52–276.
Cod: [20,875]

094 **Ad Innocentium papam** (epist. 1), MPG 52: 529–536.
Cod: [1,989]

095 **Ad Innocentium papam** (epist. 2), MPG 52: 535–536.
Cod: [570]

096 **Epistula ad episcopos, presbyteros et diaconos**, MPG 52: 541*–542*.
Cod: [680]

097 **Epistulae 18–242**, MPG 52: 623–748.
Epistulae 237–241 sunt spuriae.
Epistulae 1–17: Cf. Epistulae ad Olympiadem (2062 088).
Epistula 125: Cf. et Epistula ad Cyriacum (2062 376).
Epistula 233: Cf. et Epistula ad Antiochum (2062 344).
Cod: [47,866]

088 **Epistulae ad Olympiadem** (epist. 1–17), ed. A.-M. Malingrey, *Jean Chrysostome. Lettres à Olympias*, 2nd edn. [*Sources chrétiennes* 13 bis. Paris: Cerf, 1968]: 106–388.
Cod: [30,264]

344 **Epistula ad Antiochum** (epist. 233) [Sp.], ed. P.G. Nicolopoulos, Αἱ εἰς τὸν ᾽Ιωάννην τὸν Χρυσόστομον ἐσφαλμένως ἀποδιδόμεναι ἐπιστολαί. Athens: Tsiveriotes, 1973: 497.
Cod

376 **Epistula ad Cyriacum** (epist. 125 + recensiones), ed. Nicolopoulos, *op. cit.*, 381–391, 395–411, 413–419, 423–449.
Cod

098 **Laus Diodori episcopi**, MPG 52: 761–766.
Cod: [1,072]

099 **In sanctum pascha**, MPG 52: 765–772.
Cod: [2,811]

112 **In Genesim** (homiliae 1–67), MPG 53:21–385; 54:385–580.
Cod: [283,104]

113 **In Genesim** (sermones 1–9), MPG 54: 581–630.
Cod: [22,713]

114 **De Anna** (sermones 1–5), MPG 54: 631–676.
Cod: [20,369]

115 **De Davide et Saule** (homiliae 1–3), MPG 54: 675–708.
Cod: [14,861]

143 **Expositiones in Psalmos**, MPG 55: 39–498.
Cod: [178,466]

144 **In illud:** *Ne timueritis cum dives factus fuerit homo* (homiliae 1–2), MPG 55: 499–518.
Cod: [6,878]

145 **In Psalmum 145**, MPG 55: 519–528.
Cod: [3,258]

497 **In Isaiam**, ed. J. Dumortier, *Jean Chrysostome. Commentaire sur Isaïe* [*Sources chrétiennes* 304. Paris: Cerf, 1983]: 36–356.
Cod

498 **In illud:** *Vidi dominum* (homiliae 1–6), ed. J. Dumortier, *Jean Chrysostome. Homélies sur Ozias* [*Sources chrétiennes* 277. Paris: Cerf, 1981]: 42–228.
Cod

148 **In illud Isaiae:** *Ego dominus deus feci lumen*, MPG 56: 141–152.
Cod: [3,982]

149 **In illud:** *Domine, non est in homine*, MPG 56: 153–162.
Cod: [3,258]

150 **De prophetiarum obscuritate** (homiliae 1–2), MPG 56: 163–192.
Cod: [10,498]

180 **In illud:** *Filius ex se nihil facit*, MPG 56: 247–256.
Cod: [3,258]

175 **Contra ludos et theatra**, MPG 56: 263–270.
Cod: [2,534]

151 **In illud:** *Hoc scitote quod in novissimis diebus*, MPG 56: 271–280.
Cod: [3,258]

152 **In Matthaeum** (homiliae 1–90), MPG 57:13–472; 58:471–794.
Cod: [458,292]

153 **In Joannem** (homiliae 1–88), MPG 59: 23–482.
Cod: [166,158]

154 **In Acta apostolorum** (homiliae 1–55), MPG 60: 13–384.
Cod: [136,811]

155 **In epistulam ad Romanos** (homiliae 1–32), MPG 60: 391–682.
Cod: [129,990]

156 **In epistulam i ad Corinthios** (argumentum et homiliae 1–44), MPG 61: 9–382.
Cod: [135,026]

157 **In epistulam ii ad Corinthios** (argumentum et homiliae 1–30), MPG 61: 381–610.
Cod: [82,898]

158 **In epistulam ad Galatas commentarius**, MPG 61: 611–682.
Cod: [25,702]

159 **In epistulam ad Ephesios** (argumentum et homiliae 1–24), MPG 62: 9–176.
Cod: [60,454]

160 **In epistulam ad Philippenses** (argumentum et homiliae 1–15), MPG 62: 177–298.
Cod: [43,802]

161 **In epistulam ad Colossenses** (homiliae 1–12), MPG 62: 299–392.
Cod: [33,666]

162 **In epistulam i ad Thessalonicenses** (homiliae 1–11), MPG 62: 391–468.
Cod: [27,874]

163 **In epistulam ii ad Thessalonicenses** (homiliae 1–5), MPG 62: 467–500.
Cod: [11,946]

164 **In epistulam i ad Timotheum** (argumentum et homiliae 1–18), MPG 62: 501–600.
Cod: [35,838]

165 **In epistulam ii ad Timotheum** (homiliae 1–10), MPG 62: 599–662.
Cod: [22,806]

166 **In epistulam ad Titum** (homiliae 1–6), MPG 62: 663–700.
Cod: [13,394]

167 **In epistulam ad Philemonem** (argumentum et homiliae 1–3), MPG 62: 701–720.
Cod: [6,878]

168 **In epistulam ad Hebraeos** (argumentum et homiliae 1–34), MPG 63: 9–236.
Cod: [82,174]

169 **Homilia dicta postquam reliquiae martyrum**, MPG 63: 467–472.
Cod: [1,810]

170 **Homilia dicta praesente imperatore**, MPG 63: 473–478.
Cod: [1,810]

171 **Quod frequenter conveniendum sit**, MPG 63: 461–468.
Cod: [2,534]

172 **Adversus eos qui non adfuerant**, MPG 63: 477–486.
Cod: [3,258]

173 **De studio praesentium**, MPG 63: 485–492.
Cod: [2,534]

174 **Adversus catharos**, MPG 63: 491–494.
Cod: [724]

176 **Homilia dicta in templo sanctae Anastasiae**, MPG 63: 493–500.
Cod: [2,534]

177 **Homilia habita postquam presbyter Gothus**, MPG 63: 499–510.
Cod: [3,982]

178 **In illud:** *Pater meus usque modo operatur*, MPG 63: 511–516.
Cod: [2,172]

179 **In illud:** *Messis quidem multa*, MPG 63: 515–524.
Cod: [3,258]

181 **De Eleazaro et septem pueris**, MPG 63: 523–530.
Cod: [2,534]

182 **In poenitentiam Ninivitarum**, MPG 64: 424–433.
Cod: [3,258]

183 **Commentarius in Job** (prooemium tantum), MPG 64: 504–506.
Cod: [362]

184 **Fragmenta in Job** (in catenis), MPG 64: 505–656.
Q: [27,331]

185 **Fragmenta in Proverbia** (in catenis), MPG 64: 660–740.
Q: [14,480]

186 **Fragmenta in Jeremiam** (in catenis), MPG 64: 740–1037.
Q: [53,938]

187 **Fragmenta in epistulas catholicas**, MPG 64: 1040–1061.
Q: [3,982]

378 **De inani gloria et de educandis liberis**, ed. A.-M. Malingrey, *Jean Chrysostome. Sur la vaine gloire et l'éducation des enfants* [*Sources chrétiennes* 188. Paris: Cerf, 1972]: 64–196.
Cod: [8,375]

379 **In illud:** *Apparuit gratia dei omnibus hominibus*, ed. A. Wenger, "Une homélie inédite de Jean Chrysostome sur l'épiphanie," *Revue des études byzantines* 29 (1971) 123–135.
Cod

380 **Catechesis de juramento** (series prima), ed. A. Papadopoulos-Kerameus, *Varia Graeca sacra*. St. Petersburg: Kirschbaum, 1909 (repr. Leipzig: Zentralantiquariat der DDR, 1975): 154–166.
Cod: [3,365]

381 **Catechesis ultima ad baptizandos** (series prima), ed. Papadopoulos-Kerameus, *op. cit.*, 166–175.
Cod: [2,589]

382 **Catecheses ad illuminandos 1–8** (series tertia), ed. A. Wenger, *Jean Chrysostome. Huit catéchèses baptismales*, 2nd edn. [*Sources chrétiennes* 50 bis. Paris: Cerf, 1970]: 108–260.
Homilia 3 = Ad neophytos.
Cod: [35,167]

383 **Fragmenta ex homiliis diversis**, ed. S. Haidacher, "Chrysostomos-Fragmente im Maximos-Florilegium und in den Sacra Parallela," *Byzantinische Zeitschrift* 16 (1907) 173–186.
Ex homilia ὅτι χρὴ γενναίως φέρειν τὴν πενίαν (frr. 6–8): pp. 173–175.
Ex homilia εἰς τὴν χήραν τὴν τὰ δύο λεπτὰ προσενέγκασαν ἐν τῷ γαζοφυλακίῳ (fr. 9): p. 175.
Ex homilia in sanctum Stephanum (fr. 10): p. 176.
Ex homilia in sanctum Romanum martyrem (fr. 11): p. 176.
Ex homilia de Constantino imperatore (fr. 12): p. 176.
Ἐκ τοῦ εἰς τὰς Βασιλείας γ′ λόγου (fr. 13): pp. 176–177.
Εἰς τὴν β′ Βασιλειῶν (fr. 14): p. 177.
Ἐκ τῆς εἰς τὸν Βασίλειον ὁμιλίας (fr. 15): p. 177.
In martyrem Julianum (fr. 16): p. 177.
In Lazarum (fr. 17): p. 178.
Ἐκ τῆς πη′ ἐπιστολῆς (fr. 18): p. 178.
Fragmenta varia sine lemmate (frr. 19–56): pp. 178–186.
Q

384 **Fragmenta ex homiliis diversis**, ed. G. Bardy, "Les citations de saint Jean Chrysostome dans le florilège du cod. Vatican. graec. 1142," *Re-*

vue de l'Orient chrétien 23 (1922–1923) 430–431.

Εἰς τὸ μυστικὸν δεῖπνον: pp. 430–431.
Εἰς τὸ πάθος τοῦ κυρίου: p. 431.

386 **Fragmentum in Matth. 3.16** (ap. Nilum Ancyranum, epist. 293), MPG 79: 345.
Q

387 **Fragmentum incertum** (ap. Nilum Ancyranum, epist. 294), MPG 79: 345–348.
Q

385 **Fragmenta incerta in Eclogis,** ed. S. Haidacher, "Studien über Chrysostomus-Eklogen," *Österreichische Akademie der Wissenschfaten,* Philosoph.-hist. Kl., Sitzungsberichte, Bd. 144, Abh. 4. Vienna: Österreichische Akademie der Wissenschaften, 1902: 23–28.
Q

388 **In parabolam de ficu** (ap. Anastasium Sinaitam, *Interrogationes et responsiones*), MPG 89: 365–368.
Q

389 **De jejunio** (ap. Anastasium Sinaitam, *Interrogationes et responsiones*), MPG 89: 340.
Q

390 **In Petrum, Jacobum et Joannem** (ap. Eustratium Constantinopolitanum, *De statu animarum post mortem*), ed. L. Allacci, *De utriusque ecclesiae occidentalis perpetua...consensione.* Rome: Maronita, 1655.
Q

391 **Ex enarratione in epistulam ad Hebraeos** (ap. Joannem Damascenum, *De imaginibus*, orat. 1 & 3), MPG 94: 1269–1272, 1361–1364.
Q

392 **Ex narratione in parabolam seminis** (ap. Joannem Damascenum, *De imaginibus*, orat. 2), MPG 94: 1313.
Q

393 **Fragmentum incertum** (ap. Joannem Damascenum, *De imaginibus*, orat. 3), MPG 94: 1396–1397.
Q

394 **In sanctum Flavianum Antiochenum** (ap. Joannem Damascenum, *De imaginibus*, orat. 3), MPG 94: 1400.
Q

395 **Contra Julianum** (ap. Joannem Damascenum, *De imaginibus*, orat. 3), MPG 94: 1408.
Q

401 **Daemones non gubernare mundum** (ap. Georgium, *Chronicon*), ed. C. de Boor, *Georgii monachi chronicon,* vol. 1. Leipzig: Teubner, 1904 (repr. Stuttgart: 1978 (1st edn. corr. P. Wirth)): 108–112.
Q

116 **Comparatio regis et monachi** [Dub.], MPG 47: 387–392.
Cod: [2,249]

117 **Ascetam facetiis uti non debere** [Sp.], MPG 48: 1055–1060.
Cod: [2,625]

118 **De jejunio et eleemosyna** [Sp.], MPG 48: 1059–1062.
Cod: [1,737]

119 **De sacerdotio** (lib. 7) [Dub.], MPG 48: 1067–1070.
De sacerdotio (lib. 1–6): Cf. 2062 085.
Cod: [1,672]

120 **Christi discipulum benignum esse debere** [Sp.], MPG 48: 1069–1072.
Cod: [1,334]

121 **De fugienda simulata specie** [Sp.], MPG 48: 1073–1076.
Cod: [1,163]

122 **Contra Judaeos, gentiles et haereticos** [Dub.], MPG 48: 1075–1080.
Cod: [2,987]

123 **De sancta trinitate** [Sp.], MPG 48: 1087–1096.
Cod: [5,347]

402 **In sanctam Pelagiam** [Sp.], ed. P.F. de' Cavalieri, *Note agiografiche* 8 [*Studi e Testi* 65. Vatican City: Biblioteca Apostolica Vaticana, 1935]: 301–303.
Cod

124 **In sanctum Romanum** (homilia 2) [Sp.], MPG 50: 611–618.
Cod: [1,997]

125 **In proditionem Judae** [Dub.], MPG 50: 715–720.
Cod: [1,152]

126 **In sanctum Bassum** [Dub.], MPG 50: 719–726.
Cod: [2,157]

127 **In sanctos Petrum et Heliam** [Sp.], MPG 50: 725–736.
Cod: [4,861]

128 **De beato Abraham** [Sp.], MPG 50: 737–746.
Cod: [3,754]

129 **De sancta Thecla martyre** [Sp.], MPG 50: 745–748.
Cf. et 2062 488.
Cod: [964]

488 **De sancta Thecla martyre** (e cod. Athon. Panteleimon 58) [Sp.], ed. M. Aubineau, "Le panégyrique de Thècle attribué à Jean Chrysostome: la fin retrouvée d'un texte mutilé," *Analecta Bollandiana* 93 (1975) 351–352.
Cf. et 2062 129.
Cod

130 **De precatione** (orat. 1–2) [Sp.], MPG 50: 775–786.
Cod: [4,873]

131 **In oraculum Zachariae redditum** [Sp.], MPG 50: 785–788.
Cod: [1,138]

132 **In laudem conceptionis sancti Joannis Baptistae** [Sp.], MPG 50: 787–792.
Cod: [2,228]

133 **In annuntiationem beatae virginis** [Sp.], MPG 50: 791–796.
Cod: [1,446]

134 **In illud:** *Exiit edictum* [Dub.], MPG 50: 795–800.
Cod: [2,844]

135 **In sanctum Joannem praecursorem** [Sp.], MPG 50: 801–806.
Cod: [2,397]

136 **In sanctam theophaniam seu baptismum Christi** [Sp.], MPG 50: 805–808.
Cod: [1,404]

137 **De occursu domini, de deipara et Symeone** [Sp.], MPG 50: 807–812.
Cod: [2,207]

138 **In sancta et magna parasceue** [Dub.], MPG 50: 811–816.
Cod: [2,243]

139 **In venerabilem crucem sermo** [Sp.], MPG 50: 815–820.
Cod: [2,326]

140 **In triduanam resurrectionem domini** [Sp.], MPG 50: 821–824.
Cod: [1,796]

141 **De angusta porta et in orationem dominicam** [Sp.], MPG 51: 41–48.
Cod: [3,179]

142 **Homilia de capto Eutropio** [Sp.], MPG 52: 395–414.
Cod: [8,292]

101 **De Chananaea** [Dub.], MPG 52: 449–460.
Cod: [4,967]

102 **Epistula ad Caesarium** [Sp.], MPG 52: 755–760.
Cod: [516]

499 **Epistula ad Caesarium** [Sp.], ed. Nicolopoulos, *op. cit.*, 513–518.
Cod

100 **In ascensionem** (sermo 1) [Sp.], MPG 52: 791–794.
Cod: [775]

103 **In ascensionem** (sermo 2) [Sp.], MPG 52: 793–796.
Cod: [1,641]

104 **In ascensionem** (sermo 3) [Sp.], MPG 52: 797–800.
Cod: [1,104]

105 **In ascensionem** (sermo 4) [Sp.], MPG 52: 799–802.
Cod: [1,681]

106 **In ascensionem** (sermo 5) [Sp.], MPG 52: 801–802.
Cod: [493]

107 **In pentecosten** (sermo 1) [Sp.], MPG 52: 803–808.
Cod: [2,319]

108 **In pentecosten** (sermo 2) [Sp.], MPG 52: 807–809.
Cod: [1,227]

109 **In pentecosten** (sermo 3) [Sp.], MPG 52: 809–812.
Cod: [1,241]

110 **De adoratione pretiosae crucis** [Sp.], MPG 52: 835–840.
Cod: [2,803]

111 **De confessione pretiosae crucis** [Sp.], MPG 52: 841–844.
Cod: [1,906]

196 **In Psalmum 50** [Sp.], MPG 55: 527–532.
Q: [1,316]

197 **Prooemia in Psalmos** (fragmenta) [Sp.], MPG 55: 531–538.
Prooemium in Psalmos: pp. 531–534.
Argumentum Psalmorum: pp. 533–538.
Q: [4,969]

198 **In illud: *Verumtamen frustra conturbatur*** [Sp.], MPG 55: 559–564.
Cod: [6,405]

199 **In Psalmum 50** (homilia 1) [Sp.], MPG 55: 565–575.
Cf. et 2062 500.
Cod: [6,588]

500 **In Psalmum 50** (homilia 1) [Sp.] (*P. Berol.* 6788 A), ed. K. Treu, "Ein Berliner Chrysostomos-Papyrus (P. 6788 A)," *Studia patristica* 12 (1975) 74–75.
Cf. et 2062 199.
Pap

200 **In Psalmum 50** (homilia 2) [Sp.], MPG 55: 575–588.
Cod: [7,726]

201 **In Psalmum 75** [Sp.], MPG 55: 593–598.
Cod: [1,953]

202 **De turture seu de ecclesia sermo** [Sp.], MPG 55: 599–602.
Cod: [2,087]

203 **In Psalmum 92** [Sp.], MPG 55: 611–616.
Cod: [1,992]

204 **In Psalmum 94** [Sp.], MPG 55: 615–620.
Cod: [1,809]

205 **In Psalmum 100** [Sp.], MPG 55: 629–636.
Cod: [3,856]

206 **In Psalmos 101–107** [Sp.], MPG 55: 635–674.
Q: [22,775]

207 **In Psalmum 118** (homiliae 1–3) [Sp.], MPG 55: 675–708.
Cod: [19,377]

208 **In Psalmum 139** [Sp.], MPG 55: 707–710.
Cod: [1,749]

209 **Interpretatio in Danielem prophetam** [Sp.], MPG 56: 193–246.
Cod: [19,157]

210 **De Melchisedech** [Sp.], MPG 56: 257–262.
Cod: [2,148]

211 **De perfecta caritate** [Sp.], MPG 56: 279–290.
Cod: [5,087]

212 **De continentia** [Dub.], ed. S. Haidacher, "Drei unedierte Chrysostomus-Texte einer Baseler Handschrift," *Zeitschrift für katholische Theologie* 30 (1906) 575–581.
Cod

213 **Synopsis scripturae sacrae** [Dub.], MPG 56: 313–386.
Cod: [29,282]

214 **In natalem Christi diem** [Dub.], MPG 56: 385–394.
Cod: [2,940]

215 **In Genesim** (sermo 1) [Sp.], MPG 56: 519–522.
Cod: [1,575]

216 **In Genesim** (sermo 3) [Sp.], MPG 56: 525–538.
Cod: [7,795]

217 **Contra theatra** [Sp.], MPG 56: 541–554.
Cod: [8,442]

218 **In Job** (sermones 1–4) [Sp.], MPG 56: 563–582.
Cod: [12,496]

219 **In Eliam prophetam** [Sp.], MPG 56: 583–586.
Cod: [2,015]

220 **De Joseph et de castitate** [Sp.], MPG 56: 587–590.
Cod: [2,005]

221 **De Susanna** [Sp.], MPG 56: 589–594.
Cod: [2,493]

222 **De tribus pueris** [Sp.], MPG 56: 593–600.
Cod: [3,116]

224 **In decollationem sancti Joannis** [Sp.], MPG 59: 485–490.
Cod: [2,670]

225 **In praecursorem domini** [Sp.], MPG 59: 489–492.
Cod: [690]

226 **In Petrum et Paulum** [Sp.], MPG 59: 491–496.
Cod: [1,568]

227 **In duodecim apostolos** [Sp.], MPG 59: 495–498.
Cod: [1,040]

228 **In sanctum Thomam apostolum** [Sp.], MPG 59: 497–500.
Cod: [1,184]

229 **In sanctum Stephanum protomartyrem** [Sp.], MPG 59: 501–508.
Cod: [3,689]

230 **In illud: *Sufficit tibi gratia mea*** [Sp.], MPG 59: 507–516.
Cod: [3,868]

231 **In parabolam de filio prodigo** [Sp.], MPG 59: 515–522.
Cod: [3,562]

232 **In saltationem Herodiadis** [Sp.], MPG 59: 521–526.
Cod: [3,302]

233 **In illud: *Collegerunt Judaei*** [Sp.], MPG 59: 525–528.
Cod: [1,160]

234 **In decem virgines** [Sp.], MPG 59: 527–532.
Cod: [1,928]

235 **In Samaritanam** [Sp.], MPG 59: 535–542.
Cod: [4,655]

236 **De caeco nato** [Sp.], MPG 59: 543–554.
Cod: [7,308]

237 **De pseudoprophetis** [Sp.], MPG 59: 553–568.
Cod: [9,263]

238 **De circo** [Sp.], MPG 59: 567–570.
Cod: [1,208]

239 **In illud: *Attendite ne eleemosynam*** [Sp.], MPG 59: 571–574.
Cod: [2,023]

240 **In principium indictionis, in martyres** [Sp.], MPG 59: 575–578.
Cod: [1,785]

241 **In illud: *Simile est regnum caelorum patri familias*** [Sp.], MPG 59: 577–586.
Cod: [4,043]

242 **In parabolam de ficu** [Sp.], MPG 59: 585–590.
Cod: [2,556]

243 **De pharisaeo** [Sp.], MPG 59: 589–592.
Cod: [1,251]

244 **De Lazaro et divite** [Sp.], MPG 59: 591–596.
Cod: [1,677]

245 **In publicanum et pharisaeum** [Sp.], MPG 59: 595–600.
Cod: [1,909]

246 **De caeco et Zacchaeo** [Sp.], MPG 59: 599–610.
Cod: [4,802]

247 **In Joannem theologum** [Sp.], MPG 59: 609–614.
Cod: [2,633]

248 **De negatione Petri** [Sp.], MPG 59: 613–620.
Cod: [2,693]

249 **In secundum domini adventum** [Sp.], MPG 59: 619–628.
Cod: [3,588]

250 **Interpretatio orationis *Pater noster*** [Sp.], MPG 59: 627–628.
Cod: [480]

251 **In principium indictionis** [Sp.], MPG 59: 673–674.
Cod: [890]

252 **In venerandum crucem** [Sp.], MPG 59: 675–678.
Cod: [1,897]

253 **In exaltationem venerandae crucis** [Sp.], MPG 59: 679–682.
Cod: [1,931]

254 **In sanctum Stephanum** [Sp.], MPG 59: 699–702.
Cod: [825]

255 **In mediam hebdomadam jejuniorum** [Sp.], MPG 59: 701–704.
Cod: [728]

256 **In ramos palmarum** [Sp.], MPG 59: 703–708.
Cod: [2,988]

257 **Contra haereticos et in sanctam deiparam** [Sp.], MPG 59: 709–714.
Cod: [2,284]

258 **In latronem** [Sp.], MPG 59: 719–722.
Cod: [1,264]

259 **Sermo catecheticus in pascha** [Sp.], MPG 59: 721–724.
Cod: [378]

260 **In sanctum pascha** (sermo 1) [Sp.], ed. P. Nautin, *Homélies pascales*, vol. 2 [*Sources chrétiennes* 36. Paris: Cerf, 1953]: 55–75.
Cod

261 **In sanctum pascha** (sermo 2) [Sp.], ed. Nautin, *op. cit.*, 77–101.
Cod

262 **In sanctum pascha** (sermo 3) [Sp.], ed. Nautin, *op. cit.*, 103–117.
Cod

263 **In sanctum pascha** (sermo 4) [Sp.], MPG 59: 731–732.
Cod: [941]

264 **In sanctum pascha** (sermo 5) [Sp.], MPG 59: 731–736.
Cod: [2,008]

265 **In sanctum pascha** (sermo 6) [Sp.], ed. P. Nautin, *Homélies pascales*, vol. 1 [*Sources chrétiennes* 27. Paris: Cerf, 1950]: 117–191.
Cod

266 **In sanctum pascha** (sermo 7) [Sp.], ed. F. Floëri and P. Nautin, *Homélies pascales*, vol. 3 [*Sources chrétiennes* 48. Paris: Cerf, 1957]: 111–173.
Cod

267 **In synaxim archangelorum** [Sp.], MPG 59: 755–756.
Cod: [945]

268 **De paenitentia** [Sp.], MPG 59: 757–766.
Cod: [5,017]

269 **De paenitentia** (sermo 1) [Sp.], MPG 60: 681–700.
Cod: [11,653]

270 **De paenitentia** (sermo 2) [Sp.], MPG 60: 699–706.
Cod: [3,894]

271 **De paenitentia** (sermo 3) [Sp.], MPG 60: 705–708.
Cod: [1,411]

272 **De eleemosyna** [Sp.], MPG 60: 707–712.
Cod: [2,442]

273 **De jejunio** (sermones 1–7) [Sp.], MPG 60: 711–724.
Cod: [8,014]

274 **De patientia** (sermo 1) [Dub.], MPG 60: 723–730.
Cod: [4,330]

275 **De patientia** (sermo 2) [Dub.], MPG 60: 729–736.
Cod: [3,493]

276 **De salute animae** [Sp.], MPG 60: 735–738.
Cod: [1,914]

277 **In catechumenos** [Sp.], MPG 60: 739–742.
Cod: [1,726]

278 **De corruptoribus virginum** [Sp.], MPG 60: 741–744.
Cod: [1,873]

279 **Contra haereticos** [Sp.], MPG 60: 745–748.
Cod: [1,223]

280 **De eleemosyna** [Sp.], MPG 60: 747–752.
Cod: [2,742]

281 **Epistula ad monachos** [Sp.], ed. Nicolopoulos, *op. cit.*, 481–493.
Cod

282 **In annuntiationem sanctissimae deiparae** [Sp.], MPG 60: 755–760.
Cod: [1,875]

283 **De remissione peccatorum** [Sp.], MPG 60: 759–764.
Cod: [2,587]

284 **De non judicando proximo** [Sp.], MPG 60: 763–766.
Cod: [1,730]

285 **De paenitentia** [Sp.], MPG 60: 765–768.
Cod: [1,216]

286 **De spe** [Sp.], MPG 60: 771–774.
Cod: [1,216]

287 **De caritate** [Sp.], MPG 60: 773–776.
Cod: [769]

288 **Caritatem secundum deum rem esse deo dignam** [Sp.], MPG 61: 681–684.
Cod: [1,359]

289 **In proditionem Judae** [Sp.], MPG 61: 687–690.
Cod: [800]

290 **In illud: Memor fui dei** [Sp.], MPG 61: 689–698.
Cod: [5,551]

291 **In Rachelem et infantes** [Sp.], MPG 61: 697–700.
Cod: [1,129]

292 **In Herodem et infantes** [Sp.], MPG 61: 699–702.
Cod: [1,312]

293 **In Martham, Mariam et Lazarum** [Sp.], MPG 61: 701–706.
Cod: [3,040]

294 **In illud: Exeuntes pharisaei** [Sp.], MPG 61: 705–710.
Cod: [2,075]

295 **In meretricem et in pharisaeum** [Sp.], MPG 61: 709–712.
Cod: [680]

296 **In assumptionem domini nostri Jesu Christi** [Sp.], MPG 61: 711–712.
Cod: [912]

297 **In ramos palmarum** [Sp.], MPG 61: 715–720.
Cod: [2,341]

298 **In laudem sancti Joannis theologi** (homilia 1) [Sp.], MPG 61: 719–720.
Cod: [830]

299 **In laudem sancti Joannis theologi** (homilia 2) [Sp.], MPG 61: 719–722.
Cod: [693]

300 **In transfigurationem** [Sp.], MPG 61: 721–724.
Cod: [1,101]

301 **De siccitate** [Sp.], MPG 61: 723–726.
Cod: [1,328]

302 **In Jordanum fluvium** [Sp.], MPG 61: 725–728.
Cod: [1,353]

303 **In pharisaeum et meretricem** [Sp.], MPG 61: 727–734.
Cod: [3,530]

304 **In Christi natalem diem** [Sp.], MPG 61: 737–738.
Cod: [1,199]

305 **In illud: Ascendit dominus in templo** [Sp.], MPG 61: 739–742.
Cod: [1,838]

306 **In mediam pentecosten** [Sp.], MPG 61: 741–744.
Cod: [986]

307 **In Samaritanam, in die mediae pentecostes** [Sp.], MPG 61: 743–746.
Cod: [1,046]

308 **In illud: Pater si possibile est** [Sp.], MPG 61: 751–756.
Cod: [2,853]

309 In illud: *Homo quidam descendebat* [Sp.], MPG 61: 755-758.
Cod: [1,013]

310 In natale sancti Joannis prophetae [Sp.], MPG 61: 757-762.
Cod: [3,024]

311 In natale domini nostri Jesu Christi [Sp.], MPG 61: 763-768.
Cod: [2,058]

312 In Zacchaeum publicanum [Sp.], MPG 61: 767-768.
Cod: [1,032]

313 In centurionem [Sp.], MPG 61: 769-772.
Cod: [2,677]

314 In illud: *Exiit qui seminat* [Sp.], MPG 61: 771-776.
Cod: [1,989]

315 In drachmam et in illud: *Homo quidam habebat duos filios* [Sp.], MPG 61: 781-784.
Cod: [1,656]

316 De jejunio [Sp.], MPG 61: 787-790.
Cod: [1,452]

317 In filium viduae [Sp.], MPG 61: 789-794.
Cod: [1,936]

318 In publicanum et pharisaeum [Sp.], MPG 62: 723-728.
Cod: [2,521]

319 In ingressum sanctorum jejuniorum [Sp.], MPG 62: 727-728.
Cod: [488]

320 De jejunio, dominica quinta jejuniorum [Sp.], MPG 62: 731-732.
Cod: [856]

321 De jejunio [Sp.], MPG 62: 731-738.
Cod: [3,028]

322 De oratione [Dub.], MPG 62: 737-740.
Cod: [1,031]

323 In illud: *Ignem veni mittere in terram* [Sp.], MPG 62: 739-742.
Cod: [1,691]

324 Admonitiones spiritales [Sp.], MPG 62: 741-744.
Cod: [1,584]

325 In principium jejuniorum [Sp.], MPG 62: 745-748.
Cod: [1,418]

326 In adorationem venerandae crucis [Sp.], MPG 62: 747-754.
Cod: [3,567]

327 In resurrectionem domini [Sp.], MPG 62: 753-756.
Cod: [816]

328 In parabolam Samaritani [Sp.], MPG 62: 755-758.
Cod: [1,505]

329 De jejunio, MPG 62: 757-760.
Cod: [679]

330 De jejunio, de Davide [Sp.], MPG 62: 759-764.
Cod: [3,137]

331 In annuntiationem deiparae [Sp.], MPG 62: 763-770.
Cod: [3,119]

332 De eleemosyna [Sp.], MPG 62: 769-770.
Cod: [1,165]

333 De caritate [Sp.], MPG 62: 769-772.
Cod: [1,062]

334 In Lazarum (homilia 1) [Sp.], MPG 62: 771-776.
Cod: [2,018]

335 In Lazarum (homilia 2) [Sp.], MPG 62: 775-778.
Cod: [1,080]

336 In Lazarum (homilia 3) [Sp.], MPG 62: 777-780.
Cod: [602]

337 De mansuetudine sermo [Sp.], MPG 63: 549-556.
Cod: [2,535]

338 Eclogae i–xlviii ex diversis homiliis [Sp.], MPG 63: 567-902.
Cod: [151,482]

339 Liturgia (forma brevior juxta cod. Barber. gr. 336), ed. F.E. Brightman, *Liturgies eastern and western*, vol. 1. Oxford: Clarendon Press, 1896: 309-344.
Cod

340 Liturgia (forma brevior juxta cod. Vat. gr.), ed. N. Krasnoselčev, *Svjedjenija o njekotoryh liturgičeskich rukopisjah Vatikanskoj Biblioteki.* Kazan, 1885: 283-295.
Cod

341 Liturgia (forma brevior juxta cod. Leningr. gr. 226), ed. M.I. Orlov, *Liturgija svjatogo Vasilija Velikago.* St. Petersburg, 1909: 384-404.
Cod

342 Liturgia (forma brevior Constantinopolitana juxta cod. Sevastianov 474), ed. Krasnoselčev, *op. cit.,* 237-280.
Cod

343 Liturgia (forma integra hodierna), ed. Brightman, *op. cit.,* 353-399.
Cod

345 Oratio ante lectionem [Sp.], MPG 63: 923-924.
Cod: [81]

346 Oratio secunda [Sp.], MPG 63: 923-928.
Cod: [1,593]

347 In novam dominicam et in apostolum Thomam [Sp.], MPG 63: 927-930.
Cod: [2,007]

348 In sanctum Stephanum (homilia 1) [Sp.], MPG 63: 929-932.
Cod: [1,032]

349 In sanctum Stephanum (homilia 2) [Sp.], MPG 63: 931-934.
Cod: [404]

350 In sanctum Stephanum (homilia 3) [Sp.], MPG 63: 933-934.
Cod: [420]

351 De patientia et de consummatione huius saeculi [Sp.], MPG 63: 937-942.
Cod: [2,574]

352 De paenitentia et in lectionem de Davide et de uxore Uriae [Sp.], MPG 64: 11-16.
Cod: [1,919]

353 **De iis qui in jejunio continenter vivunt** [Sp.], MPG 64: 15–16.
Cod: [832]

354 **Sermo exhortatorius de temperantia** [Sp.], MPG 64: 17–18.
Cod: [560]

355 **Quod grave sit dei clementiam contemnere** [Dub.], MPG 64: 17–18.
Cod: [150]

356 **In sanguinis fluxu laborantem** [Sp.], MPG 64: 17–20.
Cod: [1,377]

357 **Quod mari similis sit haec vita** [Sp.], MPG 64: 19–22.
Cod: [1,229]

358 **In illud: *Simile est regnum caelorum grano sinapis*** [Sp.], MPG 64: 21–26.
Cod: [1,559]

359 **In illud: *Si qua in Christo nova creatura*** [Sp.], MPG 64: 25–34.
Cod: [6,001]

360 **In evangelii dictum et de virginitate** [Sp.], MPG 64: 37–44.
Cod: [3,457]

361 **De cognitione dei et in sancta theophania** [Sp.], MPG 64: 43–46.
Cod: [1,098]

362 **In lacum Genesareth et in sanctum Petrum apostolum** [Sp.], MPG 64: 47–52.
Cod: [2,608]

363 **De eleemosyna** [Sp.], MPG 64: 433–444.
Cod: [2,183]

364 **Ad eos qui magni aestimant opes** [Sp.], MPG 64: 453–461.
Cod: [1,242]

365 **De precatione** [Sp.], MPG 64: 461–465.
Cod: [1,176]

366 **De virtute animi** [Sp.], MPG 64: 473–480.
Cod: [1,418]

367 **Ad Eudoxiam** (epist. 1–7) [Sp.], ed. Nicolopoulos, *op. cit.*, 286, 287, 289–290, 295–297, 503–504, 507.
Q, Cod

368 **Precatio in obsessos** [Sp.], MPG 64: 1061.
Cod: [123]

369 **Precatio** [Sp.], MPG 64: 1061–1064.
Cod: [88]

370 **Precatio** [Sp.], MPG 64: 1064.
Cod: [103]

371 **Precatio** [Sp.], MPG 64: 1064–1068.
Cod: [904]

403 **De oratione Annae et quod utilis est paupertas**, *Savile* 5: 78–83.
Cod

404 **In publicanum et pharisaeum**, *Savile* 5: 261–264.
Cod

405 **Quod stantem non superbire et lapsum non desperare oportet**, *Savile* 5: 351–355.
Cod

406 **In illud: *Voluntarie enim peccantibus*,** *Savile* 5: 807–814.
Cod

407 **In vivificam sepulturam et triduanam resurrectionem Christi**, *Savile* 5: 912–916.
Cod

408 **De jejunio, et quod optimum sacrificium est beneficia dei agnoscere**, *Savile* 6: 886–889.
Cod

409 **De jejunio sanctae quadragesimae, et quod ignauorum nulla erit excusatio**, *Savile* 6: 889–893.
Cod

410 **Quod animae curam curae corporis praeferre debemus**, *Savile* 6: 893–896.
Cod

411 **De non vituperandis sacerdotibus**, *Savile* 6: 896–902.
Cod

412 **In transfigurationem domini**, *Savile* 7: 339–340.
Cod

413 **In natale domini et in sanctam Mariam genitricem** [Sp.], ed. F.J. Leroy, "Une nouvelle homélie acrostiche sur la nativité," *Muséon* 77 (1964) 163–173.
Cod

414 **Visio Danielis**, ed. A. Vassiliev, *Anecdota Graeco-Byzantina*, vol. 1. Moscow: Imperial University Press, 1893: 33–38.
Cod

415 **De cruce et latrone** [Sp.], ed. A. Wenger, "Le sermon lxxx de la collection augustinienne de Mai restitué à Sévérien de Gabala," *Augustinus Magister. Congrès international augustinien* 1. Paris: Études Augustiniennes, 1954: 177–182.
Cod

416 **In recens baptizatos et in sanctum pascha** [Sp.], ed. F. Combefis, *Sancti Ioannis Chrysostomi de educandis liberis liber aureus*. Paris: Bertier, 1656: 169–177.
Cod

417 **In infirmos**, ed. Vassiliev, *op. cit.*, 323–327.
Cod

418 **In omnes sanctos** [Dub.], ed. K.I. Dyobouniotes, "ʿΟ ὑπ᾽ ἀριθμ. 108 κῶδιξ τῆς ʿΙ. Συνόδου τῆς ᾿Εκκλησίας τῆς ῾Ελλάδος," ᾿Εκκλησιαστικὸς Φάρος 9 (1912) 303–305.
Cod

419 **In magnam feriam v** [Sp.], ed. R. Trautmann and R. Klostermann, "Noch ein griechischer Text zum Codex Suprasliensis," *Zeitschrift für slavische Philologie* 13 (1936) 338–341.
Cod

420 **De meretrice** [Sp.], ed. R. Abicht, "Quellennachweise zum Codex Suprasliensis," *Archiv für slavische Philologie* 16 (1894) 149–153.
Cod

421 **Epistula ad abbatem**, ed. Nicolopoulos, *op. cit.*, 455–478.
Cod

422 **In sancta lumina** [Sp.], ed. Combefis, *op. cit.*, 118–168.
Cod

423 **In nativitatem Joannis Baptistae** [Sp.], ed. F. Halkin, *Inédits byzantins d'Ochrida, Candie et Moscou* [*Subsidia hagiographica* 38. Brussels: Société des Bollandistes, 1963]: 87–94.
Cod

424 **In Christi ascensionem** [Sp.], ed. C. Baur, "Drei unedierte Festpredigten aus der Zeit der nestorianischen Streitigkeiten," *Traditio* 9 (1953) 122–124.
Cod

425 **In illud:** *Dominus regnavit* **et in illud:** *Dies diei dicit verbum* [Sp.], ed. F. Nau, "Le texte grec de trois homélies de Nestorius, et une homélie inédite sur le Psaume 96," *Revue de l'Orient chrétien* 15 (1910) 120–124.
Cod

426 **In assumptionem domini** [Sp.], ed. Baur, *op. cit.*, 116–119.
Cod

427 **In resurrectionem domini** [Sp.], ed. M. Aubineau, *Homélies pascales* [*Sources chrétiennes* 187. Paris: Cerf, 1972]: 318–324.
Cod

428 **Deprecatio** [Sp.], ed. M. Richard, "Témoins grecs des fragments xiii et xv de Méliton de Sardes," *Muséon* 85 (1972) 318–321.
Cod

429 **Epitimia 73** [Sp.], ed. J.B. Pitra, *Spicilegium Solesmense*, vol. 4. Paris: Didot, 1858 (repr. Graz: Akademische Druck- und Verlagsanstalt, 1963): 461–464.
Cod

430 **In illud:** *Nolite thesaurizare vobis thesauros in terra*, ed. Hippolytus Monachus, "Δύο λόγοι ἐπ' ὀνόματι τοῦ ἁγ. Ἰωάννου τοῦ Χρυσοστόμου," Νέα Σιών 20 (1925) 629–633.
Cod

431 **De utilitate tentationum**, ed. B. de Montfaucon, *Sancti patris nostri Johannis Chrysostomi opera omnia*, vol. 13. Venice, 1741: Appendix.
Cod

432 **In catenas sancti Petri** [Sp.], ed. E. Batareikh, "Discours inédit sur les chaînes de S. Pierre attribué à S. Jean Chrysostome," Χρυσοστομικά 3. Rome: Pustet, 1908: 978–1005.
Cod

433 **Stichoi** [Sp.], ed. J.B. Pitra, *Iuris ecclesiastici Graecorum historia et monumenta*, vol. 2. Rome: Congregatio de Propaganda Fide, 1868: 170.
Cod

434 **In passionem salvatoris nostri Jesu Christi**, ed. Hippolytus Monachus, "Ἐπ' ὀνόματι Ἰωάννου τοῦ Χρυσοστόμου φερόμενοι λόγοι," Νέα Σιών 18 (1923) 691–692.
Cod

435 **In ramos palmarum**, ed. Hippolytus Mona-

chus, Νέα Σιών 18, 309–313.
Cod

436 **In synaxim incorporalium**, ed. Halkin, *op. cit.*, 133–146.
Cod

437 **Encomium in sanctum Joannem evangelistam**, ed. Hippolytus Monachus, "Ἰωάννου τοῦ Χρυσοστόμου ἐγκώμιον εἰς Ἰωάννην τὸν εὐαγγελιστήν," Νέα Σιών 17 (1922) 665–667, 725–728.
Cod

438 **In sanctum pascha** [Sp.], ed. Baur, *op. cit.*, 108–110.
Cod

440 **In nativitatem** [Sp.], ed. Combefis, *op. cit.*, 104–117.
Cod

441 **Sermones animae utiles**, ed. M.N. Speranskij, "Perevodnije sborniki izrečenij v slavjano-russkoj pis'mennosti," *Čtenija v imper. Obščestvě istorii i drevnostej rossijskich pri Moskovskom Universitetě*, fasc. 2 (1905) 204–218.
Cod

442 **Oratio de hypapante** [Sp.], ed. E. Bickersteth, "Edition and translation of a hypapante homily ascribed to John Chrysostom," *Orientalia Christiana periodica* 32 (1966) 56–76.
Cod

443 **In illud:** *Credidi propter quod locutus sum*, ed. S. Haidacher, "Drei unedierte Chrysostomus-Texte einer baseler Handschrift," *Zeitschrift für katholische Theologie* 31 (1907) 351–358.
Cod

444 **In Christi natalem** [Sp.], ed. S.G. Mercati, "Antica omelia metrica εἰς τὴν Χριστοῦ γέναν," *Biblica* 1 (1920) 84–90.
Cod

445 **Encomium in sanctos martyres**, ed. M. Aubineau, "Une homélie grecque inédite 'sur tous les martyrs' attribuée à Jean Chrysostome," *Forma futuri. Studi in onore del Cardinale Michele Pellegrino*. Turin: Erasmo, 1975: 622–623.
Cod

446 **Encomium in sanctum Polycarpum**, ed. A. Hilgenfeld, "Des Chrysostomus Lobrede auf Polykarp," *Zeitschrift für wissenschaftliche Theologie* 45 (1902) 570–572.
Cod

447 **In illud:** *Quando ipsi subiciet omnia* [Sp.], ed. S. Haidacher, "Drei unedierte Chrysostomus-Texte einer Baseler Handschrift," *Zeitschrift für katholische Theologie* 31 (1907) 150–167.
Cod

448 **De descensu ad inferos et de latrone** [Sp.], ed. H. Brunell, *Sanctorum patrum orationes et epistolae selectae*, vol. 1. Rome, 1585: 145–155.
Cod

489 **De nativitate Joannis Baptistae** [Sp.], ed. C. Datema, "An unedited homily of Ps. Chryso-

stom on the birth of John the Baptist," *Byzantion* 52 (1982) 76–80.
Cod

452 **Oratio de epiphania** [Dub.], ed. A. Wenger, "Une homélie inédite (de Sévérien de Gabala?) sur l'épiphanie," *Analecta Bollandiana* 95 (1977) 81–90.
Cod

455 **Sermones duo prophylactici**, ed. G. Astruc-Morize, *Pseudochrysostomi sermo prophylacticus ii* [*Corpus Christianorum. Series Graeca.* Turnhout: Brepols, 1976]: 25–39.
Cod

463 **De nativitate** [Sp.], ed. S.J. Voicu, "Une homélie pseudo-chrysostomienne pour la Noël," *Byzantion* 43 (1973) 486–494.
Cod

465 **Oratio in patres Nicaenos** (excerptum), ed. V. Grecu, "Izvorul principal bizantin... Omiliile patriarhului Ioan xiv Caleca," *Studii şi cercetari* 35. Bucharest, 1939: 138–140.
Cod

491 **In sanctum pascha** [Sp.], ed. C. Datema and P. Allen, "Text and tradition of two Easter homilies of Ps. Chrysostom," *Jahrbuch der österreichischen Byzantinistik* 30 (1981) 98–102.
Cod

492 **In resurrectionem domini** (versio A) [Sp.], ed. C. Datema and P. Allen, "Leontius, presbyter of Constantinople – a compiler?," *Jahrbuch der österreichischen Byzantinistik* 29 (1980) 12–18.
Cod

493 **In resurrectionem domini** (versio B) [Sp.], ed. C. Datema and P. Allen, "Text and tradition of two Easter homilies of Ps. Chrysostom," *Jahrbuch der österreichischen Byzantinistik* 30 (1981) 94–97.
Cod

473 **In nativitatem Christi** (fragmenta duo) [Sp.], ed. M. Jugie, "La mort et l'assomption de la sainte Vierge dans la tradition des cinq premiers siècles," *Échos d'Orient* 25 (1926) 134, adn. 1.2.
Cod

484 **In sanctum Paulum apostolum** (excerptum), ed. L. Petit, X. Sidéridès and M. Jugie, *Oeuvres complètes de Gennade Scholarios*, vol. 3. Paris, 1930: 427–430.
Cod

494 **In operarios undecimae horae** [Sp.], ed. S.J. Voicu, "*In operarios undecimae horae*: una omelia pseudocrisostomica arianeggiante," *Augustinianum* 18 (1978) 353–356.
Cod

495 **In Ecclesiasten** [Sp.], ed. S. Leanza, *Procopii Gazaei catena in Ecclesiasten necnon Pseudochrysostomi commentarius in eundem Ecclesiasten* [*Corpus Christianorum. Series Graeca* 4. Turnhout: Brepols, 1978]: 67–97.
Cod

x01 **Ad neophytos.**
Cf. 2062 382.

x02 **Epistula ad Epiphanium** (ap. Socratem).
HE 6.14.
Cf. SOCRATES Scr. Eccl. (2057 001).

x03 **Apocalypsis apocrypha sancti Joannis altera** [Sp.].
Nau, pp. 215–221.
Cf. APOCALYPSIS JOANNIS (1158 002).

x04 **Epistula ad Theophilum Alexandrinum** (ap. Palladium).
Coleman-Norton, p. 41.
Cf. PALLADIUS Scr. Eccl. (2111 004).

x05 **Epistula ad Theophilum Alexandrinum** (ap. Palladium).
Coleman-Norton, p. 42.
Cf. PALLADIUS Scr. Eccl. (2111 004).

x06 **Epistula ad Theophili partium episcopos** (ap. Palladium).
Coleman-Norton, p. 49.
Cf. PALLADIUS Scr. Eccl. (2111 004).

x07 **Epistula ad Theophili partium episcopos** (ap. Palladium).
Coleman-Norton, p. 63.
Cf. PALLADIUS Scr. Eccl. (2111 004).

x08 **Epistula ad imperatorem** (ap. Palladium).
Coleman-Norton, p. 55.

4015 **JOANNES PHILOPONUS** Phil.
vel Joannes Grammaticus
A.D. 6: Alexandrinus
Bibliography in progress

001 **In Aristotelis categorias commentarium**, ed. A. Busse, *Philoponi (olim Ammonii) in Aristotelis categorias commentarium* [*Commentaria in Aristotelem Graeca* 13.1. Berlin: Reimer, 1898]: 1–205.
Cod: 67,259

002 **In Aristotelis analytica priora commentaria**, ed. M. Wallies, *Ioannis Philoponi in Aristotelis analytica priora commentaria* [*Commentaria in Aristotelem Graeca* 13.2. Berlin: Reimer, 1905]: 1–485.
Cod: 165,959

003 **In Aristotelis analytica posteriora commentaria** (prooemium e codd. BRL), ed. M. Wallies, *Ioannis Philoponi in Aristotelis analytica posteriora commentaria cum Anonymo in librum ii* [*Commentaria in Aristotelem Graeca* 13.3. Berlin: Reimer, 1909]: xxvii–xxx.
Cod: 1,600

004 **In Aristotelis analytica posteriora commentaria**, ed. Wallies, *CAG* 13.3, 1–440.
Cod: 147,905

005 **In Aristotelis meteorologicorum librum primum commentarium**, ed. M. Hayduck, *Ioannis Philoponi in Aristotelis meteorologicorum librum primum commentarium* [*Commentaria in Aristotelem Graeca* 14.1. Berlin: Reimer, 1901]: 1–131.
Cod: 53,855

006 **In Aristotelis libros de generatione et corruptione commentaria**, ed. H. Vitelli, *Ioannis Philoponi in Aristotelis libros de generatione et cor-*

ruptione commentaria [*Commentaria in Aristotelem Graeca* 14.2. Berlin: Reimer, 1897]: 1–314.
Cod: 108,122

007 **In libros de generatione animalium commentaria**, ed. M. Hayduck, *Ioannis Philoponi (Michaelis Ephesii) in libros de generatione animalium commentaria* [*Commentaria in Aristotelem Graeca* 14.3. Berlin: Reimer, 1903]: 1–249.
Cod: 96,011

008 **In Aristotelis de anima libros commentaria**, ed. M. Hayduck, *Ioannis Philoponi in Aristotelis de anima libros commentaria* [*Commentaria in Aristotelem Graeca* 15. Berlin: Reimer, 1897]: 1–607.
Cod: 240,874

009 **In Aristotelis physicorum libros commentaria**, ed. H. Vitelli, *Ioannis Philoponi in Aristotelis physicorum libros octo commentaria*, 2 vols. [*Commentaria in Aristotelem Graeca* 16 & 17. Berlin: Reimer, 16:1887; 17:1888]: **16**:1–495; **17**:496–908.
Cod: 308,937

010 **De aeternitate mundi**, ed. H. Rabe, *Ioannes Philoponus. De aeternitate mundi contra Proclum.* Leipzig: Teubner, 1899 (repr. Hildesheim: Olms, 1963): 1–646.
Cod: 146,246

011 **De opificio mundi**, ed. W. Reichardt, *Joannis Philoponi de opificio mundi libri vii.* Leipzig: Teubner, 1897: 1–308.
Cod: [66,220]

012 **De vocabulis quae diversum significatum exhibent secundum differentiam accentus**, ed. L.W. Daly, *Iohannis Philoponi de vocabulis quae diversum significatum exhibent secundum differentiam accentus.* Philadelphia: American Philosophical Society, 1983: 3–53, 55–139, 141–195, 197–238.
Cod

013 **Compendium** περὶ διαλέκτων, ed. O. Hoffmann, *Die griechischen Dialekte*, vol. 2. Göttingen: Vandenhoeck & Ruprecht, 1893: 204.
Cod

014 **In Nicomachi arithmeticam introductionem** (lib. 1), ed. R. Hoche, Ἰωάννου Γραμματικοῦ Ἀλεξανδρέως. Εἰς τὸ πρῶτον τῆς Νικομάχου ἀριθμητικῆς εἰσαγωγῆς. Leipzig: Teubner, 1864.
Cod

015 **In Nicomachi arithmeticam introductionem** (lib. 2), ed. R. Hoche, Ἰωάννου Γραμματικοῦ Ἀλεξανδρέως. Εἰς τὸ δεύτερον τῆς Νικομάχου ἀριθμητικῆς εἰσαγωγῆς. Berlin: Calvary, 1867: 1–37.
Cod

016 **Tonica praecepta**, ed. W. Dindorf, Ἰωάννου Ἀλεξανδρέως τονικὰ παραγγέλματα. Αἰλίου Ἡρωδιανοῦ περὶ σχημάτων. Leipzig: Reimer, 1825.
Cod

0526 **Flavius JOSEPHUS** Hist.
A.D. 1

001 **Antiquitates Judaicae**, ed. B. Niese, *Flavii Iosephi opera*, vols. 1–4. Berlin: Weidmann, 1:1887; 2:1885: 3:1892; 4:1890 (repr. 1955): 1:3–362; 2:3–392; 3:3–409; 4:3–320.
Cod: 322,395

002 **Josephi vita**, ed. Niese, *op. cit.*, vol. 4, 321–389.
Cod: 16,293

003 **Contra Apionem** (= De Judaeorum vetustate), ed. Niese, *op. cit.*, vol. 5 (1889; repr. 1955): 3–99.
Cod: 23,540

004 **De bello Judaico libri vii**, ed. Niese, *op. cit.*, vol. 6 (1895; repr. 1955): 3–628.
Cod: 129,064

1451 *JOSEPHUS ET ASENETH*
A.D. 2

001 **Confessio et precatio Aseneth**, ed. M. Philonenko, *Joseph et Aséneth.* Leiden: Brill, 1968: 128–220.
Cod: 8,641

1452 **JUBA II** <Hist.>
1 B.C.–A.D. 1: Mauretanicus

001 **Testimonia**, FGrH #275: 3A:127–130.
NQ

002 **Fragmenta**, FGrH #275: 3A:130–155.
Q

x01 **Epigramma irrisorium.**
App. Anth. 5.29: Cf. EPIGRAMMATICI in *App. Anth.* (7052 005).

2180 **JUDAS** Hist.
A.D. 3

001 **Testimonium**, FGrH #261: 2B:1229.
NQ

4050 **JULIANUS** <Epigr.>
fiq Julianus Meteorus Scholasticus
A.D. 6: Aegyptius
Cf. et JULIANUS <Epigr.> (4054).

001 **Epigrammata**, AG 5.298; **6**.12, 18–20, 25–26, 28–29, 67–68; **7**.32–33, 58–59, 69–70, 561–562, 565, 576–577, 580–582, 584–587, 590–592, 594–595, 597–601, 603, 605; **9**.398, 445–447, 652, 654, 661, 738–739, 763, 771, 793–798; **16**.87–88, 107–108, 113, 130, 139, 157, 173, 181, 203, 325, 388.
AG 6.186: Cf. Julius DIOCLES Rhet. (0162 001).
AG 9.9, 9b: Cf. Julius POLYAENUS Epigr. (1620 001).
AG 16.218: Cf. Joannes BARBUCALLUS Gramm. (4051 001).
Q: 2,122

x01 **Epigramma demonstrativum.**
App. Anth. 3.179: Cf. EPIGRAMMATICI in *App. Anth.* (7052 003).

4053 **JULIANUS** <Epigr.>
A.D. 6
001 **Epigrammata,** AG 11.367–369.
Q: 47

4054 **JULIANUS** <Epigr.>
fiq Julianus Praefectus Aegypti
Incertum
Cf. et JULIANUS <Epigr.> (4050).
001 **Epigramma,** AG 9.481.
Q: 32

0940 **JULIANUS** Med.
A.D. 2: Alexandrinus
x01 **Fragmenta ap. Galenum.**
K**13**.557; **18.1**.248, 255–257, 296 in CMG, vol.
5.10.3, pp. 34, 40–42, 68, 69.
Cf. GALENUS Med. (0057 077, 094).
x02 **Fragmentum ap. Paulum.**
CMG, vol. 9.2, pp. 280–281.
Cf. PAULUS Med. (0715 001).

2003 **Flavius Claudius JULIANUS Imperator** Phil.
A.D. 4: Constantinopolitanus
001 Ἐγκώμιον εἰς τὸν αὐτοκράτορα Κωνστάντιον,
ed. J. Bidez, *L'empereur Julien. Oeuvres com-*
plètes, vol. 1.1. Paris: Les Belles Lettres, 1932:
10–68.
Cod: [11,876]
002 Εὐσεβίας τῆς βασιλίδος ἐγκώμιον, **ed. Bidez,**
op. cit., vol. 1.1, 73–105.
Cod: [7,009]
003 Περὶ τῶν τοῦ αὐτοκράτορος πράξεων ἢ περὶ
βασιλείας, ed. Bidez, *op. cit.,* vol. 1.1, 116–180.
Cod: [13,378]
004 Ἐπὶ τῇ ἐξόδῳ τοῦ ἀγαθωτάτου Σαλουστίου
παραμυθητικὸς εἰς ἑαυτόν, ed. Bidez, *op. cit.,*
vol. 1.1, 189–206.
Cod: [3,091]
005 Ἀθηναίων τῇ βουλῇ καὶ τῷ δήμῳ, ed. Bidez,
op. cit., vol. 1.1, 213–235.
Cod: [4,782]
006 Θεμιστίῳ φιλοσόφῳ, ed. G. Rochefort, *op. cit.,*
vol. 2.1 (1963): 12–30.
Cod: [3,398]
007 Πρὸς Ἡράκλειον κυνικὸν περὶ τοῦ πῶς κυνισ-
τέον καὶ εἰ πρέπει τῷ κυνὶ μύθους πλάττειν, ed.
Rochefort, *op. cit.,* vol. 2.1, 43–90.
Cod: [9,061]
008 Εἰς τὴν μητέρα τῶν θεῶν, ed. Rochefort, *op.*
cit., vol. 2.1, 103–131.
Cod: [5,891]
009 Εἰς τοὺς ἀπαιδεύτους κύνας, ed. Rochefort, *op.*
cit., vol. 2.1, 144–173.
Cod: [5,803]
010 Συμπόσιον ἢ Κρόνια, ed. C. Lacombrade, *op.*
cit., vol. 2.2 (1964): 32–71.
Cod: [6,989]
011 Εἰς τὸν βασιλέα Ἥλιον πρὸς Σαλούστιον, ed.
Lacombrade, *op. cit.,* vol. 2.2, 100–138.
Cod: [7,672]

012 **Misopogon** (sc. Ἀντιοχικὸς ἢ Μισοπώγων),
ed. Lacombrade, *op. cit.,* vol. 2.2, 156–199.
Cod: [8,545]
013 **Epistulae,** ed. Bidez, *op. cit.,* vol. 1.2, 2nd edn.
(1960): 12–23, 26, 51–77, 84–91, 133–200,
205–207.
Cod: [20,296]
014 **Poematia et fragmenta,** ed. Bidez, *op. cit.,* vol.
1.2, 214–217.
frr. 161, 165–170, 176–178.
Q: [361]
015 **Epistulae dubiae,** ed. Bidez, *op. cit.,* vol. 1.2,
222–231.
Cod: [1,628]
016 **Epistulae spuriae,** ed. Bidez, *op. cit.,* vol. 1.2,
246–249.
Cod: [395]
017 **Contra Galilaeos,** ed. C.J. Neumann, *Juliani*
imperatoris librorum contra Christianos quae
supersunt. Leipzig: Teubner, 1880: 163–233.
Q
018 **Epigrammata,** AG **9**.365, 368; **16**.115(?).
AG 7.747: Cf. LIBANIUS Soph. (2200 011).
AG 11.108, 109: Cf. ANONYMI EPIGRAMMA-
TICI (0138 001).
Q: 125
019 **Testimonia,** FGrH #238: 2B:990–991.
NQ
020 **Fragmentum,** ed. A. Guida, "Frammenti in-
editi di Eupoli, Teleclide, Teognide, Giuliano
e Imerio da un nuovo codice del Lexicon
Vindobonense," *Prometheus* 5 (1979) 208.
Q
x01 **Aenigmata.**
App. Anth. 7.22–23: Cf. EPIGRAMMATICI in
App. Anth. (7052 007).

0737 **JULIANUS Scriptor Legis De Medicis**
fiq Julianus Imperator
A.D. 4?
001 **Lex de medicis,** ed. J.L. Ideler, *Physici et*
medici Graeci minores, vol. 2. Berlin: Reimer,
1842 (repr. Amsterdam: Hakkert, 1963): 464.
Cod: 64

1757 **JULIUS** Epic.
ante A.D. 5
001 **Fragmenta,** ed. E. Heitsch, *Die griechischen*
Dichterfragmente der römischen Kaiserzeit, vol.
1, 2nd edn. Göttingen: Vandenhoeck & Ruprecht, 1963: 77.
frr. 1–2.
Q: [35]

2956 **Sextus JULIUS AFRICANUS** Hist.
A.D. 2–3: Hierosolymitanus, Alexandrinus
001 **Chronographiae** (fragmenta), ed. M.J. Routh,
Reliquiae sacrae, vol. 2. Oxford: Oxford University Press, 1846 (repr. Hildesheim: Olms,
1974): 238–308.
Q

002 **Cesti** (fragmenta), ed. J.R. Vieillefond, *Les "Cestes" de Julius Africanus*. Florence: Sansoni, 1970: 103–323.
Q, Cod, Pap

003 **Epistula ad Origenem**, ed. W. Reichardt, *Die Briefe des Sextus Julius Africanus an Aristides und Origenes* [*Texte und Untersuchungen* 34.3. Leipzig: Hinrichs, 1909]: 78–80.
Cod

004 **Epistula ad Aristidem**, ed. Reichardt, *op. cit.*, 53–62.
Q, Cod

1453 **JUNCUS** Phil.
A.D. 2?

x01 **Fragmenta ap. Stobaeum.**
Anth. IV.50a.27; 50b.85; 50c.95; 53.35.
Cf. Joannes STOBAEUS (2037 001).

0943 **JUNIAS** Med.
ante A.D. 2?

x01 **Fragmentum ap. Oribasium.**
CMG, vol. 6.2.2, p. 299.
Cf. ORIBASIUS Med. (0722 003).

2673 **JUNIOR** Poeta
Incertum

x01 **Epigramma dedicatorium.**
App. Anth. 1.199: Cf. EPIGRAMMATICI in *App. Anth.* (7052 001).

0740 *JUSJURANDUM MEDICUM*
Incertum

001 **Jusjurandum medicum**, ed. U.C. Bussemaker, *Poetae bucolici et didactici*. Paris: Didot, 1862: 90.
Cf. et HIPPOCRATES Med. et CORPUS HIPPO-CRATICUM (0627 057).
Cod: 75

1454 **JUSTINUS** Gnost.
A.D. 2

001 **Fragmenta**, ed. W. Völker, *Quellen zur Geschichte der christlichen Gnosis*. Tübingen: Mohr, 1932: 27–33.
Q

0645 **JUSTINUS MARTYR** Apol.
A.D. 2: Samaritanus, Romanus

001 **Apologia**, ed. E.J. Goodspeed, *Die ältesten Apologeten*. Göttingen: Vandenhoeck & Ruprecht, 1915: 26–77.
Cod: [15,591]

002 **Apologia secunda**, ed. Goodspeed, *op. cit.*, 78–89.
Cod: [3,570]

003 **Dialogus cum Tryphone**, ed. Goodspeed, *op. cit.*, 90–265.
Cod: [56,248]

004 **Fragmenta operum deperditorum**, ed. J.C.T. Otto, *Corpus apologetarum Christianorum sae-*

culi secundi, vol. 3, 3rd edn. Jena: Mauke, 1879 (repr. Wiesbaden: Sändig, 1971): 250–264.
frr. 1–20.
Q: [760]

0646 **Pseudo-JUSTINUS MARTYR**
A.D. 3/5
Cf. et ACTA JUSTINI ET SEPTEM SODALIUM (0384).

001 **Oratio ad gentiles**, ed. J.C.T. Otto, *Corpus apologetarum Christianorum saeculi secundi*, vol. 3, 3rd edn. Jena: Mauke, 1879 (repr. Wiesbaden: Sändig, 1971): 2–18.
Cod: [1,114]

002 **Cohortatio ad gentiles**, ed. Otto, *op. cit.*, vol. 3, 18–126.
Cod: [11,571]

003 **De monarchia**, ed. Otto, *op. cit.*, vol. 3, 126–158.
Cod: [1,982]

004 **Epistula ad Diognetum**, ed. Otto, *op. cit.*, vol. 3, 158–210.
Cod: [2,791]

005 **De resurrectione**, ed. Otto, *op. cit.*, vol. 3, 210–248.
Cod: [3,600]

006 **Expositio rectae fidei**, ed. Otto, *op. cit.*, vol. 4, 3rd edn. (1880; repr. 1969): 2–66.
Cod: [6,100]

007 **Epistula ad Zenam et Serenum**, ed. Otto, *op. cit.*, vol. 4, 66–98.
Cod: [3,681]

008 **Confutatio dogmatum quorundam Aristotelicorum**, ed. Otto, *op. cit.*, vol. 4, 100–222.
Cod: [17,427]

009 **Quaestiones et responsiones ad orthodoxos**, ed. Otto, *op. cit.*, vol. 5, 3rd edn. (1881; repr. 1969): 2–246.
Cod: [30,419]

010 **Quaestiones Christianorum ad gentiles**, ed. Otto, *op. cit.*, vol. 5, 246–326.
Cod: [13,213]

011 **Quaestiones gentilium ad Christianos**, ed. Otto, *op. cit.*, vol. 5, 326–366.
Cod: [5,555]

012 **Fragmenta**, ed. Otto, *op. cit.*, vol. 5, 368–374.
frr. 1–7.
Q, Cod: [584]

2497 **JUSTUS** Hist.
A.D. 1: Tiberiensis

001 **Testimonia**, FGrH #734: 3C:695–699.
NQ

002 **Fragmenta**, FGrH #734: 3C:699.
Q

0944 **JUSTUS** Med.
A.D. 2

x01 **Fragmenta ap. Oribasium.**
CMG, vol. 6.1.1, pp. 298, 300.

Cf. ORIBASIUS Med. (0722 001).

x02 **Fragmentum ap. Paulum.**
CMG, vol. 9.2, p. 287.
Cf. PAULUS Med. (0715 001).

x03 **Fragmentum ap. Aëtium** (lib. 3).
CMG, vol. 8.1, p. 306.
Cf. AËTIUS Med. (0718 003).

1455 *KERYGMA PETRI*
A.D. 2
001 **Kerygma Petri,** ed. E. Klostermann, *Apocrypha I. Reste des Petrusevangeliums, der Petrusapokalypse und des Kerygma Petri,* 2nd edn. [*Kleine Texte* 3. Bonn: Marcus & Weber, 1908]: 13–16.
Q

1456 **LACO** Epigr.
Incertum
001 **Epigramma,** AG 6.203.
Q: 64

2525 **LAETUS** Hist.
vel Mochus
ante 2 B.C.?
001 **Testimonium,** FGrH #784: 3C:795.
NQ
002 **Fragmenta,** FGrH #784: 3C:795–797.
Q

1930 **LAMACHUS** Hist.
4 B.C.: fort. Smyrnaeus
001 **Testimonium,** FGrH #116: 2B:617.
NQ

0945 **LAMPON** Med.
ante A.D. 1: Pelusiota
x01 **Fragmenta ap. Galenum.**
K12.682; 13.133–134.
Cf. GALENUS Med. (0057 076).

0370 **LAMPROCLES** Lyr.
5 B.C.: Atheniensis
001 **Fragmenta,** ed. D.L. Page, *Poetae melici Graeci.* Oxford: Clarendon Press, 1962 (repr. 1967 (1st edn. corr.)): 379–380.
frr. 1–2.
Q: [27]

0918 **LAMYNTHIUS** Lyr.
5 B.C.: Milesius
001 **Titulus,** ed. D.L. Page, *Poetae melici Graeci.* Oxford: Clarendon Press, 1962 (repr. 1967 (1st edn. corr.)): 442.
NQ

0946 **LAODICUS** <Med.>
ante A.D. 1
x01 **Fragmentum ap. Galenum.**
K12.626.
Cf. GALENUS Med. (0057 076).

0469 **LAON** Comic.
3 B.C.?
001 **Fragmenta,** ed. T. Kock, *Comicorum Atticorum fragmenta,* vol. 3. Leipzig: Teubner, 1888: 382.
frr. 1–2.
Q: 31
002 **Fragmenta,** ed. A. Meineke, *Fragmenta comicorum Graecorum,* vol. 4. Berlin: Reimer, 1841 (repr. De Gruyter, 1970): 574.
Q: 32

2321 **LAOSTHENIDAS** Hist.
1 B.C.?: fort. Creticus
001 **Titulus,** FGrH #462: 3B:400.
NQ

0366 **LASUS** Lyr.
6 B.C.: Hermioneus
001 **Fragmentum,** ed. D.L. Page, *Poetae melici Graeci.* Oxford: Clarendon Press, 1962 (repr. 1967 (1st edn. corr.)): 365.
fr. 1.
Q: [15]
002 **Tituli,** ed. Page, *op. cit.,* 365.
NQ

2159 **LEANDR(I)US** Hist.
ante 3 B.C.: Milesius
001 **Fragmenta,** FGrH #492: 3B:461–464.
frr. 10–19.
Q

2944 **LEO VI SAPIENS Imperator** Phil.
A.D. 9–10: Constantinopolitanus
x01 **Epigramma.**
AG 9.581.
Cf. ANONYMI EPIGRAMMATICI (0138 001).
x02 **Epigramma** (oraculum).
App. Anth. 6.225: Cf. EPIGRAMMATICI in *App. Anth.* (7052 006).

1941 **LEO** Hist.
4 B.C.?: Byzantius
001 **Testimonia,** FGrH #132: 2B:676.
NQ
002 **Fragmenta,** FGrH #132: 2B:677.
Q

1978 **LEO** Hist.
4/3 B.C.: Pellaeus
001 **Testimonium,** FGrH #659: 3C:208–209.
NQ
002 **Fragmenta,** FGrH #659: 3C:209–211.
Q

2375 **LEO** Hist.
2 B.C.: Samius
001 **Testimonium,** FGrH #540: 3B:523.
test. 1: *Inscr. Samos* (Heraion inv. 197).
NQ

2186 **LEO** Hist.
2 B.C./A.D. 2: Alabandeus
001 **Testimonium**, FGrH #278: 3A:157–158.
NQ
002 **Fragmenta**, FGrH #279: 3A:158.
Q

0723 **LEO** Phil.
A.D. 9: Constantinopolitanus
001 **De natura hominum synopsis**, ed. R. Renehan, *Leo the physican. Epitome on the nature of man* [*Corpus medicorum Graecorum*, vol. 10.4. Berlin: Akademie-Verlag, 1969]: 16–61.
Cod: [7,014]
002 **Conspectus medicinae**, ed. F.Z. Ermerins, *Anecdota medica Graeca*. Leiden: Luchtmans, 1840 (repr. Amsterdam: Hakkert, 1963): 80–86, 89–217.
Cod: [9,787]

2710 **LEO BARDALAS** Epigr.
A.D. 13–14
x01 **Epigrammata** (*App. Anth.*).
Epigramma demonstrativum: 3.418.
Epigrammata exhortatoria et supplicatoria: 4.117–120.
App. Anth. 3.418: Cf. EPIGRAMMATICI in *App. Anth.* (7052 003).
App. Anth. 4.117–120: Cf. EPIGRAMMATICI in *App. Anth.* (7052 004).

9016 **LEO Philosophus** Gramm.
A.D. 9–10
Bibliography in progress
001 **Epigrammata**, AG **9**.200–203, 214, 361, 578–579; **15**.12.
AG 16.387c: Cf. ANONYMI EPIGRAMMATICI (0138 001).
Q: 404
x01 **Epigrammata** (*App. Anth.*).
Epigramma demonstrativum: 3.255.
Epigramma exhortatorium et supplicatorium: 4.77.
Epigramma irrisorium: 5.58.
App. Anth. 3.255: Cf. EPIGRAMMATICI in *App. Anth.* (7052 003).
App. Anth. 4.77: Cf. EPIGRAMMATICI in *App. Anth.* (7052 004).
App. Anth. 5.58: Cf. EPIGRAMMATICI in *App. Anth.* (7052 005).

1458 **LEONIDAS** Epigr.
4–3 B.C.: Tarentinus
001 **Epigrammata**, AG **5**.188, 206; **6**.4, 13, 35, 44, 110, 120, 129–131, 154, 188, 200, 202, 204–205, 211, 221, 226, 262–263, 281, 286, 288–289, 293, 296, 298, 300, 302, 305, 309, 334, 355; **7**.13, 19, 35, 67, 163, 173, 190, 198, 264, 266, 273, 283, 295, 316, 408, 422, 440, 448, 452, 455, 463, 466, 472–472b, 478, 480, 503–504, 506, 648, 652, 654–665, 715, 719, 726,

731, 736, 740; **9**.24–25, 99, 107, 179, 316, 318, 320, 322, 326, 329, 335, 337, 563, 719, 744; **10**.1; **16**.171, 182, 190, 206, 230, 236, 261, 306–307.
AG 6.189: Cf. MOERO Epic. (0220 002).
AG 7.187: Cf. PHILIPPUS Epigr. (1589 001).
AG 9.435: Cf. THEOCRITUS Bucol. (0005 005).
AG 16.213: Cf. STRATON Epigr. (1697 001).
AG 16.213: Cf. et MELEAGER Epigr. (1492 001).
Q: 4,282
x01 **Epigramma exhortatorium et supplicatorium**.
App. Anth. 4.39: Cf. EPIGRAMMATICI in *App. Anth.* (7052 004).

1457 **Julius LEONIDAS** Math. et Astrol.
A.D. 1: Alexandrinus
001 **Epigrammata**, AG **6**.321–322, 324–329; **7**.547–550, 668, 675; **9**.12, 42, 78–80, 106, 123, 344–356; **11**.9, 70, 187, 199–200, 213; **12**.20.
AG 6.323: Cf. NICODEMUS Epigr. (1536 001).
AG 7.676: Cf. ANONYMI EPIGRAMMATICI (0138 001).
Q: 1,042

0948 **LEONIDAS** Med.
vel Leonides
A.D. 1: Alexandrinus
x01 **Fragmentum ap. Paulum**.
CMG, vol. 9.2, p. 122.
Cf. PAULUS Med. (0715 001).
x02 **Fragmenta ap. Aëtium** (lib. 6–7).
CMG, vol. 8.2, pp. 123, 320.
Cf. AËTIUS Med. (0718 006–007).
x03 **Fragmenta ap. Aëtium** (lib. 15).
Zervos, *Athena* 21, pp. 17, 24, 34.
Cf. AËTIUS Med. (0718 015).
x04 **Fragmenta ap. Aëtium** (lib. 16).
Zervos, *Gynaekologie des Aëtios*, pp. 58, 60, 61, 68.
Cf. AËTIUS Med. (0718 016).

2554 **LEONIDES** Hist.
Incertum
001 **Fragmentum**, FGrH #827: 3C:899–900.
Q

LEONTEUS Trag.
A.D. 1: Argivus
AG 9.20.
Cf. ANONYMI EPIGRAMMATICI (0138).

4062 **LEONTIUS Minotaurus** Epigr.
A.D. 6
001 **Epigrammata**, AG **5**.295; **7**.149–150, 571, 573, 575, 579; **9**.614, 624, 630, 650, 681; **16**.32, 33, 37, 245, 272, 283–288, 357.
AG 9.20: Cf. ANONYMI EPIGRAMMATICI (0138 001).
Q: 672

0949 **LEPIDIANUS** Med.
ante A.D. 4
x01 **Fragmentum ap. Oribasium.**
CMG, vol. 6.2.2, p. 246.
Cf. ORIBASIUS Med. (0722 003).

1459 **LEPIDUS** Hist.
Incertum
001 **Fragmenta**, FGrH #838: 3C:905.
Q

1460 **LESBONAX** Gramm.
A.D. 1
001 **De figuris** (recensio A), ed. R. Müller, *De
Lesbonacte grammatico* [*Diss. Greifswald*
(1890)]: 33–54.
Cod
002 **De figuris** (recensio B), ed. Müller, *op. cit.*, 33–
55.
Cod

0649 **LESBONAX** Rhet.
A.D. 2
001 Πολιτικός, ed. F. Kiehr, *Lesbonactis sophistae
quae supersunt* [*Diss. Strassburg* (1906)]: 25–
27.
Cod: [345]
002 Προτρεπτικὸς **A**, ed. Kiehr, *op. cit.*, 27–32.
Cod: [1,359]
003 Προτρεπτικὸς **B**, ed. Kiehr, *op. cit.*, 32–37.
Cod: [899]

LESCHES
7 B.C.?: Mytilenensis
Cf. ILIAS PARVA (1444).
Cf. ILIU PERSIS (1445).

2629 **LESCHIDA** Epic.
3/2 B.C.
001 **Titulus**, ed. H. Lloyd-Jones and P. Parsons,
Supplementum Hellenisticum. Berlin: De Gruyter, 1983: 250.
fr. 503.
NQ: [1]

1967 **LESCHIDES** Hist.
3/2 B.C.
001 **Testimonium**, FGrH #172: 2B:895.
NQ

1461 **LEUCIPPUS** Phil.
5 B.C.: Eleaticus vel Abderita vel Milesius
001 **Testimonia**, ed. H. Diels and W. Kranz, *Die
Fragmente der Vorsokratiker*, vol. 2, 6th edn.
Berlin: Weidmann, 1952 (repr. Dublin: 1966):
70–79.
test. 1–37.
NQ
002 **Fragmenta**, ed. Diels and Kranz, *op. cit.*, 80–
81.
frr. 1–2.

fr. 1a: *P. Herc.* 1788.
Q, Pap

0470 **LEUCO** Comic.
5–4 B.C.
001 **Fragmentum**, ed. T. Kock, *Comicorum Atticorum fragmenta*, vol. 1. Leipzig: Teubner, 1880:
703–704.
fr. 1 + tituli.
Q: 15
002 **Fragmentum**, ed. A. Meineke, *Fragmenta comicorum Graecorum*, vol. 2.2. Berlin: Reimer,
1840 (repr. De Gruyter, 1970): 749.
Q: 10
003 **Fragmentum**, ed. C. Austin, *Comicorum Graecorum fragmenta in papyris reperta*. Berlin: De
Gruyter, 1973: 120–121.
fr. 102.
Pap: 16

2200 **LIBANIUS** Rhet. et Soph.
A.D. 4: Antiochenus, Constantinopolitanus,
Nicomedensis
004 **Orationes 1–64**, ed. R. Foerster, *Libanii opera*,
vols. 1–4. Leipzig: Teubner, 1.1–1.2:1903;
2:1904; 3:1906; 4:1908 (repr. Hildesheim:
Olms, 1963): **1.1**:79–320; **1.2**:354–535; **2**:9–
572; **3**:4–487; **4**:6–498.
Cod: 260,527
005 **Declamationes 1–51**, ed. Foerster, *op. cit.*, vols.
5 (1909; repr. 1963); 6 (1911; repr. 1963); 7
(1913; repr. 1963): **5**:13–564; **6**:7–658; **7**:7–
736.
Cod: 220,316
012 **Declamatio 3** (Legatio Menelai, Theorema),
ed. Foerster, *op. cit.*, vol. 5, 210–211.
Cod: 102
006 **Progymnasmata**, ed. Foerster, *op. cit.*, vol. 8
(1915; repr. 1963): 24–571.
Cod: 69,308
007 **Argumenta orationum Demosthenicarum**, ed.
Foerster, *op. cit.*, vol. 8, 600–681.
Cod: 12,379
008 **Characteres epistolici** [Sp.], ed. Foerster, *op.
cit.*, vol. 9 (1927; repr. 1963): 27–47.
Cod: 2,450
001 **Epistulae 1–1544**, ed. Foerster, *op. cit.*, vols. 10
(1921; repr. 1963) & 11 (1922; repr. 1963):
10:1–758; **11**:1–562.
Cod: 226,218
002 **Epistulae pseudepigraphae**, ed. Foerster, *op.
cit.*, vol. 11, 563–571.
Cod: 1,234
003 **Epistularum Basilii et Libanii quod fertur
commercium**, ed. Foerster, *op. cit.*, vol. 11,
572–597.
Cod: 3,269
009 **Fragmenta de declamationibus**, ed. Foerster,
op. cit., vol. 11, 637–648.
frr. 48–50.
Cod: [1,695]

013 **Fragmenta**, ed. Foerster, *op. cit.*, vol. 11, 653–662, 664–668.
frr. 54–56, 57a–b, 58–82, 84–85, 88–93.
Q, Cod: [351]

010 **Fragmentum**, *P. Rain.* 3.60.
Pap

011 **Epigramma**, AG 7.747.
Q: 15

1774 *LIBER ELCHESAI*
A.D. 2

001 **Liber Elchesai**, ed. A. Hilgenfeld, *Novum Testamentum extra canonem receptum*, fasc. 3, 2nd edn. Leipzig: Weigel, 1881: 229–240.
Q

1462 *LIBER ELDAD ET MODAD*
ante A.D. 2

001 **Fragmentum**, ed. A.-M. Denis, *Fragmenta pseudepigraphorum quae supersunt Graeca* [*Pseudepigrapha veteris testamenti Graece* 3. Leiden: Brill, 1970]: 68.
Q: [18]

1463 *LIBER ENOCH*
2/1 B.C.

001 **Apocalypsis Enochi**, ed. M. Black, *Apocalypsis Henochi Graece* [*Pseudepigrapha veteris testamenti Graece* 3. Leiden: Brill, 1970]: 19–44.
Cod: [7,714]

002 **Apocalypsis Enochi** (recensio ap. Syncellum), ed. Black, *op. cit.*, 21–26, 29–30, 32–33, 37.
Q

1859 *LIBER JANNES ET MAMBRES*
Incertum

001 **Fragmentum**, ed. A.-M. Denis, *Fragmenta pseudepigraphorum quae supersunt Graeca* [*Pseudepigrapha veteris testamenti Graece* 3. Leiden: Brill, 1970]: 69.
Q: [18]

1464 *LIBER JUBILAEORUM*
2/1 B.C.

001 **Fragmenta**, ed. A.-M. Denis, *Fragmenta pseudepigraphorum quae supersunt Graeca* [*Pseudepigrapha veteris testamenti Graece* 3. Leiden: Brill, 1970]: 70–101.
Q, Cod: [2,154]

0374 **LICYMNIUS** Lyr.
5 B.C.: Chius

001 **Fragmenta**, ed. D.L. Page, *Poetae melici Graeci*. Oxford: Clarendon Press, 1962 (repr. 1967 (1st edn. corr.)): 396–397.
frr. 2–4.
Q: [37]

002 **Titulus**, ed. Page, *op. cit.*, 396.
NQ

0203 **LIMENIUS** Lyr.
2 B.C.: Atheniensis

001 **Paean Delphicus ii et prosodium in Apollinem**, ed. J.U. Powell, *Collectanea Alexandrina*. Oxford: Clarendon Press, 1925 (repr. 1970): 149–150.
Epigr: [298]

0950 **LINGON** Med.
ante A.D. 2

x01 **Fragmentum ap. Galenum**.
K13.286.
Cf. GALENUS Med. (0057 076).

1465 **[LINUS]** Epic.
Incertum

001 **Testimonia**, ed. M.L. West, *The Orphic poems*. Oxford: Clarendon Press, 1983: 62–65.
test. 1–4, 6–9, 12.
Q

002 **Fragmenta**, ed. West, *op. cit.*, 65–67.
frr. 1–7, 9–11.
Q

2630 **LOBO** Poeta
3 B.C.?: Argivus

001 **Fragmenta et titulus**, ed. H. Lloyd-Jones and P. Parsons, *Supplementum Hellenisticum*. Berlin: De Gruyter, 1983: 251–257.
frr. 504–526.
Q: [309]

002 **Epigrammata in poetas ante Alexandrinorum aetatem condita**, ed. W. Crönert, "De Lobone Argivo," *Charites Friedrich Leo zum sechzigsten Geburtstag dargebracht*. Berlin: Weidmann, 1911: 142–145.
Q

0951 **LOGADIUS** Soph.
ante A.D. 6

x01 **Fragmentum ap. Paulum**.
CMG, vol. 9.2, p. 287.
Cf. PAULUS Med. (0715 001).

x02 **Fragmentum ap. Aëtium** (lib. 3).
CMG, vol. 8.1, p. 302.
Cf. AËTIUS Med. (0718 003).

LOGIA JESU
Cf. AGRAPHA (1776).

1466 **LOLLIANUS** Scr. Erot.
fiq Publius Hordeonius Lollianus Ephesius
A.D. 2

001 **Fragmenta**, ed. A. Henrichs, *Die Phoinikika des Lollianos* [*Papyrologische Texte und Abhandlungen* 14. Bonn: Habelt, 1972]: 82–103.
Pap

1467 **LOLLIANUS** Soph.
A.D. 2: Ephesius

001 **Fragmenta**, ed. O. Schissel, "Lollianos aus Ephesos," *Philologus* 82 (1927) 185–188.
Q

0143 **LOLLIUS BASSUS** Epigr.
A.D. 1: Smyrnaeus
001 **Epigrammata**, AG **5**.125; **7**.243, 372, 386, 391;
9.30, 53, 236, 279, 289; **10**.102; **11**.72.
AG 9.283: Cf. CRINAGORAS Epigr. (0154
001).
Q: 416

0560 **[LONGINUS]** Rhet.
A.D. 1?
001 **De sublimitate**, ed. D.A. Russell, *'Longinus'.
On the sublime.* Oxford: Clarendon Press,
1964: 1–56.
Cod: [13,669]
002 **Ars rhetorica**, ed. L. Spengel, *Rhetores Graeci*,
vol. 1. Leipzig: Teubner, 1853 (repr. Frankfurt
am Main: Minerva, 1966): 299–320.
Cod: [5,718]
003 **Excerpta**, ed. Spengel, *op. cit.*, 325–328.
Cod: [704]

0561 **LONGUS** Scr. Erot.
A.D. 2?: fort. Lesbius
001 **Daphnis et Chloe**, ed. G. Dalmeyda, *Longus.
Pastorales (Daphnis et Chloé)*. Paris: Les Belles
Lettres, 1934 (repr. 1971): 2–106.
Cod: 20,929

0734 **<LUCAS Apostolus>** Med.
post A.D. 1
001 **Σκευασία ἁλατίου**, ed. J.L. Ideler, *Physici et
medici Graeci minores*, vol. 1. Berlin: Reimer,
1841 (repr. Amsterdam: Hakkert, 1963): 297.
Cod: 122

0062 **LUCIANUS** Soph.
A.D. 2: Samosatenus
001 **Phalaris**, ed. A.M. Harmon, *Lucian*, vol. 1.
Cambridge, Mass.: Harvard University Press,
1913 (repr. 1961): 2–30.
Cod: 2,951
002 **Hippias**, ed. Harmon, *op. cit.*, vol. 1, 34–44.
Cod: 999
003 **Bacchus**, ed. Harmon, *op. cit.*, vol. 1, 48–58.
Cod: 1,048
004 **Hercules**, ed. Harmon, *op. cit.*, vol. 1, 62–70.
Cod: 780
005 **Electrum**, ed. Harmon, *op. cit.*, vol. 1, 74–78.
Cod: 625
006 **Muscae encomium**, ed. Harmon, *op. cit.*, vol.
1, 82–94.
Cod: 1,206
007 **Nigrinus**, ed. M.D. Macleod, *Luciani opera*,
vol. 1. Oxford: Clarendon Press, 1972: 31–45.
Cod: 4,114
008 **Demonax**, ed. Harmon, *op. cit.*, vol. 1, 142–
172.
Cod: 3,179
009 **De domo**, ed. Harmon, *op. cit.*, vol. 1, 176–
206.
Cod: 3,203

010 **Patriae encomium**, ed. Harmon, *op. cit.*, vol. 1,
210–218.
Cod: 984
011 **Macrobii**, ed. Harmon, *op. cit.*, vol. 1, 222–244.
Cod: 2,199
012 **Verae historiae**, ed. Macleod, *Luciani opera*,
vol. 1, 82–125.
Cod: 11,310
013 **Calumniae non temere credendum**, ed. Harmon, *op. cit.*, vol. 1, 360–392.
Cod: 3,235
014 **Lis consonantium** (= **Judicium vocalium**), ed.
Harmon, *op. cit.*, vol. 1, 396–408.
Cod: 1,188
015 **Symposium**, ed. Macleod, *Luciani opera*, vol.
1, 144–163.
Cod: 4,777
016 **Cataplus**, ed. Harmon, *op. cit.*, vol. 2 (1915;
repr. 1960): 2–56.
Cod: 4,131
017 **Juppiter confutatus**, ed. Harmon, *op. cit.*, vol.
2, 60–86.
Cod: 2,377
018 **Juppiter tragoedus**, ed. Harmon, *op. cit.*, vol. 2,
90–168.
Cod: 6,865
019 **Gallus**, ed. Harmon, *op. cit.*, vol. 2, 172–238.
Cod: 5,842
020 **Prometheus**, ed. Harmon, *op. cit.*, vol. 2, 242–
264.
Cod: 2,419
021 **Icaromenippus**, ed. Harmon, *op. cit.*, vol. 2,
268–322.
Cod: 5,372
022 **Timon**, ed. Macleod, *Luciani opera*, vol. 1,
310–336.
Cod: 6,070
023 **Charon sive contemplantes**, ed. Harmon, *op.
cit.*, vol. 2, 396–446.
Cod: 4,340
024 **Vitarum auctio**, ed. Harmon, *op. cit.*, vol. 2,
450–510.
Cod: 3,747
025 **Revivescentes sive piscator**, ed. Harmon, *op.
cit.*, vol. 3 (1921; repr. 1969): 2–80.
Cod: 6,621
026 **Bis accusatus sive tribunalia**, ed. Harmon, *op.
cit.*, vol. 3, 84–150.
Cod: 5,861
027 **De sacrificiis**, ed. Harmon, *op. cit.*, vol. 3, 154–
170.
Cod: 1,830
028 **Adversus indoctum et libros multos ementem**,
ed. Harmon, *op. cit.*, vol. 3, 174–210.
Cod: 3,916
029 **Somnium sive vita Luciani**, ed. Harmon, *op.
cit.*, vol. 3, 214–232.
Cod: 1,837
030 **De parasito sive artem esse parasiticam**, ed.
Harmon, *op. cit.*, vol. 3, 236–316.
Cod: 6,685

031 **Philopseudes sive incredulus**, ed. Harmon, *op. cit.*, vol. 3, 320–380.
Cod: 6,401

032 **Dearum judicium**, ed. Harmon, *op. cit.*, vol. 3, 384–408.
Cod: 2,090

033 **De mercede conductis potentium familiaribus**, ed. Harmon, *op. cit.*, vol. 3, 412–480.
Cod: 7,251

034 **Anacharsis**, ed. Harmon, *op. cit.*, vol. 4 (1925; repr. 1961): 2–68.
Cod: 6,527

035 **Menippus sive necyomantia**, ed. Harmon, *op. cit.*, vol. 4, 72–108.
Cod: 3,379

036 **De luctu**, ed. Harmon, *op. cit.*, vol. 4, 112–130.
Cod: 1,802

037 **Rhetorum praeceptor**, ed. Harmon, *op. cit.*, vol. 4, 134–170.
Cod: 3,572

038 **Alexander**, ed. Harmon, *op. cit.*, vol. 4, 174–252.
Cod: 7,021

039 **Imagines**, ed. Harmon, *op. cit.*, vol. 4, 256–294.
Cod: 3,329

040 **Pro imaginibus**, ed. Harmon, *op. cit.*, vol. 4, 298–334.
Cod: 3,585

041 **De Syria dea**, ed. Harmon, *op. cit.*, vol. 4, 338–410.
Cod: 6,367

042 **De morte Peregrini**, ed. Harmon, *op. cit.*, vol. 5 (1936; repr. 1972): 2–50.
Cod: 4,285

043 **Fugitivi**, ed. Harmon, *op. cit.*, vol. 5, 54–98.
Cod: 3,278

044 **Toxaris vel amicitia**, ed. Harmon, *op. cit.*, vol. 5, 102–206.
Cod: 9,918

045 **De saltatione**, ed. Harmon, *op. cit.*, vol. 5, 210–288.
Cod: 7,126

046 **Lexiphanes**, ed. Harmon, *op. cit.*, vol. 5, 292–326.
Cod: 2,929

047 **Eunuchus**, ed. Harmon, *op. cit.*, vol. 5, 330–344.
Cod: 1,341

048 **De astrologia**, ed. Harmon, *op. cit.*, vol. 5, 348–368.
Cod: 2,001

049 **Pseudologista**, ed. Harmon, *op. cit.*, vol. 5, 372–414.
Cod: 4,004

050 **Deorum concilium**, ed. Harmon, *op. cit.*, vol. 5, 418–440.
Cod: 1,902

051 **Tyrannicida**, ed. Harmon, *op. cit.*, vol. 5, 444–472.
Cod: 2,916

052 **Abdicatus**, ed. Harmon, *op. cit.*, vol. 5, 476–524.
Cod: 4,884

053 **Quomodo historia conscribenda sit**, ed. K. Kilburn, *Lucian*, vol. 6. Cambridge, Mass.: Harvard University Press, 1959 (repr. 1968): 2–72.
Cod: 7,639

054 **Dipsades**, ed. Kilburn, *op. cit.*, vol. 6, 76–84.
Cod: 945

055 **Saturnalia**, ed. Kilburn, *op. cit.*, vol. 6, 88–138.
Cod: 5,286

056 **Herodotus**, ed. Kilburn, *op. cit.*, vol. 6, 142–150.
Cod: 937

057 **Zeuxis**, ed. Kilburn, *op. cit.*, vol. 6, 154–168.
Cod: 1,611

058 **Pro lapsu inter salutandum**, ed. Kilburn, *op. cit.*, vol. 6, 172–188.
Cod: 1,631

059 **Apologia**, ed. Kilburn, *op. cit.*, vol. 6, 192–212.
Cod: 2,101

060 **Harmonides**, ed. Kilburn, *op. cit.*, vol. 6, 216–224.
Cod: 995

061 **Hesiodus**, ed. Kilburn, *op. cit.*, vol. 6, 228–236.
Cod: 942

062 **Scytha**, ed. Kilburn, *op. cit.*, vol. 6, 240–256.
Cod: 1,862

063 **Hermotimus**, ed. Kilburn, *op. cit.*, vol. 6, 260–414.
Cod: 14,455

064 **Prometheus es in verbis**, ed. Kilburn, *op. cit.*, vol. 6, 418–426.
Cod: 1,033

065 **Navigium**, ed. Kilburn, *op. cit.*, vol. 6, 430–486.
Cod: 5,504

066 **Dialogi mortuorum**, ed. Macleod, *Lucian*, vol. 7. Cambridge, Mass.: Harvard University Press, 1961: 2–174.
Cod: 11,885

067 **Dialogi marini**, ed. Macleod, *Lucian*, vol. 7, 178–236.
Cod: 4,197

068 **Dialogi deorum**, ed. Macleod, *Lucian*, vol. 7, 240–352.
Cod: 8,021

069 **Dialogi meretricii**, ed. Macleod, *Lucian*, vol. 7, 356–466.
Cod: 8,303

070 **Soloecista**, ed. Macleod, *Lucian*, vol. 8. Cambridge, Mass.: Harvard University Press, 1967: 4–44.
Cod: 1,875

071 **Podagra**, ed. Macleod, *Lucian*, vol. 8, 324–354.
Cod: 1,813

x01 **Epigrammata**.
Cf. Pseudo-LUCIANUS Soph. (0061 009–010).

x02 **Oracula Ficta**.
App. Anth. 6.296–307.
Cf. EPIGRAMMATICI in *App. Anth.* (7052 006).

0061 **Pseudo-LUCIANUS** Soph.
post A.D. 2
001 **Asinus**, ed. M.D. Macleod, *Lucian*, vol. 8.
Cambridge, Mass.: Harvard University Press,
1967: 52–144.
Cod: 9,802
002 **Amores**, ed. Macleod, *op. cit.*, 150–234.
Cod: 7,747
003 **Demosthenis encomium**, ed. Macleod, *op. cit.*,
238–300.
Cod: 5,224
004 **Halcyon**, ed. Macleod, *op. cit.*, 306–316.
Cod: 948
005 **Ocypus**, ed. Macleod, *op. cit.*, 358–376.
Cod: 1,131
006 **Cynicus**, ed. Macleod, *op. cit.*, 380–410.
Cod: 2,487
007 **Philopatris**, ed. Macleod, *op. cit.*, 416–464.
Cod: 3,402
008 **Charidemus**, ed. Macleod, *op. cit.*, 468–502.
Cod: 3,500
009 **Epigramma**, ed. Macleod, *op. cit.*, 526.
Q: 33
010 **Epigrammata**, AG **6**.17; **7**.308; **9**.120, 367;
10.26–29, 31, 35–37, 41–42, 122; **11**.274, 294,
396–397, 400–405, 410, 427–436; **16**.154,
163–164, 238.
AG 6.20: Cf. JULIANUS <Epigr.> (4050 001).
AG 6.164; 11.10, 68, 239, 278, 408: Cf. LU-
CILLIUS Epigr. (1468 001).
AG 7.339; 9.74; 10.30; 11.420: Cf. ANONYMI
EPIGRAMMATICI (0138 001).
AG 10.58: Cf. PALLADAS Epigr. (2123 001).
AG 11.17: Cf. NICARCHUS II Epigr. (1532
001).
AG 11.129: Cf. CEREALIUS Epigr. (0151 001).
Q: 1,141
x01 **Nero**.
Cf. Flavius PHILOSTRATUS Soph. (0638 005).
x02 **Epistulae**.
Cf. ANACHARSIDIS EPISTULAE (0037 001).
Cf. PHALARIDIS EPISTULAE (0053 001).
x03 **Epigramma demonstrativum**.
App. Anth. 3.132: Cf. EPIGRAMMATICI in
App. Anth. (7052 003).

2957 **LUCIANUS** Theol. et Int. Vet. Test.
A.D. 4: Antiochenus
001 **Epistula ad Antiochenos** (fragmentum), ed. L.
Dindorf, *Chronicon Paschale*, vol. 1 [*Corpus
scriptorum historiae Byzantinae*. Bonn: Weber,
1832]: 516.
Q
002 **In Job 2.9–10** (fragmentum), ed. D. Hagedorn,
Der Hiobkommentar des Arianers Julian [*Pa-
tristische Texte und Studien* 14. Berlin: De
Gruyter, 1973]: 30–33.
Q

1468 **LUCILLIUS** Epigr.
A.D. 1
001 **Epigrammata**, AG 5.68; **6**.164, 166; **9**.55, 572;

11.10–11, 68–69, 75–81, 83–85, 87–95, 99–
101, 103–107, 111–116, 131–143, 148, 153–
155, 159–161, 163–165, 171–172, 174–179,
183–185, 189–192, 194, 196–197, 205–208,
210–212, 214–217, 233–234, 239–240, 245–
247, 249, 253–254, 256–259, 264–266, 276–
279, 295, 308–315, 388–393, 408.
AG 9.573: Cf. AMMIANUS Epigr. (0109 001).
AG 9.574; 11.282, 316, 394: Cf. ANONYMI
EPIGRAMMATICI (0138 001).
AG 10.122; 11.294, 433: Cf. Pseudo-LUCI-
ANUS Soph. (0061 010).
AG 11.173: Cf. PHILIPPUS Epigr. (1589 001).
AG 11.195: Cf. DIOSCORIDES Epigr. (0173
001).
AG 11.281, 293: Cf. PALLADAS Epigr. (2123
001).
Q: 3,903

0952 **LUCIUS** Med.
A.D. 1: fort. Tarsensis
x01 **Fragmenta ap. Galenum**.
K12.488, 787, 828; **13**.287, 292–293, 295, 746,
829, 850, 852, 853–854, 857, 934, 969.
Cf. GALENUS Med. (0057 076–077).
x02 **Fragmentum ap. Aëtium** (lib. 12).
Kostomiris, p. 80.
Cf. AËTIUS Med. (0718 012).
x03 **Fragmenta ap. Aëtium** (lib. 15).
Zervos, *Athena* 21, pp. 30, 92.
Cf. AËTIUS Med. (0718 015).

2686 **LUCULLUS** Epigr.
A.D. 3/4
x01 **Epigramma sepulcrale**.
App. Anth. 2.496: Cf. EPIGRAMMATICI in
App. Anth. (7052 002).

1977 **Lucius Licinius LUCULLUS** Hist.
1 B.C.
001 **Testimonia**, FGrH #185: 2B:917.
NQ

2439 **LUPERCUS** Gramm.
A.D. 3: Berytensis
001 **Testimonium**, FGrH #636: 3C:183–184.
NQ

1469 **LYCEAS** Hist.
4 B.C.?: Naucratites
001 **Fragmenta**, FGrH #613: 3C:120–121.
Q

2212 **LYCEAS** Hist.
ante A.D. 2: fort. Argivus
001 **Fragmenta**, FGrH #312: 3B:21–22.
Q
002 **Titulus**, ed. H. Lloyd-Jones and P. Parsons,
Supplementum Hellenisticum. Berlin: De Gruyter, 1983: 257.
titul. 527.
NQ: [2]

0953 **LYCOMEDES** Med.
ante A.D. 1
x01 **Fragmentum ap. Galenum.**
K13.92.
Cf. GALENUS Med. (0057 076).

2246 **LYCON** Phil.
vel Lycus
4 B.C.: Tarentinus vel Iasensis
001 **Testimonia**, ed. H. Diels and W. Kranz, *Die
Fragmente der Vorsokratiker*, vol. 1, 6th edn.
Berlin: Weidmann, 1951 (repr. Dublin: 1966):
445-446.
test. 1-5.
NQ

1138 **LYCON** Phil.
3 B.C.: Alexandrinus (Troadis)
001 **Fragmenta**, ed. F. Wehrli, *Lykon und Ariston
von Keos* [*Die Schule des Aristoteles*, vol. 6, 2nd
edn. Basel: Schwabe, 1968]: 11-15.
Q

2444 **LYCOPHRON** Soph.
4 B.C.
001 **Testimonia**, ed. H. Diels and W. Kranz, *Die
Fragmente der Vorsokratiker*, vol. 2, 6th edn.
Berlin: Weidmann, 1952 (repr. Dublin: 1966):
307-308.
test. 1-6.
NQ

0341 **LYCOPHRON** Trag.
4-3 B.C.: Chalcidicus, Alexandrinus
001 **Fragmenta**, ed. B. Snell, *Tragicorum Graecorum fragmenta*, vol. 1. Göttingen: Vandenhoeck & Ruprecht, 1971: 275-278.
frr. 2-5 + tituli (frr. 1-1k, 4a-4c, 6-9).
Q: 138
002 **Alexandra**, ed. L. Mascialino, *Lycophronis Alexandra*. Leipzig: Teubner, 1964: 1-65.
Cod: 7,527
003 **Titulus**, ed. H. Lloyd-Jones and P. Parsons,
Supplementum Hellenisticum. Berlin: De Gruyter, 1983: 258.
titul. 531.
NQ: [1]

0381 **LYCOPHRONIDES** Lyr.
4 B.C.
001 **Fragmenta**, ed. D.L. Page, *Poetae melici
Graeci*. Oxford: Clarendon Press, 1962 (repr.
1967 (1st edn. corr.)): 446.
frr. 1-2.
Q: [52]

0034 **LYCURGUS** Orat.
4 B.C.: Atheniensis
001 **Oratio in Leocratem**, ed. N.C. Conomis (post
C. Scheibe & F. Blass), *Lycurgi oratio in Leocratem*. Leipzig: Teubner, 1970: 33-90.
Cod: 11,217

002 **Fragmenta**, ed. Conomis, *op. cit.*, 91-92, 95-
118, 120.
Ἀπολογισμὸς ὧν πεπολίτευται (fr. 1): pp. 91-
92.
Κατ' Ἀριστογείτονος (fr. 2): pp. 95-96.
Κατ' Αὐτολύκου (fr. 3): p. 97.
Πρὸς Δημάδην ὑπὲρ τῶν εὐθυνῶν (fr. 4): p. 98.
Περὶ τῆς διοικήσεως (fr. 5): pp. 98-100.
Περὶ τῆς ἱερείας (fr. 6): pp. 100-105.
Περὶ τῆς ἱερωσύνης sive Κροκωνιδῶν διαδικα-
σία πρὸς Κοιρωνίδας (fr. 7): pp. 105-107.
Κατὰ Ἰσχυρίου (fr. 8): p. 107.
Κατὰ Κηφισοδότου ὑπὲρ τῶν Δημάδου τιμῶν
(fr. 9): pp. 107-108.
Κατὰ Λυκόφρονος εἰσαγγελία Α'Β' (frr. 10-
11): pp. 109-112.
Κατὰ Λυσικλέους (fr. 12): p. 113.
Πρὸς τὰς μαντείας sive Περὶ τῶν μαντειῶν (fr.
13): pp. 113-114.
Κατὰ Μενεσαίχμου εἰσαγγελία sive Δηλιακός
(fr. 14): pp. 114-118.
Fragmenta sedis incertae (fr. 15): pp. 118, 120.
Q, Pap: 3,581

1470 **LYCUS** Hist.
4-3 B.C.: Rheginus
001 **Testimonia**, FGrH #570: 3B:664.
NQ
002 **Fragmenta**, FGrH #570: 3B:664-668.
Q
003 **Fragmenta**, ed. H.J. Mette, "Die 'Kleinen'
griechischen Historiker heute," *Lustrum* 21
(1978) 31-32.
fr. 1 bis a-b.
Q

2267 **LYCUS** Hist.
post 4 B.C.
001 **Fragmenta**, FGrH #380: 3B:249-250.
Q

0955 **LYCUS** Med.
2-1 B.C.: Neapolitanus
Cf. et ANONYMUS NEAPOLITANUS Med.
(1119).
x01 **Fragmenta ap. Oribasium.**
CMG, vol. **6.1.1**, pp. 278, 293; **6.1.2**, p. 28;
6.2.1, p. 46; **6.3**, pp. 22, 119.
Cf. ORIBASIUS Med. (0722 001, 004).
x02 **Fragmentum ap. Paulum.**
CMG, vol. 9.2, p. 17.
Cf. PAULUS Med. (0715 001).
x03 **Fragmentum ap. Aëtium** (lib. 3).
CMG, vol. 8.1, p. 349.
Cf. AËTIUS Med. (0718 003).

0954 **LYCUS** Med.
A.D. 2: Macedonius
x01 **Fragmenta ap. Galenum.**
K18.1.198, 216 in CMG, vol. 5.10.3, pp. 4, 13.
Cf. GALENUS Med. (0057 093).

2580 **Joannes Laurentius LYDUS** Hist.
A.D. 6: Philadelphius, Constantinopolitanus
001 **De magistratibus populi Romani**, ed. R. Wünsch, *Ioannis Lydi de magistratibus populi Romani libri tres.* Leipzig: Teubner, 1903 (repr. Stuttgart: 1967): 1–170.
Cod
002 **De mensibus**, ed. R. Wünsch, *Ioannis Lydi liber de mensibus.* Leipzig: Teubner, 1898 (repr. Stuttgart: 1967): 1–184.
Cod
003 **De ostentis**, ed. C. Wachsmuth, *Ioannis Laurentii Lydi liber de ostentis et calendaria Graeca omnia.* Leipzig: Teubner, 1897: 3–160.
Cod

0471 **LYNCEUS** Comic.
4/3 B.C.: Samius
001 **Fragmentum**, ed. T. Kock, *Comicorum Atticorum fragmenta*, vol. 3. Leipzig: Teubner, 1888: 274–275.
fr. 1.
Q: 158
002 **Fragmentum**, ed. A. Meineke, *Fragmenta comicorum Graecorum*, vol. 4. Berlin: Reimer, 1841 (repr. De Gruyter, 1970): 433.
Q: 157

0230 *LYRICA ADESPOTA* (CA)
Varia
001 **Fragmenta lyrica**, ed. J.U. Powell, *Collectanea Alexandrina.* Oxford: Clarendon Press, 1925 (repr. 1970): 177–179, 181–200.
Παρακλαυσίθυρον (fr. 1): pp. 177–179.
Mimi fragmenta (fr. 2): p. 181.
Κωμαστής (fr. 3): pp. 181–182.
Παῖς ἀλέκτορα ἀπολέσας (fr. 4): pp. 182–183.
Marisaeum melos (fr. 5): p. 184.
Helenae querimonia (fr. 6): p. 185.
Saltus montanus (fr. 7): p. 185.
Aphorismi erotici (fr. 8): p. 186.
Fragmentum Pseudo-Alcmanis (fr. 9): p. 186.
Laudes Homeri (fr. 10): pp. 187–188.
Cassandrae oracula (fr. 11): pp. 188–189.
Choliambi anonymi (frr. 12–15): p. 190.
Scolia (sine titulo) (frr. 16–17, 21): pp. 190–192.
Musae (scolion) (fr. 18): p. 191.
Εὐφωρατίς (scolion) (fr. 19): p. 191.
Mnemosyne (scolion) (fr. 20): pp. 191–192.
Fragmenta dithyramborum (frr. 22–25): pp. 192–193.
Partheneion (fr. 26): p. 193.
Fragmenta Phalaecea (frr. 27–30): pp. 193–194.
Ἐπῳδοί (fr. 31): p. 194.
Nautarum cantilena (fr. 32): p. 195.
Ῥοδίοις ἀνέμοις (fr. 33): pp. 195–196.
Hymnus in Fortunam (fr. 34): p. 196.
Εἰς τὴν φύσιν Πυθαγόρου (fr. 35): p. 197.
Εἰς τὴν Ἴσιν (fr. 36): p. 198.
Aulodiae (fr. 37): pp. 199–200.

Monodia (fr. 38): p. 200.
Q, Cod, Pap: [2,237]

0297 *LYRICA ADESPOTA* (PMG)
Varia
001 **Fragmenta**, ed. D.L. Page, *Poetae melici Graeci.* Oxford: Clarendon Press, 1962 (repr. 1967 (1st edn. corr.)): 484–546, 548–551.
frr. 1–9, 11–53, 55–63, 66–97, 99–127.
Q, Pap, Epigr: [3,210]

1471 *LYRICA ADESPOTA* (SLG)
Varia
001 **Fragmenta**, ed. D.L. Page, *Supplementum lyricis Graecis.* Oxford: Clarendon Press, 1974: 106–151.
frr. S317–S475, S477.
Q, Pap, Epigr: [2,933]

2402 **LYSANDER** Hist.
vel Cleon Halicarnassensis
5/4 B.C.
001 **Testimonia**, FGrH #583: 3B:694–695.
NQ

2298 **LYSANIAS** Hist.
ante A.D. 2: Mallotes
001 **Fragmentum**, FGrH #426: 3B:322.
Q

0956 **LYSIAS** Med.
ante A.D. 1
x01 **Fragmentum ap. Galenum.**
K13.49.
Cf. GALENUS Med. (0057 076).

0540 **LYSIAS** Orat.
5–4 B.C.: Atheniensis
001 **De caede Eratosthenis**, ed. U. Albini, *Lisia. I discorsi.* Florence: Sansoni, 1955: 6–16.
Cod: 2,525
002 **Epitaphius** [Sp.], ed. Albini, *op. cit.*, 320–337.
Cod: 4,251
003 **Contra Simonem**, ed. Albini, *op. cit.*, 20–29.
Cod: 2,280
004 Περὶ τραύματος ἐκ προνοίας ὑπὲρ οὗ καὶ πρὸς ὃν <ἄδηλον>, ed. Albini, *op. cit.*, 34–38.
Cod: 1,010
005 **Pro Callia**, ed. Albini, *op. cit.*, 42–43.
Cod: 292
006 **In Andocidem** [Sp.], ed. Albini, *op. cit.*, 342–353.
Cod: 2,744
007 **Areopagiticus**, ed. Albini, *op. cit.*, 48–56.
Cod: 2,119
008 Κατηγορία πρὸς τοὺς συνουσιαστὰς κακολογιῶν [Sp.], ed. Albini, *op. cit.*, 358–362.
Cod: 1,078
009 **Pro milite** [Sp.], ed. Albini, *op. cit.*, 366–370.
Cod: 926
010 **In Theomnestum 1**, ed. Albini, *op. cit.*, 60–66.
Cod: 1,544

011 **In Theomnestum 2** [Sp.], ed. Albini, *op. cit.*, 372–374.
Cod: 574

012 **In Eratosthenem**, ed. Albini, *op. cit.*, 70–90.
Cod: 5,052

013 **In Agoratum**, ed. Albini, *op. cit.*, 94–116.
Cod: 5,074

014 **In Alcibiadem 1**, ed. Albini, *op. cit.*, 120–130.
Cod: 2,501

015 **In Alcibiadem 2**, ed. Albini, *op. cit.*, 132–134.
Cod: 632

016 **Pro Mantitheo**, ed. Albini, *op. cit.*, 138–143.
Cod: 1,193

017 Πρὸς τὸ δημόσιον περὶ τῶν Ἐράτωνος χρημάτων, ed. Albini, *op. cit.*, 148–151.
Cod: 621

018 Περὶ τῆς δημεύσεως <τῶν> τοῦ Νικίου ἀδελφοῦ ἐπίλογος, ed. Albini, *op. cit.*, 156–161.
Cod: 1,410

019 Ὑπὲρ τῶν Ἀριστοφάνους χρημάτων, πρὸς τὸ δημόσιον, ed. Albini, *op. cit.*, 166–180.
Cod: 3,260

020 **Pro Polystrato** [Sp.], ed. Albini, *op. cit.*, 378–386.
Cod: 1,994

021 Ἀπολογία δωροδοκίας ἀπαράσημος, ed. Albini, *op. cit.*, 184–189.
Cod: 1,354

022 Κατὰ τῶν σιτοπωλῶν, ed. Albini, *op. cit.*, 194–199.
Cod: 1,175

023 **In Pancleonem**, ed. Albini, *op. cit.*, 204–207.
Cod: 804

024 <Ὑπὲρ τοῦ ἀδυνάτου>, ed. Albini, *op. cit.*, 212–218.
Cod: 1,485

025 [Δήμου καταλύσεως] ἀπολογία, ed. Albini, *op. cit.*, 222–230.
Cod: 2,117

026 <Περὶ τῆς Εὐάνδρου δοκιμασίας>, ed. Albini, *op. cit.*, 234–240.
Cod: 1,441

027 **In Epicratem**, ed. Albini, *op. cit.*, 244–247.
Cod: 794

028 **In Ergoclem**, ed. Albini, *op. cit.*, 252–256.
Cod: 959

029 **In Philocratem**, ed. Albini, *op. cit.*, 260–263.
Cod: 704

030 **In Nicomachum**, ed. Albini, *op. cit.*, 268–276.
Cod: 1,971

031 **In Philonem**, ed. Albini, *op. cit.*, 280–288.
Cod: 1,894

032 **In Diogitonem**, ed. Albini, *op. cit.*, 292–300.
Cod: 1,784

033 **Olympiacus**, ed. Albini, *op. cit.*, 304–306.
Cod: 457

034 Περὶ τοῦ μὴ καταλῦσαι τὴν πάτριον πολιτείαν Ἀθήνησι, ed. Albini, *op. cit.*, 310–313.
Cod: 584

035 **Fragmenta**, ed. Albini, *op. cit.*, 394–407.
Πρὸς Ἱπποθέρσην, ὑπὲρ θεραπαίνης: pp. 394–397.

Πρὸς Θεόμνηστον: pp. 397–398.
Κατὰ Θεοζοτίδου: pp. 399–400.
Πρὸς Αἰσχίνης τὸν Σωκρατικὸν χρέως: pp. 400–401.
Πρὸς Ἀρχεβιάδην: p. 402.
Κατὰ Τείσιδος: pp. 402–404.
Πρὸς τοὺς Ἱπποκράτους παῖδας: pp. 404–405.
Ὑπὲρ Φερενίκου περὶ τοῦ Ἀνδροκλείδου κλήρου: pp.405–406.
Πρὸς Κινησίαν ὑπὲρ Φανίου παρανόμων: pp. 406–407.
Q, Pap: 2,527

036 **Fragmenta**, ed. T. Thalheim, *Lysiae orationes* (editio maior), 2nd edn. Leipzig: Teubner, 1913: 328–366, 368–370.
frr. 1–102b, 109b: pp. 328–366, 368.
frr. 110–115 (epistulae): pp. 369–370.
fr. 116 (vocabula singula): p. 370.
Q, Pap: [9,016]

037 **Fragmentum**, *P. Rain.* 1.13.
Pap

2262 **LYSIMACHIDES** Hist.
1 B.C.–A.D. 1?

001 **Fragmenta**, FGrH #366: 3B:226–228.
Q

0574 **LYSIMACHUS** Hist.
4–3 B.C.: Alexandrinus

001 **Fragmenta**, FGrH #382: 3B:251–258.
fr. 21: *P. Oxy.* 15.1790.
Q, Pap

002 **Fragmenta**, ed. H.J. Mette, "Die 'Kleinen' griechischen Historiker heute," *Lustrum* 21 (1978) 27–28.
frr. 12b, 23 (olim 21).
fr. 23: *P. Oxy.* 15.1790.
Q, Pap

1965 **LYSIMACHUS** Hist.
3–2 B.C.

001 **Testimonium**, FGrH #170: 2B:895.
NQ

2427 **LYSIMACHUS** Hist.
1 B.C.–A.D. 1?

001 **Testimonia**, FGrH #621: 3C:154–155.
NQ

002 **Fragmenta**, FGrH #621: 3C:155–156.
Q

0472 **LYSIPPUS** Comic.
5 B.C.

001 **Fragmenta**, ed. T. Kock, *Comicorum Atticorum fragmenta*, vol. 1. Leipzig: Teubner, 1880: 700–703.
frr. 1–5, 7–10 + tituli.
Q: 98

002 **Fragmenta**, ed. A. Meineke, *Fragmenta comicorum Graecorum*, vol. 2.2. Berlin: Reimer, 1840 (repr. De Gruyter, 1970): 744–746, 748.
Q: 151

003 **Titulus**, ed. C. Austin, *Comicorum Graecorum fragmenta in papyris reperta.* Berlin: De Gruyter, 1973: 121.
NQ: 2

0633 **<LYSIS>** Phil.
4/2 B.C.: Tarentinus
001 **Epistula ad Hipparchum**, ed. H. Thesleff, *The Pythagorean texts of the Hellenistic period.* Åbo: Åbo Akademi, 1965: 111–114.
Q: 544
002 **Testimonia**, ed. H. Diels and W. Kranz, *Die Fragmente der Vorsokratiker*, vol. 1, 6th edn. Berlin: Weidmann, 1951 (repr. Dublin: 1966): 420–421.
test. 1–5: auctores alii nominantur Archippus et Opsimus.
NQ

1472 **LYSISTRATUS** Epigr.
5 B.C.: Atheniensis
001 **Epigramma**, AG 9.509.
Q: 6

2318 **MACARIUS** Hist.
3 B.C.?: Cous
001 **Fragmenta**, FGrH #456: 3B:384.
Q

MACARIUS Paroemiogr.
A.D. 14: Philadelphius
Cf. Macarius CHRYSOCEPHALUS Paroemiogr. (9008).

2109 **<MACARIUS>** Scr. Eccl.
A.D. 4: Aegyptius
001 **Sermones 64** (collectio B), ed. H. Berthold, *Makarios/Symeon Reden und Briefe*, 2 vols. [*Die griechischen christlichen Schriftsteller.* Berlin: Akademie-Verlag, 1973]: 1:3–265; 2:3–219.
Cod: [152,077]
002 **Homiliae spirituales 50** (collectio H), ed. H. Dörries, E. Klostermann and M. Kroeger, *Die 50 geistlichen Homilien des Makarios* [*Patristische Texte und Studien* 4. Berlin: De Gruyter, 1964]: 1–322.
Cod: [83,388]
003 **Sermones 1–22, 24–27**, ed. E. Klostermann and H. Berthold, *Neue Homilien des Makarius/Symeon* [*Texte und Untersuchungen* 72. Berlin: Akademie-Verlag, 1961]: 1–113, 128–158.
Cod: [37,197]
004 **Homiliae 7** (collectio HA), ed. G.L. Marriott, *Macarii anecdota* [*Harvard Theological Studies* 5. Cambridge, Mass.: Harvard University Press, 1918 (repr. New York: Kraus, 1969)]: 19–48.
Cod: [9,878]
005 **Epistula magna**, ed. W. Jaeger, *Two rediscovered works of ancient Christian literature:*

Gregory of Nyssa and Macarius. Leiden: Brill, 1954: 233–301.
Cod: [13,714]
006 **Sermo 23** (recensio excerpta), ed. Klostermann and Berthold, *op. cit.*, 114, 116, 118, 120, 122, 124, 126.
Cod: [527]
007 **Sermo 23** (recensio completa), ed. Klostermann and Berthold, *op. cit.*, 115, 117, 119, 121, 123, 125, 127.
Cod: [2,027]
008 **Sermo 28** (recensio expletior), ed. Klostermann and Berthold, *op. cit.*, 160, 162, 164, 166–170.
Cod: [1,880]
009 **Sermo 28** (recensio brevior), ed. Klostermann and Berthold, *op. cit.*, 161, 163, 165.
Cod: [952]
010 **Preces**, MPG 34: 445–448.
Cod: [367]
011 **Apophthegmata**, MPG 34: 236–261.
Cod: [4,878]
012 **Opusculum 1** (= **De custodia cordis**), MPG 34: 821–841.
Cod: [4,117]
013 **Sermo 17** (excerpta), ed. Klostermann and Berthold, *op. cit.*, 91–94.
Cod: [154]

1473 **MACEDONIUS I** Epigr.
1 B.C.?: Thessalonicensis
001 **Epigrammata**, AG 9.275; 11.27, 39.
Q: 85

4064 **MACEDONIUS II** Epigr.
A.D. 6: Thessalonicensis
001 **Epigrammata**, AG 5.223–225, 227, 229, 231, 233, 235, 238, 240, 243, 245, 247, 271; 6.30, 40, 56, 69–70, 73, 83, 175–176; 7.566; 9.625, 645, 648–649; 10.67, 70–71; 11.58–59, 61, 63, 366, 370, 374–375, 380; 16.51.
Q: 1,643

0202 **MACE(DONIUS)** Lyr.
Incertum
001 **Paean in Apollinem et Aesculapium** (*IG* 3.1.171b), ed. J.U. Powell, *Collectanea Alexandrina.* Oxford: Clarendon Press, 1925 (repr. 1970): 138–139.
Epigr: [159]
x01 **Epigramma exhortatorium et supplicatorium.**
App. Anth. 4.53(?): Cf. EPIGRAMMATICI in *App. Anth.* (7052 004).

0957 **MACHAERION** Med.
ante A.D. 2
x01 **Fragmentum ap. Galenum.**
K13.797.
Cf. GALENUS Med. (0057 077).
x02 **Fragmentum ap. Paulum.**
CMG, vol. 9.2, p. 364.
Cf. PAULUS Med. (0715 001).

x03 **Fragmentum ap. Aëtium** (lib. 15).
Zervos, *Athena* 21, p. 41.
Cf. AËTIUS Med. (0718 015).

MACHAON Med.
Cf. ASCLEPIUS et MACHAON Med. (0879).

0473 **MACHON** Comic.
3 B.C.: Corinthius, Sicyonius, Alexandrinus
001 **Fragmenta**, ed. A.S.F. Gow, *Machon. The fragments*. Cambridge: Cambridge University Press, 1965: 35-56.
frr. 1-21.
Q: 2,986
002 **Fragmenta**, ed. T. Kock, *Comicorum Atticorum fragmenta*, vol. 3. Leipzig: Teubner, 1888: 324-325.
frr. 1-2.
Q: 96
003 **Fragmenta**, ed. A. Meineke, *Fragmenta comicorum Graecorum*, vol. 4. Berlin: Reimer, 1841 (repr. De Gruyter, 1970): 496-497.
Q: 96

2339 **MAEANDRIUS** Hist.
ante 3 B.C.: Milesius
001 **Fragmenta**, FGrH #491: 3B:459-461.
frr. 1-9.
fr. 1a-c: *Inscr. Priene* 37.
Q, Epigr

1474 **Quintus MAECIUS** Epigr.
1 B.C.
001 **Epigrammata**, AG **5**.114, 117, 130, 133; **6**.33, 89, 230(?), 233; **9**.249, 403, 411; **16**.198.
AG 7.635: Cf. ANTIPHILUS Epigr. (0118 001).
Q: 467

5002 *MAGICA*
Varia
Bibliography in progress
001 **Papyri magicae**, ed. K. Preisendanz and A. Henrichs, *Papyri Graecae magicae. Die griechischen Zauberpapyri*, vols. 1-2, 2nd edn. Stuttgart: Teubner, 1:1973; 2:1974: 1:2-200; 2:1-266.
Pap

0474 **MAGNES** Comic.
5 B.C.
001 **Fragmenta**, ed. T. Kock, *Comicorum Atticorum fragmenta*, vol. 1. Leipzig: Teubner, 1880: 7-9.
frr. 1-7 + tituli.
Q: 55
002 **Fragmenta**, ed. A. Meineke, *Fragmenta comicorum Graecorum*, vol. 2.1. Berlin: Reimer, 1839 (repr. De Gruyter, 1970): 9-11.
Q: 46
003 **Fragmentum**, ed. J. Demiańczuk, *Supplementum comicum*. Krakau: Nakładem Akademii,

1912 (repr. Hildesheim: Olms, 1967): 54.
fr. 1.
Q: 2

2157 **MAGNUS** Hist.
A.D. 4: Carrhaeus
001 **Testimonia**, FGrH #225: 2B:951-952.
NQ
002 **Fragmenta**, FGrH #225: 2B:952-954.
Q

0961 **MAGNUS** Med.
A.D. 1: Philadelphius
x01 **Fragmenta ap. Galenum**.
K13.80, 829, 831.
Cf. GALENUS Med. (0057 076-077).

0962 **MAGNUS** Med.
ante A.D. 2: Tarsensis
x01 **Fragmentum ap. Galenum**.
K13.313.
Cf. GALENUS Med. (0057 076).

0965 **MAGNUS** Med.
A.D. 2: Ephesius
x01 **Fragmentum ap. Galenum**.
K8.640-641.
Cf. GALENUS Med. (0057 059).
x02 **Fragmentum ap. Oribasium**.
CMG, vol. 6.2.2, p. 217.
Cf. ORIBASIUS Med. (0722 003).

0959 **MAGNUS** Med.
ante A.D. 6
001 **Epigramma**, AG 16.270.
Q: 25
x01 **Fragmentum ap. Aëtium** (lib. 7).
CMG, vol. 8.2, p. 372.
Cf. AËTIUS Med. (0718 007).
x02 **Fragmentum ap. Alexandrum Trallianum**.
Puschmann, vol. 2, pp. 177-179.
Cf. ALEXANDER Med. (0744 003).
x03 **Fragmentum ap. Paulum**.
CMG, vol. 9.2, p. 341.
Cf. PAULUS Med. (0715 001).

0960 **MAGNUS ὁ ἀρχιατρός** Med.
A.D. 2
x01 **Fragmentum ap. Galenum**.
K14.262.
Cf. GALENUS Med. (0057 079).

0963 **MAGNUS ὁ κλινικός** Med.
ante A.D. 2
x01 **Fragmentum ap. Galenum**.
K12.829.
Cf. GALENUS Med. (0057 076).

1807 **MAGO** <Med.>
3/2 B.C.: Carthaginiensis
x01 **Fragmentum ap. Hippiatrica**.

Oder & Hoppe, vol. 1, pp. 141–142.
Cf. HIPPIATRICA (0738 001).

0920 **[MAIA]** Med.
Incertum
x01 **Fragmentum ap. Galenum.**
K13.840.
Cf. GALENUS Med. (0057 077).

1475 **MAIISTAS** Epic.
3 B.C.
001 **Aretalogia** (*IG* 11.4.1299), ed. J.U. Powell, *Collectanea Alexandrina.* Oxford: Clarendon Press, 1925 (repr. 1970): 69–71.
Epigr: [456]

2382 **MALACUS** Hist.
ante A.D. 3
001 **Fragmentum,** FGrH #552: 3B:539.
Q

2582 **MALCHUS** Hist.
A.D. 5–6: Philadelphius, Constantinopolitanus
001 **Fragmenta,** FHG 4: 111–132.
Q

1476 **MAMERCUS** Eleg.
4 B.C.
001 **Epigramma,** ed. E. Diehl, *Anthologia lyrica Graeca,* fasc. 1, 3rd edn. Leipzig: Teubner, 1949: 112.
Q: [10]
x01 **Epigramma dedicatorium.**
App. Anth. 1.84: Cf. EPIGRAMMATICI in *App. Anth.* (7052 001).

2583 **MANETHO** Astrol.
A.D. 4?
001 'Αποτελεσματικά, ed. A. Koechly, *Poetae bucolici et didactici.* Paris: Didot, 1862: 41–101.
Cod

1477 **MANETHO** Hist.
3 B.C.: Aegyptius
001 **Testimonia,** FGrH #609: 3C:5–10.
NQ
002 **Fragmenta,** FGrH #609: 3C:11–13, 16–55, 80–112.
frr. 1–24 = Manetho.
frr. 25–28 = Pseudo-Manetho.
fr. 11: *P. Baden* 59.
Q, Pap

1478 **Pseudo-MANETHO** Hist.
Incertum
001 **Fragmenta,** FGrH #610: 3C:112–118.
Cf. et MANETHO Hist. (1477 002).
Q

0966 **MANETHO** Med.
3 B.C.?
x01 **Fragmentum ap. Paulum.**

CMG, vol. 9.2, p. 324.
Cf. PAULUS Med. (0715 001).

0967 **MANTIAS** Med.
2 B.C.
x01 **Fragmenta ap. Galenum.**
K13.162, 751.
Cf. GALENUS Med. (0057 076–077).

0200 *MANTISSA PROVERBIORUM*
Incertum
001 **Mantissa proverbiorum,** ed. E.L. von Leutsch, *Corpus paroemiographorum Graecorum,* vol. 2. Göttingen: Vandenhoeck & Ruprecht, 1851 (repr. Hildesheim: Olms, 1958): 745–779.
Cod: [4,339]

2716 **MANUEL** Epigr.
A.D. 9
x01 **Epigramma exhortatorium et supplicatorium.**
App. Anth. 4.115: Cf. EPIGRAMMATICI in *App. Anth.* (7052 004).

2585 **MARCELLINUS** Biogr.
A.D. 4?
001 **Vita Thucydidis,** ed. H.S. Jones, *Thucydidis historiae,* vol. 1. Oxford: Clarendon Press, 1942 (1st edn. rev.) (repr. 1958): xi–xx.
Cod

0667 **MARCELLINUS I** Med.
A.D. 2
001 **De pulsibus,** ed. H. Schöne, "Marcellinos' Pulslehre. Ein griechisches Anekdoton," *Festschrift zur 49. Versammlung deutscher Philologen und Schulmänner.* Basel: Birkhäuser, 1907: 455–471.
Cod: 5,080

0968 **MARCELLINUS II** Med.
ante A.D. 1
x01 **Fragmentum ap. Galenum.**
K13.90.
Cf. GALENUS Med. (0057 076).
x02 **Fragmentum ap. Alexandrum Trallianum.**
Puschmann, vol. 2, p. 357.
Cf. ALEXANDER Med. (0744 003).

2676 **MARCELLUS** Epigr.
A.D. 2?
x01 **Epigrammata dedicatoria.**
App. Anth. 1.263–264: Cf. EPIGRAMMATICI in *App. Anth.* (7052 001).

2458 **MARCELLUS** Hist.
Incertum
001 **Fragmenta,** FGrH #671: 3C:283–284.
Q

0281 **MARCELLUS** Poet. Med.
A.D. 2: Sidetes
001 **De piscibus fragmentum,** ed. E. Heitsch, *Die*

*griechischen Dichterfragmente der römischen
Kaiserzeit*, vol. 2. Göttingen: Vandenhoeck &
Ruprecht, 1964: 17–22.
Cod: [654]

x01 **Fragmentum ap. Paulum.**
CMG, vol. 9.1, p. 331.
Cf. PAULUS Med. (0715 001).

x02 **Fragmentum ap. Aëtium** (lib. 6).
CMG, vol. 8.2, p. 151.
Cf. AËTIUS Med. (0718 006).

2041 **MARCELLUS** Theol.
A.D. 4: Ancyranus

001 **Fragmenta**, ed. E. Klostermann and G.C. Hansen, *Eusebius Werke*, vol. 4, 2nd edn. [*Die
griechischen christlichen Schriftsteller* 14. Berlin: Akademie-Verlag, 1972]: 185–215.
Fragmenta e libro contra Asterium (frr. 1–128):
pp. 185–214.
Epistula ad Julium papam (fr. 129): pp. 214–
215.
Q: [11,952]

002 **De sancta ecclesia**, ed. G. Mercati, *Anthimi
Nicomediensis episcopi et martyris de sancta ecclesia* in *Note di letteratura biblica e cristiana
antica* [*Studi e Testi* 5. Rome: Biblioteca Apostolica Vaticana, 1905]: 87–98.
Q

004 **Expositio fidei**, ed. H. Nordberg, *Athanasiana
I* [*Commentationes humanarum litterarum*
30.2. Helsinki: Centraltryckeriet, 1962]: 49–56.
Cod: [1,140]

005 **De incarnatione et contra Arianos**, MPG 26:
984–1028.
Cod

x01 **Sermo major de fide.**
Athanasius, *Sermo major de fide* [Sp.].
Cf. ATHANASIUS Theol. (2035 023).

x02 **Contra theopaschitas.**
Athanasius, *Epist. ad Liberium* [Sp.].
Cf. ATHANASIUS Theol. (2035 033).

1479 *MARCI AURELII EPISTULA*
post A.D. 2
Cf. et MARCUS AURELIUS ANTONINUS Imperator <Phil.> (0562).

001 **Epistula ad senatum, qua testatur Christianos
victoriae causam fuisse**, ed. J.C.T. Otto, *Corpus apologetarum Christianorum saeculi
secundi*, vol. 1, 3rd edn. Jena: Mauke, 1876
(repr. Wiesbaden: Sändig, 1969): 246–252.
Cod: [453]

4003 **MARCIANUS** Geogr.
A.D. 3/5: Heracleensis

001 **Periplus maris exteri**, ed. K. Müller, *Geographi
Graeci minores*, vol. 1. Paris: Didot, 1855 (repr.
Hildesheim: Olms, 1965): 515–562.
Cod: [12,112]

002 **Menippi periplus maris interni** (epitome Marciani), ed. Müller, *op. cit.*, 563–572.
Cod: [2,441]

003 **Artemidori geographia** (epitome Marciani), ed.
Müller, *op. cit.*, 574–576.
Q: [512]

0969 **MARCIANUS** Med.
ante A.D. 4: Africanus

x01 **Fragmentum ap. Oribasium.**
CMG, vol. 6.2.2, p. 243.
Cf. ORIBASIUS Med. (0722 003).

x02 **Fragmentum ap. Aëtium** (lib. 7).
CMG, vol. 8.2, p. 387.
Cf. AËTIUS Med. (0718 007).

x03 **Fragmentum ap. Aëtium** (lib. 8).
CMG, vol. 8.2, p. 485.
Cf. AËTIUS Med. (0718 008).

x04 **Fragmentum ap. Aëtium** (lib. 9).
Zervos, *Athena* 23, pp. 331, 389.
Cf. AËTIUS Med. (0718 009).

x05 **Fragmentum ap. Aëtium** (lib. 11).
Daremberg-Ruelle, p. 571.
Cf. AËTIUS Med. (0718 011).

x06 **Fragmentum ap. Aëtium** (lib. 12).
Kostomiris, p. 28.
Cf. AËTIUS Med. (0718 012).

1035 **MARCINUS** Med.
ante A.D. 6: Thrax

x01 **Fragmentum ap. Alexandrum Trallianum.**
Puschmann, vol. 1, p. 565.
Cf. ALEXANDER Med. (0744 003).

2958 **MARCION** Theol.
A.D. 2: Sinopensis

003 **Apostolicum**, ed. A. von Harnack, *Marcion:
Das Evangelium vom fremden Gott*, 2nd edn.
[*Texte und Untersuchungen* 45. Leipzig: Hin-
richs, 1924]: 67*–127*.
Q

002 **Evangelium**, ed. von Harnack, *op. cit.*, 183*–
240*.
Q

001 **Antitheses**, ed. von Harnack, *op. cit.*, 256*–
313*.
Q

1823 **MARCUS** Gnost.
A.D. 2

001 **Fragmenta**, ed. W. Völker, *Quellen zur Ge-
schichte der christlichen Gnosis*. Tübingen:
Mohr, 1932: 136–141.
Q

0970 **MARCUS** Med.
ante A.D. 2

x01 **Fragmentum ap. Galenum.**
K12.750.
Cf. GALENUS Med. (0057 076).

0562 **MARCUS AURELIUS ANTONINUS** Imperator Phil.
A.D. 2

Cf. et MARCI AURELII EPISTULA (1479).

001 Tὰ εἰς ἑαυτόν, ed. A.S.L. Farquharson, *The meditations of the emperor Marcus Aurelius*, vol. 1. Oxford: Clarendon Press, 1944 (repr. 1968): 4–250.
Cod: 29,724

0972 **MARCUS TELENTIUS** Med.
ante A.D. 2
x01 **Fragmentum ap. Galenum.**
K13.973.
Cf. GALENUS Med. (0057 077).

MARGITES
Cf. [HOMERUS] <Epic.> (0253).

1480 **MARIA JUDAEA** Alchem.
3/2 B.C.
001 **Fragmenta,** ed. M. Berthelot, *Collection des anciens alchimistes grecs.* Paris: Steinheil, 1887 (repr. London: Holland Press, 1963): 93, 102, 103, 146, 149, 152, 157, 169, 173, 182, 192, 193, 195, 196–197, 198, 200, 201, 236–237, 351, 356, 357, 382, 404.
Q

4073 **MARIANUS** Epigr.
A.D. 5–6
001 **Epigrammata,** AG **9.**626–627, 657, 668–669; **16.**201.
Q: 343

4074 **MARINUS** Epigr.
fiq Marinus Phil.
Incertum
Cf. et MARINUS Phil. (4075).
001 **Epigrammata,** AG 1.23, 28.
Q: 54

0973 **MARINUS** Med.
A.D. 2: fort. Alexandrinus
x01 **Fragmentum ap. Galenum.**
K13.25.
Cf. GALENUS Med. (0057 076).

4075 **MARINUS** Phil.
A.D. 5: Palaestinus
001 **Epigrammata,** AG 9.196–197.
Q: 53

2432 *MARMOR PARIUM*
3 B.C.
001 **Marmor Parium** (*IG* 12.5, 444), FGrH #239: 2B:992–1005.
Epigr

1481 **MARSYAS Pellaeus et MARSYAS Philippeus**
Hist.
post 4 B.C.: Pellaeus, Philippeus
001 **Testimonia,** FGrH #135–136: 2B:736–737.
NQ

002 **Fragmenta Marsyae Pellaei,** FGrH #135–136: 2B:737.
Q
003 **Fragmenta Marsyae Philippei,** FGrH #135–136: 2B:737–739.
Q
004 **Fragmenta Marsyae Pellaei vel Marsyae Philippei,** FGrH #135–136: 2B:739–741.
Q

2011 *MARTYRIUM AGAPAE, IRENAE, CHIONAE ET SODALIUM*
post A.D. 4
001 **Martyrium Agapae, Irenae, Chionae et sodalium,** ed. H. Musurillo, *The acts of the Christian martyrs.* Oxford: Clarendon Press, 1972: 280–292.
Cod: [1,885]

0390 *MARTYRIUM CARPI, PAPYLI ET AGATHONICAE*
A.D. 2
001 **Martyrium sanctorum Carpi, Papyli et Agathonicae,** ed. H. Musurillo, *The acts of the Christian martyrs.* Oxford: Clarendon Press, 1972: 22–28.
Cod: [989]

2008 *MARTYRIUM CONONIS*
post A.D. 4
001 **Martyrium Cononis,** ed. H. Musurillo, *The acts of the Christian martyrs.* Oxford: Clarendon Press, 1972: 186–192.
Cod: [982]

2010 *MARTYRIUM DASII*
post A.D. 4
001 **Martyrium Dasii,** ed. H. Musurillo, *The acts of the Christian martyrs.* Oxford: Clarendon Press, 1972: 272–278.
Cod: [1,154]

1483 *MARTYRIUM ET ASCENSIO ISAIAE*
A.D. 2
001 **Fragmenta,** ed. A.-M. Denis, *Fragmenta pseudepigraphorum quae supersunt Graeca* [*Pseudepigrapha veteris testamenti Graece* 3. Leiden: Brill, 1970]: 105–114.
Q, Cod, Pap: [1,401]

2009 *MARTYRIUM MARINI*
post A.D. 3
001 **Martyrium Marini,** ed. H. Musurillo, *The acts of the Christian martyrs.* Oxford: Clarendon Press, 1972: 240–242.
Q: [274]

MARTYRIUM PAULI
Cf. ACTA PAULI (0388 002).

2016 *MARTYRIUM PERPETUAE*
post A.D. 3

001 **Martyrium Perpetuae**, ed. J.A. Robinson, *The passion of S. Perpetua* [*Texts and Studies* 1.2. Cambridge: Cambridge University Press, 1891 (repr. Nendeln, Liechtenstein: Kraus, 1967)]: 61–95.
Cod: [4,063]

MARTYRIUM PETRI
Cf. ACTA PETRI (0389 001).

2005 **MARTYRIUM PIONII**
A.D. 4?
001 **Martyrium Pionii presbyteri et sodalium**, ed. H. Musurillo, *The acts of the Christian martyrs*. Oxford: Clarendon Press, 1972: 136–166.
Cod: [4,527]

1484 **MARTYRIUM POLYCARPI**
fort. auctore Pseudo-Pionio
post A.D. 2
001 **Martyrium Polycarpi**, ed. H. Musurillo, *The acts of the Christian martyrs*. Oxford: Clarendon Press, 1972: 2–20.
Epilogus Mosquensis = pp. 18–20.
Cod: [2,837]

2007 **MARTYRIUM POTAMIAENAE ET BASILIDIS**
post A.D. 3
001 **Martyrium Potamiaenae et Basilidis**, ed. H. Musurillo, *The acts of the Christian martyrs*. Oxford: Clarendon Press, 1972: 132–134.
Q: [420]

1485 **MARTYRIUM PTOLEMAEI ET LUCII**
A.D. 2
001 **Martyrium Ptolemaei et Lucii**, ed. H. Musurillo, *The acts of the Christian martyrs*. Oxford: Clarendon Press, 1972: 38–40.
Cod: [511]

1888 **MATRIS** Hist.
3 B.C.?: Thebanus
001 **Testimonia**, FGrH #39: 1A:260, *15 addenda.
NQ
002 **Fragmenta**, FGrH #39: 1A:260.
Q

1486 **MATRON** Parodius
4 B.C.: Pitanaeus
001 **Convivium Atticum**, ed. P. Brandt, *Corpusculum poesis epicae Graecae Ludibundae*, fasc. 1. Leipzig: Teubner, 1888: 60–71.
Q: [894]
002 **Fragmenta**, ed. Brandt, *op. cit.*, 91–93.
frr. 1–6.
Q: [136]
003 **Fragmenta**, ed. H. Lloyd-Jones and P. Parsons, *Supplementum Hellenisticum*. Berlin: De Gruyter, 1983: 259–262, 266–268.
frr. 534–540.
Q: [952]

1560 **MATTHIAE TRADITIONES**
fiq *Evangelium apocryphum secundum Matthiam*
ante A.D. 2
001 **Matthiae traditiones**, ed. E. Preuschen, *Antilegomena*, 2nd edn. Gieszen: Töpelmann, 1905: 13–15.
Q: [512]

2709 **Joannes MAUROPUS** Rhet.
A.D. 11: Paphlagonius
Bibliography in progress
x01 **Epigramma demonstrativum**.
App. Anth. 3.411: Cf. EPIGRAMMATICI in *App. Anth.* (7052 003).

1040 **MAXIMIANUS** Med.
ante A.D. 6
x01 **Fragmentum ap. Alexandrum Trallianum**.
Puschmann, vol. 2, p. 57.
Cf. ALEXANDER Med. (0744 003).

1487 **MAXIMUS** Astrol.
A.D. 2/4?
001 Περὶ καταρχῶν, ed. A. Ludwich, *Maximi et Ammonis carminum de actionum auspiciis reliquiae*. Leipzig: Teubner, 1877: 3–48.
Cod: [4,109]
002 Περὶ καταρχῶν (epitome), ed. Ludwich, *op. cit.*, 79–96.
Cod: [2,311]

2675 **MAXIMUS** Epigr.
post A.D. 2: fort. Apamensis
x01 **Epigramma dedicatorium**.
App. Anth. 1.248(?): Cf. EPIGRAMMATICI in *App. Anth.* (7052 001).

1488 **MAXIMUS** Scr. Eccl.
A.D. 2
001 **Fragmentum ex libro de materia**, ed. M.J. Routh, *Reliquiae sacrae*, vol. 2, 2nd edn. Oxford: Oxford University Press, 1846 (repr. Hildesheim: Olms, 1974): 87–107.
Q: [3,283]

0563 **MAXIMUS** Soph.
A.D. 2: Tyrius
001 **Philosophumena**, ed. H. Hobein, *Maximi Tyrii philosophumena*. Leipzig: Teubner, 1910: 1–484.
Cod: [68,464]

2025 **MAXIMUS** Soph.
A.D. 4?: Byzantius vel Epirota
001 Περὶ τῶν ἀλύτων ἀντιθέσεων, ed. C. Walz, *Rhetores Graeci*, vol. 5. Stuttgart: Cotta, 1833 (repr. Osnabrück: Zeller, 1968): 577–590.
Cod: 3,025

1939 **MEDIUS** Hist.
post 4 B.C.?: Larissaeus

001 **Testimonia**, FGrH #129: 2B:670–671.
NQ

002 **Fragmentum**, FGrH #129: 2B:671–672.
Q

1489 **MEGASTHENES** Hist.
4–3 B.C.

001 **Testimonia**, FGrH #715: 3C:603–604.
NQ

002 **Fragmenta**, FGrH #715: 3C:604–639.
Q

0976 **MEGES** Med.
A.D. 1: Sidonius

x01 **Fragmentum ap. Galenum.**
K12.845.
Cf. GALENUS Med. (0057 076).

x02 **Fragmentum ap. Oribasium.**
CMG, vol. 6.2.1, pp. 142–144.
Cf. ORIBASIUS Med. (0722 001).

1490 **<MEGILLUS>** Phil.
3/2 B.C.: Lacon

001 **Fragmentum**, ed. H. Thesleff, *The Pythagorean texts of the Hellenistic period*. Åbo: Åbo Akademi, 1965: 115.
Q: 67

1365 **MELAMPUS Scriptor De Divinatione**
3 B.C.

001 Περὶ ἐλαιῶν τοῦ σώματος, ed. J.G.F. Franz, *Scriptores physiognomoniae veteres*. Altenburg: Richter, 1780: 501–508.
Cod

002 Περὶ παλμῶν ἀρχομένου ἀπὸ κεφαλῆς ἕως ποδῶν (*Cod. Berol.* 1577), ed. H. Diels, "Anonyme Version des Phillippsianus," *Abhandlungen der königlich preussischen Akademie der Wissenschaften*, Philol.-hist. Kl., Abh. 4. Berlin: Reimer, 1908: 7–9.
Cf. et 1365 006.
Cod

006 Περὶ παλμῶν ἀρχομένου ἀπὸ κεφαλῆς ἕως ποδῶν (*P. Flor.* 3.391), ed. Diels, *AAB* 4 (1908), 12–15.
Cf. et 1365 002.
Pap

003 Περὶ παλμῶν μαντικὴ πρὸς Πτολεμαῖον βασιλέα (versio A), ed. H. Diels, "Die griechischen Zuckungsbücher (Melampus περὶ παλμῶν)," *Abhandlungen der königlich preussischen Akademie der Wissenschaften*, Philol.-hist. Kl., Abh. 4. Berlin: Reimer, 1907: 21–32.
Cod

004 Περὶ παλμῶν τί σημαίνουσιν ἐν ἑκάστῳ μέρει (versio P), ed. Diels, *AAB* 4 (1907), 35–38.
Cod

005 **Lunarium**, ed. D. Bassi, F. Cumont, A. Martini and A. Olivieri, *Codices Italici* [*Catalogus codicum astrologorum Graecorum* 4. Brussels: Lamertin, 1903]: 110–113.
Cod

0373 **MELANIPPIDES** Lyr.
5 B.C.: Melius

001 **Fragmenta**, ed. D.L. Page, *Poetae melici Graeci*. Oxford: Clarendon Press, 1962 (repr. 1967 (1st edn. corr.)): 392–395.
frr. 1–7.
Q: [127]

1491 **MELANTHIUS** Hist.
4 B.C.?: fort. Atheniensis

001 **Fragmenta**, FGrH #326: 3B:86–87.
Q

0344 **MELANTHIUS** Trag.
2 B.C.: Rhodius

001 **Fragmentum**, ed. B. Snell, *Tragicorum Graecorum fragmenta*, vol. 1. Göttingen: Vandenhoeck & Ruprecht, 1971: 303.
fr. 1.
Q: [8]

0254 **MELANTHIUS** Trag. et Eleg.
5 B.C.: Atheniensis

001 **Fragmentum**, ed. M.L. West, *Iambi et elegi Graeci*, vol. 2. Oxford: Clarendon Press, 1972: 81.
fr. 1.
Q: [13]

002 **Titulus**, ed. B. Snell, *Tragicorum Graecorum fragmenta*, vol. 1. Göttingen: Vandenhoeck & Ruprecht, 1971: 138.
NQ

1492 **MELEAGER** Epigr.
2–1 B.C.: Gadarensis

001 **Epigrammata**, AG **4**.1; **5**.8, 24, 57, 96, 136–137, 139–141, 143–144, 147–149, 151–152, 154–157, 160, 163, 165–166, 171–180, 182, 184, 187, 190–192, 195, 196–198, 204, 208, 212, 214–215; **6**.162–163; **7**.13, 79, 182, 195–196, 207, 352, 417–419, 421, 428, 461, 468, 470, 476, 535; **9**.16, 331, 363; **11**.223; **12**.23, 33, 41, 47–49, 52–54, 56–57, 59–60, 63, 65, 68, 70, 72, 74, 76, 78, 80–86, 92, 94–95, 101, 106, 109–110, 113–114, 117, 119, 122, 125–128, 132–133, 137, 141, 144, 147, 154, 157–159, 164–165, 167, 256–257; **16**.134, 213.
AG 5.2, 82, 99, 168, 195b; 12.79: Cf. ANONYMI EPIGRAMMATICI (0138 001).
AG 5.189: Cf. ASCLEPIADES Epigr. (0137 001).
AG 7.31: Cf. DIOSCORIDES Epigr. (0173 001).
AG 12.234–235; 16.213: Cf. (et) STRATON Epigr. (1697 001).
Q: 5,928

0730 **MELETIUS** Med.
A.D. 7/9

001 **De natura hominis**, ed. J.A. Cramer, *Anecdota Graeca e codd. manuscriptis bibliothecarum Oxoniensium*, vol. 3. Oxford: Oxford University

Press, 1836 (repr. Amsterdam: Hakkert, 1963):
5–157.
Cod: 41,310

002 **Hypothesis ad opus De natura hominis** (e cod.
Barocciano 131), ed. Cramer, *op. cit.*, 1–4.
Cod

0977 **MELETUS** Med.
ante A.D. 1
x01 **Fragmentum ap. Galenum.**
K12.946.
Cf. GALENUS Med. (0057 076).

1848 **MELETUS Junior** Trag.
Incertum
001 **Titulus**, ed. B. Snell, *Tragicorum Graecorum
fragmenta*, vol. 1. Göttingen: Vandenhoeck &
Ruprecht, 1971: 188.
NQ

1493 **MELINNO** Lyr.
2 B.C.?: Lesbia
001 **Εἰς 'Ρώμην**, ed. H. Lloyd-Jones and P. Parsons, *Supplementum Hellenisticum*. Berlin: De
Gruyter, 1983: 268–269.
fr. 541.
Q: [102]

0051 **<MELISSA>** Phil.
3 B.C.?
001 **Fragmentum epistulae ad Clearetam**, ed. H.
Thesleff, *The Pythagorean texts of the Hellenistic period*. Åbo: Åbo Akademi, 1965: 115–116.
Q: 221

2282 **MELISSEUS** Hist.
ante 4 B.C.?
001 **Fragmenta**, FGrH #402: 3B:297.
Q

1494 **MELISSUS** Phil.
5 B.C.: Samius
001 **Testimonia**, ed. H. Diels and W. Kranz, *Die
Fragmente der Vorsokratiker*, vol. 1, 6th edn.
Berlin: Weidmann, 1951 (repr. Dublin: 1966):
258–267.
test. 1–14.
NQ
002 **Fragmenta**, ed. Diels and Kranz, *op. cit.*, 268–
276.
frr. 1–12.
Q

2955 **MELITIUS et MELITIANI** Theol.
A.D. 4: Lycopolitanus (Melitius)
001 **Epistulae Melitianorum**, ed. H.I. Bell, *Jews
and Christians in Egypt. The Jewish troubles in
Alexandria and the Athanasian controversy*.
Oxford: Oxford University Press, 1924: 38–99.
Pap
x01 **Breviarium a Melitio datum Alexandro episcopo.**

Opitz, pp. 149–151.
Cf. ATHANASIUS Theol. (2035 005).

1495 **MELITO** Apol.
A.D. 2: Sardianus
001 **De pascha**, ed. O. Perler, *Méliton de Sardes.
Sur la Pâque et fragments* [*Sources chrétiennes*
123. Paris: Cerf, 1966]: 60–126.
Cod: [4,553]
002 **Fragmentum** (*P. Bodmer* 12), ed. Perler, *op.
cit.*, 128.
Pap: [30]
003 **Fragmenta**, ed. Perler, *op. cit.*, 218–224, 226,
228–236.
frr. 1–4, 6–7, 8b–12.
Q: [1,381]
x01 **Deprecatio.**
Richard, *Muséon* 85, pp. 318–321.
Cf. JOANNES CHRYSOSTOMUS Scr. Eccl.
(2062 428).

2250 **MELITO** Hist.
A.D. 2?: fort. Atheniensis
001 **Fragmentum**, FGrH #345: 3B:208.
Q

0978 **MELITO** Med.
A.D. 1
x01 **Fragmentum ap. Galenum.**
K13.843.
Cf. GALENUS Med. (0057 077).

0825 **MELITO** Trag.
A.D. 1
001 **Titulus**, ed. B. Snell, *Tragicorum Graecorum
fragmenta*, vol. 1. Göttingen: Vandenhoeck &
Ruprecht, 1971: 314.
NQ

1496 **MEMNON** Hist.
1 B.C.–A.D. 1?: fort. Heracleota
001 **Testimonium**, FGrH #434: 3B:336–337.
NQ
002 **Fragmenta**, FGrH #434: 3B:337–368.
Cod

1497 **MENAECHMUS** Hist.
4 B.C.: Sicyonius
001 **Testimonia**, FGrH #131: 2B:673.
NQ
002 **Fragmenta**, FGrH #131: 2B:673–676.
Q
x01 **Sicyonis historia** (*P. Oxy.* 11.1365).
FGrH #551, fr. 1b (= FGrH #105, fr. 2).
Cf. ADDITAMENTA (FGrH) (2433 024).
Cf. ANONYMI HISTORICI (FGrH) (1139 004).

0541 **MENANDER** Comic.
4–3 B.C.: Atheniensis
Cf. et MENANDRI ET PHILISTIONIS SENTENTIAE (1791).
001 **Aspis**, ed. F.H. Sandbach, *Menandri reliquiae*

selectae. Oxford: Clarendon Press, 1972: 3–25.
Pap: 3,263

002 **Aspidis fragmenta aliunde nota**, ed. Sandbach, *op. cit.*, 25–26.
frr. 1–2.
Q: 37

003 **Georgus**, ed. Sandbach, *op. cit.*, 29–33.
Pap: 688

004 **Georgi fragmenta aliunde nota**, ed. Sandbach, *op. cit.*, 34–35.
frr. 1–7.
Q, Pap: 131

005 **Dis exapaton**, ed. Sandbach, *op. cit.*, 39–41.
Pap: 402

006 **Dis exapatontis fragmenta aliunde nota**, ed. Sandbach, *op. cit.*, 41–42.
frr. 1–5.
Q, Pap: 34

007 **Dyscolus**, ed. Sandbach, *op. cit.*, 47–91.
Pap: 6,693

008 **Epitrepontum fragmenta**, ed. Sandbach, *op. cit.*, 97–98, 120–121, 130.
frr. 1–10.
Q: 105

009 **Epitrepontes**, ed. Sandbach, *op. cit.*, 98–130.
Pap: 4,493

010 **Heros**, ed. Sandbach, *op. cit.*, 135–139.
Pap: 532

011 **Herois fragmenta aliunde nota**, ed. Sandbach, *op. cit.*, 139–141.
frr. 1–8, 10.
Q: 82

012 **Theophorumene**, ed. Sandbach, *op. cit.*, 145.
Pap: 118

013 **Theophorumenae fragmentum dubium**, ed. Sandbach, *op. cit.*, 146.
Pap: 104

014 **Theophorumenae fragmenta aliunde nota**, ed. Sandbach, *op. cit.*, 147–148.
frr. 1–5.
Q: 153

015 **Carchedonius**, ed. Sandbach, *op. cit.*, 153–154.
Pap: 153

016 **Carchedonii fragmenta aliunde nota**, ed. Sandbach, *op. cit.*, 154–155.
frr. 1–7.
Q: 46

017 **Citharista**, ed. Sandbach, *op. cit.*, 159–161.
Pap: 398

018 **Citharistae fragmenta aliunde nota**, ed. Sandbach, *op. cit.*, 162–164.
frr. 1–12.
Q, Pap: 161

019 **Colax**, ed. Sandbach, *op. cit.*, 167–171.
Pap: 625

020 **Colacis fragmenta aliunde nota**, ed. Sandbach, *op. cit.*, 172–173.
frr. 2–7.
Q: 103

021 **Coneazomenae**, ed. Sandbach, *op. cit.*, 177–178.
Pap: 126

022 **Coneazomenarum fragmenta aliunde nota**, ed. Sandbach, *op. cit.*, 178.
fr. 1.
Q: 15

023 **Misumenus**, ed. Sandbach, *op. cit.*, 181, 183–194.
Pap: 1,594

024 **Misumeni fragmenta**, ed. Sandbach, *op. cit.*, 182–183, 194–195.
frr. 2–11.
Q: 78

025 **Periciromene**, ed. Sandbach, *op. cit.*, 199–221.
Pap: 3,152

026 **Periciromenae fragmenta aliunde nota**, ed. Sandbach, *op. cit.*, 221.
frr. 1–2.
Q: 13

027 **Perinthia**, ed. Sandbach, *op. cit.*, 225–226.
Pap: 152

028 **Perinthiae fragmenta aliunde nota**, ed. Sandbach, *op. cit.*, 226–228.
frr. 1–10.
Q: 93

029 **Samia**, ed. Sandbach, *op. cit.*, 231–265.
Pap: 5,424

030 **Samiae fragmentum aliunde notum**, ed. Sandbach, *op. cit.*, 265.
Q: 10

031 **Sicyonius**, ed. Sandbach, *op. cit.*, 269–284.
Pap: 2,212

032 **Sicyonii fragmenta aliunde nota**, ed. Sandbach, *op. cit.*, 284–286.
frr. 1–6, 10–11.
Q, Pap: 104

033 **Phasma**, ed. Sandbach, *op. cit.*, 289–293.
Pap: 637

034 **Fabula incerta**, ed. Sandbach, *op. cit.*, 297–299.
Pap: 342

035 **Fragmentum dubium**, ed. Sandbach, *op. cit.*, 300.
Pap: 69

036 **Fragmenta longiora apud alios auctores servata**, ed. Sandbach, *op. cit.*, 303–324.
frr. 59–60, 97, 208–210, 215, 250–251, 264, 276, 286–287, 303–304, 333–336, 397, 416a–b, 417, 451, 538, 568, 581, 592, 612, 614, 620, 656, 714, 718, 722, 740, 745, 754, 794, 795.
Q, Pap: 2,238

037 **Fragmenta**, ed. C. Austin, *Comicorum Graecorum fragmenta in papyris reperta*. Berlin: De Gruyter, 1973: 121–196.
frr. 103–104, 106–107, 110–111, 113, 119, 121–122, 124, 128–129, 131–135, 138, 140, 142–143, 145–148, 151, 157–159, 163, 165, 167–168, 171, 173, 180–181, 183, 186–187, 190, 193, 195, 202–204 + tituli.
Pap: 4,141

038 **Misumeni nova fragmenta**, ed. E.G. Turner, "New fragments of the *Misoumenos* of Menander," *Bulletin of the Institute of Classical Studies*, suppl. 17 (1965) 25–73.
Pap: 1,254

039 **Fragmenta**, ed. T. Kock, *Comicorum Attico-rum fragmenta*, vol. 3. Leipzig: Teubner, 1888: 3–152, 155–164, 166–241, 246–271.
frr. 1, 3–6, 8–33, 36, 39, 41–42, 48, 50–55, 59–100, 102–107, 109–120, 123–132, 134–151, 153–162, 164–171, 173–181, 183–185, 187–189, 191–258, 260–275, 278–314, 316–333, 335–389, 391–411, 413, 415–443, 445–458, 460–463, 465–494, 497–544, 546–720, 722–734, 736–749, 751–864, 866–895, 897–907, 912–930, 962–963, 965–986, 988–1116, 1121, 1127 + tituli.
Q: 12,000

040 **Fragmenta**, ed. A. Meineke, *Fragmenta comico-rum Graecorum*, vol. 4. Berlin: Reimer, 1841 (repr. De Gruyter, 1970): 69–79, 81–189, 191–215, 217–296, 298–300, 302, 305, 307, 321–332, 876.
Q: 10,779

041 **Fragmenta**, ed. J. Demiańczuk, *Supplementum comicum*. Krakau: Nakładem Akademii, 1912 (repr. Hildesheim: Olms, 1967): 54–62.
frr. 1–18, 20–24.
Q: 246

042 **Sententiae ex codicibus Byzantinis**, ed. S. Jae-kel, *Menandri sententiae*. Leipzig: Teubner, 1964: 33–83.
Cod: 5,299

044 **Epigrammata**, AG 7.72; **11.438**.
AG 11.286: Cf. PALLADAS Epigr. (2123 001).
Q: 24

045 **Fragmenta**, ed. A. Körte and A. Thierfelder, *Menandri quae supersunt*, vol. 2, 2nd edn. Leipzig: Teubner, 1959: 14–251, 267–271, 295, 298.
frr. 1–3, 5–8, 10–28, 30, 33–40, 42–43, 45–50, 53–73, 76–90, 93–94, 97–98a, 100–101, 104–106, 109–125, 127–139, 141–159, 161–164, 166, 171–181, 185–190, 192–216, 218–224, 226–231, 235, 238–244, 248–259, 263–267, 269–272, 274–282, 284, 286–292, 294–298, 300–309, 311–331, 333–354, 358–368, 371–376, 380–390, 392, 394–398, 401–405, 407–412, 416–428, 431–443, 446–456, 459, 462–703, 705–722, 724–807, 809, 932–937, 939–941, 944–950, addenda 317a, 669a, 715a.
Q: 9,889

046 **Epigramma**, ed. Meineke, *op. cit.*, vol. 4, 335.
Q: 19

047 **Sententiae**, ed. Meineke, *op. .cit.*, vol. 4, 340–362.
Q: 4,515

048 **Sententiae ex papyris**, ed. Jaekel, *op. cit.*, 3–25.
Pap: 1,568

049 **Fragmenta**, ed. Meineke, *op. cit.*, vol. 5.1 (1857; repr. 1970): ccxliv, ccxlviii, ccli, ccliii, cclxiii, cclxxix, cclxxxiv, ccxcii–ccxciii, 109–110.
Q: [100]

1498 **MENANDER** Hist.
ante 2 B.C.: Ephesius

001 **Testimonia**, FGrH #783: 3C:788–789.
NQ

002 **Fragmenta**, FGrH #783: 3C:789–795.
Q

2586 **MENANDER** Rhet.
A.D. 3/4: Laodicensis

001 Διαίρεσις τῶν ἐπιδεικτικῶν (olim sub auctore Genethlio), ed. D.A. Russell and N.G. Wilson, *Menander rhetor*. Oxford: Clarendon Press, 1981: 2–74.
Cod

002 Περὶ ἐπιδεικτικῶν, ed. Russell and Wilson, *op. cit.*, 76–224.
Cod

4076 **MENANDER Protector** Hist.
A.D. 6: Constantinopolitanus

001 **Epigramma**, AG 1.101.
Q: 47

002 **Fragmenta**, ed. L. Dindorf, *Historici Graeci minores*, vol. 2. Leipzig: Teubner, 1871: 1–131.
Q

1791 *MENANDRI ET PHILISTIONIS SENTEN-TIAE*
Incertum
Cf. et MENANDER Comic. (0541 042, 045).

001 **Comparatio Menandri et Philistionis**, ed. S. Jaekel, *Menandri sententiae*. Leipzig: Teubner, 1964: 87–120.
Q: 4,287

002 **Sententiae Menandri et Philistionis**, ed. A. Meineke, *Fragmenta comicorum Graecorum*, vol. 4. Berlin: Reimer, 1841 (repr. De Gruyter, 1970): 335–338.
Q: 359

1499 **MENECLES** Hist.
2 B.C.: Barcaeus

001 **Fragmenta**, FGrH #270: 3A:83–84.
Q

2325 **MENECLES** Hist.
2 B.C.: Teius

001 **Testimonium**, FGrH #466: 3B:402–403.
test. 1: *Inscr. Cret.* 1.280.
NQ

MENECLES Perieg.
Cf. CALLICRATES-MENECLES Perieg. (1236).

2684 **MENECLES** Phil.
post 3 B.C.

x01 **Epigramma sepulcrale.**
App. Anth. 2.383: Cf. EPIGRAMMATICI in *App. Anth.* (7052 002).

0523 **MENECRATES** Comic.
post 5 B.C.

001 **Titulus**, ed. T. Kock, *Comicorum Atticorum*

fragmenta, vol. 3. Leipzig: Teubner, 1888: 383.
NQ: 5

002 **Titulus**, ed. A. Meineke, *Fragmenta comicorum Graecorum*, vol. 1. Berlin: Reimer, 1839 (repr. De Gruyter, 1970): 493.
NQ

003 **Fragmentum**, ed. J. Demiańczuk, *Supplementum comicum*. Krakau: Nakładem Akademii, 1912 (repr. Hildesheim: Olms, 1967): 63.
fr. 1.
Q: 8

1501 **MENECRATES** Epigr.
4–3 B.C.: Samius
001 **Epigrammata**, AG 9.54–55.
Q: 35

1502 **MENECRATES** Epigr.
1 B.C.: Smyrnaeus
001 **Epigramma**, AG 9.390.
Q: 42

1503 **MENECRATES** Hist.
4 B.C.: Xanthius
001 **Fragmenta**, FGrH #769: 3C:761–762.
Q

2475 **MENECRATES** Hist.
post 4 B.C.?
001 **Fragmenta**, FGrH #701: 3C:555.
Q

0639 **MENECRATES** Med.
4 B.C.: Syracusanus
001 **Epistula** [Sp.], ed. R. Hercher, *Epistolographi Graeci*. Paris: Didot, 1873 (repr. Amsterdam: Hakkert, 1965): 399.
Q: [58]

0980 **Tiberius Claudius MENECRATES** Med.
A.D. 1
x01 **Fragmenta ap. Galenum**.
K12.846, 946.
Cf. GALENUS Med. (0057 076).

1500 **MENECRATES** Poet. Phil.
4 B.C.: Ephesius
001 **Fragmentum et titulus**, ed. H. Lloyd-Jones and P. Parsons, *Supplementum Hellenisticum*. Berlin: De Gruyter, 1983: 269–270.
frr. (+ titul.) 543–544.
Q: [9]

0982 **MENECRITUS** Med.
ante A.D. 4
x01 **Fragmentum ap. Oribasium**.
CMG, vol. 6.2.1, p. 286.
Cf. ORIBASIUS Med. (0722 001).

1504 **MENELAUS** Epic.
post 1 B.C.?: Aegaeus
001 **Testimonia**, FGrH #384: 3B:261–262.
NQ

002 **Fragmenta**, FGrH #384: 3B:262.
Q

003 **Fragmenta et titulus**, ed. H. Lloyd-Jones and P. Parsons, *Supplementum Hellenisticum*. Berlin: De Gruyter, 1983: 271–272.
frr. (+ titul.) 551–555.
Q: [12]

0983 **MENELAUS** Med.
ante A.D. 2
x01 **Fragmentum ap. Galenum**.
K14.173.
Cf. GALENUS Med. (0057 078).

0984 **MENEMACHUS** Med.
A.D. 1: Aphrodisiensis
x01 **Fragmenta ap. Oribasium**.
CMG, vol. **6.1.1**, p. 220; **6.1.2**, p. 58.
Cf. ORIBASIUS Med. (0722 001).

1505 **MENESTHENES** Hist.
ante A.D. 3
001 **Fragmentum**, FHG 4: 451–452.
Q

0985 **MENESTHEUS** Med.
ante A.D. 2
x01 **Fragmentum ap. Galenum**.
K13.830.
Cf. GALENUS Med. (0057 077).

2228 **MENESTOR** Phil.
5 B.C.: Sybarita
001 **Testimonia**, ed. H. Diels and W. Kranz, *Die Fragmente der Vorsokratiker*, vol. 1, 6th edn. Berlin: Weidmann, 1951 (repr. Dublin: 1966): 375–376.
test. 1–7.
NQ

1787 **[MENIPPUS]** Comic.
Incertum
001 **Tituli**, ed. T. Kock, *Comicorum Atticorum fragmenta*, vol. 3. Leipzig: Teubner, 1888: 383.
NQ: 3

002 **Tituli**, ed. A. Meineke, *Fragmenta comicorum Graecorum*, vol. 1. Berlin: Reimer, 1839 (repr. De Gruyter, 1970): 494.
NQ

0079 **MENIPPUS** Geogr.
1 B.C.: Pergamenus
002 **Fragmenta**, ed. K. Müller, *Geographi Graeci minores*, vol. 1. Paris: Didot, 1855 (repr. Hildesheim: Olms, 1965): 572–573.
Q

x01 **Menippi periplus Maris Interni** (epitome Marciani).
GGM, vol. 1, pp. 563–572.
Cf. MARCIANUS Geogr. (4003 002).

2517 **MENIPPUS** Hist.
ante 1 B.C.

001 **Titulus**, FGrH #766: 3C:758.
NQ

0986 **MENIPPUS** Med.
ante A.D. 1
x01 **Fragmentum ap. Galenum.**
K14.172.
Cf. GALENUS Med. (0057 078).

0052 **MENIPPUS** Phil.
3 B.C.: Gadarensis
001 **Epistula** [Sp.], ed. R. Hercher, *Epistolographi Graeci*. Paris: Didot, 1873 (repr. Amsterdam: Hakkert, 1965): 400.
Q: [62]

MENO Med.
Cf. ANONYMUS LONDINENSIS (0643 001).

1506 **MENODOTUS** Hist.
3 B.C.?: Samius
001 **Fragmenta**, FGrH #541: 3B:524–526.
Q

1916 **MENODOTUS** Hist.
2 B.C.: Perinthius
Cf. et MENODOTUS Hist. (1506).
001 **Testimonium**, FGrH #82: 2A:189.
NQ

0989 **MENOETIUS** Med.
ante A.D. 2
x01 **Fragmenta ap. Galenum.**
K13.509, 511–512.
Cf. GALENUS Med. (0057 077).

2631 **MENOPHILUS** Poeta
Incertum: Damascenus
001 **Fragmentum**, ed. H. Lloyd-Jones and P. Parsons, *Supplementum Hellenisticum*. Berlin: De Gruyter, 1983: 272–273.
fr. 558.
Q: [104]

2202 **[MENYLLUS]** Hist.
Incertum
001 **Fragmenta**, FGrH #295: 3A:178–179.
Q

1021 ***MEROPIS***
6 B.C.
001 **Fragmenta** (*P. Cologne* inv. 5604), ed. L. Koenen and R. Merkelbach, *Collectanea papyrologica. Texts published in honor of H.C. Youtie*, vol. 1 (ed. A.E. Hanson) [*Papyrologische Texte und Abhandlungen* 19. Bonn: Habelt, 1976]: 9, 11, 13, 15.
Pap

0268 **MESOMEDES** Lyr.
A.D. 2: Creticus
001 **Fragmenta**, ed. E. Heitsch, *Die griechischen Dichterfragmente der römischen Kaiserzeit*, vol.

1, 2nd edn. Göttingen: Vandenhoeck & Ruprecht, 1963: 25–32.
frr. 1–13.
Q, Cod: [914]
002 **Epigrammata**, AG **14**.63; **16**.323.
Q: 103

0475 **METAGENES** Comic.
5 B.C.
001 **Fragmenta**, ed. T. Kock, *Comicorum Atticorum fragmenta*, vol. 1. Leipzig: Teubner, 1880: 704–710.
frr. 1–10, 12–16, 19.
Q: 222
002 **Fragmenta**, ed. A. Meineke, *Fragmenta comicorum Graecorum*, vol. 2.2. Berlin: Reimer, 1840 (repr. De Gruyter, 1970): 751–756, 758–759.
p. 758: fr. 3 supplied from vol. 5.1, p. 115.
Q: 223

2708 **METHODIUS** Scr. Eccl.
A.D. 9: Constantinopolitanus
x01 **Epigramma demonstrativum.**
App. Anth. 3.310: Cf. EPIGRAMMATICI in *App. Anth.* (7052 003).

2959 **METHODIUS** Scr. Eccl.
A.D. 3–4: Olympius
001 **Symposium** *sive* **Convivium decem virginum**, ed. H. Musurillo and V.-H. Debidour, *Méthode d'Olympe. Le banquet* [*Sources chrétiennes* 95. Paris: Cerf, 1963]: 42–332.
Cod
002 **De libero arbitrio**, ed. G.N. Bonwetsch, *Methodius* [*Die griechischen christlichen Schriftsteller* 27. Leipzig: Hinrichs, 1917]: 145–206.
Cod
003 **De resurrectione**, ed. Bonwetsch, *op. cit.*, 226, 242–352, 361–363, 368–371, 373–382, 384–386, 388, 391–400, 403, 405, 410–416, 420.
Cod
004 **De lepra ad Sistelium**, ed. Bonwetsch, *op. cit.*, 455–464, 466–467, 469.
Cod
005 **De creatis** (fragmenta ap. Photium, *Bibl.* cod. 235), ed. Bonwetsch, *op. cit.*, 493–500.
Q
006 **Adversus Porphyrium** (fragmenta), ed. Bonwetsch, *op. cit.*, 503–507.
Q
007 **Fragmenta in Job** (fragmenta in catenis), ed. Bonwetsch, *op. cit.*, 511–519.
Q
008 **De martyribus** (fragmenta), ed. Bonwetsch, *op. cit.*, 520.
Q
009 **Fragmentum de resurrectione** (e cod. Vat. gr. 2022) [Sp.], ed. Bonwetsch, *op. cit.*, 423–424.
Cod
010 **Fragmenta incerta** [Sp.], ed. Bonwetsch, *op. cit.*, 520–521.
Q
011 **In Genesim** (fragmentum in catenis), ed. R.

Devreesse, *Les anciens commentateurs de
l'Octateuque et des Rois* [*Studi e Testi* 201.
Vatican City: Biblioteca Apostolica Vaticana,
1959]: 54.
Q

012 **Sermo de Simeone et Anna** [Sp.], MPG 18:
348–381.
Cod

013 **Sermo in ramos palmarum** [Sp.], MPG 18:
384–397.
Cod

014 **Apocalypsis** (recensio 1) [Sp.], ed. A. Lolos,
Die Apokalypse des Ps.-Methodios [*Beiträge zur
klassischen Philologie* 83. Meisenheim am
Glan: Hain, 1976]: 46–140.
Cod

015 **Apocalypsis** (recensio 2) [Sp.], ed. Lolos, *Beiträge zur klassischen Philologie* 83, 47–141.
Cod

016 **Apocalypsis** (recensio 3) [Sp.], ed. A. Lolos,
*Die dritte und vierte Redaktion des Ps.-Metho-
dios* [*Beiträge zur klassischen Philologie* 94.
Meisenheim am Glan: Hain, 1978]: 22, 25–38,
40–75.
Cod

017 **Apocalypsis** (recensio 4) [Sp.], ed. Lolos, *Beiträge zur klassischen Philologie* 94: 23, 39–69,
76–78.
Cod

1507 **<METOPUS>** Phil.
3 B.C.: Metapontinus
001 **Fragmenta**, ed. H. Thesleff, *The Pythagorean
texts of the Hellenistic period.* Åbo: Åbo Akademi, 1965: 116–121.
Q: 1,441

4077 **METRODORUS** Gramm.
Incertum
001 **Epigrammata**, AG 9.360, 712.
Q: 93

1976 **METRODORUS** Hist.
1 B.C.: Scepsius
001 **Testimonia**, FGrH #184: 2B:912–914.
NQ
002 **Fragmenta**, FGrH #184: 2B:914–917.
Q

1508 **METRODORUS** Phil.
4 B.C.: Chius
001 **Fragmenta**, FGrH #43: 1A:266, *15 addenda.
Q
002 **Testimonia**, ed. H. Diels and W. Kranz, *Die
Fragmente der Vorsokratiker*, vol. 2, 6th edn.
Berlin: Weidmann, 1952 (repr. Dublin: 1966):
231–233.
test. 1–25.
NQ
003 **Fragmenta**, ed. Diels and Kranz, *op. cit.*, 233–
234.
frr. 1–6.
Q

1773 **METRODORUS** Phil.
4–3 B.C.: Lampsacenus
001 **Fragmenta**, ed. A. Körte, "Metrodori Epicurei
fragmenta," *Jahrbücher für classische Philologie*, suppl. 17. Leipzig: Teubner, 1890: 537–
552, 554–565.
Q

1811 **METRODORUS Major** Phil.
6 B.C.: Lampsacenus
001 **Testimonia**, ed. H. Diels and W. Kranz, *Die
Fragmente der Vorsokratiker*, vol. 2, 6th edn.
Berlin: Weidmann, 1952 (repr. Dublin: 1966):
49–50.
test. 1–6.
NQ

2531 **METROPHANES** Hist.
A.D. 3/4?
001 **Testimonium**, FGrH #796: 3C:834.
NQ
002 **Fragmentum**, FGrH #796: 3C:835.
Q

9017 **MICHAEL** Epigr.
A.D. 10
001 **Epigramma**, AG 1.122.
Q: 24

2704 **MICHAEL** Epigr.
Incertum
x01 **Epigrammata demonstrativa.**
App. Anth. 3.275–276: Cf. EPIGRAMMATICI
in *App. Anth.* (7052 003).

4034 **MICHAEL** Phil.
A.D. 11–12: Ephesius
001 **In ethica Nicomachea ix–x commentaria**, ed.
G. Heylbut, *Eustratii et Michaelis et anonyma
in ethica Nicomachea commentaria* [*Commentaria in Aristotelem Graeca* 20. Berlin: Reimer,
1892]: 461–620.
Cod: [70,539]
002 **In parva naturalia commentaria**, ed. P. Wendland, *Michaelis Ephesii in parva naturalia commentaria* [*Commentaria in Aristotelem Graeca*
22.1. Berlin: Reimer, 1903]: 1–149.
Cod: [55,383]
003 **In libros de partibus animalium commentaria**,
ed. M. Hayduck, *Michaelis Ephesii in libros de
partibus animalium, de animalium motione, de
animalium incessu commentaria* [*Commentaria
in Aristotelem Graeca* 22.2. Berlin: Reimer,
1904]: 1–99.
Cod: [43,969]
004 **In libros de animalium motione commentarium**, ed. Hayduck, *CAG* 22.2, 103–131.
Cod: [10,755]
005 **In librum de animalium incessu commentarium**, ed. Hayduck, *CAG* 22.2, 135–170.
Cod: [14,823]
006 **In librum quintum ethicorum Nicomacheorum
commentarium**, ed. M. Hayduck, *Michaelis*

Ephesii in librum quintum ethicorum Nico-
macheorum commentarium [*Commentaria in*
Aristotelem Graeca 22.3. Berlin: Reimer, 1901]:
1–72.
Cod: [31,140]

4078 **MICHAELIUS** Gramm.
A.D. 6
001 **Epigramma**, AG 16.316.
Q: 39

1509 **<MILON>** <Phil.>
Incertum: Crotoniensis
001 **Fragmentum**, ed. H. Thesleff, *The Pythagorean*
texts of the Hellenistic period. Åbo: Åbo Akademi, 1965: 122–123.
Q: 65

1510 *MIMI ANONYMI*
ante A.D. 3
001 **Fragmentum** (*P. Oxy.* 3.413), ed. D.L. Page,
Select papyri, vol. 3 [*Literary papyri*]. London:
Heinemann, 1941 (repr. 1970): 338–348.
Pap: [1,340]
002 **Fragmentum** (*P. Oxy.* 3.413), ed. Page, *op. cit.*,
352–360.
Pap
003 **Fragmentum** (*P. Lit. Lond.* 97), ed. Page, *op.*
cit., 362–366.
Pap
004 **Fragmentum** (*P. Lit. Lond.* 52), ed. Page, *op.*
cit., 368–370.
Pap

0255 **MIMNERMUS** Eleg.
7 B.C.: Smyrnaeus
001 **Fragmenta**, ed. M.L. West, *Iambi et elegi*
Graeci, vol. 2. Oxford: Clarendon Press, 1972:
81–90.
frr. 1–9, 11–12, 13a–17, 22, 24–26.
Q: [645]
002 **Epigramma**, AG 9.50.
AG 7.405: Cf. PHILIPPUS Epigr. (1589 001).
Q: 15
003 **Fragmenta**, FGrH #578: 3B:688–690.
Q

1511 **MIMNERMUS** Trag.
ante 4 B.C.?
001 **Fragmenta**, ed. A. Nauck, *Tragicorum Grae-*
corum fragmenta. Leipzig: Teubner, 1889
(repr. Hildesheim: Olms, 1964): 829–830.
frr. 1–2.
Q: [34]

0991 **MINUCIANUS** Med.
1 B.C.–A.D. 1
x01 **Fragmentum ap. Galenum.**
K13.930.
Cf. GALENUS Med. (0057 077).

1512 *MINYAS*
ante 5 B.C.

001 **Fragmentum**, ed. G. Kinkel, *Epicorum Graeco-*
rum fragmenta, vol. 1. Leipzig: Teubner, 1877:
215.
fr. 1.
Q: [16]

0992 **MITHRIDATES VI Eupator** <Med.>
2–1 B.C.
x01 **Fragmenta ap. Galenum.**
K**13**.23, 52–53, 54–56, 329–330; **14**.148, 152–
155, 164.
Cf. GALENUS Med. (0057 076, 078).
x02 **Fragmentum ap. Paulum.**
CMG, vol. 9.2, p. 297.
Cf. PAULUS Med. (0715 001).

0039 *MITHRIDATIS EPISTULA*
1 B.C.?
Cf. et BRUTI EPISTULAE (1803).
001 **Epistula**, ed. R. Hercher, *Epistolographi Graeci.*
Paris: Didot, 1873 (repr. Amsterdam: Hakkert,
1965): 177–178.
Cod: [349]

1513 **MNASALCES** Epigr.
3 B.C.: Sicyonius
001 **Epigrammata**, AG **6**.9, 110, 125, 128, 264, 268;
7.54, 171, 192, 194, 212, 242, 488, 491; **9**.70,
324, 333; **12**.138.
AG 7.490: Cf. ANYTE Epigr. (0121 001).
Q: 486
x01 **Epigrammata** (*App. Anth.*).
Epigramma demonstrativum: 3.71.
Epigramma irrisorium: 5.14.
App. Anth. 3.71: Cf. EPIGRAMMATICI in *App.*
Anth. (7052 003).
App. Anth. 5.14: Cf. EPIGRAMMATICI in *App.*
Anth. (7052 005).

0993 **MNASEAS** Med.
vel Mnasaeus
A.D. 1
x01 **Fragmentum ap. Galenum.**
K13.445.
Cf. GALENUS Med. (0057 077).
x02 **Fragmenta ap. Oribasium.**
CMG, vol. **6**.2.2, p. 271; **6**.3, pp. 83, 87, 492.
Cf. ORIBASIUS Med. (0722 003–005).
x03 **Fragmentum ap. Paulum.**
CMG, vol. 9.2, p. 353.
Cf. PAULUS Med. (0715 001).
x04 **Fragmentum ap. Aëtium** (lib. 15).
Zervos, *Athena* 21, p. 83.
Cf. AËTIUS Med. (0718 015).
x05 **Fragmentum ap. Alexandrum Trallianum.**
Puschmann, vol. 2, pp. 107–109.
Cf. ALEXANDER Med. (0744 003).

1514 **MNASEAS** Perieg.
3 B.C.: Patrensis
001 **Fragmenta**, FHG 3: 149–158.
Q
002 **Fragmenta**, ed. H.J. Mette, "Die 'Kleinen'

griechischen Historiker heute," *Lustrum* 21
(1978) 39–40.
frr. 25 bis a–b, 34 bis, 51.
fr. 51: *P. Oxy.* 13.1611.
Q, Pap

0476 **MNESIMACHUS** Comic.
4 B.C.
001 **Fragmenta**, ed. T. Kock, *Comicorum Attico-rum fragmenta*, vol. 2. Leipzig: Teubner, 1884:
436–438, 441–442.
frr. 1–4, 7–11.
Q: 448
002 **Fragmenta**, ed. A. Meineke, *Fragmenta comico-rum Graecorum*, vol. 3. Berlin: Reimer, 1840
(repr. De Gruyter, 1970): 567–570, 576–579.
Q: 451

2565 **MNESIMACHUS** Hist.
4/3 B.C.?: Phaselinus
001 **Fragmenta**, FGrH #841: 3C:927–928.
Q

1959 **MNESIPTOLEMUS** Hist.
3–2 B.C.: Cumaeus
001 **Testimonia**, FGrH #164: 2B:890.
NQ

0701 **MNESITHEUS** Med.
4 B.C.: Atheniensis
Cf. et MNESITHEUS Med. (0805).
x01 **Fragmenta ap. Galenum.**
K6.512–513, 645–646 in CMG, vol. 5.4.2, pp.
235–236, 321–322.
Cf. GALENUS Med. (0057 037).
x02 **Fragmenta ap. Oribasium.**
CMG, vol. **6.1.1**, pp. 62–64, 261, 288–290;
6.2.2, p. 135.
Cf. ORIBASIUS Med. (0722 001–002).
x03 **Fragmenta ap. Athenaeum.**
Deipnosophistae 1.32d; 2.54b–c, 59b; **3**.80c–e,
92b–c, 106d; **11**.483f–484b.
Cf. ATHENAEUS Soph. (0008 001).

0805 **MNESITHEUS** Med.
fiq Mnesitheus Atheniensis vel Mnesitheus
Cyzicenus
4/3 B.C.?
Cf. et MNESITHEUS Med. (0701).
Cf. et MNESITHEUS Med. (0702).
x01 **Fragmentum ap. Oribasium.**
CMG, vol. 6.2.2, p. 84.
Cf. ORIBASIUS Med. (0722 002).

0702 **MNESITHEUS** Med.
3 B.C.?: Cyzicenus
Cf. et MNESITHEUS Med. (0805).
x01 **Fragmentum ap. Oribasium.**
CMG, vol. 6.1.1, p. 100.
Cf. ORIBASIUS Med. (0722 001).

1890 **MODERATUS** Phil.
A.D. 1: Gaditanus

001 **Fragmenta**, ed. F.W.A. Mullach, *Fragmenta
philosophorum Graecorum*, vol. 2. Paris: Didot,
1867 (repr. Aalen: Scientia, 1968): 48–49.
Q
x01 **Fragmenta ap. Porphyrium.**
VP 48.
Cf. PORPHYRIUS Phil. (2034 002).
x02 **Fragmenta ap. Simplicium.**
CAG 9, pp. 230–231.
Cf. SIMPLICIUS Phil. (4013 004).

1515 **MOERIS** Attic.
A.D. 2
001 **Lexicon Atticum**, ed. I. Bekker, *Harpocration
et Moeris*. Berlin: Reimer, 1833: 187–214.
Cod

0220 **MOERO** Epic.
4–3 B.C.: Byzantia
001 **Fragmenta**, ed. J.U. Powell, *Collectanea Alex-andrina*. Oxford: Clarendon Press, 1925 (repr.
1970): 21–22.
frr. 1–3.
Q: [128]
002 **Epigrammata**, AG 6.119, 189.
Q: 53

1516 **MOLPIS** Hist.
2–1 B.C.: Lacon
001 **Testimonium**, FGrH #590: 3B:704.
NQ
002 **Fragmenta**, FGrH #590: 3B:704–705.
Q

2968 **MONIMUS** Phil.
4 B.C.: Syracusanus
001 **Fragmenta**, ed. F.W.A. Mullach, *Fragmenta
philosophorum Graecorum*, vol. 2. Paris: Didot,
1867 (repr. Aalen: Scientia, 1968): 345.
Q

0277 ***MONODIA***
ante A.D. 2
001 **Mirmillonis amatrix** (*P. Ryl.* 1.15), ed. E.
Heitsch, *Die griechischen Dichterfragmente der
römischen Kaiserzeit*, vol. 1, 2nd edn. Göttin-gen: Vandenhoeck & Ruprecht, 1963: 45.
Pap: [99]

1044 **MONOIMUS** Gnost.
A.D. 2: Arabius
x01 **Fragmenta.**
Hippolytus, *Refut.* 8.12.1–8.15.2.
Cf. HIPPOLYTUS Scr. Eccl. (2115 001).

1771 **MONTANUS et MONTANISTAE** Theol.
A.D. 2: Phrygius (Montanus)
001 **Oracula**, ed. P. de Labriolle, *La crise mon-taniste*. Paris: Leroux, 1913: 37–38, 43, 45–46,
60–61, 68–69, 71, 73, 86–87, 95–97.
Q
x01 **Fragmenta ap. Epiphanium.**
Haer. 48.10,11.

Cf. EPIPHANIUS Scr. Eccl. (2021 002).

x02 **Fragmenta ap. Didymum** (*Trin.* 3.41).
MPG 39.984.
Cf. DIDYMUS CAECUS Scr. Eccl. (2102 043).

x03 **Fragmenta** (in *Doctrina patrum*).
Diekamp, p. 306, fr. 14.
Cf. DOCTRINA PATRUM (7051 001).

0314 **MORSIMUS** Trag.
5 B.C.: Atheniensis
001 **Fragmentum,** ed. B. Snell, *Tragicorum Graeco-rum fragmenta,* vol. 1. Göttingen: Vanden-hoeck & Ruprecht, 1971: 148.
fr. 1.
Q: [10]

0575 **<MOSCHION>** Gnom.
Incertum
001 **Sententiae,** ed. H. Schenkl, *Epicteti dissertati-ones ab Arriano digestae.* Leipzig: Teubner, 1916 (repr. Stuttgart: 1965): 493–494.
frr. 1–25.
Q: [583]
002 **Hypothecae,** ed. Schenkl, *op. cit.,* 495–496.
frr. 1–18.
Q

1517 **MOSCHION** Paradox.
3 B.C.?
001 **Fragmenta,** FGrH #575: 3B:675–678.
Q

0339 **MOSCHION** Trag.
3 B.C.
001 **Fragmenta,** ed. B. Snell, *Tragicorum Grae-corum fragmenta,* vol. 1. Göttingen: Vanden-hoeck & Ruprecht, 1971: 264–268.
frr. 1–10, 12.
Q: [442]

0994 **MOSCHION** ὁ διορθωτής Med.
1 B.C.
Cf. et APHRODAS et MOSCHION Med. (0866).
x01 **Fragmenta ap. Galenum.**
K13.528, 537–539, 646–649, 853.
Cf. GALENUS Med. (0057 077).
x02 **Fragmentum ap. Aëtium** (lib. 15).
Zervos, *Athena* 21, p. 63.
Cf. AËTIUS Med. (0718 015).
x03 **Fragmentum ap. Alexandrum Trallianum.**
Puschmann, vol. 1, p. 571.
Cf. ALEXANDER Med. (0744 003).
x04 **Fragmentum ap. Hippiatrica.**
Oder & Hoppe, vol. 2, p. 194.
Cf. HIPPIATRICA (0738 006).

0035 **MOSCHUS** Bucol.
2 B.C.: Syracusanus
001 **Eros drapeta,** ed. A.S.F. Gow, *Bucolici Graeci.* Oxford: Clarendon Press, 1952 (repr. 1969): 132–133.
Cod: [255]

002 **Europa,** ed. Gow, *op. cit.,* 133–139.
Cod: [1,174]
003 **Epitaphius Bionis** [Sp.], ed. Gow, *op. cit.,* 140–145.
Cod: [972]
004 **Megara** [Sp.], ed. Gow, *op. cit.,* 146–150.
Cod: [917]
005 **Fragmenta,** ed. Gow, *op. cit.,* 151–152.
Q: [270]
006 **Epigrammata,** AG **9.**440; **16.**200.
Q: 284

2181 **MOSES** Alchem.
A.D. 2?
001 **Fragmenta,** ed. M. Berthelot, *Collection des anciens alchimistes grecs.* Paris: Steinheil, 1887 (repr. London: Holland Press, 1963): 38–39, 300–315.
Cod

2414 **MOSMES** (?) Hist.
post 4 B.C.?
001 **Fragmentum,** FGrH #614: 3C:122.
Q

1518 **Quintus MUCIUS SCAEVOLA** Epigr.
1 B.C.
001 **Epigramma,** AG 9.217.
Q: 41

1519 **MUNDUS MUNATIUS** Epigr.
A.D. 1?
001 **Epigramma,** AG 9.103.
Q: 53

0808 **MUSA** Med.
fiq Antonius Musa vel Petronius
A.D. 1?
Cf. et ANTONIUS MUSA Med. (0669).
Cf. et PETRONIUS Med. (1026).
x01 **Fragmenta ap. Galenum.**
K12.956; **13.**832.
Cf. GALENUS Med. (0057 076–077).
x02 **Fragmenta ap. Oribasium.**
CMG, vol. **6.2.2,** p. 192; **6.3,** pp. 93, 494.
Cf. ORIBASIUS Med. (0722 003–005).
x03 **Fragmentum ap. Paulum.**
CMG, vol. 9.2, p. 317.
Cf. PAULUS Med. (0715 001).

0576 **MUSAEUS** Epic.
2 B.C.?: Ephesius
001 **Testimonium,** FGrH #455: 3B:383.
NQ
002 **Fragmentum,** FGrH #455: 3B:383.
Q
003 **Tituli,** ed. H. Lloyd-Jones and P. Parsons, *Supplementum Hellenisticum.* Berlin: De Gruy-ter, 1983: 274.
frr. 560–561.
NQ: [6]

2691 **[MUSAEUS]** Phil.
Incertum: Eleusinius

001 **Testimonia**, ed. H. Diels and W. Kranz, *Die Fragmente der Vorsokratiker*, vol. 1, 6th edn. Berlin: Weidmann, 1951 (repr. Dublin: 1966): 20–22.
test. 1–11.
NQ

002 **Fragmenta**, ed. Diels and Kranz, *op. cit.*, 22–27.
frr. 1–22.
Q

4082 **MUSAEUS Grammaticus** Epic.
A.D. 5/6

001 **Hero et Leander**, ed. H. Färber, *Hero und Leander*. Munich: Heimeran, 1961: 6–26.
Cod: [2,185]

1520 **MUSICIUS** Epigr.
ante A.D. 3

001 **Epigramma**, AG 9.39.
Q: 28

0628 **Gaius MUSONIUS RUFUS** Phil.
A.D. 1: Volsiniensis

001 **Dissertationum a Lucio digestarum reliquiae**, ed. C.E. Lutz, *Musonius Rufus "The Roman Socrates."* New Haven: Yale University Press, 1947: 32–128.
frr. 1–21.
fr. 15: *P. Rendel Harris* 1 (inv. 3).
Q, Pap: [16,462]

002 **Fragmenta minora**, ed. Lutz, *op. cit.*, 131–141, 144.
frr. 22–48, 50–51, 53.
Q: [1,225]

003 **Epistulae spuriae**, ed. O. Hense, *C. Musonii Rufi reliquiae*. Leipzig: Teubner, 1905: 137–143.
Cod: [1,351]

004 **Fragmentum**, ed. G.D. Kilpatrick, "A fragment of Musonius," *Classical Review* 63 (1949) 94.
Q: [23]

0509 **<MYIA>** Phil.
3/2 B.C.

001 **Epistula ad Phyllidem**, ed. H. Thesleff, *The Pythagorean texts of the Hellenistic period*. Åbo: Åbo Akademi, 1965: 123–124.
Q: 301

1522 **MYRINUS** Epigr.
1 B.C.?

001 **Epigrammata**, AG **6**.108, 254; 7.703; **11**.67.
Q: 137

1523 **MYRON** Hist.
3 B.C.?: Prienaeus

001 **Testimonium**, FGrH #106: 2B:509.
NQ

002 **Fragmenta**, FGrH #106: 2B:509–515.
Q

2331 **MYRSILUS** Hist.
3 B.C.: Methymnaeus

001 **Testimonia**, FGrH #477: 3B:437.
NQ

002 **Fragmenta**, FGrH #477: 3B:437–442.
Q

0477 **MYRTILUS** Comic.
5 B.C.

001 **Fragmenta**, ed. T. Kock, *Comicorum Atticorum fragmenta*, vol. 1. Leipzig: Teubner, 1880: 253–254.
frr. 3–4 + tituli.
Q: 19

002 **Fragmenta**, ed. A. Meineke, *Fragmenta comicorum Graecorum*, vol. 2.1. Berlin: Reimer, 1839 (repr. De Gruyter, 1970): 418–419.
Q: 18

003 **Fragmentum**, ed. Kock, *op. cit.*, vol. 3 (1888): 717.
fr. 3b.
Q: 7

1524 **NAUMACHIUS** Epic.
A.D. 2

001 **Fragmentum**, ed. E. Heitsch, *Die griechischen Dichterfragmente der römischen Kaiserzeit*, vol. 1, 2nd edn. Göttingen: Vandenhoeck & Ruprecht, 1963: 92–94.
Q: [525]

0478 **NAUSICRATES** Comic.
4 B.C.

001 **Fragmenta**, ed. T. Kock, *Comicorum Atticorum fragmenta*, vol. 2. Leipzig: Teubner, 1884: 295–296.
frr. 1–3.
Q: 132

002 **Fragmenta**, ed. A. Meineke, *Fragmenta comicorum Graecorum*, vol. 4. Berlin: Reimer, 1841 (repr. De Gruyter, 1970): 575, 578.
Q: 87

003 **Fragmentum**, ed. J. Demiańczuk, *Supplementum comicum*. Krakau: Nakładem Akademii, 1912 (repr. Hildesheim: Olms, 1967): 64.
fr. 1.
Q: 2

2334 **NAUSIPHANES** Phil.
4–3 B.C.: Teius

001 **Testimonia**, ed. H. Diels and W. Kranz, *Die Fragmente der Vorsokratiker*, vol. 2, 6th edn. Berlin: Weidmann, 1952 (repr. Dublin: 1966): 246–247.
test. 1–9.
NQ

002 **Fragmenta**, ed. Diels and Kranz, *op. cit.*, 248–250.
frr. 1–4.
Q

0269 *NAUTARUM CANTIUNCULAE*
ante A.D. 2/3

001 **Fragmentum** (*P. Oxy.* 3.425), ed. E. Heitsch, *Die griechischen Dichterfragmente der römischen Kaiserzeit*, vol. 1, 2nd edn. Göttingen: Vandenhoeck & Ruprecht, 1963: 33.
Pap: [23]

002 **Ad Rhodios ventos** (*P. Oxy.* 11.1383), ed. Heitsch, *op. cit.*, 33.
Pap: [42]

1525 **NEANTHES** Hist.
3 B.C.: Cyzicenus

001 **Testimonia**, FGrH #84: 2A:191.
NQ

002 **Fragmenta**, FGrH #84: 2A:192–202.
fr. 34: *P. Herc.* 327, fr. 4.
Q, Pap

1966 **NEANTHES Junior** Hist.
3–2 B.C.: Cyzicenus

001 **Fragmentum**, FGrH #171: 2B:895.
Q

1942 **NEARCHUS** Hist.
4–3 B.C.?: Cretensis

001 **Testimonia**, FGrH #133: 2B:677–680.
test. 2: *Inscr. Delphi.*
NQ

002 **Fragmenta**, FGrH #133: 2B:681–722.
Q

0995 **[NECHEPSO et PETOSIRIS]** Astrol.
ante 2 B.C.: Aegyptius

001 **Fragmenta**, ed. E. Riess, "Nechepsonis et Petosiridis fragmenta magica," *Philologus*, suppl. 6 (1891–1893) 332–387.
Q, Cod

002 **Testimonium**, FGrH #663: 3C:214.
NQ

x01 **Fragmentum ap. Aëtium** (lib. 2).
CMG, vol. 8.1, p. 164.
Cf. AËTIUS Med. (0718 002).

x02 **Fragmentum ap. Aëtium** (lib. 15).
Zervos, *Athena* 21, p. 42.
Cf. AËTIUS Med. (0718 015).

0996 **NEILAMMON** Med.
ante A.D. 7

x01 **Fragmentum ap. Paulum.**
CMG, vol. 9.2, p. 338.
Cf. PAULUS Med. (0715 001).

4079 **NEILUS** Epigr.
A.D. 5

001 **Epigrammata**, AG 1.33; **16**.247.
Q: 49

0743 **NEMESIUS** Theol.
A.D. 4: Emesenus

001 **De natura hominis**, ed. B. Einarson, *Nemesius of Emesa* [*Corpus medicorum Graecorum* (in press)]: 35–368.
N.B.: Text in the TLG data bank is based upon the editor's 1974 typescript.
Cod: 37,929

0307 **NEOPHRON** Trag.
5 B.C.

001 **Fragmenta**, ed. B. Snell, *Tragicorum Graecorum fragmenta*, vol. 1. Göttingen: Vandenhoeck & Ruprecht, 1971: 92–94.
frr. 1–3.
Q: [155]

1526 **NEOPTOLEMUS** Gramm.
3 B.C.: Parianus

001 **Fragmenta**, ed. J.U. Powell, *Collectanea Alexandrina*. Oxford: Clarendon Press, 1925 (repr. 1970): 27–28.
frr. 2, 3, 6.
Q: [39]

002 **Testimonium**, FGrH #702: 3C:555.
NQ

003 **Fragmenta**, FGrH #702: 3C:556.
Q

004 **Fragmenta**, ed. H.J. Mette, "Neoptolemos von Parion," *Rheinisches Museum* 123 (1980) 1–13.
Q

1527 **NEPUALIUS** Phil.
vel Neptunalius vel Neptunianus
A.D. 2?

001 Περὶ τῶν κατὰ ἀντιπάθειαν καὶ συμπάθειαν, ed. W. Gemoll, *Nepualii fragmentum περὶ τῶν κατὰ ἀντιπάθειαν καὶ συμπάθειαν et Democriti περὶ συμπαθειῶν καὶ ἀντιπαθειῶν* [*Städtisches Realprogymnasium zu Striegau* (1884)]: 1–3.
Cod

0998 **Tiberius Claudius NERO Imperator** <Med.>
A.D. 1

x01 **Fragmentum ap. Paulum.**
CMG, vol. 9.2, p. 359.
Cf. PAULUS Med. (0715 001).

2456 **NESSAS** Phil.
5 B.C.: Chius

001 **Testimonia**, ed. H. Diels and W. Kranz, *Die Fragmente der Vorsokratiker*, vol. 2, 6th edn. Berlin: Weidmann, 1952 (repr. Dublin: 1966): 230.
test. 1–2.
NQ

002 **Fragmenta**, ed. Diels and Kranz, *op. cit.*, 230.
frr. 1–2.
Q

1528 **NESTOR** Epic.
A.D. 2–3: Larandensis

001 **Epigrammata**, AG 9.128–129, 364, 537.
AG 9.536: Cf. ANONYMI EPIGRAMMATICI (0138 001).
Q: 108

x01 **Epigramma dedicatorium.**

App. Anth. 1.299?: Cf. EPIGRAMMATICI in *App. Anth.* (7052 001).

0218 **NICAENETUS** Epic.
3 B.C.: Abderita
001 **Fragmenta**, ed. J.U. Powell, *Collectanea Alexandrina.* Oxford: Clarendon Press, 1925 (repr. 1970): 1, 3–4.
frr. 1, 3–7.
Q: [245]
002 **Epigrammata**, AG **6**.225; **7**.502; **13**.29; **16**.191.
Q: 125
x01 **Epigramma exhortatorium et dedicatorium.**
App. Anth. 4.40: Cf. EPIGRAMMATICI in *App. Anth.* (7052 004).

0022 **NICANDER** Epic.
2 B.C.: Colophonius
Cf. et NICANDER Colophonius Hist. (1933).
001 **Theriaca**, ed. A.S.F. Gow and A.F. Scholfield, *Nicander. The poems and poetical fragments.* Cambridge: Cambridge University Press, 1953: 28–92.
Cod, Pap: 6,380
002 **Alexipharmaca**, ed. Gow and Scholfield, *op. cit.*, 94–136.
Cod: 4,149
003 **Fragmenta**, ed. Gow and Scholfield, *op. cit.*, 138–166.
Oetaica (frr. 16, 18): p. 138.
Thebaica (fr. 19): p. 138.
Sicelia (frr. 21–22): pp. 138–140.
Europia (frr. 26–27): p. 140.
Ophiaca (frr. 31–32): p. 142.
Heteroeumena (frr. 43, 50, 59, 62): pp. 142–144.
Georgica (frr. 68–76, 78–87, 90–91): pp. 144–160.
Cynegetica (?) (frr. 98, 100): p. 162.
Hymnus in Attalum (?) (fr. 104): p. 162.
Epigrammata (frr. 105–107): pp. 162–164.
Incertae sedis fragmenta (frr. 108–112): pp. 164–166.
Q: 1,332
004 **Fragmenta prosaica**, ed. O. Schneider, *Nicandrea.* Leipzig: Teubner, 1856.
Q
005 **Fragmenta**, ed. H. Lloyd-Jones and P. Parsons, *Supplementum Hellenisticum.* Berlin: De Gruyter, 1983: 274, 277–278.
frr. 562–563a.
fr. 562: *P. Oxy.* 37.2812.
fr. 563: *P. Oxy.* 19.2221.
fr. 563a: *P. Mil. Vogl.* 2.45.
Pap: [150]
006 **Epigrammata**, AG **7**.435, 526; **9**.503b.
AG 11.7: Cf. NICARCHUS II Epigr. (1532 001).
Q: 80
x01 **Fragmenta.**
FGrH #271–272.
Cf. NICANDER Hist. (1933 001–002).

1529 **NICANDER** Gramm.
3/1 B.C.: Thyatirius
001 **Testimonium**, FGrH #343: 3B:205.
NQ
002 **Fragmenta**, FGrH #343: 3B:205–207.
Q

1933 **NICANDER** Hist.
2 B.C.: Colophonius
Cf. et NICANDER Epic. (0022).
001 **Testimonia**, FGrH #271–272: 3A:85–86.
NQ
002 **Fragmenta**, FGrH #271–272: **3A**:87–95; **3B**:753 addenda.
Q

2474 **NICANDER** Hist.
2 B.C.?: Chalcedonius
001 **Fragmenta**, FGrH #700: 3C:554–555.
Q

1530 **NICANOR** Gramm.
A.D. 2: Alexandrinus
001 **Testimonium**, FGrH #628: 3C:178.
NQ
002 **Fragmenta**, FGrH #628: 3C:178–179.
Q
003 Περὶ 'Ιλιακῆς στιγμῆς, ed. L. Friedländer, *Nicanoris περὶ 'Ιλιακῆς στιγμῆς reliquiae emendatiores*, 2nd edn. Berlin: Borntraeger, 1857 (repr. Hakkert, 1967): 141–278.
Q
004 Περὶ 'Οδυσσειακῆς στιγμῆς, ed. O. Carnuth, *Nicanoris περὶ 'Οδυσσειακῆς στιγμῆς reliquiae emendatiores.* Berlin: Borntraeger, 1875 (repr. Hakkert, 1967): 21–68.
Q

1948 **NICANOR** Hist.
ante 2 B.C.
001 **Fragmenta**, FGrH #146: 2B:814–815.
Q

1531 **NICARCHUS I** Epigr.
4–3 B.C.
001 **Epigrammata**, AG **6**.31, 285; **7**.159, 166; **9**.330.
Q: 245

1532 **NICARCHUS II** Epigr.
A.D. 1
001 **Epigrammata**, AG **5**.38–40; **9**.576; **11**.1, 7, 17–18, 71, 73–74, 82, 96, 102, 110, 124, 162, 169–170, 186, 241–243, 251–252, 328–332, 395, 398, 406–407, 415.
AG 5.67: Cf. CAPITO Epigr. (0149 001).
AG 5.98: Cf. ARCHIAS Epigr. (0126 001).
AG 11.72: Cf. LOLLIUS BASSUS Epigr. (0143 001).
AG 11.118–122: Cf. CALLICTER Epigr. (0148 001).

AG 11.244: Cf. ANONYMI EPIGRAMMATICI
(0138 001).
Q: 1,355

2494 **NICARCHUS** Hist.
A.D. 1?
001 **Fragmentum**, FGrH #731: 3C:691–692.
Q

2361 **NICASYLUS** Hist.
Incertum
001 **Titulus**, FGrH #519: 3B:492.
NQ

4145 **NICEPHORUS GREGORAS** Polyhist.
A.D. 13–14: Heracleensis, Constantinopoli-
tanus
x01 **Epigramma sepulcrale**.
App. Anth. 2.774: Cf. EPIGRAMMATICI in
App. Anth. (7052 002).

2633 **NICERATUS** Epic.
5 B.C.: Heracleota
001 **Titulus**, ed. H. Lloyd-Jones and P. Parsons,
Supplementum Hellenisticum. Berlin: De Gruyter, 1983: 278.
fr. 564.
NQ: [1]

NICERATUS Epigr.
AG 13.29.
Cf. NICAENETUS Epic. (0218 002).

0999 **NICERATUS** Med.
1 B.C.–A.D. 1
x01 **Fragmenta ap. Galenum**.
K13.87, 96, 98, 110, 180, 232, 233–234.
Cf. GALENUS Med. (0057 076).

2705 **NICETAS DAVID** Scr. Eccl.
A.D. 10: Dadybrensis
Bibliography in progress
x01 **Epigramma demonstrativum**.
App. Anth. 3.285: Cf. EPIGRAMMATICI in
App. Anth. (7052 003).

0046 *NICIAE EPISTULA*
Incertum
001 **Epistula**, ed. R. Hercher, *Epistolographi Graeci.*
Paris: Didot, 1873 (repr. Amsterdam: Hakkert,
1965): 405–406.
Q: [768]

1533 **NICIAS** Epigr.
3 B.C.: Milesius
001 **Epigrammata**, AG **6**.122, 127, 270; **7**.200;
9.315, 564; **16**.188.
AG 11.398: Cf. NICARCHUS II Epigr. (1532
001).
Q: 181
002 **Fragmentum**, ed. H. Lloyd-Jones and P. Par-

sons, *Supplementum Hellenisticum.* Berlin: De
Gruyter, 1983: 279.
fr. 566.
Q: [15]

1837 **NICIAS** Gramm.
1 B.C.?: fort. Cous
001 **Fragmenta**, ed. R. Berndt, "Die Fragmente des
Grammatikers Nicias," *Philologische Wochenschrift* 30 (1910) coll. 508–510.
Q

2217 **NICIAS** Hist.
ante A.D. 3
001 **Fragmentum**, FGrH #318: 3B:31.
Q

1902 **<NICIAS>** Hist.
Incertum: Mallotes
001 **Fragmenta**, FGrH #60: 1A:298.
Q

0479 **NICO** Comic.
post 5 B.C.
001 **Fragmentum**, ed. T. Kock, *Comicorum Atticorum fragmenta*, vol. 3. Leipzig: Teubner, 1888:
389.
fr. 1.
Q: 19
002 **Fragmentum**, ed. A. Meineke, *Fragmenta comicorum Graecorum*, vol. 4. Berlin: Reimer,
1841 (repr. De Gruyter, 1970): 578.
Q: 20

1937 **NICOBULE** Hist.
4 B.C.
001 **Testimonia**, FGrH #127: 2B:667.
NQ
002 **Fragmenta**, FGrH #127: 2B:667.
Q

0480 **NICOCHARES** Comic.
4 B.C.
001 **Fragmenta**, ed. T. Kock, *Comicorum Atticorum fragmenta*, vol. 1. Leipzig: Teubner, 1880:
770–774.
frr. 1–3, 5, 7–9, 11–12, 14–21 + tituli.
Q: 116
002 **Fragmenta**, ed. A. Meineke, *Fragmenta comicorum Graecorum*, vol. 2.2. Berlin: Reimer, 1840
(repr. De Gruyter, 1970): 842–846.
Q: 88
003 **Fragmenta**, ed. J. Demiańczuk, *Supplementum
comicum.* Krakau: Nakładem Akademii, 1912
(repr. Hildesheim: Olms, 1967): 64–66.
frr. 1–5, 7.
Q: 30

2279 **NICOCHARES** Hist.
ante 4 B.C.

001 **Testimonium**, FGrH #398: 3B:292.
NQ

1534 **NICOCLES** Hist.
ante 1 B.C.: Lacon
001 **Fragmenta**, FGrH #587: 3B:701–702.
Q

1535 **NICOCRATES** Hist.
ante 2 B.C.
001 **Fragmenta**, FGrH #376: 3B:242–244.
fr. 1: *P. Mich.* 4913.
Q, Pap

1536 **NICODEMUS** Epigr.
Incertum: Heracleensis
001 **Epigrammata**, AG **6**.314–320, 323; **9**.53.
Q: 131

0481 **NICOLAUS** Comic.
4 B.C.?
001 **Fragmenta**, ed. T. Kock, *Comicorum Attico-rum fragmenta*, vol. 3. Leipzig: Teubner, 1888: 383–384, 386.
frr. 1–2.
Q: 277
002 **Fragmentum**, ed. A. Meineke, *Fragmenta co-micorum Graecorum*, vol. 4. Berlin: Reimer, 1841 (repr. De Gruyter, 1970): 579–580.
Q: 275

2713 **NICOLAUS** Epigr.
A.D. 14?
x01 **Epigrammata exhortatoria et supplicatoria.**
App. Anth. 4.106–107: Cf. EPIGRAMMATICI in *App. Anth.* (7052 004).

0577 **NICOLAUS** Hist.
1 B.C.: Damascenus
001 **Testimonia**, FGrH #90: 2A:324–328.
NQ
002 **Fragmenta**, FGrH #90: 2A:328–430.
Q

1001 **NICOLAUS** Med.
ante A.D. 2
x01 **Fragmentum ap. Galenum.**
K13.831.
Cf. GALENUS Med. (0057 077).
x02 **Fragmentum ap. Paulum.**
CMG, vol. 9.2, p. 358.
Cf. PAULUS Med. (0715 001).

4144 **NICOLAUS** Med.
A.D. 13
x01 **Epigrammata sepulcralia.**
App. Anth. 2.771–773: Cf. EPIGRAMMATICI in *App. Anth.* (7052 002).

0482 **NICOMACHUS** Comic.
3 B.C.
001 **Fragmenta**, ed. T. Kock, *Comicorum Attico-*

rum fragmenta, vol. 3. Leipzig: Teubner, 1888: 386–389.
frr. 1–4.
Q: 335
002 **Fragmenta**, ed. A. Meineke, *Fragmenta comico-rum Graecorum*, vol. 4. Berlin: Reimer, 1841 (repr. De Gruyter, 1970): 583–584, 587–588.
Q: 311

1537 **NICOMACHUS** Epigr.
ante 2 B.C.
001 **Epigramma**, AG 7.299.
Q: 29

1538 **NICOMACHUS** Hist.
ante A.D. 2
001 **Fragmentum**, FGrH #662: 3C:213–214.
Q

1961 **NICOMACHUS** Hist.
A.D. 3–4?
001 **Fragmentum**, FGrH #215: 2B:946.
Q

0358 **NICOMACHUS** Math.
A.D. 2: Gerasenus
001 **Introductio arithmetica**, ed. R. Hoche, *Nico-machi Geraseni Pythagorei introductionis arith-meticae libri ii*. Leipzig: Teubner, 1866: 1–70, 73–147.
Cod: [24,287]
002 **Harmonicum enchiridion**, ed. K. Jan, *Musici scriptores Graeci*. Leipzig: Teubner, 1895 (repr. Hildesheim: Olms, 1962): 236–265.
Cod: [5,244]
003 **Theologoumena arithmeticae**, ed. V. de Falco, *[Iamblichi] theologoumena arithmeticae*. Leip-zig: Teubner, 1922: 17–30, 42, 56–71.
Q: [5,911]
004 **Excerpta**, ed. Jan, *op. cit.*, 266–282.
Cod: [2,483]

NICOMACHUS Med.
Cf. ALCIMION vel NICOMACHUS Med. (0823).

0342 **NICOMACHUS** Trag.
3 B.C.: Alexandrinus (Troadis)
001 **Fragmenta**, ed. B. Snell, *Tragicorum Grae-corum fragmenta*, vol. 1. Göttingen: Vanden-hoeck & Ruprecht, 1971: 285–287.
frr. 1, 7, 13–16.
Q: [31]

1843 **NICOMACHUS** Trag.
Incertum: Atheniensis
001 **Tituli**, ed. B. Snell, *Tragicorum Graecorum fragmenta*, vol. 1. Göttingen: Vandenhoeck & Ruprecht, 1971: 155.
NQ

NICOMEDES Epigr.
AG 9.53.

Cf. NICODEMUS Epigr. (1536 001).
Cf. LOLLIUS BASSUS Epigr. (0143 001).

2520 **NICOMEDES** Hist.
4 B.C.?: Acanthius
001 **Fragmenta**, FGrH #772: 3C:766–767.
Q

2674 **NICOMEDES** Med.
vel Nicodemus
A.D. 2
x01 **Epigramma dedicatorium.**
App. Anth. 1.247(?): Cf. EPIGRAMMATICI in
App. Anth. (7052 001).

NICOMEDES Rex Bithyniae <Med.>
Cf. CODAMUS vel NICOMEDES Rex Bithyniae
<Med.> (0838).

0483 **NICOPHON** Comic.
5–4 B.C.: Atheniensis
001 **Fragmenta**, ed. T. Kock, *Comicorum Atticorum fragmenta*, vol. 1. Leipzig: Teubner, 1880:
775–780.
frr. 1–29.
Q: 183
002 **Fragmenta**, ed. A. Meineke, *Fragmenta comicorum Graecorum*, vol. 2.2. Berlin: Reimer, 1840
(repr. De Gruyter, 1970): 848–854.
Q: 155

0484 **NICOSTRATUS** Comic.
4 B.C.
001 **Fragmenta**, ed. T. Kock, *Comicorum Atticorum fragmenta*, vol. 2. Leipzig: Teubner, 1884:
219–230, 581.
frr. 1–13, 15–22, 24–36, 38–40, 42 + titulus.
Q: 562
002 **Fragmenta**, ed. A. Meineke, *Fragmenta comicorum Graecorum*, vol. 3. Berlin: Reimer, 1840
(repr. De Gruyter, 1970): 278–290.
Q: 527
003 **Fragmentum**, ed. J. Demiańczuk, *Supplementum comicum*. Krakau: Nakładem Akademii,
1912 (repr. Hildesheim: Olms, 1967): 66.
fr. 1.
Q: 9
004 **Titulus**, ed. Kock, *op. cit.*, vol. 3 (1888): 739.
NQ: [2]
005 **Fragmenta**, ed. Meineke, *op. cit.*, vol. 5.1
(1857; repr. 1970): 84.
Q: [21]

2523 **NICOSTRATUS** Hist.
ante 2 B.C.
001 **Fragmentum**, FGrH #778: 3C:772.
Q

2144 **NICOSTRATUS** Hist.
A.D. 3: Trapezius
001 **Testimonium**, FGrH #98: 2A:452.
NQ

1005 **NICOSTRATUS** Med.
ante A.D. 2
x01 **Fragmenta ap. Galenum.**
K13.139, 279, 299, 308, 985; 14.208.
Cf. GALENUS Med. (0057 076–078).

1539 **NICOSTRATUS** Soph.
A.D. 2: Macedo
x01 **Fragmenta ap. Stobaeum.**
Anth. IV.22.102; 23.62–65.
Cf. Joannes STOBAEUS (2037 001).

0997 **NILEUS** Med.
vel Neileus vel Neilus
3 B.C.
x01 **Fragmenta ap. Galenum.**
K12.765–766; 13.182.
Cf. GALENUS Med. (0057 076).
x02 **Fragmenta ap. Oribasium.**
CMG, vol. 6.2.2, pp. 203, 245; 6.3, p. 100.
Cf. ORIBASIUS Med. (0722 003–004).
x03 **Fragmenta ap. Paulum.**
CMG, vol. 9.2, pp. 342, 371.
Cf. PAULUS Med. (0715 001).
x04 **Fragmentum ap. Aëtium** (lib. 7).
CMG, vol. 8.2, p. 375.
Cf. AËTIUS Med. (0718 007).
x05 **Fragmentum ap. Aëtium** (lib. 9).
Zervos, *Athena* 23, p. 308.
Cf. AËTIUS Med. (0718 009).

1804 ***NINUS***
2 B.C.?
001 **Fragmenta A–B** (*P. Berol.* 6926), ed. F. Zimmermann, *Griechische Roman-Papyri und verwandte Texte*. Heidelberg: Bilabel, 1936: 14–
35.
Pap: [1,454]
002 **Fragmentum C** (*PSI* 1305), ed. M. Norsa, *PSI*
13 (1949): 82–86.
Pap

2045 **NONNUS** Epic.
A.D. 6: Panopolitanus
001 **Dionysiaca**, ed. R. Keydell, *Nonni Panopolitani
Dionysiaca*, 2 vols. Berlin: Weidmann, 1959:
1:1–500; 2:1–509.
Cod: [129,086]
002 **Paraphrasis sancti evangelii Joannei**, ed. A.
Scheindler, *Paraphrasis s. evangelii Ioannei*.
Leipzig: Teubner, 1881: 3–228.
Cod: [23,187]
003 **Epigramma**, AG 10.120.
Q: 14

1006 **NONNUS** Med.
ante A.D. 6
x01 **Fragmentum ap. Aëtium** (lib. 7).
CMG, vol. 8.2, p. 382.
Cf. AËTIUS Med. (0718 007).

1540 **NOSSIS** Epigr.
4 B.C.: Locra

001 **Epigrammata**, AG 5.170; 6.132, 265, 273(?), 275, 353–354; 7.414, 718; 9.332, 604–605.
Q: 336

1541 *NOSTOI*
post 7 B.C.
Cf. et ATRIDARUM REDITUS (1212).
001 **Fragmenta**, ed. T.W. Allen, *Homeri opera*, vol. 5. Oxford: Clarendon Press, 1912 (repr. 1969): 140–142.
frr. 2, 6, 8, 11.
Q

0031 *NOVUM TESTAMENTUM*
A.D. 1
001 **Evangelium secundum Matthaeum**, ed. K. Aland, M. Black, C.M. Martini, B.M. Metzger and A. Wikgren, *The Greek New Testament*, 2nd edn. Stuttgart: Württemberg Bible Society, 1968: 1–117.
Cod: 19,521
002 **Evangelium secundum Marcum**, ed. Aland, Black, Martini, Metzger, and Wikgren, *op. cit.*, 118–198.
Cod: 12,076
003 **Evangelium secundum Lucam**, ed. Aland, Black, Martini, Metzger, and Wikgren, *op. cit.*, 199–319.
Cod: 20,728
004 **Evangelium secundum Joannem**, ed. Aland, Black, Martini, Metzger, and Wikgren, *op. cit.*, 320–415.
Cod: 16,576
005 **Acta apostolorum**, ed. Aland, Black, Martini, Metzger, and Wikgren, *op. cit.*, 416–528.
Cod: 19,551
006 **Epistula Pauli ad Romanos**, ed. Aland, Black, Martini, Metzger, and Wikgren, *op. cit.*, 529–577.
Cod: 7,573
007 **Epistula Pauli ad Corinthios i**, ed. Aland, Black, Martini, Metzger, and Wikgren, *op. cit.*, 578–620.
Cod: 7,266
008 **Epistula Pauli ad Corinthios ii**, ed. Aland, Black, Martini, Metzger, and Wikgren, *op. cit.*, 621–647.
Cod: 4,761
009 **Epistula Pauli ad Galatas**, ed. Aland, Black, Martini, Metzger, and Wikgren, *op. cit.*, 648–663.
Cod: 2,379
010 **Epistula Pauli ad Ephesios**, ed. Aland, Black, Martini, Metzger, and Wikgren, *op. cit.*, 664–680.
Cod: 2,605
011 **Epistula Pauli ad Philippenses**, ed. Aland, Black, Martini, Metzger, and Wikgren, *op. cit.*, 681–691.
Cod: 1,731
012 **Epistula Pauli ad Colossenses**, ed. Aland, Black, Martini, Metzger, and Wikgren, *op. cit.*, 692–703.
Cod: 1,684
013 **Epistula Pauli ad Thessalonicenses i**, ed. Aland, Black, Martini, Metzger, and Wikgren, *op. cit.*, 704–713.
Cod: 1,574
014 **Epistula Pauli ad Thessalonicenses ii**, ed. Aland, Black, Martini, Metzger, and Wikgren, *op. cit.*, 714–719.
Cod: 879
015 **Epistula Pauli ad Timotheum i**, ed. Aland, Black, Martini, Metzger, and Wikgren, *op. cit.*, 720–730.
Cod: 1,717
016 **Epistula Pauli ad Timotheum ii**, ed. Aland, Black, Martini, Metzger, and Wikgren, *op. cit.*, 731–738.
Cod: 1,337
017 **Epistula Pauli ad Titum**, ed. Aland, Black, Martini, Metzger, and Wikgren, *op. cit.*, 739–743.
Cod: 720
018 **Epistula Pauli ad Philemonem**, ed. Aland, Black, Martini, Metzger, and Wikgren, *op. cit.*, 744–746.
Cod: 365
019 **Epistula Pauli ad Hebraeos**, ed. Aland, Black, Martini, Metzger, and Wikgren, *op. cit.*, 747–778.
Cod: 5,286
020 **Epistula Jacobi**, ed. Aland, Black, Martini, Metzger, and Wikgren, *op. cit.*, 779–790.
Cod: 1,857
021 **Epistula Petri i**, ed. Aland, Black, Martini, Metzger, and Wikgren, *op. cit.*, 791–804.
Cod: 1,790
022 **Epistula Petri ii**, ed. Aland, Black, Martini, Metzger, and Wikgren, *op. cit.*, 805–812.
Cod: 1,180
023 **Epistula Joannis i**, ed. Aland, Black, Martini, Metzger, and Wikgren, *op. cit.*, 813–826.
Cod: 2,250
024 **Epistula Joannis ii**, ed. Aland, Black, Martini, Metzger, and Wikgren, *op. cit.*, 827–829.
Cod: 264
025 **Epistula Joannis iii**, ed. Aland, Black, Martini, Metzger, and Wikgren, *op. cit.*, 830–831.
Cod: 235
026 **Epistula Juda**, ed. Aland, Black, Martini, Metzger, and Wikgren, *op. cit.*, 832–835.
Cod: 489
027 **Apocalypsis Joannis**, ed. Aland, Black, Martini, Metzger, and Wikgren, *op. cit.*, 836–895.
Cod: 10,224

1543 **NUMENIUS** Epigr.
ante A.D. 2: Tarsensis
001 **Epigramma**, AG 12.28.
AG 12.60: Cf. MELEAGER Epigr. (1492 001).

AG 12.237: Cf. STRATON Epigr. (1697 001).
Q: 18

0704 **NUMENIUS** Med.
fiq Numenius Heracleota
3 B.C.?
Cf. et NUMENIUS Poet. Didac. (0703).
x01 **Fragmentum ap. Philumenum.**
CMG, vol. 10.1.1, p. 22.
Cf. PHILUMENUS Med. (0671 001).

1542 **NUMENIUS** Phil.
A.D. 2: Apamensis
001 **Fragmenta**, ed. É. des Places, *Numénius. Frag-
ments.* Paris: Les Belles Lettres, 1974: 42–94,
99–102.
Περὶ τἀγαθοῦ (frr. 1–22): pp. 1–61.
Περὶ τῶν παρὰ Πλάτωνι ἀπορρήτων (fr. 23):
pp. 61–62.
Περὶ τῆς τῶν Ἀκαδημαϊκῶν πρὸς Πλάτωνα
διαστάσεως (frr. 24–28): pp. 62–80.
Περὶ ἀφθαρσίας ψυχῆς (fr. 29): p. 80.
Incertorum operum fragmenta (frr. 30–33, 35–
51, 53–54, 56–59): pp. 80–94, 99–101.
Fragmentum dubium (fr. 60): pp. 101–102.
Q: [10,609]

0703 **NUMENIUS** Poet. Didac.
fiq Numenius Med.
3 B.C.: Heracleota
Cf. et NUMENIUS Med. (0704 001).
001 **Fragmenta et tituli**, ed. H. Lloyd-Jones and P.
Parsons, *Supplementum Hellenisticum.* Berlin:
De Gruyter, 1983: 279–285.
frr. (+ titul.) 568–592.
Q: [327]

1544 **NYMPHIS** Hist.
4–3 B.C.: Heracleota
001 **Testimonia**, FGrH #432: 3B:328–329.
NQ
002 **Fragmenta**, FGrH #432: 3B:329–334, 758 addenda.
Q

0578 **NYMPHODORUS** Hist.
4 B.C.: Syracusanus
001 **Testimonia**, FGrH #572: 3B:668–669.
NQ
002 **Fragmenta**, FGrH #572: 3B:669–674.
Q

1007 **NYMPHODOTUS** Med.
ante A.D. 2
x01 **Fragmentum ap. Galenum.**
K13.926.
Cf. GALENUS Med. (0057 077).
x02 **Fragmentum ap. Oribasium.**
CMG, vol. 6.2.2, p. 217.
Cf. ORIBASIUS Med. (0722 003).
x03 **Fragmentum ap. Paulum.**
CMG, vol. 9.2, p. 322.

Cf. PAULUS Med. (0715 001).

1545 **OCELLUS** Phil.
5 B.C.: Lucanus
001 **De universi natura** [Sp.], ed. R. Harder, *Ocellus Lucanus* [*Neue philologische Untersuchungen*, vol. 1. Berlin: Weidmann, 1926]: 11–
25.
Cod: [4,273]
002 **Fragmenta** [Sp.], ed. Harder, *op. cit.*, 26–27.
frr. 1–3.
Q: [333]
003 **Testimonia**, ed. H. Diels and W. Kranz, *Die
Fragmente der Vorsokratiker*, vol. 1, 6th edn.
Berlin: Weidmann, 1951 (repr. Dublin: 1966):
440–441.
test. 1–8.
NQ

1243 *ODAE SALOMONIS*
A.D. 1–2
001 **Oda Salomonis** (11.1–24) (*P. Bodmer* 11), ed.
M. Testuz, *Papyrus Bodmer X–XII.* Geneva:
Bibliotheca Bodmeriana, 1959: 60–68.
Pap

1546 *OECHALIAE HALOSIS*
fort. auctore Creophylo Samio vel Chio
Incertum
001 **Fragmentum**, ed. T.W. Allen, *Homeri opera*,
vol. 5. Oxford: Clarendon Press, 1912 (repr.
1969): 146.
fr. 1.
Q

2866 **OECUMENIUS** Rhet. et Phil.
A.D. 6
Bibliography in progress
001 **Commentarius in Apocalypsin**, ed. H.C. Hos-
kier, *The complete commentary of Oecumenius
on the Apocalypse.* Ann Arbor: University of
Michigan Press, 1928: 29–260.
Cod
002 **Fragmenta in epistulam ad Romanos** (in catenis), ed. K. Staab, *Pauluskommentar aus der
griechischen Kirche aus Katenenhandschriften
gesammelt.* Münster: Aschendorff, 1933: 423–
432.
Q
003 **Fragmenta in epistulam i ad Corinthios** (in
catenis), ed. Staab, *op. cit.*, 432–443.
Q
004 **Fragmenta in epistulam ii ad Corinthios** (in
catenis), ed. Staab, *op. cit.*, 444–446.
Q
005 **Fragmenta in epistulam ad Galatas** (in catenis), ed. Staab, *op. cit.*, 446–448.
Q
006 **Fragmenta in epistulam ad Ephesios** (in catenis), ed. Staab, *op. cit.*, 448–452.
Q

007 **Fragmenta in epistulam ad Philippenses** (in catenis), ed. Staab, *op. cit.*, 452–453.
Q

008 **Fragmenta in epistulam ad Colossenses** (in catenis), ed. Staab, *op. cit.*, 453–455.
Q

009 **Fragmenta in epistulam i ad Thessalonicenses** (in catenis), ed. Staab, *op. cit.*, 456–457.
Q

010 **Fragmenta in epistulam ii ad Thessalonicenses** (in catenis), ed. Staab, *op. cit.*, 457–458.
Q

011 **Fragmenta in epistulam i ad Timotheum** (in catenis), ed. Staab, *op. cit.*, 458–460.
Q

012 **Fragmenta in epistulam ii ad Timotheum** (in catenis), ed. Staab, *op. cit.*, 460–461.
Q

013 **Fragmenta in epistulam ad Titum** (in catenis), ed. Staab, *op. cit.*, 461.
Q

014 **Fragmentum in epistulam ad Philemonem** (in catenis), ed. Staab, *op. cit.*, 462.
Q

015 **Fragmenta in epistulam ad Hebraeos** (in catenis), ed. Staab, *op. cit.*, 462–469.
Q

1547 **OEDIPODEA**
fort. auctore Cinaethone Lacedaemonio
post 7 B.C.
001 **Fragmenta**, ed. T.W. Allen, *Homeri opera*, vol. 5. Oxford: Clarendon Press, 1912 (repr. 1969): 112.
frr. 1–2.
Q

0971 **OENIADES** Lyr.
4 B.C.: Thebanus
001 **Titulus**, ed. D.L. Page, *Poetae melici Graeci.* Oxford: Clarendon Press, 1962 (repr. 1967 (1st edn. corr.)): 443.
NQ

1548 **OENOMAUS** Phil.
A.D. 2: Gadarensis
001 **Fragmenta**, ed. F.W.A. Mullach, *Fragmenta philosophorum Graecorum*, vol. 2. Paris: Didot, 1867 (repr. Aalen: Scientia, 1968): 361–385.
Q

002 **Epigramma**, AG 9.749.
Q: 15

2234 **OENOPIDES** Phil.
5 B.C.: Chius
001 **Testimonia**, ed. H. Diels and W. Kranz, *Die Fragmente der Vorsokratiker*, vol. 1, 6th edn. Berlin: Weidmann, 1951 (repr. Dublin: 1966): 393–395.
test. 1–14.
NQ

2373 **OLYMPICHUS** Hist.
ante 2 B.C.: Samius
001 **Fragmentum**, FGrH #537: 3B:522.
Q

1008 **OLYMPICUS** Med.
A.D. 2: Milesius
x01 **Fragmentum ap. Galenum**.
K10.67–68.
Cf. GALENUS Med. (0057 066).

2589 **OLYMPIODORUS** Alchem.
fiq Olympiodorus Phil.
A.D. 6?
Cf. et OLYMPIODORUS Phil. (4019).
001 Εἰς τὸ κατ' ἐνέργειαν Ζοσίμου ὅσα ἀπὸ Ἑρμοῦ καὶ τῶν φιλοσόφων ἦσαν εἰρημένα (= **De arte sacra**), ed. M. Berthelot, *Collection des anciens alchimistes grecs.* Paris: Steinheil, 1887 (repr. London: Holland Press, 1963): 69–104.
Cod

002 **Fragmenta**, ed. Berthelot, *op. cit.*, 104–106.
Cod

2590 **OLYMPIODORUS** Hist.
A.D. 5: Thebanus (Aegypti)
001 **Fragmenta**, ed. L. Dindorf, *Historici Graeci minores*, vol. 1. Leipzig: Teubner, 1870: 450–471.
Q

002 **Blemyomachia** (*P. Berol.* 5003), ed. H. Livrea, *Anonymi fortasse Olympiodori Thebani Blemyomachia (P. Berol. 5003).* Meisenheim am Glan: Hain, 1978: 36–53.
Pap

4019 **OLYMPIODORUS** Phil.
fiq Olympiodorus Alchem.
A.D. 6: Alexandrinus
Cf. et OLYMPIODORUS Alchem. (2589).
001 **Prolegomena**, ed. A. Busse, *Olympiodori prolegomena et in categorias commentarium* [*Commentaria in Aristotelem Graeca* 12.1. Berlin: Reimer, 1902]: 1–25.
Cod: [10,857]

002 **In Aristotelis categorias commentarium**, ed. Busse, *op. cit.*, 26–148.
Cod: [53,961]

003 **In Aristotelis meteora commentaria**, ed. G. Stüve, *Olympiodori in Aristotelis meteora commentaria* [*Commentaria in Aristotelem Graeca* 12.2. Berlin: Reimer, 1900]: 1–338.
Cod: [122,034]

004 **In Platonis Alcibiadem commentarii**, ed. L.G. Westerink, *Olympiodorus. Commentary on the first Alcibiades of Plato.* Amsterdam: Hakkert, 1956 (repr. 1982): 1–144.
Cod

005 **In Platonis Gorgiam commentaria**, ed. L.G. Westerink, *Olympiodori in Platonis Gorgiam commentaria.* Leipzig: Teubner, 1970: 1–268.
Cod

006 **In Platonis Phaedonem commentaria**, ed. L.G. Westerink, *The Greek commentaries on Plato's Phaedo*, vol. 1 (Olympiodorus). Amsterdam: North-Holland, 1976: 39–181.
Cod

x01 **In Philebum.**
Cf. DAMASCIUS Phil. (4066 006).

x02 **Epigramma demonstrativum.**
App. Anth. 3.177: Cf. EPIGRAMMATICI in *App. Anth.* (7052 003).

1022 **OLYMPIUS** Med.
A.D. 1?

x01 **Fragmentum ap. Aëtium** (lib. 11).
Daremberg-Ruelle, p. 579.
Cf. AËTIUS Med. (0718 011).

1990 **OLYMPUS** Hist.
1 B.C.

001 **Fragmentum**, FGrH #198: 2B:929–930.
Q

0648 **ONASANDER** Tact.
vel Onosander
A.D. 1

001 **Strategicus**, ed. W.A. Oldfather, A.S. Pease and J.B. Titchener, *Aeneas Tacticus, Asclepiodotus, Onasander.* Cambridge, Mass.: Harvard University Press, 1923 (repr. 1962): 368–526.
Cod: [12,630]

1999 **ONASIMUS** Hist.
A.D. 3–4?: Cyprius vel Lacedaemonius

001 **Testimonium**, FGrH #216: 2B:946.
NQ

002 **Fragmenta**, FGrH #216: 2B:947.
Q

1889 **ONASUS** Hist.
2 B.C./A.D. 1

001 **Fragmenta**, FGrH #41: 1A:263.
Q

1549 **<ONATAS>** Phil.
vel Onatus
fiq Onetor Atheniensis
3 B.C.: Crotoniensis

001 **Fragmenta**, ed. H. Thesleff, *The Pythagorean texts of the Hellenistic period.* Åbo: Åbo Akademi, 1965: 139–140.
Q: 457

1943 **ONESICRITUS** Hist.
4–3 B.C.: Astypaleius

001 **Testimonia**, FGrH #134: 2B:723–725.
NQ

002 **Fragmenta**, FGrH #134: 2B:725–736.
Q

2362 **ONOMASTUS** Hist.
Incertum

001 **Titulus**, FGrH #520: 3B:492.
NQ

0485 **OPHELIO** Comic.
4 B.C.

001 **Fragmenta**, ed. T. Kock, *Comicorum Atticorum fragmenta*, vol. 2. Leipzig: Teubner, 1884: 293–294.
frr. 1–3, 5 + tituli.
Q: 36

002 **Fragmenta**, ed. A. Meineke, *Fragmenta comicorum Graecorum*, vol. 3. Berlin: Reimer, 1840 (repr. De Gruyter, 1970): 380–381.
Q: 31

0023 **OPPIANUS** Epic.
A.D. 2: Anazarbensis

001 **Halieutica**, ed. A.W. Mair, *Oppian, Colluthus, Tryphiodorus.* Cambridge, Mass.: Harvard University Press, 1928 (repr. 1963): 200–514.
Cod: 22,909

0024 **OPPIANUS** Epic.
A.D. 2–3: Apamensis

001 **Cynegetica**, ed. A.W. Mair, *Oppian, Colluthus, Tryphiodorus.* Cambridge, Mass.: Harvard University Press, 1928 (repr. 1963): 2–198.
Cod: [13,594]

5001 *ORACULA*
Varia
Cf. et ORACULA CHALDAICA (1550).
Cf. et ORACULA SIBYLLINA (1551).

x01 **Oracula.**
App. Anth. 6.1–323: Cf. EPIGRAMMATICI in *App. Anth.* (7052 006).
App. Anth. 6.24b, 107 addenda: Cf. EPIGRAMMATICI in *App. Anth.* (7052 008).
Ammon: 178–179.
Amphilytus Acarnan: 207.
Apollo anonymus: 144, 155.
Apollo Chalcedonius: 143.
Apollo Clarius: 134–139.
Apollo Colophonius: 140.
Apollo incertus: 156–173.
Apollo Ismenius: 132–133.
Apollo Milesius: 123–131.
Apollo Pythius: 1–122; 24b, 107 addenda.
Apollo Sarpedonius: 141–142.
Asclepius: 180–181.
Bacis: 205–206.
Diopithes: 220.
Euclus: 221.
Hecate: 193–204.
Hermes: 182.
Musaeus: 222.
Oracula ficta: 277, 291–323.
Oracula varia: 226–263, 265–276.
Pan: 191–192.
Peliades: 223.
Phaennis: 224.
Serapis: 183–189.

Sibylla: 208–219.
Trophonius: 190.
Vergilius: 264.
Zeus Belus: 174.
Zeus Dodonaeus: 175–177.
x02 **Oraculum Herophilae Sibyllae.**
  App. Anth. 3.123: Cf. EPIGRAMMATICI in
  App. Anth. (7052 003).
x03 **Oraculum Leonis Imperatoris.**
  Cf. LEO VI SAPIENS Imperator Phil. (2944
  x02).

1550 *ORACULA CHALDAICA*
  A.D. 2
  001 **Oracula** (fragmenta), ed. É des Places, *Oracles
    chaldaïques.* Paris: Les Belles Lettres, 1971:
    66–121.
    Q: 2,791

1551 *ORACULA SIBYLLINA*
  2 B.C.–A.D. 4
  001 **Oracula**, ed. J. Geffcken, *Die Oracula Sibyllina*
    [*Die griechischen christlichen Schriftsteller* 8.
    Leipzig: Hinrichs, 1902]: 1–226.
    Cod: 29,475
  002 **Fragmenta**, ed. Geffcken, *op. cit.*, 227–233.
    Q: 663
  003 **Fragmentum**, *P. Flor.* 3.389.
    Pap
  x01 **Aenigmata.**
    App. Anth. 7.25–26: Cf. EPIGRAMMATICI in
    App. Anth. (7052 007).

1552 *ORATIO JOSEPHI*
  ante A.D. 3
  001 **Fragmenta**, ed. A.-M. Denis, *Fragmenta pseud-
    epigraphorum quae supersunt Graeca* [*Pseudepi-
    grapha veteris testamenti Graece* 3. Leiden:
    Brill, 1970]: 61–62.
    Q: [164]

1858 *ORATIO MANASSIS*
  1 B.C./A.D. 4?
  001 **Oratio**, ed. A.-M. Denis, *Fragmenta pseudepi-
    graphorum quae supersunt Graeca* [*Pseudepi-
    grapha veteris testamenti Graece* 3. Leiden:
    Brill, 1970]: 115–117.
    Q: [370]

1010 **ORESTINUS** Med.
  1 B.C.?
  x01 **Fragmentum ap. Galenum.**
    K12.402.
    Cf. GALENUS Med. (0057 076).

0722 **ORIBASIUS** Med.
  A.D. 4: Pergamenus
  001 **Collectiones medicae** (libri 1–14), ed. J. Rae-
    der, *Oribasii collectionum medicarum reliquiae*,
    vols. 1–2 [*Corpus medicorum Graecorum*, vols.
    6.1.1–6.1.2. Leipzig: Teubner, 6.1.1:1928;
    6.1.2:1929]: **6.1.1**:4–27, 30–65, 67–91, 93–109,

111–153,   155–192,   194–245,   247–300;
  6.1.2:4–237.
  Cod: [164,025]
002 **Collectiones medicae** (libri incerti), ed. J. Raeder, *Oribasii collectionum medicarum reliquiae*,
  vol. 4 [*Corpus medicorum Graecorum*, vol.
  6.2.2. Leipzig: Teubner, 1933]: 75–180.
  Cod: [39,120]
003 **Eclogae medicamentorum**, ed. Raeder, *CMG*
  6.2.2, 185–307.
  Cod: [44,195]
004 **Synopsis ad Eustathium filium**, ed. J. Raeder,
  *Oribasii synopsis ad Eustathium et libri ad
  Eunapium* [*Corpus medicorum Graecorum*, vol.
  6.3. Leipzig: Teubner, 1926 (repr. Amsterdam:
  Hakkert, 1964)]: 5–313.
  Cod: [78,697]
005 **Liber ad Eunapium 1**, ed. Raeder, *CMG* 6.3,
  317–318, 320–347.
  Cod: [10,020]
006 **Liber ad Eunapium 2**, ed. Raeder, *CMG* 6.3,
  349–393.
  Cod: [15,062]
007 **Collectiones medicae** (liber 15), ed. Raeder,
  CMG 6.1.2, 239–297.
  Cod: [18,220]
008 **Collectiones medicae** (libri 16, 24–25, 43–50),
  ed. J. Raeder, *Oribasii collectionum medicarum
  reliquiae*, vols. 2–4 [*Corpus medicorum Graecorum*, vols. 6.1.2–6.2.2. Leipzig: Teubner,
  6.1.2:1929; 6.2.1:1931; 6.2.2:1933]: **6.1.2**:298;
  6.2.1:4–291; **6.2.2**:4–69.
  Cod: [120,441]
009 **Libri ad Eunapium 3–4**, ed. Raeder, *CMG* 6.3,
  396–433, 436–498.
  Cod: [32,954]
010 **Testimonia**, FGrH #221: 2B:950.
  NQ

2042 **ORIGENES** Theol.
  A.D. 2–3: Alexandrinus, Caesariensis
047 **Commentarii in Genesim** (fragmenta), MPG
  12: 45–92.
  Q: [7,079]
048 **Selecta in Genesim**, MPG 12: 92–145.
  Q: [10,069]
022 **Homiliae in Genesim** (in catenis), ed. W.A.
  Baehrens, *Origenes Werke*, vol. 6 [*Die griechischen christlichen Schriftsteller* 29. Leipzig:
  Teubner, 1920]: 23–30.
  Q: 1,079
049 **Fragmenta ex commentariis in Exodum**, MPG
  12: 264–281.
  Q: [3,486]
050 **Selecta in Exodum**, MPG 12: 281–297.
  Q: [3,300]
067 **Adnotationes in Exodum**, MPG 17: 16–17.
  Q: [270]
023 **Homiliae in Exodum**, ed. Baehrens, *GCS* 29,
  217–218, 221–230.
  Q: 944

051 **Selecta in Leviticum**, MPG 12: 397–404.
Q: [1,546]

068 **Adnotationes in Leviticum**, MPG 17: 17–22.
Q: [678]

024 **Homiliae in Leviticum**, ed. Baehrens, *GCS* 29, 332–334, 395, 402–407, 409–416.
Q: 1,517

052 **Selecta in Numeros**, MPG 12: 576–584.
Q: [1,764]

069 **Adnotationes in Numeros**, MPG 17: 21–24.
Q: [244]

053 **Selecta in Deuteronomium**, MPG 12: 805–817.
Q: [2,510]

070 **Adnotationes in Deuteronomium**, MPG 17: 24–36.
Q: [2,328]

025 **Homiliae in librum Jesu Nave**, ed. W.A. Baehrens, *Origenes Werke*, vol. 7 [*Die griechischen christlichen Schriftsteller* 30. Leipzig: Teubner, 1921]: 290–291, 293, 298–302, 305, 308, 310, 312, 394–398, 406–445, 448–456, 460–463.
Cf. et 2042 080.
Q: 4,452

054 **Selecta in Jesum Nave**, MPG 12: 820–824.
Q: [974]

071 **Adnotationes in Jesum Nave**, MPG 17: 36–37.
Q: [195]

055 **Selecta in Judices**, MPG 12: 949.
Q: [285]

072 **Adnotationes in Judices**, MPG 17: 37–40.
Q: [213]

056 **In Ruth** (fragmentum), MPG 12: 989.
Q: [54]

013 **De engastrimytho** (= Homilia in i Reg. [i Sam.] 28.3-25), ed. E. Klostermann, *Origenes Werke*, vol. 3 [*Die griechischen christlichen Schriftsteller* 6. Leipzig: Hinrichs, 1901]: 283–294.
Cod: [3,932]

014 **Fragmenta in librum primum Regnorum** (in catenis), ed. Klostermann, *GCS* 6, 295–303.
Q: [2,113]

015 **Fragmentum in librum primum Regnorum** (in catenis), ed. Klostermann, *GCS* 6, 304.
Q: [93]

057 **Selecta in Job** (e codd. Paris.), MPG 12: 1032–1049.
Q: [3,614]

073 **Enarrationes in Job** (e codd. Marc. gr. 21, 538), MPG 17: 57–105.
Q: [8,921]

086 **Homiliae in Job** (fragmenta e codd. Vat.), ed. J. Pitra, *Analecta sacra spicilegio Solesmensi parata*, vol. 2. Paris: Tusculum, 1884 (repr. Farnborough: Gregg Press, 1966): 361–391.
Q

058 **Selecta in Psalmos** [Dub.], MPG 12: 1053–1320, 1368–1369, 1388–1389, 1409–1685.
Q, Cod: [107,596]

074 **Excerpta in Psalmos** [Dub.], MPG 17: 105–149.
Q: [9,156]

044 **Fragmenta in Psalmos 1–150** [Dub.], ed. Pitra, *op. cit.*, vols. 2 & 3 (Venice: Lazarus Monastery, 1883): **2**:444–483; **3**:1–236, 242–245, 248–364.
Cod: 86,530

059 **Fragmenta ex commentariis in Proverbia**, MPG 13: 17–33.
Q: [3,471]

075 **Expositio in Proverbia**, MPG 17: 161–252.
Q: [18,593]

026 **Libri x in Canticum canticorum** (fragmenta), ed. W.A. Baehrens, *Origenes Werke*, vol. 8 [*Die griechischen christlichen Schriftsteller* 33. Leipzig: Teubner, 1925]: 90–92, 96, 98, 101, 108–109, 111, 126, 128–132, 141–146, 154–155, 161–162, 165–166, 168–169, 174–175, 178–184, 191–194, 199–202, 220–221, 224, 226, 230–233, 235–237, 240–241.
Cf. et 2042 081.
Q: 2,806

076 **Scholia in Canticum canticorum**, MPG 17: 253–288.
Q: [7,228]

081 **Libri x in Canticum canticorum** (addenda), ed. Baehrens, *GCS* 33, liii–liv.
cf. et 2042 026.
Q

060 **In Canticum canticorum** (libri duo quos scripsit in adulescentia), MPG 13: 36.
Q: [174]

009 **In Jeremiam** (homiliae 1–11), ed. P. Nautin, *Origène. Homélies sur Jérémie*, vol. 1 [*Sources chrétiennes* 232. Paris: Cerf, 1976]: 196–430.
Cod: 24,992

021 **In Jeremiam** (homiliae 12–20), ed. Klostermann, *GCS* 6, 85–194.
Cf. et 2042 084.
Cod: 33,153

084 **Fragmenta in Jeremiam** (e *Philocalia*), ed. Klostermann, *GCS* 6, 195–198.
Cf. et 2042 021.
Q: 757

010 **Fragmenta in Jeremiam** (in catenis), ed. Klostermann, *GCS* 6, 199–232.
Q: [8,946]

011 **Fragmenta in Lamentationes** (in catenis), ed. Klostermann, *GCS* 6, 235–278.
Q: [11,405]

012 **Fragmentum in Lamentationes** (in catenis), ed. Klostermann, *GCS* 6, 279.
Q: [183]

061 **Fragmenta ex commentariis in Ezechielem**, MPG 13: 664–665.
Q: [468]

027 **Homiliae in Ezechielem**, ed. Baehrens, *GCS* 33, 319–320, 323, 327–329, 336–337, 340, 354–355, 378, 390, 396, 426–427, 434–435, 450–452.

Cf. et 2042 082.
Cod: 1,384

062 **Selecta in Ezechielem**, MPG 13: 768–825.
Q: [12,047]

063 **Fragmentum ex commentariis in Osee**, MPG 13: 825–828.
Q: [577]

029 **Commentarium in evangelium Matthaei** (lib. 10–11), ed. R. Girod, *Origène. Commentaire sur l'évangile selon Matthieu*, vol. 1 [*Sources chrétiennes* 162. Paris: Cerf, 1970]: 140–386.
Cod: 22,406

030 **Commentarium in evangelium Matthaei** (lib. 12–17), ed. E. Klostermann, *Origenes Werke*, vol. 10.1–10.2 [*Die griechischen christlichen Schriftsteller* 40.1–40.2. Leipzig: Teubner, 10.1:1935; 10.2:1937]: **10.1**:69–304; **10.2**:305–703.
Cod: 95,260

028 **Commentariorum series in evangelium Matthaei** (Mt. 22.34–27.63), ed. E. Klostermann, *Origenes Werke*, vol. 11 [*Die griechischen christlichen Schriftsteller* 38.2. Leipzig: Teubner, 1933]: 4, 21–22, 42–43, 54, 83–84, 86, 93–101, 103, 108, 110, 112–114, 118–128, 130–138, 140, 144–151, 156–157, 159–163, 166, 171, 178, 180, 189, 191–192, 206, 219–220, 222, 227, 229–230, 233, 236–242, 244–248, 250–255, 257–266, 270–278, 283–284, 287, 293–295.
Q: 4,732

031 **Fragmenta ex commentariis in evangelium Matthaei**, ed. E. Klostermann and E. Benz, *Origenes Werke*, vol. 12 [*Die griechischen christlichen Schriftsteller* 41.1. Leipzig: Teubner, 1941]: 3–5.
Cf. et 2042 085.
Q: 495

085 **Fragmenta ex commentariis in evangelium Matthaei** (in catenis), ed. Klostermann and Benz, *GCS* 41.1, 13–235.
Cf. et 2042 031.
Q

016 **Homiliae in Lucam**, ed. M. Rauer, *Origenes Werke*, vol. 9, 2nd edn. [*Die griechischen christlichen Schriftsteller* 49 (35). Berlin: Akademie-Verlag, 1959]: 3–51, 54–90, 92–96, 99–109, 111, 114–123, 125–130, 132–139, 141–145, 154–155, 157–158, 160–166, 168–174, 177–179, 181, 183, 186–203, 205–206, 209–212, 214–222.
Cod: [12,531]

017 **Fragmenta in Lucam**, ed. Rauer, *GCS* 49 (35), 227–336.
Q: [22,334]

078 **Scholia in Lucam**, MPG 17: 312–369.
Cod: [12,121]

005 **Commentarii in evangelium Joannis** (lib. 1, 2, 4, 5, 6, 10, 13), ed. C. Blanc, *Origène. Commentaire sur saint Jean*, 3 vols. [*Sources chrétiennes* 120, 157, 222. Paris: Cerf, 1:1966;

2:1970; 3:1975]: **1**:56–390; **2**:128–580; **3**:34–282.
Lib. 19, 20, 28, 32: Cf. 2042 079.
Cod: 96,316

006 **Fragmenta in evangelium Joannis**, ed. E. Preuschen, *Origenes Werke*, vol. 4 [*Die griechischen christlichen Schriftsteller* 10. Leipzig: Hinrichs, 1903]: 483–574.
Q: [24,268]

079 **Commentarii in evangelium Joannis** (lib. 19, 20, 28, 32), ed. Preuschen, *GCS* 10, 298–480.
Lib. 1, 2, 4, 5, 6, 10, 13: Cf. 2042 005.
Cod: 61,431

064 **Fragmentum ex homiliis in Acta apostolorum**, MPG 14: 829–832.
Q: [197]

039 **Commentarii in Romanos** (Cod. Athon. Laura 184 B64), ed. O. Bauernfeind, *Der Römerbrieftext des Origenes nach dem codex von der Goltz* [*Texte und Untersuchungen* 44.3. Leipzig: Hinrichs, 1923]: 91–119.
Cod: 5,761

036 **Commentarii in epistulam ad Romanos** (I.1–XII.21) (in catenis), ed. A. Ramsbotham, "Documents: The commentary of Origen on the epistle to the Romans," *Journal of Theological Studies* 13 & 14 (1912) **13**:210–224, 357–368; **14**:10–22.
Q: 13,938

037 **Commentarii in epistulam ad Romanos** (e cod. Vindob. gr. 166), ed. K. Staab, "Neue Fragmente aus dem Kommentar des Origenes zum Römerbrief," *Biblische Zeitschrift* 18 (1928) 74–82.
Q: 1,692

038 **Commentarii in Romanos** (III.5–V.7) (*P. Cairo* 88748 + Cod. Vat. gr. 762), ed. J. Scherer, *Le commentaire d'Origène sur Rom. III.5–V.7.* Cairo: L'Institut Français d'Archéologie Orientale, 1957: 124–232.
Q, Cod, Pap: 11,868

034 **Fragmenta ex commentariis in epistulam i ad Corinthios** (e catenis), ed. C. Jenkins, "Documents: Origen on I Corinthians," *Journal of Theological Studies* 9 & 10 (1908) **9**:232–247, 353–372, 500–514; **10**:29–51.
Q: 26,284

035 **Fragmenta ex commentariis in epistulam ad Ephesios** (e catenis), ed. J.A.F. Gregg, "Documents: The commentary of Origen upon the epistle to the Ephesians," *Journal of Theological Studies* 3 (1902) 234–244, 398–420, 554–576.
Q: 18,328

065 **Ex homiliis in epistulam ad Hebraeos**, MPG 14: 1308–1309.
Q: [187]

042 **Scholia in Apocalypsem** (scholia 1, 3–39), ed. C. Diobouniotis and A. von Harnack, *Der Scholien-Kommentar des Origenes zur Apokalypse Johannis* [*Texte und Untersuchungen*

38.3. Leipzig: Hinrichs, 1911]: 21–44.
Cod: 5,262

043 **Scholia in Apocalypsem** (scholia 28–38), ed.
C.H. Turner, "Document: Origen, scholia in
Apocalypsin," *Journal of Theological Studies* 25
(1923) 1–15.
Cod: 1,888

007 **Exhortatio ad martyrium**, ed. P. Koetschau,
Origenes Werke, vol. 1 [*Die griechischen christlichen Schriftsteller* 2. Leipzig: Hinrichs, 1899]:
3–47.
Cod: [13,566]

001 **Contra Celsum**, ed. M. Borret, *Origène. Contre
Celse*, 4 vols. [*Sources chrétiennes* 132, 136,
147, 150. Paris: Cerf, 1:1967; 2:1968; 3–
4:1969]: 1:64–476; 2:14–434; 3:14–382; 4:14–
352.
Cod: 166,590

008 **De oratione**, ed. P. Koetschau, *Origenes Werke*,
vol. 2 [*Die griechischen christlichen Schriftsteller* 3. Leipzig: Hinrichs, 1899]: 297–403.
Cod: [30,665]

046 **De resurrectione libri ii** (fragmentum), MPG
11: 96.
Q: [264]

018 **Dialogus cum Heraclide**, ed. J. Scherer, *Entre-
tien d'Origène avec Héraclide* [*Sources chrétiennes* 67. Paris: Cerf, 1960]: 52–110.
Cod: 5,607

002 **De principiis**, ed. H. Görgemanns and H.
Karpp, *Origenes vier Bücher von den Prinzi-
pien*. Darmstadt: Wissenschaftliche Buchgesellschaft, 1976: 462–560, 668–764.
Q, Cod: [14,778]

003 **Fragmenta de principiis**, ed. Görgemanns and
Karpp, *op. cit.*, 92, 94, 96, 136, 146, 154, 162,
164, 168, 192, 220, 226, 240, 244, 262, 284–
286, 310, 364, 388, 392, 400, 648, 730, 774,
782, 784, 786, 794, 796, 808, 810, 812.
Q: [1,740]

004 **Fragmenta alia de principiis**, ed. Görgemanns
and Karpp, *op. cit.*, 228, 392, 394.
Q: [105]

033 **Epistula ad Gregorium Thaumaturgum**, ed. P.
Koetschau, *Des Gregorios Thaumaturgos Dank-
rede an Origenes*. Freiburg: Mohr, 1894: 40–
44.
Q: 858

040 **Epistula ad ignotum (Fabianum Romanum)**,
ed. P. Nautin, *Lettres et écrivains chrétiens des
2ᵉ et 3ᵉ siècles* [*Patristica* 2. Paris: Cerf, 1961]:
250–251.
Q: 123

045 **Epistula ad Africanum**, MPG 11: 48–85.
Cod: [5,407]

041 **Epistula quibusdam qui ei obtrectabant (ad
Alexandrum Hierosolymitanum)**, ed. Nautin,
Patristica 2, 126.
Q: 118

083 **Hexapla**, ed. F. Field, *Origenis hexaplorum*

quae supersunt, 2 vols. Oxford: Oxford University Press, 1875 (repr. Hildesheim: Olms,
1964): 1:7–806; 2:4–1034.
Cod

019 **Philocalia** (*sive* **Ecloga de operibus Origenis a
Basilio et Gregorio Nazianzeno facta**) (cap. 1–
27), ed. J.A. Robinson, *The philocalia of Origen*. Cambridge: Cambridge University Press,
1893: 1–256.
Cod: 65,752

020 **Philocalia** (*sive* **Ecloga de operibus Origenis a
Basilio et Gregorio Nazianzeno facta**) (cap. 23,
25–27), ed. É. Junod, *Origène. Philocalie 21–
27: sur le libre arbitre* [*Sources chrétiennes* 226.
Paris: Cerf, 1976]: 130–314.
Cod: 14,424

032 **Fragmenta in evangelium Matthaei**, ed. E.
Klostermann and E. Benz, *Zur Überlieferung
der Matthäuserklärung des Origenes* [*Texte und
Untersuchungen* 47.2. Leipzig: Hinrichs, 1931]:
4–8.
Q: 517

066 **Adnotationes in Genesim**, MPG 17: 12–16.
Q: [681]

077 **Scholia in Matthaeum**, MPG 17: 289–309.
Cod: [4,452]

080 **Homiliae in librum Jesu Nave** (addendum), ed.
W.A. Baehrens, *Origenes Werke*, vol. 7 [*Die
griechischen christlichen Schriftsteller* 30. Leip-
zig: Teubner, 1921]: 621.
Cf. et 2042 025.
Q

082 **Homiliae in Ezechielem** (addendum), ed.
Baehrens, *GCS* 33, lv.
Cf. et 2042 027.
Q

0924 **ORIGENIA** Med.
ante A.D. 1

x01 **Fragmenta ap. Galenum.**
K13.58, 85, 143.
Cf. GALENUS Med. (0057 076).

1011 **ORION** Med.
ante A.D. 1

x01 **Fragmentum ap. Galenum.**
K13.1038.
Cf. GALENUS Med. (0057 077).

0579 *ORPHICA*
Varia

001 **Hymni**, ed. W. Quandt, *Orphei hymni*, 3rd
edn. Berlin: Weidmann, 1962 (repr. 1973): 1–
57.
Cod: 6,844

002 **Argonautica**, ed. G. Dottin, *Les argonautiques
d'Orphée*. Paris: Les Belles Lettres, 1930: 3–
54.
Cod: 9,013

003 **De lapidibus**, ed. E. Abel, *Orphei lithica*. Ber-

lin: Calvary, 1881: 15-38.
Cod: 5,025

004 **De lapidibus epitome**, ed. Abel, *op. cit.*, 138-
153.
Cod: 2,767

005 **Fragmenta**, ed. O. Kern, *Orphicorum fragmenta*. Berlin: Weidmann, 1922 (repr. 1972):
80-344 (passim).
Q, Pap, Epigr

007 **Fragmentum astrologicum**, ed. M.A. Sangin,
Codices Rossici [*Catalogus codicum astrologorum
Graecorum* 12. Brussels: Lamertin, 1936]: 158-
161.
Cod

008 **Fragmenta**, ed. A. Giannini, *Paradoxographorum Graecorum reliquiae*. Milan: Istituto Editoriale Italiano, 1965: 384-385.
Q

009 **Testimonia**, ed. H. Diels and W. Kranz, *Die
Fragmente der Vorsokratiker*, vol. 1, 6th edn.
Berlin: Weidmann, 1951 (repr. Dublin: 1966):
1-6.
test. 1-16.
NQ

010 **Fragmenta**, ed. Diels and Kranz, *op. cit.*, 6-20.
frr. 1-23.
fr. 15a: *P. Berol.* 44.
fr. 19: *IG* 14.641.
fr. 23: *P. Gurob* 1.
Q, Pap, Epigr

x01 **Epigrammata** (*App. Anth.*).
Epigramma dedicatorium: 1.1(?).
Epigramma exhortatorium et supplicatorium:
4.47(?).
App. Anth. 1.1(?): Cf. EPIGRAMMATICI in
App. Anth. (7052 001).
App. Anth. 4.47(?): Cf. EPIGRAMMATICI in
App. Anth. (7052 004).

x02 **Hieros logos**.
PsVTGr 3.164-167.
Cf. PSEUDO-AUCTORES HELLENISTAE (1639
001).
Q

2480 **ORTHAGORAS** Hist.
1 B.C.?

001 **Fragmenta**, FGrH #713: 3C:601-603.
Q

1016 **<OSTANES Magus>**
5 B.C.

001 **Fragmenta**, ed. J. Bidez and F. Cumont, *Les
mages hellénisés*, vol. 2. Paris: Les Belles
Lettres, 1938: 302, 318, 322, 329-330, 331,
334-335.
Q

1012 **OTHO** Med.
ante 1 B.C.: Siculus

x01 **Fragmentum ap. Galenum**.
K12.403.

Cf. GALENUS Med. (0057 076).

1013 **PACCIUS ANTIOCHUS** Med.
fiq Antiochus Romanus
A.D. 1
Cf. et ANTIOCHUS Med. (0778).

x01 **Fragmenta ap. Galenum**.
K12.751, 760, 772, 782; 13.284, 984.
Cf. GALENUS Med. (0057 076-077).

1203 *PAEANES* (CA)
4-2 B.C.

001 **Paean Erythraeus in Aesculapium**, ed. J.U.
Powell, *Collectanea Alexandrina*. Oxford:
Clarendon Press, 1925 (repr. 1970): 136.
Epigr: [94]

002 **Paean Erythraeus ad urbem dium repertus**, ed.
Powell, *op. cit.*, 137.
Epigr: [103]

003 **Fragmentum Erythraeum paeanis in Apollinem**, ed. Powell, *op. cit.*, 140.
Epigr: [60]

004 **Fragmentum Erythraeum paeanis in Seleucum**, ed. Powell, *op. cit.*, 140.
Epigr: [16]

005 **Paean Delphicus i in Apollinem**, ed. Powell,
op. cit., 141-142.
Epigr: [200]

006 **Fragmentum paeanis in Titum Flamininum**,
ed. Powell, *op. cit.*, 173.
Q: [29]

2665 **Mettius PAEON** Epigr.
Incertum: Sidetes

x01 **Epigrammata dedicatoria**.
App. Anth. 1.187-188: Cf. EPIGRAMMATICI
in *App. Anth.* (7052 001).

2512 **PAEON** Hist.
3 B.C.?: Amathusiacus

001 **Fragmenta**, FGrH #757: 3C:737.
Q

2450 **PALAEPHATUS** Gramm.
Incertum: Aegyptius

001 **Testimonium**, FGrH #660: 3C:211-212.
NQ

002 **Fragmentum**, FGrH #660: 3C:212.
Q

1553 **PALAEPHATUS** Myth.
4 B.C.?

001 **De incredibilibus**, ed. N. Festa, *Palaephati
περὶ ἀπίστων* [*Mythographi Graeci* 3.2. Leipzig: Teubner, 1902]: 1-72.
Cod: [7,855]

002 **Testimonia**, FGrH #44: 1A:266-267, *16-*17
addenda.
NQ

003 **Fragmenta**, FGrH #44: 1A:267-268, *17-*19.
fr. 3 bis: *P. Oxy.* 13.1611.
Q

2123 **PALLADAS** Epigr.
A.D. 4–5: Alexandrinus
001 **Epigrammata**, AG **5.**71–72, 257; **6.**60–61, 85;
7.607, 610, 681–688; **9.**5–6, 119, 165–176,
180–183, 377–379, 393–395, 397, 400–401,
441, 484, 486–487, 489, 502–503, 508, 528,
773; **10.**32, 34, 44–63, 65, 72–73, 75, 77–99;
11.54–55, 62, 204, 255, 263, 280–281, 283–
293, 299–307, 317, 323, 340–341, 349, 351,
353, 355, 357, 371, 373, 377–378, 381, 383–
387; **15.**20; **16.**20, 194, 207, 282, 317.
AG 7.339; 9.134–135, 399, 501; 11.273, 343:
Cf. ANONYMI EPIGRAMMATICI (0138 001).
AG 9.9b: Cf. Julius POLYAENUS Epigr. (1620
001).
AG 9.57: Cf. PAMPHILUS Epigr. (1554 001).
AG 9.118: Cf. <BESANTINUS> Epigr. (0144
001).
AG 9.120; 11.294, 430: Cf. Pseudo-LUCIANUS
Soph. (0061 010).
AG 9.503b: Cf. NICANDER Epic. (0022 006).
AG 10.121: Cf. RARUS Epigr. (1653 001).
AG 11.295, 310: Cf. LUCILLIUS Epigr. (1468
001).
Q: 4,582
x01 **Epigramma demonstrativum** (auctore Pallada
vel Agathia).
App. Anth. 3.145(?): Cf. EPIGRAMMATICI in
App. Anth. (7052 003).
Cf. et AGATHIAS Scholasticus Hist. et Epigr.
(4024 x01).

2564 **PALLADIUS** Hist.
A.D. 4: Methonaeus
001 **Testimonia**, FGrH #837: 3C:904.
NQ
002 **Titulus**, FGrH #837: 3C:904.
NQ

0726 **PALLADIUS** Med.
A.D. 6: Alexandrinus
001 **Commentarii in Hippocratis librum sextum de
morbis popularibus**, ed. F.R. Dietz, *Scholia in
Hippocratem et Galenum*, vol. 2. Königsberg:
Borntraeger, 1834 (repr. Amsterdam: Hakkert,
1966): 1–39, 73–88, 92–204.
Cod: [46,406]
002 **Synopsis de febribus**, ed. J.L. Ideler, *Physici et
medici Graeci minores*, vol. 1. Berlin: Reimer,
1841 (repr. Amsterdam: Hakkert, 1963): 107–
120.
Cf. et THEOPHILUS Protospatharius et STE-
PHANUS ATHENIENSIS Med. (0746 001).
Cod: [3,714]
003 Περὶ βρώσεως καὶ πόσεως, ed. Dietz, *op. cit.*,
vii–viii.
Cod: [134]
004 **Scholia in Hippocratis de fracturis**, ed. D.
Irmer, *Palladius. Kommentar zu Hippokrates
'De fracturis' und seine Parallelversion unter
dem Namen des Stephanus von Alexandria
[Hamburger philologische Studien* 45. Ham-

burg: Buske, 1977]: 16–88.
Cod

2111 **PALLADIUS** Scr. Eccl.
A.D. 4–5
001 **Historia Lausiaca**, ed. G.J.M. Bartelink, *Palla-
dio. La storia Lausiaca*. Verona: Fondazione
Lorenzo Valla: 4–292.
Cod: [29,426]
002 **Prooemium ad historiam Lausiacam**, ed. C.
Butler, *The Lausiac history of Palladius*, vol. 2.
Cambridge: Cambridge University Press, 1904
(repr. Hildesheim: Olms, 1967): 3–5.
Cod: [643]
003 **Epistula ad Lausum**, ed. Butler, *op. cit.*, 6–7.
Cod: [327]
004 **Dialogus de vita Joannis Chrysostomi**, ed. P.R.
Coleman-Norton, *Palladii dialogus de vita S.
Joanni Chrysostomi*. Cambridge: Cambridge
University Press, 1928: 3–147.
Cod: [36,972]
005 **De gentibus Indiae et Bragmanibus** [Sp.], ed.
W. Berghoff, *Palladius. De gentibus Indiae et
Bragmanibus*. Meisenheim am Glan: Hain,
1967: 2–55.
Cod: [7,146]

1828 **PAMPHILA** Hist.
A.D. 1: Epidauria
001 **Fragmenta**, FHG 3: 520–522.
Q

1554 **PAMPHILUS** Epigr.
fiq Pamphilus Alexandrinus Gramm.
2 B.C.
001 **Epigrammata**, AG 7.201; **9.**57.
Q: 44

PAMPHILUS Gramm.
2 B.C.: Alexandrinus
Cf. PAMPHILUS Epigr. (1554).

1014 **PAMPHILUS** Med.
ante A.D. 2: Romanus
x01 **Fragmentum ap. Galenum**.
K13.68.
Cf. GALENUS Med. (0057 076).

1015 **PAMPHILUS** <Med.>
ante A.D. 6
x01 **Fragmentum ap. Aëtium** (lib. 16).
Zervos, *Gynaekologie des Aëtios*, p. 171.
Cf. AËTIUS Med. (0718 016).

2634 **PAMPHILUS** Poeta
ante 4 B.C.: Siculus
001 **Fragmentum**, ed. H. Lloyd-Jones and P. Parsons, *Supplementum Hellenisticum*. Berlin: De
Gruyter, 1983: 286.
fr. 597.
Q: [14]

2961 **PAMPHILUS** Scr. Eccl.
A.D. 3–4: Caesariensis
001 **Fragmentum in Psalmum 71** (in catenis) [Sp.],
ed. J. Pitra, *Analecta sacra spicilegio Solesmense
parata*, vol. 3. Venice: St. Lazarus Monastery,
1883: 469–470.
Q

1399 **PAMPHILUS** Trag.
4 B.C.: Atheniensis
001 **Titulus**, ed. B. Snell, *Tragicorum Graecorum
fragmenta*, vol. 1. Göttingen: Vandenhoeck &
Ruprecht, 1971: 189.
NQ

4038 **PAMPREPIUS** Epic.
A.D. 5: Panopolitanus
001 **Fragmenta** (*P. Vindob.* 29788 A–C), ed. E.
Heitsch, *Die griechischen Dichterfragmente der
römischen Kaiserzeit*, vol. 1, 2nd edn. Göttingen: Vandenhoeck & Ruprecht, 1963: 109–
120.
frr. 1–4.
Pap: [1,629]
002 **Testimonium**, FGrH #749: 3C:732.
NQ
003 **Titulus**, FGrH #749: 3C:732.
NQ

1359 **PANAETIUS** Phil.
2 B.C.: Rhodius
001 **Fragmenta**, ed. M. van Straaten, *Panaetii Rhodii fragmenta*, 3rd edn. Leiden: Brill, 1962:
19–20, 24, 28–31, 33, 42–44, 48–52.
Q

0256 **PANARCES** <Iamb.>
5 B.C.
001 **Fragmenta**, ed. M.L. West, *Iambi et elegi
Graeci*, vol. 2. Oxford: Clarendon Press, 1972:
91.
Q: [61]

1555 **PANCRATES** Epic.
A.D. 2
001 **Fragmenta**, ed. E. Heitsch, *Die griechischen
Dichterfragmente der römischen Kaiserzeit*, vol.
1, 2nd edn. Göttingen: Vandenhoeck & Ruprecht, 1963: 52–54.
frr. 1–4.
fr. 1: *P. Brit. Mus.* 1109b.
fr. 2: *P. Oxy.* 8.1085.
Q, Pap: [321]
002 **Testimonium**, FGrH #625: 3C:160.
NQ
003 **Fragmentum**, FGrH #625: 3C:160.
Q

1556 **PANCRATES** Epigr.
3/2 B.C.: Arcadius
001 **Fragmenta**, ed. H. Lloyd-Jones and P. Parsons,
Supplementum Hellenisticum. Berlin: De Gruy-

ter, 1983: 286–287.
frr. 598–600, 602.
Q: [50]
002 **Epigrammata**, AG 6.117, 356; 7.653.
Q: 78

2120 **PANTELEIUS** Epic.
ante A.D. 5
001 **Fragmentum**, ed. E. Heitsch, *Die griechischen
Dichterfragmente der römischen Kaiserzeit*, vol.
1, 2nd edn. Göttingen: Vandenhoeck & Ruprecht, 1963: 81–82.
Q: [61]

1557 **PANYASSIS** Epic.
5 B.C.: Halicarnassensis
001 **Fragmenta**, ed. V.J. Matthews, *Panyassis of
Halikarnassos*. Leiden: Brill, 1974: 43, 48, 50,
74–76, 88, 91, 100, 131, 135, 138, 142.
frr. 1–2, 4, 5, 12–16, 18, 28–30, 32.
Q: [453]
002 **Testimonium**, FGrH #440: 3B:371.
NQ

1558 **PAPIAS** Scr. Eccl.
A.D. 2: Hierapolitanus
001 **Fragmenta**, ed. K. Bihlmeyer and W. Schneemelcher (post F.X. Funk), *Die apostolischen
Väter*, 3rd edn. Tübingen: Mohr, 1970: 134–
139.
Q: [1,783]

2032 **PAPPUS** Math.
A.D. 4: Alexandrinus
001 **Synagoge**, ed. F. Hultsch, *Pappi Alexandrini
collectionis quae supersunt*, 3 vols. Berlin:
Weidmann, 1:1876; 2:1877; 3:1878: **1**:2–470;
2:474–1020; **3**:1022–1134.
Cod: [142,719]
002 **Commentaria in Ptolemaei syntaxin mathematicam 5–6**, ed. A. Rome, *Commentaires de
Pappus et de Théon d'Alexandrie sur l'Almageste*, vol. 1 [*Studi e Testi* 54. Rome: Biblioteca
Apostolica Vaticana, 1931]: 1–314.
Cod: [66,585]

Παραδόσεις τοῦ Ματθίου
Cf. MATTHIAE TRADITIONES (1560).

0580 *PARADOXOGRAPHUS FLORENTINUS*
A.D. 2?
001 **Mirabilia de aquis**, ed. A. Giannini, *Paradoxo-
graphorum Graecorum reliquiae*. Milan: Istituto
Editoriale Italiano, 1965: 316–328.
Cod: [1,233]

0581 *PARADOXOGRAPHUS PALATINUS*
A.D. 3?
001 **Admiranda**, ed. A. Giannini, *Paradoxographorum Graecorum reliquiae*. Milan: Istituto Editoriale Italiano, 1965: 354–360.
Cod: [616]

0582 **PARADOXOGRAPHUS VATICANUS**
A.D. 2?
001 **Admiranda**, ed. A. Giannini, *Paradoxographo-rum Graecorum reliquiae*. Milan: Istituto Editoriale Italiano, 1965: 332–350.
Cod: [1,607]

1772 **PARALEIPOMENA JEREMIOU**
A.D. 2?
001 **Paraleipomena Jeremiou**, ed. R.A. Kraft and A.-E. Purintun, *Texts and translations 1. Pseudepigrapha series 1*. Missoula, Montana: Society of Biblical Literature, 1972: 12–48.
Cod: [4,195]

1785 **PARAMONUS** Comic.
Incertum
001 **Tituli**, ed. T. Kock, *Comicorum Atticorum fragmenta*, vol. 3. Leipzig: Teubner, 1888: 355.
NQ: 3

1561 **PARDALAS** Epigr.
Incertum: Sardianus
x01 **Epigramma dedicatorium**.
App. Anth. 1.190: Cf. EPIGRAMMATICI in *App. Anth.* (7052 001).

PARMENIDES Epigr.
AG 9.113.
Cf. PARMENION Epigr. (1563 001).

1562 **PARMENIDES** Poet. Phil.
5 B.C.
001 **Testimonia**, ed. H. Diels and W. Kranz, *Die Fragmente der Vorsokratiker*, vol. 1, 6th edn. Berlin: Weidmann, 1951 (repr. Dublin: 1966): 217–227.
test. 1–54.
NQ
002 **Fragmenta**, ed. Diels and Kranz, *op. cit.*, 227–246.
frr. 1–25.
Q

1563 **PARMENION** Epigr.
1 B.C.: Macedo
001 **Epigrammata**, AG **5**.33–34; **7**.183–184, 239; **9**.27, 43, 69, 113–114, 304, 342; **11**.4, 65; **16**.216, 222.
AG 7.240: Cf. ADAEUS Epigr. (0102 001).
AG 11.5: Cf. CALLICTER Epigr. (0148 001).
Q: 366

1564 **PARMENISCUS** Gramm.
2–1 B.C.
001 **Fragmenta**, ed. M. Breithaupt, *De Parmenisco grammatico*. Leipzig: Teubner, 1915: 2–54.
Q

2225 **PARM(EN)ISCUS** Phil.
6 B.C.: Metapontinus
001 **Testimonia**, ed. H. Diels and W. Kranz, *Die*

Fragmente der Vorsokratiker, vol. 1, 6th edn. Berlin: Weidmann, 1951 (repr. Dublin: 1966): 112–113.
test. 1–3.
NQ

1565 **[PARMENO]** Epigr.
3 B.C.
001 **Epigramma**, AG 13.18.
Q: 35

1566 **PARMENO** Iamb.
3 B.C.: Byzantius
001 **Fragmenta**, ed. J.U. Powell, *Collectanea Alexandrina*. Oxford: Clarendon Press, 1925 (repr. 1970): 237.
frr. 1–3.
Q: [36]
002 **Fragmentum**, ed. H. Lloyd-Jones and P. Parsons, *Supplementum Hellenisticum*. Berlin: De Gruyter, 1983: 288.
fr. 604a.
Q: [26]
x01 **Epigramma demonstrativum**.
App. Anth. 3.124: Cf. EPIGRAMMATICI in *App. Anth.* (7052 003).

1801 **PARODICA ANONYMA**
Varia
001 **Incertorum fragmenta**, ed. P. Brandt, *Corpusculum poesis epicae Graecae Ludibundae*, fasc. 1. Leipzig: Teubner, 1888: 96–99, 101–104, 107, 109–110.
frr. 1–9.
Q: [376]
002 **Fragmenta dubia**, ed. Brandt, *op. cit.*, 112–113.
frr. 1–3.
Q: [25]

2227 **PARON** Phil.
6 B.C.
001 **Testimonium**, ed. H. Diels and W. Kranz, *Die Fragmente der Vorsokratiker*, vol. 1, 6th edn. Berlin: Weidmann, 1951 (repr. Dublin: 1966): 217.
NQ

1567 **PARRHASIUS** Epigr.
5/4 B.C.: Ephesius
001 **Epigrammata**, ed. E. Diehl, *Anthologia lyrica Graeca*, fasc. 1, 3rd edn. Leipzig: Teubner, 1949: 110–111.
frr. 1–3.
Q: [65]
x01 **Epigrammata demonstrativa**.
App. Anth. 3.20–22: Cf. EPIGRAMMATICI in *App. Anth.* (7052 003).

1568 **PARTHAX** Hist.
ante A.D. 2
001 **Fragmenta**, FGrH #825: 3C:898.
Q

0655 **PARTHENIUS** Myth.
1 B.C.: Nicaenus
001 **Narrationes amatoriae**, ed. E. Martini, *Parthenii Nicaeni quae supersunt* [*Mythographi Graeci* 2.1, suppl. Leipzig: Teubner, 1902]: 41–92.
Cod: 7,148
002 **Poesis reliquiae**, ed. Martini, *op. cit.*, 11–37.
Elegiarum reliquiae (frr. 1–10): pp. 11–17.
Carmina forma incerta (frr. 11–21): pp. 18–22, 24, 26.
Incertae sedis fragmenta (frr. 22–46): pp. 26–37.
Q: 221
003 **Fragmenta et tituli**, ed. H. Lloyd-Jones and P. Parsons, *Supplementum Hellenisticum*. Berlin: De Gruyter, 1983: 291–300, 302–304, 306–315.
frr. (+ titul.) 606–612b, 614–636, 639–664, 666.
frr. 609–612b, 614: *P. Gen.* 97.
fr. 626: *P. Lit. Lond.* 64.
Q, Pap: [289]

1017 **PASIO** Med.
ante A.D. 1
x01 **Fragmentum ap. Oribasium**.
CMG, vol. 6.3, p. 95.
Cf. ORIBASIUS Med. (0722 004).
x02 **Fragmentum ap. Paulum**.
CMG, vol. 9.2, p. 318.
Cf. PAULUS Med. (0715 001).
x03 **Fragmentum ap. Aëtium** (lib. 15).
Zervos, *Athena* 21, p. 89.
Cf. AËTIUS Med. (0718 015).

PASTOR HERMAE
Cf. HERMAS Scr. Eccl. (1419 001).

2479 **PATROCLES** Hist.
4/3 B.C.
001 **Testimonia**, FGrH #712: 3C:597–598.
NQ
002 **Fragmenta**, FGrH #712: 3C:598–601.
Q

0324 **PATROCLES** Trag.
4 B.C.: Thurius
001 **Fragmenta**, ed. B. Snell, *Tragicorum Graecorum fragmenta*, vol. 1. Göttingen: Vandenhoeck & Ruprecht, 1971: 197.
frr. 1–2.
Q: [51]

1018 **PATROCLUS** Med.
1 B.C.?
x01 **Fragmentum ap. Galenum**.
K13.1019.
Cf. GALENUS Med. (0057 077).

PAULI ET CORINTHIORUM EPISTULAE
P. Bodmer 10
Cf. ACTA PAULI (0388 003).

1020 **PAULINUS** Med.
ante A.D. 1
x01 **Fragmentum ap. Galenum**.
K13.211–213.
Cf. GALENUS Med. (0057 076).

2053 **PAULUS** Astrol.
A.D. 4: Alexandrinus
001 **Elementa apotelesmatica**, ed. E. Boer, *Pauli Alexandrini elementa apotelesmatica*. Leipzig: Teubner, 1958: 1–100.
Cod: [16,212]
002 **Anacephalaeosis**, ed. Boer, *op. cit.*, xxi–xxiv.
Cod: [1,016]

1019 **PAULUS** Med.
A.D. 4?
x01 **Fragmentum ap. Oribasium**.
CMG, vol. 6.2.2, p. 287.
Cf. ORIBASIUS Med. (0722 004).

0715 **PAULUS** Med.
A.D. 7: Aegineta
001 **Epitomae medicae libri septem**, ed. J.L. Heiberg, *Paulus Aegineta*, 2 vols. [*Corpus medicorum Graecorum*, vols. 9.1 & 9.2. Leipzig: Teubner, 9.1:1921; 9.2:1924]: **9.1**:3–388; **9.2**:5–411.
Cod: 206,386

4039 **PAULUS Silentiarius** Poet. Christ.
A.D. 6
Bibliography in progress
001 **Descriptio Sanctae Sophiae**, ed. P. Friedländer, *Johannes von Gaza und Paulus Silentiarius*. Leipzig: Teubner, 1912: 227–256.
Cod
002 **Descriptio ambonis**, ed. Friedländer, *op. cit.*, 257–265.
Cod
003 **In thermas Pythicas** [Sp.], MPG 86: 2263–2268.
Cod
004 **Epigrammata**, AG **5**.217, 219, 221, 226, 228, 230, 232, 234, 236, 239, 241, 244, 246, 248, 250, 252, 254–256, 258–260, 262, 264, 266, 268, 270, 272, 274–275, 279, 281, 283, 286, 288, 290–291, 293, 300–301; **6**.54, 57, 64–66, 71, 75, 81–82, 84, 168; **7**.4, 307, 560, 563, 588, 604, 606, 609; **9**.396, 443, 620, 651, 658, 663–664, 764–765, 770, 782; **10**.15, 74, 76; **11**.60; **16**.57, 77, 118, 277–278.
AG 7.600: Cf. JULIANUS <Epigr.> (4050 001).
AG 9.444: Cf. ERATOSTHENES Scholasticus Epigr. (4063 001).
AG 9.766–769: Cf. AGATHIAS Scholasticus Hist. et Epigr. (4024 002).
Q: 3,434
x01 **In thermas Pythicas** [Sp.].
App. Anth. 4.75: Cf. EPIGRAMMATICI in *App. Anth.* (7052 004).

047 *PAUSANIAE ET XERXIS EPISTULAE*
Incertum
001 **Epistulae**, ed. R. Hercher, *Epistolographi Graeci*. Paris: Didot, 1873 (repr. Amsterdam: Hakkert, 1965): 407.
Q: [150]

569 **PAUSANIAS** Attic.
A.D. 2
001 Ἀττικῶν ὀνομάτων συναγωγή, ed. H. Erbse, *Untersuchungen zu den attizistischen Lexika* [*Abhandlungen der deutschen Akademie der Wissenschaften zu Berlin*, Philosoph.-hist. Kl. Berlin: Akademie-Verlag, 1950]: 152–221.
Q: [22,920]

PAUSANIAS Geogr.
2 B.C.?: Damascenus
Cf. Pseudo-SCYMNUS (0068).

2401 **PAUSANIAS** Hist.
4 B.C.: Lacedaemonius
001 **Testimonia**, FGrH #582: 3B:693–694.
NQ

2407 **PAUSANIAS** Hist.
post 1 B.C.?: Lacon
001 **Testimonium**, FGrH #592: 3B:707.
NQ

2573 **PAUSANIAS** Hist.
A.D. 4: Antiochenus vel Damascenus
001 **Testimonium**, FGrH #854: 3C:938.
NQ
002 **Fragmenta**, FGrH #854: 3C:938–942.
Q

0525 **PAUSANIAS** Perieg.
A.D. 2: fort. Lydius
001 **Graeciae descriptio**, ed. F. Spiro, *Pausaniae Graeciae descriptio*, 3 vols. Leipzig: Teubner, 1903 (repr. Stuttgart: 1:1967): 1:1–420; 2:1–389; 3:1–217.
Cod: 224,602

2266 **PAXAMUS** Hist.
Incertum
001 **Testimonium**, FGrH #377: 3B:245.
NQ

0275 Πειραζομένη
ante A.D. 3
001 **Fragmentum** (*P. Brit. Mus.* 2208), ed. E. Heitsch, *Die griechischen Dichterfragmente der römischen Kaiserzeit*, vol. 1, 2nd edn. Göttingen: Vandenhoeck & Ruprecht, 1963: 41–42.
Pap: [152]

2019 **PELAGIUS** Alchem.
A.D. 3?
001 **Fragmenta**, ed. M. Berthelot, *Collection des anciens alchimistes grecs*. Paris: Steinheil, 1887

(repr. London: Holland Press, 1963): 89, 199, 253–261.
Cod

1571 **<PEMPELUS>** Phil.
3/2 B.C.
001 **Fragmenta**, ed. H. Thesleff, *The Pythagorean texts of the Hellenistic period*. Åbo: Åbo Akademi, 1965: 141–142.
Q: 227

0629 **PERIANDER** <Phil.>
7–6 B.C.: Corinthius
Cf. et <SEPTEM SAPIENTES> (1667).
001 **Epistulae** [Sp.], ed. R. Hercher, *Epistolographi Graeci*. Paris: Didot, 1873 (repr. Amsterdam: Hakkert, 1965): 408.
Q: [113]

1572 **<PERICTIONE>** Phil.
4/2 B.C.
001 **Fragmenta**, ed. H. Thesleff, *The Pythagorean texts of the Hellenistic period*. Åbo: Åbo Akademi, 1965: 142–146.
Q: 1,176

1023 **PERIGENES** Med.
1 B.C.?
x01 **Fragmenta** ap. Galenum.
K13.33–34, 69–70, 73.
Cf. GALENUS Med. (0057 076).

0064 *PERIPLUS HANNONIS*
4 B.C.
001 **Periplus Hannonis**, ed. K. Müller, *Geographi Graeci minores*, vol. 1. Paris: Didot, 1855 (repr. Hildesheim: Olms, 1965): 1–14.
Cod: [682]

0071 *PERIPLUS MARIS ERYTHRAEI*
fort. auctore Arriano
post A.D. 2
001 **Anonymi (Arriani, ut fertur) periplus maris Erythraei**, ed. K. Müller, *Geographi Graeci minores*, vol. 1. Paris: Didot, 1855 (repr. Hildesheim: Olms, 1965): 257–305.
Cod: [6,561]

0077 *PERIPLUS MARIS MAGNI*
post A.D. 3
001 **Stadiasmus sive periplus Maris Magni**, ed. K. Müller, *Geographi Graeci minores*, vol. 1. Paris: Didot, 1855 (repr. Hildesheim: Olms, 1965): 427–514.
Cod: [5,983]

PERIPLUS MARIS RUBRI
Cf. PERIPLUS MARIS ERYTHRAEI (0071).

0075 *PERIPLUS PONTI EUXINI*
post A.D. 6
001 **Anonymi (Arriani, ut fertur) periplus ponti**

Euxini, ed. K. Müller, *Geographi Graeci minores*, vol. 1. Paris: Didot, 1855 (repr. Hildesheim: Olms, 1965): 402–423.
Cod: [5,791]

1573 **PERITAS** Epigr.
Incertum
001 **Epigramma**, AG 16.236.
Q: 28

2403 **PERSAEUS** Hist.
4–3 B.C.: Citieus
001 **Testimonia**, FGrH #584: 3B:696–697.
NQ
002 **Fragmenta**, FGrH #584: 3B:697–700.
Q

1574 **PERSAEUS** Phil.
4–3 B.C.: Citiensis
001 **Fragmenta**, ed. J. von Arnim, *Stoicorum veterum fragmenta*, vol. 1. Leipzig: Teubner, 1905 (repr. Stuttgart: 1968): 96–102.
Q

1575 **PERSES** Epigr.
4 B.C.: Thebanus
001 **Epigrammata**, AG **6**.112, 272, 274; **7**.445, 487, 501, 539, 730; **9**.334.
Q: 257

2722 **PERSEUS** Epigr.
Incertum
x01 **Problema**.
App. Anth. 7.4(?): Cf. EPIGRAMMATICI in *App. Anth.* (7052 007).

2635 **PERSINUS** Poeta
4 B.C.: Ephesius vel Milesius
001 **Titulus**, ed. H. Lloyd-Jones and P. Parsons, *Supplementum Hellenisticum*. Berlin: De Gruyter, 1983: 316.
fr. 666c.
NQ: [1]

2323 **PETELLIDAS** Hist.
ante 1 B.C.: Creticus
001 **Fragmentum**, FGrH #464: 3B:401–402.
Q

1024 **PETINUS** Med.
ante A.D. 1
x01 **Fragmentum ap. Galenum**.
K13.57.
Cf. GALENUS Med. (0057 076).

[PETOSIRIS]
Cf. [NECHEPSO et PETOSIRIS] Astrol. (0995).

2247 **PETRON** Phil.
6 B.C.
001 **Testimonium**, ed. H. Diels and W. Kranz, *Die Fragmente der Vorsokratiker*, vol. 1, 6th edn.

Berlin: Weidmann, 1951 (repr. Dublin: 1966): 106.
NQ

1025 **PETRONAS** Med.
5 B.C.: Aegineta
x01 **Fragmentum ap. Galenum**.
K15.436 in CMG, vol. 5.9.1, p. 126.
Cf. GALENUS Med. (0057 087).

1026 **PETRONIUS** Med.
fort. Musa.
A.D. 1
Cf. et MUSA Med. (0808).
x01 **Fragmentum ap. Galenum**.
K13.831.
Cf. GALENUS Med. (0057 077).

2678 **<PETRONIUS APOLLODORUS>** Epigr.
A.D. 4
x01 **Epigramma dedicatorium**.
App. Anth. 1.340: Cf. EPIGRAMMATICI in *App. Anth.* (7052 001).

1027 **PETRUS** Med.
ante A.D. 6
x01 **Fragmentum ap. Aëtium** (lib. 7).
CMG, vol. 8.2, p. 386.
Cf. AËTIUS Med. (0718 007).

2962 **PETRUS** Scr. Eccl.
A.D. 3–4: Alexandrinus
001 **De deitate** (fragmentum), ed. M. Richard, "Le florilège du cod. Vatopédi 236 sur le corruptible et l'incorruptible," *Muséon* 86 (1973) 268–269.
Q
002 **De adventu domini** (tragmentum), MPG 18: 521.
Q
003 **De anima** (fragmenta), ed. W. Bienert, "Neue Fragmente des Dionysius und des Petrus von Alexandrien aus Cod. Vatop. 236," Κληρονομία 5 (1973) 311–312.
Cod
004 **Epistula canonica** (e Περὶ μετανοίας) (canones 1–14), FONTI II: 578–596.
Cod
005 **De paschate ad Tricentium** (fragmenta), MPG 18: 512–517.
Q
006 **De paschate ad Tricentium** (canon 15 epistulae canonicae) (fragmentum), FONTI II: 597.
Cod
007 **Epistula ad clericos suos** (fragmentum), ed. M. Richard, "Quelques nouveaux fragments des pères anténicéens et nicéens," *Symbolae Osloenses* 38 (1963) 80.
Q
008 **Epistula festalis** (fragmenta), ed. Richard, *Muséon* 86, 267–268.
Q

011 **Didascalia** (fragmentum) [Sp.], ed. J.M. Heer, "Ein neues Fragment der Didaskalie des Märtyrerbischofs Petros von Alexandrien," *Oriens Christianus* 2 (1902) 344–351.
Q

012 **Didascalia** (fragmenta) [Sp.], ed. K. Holl, *Fragmente vornicänischer Kirchenväter aus den Sacra Parallela* [*Texte und Untersuchungen* 20. Leipzig: Hinrichs, 1899]: 234.
Q

013 **Didascalia** (fragmentum ap. Eliam Cretensem) [Sp.], MPG 36: 895.
Q

x01 **De deitate** (fragmenta).
ACO **1.1.2**, p. 39; **1.1.7**, pp. 36, 89, 90.
Cf. CONCILIA OECUMENICA (ACO) (5000 001).

x02 **De anima** (fragmentum).
ACO 3, p. 197.
Cf. CONCILIA OECUMENICA (ACO) (5000 004).

PHACELLUS (?) Epigr.
AG 7.650.
Cf. PHALAECUS Epigr. (1581 001).

1576 **PHAEDIMUS** <Epic.>
Incertum
001 **Fragmentum**, ed. G. Kinkel, *Epicorum Graecorum fragmenta*, vol. 1. Leipzig: Teubner, 1877: 214.
Q: [6]

1577 **PHAEDIMUS** Epigr.
3 B.C.: Macedo vel Paphlagonius
001 **Epigrammata**, AG **6**.271; **7**.739; **13**.2, 22.
Q: 140
002 **Fragmentum**, ed. H. Lloyd-Jones and P. Parsons, *Supplementum Hellenisticum*. Berlin: De Gruyter, 1983: 316.
fr. 669.
Q: [7]

PHAEDRI EPISTULA
Epist. Graec., p. 627.
Cf. SOCRATICORUM EPISTULAE (0637 001).

1578 **PHAENIAS** Phil.
vel Phanias
4 B.C.: Eresius
001 **Fragmenta**, ed. F. Wehrli, *Phainias von Eresos. Chamaileon. Praxiphanes* [*Die Schule des Aristoteles*, vol. 9, 2nd edn. Basel: Schwabe, 1969]: 10–21.
Q

1579 **PHAËNNUS** Epigr.
3 B.C.
001 **Epigrammata**, AG 7.197, 437.
Q: 49

2366 **PHAENNUS** Hist.
Incertum

001 **Titulus**, FGrH #525: 3B:503.
NQ

1580 **PHAESTUS** Epic.
post 4 B.C.
001 **Fragmentum**, ed. J.U. Powell, *Collectanea Alexandrina*. Oxford: Clarendon Press, 1925 (repr. 1970): 28.
Q: [7]
002 **Fragmenta**, FGrH #593: 3B:707.
Q
003 **Fragmentum**, ed. H. Lloyd-Jones and P. Parsons, *Supplementum Hellenisticum*. Berlin: De Gruyter, 1983: 316.
fr. 670.
Q: [7]

1581 **PHALAECUS** Epigr.
4 B.C.: Phoceus
001 **Epigrammata**, AG **6**.165; **7**.650; **13**.5–6, 27.
Q: 225
x01 **Epigramma dedicatorium** (*App. Anth.*).
App. Anth. 1.117: Cf. EPIGRAMMATICI in *App. Anth.* (7052 001).

0053 *PHALARIDIS EPISTULAE*
A.D. 2?
001 **Epistulae**, ed. R. Hercher, *Epistolographi Graeci*. Paris: Didot, 1873 (repr. Amsterdam: Hakkert, 1965): 409–459.
Cod: [18,244]

2667 **PHALERNUS** Poeta et Soph.
A.D. 2–3
x01 **Epigramma dedicatorium**.
App. Anth. 1.191: Cf. EPIGRAMMATICI in *App. Anth.* (7052 001).

1582 **PHANIAS** Gramm.
3 B.C.
001 **Epigrammata**, AG **6**.294–295, 297, 299, 304, 307; **7**.537; **12**.31.
Q: 357

0975 **PHANIUS** Med.
ante A.D. 1
x01 **Fragmentum ap. Galenum**.
K13.840.
Cf. GALENUS Med. (0057 077).

0214 **PHANOCLES** Eleg.
3 B.C.?
001 **Fragmenta**, ed. J.U. Powell, *Collectanea Alexandrina*. Oxford: Clarendon Press, 1925 (repr. 1970): 106–108.
frr. 1–3.
Q: [207]
x01 **Fragmentum papyraceum** (*P. Sorbonne* inv. 2254) (fort. auctore Phanocle).
SH, pp. 478–479, fr. 970.
Cf. ADESPOTA PAPYRACEA (SH) (2648 002).

1583 **PHANODEMUS** Hist.
      4 B.C.: Atheniensis
  001 **Testimonia**, FGrH #325: 3B:77–78, 757 ad-
      denda.
      test. 2: *IG²* 2.223.
      test. 3a: *IG* 7.4252.
      test. 3b: *IG* 7.4253.
      test. 4: *IG* 7.4254.
      test. 5: *Inscr. Delphi.*
      test. 8: *P. Oxy.* 17.2082.
      NQ
  002 **Fragmenta**, FGrH #325: 3B:79–85.
      Q, Cod

2278 **PHANODICUS** Hist.
      2 B.C.?
  001 **Fragmenta**, FGrH #397: 3B:291–292.
      Q

2471 **PHARNUCHUS** Hist.
      1 B.C.–A.D. 1?: Nisibenus
  001 **Testimonium**, FGrH #694: 3C:533.
      NQ

0979 **Apius PHASCUS** Med.
      ante A.D. 2
  x01 **Fragmentum ap. Galenum.**
      K12.841–842.
      Cf. GALENUS Med. (0057 076).

0486 **PHERECRATES** Comic.
      5 B.C.
  001 **Fragmenta**, ed. T. Kock, *Comicorum Attico-
      rum fragmenta*, vol. 1. Leipzig: Teubner, 1880:
      145–175, 177–188, 190–209.
      frr. 1–13, 15–17, 19–56, 58–65, 67–73, 75–91,
      93–98, 100–109, 113–132, 134–138, 141–191,
      195–249 + tituli.
      Q: 2,483
  002 **Fragmenta**, ed. A. Meineke, *Fragmenta comico-
      rum Graecorum*, vol. 2.1. Berlin: Reimer, 1839
      (repr. De Gruyter, 1970): 252–272, 274–300,
      305, 309–316, 318–327, 335–355, 357–360.
      p. 338, fr. 7: line 7 supplied from vol. 5.1, p.
      lvii.
      Q: 2,340
  003 **Fragmenta**, ed. J. Demiańczuk, *Supplementum
      comicum*. Krakau: Nakładem Akademii, 1912
      (repr. Hildesheim: Olms, 1967): 66–71.
      frr. 1–22.
      Q: 94
  004 **Fragmentum**, ed. C. Austin, *Comicorum Grae-
      corum fragmenta in papyris reperta*. Berlin: De
      Gruyter, 1973: 196.
      fr. 205.
      Pap: 12
  005 **Fragmentum**, ed. Kock, *op. cit.*, vol. 3 (1888):
      716.
      fr. 155b.
      Q: 16
  006 **Fragmenta**, ed. Meineke, *op. cit.*, vol. 5.1

(1857; repr. 1970): li.
Q: [23]

1584 **PHERECYDES** Hist.
      5 B.C.: Atheniensis
      Cf. et ANTIOCHUS-PHERECYDES Hist. (2221).
  001 **Testimonia**, FGrH #3: 1A:58–59.
      NQ
  002 **Fragmenta**, FGrH #3: 1A:59–104, *5 addenda.
      Q

2329 **PHERECYDES** Hist.
      4 B.C./A.D. 2: Lerius
  001 **Testimonium**, FGrH #475: 3B:434.
      NQ
  002 **Fragmenta**, FGrH #475: 3B:434–435.
      Q

0630 **PHERECYDES** Phil. et Myth.
      6 B.C.: Syrius
      Cf. et PHERECYDIS EPISTULA (1585).
  001 **Testimonia**, ed. H. Diels and W. Kranz, *Die
      Fragmente der Vorsokratiker*, vol. 1, 6th edn.
      Berlin: Weidmann, 1951 (repr. Dublin: 1966):
      43–46.
      test. 1–12.
      NQ
  002 **Fragmenta**, ed. Diels and Kranz, *op. cit.*, 47–
      51.
      frr. 1–14.
      Q, Pap

1585 ***PHERECYDIS EPISTULA***
      Incertum
      Cf. et PHERECYDES Phil. et Myth. (0630).
  001 **Epistula**, ed. R. Hercher, *Epistolographi Graeci.*
      Paris: Didot, 1873 (repr. Amsterdam: Hakkert,
      1965): 460.
      Q: [127]

2636 **PHERENICUS** Epic.
      2 B.C./A.D. 2?: Heracleota
  001 **Fragmentum**, ed. H. Lloyd-Jones and P. Par-
      sons, *Supplementum Hellenisticum*. Berlin: De
      Gruyter, 1983: 317.
      fr. 671.
      Q: [29]

1880 **PHIDALIUS** Hist.
      Incertum: Corinthius
  001 **Fragmenta**, FGrH #30: 1A:214.
      NQ

1586 **PHILAENIS Scriptor De Aphrodisiis**
      3 B.C.?: Samia
  001 **Fragmenta**, *P. Oxy.* 39.2891.
      Pap

1079 **PHILAGRIUS** Med.
      A.D. 4–5: Epirotes
  x01 **Fragmentum ap. Oribasium.**

CMG, vol. **6.1.1**, pp. 133–138; **6.3**, pp. 109, 111, 312.
Cf. ORIBASIUS Med. (0722 001, 004).

x02 **Fragmentum ap. Paulum.**
CMG, vol. 9.2, pp. 285, 333, 366.
Cf. PAULUS Med. (0715 001).

x03 **Fragmentum ap. Aëtium** (lib. 3).
CMG, vol. 8.1, p. 299.
Cf. AËTIUS Med. (0718 003).

x04 **Fragmentum ap. Aëtium** (lib. 5).
CMG, vol. 8.2, p. 112.
Cf. AËTIUS Med. (0718 005).

x05 **Fragmentum ap. Aëtium** (lib. 7).
CMG, vol. 8.2, pp. 374, 376, 381.
Cf. AËTIUS Med. (0718 007).

x06 **Fragmentum ap. Aëtium** (lib. 8).
CMG, vol. 8.2, pp. 475, 516.
Cf. AËTIUS Med. (0718 008).

x07 **Fragmentum ap. Aëtium** (lib. 9).
Zervos, *Athena* 23, p. 305.
Cf. AËTIUS Med. (0718 009).

x08 **Fragmentum ap. Aëtium** (lib. 11).
Daremberg-Ruelle, pp. 95, 123, 573–574.
Cf. AËTIUS Med. (0718 011).

x09 **Fragmentum ap. Aëtium** (lib. 12).
Kostomiris, pp. 46, 50, 52, 85, 88, 89, 111.
Cf. AËTIUS Med. (0718 012).

x10 **Fragmentum ap. Aëtium** (lib. 15).
Zervos, *Athena* 21, p. 29.
Cf. AËTIUS Med. (0718 015).

x11 **Fragmentum ap. Aëtium** (lib. 16).
Zervos, *Gynaekologie des Aëtios*, pp. 103–105.
Cf. AËTIUS Med. (0718 016).

PHILAGRIUS Scriptor Facetiarum
A.D. 4?
Cf. HIEROCLES et PHILAGRIUS Scriptores
Facetiarum (2404).

2013 ***PHILEAE EPISTULA***
A.D. 4
Cf. et ACTA PHILEAE (2014).

001 **Phileae epistula**, ed. H. Musurillo, *The acts of the Christian martyrs*. Oxford: Clarendon Press, 1972: 320–324.
Q: [703]

2966 **PHILEAS** Scr. Eccl.
A.D. 3–4: Thmuitanus

001 **Apologia** (fragmenta), ed. V. Martin, *Papyrus Bodmer XX. Apologie de Philéas évêque de Thmouis*. Geneva: Bibliotheca Bodmeriana, 1964.
Pap

x01 **Epistula ad Thmuitanos** (ap. Eusebium).
HE 8.10.2–10.
Cf. EUSEBIUS Scr. Eccl. (2018 002).

0487 **PHILEMON** Comic.
4–3 B.C.: Syracusanus

001 **Fragmenta**, ed. T. Kock, *Comicorum Attico-*

rum fragmenta, vol. 2. Leipzig: Teubner, 1884: 478–539.
frr. 2–18, 20–39, 41–44, 46–77, 79–86, 88–211, 213, 219–220, 222–240, 243–247 + tituli.
fr. 89: *P. Cairo* inv. 56226.
fr. 233: Tabula lignea Cairensis.
Q, Pap: 4,361

002 **Fragmenta**, ed. A. Meineke, *Fragmenta comicorum Graecorum*, vol. 4. Berlin: Reimer, 1839 (repr. De Gruyter, 1970): 3–64, 67.
Q: 4,192

003 **Fragmenta**, ed. J. Demiańczuk, *Supplementum comicum*. Krakau: Nakładem Akademii, 1912 (repr. Hildesheim: Olms, 1967): 71–72.
frr. 1–3.
fr. 3: *P. Oxy.* 9.39 (col. 7, v. 32).
Q, Pap: 56

004 **Fragmenta**, ed. C. Austin, *Comicorum Graecorum fragmenta in papyris reperta*. Berlin: De Gruyter, 1973: 197–200.
frr. 206, 212–214.
Pap: 136

006 **Titulus**, ed. Kock, *op. cit.*, vol. 3 (1888): 749.
NQ: 2

007 **Fragmentum**, ed. Kock, *op. cit.*, vol. 3, 750.
fr. 224b.
Q: 2

008 **Epigramma**, AG 9.450.
AG 10.82: Cf. PALLADAS Epigr. (2123 001).
Q: 17

009 **Fragmenta**, ed. Meineke, *op. cit.*, vol. 5.1 (1857; repr. 1970): ccxxxiv, ccxxxviii–ccxxxix.
Q: [82]

x01 **Sententia ap. Menandrum** (tabula lignea Cairensis).
Menandri sententiae, fr. 15.
Cf. MENANDER Comic. (0541 048).

0488 **PHILEMON Junior** Comic.
3 B.C.

001 **Fragmenta**, ed. T. Kock, *Comicorum Atticorum fragmenta*, vol. 2. Leipzig: Teubner, 1884: 540.
frr. 1–3 + titulus.
Q: 106

002 **Fragmenta**, ed. A. Meineke, *Fragmenta comicorum Graecorum*, vol. 4. Berlin: Reimer, 1841 (repr. De Gruyter, 1970): 68.
Q: 91

1384 **PHILEMON III** Comic.
3 B.C.?

001 **Titulus**, ed. T. Kock, *Comicorum Atticorum fragmenta*, vol. 2. Leipzig: Teubner, 1884: 540.
NQ: [1]

2718 **Manuel PHILES** Poeta
A.D. 13–14: Ephesius, Constantinopolitanus
Bibliography in progress

x01 **Epigrammata** (*App. Anth.*).
Epigramma exhortatorium et supplicatorium: 4.141.

Epigramma irrisorium: 5.79.
App. Anth. 4.141: Cf. EPIGRAMMATICI in *App. Anth.* (7052 004).
App. Anth. 5.79: Cf. EPIGRAMMATICI in *App. Anth.* (7052 005).

0489 **PHILETAERUS** Comic.
4 B.C.
001 **Fragmenta**, ed. T. Kock, *Comicorum Atticorum fragmenta*, vol. 2. Leipzig: Teubner, 1884: 230–235.
frr. 1, 3–18, 20 + tituli.
Q: 324
002 **Fragmenta**, ed. A. Meineke, *Fragmenta comicorum Graecorum*, vol. 3. Berlin: Reimer, 1840 (repr. De Gruyter, 1970): 292–299.
Q: 307
003 **Fragmentum**, ed. J. Demiańczuk, *Supplementum comicum.* Krakau: Nakładem Akademii, 1912 (repr. Hildesheim: Olms, 1967): 72.
fr. 1.
Q: 2

0212 **PHILETAS** Eleg. et Gramm.
vel Philitas
4–3 B.C.: Cous
001 **Fragmenta**, ed. J.U. Powell, *Collectanea Alexandrina.* Oxford: Clarendon Press, 1925 (repr. 1970): 90–95.
frr. 1–4, 6–14, 16–26.
Q: [322]
002 **Fragmenta poetica**, ed. W. Kuchenmüller, *Philetae Coi reliquiae* [*Diss. Berlin* (1928)]: 38–41, 49–50, 52, 58, 61, 64, 66, 68, 72, 74, 76–78, 80–87.
frr. 1–8, 10–28.
Q
003 **Fragmenta grammatica**, ed. Kuchenmüller, *op. cit.*, 91–96, 98–100, 102–111.
frr. 29–59.
Q
004 **Fragmenta**, ed. H. Lloyd-Jones and P. Parsons, *Supplementum Hellenisticum.* Berlin: De Gruyter, 1983: 318–320.
frr. 673–674, 675a–675d.
fr. 673: *P. Oxy.* 20.2258a.
fr. 674: *P. Oxy.* 20.2260.
Q, Pap: [34]
x01 **Epigramma exhortatorium et supplicatorium.**
App. Anth. 4.36: Cf. EPIGRAMMATICI in *App. Anth.* (7052 004).

1587 **PHILIADES** Eleg.
5 B.C.: Megareus
001 **Fragmentum**, ed. E. Diehl, *Anthologia lyrica Graeca*, fasc. 1, 3rd edn. Leipzig: Teubner, 1949: 87.
Q: [12]
x01 **Epigramma demonstrativum.**
App. Anth. 3.19: Cf. EPIGRAMMATICI in *App. Anth.* (7052 003).

1588 **PHILICUS** Lyr.
3 B.C.: Corcyraeus
001 **Fragmenta**, ed. H. Lloyd-Jones and P. Parsons, *Supplementum Hellenisticum.* Berlin: De Gruyter, 1983: 321–324.
frr. 676–680.
frr. 678–680: *PSI* 1282.
Q, Pap: [585]

2692 **PHILINNA** Poeta
ante 1 B.C.: Thessala
x01 **Incantamenta hexametrica** (fort. auctore Philinna).
SH, p. 399, fr. 900.
Cf. ADESPOTA PAPYRACEA (SH) (2648 001).

1969 **PHILINUS** Hist.
3 B.C.: Agrigentinus
001 **Testimonia**, FGrH #174: 2B:897.
NQ
002 **Fragmenta**, FGrH #174: 2B:897–900.
Q

1030 **PHILINUS** Med.
3 B.C.: Cous
x01 **Fragmenta ap. Galenum.**
K13.113, 842.
Cf. GALENUS Med. (0057 076–077).
x02 **Fragmentum ap. Philumenum.**
CMG, vol. 10.1.1, p. 10.
Cf. PHILUMENUS Med. (0671 001).

0490 **PHILIPPIDES** Comic.
4 B.C.
001 **Fragmenta**, ed. T. Kock, *Comicorum Atticorum fragmenta*, vol. 3. Leipzig: Teubner, 1888: 301–312.
frr. 1–29, 31–40 + titulus.
Q: 463
002 **Fragmenta**, ed. A. Meineke, *Fragmenta comicorum Graecorum*, vol. 4. Berlin: Reimer, 1841 (repr. De Gruyter, 1970): 467–477, 478.
478: fr. 18 supplied from vol. 5.1, p. cccxv.
Q: 439

1781 **PHILIPPUS** Comic.
4 B.C.
001 **Fragmentum**, ed. T. Kock, *Comicorum Atticorum fragmenta*, vol. 2. Leipzig: Teubner, 1884: 215.
fr. 1.
Q: 4
002 **Fragmentum**, ed. A. Meineke, *Fragmenta comicorum Graecorum*, vol. 1. Berlin: Reimer, 1839 (repr. De Gruyter, 1970): 342.
Q

1589 **PHILIPPUS** Epigr.
A.D. 1: Thessalonicensis
001 **Epigrammata**, AG **4**.2; **6**.5, 36, 38, 62, 90, 92, 94, 99, 101–104, 107, 203, 231, 236, 240, 247,

251, 259; **7.**186-187, 234, 362, 382-383, 385, 394, 405, 554, 692; **9.**11, 22, 56, 83, 85, 88-89, 232, 240, 247, 253-255, 262, 264-265, 267, 274, 285, 290, 293, 299, 307, 311, 416, 438, 543, 561, 575, 708-709, 742, 777-778; **11.**33, 36, 173, 321, 347; **13.**1; **16.**25, 52, 81, 93, 104, 137, 141, 177, 193, 215, 240.
AG 6.114: Cf. SIMIAS Gramm. (0211 002).
AG 7.237: Cf. ALPHEUS Epigr. (0108 001).
AG 9.266, 269: Cf. ANTIPATER Epigr. (0114 001).
AG 9.562: Cf. CRINAGORAS Epigr. (0154 001).
AG 9.563: Cf. LEONIDAS Epigr. (1458 001).
Q: 3,413

1590 **PHILIPPUS** Hist.
3 B.C.?: Theangelius
001 **Fragmenta,** FGrH #741: 3C:718.
Q

2142 **PHILIPPUS** Hist.
A.D. 2: Pergamenus
001 **Testimonium,** FGrH #95: 2A:446.
test. 1: *IG* 4.1153.
NQ
002 **Fragmentum,** FGrH #95: 2A:446.
fr. 1: *IG* 4.1153.
Epigr

2188 **PHILIPPUS** Hist.
A.D. 4?: Amphipolitanus
001 **Testimonia,** FGrH #280: 3A:159.
NQ
002 **Fragmentum,** FGrH #280: 3A:159.
Q

0990 **PHILIPPUS** <Med.>
fiq Philippus Xerus Rheginus
ante A.D. 2: Macedo
x01 **Fragmentum ap. Galenum.**
K14.149-150.
Cf. GALENUS Med. (0057 078).

1031 **PHILIPPUS** Med.
A.D. 2
x01 **Fragmenta ap. Galenum.**
K13.88, 105, 304.
Cf. GALENUS Med. (0057 076).
x02 **Fragmentum ap. Paulum.**
CMG, vol. 9.2, p. 317.
Cf. PAULUS Med. (0715 001).

0048 **PHILIPPUS II Rex Macedonum** <Epist.>
5-4 B.C.
001 **Epistulae,** ed. R. Hercher, *Epistolographi Graeci.* Paris: Didot, 1873 (repr. Amsterdam: Hakkert, 1965): 461-467.
Q: [2,374]
x01 **Epigramma irrisorium.**

App. Anth. 5.10: Cf. EPIGRAMMATICI in *App. Anth.* (7052 005).

0491 **PHILISCUS** Comic.
fiq Philiscus Corcyraeus Epigr.
4 B.C.?
Cf. et PHILISCUS Epigr. (2131).
001 **Fragmenta,** ed. T. Kock, *Comicorum Atticorum fragmenta,* vol. 2. Leipzig: Teubner, 1884: 443-444.
frr. 1-5 + tituli.
Q: 60
002 **Fragmenta,** ed. A. Meineke, *Fragmenta comicorum Graecorum,* vol. 3. Berlin: Reimer, 1840 (repr. De Gruyter, 1970): 579-580.
Q: 44
003 **Fragmentum,** ed. C. Austin, *Comicorum Graecorum fragmenta in papyris reperta.* Berlin: De Gruyter, 1973: 200.
fr. 215.
Pap: 112

2131 **PHILISCUS** Epigr.
fiq Philiscus Comic.
3 B.C.: Corcyraeus
Cf. et PHILISCUS Comic. (0491).
001 **Epigramma,** AG 11.441.
Q: 8

0257 **PHILISCUS** Rhet.
5-4 B.C.: Milesius
001 **Fragmentum,** ed. M.L. West, *Iambi et elegi Graeci,* vol. 2. Oxford: Clarendon Press, 1972: 93.
Q: [69]
002 **Fragmentum,** FGrH #337 bis: 3B:757 addenda.
Q
x01 **Epigramma sepulcrale.**
App. Anth. 2.124: Cf. EPIGRAMMATICI in *App. Anth.* (7052 002).

0335 **PHILISCUS** Trag.
4 B.C.: Aegineta
001 **Fragmentum,** ed. B. Snell, *Tragicorum Graecorum fragmenta,* vol. 1. Göttingen: Vandenhoeck & Ruprecht, 1971: 259.
fr. 1.
Q: [14]

1870 **PHILISTIDES** Hist.
5 B.C.?: Mallotes
001 **Testimonia,** FGrH #11: 1A:165, *9 addenda.
NQ
002 **Fragmenta,** FGrH #11: 1A:165-166.
Q

1591 **PHILISTUS** Hist.
5-4 B.C.: Syracusanus
001 **Testimonia,** FGrH #556: 3B:551-558.
NQ

002 **Fragmenta**, FGrH #556: 3B:558–567.
fr. 77: *P. Oxy.* 1.222.
Q, Pap

2422 **PHILISTUS** Hist.
post 4 B.C.?: Naucratites
001 **Testimonia**, FGrH #615: 3C:122.
NQ

1592 **PHILITAS** Epigr.
ante 1 B.C.: Samius
001 **Epigrammata**, AG 6.210; 7.481.
Q: 64

1594 **PHILO** Epic.
2 B.C.: Judaeus
002 **Fragmenta**, ed. H. Lloyd-Jones and P. Parsons,
Supplementum Hellenisticum. Berlin: De Gruyter, 1983: 328–330.
frr. 681–686.
Q: [144]

1593 **PHILO** <Epigr.>
fiq (H)eren(n)ius Philo
A.D. 1?
Cf. et (H)EREN(N)IUS PHILO Hist. et Gramm.
(1416).
001 **Epigramma**, AG 11.419.
Q: 16

2457 **PHILO** Hist.
3 B.C.
001 **Testimonium**, FGrH #670: 3C:283.
NQ
002 **Fragmenta**, FGrH #670: 3C:283.
Q

1599 **PHILO** Mech.
3–2 B.C.: Byzantius
001 **Belopoeica**, ed. H. Diels and E. Schramm,
Philons Belopoiika [*Abhandlungen der preuss-
ischen Akademie der Wissenschaften*, Philo-
soph.-hist. Kl., no. 16. Berlin: Reimer, 1919]:
7–68.
Cod: [11,014]
002 **Parasceuastica et poliorcetica**, ed. H. Diels and
E. Schramm, *Exzerpte aus Philons Mechanik B.
VII und VIII* [*Abhandlungen der preussischen
Akademie der Wissenschaften*, Philosoph.-hist.
Kl., no. 12. Berlin: Reimer, 1920]: 17–84.
Cod: [9,739]

0706 **PHILO** Med.
A.D. 1/2: Tarsensis
001 **Fragmentum**, ed. H. Lloyd-Jones and P. Par-
sons, *Supplementum Hellenisticum*. Berlin: De
Gruyter, 1983: 332–333.
fr. 690.
Q: [152]
x01 **Fragmentum ap. Galenum**.
K13.267–269.
Cf. GALENUS Med. (0057 076).

x02 **Fragmenta ap. Oribasium**.
CMG 6.3, pp. 112, 496.
Cf. ORIBASIUS Med. (0722 004–005).
x03 **Fragmentum ap. Paulum**.
CMG 9.2, p. 300.
Cf. PAULUS Med. (0715 001).
x04 **Fragmentum ap. Aëtium** (lib. 9).
Zervos, *Athena* 23, p. 349.
Cf. AËTIUS Med. (0718 009).

2595 **PHILO** Paradox.
A.D. 4/6: Byzantius
001 **De septem orbis spectaculis**, ed. R. Hercher,
*Aeliani de natura animalium, varia historia,
epistolae et fragmenta. Porphyrii philosophi de
abstinentia et de antro nympharum. Philonis
Byzantii de septem orbis spectaculis*. Paris: Didot, 1858: 101–105.
Cod

2638 **PHILO** Poeta
5 B.C.?: Metapontinus vel Nicomedensis
001 **Fragmentum**, ed. H. Lloyd-Jones and P. Parsons, *Supplementum Hellenisticum*. Berlin: De
Gruyter, 1983: 332.
fr. 689a.
Q: [4]

0018 **PHILO JUDAEUS** Phil.
1 B.C.–A.D. 1: Alexandrinus
Bibliography in progress
001 **De opificio mundi**, ed. L. Cohn, *Philonis Alexandrini opera quae supersunt*, vol. 1. Berlin:
Reimer, 1896 (repr. De Gruyter, 1962): 1–60.
Cod: 13,672
002 **Legum allegoriarum libri i–iii**, ed. Cohn, *op.
cit.*, vol. 1, 61–169.
Cod: 33,081
003 **De cherubim**, ed. Cohn, *op. cit.*, vol. 1, 170–
201.
Cod: 7,831
004 **De sacrificiis Abelis et Caini**, ed. Cohn, *op.
cit.*, vol. 1, 202–257.
Cod: 9,828
005 **Quod deterius potiori insidiari soleat**, ed.
Cohn, *op. cit.*, vol. 1, 258–298.
Cod: 11,566
006 **De posteritate Caini**, ed. P. Wendland, *op. cit.*,
vol. 2 (1897; repr. 1962): 1–41.
Cod: 11,366
007 **De gigantibus**, ed. Wendland, *op. cit.*, vol. 2,
42–55.
Cod: 3,341
008 **Quod deus sit immutabilis**, ed. Wendland, *op.
cit.*, vol. 2, 56–94.
Cod: 9,216
009 **De agricultura**, ed. Wendland, *op. cit.*, vol. 2,
95–132
Cod: 9,200
010 **De plantatione**, ed. Wendland, *op. cit.*, vol. 2,
133–169.
Cod: 9,171

011 **De ebrietate**, ed. Wendland, *op. cit.*, vol. 2, 170-214.
Cod: 11,964

012 **De sobrietate**, ed. Wendland, *op. cit.*, vol. 2, 215-228.
Cod: 3,719

013 **De confusione linguarum**, ed. Wendland, *op. cit.*, vol. 2, 229-267.
Cod: 10,751

014 **De migratione Abrahami**, ed. Wendland, *op. cit.*, vol. 2, 268-314.
Cod: 13,146

015 **Quis rerum divinarum heres sit**, ed. Wendland, *op. cit.*, vol. 3 (1898; repr. 1962): 1-71.
Cod: 16,515

016 **De congressu eruditionis gratia**, ed. Wendland, *op. cit.*, vol. 3, 72-109.
Cod: 9,258

017 **De fuga et inventione**, ed. Wendland, *op. cit.*, vol. 3, 110-155.
Cod: 11,419

018 **De mutatione nominum**, ed. Wendland, *op. cit.*, vol. 3, 156-203.
Cod: 13,715

019 **De somniis** (lib. i-ii), ed. Wendland, *op. cit.*, vol. 3, 204-306.
Cf. et 0018 039.
Cod: 27,040

020 **De Abrahamo**, ed. Cohn, *op. cit.*, vol. 4 (1902; repr. 1962): 1-60.
Cod: 13,617

021 **De Josepho**, ed. Cohn, *op. cit.*, vol. 4, 61-118.
Cod: 13,088

022 **De vita Mosis** (lib. i-ii), ed. Cohn, *op. cit.*, vol. 4, 119-268.
Cod: 32,002

023 **De decalogo**, ed. Cohn, *op. cit.*, vol. 4, 269-307.
Cod: 8,619

024 **De specialibus legibus** (lib. i-iv), ed. Cohn, *op. cit.*, vol. 5 (1906; repr. 1962): 1-265.
Cod: 58,217

025 **De virtutibus**, ed. Cohn, *op. cit.*, vol. 5, 266-335.
Cod: 12,421

026 **De praemiis et poenis + De exsecrationibus**, ed. Cohn, *op. cit.*, vol. 5, 336-376.
Cod: 9,303

027 **Quod omnis probus liber sit**, ed. Cohn and S. Reiter, vol. 6 (1915; repr. 1962): 1-45.
Cod: 7,769

028 **De vita contemplativa**, ed. Cohn and Reiter, *op. cit.*, vol. 6, 46-71.
Cod: 4,701

029 **De aeternitate mundi**, ed. Cohn and Reiter, *op. cit.*, vol. 6, 72-119.
Cod: 9,401

030 **In Flaccum**, ed. Cohn and Reiter, *op. cit.*, vol. 6, 120-154.
Cod: 9,102

031 **Legatio ad Gaium**, ed. Cohn and Reiter, *op. cit.*, vol. 6, 155-223.
Cf. et 0018 039.
Cod: 17,824

032 **Hypothetica**, ed. Cohn and Reiter, *op. cit.* (editio minor), vol. 6 (1915): 191-200.
Q

033 **De providentia**, ed. F.H. Colson, *Philo*, vol. 9. Cambridge, Mass: Harvard University Press, 1941 (repr. 1967): 454-506.
Q

034 **Quaestiones in Genesim** (fragmenta), ed. F. Petit, *Les oeuvres de Philon d'Alexandrie*, vol. 33. Paris: Cerf, 1978: 41-228.
Q

035 **Quaestiones in Exodum** (fragmenta), ed. Petit, *op. cit.*, 233-306.
Q

036 **De ebrietate ii**, ed. P. Wendland, *Neu entdeckte Fragmente Philos nebst einer Untersuchung über die ursprüngliche Gestalt der Schrift de sacrificiis Abelis et Caini*. Berlin: Reimer, 1891: 22-25.
Cf. et 0018 011.
Cod

038 Περὶ ἀριθμῶν, ed. K. Staehle, *Die Zahlenmystik bei Philon von Alexandreia*. Leipzig: Teubner, 1931: 19-75.
Q

039 **Fragmenta**, ed. H. Lewy, "Neue Philontexte in der Überarbeitung des Ambrosius. Mit einem Anhang: Neu gefundene griechische Philonfragmente," *Sitzungsberichte der preussischen Akademie der Wissenschaften zu Berlin*, Philosoph.-hist. Kl., 1932. Berlin: De Gruyter, 1932: 80-84.
Legatio ad Gaium (frr. 17-18): pp. 80-81.
De somniis (fr. 19): p. 81.
Fragmenta incertae sedis (frr. 20-32): pp. 81-84.

040 **Fragmenta**, ed. J.R. Harris, *Fragments of Philo Judaeus*. Cambridge: Cambridge University Press, 1886: 6-11, 75-85, 87-110.
Q

041 **De deo** (*P. Berol.* inv. 17027), ed. K. Stahlschmidt, "Eine unbekannte Schrift Philons von Alexandrien (oder eines ihm nahestehenden Verfassers)," *Aegyptus* 22 (1942) 162-165.
Pap

042 **Fragmenta incerti operis**, *P. Oxy.* 18.2158.
Pap

2492 **PHILO Senior** Hist.
1 B.C.

001 **Testimonia**, FGrH #729: 3C:689-690.
NQ

002 **Fragmenta**, FGrH #729: 3C:690-691.
Q

0583 **PHILOCHORUS** Hist.
4-3 B.C.: Atheniensis

001 **Testimonia**, FGrH #328: 3B:97-98.
NQ

002 **Fragmenta**, FGrH #328: 3B:98–160.
fr. 98: *P. Oxy.* 10.1241.
fr. 229: *P. Oxy.* 6.853.
Q, Pap

003 **Fragmentum** (*P. Oslo* 1662), ed. H.J. Mette,
"Die 'Kleinen' griechischen Historiker heute,"
Lustrum 21 (1978) 26.
fr. 34c.
Pap

1794 **PHILOCLES** Comic.
Incertum
001 **Titulus**, ed. T. Kock, *Comicorum Atticorum
fragmenta*, vol. 3. Leipzig: Teubner, 1888: 366.
NQ: 2

1034 **PHILOCLES** Med.
ante A.D. 1
x01 **Fragmentum ap. Galenum.**
K13.1034–1035.
Cf. GALENUS Med. (0057 077).

0312 **PHILOCLES** Trag.
5 B.C.
001 **Fragmenta**, ed. B. Snell, *Tragicorum Graecorum fragmenta*, vol. 1. Göttingen: Vandenhoeck & Ruprecht, 1971: 141–142.
frr. 1, 3–5.
Q: [25]

2415 **PHILOCRATES** Hist.
4 B.C.?
001 **Fragmenta**, FGrH #601: 3B:733.
Q

0205 **PHILODAMUS** Lyr.
4 B.C.: Scarpheus
001 **Paean in Dionysum**, ed. J.U. Powell, *Collectanea Alexandrina*. Oxford: Clarendon Press,
1925 (repr. 1970): 165–169.
Epigr: [593]

002 **Paean in Dionysum** (fragmenta incerti ordinis),
ed. Powell, *op. cit.*, 169–170.
Epigr: [22]

1595 **PHILODEMUS** Phil.
1 B.C.: Gadarensis
001 Κατὰ τῆς ἀποδείξεως ἐκ τῶν Ζήνωνος σχολῶν
(*P. Herc.* 1389, subscriptio), ed. D. Comparetti,
"Relazione sui papiri Ercolanesi," *Atti della R.
Accademia dei Lincei*, ser. 3, vol. 5. Rome:
Salviucci, 1880: 178.
Pap

010 Περὶ αἱρέσεων καὶ φυγῶν (*P. Herc.* 1251), ed.
W. Schmid, *Ethica Epicurea. Pap. Herc. 1251*
[*Studia Herculanensia* 1. Leipzig: Harrassowitz,
1939]: 9–53.
Pap

020 Περὶ αἰσθήσεως (?) (*P. Herc.* 19/698), ed. W.
Scott, *Fragmenta Herculanensia*. Oxford: Cla-
rendon Press, 1885: 257–299.
Pap

030 Περὶ βίων καὶ ἠθῶν (*P. Herc.* 168, col. 1), ed.

E. Bignone, "Epicurea," *Atti della Accademia
delle Scienze di Torino* 47 (1912) 671–673.
Pap

031 Περὶ βίων καὶ ἠθῶν (*P. Herc.* 168, col. 2), ed.
E. Bignone, "Philodemea," *Rivista di filologia e
di istruzione classica* 47 (1919) 416–418.
Pap

040 Περὶ γάμου (?) (*P. Herc.* 312), ed. W. Crönert,
Kolotes und Menedemos. Leipzig: Avenarius,
1906 (repr. Amsterdam: Hakkert, 1965): 126.
Pap

050 Περὶ Ἐπικούρου (*P. Herc.* 1232, subscriptio),
ed. W. Crönert, "Neues über Epikur und einige herkulanensische Rollen," *Rheinisches Museum* 56 (1901) 615.
Pap

053 Περὶ Ἐπικούρου (lib. ii) (*P. Herc.* 1289, sub-
scriptio et coll. 10.1–14, 11.1–8), ed. Crönert,
RhM 56, 615–616.
Pap

054 Περὶ Ἐπικούρου (lib. ii) (*P. Herc.* 1289, frr. 1–
10), ed. D. Bassi, "Φιλοδήμου περὶ Ἐπικούρου
<Α?>, Β," *Miscellanea Ceriani*. Milan: Hoepli,
1910: 513–529.
Pap

055 Περὶ Ἐπικούρου (lib. ii) (*P. Herc.* 1289, fr. 1;
fr. 6, coll. 2–6; subscriptio), ed. A. Vogliano,
*Epicuri et Epicureorum scripta in Herculanensi-
bus papyris servata*. Berlin: Weidmann, 1928:
59–61.
Pap

060 Περὶ ἐπιχαιρεκακίας (?) (*P. Herc.* 1678), ed. D.
Bassi, "Papiro Ercolanese inedito 1678 (Φιλο-
δήμου περὶ ἐπιχαιρεκακίας)," *Rivista Indo-
Greco-Italica* 4 (1920) 65 (n. 1), 66–67 (+ nn.).
Pap

070 Περὶ ἔρωτος (?) (*P. Herc.* 1167, 1384, fragmenta), ed. F. Sbordone, "Nuovi frammenti
dei papiri Ercolanesi," *Parola del passato* 103
(1965) 311–312.
Pap

080 Περὶ εὐσεβείας (*P. Herc.* 229, 242, 243, 247,
248, 433, 1077, 1088, 1098, 1428, 1609, 1610,
1648), ed. T. Gomperz, *Philodem. Über Fröm-
migkeit* [*Herkulanische Studien* 2. Leipzig:
Teubner, 1866]: 5–151.
New edition in preparation by A. Henrichs and
D. Obbink.
Pap

081 Περὶ εὐσεβείας (*P. Herc.* 242, 243, 247, 248,
433, 1088, 1428, 1602, 1609, 1610, 1648), ed.
A. Schober, *Philodemi περὶ εὐσεβείας libelli
partem priorem restituit* [*Diss. Königsberg* (un-
published) (1923)]: 1–103.
New edition in preparation by A. Henrichs and
D. Obbink.
Pap

082 Περὶ εὐσεβείας (*P. Herc.* 242; 243; 247; 248;
433; 1428, fr. 3; 1609), ed. A. Henrichs,
"Philodems de pietate als mythographische
Quelle," *Cronache Ercolanesi* 5 (1975) 8–13,
18–19, 21–22, 35.
Pap

088 Περὶ εὐσεβείας (*P. Herc.* 243, fr. 2.1–27b), ed. A. Henrichs, "Die Kekropidensage im P. Herc. 243: von Kallimachos zu Ovid," *Cronache Ercolanesi* 13 (1983) 37.
Pap

089 Περὶ εὐσεβείας (*P. Herc.* 243, fr. 6.1-19), ed. A. Henrichs, "Ein neues Likymniosfragment bei Philodem," *Zeitschrift für Papyrologie und Epigraphik* 57 (1984) 53–57.
Pap

091 Περὶ εὐσεβείας (*P. Herc.* 243, frr. 3.1–28, 4.3–12; 247, fr. 6a.1-22; 433, fr. 2a.1-21; 1088, fr. 2b.3-10; 1428, frr. 11.1-7, 23.1-9, 23a.1-11; 1610, fr. 3.3-19), ed. A. Henrichs, "Toward a new edition of Philodemus' treatise 'On piety'," *Greek, Roman and Byzantine studies* 13 (1972) 72-73, 77, 78 (n. 32), 80, 84, 86-87, 92, 94.
Pap

095 Περὶ εὐσεβείας (*P. Herc.* 1088, fr. 2a.1-30; 2b.1-7), ed. W. Luppe, "Atlas-Zitate im 1. Buch von Philodems 'de pietate'," *Cronache Ercolanesi* 13 (1983) 45-48, 50-52.
Pap

096 Περὶ εὐσεβείας (*P. Herc.* 1098, fr. 9.13-14), ed. D. Sedley, "The structure of Epicurus' 'On nature'," *Cronache Ercolanesi* 4 (1974) 91.
Pap

098 Περὶ εὐσεβείας (*P. Herc.* 1428, coll. 1-15), ed. A. Henrichs, "Die Kritik der stoischen Theologie im P. Herc. 1428," *Cronache Ercolanesi* 4 (1974) 12-26.
Pap

099 Περὶ εὐσεβείας (*P. Herc.* 1428, frr. 16 et 19), ed. A. Henrichs, "Two doxographical notes: Democritus and Prodicus on religion," *Harvard studies in classical philology* 79 (1975) 96, 107.
Pap

100 Περὶ εὐσεβείας (*P. Herc.* 1428, fr. 16), ed. M. Marcovich, "Democritus on gods: P. Herc. 1428, fr. 16," *Zeitschrift für Papyrologie und Epigraphik* 19 (1975) 244.
Pap

101 Περὶ εὐσεβείας (*P. Herc.* 1428, fr. 16), ed. M. Gigante and G. Indelli, "Democrito nei papiri ercolanesi di Filodemo" in *Democrito e l'atomismo antico* (ed. F. Romano), *Siculorum Gymnasium*, n.s. 31.1 (1980) 451 (n. 3).
Pap

102 Περὶ εὐσεβείας (*P. Herc.* 1602, fr. 7.7, 13-19), ed. A. Henrichs, "Ein Meropiszitat in Philodems de pietate," *Cronache Ercolanesi* 7 (1977) 124.
Pap

113 Περὶ θανάτου (*P. Herc.* 807, col. 18), ed. A. Ievolo, "Testimonianze biografiche e motivi dossografici di Teofrasto nei papiri ercolanesi," *Cronache Ercolanesi* 3 (1973) 96.
Pap

115 Περὶ θανάτου (*P. Herc.* 1050), ed. S. Mekler, "Φιλόδημος περὶ θανάτου δ. Philodemos über den Tod, viertes Buch. Nach der Oxforder und

Neapolitaner Abschrift," *Sitzungsberichte der kaiserlichen Akademie der Wissenchaften*, Philol.-hist. Kl., Bd. 110. Vienna: Gerold, 1886: 305-354.
Pap

116 Περὶ θανάτου (*P. Herc.* 1050), ed. T. Kuiper, *Philodemus over den Dood*. Amsterdam: Paris, 1925: 1-165.
Pap

117 Περὶ θανάτου (*P. Herc.* 1050, col. 3a.3-13), ed. M. Gigante, "Filodemo de morte iv.3," *Rendiconti dell'Accademia di Archeologia, Lettere e Belle Arti di Napoli* 28 (1953) 129.
Pap

118 Περὶ θανάτου (*P. Herc.* 1050, coll. 1.1-24, 2.1-23, 3.26-39, 3a.1-13), ed. Gigante, *RAAN* 28, 119-122, 124-125.
Pap

119 Περὶ θανάτου (*P. Herc.* 1050, coll. 4-9), ed. M. Gigante, "Philodemi de morte IV coll. 4-9," *Parola del passato* 58 (1958) 51-58.
Pap

132 Περὶ θεῶν (lib. i) (*P. Herc.* 26), ed. H. Diels, *Philodemos über die Götter, erstes Buch* [*Abhandlungen der königlich preussischen Akademie der Wissenschaften*, Philosoph.-hist. Kl., 1915, no. 7. Berlin: Reimer, 1916 (repr. Leipzig: Zentralantiquariat der DDR, 1970)]: 4, 9-42, 44-45, 51 (nn. 1, 3-4, 7), 52 (n. 3), 53 + n. 2), 54 (+ n. 1), 55 (n. 1), 56 (n. 5), et passim.
Pap

135 Περὶ θεῶν (lib. iii) (*P. Herc.* 89, subscriptio et fragmenta), ed. Crönert, *Kolotes und Menedemos*, 113 (n. 512).
Pap

138 Περὶ θεῶν (lib. iii) (*P. Herc.* 152/157), ed. H. Diels, *Philodemos über die Götter, drittes Buch* [*Abhandlungen der königlich preussischen Akademie der Wissenschaften*, Philosoph.-hist. Kl., 1916, no. 4. Berlin: Reimer, 1917 (repr. Leipzig: Zentralantiquariat der DDR, 1970)]: 13-69.
Pap

139 Περὶ θεῶν (lib. iii) (*P. Herc.* 152/157, fragmenta), ed. R. Philippson, "Nachträgliches zur epikureischen Götterlehre," *Hermes* 53 (1918) 381, 384-387.
Pap

141 Περὶ θεῶν (lib. iii) (*P. Herc.* 152/157, fr. 75), ed. G. Arrighetti, "Filodemo. Gli dèi iii fr. 75 (Antifane, gli stoici e i πράγματα)," *Cronache Ercolanesi* 13 (1983) 29.
Pap

143 Περὶ θεῶν (?) (*P. Herc.* 1638, frr. 1-3), ed. D. Bassi, "Frammenti inediti di opere di Filodemo (περὶ μουσικῆς–περὶ θεῶν?–περὶ ῥητορικῆς) in papiri Ercolanesi," *Rivista di filologia e di istruzione classica* 38 (1910) 327.
Pap

150 Περὶ κακιῶν (*P. Herc.* 253, fr. 12.1-8), ed. A. Körte, "Augusteer bei Philodem," *Rheinisches Museum* 45 (1890) 172.
Pap

151 Περὶ κακιῶν (*P. Herc.* 253, col. 12.4–5), ed. Crönert, *Kolotes und Menedemos*, 127 (n. 534). Pap

164 Περὶ κολακείας (*P. Herc.* 222, fragmenta), ed. T. Gargiulo, "P. Herc. 222: Filodemo sull'adulazione," *Cronache Ercolanesi* 11 (1981) 106–109. Pap

168 Περὶ κολακείας (*P. Herc.* 223, frr. 1–8), ed. M. Gigante and G. Indelli, "Bione e l'epicureismo," *Cronache Ercolanesi* 8 (1978) 127–131. Pap

172 Περὶ κολακείας (*P. Herc.* 1082), ed. L. Spengel, "Die herculanensischen Rollen," *Philologus*, suppl. 2 (1863) 526–527. Pap

173 Περὶ κολακείας (*P. Herc.* 1082, col. 11.1–7), ed. Crönert, *Kolotes und Menedemos*, 127 (n. 534). Pap

175 Περὶ κολακείας (*P. Herc.* 1089, coll. 1–9), ed. E.A. Méndez, "P. Herc. 1089: Filodemo 'sobre la adulación'," *Cronache Ercolanesi* 13 (1983) 125–126. Pap

179 Περὶ κολακείας (*P. Herc.* 1457, fragmenta), ed. Crönert, *Kolotes und Menedemos*, 91 (n. 447), 130 (n. 542), 178 (n. 34), 182 (n. 91, line 38 + n. 447). Pap

181 Περὶ κολακείας (*P. Herc.* 1457, frr. 11.1–9; 12.4–8; 16.8–9, 13; 3.31–37), ed. U.E. Paoli, "Papiro Ercolanese 1457," *Rivista di filologia e di istruzione classica* 43 (1915) 312, 314–315. Pap

182 Περὶ κολακείας (*P. Herc.* 1457, col. 5, fr. 6–col. 7, v. 20), ed. E. Kondo, "I caratteri di Teofrasto nei papiri ercolanesi," *Cronache Ercolanesi* 1 (1971) 74–75. Pap

185 Περὶ κολακείας (*P. Herc.* 1457, fragmenta), ed. E. Kondo, "Per l'interpretazione del pensiero filodemeo sulla adulazione nel P. Herc. 1457," *Cronache Ercolanesi* 4 (1974) 45, 46 (nn. 26–27), 47 (nn. 30, 33, 42–44), 48 (+ nn. 46, 49–51), 49 (+ nn. 61, 63), 50 (+ n. 65), 51, 52 (+ n. 83), 53 (+ n. 89), 54–55. Pap

190 Περὶ κολακείας (*P. Herc.* 1675, subscriptio et fragmenta), ed. V. de Falco, "Appunti sul περὶ κολακείας di Filodemo, Pap. erc. 1675," *Rivista Indo-Greco-Italica* 10 (1926) 15–26. Pap

199 Περὶ μαθήσεως (?) (*P. Herc.* 862), ed. Scott, *Fragmenta Herculanensia*, 313–325. Pap

200 Περὶ μανίας (*P. Herc.* 57), ed. D. Bassi, "Notizie di papiri Ercolanesi inediti," *Rivista di filologia e di istruzione classica* 45 (1917) 457–458, 460–465. Pap

221 Περὶ μουσικῆς (*P. Herc.* 225, 411, 424, 1094, 1497, 1572, 1575, 1576, 1578, 1583), ed. D.A.

van Krevelen, *Philodemus. De muziek met vertaling en commentaar.* Hilversum: Schipper, 1939: 2–228. Pap

222 Περὶ μουσικῆς (lib. i) (*P. Herc.* 225, 411, 424, 1094, 1572, 1583), ed. G.M. Rispoli, "Il primo libro del περὶ μουσικῆς di Filodemo," *Ricerche sui papiri Ercolanesi* 1. Naples: Giannini, 1969: 39–241. Pap

241 Περὶ οἰκονομίας (*P. Herc.* 1424), ed. C. Jensen, *Philodemi περὶ οἰκονομίας qui dicitur libellus.* Leipzig: Teubner, 1906: 1–76. Pap

251 Περὶ ὁμιλίας (*P. Herc.* 873), ed. F. Amoroso, "Filodemo sulla conversazione," *Cronache Ercolanesi* 5 (1975) 65–68. Pap

261 Περὶ ὀργῆς (*P. Herc.* 182), ed. K. Wilke, *Philodemi de ira liber.* Leipzig: Teubner, 1914: 1–100. Pap

264 Περὶ ὀργῆς (*P. Herc.* 182, fragmenta), ed. R. Philippson, "Philodems Buch über den Zorn. Ein Beitrag zu seiner Wiederherstellung und Auslegung," *Rheinisches Museum* 71 (1916) 427–459. Pap

271 Περὶ παρρησίας (*P. Herc.* 1471), ed. A. Olivieri, *Philodemi περὶ παρρησίας libellus.* Leipzig: Teubner, 1914: 1–68. Pap

274 Περὶ παρρησίας (*P. Herc.* 1471, fragmenta), ed. M. Gigante, "Philodème: sur la liberté de parole," *Actes du 8ᵉ Congrès de l'Association G. Budé.* Paris: Les Belles Lettres, 1969: 196–217. Pap

275 Περὶ παρρησίας (*P. Herc.* 1471, col. 12), ed. M. Gigante, "Testimonianze di Filodemo su Maison," *Cronache Ercolanesi* 1 (1971) 67. Pap

281 Περὶ πλούτου (*P. Herc.* 163), ed. A. Tepedino Guerra, "Il primo libro 'sulla ricchezza' di Filodemo," *Cronache Ercolanesi* 8 (1978) 61–74. Pap

290 Περὶ ποιημάτων (lib. i–iii) (*P. Herc.* 460 + 1073, 994, 1074 + 1081 + 1676), ed. F. Sbordone, "Eufonia e synthesis nella poetica di Filodemo," *Museum philologum Londiniense* 2 (1977) 257–258. Pap

294 Περὶ ποιημάτων (lib. i) (*P. Herc.* 994), ed. F. Sbordone, Φιλοδήμου περὶ ποιημάτων *tractatus tres* [*Ricerche sui papiri Ercolanesi* 2. Naples: Giannini, 1976]: 2–113. Pap

296 Περὶ ποιημάτων (lib. i) (*P. Herc.* 994), ed. M.L. Nardelli, "P. Herc. 994, col. X," *Cronache Ercolanesi* 12 (1982) 135–136. Pap

301 Περὶ ποιημάτων (lib. ii) (*P. Herc.* 460, 1073),

ed. F. Sbordone, Φιλοδήμου περὶ ποιημάτων *tractatus tres* [*Ricerche sui papiri Ercolanesi* 2. Naples: Giannini, 1976]: 117–187.
Pap

304 Περὶ ποιημάτων (lib. ii) (?) (*P. Herc.* 407, 466, fragmenta), ed. R. Schächter, "De Homero in Philodemi περὶ ποιημάτων libro ii laudato," *Eos* 31 (1928) 445.
Pap

310 Περὶ ποιημάτων (lib. ii) (?) (*P. Herc.* 466, fragmentum), ed. F. Sbordone, "Il papiro Ercolanese 444," *Rendiconti dell'Accademia di Archeologia, Lettere e Belle Arti di Napoli* 35 (1960) 109.
Pap

316 Περὶ ποιημάτων (lib. iii) (*P. Herc.* 1074, 1081, 1676), ed. F. Sbordone, Φιλοδήμου περὶ ποιημάτων *tractatus tres* [*Ricerche sui papiri Ercolanesi* 2. Naples: Giannini, 1976]: 191–267.
Pap

317 Περὶ ποιημάτων (lib. iii) (*P. Herc.* 1074.23 + 1081.25, 1091.16 + 1074.22), ed. H.J. Mette, "Zu Philodem, περὶ ποιημάτων," *Zeitschrift für Papyrologie und Epigraphik* 34 (1979) 59–61.
Pap

319 Περὶ ποιημάτων (lib. iii) (*P. Herc.* 1081, fragmenta), ed. C. Jensen, *Philodemos über die Gedichte, fünftes Buch*. Berlin: Weidmann, 1923 (repr. 1973): 143, 147.
Pap

326 Περὶ ποιημάτων (lib. iv) (*P. Herc.* 207), ed. F. Sbordone, "Il quarto libro del περὶ ποιημάτων di Filodemo," *Ricerche sui papiri Ercolanesi* 1. Naples: Giannini, 1969: 299–337.
Pap

328 Περὶ ποιημάτων (lib. iv) (?) (*P. Herc.* 1581, fragmenta), ed. M.L. Nardelli, "La catarsi poetica nel P. Herc. 1581," *Cronache Ercolanesi* 8 (1978) 99–101.
Pap

330 Περὶ ποιημάτων (lib. v) (*P. Herc.* 228, frr. 4, 6), ed. Jensen, *Philodemos über die Gedichte, fünftes Buch*, 154–155.
Pap

332 Περὶ ποιημάτων (lib. v) (*P. Herc.* 228, fr. 2, col. 2; fr. 3, col. 1), ed. C. Coppola, "Frammenti inediti del P. Herc. 228," *Cronache Ercolanesi* 13 (1983) 103.
Pap

336 Περὶ ποιημάτων (lib. v) (*P. Herc.* 1425, 1538), ed. Jensen, *Philodemos über die Gedichte, fünftes Buch*, 3–79.
Pap

338 Περὶ ποιημάτων (lib. v) (*P. Herc.* 1425, 1538, fragmenta), ed. C. Jensen, "Herakleides vom Pontus bei Philodem und Horaz," *Sitzungsberichte der königlich preussischen Akademie der Wissenschaften zu Berlin*. Berlin: Reimer, 1936: 292–320.
Pap

344 Περὶ ποιημάτων (loci incerti) (*P. Herc.* 403,

fragmenta), ed. F. Sbordone, "Ancora un papiro ercolanese della *Poetica* di Filodemo: n. 403," *Studi filologici e storici in onore di Vittorio de Falco*. Naples: Libreria Scientifica, 1971: 344–348, 350–351.
Pap

346 Περὶ ποιημάτων (loci incerti) (*P. Herc.* 444, fragmenta), ed. F. Sbordone, "Il papiro Ercolanese 444," *Rendiconti dell'Accademia di Archeologia, Lettere e Belle Arti di Napoli* 35 (1960) 101–107.
Pap

348 Περὶ ποιημάτων (?) (*P. Herc.* 1275, subscriptio), ed. D. Comparetti, "Relazione sui papiri Ercolanesi," *Atti della R. Accademia dei Lincei*, ser. 3, vol. 5. Rome: Salviucci, 1880: 178.
Pap

350 Περὶ ποιημάτων (?) (*P. Herc.* 1677, fragmenta), ed. T. Gomperz, "Philodem und die ästhetischen Schriften der herculanischen Bibliothek," *Sitzungsberichte der philosophisch-historischen Classe der kaiserlichen Akademie der Wissenschaften* 123. Vienna: Tempsky, 1891: 69.
Pap

362 Περὶ προνοίας (*P. Herc.* 1670), ed. D. Bassi, "Notizie di papiri Ercolanesi inediti," *Rivista di filologia e di istruzione classica* 44 (1916) 51–62.
Pap

366 Περὶ προνοίας (*P. Herc.* 1670, fragmenta), ed. M. Ferrario, "Filodemo sulla provvidenza (*P. Herc.* 1670)," *Cronache Ercolanesi* 2 (1972) 75, 76 (+ n. 48), 77 (+ n. 59), 78 (+ nn. 67–68, 71–72), 79–82, 84–92, 94.
Pap

370 Περὶ ῥητορικῆς (*P. Herc.* 220, 221, 224, 240, 245, 250, 380, 398, 408, 409, 425, 426, 455, 467, 468, 473, 1004, 1007, 1015/832, 1078/1080, 1079, 1086, 1095, 1114, 1117, 1423, 1426, 1427, 1506, 1573, 1580, 1612, 1633, 1669, 1672, 1674), ed. S. Sudhaus, *Philodemi volumina rhetorica*, vols. 1–2. Leipzig: Teubner, 1:1892; 2:1896 (repr. Amsterdam: Hakkert, 1964): 1:1–385; 2:1–303.
Pap

372 Περὶ ῥητορικῆς (*P. Herc.* 224, fr. 12.1–13), ed. Crönert, *Kolotes und Menedemos*, 67.
Pap

374 Περὶ ῥητορικῆς (*P. Herc.* 232, fragmenta), ed. Bassi, *RFIC* 38, 340.
Pap

376 Περὶ ῥητορικῆς (*P. Herc.* 410, coll. 1–4), ed. Bassi, *RFIC* 38, 341–342.
Pap

380 Περὶ ῥητορικῆς (*P. Herc.* 449, frr. 1, 3–4), ed. Bassi, *RFIC* 38, 342–343.
Pap

382 Περὶ ῥητορικῆς (*P. Herc.* 453, coll. 1–4 et fragmentum), ed. Bassi, *RFIC* 38, 343–345.
Pap

384 Περὶ ῥητορικῆς (*P. Herc.* 463), ed. F. Longo

Auricchio, "Frammenti inediti di un libro della retorica di Filodemo (P. Herc. 463)," *Cronache Ercolanesi* 12 (1982) 69–74.
Pap

386 Περὶ ῥητορικῆς (*P. Herc.* 470, coll. 1–5), ed. Bassi, *RFIC* 38, 345–346.
Pap

388 Περὶ ῥητορικῆς (*P. Herc.* 1001, fragmenta), ed. Bassi, *RFIC* 44, 482–483.
Pap

392 Περὶ ῥητορικῆς (*P. Herc.* 1004, fragmenta), ed. M.G. Cappelluzzo, "Per una nuova edizione di un libro della retorica filodemea," *Cronache Ercolanesi* 6 (1976) 70–76.
Pap

400 Περὶ ῥητορικῆς (*P. Herc.* 1118, frr. 1–3), ed. Bassi, *RFIC* 38, 346–347.
Pap

402 Περὶ ῥητορικῆς (*P. Herc.* 1119, frr. 1, 3–5, 8–12), ed. Bassi, *RFIC* 38, 347.
Pap

410 Περὶ ῥητορικῆς (?) (*P. Herc.* 1574, coll. 1–6), ed. Bassi, *RFIC* 38, 348–351.
Pap

412 Περὶ ῥητορικῆς (*P. Herc.* 1605, fragmenta), ed. Bassi, *RFIC* 38, 351.
Pap

414 Περὶ ῥητορικῆς (*P. Herc.* 1606, frr. 1–4), ed. Bassi, *RFIC* 38, 352 (+ n.).
Pap

416 Περὶ ῥητορικῆς (?) (*P. Herc.* 1636, fragmenta), ed. Bassi, *RFIC* 44, 481–482.
Pap

418 Περὶ ῥητορικῆς (*P. Herc.* 1641, frr. 1–3), ed. Bassi, *RFIC* 38, 352.
Pap

424 Περὶ ῥητορικῆς (lib. i–ii) (*P. Herc.* 408, 409, 425, 1079, 1086, 1117, 1573, 1580, 1672, 1674), ed. F. Longo Auricchio, Φιλοδήμου περὶ ῥητορικῆς libri primi et secundi [*Ricerche sui papiri Ercolanesi* 3. Naples: Giannini, 1977]: 3–279.
Pap

426 Περὶ ῥητορικῆς (lib. i) (*P. Herc.* 1790, frr. c + d², g¹ + h², r² + q¹, s² + t¹, u² + v¹), ed. F. Sbordone, "Recenti tentativi di svolgimento dei papiri ercolanesi," *Cronache Ercolanesi* 1 (1971) 33–35.
Pap

431 Περὶ ῥητορικῆς (lib. ii) (*P. Herc.* 1674, coll. 44.19–49, 48.23–49.27), ed. F. Longo Auricchio, "I filosofi megarici nella 'retorica' di Filodemo," *Cronache Ercolanesi* 5 (1975) 77–78.
Pap

432 Περὶ ῥητορικῆς (lib. iv) (*P. Herc.* 1673, col. 13.13–23), ed. A. Ievolo, "Testimonianze biografiche e motivi dossografici di Teofrasto nei papiri ercolanesi," *Cronache Ercolanesi* 3 (1973) 95.
Pap

437 Περὶ ῥητορικῆς (lib. iv, pars ii) (*P. Herc.* 1007,

fragmenta), ed. M. Gigante, "Testimonianze di Filodemo su Maison," *Cronache Ercolanesi* 1 (1971) 65–66.
Pap

442 Περὶ ῥητορικῆς (lib. v) (*P. Herc.* 1669, frr. 1–39b), ed. M. Ferrario, "Frammenti del v libro della 'retorica' di Filodemo," *Cronache Ercolanesi* 10 (1980) 65–79.
Pap

472 Περὶ σημειώσεων (*P. Herc.* 1065), ed. P.H. De Lacy, E.A. De Lacy, M. Gigante, F. Longo Auricchio and A. Tepedino Guerra, *Philodemus: On methods of inference*, rev. edn. [*La scuola di Epicuro* 1. Naples: Bibliopolis, 1978]: 29–87.
Pap

480 Περὶ τῆς Σωκράτους αἱρέσεως (?) (*P. Herc.* 495 (?), 558 (?), fragmenta), ed. W. Crönert, "Herculanensische Bruchstücke einer Geschichte des Sokrates und seiner Schule," *Rheinisches Museum* 57 (1902) 286–290, 292–298.
Pap

482 Περὶ τῆς Σωκράτους αἱρέσεως (?) (*P. Herc.* 495 (?), fragmentum), ed. Bassi, *RFIC* 44, 484.
Pap

492 Περὶ τοῦ καθ᾽ Ὅμηρον ἀγαθοῦ βασιλέως (*P. Herc.* 1507), ed. T. Dorandi, *Filodemo. Il buon re secondo Omero* [*La scuola di Epicuro*, vol. 3. Naples: Bibliopolis, 1982]: 75–120.
Pap

500 Περὶ τῶν Ζήνωνος σχολῶν (*P. Herc.* 300, fr. 9n + *P. Herc.* 1003, subscriptio et fragmenta), ed. W. Crönert, "Die λογικὰ ζητήματα des Chrysippos," *Hermes* 36 (1901) 572–576.
Pap

512 Περὶ τῶν Στωικῶν (*P. Herc.* 155, 339), ed. T. Dorandi, "Filodemo. Gli stoici (P. Herc. 155 e 339)," *Cronache Ercolanesi* 12 (1982) 99–103. olim Περὶ τῶν φιλοσόφων.
Pap

520 Περὶ ὕβρεως (?) (*P. Herc.* 1017, fragmentum), ed. D. Bassi, "Φιλοδήμου περὶ ὕβρεως?," *Rivista Indo-Greco-Italica* 5 (1921) 16.
Pap

532 Περὶ ὑπερηφανίας (*P. Herc.* 1008, fr. 1 + coll. 1–24), ed. C. Jensen, *Philodemi περὶ κακιῶν liber decimus.* Leipzig: Teubner, 1911: 3–43. Cf. et 1595 534.
Pap

534 Περὶ ὑπερηφανίας (*P. Herc.* 1008, fr. 1 + coll. 1–10), ed. C. Jensen, Ein neuer Brief Epikurs [*Abhandlungen der Gesellschaft der Wissenschaften zu Göttingen*, Philol.-hist. Kl., ser. 3, no. 5. Berlin: Weidmann, 1933]: 13–33.
Pap

536 Περὶ ὑπερηφανίας (*P. Herc.* 1008, subscriptio), ed. M. Capasso, "Il presunto papiro di Fania," *Cronache Ercolanesi* 8 (1978) 157.
Pap

551 Περὶ φιλαργυρίας (?) (*P. Herc.* 465, fr. 12.15–21), ed. Crönert, *RhM* 56, 625.
Pap

553 Περὶ φιλαργυρίας (?) (*P. Herc.* 1645, fragmentum), ed. W. Crönert, "Fälschungen in den Abschriften der herculanensischen Rollen," *Rheinisches Museum* 53 (1898) 594.
Pap

560 Περὶ φιλοδοξίας (?) (*P. Herc.* 1025, fragmentum), ed. Crönert, *Kolotes und Menedemos*, 91 (n. 447).
Pap

572 Περὶ χάριτος (*P. Herc.* 1414), ed. A. Tepedino Guerra, "Filodemo sulla gratitudine," *Cronache Ercolanesi* 7 (1977) 100–102.
Pap

582 Πραγματεῖαι (*P. Herc.* 310 (?), 1418), ed. C. Diano, *Lettere di Epicuro e dei suoi*. Florence: Sansoni, 1946: 7–20, 27 (+ n. 1), 29–30 (+ app. crit.), 32, 40.
Pap

588 Πραγματεῖαι (*P. Herc.* 1418), ed. L. Spina, "Il trattato di Filodemo su Epicuro e altri (*P. Herc.* 1418)," *Cronache Ercolanesi* 7 (1977) 49–68.
Pap

595 Πρὸς τοὺς [σοφιστάς] (*P. Herc.* 1005, fragmenta), ed. F. Sbordone, *Philodemi adversus [sophistas]*. Naples: Loffredo, 1947: 3–113, 131–133.
Pap

602 Σύνταξις τῶν φιλοσόφων (*P. Herc.* 164, 1021), ed. S. Mekler, *Academicorum philosophorum index Herculanensis*, 2nd edn. Berlin: Weidmann, 1958: 3–113.
Pap

606 Σύνταξις τῶν φιλοσόφων (*P. Herc.* 327, frr. 1–6b), ed. Crönert, *Kolotes und Menedemos*, 128.
Pap

610 Σύνταξις τῶν φιλοσόφων (*P. Herc.* 1018), ed. A. Traversa, *Index stoicorum Herculanensis*. Genoa: University of Genoa Press, 1952: 1–110, 117.
Pap

616 Σύνταξις τῶν φιλοσόφων (*P. Herc.* 1021, coll. 1*.1–2.5, 2.36–43, 3.1–14, 3.34–5.19, 10.16–24), ed. K. Gaiser, "La biografia di Platone in Filodemo: nuovi dati dal P. Herc. 1021," *Cronache Ercolanesi* 13 (1983) 55–60.
Pap

618 Σύνταξις τῶν φιλοσόφων (*P. Herc.* 1508, coll. 3–5, fragmenta), ed. Crönert, *Kolotes und Menedemos*, 131.
Pap

632 Incerti operis de Epicuro fragmenta (*P. Herc.* 671, 861, fragmenta), ed. W. Crönert, "Die λογικὰ ζητήματα des Chrysippos," *Hermes* 36 (1901) 577–578.
Pap

636 Incerti operis de Epicuro fragmentum (*P. Herc.* 986, frr. 2.4–8, 12.8–10, 14.6, 21.1–8, 24.6–10), ed. Crönert, *RhM* 56, 618–619.
Pap

638 Incerti operis de Epicuro fragmenta (*P. Herc.*

998, frr. 11.2–8, 12.4–8, 16.4–7), ed. Crönert, *RHM* 56, 619–620.
Pap

640 Incerti operis de Epicuro fragmentum (*P. Herc.* 1036), ed. Crönert, *RhM* 56, 625.
Pap

642 Incerti operis de Epicuro fragmentum (*P. Herc.* 1084, fr. 1.1–16), ed. Crönert, *RhM* 56, 616–617.
Pap

644 Incerti operis de Epicuro fragmentum (*P. Herc.* 1188), ed. Crönert, *RhM* 56, 625 (+ n. 3).
Pap

646 Incerti operis de Epicuro fragmentum (*P. Herc.* 1188), ed. Crönert, *Kolotes und Menedemos*, 184 (n. 133).
Pap

648 Incerti operis de Epicuro fragmenta (*P. Herc.* 1735, frr. 2 + 1, 10 + 3), ed. F. Sbordone, "Recenti tentativi di svolgimento dei papiri ercolanesi," *Cronache Ercolanesi* 1 (1971) 31–32.
Pap

660 Incerti operis fragmenta (*P. Herc.* 118, fragmenta), ed. Crönert, *RhM* 56, 615.
Pap

662 Incerti operis fragmenta (*P. Herc.* 300 (?), fr. 6), ed. H. Usener, *Epicurea*. Leipzig: Teubner, 1887 (repr. Stuttgart: 1966): 346.
fr. 161a.
Pap

664 Incerti operis fragmenta (*P. Herc.* 415, fragmenta), ed. D. Bassi, "Papiri ercolanesi inediti," *Classici e Neolatini* 3 (1908) 18–19.
Pap

666 Incerti operis fragmenta (*P. Herc.* 421, fragmenta), ed. Bassi, *Classici et Neolatini* 3, 10.
Pap

668 Incerti operis fragmenta (*P. Herc.* 461, frr. 1+2, 3+4, 6+5, 8+9), ed. Sbordone, *CronErc* 1, 38–39.
Pap

672 Incerti operis fragmentum (*P. Herc.* 1504), ed. Sbordone, *CronErc* 1, 30.
Pap

674 Incerti operis fragmenta (*P. Herc.* 1692, coll. 1–5), ed. Bassi, *RFIC* 38, 335–340.
Pap

678 Incerti operis fragmentum (*P. Herc.* 1784, fragmentum), ed. F. Sbordone, "Nuovi frammenti dei papiri Ercolanesi," *Parola del passato* 103 (1965) 313.
Pap

730 Epigrammata, AG 5.4, 13, 25, 46, 107, 112, 115, 120–121, 123–124, 126, 131–132, 306, 308(?); 6.246(?), 349; 7.222; 9.412, 570; 10.21, 103; 11.30, 34–35, 41, 44, 318; 12.173; 16.234.
AG 5.8, 24: Cf. MELEAGER Epigr. (1492 001).
AG 5.80: Cf. PLATO Phil. (0059 039).
AG 5.113; 6.246(?): Cf. (et) Marcus ARGENTARIUS Rhet. et Epigr. (0132 001).

AG 5.114: Cf. Quintus MAECIUS Epigr. (1474 001).

AG 5.308(?): Cf. et ANTIPHILUS Epigr. (0118 001).

Q

x01 **Vita Philonidis** (*P. Herc.* 1044).
Crönert, pp. 942–959.
Cf. ANONYMUS EPICUREUS Phil. (1779 003).

1596 **PHILOLAUS** Phil.
5 B.C.: Crotoniensis

001 **Testimonia**, ed. H. Diels and W. Kranz, *Die Fragmente der Vorsokratiker*, vol. 1, 6th edn. Berlin: Weidmann, 1951 (repr. Dublin: 1966): 398–406.
test. 1–29.
NQ

002 **Fragmenta**, ed. Diels and Kranz, *op. cit.*, 406–419.
frr. 1–23.
Q

003 **Fragmenta** [Sp.], ed. H. Thesleff, *The Pythagorean texts of the Hellenistic period.* Åbo: Åbo Akademi, 1965: 149–151.
Q: 258

x01 **Epigramma**.
AG 7.126.
Cf. DIOGENES LAERTIUS Biogr. (0004 002).

1598 **PHILOMNESTUS** Hist.
ante A.D. 3

001 **Fragmenta**, FGrH #527: 3B:504.
Q

0492 **PHILONIDES** Comic.
5 B.C.

001 **Fragmenta**, ed. T. Kock, *Comicorum Atticorum fragmenta*, vol. 1. Leipzig: Teubner, 1880: 254–257.
frr. 1–18 + tituli.
Q: 105

002 **Fragmenta**, ed. A. Meineke, *Fragmenta comicorum Graecorum*, vol. 2.1. Berlin: Reimer, 1839 (repr. De Gruyter, 1970): 421–424.
Q: 51

003 **Fragmenta**, ed. J. Demiańczuk, *Supplementum comicum.* Krakau: Nakładem Akademii, 1912 (repr. Hildesheim: Olms, 1967): 73.
frr. 1–2.
Q: 24

1934 **PHILONIDES** Hist.
post 4 B.C.: Cretensis

001 **Testimonia**, FGrH #121: 2B:627.
test. 1a: *Inscr. Olympia* 5.276.
NQ

002 **Fragmentum**, FGrH #121: 2B:627.
Q

1036 **PHILONIDES** Med.
A.D. 1: Dyrrachinus, Siculus

x01 **Fragmentum ap. Galenum**.
K13.978.
Cf. GALENUS Med. (0057 077).

x02 **Fragmentum ap. Athenaeum**.
Deipnosophistae 15.675a–e.
Cf. ATHENAEUS Soph. (0008 001).

PHILONIDES Epicureus Phil.
P. Herc. 1044.
Cf. VITA PHILONIDIS (1748 x01).

0493 **PHILOSTEPHANUS** Comic.
Incertum

001 **Fragmentum**, ed. T. Kock, *Comicorum Atticorum fragmenta*, vol. 3. Leipzig: Teubner, 1888: 393.
fr. 1.
Q: 28

002 **Fragmentum**, ed. A. Meineke, *Fragmenta comicorum Graecorum*, vol. 4. Berlin: Reimer, 1841 (repr. De Gruyter, 1970): 589.
Q: 28

0584 **PHILOSTEPHANUS** Hist.
3 B.C.: Cyrenaeus

001 **De mirabilibus fluviis**, ed. A. Giannini, *Paradoxographorum Graecorum reliquiae.* Milan: Istituto Editoriale Italiano, 1965: 21–23.
Q

002 **Fragmenta**, FHG 3: 28–34.
frr. 1–37.
Q

003 **Fragmenta**, ed. H. Lloyd-Jones and P. Parsons, *Supplementum Hellenisticum.* Berlin: De Gruyter, 1983: 335.
frr. 691, 693.
Q: [28]

x01 **Epigramma**.
App. Anth. 3.66b addenda: Cf. EPIGRAMMATICI in *App. Anth.* (7052 008).

2058 **PHILOSTORGIUS** Scr. Eccl.
A.D. 4–5
Bibliography in progress

001 **Historia ecclesiastica**, ed. F. Winkelmann (post J. Bidez), *Philostorgius. Kirchengeschichte* [*Die griechischen christlichen Schriftsteller* 21, 2nd edn. Berlin: Akademie-Verlag, 1972]: 1–150.
Cod

002 **Fragmenta ex vita Constantini** (Cod. Angelicus 22), ed. Winkelmann (post Bidez), *op. cit.*, 8–17, 20–24, 26.
Cod

003 **Fragmenta ex passione Artemi**, ed. Winkelmann, (post Bidez), *op. cit.*, 151–157 et passim.
Cod

004 **Supplementa Philostorgiana**, MPG 65: 624–628.
Cod

005 **Fragmenta ex Suda**, MPG 65: 629–637.
Cod

006 **Epigramma**, AG 9.193.
AG 9.194: Cf. ANONYMI EPIGRAMMATICI
(0138 001).
Q: 10

2527 **PHILOSTRATUS** Hist.
1 B.C.?
001 **Fragmentum**, FGrH #789: 3C:801–802.
Q

2145 **PHILOSTRATUS** Hist.
A.D. 3: Atheniensis
001 **Testimonium**, FGrH #99: 2A:452.
NQ
002 **Fragmentum**, FGrH #99: 2A:452.
Q

0638 **Flavius PHILOSTRATUS** Soph.
A.D. 2–3
001 **Vita Apollonii**, ed. C.L. Kayser, *Flavii Philostrati opera*, vol. 1. Leipzig: Teubner, 1870
(repr. Hildesheim: Olms, 1964): 1–344.
Cod: [87,068]
002 **Apollonii epistulae**, ed. Kayser, *op. cit.*, vol. 1,
345–368.
Cod: [5,519]
003 **Vitae sophistarum**, ed. Kayser, *op. cit.*, vol. 2
(1871; repr. 1964): 1–127.
Cod: [29,914]
004 **Heroicus**, ed. Kayser, *op. cit.*, vol. 2, 128–219.
Cod: [22,611]
005 **Nero**, ed. Kayser, *op. cit.*, vol. 2, 220–224.
Cod: [1,045]
006 **Epistulae et dialexeis**, ed. Kayser, *op. cit.*, vol.
2, 225–260.
Cod: [7,783]
007 **De gymnastica**, ed. Kayser, *op. cit.*, vol. 2,
261–293.
Cod: [7,931]
009 **Epigramma**, AG 16.110.
Q: 48

0652 **PHILOSTRATUS Junior** Soph.
A.D. 3: Lemnius
001 **Imagines**, ed. C.L. Kayser, *Flavii Philostrati
opera*, vol. 2. Leipzig: Teubner, 1871 (repr.
Hildesheim: Olms, 1964): 390–420.
Cod: [7,449]

1600 **PHILOSTRATUS Major** Soph.
A.D. 2–3: Lemnius
001 **Imagines**, ed. O. Benndorf and K. Schenkl,
Philostrati maioris imagines. Leipzig: Teubner,
1893: 3–129.
Cod: [23,433]

1037 **PHILOTAS** Med.
A.D. 2?
x01 **Fragmenta ap. Galenum**.
K12.752, 838; **13**.745.
Cf. GALENUS Med. (0057 076–077).

1601 **PHILOXENUS** Epigr.
3 B.C.
001 **Epigramma**, AG 9.319.
Q: 25

1602 **PHILOXENUS** Gramm.
1 B.C.: Alexandrinus
001 **Fragmenta**, ed. C. Theodoridis, *Die Fragmente
des Grammatikers Philoxenos*. Berlin: De Gruyter, 1976: 93–387.
Q

0379 **PHILOXENUS** Lyr.
5–4 B.C.: Cytherius
001 **Fragmenta**, ed. D.L. Page, *Poetae melici
Graeci*. Oxford: Clarendon Press, 1962 (repr.
1967 (1st edn. corr.)): 423, 426–428, 430–432.
frr. 2, 6–11, 15–20.
Q: [111]
002 **Tituli**, ed. D.L. Page, *Poetae melici Graeci*.
Oxford: Clarendon Press, 1962 (repr. 1967 (1st
edn. corr.)): 423, 428–429.
NQ

0380 **PHILOXENUS** Lyr.
5–4 B.C.: fort. Leucadius
001 **Fragmenta**, ed. D.L. Page, *Poetae melici
Graeci*. Oxford: Clarendon Press, 1962 (repr.
1967 (1st edn. corr.)): 433–441.
frr. a–e.
Q: [815]
002 **Fragmentum** [Sp.], ed. J.U. Powell, *Collectanea
Alexandrina*. Oxford: Clarendon Press, 1925
(repr. 1970): 251.
fr. 9.
Q: [14]

1039 **Claudius PHILOXENUS** Med.
2–1 B.C.: Alexandrinus
x01 **Fragmenta ap. Galenum**.
K12.683–684, 731, 735, 736, 743; **13**.539–540,
645, 742–743, 819–820.
Cf. GALENUS Med. (0057 076–077).
x02 **Fragmentum ap. Paulum**.
CMG, vol. 9.2, p. 303.
Cf. PAULUS Med. (0715 001).

2344 **PHILTEAS** Hist.
ante 4 B.C.?
001 **Testimonium**, FGrH #498: 3B:469.
NQ
002 **Fragmenta**, FGrH #498: 3B:469–470.
Q

0671 **PHILUMENUS** Med.
A.D. 2: Alexandrinus
Cf. et HERODOTUS et PHILUMENUS Med.
(0910).
001 **De venenatis animalibus eorumque remediis**,
ed. M. Wellmann, *Philumeni de venenatis animalibus eorumque remediis* [*Corpus medicorum*

Graecorum, vol. 10.1.1. Leipzig: Teubner,
1908]: 4–40.
Cod: [9,385]

0494 **PHILYLLIUS** Comic.
5–4 B.C.
001 **Fragmenta**, ed. T. Kock, *Comicorum Atticorum fragmenta*, vol. 1. Leipzig: Teubner, 1880:
781–789.
frr. 1–8, 10–15, 17–23, 25–33 + tituli.
Q: 238
002 **Fragmenta**, ed. A. Meineke, *Fragmenta comicorum Graecorum*, vol. 2.2. Berlin: Reimer, 1840
(repr. De Gruyter, 1970): 857–865.
Q: 207
003 **Fragmenta**, ed. J. Demiańczuk, *Supplementum
comicum*. Krakau: Nakładem Akademii, 1912
(repr. Hildesheim: Olms, 1967): 73–74.
frr. 1–2.
Q: 4
004 **Titulus**, ed. C. Austin, *Comicorum Graecorum
fragmenta in papyris reperta*. Berlin: De Gruyter, 1973: 201.
NQ: 2

1603 <**PHINTYS**> Phil.
3 B.C.
001 **Fragmenta**, ed. H. Thesleff, *The Pythagoréan
texts of the Hellenistic period*. Åbo: Åbo Akademi, 1965: 151–154.
Q: 741

0585 **Publius Aelius PHLEGON** Paradox.
A.D. 2: Trallianus
001 **De Mirabilibus**, ed. A. Giannini, *Paradoxographorum Graecorum reliquiae*. Milan: Istituto
Editoriale Italiano, 1965: 170–218.
Cod: [5,247]
002 **Testimonia**, FGrH #257: 2B:1159–1160.
NQ
003 **Fragmenta**, FGrH #257: **2B**:1160–1194;
3B:744–745 addenda.
Cf. et 0585 x02.
Q, Cod
x01 **Fragmentum ap. Paradoxographum Florenti-
num 35** [Dub.].
PGR, p. 324.
PARADOXOGRAPHUS FLORENTINUS (0580
001).
x02 **Chronicon Olympicum** (fort. auctore Phle-
gonte).
FGrH #257a.
Cf. ANONYMI HISTORICI (FGrH) (1139 019).
x03 **Victores Olympici** (fort. auctore Phlegonte vel
Eratosthene).
FGrH #415.
Cf. ANONYMI HISTORICI (FGrH) (1139 026).

2124 **PHOCAS Diaconus** Epigr.
Incertum
001 **Epigramma**, AG 9.772.
Q: 13

2272 **PHOCUS** Phil.
Incertum: Samius
001 **Titulus**, ed. H. Diels and W. Kranz, *Die Frag-
mente der Vorsokratiker*, vol. 1, 6th edn. Berlin:
Weidmann, 1951 (repr. Dublin: 1966): 41.
NQ

PHOCYLIDEA
Cf. Pseudo-PHOCYLIDES Gnom. (1605).

1604 **PHOCYLIDES** Eleg. et Gnom.
6 B.C.: Milesius
001 **Sententiae**, ed. E. Diehl, *Anthologia lyrica
Graeca*, fasc. 1, 3rd edn. Leipzig: Teubner,
1949: 57–60.
frr. 1–[17].
Q: [270]
002 **Epigramma**, AG 10.117.
Q: 30

1605 **Pseudo-PHOCYLIDES** Gnom.
A.D. 1/2
001 **Sententiae**, ed. D. Young (post E. Diehl), *Theognis*. Leipzig: Teubner, 1971: 95–112.
Cod: [1,606]

2596 **PHOEBAMMON** Soph.
A.D. 5/6: Antinoupolitanus
Bibliography in progress
001 **De figuris**, ed. L. Spengel, *Rhetores Graeci*, vol.
3. Leipzig: Teubner, 1856 (repr. Frankfurt am
Main: Minerva, 1966): 43–56.
Cod

0495 **PHOENICIDES** Comic.
3 B.C.
001 **Fragmenta**, ed. T. Kock, *Comicorum Atticorum fragmenta*, vol. 3. Leipzig: Teubner, 1888:
333–334.
frr. 1–4 + titulus.
Q: 200
002 **Fragmenta**, ed. A. Meineke, *Fragmenta comicorum Graecorum*, vol. 4. Berlin: Reimer, 1841
(repr. De Gruyter, 1970): 509–511.
Q: 200
003 **Titulus**, ed. C. Austin, *Comicorum Graecorum
fragmenta in papyris reperta*. Berlin: De Gruyter, 1973: 201.
NQ: 1

1606 **PHOENIX** Iamb.
3 B.C.: Colophonius
001 **Fragmenta**, ed. J.U. Powell, *Collectanea Alexandrina*. Oxford: Clarendon Press, 1925 (repr.
1970): 231–236.
frr. 1–6.
fr. 6: *P. Heidelb.* inv. 310.
Q, Pap: [473]
002 **Fragmenta** (*P. Strassb.* [W.G. 304–307]), ed.
A.D. Knox, *Herodes, Cercidas, and the Greek
choliambic poets*. Cambridge, Mass.: Harvard

University Press, 1929 (repr. 1967): 256–262.
frr. 4–6, 8.
Pap

1788 PHORMIS Comic.
vel Phormus
Incertum
001 **Fragmentum**, ed. T. Kock, *Comicorum Atticorum fragmenta*, vol. 3. Leipzig: Teubner, 1888: 393.
fr. 1.
Q: 3
002 **Titulus**, ed. G. Kaibel, *Comicorum Graecorum fragmenta*, vol. 1.1 [*Poetarum Graecorum fragmenta*, vol. 6.1. Berlin: Weidmann, 1899]: 148.
NQ: 2

1607 PHORONIS
7 B.C.?
001 **Fragmenta**, ed. G. Kinkel, *Epicorum Graecorum fragmenta*, vol. 1. Leipzig: Teubner, 1877: 210–211.
frr. 1–2, 4–5.
Q: [78]

4040 PHOTIUS Scr. Eccl.
A.D. 9: Constantinopolitanus
Bibliography in progress
001 **Bibliotheca**, ed. R. Henry, *Photius. Bibliothèque*, 8 vols. Paris: Les Belles Lettres, 1:1959; 2:1960; 3:1962; 4:1965; 5:1967; 6:1971; 7:1974; 8:1977: 1:1–191; 2:8–203; 3:8–227; 4:8–174; 5:8–201; 6:8–194; 7:8–228; 8:8–214.
Cod: 360,682
002 **Quaestiones ad Amphilochium**, MPG 101: 45–1172.
Cod
003 **Contra Manichaeos**, MPG 102: 16–264.
Cod
004 **De spiritus sancti mystagogia**, MPG 102: 280–400.
Cod
005 **Homilia 1: In sanctae Mariae nativitatem**, MPG 102: 548–561.
Cod
006 **Homilia 3: In dedicatione novae basilicae**, MPG 102: 564–573.
Cod
007 **Homilia 4: Sancti Athanasii encomium**, MPG 102: 576.
Cod
008 **Carmina**, MPG 102: 576–584.
Cod
009 **Epistulae**, MPG 102: 585–989.
Cod
010 **Syntagma canonum**, MPG 104: 441–976.
Cod
011 **Epigramma**, AG 9.203.
Q: 65
012 **Interrogationes decem**, MPG 104: 1220–1232.
Cod

013 **Nomocanon**, MPG 104: 980–1217.
Cod
014 **Fragmenta in epistulam ad Romanos** (in catenis), ed. K. Staab, *Pauluskommentar aus der griechischen Kirche aus Katenenhandschriften gesammelt*. Münster: Aschendorff, 1933: 470–544.
Q
015 **Fragmenta in epistulam i ad Corinthios** (in catenis), ed. Staab, *op. cit.*, 544–583.
Q
016 **Fragmenta in epistulam ii ad Corinthios** (in catenis), ed. Staab, *op. cit.*, 583–604.
Q
017 **Fragmenta in epistulam ad Galatas** (in catenis), ed. Staab, *op. cit.*, 604–610.
Q
018 **Fragmenta in epistulam ad Ephesios** (in catenis), ed. Staab, *op. cit.*, 611–621.
Q
019 **Fragmenta in epistulam ad Philippenses** (in catenis), ed. Staab, *op. cit.*, 621–630.
Q
020 **Fragmenta in epistulam ad Colossenses** (in catenis), ed. Staab, *op. cit.*, 631–633.
Q
021 **Fragmenta in epistulam i ad Thessalonicenses** (in catenis), ed. Staab, *op. cit.*, 633–636.
Q
022 **Fragmenta in epistulam ii ad Thessalonicenses** (in catenis), ed. Staab, *op. cit.*, 636.
Q
023 **Fragmenta in epistulam i ad Timotheum** (in catenis), ed. Staab, *op. cit.*, 636–637.
Q
024 **Fragmentum in epistulam ii ad Timotheum** (in catenis), ed. Staab, *op. cit.*, 637.
Q
025 **Fragmentum in epistulam ad Philemonem** (in catenis), ed. Staab, *op. cit.*, 637.
Q
026 **Fragmenta in epistulam ad Hebraeos** (in catenis), ed. Staab, *op. cit.*, 637–652.
Q
028 **Commentarii in Matthaeum** (in catenis), ed. J. Reuss, *Matthäus-Kommentare aus der griechischen Kirche* [*Texte und Untersuchungen* 61. Berlin: Akademie-Verlag, 1957]: 270–337.
Q
027 **Commentarii in Joannem** (in catenis), ed. J. Reuss, *Johannes-Kommentare aus der griechischen Kirche* [*Texte und Untersuchungen* 89. Berlin: Akademie-Verlag, 1966]: 359–412.
Q

1608 PHRYNICHUS Attic.
A.D. 2: Arabius
001 **Praeparatio sophistica**, ed. J. de Borries, *Phrynichi sophistae praeparatio sophistica*. Leipzig: Teubner, 1911: 1–129.
Cod: [16,663]
002 **Eclogae**, ed. E. Fischer, *Die Ekloge des Phry-*

nichos. Berlin: De Gruyter, 1974: 60–109.
Cod: [9,573]

003 **Eclogae** (familia q), ed. Fischer, *op. cit.*, 109–124.
Cod: [3,910]

004 **Eclogae** (familia T), ed. Fischer, *op. cit.*, 124–130.
Cod: [1,512]

005 **Fragmenta**, ed. de Borries, *op. cit.*, 130–180.
frr. 1–370.
Q, Cod: [8,184]

0496 **PHRYNICHUS** Comic.
5 B.C.: Atheniensis

001 **Fragmenta**, ed. T. Kock, *Comicorum Atticorum fragmenta*, vol. 1. Leipzig: Teubner, 1880: 369–391.
frr. 1–3, 5–10, 13–15, 18–25, 27–29, 31–40, 43, 45–46, 48, 50–70, 73–95.
Q: 550

002 **Fragmenta**, ed. A. Meineke, *Fragmenta comicorum Graecorum*, vol. 2.1. Berlin: Reimer, 1839 (repr. De Gruyter, 1970): 580–584, 586–590, 592–606.
Q: 502

003 **Fragmenta**, ed. J. Demiańczuk, *Supplementum comicum*. Krakau: Nakładem Akademii, 1912 (repr. Hildesheim: Olms, 1967): 74–76.
frr. 1–8.
Q: 36

004 **Tituli**, ed. C. Austin, *Comicorum Graecorum fragmenta in papyris reperta*. Berlin: De Gruyter, 1973: 201.
NQ: 3

005 **Fragmentum**, ed. Meineke, *op. cit.*, vol. 5.1 (1857; repr. 1970): xcvi.
Q: [8]

0303 **PHRYNICHUS** Trag.
6 B.C.: Atheniensis

001 **Fragmenta**, ed. B. Snell, *Tragicorum Graecorum fragmenta*, vol. 1. Göttingen: Vandenhoeck & Ruprecht, 1971: 72–79.
frr. 1, 1a, 2, 3a, 4, 5–14, 16–17, 20–24.
Q: [223]

x01 **Epigramma demonstrativum.**
App. Anth. 3.18: Cf. EPIGRAMMATICI in *App. Anth.* (7052 003).

0876 **PHRYNICHUS II** Trag.
Incertum: Atheniensis

001 **Tituli**, ed. B. Snell, *Tragicorum Graecorum fragmenta*, vol. 1. Göttingen: Vandenhoeck & Ruprecht, 1971: 323.
NQ

1609 **PHYLARCHUS** Hist.
3 B.C.: Atheniensis

001 **Testimonia**, FGrH #81: 2A:161–162.
NQ

002 **Fragmenta**, FGrH #81: 2A:162–189.
Q

003 **Fragmentum**, ed. H. Lloyd-Jones and P. Parsons, *Supplementum Hellenisticum*. Berlin: De Gruyter, 1983: 336.
fr. 694a.
Q: [17]

1038 **PHYLOTIMUS** Med.
3 B.C.: Cous

x01 **Fragmenta ap. Galenum.**
K6.720, 726–727 in CMG, vol. 5.4.2, pp. 368, 372.
Cf. GALENUS Med. (0057 037).

x02 **Fragmenta ap. Oribasium.**
CMG, vol. 6.1.1, pp. 64, 107, 151.
Cf. ORIBASIUS Med. (0722 001).

x03 **Fragmenta ap. Athenaeum.**
Deipnosophistae 2.53f; **3.79a.**
Cf. ATHENAEUS Soph. (0008 001).

2654 *PHYSIOLOGUS GRAECUS*
A.D. 2/4?

001 **Physiologus**, ed. F. Sbordone, *Physiologus*. Rome: Dante Alighieri-Albrighi, Segati, 1936 (repr. Hildesheim: Olms, 1976): 1–325.
Cod

002 **Physiologus**, ed. D. Offermanns, *Der Physiologus nach den Handschriften G und M*. Meisenheim am Glan: Hain, 1966.
Cod

003 **Physiologus**, ed. D. Kaimakis, *Der Physiologus nach der ersten Redaktion*. Meisenheim am Glan: Hain, 1974: 6a–141a, 143b, 148b.
Cod

2963 **PIERIUS** Scr. Eccl.
A.D. 3–4: Alexandrinus

001 **Fragmentum** (ap. Philippum Sidensem), ed. C. de Boor, *Neue Fragmente des Papias, Hegesippus und Pierius in bisher unbekannten Excerpten aus der Kirchengeschichte des Philippus Sidetes* [*Texte und Untersuchungen* 5.2. Leipzig: Hinrichs, 1888]: 170–171.
Q

0258 **PIGRES** Eleg.
6–5 B.C.

001 **Fragmentum**, ed. M.L. West, *Iambi et elegi Graeci*, vol. 2. Oxford: Clarendon Press, 1972: 93.
Q: [15]

0033 **PINDARUS** Lyr.
6–5 B.C.: Boeotus

001 **Olympia**, ed. H. Maehler (post B. Snell), *Pindari carmina cum fragmentis*, pt. 1, 5th edn. Leipzig: Teubner, 1971: 2–6, 8–15, 17–34, 36–40, 42–56, 58.
Cod: 6,102

002 **Pythia**, ed. Maehler (post Snell), *op. cit.*, 59–64, 66–91, 93–121.
Cod: 7,719

003 **Nemea**, ed. Maehler (post Snell), *op. cit.*, 122–
139, 141–143, 145–162.
Cod: 5,119

004 **Isthmia**, ed. Maehler (post Snell), *op. cit.*, 163–
181, 183–184, 186–190.
Cod: 3,066

005 **Fragmenta**, ed. Maehler (post Snell), *op. cit.*,
pt. 2, 4th edn. (1975): 1–161, 215–216.
Isthmia, frr. 1–2, 4–8, 10–14, 15 (= 6a(d)), 16–
27, 28 (= 6a(c)): pp. 1–7.
Hymni, frr. 29–30, 32–40, 42–47, 49, 50–51,
(= 33a), 51a–51b, 51d, 51f: pp. 8–15.
Paeanes, frr. 52a–52w, 57, 59–61, 66–67, 70:
pp. 16–71.
Dithyrambi, frr. 70a–70d, 71–72, 74, 74a, 75–
78, 80, 81 (= post 70b), 82, 83 (= 75), 84–85,
86, 86a, pp. 72–84 70b), 82, 83 (= 75), 84–85,
86, 86a, 87 (= 33c), 88 (= 33D): pp. 72–84.
Prosodia, frr. 89a–89b, 92–94: pp. 85–86.
Parthenia, frr. 94a–97, 99, 104b, 104c–104d (=
94a–94b): pp. 87–94.
Hyporchemata, frr. 105–106, 107a–107b, 108–
113, 116–117 (= 94c): pp. 95–99.
Encomia, frr. 118–128: pp. 100–104.
Threni, frr. 128a–131b, 133–138, 139 (=
128c): pp. 105–112.
Fragmenta incertorum librorum, frr. 140a–141,
142 (= 108b), 143–144, 145 (= 35a), 146, 147
(= 33b), 148, 150–153, 155–166, 167 (= 128f),
168b, 169a–169b, 170–173, 177, 178 (= 35c),
179–185, 187–196, 198a–198b, 199, 201–207,
209–215c, 216 (= 35b), 217, 219–234, 236–
246b, 247 (= 85a), 248, 249b (= post 70b),
250a, 252 (= prae 165), 255–256, 258 (= 243),
259–260, 273, 277–278 (= 223), 282, 287–288,
292, 294–297, 299–300, 302–307, 309–311,
313–314, 317–321, 325–327, 329–332: pp.
113–151.
Fragmenta dubia, frr. 333–335, 337–342, 346–
359: pp. 152–161.
Fragmenta addenda et corrigenda, frr. 52w(k),
94e, 124e, 169b: pp. 215–216.
Q, Pap: 9,106

x01 **Epigramma sepulcrale.**
App. Anth. 2.10: Cf. EPIGRAMMATICI in *App.
Anth.* (7052 002).

1610 **PINYTUS** Epigr.
A.D. 1: Bithynius
001 **Epigramma**, AG 7.16.
Q: 16

0288 **PISANDER** Epic.
7/6 B.C.: Camirensis
002 **Fragmenta**, ed. G. Kinkel, *Epicorum Graecorum fragmenta*, vol. 1. Leipzig: Teubner,
1877: 251–252.
frr. 7–11.
Q: [30]
003 **Epigramma**, AG 7.304.
Q: 30

0522 **PISANDER** Epic.
A.D. 3?: Larandensis
001 **Fragmenta**, ed. E. Heitsch, *Die griechischen
Dichterfragmente der römischen Kaiserzeit*, vol.
2. Göttingen: Vandenhoeck & Ruprecht, 1964:
46–47.
frr. 7, 16–20.
Q: [37]

0393 **PISANDER** Myth.
2 B.C.
001 **Testimonia**, FGrH #16: 1A:*10 addenda.
NQ
002 **Fragmenta**, FGrH #16: 1A:181–182, *11 addenda.
Q

0049 *PISISTRATI EPISTULA*
Incertum
001 **Epistula**, ed. R. Hercher, *Epistolographi Graeci*.
Paris: Didot, 1873 (repr. Amsterdam: Hakkert,
1965): 490.
Q: [213]

2395 **PISISTRATUS** Hist.
Incertum: Liparaeus
001 **Fragmentum**, FGrH #574: 3B:674.
Q

1612 **PISO** Epigr.
A.D. 1–2
001 **Epigramma**, AG 11.424.
Q: 13

1613 *PITTACI EPISTULA*
Incertum
Cf. et PITTACUS <Lyr.>. (0631).
001 **Epistula**, ed. R. Hercher, *Epistolographi Graeci*.
Paris: Didot, 1873 (repr. Amsterdam: Hakkert,
1965): 491.
Q: [54]

0631 **PITTACUS** <Lyr.>
7–6 B.C.: Mytilenensis
Cf. et <SEPTEM SAPIENTES> (1667).
001 **Fragmentum**, ed. T. Bergk, *Poetae lyrici
Graeci*, vol. 3, 4th edn. Leipzig: Teubner,
1882: 198.
Q: [23]
002 **Epigramma**, AG 11.440.
Q: 8

2677 **PIUS** Gramm.
A.D. 2–3
001 **Fragmenta**, ed. E. Hiller, "Der Grammatiker
Pius und die ἀπολογίαι πρὸς τὰς ἀθετήσεις
Ἀριστάρχου," *Philologus* 28 (1869) 86–115
(passim).
Q

4146 **Maximus PLANUDES** Polyhist.
A.D. 13–14: Nicomedensis

x01 **Epigrammata** (*App. Anth.*).
Epigramma sepulcrale: 2.775.
Epigramma demonstrativum: 3.422.
Epigrammata irrisoria: 5.80–82.
App. Anth. 2.775: Cf. EPIGRAMMATICI in
App. Anth. (7052 002).
App. Anth. 3.422: Cf. EPIGRAMMATICI in
App. Anth. (7052 003).
App. Anth. 5.80–82: Cf. EPIGRAMMATICI in
App. Anth. (7052 005).

0497 **PLATO** Comic.
　　　5–4 B.C.: Atheniensis
001 **Fragmenta**, ed. T. Kock, *Comicorum Attico-*
rum fragmenta, vol. 1. Leipzig: Teubner, 1880:
601–627, 629–659, 661–667.
frr. 1–59, 62–69, 71–74, 76–79, 82–98, 104–
124, 126–131, 134–138, 142–164, 166–169,
171–178, 180–202, 205–209, 211, 221–259,
263, 265, 267.
Q: 2,013
002 **Fragmenta**, ed. A. Meineke, *Fragmenta comico-*
rum Graecorum, vol. 2.2. Berlin: Reimer, 1840
(repr. De Gruyter, 1970): 615–622, 624–641,
643–650, 652–657, 659–662, 664–677, 679–
687, 693.
p. 693: fr. 45 supplied from vol. 5.1, p. cix.
Q: 1,824
003 **Fragmenta**, ed. J. Demiańczuk, *Supplementum*
comicum. Krakau: Nakładem Akademii, 1912
(repr. Hildesheim: Olms, 1967): 76–82.
frr. 1–28.
fr. 28: *P. Berol.* inv. 9772.
Q, Pap: 102
004 **Fragmenta**, ed. C. Austin, *Comicorum Grae-*
corum fragmenta in papyris reperta. Berlin: De
Gruyter, 1973: 202–203.
frr. 216–217.
Pap: 32
006 **Fragmentum**, ed. Kock, *op. cit.*, vol. 3 (1888):
729.
fr. 207b.
Q: 4
007 **Fragmenta**, ed. Meineke, *op. cit.*, vol. 5.1
(1857; repr. 1970): xcvi, xcix, cix.
Q: [12]
005 **Epigramma**, AG 9.359.
Q: 82

1042 **PLATO** Med.
　　　ante A.D. 1
x01 **Fragmentum ap. Galenum**.
K13.60.
Cf. GALENUS Med. (0057 076).

0059 **PLATO** Phil.
　　　5–4 B.C.: Atheniensis
　　　Cf. et SOCRATICORUM EPISTULAE (0637).
001 **Euthyphro**, ed. J. Burnet, *Platonis opera*, vol. 1.
Oxford: Clarendon Press, 1900 (repr. 1967): St
I.2a–16a.
Cod: 5,463

002 **Apologia Socratis**, ed. Burnet, *op. cit.*, vol. 1, St
I.17a–42a.
Cod: 8,854
003 **Crito**, ed. Burnet, *op. cit.*, vol. 1, St I.43a–54e.
Cod: 4,329
004 **Phaedo**, ed. Burnet, *op. cit.*, vol. 1, St I.57a–
118a.
Cod: 22,633
005 **Cratylus**, ed. Burnet, *op. cit.*, vol. 1, St I.383a–
440e.
Cod: 19,201
006 **Theaetetus**, ed. Burnet, *op. cit.*, vol. 1, St
I.142a–210d.
Cod: 23,803
007 **Sophista**, ed. Burnet, *op. cit.*, vol. 1, St I.216a–
268d.
Cod: 17,414
008 **Politicus**, ed. Burnet, *op. cit.*, vol. 1, St II.257a–
311c.
Cod: 18,592
009 **Parmenides**, ed. Burnet, *op. cit.*, vol. 2 (1901;
repr. 1967): St III.126a–166c.
Cod: 16,434
010 **Philebus**, ed. Burnet, *op. cit.*, vol. 2, St II.11a–
67b.
Cod: 19,055
011 **Symposium**, ed. Burnet, *op. cit.*, vol. 2, St
III.172a–223d.
Cod: 17,530
012 **Phaedrus**, ed. Burnet, *op. cit.*, vol. 2, St
III.227a–279c.
Cod: 17,221
013 **Alcibiades i**, ed. Burnet, *op. cit.*, vol. 2, St
II.103a–135c.
Cod: 11,317
014 **Alcibiades ii**, ed. Burnet, *op. cit.*, vol. 2, St
II.138a–151c.
Cod: 4,422
015 **Hipparchus**, ed. Burnet, *op. cit.*, vol. 2, St
II.225a–232c.
Cod: 2,426
016 **Amatores**, ed. Burnet, *op. cit.*, vol. 2, St
I.132a–139a.
Cod: 2,424
017 **Theages**, ed. Burnet, *op. cit.*, vol. 3 (1903; repr.
1968): St I.121a–131a.
Cod: 3,650
018 **Charmides**, ed. Burnet, *op. cit.*, vol. 3, St
II.153a–176d.
Cod: 8,410
019 **Laches**, ed. Burnet, *op. cit.*, vol. 3, St II.178a–
201c.
Cod: 8,021
020 **Lysis**, ed. Burnet, *op. cit.*, vol. 3, St II.203a–
223b.
Cod: 7,319
021 **Euthydemus**, ed. Burnet, *op. cit.*, vol. 3, St
I.271a–307c.
Cod: 13,030
022 **Protagoras**, ed. Burnet, *op. cit.*, vol. 3, St
I.309a–362a.
Cod: 18,079

023 **Gorgias**, ed. Burnet, *op. cit.*, vol. 3, St I.447a–527e.
Cod: 27,824

024 **Meno**, ed. Burnet, *op. cit.*, vol. 3, St II.70a–100c.
Cod: 10,396

025 **Hippias major**, ed. Burnet, *op. cit.*, vol. 3, St III.281a–304e.
Cod: 8,911

026 **Hippias minor**, ed. Burnet, *op. cit.*, vol. 3, St I.363a–376c.
Cod: 4,505

027 **Ion**, ed. Burnet, *op. cit.*, vol. 3, St I.530a–542b.
Cod: 4,091

028 **Menexenus**, ed. Burnet, *op. cit.*, vol. 3, St II.234a–249e.
Cod: 4,908

029 **Clitophon**, ed. Burnet, *op. cit.*, vol. 4 (1902; repr. 1968): St III.406a–410e.
Cod: 1,575

030 **Respublica**, ed. Burnet, *op. cit.*, vol. 4, St II.327a–621d.
Cod: 89,358

031 **Timaeus**, ed. Burnet, *op. cit.*, vol. 4, St III.17a–92c.
Cod: 24,104

032 **Critias**, d. Burnet, *op. cit.*, vol. 4, St III.106a–121c.
Cod: 5,040

033 **Minos**, ed. Burnet, *op. cit.*, vol. 5 (1907; repr. 1967): St II.313a–321d.
Cod: 3,078

034 **Leges**, ed. Burnet, *op. cit.*, vol. 5, St II.624a–969d.
Cod: 106,297

035 **Epinomis**, ed. Burnet, *op. cit.*, vol. 5, St II.973a–992e.
Cod: 6,389

036 **Epistulae**, ed. Burnet, *op. cit.*, vol. 5, St III.309a–363e.
Cod: 17,213

037 **Definitiones**, ed. Burnet, *op. cit.*, vol. 5, St III.411a–416a.
Cod: 1,738

038 **Spuria**, ed. Burnet, *op. cit.*, vol. 5, St III.364a–406a.
De justo: 372a–375d.
De virtute: 376a–379d.
Demodocus: 380a–386b.
Sisyphus: 387b–391d.
Eryxias: 392a–406a.
Axiochus: 364a–372a.
Cod: 14,839

039 **Epigrammata**, AG **5**.78–80; **6**.1, 43; **7**.99–100, 256, 259, 265, 268–269, 669–670; **9**.3, 44, 51, 506, 747, 823; **16**.13, 160–161, 210, 248.
AG 7.35: Cf. LEONIDAS Epigr. (1458 001).
AG 7.217: Cf. ASCLEPIADES Epigr. (0137 001).
AG 9.39: Cf. MUSICIUS Epigr. (1520 001).
AG 9.45: Cf. STATYLLIUS FLACCUS Epigr. (1694 001).

AG 9.759, 826; 16.12, 162: Cf. ANONYMI EPIGRAMMATICI (0138 001).
AG 9.827: Cf. AMMONIUS Epigr. (0289 002).
AG 16.11: Cf. HERMOCREON Epigr. (1422 001).
Q: 639

040 **Fragmenta tragica**, ed. B. Snell, *Tragicorum Graecorum fragmenta*, vol. 1. Göttingen: Vandenhoeck & Ruprecht, 1971: 186.
frr. 1–3.
Q: 10

041 **Epigrammata**, ed. E. Diehl, *Anthologia lyrica Graeca*, fasc. 1, 3rd edn. Leipzig: Teubner, 1949: 102–110.
frr. 1–33.
Q: 766

x01 **Epigramma demonstrativum**.
App. Anth. 3.33: Cf. EPIGRAMMATICI in *App. Anth.* (7052 003).

1614 **PLATO Junior** Epigr.
Incertum

001 **Epigrammata**, AG 9.13, 748, 751.
AG 9.13b: Cf. ANTIPHILUS Epigr. (0118 001).
AG 16.210: Cf. PLATO Phil. (0059 039).
Q: 48

1615 **PLATONIUS** Gramm.
Incertum

001 **Fragmenta de comoedia Graeca**, ed. G. Kaibel, *Comicorum Graecorum fragmenta*, vol. 1.1 [*Poetarum Graecorum fragmenta* 6.1. Berlin: Weidmann, 1899]: 3–6.
Περὶ διαφορᾶς κωμῳδιῶν: pp. 3–5.
Περὶ διαφορᾶς χαρακτήρων: p. 6.
Cod: [951]

1043 **PLATYSEMUS** Med.
ante A.D. 4

x01 **Fragmentum ap. Oribasium**.
CMG, vol. 6.2.2, p. 263.
Cf. ORIBASIUS Med. (0722 003).

1895 **PLESIMACHUS** Hist.
Incertum

001 **Fragmentum**, FGrH #52: 1A:295.
Q

2000 **PLOTINUS** Phil.
A.D. 3: Lycopolitanus, Alexandrinus, Romanus

001 **Enneades**, ed. P. Henry and H.-R. Schwyzer, *Plotini opera*, 3 vols. Leiden: Brill, 1:1951; 2:1959; 3:1973: 1:48–142, 145–253, 255–417; 2:3–258, 260–427; 3:2–328.
Cod: 216,398

0007 **PLUTARCHUS** Biogr. et Phil.
A.D. 1–2: Chaeronensis

001 **Theseus**, ed. K. Ziegler, *Plutarchi vitae parallelae*, vol. 1.1, 4th edn. Leipzig: Teubner, 1969: 1–35.
Cod: 7,972

002 **Romulus**, ed. Ziegler, *Vitae*, vol. 1.1, 35–76.
Cod: 9,727

003 **Comparatio Thesei et Romuli**, ed. Ziegler, *Vitae*, vol. 1.1, 76–81.
Cod: 1,206

007 **Solon**, ed. Ziegler, *Vitae*, vol. 1.1, 82–123.
Cod: 9,051

008 **Publicola**, ed. Ziegler, *Vitae*, vol. 1.1, 124–152.
Cod: 6,168

009 **Comparatio Solonis et Publicolae**, ed. Ziegler, *Vitae*, vol. 1.1, 152–156.
Cod: 999

010 **Themistocles**, ed. Ziegler, *Vitae*, vol. 1.1, 157–197.
Cod: 8,453

011 **Camillus**, ed. Ziegler, *Vitae*, vol. 1.1, 197–248.
Cod: 11,602

024 **Aristides**, ed. Ziegler, *Vitae*, vol. 1.1, 249–287.
Cod: 8,606

025 **Cato Maior**, ed. Ziegler, *Vitae*, vol. 1.1, 287–324.
Cod: 8,493

026 **Comparatio Aristidis et Catonis**, ed. Ziegler, *Vitae*, vol. 1.1, 324–331.
Cod: 1,536

035 **Cimon**, ed. Ziegler, *Vitae*, vol. 1.1, 332–359.
Cod: 6,271

036 **Lucullus**, ed. Ziegler, *Vitae*, vol. 1.1, 359–419.
Cod: 14,069

037 **Comparatio Cimonis et Luculli**, ed. Ziegler, *Vitae*, vol. 1.1, 419–423.
Cod: 1,037

012 **Pericles**, ed. Ziegler, *Vitae*, vol. 1.2, 3rd edn. (1964): 1–47.
Cod: 10,584

013 **Fabius Maximus**, ed. Ziegler, *Vitae*, vol. 1.2, 47–81.
Cod: 8,046

014 **Comparatio Periclis et Fabii Maximi**, ed. Ziegler, *Vitae*, vol. 1.2, 81–84.
Cod: 756

038 **Nicias**, ed. Ziegler, *Vitae*, vol. 1.2, 85–125.
Cod: 9,517

039 **Crassus**, ed. Ziegler, *Vitae*, vol. 1.2, 126–177.
Cod: 10,692

040 **Comparatio Niciae et Crassi**, ed. Ziegler, *Vitae*, vol. 1.2, 177–182.
Cod: 1,270

016 **Marcius Coriolanus**, ed. Ziegler, *Vitae*, vol. 1.2, 183–226.
Cod: 9,765

015 **Alcibiades**, ed. Ziegler, *Vitae*, vol. 1.2, 226–274.
Cod: 10,624

017 **Comparatio Alcibiadis et Marcii Coriolani**, ed. Ziegler, *Vitae*, vol. 1.2, 274–279.
Cod: 1,129

054 **Demosthenes**, ed. Ziegler, *Vitae*, vol. 1.2, 280–312.
Cod: 7,370

055 **Cicero**, ed. Ziegler, *Vitae*, vol. 1.2, 312–368.
Cod: 12,578

056 **Comparatio Demosthenis et Ciceronis**, ed. Ziegler, *Vitae*, vol. 1.2, 368–373.
Cod: 1,039

049 **Phocion**, ed. Ziegler, *Vitae*, vol. 2.1, 2nd edn. (1964): 1–31.
Cod: 8,422

050 **Cato Minor**, ed. Ziegler, *Vitae*, vol. 2.1, 32–92.
Cod: 17,099

060 **Dion**, ed. Ziegler, *Vitae*, vol. 2.1, 93–135.
Cod: 12,217

061 **Brutus**, ed. Ziegler, *Vitae*, vol. 2.1, 135–179.
Cod: 12,354

062 **Comparatio Dionis et Bruti**, ed. Ziegler, *Vitae*, vol. 2.1, 179–183.
Cod: 963

019 **Aemilius Paullus**, ed. Ziegler, *Vitae*, vol. 2.1, 184–222.
Cod: 10,177

018 **Timoleon**, ed. Ziegler, *Vitae*, vol. 2.1, 222–255.
Cod: 9,148

020 **Comparatio Aemilii Paulli et Timoleontis**, ed. Ziegler, *Vitae*, vol. 2.1, 255–256.
Cod: 495

042 **Sertorius**, ed. Ziegler, *Vitae*, vol. 2.1, 257–281.
Cod: 6,878

041 **Eumenes**, ed. Ziegler, *Vitae*, vol. 2.1, 281–301.
Cod: 5,684

043 **Comparatio Eumenis et Sertorii**, ed. Ziegler, *Vitae*, vol. 2.1, 301–302.
Cod: 412

027 **Philopoemen**, ed. Ziegler, *Vitae*, vol. 2.2, 2nd edn. (1968): 1–27.
Cod: 5,997

028 **Titus Flamininus**, ed. Ziegler, *Vitae*, vol. 2.2, 28–56.
Cod: 6,140

029 **Comparatio Philopoemenis et Titi Flaminini**, ed. Ziegler, *Vitae*, vol. 2.2, 56–59.
Cod: 576

021 **Pelopidas**, ed. Ziegler, *Vitae*, vol. 2.2, 60–105.
Cod: 9,850

022 **Marcellus**, ed. Ziegler, *Vitae*, vol. 2.2, 105–147.
Cod: 8,830

023 **Comparatio Pelopidae et Marcelli**, ed. Ziegler, *Vitae*, vol. 2.2, 148–151.
Cod: 848

047 **Alexander**, ed. Ziegler, *Vitae*, vol. 2.2, 152–253.
Cod: 20,808

048 **Caesar**, ed. Ziegler, *Vitae*, vol. 2.2, 253–337.
Cod: 16,522

057 **Demetrius**, ed. Ziegler, *Vitae*, vol. 3.1, 2nd edn. (1971): 1–60.
Cod: 12,745

058 **Antonius**, ed. Ziegler, *Vitae*, vol. 3.1, 60–148.
Cod: 19,144

059 **Comparatio Demetrii et Antonii**, ed. Ziegler, *Vitae*, vol. 3.1, 149–152.
Cod: 924

030 **Pyrrhus**, ed. Ziegler, *Vitae*, vol. 3.1, 153–203.
Cod: 11,321

031 **Marius**, ed. Ziegler, *Vitae*, vol. 3.1, 203–263.
Cod: 13,323

063 **Aratus**, ed. Ziegler, *Vitae*, vol. 3.1, 264–317.
Cod: 12,262

064 **Artaxerxes**, ed. Ziegler, *Vitae*, vol. 3.1, 318–351.
Cod: 7,653

051 **Agis et Cleomenes**, ed. Ziegler, *Vitae*, vol. 3.1, 352–415.
Cod: 13,975

052 **Tiberius et Gaius Gracchus**, ed. Ziegler, *Vitae*, vol. 3.1, 416–458.
Cod: 9,550

053 **Comparatio Agidis et Cleomenis cum Tiberio et Gaio Graccho**, ed. Ziegler, *Vitae*, vol. 3.1, 458–463.
Cod: 1,005

004 **Lycurgus**, ed. B. Perrin, *Plutarch's lives*, vol. 1. Cambridge, Mass.: Harvard University Press, 1914 (repr. 1967): 204–302.
Cod: 9,749

005 **Numa**, ed. Perrin, *Plutarch's lives*, vol. 1, 306–382.
Cod: 7,773

006 **Comparatio Lycurgi et Numae**, ed. Perrin, *Plutarch's lives*, vol. 1, 382–400.
Cod: 1,642

032 **Lysander**, ed. Perrin, *Plutarch's lives*, vol. 4 (1916; repr. 1968): 234–320.
Cod: 8,425

033 **Sulla**, ed. Perrin, *Plutarch's lives*, vol. 4, 324–444.
Cod: 11,958

034 **Comparatio Lysandri et Sullae**, ed. Perrin, *Plutarch's lives*, vol. 4, 444–456.
Cod: 1,270

044 **Agesilaus**, ed. Perrin, *Plutarch's lives*, vol. 5 (1917; repr. 1968): 2–112.
Cod: 11,137

045 **Pompeius**, ed. Perrin, *Plutarch's lives*, vol. 5, 116–324.
Cod: 20,853

046 **Comparatio Agesilai et Pompeii**, ed. Perrin, *Plutarch's lives*, vol. 5, 326–336.
Cod: 1,125

065 **Galba**, ed. Perrin, *Plutarch's lives*, vol. 11 (1926; repr. 1962): 206–272.
Cod: 6,395

066 **Otho**, ed. Perrin, *Plutarch's lives*, vol. 11, 276–318.
Cod: 4,295

081 **Regum et imperatorum apophthegmata** (172b–208a), ed. W. Nachstädt, *Plutarchi moralia*, vol. 2.1. Leipzig: Teubner, 1935 (repr. 1971): 1–109.
Cod: 16,811

082 **Apophthegmata Laconica** (208b–242d), ed. Nachstädt, *Plutarchi moralia*, vol. 2.1, 110–165, 167–224.
Cod: 17,043

083 **Mulierum virtutes** (242e–263c), ed. Nachstädt, *Plutarchi moralia*, vol. 2.1, 225–272.
Cod: 9,861

084 **Aetia Romana et Graeca** (263d–304f), ed. J.B. Titchener, *Plutarchi moralia*, vol. 2.1, 273–366.
Cod: 20,354

085 **Parallela minora** (305a–316b), ed. Nachstädt, *Plutarchi moralia*, vol. 2.2 (1935; repr. 1971): 1–42.
Cod: 5,175

086 **De fortuna Romana** (316c–326c), ed. Nachstädt, *Plutarchi moralia*, vol. 2.2, 43–74.
Cod: 4,981

087 **De Alexandri magni fortuna aut virtute** (326d–345b), ed. Nachstädt, *Plutarchi moralia*, vol. 2.2, 75–120.
Cod: 8,721

088 **De gloria Atheniensium** (345c–351b), ed. Nachstädt, *Plutarchi moralia*, vol. 2.2, 121–136.
Cod: 2,842

089 **De Iside et Osiride** (351c–384c), ed. W. Sieveking, *Plutarchi moralia*, vol. 2.3 (1935; repr. 1971): 1–80.
Cod: 16,666

090 **De E apud Delphos** (384d–394c), ed. Sieveking, *Plutarchi moralia*, vol. 3 (1929; repr. 1972): 1–24.
Cod: 5,116

091 **De Pythiae oraculis** (394d–409d), ed. Sieveking, *Plutarchi moralia*, vol. 3, 25–59.
Cod: 7,521

092 **De defectu oraculorum** (409e–438d), ed. Sieveking, *Plutarchi moralia*, vol. 3, 59–122.
Cod: 14,195

093 **An virtus doceri possit** (439a–440c), ed. M. Pohlenz, *Plutarchi moralia*, vol. 3 (1929; repr. 1972): 123–127.
Cod: 691

094 **De virtute morali** (440d–452d), ed. Pohlenz, *Plutarchi moralia*, vol. 3, 127–156.
Cod: 6,116

095 **De cohibenda ira** (452f–464d), ed. Pohlenz, *Plutarchi moralia*, vol. 3, 157–186.
Cod: 5,792

096 **De tranquillitate animi** (464e–477f), ed. Pohlenz, *Plutarchi moralia*, vol. 3, 187–220.
Cod: 6,469

097 **De fraterno amore** (478a–492d), ed. Pohlenz, *Plutarchi moralia*, vol. 3, 221–254.
Cod: 6,970

098 **De amore prolis** (493a–497e), ed. Pohlenz, *Plutarchi moralia*, vol. 3, 255–267.
Cod: 2,348

099 **An vitiositas ad infelicitatem sufficiat** (498a–500a), ed. Pohlenz, *Plutarchi moralia*, vol. 3, 268–273.
Cod: 923

100 **Animine an corporis affectiones sint peiores** (500b–502a), ed. Pohlenz, *Plutarchi moralia*, vol. 3, 273–279.
Cod: 910

101 **De garrulitate** (502b–515a), ed. Pohlenz, *Plutarchi moralia*, vol. 3, 279–311.
Cod: 6,250

102 **De curiositate** (515b–523b), ed. Pohlenz, *Plutarchi moralia*, vol. 3, 311–332.
Cod: 3,975

103 **De cupiditate divitiarum** (523c–528b), ed. Pohlenz, *Plutarchi moralia*, vol. 3, 332–346.
Cod: 2,361

104 **De vitioso pudore** (528c–536d), ed. Pohlenz, *Plutarchi moralia*, vol. 3, 346–365.
Cod: 3,861

105 **De invidia et odio** (536e–538e), ed. Pohlenz, *Plutarchi moralia*, vol. 3, 365–371.
Cod: 1,056

106 **De laude ipsius** (539a–547f), ed. Pohlenz, *Plutarchi moralia*, vol. 3, 371–393.
Cod: 4,281

107 **De sera numinis vindicta** (548a–568a), ed. Pohlenz, *Plutarchi moralia*, vol. 3, 394–444.
Cod: 9,781

108 **De fato** (568b–574f), ed. Sieveking, *Plutarchi moralia*, vol. 3, 445–460.
Cod: 3,572

109 **De genio Socratis** (575a–598f), ed. Sieveking, *Plutarchi moralia*, vol. 3, 460–511.
Cod: 12,039

110 **De exilio** (599a–607f), ed. Sieveking, *Plutarchi moralia*, vol. 3, 512–532.
Cod: 4,375

111 **Consolatio ad uxorem** (608a–612b), ed. Sieveking, *Plutarchi moralia*, vol. 3, 533–542.
Cod: 2,047

112 **Quaestiones convivales** (612c–748d), ed. C. Hubert, *Plutarchi moralia*, vol. 4 (1938; repr. 1971): 1–335.
Cod: 66,199

113 **Amatorius** (748e–771e), ed. Hubert, *Plutarchi moralia*, vol. 4, 336–396.
Cod: 11,677

114 **Amatoriae narrationes** (771e–775e), ed. Hubert, *Plutarchi moralia*, vol. 4, 396–405.
Cod: 1,877

121 **Vitae decem oratorum** (832b–852e), ed. J. Mau, *Plutarchi moralia*, vol. 5.2.1 (1971): 1–49.
Cod: 9,754

125 **Aetia physica** (911c–919e), ed. Hubert, *Plutarchi moralia*, vol. 5.3, 2nd edn. (1960): 1–26.
Cod: 4,437

126 **De facie in orbe lunae** (920b–945e), ed. Pohlenz, *Plutarchi moralia*, vol. 5.3, 31–89.
Cod: 13,440

127 **De primo frigido** (945f–955c), ed. Hubert, *Plutarchi moralia*, vol. 5.3, 90–114.
Cod: 5,278

128 **Aqua an ignis utilior** (955d–958e), ed. Hubert, *Plutarchi moralia*, vol. 6.1 (1954; repr. 1959): 1–10.
Cod: 1,718

129 **De sollertia animalium** (959a–985c), ed. Hubert, *Plutarchi moralia*, vol. 6.1, 11–75.
Cod: 13,178

130 **Bruta ratione uti** (985d–992e), ed. Hubert, *Plutarchi moralia*, vol. 6.1, 76–93.
Cod: 3,610

131 **De esu carnium i** (993a–996c), ed. Hubert, *Plutarchi moralia*, vol. 6.1, 94–104.
Cod: 1,690

132 **De esu carnium ii** (996d–999b), ed. Hubert, *Plutarchi moralia*, vol. 6.1, 105–112.
Cod: 1,330

133 **Platonicae quaestiones** (999c–1011e) ed. Hubert, *Plutarchi moralia*, vol. 6.1, 113–142.
Cod: 6,581

134 **De animae procreatione in Timaeo** (1012b–1030c), ed. Hubert, *Plutarchi moralia*, vol. 6.1, 143–188.
Cod: 9,925

135 **Epitome libri de animae procreatione in Timaeo** (1030d–1032f), ed. Hubert, *Plutarchi moralia*, vol. 6.1, 189–194.
Cod: 1,248

136 **De Stoicorum repugnantiis** (1033a–1057b), ed. R. Westman (post M. Pohlenz), *Plutarchi moralia*, vol. 6.2, 2nd edn. (1959): 2–58.
Cod: 12,602

137 **Stoicos absurdiora poetis dicere** (1057c–1058e), ed. Westman (post Pohlenz), *Plutarchi moralia*, vol. 6.2, 59–61.
Cod: 540

138 **De communibus notitiis contra Stoicos** (1058e–1086b), ed. Westman (post Pohlenz), *Plutarchi moralia*, vol. 6.2, 62–122.
Cod: 14,372

139 **Non posse suaviter vivi secundum Epicurum** (1086c–1107c), ed. Westman (post Pohlenz), *Plutarchi moralia*, vol. 6.2, 124–172.
Cod: 10,278

140 **Adversus Colotem** (1107d–1127e), ed. Westman (post Pohlenz), *Plutarchi moralia*, vol. 6.2, 173–215.
Cod: 10,441

141 **De latenter vivendo** (1128a–1130e), ed. Westman (post Pohlenz), *Plutarchi moralia*, vol. 6.2, 216–223.
Cod: 1,325

143 **De libidine et aegritudine**, ed. Ziegler and Pohlenz, *Plutarchi moralia*, vol. 6.3, 3rd edn. (1966): 51–59.
Cod: 1,727

144 **Parsne an facultas animi sit vita passiva**, ed. Ziegler and Pohlenz, *Plutarchi moralia*, vol. 6.3, 60–64.
Cod: 1,139

145 **Fragmenta**, ed. F.H. Sandbach, *Plutarchi moralia*, vol. 7 (1967): 13–138.
Q, Cod: 23,639

067 **De liberis educandis** (1a–14c), ed. F.C. Babbitt, *Plutarch's moralia*, vol. 1. Cambridge, Mass.: Harvard University Press, 1927 (repr. 1969): 4–68.
Cod: 6,339

068 **Quomodo adolescens poetas audire debeat** (14d–37b), ed. Babbitt, *Plutarch's moralia*, vol. 1, 74–196.
Cod: 10,493

069 **De recta ratione audiendi** (37b–48d), ed. Bab-

bitt, *Plutarch's moralia*, vol. 1, 204–258.
Cod: 5,299

070 **Quomodo adulator ab amico internoscatur**
(48e–74e), ed. Babbitt, *Plutarch's moralia*, vol.
1, 264–394.
Cod: 12,265

071 **Quomodo quis suos in virtute sentiat profectus**
(75a–86a), ed. Babbitt, *Plutarch's moralia*, vol.
1, 400–456.
Cod: 5,270

072 **De capienda ex inimicis utilitate** (86b–92f), ed.
Babbitt, *Plutarch's moralia*, vol. 2 (1928; repr.
1962): 4–40.
Cod: 3,145

073 **De amicorum multitudine** (93a–97b), ed. Babbitt, *Plutarch's moralia*, vol. 2, 46–68.
Cod: 1,905

074 **De fortuna** (97c–100a), ed. Babbitt, *Plutarch's
moralia*, vol. 2, 74–88.
Cod: 1,314

075 **De virtute et vitio** (100b–101e), ed. Babbitt,
Plutarch's moralia, vol. 2, 94–100.
Cod: 695

076 **Consolatio ad Apollonium** (101f–122a), ed.
Babbitt, *Plutarch's moralia*, vol. 2, 108–210.
Cod: 9,580

077 **De tuenda sanitate praecepta** (122b–137e), ed.
Babbitt, *Plutarch's moralia*, vol. 2, 216–292.
Cod: 7,141

078 **Conjugalia praecepta** (138a–146a), ed. Babbitt,
Plutarch's moralia, vol. 2, 298–342.
Cod: 3,853

079 **Septem sapientium convivium** (146b–164d),
ed. Babbitt, *Plutarch's moralia*, vol. 2, 348–
448.
Cod: 8,983

080 **De superstitione** (164e–171f), ed. Babbitt, *Plutarch's moralia*, vol. 2, 454–494.
Cod: 3,469

115 **Maxime cum principibus philosopho esse dis-
serendum** (776a–779c), ed. H.N. Fowler, *Plutarch's moralia*, vol. 10 (1936; repr. 1969): 28–
46.
Cod: 1,596

116 **Ad principem ineruditum** (779d–782f), ed.
Fowler, *Plutarch's moralia*, vol. 10, 52–70.
Cod: 1,649

117 **An seni respublica gerenda sit** (783b–797f),
ed. Fowler, *Plutarch's moralia*, vol. 10, 76–
152.
Cod: 6,968

118 **Praecepta gerendae reipublicae** (798a–825f),
ed. Fowler, *Plutarch's moralia*, vol. 10, 158–
298.
Cod: 12,890

119 **De unius in republica dominatione, populari
statu, et paucorum imperio** (826a–827c), ed.
Fowler, *Plutarch's moralia*, vol. 10, 304–310.
Cod: 582

120 **De vitando aere alieno** (827d–832a), ed. Fowler, *Plutarch's moralia*, vol. 10, 316–338.
Cod: 2,087

122 **Comparationis Aristophanis et Menandri compendium** (853a–854d), ed. Fowler, *Plutarch's
moralia*, vol. 10, 462–472.
Cod: 763

123 **De Herodoti malignitate** (854e–874c), ed. L.
Pearson, *Plutarch's moralia*, vol. 11 (1965;
repr. 1970): 8–128.
Cod: 9,433

146 Παροιμίαι αἷς 'Αλεξανδρεῖς ἐχρῶντο, ed. E.L.
von Leutsch and F.G. Schneidewin, *Corpus
paroemiographorum Graecorum*, vol. 1. Göttingen: Vandenhoeck & Ruprecht, 1839 (repr.
Hildesheim: Olms, 1965): 321–342.
Q, Cod: 2,807

147 'Εκλογὴ περὶ τῶν ἀδυνάτων, ed. von Leutsch
and Schneidewin, *op. cit.*, 343–348.
Q, Cod: 172

148 **Fragmenta**, FGrH #388: 3B:264–265.
Q: [450]

0094 **Pseudo-PLUTARCHUS**
post A.D. 2

001 **De fluviis**, ed. K. Müller, *Geographi Graeci
minores*, vol. 2. Paris: Didot, 1861 (repr. Hildesheim: Olms, 1965): 637–665.
Cod: 6,879

002 **De musica** (1131b–1147a), ed. K. Ziegler, *Plu-
tarchi moralia*, vol. 6.3, 3rd edn. Leipzig:
Teubner, 1966: 1–37.
Cod: 8,504

003 **Placita philosophorum** (874d–911c), ed. J.
Mau, *Plutarchi moralia*, vol. 5.2.1. Leipzig:
Teubner, 1971: 50–153.
Cod: 17,824

004 **Titulus**, ed. A. Giannini, *Paradoxographorum
Graecorum reliquiae*. Milan: Istituto Editoriale
Italiano, 1965: 396.
NQ: [10]

x01 **Stromata.**
Plutarchi moralia, vol. 7, pp. 110–114.
Cf. PLUTARCHUS Biogr. et Phil. (0007 145)
(fr. 179).

x02 **Apophthegmata Romana.**
Ofenloch, pp. 206–210.
Cf. Pseudo-CAECILIUS Rhet. (1234 001).

x03 **[Plutarchi] vita Homeri.**
Allen, vol. 5, pp. 239–245.
VITAE HOMERI (1805 002).

0987 **PODANITES** Med.
ante A.D. 2

x01 **Fragmentum ap. Galenum.**
K13.115.
Cf. GALENUS Med. (0057 076).

0625 **POLEMAEUS** Trag.
1 B.C.: Ephesius

001 **Tituli**, ed. B. Snell, *Tragicorum Graecorum
fragmenta*, vol. 1. Göttingen: Vandenhoeck &
Ruprecht, 1971: 309.
frr. 1–2.
NQ

0586 **POLEMON** Perieg.
3–2 B.C.: Iliensis
001 **Fragmenta**, FHG 3: 108–148.
Q
002 **Testimonium et fragmenta**, ed. H.J. Mette,
"Die 'Kleinen' griechischen Historiker heute,"
Lustrum 21 (1978) 40–41.
frr. 4 bis, 37 bis, 65 bis, 75 bis.
testimonium: *IG* 8.281.
fr. 4 bis: *P. Oxy.* 13.1611.
fr. 65 bis: *P. Oxy.* 18.2176.
Q, Pap, Epigr

1617 **Marcus Antonius POLEMON** Soph.
A.D. 1–2
001 **Declamationes**, ed. H. Hinck, *Polemonis declamationes quae exstant duae.* Leipzig: Teubner,
1873: 3–39.
In Cynaegirum: pp. 3–17.
In Callimachum: pp. 17–39.
Cod: [6,269]
002 **Fragmentum physiognomonicum**, ed. J.A. Cramer, *Anecdota Graeca e codd. manuscriptis
bibliothecarum Oxoniensium*, vol. 4. Oxford:
Oxford University Press, 1836 (repr. Amsterdam: Hakkert, 1963): 255.
Q: [30]

1616 **POLEMON I** <Epigr.>
vel Polemon II
1 B.C./A.D. 1
001 **Epigrammata**, AG 5.68; **9.**746; 11.38.
Q: 88
x01 **Epigrammata** (*App. Anth.*).
Epigramma demonstrativum: 3.106.
Epigramma irrisorium: 5.30.
App. Anth. 3.106: Cf. EPIGRAMMATICI in
App. Anth. (7052 003).
App. Anth. 5.30: Cf. EPIGRAMMATICI in *App.
Anth.* (7052 005).

0498 **POLIOCHUS** Comic.
5/3 B.C.
001 **Fragmenta**, ed. T. Kock, *Comicorum Atticorum fragmenta*, vol. 3. Leipzig: Teubner, 1888:
390.
frr. 1–2.
Q: 58
002 **Fragmenta**, ed. A. Meineke, *Fragmenta comicorum Graecorum*, vol. 4. Berlin: Reimer, 1841
(repr. De Gruyter, 1970): 589–590.
Q: 59

2477 **POLLES** Hist.
Incertum: Aegaeus
001 **Testimonia**, FGrH #705: 3C:565.
NQ

1045 **POLLES** Med.
fiq Polles Aegaeus Phil.
ante A.D. 4
x01 **Fragmentum ap. Oribasium**.

CMG, vol. 6.2.1, p. 177 scholia.
Cf. ORIBASIUS Med. (0722 001).
x02 **Fragmenta ap. Oribasium**.
CMG, vol. 6.3, pp. 65, 67–68.
Cf. ORIBASIUS Med. (0722 004).
x03 **Fragmenta ap. Aëtium** (lib. 15).
Zervos, *Athena* 21, pp. 73, 74, 75, 77, 78, 79,
82.
Cf. AËTIUS Med. (0718 015).

1618 **POLLIANUS** Epigr.
A.D. 2
001 **Epigrammata**, AG 11.127–128, 130, 167;
16.150.
Q: 179

1985 **Asinius POLLIO** Hist.
1 B.C.–A.D. 1: Trallianus
001 **Testimonium**, FGrH #193: 2B:928.
NQ

0542 **Julius POLLUX** Gramm.
A.D. 2
001 **Onomasticon**, ed. E. Bethe, *Pollucis onomasticon*, 2 vols. [*Lexicographi Graeci* 9.1–9.2. Leipzig: Teubner, 9.1:1900; 9.2:1931 (repr. Stuttgart: 1967)]: **9.1**:1–305; **9.2**:1–248.
Cod: [139,776]

1869 **POLUS** Rhet. et Hist.
5 B.C.: Agragantinus
001 **Testimonium**, FGrH #7: 1A:158.
NQ

1619 **POLUS LUCANUS** Phil.
Incertum
x01 **Fragmentum ap. Stobaeum**.
Anth. III.9.51.
Cf. Joannes STOBAEUS (2037 001).

1620 **Julius POLYAENUS** Epigr.
fiq Gaius Julius Polyaenus Soph. et Hist.
1 B.C.
Cf. et Gaius Julius POLYAENUS Soph. et Hist.
(1988).
001 **Epigrammata**, AG 9.7–9b.
Q: 101

1621 **POLYAENUS** Epigr.
A.D. 2: Sardianus
001 **Epigramma**, AG 9.1.
Q: 38

0616 **POLYAENUS** Rhet.
A.D. 2: Macedo
001 **Strategemata**, ed. E. Woelfflin and J. Melber,
Polyaeni strategematon libri viii. Leipzig:
Teubner, 1887 (repr. Stuttgart: 1970): 3–425.
Cod: [63,717]
002 **Excerpta Polyaeni**, ed. Woelfflin and Melber,
op. cit., 431–504.
Cod: [16,356]

003 **Testimonia**, FGrH #639: 3C:185.
NQ

004 **Fragmenta**, FGrH #639: 3C:185–186.
Q

1988 **Gaius Julius POLYAENUS** Soph. et Hist.
fiq Julius Polyaenus Epigr.
1 B.C.: Sardianus
Cf. et Julius POLYAENUS Epigr. (1620).

001 **Testimonium**, FGrH #196: 2B:929.
NQ

1886 **POLYARCHUS** Hist.
vel Polyanthus
ante A.D. 2: Cyrenaeus

001 **Fragmenta**, FGrH #37: 1A:259.
Q

0543 **POLYBIUS** Hist.
3–2 B.C.: Megalopolitanus

001 **Historiae**, ed. T. Buettner-Wobst, *Polybii histo-riae*, vols. 1–4. Leipzig: Teubner, 1:1905; 2:1889; 3:1893; 4:1904 (repr. Stuttgart: 1:1962; 2–3:1965; 4:1967): **1**:1–361; **2**:1–380; **3**:1–430; **4**:1–512.
Q, Cod: 327,437

002 **Fragmenta ex incertis libris**, ed. Buettner-Wobst, *op. cit.*, vol. 4, 513–545.
frr. 1–237.
Q: 4,229

003 **Testimonium**, FGrH #173: 2B:896.
NQ

2177 **Tiberius Claudius POLYBIUS** Hist.
1 B.C.–A.D. 1

001 **Fragmentum**, FGrH #254: 2B:1153.
Q

0605 **POLYBIUS** Rhet.
Incertum: Sardianus

001 **Fragmenta de figuris**, ed. L. Spengel, *Rhetores Graeci*, vol. 3. Leipzig: Teubner, 1856 (repr. Frankfurt am Main: Minerva, 1966): 105–109.
Cod: [745]

002 **De barbarismo et soloecismo**, ed. A. Nauck, *Lexicon Vindobonense*. St. Petersburg: Eggers, 1867 (repr. Hildesheim: Olms, 1965): 283–289.
Cod: [999]

1622 **POLYCARPUS** Scr. Eccl.
A.D. 1–2: Smyrnaeus

001 **Epistula ad Philippenses**, ed. K. Bihlmeyer and W. Schneemelcher (post F.X. Funk), *Die apostolischen Väter*, 3rd edn. Tübingen: Mohr, 1970: 114–120.
Cod: [1,176]

1624 **POLYCHARMUS** Hist.
post 4 B.C.?: Naucratites
Cf. et POLYCHARMUS Hist. (1623).

001 **Fragmentum**, FGrH #640: 3C:187.
Q

1623 **POLYCHARMUS** Hist.
fiq Polycharmus Naucratites
2 B.C.?
Cf. et POLYCHARMUS Hist. (1624).

001 **Fragmenta**, FGrH #770: 3C:762–765.
Q

1938 **POLYCLITUS** Hist.
post 4 B.C.: Larissaeus

001 **Testimonia**, FGrH #128: 2B:668.
NQ

002 **Fragmenta**, FGrH #128: 2B:668–670.
Q

1625 **POLYCLITUS** Phil.
5 B.C.: Argivus

001 **Testimonia**, ed. H. Diels and W. Kranz, *Die Fragmente der Vorsokratiker*, vol. 1, 6th edn. Berlin: Weidmann, 1951 (repr. Dublin: 1966): 391.
test. 1–3.
NQ

002 **Fragmenta**, ed. Diels and Kranz, *op. cit.*, 392–393.
frr. 1–2.
Q

2410 **POLYCRATES** Hist.
4 B.C.: Atheniensis

001 **Testimonium**, FGrH #597: 3B:730.
NQ

1627 **POLYCRATES** Hist.
ante 1 B.C.: Lacon

001 **Fragmentum**, FGrH #588: 3B:702–703.
Q

1626 **POLYCRATES** Scr. Eccl.
A.D. 2: Ephesinus

001 **Fragmentum synodicae epistulae**, ed. M.J. Routh, *Reliquiae sacrae*, vol. 2, 2nd edn. Oxford: Oxford University Press, 1846 (repr. Hildesheim: Olms, 1974): 13–16.
Q: [356]

2385 **POLYCRITUS** Hist.
4 B.C.?: Mendaeus

001 **Testimonia**, FGrH #559: 3B:568.
NQ

002 **Fragmenta**, FGrH #559: 3B:568–570.
Q

003 **Titulus**, ed. H. Lloyd-Jones and P. Parsons, *Supplementum Hellenisticum*. Berlin: De Gruyter, 1983: 337.
titul. 696.
NQ: [1]

1041 **POLYDEUCES** Med.
ante A.D. 6

x01 **Fragmentum ap. Alexandrum Trallianum.**
Puschmann, vol. 2, p. 15.
Cf. ALEXANDER Med. (0744 003).

2327 **POLYGNOSTUS** Hist.
Incertum
001 **Fragmentum,** FGrH #473: 3B:433.
Q

1048 **POLYIDUS** Med.
ante A.D. 1
x01 **Fragmenta ap. Galenum.**
K13.826, 834.
Cf. GALENUS Med. (0057 077).
x02 **Fragmenta ap. Oribasium.**
CMG, vol. **6.2.2,** p. 216; **6.3,** p. 494.
Cf. ORIBASIUS Med. (0722 003, 005).
x03 **Fragmentum ap. Paulum.**
CMG, vol. 9.2, p. 318.
Cf. PAULUS Med. (0715 001).

0331 **<POLYIDUS>** Trag.
4 B.C.
001 **Fragmentum,** ed. B. Snell, *Tragicorum Grae-*
corum fragmenta, vol. 1. Göttingen: Vandenhoeck & Ruprecht, 1971: 249.
fr. 2.
Q: [21]

1839 **POLYPHRASMON** Trag.
5 B.C.
001 **Titulus,** ed. B. Snell, *Tragicorum Graecorum*
fragmenta, vol. 1. Göttingen: Vandenhoeck &
Ruprecht, 1971: 85.
NQ

1628 **POLYSTRATUS** Epigr.
2 B.C.: Aegyptius
001 **Epigrammata,** AG **7.**297; **12.**91.
Q: 80

1629 **POLYSTRATUS** Phil.
3–2 B.C.
001 Περὶ ἀλόγου καταφρονήσεως (*P. Herc.*
336/1150), ed. K. Wilke, *Polystrati Epicurei*
περὶ ἀλόγου καταφρονήσεως libellus. Leipzig:
Teubner, 1905: 3–33.
Pap: 2,688
002 **Fragmenta** (*P. Herc.* 346), ed. A. Vogliano,
Epicuri et Epicureorum scripta in Herculanensi-
bus papyris servata. Berlin: Weidmann, 1928:
77–89.
Pap: 2,496

0499 **POLYZELUS** Comic.
5–4 B.C.
001 **Fragmenta,** ed. T. Kock, *Comicorum Attico-*
rum fragmenta, vol. 1. Leipzig: Teubner, 1880:
789–793.
frr. 2–4, 6–12 + tituli.
Q: 110
002 **Fragmenta,** ed. A. Meineke, *Fragmenta comico-*

rum Graecorum, vol. 2.2. Berlin: Reimer, 1840
(repr. De Gruyter, 1970): 867, 869–872.
Q: 90
003 **Fragmentum,** ed. J. Demiańczuk, *Supplemen-*
tum comicum. Krakau: Nakładem Akademii,
1912 (repr. Hildesheim: Olms, 1967): 82.
fr. 1.
Q: 3

1630 **POLYZELUS** Hist.
3 B.C.?: Rhodius
001 **Fragmenta,** FGrH #521: 3B:492–494.
Q

POMPEIUS <Epigr.>
AG 9.647.
Cf. ANONYMI EPIGRAMMATICI (0138 001).

0346 **POMPEIUS MACER** <Trag.>
1 B.C.–A.D. 1
001 **Fragmentum,** ed. B. Snell, *Tragicorum Grae-*
corum fragmenta, vol. 1. Göttingen: Vandenhoeck & Ruprecht, 1971: 313.
fr. 1.
Q: [43]

1631 **POMPEIUS MACER Junior** Epigr.
1 B.C.–A.D. 1
001 **Epigrammata,** AG 7.219; **9.**28.
Q: 79

1051 **POMPEIUS SABINUS** Med.
A.D. 2
Cf. et SABINUS Med. (1066).
x01 **Fragmentum ap. Galenum.**
K13.1027.
Cf. GALENUS Med. (0057 077).

2034 **PORPHYRIUS** Phil.
vel Malchus
A.D. 3: Tyrius, Romanus
001 **Vita Plotini,** ed. P. Henry and H.-R. Schwyzer,
Plotini opera, vol. 1. Leiden: Brill, 1951: 1–41.
Cod: 8,123
002 **Vita Pythagorae,** ed. A. Nauck, *Porphyrii*
philosophi Platonici opuscula selecta, 2nd edn.
Leipzig: Teubner, 1886 (repr. Hildesheim:
Olms, 1963): 17–52.
Cod: 6,077
003 **De abstinentia,** ed. Nauck, *op. cit.,* 85–269.
Cod: 36,196
004 **De antro nympharum,** ed. Seminar Classics
609, *Porphyry. The cave of the nymphs in the*
Odyssey [*Arethusa Monographs* 1. Buffalo: De-
partment of Classics, State University of New
York, 1969]: 2–34.
Cod: 4,993
005 **Ad Marcellam,** ed. W. Pötscher, *Porphyrios.*
Πρὸς Μαρκέλλαν. Leiden: Brill, 1969: 6–38.
Cod: 4,676
006 **Isagoge sive quinque voces,** ed. A. Busse,
Porphyrii isagoge et in Aristotelis categorias

commentarium [*Commentaria in Aristotelem Graeca* 4.1. Berlin: Reimer, 1887]: 1–22.
Cod: 5,907

007 **In Aristotelis categorias expositio per interrogationem et responsionem**, ed. Busse, *op. cit.*, 55–142.
Cod: 31,265

008 **Sententiae ad intelligibilia ducentes**, ed. E. Lamberz, *Porphyrii sententiae ad intelligibilia ducentes*. Leipzig: Teubner, 1975: 1–59.
Cod: 7,813

009 **In Platonis Timaeum commentaria** (fragmenta), ed. A.R. Sodano, *Porphyrii in Platonis Timaeum commentariorum fragmenta*. Naples, 1964: 1–48, 60–69.
Cod: 10,834

010 **Chronica**, FHG 3: 689–702, 706–707, 711–717, 719–725.
Q: 5,886

011 **De philosophia ex oraculis**, ed. G. Wolff, *Porphyrii de philosophia ex oraculis haurienda*. Berlin: Springer, 1856 (repr. Hildesheim: Olms, 1962): 109–185.
Cod: 3,921

012 Περὶ ἀγαλμάτων, ed. J. Bidez, *Vie de Porphyre le philosophe néo-platonicien*. Leipzig: Teubner, 1913 (repr. Hildesheim: Olms, 1964).
Cod: 3,106

013 **Epistula ad Anebonem**, ed. A.R. Sodano, *Porfirio. Lettera ad Anebo*. Naples: L'Arte Tipografica, 1958: 1–31.
Cod: 3,924

014 **Quaestionum Homericarum ad Iliadem pertinentium reliquiae**, ed. H. Schrader, *Porphyrii quaestionum Homericarum ad Iliadem pertinentium reliquias*, fasc. 1 & 2. Leipzig: Teubner, 1:1880; 2:1882: 1:1–180; 2:183–278.
Cod: [74,492]

015 **Zetemata codicis Vaticani**, ed. Schrader, *Porphyrii quaestionum Homericarum ad Iliadem pertinentium reliquias*, fasc. 2, 281–335.
Cod: [13,244]

016 **Quaestionum Homericarum ad Odysseam pertinentium reliquiae**, ed. H. Schrader, *Porphyrii quaestionum Homericarum ad Odysseam pertinentium reliquias*. Leipzig: Teubner, 1890: 1–134.
Cod: [27,868]

017 **Quaestionum Homericarum liber i** (recensio V), ed. A.R. Sodano, *Porphyrii quaestionum Homericarum liber i*. Naples: Giannini, 1970: 1–134.
Cod: [13,089]

018 **Quaestionum Homericarum liber i** (recensio X), ed. Sodano, *Porphyrii quaestionum Homericarum liber i*, 3–37, 39–134.
Cod: [12,546]

019 **Quaestionum Homericarum liber i** (recensio T), ed. Sodano, *Porphyrii quaestionum Homericarum liber i*, 86–89, 95–97.
Cod: [159]

020 **Quaestionum Homericarum liber i** (recensio

B), ed. Sodano, *Porphyrii quaestionum Homericarum liber i*, 86–89, 95–97.
Cod: [125]

021 Εἰς τὰ ἁρμονικὰ Πτολεμαίου ὑπόμνημα, ed. I. Düring, *Porphyrios. Kommentar zur Harmonielehre des Ptolemaios*. Göteborg: Elanders, 1932: 3–174.
Cod: 58,903

022 **Commentarium in Platonis Timaeum** (fragmentum incertum), ed. Sodano, *Porphyrii in Platonis Timaeum commentariorum fragmenta*, 116–118.
Cod: 290

023 **Contra Christianos** (fragmenta), ed. A. von Harnack, *Porphyrius. Gegen die Christen* [*Abhandlungen der königlich preussischen Akademie der Wissenschaften*, Philosoph.-hist. Kl. 1. Berlin: Reimer, 1916]: 45, 47–51, 54–67, 75–85, 87–94, 96–103.
Q

024 **Testimonia**, FGrH #260: 2B:1197–1198.
NQ

025 **Fragmenta**, FGrH #260: 2B:1208–1213, 1220–1229.
Q

026 **Symmikta zetemata** (fragmenta), ed. H. Dörrie, *Porphyrios. Symmikta Zetemata* [*Zetemata* 20. Munich: Beck, 1959]: passim.
Q

027 **Historia philosophiae** (fragmenta), ed. Nauck, *op. cit.*, 3–16.
Q

028 **Introductio in tetrabiblum Ptolemaei**, ed. A. Boer and S. Weinstock, *Codices Romani* [*Catalogus codicum astrologorum Graecorum* 5.4. Brussels: Academia, 1940]: 190–228.
Cod

029 **In Platonis Parmenidem commentaria** (fragmenta), ed. P. Hadot, *Porphyre et Victorinus*, vol. 2. Paris: Études Augustiniennes, 1968: 64–113.
Cod

x01 **Ad Gaurum quomodo animetur fetus.**
Kalbfleisch, pp. 33–62.
Cf. Pseudo-GALENUS Med. (0530 006).

0500 **POSIDIPPUS** Comic.
3 B.C.

001 **Fragmenta**, ed. T. Kock, *Comicorum Atticorum fragmenta*, vol. 3. Leipzig: Teubner, 1888: 335–348.
frr. 1–7, 9–34, 36–44.
Q: 641

002 **Fragmenta**, ed. A. Meineke, *Fragmenta comicorum Graecorum*, vol. 4. Berlin: Reimer, 1841 (repr. De Gruyter, 1970): 513–521, 523–527.
Q: 599

003 **Fragmentum**, ed. C. Austin, *Comicorum Graecorum fragmenta in papyris reperta*. Berlin: De Gruyter, 1973: 203–204.
fr. 218 + titulus.
Pap: 56

POSIDIPPUS Eleg.
3 B.C.: Thebanus
Cf. POSIDIPPUS Pellaeus Epigr. (1632 003).

1632 **POSIDIPPUS** Epigr.
fiq Posidippus Hist.
3 B.C.: Pellaeus
Cf. et POSIDIPPUS Hist. (2310).

001 **Epigrammata**, AG 5.134, 183, 186, 194, 202,
209, 211, 213; 7.170, 267; 9.359; 12.45, 77, 98,
120, 131, 168; 16.68, 119, 275.
AG 5.215: Cf. MELEAGER Epigr. (1492 001).
AG 12.17: Cf. ANONYMI EPIGRAMMATICI
(0138 001).
Q: 777

002 **Epigrammata** (*P. Didot* 28–34), ed. D.L. Page,
Select papyri, vol. 3 [*Literary papyri*]. Cambridge, Mass.: Harvard University Press, 1941
(repr. 1970): 444–448.
fr. 104.
Pap

004 **Fragmenta et tituli**, ed. H. Lloyd-Jones and P.
Parsons, *Supplementum Hellenisticum*. Berlin:
De Gruyter, 1983: 338, 340–341, 343.
frr. 698–700, 705–706.
fr. 705: *P. Berol.* 17 (= *Tabula cerata Berol.*
14283).
Q, Pap: [175]

x01 **Epigrammata** (*App. Anth.*).
Epigramma dedicatorium: 1.116.
Epigrammata demonstrativa: 3.77–81.
Epigramma irrisorium: 5.15.
App. Anth. 1.116: Cf. EPIGRAMMATICI in
App. Anth. (7052 001).
App. Anth. 3.77–81: Cf. EPIGRAMMATICI in
App. Anth. (7052 003).
App. Anth. 5.15: Cf. EPIGRAMMATICI in *App.
Anth.* (7052 005).

x02 **Fragmentum elegiacum** (*P. Lit. Lond.* 60)
(fort. auctore Posidippo).
SH, pp. 463–464, fr. 961.
Cf. ADESPOTA PAPYRACEA (SH) (2648 002).

x03 **Epigrammata** [Dub.] (*P. Cairo* inv. 65445).
SH, pp. 491, 493, frr. 978–979.
Cf. ADESPOTA PAPYRACEA (SH) (2648 003).

2310 **POSIDIPPUS** Hist.
fiq Posidippus Pellaeus
4–3 B.C.?
Cf. et POSIDIPPUS Epigr. (1632).
001 **Fragmenta**, FGrH #447: 3B:376.
Q

2639 **POSIDONIUS** Epic.
ante A.D. 2: Corinthius
001 **Titulus**, ed. H. Lloyd-Jones and P. Parsons,
Supplementum Hellenisticum. Berlin: De Gruyter, 1983: 344.
fr. 709.
NQ: [1]

1964 **POSIDONIUS** Hist.
2 B.C.

001 **Fragmenta**, FGrH #169: 2B:893–894.
Q

2187 **POSIDONIUS** Hist.
A.D. 2?: Olbiopolitanus
001 **Testimonia**, FGrH #279: 3A:158.
NQ

1866 **POSIDONIUS** Med.
A.D. 4–5?
x01 **Fragmenta ap. Aëtium** (lib. 6).
CMG, vol. 8.2, pp. 125, 133, 147, 150, 152,
158, 159.
Cf. AËTIUS Med. (0718 006).

1052 **POSIDONIUS** Phil.
2–1 B.C.: Apamensis, Rhodius
001 **Testimonia et fragmenta**, ed. W. Theiler, *Posi-
donios. Die Fragmente*, vol. 1. Berlin: De Gruyter, 1982: 16–72, 75–238, 242–244, 255–269,
279–280, 285, 290–297, 307, 310–346, 348–
350, 354–357, 375–386.
Q

002 **Testimonia**, FGrH #87: 2A:222–224.
NQ

003 **Fragmenta**, FGrH #87: 2A:225–317.
Q

2333 **POSSIS** Hist.
3–2 B.C.?: Magnes
001 **Fragmenta**, FGrH #480: 3B:444.
Q

002 **Titulus**, ed. H. Lloyd-Jones and P. Parsons,
Supplementum Hellenisticum. Berlin: De Gruyter, 1983: 344.
fr. 710.
NQ: [2]

2544 Aelius **POSTUMIUS ALBINUS** Hist.
2 B.C.: Romanus
001 **Testimonia**, FGrH #812: 3C:881–882.
NQ

002 **Fragmenta**, FGrH #812: 3C:882–883.
Q

1949 **POTAMON** Hist.
1 B.C.–A.D. 1: Mytilenensis
001 **Testimonia**, FGrH #147: 2B:815.
NQ

002 **Fragmentum**, FGrH #147: 2B:816.
Q

0663 ***PRAECEPTA SALUBRIA***
fort. auctore Asclepiade Bithynio
1 B.C.?
001 **Praecepta salubria**, ed. U.C. Bussemaker, *Poetae bucolici et didactici*. Paris: Didot, 1862:
132–134.
Cod: 583

0278 ***PRAELUSIO MIMI***
A.D. 2

001 **Fragmentum** (*P. Giessen* 1.1), ed. E. Heitsch, *Die griechischen Dichterfragmente der römischen Kaiserzeit*, vol. 1, 2nd edn. Göttingen: Vandenhoeck & Ruprecht, 1963: 46.
Pap: [70]

1053 **PRASION** Med.
ante A.D. 2
x01 **Fragmentum ap. Galenum.**
K13.854.
Cf. GALENUS Med. (0057 077).

1833 **PRATINAS** Trag.
6–5 B.C.: Phliasius
001 **Fragmenta**, ed. B. Snell, *Tragicorum Graecorum fragmenta*, vol. 1. Göttingen: Vandenhoeck & Ruprecht, 1971: 81–82.
frr. 1, 3, 4–6 + tituli.
Q: [153]
002 **Fragmenta**, ed. D.L. Page, *Poetae melici Graeci*. Oxford: Clarendon Press, 1962 (repr. 1967 (1st edn. corr.)): 367–369.
frr. 1–5.
Q: [141]

2151 **PRAXAGORAS** Hist.
A.D. 4: Atheniensis
001 **Testimonium**, FGrH #219: 2B:948–949.
NQ

0672 **PRAXAGORAS** Med.
4 B.C.: Cous
x01 **Fragmenta ap. Galenum.**
K2.906 in CMG, vol. **5.2.1**, p. 54; K**17.2.838; 18.1.7.**
Cf. GALENUS Med. (0057 016, 092).

0372 **PRAXILLA** Lyr.
5 B.C.: Sicyonia
001 **Fragmenta**, ed. D.L. Page, *Poetae melici Graeci*. Oxford: Clarendon Press, 1962 (repr. 1967 (1st edn. corr.)): 387–388, 390.
frr. 1–4, 8.
Q: [74]

2335 **PRAXION** Hist.
4 B.C.?: fort. Megareus
001 **Fragmentum**, FGrH #484: 3B:448–449.
Q

0089 **PRAXIPHANES** Phil.
4–3 B.C.: Mytilenensis, Rhodius
001 **Fragmenta**, ed. F. Wehrli, *Phainias von Eresos. Chamaileon, Praxiphanes* [*Die Schule des Aristoteles*, vol. 9, 2nd edn. Basel: Schwabe, 1969]: 93–100.
Q, Pap

1633 **PRAXITELES** <Epigr.>
4 B.C.: Cous
001 **Epigramma**, ed. E. Diehl, *Anthologia lyrica*

Graeca, fasc. 1, 3rd edn. Leipzig: Teubner, 1949: 135.
Q: [23]

1054 **PRIMION** Med.
ante A.D. 1
x01 **Fragmentum ap. Galenum.**
K13.695.
Cf. GALENUS Med. (0057 077).

1055 **PRISCIANUS** Med.
ante A.D. 4
x01 **Fragmentum ap. Oribasium.**
CMG, vol. 6.2.1, p. 218.
Cf. ORIBASIUS Med. (0722 003).

4014 **PRISCIANUS** Phil.
A.D. 6: Lydus
001 **Metaphrasis in Theophrastum**, ed. I. Bywater, *Prisciani Lydi quae extant* [*Commentaria in Aristotelem Graeca*, suppl. 1.2. Berlin: Reimer, 1886]: 1–37.
Cod: [14,842]

2641 **PRISCUS** Epic.
fiq Clutorius Priscus
1 B.C.–A.D. 1?
001 **Titulus**, ed. H. Lloyd-Jones and P. Parsons, *Supplementum Hellenisticum*. Berlin: De Gruyter, 1983: 344.
fr. 710a.
NQ: [1]

1056 **PROCLUS** Med.
1 B.C.
x01 **Fragmentum ap. Oribasium.**
CMG, vol. 6.3, p. 95.
Cf. ORIBASIUS Med. (0722 004).
x02 **Fragmentum ap. Paulum.**
CMG, vol. 9.2, p. 313.
Cf. PAULUS Med. (0715 001).

4036 **PROCLUS** Phil.
A.D. 5: Atheniensis
Bibliography in progress
001 **In Platonis rem publicam commentarii**, ed. W. Kroll, *Procli Diadochi in Platonis rem publicam commentarii*, 2 vols. Leipzig: Teubner, 1:1899; 2:1901 (repr. Amsterdam: Hakkert, 1965): 1:1–296; 2:1–368.
Cod: [169,502]
002 **Hypotyposis astronomicarum positionum**, ed. C. Manitius, *Procli Diadochi hypotyposis astronomicarum positionum*. Leipzig: Teubner, 1909 (repr. Stuttgart: 1974): 2–238.
Cod: [25,005]
003 **Epigramma**, AG 7.341.
Q: 27
004 **Theologia Platonica** (lib. 1–3), ed. D. Saffrey and L.G. Westerink, *Proclus. Théologie platonicienne*, 3 vols. Paris: Les Belles Lettres,

1:1968; 2:1974; 3:1978: **1**:1–125; **2**:1–73; **3**:1–
102.
Cf. et 4036 019 (= Theologia Platonica, lib. 4).
Cod: [69,954]
005 **Institutio theologica**, ed. E.R. Dodds, *Proclus.*
The elements of theology, 2nd edn. Oxford:
Clarendon Press, 1963 (repr. 1977): 2–184.
Cod: [31,532]
006 **Institutio physica**, ed. A. Ritzenfeld, *Procli*
Diadochi Lycii institutio physica. Leipzig:
Teubner, 1912: 2–58.
Cod: [7,711]
007 **In Platonis Alcibiadem i**, ed. L.G. Westerink,
Proclus Diadochus. Commentary on the first
Alcibiades of Plato. Amsterdam: North-Hol-
land, 1954: 1–158.
Cod: [70,523]
008 **In Platonis Parmenidem**, ed. V. Cousin, *Procli*
philosophi Platonici opera inedita, pt. 3. Paris:
Durand, 1864 (repr. Hildesheim: Olms, 1961):
617–1244.
Cod: [167,300]
009 **In Platonis Cratylum commentaria**, ed. G. Pasquali, *Procli Diadochi in Platonis Cratylum*
commentaria. Leipzig: Teubner, 1908: 1–113.
Cod: [29,792]
010 **In Platonis Timaeum commentaria**, ed. E.
Diehl, *Procli Diadochi in Platonis Timaeum*
commentaria, 3 vols. Leipzig: Teubner, 1:1903;
2:1904; 3:1906 (repr. Amsterdam: Hakkert,
1965): **1**:1–458; **2**:1–317; **3**:1–358.
Cod: [370,000]
011 **In primum Euclidis elementorum librum com-**
mentarii, ed. G. Friedlein, *Procli Diadochi in*
primum Euclidis elementorum librum commen-
tarii. Leipzig: Teubner, 1873: 3–436.
Cod: [93,579]
012 **De decem dubitationibus circa providentiam**,
ed. H. Boese, *Procli Diadochi tria opuscula.*
Berlin: De Gruyter, 1960: 5–108.
Cod: [13,913]
013 **De providentia et fato et eo quod in nobis ad**
Theodorum mechanicum, ed. Boese, *op. cit.*,
117–137, 141–155, 159–163, 169–171.
Cod: [5,544]
014 **De malorum subsistentia**, ed. Boese, *op. cit.*,
173–191, 211–265.
Cod: [9,727]
015 **Hymni 1–7**, ed. E. Vogt, *Procli hymni.* Wiesbaden: Harrassowitz, 1957: 27–33.
Cod: [1,092]
016 **Hymnorum fragmenta**, ed. Vogt, *op. cit.*, 33.
frr. 1–2.
Q: [12]
017 **Epigrammata**, ed. Vogt, *op. cit.*, 34.
Q, Cod: [69]
018 **De sacrificio et magia**, ed. J. Bidez, *Catalogue*
des manuscrits alchimiques grecs, vol. 6. Brussels: Lamertin, 1928: 148–151.
Cod: [1,049]
019 **Theologia Platonica** (lib. 4), ed. D. Saffrey and
L.G. Westerink, *Proclus. Théologie platonici-*

enne, vol. 4. Paris: Les Belles Lettres, 1981: 1–
113.
Cf. et 4036 004 (= Theologia Platonica, lib. 1–
3).
Cod: [12,209]
020 **Excerpta e Platonica Procli theologia**, ed. Cousin, *op. cit.*, 1243–1258.
Cod: [4,262]
021 **Eclogae de philosophia chaldaica**, ed. É. des
Places, *Oracles chaldaïques.* Paris: Les Belles
Lettres, 1971: 206–212.
Cod
022 **Paraphrasis Ptolemaei tetrabiblou** [Dub.], ed.
L. Allati, *Procli diadochi paraphrasis in Ptole-*
maei libros iv de siderum effectionibus. Leiden:
Elzevir, 1635.
Cod
023 **Chrestomathia** [Dub.], ed. A. Severyns, *Re-*
cherches sur la Chrestomathie de Proclus, vol. 4.
Paris: Les Belles Lettres, 1963: 67–74, 77–85,
87–97.
Vita Homeri: pp. 67–74.
Cyclicorum enarrationes: pp. 77–85, 87–97.
Cod
x01 **Scholia in Platonis Parmenidem.**
Cf. SCHOLIA (4101 001).
x02 **Scholia in Hesiodem.**
Cf. SCHOLIA (4101 002).
x03 **Characteres epistolici.**
Foerster, vol. 9, pp. 27–47.
Cf. LIBANIUS Soph. (2200 008).
x05 **Epigramma demonstrativum.**
App. Anth. 3.166: Cf. EPIGRAMMATICI in
App. Anth. (7052 003).

4029 **PROCOPIUS** Hist.
A.D. 6: Caesariensis
001 **De bellis**, ed. G. Wirth (post J. Haury), *Proco-*
pii Caesariensis opera omnia, vols. 1–2. Leipzig: Teubner, 1:1962; 2:1963: **1**:1, 4–145, 148–
305, 307–417, 419–552; **2**:1, 4–147, 150–294,
197–484, 487–678.
Lib. 1–2 = De bello Persico, lib. 1–2.
Lib. 3–4 = De bello Vandalico, lib. 1–2.
Lib. 5–8 = De bello Gothico, lib. 1–4.
Cod: [232,038]
002 **Historia arcana** (= **Anecdota**), ed. Wirth (post
Haury), *op. cit.*, vol. 3 (1963): 4–186.
Cod: [33,489]
003 **De aedificiis** (lib. 1–6), ed. Wirth (post Haury),
op. cit., vol. 4 (1964): 1, 5–186.
Cod: [37,317]

1634 **PRODICUS** Phil.
5–4 B.C.: Ceus
001 **Testimonia**, ed. H. Diels and W. Kranz, *Die*
Fragmente der Vorsokratiker, vol. 2, 6th edn.
Berlin: Weidmann, 1952 (repr. Dublin: 1966):
308–312.
test. 1–20.
NQ

002 **Fragmenta**, ed. Diels and Kranz, *op. cit.*, 312–319.
frr. 1–11.
Q

2721 **Theodorus PRODROMUS** Polyhist.
A.D. 12: Constantinopolitanus
Bibliography in progress
x01 **Epigramma irrisorium.**
App. Anth. 5.78: Cf. EPIGRAMMATICI in *App. Anth.* (7052 005).

1057 **PROËCHIUS** Med.
fiq Proëchius Arsinoeticus Episcopus
A.D. 5
x01 **Fragmentum ap. Paulum.**
CMG, vol. 9.2, p. 339.
Cf. PAULUS Med. (0715 001).

2300 **PROMATHIDAS** Hist.
4–3 B.C.: fort. Heracleota
001 **Testimonia**, FGrH #430: 3B:325.
NQ
002 **Fragmenta**, FGrH #430: 3B:325–327.
frr. 1–6: Promathidas.
frr. 7–8: Promathidas Junior.
Q
003 **Titulus**, ed. H. Lloyd-Jones and P. Parsons, *Supplementum Hellenisticum.* Berlin: De Gruyter, 1983: 345.
fr. 711 (auctore Promathida vel Promathida Juniore).
NQ: [1]

PROMATHIDAS Junior Hist.
1 B.C.
Cf. PROMATHIDAS Hist. (2300 002–003).

2548 **PROMATHION** Hist.
3 B.C.?
001 **Fragmentum**, FGrH #817: 3C:893–894.
Q

0397 **PRONOMUS** Lyr.
5 B.C.: Thebanus
001 **Titulus**, ed. D.L. Page, *Poetae melici Graeci.* Oxford: Clarendon Press, 1962 (repr. 1967 (1st edn. corr.)): 396.
NQ

2729 **PRORUS** Phil.
5 B.C.: Cyrenaeus
001 **Titulus**, ed. H. Thesleff, *The Pythagorean texts of the Hellenistic period.* Åbo: Åbo Akademi, 1965: 154.
Cf. et CLINIAS Phil. (1277 002).
NQ: [3]

1790 **PROTAGORAS** Astrol.
fiq Protagoras Cyzicenus
3 B.C.: Nicaeensis
001 **Fragmenta**, ed. D. Bassi, F. Cumont, A. Mar-

tini and A. Olivieri, *Codices Italici [Catalogus codicum astrologorum Graecorum* 4. Brussels: Lamertin, 1903]: 150–151.
Cod

1635 **PROTAGORAS** Soph.
5 B.C.: Abderita
001 **Testimonia**, ed. H. Diels and W. Kranz, *Die Fragmente der Vorsokratiker*, vol. 2, 6th edn. Berlin: Weidmann, 1952 (repr. Dublin: 1966): 253–262.
test. 1–30.
NQ
002 **Fragmenta**, ed. Diels and Kranz, *op. cit.*, 262–268.
frr. 1–12.
Q
003 **Fragmentum**, ed. J. Mejer, "The alleged new fragment of Protagoras," *Hermes* 100.2 (1972) 175.
Q

1636 **PROTAGORIDES** Hist.
2 B.C.?: Cyzicenus
001 **Testimonia**, FGrH #853: 3C:937.
NQ
002 **Fragmenta**, FGrH #853: 3C:937.
Q

1058 **PROTEUS** Med.
ante A.D. 2
x01 **Fragmentum ap. Galenum.**
K12.787.
Cf. GALENUS Med. (0057 076).
x02 **Fragmentum ap. Paulum.**
CMG, vol. 9.2, p. 343.
Cf. PAULUS Med. (0715 001).

1637 ***PROTEVANGELIUM JACOBI***
A.D. 2
001 **Protevangelium Jacobi**, ed. É. Strycker, *La forme la plus ancienne du protévangile de Jacques.* Brussels: Société des Bollandistes, 1961: 64–190.
Cod, Pap: [4,975]

1638 **PROXENUS** Hist.
3 B.C.: Epirota
001 **Fragmenta**, FGrH #703: 3C:556–560.
Q

2297 **PROXENUS** Hist.
3 B.C.?: Chalcidensis
001 **Fragmenta**, FGrH #425: 3B:322.
Q

1059 **PROXENUS** Med.
ante A.D. 1
x01 **Fragmentum ap. Galenum.**
K13.61.
Cf. GALENUS Med. (0057 076).

PSALMUS NAASSENUS
Heitsch, vol. 1, pp. 155-156.
Cf. HYMNI ANONYMI (0742 001).

1914 **PSAON** Hist.
3 B.C.: Plataeeus
001 **Testimonia**, FGrH #78: 2A:158-159.
NQ

PSELLUS Epigr.
fiq Michael PSELLUS
AG 14.5, 35, 58.
Cf. ANONYMI EPIGRAMMATICI (0138 001).

2702 **Michael PSELLUS** Polyhist.
A.D. 11: Constantinopolitanus
Bibliography in progress
x01 **Epigrammata** (*App. Anth.*).
Epigramma demonstrativum: 3.267.
Problemata: 7.34-45.
App. Anth. 3.267: Cf. EPIGRAMMATICI in
App. Anth. (7052 003).
App. Anth. 7.34-45: Cf. EPIGRAMMATICI in
App. Anth. (7052 007).

PSEUDEPICHARMEA
Cf. EPICHARMUS Comic. et PSEUDEPICHAR-
MEA (0521).

1639 **PSEUDO-AUCTORES HELLENISTAE**
Varia
001 **Fragmenta**, ed. A.-M. Denis, *Fragmenta pseud-*
epigraphorum quae supersunt Graeca [*Pseudepi-*
grapha veteris testamenti Graece 3. Leiden:
Brill, 1970]: 161-173.
Aeschylus: pp. 161-162.
Sophocles: pp. 162-163, 167-168, 173.
Euripides: pp. 163, 171.
Orpheus: pp. 163-167.
Pythagoras: p. 167.
Diphilus: pp. 168-169, 171.
Menander: pp. 169-170.
Hesiodus: p. 173.
(Hesiodus), Homerus, Callimachus/Linus: pp.
171-172.
Q: [880]

Pseudo-BEROSSUS Hist.
Incertum: Cous
Cf. BEROS(S)US Hist. (1222).

PSEUDO-CALLISTHENES
Cf. HISTORIA ALEXANDRI MAGNI (1386).

2233 **Pseudo-POLEMON**
A.D. 2
001 **Physiognomonica**, ed. R. Foerster, *Scriptores*
physiognomonici Graeci et Latini, vol. 1. Leipzig: Teubner, 1893: 427-431.
Cod
002 **Epitome Adamantiana**, ed. Foerster, *op. cit.*,

298-347, 351-397, 401-426.
Cod

0050 **PTOLEMAEI II PHILADELPHI ET ELEA-**
ZARI EPISTULAE
Incertum
001 **Epistulae**, ed. R. Hercher, *Epistolographi*
Graeci. Paris: Didot, 1873 (repr. Amsterdam:
Hakkert, 1965): 599-600.
Q: [443]

1640 **PTOLEMAEUS** Epigr.
ante 1 B.C.
001 **Epigramma**, AG 7.314.
Q: 17

1641 **PTOLEMAEUS** Gnost.
A.D. 2
001 **Epistula ad Floram**, ed. G. Quispel, *Ptolémée.*
Lettre à Flora, 2nd edn. [*Sources chrétiennes* 24
bis. Paris: Cerf, 1966]: 50-72.
Q: [2,178]

1643 **PTOLEMAEUS** Gramm.
2 B.C./A.D. 2: Ascalonita
001 Περὶ προσῳδίας Ὁμηρικῆς (fragmenta), ed. M.
Baege, *De Ptolemaeo Ascalonita* [*Diss. Halle*
(1883)]: 173-198.
Q
002 **Fragmenta**, ed. Baege, *op. cit.*, 198-200.
Περὶ μέτρων: p. 198.
Περὶ τῆς Κρατητείου αἱρέσεως: p. 198.
Fragmenta incertae sedis: pp. 199-200.
Q
003 Περὶ διαφορᾶς λέξεων, ed. H. Heylbut, "Ptolemaeus περὶ διαφορᾶς λέξεων," *Hermes* 22
(1887) 388-410.
Cod

1646 **PTOLEMAEUS** Hist.
3-2 B.C.: Megalopolitanus
001 **Testimonia**, FGrH #161: 2B:887.
NQ
002 **Fragmenta**, FGrH #161: 2B:888.
Q

1991 **PTOLEMAEUS** Hist.
1 B.C.-A.D. 1
001 **Fragmentum**, FGrH #199: 2B:930.
Q

1647 **PTOLEMAEUS** Hist.
ante A.D. 1: Mendesicus
001 **Testimonia**, FGrH #611: 3C:118.
NQ
002 **Fragmenta**, FGrH #611: 3C:119.
Q

0363 **Claudius PTOLEMAEUS** Math.
A.D. 2: Alexandrinus
001 **Syntaxis mathematica**, ed. J.L. Heiberg, *Clau-*
dii Ptolemaei opera quae exstant omnia, vols.

1.1–1.2. Leipzig: Teubner, 1.1:1898; 1.2:1903:
1.1:3–546; **1.2**:1–608.
Cod: [232,036]

002 **Phaseis**, ed. Heiberg, *op. cit.*, vol. 2 (1907): 3–67.
Cod: [10,028]

003 **Hypotheses**, ed. Heiberg, *op. cit.*, vol. 2, 70–106.
Cod: [4,559]

004 **Inscriptio Canobi**, ed. Heiberg, *op. cit.*, vol. 2, 149–155.
Cod: [1,235]

005 **Ψηφοφορία**, ed. Heiberg, *op. cit.*, vol. 2, 159–185.
Cod: [5,264]

006 **De analemmate**, ed. Heiberg, *op. cit.*, vol. 2, 194–216.
Cod: [2,375]

007 **Apotelesmatica** (=**Tetrabiblos**), ed. F. Boll and E. Boer, *Claudii Ptolemaei opera quae exstant omnia*, vol. 3.1. Leipzig: Teubner, 1940 (repr. 1957): 1–213.
Cod: [40,412]

008 **De judicandi facultate et animi principatu**, ed. F. Lammert, *Claudii Ptolemaei opera quae exstant omnia*, vol. 3.2, 2nd edn. Leipzig: Teubner, 1961: 3–25.
Cod: [4,160]

009 **Geographia** (lib. 1–3), ed. K. Müller, *Claudii Ptolemaei geographia*, vol. 1.1. Paris: Didot, 1883: 1–570.
Cf. et 0363 014.
Cod: [90,475]

010 **Harmonica**, ed. I. Düring, *Die Harmonielehre des Klaudios Ptolemaios* [*Göteborgs Högskolas Årsskrift* 36. Göteborg: Elanders, 1930]: 2–111.
Cod: [31,901]

011 **Musica**, ed. K. Jan, *Musici scriptores Graeci.* Leipzig: Teubner, 1895 (repr. Hildesheim: Olms, 1962): 411–420.
Cod: [1,141]

012 **Fragmenta**, ed. Heiberg, *op. cit.*, vol. 2, 263–270.
frr. 1–8.
Q

013 **Epigramma**, AG 9.577.
Q: 25

014 **Geographia** (lib. 4–8), ed. C.F.A. Nobbe, *Claudii Ptolemaei geographia*, vols. 1–2. Leipzig: Teubner, 1:1843; 2:1845 (repr. Hildesheim: Olms, 1966): 1:222–284; 2:1–264.
Cf. et 0363 009.
Cod

x01 **Epigramma demonstrativum.**
App. Anth. 3.120: Cf. EPIGRAMMATICI in *App. Anth.* (7052 003).

1642 **Pseudo-PTOLEMAEUS**
post A.D. 2

001 **Fructus sive centiloquium**, ed. E. Boer, *Claudii Ptolemaei opera quae exstant omnia*, vol. 3.2,

2nd edn. Leipzig: Teubner, 1961: 37–61.
Cod: [2,825]

1060 **PTOLEMAEUS** Med.
2–1 B.C.: Cyrenaeus

x01 **Fragmenta ap. Galenum.**
K**12**.584, 789; **13**.101, 849.
Cf. GALENUS Med. (0057 076–077).

1644 **PTOLEMAEUS** Phil. et Gramm.
A.D. 1–2: Chennus

001 Καινὴ ἱστορία (fragmenta), ed. A. Chatzis, *Der Philosoph und Grammatiker Ptolemaios Chennos.* Paderborn: Schöningh, 1914 (repr. New York: Johnson Reprint, 1967): 10–45.
Q

002 **Fragmenta**, ed. Chatzis, *op. cit.*, 46–51.
Fragmentum incertae sedis (fr. 1): p. 46.
Fragmenta probabili modo ad Καινὴν ἱστορίαν referenda (frr. 2–7): pp. 46–50.
Fragmenta dubia (frr. 8–11): pp. 50–51.
Q

003 **Reliquarum scriptionum fragmenta**, ed. Chatzis, *op. cit.*, 53–56.
frr. 1–7.
Q

004 **Titulus**, ed. A. Giannini, *Paradoxographorum Graecorum reliquiae.* Milan: Istituto Editoriale Italiano, 1965: 396.
NQ

1944 **PTOLEMAEUS I SOTER** Hist.
4–3 B.C.

001 **Testimonia**, FGrH #138: 2B:752–753.
NQ

002 **Fragmenta**, FGrH #138: 2B:753–769.
Q

2693 **PTOLEMAEUS III EUERGETES I** <Epigr.>
3 B.C.

001 **Epigramma**, ed. H. Lloyd-Jones and P. Parsons, *Supplementum Hellenisticum.* Berlin: De Gruyter, 1983: 345.
fr. 712.
Q: [28]

x01 **Epigramma demonstrativum.**
App. Anth. 3.39: Cf. EPIGRAMMATICI in *App. Anth.* (7052 003).

0604 **PTOLEMAEUS IV PHILOPATOR** Trag.
3 B.C.

001 **Titulus**, ed. B. Snell, *Tragicorum Graecorum fragmenta*, vol. 1. Göttingen: Vandenhoeck & Ruprecht, 1971: 283.
NQ

1645 **PTOLEMAEUS VIII EUERGETES II** <Hist.>
2 B.C.

001 **Testimonia**, FGrH #234: 2B:983.
NQ

002 **Fragmenta**, FGrH #234: 2B:983–987.
Q

1814 **PTOLEMAIS** Phil.
post 4 B.C.: Cyrenensis
001 **Fragmenta de musica**, ed. H. Thesleff, *The Pythagorean texts of the Hellenistic period.* Åbo: Åbo Akademi, 1965: 242–243.
Q: 459

1061 **PUBLIUS** Med.
1 B.C.
x01 **Fragmenta ap. Galenum**.
K13.281, 533, 842, 852.
Cf. GALENUS Med. (0057 076–077).

1062 **PYRAMUS** Med.
ante A.D. 2
x01 **Fragmentum ap. Galenum**.
K12.777.
Cf. GALENUS Med. (0057 076).

2349 **PYRANDER** Hist.
Incertum
001 **Fragmentum**, FGrH #504: 3B:481.
Q

1648 **PYRGION** Hist.
ante A.D. 3
001 **Fragmentum**, FGrH #467: 3B:403.
Q

2563 **PYRRHO** Hist.
ante A.D. 2: Liparaeus
001 **Fragmentum**, FGrH #836: 3C:903.
Q

2160 **PYRRHUS** Hist.
3 B.C.: fort. Epirotes
001 **Fragmenta**, FGrH #229: 2B:973.
Q

1649 **PYTHAENETUS** Hist.
3–2 B.C.?
001 **Fragmenta**, FGrH #299: 3B:2–3.
Q

0632 **<PYTHAGORAS>** Phil.
6–5 B.C.
001 **Carmen aureum**, ed. D. Young (post E. Diehl), *Theognis.* Leipzig: Teubner, 1971: 86–94.
Cod: 553
002 **Fragmenta**, ed. H. Thesleff, *The Pythagorean texts of the Hellenistic period.* Åbo: Åbo Akademi, 1965: 157–159, 162–165, 168–174, 185–186.
Q: 1,757
004 **Fragmenta astrologica**, ed. J. Heeg, *Codices Romani [Catalogus codicum astrologorum Graecorum* 5.3. Brussels: Lamertin, 1910]: 114.
Cf. et 0632 007.
Cod
006 **Testimonia**, ed. H. Diels and W. Kranz, *Die Fragmente der Vorsokratiker*, vol. 1, 6th edn.

Berlin: Weidmann, 1951 (repr. Dublin: 1966): 96–105.
test. 1–21.
NQ
007 **Fragmenta astrologica**, ed. K.O. Zuretti, *Codices Hispanienses [Catalogus codicum astrologorum Graecorum* 11.2. Brussels: Lamertin, 1934]: 124–125, 135–138, 139–144.
Cf. et 0632 004.
Cod
005 **Epigramma**, AG 7.746.
Q: 8
x01 **Fragmentum**.
PsVTGr 3.167.
Cf. PSEUDO-AUCTORES HELLENISTAE (1639 001).
Q

2239 **PYTHAGORISTAE** (D-K) Phil.
Varia
001 **Testimonia et fragmenta**, ed. H. Diels and W. Kranz, *Die Fragmente der Vorsokratiker*, vol. 1, 6th edn. Berlin: Weidmann, 1951 (repr. Dublin: 1966): 446–480.
Q

2682 **PYTHEAS** Epigr.
ante A.D. 3: Arcadius
x01 **Epigramma sepulcrale**.
App. Anth. 2.156: Cf. EPIGRAMMATICI in *App. Anth.* (7052 002).

1650 **PYTHEAS** Perieg.
4 B.C.: Massiliensis
001 **Fragmenta**, ed. H.J. Mette, *Pytheas von Massalia.* Berlin: De Gruyter, 1952: 17–29, 34–35. frr. 1–9b, 14–15.
Q: 3,710

1651 **PYTHERMUS** Hist.
3–2 B.C.: Ephesius
001 **Fragmenta**, FGrH #80: 2A:160–161.
Q

PYTHERMUS Lyr.
6 B.C.: Teius
PMG, p. 479, fr. 27.
Cf. CARMINA CONVIVIALIA (0296 001).

2179 **PYTHEUS-SATYRUS** Hist.
4 B.C.
001 **Testimonium**, FGrH #429: 3B:325.
NQ
002 **Fragmenta**, FGrH #429: 3B:325.
Q

1834 **PYTHION** Med.
ante A.D. 1
x01 **Fragmentum ap. Galenum**.
K13.536.
Cf. GALENUS Med. (0057 077).

1063 **PYTHIUS** Med.
      ante A.D. 1
x01   **Fragmentum ap. Galenum.**
      K12.879–880.
      Cf. GALENUS Med. (0057 076).

2560 **PYTHOCLES** Hist.
      Incertum: Samius
001   **Fragmenta,** FGrH #833: 3C:902.
      Q

0337 **PYTHON** Trag.
      4 B.C.
001   **Fragmentum,** ed. B. Snell, *Tragicorum Grae-*
      corum fragmenta, vol. 1. Göttingen: Vanden-
      hoeck & Ruprecht, 1971: 260.
      fr. 1.
      Q: [124]

1652 **QUADRATUS** Apol.
      A.D. 2: Atheniensis
x01   **Fragmentum ap. Eusebium.**
      HE 4.3.1–2.
      Cf. EUSEBIUS Scr. Eccl. et Theol. (2018 002).

1064 **QUADRATUS** Med.
      ante A.D. 1
x01   **Fragmentum ap. Galenum.**
      K13.1034.
      Cf. GALENUS Med. (0057 077).

2046 **QUINTUS** Epic.
      A.D. 4: Smyrnaeus
001   **Posthomerica,** ed. F. Vian, *Quintus de Smyrne.*
      La suite d'Homère, 3 vols. Paris: Les Belles
      Lettres, 1:1963; 2:1966; 3:1969: 1:12–44, 56–
      81, 96–126, 136–159; 2:18–44, 67–92, 105–
      134, 144–163, 180–202; 3.16–36, 48–68, 88–
      111, 128–151, 176–203.
      Cod: 62,202
x01   **Epigramma.**
      AG 16.92: Cf. ANONYMI EPIGRAMMATICI
      (0138 001).

1065 **QUINTUS** Med.
      A.D. 2
x01   **Fragmentum ap. Oribasium.**
      CMG, vol. 6.3, p. 115.
      Cf. ORIBASIUS Med. (0722 004).

1653 **RARUS** Epigr.
      Incertum
001   **Epigramma,** AG 10.121.
      Q: 41

1068 ***RES GESTAE DIVI AUGUSTI***
      A.D. 1
001   **Res gestae** (monumentum Ancyranum), ed. H.
      Volkmann, *Das Monumentum Ancyranum,* 3rd
      edn. [*Kleine Texte* 29–30. Berlin: De Gruyter,
      1969].
      Epigr

0219 **RHIANUS** Epic.
      3 B.C.: Benaeus
001   **Fragmenta,** ed. J.U. Powell, *Collectanea Alex-*
      andrina. Oxford: Clarendon Press, 1925 (repr.
      1970): 9–21.
      frr. 1, 10, 13, 16, 19–20, 25, 30–32, 34, 36,
      38–39, 41, 47, 50–51, 54–58, 60, 66–76.
      Q: [770]
002   **Epigrammata,** AG **6.**34, 173, 278; **7.**315; **12.**38,
      58, 93, 121, 142(?), 146.
      Q: 393
003   **Fragmentum et titulus,** ed. H. Lloyd-Jones and
      P. Parsons, *Supplementum Hellenisticum.* Ber-
      lin: De Gruyter, 1983: 347.
      frr. 715–716.
      Q: [3]
004   **Testimonia,** FGrH #265: 3A:64.
      NQ
005   **Fragmenta,** FGrH #265: 3A:65–73.
      Q
006   **Fragmenta,** ed. H.J. Mette, "Die 'Kleinen'
      griechischen Historiker heute," *Lustrum* 21
      (1978) 24–25.
      frr. 41 bis a–b, 41 ter a–b, 41 quater, 47 bis.
      fr. 41 ter a–b: *P. Oxy.* 39.2883.
      fr. 41 quater: *P. Oxy.* 30.2522.
      fr. 47 bis: *P. Oxy.* 27.2463.
      Q, Pap
x01   **Fragmentum hexametricum** (*P. Oxy.* 30.2522).
      SH, pp. 425–426, fr. 923.
      Cf. ADESPOTA PAPYRACEA (SH) (2648 001).
x02   **Fragmentum hexametricum** (*P. Oxy.* 39.2883).
      SH, p. 447, fr. 946.
      Cf. ADESPOTA PAPYRACEA (SH) (2648 001).
x03   **Fragmenta hexametrica** [Dub.] (*P. Oxy.*
      37.2819).
      SH, pp. 442–445, frr. 941–945.
      Cf. ADESPOTA PAPYRACEA (SH) (2648 001).
x04   **Epigramma irrisorium.**
      App. Anth. 5.21: Cf. EPIGRAMMATICI in *App.*
      Anth. (7052 005).

1654 **RHINTHON** Comic.
      vel Rhinton
      3 B.C.: Syracusanus
001   **Fragmenta,** ed. G. Kaibel, *Comicorum Grae-*
      corum fragmenta, vol. 1.1 [*Poetarum Graeco-*
      rum fragmenta, vol. 6.1. Berlin: Weidmann,
      1899]: 185–187.
      frr. 3, 7, 8, 10, 12 + tituli.
      Q: 63
002   **Titulus,** ed. C. Austin, *Comicorum Graecorum*
      fragmenta in papyris reperta. Berlin: De Gruy-
      ter, 1973: 204.
      NQ: 1

1655 **RHODO** Scr. Eccl.
      A.D. 2
x01   **Fragmentum ap. Eusebium.**
      HE 5.13.2–7.
      Cf. EUSEBIUS Scr. Eccl. et Theol. (2018 002).

1067 **RIPALUS** Med.
ante A.D. 2
x01 **Fragmentum ap. Galenum.**
K13.64.
Cf. GALENUS Med. (0057 076).

1656 **RUFINUS** Epigr.
A.D. 2: fort. Samius
001 **Epigrammata,** AG 5.9, 12, 14–15, 18–19, 21–
22, 27–28, 35–37, 41–44, 47–48, 60–62, 66,
69–71, 73–77, 87–88, 92–94, 97, 103.
AG 5.23: Cf. CALLIMACHUS Philol. (0533
001).
AG 5.50, 90, 95: Cf. ANONYMI EPIGRAMMA-
TICI (0138 001).
AG 5.89: Cf. Marcus ARGENTARIUS Rhet. et
Epigr. (0132 001).
Q: 1,372

4041 **RUF(IN)US** Epigr.
Incertum
001 **Epigramma,** AG 5.284.
Q: 14

2688 **RUFUS** Epigr.
A.D. 3?
x01 **Epigramma sepulcrale.**
App. Anth. 2.625: Cf. EPIGRAMMATICI in
App. Anth. (7052 002).

2553 **RUFUS** Hist.
A.D. 2–3?
001 **Testimonia,** FGrH #826: 3C:898–899.
NQ
002 **Fragmentum,** FGrH #826: 3C:899.
Q

0564 **RUFUS** Med.
A.D. 1–2: Ephesius
001 **De renum et vesicae morbis,** ed. C. Daremberg and C.É. Ruelle, *Oeuvres de Rufus
d'Éphèse.* Paris: Imprimerie Nationale, 1879
(repr. Amsterdam: Hakkert, 1963): 1–63.
Cod: 7,052
002 **De satyriasmo et gonorrhoea,** ed. Daremberg
and Ruelle, *op. cit.,* 64–84.
Cod: 2,392
003 **De corporis humani appellationibus,** ed. Daremberg and Ruelle, *op. cit.,* 133–167.
Cod: 4,985
004 **De partibus corporis humani,** ed. Daremberg
and Ruelle, *op. cit.,* 168–185.
Cod: 2,327
005 **De ossibus,** ed. Daremberg and Ruelle, *op. cit.,*
186–194.
Cod: 1,087
006 **Quaestiones medicinales,** ed. H. Gärtner, *Rufus von Ephesos. Die Fragen des Arztes an den
Kranken* [*Corpus medicorum Graecorum, supplementum,* vol. 4. Berlin: Akademie-Verlag,
1962]: 24–46.
Cod: 3,481

007 **Synopsis de pulsibus,** ed. Daremberg and Ruelle, *op. cit.,* 219–232.
Cod: 1,823
x01 **Fragmenta ap. Galenum.**
K12.425; **13.**92.
Cf. GALENUS Med. (0057 076).
x02 **Fragmenta ap. Oribasium.**
CMG **6.1.1,** pp. 20, 59, 61, 97, 117, 126, 127,
128, 189, 227, 267, 270, 290, 291, 297; **6.2.1,**
pp. 102, 131, 133, 150, 165, 166, 167, 168,
184, 191; **6.2.2,** pp. 43, 106, 109, 117, 136;
6.3, pp. 8, 14, 16, 17, 19, 92, 108, 119, 120,
148, 162, 199, 236, 237, 266, 328, 496.
Cf. ORIBASIUS Med. (0722 001, 002, 004,
005).
x03 **Fragmenta ap. Paulum.**
CMG **9.1,** pp. 62, 65, 108, 184; **9.2,** p. 287.
Cf. PAULUS Med. (0715 001).
x04 **Fragmenta ap. Aëtium** (lib. 1–3).
CMG 8.1, pp. 121, 180, 183, 265–268, 305,
307, 337.
Cf. AËTIUS Med. (0718 001–003).
x05 **Fragmenta ap. Aëtium** (lib. 5, 6, 8).
CMG 8.2, pp. 82, 146, 151, 410.
Cf. AËTIUS Med. (0718 005, 006, 008).
x06 **Fragmenta ap. Aëtium** (lib. 11).
Daremberg-Ruelle, pp. 87–88, 98–104, 109–
112, 113–117, 126.
Cf. AËTIUS Med. (0718 011).
x07 **Fragmenta ap. Aëtium** (lib. 12).
Kostomiris, pp. 47, 48.
Cf. AËTIUS Med. (0718 012).
x08 **Fragmenta ap. Aëtium** (lib. 16).
Zervos, *Gynaekologie des Aëtios,* p. 160.
Cf. AËTIUS Med. (0718 016).

0606 **RUFUS** Soph.
A.D. 2: Perinthius
001 **Ars rhetorica,** ed. L. Spengel, *Rhetores Graeci,*
vol. 1. Leipzig: Teubner, 1853 (repr. Frankfurt
am Main: Minerva, 1966): 463–470.
Cod: [1,551]

2546 **Publius RUTILIUS RUFUS** Hist.
2–1 B.C.
001 **Testimonia,** FGrH #815: 3C:887–889.
NQ
002 **Fragmenta,** FGrH #815: 3C:889–892.
Q

1066 **SABINUS** Med.
fiq Pompeius Sabinus
A.D. 1–2
Cf. et POMPEIUS SABINUS Med. (1051).
x01 **Fragmentum ap. Galenum.**
K15.25 in CMG, vol. 5.9.1, p. 15.
Cf. GALENUS Med. (0057 085).
x02 **Fragmentum ap. Oribasium.**
CMG, vol. 6.1.2, p. 15.
Cf. ORIBASIUS Med. (0722 001).

2049 **SALLUSTIUS** Phil.
A.D. 4

001 **De deis et mundo**, ed. G. Rochefort, *Saloustios. Des dieux et du monde*. Paris: Les Belles Lettres, 1960: 2–25.
Cod: [5,427]

1825 *SALOMONIS EPISTULAE*
ante 2 B.C.
x01 **Epistulae**.
FGrH #723, fr. 2
Cf. EUPOLEMUS Hist. (2486 002).
Q

1657 *SAMIORUM ANNALES*
fort. auctore Aethlio Samio
5–4 B.C.?
Cf. et AETHLIUS Hist. (0686).
001 **Fragmenta**, FGrH #544: 3B:527.
Q

1658 **SAMUS** Epigr.
vel Samius
3 B.C.: Macedonius
001 **Epigramma**, AG 6.116.
AG 7.647: Cf. SIMONIDES Lyr. (0261 001).
Q: 35
x01 **Epigramma demonstrativum**.
App. Anth. 3.72: Cf. EPIGRAMMATICI in *App. Anth.* (7052 003).

0501 **SANNYRION** Comic.
5 B.C.
001 **Fragmenta**, ed. T. Kock, *Comicorum Atticorum fragmenta*, vol. 1. Leipzig: Teubner, 1880: 793–795.
frr. 1–4, 6–8, 10–11.
Q: 71
002 **Fragmenta**, ed. A. Meineke, *Fragmenta comicorum Graecorum*, vol. 2.2. Berlin: Reimer, 1840 (repr. De Gruyter, 1970): 873–875.
Q: 69
003 **Fragmenta**, ed. J. Demiańczuk, *Supplementum comicum*. Krakau: Nakładem Akademii, 1912 (repr. Hildesheim: Olms, 1967): 83.
frr. 1–3.
Q: 5
004 **Titulus**, ed. C. Austin, *Comicorum Graecorum fragmenta in papyris reperta*. Berlin: De Gruyter, 1973: 204.
NQ: 2
005 **Titulus**, ed. Kock, *op. cit.*, vol. 3 (1888): 731.
NQ: [1]

0009 **SAPPHO** Lyr.
7–6 B.C.: Lesbia
Cf. et SAPPHO et ALCAEUS Lyr. (1815).
Cf. et SAPPHUS vel ALCAEI FRAGMENTA (0387).
001 **Fragmenta**, ed. E. Lobel and D.L. Page, *Poetarum Lesbiorum fragmenta*. Oxford: Clarendon Press, 1955 (repr. 1968 (1st edn. corr.)): 2, 5–68, 70–103, 108–110.
frr. 1–88, 90–192, 210–211, 213.
Q, Pap, Epigr: [5,135]

004 **Fragmentis addenda**, ed. Lobel and Page, *op. cit.*, 338–339.
frr. 214, 29(25)+24a.
Pap: [92]
003 **Fragmenta**, ed. D.L. Page, *Supplementum lyricis Graecis*. Oxford: Clarendon Press, 1974: 74–76, 150.
frr. S259–S261, S476.
Pap: [201]
002 **Epigrammata**, AG 6.269(?); 7.489, 505.
Q

1815 **SAPPHO et ALCAEUS** Lyr.
7–6 B.C.
Cf. et ALCAEUS Lyr. (0383).
Cf. et SAPPHO Lyr. (0009).
Cf. et SAPPHUS vel ALCAEI FRAGMENTA (0387).
001 **Fragmenta**, ed. D.L. Page, *Supplementum lyricis Graecis*. Oxford: Clarendon Press, 1974: 87–97.
frr. S273–S286: *P. Oxy.* 29.2506.
Pap: [707]

0387 *SAPPHUS vel ALCAEI FRAGMENTA*
7–6 B.C.
Cf. et ALCAEUS Lyr. (0383).
Cf. et SAPPHO Lyr. (0009).
Cf. et SAPPHO et ALCAEUS Lyr. (1815).
001 **Fragmenta**, ed. E. Lobel and D.L. Page, *Poetarum Lesbiorum fragmenta*. Oxford: Clarendon Press, 1955 (repr. 1968 (1st edn. corr.)): 292–297.
frr. 1–8, 10–14, 16–27.
Q, Pap: [179]
002 **Fragmenta**, ed. D.L. Page, *Supplementum lyricis Graecis*. Oxford: Clarendon Press, 1974: 98–102.
frr. S287–S312.
Pap: [333]

1659 **SATRIUS** Epigr.
fiq Satyrus
1 B.C.
Cf. et SATYRUS Epigr. (1660).
001 **Epigramma**, AG 6.11.
Q: 35

0608 **SATYRUS** Biogr.
3/2 B.C.: Oxyrhynchites
001 **Vita Euripidis** (*P. Oxy.* 9.1176), ed. G. Arrighetti, *Satiro. Vita di Euripide*. Pisa: Libreria Goliardica Editrice, 1964: 37–81.
Pap: [817]
002 **Fragmenta**, FHG 3: 159–164.
Q

1660 **SATYRUS** Epigr.
1 B.C.
Cf. et SATRIUS Epigr. (1659).
001 **Epigrammata**, AG 10.6, 11, 13; 16.153, 195.
Q: 148

1661 **SATYRUS** Hist.
3 B.C.: Alexandrinus
001 **Fragmentum** (*P. Oxy.* 27.2465), ed. H.J.
Mette, "Die 'Kleinen' griechischen Historiker
heute," *Lustrum* 21 (1978) 33–35.
fr. 1b.
Pap
002 **Fragmentum**, FGrH #631: 3C:180–182.
Q

1069 **SATYRUS** Med.
A.D. 2
x01 **Fragmentum ap. Galenum.**
K16.524 in CMG, vol. 5.9.2, p. 20.
Cf. GALENUS Med. (0057 088).

1873 **SATYRUS "Zeta"** Hist.
2 B.C.
001 **Fragmenta**, FGrH #20: 1A:184–185.
Q

2330 **SCAMON** Hist.
4 B.C.: Mytilenensis
001 **Testimonia**, FGrH #476: 3B:435–436.
NQ
002 **Fragmenta**, FGrH #476: 3B:436–437.
Q

4101 **SCHOLIA**
Varia
Bibliography in progress
001 **Scholia in Platonis Parmenidem**, ed. V. Cousin, *Procli philosophi Platonici opera inedita*, pt.
3. Paris, 1864 (repr. Hildesheim: Olms, 1961):
1257–1314.
Cod: [15,162]
002 **Scholia in Hesiodem**, ed. A. Pertusi, *Scholia
vetera in Hesiodi opera et dies*. Milan: Societa
Editrice Vita e Pensiero, 1955: 1–259.
Cod: [52,000]
003 **Scholia in opticorum recensionem Theonis**,
ed. J.L. Heiberg, *Euclidis opera omnia*, vol. 7.
Leipzig: Teubner, 1895: 251–284.
Cod
004 **Introductio in prolegomena Hermogenis artis
rhetoricae**, ed. C. Walz, *Rhetores Graeci*, vol. 4.
Stuttgart: Cotta, 1833 (repr. Osnabrück: Zeller,
1968): 1–38.
Cod: [8,918]

2514 **Publius Cornelius SCIPIO** Hist.
3–2 B.C.: Romanus
001 **Testimonia**, FGrH #811: 2B:880–881.
NQ

2163 **Publius Cornelius SCIPIO Major** Hist.
3–2 B.C.: Romanus
001 **Fragmentum**, FGrH #232: 2B:979–980.
Q

2164 **Publius Cornelius SCIPIO NASICA CORCU-
LUM** Hist.
2 B.C.: Romanus

001 **Fragmenta**, FGrH #233: 2B:981–982.
Q

1662 **SCIRAS** Comic.
3 B.C.
001 **Fragmentum**, ed. G. Kaibel, *Comicorum Graecorum fragmenta*, vol. 1.1 [*Poetarum Graecorum fragmenta*, vol. 6.1. Berlin: Weidmann,
1899]: 190.
fr. 1.
Q: 12

0353 <**SCLERIAS**> Trag.
Incertum
001 **Fragmenta**, ed. B. Snell, *Tragicorum Graecorum fragmenta*, vol. 1. Göttingen: Vandenhoeck & Ruprecht, 1971: 323–324.
frr. 1–2, 4.
Q: [46]

0273 *SCOLIA ALPHABETICA*
ante A.D. 3
001 **Fragmenta** (*P. Oxy.* 15.1795), ed. E. Heitsch,
*Die griechischen Dichterfragmente der röm-
ischen Kaiserzeit*, vol. 1, 2nd edn. Göttingen:
Vandenhoeck & Ruprecht, 1963: 38–40.
Cf. et ANONYMI AULODIA (1836 001).
Cf. et LYRICA ADESPOTA (CA) (0230 001).
Pap: [303]
002 **Fragmenta** (*P. Oxy.* 1.15), ed. Heitsch, *op. cit.*,
40–41.
Pap: [98]

SCOLIA ANONYMA
PMG, pp. 472–482, frr. 1–25, 28–31, 33.
CA, pp. 190–192, frr. 16–17, 21.
Cf. CARMINA CONVIVIALIA (0296 001).
Cf. LYRICA ADESPOTA (CA) (0230 001).

2238 **SCOPAS** (?) Hist.
ante 2 B.C.
001 **Testimonium**, FGrH #413: 3B:305.
NQ
002 **Fragmentum**, FGrH #413: 3B:306.
Q

0065 **SCYLAX** Perieg.
5/4 B.C.: Caryandensis
001 **Periplus Scylacis**, ed. K. Müller, *Geographi
Graeci minores*, vol. 1. Paris: Didot, 1855 (repr.
Hildesheim: Olms, 1965): 15–96.
Cod: [9,062]
002 **Testimonia**, FGrH #709: 3C:587–589.
NQ
003 **Fragmenta**, FGrH #709: 3C:589–592.
Q

0068 **Pseudo-SCYMNUS** Geogr.
vel Pausanias Damascenus
1 B.C.
001 **Ad Nicomedem regem, vv. 1–980** (*sub titulo
Orbis descriptio*), ed. K. Müller, *Geographi*

Graeci minores, vol. 1. Paris: Didot, 1855 (repr. Hildesheim: Olms, 1965): 196–237.
Cod: [5,805]

002 **Ad Nicomedem regem, vv. 722–1026**, ed. A. Diller, *The tradition of the minor Greek geographers*. Lancaster, Pennsylvania: American Philological Association, 1952: 165–176.
Cod: [1,688]

0259 **SCYTHINUS** Poet. Phil.
4 B.C.: Teius

001 **Fragmenta**, ed. M.L. West, *Iambi et elegi Graeci*, vol. 2. Oxford: Clarendon Press, 1972: 96.
frr. 1–2.
Q: [58]

002 **Testimonia**, FGrH #13: 1A:176.
NQ

004 **Fragmentum**, FGrH #13: 1A:176–177.
Q

003 **Epigrammata**, AG 12.22, 232.
Q: 98

0274 **SECUNDUS** Epigr.
A.D. 1: Tarentinus

001 **Epigrammata**, AG 9.36, 260, 301; 16.214.
Q: 164

SECUNDUS Phil.
A.D. 2: Atheniensis
Cf. VITA ET SENTENTIAE SECUNDI (1521).

1810 **SELEUCUS** Gramm.
A.D. 1: Alexandrinus

001 **Fragmenta**, ed. R. Reitzenstein, *Geschichte der griechischen Etymologika*. Leipzig: Teubner, 1897 (repr. Amsterdam: Hakkert, 1964): 157–165.
Q: [2,151]

002 Περὶ Ἑλληνισμοῦ (fragmentum), ed. H. Funaioli, *Grammaticae Romanae fragmenta*, vol. 1. Leipzig: Teubner, 1907: 450–451.
Q

003 **Testimonia**, FGrH #341: 3B:197.
NQ

004 **Fragmenta**, FGrH #341 & #634: **3B**:197–198; **3C**:183.
Q

005 **Fragmenta**, ed. M. Müller, *De Seleuco Homerico* [*Diss. Göttingen* (1891)]: 34–53.
Q

2524 **SELEUCUS** Gramm.
Incertum: Emesenus

001 **Testimonium**, FGrH #780: 3C:777.
NQ

0209 **SELEUCUS** Lyr.
2 B.C.

001 Ἱλαρὰ ᾄσματα, ed. J.U. Powell, *Collectanea Alexandrina*. Oxford: Clarendon Press, 1925 (repr. 1970): 176.
Q: [17]

2464 **SEMERONIUS** Hist.
Incertum: Babylonius

001 **Fragmentum**, FGrH #686: 3C:410.
Q

0260 **SEMONIDES** Eleg. et Iamb.
7 B.C.: Samius, Amorginus

001 **Fragmenta**, ed. M.L. West, *Iambi et elegi Graeci*, vol. 2. Oxford: Clarendon Press, 1972: 97–109, 111–112.
frr. 1–28, 30–31a, 41–42.
Q: [1,131]

002 **Testimonia**, FGrH #534: 3B:520.
NQ

1663 **SEMUS** Gramm.
3–2 B.C.?: Delius

001 **Testimonium**, FGrH #396: 3B:285.
NQ

002 **Fragmenta**, FGrH #396: 3B:285–291.
Q

2431 **Lucius Annaeus SENECA** Phil.
1 B.C.– A.D. 1: Cordubensis

001 **Fragmenta**, FGrH #644: 3C:189–190.
Q

SENECA Iatrosophista <Epigr.>
AG 1.90.
Cf. SOPHRONIUS Soph. (4042 016).

1664 **SENIORES ALEXANDRINI** Scr. Eccl.
A.D. 2

001 **Fragmenta**, ed. J. Pitra, *Analecta sacra spicilegio Solesmensi parata*, vol. 2. Paris: Tusculum, 1884 (repr. Farnborough: Gregg Press, 1966): 335–345.
Cod: [1,745]

1665 **SENIORES APUD IRENAEUM** Scr. Eccl.
A.D. 2–3

001 **Reliquiae plurium anonymorum**, ed. M.J. Routh, *Reliquiae sacrae*, vol. 1, 2nd edn. Oxford: Oxford University Press, 1846 (repr. Hildesheim: Olms, 1974): 47–48, 56–59.
Q: [486]

1759 ***SENTENTIAE PYTHAGOREORUM***
A.D. 2–3?

001 **Sententiae Pythagoreorum** (fort. auctore vel collectore Demophilo), ed. A. Elter, *Gnomica homoeomata*, pt. 5 [*Programm zur Feier des Geburtstages seiner Majestät des Kaisers und Königs am 27. Januar 1904*. Bonn: Georg, 1905]: coll. 1–36.
Q, Cod: [3,376]

002 **Sententiae Pythagoreorum**, ed. H. Chadwick, *The sentences of Sextus*. Cambridge: Cambridge University Press, 1959: 84–94.
Cod: [1,945]

1666 ***SENTENTIAE SEXTI***
A.D. 2/3

001 **Sententiae Sexti**, ed. H. Chadwick, *The sentences of Sextus*. Cambridge: Cambridge University Press, 1959: 12–72.
Cod: [4,911]

1667 **<SEPTEM SAPIENTES>** Phil.
Varia
Cf. et BIAS <Phil.> (1223).
Cf. et CHILON <Phil.> (1261).
Cf. et CLEOBULUS Lyr. (1274).
Cf. et PERIANDER <Phil.> (0629).
Cf. et PITTACUS <Lyr.> (0631).
Cf. et SOLON Nomographus (0263).
Cf. et THALES Phil. (1705).

001 **Testimonia**, ed. H. Diels and W. Kranz, *Die Fragmente der Vorsokratiker*, vol. 1, 6th edn. Berlin: Weidmann, 1951 (repr. Dublin: 1966): 61–62.
test. 1–3.
NQ

002 **Apophthegmata** (ex collectione Demetrii Phalerei) (ap. Stobaeum), ed. Diels and Kranz, *op. cit.*, 63–66.
Q

003 **Apophthegmata** (ex collectione Demetrii Phalerei) (ap. Stobaeum), ed. F.W.A. Mullach, *Fragmenta philosophorum Graecorum*, vol. 1. Paris: Didot, 1860 (repr. Aalen: Scientia, 1968): 212–214.
Q

004 **Sententiae**, ed. Mullach, *op. cit.*, 215–216.
Cod

005 **Praecepta** (sub auctore Sosiade) (ap. Stobaeum), ed. Mullach, *op. cit.*, 217–218.
Q

006 **Apophthegmata** (ap. auctores diversos), ed. Mullach, *op. cit.*, 219–235.
Q

0527 *SEPTUAGINTA*
Varia
001 **Genesis**, ed. A. Rahlfs, *Septuaginta*, vol. 1, 9th edn. Stuttgart: Württembergische Bibelanstalt, 1935 (repr. 1971): 1–86.
Cod: 34,301

002 **Exodus**, ed. Rahlfs, *op. cit.*, vol. 1, 86–158.
Cod: 26,553

003 **Leviticus**, ed. Rahlfs, *op. cit.*, vol. 1, 158–209.
Cod: 20,335

004 **Numeri**, ed. Rahlfs, *op. cit.*, vol. 1, 210–283.
Cod: 26,811

005 **Deuteronomium**, ed. Rahlfs, *op. cit.*, vol. 1, 284–354.
Cod: 24,297

006 **Josue** (Cod. Vaticanus + Cod. Alexandrinus), ed. Rahlfs, *op. cit.*, vol. 1, 354–405.
Cod. Vat. + Cod. Alex.: 354–381, 384–388, 392–405.
Cod. Vat. solum: 382–384, 388–392.
Cod: 15,847

007 **Josue** (Cod. Alexandrinus), ed. Rahlfs, *op. cit.*,
vol. 1, 382–384, 388–392.
Cod: 1,195

008 **Judices** (Cod. Alexandrinus), ed. Rahlfs, *op. cit.*, vol. 1, 405–495.
Cod: 16,883

009 **Judices** (Cod. Vaticanus), ed. Rahlfs, *op. cit.*, vol. 1, 405–495.
Cod: 16,519

010 **Ruth**, ed. Rahlfs, *op. cit.*, vol. 1, 495–501.
Cod: 2,200

011 **Regnorum i** (Samuelis i in textu Masoretico), ed. Rahlfs, *op. cit.*, vol. 1, 502–564.
Cod: 21,243

012 **Regnorum ii** (Samuelis ii in textu Masoretico), ed. Rahlfs, *op. cit.*, vol. 1, 565–622.
Cod: 18,914

013 **Regnorum iii** (Regum i in textu Masoretico), ed. Rahlfs, *op. cit.*, vol. 1, 623–693.
Cod: 22,061

014 **Regnorum iv** (Regum ii in textu Masoretico), ed. Rahlfs, *op. cit.*, vol. 1, 693–752.
Cod: 19,990

015 **Paralipomenon i**, ed. Rahlfs, *op. cit.*, vol. 1, 752–811.
Cod: 17,451

016 **Paralipomenon ii**, ed. Rahlfs, *op. cit.*, vol. 1, 811–873.
Cod: 22,679

017 **Esdras i** (liber apocryphus), ed. Rahlfs, *op. cit.*, vol. 1, 873–903.
Cod: 9,624

018 **Esdras ii** (Ezra et Nehemias in textu Masoretico), ed. Rahlfs, *op. cit.*, vol. 1, 903–950.
Cod: 14,219

019 **Esther**, ed. Rahlfs, *op. cit.*, vol. 1, 951–973.
Cod: 6,237

020 **Judith**, ed. Rahlfs, *op. cit.*, vol. 1, 973–1002.
Cod: 9,736

021 **Tobias** (Cod. Vaticanus + Cod. Alexandrinus), ed. Rahlfs, *op. cit.*, vol. 1, 1002–1039.
Cod: 5,856

022 **Tobias** (Cod. Sinaiticus), ed. Rahlfs, *op. cit.*, vol. 1, 1002–1039.
Cod: 7,636

023 **Machabaeorum i**, ed. Rahlfs, *op. cit.*, vol. 1, 1039–1099.
Cod: 19,535

024 **Machabaeorum ii**, ed. Rahlfs, *op. cit.*, vol. 1, 1099–1139.
Cod: 12,762

025 **Machabaeorum iii**, ed. Rahlfs, *op. cit.*, vol. 1, 1139–1156.
Cod: 5,484

026 **Machabaeorum iv**, ed. Rahlfs, *op. cit.*, vol. 1, 1157–1184.
Cod: 8,489

027 **Psalmi**, ed. Rahlfs, *op. cit.*, vol. 2, 9th edn. (1935; repr. 1971): 1–164.
Cod: 35,353

028 **Odae**, ed. Rahlfs, *op. cit.*, vol. 2, 164–183.
Cod: 4,234

029 **Proverbia**, ed. Rahlfs, *op. cit.*, vol. 2, 183–238.
Cod: 11,265

030 **Ecclesiastes**, ed. Rahlfs, *op. cit.*, vol. 2, 238–260.
Cod: 4,573

031 **Canticum**, ed. Rahlfs, *op. cit.*, vol. 2, 260–270.
Cod: 2,037

032 **Job**, ed. Rahlfs, *op. cit.*, vol. 2, 271–345.
Cod: 13,664

033 **Sapientia**, ed. Rahlfs, *op. cit.*, vol. 2, 345–376.
Cod: 6,985

034 **Siracides**, ed. Rahlfs, *op. cit.*, vol. 2, 377–471.
Cod: 18,760

035 **Psalmi Salomonis**, ed. Rahlfs, *op. cit.*, vol. 2, 471–489.
Cod: 4,969

036 **Osee**, ed. Rahlfs, *op. cit.*, vol. 2, 490–501.
Cod: 4,204

037 **Amos**, ed. Rahlfs, *op. cit.*, vol. 2, 502–511.
Cod: 3,409

038 **Michaeas**, ed. Rahlfs, *op. cit.*, vol. 2, 512–519.
Cod: 2,515

039 **Joel**, ed. Rahlfs, *op. cit.*, vol. 2, 519–524.
Cod: 1,693

040 **Abdias**, ed. Rahlfs, *op. cit.*, vol. 2, 524–526.
Cod: 505

041 **Jonas**, ed. Rahlfs, *op. cit.*, vol. 2, 526–529.
Cod: 1,136

042 **Nahum**, ed. Rahlfs, *op. cit.*, vol. 2, 530–533.
Cod: 1,006

043 **Habacuc**, ed. Rahlfs, *op. cit.*, vol. 2, 533–537.
Cod: 1,162

044 **Sophonias**, ed. Rahlfs, *op. cit.*, vol. 2, 538–542.
Cod: 1,289

045 **Aggaeus**, ed. Rahlfs, *op. cit.*, vol. 2, 542–545.
Cod: 1,005

046 **Zacharias**, ed. Rahlfs, *op. cit.*, vol. 2, 545–561.
Cod: 5,243

047 **Malachias**, ed. Rahlfs, *op. cit.*, vol. 2, 561–565.
Cod: 1,490

048 **Isaias**, ed. Rahlfs, *op. cit.*, vol. 2, 566–656.
Cod: 28,804

049 **Jeremias**, ed. Rahlfs, *op. cit.*, vol. 2, 656–748.
Cod: 30,810

050 **Baruch**, ed. Rahlfs, *op. cit.*, vol. 2, 748–756.
Cod: 2,803

051 **Threni** *seu* **Lamentationes**, ed. Rahlfs, *op. cit.*, vol. 2, 756–766.
Cod: 2,422

052 **Epistula Jeremiae**, ed. Rahlfs, *op. cit.*, vol. 2, 766–770.
Cod: 1,370

053 **Ezechiel**, ed. Rahlfs, *op. cit.*, vol. 2, 770–863.
Cod: 31,394

054 **Susanna** (translatio Graeca), ed. Rahlfs, *op. cit.*, vol. 2, 864–870.
Cod: 853

055 **Susanna** (Theodotionis versio), ed. Rahlfs, *op. cit.*, vol. 2, 864–870.
Cod: 1,230

056 **Daniel** (translatio Graeca), ed. Rahlfs, *op. cit.*, vol. 2, 870–936.
Cod: 11,398

057 **Daniel** (Theodotionis versio), ed. Rahlfs, *op. cit.*, vol. 2, 870–936.
Cod: 11,096

058 **Bel et Draco** (translatio Graeca), ed. Rahlfs, *op. cit.*, vol. 2, 936–941.
Cod: 960

059 **Bel et Draco** (Theodotionis versio), ed. Rahlfs, *op. cit.*, vol. 2, 936–941.
Cod: 939

1669 **SERAPION** Astrol.
fiq Serapion Alexandrinus
1 B.C.?: Antiochenus

001 **Fragmenta**, ed. A. Olivieri, *Codices Florentini* [*Catalogus codicum astrologorum Graecorum* 1. Brussels: Lamertin, 1898]: 99–102.
Cod

002 **Fragmenta**, ed. F. Cumont and F. Boll, *Codices Romani* [*Catalogus codicum astrologorum Graecorum* 5.1. Brussels: Lamertin, 1904]: 179–180.
Cod

003 **Fragmenta**, ed. J. Heeg, *Codices Romani* [*Catalogus codicum astrologorum Graecorum* 5.3. Brussels: Lamertin, 1910]: 96–97, 125.
Cod

004 **Fragmenta**, ed. P. Boudreaux, *Codices Parisini* [*Catalogus codicum astrologorum Graecorum* 8.4. Brussels: Lamertin, 1921]: 225–232.
Cod

1668 **SERAPION** Epigr.
ante A.D. 1: Alexandrinus

001 **Epigramma**, AG 7.400.
Q: 27

1070 **SERAPION** Med.
3 B.C.: Alexandrinus

x01 **Fragmenta ap. Galenum.**
K13.509–510, 833.
Cf. GALENUS Med. (0057 077).

x02 **Fragmentum ap. Oribasium.**
CMG, vol. 6.2.2, p. 285.
Cf. ORIBASIUS Med. (0722 003).

x03 **Fragmentum ap. Paulum.**
CMG, vol. 9.2, p. 360.
Cf. PAULUS Med. (0715 001).

x04 **Fragmentum ap. Aëtium** (lib. 15).
Zervos, *Athena* 21, p. 88.
Cf. AËTIUS Med. (0718 015).

1670 **SERAPION** Scr. Eccl.
A.D. 2–3: Antiochenus

001 **Fragmenta**, ed. M.J. Routh, *Reliquiae sacrae*, vol. 1, 2nd edn. Oxford: Oxford University Press, 1846 (repr. Hildesheim: Olms, 1974): 451–453.

Fragmentum ex epistula ad Caricum et Pontium: pp. 451-452.
Fragmentum ex libro de evangelio, quod sub nomine Petri ferebatur: pp. 452-453.
Q: [350]

0347 **SERAPION** Trag.
A.D. 1
001 **Fragmentum**, ed. B. Snell, *Tragicorum Graecorum fragmenta*, vol. 1. Göttingen: Vandenhoeck & Ruprecht, 1971: 315.
fr. 1.
Q: [15]

2055 **SERENUS** Geom.
A.D. 4: Antinoensis
001 **De sectione cylindri**, ed. J.L. Heiberg, *Sereni Antinoensis opuscula*. Leipzig: Teubner, 1896: 2-116.
Cod: [12,940]
002 **De sectione coni**, ed. Heiberg, *op. cit.*, 120-302.
Cod: [20,012]

1671 **SERENUS** Gnom.
fiq Aelius Serenus Gramm.
A.D. 2?: fort. Atheniensis
x01 **Fragmenta ap. Stobaeum.**
Anth. III.5.36-38; 6.17-19; 7.62; 11.23; 13.48-49, 58; 29.96; 39.27; **IV**.2.26; 6.20; 19.48; 22f.134; 24a.11.
Cf. Joannes STOBAEUS (2037 001).

1072 **SERGIUS** Med.
ante A.D. 2: Babylonius
x01 **Fragmenta ap. Galenum.**
K12.746, 751.
Cf. GALENUS Med. (0057 076).

1073 **Clemens SERTORIUS** Med.
ante A.D. 2
x01 **Fragmentum ap. Galenum.**
K13.1037.
Cf. GALENUS Med. (0057 077).

1672 **SERVIUS** Hist.
Incertum
001 **Fragmentum**, FGrH #47: 1A:272.
Q

1820 **SEUTHES** Astrol.
ante A.D. 2
001 **Fragmenta**, ed. W. Kroll, *Codices Romani* [*Catalogus codicum astrologorum Graecorum*, vol. 5.2. Brussels: Lamertin, 1906]: 114.
Q

4139 **SEVERIANUS** Scr. Eccl.
A.D. 4: Gabalensis
Bibliography in progress

039 **Fragmenta in epistulam ad Romanos** (in catenis), ed. K. Staab, *Pauluskommentar aus der griechischen Kirche aus Katenenhandschriften gesammelt*. Münster: Aschendorff, 1933: 213-225.
Q

040 **Fragmenta in epistulam i ad Corinthios** (in catenis), ed. Staab, *op. cit.*, 225-277.
Q

041 **Fragmenta in epistulam ii ad Corinthios** (in catenis), ed. Staab, *op. cit.*, 278-298.
Q

042 **Fragmenta in epistulam ad Galatas** (in catenis), ed. Staab, *op. cit.*, 298-304.
Q

043 **Fragmenta in epistulam ad Ephesios** (in catenis), ed. Staab, *op. cit.*, 304-313.
Q

044 **Fragmenta in epistulam ad Philippenses** (in catenis), ed. Staab, *op. cit.*, 313-314.
Q

045 **Fragmenta in epistulam ad Colossenses** (in catenis), ed. Staab, *op. cit.*, 314-328.
Q

046 **Fragmenta in epistulam i ad Thessalonicenses** (in catenis), ed. Staab, *op. cit.*, 328-331.
Q

047 **Fragmenta in epistulam ii ad Thessalonicenses** (in catenis), ed. Staab, *op. cit.*, 332-336.
Q

048 **Fragmenta in epistulam i ad Timotheum** (in catenis), ed. Staab, *op. cit.*, 336-341.
Q

049 **Fragmenta in epistulam ii ad Timotheum** (in catenis), ed. Staab, *op. cit.*, 342-344.
Q

050 **Fragmenta in epistulam ad Titum** (in catenis), ed. Staab, *op. cit.*, 344-345.
Q

051 **Fragmenta in epistulam ad Philemonem** (in catenis), ed. Staab, *op. cit.*, 345.
Q

052 **Fragmenta in epistulam ad Hebraeos** (in catenis), ed. Staab, *op. cit.*, 345-351.
Q

1074 **SEVERUS** Med.
fiq Severus Iatrosophista
A.D. 1
Cf. et SEVERUS Iatrosophista Med. (0748).
x01 **Fragmentum ap. Galenum.**
K12.734.
Cf. GALENUS Med. (0057 076).
x02 **Fragmentum ap. Paulum.**
CMG, vol. 9.2, p. 337.
Cf. PAULUS Med. (0715 001).
x03 **Fragmenta ap. Aëtium** (lib. 7).
CMG, vol. 8.2, pp. 279, 296, 331, 337, 341, 396.
Cf. AËTIUS Med. (0718 007).

x04 **Fragmentum ap. Alexandrum Trallianum.**
Puschmann, vol. 2, p. 44.
Cf. ALEXANDER Med. (0744 003).

2970 **SEVERUS** Phil.
A.D. 2
001 Περὶ ψυχῆς (fragmentum), ed. F.W.A. Mullach, *Fragmenta philosophorum Graecorum*,
vol. 2. Paris: Didot, 1867 (repr. Aalen: Scientia, 1968): 204–205.
Q

0748 **SEVERUS Iatrosophista** Med.
A.D. 1?
Cf. et SEVERUS Med. (1074).
001 **De instrumentis infusoriis seu clysteribus ad
Timotheum**, ed. F.R. Dietz, *Severi iatrosophis-
tae de clysteribus liber* [*Diss. med. Königsberg*
(1836)]: 3–43.
Cod: [9,132]

SEXTUS Phil.
Cf. SENTENTIAE SEXTI (1666).

SEXTUS JULIUS AFRICANUS Hist.
Cf. Sextus JULIUS AFRICANUS Hist. (2956).

0544 **SEXTUS EMPIRICUS** Phil.
A.D. 2–3
001 **Pyrrhoniae hypotyposes**, ed. H. Mutschmann,
Sexti Empirici opera, vol. 1. Leipzig: Teubner,
1912: 3–131, 133–209.
Cod: 52,696
002 **Adversus mathematicos**, ed. Mutschmann and
J. Mau, *Sexti Empirici opera*, vols. 2 & 3 (2nd
edn.). Leipzig: Teubner, 2:1914; 3:1961: 2:3–
429; **3**:1–177.
Lib. 1 (Adversus mathematicos et grammati-
cos): vol. 3, pp. 1–82.
Lib. 2 (Adversus rhetores): vol. 3, pp. 83–106.
Lib. 3 (Adversus geometras): vol. 3, pp. 107–
132.
Lib. 4 (Adversus arithmeticos): vol. 3, pp. 133–
140.
Lib. 5 (Adversus astrologos): vol. 3, pp. 141–
162.
Lib. 6 (Adversus musicos): vol. 3, pp. 163–177.
Lib. 7 (Adversus dogmaticos 1) (= Adversus
logicos 1): vol. 2, pp. 3–10.
Lib. 8 (Adversus dogmaticos 2) (= Adversus
logicos 2): vol. 2, pp. 104–212.
Lib. 9 (Adversus dogmaticos 3) (= Adversus
physicos 1): vol. 2, pp. 213–302.
Lib. 10 (Adversus dogmaticos 4) (= Adversus
physicos 2): vol. 2, pp. 303–374.
Lib. 11 (Adversus dogmaticos 5) (= Adversus
ethicos): vol. 2, pp. 375–429.
Cod: 155,211

2960 **SIBYLLA TIBURTINA**
A.D. 4: Tiburtina

001 **Prophetia**, ed. P.J. Alexander, *The oracle of
Baalbek. The Tiburtine Sibyl in Greek dress*
[*Dumbarton Oaks Studies* 10. Washington,
D.C.: Dumbarton Oaks, 1967]: 9–22.
Cod

1970 **SILENUS** Hist.
3 B.C.: fort. Calactinus
001 **Testimonia**, FGrH #175: 2B:900.
NQ
002 **Fragmenta**, FGrH #175: 2B:900–903.
Q

1877 **SILENUS** Hist.
3/2 B.C.?: Chius
001 **Fragmenta**, FGrH #27: 1A:211–212.
Q

0603 **SILENUS** Trag.
2 B.C.
001 **Titulus**, ed. B. Snell, *Tragicorum Graecorum
fragmenta*, vol. 1. Göttingen: Vandenhoeck &
Ruprecht, 1971: 309.
NQ

0211 **SIMIAS** Gramm.
vel Simmias
4–3 B.C.: Rhodius
001 **Fragmenta**, ed. J.U. Powell, *Collectanea Alexandrina*. Oxford: Clarendon Press, 1925 (repr.
1970): 109, 111–117, 119.
frr. 1, 3–4, 6–26.
Q: [700]
002 **Epigrammata**, AG **6**.113–114; **7**.21–22, 60,
193, 203, 647; **15**.22, 24, 27.
AG 6.116: Cf. SAMUS Epigr. (1658 001).
AG 7.20: Cf. SIMONIDES Lyr. (0261 003).
Q: 561
x01 **Fragmentum hexametricum** (*P. Mich.* 3.139)
(fort. auctore Simia Rhodio).
SH, p. 411, fr. 906.
Cf. ADESPOTA PAPYRACEA (SH) (2648 001).

1673 **SIMMIAS** Epigr.
5–4 B.C.: Thebanus
001 **Epigrammata**, AG 7.21–22, 60.
Q: 105

0988 **SIMMIAS** Med.
ante A.D. 2: Medus
x01 **Fragmentum ap. Galenum.**
K14.180.
Cf. GALENUS Med. (0057 078).

2600 **SIMON Scriptor De Re Equestri**
5 B.C.: Atheniensis
001 **De forma et delectu equorum**, ed. K. Widdra,
Ξενοφῶντος περὶ ἱππικῆς. Leipzig: Teubner,
1964: 41–44.
Cod
002 **Fragmenta**, ed. F. Ruehl, *Xenophontis scripta*

minora, vol. 2. Leipzig: Teubner, 1912: 196–197.
frr. 1–6.
Q

1674 <SIMON MAGUS> Gnost.
A.D. 1
001 **Apophasis megale** (fragmenta), ed. W. Völker, *Quellen zur Geschichte der christlichen Gnosis.* Tübingen: Mohr, 1932: 1–11.
Q

1906 **SIMONIDES** Epic.
Incertum: Carystius vel Eretrius
001 **Testimonium,** FGrH #55c: 1A:*20 addenda.
Q
002 **Tituli,** ed. H. Lloyd-Jones and P. Parsons, *Supplementum Hellenisticum.* Berlin: De Gruyter, 1983: 348.
frr. 720–722.
NQ: [7]

1958 **SIMONIDES** Hist.
3–2 B.C.: Magnes
001 **Testimonium,** FGrH #163: 2B:889.
NQ

0261 **SIMONIDES** Lyr.
6–5 B.C.: Ceus
001 **Fragmenta,** ed. M.L. West, *Iambi et. elegi Graeci,* vol. 2. Oxford: Clarendon Press, 1972: 113–117.
frr. 2–17.
Q: [280]
002 **Fragmenta,** ed. D.L. Page, *Poetae melici Graeci.* Oxford: Clarendon Press, 1962 (repr. 1967 (1st edn. corr.)): 238–241, 244–274, 276–277, 279, 281–290, 292–309, 311–318.
frr. 1–4, 6–7, 9–12, 14–22, 26, 28, 33, 36–41, 45–46, 48, 50, 54–55, 59, 62, 66–67, 70, 72, 74, 76, 78–82, 85, 87–90, 92–98, 100, 103, 107, 109–111, 113, 115, 117–121, 125–126, 128, 131, 133–134.
Q, Pap: [4,448]
003 **Epigrammata,** AG 5.159; **6.**2, 50, 52, 197, 212–217; **7.**20, 24–25, 77, 177, 248–251, 253–254b, 258, 270, 296, 300–302, 344, 348–349, 431, 442–443, 496, 507, 508–516, 647, 650b, 677; **9.**700, 757–758; **10.**105; **13.**11, 14, 19–20, 26, 28, 30; **16.**2–3, 23–24, 26, 60, 82, 204, 232.
AG 5.161: Cf. HEDYLUS Epigr. (0198 001).
AG 6.144: Cf. ANACREON Lyr. (0237 004).
AG 7.22: Cf. SIMIAS Epigr. (0211 002).
AG 7.187: Cf. PHILIPPUS Epigr. (1589 001).
AG 7.257, 347, 507b: Cf. ANONYMI EPIGRAMMATICI (0138 001).
AG 7.344b: Cf. CALLIMACHUS Philol. (0533 001).
AG 7.345: Cf. AESCHRION Lyr. (0679 001).
AG 9.147: Cf. ANTAGORAS Epic. (0215 002).
Q: 1,688

004 **Testimonium,** FGrH #8: 1A:158.
NQ
005 **Fragmenta,** FGrH #8: 1A:159, *8–*9 addenda.
fr. 7: *P. Giessen* 307.
Q, Pap
x01 **Epigrammata** (*App. Anth.*).
Epigrammata dedicatoria: 1.23, 24(?), 25.
Epigrammata sepulcralia: 2.4–6.
Epigrammata demonstrativa: 3.6–14.
Epigrammata exhortatoria et supplicatoria: 4.2–6.
Epigrammata irrisoria: 5.3.
App. Anth. 1.23, 24(?), 25: Cf. EPIGRAMMATICI in *App. Anth.* (7052 001).
App. Anth. 2.4–6: Cf. EPIGRAMMATICI in *App. Anth.* (7052 002).
App. Anth. 3.6–14: Cf. EPIGRAMMATICI in *App. Anth.* (7052 003).
App. Anth. 4.2–6: Cf. EPIGRAMMATICI in *App. Anth.* (7052 004).
App. Anth. 5.3: Cf. EPIGRAMMATICI in *App. Anth.* (7052 005).

SIMONIS EPISTULA
Epist. Graec., p. 618.
Cf. SOCRATICORUM EPISTULAE (0637 001).

4013 **SIMPLICIUS** Phil.
A.D. 6: Atheniensis
Bibliography in progress
001 **In Aristotelis quattuor libros de caelo commentaria,** ed. J.L. Heiberg, *Simplicii in Aristotelis de caelo commentaria* [*Commentaria in Aristotelem Graeca* 7. Berlin: Reimer, 1894]: 1–361, 365–731.
Cod: 268,077
002 **De caelo i** (interpretatio Graeca ex Kc), ed. Heiberg, *op. cit.,* 361–364.
Cod: 491
003 **In Aristotelis categorias commentarium,** ed. K. Kalbfleisch, *Simplicii in Aristotelis categorias commentarium* [*Commentaria in Aristotelem Graeca* 8. Berlin: Reimer, 1907]: 1–438.
Cod: 171,044
004 **In Aristotelis physicorum libros commentaria,** ed. H. Diels, *Simplicii in Aristotelis physicorum libros octo commentaria,* 2 vols. [*Commentaria in Aristotelem Graeca* 9 & 10. Berlin: Reimer, 9:1882; 10:1895]: **9:**1–800; **10:**801–1366.
Cod: 537,085
005 **In libros Aristotelis de anima commentaria,** ed. M. Hayduck, *Simplicii in libros Aristotelis de anima commentaria* [*Commentaria in Aristotelem Graeca* 11. Berlin: Reimer, 1882]: 1–329.
Cod: 139,473
006 **Commentarius in Epicteti enchiridion,** ed. F. Dübner, *Theophrasti characteres.* Paris: Didot, 1842: 1–138.
Cod

2245 **SIMUS** Phil.
4 B.C.

001 **Testimonia**, ed. H. Diels and W. Kranz, *Die Fragmente der Vorsokratiker*, vol. 1, 6th edn. Berlin: Weidmann, 1951 (repr. Dublin: 1966): 444–445.
test. 1–3: auctores alii nominantur Myonides et Euphranor.
NQ

0398 **SIMYLUS** Comic.
4/3 B.C.
001 **Fragmentum**, ed. T. Kock, *Comicorum Atticorum fragmenta*, vol. 2. Leipzig: Teubner, 1884: 444.
fr. 1 + titulus.
Q: 4
002 **Fragmentum**, ed. A. Meineke, *Fragmenta comicorum Graecorum*, vol. 1. Berlin: Reimer, 1839 (repr. De Gruyter, 1970): 424.
Q

1675 **SIMYLUS** Eleg.
3 B.C.?
002 **Fragmenta**, ed. H. Lloyd-Jones and P. Parsons, *Supplementum Hellenisticum*. Berlin: De Gruyter, 1983: 349–350.
frr. 724–725.
Q: [66]

1676 **SIMYLUS** Iamb.
4 B.C./A.D. 2
001 **Fragmenta**, ed. A. Meineke, *Fragmenta comicorum Graecorum*, vol. 1. Berlin: Reimer, 1839 (repr. De Gruyter, 1970): xiii–xv.
Q
002 **Fragmenta**, ed. H. Lloyd-Jones and P. Parsons, *Supplementum Hellenisticum*. Berlin: De Gruyter, 1983: 350–351.
frr. 726–728.
Q: [142]

1893 **SISYPHUS** Hist.
3 B.C.: Cous
001 **Testimonium**, FGrH #50: 1A:284.
NQ
002 **Fragmenta**, FGrH #50: 1A:284–294.
Q

2644 **SMINTHES** Astron.
4 B.C.?
001 **Titulus**, ed. H. Lloyd-Jones and P. Parsons, *Supplementum Hellenisticum*. Berlin: De Gruyter, 1983: 351.
fr. 729.
NQ: [1]

1677 **SOCRATES** Epigr.
Incertum
001 **Epigramma**, AG 14.1.
Q: 56

1678 **SOCRATES** Hist.
ante 1 B.C.: Argivus

001 **Testimonium**, FGrH #310: 3B:15.
NQ
002 **Fragmenta**, FGrH #310: 3B:15–20.
Q

1679 **SOCRATES** Hist.
1 B.C.: Rhodius
001 **Fragmenta**, FGrH #192: 2B:927–928.
Q

1000 **SOCRATES** Med.
A.D. 1?
x01 **Fragmentum ap. Pseudo-Galenum.**
K14.501.
Cf. Pseudo-GALENUS Med. (0530 029).

0262 **SOCRATES** Phil.
5–4 B.C.: Atheniensis
Cf. et SOCRATIS EPISTULAE (0636).
001 **Fragmenta**, ed. M.L. West, *Iambi et elegi Graeci*, vol. 2. Oxford: Clarendon Press, 1972: 118–119.
frr. 1–3.
Q: [34]
x01 **Epigramma exhortatorium et supplicatorium.**
App. Anth. 4.16(?): Cf. EPIGRAMMATICI in *App. Anth.* (7052 004).

2057 **SOCRATES Scholasticus** Hist.
A.D. 4–5: Constantinopolitanus
001 **Historia ecclesiastica**, ed. W. Bright, *Socrates' ecclesiastical history*, 2nd edn. Oxford: Clarendon Press, 1893: 1–330.
Cod: [109,855]

0637 *SOCRATICORUM EPISTULAE*
Incertum
Cf. et SOCRATIS EPISTULAE (0636).
001 **Epistulae**, ed. R. Hercher, *Epistolographi Graeci*. Paris: Didot, 1873 (repr. Amsterdam: Hakkert, 1965): 616–629, 634–635.
Cod: [6,166]

1003 **SOCRATION** Med.
ante A.D. 2
x01 **Fragmentum ap. Galenum.**
K12.835–836.
Cf. GALENUS Med. (0057 076).

0636 *SOCRATIS EPISTULAE*
Incertum
Cf. et SOCRATES Phil. (0262).
Cf. et SOCRATICORUM EPISTULAE (0637).
001 **Epistulae**, ed. R. Hercher, *Epistolographi Graeci*. Paris: Didot, 1873 (repr. Amsterdam: Hakkert, 1965): 609–616.
Cod: [3,049]

1680 **<SODAMUS>** Eleg.
Incertum: Tegeates
001 **Fragmentum**, ed. E. Diehl, *Anthologia lyrica*

Graeca, fasc. 1, 3rd edn. Leipzig: Teubner, 1949: 127.
Q: [16]

1786 **SOGENES** Comic.
Incertum
001 **Titulus**, ed. T. Kock, *Comicorum Atticorum fragmenta*, vol. 3. Leipzig: Teubner, 1888: 355.
NQ: 2

1075 **SOLON** Med.
ante A.D. 1: Smyrnaeus
x01 **Fragmentum ap. Galenum**.
K12.630.
Cf. GALENUS Med. (0057 076).

0263 **SOLON** Nomographus
7–6 B.C.: Atheniensis
Cf. et <SEPTEM SAPIENTES> (1667).
Cf. et SOLONIS EPISTULAE (1681).
Cf. et SOLONIS LEGES (1808).
001 **Fragmenta**, ed. M.L. West, *Iambi et elegi Graeci*, vol. 2. Oxford: Clarendon Press, 1972: 120–144.
frr. 1–4a, 4c, 5–7, 9–21, 22a, 23–28, 31–34, 36–40, 43.
Q: 1,869
x01 **Epigrammata** (*App. Anth.*).
Epigramma demonstrativum: 3.5.
Epigramma exhortatorium et supplicatorium: 4.1.
App. Anth. 3.5: Cf. EPIGRAMMATICI in *App. Anth.* (7052 003).
App. Anth. 4.1: Cf. EPIGRAMMATICI in *App. Anth.* (7052 004).

1681 *SOLONIS EPISTULAE*
Incertum
Cf. et SOLON Nomographus (0263).
001 **Epistulae**, ed. R. Hercher, *Epistolographi Graeci*. Paris: Didot, 1873 (repr. Amsterdam: Hakkert, 1965): 636–637.
Q: [461]

1808 *SOLONIS LEGES*
6 B.C.
Cf. et SOLON Nomographus (0263).
001 **Fragmenta**, ed. E. Ruschenbusch, Σόλωνος νόμοι [*Historia Einzelschriften* 9 (1966)]: 70–126.
Q, Pap, Epigr

1682 **SOPATER** Comic.
4–3 B.C.: Paphius
001 **Fragmenta**, ed. G. Kaibel, *Comicorum Graecorum fragmenta*, vol. 1.1 [*Poetarum Graecorum fragmenta*, vol. 6.1. Berlin: Weidmann, 1899]: 192–197.
frr. 1–21, 23–25.
Q: 314

2031 **SOPATER** Rhet.
A.D. 4: Atheniensis

001 Διαίρεσις ζητημάτων, ed. C. Walz, *Rhetores Graeci*, vol. 8. Stuttgart: Cotta, 1835 (repr. Osnabrück: Zeller, 1968): 2–385.
Cod: 92,268
002 **Scholia ad Hermogenis status seu artem rhetoricam**, ed. Walz, *op. cit.*, vol. 5 (1833; repr. 1968): 1–211.
Cod: 55,814
003 **Prolegomena in Aristidem**, ed. W. Dindorf, *Aristides*, vol. 3. Leipzig: Reimer, 1829 (repr. Hildesheim: Olms, 1964): 737–757.
Cod: 5,343
004 **Prolegomena in Aristidem**, ed. F.W. Lenz, *The Aristeides prolegomena* [*Mnemosyne*, suppl. 5. Leiden: Brill, 1959]: 111–119, 121–125, 127–151, 153–155, 157–166, 169–172.
Cod
005 **Progymnasmatum fragmenta**, ed. H. Rabe, *Aphthonii progymnasmata*. Leipzig: Teubner, 1926: 59–69.
Cod
006 **Paraphrases**, ed. S. Glöckner, "Aus Sopatros μεταποιήσεις," *Rheinisches Museum* 65 (1910) 505–514.
Cod

1683 **SOPHAENETUS** Hist.
5–4 B.C.: Stymphalicus
001 **Testimonia**, FGrH #109: 2B:523.
NQ
002 **Fragmenta**, FGrH #109: 2B:523.
Q

1684 *SOPHIA JESU CHRISTI*
A.D. 2
001 **Fragmentum**, *P. Oxy.* 8.1081.
Pap

0502 **SOPHILUS** Comic.
4 B.C.?
001 **Fragmenta**, ed. T. Kock, *Comicorum Atticorum fragmenta*, vol. 2. Leipzig: Teubner, 1884: 444–447.
frr. 3–8 + tituli.
Q: 101
002 **Fragmenta**, ed. A. Meineke, *Fragmenta comicorum Graecorum*, vol. 3. Berlin: Reimer, 1840 (repr. De Gruyter, 1970): 581–583.
Q: 95
x01 **Problema**.
App. Anth. 7.5: Cf. EPIGRAMMATICI in *App. Anth.* (7052 007).

0011 **SOPHOCLES** Trag.
5 B.C.: Atheniensis
001 **Trachiniae**, ed. A. Dain and P. Mazon, *Sophocle*, vol. 1. Paris: Les Belles Lettres, 1955 (repr. 1967 (1st edn. rev.)): 14–60.
Cod: 7,439
002 **Antigone**, ed. Dain and Mazon, *op. cit.*, vol. 1, 72–122.
Cod: 7,560
003 **Ajax**, ed. Dain and Mazon, *op. cit.*, vol. 2

(1958; repr. 1968 (1st edn. rev.)): 10–59.
Cod: 8,045

004 **Oedipus tyrannus**, ed. Dain and Mazon, *op. cit.*, vol. 2, 72–128.
Cod: 9,472

005 **Electra**, ed. Dain and Mazon, *op. cit.*, vol. 2, 138–194.
Cod: 8,920

006 **Philoctetes**, ed. Dain and Mazon, *op. cit.*, vol. 3 (1960; repr. 1967 (1st edn. rev.)): 10–66.
Cod: 8,977

007 **Oedipus Coloneus**, ed. Dain and Mazon, *op. cit.*, vol. 3, 78–152.
Cod: 10,656

008 **Fragmenta**, ed. S. Radt, *Tragicorum Graecorum fragmenta*, vol. 4. Göttingen: Vandenhoeck & Ruprecht, 1977: 99–120, 122–324, 326–338, 340–353, 355–380, 382–390, 392–435, 437–445, 447–484, 486–656.
frr. 1–25a, 28–72, 74–100a, 108–120, 122–141, 143–150, 152–159, 162–179, 180a–185, 187–190, 198a–203, 205–223b, 225–227, 235–289, 291–312, 314–314b, 316, 318–324, 326–334, 337–342, 345–360, 363–364, 367–371, 373–375, 377–412, 414–418, 420–445a, 447–450, 451a, 453–458, 460–469, 471–496, 498–527, 528a–546, 549–573, 576–644, 646–648, 650–655, 658–703, 706–730, 730a–g (ed. R. Kannicht), 732, 734–741, 743–747, 749–800, 803–804, 806–808, 811–829, 831–849, 851–881, 883–885a, 887–890, 892–898, 900–982, 984–985, 987–1027b, 1029–1032, 1034–1056, 1058–1063, 1065–1066, 1068, 1070, 1072–1079, 1081–1095, 1097–1112, 1114–1115, 1116a, 1117, 1119, 1122, 1124–1125, 1130–1133, 1135–1154.
Q, Pap: 16,027

009 **Fragmenta**, ed. M.L. West, *Iambi et elegi Graeci*, vol. 2. Oxford: Clarendon Press, 1972: 145–146.
frr. 1, 4–5.
Q: 46

010 **Fragmenta**, ed. D.L. Page, *Poetae melici Graeci*. Oxford: Clarendon Press, 1962 (repr. 1967 (1st edn. corr.)): 380–381.
fr. 1.
Q, Epigr: 52

x01 **Epigrammata** (*App. Anth.*).
Epigramma exhortatorium et supplicatorium: 4.12.
Epigramma irrisorium: 5.5.
App. Anth. 4.12: Cf. EPIGRAMMATICI in *App. Anth.* (7052 004).
App. Anth. 5.5: Cf. EPIGRAMMATICI in *App. Anth.* (7052 005).

0326 **SOPHOCLES Junior** Trag.
4 B.C.

001 **Fragmentum**, ed. B. Snell, *Tragicorum Graecorum fragmenta*, vol. 1. Göttingen: Vandenhoeck & Ruprecht, 1971: 208.
fr. 1.
Q: [5]

4030 **SOPHONIAS** Phil.
A.D. 13–14

001 **In libros Aristotelis de anima paraphrasis**, ed. M. Hayduck, *Sophoniae in libros Aristotelis de anima paraphrasis* [*Commentaria in Aristotelem Graeca* 23.1. Berlin: Reimer, 1883]: 1–152.
Cod: [75,231]

x01 **In parva naturalia commentaria.**
CAG 5.6, pp. 1–44.
Cf. THEMISTIUS Phil. et Rhet. (2001 041).

0524 **SOPHRON** Mimogr.
5 B.C.

001 **Fragmenta**, ed. G. Kaibel, *Comicorum Graecorum fragmenta*, vol. 1.1 [*Poetarum Graecorum fragmenta*, vol. 6.1. Berlin: Weidmann, 1899]: 154–179.
frr. 1–3, 5–6, 10–12, 14–16, 18–30, 32–37, 39, 41–42, 46, 48–50, 52–64, 66–68, 70, 72–75, 81–92, 94–101, 104–106, 110, 117–118, 120–121, 123, 125–127, 129, 131, 134–135, 144, 149–150, 156–158, 163, 165–166, 168.
Q: 643

002 **Fragmenta**, ed. J. Demiańczuk, *Supplementum comicum*. Krakau: Nakładem Akademii, 1912 (repr. Hildesheim: Olms, 1967): 125–126.
frr. 1–2.
Q: 34

003 **Fragmentum**, ed. D.L. Page, *Select papyri*, vol. 3 [*Literary papyri*]. London: Heinemann, 1941 (repr. 1970): 330.
PSI 1214.
Pap

004 **Titulus**, *P. Oxy.* 2.301.
NQ

4149 **SOPHRONIUS** Gramm.
A.D. 9: Alexandrinus

001 **Excerpta ex Joannis Characis commentariis in Theodosii Alexandrini canones**, ed. A. Hilgard, *Grammatici Graeci*, vol. 4.2. Leipzig: Teubner, 1894 (repr. Hildesheim: Olms, 1965): 375–434.
Cod

4042 **SOPHRONIUS** Soph.
A.D. 6–7: Damascenus

001 **Epistula Synodica**, MPG 87.3: 3148–3200.
Cod

002 **Orationes**, MPG 87.3: 3217–3364.
In sanctissimae deiparae annuntiationem (orat. 2): col. 3217–3288.
In exaltationem sanctae crucis (orat. 4): col. 3301–3309.
De festo sanctae crucis (orat. 5): col. 3309–3316.
Encomium in sanctum Joannem Baptistam (orat. 7): col. 3321–3354.
In sanctos apostolos Petrum et Paulum (orat. 8): col. 3356–3364.
Encomium de sancto Joanne evangelista (orat. 9): col. 3364.
Cod

003 **De peccatorum confessione,** MPG 87.3: 3365–3372.
Cod

004 **Fragmentum de baptismate apostolorum,** MPG 87.3: 3372.
Cod

005 **Laudes in sanctos Cyrum et Joannem,** MPG 87.3: 3380–3424.
Cod

006 **Narratio miraculorum sanctorum Cyri et Joannis,** MPG 87.3: 3424–3676.
Cod

007 **De sanctis Cyro et Joanne,** MPG 87.3: 3677–3689.
Cod

008 **Alia vita acephala sanctorum martyrum Cyri et Joannis,** MPG 87.3: 3689–3696.
Cod

009 **Vita Mariae Aegyptiae,** MPG 87.3: 3697–3726.
Cod

010 **Anacreontica,** MPG 87.3: 3733–3838.
Cod

011 **Triodium,** MPG 87.3: 3840–3981.
Cod

012 **Commentarius,** MPG 87.3: 3981–4001.
Cod

013 **Oratio,** MPG 87.3: 4001–4004.
Cod

014 **Troparium horarum,** MPG 87.3: 4005–4009.
Cod

015 **Fragmentum dogmaticum,** MPG 87.3: 4009–4012.
Cod

016 **Epigrammata,** AG 1.90, 123; 7.679–680; 9.787.
Q: 211

0565 **SORANUS** Med.
A.D. 1–2: Ephesius

001 **Gynaeciorum libri iv,** ed. J. Ilberg, *Sorani Gynaeciorum libri iv, de signis fracturarum, de fasciis, vita Hippocratis secundum Soranum* [*Corpus medicorum Graecorum,* vol. 4. Leipzig: Teubner, 1927]: 3–152.
Cod: 42,415

002 **De signis fracturarum,** ed. Ilberg, *op. cit.,* 155–158.
Cod: 1,157

003 **De fasciis,** ed. Ilberg, *op. cit.,* 159–171.
Cod: 2,767

004 **Vita Hippocratis,** ed. Ilberg, *op. cit.,* 175–178.
Cod: 701

2481 **SOSANDER** Perieg.
ante 1 B.C.

001 **Testimonium,** FGrH #714: 3C:603.
NQ

1076 **SOSANDRUS** Med.
ante A.D. 2

x01 **Fragmentum ap. Galenum.**
K12.733.
Cf. GALENUS Med. (0057 076).

x02 **Fragmentum ap. Aëtium** (lib. 7).
CMG, vol. 8.2, p. 328.
Cf. AËTIUS Med. (0718 007).

1686 **SOSIBIUS** Gramm.
fiq Sosibius Lacon
3 B.C.

x01 **Fragmentum,** FGrH #595, fr. 26: 3B:718–719.
Cf. SOSIBIUS Gramm. (1685 002).
Q

1685 **SOSIBIUS** Gramm.
fiq Sosibius ὁ λυτικός
3–2 B.C.: Lacon

001 **Testimonia,** FGrH #595: 3B:713–714.
NQ

002 **Fragmenta,** FGrH #595: 3B:714–718.
frr. 1–25.
fr. 26: altero auctore Sosibio Gramm. (1686).
Q

003 **Fragmentum** (*P. Oxy.* 24.2389), ed. H.J. Mette, "Die 'Kleinen' griechischen Historiker heute," *Lustrum* 21 (1978) 32.
fr. 6 bis.
Pap

0503 **SOSICRATES** Comic.
3 B.C.?

001 **Fragmenta,** ed. T. Kock, *Comicorum Atticorum fragmenta,* vol. 3. Leipzig: Teubner, 1888: 391–392.
frr. 1–5, 7.
Q: 77

002 **Fragmenta,** ed. A. Meineke, *Fragmenta comicorum Graecorum,* vol. 4. Berlin: Reimer, 1841 (repr. De Gruyter, 1970): 591–592.
Q: 67

1687 **SOSICRATES** Hist.
2 B.C.: fort. Rhodius

001 **Testimonia,** FGrH #461: 3B:398–399.
NQ

002 **Fragmenta,** FGrH #461: 3B:399–400.
Q

1077 **SOSICRATES** Med.
ante A.D. 1

x01 **Fragmentum ap. Galenum.**
K13.114.
Cf. GALENUS Med. (0057 076).

0504 **SOSIPATER** Comic.
3 B.C.?

001 **Fragmentum,** ed. T. Kock, *Comicorum Atticorum fragmenta,* vol. 3. Leipzig: Teubner, 1888: 314–316.
fr. 1.
Cod: 378

002 **Fragmentum,** ed. A. Meineke, *Fragmenta comicorum Graecorum,* vol. 4. Berlin: Reimer, 1841 (repr. De Gruyter, 1970): 482–484.
Cod: 381

0338 **SOSIPHANES** Trag.
4 B.C.: Syracusanus
001 **Fragmenta**, ed. B. Snell, *Tragicorum Grae-corum fragmenta*, vol. 1. Göttingen: Vanden-hoeck & Ruprecht, 1971: 261–263.
frr. 1–5, 7.
Q: [100]

0340 **SOSITHEUS** Trag.
3 B.C.
001 **Fragmenta**, ed. B. Snell, *Tragicorum Grae-corum fragmenta*, vol. 1. Göttingen: Vanden-hoeck & Ruprecht, 1971: 270–272.
frr. 1, 2, 3–4.
Q: [169]

2568 **SOSTHENES** Hist.
Incertum: Cnidius
001 **Fragmenta**, FGrH #846: 3C:931–932.
Q

1688 **SOSTRATUS** Gramm.
1 B.C.: Nyssensis
001 **Fragmenta**, FGrH #23: 1A:186–188, *11–*12 addenda.
Q
002 **Titulus**, ed. H. Lloyd-Jones and P. Parsons, *Supplementum Hellenisticum*. Berlin: De Gruy-ter, 1983: 353.
fr. 735.
NQ: [2]

2694 **SOSTRATUS** Poeta
vel Sosicrates
1 B.C.?: Phanagorita
001 **Tituli**, ed. H. Lloyd-Jones and P. Parsons, *Supplementum Hellenisticum*. Berlin: De Gruy-ter, 1983: 352.
fr. 732–733.
NQ: [2]

1689 **SOSYLUS** Hist.
3 B.C.: Lacedaemonius
001 **Testimonia**, FGrH #176: 2B:903.
NQ
002 **Fragmenta**, FGrH #176: 2B:903–906.
fr. 1: *P. Würzburg*.
Q, Pap

1690 *SOTADEA*
Incertum
Cf. et SOTADES Iamb. (1691).
001 **Fragmenta**, ed. J.U. Powell, *Collectanea Alex-andrina*. Oxford: Clarendon Press, 1925 (repr. 1970): 240–244.
frr. 6–23.
Q: [541]

0505 **SOTADES** Comic.
4 B.C.
001 **Fragmenta**, ed. T. Kock, *Comicorum Attico-rum fragmenta*, vol. 2. Leipzig: Teubner, 1884: 447–449.
frr. 1–3.
Q: 211
002 **Fragmenta**, ed. A. Meineke, *Fragmenta comico-rum Graecorum*, vol. 3. Berlin: Reimer, 1840 (repr. De Gruyter, 1970): 585–586, 588.
Q: 210
003 **Fragmentum**, ed. J. Demiańczuk, *Supplemen-tum comicum*. Krakau: Nakładem Akademii, 1912 (repr. Hildesheim: Olms, 1967): 83.
fr. 1.
Q: 33

1691 **SOTADES** Iamb.
3 B.C.
Cf. et SOTADEA (1690).
001 **Fragmenta**, ed. J.U. Powell, *Collectanea Alex-andrina*. Oxford: Clarendon Press, 1925 (repr. 1970): 238–239.
frr. 1–4.
Q: [75]

2258 **SOTADES** Phil.
Incertum: Atheniensis
001 **Testimonium**, FGrH #358: 3B:218.
NQ

2442 **SOTERICHUS** Epic. et Hist.
A.D. 3–4: Oasites
001 **Testimonia**, FGrH #641: 3C:187–188.
NQ
002 **Fragmentum**, FGrH #641: 3C:188.
Q

1071 **SOTION** Biogr.
3–2 B.C.: Alexandrinus
001 **Fragmenta**, ed. F. Wehrli, *Sotion* [*Die Schule des Aristoteles*, suppl. 2. Basel: Schwabe, 1978]: 23–31.
Q

0587 **SOTION** <Paradox.>
A.D. 1
001 **Fragmenta**, ed. A. Westermann, *Scriptores re-rum mirabilium Graeci*. Braunschweig: Wester-mann, 1839 (repr. Amsterdam: Hakkert, 1963): 183–191.
Cod

2048 **Salaminius Hermias SOZOMENUS** Scr. Eccl.
A.D. 5
001 **Historia ecclesiastica**, ed. J. Bidez and G.C. Hansen, *Sozomenus. Kirchengeschichte* [*Die griechischen christlichen Schriftsteller* 50. Ber-lin: Akademie-Verlag, 1960]: 1–408.
Cod: [119,602]

1692 **SPEUSIPPUS** Phil.
4 B.C.: Atheniensis
001 **Epistulae**, ed. R. Hercher, *Epistolographi*

Graeci. Paris: Didot, 1873 (repr. Amsterdam: Hakkert, 1965): 632–634.
Cod: [492]

002 **Epistula ad Philippum regem**, ed. E. Bickermann and J. Sykutris, *Speusipps Brief an König Philipp.* Leipzig: Hirzel, 1928: 7–12.
Cod

003 **Fragmenta**, ed. P. Lang, *De Speusippi academici scriptis.* Bonn: Georg, 1911 (repr. Hildesheim: Olms, 1965): 51–87.
Q

004 **Epigramma**, AG 16.31.
Q: 16

1693 **SPHAERUS** Phil.
3 B.C.: Borysthenius

001 **Fragmenta**, ed. J. von Arnim, *Stoicorum veterum fragmenta*, vol. 1. Leipzig: Teubner, 1905 (repr. Stuttgart: 1968): 139–142.
Q

002 **Testimonia**, FGrH #585: 3B:700–701.
NQ

003 **Fragmenta**, FGrH #585: 3B:701.
Q

1846 **SPINTHARUS** Trag.
Incertum

001 **Tituli**, ed. B. Snell, *Tragicorum Graecorum fragmenta*, vol. 1. Göttingen: Vandenhoeck & Ruprecht, 1971: 168.
NQ

STADIASMUS
Cf. PERIPLUS MARIS MAGNI (0077).

2182 **STAPHYLUS** Hist.
ante 2 B.C.: Naucratites

001 **Testimonium**, FGrH #269: 3A:80.
NQ

002 **Fragmenta**, FGrH #269: 3A:80–82.
Q

STASINUS Epic.
Cf. CYPRIA (1296).

1694 **STATYLLIUS FLACCUS** Epigr.
fiq Tullius Flaccus
1 B.C.?

001 **Epigrammata**, AG **5**.5; **6**.193, 196; **7**.290, 542, 650; **9**.37, 44–45, 98, 117; **12**.12, 25–27; **16**.211.
AG 6.165: Cf. PHALAECUS Epigr. (1581 001).
AG 7.294: Cf. TULLIUS LAUREA Epigr. (1743 001).
Q: 557

9021 **STEPHANUS** Alchem.
fiq Stephanus Phil.
A.D. 7: Alexandrinus
Cf. et STEPHANUS Phil. (9019).

001 **De magna et sacra arte**, ed. J.L. Ideler, *Physici et medici Graeci minores*, vol. 2. Berlin: Rei-

mer, 1842 (repr. Amsterdam: Hakkert, 1963): 199–253.
Cod

0506 **STEPHANUS** Comic.
4–3 B.C.

001 **Fragmentum**, ed. T. Kock, *Comicorum Atticorum fragmenta*, vol. 3. Leipzig: Teubner, 1888: 360.
fr. 1.
Q: 38

002 **Fragmentum**, ed. A. Meineke, *Fragmenta comicorum Graecorum*, vol. 4. Berlin: Reimer, 1841 (repr. De Gruyter, 1970): 544.
Q: 37

4028 **STEPHANUS** Gramm.
A.D. 6: Byzantius

001 **Ethnica**, ed. A. Meineke, *Stephan von Byzanz. Ethnika.* Berlin: Reimer, 1849 (repr. Graz: Akademische Druck- und Verlagsanstalt, 1958): 1–713.
Cod: [104,030]

002 **Epigramma**, AG 9.385.
Q: 179

9020 **STEPHANUS** Gramm.
A.D. 12?: fort. Constantinopolitanus

001 **In artem rhetoricam commentaria**, ed. H. Rabe, *Stephani in artem rhetoricam commentarium* [*Commentaria in Aristotelem Graeca* 21.2. Berlin: Reimer, 1896]: 263–322.
Cod

0724 **STEPHANUS** Med.
fiq Stephanus Alexandrinus
A.D. 7: Atheniensis
Cf. et STEPHANUS ALEXANDRINUS Med. (0736).
Cf. et THEOPHILUS Protospatharius et STEPHANUS ATHENIENSIS Med. (0746).
Cf. et THEOPHILUS Protospatharius, DAMASCIUS et STEPHANUS ATHENIENSIS Med. (0728).

001 **Commentarii in priorem Galeni librum therapeuticum ad Glauconem**, ed. F.R. Dietz, *Scholia in Hippocratem et Galenum*, vol. 1. Königsberg: Borntraeger, 1834 (repr. Amsterdam: Hakkert, 1966): 233–344.
Cod: 29,900

002 **Scholia in Hippocratis prognosticon**, ed. J.M. Duffy, *Commentary on Hippocrates' Prognosticon* [*Diss.* SUNY Buffalo (1975)]: 1–243.
Cod: 51,411

003 **Collyrium ophthalmicum**, ed. W. Studemund, *Index lectionum in universitate litterarum Vratislaviensi per hiemem anni 1888–1889.* Breslau: Breslau University Press, 1889: 12–14.
Cod: 1,062

004 **Scholia in Hippocratis de fracturis**, ed. D. Irmer, *Palladius. Kommentar zu Hippokrates 'De fracturis' und seine Parallelversion unter*

dem Namen des Stephanus von Alexandria
[*Hamburger philologische Studien* 45. Hamburg: Buske, 1977]: 17–89.
Cod

0736 **STEPHANUS** Med.
fiq Stephanus Atheniensis
A.D. 7: Alexandrinus
Cf. et STEPHANUS ATHENIENSIS Med. (0724).
001 **In Magni sophistae librum de urinis**, ed. U.C. Bussemaker, "In Magni sophistae librum de urinis," *Revue de Philologie* 1 (1845) 423–438, 543–560.
Cod: 8,366

9019 **STEPHANUS** Phil.
fiq Stephanus Alchem.
A.D. 7: Alexandrinus, Constantinopolitanus
Cf. et STEPHANUS Alchem. (9021).
001 **In librum Aristotelis de interpretatione commentarium**, ed. M. Hayduck, *Stephani in librum Aristotelis de interpretatione commentarium* [*Commentaria in Aristotelem Graeca* 18.3. Berlin: Reimer, 1885]: 1–68.
Cod

0292 **STESICHORUS** Lyr.
7–6 B.C.: Himeraeus
001 **Fragmenta**, ed. D.L. Page, *Poetae melici Graeci*. Oxford: Clarendon Press, 1962 (repr. 1967 (1st edn. corr.)): 97–102, 104, 106, 109, 112–121, 123–132, 135, 137.
frr. 1–2, 4, 7–8, 10–11, 15–16, 23, 32–35, 37, 40, 44–46, 51, 55–56, 58, 63, 65–68, 70, 72–73, 76–80, 82–84, 87, 89, 97, 101.
Q, Pap: [715]
002 **Fragmenta**, ed. D.L. Page, *Supplementum lyricis Graecis*. Oxford: Clarendon Press, 1974: 6–43.
frr. S7–S84: *P. Oxy.* 2617.
frr. S88–S132: *P. Oxy.* 2619.
frr. S133–S147: *P. Oxy.* 2803.
frr. S148–S150: *P. Oxy.* 2618.
Pap: [2,778]
003 **Tituli**, ed. Page, PMG, 107–108, 111–112, 115, 118, 136, 138.
NQ

0981 **STESICHORUS II** Lyr.
4 B.C.: Himeraeus
001 **Titulus**, ed. D.L. Page, *Poetae melici Graeci*. Oxford: Clarendon Press, 1962 (repr. 1967 (1st edn. corr.)): 443.
NQ

2171 **STESICLIDES** Hist.
vel Ctesicles
2–1 B.C.?: Atheniensis
001 **Fragmenta**, FGrH #245: 2B:1128–1129.
Q

1923 **STESIMBROTUS** Hist.
5 B.C.: Thasius
001 **Testimonia**, FGrH #107: 2B:515–516.
NQ
002 **Fragmenta**, FGrH #107: **2B**:516–522; **3B**:742 addenda.
Q

0315 **STHENELUS** Trag.
5 B.C.
001 **Fragmentum**, ed. B. Snell, *Tragicorum Graecorum fragmenta*, vol. 1. Göttingen: Vandenhoeck & Ruprecht, 1971: 151.
fr. 1.
Q: [9]
002 **Fragmentum**, ed. H. Lloyd-Jones and P. Parsons, *Supplementum Hellenisticum*. Berlin: De Gruyter, 1983: 354.
fr. 736.
Q: [6]

1695 **<STHENIDAS>** Phil.
3 B.C./A.D. 2
001 **Fragmentum**, ed. H. Thesleff, *The Pythagorean texts of the Hellenistic period*. Åbo: Åbo Akademi, 1965: 187–188.
Q: 197

2037 **Joannes STOBAEUS Anthologus**
A.D. 5
001 **Anthologium**, ed. C. Wachsmuth and O. Hense, *Ioannis Stobaei anthologium*, 5 vols. Berlin: Weidmann, 1–2:1884; 3:1894; 4:1909; 5:1912 (repr. 1958): 1:15–502; 2:3–264; 3:3–764; 4:1–675; 5:676–1143.
Cod: [393,445]

0099 **STRABO** Geogr.
1 B.C.–A.D. 1: Amasiotes
001 **Geographica**, ed. A. Meineke, *Strabonis geographica*, 3 vols. Leipzig: Teubner, 1877 (repr. Graz: Akademische Druck- und Verlagsanstalt, 1969): 1:xiii–xv, 1–396; 2:397–814; 3:815–1173.
Cod: 299,836
002 **Testimonia**, FGrH #91: 2A:430.
NQ
003 **Fragmenta**, FGrH #91: 2A:430–436.
Q

0507 **STRATON** Comic.
4–3 B.C.
001 **Fragmentum**, ed. T. Kock, *Comicorum Atticorum fragmenta*, vol. 3. Leipzig: Teubner, 1888: 361–362.
fr. 1.
Q: 302
002 **Fragmentum**, ed. A. Meineke, *Fragmenta comicorum Graecorum*, vol. 4. Berlin: Reimer, 1841 (repr. De Gruyter, 1970): 545–546.
Q: 302
003 **Fragmentum**, ed. C. Austin, *Comicorum Grae-*

corum fragmenta in papyris reperta. Berlin: De
Gruyter, 1973: 205–206.
fr. 219.
Pap: 326

1697 **STRATON** Epigr.
A.D. 2: Sardianus
  001 **Epigrammata**, AG 11.19, 21–22, 117, 225;
  12.1–11, 13, 15–16, 21, 175–229, 231, 234–
  255, 258; **16**.213.
  AG 11.118–122: Cf. CALLICTER Epigr. (0148
  001).
  Q: 3,302

1963 **STRATON** Hist.
2 B.C.
  001 **Testimonium**, FGrH #168: 2B:893.
  NQ

1080 **STRATON** Med.
3 B.C.: Alexandrinus
  x01 **Fragmenta ap. Philumenum**.
  CMG, vol. 10.1.1, pp. 9, 28, 30, 36, 40.
  Cf. PHILUMENUS Med. (0671 001).

1081 **STRATON** Med.
A.D. 1: Berytensis
  x01 **Fragmenta ap. Galenum**.
  K13.290, 303.
  Cf. GALENUS Med. (0057 076).
  x02 **Fragmenta ap. Alexandrum Trallianum**.
  Puschmann, vol. 1, pp. 563, 565, 571.
  Cf. ALEXANDER Med. (0744 003).

1696 **STRATON** Phil.
3 B.C.: Lampsacenus
  001 **Fragmenta**, ed. F. Wehrli, *Straton von Lamp-
  sakos* [*Die Schule des Aristoteles*, vol. 5, 2nd
  edn. Basel: Schwabe, 1969]: 12–42.
  Q

2645 **STRATONICUS** Poeta
5–4 B.C.: Atheniensis
  001 **Fragmentum**, ed. H. Lloyd-Jones and P. Parsons, *Supplementum Hellenisticum*. Berlin: De
  Gruyter, 1983: 354.
  fr. 737.
  Q: [11]

0508 **STRATTIS** Comic.
5 B.C.: Atheniensis
  001 **Fragmenta**, ed. T. Kock, *Comicorum Atticorum fragmenta*, vol. 1. Leipzig: Teubner, 1880:
  711–715, 717–733.
  frr. 1–4, 8–9, 11, 13–14, 22–48, 51–63, 66–67,
  71–75, 77–80 + tituli.
  Q: 627
  002 **Fragmenta**, ed. A. Meineke, *Fragmenta comicorum Graecorum*, vol. 2.2. Berlin: Reimer, 1840
  (repr. De Gruyter, 1970): 763–764, 766–768,
  771–776, 778–781, 783–788.
  Q: 571

  003 **Fragmenta**, ed. J. Demiańczuk, *Supplementum
  comicum*. Krakau: Nakładem Akademii, 1912
  (repr. Hildesheim: Olms, 1967): 84–86.
  frr. 1–10.
  Q: 40
  004 **Fragmenta**, ed. C. Austin, *Comicorum Graecorum fragmenta in papyris reperta.* Berlin: De
  Gruyter, 1973: 207–216.
  fr. 220 + tituli.
  Pap: 713
  005 **Fragmenta**, ed. Meineke, *op. cit.*, vol. 5.1
  (1857; repr. 1970): cxvi.
  Q: [7]

1931 **STRATTIS** Hist.
post 4 B.C.: Olynthius
  001 **Testimonium**, FGrH #118: 2B:622.
  NQ

STYLIANUS <Epigr.>
A.D. 9–10: Neocaesariensis
AG 16.387c.
Cf. ANONYMI EPIGRAMMATICI (0138 001).

9010 *SUDA*
A.D. 10
  001 **Lexicon**, ed. A. Adler, *Suidae lexicon*, 4 vols.
  [*Lexicographi Graeci* 1.1–1.4. Leipzig: Teubner, 1.1:1928; 1.2:1931; 1.3:1933; 1.4:1935
  (repr. Stuttgart: 1.1:1971; 1.2:1967; 1.3:1967;
  1.4:1971)]: **1.1**:1–549; **1.2**:1–740; **1.3**:1–632;
  1.4:1–854.
  Cod: [677,708]
  002 **Onomasticon tacticon**, ed. Adler, *op. cit.*, vol.
  1.4, 855–864.
  Cod: [2,511]

1760 **Gaius SUETONIUS TRANQUILLUS** Hist.
et Gramm.
A.D. 1–2: Romanus
  001 Περὶ βλασφημιῶν καὶ πόθεν ἑκάστη, ed. J.
  Taillardat, *Suétone*. Περὶ βλασφημιῶν. Περὶ
  παιδιῶν. Paris: Les Belles Lettres, 1967: 48–
  63.
  Cod: [1,400]
  002 Περὶ τῶν παρ' Ἕλλησι παιδιῶν, ed. Taillardat,
  op. cit., 64–73.
  Cod

2416 **SUIDAS** Hist.
4/3 B.C.?: Thessalius
  001 **Fragmenta**, FGrH #602: 3B:733–736.
  Q

2660 **Lucius Cornelius SULLA FELIX** <Epigr.>
2–1 B.C.
  x01 **Epigramma dedicatorium**.
  App. Anth. 1.153: Cf. EPIGRAMMATICI in
  App. Anth. (7052 001).

1920 **Gaius SULPICIUS GALBA** Hist.
1 B.C.

001 **Testimonia,** FGrH #92: 2A:436.
NQ

002 **Fragmenta,** FGrH #92: 2A:436.
Q

1761 **SULPICIUS MAXIMUS** Epic.
A.D. 1

001 **Epigrammata,** ed. R. Cagnat, *Inscriptiones Graecae ad res Romanas pertinentes,* vol. 1. Rome: Bretschneider, 1964: 116–118.
Epigr

x01 **Epigramma sepulcrale.**
App. Anth. 2.267: Cf. EPIGRAMMATICI in *App. Anth.* (7052 002).

1826 *SURONIS EPISTULA*
ante 2 B.C.

x01 **Epistula.**
FGrH #723, fr. 2
Cf. EUPOLEMUS Hist. (2486 002).
Q

0264 **SUSARION** Comic.
6/5 B.C.: Megarensis

001 **Fragmentum,** ed. T. Kock, *Comicorum Atticorum fragmenta,* vol. 1. Leipzig: Teubner, 1880: 3.
fr. 1.
Q: 31

002 **Fragmentum,** ed. M.L. West, *Iambi et elegi Graeci,* vol. 2. Oxford: Clarendon Press, 1972: 147.
Q: [34]

003 **Fragmentum,** ed. A. Meineke, *Fragmenta comicorum Graecorum,* vol. 2.1. Berlin: Reimer, 1839 (repr. De Gruyter, 1970): 3.
Q: 31

SYMEON Scr. Eccl.
A.D. 4: Mesopotamius
Cf. <MACARIUS> Scr. Eccl. (2109).

1769 **SYMMACHUS** Int. Vet. Test.
A.D. 2

001 **Fragmenta,** ed. J. Reider, *An index to Aquila* (rev. N. Turner). Leiden: Brill, 1966: passim.
Q

1082 **SYNERUS** Med.
ante A.D. 2

x01 **Fragmentum ap. Galenum.**
K12.774–775.
Cf. GALENUS Med. (0057 076).

4043 **SYNESIUS** Epigr.
A.D. 6

001 **Epigramma,** AG 16.267.
Q: 49

2006 **SYNESIUS** Phil.
A.D. 4–5: Cyrenensis

001 **Epistulae,** ed. R. Hercher, *Epistolographi*

Graeci. Paris: Didot, 1873 (repr. Amsterdam: Hakkert, 1965): 638–739.
Cod: [40,238]

002 **Oratio de regno,** ed. N. Terzaghi, *Synesii Cyrenensis opuscula.* Rome: Polygraphica, 1944: 5–62.
Cod: [9,385]

003 **Aegyptii sive de providentia,** ed. Terzaghi, *op. cit.,* 63–131.
Cod: [12,027]

004 **Sermo de dono astrolabii,** ed. Terzaghi, *op. cit.,* 132–142.
Cod: [1,794]

005 **De insomniis,** ed. Terzaghi, *op. cit.,* 143–189.
Cod: [7,740]

006 **Calvitii encomium,** ed. Terzaghi, *op. cit.,* 190–232.
Cod: [7,580]

007 **Dion,** ed. Terzaghi, *op. cit.,* 233–278.
Cod: [8,336]

008 **Homiliae,** ed. Terzaghi, *op. cit.,* 279–282.
Cod: [668]

009 **Catastasis,** ed. Terzaghi, *op. cit.,* 283–293.
Cod: [1,877]

010 **Hymni,** ed. A. Dell'Era, *Sinesio di Cirene. Inni.* Rome: Tumminelli, 1968: 33–169.
Cod: [4,271]

011 **Epigrammata,** AG 16.76, 79.
Q: 18

x01 **Epigramma exhortatorium et supplicatorium.**
App. Anth. 4.74: Cf. EPIGRAMMATICI in *App. Anth.* (7052 004).

2047 *SYRIANI, SOPATRI ET MARCELLINI SCHOLIA AD HERMOGENIS STATUS*
post A.D. 7

001 **Scholia ad Hermogenis status,** ed. C. Walz, *Rhetores Graeci,* vol. 4. Stuttgart: Cotta, 1833 (repr. Osnabrück: Zeller, 1968): 39–846.
Cod: [193,499]

4017 **SYRIANUS** Phil.
A.D. 5: Atheniensis

001 **In metaphysica commentaria,** ed. W. Kroll, *Syriani in metaphysica commentaria* [*Commentaria in Aristotelem Graeca* 6.1. Berlin: Reimer, 1902]: 1–195.
Cod: [82,772]

002 **Commentarium in libros** περὶ ἰδεῶν, ed. H. Rabe, *Syriani in Hermogenem commentaria,* vol. 1. Leipzig: Teubner, 1892: 1–112.
Cod

003 **Commentarium in librum** περὶ στάσεων, ed. Rabe, *op. cit.,* vol. 2 (1893): 1–203.
Cod

x01 **Epigramma.**
AG 9.358.
Cf. et ANONYMI EPIGRAMMATICI (0138 001).

2540 **SYRISCUS** Hist.
3 B.C.: Cherronensis

001 **Testimonium,** FGrH #807: 3C:844.

test. 1: *Inscr. Cherronesos.*
NQ

1827 **SYRUS** Astrol.
A.D. 2?
001 **Fragmenta**, ed. A. Olivieri, *Codices Florentini*
[*Catalogus codicum astrologorum Graecorum*,
vol. 1. Brussels: Lamertin, 1898]: 131–134,
171–172.
Cod

1766 **TATIANUS** Apol.
A.D. 2: Syrius
001 **Oratio ad Graecos**, ed. E.J. Goodspeed, *Die
ältesten Apologeten*. Göttingen: Vandenhoeck &
Ruprecht, 1915: 268–305.
Cod: [10,690]
002 **Diatesseron**, ed. C.B. Welles, *The excavations
at Dura-Europos: final report* 5, pt. 1. New
Haven: Yale University Press, 1959: 74.
Pap: [86]

2476 **TAURON** Hist.
4 B.C.?
001 **Testimonium**, FGrH #710: 3C:592.
NQ
002 **Fragmentum**, FGrH #710: 3C:592.
Q

1084 **TELAMON** Med.
ante A.D. 2
x01 **Fragmentum ap. Galenum**.
K13.528.
Cf. GALENUS Med. (0057 077).

1597 **<TELAUGES>** Phil.
Incertum: Samius
001 **Titulus**, ed. H. Thesleff, *The Pythagorean texts
of the Hellenistic period*. Åbo: Åbo Akademi,
1965: 189.
NQ: 3

0510 **TELECLIDES** Comic.
5 B.C.
001 **Fragmenta**, ed. T. Kock, *Comicorum Atticorum fragmenta*, vol. 1. Leipzig: Teubner, 1880:
209–224.
frr. 1–5, 10, 13–14, 19–21, 23–28, 30–33, 35–
45, 47–66.
Q: 428
002 **Fragmenta**, ed. A. Meineke, *Fragmenta comicorum Graecorum*, vol. 2.1. Berlin: Reimer, 1839
(repr. De Gruyter, 1970): 361–366, 368–375.
p. 369: fr. 8 supplied from vol. 5.1, p. lx.
Q: 389
003 **Fragmenta**, ed. J. Demiańczuk, *Supplementum
comicum*. Krakau: Nakładem Akademii, 1912
(repr. Hildesheim: Olms, 1967): 86.
frr. 1–2.
Q: 6
005 **Fragmentum**, ed. A. Guida, "Frammenti inediti di Eupoli, Teleclide, Teognide, Giuliano

e Imerio da un nuovo codice del Lexicon
Vindobonense," *Prometheus* 5 (1979) 202.
Q

2264 **TELEPHANES** Hist.
ante A.D. 3
001 **Fragmentum**, FGrH #371: 3B:233.
Q

1049 **TELEPHANES** Med.
ante A.D. 2
x01 **Fragmentum ap. Galenum**.
K13.532.
Cf. GALENUS Med. (0057 077).

1698 **TELEPHUS** Gramm.
A.D. 2: Pergamenus
001 **Testimonia**, FGrH #505: 3B:482.
NQ
002 **Fragmenta**, FGrH #505: 3B:483.
Q

1699 **TELES** Phil.
3 B.C.: fort. Megarensis
001 Περὶ τοῦ δοκεῖν καὶ τοῦ εἶναι, ed. O. Hense,
Teletis reliquiae, 2nd edn. Tübingen: Mohr,
1909 (repr. Hildesheim: Olms, 1969): 3–4.
Q: [359]
002 Περὶ αὐταρκείας, ed. Hense, *op. cit.*, 5–20.
Q: [1,632]
003 Περὶ φυγῆς, ed. Hense, *op. cit.*, 21–32.
Q: [1,396]
004 Περὶ συγκρίσεως πενίας καὶ πλούτου (e Sto-
baeo, *Anth.* 97.31), ed. Hense, *op. cit.*, 33–44.
Q: [1,310]
005 Περὶ συγκρίσεως πενίας καὶ πλούτου (e Sto-
baeo, *Anth.* 95.21), ed. Hense, *op. cit.*, 45–48.
Q: [486]
006 Περὶ τοῦ μὴ εἶναι τέλος ἡδονήν, ed. Hense, *op.
cit.*, 49–51.
Q: [239]
007 Περὶ περιστάσεων, ed. Hense, *op. cit.*, 52–54.
Q: [229]
008 Περὶ ἀπαθείας, ed. Hense, *op. cit.*, 55–62.
Q: [1,045]

2211 **TELESARCHUS** Hist.
3–2 B.C.?
001 **Fragmentum**, FGrH #308: 3B:15.
Q

0369 **TELESILLA** Lyr.
5 B.C.: Argiva
001 **Fragmenta**, ed. D.L. Page, *Poetae melici
Graeci*. Oxford: Clarendon Press, 1962 (repr.
1967 (1st edn. corr.)): 372–374.
frr. 1–2, 6–8, 10.
Q: [24]

0377 **TELESTES** Lyr.
5 B.C.: Selinuntius
001 **Fragmenta**, ed. D.L. Page, *Poetae melici*

Graeci. Oxford: Clarendon Press, 1962 (repr. 1967 (1st edn. corr.)): 419–421.
frr. 1–2, 4, 6–7.
Q: [137]

002 **Titulus**, ed. Page, *op. cit.*, 421.
NQ

1903 **TELLIS** Hist.
3 B.C.

001 **Testimonium**, FGrH #61: 1A:298.
NQ

002 **Fragmenta**, FGrH #61: 1A:299.
Q

0299 **<TERPANDER>** Lyr.
7 B.C.: Lesbius

001 **Fragmenta**, ed. D.L. Page, *Poetae melici Graeci*. Oxford: Clarendon Press, 1962 (repr. 1967 (1st edn. corr.)): 362.
frr. 1–2.
Q: [21]

002 **Fragmentum**, ed. D.L. Page, *Supplementum lyricis Graecis*. Oxford: Clarendon Press, 1974: 4.
fr. S6: *P. Oxy.* 2737.
Pap: [4]

1700 *TESTAMENTA XII PATRIARCHARUM*
2 B.C./A.D. 3

001 **Testamenta xii patriarcharum**, ed. M. de Jonge, *Testamenta xii patriarcharum*, 2nd edn. [*Pseudepigrapha veteris testamenti Graece* 1. Leiden: Brill, 1970]: 1–86.
Cod: [19,845]

1701 *TESTAMENTUM ABRAHAE*
A.D. 1

001 **Testamentum Abrahae** (recensio A), ed. M.R. James, *The testament of Abraham* [*Texts and Studies* 2.2. Cambridge: Cambridge University Press, 1892]: 77–104.
Cod: [7,131]

002 **Testamentum Abrahae** (recensio B), ed. James, *op. cit.*, 105–119.
Cod: [3,301]

TESTAMENTUM ADAM
Cf. APOCALYPSIS ADAM (1153).

1702 *TESTAMENTUM JOBI*
A.D. 2/3

001 **Testamentum Jobi**, ed. S.P. Brock, *Testamentum Jobi* [*Pseudepigrapha veteris testamenti Graece* 2. Leiden: Brill, 1967]: 19–59.
Cod: [6,775]

TESTAMENTUM MOSIS
Cf. ASSUMPTIO MOSIS (1201).

2679 *TESTAMENTUM SALOMONIS*
A.D. 3?

001 **Testamentum Salomonis**, ed. C.C. McCown,

The testament of Solomon. Leipzig: Hinrichs, 1922: 5–120.
Cod

2015 *TESTAMENTUM XL MARTYRUM*
post A.D. 4

001 **Testamentum xl martyrum**, ed. H. Musurillo, *The acts of the Christian martyrs*. Oxford: Clarendon Press, 1972: 354–360.
Cod: [1,057]

1703 **TEUCER** Astrol.
A.D. 1: Babylonius

001 **Fragmenta**, ed. F. Boll, *Codices Germanici* [*Catalogus codicum astrologorum Graecorum* 7. Brussels: Lamertin, 1908]: 194–213.
Q

002 **Fragmenta**, ed. S. Weinstock, *Codices Britannici* [*Catalogus codicum astrologorum Graecorum* 9.2. Brussels: Academia, 1953]: 180–186.
Cod

1704 **TEUCER** Hist.
1 B.C.: Cyzicenus

001 **Testimonium**, FGrH #274: 3A:126.
NQ

002 **Fragmenta**, FGrH #274: 3A:126–127.
Q

2288 **TEUPALUS** Hist.
Incertum: Eleus

001 **Testimonium**, FGrH #408: 3B:301.
NQ

1705 **THALES** Phil.
6 B.C.: Milesius
Cf. et <SEPTEM SAPIENTES> (1667).

001 **Epistulae**, ed. R. Hercher, *Epistolographi Graeci*. Paris: Didot, 1873 (repr. Amsterdam: Hakkert, 1965): 740.
Q: [203]

002 **Testimonia**, ed. H. Diels and W. Kranz, *Die Fragmente der Vorsokratiker*, vol. 1, 6th edn. Berlin: Weidmann, 1951 (repr. Dublin: 1966): 67–79.
test. 1–23.
NQ

003 **Fragmenta**, ed. Diels and Kranz, *op. cit.*, 80–81.
frr. 1–4.
Q

x01 **Epigramma dedicatorium**.
App. Anth. 1.21(?): Cf. EPIGRAMMATICI in *App. Anth.* (7052 001).

1707 **Antonius THALLUS** Epigr.
fiq Antonius Argivus
A.D. 1: Milesius
Cf. et ANTONIUS Argivus Epigr. (0120).

001 **Epigrammata**, AG 6.91, 235; 7.188, 373; 9.220.
Q: 203

1706 **THALLUS** Hist.
      A.D. 1/2: fort. Samaritanus
  001 **Testimonia**, FGrH #256: 2B:1157.
      NQ
  002 **Fragmenta**, FGrH #256: 2B:1157–1158.
      Q

0925 **THAMYRAS** Med.
      ante A.D. 2
  x01 **Fragmentum ap. Galenum**.
      K13.300.
      Cf. GALENUS Med. (0057 076).

1085 **THARSEUS** Med.
      ante A.D. 1
  x01 **Fragmentum ap. Galenum**.
      K13.741–742.
      Cf. GALENUS Med. (0057 077).

4044 **THEAETETUS** Epigr.
      A.D. 6
  001 **Epigrammata**, AG **6**.27; **9**.659; **10**.16; **16**.32b,
      221, 233.
      Q: 252

1708 **THEAETETUS** Poeta
      3 B.C.: Cyrenaeus
  001 **Epigrammata**, AG **6**.357; 7.444, 499, 727.
      AG 13.29: Cf. NICAENETUS Epic. (1528 001).
      Q: 151
  x01 **Epigrammata** (*App. Anth.*).
      Epigramma sepulcrale: 2.28.
      Epigramma demonstrativum: 3.35.
      App. Anth. 2.28: Cf. EPIGRAMMATICI in *App.
      Anth.* (7052 002).
      App. Anth. 3.35: Cf. EPIGRAMMATICI in *App.
      Anth.* (7052 003).

1709 **THEAGENES** Hist.
      3 B.C.?: Macedo
  001 **Testimonium**, FGrH #774: 3C:768.
      NQ
  002 **Fragmenta**, FGrH #774: 3C:768–770.
      Q

2275 **THEAGENES** Phil.
      6 B.C.: Rheginus
  001 **Testimonia**, ed. H. Diels and W. Kranz, *Die
      Fragmente der Vorsokratiker*, vol. 1, 6th edn.
      Berlin: Weidmann, 1951 (repr. Dublin: 1966):
      51–52.
      test. 1–4.
      NQ

1710 **<THEAGES>** Phil.
      3 B.C.?
  001 **Fragmenta**, ed. H. Thesleff, *The Pythagorean
      texts of the Hellenistic period*. Åbo: Åbo Aka-
      demi, 1965: 190–193.
      Q: 1,145

0054 **<THEANO>** Phil.
      post 4 B.C.?
  001 **Fragmenta**, ed. H. Thesleff, *The Pythagorean
      texts of the Hellenistic period*. Åbo: Åbo Aka-
      demi, 1965: 195–201.
      Q: 1,915

1711 **<THEARIDAS>** Phil.
      3 B.C.
  001 **Fragmentum**, ed. H. Thesleff, *The Pythagorean
      texts of the Hellenistic period*. Åbo: Åbo Aka-
      demi, 1965: 201.
      Q: 32

1712 ***THEBAÏS***
      7/6 B.C.
  001 **Fragmenta**, ed. T.W. Allen, *Homeri opera*, vol.
      5. Oxford: Clarendon Press, 1912 (repr. 1969):
      113–114.
      frr. 1–5.
      Q

1713 **THEMISON** Hist.
      ante 3 B.C.?
  001 **Fragmenta**, FGrH #374: 3B:241.
      Q

1088 **THEMISON** Med.
      1 B.C.–A.D. 1: Laodicensis
  x01 **Fragmentum ap. Galenum**.
      K13.158–159.
      Cf. GALENUS Med. (0057 076).
  x02 **Fragmenta ap. Soranum**.
      CMG, vol. 4, pp. 10, 25.
      Cf. SORANUS Med. (0565 001).

2001 **THEMISTIUS** Phil. et Rhet.
      A.D. 4: Constantinopolitanus
  001 Περὶ φιλανθρωπίας ἢ Κωνστάντιος, ed. H.
      Schenkl and G. Downey, *Themistii orationes
      quae supersunt*, vol. 1. Leipzig: Teubner, 1965:
      4–25.
      Cod: [4,778]
  002 Εἰς Κωνστάντιον τὸν αὐτοκράτορα, ὅτι μά-
      λιστα φιλόσοφος ὁ βασιλεύς, ἢ χαριστήριος,
      ed. Schenkl and Downey, *op. cit.*, vol. 1, 28–
      56.
      Cod: [4,700]
  003 Πρεσβευτικὸς ὑπὲρ Κωνσταντινουπόλεως ῥη-
      θεὶς ἐν 'Ρώμῃ, ed. Schenkl and Downey, *op.
      cit.*, vol. 1, 58–68.
      Cod: [2,347]
  004 Εἰς τὸν αὐτοκράτορα Κωνστάντιον, ed. Schenkl
      and Downey, *op. cit.*, vol. 1, 70–89.
      Cod: [3,977]
  005 'Υπατικὸς εἰς τὸν αὐτοκράτορα 'Ιοβιανόν, ed.
      Schenkl and Downey, *op. cit.*, vol. 1, 92–104.
      Cod: [2,205]
  006 Φιλάδελφοι ἢ περὶ φιλανθρωπίας, ed. Schenkl
      and Downey, *op. cit.*, vol. 1, 106–125.
      Cod: [3,695]

007 Περὶ τῶν ἠτυχηκότων ἐπὶ Οὐάλεντος, ed. Schenkl and Downey, *op. cit.*, vol. 1, 128–151.
Cod: [4,631]

008 Πενταετηρικός, ed. Schenkl and Downey, *op. cit.*, vol. 1, 154–180.
Cod: [5,491]

009 Προτρεπτικὸς Οὐαλεντινιανῷ νέῳ, ed. Schenkl and Downey, *op. cit.*, vol. 1, 182–194.
Cod: [2,358]

010 Ἐπὶ τῆς εἰρήνης Οὐάλεντι, ed. Schenkl and Downey, *op. cit.*, vol. 1, 196–214.
Cod: [3,572]

011 Δεκετηρικὸς ἢ περὶ τῶν πρεπόντων λόγων τῷ βασιλεῖ, ed. Schenkl and Downey, *op. cit.*, vol. 1, 216–230.
Cod: [3,657]

013 Ἐρωτικὸς ἢ περὶ κάλλους βασιλικοῦ, ed. Schenkl and Downey, *op. cit.*, vol. 1, 232–257.
Cod: [5,583]

014 Πρεσβευτικὸς εἰς Θεοδόσιον αὐτοκράτορα, ed. Schenkl and Downey, *op. cit.*, vol. 1, 260–265.
Cod: [975]

015 Εἰς Θεοδόσιον· τίς ἡ βασιλικωτάτη τῶν ἀρετῶν, ed. Schenkl and Downey, *op. cit.*, vol. 1, 268–286.
Cod: [4,273]

016 Χαριστήριος τῷ αὐτοκράτορι ὑπὲρ τῆς εἰρήνης καὶ τῆς ὑπατείας τοῦ στρατηγοῦ Σατορνίνου, ed. Schenkl and Downey, *op. cit.*, vol. 1, 288–304.
Cod: [3,800]

017 Ἐπὶ τῇ χειροτονίᾳ τῆς πολιαρχίας, ed. Schenkl and Downey, *op. cit.*, vol. 1, 306–309.
Cod: [839]

018 Περὶ τῆς τοῦ βασιλέως φιληκοΐας, ed. Schenkl and Downey, *op. cit.*, vol. 1, 312–325.
Cod: [2,532]

019 Ἐπὶ τῇ φιλανθρωπίᾳ τοῦ αὐτοκράτορος Θεοδοσίου, ed. Schenkl and Downey, *op. cit.*, vol. 1, 328–339.
Cod: [2,236]

020 Ἐπιτάφιος ἐπὶ τῷ πατρί, ed. Schenkl, Downey, and Norman, *op. cit.*, vol. 2 (1971): 2–15.
Cod: [2,316]

021 Βασανιστὴς ἢ φιλόσοφος, ed. Schenkl, Downey, and Norman, *op. cit.*, vol. 2, 18–49.
Cod: [6,361]

022 Περὶ φιλίας, ed. Schenkl, Downey, and Norman, *op. cit.*, vol. 2, 52–73.
Cod: [5,143]

023 Σοφιστής, ed. Schenkl, Downey, and Norman, *op. cit.*, vol. 2, 76–95.
Cod: [4,811]

024 Προτρεπτικὸς Νικομηδεῦσιν εἰς φιλοσοφίαν, ed. Schenkl, Downey, and Norman, *op. cit.*, vol. 2, 98–111.
Cod: [2,477]

025 Πρὸς τὸν ἀξιώσαντα λέγειν ἐκ τοῦ παραχρῆμα, ed. Schenkl, Downey, and Norman, *op. cit.*, vol. 2, 114–115.
Cod: [370]

026 <Ὑπὲρ τοῦ λέγειν ἢ πῶς τῷ φιλοσόφῳ λεκτέον>, ed. Schenkl, Downey, and Norman, *op. cit.*, vol. 2, 118–151.
Cod: [5,816]

027 Περὶ τοῦ μὴ δεῖν τοῖς τόποις ἀλλὰ τοῖς ἀνδράσι προσέχειν, ed. Schenkl, Downey, and Norman, *op. cit.*, vol. 2, 154–167.
Cod: [2,821]

028 Ἡ ἐπὶ τῷ λόγῳ διάλεξις, ed. Schenkl, Downey, and Norman, *op. cit.*, vol. 2, 170–172.
Cod: [676]

029 Πρὸς τοὺς οὐκ ὀρθῶς ἐξηγουμένους τὸν σοφιστήν, ed. Schenkl, Downey, and Norman, *op. cit.*, vol. 2, 174–179.
Cod: [1,289]

030 Θέσις εἰ γεωργητέον, ed. Schenkl, Downey, and Norman, *op. cit.*, vol. 2, 182–186.
Cod: [1,023]

031 Περὶ προεδρίας εἰς τὴν σύγκλητον, ed. Schenkl, Downey, and Norman, *op. cit.*, vol. 2, 188–192.
Cod: [990]

032 Μετριοπαθὴς ἢ φιλότεκνος, ed. Schenkl, Downey, and Norman, *op. cit.*, vol. 2, 194–204.
Cod: [2,491]

033 <Περὶ τῶν ὀνομάτων τοῦ βασιλέως καὶ τοῦ ὑπάτου>, ed. Schenkl, Downey, and Norman, *op. cit.*, vol. 2, 206–210.
Cod: [1,021]

034 Πρὸς τοὺς αἰτιασαμένους ἐπὶ τῷ δέξασθαι τὴν ἀρχήν, ed. Schenkl, Downey, and Norman, *op. cit.*, vol. 2, 212–232.
Cod: [4,248]

035 <Φ>ιλόπολις, ed. Schenkl, Downey, and Norman, *op. cit.*, vol. 3 (1974): 1.
Cod: [134]

036 Περὶ ψυχῆς (fragmenta), ed. Schenkl, Downey, and Norman, *op. cit.*, vol. 3, 2–4.
Q: [200]

037 Περὶ φρονήσεως (fragmentum), ed. Schenkl, Downey, and Norman, *op. cit.*, vol. 3, 4–5.
Cod: [270]

038 **Analyticorum posteriorum paraphrasis**, ed. M. Wallies, *Themistii analyticorum posteriorum paraphrasis* [*Commentaria in Aristotelem Graeca* 5.1. Berlin: Reimer, 1900]: 1–66.
Cod: [25,395]

039 **In Aristotelis physica paraphrasis**, ed. H. Schenkl, *Themistii in Aristotelis physica paraphrasis* [*Commentaria in Aristotelem Graeca* 5.2. Berlin: Reimer, 1900]: 1–236.
Cod: [89,225]

040 **In libros Aristotelis de anima paraphrasis**, ed. R. Heinze, *Themistii in libros Aristotelis de anima paraphrasis* [*Commentaria in Aristotelem Graeca* 5.3. Berlin: Reimer, 1899]: 1–126.
Cod: [58,759]

041 **(Sophoniae) in parva naturalia commentarium**, ed. P. Wendland, *Themistii (Sophoniae) in*

parva naturalia commentarium [*Commentaria in Aristotelem Graeca* 5.6. Berlin: Reimer, 1903]: 1–44.
Cod: [16,301]

042 **Quae fertur in Aristotelis analyticorum priorum librum i paraphrasis**, ed. M. Wallies, *Themistii quae fertur in Aristotelis analyticorum priorum librum i paraphrasis* [*Commentaria in Aristotelem Graeca* 23.3. Berlin: Reimer, 1884]: 1–164.
Cod: [79,760]

x01 **Epigramma**.
AG 11.292.
Cf. PALLADAS Epigr. (2123 001).

0055 **THEMISTOCLIS EPISTULAE**
Incertum

001 **Epistulae**, ed. R. Hercher, *Epistolographi Graeci*. Paris: Didot, 1873 (repr. Amsterdam: Hakkert, 1965): 741–762.
Cod: [8,862]

1924 **THEMISTOGENES** Hist.
4 B.C.?: Syracusanus

001 **Testimonia**, FGrH #108: 2B:522.
NQ

2515 **THEOCHRESTUS** Hist.
post 4 B.C.?: fort. Cyrenaeus

001 **Testimonium**, FGrH #761: 3C:742.
NQ

002 **Fragmenta**, FGrH #761: 3C:742–743.
Q

0206 **THEOCLES** Lyr.
3 B.C.?

001 **Ithyphalli**, ed. J.U. Powell, *Collectanea Alexandrina*. Oxford: Clarendon Press, 1925 (repr. 1970): 173.
Q: [20]

1947 **THEOCLIUS** Hist.
vel Theocles vel Theoclus vel Theoclytus vel Theo Chius
A.D. 3-4?

001 **Fragmentum**, FGrH #214: 2B:945–946.
Q

0005 **THEOCRITUS** Bucol.
4–3 B.C.: Syracusanus

001 **Idyllia**, ed. A.S.F. Gow, *Theocritus*, vol. 1, 2nd edn. Cambridge: Cambridge University Press, 1952 (repr. 1965): 4–236.
Cod, Pap: 20,501

002 **Epigrammata**, ed. Gow, *op. cit.*, 240–254.
Q: 972

003 **Syrinx**, ed. Gow, *op. cit.*, 256.
Cod: 80

004 **Fragmentum**, ed. Gow, *op. cit.*, 238.
fr. 3.
Q: 42

005 **Epigrammata**, AG 6.336–340; 7.262, 658;

9.338, 432–435, 437, 598–600; **13**.3; **15**.21.
AG 6.177: Cf. ANONYMI EPIGRAMMATICI (0138 001).
AG 7.534: Cf. AUTOMEDON Epigr. (0140 001).
AG 7.659–664: Cf. LEONIDAS Epigr. (1458 001).
Q: 751

1714 **THEOCRITUS** Soph.
4 B.C.: Chius

001 **Fragmentum**, ed. E. Diehl, *Anthologia lyrica Graeca*, fasc. 1, 3rd edn. Leipzig: Teubner, 1949: 127.
Q: [26]

002 **Testimonium**, FGrH #760: 3C:742.
NQ

003 **Fragmentum**, ed. H. Lloyd-Jones and P. Parsons, *Supplementum Hellenisticum*. Berlin: De Gruyter, 1983: 355.
fr. 738.
Q: [24]

x01 **Epigramma sepulcrale**.
App. Anth. 2.46: Cf. EPIGRAMMATICI in *App. Anth.* (7052 002).

0329 **THEODECTAS** Trag.
4 B.C.

001 **Fragmenta**, ed. B. Snell, *Tragicorum Graecorum fragmenta*, vol. 1. Göttingen: Vandenhoeck & Ruprecht, 1971: 230–237.
frr. 1a, 2–3, 4–5, 6–12, 13–20.
Q: [484]

x01 **Aenigmata**.
App. Anth. 7.12–14: Cf. EPIGRAMMATICI in *App. Anth.* (7052 007).

1928 **THEODECTES** Hist.
4 B.C.: Phaselinus

001 **Testimonium**, FGrH #113: 2B:525.
NQ

2125 **THEODORETUS** Gramm.
A.D. 4

001 **Epigramma**, AG 16.34.
Q: 13

4089 **THEODORETUS** Scr. Eccl. et Theol.
A.D. 4–5: Cyrrhensis

001 **Graecarum affectionum curatio**, ed. P. Canivet, *Théodoret de Cyr. Thérapeutique des maladies helléniques*, 2 vols. [*Sources chrétiennes* 57. Paris: Cerf, 1958]: 1:100–287; 2:296–446.
Cod: [71,342]

002 **Eranistes**, ed. G.H. Ettlinger, *Theodoret of Cyrus. Eranistes*. Oxford: Clarendon Press, 1975: 61–266.
Cod: [59,985]

003 **Historia ecclesiastica**, ed. L. Parmentier and F. Scheidweiler, *Theodoret. Kirchengeschichte*, 2nd edn. [*Die griechischen christlichen Schrift-*

steller 44. Berlin: Akademie-Verlag, 1954]: 1–349.
Cod: [75,246]

004 **Historia religiosa** (= **Philotheus**), ed. P. Canivet and A. Leroy-Molinghen, *Théodoret de Cyr. L'histoire des moines de Syrie*, 2 vols. [*Sources chrétiennes* 234, 257. Paris: Cerf, 1:1977; 2:1979]: **1**:124–144, 160–508; **2**:8–250, 254–314.
Philotheus 31 = Oratio de divina et sancta caritate.
Cod: [50,751]

005 **Epistulae: Collectio Patmensis** (epistulae 1–52), ed. Y. Azéma, *Théodoret de Cyr. Correspondance I* [*Sources chrétiennes* 40. Paris: Cerf, 1955]: 74–121.
Cod: [8,988]

006 **Epistulae: Collectio Sirmondiana** (epistulae 1–95), ed. Y. Azéma, *Théodoret de Cyr. Correspondance II* [*Sources chrétiennes* 98. Paris: Cerf, 1964]: 20–248.
Cod: [22,584]

007 **Epistulae: Collectio Sirmondiana** (epistulae 96–147), ed. Y. Azéma, *Théodoret de Cyr. Correspondance III* [*Sources chrétienes* 111. Paris: Cerf, 1965]: 10–232.
Cod: [24,482]

008 **Commentaria in Isaiam** (1–3), ed. J.-N. Guinot, *Théodoret de Cyr. Commentaire sur Isaïe*, vol. 1 [*Sources chrétiennes* 276. Paris: Cerf, 1980]: 136–330.
Cf. et 4089 009.
Cod

009 **Interpretatio in Isaiam** (4–20), ed. A. Möhle, *Theodoret von Kyros. Kommentar zu Jesaia* [*Mitteilungen des Septuaginta-Unternehmens* 5. Berlin: Weidmann, 1932]: 50–263.
Cf. et 4089 008.
Cod: [50,137]

010 **Ad quaesita magorum** (fragmentum) [Sp.], ed. M. Brok, "Le livre contre les mages de Théodoret de Cyr," *Mélanges de science religieuse* 10 (1953) 183–184.
Cod: [724]

016 **Quaestiones et responsiones ad orthodoxos** [Dub.], ed. A. Papadopoulos-Kerameus, Θεοδωρήτου ἐπισκόπου πόλεως Κύρρου πρὸς τὰς ἐπενεχθείσας αὐτῷ ἐπερωτήσεις παρά τινος τὸν ἐξ Αἰγύπτου ἐπίσκοπον ἀποκρίσεις. St. Petersburg: Kirschbaum, 1895: 1–150.
Cod: [27,331]

017 **Homilia in nativitate Joannis Baptistae** [Sp.], ed. V. Latyšev, "Θεοδώρου τοῦ Δαφνοπάτου λόγοι δύο," *Pravoslavnyj Palestinskij Sbornik* 59 (1910) 3–14.
Cod: [3,077]

020 **De sancta trinitate**, MPG 75: 1148–1189.
Cod: [8,742]

021 **De incarnatione domini**, MPG 75: 1420–1477.
Cod: [11,893]

022 **Quaestiones in Octateuchum**, ed. N. Fernández Marcos and A. Sáenz-Badillos, *Theodoreti Cyrensis quaestiones in Octateuchum* [*Textos y Estudios <<Cardenal Cisneros>>* 17. Madrid: Poliglota Matritense, 1979]: 3–318.
Quaestiones in Genesim: pp. 3–99.
Quaestiones in Exodum: pp. 100–152.
Quaestiones in Leviticum: pp. 153–189.
Quaestiones in Numeros: pp. 190–226.
Quaestiones in Deuteronomium: pp. 227–267.
Quaestiones in Josuam: pp. 268–288.
Quaestiones in Judices: pp. 289–311.
Quaestiones in Ruth: pp. 312–318.
Cod: [75,114]

023 **Quaestiones in libros Regnorum et Paralipomenon**, MPG 80: 528–858.
Cod: [53,517]

024 **Interpretatio in Psalmos**, MPG 80: 857–1997.
Cod: [194,467]

025 **Explanatio in Canticum canticorum**, MPG 81: 28–213.
Cod: [36,779]

026 **Interpretatio in Jeremiam**, MPG 81: 496–805.
Cod: [52,586]

027 **Interpretatio in Ezechielem**, MPG 81: 808–1256.
Cod: [84,473]

028 **Interpretatio in Danielem**, MPG 81: 1256–1546.
Cod: [54,932]

029 **Interpretatio in xii prophetas minores**, MPG 81: 1545–1988.
Cod: [83,548]

030 **Interpretatio in xii epistulas sancti Pauli**, MPG 82: 36–877.
Cod: [160,901]

031 **Haereticarum fabularum compendium**, MPG 83: 336–556.
Cod: [41,510]

032 **De providentia orationes decem**, MPG 83: 556–773.
Cod: [43,581]

033 **Libellus contra Nestorium ad Sporacium** [Sp.], MPG 83: 1153–1164.
Cod: [2,172]

034 **Ad eos qui in Euphratesia et Osrhoena regione, Syria, Phoenicia et Cilicia vitam monasticam degunt** (ex epistula 151), MPG 83: 1416–1433.
Cod: [3,658]

035 **Quod unicus filius sit dominus noster Jesus Christus** (ex epistula 151) [Dub.], MPG 83: 1433–1440.
Cod: [1,940]

036 **Libri v contra Cyrillum et concilium Ephesinum** (**Pentalogus**) (fragmenta Graeca), MPG 84: 65–88.
Cod: [4,163]

037 **Contra Judaeos** (fragmentum) [Sp.], ed. M. Brok, "Un soi-disant fragment du 'Traité contre les Juifs' de Théodoret," *Revue d'histoire ecclésiastique* 45 (1950) 490–494.
Cod: [1,374]

x01 **Expositio rectae fidei.**

Otto, vol. 4, pp. 2–66.
Cf. Pseudo-JUSTINUS MARTYR (0646 006).

x02 **Sermones quinque in Joannem Chryso-
stomum.**
Photius, *Bibliotheca* 273.
Cf. PHOTIUS Scr. Eccl. (4040 001).

x03 **Ex sermone Chalcedone, cum essent abituri,
habito.**
ACO 1.1.7, pp. 82–83.
Cf. CONCILIA OECUMENICA (ACO) (5000
001).

x04 **Epistula ad Alexandrum Hierapolitanum** (=
epistula 169 e collectione conciliari).
ACO 1.1.7, pp. 79–80.
Cf. CONCILIA OECUMENICA (ACO) (5000
001).

x05 **Epistula ad Joannem Antiochenum** (= epistula
150 e collectione conciliari).
ACO 1.1.6, pp. 107–108.
Cf. CONCILIA OECUMENICA (ACO) (5000
001).

x06 **Theodoreti impugnatio xii anathematismorum
Cyrilli et Cyrilli apologia.**
ACO 1.1.6, pp. 108–144.
Cf. CONCILIA OECUMENICA (ACO) (5000
001).

x07 **Epistula ad Joannem Antiochenum** (= epistula
171 e collectione conciliari).
ACO 1.1.7, pp. 163–164.
Cf. CONCILIA OECUMENICA (ACO) (5000
001).

1715 **THEODORIDAS** Epigr.
3 B.C.: Syracusanus
001 **Epigrammata**, AG **6.**155–157, 222, 224; **7.**282,
406, 439, 479, 527–529, 722, 732, 738; **9.**743;
13.8, 21; **16.**132.
Q: 525
002 **Fragmenta et tituli**, ed. H. Lloyd-Jones and P.
Parsons, *Supplementum Hellenisticum*. Berlin:
De Gruyter, 1983: 356–358.
frr. 739, 741–746, 748.
Q: [43]

1094 **THEODORIDES** Trag.
4 B.C.
001 **Tituli**, ed. B. Snell, *Tragicorum Graecorum
fragmenta*, vol. 1. Göttingen: Vandenhoeck &
Ruprecht, 1971: 249.
NQ

1716 **THEODORUS** Epigr.
4–3 B.C.
001 **Epigramma**, AG 6.282.
Q: 37

2728 **THEODORUS** Epigr.
A.D. 4?
x01 **Epigramma.**
App. Anth. 2.705b addenda: Cf. EPIGRAMMA-
TICI in *App. Anth.* (7052 008).

4045 **THEODORUS** Epigr.
A.D. 6
001 **Epigramma**, AG 7.556.
Q: 16

1717 **THEODORUS** Gramm.
A.D. 2: Bithynius
001 **Epigramma**, AG 11.198.
Q: 12

2251 **THEODORUS** Hist.
5–4 B.C.?: Phocaeus
001 **Testimonium**, FGrH #406: 3B:300.
NQ

1892 **THEODORUS** Hist.
post 4 B.C.: Iliensis
001 **Fragmenta**, FGrH #48: 1A:273.
Q

2161 **THEODORUS** Hist.
3 B.C.: fort. Rhodius
001 **Fragmentum**, FGrH #230: 2B:974.
Q

2551 **THEODORUS** Hist.
ante 2 B.C.
001 **Testimonium**, FGrH #822: 3C:896.
NQ

1987 **THEODORUS** Hist.
1 B.C.
001 **Testimonium**, FGrH #195: 2B:929.
NQ

2570 **THEODORUS** Hist.
1 B.C.: Gadarensis
001 **Testimonia**, FGrH #850: 3C:935–936.
NQ
002 **Tituli**, FGrH #850: 3C:936.
NQ

1904 **THEODORUS** Hist.
ante A.D. 2: Samothracenus
001 **Fragmenta**, FGrH #62: 1A:299.
Q

2150 **THEODORUS** Hist.
Incertum
001 **Testimonium**, FGrH #542: 3B:526.
NQ

2237 **THEODORUS** Math.
5 B.C.: Cyrenaeus
001 **Testimonia**, ed. H. Diels and W. Kranz, *Die
Fragmente der Vorsokratiker*, vol. 1, 6th edn.
Berlin: Weidmann, 1951 (repr. Dublin: 1966):
397.
test. 1–5.
NQ
002 **Testimonia**, ed. M. Winiarczyk, *Diagorae Melii*

et Theodori Cyrenaei reliquiae. Leipzig: Teubner, 1981: 31–45.
NQ

1090 THEODORUS Med.
A.D. 1: fort. Macedo
x01 **Fragmenta ap. Aëtium** (lib. 6, 8).
CMG, vol. 8.2, pp. 236, 476.
Cf. AËTIUS Med. (0718 006, 008).
x02 **Fragmentum ap. Aëtium** (lib. 16).
Zervos, *Gynaekologie des Aëtios,* p. 67.
Cf. AËTIUS Med. (0718 016).
x03 **Fragmenta ap. Philumenum.**
CMG, vol. 10.1.1, pp. 8–10, 39.
Cf. PHILUMENUS Med. (0671 001).

1028 THEODORUS Med.
fiq Theodorus Moschion vel Theodorus Priscianus
A.D. 4–5?
x01 **Fragmentum ap. Alexandrum Trallianum.**
Puschmann, vol. 1, p. 559.
Cf. ALEXANDER Med. (0744 003).

2947 THEODORUS Phil.
A.D. 3–4: Asinaeus
001 **Testimonia,** ed. W. Deuse, *Theodoros von Asine.* Wiesbaden: Steiner, 1973: 30–56.
NQ

2696 THEODORUS Poeta
ante 4 B.C.: Colophonius
001 **Titulus,** ed. H. Lloyd-Jones and P. Parsons, *Supplementum Hellenisticum.* Berlin: De Gruyter, 1983: 360.
fr. 753.
NQ: [1]

2695 THEODORUS Poeta
Incertum: fort. Smyrnaeus
001 **Titulus,** ed. H. Lloyd-Jones and P. Parsons, *Supplementum Hellenisticum.* Berlin: De Gruyter, 1983: 359.
titul. 749.
NQ: [1]

4126 THEODORUS Scr. Eccl.
A.D. 4: Heracleensis
Cf. et THEODORUS Heracleensis vel THEODORUS Mopsuestenus Scr. Eccl. (2967).
Bibliography in progress
002 **Fragmenta in Matthaeum** (in catenis), ed. J. Reuss, *Matthäus-Kommentare aus der griechischen Kirche* [*Texte und Untersuchungen* 61. Berlin: Akademie-Verlag, 1957]: 55–95.
Q
004 **Fragmenta in Joannem** (in catenis), ed. J. Reuss, *Johannes-Kommentare aus der griechischen Kirche* [*Texte und Untersuchungen* 89. Berlin: Akademie-Verlag, 1966]: 67–176.
Q

4135 THEODORUS Theol.
A.D. 4–5: Mopsuestenus
Cf. et THEODORUS Heracleensis vel THEODORUS Mopsuestenus Scr. Eccl. (2967).
Bibliography in progress
009 **Fragmenta in Matthaeum** (in catenis), ed. J. Reuss, *Matthäus-Kommentare aus der griechischen Kirche* [*Texte und Untersuchungen* 61. Berlin: Akademie-Verlag, 1957]: 96–135.
Q
015 **Fragmenta in epistulam ad Romanos** (in catenis), ed. K. Staab, *Pauluskommentar aus der griechischen Kirche aus Katenenhandschriften gesammelt.* Münster: Aschendorff, 1933: 113–172.
Q
016 **Fragmenta in epistulam i ad Corinthios** (in catenis), ed. Staab, *op. cit.,* 172–196.
Q
017 **Fragmenta in epistulam ii ad Corinthios** (in catenis), ed. Staab, *op. cit.,* 196–200.
Q
018 **Fragmenta in epistulam ad Hebraeos** (in catenis), ed. Staab, *op. cit.,* 200–212.
Q

0611 THEODORUS Trag.
2 B.C.
001 **Tituli,** ed. B. Snell, *Tragicorum Graecorum fragmenta,* vol. 1. Göttingen: Vandenhoeck & Ruprecht, 1971: 304.
frr. 1–2.
NQ

2967 THEODORUS Heracleensis vel THEODORUS Mopsuestenus Scr. Eccl.
A.D. 4–5
Cf. et THEODORUS Scr. Eccl. (4126).
Cf. et THEODORUS Theol. (4135).
Bibliography in progress
001 **Fragmenta in Matthaeum,** ed. J. Reuss, *Matthäus-Kommentare aus der griechischen Kirche* [*Texte und Untersuchungen* 61. Berlin: Akademie-Verlag, 1957]: 136–150.
Q

1718 THEODORUS ὁ Παναγής Gramm.
1 B.C.?: Atheniensis
001 **Fragmenta,** FGrH #346: 3B:208–209.
Q

2714 THEODORUS STUDITES Scr. Eccl.
A.D. 8–9: Bithynius, Constantinopolitanus
Bibliography in progress
x01 **Epigramma exhortatorium et supplicatorium.**
App. Anth. 4.111: Cf. EPIGRAMMATICI in *App. Anth.* (7052 004).

2020 THEODOSIUS Gramm.
A.D. 4–5: Alexandrinus
001 **Canones isagogici de flexione nominum,** ed. A. Hilgard, *Grammatici Graeci,* vol. 4.1. Leipzig:

Teubner, 1894 (repr. Hildesheim: Olms, 1965): 3–42.
Cod: [7,562]

002 **Canones isagogici de flexione verborum**, ed. Hilgard, *op. cit.*, 43–99.
Cod: [11,392]

003 Περὶ γραμματικῆς [Sp.], ed. K. Göttling, *Theodosii Alexandrini grammatica*. Leipzig: Libraria Dykiana, 1822: 1–197.
Cod

004 Περὶ τόνου [Sp.], ed. Göttling, *op. cit.*, 198–201.
Cod

005 **Epitome catholicae Herodiani** [Sp.], ed. Göttling, *op. cit.*, 202–205.
Cod

1719 **THEODOSIUS** Math. et Astron.
2–1 B.C.: Tripolites

001 **Sphaerica**, ed. J.L. Heiberg, *Theodosius Tripolites. Sphaerica [Abhandlungen der Gesellschaft der Wissenschaften zu Göttingen*, Philol.-hist. Kl., N.F. 19.3. Berlin: Weidmann, 1927]: 2–164.
Cod: [28,835]

002 **De habitationibus**, ed. R. Fecht, *Theodosii de habitationibus liber, de diebus et noctibus libri duo [Abhandlungen der Gesellschaft der Wissenschaften zu Göttingen*, Philol.-hist. Kl., N.F. 19.4. Berlin: Weidmann, 1927]: 14–42.
Cod: [4,534]

003 **De diebus et noctibus**, ed. Fecht, *op. cit.*, 54–154.
Cod: [19,566]

1091 **THEODOSIUS** Med.
A.D. 2–3?

x01 **Fragmentum ap. Aëtium** (lib. 6).
CMG, vol. 8.2, p. 198.
Cf. AËTIUS Med. (0718 006).

x02 **Fragmentum ap. Alexandrum Trallianum**.
Puschmann, vol. 2, p. 565.
Cf. ALEXANDER Med. (0744 003).

1770 **THEODOTION** Int. Vet. Test.
A.D. 2

001 **Fragmenta**, ed. J. Reider, *An index to Aquila* (rev. N. Turner). Leiden: Brill, 1966: passim.
Q

THEODOTUS Gnost.
A.D. 2
Cf. CLEMENS ALEXANDRINUS Theol. (0555 007).

2495 **THEODOTUS** Hist.
ante 2 B.C.

001 **Fragmenta**, FGrH #732: 3C:692–694.
Q

1720 **THEODOTUS** Hist.
ante 1 B.C.

002 **Fragmenta**, ed. H. Lloyd-Jones and P. Parsons, *Supplementum Hellenisticum*. Berlin: De Gruyter, 1983: 360–362.
frr. 757–764.
Q: [376]

1721 **THEODOTUS Coriarius Ebionites** Scr. Eccl.
A.D. 2–3

x01 **Fragmentum**.
Epiphanius, *Haer.* 54.
Cf. EPIPHANIUS Scr. Eccl. (2021 002).

1722 **THEOGENES** Hist.
ante 3 B.C.

001 **Fragmenta**, FGrH #300: 3B:3–4.
Q

0511 **THEOGNETUS** Comic.
3 B.C.?

001 **Fragmenta**, ed. T. Kock, *Comicorum Atticorum fragmenta*, vol. 3. Leipzig: Teubner, 1888: 364–365.
frr. 1–2 + titulus.
Q: 91

002 **Fragmenta**, ed. A. Meineke, *Fragmenta comicorum Graecorum*, vol. 4. Berlin: Reimer, 1841 (repr. De Gruyter, 1970): 549–550.
Q: 90

003 **Titulus**, ed. C. Austin, *Comicorum Graecorum fragmenta in papyris reperta*. Berlin: De Gruyter, 1973: 216.
NQ: 4

0002 **THEOGNIS** Eleg.
6 B.C.: Megarensis

001 **Elegiae**, ed. D. Young (post E. Diehl), *Theognis*, 2nd edn. Leipzig: Teubner, 1971: 1–83.
Cod: 9,928

002 **Fragmenta sedis incertae**, ed. Young, *op. cit.*, 83.
Cod: 50

003 **Fragmenta dubia**, ed. Young, *op. cit.*, 84–85.
frr. 1–10.
Q: 192

004 **Epigrammata**, AG 10.40, 113.
AG 9.118: Cf. <BESANTINUS> Epigr. (0144 001).
Q: 29

2367 **THEOGNIS** Hist.
ante A.D. 3: Rhodius

001 **Fragmenta**, FGrH #526: 3B:503–504.
Q

0313 **THEOGNIS** Trag.
5 B.C.

001 **Fragmentum**, ed. B. Snell, *Tragicorum Graecorum fragmenta*, vol. 1. Göttingen: Vandenhoeck & Ruprecht, 1971: 146.
fr. 1.
Q: [4]

2964 **THEOGNOSTUS** Scr. Eccl.
A.D. 3: Alexandrinus
001 **Hypothyposes** (fragmenta), ed. A. von Harnack, *Die Hypothyposen des Theognostus [Texte und Untersuchungen* 24.3. Leipzig: Hinrichs, 1903]: 75–78.
Q, Cod
002 **Fragmentum** (Dub.), ed. J.A. Munitiz, "A fragment attributed to Theognostus," *Journal of Theological Studies*, n.s. 30 (1979) 56–66.
Q

1723 **THEOLYTUS** Epic.
ante 3 B.C.?: Methymnaeus
001 **Fragmentum**, ed. J.U. Powell, *Collectanea Alexandrina*. Oxford: Clarendon Press, 1925 (repr. 1970): 9.
Q: [22]

2332 **THEOLYTUS** Hist.
4–3 B.C.?: fort. Methymnaeus
001 **Fragmenta**, FGrH #478: 3B:442–443.
Q

2033 **THEON** Math.
A.D. 4: Alexandrinus
Cf. et EUCLIDES Geom. (1799 010).
Bibliography in progress
001 **Commentaria in Ptolemaei syntaxin mathematicam i–ii**, ed. A. Rome, *Commentaires de Pappus et de Théon d'Alexandrie sur l'Almageste*, vol. 2 [*Studi e Testi* 72. Vatican City: Biblioteca Apostolica Vaticana, 1936]: 317–804.
Cod
002 **Commentaria in Ptolemaei syntaxin mathematicam iii–iv**, ed. A. Rome, *Commentaires de Pappus et de Théon d'Alexandrie sur l'Almageste*, vol. 3 [*Studi e Testi* 106. Vatican City: Biblioteca Apostolica Vaticana, 1943]: 807–1085.
Cod
003 **Commentaria in Ptolemaei canones**, ed. M. Halma, *Tables manuelles astronomiques de Ptolemée et de Théon*, pt. 3. Paris: Merlin, 1825: 38–58.
Cod
005 Γένος Ἀράτου [Dub.], ed. E. Maass, *Commentariorum in Aratum reliquiae*, 2nd edn. Berlin: Weidmann, 1898 (repr. 1958): 146–151.
Cod
006 **Testimonia**, FGrH #651: 3C:204.
NQ
007 **Epigrammata**, AG 7.292; 9.41, 491.
Q: 63
x01 **Opticorum recensio Theonis**.
Heiberg, vol. 7, pp. 144–246.
Cf. EUCLIDES Geom. (1799 010).
x02 **Scholia in opticorum recensionem Theonis**.
Heiberg, vol. 7, pp. 251–284.
Cf. SCHOLIA (4101 003).
x03 **Epigrammata demonstrativa**.
App. Anth. 3.146, 147(?): Cf. EPIGRAMMATICI

in *App. Anth.* (7052 003).
App. Anth. 3.147: Cf. et HERMETICA (1286 x01).

1092 **THEON** Med.
A.D. 2: Alexandrinus
x01 **Fragmentum ap. Galenum**.
K6.96–97 in CMG, vol. 5.4.2, p. 44.
Cf. GALENUS Med. (0057 036).

1724 **THEON** Phil.
A.D. 2: Smyrnaeus
001 **De utilitate mathematicae**, ed. E. Hiller, *Theonis Smyrnaei philosophi Platonici expositio rerum mathematicarum ad legendum Platonem utilium*. Leipzig: Teubner, 1878: 1–205.
Cod: 38,865

0607 **Aelius THEON** Rhet.
A.D. 1/2: Alexandrinus
001 **Progymnasmata**, ed. L. Spengel, *Rhetores Graeci*, vol. 2. Leipzig: Teubner, 1854 (repr. Frankfurt am Main: Minerva, 1966): 59–130.
Cod: [19,032]

2965 **THEONAS** Scr. Eccl.
A.D. 3–4: Alexandrinus
001 **Epistula contra Manichaeos** (fragmenta) (*P. Ryl.* 3.469), ed. C.H. Roberts, *Catalogue of the Greek and Latin papyri in the John Rylands Library*, vol. 3 [*Theological and literary texts*]. Manchester: Manchester University Press, 1938: 41–43.
Pap

THEOPHANES <Epigr.>
AG 7.537, 539.
Cf. PHANIAS Gramm. (1582 001).
Cf. PERSES Epigr. (1575 001).

1981 **THEOPHANES** Hist.
1 B.C.: Mytilenensis
001 **Testimonia**, FGrH #188: 2B:919–921.
NQ
002 **Fragmenta**, FGrH #188: 2B:921–923.
Q

4046 **THEOPHANES Confessor** Hist.
A.D. 8–9
001 **Chronographia**, ed. C. de Boor, *Theophanis chronographia*, vol. 1. Leipzig: Teubner, 1883: 3–503.
Cod
002 **Epigrammata**, AG 15.14, 35.
Q: 57

2707 **THEOPHANES GRAPTOS** Poeta
A.D. 8–9: Hierosolymitanus
Bibliography in progress
x01 **Epigramma demonstrativum**.
App. Anth. 3.309: Cf. EPIGRAMMATICI in *App. Anth.* (7052 003).

1725 **THEOPHILUS** Apol.
A.D. 2: Antiochenus
001 **Ad Autolycum**, ed. R.M. Grant, *Theophilus of Antioch. Ad Autolycum*. Oxford: Clarendon Press, 1970: 2–146.
Cod: 21,963
002 **In Canticum canticorum** (fragmentum), ed. M. Richard, "Les fragments exégétiques de Théophile d'Alexandrie et de Théophile d'Antioche," *Revue Biblique* 47 (1938) 392.
no. 11.
Q

0512 **THEOPHILUS** Comic.
4 B.C.
001 **Fragmenta**, ed. T. Kock, *Comicorum Atticorum fragmenta*, vol. 2. Leipzig: Teubner, 1884: 473–477.
frr. 1–12.
Q: 308
002 **Fragmenta**, ed. A. Meineke, *Fragmenta comicorum Graecorum*, vol. 3. Berlin: Reimer, 1840 (repr. De Gruyter, 1970): 626–631.
Q: 309

2496 **THEOPHILUS** Hist.
ante 2 B.C.?
001 **Fragmentum**, FGrH #733: 3C:695.
Q

2203 **[THEOPHILUS]** Hist.
Incertum
001 **Fragmenta**, FGrH #296: 3A:179–180.
Q

2394 **THEOPHILUS** Hist.
Incertum
001 **Fragmentum**, FGrH #573: 3B:674.
Q

1093 **THEOPHILUS** Med.
ante A.D. 6
x01 **Fragmentum ap. Aëtium** (lib. 7)
CMG, vol. 8.2, p. 382.
Cf. AËTIUS Med. (0718 007).
x02 **Fragmentum ap. Alexandrum Trallianum**.
Puschmann, vol. 2, p. 19.
Cf. ALEXANDER Med. (0744 003).

4115 **THEOPHILUS** Scr. Eccl.
A.D. 4: Alexandrinus
Bibliography in progress
029 **Fragmenta in Matthaeum** (in catenis), ed. J. Reuss, *Matthäus-Kommentare aus der griechischen Kirche* [*Texte und Untersuchungen* 61. Berlin: Akademie-Verlag, 1957]: 151–152.
Q
030 **Fragmenta in Joannem** (in catenis), ed. J. Reuss, *Johannes-Kommentare aus der griechischen Kirche* [*Texte und Untersuchungen* 89. Berlin: Akademie-Verlag, 1966]: 187.
Q

1050 **THEOPHILUS et NARCISSUS** Scr. Eccl.
A.D. 2: Caesariensis (Theophilus), Hierosolymitanus (Narcissus)
001 **Epistula de pascha** (fragmentum), ed. P. Nautin, *Lettres et écrivains chrétiens des 2ᵉ et 3ᵉ siècles* [*Patristica* 2. Paris: Cerf, 1961]: 85–87.
Q

2706 **THEOPHILUS Imperator**
A.D. 9
x01 **Epigramma demonstrativum**.
App. Anth. 3.308: Cf. EPIGRAMMATICI in *App. Anth.* (7052 003).

0729 **THEOPHILUS Protospatharius** Med.
A.D. 7
Cf. et THEOPHILUS Protospatharius, DAMASCIUS et STEPHANUS ATHENIENSIS Med. (0728).
Cf. et THEOPHILUS Protospatharius et STEPHANUS ATHENIENSIS Med. (0746).
002 **De urinis**, ed. J.L. Ideler, *Physici et medici Graeci minores*, vol. 1. Berlin: Reimer, 1841 (repr. Amsterdam: Hakkert, 1963): 261–283.
Cod: 6,419
003 **De excrementis**, ed. Ideler, *op. cit.*, 397–408.
Cod: 3,299
004 **De pulsibus**, ed. F.Z. Ermerins, *Anecdota medica Graeca*. Leiden: Luchtmans, 1840 (repr. Amsterdam: Hakkert, 1963): 3–77.
Cod: 7,009
005 **De corporis humani fabrica libri quinque**, ed. G.A. Greenhill, *Theophili Protospatharii de corporis humani fabrica libri v*. Oxford: Oxford University Press, 1842: 1–272.
Cod: 30,544

0746 **THEOPHILUS Protospatharius et STEPHANUS ATHENIENSIS** Med.
A.D. 7
Cf. et STEPHANUS ATHENIENSIS Med. (0724).
Cf. et THEOPHILUS Protospatharius Med. (0729).
Cf. et THEOPHILUS Protospatharius, DAMASCIUS et STEPHANUS ATHENIENSIS Med. (0728).
001 **De febrium differentia**, ed. D. Sicurus, *Theophili et Stephani Atheniensis de febrium differentia ex Hippocrate et Galeno*. Florence: Bengini, 1862: 5–46.
Cf. et PALLADIUS Med. (0726 002).
Cod: 12,966

0728 **THEOPHILUS Protospatharius, DAMASCIUS et STEPHANUS ATHENIENSIS** Med.
A.D. 7
Cf. et STEPHANUS ATHENIENSIS Med. (0724).
Cf. et THEOPHILUS Protospatharius Med. (0729).

Cf. et THEOPHILUS Protospatharius et
STEPHANUS ATHENIENSIS Med. 0746).

001 **Commentarii in Hippocratis aphorismos**, ed.
F.R. Dietz, *Scholia in Hippocratem et Galenum*, vol. 2. Königsberg: Borntraeger, 1834
(repr. Amsterdam: Hakkert, 1966): 236, 238–
240, 244–544.
Cod: 72,392

0093 **THEOPHRASTUS** Phil.
4–3 B.C.: Eresius

001 **Historia plantarum**, ed. A. Hort, *Theophrastus.
Enquiry into plants*, 2 vols. Cambridge, Mass.:
Harvard University Press, 1916 (repr. 1:1968;
2:1961): 1:2–474; 2:2–320.
Cod: 73,980

002 **De causis plantarum** (lib. 1), ed. R.E. Dengler,
Theophrastus. De causis plantarum, book one.
Philadelphia: University of Pennsylvania Press,
1927: 12–138.
Cf. et 0093 014.
Cod: 12,284

003 **De sensu et sensibilibus** (= fr. 1, Wimmer),
ed. H. Diels, *Doxographi Graeci*. Berlin: Reimer, 1879 (repr. De Gruyter, 1965): 499–527.
Cod: 9,212

004 **De lapidibus** (= fr. 2, Wimmer), ed. D.E.
Eichholz, *Theophrastus. De lapidibus*. Oxford:
Clarendon Press, 1965: 56–84.
Cod: 4,379

005 **De igne** (= fr. 3, Wimmer), ed. V. Coutant,
Theophrastus. De igne. Assen: Royal Vangor-
cum, 1971: 3–51.
Cod: 6,390

006 **Metaphysica** (= fr. 12, Wimmer), ed. W.D.
Ross and F.H. Fobes, *Theophrastus. Meta-
physics*. Oxford: Clarendon Press, 1929 (repr.
Hildesheim: Olms, 1967): 2–38.
Cod: 3,559

007 **De pietate**, ed. W. Pötscher, *Theophrastos.
Περὶ εὐσεβείας* [*Philosophia Antiqua* 11. Lei-
den: Brill, 1964]: 146–184.
Cod: 4,526

008 **Physicorum opiniones**, ed. Diels, *op. cit.*, 475–
495.
Q: 4,897

009 **Characteres**, ed. P. Steinmetz, *Theophrast.
Charaktere*, vol. 1 [*Das Wort der Antike* 7.
Munich: Hueber, 1960]: 62–106.
Cod: 6,876

010 **Fragmenta**, ed. F. Wimmer, *Theophrasti Eresii
opera, quae supersunt, omnia*. Paris: Didot,
1866 (repr. Frankfurt am Main: Minerva,
1964): 364–410, 417–462.
De odoribus (fr. 4): pp. 364–376.
De ventis (fr. 5): pp. 376–389.
De signis tempestatum (fr. 6): pp. 389–398.
De lassitudine (fr. 7): pp. 398–401.
De vertigine (fr. 8): pp. 401–403.
De sudore (fr. 9): pp. 403–408.
De animi defectione (fr. 10): p. 409.

De nervorum resolutione (fr. 11): pp. 409–410.
Fragmenta varia (frr. 13–190): pp. 417–462.
Q, Cod: 36,234

011 **Περὶ λέξεως** (fragmentum), *P. Hamb.* 128.
Pap

012 **De aqua** (fragmentum), *P. Hibeh* 1.16.
Pap

013 **De animalibus** (fragmentum), *P. Lit. Lond.*
164.
Pap

014 **De causis plantarum** (lib. 2–6), ed. Wimmer,
op. cit., 192–319.
Cf. et 0093 002.
Cod: 59,608

015 **De eligendis magistratibus** (fragmentum), ed.
W. Aly, *Fragmentum Vaticanum de eligendis
magistratibus e codice bis rescripto Vat. gr. 2306*
[*Studi e Testi* 104. Vatican City: Biblioteca
Apostolica Vaticana, 1943].
Cod

0513 **THEOPOMPUS** Comic.
5–4 B.C.

001 **Fragmenta**, ed. T. Kock, *Comicorum Atticorum fragmenta*, vol. 1. Leipzig: Teubner, 1880:
733–756.
frr. 2–15, 17, 19–27, 29–30, 32–38, 40–44, 46–
48, 50–56, 58–64, 66–77, 79–99 + tituli.
Q: 674

002 **Fragmenta**, ed. A. Meineke, *Fragmenta comicorum Graecorum*, vol. 2.2. Berlin: Reimer, 1840
(repr. De Gruyter, 1970): 792–813, 815–819.
Q: 637

003 **Fragmenta**, ed. J. Demiańczuk, *Supplementum
comicum*. Krakau: Nakładem Akademii, 1912
(repr. Hildesheim: Olms, 1967): 86–87.
frr. 1–3.
Q: 28

004 **Titulus**, ed. C. Austin, *Comicorum Graecorum
fragmenta in papyris reperta*. Berlin: De Gruyter, 1973: 217.
NQ: 2

1726 **THEOPOMPUS** Epic.
post 4 B.C.: Colophonius

001 **Fragmentum**, ed. J.U. Powell, *Collectanea Alexandrina*. Oxford: Clarendon Press, 1925
(repr. 1970): 28.
Q: [10]

002 **Fragmentum**, ed. H. Lloyd-Jones and P. Parsons, *Supplementum Hellenisticum*. Berlin: De
Gruyter, 1983: 365.
fr. 765.
Q: [11]

0566 **THEOPOMPUS** Hist.
4 B.C.: Chius

001 **Testimonia**, FGrH #115: **2B**:526–536; **3B**:742
addenda.
NQ

002 **Fragmenta**, FGrH #115: **2B**:536–617; **3B**:742
addenda.
fr. 165: *P. Oxy.* 7.1012.
fr. 305: *Inscr. Priene* 37.
Q, Pap, Epigr

003 **Fragmentum** (*P. Cologne* 5861), ed. H.J. Mette,
"Die 'Kleinen' griechischen Historiker heute,"
Lustrum 21 (1978) 17.
fr. 382 bis.
Pap

x01 **Fragmenta**.
FGrH #105, frr. 3, 4, 6.
Cf. ANONYMI HISTORICI (FGrH) (1139 004).

1874 **Gaius Julius THEOPOMPUS** Myth.
1 B.C.: Cnidius

001 **Testimonia**, FGrH #21: 1A:185–186.
NQ

4047 **THEOSEBEIA** Epigr.
A.D. 5

001 **Epigramma**, AG 7.559.
Q: 27

1727 **THEOTIMUS** Hist.
2 B.C.?

001 **Fragmenta**, FGrH #470: 3B:425–427.
Q

2561 **THEOTIMUS** Hist.
Incertum

001 **Fragmenta**, FGrH #834: 3C:902–903.
Q

1728 **THESEUS** Hist.
A.D. 1?

001 **Testimonium**, FGrH #453: 3B:381.
NQ

002 **Fragmenta**, FGrH #453: 3B:381–382.
Q

0301 **THESPIS** Trag.
6 B.C.: Atheniensis

001 **Fragmenta**, ed. B. Snell, *Tragicorum Graecorum fragmenta*, vol. 1. Göttingen: Vandenhoeck & Ruprecht, 1971: 65–66.
frr. 1c, 2–5.
Q: [77]

1004 **THESSALUS** Med. et Astrol.
A.D. 1: Trallianus

001 **De virtutibus herbarum** (cod. Paris. gr. 2502 et
cod. Vindobonensis med. gr. 23), ed. H.-V.
Friedrich, *Thessalos von Tralles* [*Beiträge zur
klassischen Philologie* 28. Meisenheim am
Glan: Hain, 1968]: 43–44, 56, 59, 62, 65, 137,
142, 147, 175, 179, 183, 187, 219, 223, 227,
231, 235, 239, 243, 247, 251, 255, 259, 263,
267.
Cod

002 **De virtutibus herbarum** (cod. Matritensis bibl.

nat. 4631 [olim 110]), ed. Friedrich, *op. cit.*,
45, 47, 49, 51, 53, 55, 58, 61, 64, 68, 73, 78,
83, 88, 93, 98, 103.
Cod

003 **De virtutibus herbarum** (cod. Monacensis
542), ed. Friedrich, *op. cit.*, 69, 74, 79, 84, 89,
94, 99, 104, 108, 112, 116, 120, 124, 128, 132,
136, 141, 146, 151, 155, 159, 163, 167, 171.
Cod

004 **De virtutibus herbarum** (codd. BHL), ed.
Friedrich, *op. cit.*, 195, 199, 203, 207, 211,
215.
Cod

005 **De virtutibus herbarum** (codd. ADE), ed.
Friedrich, *op. cit.*, 195, 196, 268.
Cod

x01 **Fragmenta ap. Galenum**.
K1.176; **10**.7–8, 73, 250–252.
Cf. GALENUS Med. (0057 066) et Pseudo-
GALENUS Med. (0530 043).

1095 **THEUDAS** Med.
ante A.D. 1

x01 **Fragmentum ap. Galenum**.
K13.925.
Cf. GALENUS Med. (0057 077).

0816 **THEUDO[TUS]** Trag.
1 B.C.

001 **Titulus**, ed. B. Snell, *Tragicorum Graecorum
fragmenta*, vol. 1. Göttingen: Vandenhoeck &
Ruprecht, 1971: 310.
NQ

2400 **THIBRON** Hist.
5/4 B.C.?: Lacedaemonius

001 **Testimonium**, FGrH #581: 3B:692–693.
NQ

4048 **THOMAS** Epigr.
A.D. 6

001 **Epigramma**, AG 16.379.
Q: 25

4049 **THOMAS** Epigr.
A.D. 6

001 **Epigramma**, AG 16.315.
Q: 23

2231 **THRASYALCES** Phil.
5/4 B.C.: Thasius

001 **Testimonia**, ed. H. Diels and W. Kranz, *Die
Fragmente der Vorsokratiker*, vol. 1, 6th edn.
Berlin: Weidmann, 1951 (repr. Dublin: 1966):
377.
test. 1–2.
NQ

0056 ***THRASYBULI EPISTULA***
Incertum

001 **Epistula**, ed. R. Hercher, *Epistolographi Graeci*.

Paris: Didot, 1873 (repr. Amsterdam: Hakkert, 1965): 787.
Q: [67]

1762 **THRASYLLUS** Astrol.
fiq Thrasyllus Hist.
A.D. 1 : Alexandrinus
Cf. et THRASYLLUS Hist. (2428).
001 **Fragmenta**, ed. W. Kroll and A. Olivieri, *Codices Parisini* [*Catalogus codicum astrologorum Graecorum* 8.3. Brussels: Lamertin, 1912]: 99–101.
Cod

2176 **THRASYLLUS** Hist.
1 B.C.–A.D. 1 : Rhodius
001 **Fragmentum**, FGrH #253: 2B:1152–1153.
Q

2428 **THRASYLLUS** Hist.
fiq Thrasyllus Astrol.
A.D. 1?: Mendesicus
Cf. et THRASYLLUS Astrol. (1762).
001 **Fragmenta**, FGrH #622: 3C:156–157.
Q

1729 **THRASYMACHUS** Phil.
5 B.C.: Chalcedonius
001 **Testimonia**, ed. H. Diels and W. Kranz, *Die Fragmente der Vorsokratiker*, vol. 2, 6th edn. Berlin: Weidmann, 1952 (repr. Dublin: 1966): 319–321.
test. 1–14.
NQ
002 **Fragmenta**, ed. Diels and Kranz, *op. cit.*, 321–326.
frr. 1–8.
Q

1097 **THREPTUS** Med.
ante A.D. 2
x01 **Fragmentum ap. Galenum**.
K13.828.
Cf. GALENUS Med. (0057 077).

0003 **THUCYDIDES** Hist.
5 B.C.: Atheniensis
001 **Historiae**, ed. H.S. Jones and J.E. Powell, *Thucydidis historiae*, 2 vols. Oxford: Clarendon Press, 1:1942 (1st edn. rev.); 2:1942 (2nd edn. rev.) (repr. 1:1970; 2:1967).
Cod: 153,260
002 **Epigramma**, AG 7.45.
Q: 32

0514 **THUGENIDES** Comic.
5 B.C.
001 **Fragmenta**, ed. T. Kock, *Comicorum Atticorum fragmenta*, vol. 3. Leipzig: Teubner, 1888: 377–378.
frr. 1–5.
Q: 16

002 **Fragmenta**, ed. A. Meineke, *Fragmenta comicorum Graecorum*, vol. 4. Berlin: Reimer, 1841 (repr. De Gruyter, 1970): 593.
Q: 9
003 **Fragmentum**, ed. J. Demiańczuk, *Supplementum comicum*. Krakau: Nakładem Akademii, 1912 (repr. Hildesheim: Olms, 1967): 87.
fr. 1.
Q: 6

1730 **THYILLUS** Epigr.
1 B.C.
001 **Epigrammata**, AG **6**.170; **7**.223; **10**.5.
Q: 121

1731 **THYMOCLES** Epigr.
3 B.C.?
001 **Epigramma**, AG 12.32.
Q: 30

2126 **TIBERIUS** Epigr.
A.D. 4/5
001 **Epigrammata**, AG 9.2, 370.
AG 9.371: Cf. ANONYMI EPIGRAMMATICI (0138 001).
Q: 83

2601 **TIBERIUS** Rhet.
A.D. 3/4
001 **De figuris Demosthenicis**, ed. G. Ballaira, *Tiberii de figuris Demosthenicis*. Rome: Ateneo, 1968: 7–45.
Cod
002 **Fragmenta**, ed. Ballaira, *op. cit.*, 55–57.
Q

1098 **TIBERIUS Imperator** <Med.>
A.D. 1
x01 **Fragmentum ap. Galenum**.
K13.836.
Cf. GALENUS Med. (0057 077).
x02 **Epigramma**.
AG 9.387: Cf. HADRIANUS Imperator (0195 001).

1732 **TIMACHIDAS** Hist.
1 B.C.: Rhodius
001 **Anagraphe Lindia**, FGrH #532: 3B:506–514.
Epigr
002 **Fragmenta et tituli**, ed. H. Lloyd-Jones and P. Parsons, *Supplementum Hellenisticum*. Berlin: De Gruyter, 1983: 366–367.
frr. (+ titul.) 769–773.
Q: [24]

1105 **TIMAEUS** Astrol.
ante 2 B.C.
001 **Fragmentum**, ed. A. Olivieri, *Codices Florentini* [*Catalogus codicum astrologorum Graecorum* 1. Brussels: Lamertin, 1898]: 97–99.
Cod

2602 **TIMAEUS** Gramm.
A.D. 1/4
001 **Lexicon Platonicum**, ed. K.F. Hermann, *Platonis dialogi secundum Thrasylli tetralogias dispositi*, vol. 6. Leipzig: Teubner, 1853: 397–408.
Cod

1733 **TIMAEUS** Hist.
4–3 B.C.: Tauromenitanus
001 **Testimonia**, FGrH #566: 3B:581–591.
NQ
002 **Fragmenta**, FGrH #566: 3B:592–658.
Q
003 **Fragmenta**, ed. H.J. Mette, "Die 'Kleinen' griechischen Historiker heute," *Lustrum* 21 (1978) 31.
fr. 88 bis a–b.
fr. 88 bis a: *P. Oxy.* 32.2637.
Q, Pap

2569 **<TIMAEUS>** Hist.
post 4 B.C.?
001 **Testimonium**, FGrH #848: 3C:935.
NQ
002 **Titulus**, FGrH #848: 3C:935.
NQ

1734 **TIMAEUS** Phil.
3/2 B.C.?: Locrus
001 **Fragmenta** [Sp.], ed. W. Marg, *The Pythagorean texts of the Hellenistic period* (ed. H. Thesleff). Åbo: Åbo Akademi, 1965: 203, 205–225.
Cod: 4,578
002 **Testimonia**, ed. H. Diels and W. Kranz, *Die Fragmente der Vorsokratiker*, vol. 1, 6th edn. Berlin: Weidmann, 1951 (repr. Dublin: 1966): 441.
test. 1–4.
NQ

1918 **TIMAGENES** Hist.
1 B.C.: Alexandrinus
001 **Testimonia**, FGrH #88: 2A:318–319.
NQ
002 **Fragmenta**, FGrH #88: 2A:319–323.
Q

2268 **TIMAGORAS** Hist.
Incertum
001 **Fragmenta**, FGrH #381: 3B:250.
Q

0889 **TIMESITHEUS** Trag.
Incertum
001 **Tituli**, ed. B. Snell, *Tragicorum Graecorum fragmenta*, vol. 1. Göttingen: Vandenhoeck & Ruprecht, 1971: 324–325.
NQ

1960 **TIMOCHARES** Hist.
2 B.C.
001 **Fragmentum**, FGrH #165: 2B:891.
Q

0515 **TIMOCLES** Comic.
4 B.C.
001 **Fragmenta**, ed. T. Kock, *Comicorum Atticorum fragmenta*, vol. 2. Leipzig: Teubner, 1884: 451–466.
frr. 1–16, 18–25, 27–38 + tituli.
Q: 1,093
002 **Fragmenta**, ed. A. Meineke, *Fragmenta comicorum Graecorum*, vol. 3. Berlin: Reimer, 1840 (repr. De Gruyter, 1970): 590–600, 602–613.
p. 613, fr. 5: line 2 supplied from vol. 5.1, p. 96.
Q: 1,119
003 **Fragmenta**, ed. J. Demiańczuk, *Supplementum comicum*. Krakau: Nakładem Akademii, 1912 (repr. Hildesheim: Olms, 1967): 88–89.
frr. 1–3.
Q: 79
004 **Fragmentum**, ed. C. Austin, *Comicorum Graecorum fragmenta in papyris reperta*. Berlin: De Gruyter, 1973: 217–218.
fr. 222.
Pap: 104

0333 **TIMOCLES** Trag.
4 B.C.
001 **Fragmentum**, ed. B. Snell, *Tragicorum Graecorum fragmenta*, vol. 1. Göttingen: Vandenhoeck & Ruprecht, 1971: 252.
fr. 1.
Q: [12]

1099 **TIMOCLIANUS** Med.
ante A.D. 4
x01 **Fragmentum ap. Oribasium.**
CMG, vol. 6.2.2, p. 240.
Cf. ORIBASIUS Med. (0722 003).

2388 **TIMOCRATES** Hist.
A.D. 1?
001 **Fragmentum**, FGrH #563: 3B:577.
Q

2459 **TIMOCRATES** Hist.
Incertum: Adramyttenus
001 **Testimonium**, FGrH #672: 3C:284.
NQ

1100 **TIMOCRATES** Med.
ante A.D. 2
x01 **Fragmentum ap. Galenum.**
K12.887.
Cf. GALENUS Med. (0057 076).

0265 **TIMOCREON** Lyr.
5 B.C.: Rhodius
001 **Fragmenta**, ed. M.L. West, *Iambi et elegi*

Graeci, vol. 2. Oxford: Clarendon Press, 1972: 149.
frr. 7, 9, 10.
Q: [28]

002 **Fragmenta**, ed. D.L. Page, *Poetae melici Graeci*. Oxford: Clarendon Press, 1962 (repr. 1967 (1st edn. corr.)): 375–378.
frr. 1–6.
Q: [187]

003 **Epigramma**, AG 13.31.
AG 16.11: Cf. HERMOCREON Epigr. (1422 001).
Q: 15

2363 **TIMOCRITUS** Hist.
Incertum
001 **Titulus**, FGrH #522: 3B:494.
NQ

2301 **TIMOGENES** Hist. et Rhet.
vel Timagenes
Incertum: Milesius
001 **Testimonium**, FGrH #435: 3B:368.
NQ

2533 **TIMOLAUS** Hist.
Incertum
001 **Fragmentum**, FGrH #798: 3C:836.
Q

2697 **TIMOLAUS** Rhet.
4 B.C.: Macedo, Larissaeus
001 **Fragmentum**, ed. H. Lloyd-Jones and P. Parsons, *Supplementum Hellenisticum*. Berlin: De Gruyter, 1983: 395.
fr. 849.
Q: [36]

2509 **TIMOMACHUS** Hist.
4/3 B.C.?
001 **Fragmenta**, FGrH #754: 3C:736.
Q

1735 **TIMON** Phil.
4–3 B.C.: Phliasius
001 **Fragmenta**, ed. H. Diels, *Poetarum philosophorum fragmenta* [*Poetarum Graecorum fragmenta* 3.1. Berlin: Weidmann, 1901]: 184–206.
Q

002 **Epigrammata**, AG 10.38; 11.296.
AG 7.313: Cf. ANONYMI EPIGRAMMATICI (0138 001).
Q: 24

003 **Fragmenta et tituli**, ed. H. Lloyd-Jones and P. Parsons, *Supplementum Hellenisticum*. Berlin: De Gruyter, 1983: 368–394.
frr. (+ titul.) 775–846.
Q: [1119]

1736 **TIMONAX** Hist.
4/3 B.C.?

001 **Fragmenta**, FGrH #842: 3C:928–929.
Q

2386 **TIMONIDES** Hist.
4 B.C.: Leucadius
001 **Testimonia**, FGrH #561: 3B:574.
NQ
002 **Fragmenta**, FGrH #561: 3B:574–576.
Q

1002 **TIMOSTHENES** Geogr.
3 B.C.: Rhodius
001 **Fragmenta**, ed. E.A. Wagner, *Die Erdbeschreibung des Timosthenes von Rhodus* [*Diss. Leipzig* (1888)]: 10–11, 64–73.
Q

2256 **TIMOSTHENES** Hist.
2–1 B.C.?
001 **Fragmentum**, FGrH #354: 3B:217.
Q

0516 **TIMOSTRATUS** Comic.
2 B.C.: Atheniensis
001 **Fragmenta**, ed. T. Kock, *Comicorum Atticorum fragmenta*, vol. 3. Leipzig: Teubner, 1888: 355–357.
frr. 1–7 + tituli.
Q: 44
002 **Tituli**, ed. A. Meineke, *Fragmenta comicorum Graecorum*, vol. 4. Berlin: Reimer, 1841 (repr. De Gruyter, 1970): 595.
NQ: 5
003 **Fragmenta**, ed. Meineke, *op. cit.*, vol. 5.1 (1857; repr. 1970): cccxxvii–cccxxviii.
Q: [23]

0517 **TIMOTHEUS** Comic.
4/3 B.C.?: Atheniensis
001 **Fragmenta**, ed. T. Kock, *Comicorum Atticorum fragmenta*, vol. 2. Leipzig: Teubner, 1884: 450.
frr. 1–2 + titulus.
Q: 45
002 **Fragmenta**, ed. A. Meineke, *Fragmenta comicorum Graecorum*, vol. 3. Berlin: Reimer, 1840 (repr. De Gruyter, 1970): 589.
Q: 41

2449 **TIMOTHEUS** Gramm.
A.D. 6: Gazaeus
001 **Testimonia**, FGrH #652: 3C:204–205.
NQ

2213 **[TIMOTHEUS]** Hist.
Incertum
001 **Fragmenta**, FGrH #313: 3B:22.
Q

0376 **TIMOTHEUS** Lyr.
5–4 B.C.: Milesius
001 **Fragmenta**, ed. D.L. Page, *Poetae melici*

Graeci. Oxford: Clarendon Press, 1962 (repr. 1967 (1st edn. corr.)): 400–413, 415–418.
frr. 2, 4–5, 10–15, 20–28.
fr. 15 = *Persae* (*P. Berol.* 9865).
Q, Pap: [1,185]

002 **Tituli**, ed. Page, *op. cit.*, 399–400, 402, 414–415.
NQ

x01 **Epigramma**.
AG 7.45.
Cf. THUCYDIDES Hist. (0003 002).

1101 **TIMOTHEUS** Med.
4/3 B.C.?: Metapontinus

x01 **Fragmentum ap. Anonymum Londinensem**.
Iatrica 8.10–32.
Cf. ANONYMUS LONDINENSIS (0643 001).

0467 **TIMOTHEUS** Trag.
4 B.C.

001 **Tituli**, ed. B. Snell, *Tragicorum Graecorum fragmenta*, vol. 1. Göttingen: Vandenhoeck & Ruprecht, 1971: 196.
fr. 1.
NQ

1793 **TIMOXENUS** Comic.
Incertum

001 **Titulus**, ed. T. Kock, *Comicorum Atticorum fragmenta*, vol. 3. Leipzig: Teubner, 1888: 366.
NQ: 2

1737 ***TITANOMACHIA***
fort. auctore Arctino Milesio vel Eumelo Corinthio
post 7 B.C.

001 **Fragmenta**, ed. T.W. Allen, *Homeri opera*, vol. 5. Oxford: Clarendon Press, 1912 (repr. 1969): 111.
frr. 4–6.
Q

1102 **TITUS Imperator** <Med.>
A.D. 1

x01 **Fragmentum ap. Galenum**.
K13.360.
Cf. GALENUS Med. (0057 076).

1738 ***TRAGICA ADESPOTA***
Varia

001 **Fragmenta**, ed. A. Nauck, *Tragicorum Graecorum fragmenta*. Leipzig: Teubner, 1889 (repr. Hildesheim: Olms, 1964): 837–958.
frr. 1–2, 4–12, 14, 16–18, 20, 22–48, 51–53, 55–144, 147–155, 157–249, 251–289, 291–431, 433–460, 462–577, 579–602.
Q, Pap, Epigr: [4,580]

002 **Fragmenta**, ed. B. Snell, *Tragicorum Graecorum fragmenta. Supplementum*. Hildesheim: Olms, 1964: 21–41.
frr. 1a–1b, 5a–5c, 12a, 14a–14b, 21a, 27a, 34a–34e, 37a–37b, 40a, 59a, 76a, 83a, 84a, 88a,
89a, 97a, 103a, 109a, 116.1, 123a, 126a, 144a, 145a, 146a, 151a, 197a–197d, 198a, 204a, 210a, 225a, 226a, 228a–228c, 233a, 234a, 239a, 242a, 270a, 279a–279b, 279d–279g, 287a, 290a, 295a, 302a, 307a–307b, 323a–323h, 327a, 328a–328d, 336a–336b, 337a, 339a, 340a, 348a–348e, 365a, 369a, 374.3–4, 384a, 416a, 427a, 437a, 438a, 443a–443d, 445a, 456a, 546a, 561b, 562a, 564a–564d, 566a–566e, 581a, 583a, 584, 587a–587c, 593a, 594a–594b, 605, 606, [608], 609, 611, 616.
Q, Pap, Epigr: [738]

003 **Fragmenta**, ed. R. Kannicht and B. Snell, *Tragicorum Graecorum fragmenta*, vol. 2. Göttingen: Vandenhoeck & Rupecht, 1981: 3–173, 177–218, 220–319.
frr. 1–3f, 5–8m, 9a–11, 12a, 13a–14c, 16–18, 20–21a, 26, 27a, 33, 34a–34c, 34e–43, 45–48, 51–51a, 53, 55–57, 59–61c, 63–63a, 67–67a, 69–71, 73, 75a–83b, 84a–89a, 90–93, 95–97, 99–101, 102a, 103a–103d, 105, 107a–110a, 114–115, 117, 118a–118b, 120a–120b, 122, 123a–130, 137–138, 144a–145c, 146a–151a, 152a–153, 155, 158–168, 170–178, 181, 182a–186, 188–197, 197b–197d, 198a–204a, 206, 207a–208, 210a–211, 213–216, 218–228c, 230–240, 242a, 244–248, 250–270, 271–276, 278, 279a–279u, 281–283, 285–286, 288–289, 290–295a, 296–297, 302a–306, 307a–307b, 323–323a, 323h–327s, 328c–347a, 348a–348h, 349, 351–357, 359–361, 363, 365–372, 375–376, 378a–384a, 386, 388, 391–393, 397–402, 404–410a, 412–413, 415–416b, 418a–427, 428–429, 430a–430b, 432a, 433, 438a, 439, 440a–442, 443a–443d, 445–445a, 447–450a, 451–456, 457–458, 460–460a, 462–469, 471, 473–504, 506–514, 515a, 516a–521, 523, 525a–537, 539–540, 543–544, 546a, 548–549, 551–553, 556–560, 561, 562–563, 564a–566a, 566c–573, 579–581a, 583a, 585–585b, 586a, 587, 587b–597, 599, 601–602a, 617–710, 712–734b.
Q, Pap: [8,500]

1739 **TRAJANUS Imperator**
A.D. 1–2

001 **Epigrammata**, AG **9**.388/389; **11**.418.
AG 6.332: Cf. HADRIANUS Imperator (0195 001).
AG 9.388/389: Cf. et ANONYMI EPIGRAMMATICI (0138 001).
Q: 56

0647 **TRIPHIODORUS** Epic. et Gramm.
A.D. 3/5: Aegyptius

001 ῞Αλωσις ᾿Ιλίου, ed. A.W. Mair, *Oppian, Colluthus, Tryphiodorus*. Cambridge, Mass.: Harvard University Press, 1928 (repr. 1963): 580–632.
Cod: [4,260]

2127 **TROILUS** Gramm.
A.D. 4: Sidonius

001 **Prolegomena rhetoricae**, ed. C. Walz, *Rhetores Graeci*, vol. 6. Stuttgart: Cotta, 1834 (repr. Osnabrück: Zeller, 1968): 42–55.
Cod

002 **Epigramma**, AG 16.55.
Q: 17

0588 **TROPHILUS** <Paradox.>
vel Herophilus vel Pamphilus
fiq Herophilus Med.
A.D. 1
Cf. et HEROPHILUS Med. (0928).

001 **Fragmenta**, ed. A. Giannini, *Paradoxographorum Graecorum reliquiae*. Milan: Istituto Editoriale Italiano, 1965: 392–393.
Q

1740 **TRYPHON** Epigr.
1 B.C./A.D. 1?

001 **Epigramma**, AG 9.488.
Q: 25

1104 **TRYPHON** Med.
1 B.C.–A.D. 1: Creticus
x01 **Fragmentum ap. Galenum**.
K13.253.
Cf. GALENUS Med. (0057 076).

1103 **TRYPHON** ὁ ἀρχαῖος Med.
1 B.C.–A.D. 1
x01 **Fragmenta ap. Galenum**.
K12.784, 843.
Cf. GALENUS Med. (0057 076).

0609 **TRYPHON I** Gramm.
1 B.C.: Alexandrinus, Romanus
001 **Περὶ τρόπων**, ed. L. Spengel, *Rhetores Graeci*, vol. 3. Leipzig: Teubner, 1856 (repr. Frankfurt am Main: Minerva, 1966): 191–206.
Cod: 3,060

002 **Περὶ παθῶν**, ed. R. Schneider, *Excerpta περὶ παθῶν* [*Programm Gymnasium Duisburg* (1895)]: 4–21.
Cod: 2,750

003 **Fragmenta**, ed. A. von Velsen, *Tryphonis grammatici Alexandrini fragmenta*. Berlin: Nikolaus, 1853 (repr. Amsterdam: Hakkert, 1965): 5, 7–71, 73–78, 80–82, 84, 86, 88–102.
Q: 8,700

004 **Περὶ μέτρων**, ed. H. zur Jacobsmühlen, *Pseudo-Hephaestion. De metris* [*Dissertationes philologicae Argentoratenses selectae* 10. Strassburg: Trübner, 1886].
Q

005 **Ars grammatica** (*P. Lit. Lond.* 182 = Brit. Mus. inv. 126), ed. F.G. Kenyon, *Classical texts from papyri in the British Museum*. London: British Museum, 1891: 111–116.
Pap

006 **De dialecto Lacedaemonia** (titulus), *P. Oxy.* 24.2396.
Pap

007 **Περὶ πνευμάτων**, ed. L.C. Valckenaer, *Joannis Scapulae lexicon Graeco-Latinum*. Oxford: Clarendon Press, 1820.
Cod

x01 **Fragmentum grammaticum** (*P. Lit. Lond.* 182 = *P. Lond.* 126)
Wouters, pp. 67–73.
Cf. ANONYMI GRAMMATICI (0072 004).

1763 **TRYPHON II** Gramm.
1 B.C.?
001 **De tropis**, ed. M.L. West, "Tryphon. De tropis," *Classical Quarterly* n.s. 15 (1965) 236–248.
Cod: [2,449]

1741 <**TUDICIUS GALLUS**> Epigr.
Incertum
001 **Epigramma**, AG 5.49.
Q: 31

TULLIUS BASSUS Med.
Cf. Julius BASSUS Med. (0941).

TULLIUS FLACCUS Epigr.
fiq Statyllius Flaccus
AG 9.37.
Cf. STATYLLIUS FLACCUS Epigr. (1694 001).

1742 **TULLIUS GEMINUS** Epigr.
A.D. 1?
001 **Epigrammata**, AG **6**.260; 7.73; **9**.288, 414, 707, 740; **16**.30, 103, 205.
AG 7.72: Cf. MENANDER Comic. (0541 044).
AG 7.746: Cf. <PYTHAGORAS> Phil. (0632 005).
AG 9.410: Cf. TULLIUS SABINUS Gramm. (1745 001).
Q: 343

1743 **TULLIUS LAUREA** Epigr.
1 B.C.
001 **Epigrammata**, AG 7.17, 294; **12**.24.
Q: 154

1745 **TULLIUS SABINUS** Gramm.
A.D. 1?: Sabinus
001 **Epigrammata**, AG **6**.158; **9**.410.
Q: 68

1106 **TURPILIANUS** Med.
ante A.D. 1
x01 **Fragmentum ap. Galenum**.
K13.736.
Cf. GALENUS Med. (0057 077).

1744 **TYMNES** Epigr.
3 B.C.
001 **Epigrammata**, AG **6**.151; 7.199, 211, 433, 477, 729; **16**.237.
Q: 205

0367 **TYNNICHUS** Lyr.
6/5 B.C.: Chalcidensis
001 **Fragmentum**, ed. D.L. Page, *Poetae melici Graeci*. Oxford: Clarendon Press, 1962 (repr. 1967 (1st edn. corr.)): 366.
fr. 1.
Q: [5]

1266 **TYRANNION** Gramm.
1 B.C.: Amisenus
001 **Fragmenta**, ed. W. Haas, *Die Fragmente des Grammatikers Dionysios Thrax [Sammlung griechischer und lateinischer Grammatiker 3.* Berlin: De Gruyter, 1977]: 101-137, 139-140, 142-162, 164-166, 168-169, 172-174, 176.
Q, Pap

1611 **TYRANNION Junior** Gramm.
vel Diocles Gramm.
1 B.C.-A.D. 1: Romanus
001 **Fragmenta**, ed. W. Haas, *Die Fragmente des Grammatikers Dionysios Thrax [Sammlung griechischer und lateinischer Grammatiker 3.* Berlin: De Gruyter, 1977]: 177-180.
Q, Pap

0266 **TYRTAEUS** Eleg.
7 B.C.: Lacedaemonius
001 **Fragmenta**, ed. M.L. West, *Iambi et elegi Graeci*, vol. 2. Oxford: Clarendon Press, 1972: 150-163.
frr. 2, 4-7, 10-14, 17-24.
fr. 2: *P. Oxy.* 38.2824.
frr. 18-23: *P. Berol.* 11675.
Q, Pap: [1,243]
002 **Fragmenta**, FGrH #580: 3B:690-692.
Q

1824 *UAPHRIS EPISTULA*
ante 2 B.C.
x01 **Epistula**.
FGrH #723, fr. 2
Cf. EUPOLEMUS Hist. (2486 002).

2462 **<ULPIANUS>** Soph.
A.D. 4?: fort. Emesenus
001 **Testimonium**, FGrH #676: 3C:344.
NQ
002 **Fragmenta**, FGrH #676: 3C:344.
Q

2670 **URANIUS** Epigr.
A.D. 2?
x01 **Epigramma dedicatorium**.
App. Anth. 1.194: Cf. EPIGRAMMATICI in *App. Anth.* (7052 001).

2461 **URANIUS** Hist.
A.D. 6?: Syrius
001 **Testimonia**, FGrH #675: 3C:339-340.
NQ

002 **Fragmenta**, FGrH #675: 3C:340-344.
Q

1089 **URBANUS** Med.
vel Orbanus
ante A.D. 2: Indus
x01 **Fragmentum ap. Galenum**.
K14.109-111.
Cf. GALENUS Med. (0057 078).

1107 **Terentius VALENS** Med.
ante A.D. 2
x01 **Fragmenta ap. Galenum**.
K12.766; **13**.115, 279, 292, 827.
Cf. GALENUS Med. (0057 076-077).

1746 **VALENTINUS** Gnost.
A.D. 2
001 **Valentini hymnus**, ed. E. Heitsch, *Die griechischen Dichterfragmente der römischen Kaiserzeit*, vol. 1, 2nd edn. Göttingen: Vandenhoeck & Ruprecht, 1963: 155.
Q: [35]
002 **Fragmenta**, ed. W. Völker, *Quellen zur Geschichte der christlichen Gnosis*. Tübingen: Mohr, 1932: 57-60.
frr. 1-9.
Q

1950 **VARRO** Hist.
post 4 B.C.
001 **Testimonium**, FGrH #149: 2B:818.
NQ

1802 *VERSUS HEROICI*
Varia
Cf. et HOMERUS Epic. (0012).
Cf. et HYMNI HOMERICI (0013).
001 **Fragmenta**, ed. T.W. Allen, *Homeri opera*, vol. 5. Oxford: Clarendon Press, 1912 (repr. 1969): 148-151.
frr. 1-2, 4-23, 25.
Q

1764 **VETTIUS VALENS** Astrol.
A.D. 2: Antiochenus
001 **Anthologiarum libri ix**, ed. W. Kroll, *Vettii Valentis anthologiarum libri*. Berlin: Weidmann, 1908 (repr. 1973): 1-363.
Cod: [116,535]
002 **Additamenta vetusta**, ed. Kroll, *op. cit.*, 364-372.
Cod: [3,500]
003 **Fragmenta**, ed. W. Kroll and A. Olivieri, *Codices Veneti [Catalogus codicum astrologorum Graecorum 2.* Brussels: Lamertin, 1900]: 161-163, 170, 174.
Q
004 **Fragmenta**, ed. D. Bassi, F. Cumont, A. Martini and A. Olivieri, *Codices Italici [Catalogus codicum astrologorum Graecorum*, vol. 4. Brus-

sels: Lamertin, 1903]: 146–149.
Cod

005 **Fragmenta**, ed. W. Kroll, *Codices Romani*
[Catalogus codicum astrologorum Graecorum,
vol. 5.2. Brussels: Lamertin, 1906]: 52–53,
113, 120–121.
Cod

006 **Fragmenta**, ed. J. Heeg, *Codices Romani [Catalogus codicum astrologorum Graecorum*, vol.
5.3. Brussels: Lamertin, 1910]: 112, 117–118.
Q

007 **Fragmenta**, ed. F. Cumont, *Codices Parisini*
[Catalogus codicum astrologorum Graecorum,
vol. 8.1. Brussels: Lamertin, 1929]: 163–171,
240, 249.
Q, Cod

VETUS TESTAMENTUM
Cf. SEPTUAGINTA (0527).

1747 *VITA ADAM ET EVAE*
1 B.C./A.D. 1

001 **Vita Adam et Evae** (*sub titulo* **Apocalypsis
Mosis**), ed. C. Tischendorf, *Apocalypses apocryphae*. Leipzig: Mendelssohn, 1866: 1–23.
Cod: [4,756]

1765 *VITA AESOPI*
A.D. 1
Cf. et AESOPUS Scr. Fab. et AESOPICA (0096).

001 **Vita G** (e cod. 397 Bibliothecae Pierponti Morgan), ed. B.E. Perry, *Aesopica*, vol. 1. Urbana:
University of Illinois Press, 1952: 35–77.
Cod: 17,236

002 **Vita W** (vita Aesopi Westermanniana), ed.
Perry, *op. cit.*, 81–107.
Cod: [14,544]

1521 *VITA ET SENTENTIAE SECUNDI*
A.D. 2

001 **Vita**, ed. B.E. Perry, *Secundus the silent philosopher [American Philological Association Philological Monographs* 22. Ithaca, New York:
American Philological Association, 1964]: 68–78.
Cod: 1,167

002 **Sententiae**, ed. Perry, *op. cit.*, 78–90.
Cod: 587

VITA PHILONIDIS
ante A.D. 1
Cf. ANONYMUS EPICUREUS Phil. (1779 003).

1749 *VITAE HESIODI PARTICULA*
Incertum
Cf. et HESIODUS Epic. (0020).

001 **Vitae Hesiodi particula**, ed. T.W. Allen, *Homeri opera*, vol. 5. Oxford: Clarendon Press,
1912 (repr. 1969): 222–224.
Cod: 441

1805 *VITAE HOMERI*
Varia
Cf. et CERTAMEN HOMERI ET HESIODI
(1252).

001 **Vita Herodotea**, ed. T.W. Allen, *Homeri opera*,
vol. 5. Oxford: Clarendon Press, 1912 (repr.
1969): 192–218.
Cod: 4,479

002 **<Plutarchi>** vita, ed. Allen, *op. cit.*, 239–245.
Cod: 978

003 **Vita Proculea** (e *Chrestomathia*), ed. Allen, *op.
cit.*, 99–102.
Cod: 589

004 **Vita quarta**, ed. Allen, *op. cit.*, 245–246.
Cod: 188

005 **Vita quinta**, ed. Allen, *op. cit.*, 247–250.
Cod: 408

006 **Vita sexta**, ed. Allen, *op. cit.*, 250–253.
Cod: 555

007 **Vita septima** (Eustathii vita, *Od.* 1713.17), ed.
Allen, *op. cit.*, 253–254.
Q: 129

008 **Tzetzis vita** (*Chil.* 13.626–665), ed. Allen, *op.
cit.*, 254–255.
Q: 277

009 **Eustathii vita** (*Il.* 4.17), ed. Allen, *op. cit.*, 255.
Q: 95

010 **Suidae vita**, ed. Allen, *op. cit.*, 256–267.
Cod: 1,725

1750 *VITAE PROPHETARUM*
Varia

001 **Enumeratio lxxii prophetarum et prophetissarum** (Epiphanii textus), ed. T. Schermann,
Prophetarum vitae fabulosae. Leipzig: Teubner,
1907: 1–3.
Dup. EPIPHANIUS Scr. Eccl. (2021 020).
Cod

002 **De prophetarum vita et obitu** (Epiphanii recensio prior), ed. Schermann, *op. cit.*, 4–25.
Dup. EPIPHANIUS Scr. Eccl. (2021 021).
Cod

003 **De prophetarum vita et obitu** (Dorothei recensio), ed. Schermann, *op. cit.*, 26–55.
Cod

004 **De prophetarum vita et obitu** (Epiphanii recensio altera), ed. Schermann, *op. cit.*, 55–67.
Dup. EPIPHANIUS Scr. Eccl. (2021 022).
Cod

005 **De prophetarum vita et obitu** (recensio anonyma), ed. Schermann, *op. cit.*, 68–98.
Cod

006 **De prophetarum vita et obitu** (recensio scholiis Hesychii aliorumque patrum in prophetas
adjecta), ed. Schermann, *op. cit.*, 99–104.
Cod

007 **Index apostolorum** (Epiphanii textus), ed.
Schermann, *op. cit.*, 107–117.
Dup. EPIPHANIUS Scr. Eccl. (2021 023).
Cod

008 **Index discipulorum** (Epiphanii textus), ed.

Schermann, *op. cit.*, 118–126.
Dup. EPIPHANIUS Scr. Eccl. (2021 024).
Cod

009 **Appendices ad indices apostolorum discipulo-rumque** (Epiphanii textus), ed. Schermann, *op. cit.*, 126–131.
Dup. EPIPHANIUS Scr. Eccl. (2021 043).
Cod

010 **Index apostolorum discipulorumque Domini** (textus Pseudo-Dorothei), ed. Schermann, *op. cit.*, 132–160.
Cod

011 **De baptismate apostolorum et beatae Mariae virginis**, ed. Schermann, *op. cit.*, 160–163.
Cod

012 **Index apostolorum discipulorumque Domini** (textus Pseudo-Hippolyti), ed. Schermann, *op. cit.*, 164–170.
Cod

013 **Index anonymus Graeco-Syrus**, ed. Schermann, *op. cit.*, 171–177.
Cod

014 **Index apostolorum discipulorumque Domini** (textus Pseudo-Symeonis logothetae), ed. Schermann, *op. cit.*, 177–183.
Q

015 **Index apostolorum discipulorumque** (in menologio Basilii II imperatoris) (forma brevior), ed. Schermann, *op. cit.*, 184–185.
Q

016 **Index apostolorum discipulorumque** (in synaxariis Graecis) (forma longior), ed. Schermann, *op. cit.*, 185–194.
Q

017 **Index apostolorum discipulorumque** (forma abbreviata), ed. Schermann, *op. cit.*, 194–197.
Cod

018 **Textus mixtus apostolorum indicum** (inter recensionem Hippolyti et Dorothei), ed. Schermann, *op. cit.*, 197–200.
Cod

019 **Textus mixtus apostolorum indicum** (inter recensionem Hippolyti et Dorothei et textum Epiphanii), ed. Schermann, *op. cit.*, 200–202.
Cod

020 **De apostolorum parentibus** (textus anonymus), ed. Schermann, *op. cit.*, 203–204.
Cod

021 **Versus in duodecim apostolos** (textus Joannis Euchaitensis), ed. Schermann, *op. cit.*, 204–205.
Cod

022 **Index apostolorum** (homilia Pseudo-Chrysostomi in xii apostolos), ed. Schermann, *op. cit.*, 206.
Cod

1751 **XANTHUS** Hist.
5 B.C.: Lydius
001 **Testimonia**, FGrH #765: 3C:750–751.
NQ

002 **Fragmenta**, FGrH #765: 3C:751–758.
Q

003 **Fragmentum**, ed. H.J. Mette, "Die 'Kleinen' griechischen Historiker heute," *Lustrum* 21 (1978) 38.
fr. 2 bis.
Q

1752 **XENAGORAS** Hist. et Geogr.
4/1 B.C.: fort. Heracleensis
001 **Testimonia**, FGrH #240: 2B:1005.
NQ

002 **Fragmenta**, FGrH #240: **2B**:1005–1010; **3B**:744 addenda.
Q

0518 **XENARCHUS** Comic.
4 B.C.
001 **Fragmenta**, ed. T. Kock, *Comicorum Atticorum fragmenta*, vol. 2. Leipzig: Teubner, 1884: 467–473.
frr. 1–14.
Q: 464

002 **Fragmenta**, ed. A. Meineke, *Fragmenta comicorum Graecorum*, vol. 3. Berlin: Reimer, 1840 (repr. De Gruyter, 1970): 614, 616–617, 620–625.
Q: 469

1830 **XENARCHUS** Phil.
1 B.C.–A.D. 1: Seleuciensis
x01 **Fragmenta ap. Simplicium**.
CAG, vol. 7, pp. 13, 14, 21–22, 23–24, 50, 55, 56, 70, 286.
Cf. SIMPLICIUS Phil. (4013 001).

2355 **XENIADES** Phil.
5 B.C.?: Corinthius
001 **Testimonium**, ed. H. Diels and W. Kranz, *Die Fragmente der Vorsokratiker*, vol. 2, 6th edn. Berlin: Weidmann, 1952 (repr. Dublin: 1966): 271.
NQ

1753 **XENION** Hist.
post 4 B.C.?
001 **Fragmenta**, FGrH #460: 3B:397–398.
Q

0519 **XENO** Comic.
3 B.C.
001 **Fragmentum**, ed. T. Kock, *Comicorum Atticorum fragmenta*, vol. 3. Leipzig: Teubner, 1888: 390.
fr. 1.
Q: 13

002 **Fragmentum**, ed. A. Meineke, *Fragmenta comicorum Graecorum*, vol. 4. Berlin: Reimer, 1841 (repr. De Gruyter, 1970): 596.
Q: 11

2558 **XENO** Hist.
Incertum

001 **Testimonium**, FGrH #824: 3C:898.
NQ

0316 **XENOCLES** Trag.
5 B.C.
001 **Fragmentum**, ed. B. Snell, *Tragicorum Graecorum fragmenta*, vol. 1. Göttingen: Vandenhoeck & Ruprecht, 1971: 153.
fr. 2.
Q: [26]

XENOCRATES Epigr.
AG 7.291; 16.186.
Cf. XENOCRITUS Epigr. (0091 001).

2174 **XENOCRATES** Hist.
Incertum
001 **Fragmentum**, FGrH #248: 2B:1130.
Q

1009 **XENOCRATES** Med.
A.D. 1: Aphrodisiensis
001 **De lapidibus**, ed. M. Wellmann, "Die Stein-
und Gemmenbücher der Antike," *Quellen und
Studien zur Geschichte der Naturwissenschaften
und Medizin* 4.4 (1935) 86–149 (passim).
Q
x01 **Fragmenta ap. Galenum.**
K12.261; **13**.90–91, 846, 931.
Cf. GALENUS Med. (0057 076–077).
x02 **Fragmenta ap. Oribasium.**
CMG, vol. **6.1.1**, pp. 47–57; **6.1.2**, p. 296.
Cf. ORIBASIUS Med. (0722 001, 007).

0091 **XENOCRITUS** Epigr.
ante 1 B.C.: Rhodius
001 **Epigrammata**, AG 7.291; **16**.186.
Q: 81

2306 **XENOMEDES** Hist.
5 B.C.?: Ceus
001 **Testimonia**, FGrH #442: 3B:372.
NQ
002 **Fragmenta**, FGrH #442: 3B:372–374.
Q

0267 **XENOPHANES** Poet. Phil.
6–5 B.C.: Colophonius
001 **Fragmenta**, ed. M.L. West, *Iambi et elegi
Graeci*, vol. 2. Oxford: Clarendon Press, 1972:
164–170.
frr. B1–3, 5–9, A14, B14, 45.
Q: [510]
002 **Fragmenta** (Silli et De natura), ed. E. Diehl,
Anthologia lyrica Graeca, fasc. 1, 3rd edn.
Leipzig: Teubner, 1949: 68–74.
frr. 9–11, 13–34.
Q: [371]
003 **Epigramma**, AG 7.120.
AG 7.119: Cf. ANONYMI EPIGRAMMATICI
(0138 001).
Q: 26

004 **Testimonium**, FGrH #450: 3B:378.
NQ
005 **Testimonia**, ed. H. Diels and W. Kranz, *Die
Fragmente der Vorsokratiker*, vol. 1, 6th edn.
Berlin: Weidmann, 1951 (repr. Dublin: 1966):
113–126.
test. 1–52.
NQ
006 **Fragmenta**, ed. Diels and Kranz, *op. cit.*, 126–
138.
frr. 1–42, 45.
Q

2518 **XENOPHILUS** Hist.
post 4 B.C.?
001 **Fragmentum**, FGrH #767: 3C:758.
Q

2241 **XENOPHILUS** Phil. et Mus.
4 B.C.: Chalcidensis
001 **Testimonia**, ed. H. Diels and W. Kranz, *Die
Fragmente der Vorsokratiker*, vol. 1, 6th edn.
Berlin: Weidmann, 1951 (repr. Dublin: 1966):
442–443.
test. 1–3.
NQ

0032 **XENOPHON** Hist.
5–4 B.C.: Atheniensis
Cf. et XENOPHONTIS EPISTULAE (1754).
001 **Hellenica**, ed. E.C. Marchant, *Xenophontis opera omnia*, vol. 1. Oxford: Clarendon Press,
1900 (repr. 1968).
Cod: 67,924
002 **Memorabilia**, ed. Marchant, *op. cit.*, vol. 2, 2nd
edn. (1921; repr. 1971).
Cod: 36,426
003 **Oeconomicus**, ed. Marchant, *op. cit.*, vol. 2.
Cod: 18,123
004 **Symposium**, ed. Marchant, *op. cit.*, vol. 2.
Cod: 9,655
005 **Apologia Socratis**, ed. Marchant, *op. cit.*, vol. 2.
Cod: 2,027
006 **Anabasis**, ed. Marchant, *op. cit.*, vol. 3 (1904;
repr. 1961).
Cod: 58,285
007 **Cyropaedia**, ed. Marchant, *op. cit.*, vol. 4
(1910; repr. 1970).
Cod: 80,684
008 **Hiero**, ed. Marchant, *op. cit.*, vol. 5 (1920; repr.
1969).
Cod: 6,068
009 **Agesilaus**, ed. Marchant, *op. cit.*, vol. 5.
Cod: 7,558
010 **De republica Lacedaemoniorum**, ed. Marchant, *op. cit.*, vol. 5.
Cod: 5,024
011 **De vectigalibus**, ed. Marchant, *op. cit.*, vol. 5.
Cod: 3,932
012 **Hipparchicus**, ed. Marchant, *op. cit.*, vol. 5.
Cod: 5,894

013 **De re equestri**, ed. Marchant, *op. cit.*, vol. 5.
Cod: 7,103

014 **Cynegeticus**, ed. Marchant, *op. cit.*, vol. 5.
Cod: 9,256

015 **Atheniensium respublica** [Sp.], ed. Marchant,
op. cit., vol. 5.
Cod: 3,250

1926 **XENOPHON** Hist.
post 4 B.C.: Atheniensis
001 **Testimonium**, FGrH #111: 2B:524.
NQ

1973 **XENOPHON** Hist.
3–2 B.C.
001 **Testimonium**, FGrH #179: 2B:906.
NQ

2376 **XENOPHON** Hist.
A.D. 2: fort. Samius
001 **Testimonium**, FGrH #540a: 3B:523.
test. 1: *Inscr. Samos* (Heraion inv. 183).
NQ

1876 **XENOPHON** Hist.
ante A.D. 3
001 **Testimonium**, FGrH #24: 1A:188.
NQ

2510 **XENOPHON** Hist.
Incertum: Cyprius
001 **Testimonium**, FGrH #755: 3C:736.
NQ

1108 **XENOPHON** Med.
4/3 B.C.: Cous
x01 **Fragmentum ap. Oribasium**.
CMG, vol. 6.2.1, p. 166.
Cf. ORIBASIUS Med. (0722 001).
x02 **Fragmentum ap. Erotianum**.
Nachmanson, p. 108.
Cf. EROTIANUS Gramm. et Med. (0716 002).

0641 **XENOPHON** Scr. Erot.
A.D. 2/3: Ephesius
001 **Ephesiaca**, ed. G. Dalmeyda, *Xénophon
d'Éphèse. Les Éphésiaques ou le roman d'Habro-
comès et d'Anthia*. Paris: Les Belles Lettres,
1926 (repr. 1962): 3–77.
Cod: 17,197
002 **Testimonium**, FGrH #419: 3B:316.
NQ

1754 ***XENOPHONTIS EPISTULAE***
Incertum
Cf. et XENOPHON Hist. (0032).
001 **Epistulae**, ed. R. Hercher, *Epistolographi
Graeci*. Paris: Didot, 1873 (repr. Amsterdam:
Hakkert, 1965): 788–791.
Q: [1,201]
x01 **Epistulae ad Socraticos**.
Epist. Graec., pp. 621–622, 623–625.
Cf. SOCRATICORUM EPISTULAE (0637 001).

2229 **XUTHUS** Phil.
5 B.C.: Crotoniensis
001 **Testimonium**, ed. H. Diels and W. Kranz, *Die
Fragmente der Vorsokratiker*, vol. 1, 6th edn.
Berlin: Weidmann, 1951 (repr. Dublin: 1966):
376.
NQ

0601 **<ZALEUCUS Nomographus>** <Phil.>
4/2 B.C.?: Locrus
001 **Fragmenta**, ed. H. Thesleff, *The Pythagorean
texts of the Hellenistic period*. Åbo: Åbo Akademi, 1965: 225–229.
Q: 698

0076 **ZELOTUS** Epigr.
Incertum
001 **Epigramma**, AG 9.30.
AG 9.31: Cf. ANONYMI EPIGRAMMATICI
(0138 001).
Q: 19

2276 **ZENIS** Hist.
4 B.C.?: Chius
001 **Fragmentum**, FGrH #393: 3B:284.
Q

2528 **ZENO** Hist.
3 B.C.: Sidonius
001 **Testimonium**, FGrH #791: 3C:824–825.
NQ
002 **Titulus**, FGrH #791: 3C:825.
NQ

1956 **ZENO** Hist.
3 B.C.?
001 **Testimonium**, FGrH #158: 2B:883.
NQ

2364 **ZENO** Hist.
2 B.C.: Rhodius
001 **Testimonia**, FGrH #523: 3B:494–495.
NQ
002 **Fragmenta**, FGrH #523: 3B:495–502.
Q

1109 **ZENO** Med.
2 B.C.
x01 **Fragmentum ap. Pseudo-Galenum**.
K19.409.
Cf. Pseudo-GALENUS Med. (0530 041).

1110 **ZENO** Med.
1 B.C.: Laodicensis
x01 **Fragmenta ap. Galenum**.
K14.163, 171.
Cf. GALENUS Med. (0057 078).
x02 **Fragmentum ap. Philumenum**.
CMG, vol. 10.1.1, p. 14.
Cf. PHILUMENUS Med. (0671 001).

0595 **ZENO** Phil.
5 B.C.: Eleaticus

001 **Testimonia**, ed. H. Diels and W. Kranz, *Die Fragmente der Vorsokratiker*, vol. 1, 6th edn. Berlin: Weidmann, 1951 (repr. Dublin: 1966): 247–255.
test. 1–30.
NQ

002 **Fragmenta**, ed. Diels and Kranz, *op. cit.*, 255–258.
frr. 1–4.
Q

0635 **ZENO** Phil.
4–3 B.C.: Citieus
Cf. et ZENONIS EPISTULA (0125).

001 **Fragmenta**, ed. J. von Arnim, *Stoicorum veterum fragmenta*, vol. 1. Leipzig: Teubner, 1905 (repr. Stuttgart: 1968): 3–71.
Q

002 **Fragmenta**, ed. H. Lloyd-Jones and P. Parsons, *Supplementum Hellenisticum*. Berlin: De Gruyter, 1983: 396.
frr. 852–852a.
Q: [23]

2294 **ZENO** Phil.
3–2 B.C.: Tarsensis

001 **Fragmenta**, ed. J. von Arnim, *Stoicorum veterum fragmenta*, vol. 3. Leipzig: Teubner, 1903 (repr. Stuttgart: 1968): 209.
Q

2134 **ZENO** Phil.
2–1 B.C.: Sidonius

001 **Fragmenta**, ed. A. Angeli and M. Colaizzo, "I frammenti di Zenone Sidonio," *Cronache Ercolanesi* 9 (1979) 72, 75–82, 85.
frr. 1–4, 11–28.
Pap

002 **Fragmenta incerta**, ed. Angeli and Colaizzo, *op. cit.*, 85–86.
frr. 1–7.
Pap

2167 **ZENOBIA** Hist.
A.D. 3: Palmyrena

001 **Testimonium**, FGrH #626: 3C:161.
NQ

0596 **ZENOBIUS** Gramm.
fiq Zenobius Sophista
A.D. 2?
Cf. et ZENOBIUS Sophista <Paroemiogr.> (0098).

001 **Epigramma**, AG 9.711.
Q: 16

0098 **ZENOBIUS Sophista** <Paroemiogr.>
A.D. 2
Cf. et ZENOBIUS Gramm. (0596).

001 **Epitome collectionum Lucilli Tarrhaei et Didymi**, ed. E.L. von Leutsch and F.G. Schneidewin, *Corpus paroemiographorum Graecorum*, vol. 1. Göttingen: Vandenhoeck &

Ruprecht, 1839 (repr. Hildesheim: Olms, 1965): 1–175.
Cod: [21,285]

0597 **ZENODORUS** Gramm.
fiq Zenodotus Ephesius
2–1 B.C.?
Cf. et ZENODOTUS Gramm. (0590).

001 Περὶ συνηθείας, ed. E. Miller, *Mélanges de littérature grecque*. Paris: Imprimerie Impériale, 1868 (repr. Amsterdam: Hakkert, 1965): 253–258.
Cod

0599 **ZENODORUS** Math.
3 B.C.?

x01 **Fragmenta ap. Theonem Alexandrinum**.
Rome, pp. 355–600 (passim).
Cf. THEON Alexandrinus Math. (2033 001).

0600 **ZENODOTUS** <Epigr.>
2 B.C.

001 **Epigramma**, AG 7.117.
Q: 40

0590 **ZENODOTUS** Gramm.
4–3 B.C.: Ephesius
Cf. et ZENODORUS Gramm. (0597).

001 **Fragmenta**, ed. H. Duentzer, *De Zenodoti studiis Homericis*. Göttingen: Dieterich, 1848: passim.
Q

002 **Fragmenta**, ed. A. Römer, *Über die Homerrecension des Zenodot*. [*Abhandlungen der königlich bayerischen Akademie der Wissenschaften*, Philosoph.-philol. Kl., Bd. 17. Munich: Franz, 1886]: passim.
Q

003 **Fragmenta**, FGrH #19: 1A:183–184.
Q

004 **Epigrammata**, AG 7.315; 16.14.
Q: 59

2550 **ZENODOTUS** Hist.
2 B.C.: Troezenius

001 **Fragmenta**, FGrH #821: 3C:895–896.
Q

0354 **ZENODOTUS** Trag.
Incertum

001 **Fragmentum**, ed. B. Snell, *Tragicorum Graecorum fragmenta*, vol. 1. Göttingen: Vandenhoeck & Ruprecht, 1971: 325.
Q: [15]

0125 *ZENONIS EPISTULA*
Incertum
Cf. et ZENO Phil. (0635).

001 **Epistula**, ed. R. Hercher, *Epistolographi Graeci*. Paris: Didot, 1873 (repr. Amsterdam: Hakkert, 1965): 792.
Q: [123]

1111 **ZENOPHILUS** Med.
ante A.D. 4
x01 **Fragmentum ap. Oribasium.**
CMG, 6.3, p. 116.
Cf. ORIBASIUS Med. (0722 005).
x02 **Fragmentum ap. Aëtium** (lib. 11).
Daremberg-Ruelle, p. 574.
Cf. AËTIUS Med. (0718 011).

2647 **ZENOTHEMIS** Geogr.
2 B.C.?
001 **Fragmentum,** ed. H. Lloyd-Jones and P. Parsons, *Supplementum Hellenisticum.* Berlin: De Gruyter, 1983: 397.
fr. 855.
Q: [12]

0127 **ZEUXIS** Epigr.
5 B.C.: Heracleota
001 **Epigramma,** ed. E. Diehl, *Anthologia lyrica Graeca,* fasc. 1, 3rd edn. Leipzig: Teubner, 1949: 111–112.
Q: [25]
x01 **Epigramma demonstrativum.**
App. Anth. 3.29: Cf. EPIGRAMMATICI in *App. Anth.* (7052 003).

1113 **ZEUXIS** Med.
ante A.D. 1
x01 **Fragmentum ap. Galenum.**
K12.834.
Cf. GALENUS Med. (0057 076).

1112 **ZEUXIS Major** Med.
2 B.C.: Tarentinus
x01 **Fragmentum ap. Galenum.**
K17.2.165–166 in CMG, vol. 5.10.2.2, p. 217.
Cf. GALENUS Med. (0057 091).

1114 **ZOILUS** Med.
ante A.D. 1
x01 **Fragmenta ap. Galenum.**
K12.632, 763–764, 771–772; **14**.178.
Cf. GALENUS Med. (0057 076, 078).
x02 **Fragmentum ap. Aëtium** (lib. 7).
CMG, vol. 8.2, p. 392.
Cf. AËTIUS Med. (0718 007).
x03 **Fragmentum ap. Alexandrum Trallianum.**
Puschmann, vol. 2, p. 39.
Cf. ALEXANDER Med. (0744 003).

0128 **ZOILUS** Phil. et Rhet.
4 B.C.: Amphipolitanus
001 **Testimonia,** FGrH #71: **2A**:109–110; **3B**:741
addenda.
NQ
002 **Fragmenta,** FGrH #71: 2A:110–112.
Q

0130 **ZOPYRUS** Hist.
4–3 B.C.?: fort. Magnes
001 **Fragmenta,** FGrH #494: 3B:465–466.
Q

0129 **ZOPYRUS** Hist.
Incertum
001 **Fragmenta,** FGrH #336: 3B:187–188.
Q

1116 **ZOPYRUS** Med.
2–1 B.C.: Alexandrinus
x01 **Fragmenta ap. Galenum.**
K14.115, 150–151.
Cf. GALENUS Med. (0057 078).
x02 **Fragmenta ap. Oribasium.**
CMG, vol. 6.1.2, pp. 217, 222, 223, 226, 228, 231, 235.
Cf. ORIBASIUS Med. (0722 001).

0355 **ZOPYRUS** Trag.
3 B.C.?
001 **Fragmentum,** ed. B. Snell, *Tragicorum Graecorum fragmenta,* vol. 1. Göttingen: Vandenhoeck & Ruprecht, 1971: 325.
Q: [14]

1829 **<ZOROASTER Magus>**
Incertum
001 **Fragmenta,** ed. J. Bidez and F. Cumont, *Les mages hellénisés,* vol. 2. Paris: Les Belles Lettres, 1938: 59–60, 157, 158, 159, 161–162, 174–175, 179–187, 188–195, 209–218, 220–226, 232–233.
Q, Cod

1755 **ZOSIMUS** Epigr.
1 B.C.?: Thasius
001 **Epigrammata,** AG **6**.15, 183–185; **9**.40.
Q: 195

2687 **ZOSIMUS** Epigr.
A.D. 3/4
x01 **Epigrammata sepulcralia.**
App. Anth. 2.497–498: Cf. EPIGRAMMATICI in *App. Anth.* (7052 002).

4084 **ZOSIMUS** Hist.
A.D. 5?: Constantinopolitanus
001 **Historia nova,** ed. F. Paschoud, *Zosime. Histoire nouvelle,* 2 vols. in 3. Paris: Les Belles Lettres, 1:1971; 2.1–2.2:1979: **1**:8–64, 70–128; **2.1**:8–58; **2.2**:262–330.
Cod: [46,951]

1117 **ZOSIMUS** Med.
ante A.D. 2
x01 **Fragmentum ap. Galenum.**
K12.753.
Cf. GALENUS Med. (0057 076).
x02 **Fragmentum ap. Oribasium.**
CMG, vol. 6.2.2, p. 232.
Cf. ORIBASIUS Med. (0722 003).
x03 **Fragmentum ap. Paulum.**
CMG, vol. 9.2, p. 378.
Cf. PAULUS Med. (0715 001).

INDEX OF TLG AUTHOR NUMBERS

The authors in this index are listed in order of their TLG author numbers. This arrangement is intended primarily for those who consult TLG machine-readable texts and require a reference system which translates author numbers into author names.

0001 **APOLLONIUS RHODIUS** Epic.
0002 **THEOGNIS** Eleg.
0003 **THUCYDIDES** Hist.
0004 **DIOGENES LAERTIUS** Biogr.
0005 **THEOCRITUS** Bucol.
0006 **EURIPIDES** Trag.
0007 **PLUTARCHUS** Biogr. et Phil.
0008 **ATHENAEUS** Soph.
0009 **SAPPHO** Lyr.
0010 **ISOCRATES** Orat.
0011 **SOPHOCLES** Trag.
0012 **HOMERUS** Epic.
0013 **HYMNI HOMERICI**
0014 **DEMOSTHENES** Orat.
0015 **HERODIANUS** Hist.
0016 **HERODOTUS** Hist.
0017 **ISAEUS** Orat.
0018 **PHILO JUDAEUS** Phil.
0019 **ARISTOPHANES** Comic.
0020 **HESIODUS** Epic.
0022 **NICANDER** Epic.
0023 **OPPIANUS** Epic.
0024 **OPPIANUS** Epic.
0026 **AESCHINES** Orat.
0027 **ANDOCIDES** Orat.
0028 **ANTIPHON** Orat.
0029 **DINARCHUS** Orat.
0030 **HYPERIDES** Orat.
0031 **NOVUM TESTAMENTUM**
0032 **XENOPHON** Hist.
0033 **PINDARUS** Lyr.
0034 **LYCURGUS** Orat.
0035 **MOSCHUS** Bucol.
0036 **BION** Bucol.
0037 **ANACHARSIDIS EPISTULAE**
0038 **ARCESILAI EPISTULA**
0039 **MITHRIDATIS EPISTULA**
0040 **CALANI EPISTULA**
0041 **CHION** <Epist.>
0042 **ALEXANDRI MAGNI EPISTU-LAE**
0043 **AMASIS EPISTULAE**
0044 **ANTIOCHI REGIS EPISTULAE**
0045 **ARTAXERXIS EPISTULAE**
0046 **NICIAE EPISTULA**
0047 **PAUSANIAE ET XERXIS EPIS-TULAE**
0048 **PHILIPPUS II Rex Macedonum** <Epist.>
0049 **PISISTRATI EPISTULA**
0050 **PTOLEMAEI II PHILADELPHI ET ELEAZARI EPISTULAE**
0051 <**MELISSA**> Phil.
0052 **MENIPPUS** Phil.
0053 **PHALARIDIS EPISTULAE**
0054 <**THEANO**> Phil.

0055 **THEMISTOCLIS EPISTULAE**
0056 **THRASYBULI EPISTULA**
0057 **GALENUS** Med.
0058 **AENEAS** Tact.
0059 **PLATO** Phil.
0060 **DIODORUS SICULUS** Hist.
0061 **Pseudo-LUCIANUS** Soph.
0062 **LUCIANUS** Soph.
0063 **DIONYSIUS THRAX** Gramm.
0064 **PERIPLUS HANNONIS**
0065 **SCYLAX** Perieg.
0066 **DICAEARCHUS** Phil.
0067 **AGATHARCHIDES** Geogr.
0068 **Pseudo-SCYMNUS** Geogr.
0069 **DIONYSIUS** Geogr.
0070 **ISIDORUS** Geogr.
0071 **PERIPLUS MARIS ERYTHRAEI**
0072 **ANONYMI GRAMMATICI**
0074 **Flavius ARRIANUS** Hist. et Phil.
0075 **PERIPLUS PONTI EUXINI**
0076 **ZELOTUS** Epigr.
0077 **PERIPLUS MARIS MAGNI**
0079 **MENIPPUS** Geogr.
0080 **ARTEMIDORUS** Geogr.
0081 **DIONYSIUS HALICARNASSEN-SIS** Rhet. et Hist.
0082 **APOLLONIUS DYSCOLUS** Gramm.
0083 **DIONYSIUS** Geogr.
0084 **DIONYSIUS** Perieg.
0085 **AESCHYLUS** Trag.
0086 **ARISTOTELES** Phil. et **CORPUS ARISTOTELICUM**
0087 **Aelius HERODIANUS et Pseudo-HERODIANUS** Gramm. et Rhet.
0088 **ARISTOXENUS** Mus.
0089 **PRAXIPHANES** Phil.
0090 **AGATHEMERUS** Geogr.
0091 **XENOCRITUS** Epigr.
0092 **ANONYMI GEOGRAPHIAE EX-POSITIO COMPENDIARIA**
0093 **THEOPHRASTUS** Phil.
0094 **Pseudo-PLUTARCHUS**
0096 **AESOPUS** Scr. Fab. et **AESOPICA**
0097 <**DIOGENIANUS**> Paroemiogr.
0098 **ZENOBIUS Sophista** <Paroemi-ogr.>
0099 **STRABO** Geogr.
0101 **ACERATUS** Gramm.
0102 **ADAEUS** Epigr.
0103 **AEMILIANUS** Rhet.
0104 **AESCHINES** Rhet.
0105 **AGIS** Epigr.
0106 **ALCAEUS** Epigr.
0107 **ALEXANDER** Epigr.
0108 **ALPHEUS** Epigr.

0109 **AMMIANUS** Epigr.
0110 **AMMONIDES** Epigr.
0111 **ANDRONICUS** Epigr.
0112 **ANTIOCHUS** Epigr.
0113 **ANTIPATER** Epigr.
0114 **ANTIPATER** Epigr.
0115 **ABGARI EPISTULA**
0116 **ABYDENUS** Hist.
0117 **ANTIPHANES** Epigr.
0118 **ANTIPHILUS** Epigr.
0119 **ANTISTIUS** <Epigr.>
0120 **ANTONIUS** Epigr.
0121 **ANYTE** Epigr.
0122 **APOLLINARIUS** Epigr.
0124 **APOLLONIDES** Epigr.
0125 **ZENONIS EPISTULA**
0126 **Aulus Licinius ARCHIAS** Epigr.
0127 **ZEUXIS** Epigr.
0128 **ZOILUS** Phil. et Rhet.
0129 **ZOPYRUS** Hist.
0130 **ZOPYRUS** Hist.
0131 **ARCHIMELUS** Epigr.
0132 **Marcus ARGENTARIUS** Rhet. et Epigr.
0133 **ARISTODICUS** Epigr.
0134 **ARISTON** Epigr.
0135 **ARTEMIDORUS** Gramm.
0136 **ARTEMON** Epigr.
0137 **ASCLEPIADES** Epigr.
0138 **ANONYMI EPIGRAMMATICI**
0139 **ANTIGENES** Lyr.
0140 **AUTOMEDON** Epigr.
0141 **ATHENAEUS** Epigr.
0142 **[BACIS]**
0143 **LOLLIUS BASSUS** Epigr.
0144 <**BESANTINUS**> Epigr.
0145 **BIANOR** Epigr.
0146 **BOETHUS** Epigr.
0147 **CALLEAS** Epigr.
0148 **CALLICTER** Epigr.
0149 **CAPITO** Epigr.
0150 **CARPHYLLIDES** Epigr.
0151 **CEREALIUS** Epigr.
0152 **CHAEREMON** Epigr.
0153 **CORNELIUS LONG(IN)US** Epigr.
0154 **CRINAGORAS** Epigr.
0156 **CYLLENIUS** Epigr.
0157 **CYRILLUS** Epigr.
0158 **DAMAGETUS** Epigr.
0159 **DEMETRIUS** Epigr.
0160 **DEMIURGUS** Epigr.
0161 **DEMOCRITUS** Epigr.
0162 **Julius DIOCLES** Rhet.
0163 **DIODORUS** Epigr.
0164 **DIODORUS ZONAS** Rhet.

0368 **CYDIAS** Lyr.
0369 **TELESILLA** Lyr.
0370 **LAMPROCLES** Lyr.
0371 **DIAGORAS** Lyr.
0372 **PRAXILLA** Lyr.
0373 **MELANIPPIDES** Lyr.
0374 **LICYMNIUS** Lyr.
0375 **CINESIAS** Lyr.
0376 **TIMOTHEUS** Lyr.
0377 **TELESTES** Lyr.
0378 **ARIPHRON** Lyr.
0379 **PHILOXENUS** Lyr.
0380 **PHILOXENUS** Lyr.
0381 **LYCOPHRONIDES** Lyr.
0382 **CASTORION** Lyr.
0383 **ALCAEUS** Lyr.
0384 **ACTA JUSTINI ET SEPTEM SODALIUM**
0385 **DIO CASSIUS** Hist.
0386 **CHILONIS EPISTULA**
0387 **SAPPHUS vel ALCAEI FRAGMENTA**
0388 **ACTA PAULI**
0389 **ACTA PETRI**
0390 **MARTYRIUM CARPI, PAPYLI ET AGATHONICAE**
0391 **ACTA SCILITANORUM MARTYRUM**
0392 **ACUSILAUS** Hist.
0393 **PISANDER** Myth.
0394 **APOLLONIUS** Comic.
0395 **DIOPHANTUS** Comic.
0396 **EUPHANES** Comic.
0397 **PRONOMUS** Lyr.
0398 **SIMYLUS** Comic.
0399 **EUDOXUS** Comic.
0400 **ALCAEUS** Comic.
0401 **ALEXANDER** Comic.
0402 **ALEXIS** Comic.
0403 **AMIPSIAS** Comic.
0404 **AMPHIS** Comic.
0405 **ANAXANDRIDES** Comic.
0406 **ANAXILAS** Comic.
0407 **ANAXIPPUS** Comic.
0408 **COMICA ADESPOTA (CAF)**
0409 **ANTIDOTUS** Comic.
0410 **ANTIPHANES** Comic.
0411 **APOLLODORUS** Comic.
0412 **APOLLODORUS Carystius vel APOLLODORUS Gelous** Comic.
0413 **APOLLODORUS** Comic.
0414 **APOLLOPHANES** Comic.
0415 **ARAROS** Comic.
0416 **ARCHEDICUS** Comic.
0417 **ARCHIPPUS** Comic.
0418 **ARISTAGORAS** Comic.
0419 **ARISTOMENES** Comic.
0420 **ARISTONYMUS** Comic.
0421 **ARISTOPHON** Comic.
0422 **ATHENIO** Comic.
0423 **AUTOCRATES** Comic.
0424 **AXIONICUS** Comic.
0425 **BATO** Comic.
0426 **CALLIAS** Comic.
0427 **<CALLIPPUS>** Comic.
0428 **CANTHARUS** Comic.
0429 **CEPHISODORUS** Comic.
0430 **CHARICLIDES** Comic.
0431 **CHIONIDES** Comic.

0432 **CLEARCHUS** Comic.
0433 **CRATES** Comic.
0434 **CRATINUS** Comic.
0435 **CRATINUS Junior** Comic.
0436 **CRITO** Comic.
0437 **CROBYLUS** Comic.
0438 **DAMOXENUS** Comic.
0439 **DEMETRIUS** Comic.
0440 **DEMETRIUS Junior** Comic.
0441 **DEMONICUS** Comic.
0442 **DEXICRATES** Comic.
0443 **DIOCLES** Comic.
0444 **DIODORUS** Comic.
0445 **DIONYSIUS** Comic.
0446 **DIOXIPPUS** Comic.
0447 **DIPHILUS** Comic.
0448 **DROMO** Comic.
0449 **ECPHANTIDES** Comic.
0450 **EPHIPPUS** Comic.
0451 **EPICRATES** Comic.
0452 **EPIGENES** Comic.
0453 **EPILYCUS** Comic.
0454 **EPINICUS** Comic.
0455 **ERIPHUS** Comic.
0456 **EUANGELUS** Comic.
0457 **EUBULIDES** Comic.
0458 **EUBULUS** Comic.
0459 **EUNICUS** Comic.
0460 **EUPHRO** Comic.
0461 **EUPOLIS** Comic.
0462 **EUTHYCLES** Comic.
0463 **HEGEMON** Parodius
0464 **HEGESIPPUS** Comic.
0465 **HENIOCHUS** Comic.
0466 **HERACLIDES** Comic.
0467 **TIMOTHEUS** Trag.
0468 **HIPPARCHUS** Comic.
0469 **LAON** Comic.
0470 **LEUCO** Comic.
0471 **LYNCEUS** Comic.
0472 **LYSIPPUS** Comic.
0473 **MACHON** Comic.
0474 **MAGNES** Comic.
0475 **METAGENES** Comic.
0476 **MNESIMACHUS** Comic.
0477 **MYRTILUS** Comic.
0478 **NAUSICRATES** Comic.
0479 **NICO** Comic.
0480 **NICOCHARES** Comic.
0481 **NICOLAUS** Comic.
0482 **NICOMACHUS** Comic.
0483 **NICOPHON** Comic.
0484 **NICOSTRATUS** Comic.
0485 **OPHELIO** Comic.
0486 **PHERECRATES** Comic.
0487 **PHILEMON** Comic.
0488 **PHILEMON Junior** Comic.
0489 **PHILETAERUS** Comic.
0490 **PHILIPPIDES** Comic.
0491 **PHILISCUS** Comic.
0492 **PHILONIDES** Comic.
0493 **PHILOSTEPHANUS** Comic.
0494 **PHILYLLIUS** Comic.
0495 **PHOENICIDES** Comic.
0496 **PHRYNICHUS** Comic.
0497 **PLATO** Comic.
0498 **POLIOCHUS** Comic.
0499 **POLYZELUS** Comic.
0500 **POSIDIPPUS** Comic.

0501 **SANNYRION** Comic.
0502 **SOPHILUS** Comic.
0503 **SOSICRATES** Comic.
0504 **SOSIPATER** Comic.
0505 **SOTADES** Comic.
0506 **STEPHANUS** Comic.
0507 **STRATON** Comic.
0508 **STRATTIS** Comic.
0509 **<MYIA>** Phil.
0510 **TELECLIDES** Comic.
0511 **THEOGNETUS** Comic.
0512 **THEOPHILUS** Comic.
0513 **THEOPOMPUS** Comic.
0514 **THUGENIDES** Comic.
0515 **TIMOCLES** Comic.
0516 **TIMOSTRATUS** Comic.
0517 **TIMOTHEUS** Comic.
0518 **XENARCHUS** Comic.
0519 **XENO** Comic.
0520 **ARCESILAUS** Comic.
0521 **EPICHARMUS** Comic. et **PSEUDEPICHARMEA**
0522 **PISANDER** Epic.
0523 **MENECRATES** Comic.
0524 **SOPHRON** Mimogr.
0525 **PAUSANIAS** Perieg.
0526 **Flavius JOSEPHUS** Hist.
0527 **SEPTUAGINTA**
0528 **AËTIUS** Doxogr.
0529 **ARIUS DIDYMUS** Doxogr.
0530 **Pseudo-GALENUS** Med.
0531 **HERMIAS** Phil.
0532 **ACHILLES TATIUS** Scr. Erot.
0533 **CALLIMACHUS** Philol.
0534 **CALLISTHENES** Hist.
0535 **DEMADES** Orat. et Rhet.
0536 **EPHORUS** Hist.
0537 **EPICURUS** Phil.
0538 **HECATAEUS** Hist.
0539 **HELLANICUS** Hist.
0540 **LYSIAS** Orat.
0541 **MENANDER** Comic.
0542 **Julius POLLUX** Gramm.
0543 **POLYBIUS** Hist.
0544 **SEXTUS EMPIRICUS** Phil.
0545 **Claudius AELIANUS** Soph.
0546 **AELIANUS** Tact.
0547 **ANAXIMENES** Hist. et Rhet.
0548 **APOLLODORUS** Myth.
0549 **APOLLODORUS** Gramm.
0550 **APOLLONIUS** Geom.
0551 **APPIANUS** Hist.
0552 **ARCHIMEDES** Geom.
0553 **ARTEMIDORUS** Onir.
0554 **CHARITON** Scr. Erot.
0555 **CLEMENS ALEXANDRINUS** Theol.
0556 **ASCLEPIODOTUS** Tact.
0557 **EPICTETUS** Phil.
0558 **HELLENICA**
0559 **HERON** Mech.
0560 **[LONGINUS]** Rhet.
0561 **LONGUS** Scr. Erot.
0562 **MARCUS AURELIUS ANTONINUS Imperator** Phil.
0563 **MAXIMUS** Soph.
0564 **RUFUS** Med.
0565 **SORANUS** Med.
0566 **THEOPOMPUS** Hist.

0567 **HERACLEON** Gramm.
0568 **ANTIGONUS** Paradox.
0569 **APOLLONIUS** Paradox.
0570 **ARCHELAUS** Paradox.
0571 **ARISTOCLES** Paradox.
0572 **GAIUS** Scr. Eccl.
0574 **LYSIMACHUS** Hist.
0575 **<MOSCHION>** Gnom.
0576 **MUSAEUS** Epic.
0577 **NICOLAUS** Hist.
0578 **NYMPHODORUS** Hist.
0579 **ORPHICA**
0580 **PARADOXOGRAPHUS FLORENTINUS**
0581 **PARADOXOGRAPHUS PALATINUS**
0582 **PARADOXOGRAPHUS VATICANUS**
0583 **PHILOCHORUS** Hist.
0584 **PHILOSTEPHANUS** Hist.
0585 **Publius Aelius PHLEGON** Paradox.
0586 **POLEMON** Perieg.
0587 **SOTION** <Paradox.>
0588 **TROPHILUS** <Paradox.>
0589 **EPISTULAE PRIVATAE**
0590 **ZENODOTUS** Gramm.
0591 **ANTISTHENES** Rhet. et Phil.
0592 **HERMOGENES** Rhet.
0593 **GORGIAS** Rhet. et Soph.
0594 **ALEXANDER** Rhet.
0595 **ZENO** Phil.
0596 **ZENOBIUS** Gramm.
0597 **ZENODORUS** Gramm.
0598 **ANONYMI RHETORES**
0599 **ZENODORUS** Math.
0600 **ZENODOTUS** <Epigr.>
0601 **<ZALEUCUS Nomographus>** <Phil.>
0602 **COMICA ADESPOTA (FCG)**
0603 **SILENUS** Trag.
0604 **PTOLEMAEUS IV PHILOPATOR** Trag.
0605 **POLYBIUS** Rhet.
0606 **RUFUS** Soph.
0607 **Aelius THEON** Rhet.
0608 **SATYRUS** Biogr.
0609 **TRYPHON I** Gramm.
0610 **ALCIDAMAS** Rhet.
0611 **THEODORUS** Trag.
0612 **DIO CHRYSOSTOMUS** Soph.
0613 **<DEMETRIUS>** Rhet.
0614 **Valerius BABRIUS** Scr. Fab.
0615 **ASPASIUS** Phil.
0616 **POLYAENUS** Rhet.
0617 **ANAXIMENES** Phil.
0618 **ANTIGONI EPISTULA**
0619 **APOLLONIUS** Phil.
0620 **ARCHYTAS** Phil.
0621 **[ATH]ENODORUS** Trag.
0622 **CLEOBULI EPISTULA**
0623 **CRATETIS EPISTULAE**
0624 **DEMETRIUS** Phil. et Hist.
0625 **POLEMAEUS** Trag.
0626 **HERACLITUS** Phil.
0627 **HIPPOCRATES** Med. et **CORPUS HIPPOCRATICUM**
0628 **Gaius MUSONIUS RUFUS** Phil.
0629 **PERIANDER** <Phil.>

0630 **PHERECYDES** Phil. et Myth.
0631 **PITTACUS** <Lyr.>
0632 **<PYTHAGORAS>** Phil.
0633 **<LYSIS>** Phil.
0635 **ZENO** Phil.
0636 **SOCRATIS EPISTULAE**
0637 **SOCRATICORUM EPISTULAE**
0638 **Flavius PHILOSTRATUS** Soph.
0639 **MENECRATES** Med.
0640 **ALCIPHRON** Rhet. et Soph.
0641 **XENOPHON** Scr. Erot.
0642 **ANONYMI IN SOPHISTICOS ELENCHOS PARAPHRASIS**
0643 **ANONYMUS LONDINENSIS** Med.
0644 **ARISTOPHANES** Gramm.
0645 **JUSTINUS MARTYR** Apol.
0646 **Pseudo-JUSTINUS MARTYR**
0647 **TRIPHIODORUS** Epic. et Gramm.
0648 **ONASANDER** Tact.
0649 **LESBONAX** Rhet.
0650 **HERODAS** Mimogr.
0651 **ANTONINUS LIBERALIS** Myth.
0652 **PHILOSTRATUS Junior** Soph.
0653 **ARATUS** Epic. et Astron.
0654 **Lucius Annaeus CORNUTUS** Phil.
0655 **PARTHENIUS** Myth.
0656 **DIOSCORIDES PEDANIUS** Med.
0657 **CRATEUAS** Med.
0658 **HELIODORUS** Scr. Erot.
0659 **COMICA ADESPOTA (Suppl. Com.)**
0660 **APOLLONIUS** Med.
0661 **ARCHIGENES** Med.
0662 **COMICA ADESPOTA (CGFPR)**
0663 **PRAECEPTA SALUBRIA**
0664 **DIOCLES** Med.
0665 **ADRIANUS** Hist.
0666 **ADRIANUS** Rhet.
0667 **MARCELLINUS I** Med.
0668 **AEGIMIUS**
0669 **ANTONIUS MUSA** Med.
0670 **AELIUS PUBLIUS JULIUS** <Epist.>
0671 **PHILUMENUS** Med.
0672 **PRAXAGORAS** Med.
0673 **AESCHINES SOCRATICUS** Phil.
0674 **AELIUS PROMOTUS** Med.
0675 **AGATHINUS** Med.
0676 **AGLAÏS** Poet. Med.
0677 **ANDREAS** Med.
0678 **ANDRON** Med.
0679 **AESCHRION** Lyr.
0680 **APOLLONIUS** Med.
0681 **ASCLEPIADES Pharmacion** Med.
0682 **ATHENAEUS** Med.
0683 **AETHIOPIS**
0684 **CLEOPATRA VII PHILOPATOR** <Med.>
0685 **Titus Statilius CRITO** Med.
0686 **AETHLIUS** Hist.
0687 **AGACLYTUS** Hist.
0688 **AGATHOCLES** Hist.
0689 **DEMOSTHENES Philalethes** Med.
0690 **ERASISTRATUS** Med.
0691 **HARPOCRATIONIS EPISTULA**

0692 **HELIODORUS** Med.
0693 **ALBINUS** Phil.
0694 **HERACLIDES** Med.
0695 **ALCIMUS** Hist.
0696 **ALCMAEONIS**
0697 **Cornelius ALEXANDER** Polyhist.
0698 **ALEXANDER** Rhet.
0699 **ALEXION** Gramm.
0700 **APOLLODORUS** Trag.
0701 **MNESITHEUS** Med.
0702 **MNESITHEUS** Med.
0703 **NUMENIUS** Poet. Didac.
0704 **NUMENIUS** Med.
0705 **ANONYMUS SENEX** Med.
0706 **PHILO** Med.
0707 **ALEXIS** Hist.
0708 **<AMMONIUS>** Gramm.
0709 **AMMONIUS** Hist.
0710 **AMPHIARAI EXILIUM (?)**
0711 **AMPHITHEUS (?)** Hist.
0712 **AMYNTAS** Hist.
0713 **ANAXAGORAS** Phil.
0714 **ANAXARCHUS** Phil.
0715 **PAULUS** Med.
0716 **EROTIANUS** Gramm. et Med.
0717 **HYPSICLES** Math. et Astron.
0718 **AËTIUS** Med.
0719 **ARETAEUS** Med.
0720 **HARMODIUS** Trag.
0721 **ANONYMI MEDICI**
0722 **ORIBASIUS** Med.
0723 **LEO** Phil.
0724 **STEPHANUS** Med.
0725 **ANAXIMANDER** Phil.
0726 **PALLADIUS** Med.
0727 **JOANNES** Med.
0728 **THEOPHILUS Protospatharius, DAMASCIUS et STEPHANUS,**
0729 **THEOPHILUS Protospatharius** Med.
0730 **MELETIUS** Med.
0731 **ADAMANTIUS JUDAEUS** Med.
0732 **ALEXANDER** Phil.
0733 **CASSIUS** Med.
0734 **<LUCAS Apostolus>** Med.
0735 **EUDEMUS** Med.
0736 **STEPHANUS** Med.
0737 **JULIANUS Scriptor Legis De Medicis**
0738 **HIPPIATRICA**
0739 **APOLLONIUS** Med.
0740 **JUSJURANDUM MEDICUM**
0741 **APOLLONIUS** Med.
0742 **HYMNI ANONYMI**
0743 **NEMESIUS** Theol.
0744 **ALEXANDER** Med.
0745 **HIEROPHILUS** Soph. et Phil.
0746 **THEOPHILUS Protospatharius et STEPHANUS ATHENIENSIS** Med.
0747 **APOLLONIUS Archistrator** Med.
0748 **SEVERUS Iatrosophista** Med.
0749 **ANTYLLUS** Med.
0750 **HELIODORUS** Trag.
0751 **Pseudo-HIPPOCRATES** Med.
0752 **EUTECNIUS** Soph.
0753 **AENEAS** Med.
0754 **ABASCANTUS** Med.
0755 **ACACIUS** Med.

0756 **ACHILLAS** Med.
0757 **ACHOLIUS** Med.
0758 **AMARANTUS** Gramm.
0759 **ANTHUS** Med.
0760 **APHRODISEUS** Med.
0761 **AGAPETUS** Med.
0762 **AGATHOCLES** Med.
0763 Julius **AGRIPPA** Med.
0764 **ALCAMENES** Med.
0765 **ALCIMION** Med.
0766 **ALCMAEON** Phil.
0767 **ALEXANDER Philalethes** Med.
0768 **AMMONIUS Lithotomus** Med.
0769 **APION** Med.
0770 **AMYTHAON** Med.
0771 **AMPHION** Med.
0772 **ANDROMACHUS Minor** Med.
0773 **ANDRONICUS** Med.
0774 **AXIORIUS** Med.
0775 **ANTHAEUS** Med.
0776 **ANTIGONUS** Med.
0777 **ANTIOCHUS Philometor** <Med.>
0778 **ANTIOCHUS** Med.
0779 **ANTIPATER** Med.
0780 **ANTIPHANES** Med.
0781 Pomponius **BASSUS** <Med.>
0782 **APOLLONIUS** Med.
0783 **APHRODAS** Med.
0784 **APHTHONIUS** Soph.
0785 **APOLLINARIUS** Med.
0786 **APOLLODORUS** Med.
0787 **BLASTUS** Med.
0788 **CHARICLES** Med.
0789 Claudius **APOLLONIUS** Med.
0790 **APOLLONIUS MYS** Med.
0791 **APOLLONIUS Ther** Med.
0792 **APOLLONIUS** Med.
0793 **DIONYSIUS** Med.
0794 **APOLLOPHANES** Med.
0795 **AQUILA SECUNDILLA** Med.
0796 **ARCHIBIUS** Med.
0797 **GALLUS** Med.
0798 **ARISTARCHUS** Med.
0799 **ANONYMUS NAUCRATITES** Med.
0800 **ANONYMUS OLYMPIONICES** Med.
0801 **ARISTION** Med.
0802 **ARISTOCLES** Med.
0803 **ARISTOCRATES** Gramm.
0804 Marcus **GALLUS** Med.
0805 **MNESITHEUS** Med.
0806 **ARISTOXENUS** Med.
0807 **ARRHABIANUS** Med.
0808 **MUSA** Med.
0809 **ARTEMIDORUS CAPITO** Med.
0810 **APOLLONIUS et ALCIMION** Med.
0811 **ASCLEPIADES** Med.
0812 **ASCLEPIUS** Med.
0813 **ASPASIUS** Med.
0814 **ASTERIUS** Med.
0815 **ATIMETRUS** Med.
0816 **THEUDO[TUS]** Trag.
0817 **APOLLONIUS Organicus** Med.
0818 **AZANITES** Med.
0819 **BACCHIUS** Med.
0820 **BAPHULLUS vel HERAS** Med.
0821 **CLEOPHANTUS** Med.

0822 **GAIUS** Med.
0823 **ALCIMION vel NICOMACHUS** Med.
0824 **CALLINICUS** Med.
0825 **MELITO** Trag.
0826 **CASTUS** Med.
0827 **CEPHISOPHON** Med.
0828 **CHARITON** Med.
0829 **CHARIXENES** Med.
0830 **CHRYSERMUS** Med.
0831 **CHRYSIPPUS** Med.
0832 **ANTIPATER et CLEOPHAN-TUS** Med.
0833 **ANAXION** Trag.
0834 Flavius **CLEMENS** <Med.>
0835 **CLEOBULUS** Med.
0836 **CLEON** Med.
0837 **CLEONIACUS** Med.
0838 **CODAMUS vel NICOMEDES Rex Bithyniae** <Med.>
0839 **CODIUS TUCUS** Med.
0840 **CONSTANTINUS** Med.
0841 **CORNELIUS** Med.
0842 **CRATERUS** Med.
0843 **CRATIPPUS** Med.
0844 **CRISPUS** Med.
0845 **CTESIAS** Hist. et Med.
0846 **CTESIPHON** Med.
0847 **CYRUS** Med.
0848 Servilius **DAMOCRATES** Poet. Med.
0849 Claudius **DAMONICUS** Med.
0850 **ANTONIUS** Med.
0851 **DARIUS** Med.
0852 **ANTYLLUS et HELIODORUS** Med.
0853 **ANTYLLUS et POSIDONIUS** Med.
0854 **DIAGORAS** Med.
0855 **DIDYMUS** Med.
0856 **DIEUCHES** Med.
0857 **DIODORUS CRONUS** Med.
0858 **APELLES** Med.
0859 **DIOGENES** Med.
0860 **DIOMEDES** Med.
0861 **DION** Med.
0862 **DIONYSIUS CYRTUS** Med.
0863 **DIONYSIUS Empiricus** Med.
0864 **DIONYSIUS** Med.
0865 **DIONYSIUS** Med.
0866 **APHRODAS et MOSCHION** Med.
0867 **DIOPHANTUS** Med.
0868 **DIOSCORUS** Med.
0869 **ARCHIGENES et POSIDONIUS** Med.
0870 **DIOSCORIDES Phacas** Med.
0871 **ARISTARCHUS** Med.
0872 **DIPHILUS** Med.
0873 **DOMITIUS NIGRINUS** Med.
0874 **DOROTHEUS** Med.
0875 **DOSITHEUS** Med.
0876 **PHRYNICHUS II** Trag.
0877 **DELETIUS** Med.
0878 Aristus **ARISTARCHUS** Med.
0879 **ASCLEPIUS et MACHAON** Med.
0880 **EPIDAURUS** Med.
0881 **EPIGONUS** Med.
0882 **CRITO et HERODOTUS** Med.
0883 **HERACLAS** Med.

0884 **DIOCLES** Med.
0885 **Pseudo-ESDRAS**
0886 **EUANGELUS** Med.
0887 **EUBULUS** Med.
0888 **EUDEMUS** Poet. Med.
0889 **TIMESITHEUS** Trag.
0890 **EUMERUS** Med.
0891 **EUGENIUS** Med.
0892 **EUGERASIA** Med.
0893 **EUNOMUS** Med.
0894 **EUPHRANOR** Med.
0895 **EURYPHON** Med.
0896 **EUSCHEMUS** Med.
0897 **EUTHYDEMUS** Med.
0898 **EUTONIUS** Med.
0899 **EUTYCHIANUS** Med.
0900 **CLEOMENES** Lyr.
0901 **FLAVIANUS** Med.
0902 **FLAVIUS** Med.
0903 **EUDEMUS Senior** Med.
0904 **GAIUS** Med.
0905 Aelius **GALLUS** Med.
0906 **GEMELLUS** Med.
0907 **GENNADIUS** Med.
0908 **GLAUCIAS** Med.
0909 **HALIEUS** Med.
0910 **HERODOTUS et PHILUMENUS** Med.
0911 **GLYTUS** Med.
0912 **HARPALUS** Med.
0913 **HARPOCRATION** Med.
0914 **HARPOCRAS** Med.
0915 **HERACLIDES** Med.
0916 **HERACLIDES** Med.
0917 **HERAS** Med.
0918 **LAMYNTHIUS** Lyr.
0919 **HERMIAS** Med.
0920 **[MAIA]** Med.
0921 **HERMOGENES** Med.
0922 **EPIGONUS vel HERMON** Med.
0923 **HERMOPHILUS** Med.
0924 **ORIGENIA** Med.
0925 **THAMYRAS** Med.
0926 **HERODOTUS** Med.
0927 **HERON** Med.
0928 **HEROPHILUS** Med.
0929 **HICESIUS** Med.
0930 **HIERAX** Med.
0931 **ANTONINUS** Med.
0932 **HYBRISTUS** Med.
0933 **HYGIENUS** Med.
0934 **JACOBUS Psychrestus** Med.
0935 **ICODOTUS** Med.
0936 **IDIUS** Med.
0937 **ARCHELAUS** Med.
0938 **ISIDORUS** Med.
0939 **ISIDORUS** Med.
0940 **JULIANUS** Med.
0941 Julius **BASSUS** Med.
0942 **CANDIDUS** <Med.>
0943 **JUNIAS** Med.
0944 **JUSTUS** Med.
0945 **LAMPON** Med.
0946 **LAODICUS** <Med.>
0947 Lecanius **ARIUS** Med.
0948 **LEONIDAS** Med.
0949 **LEPIDIANUS** Med.
0950 **LINGON** Med.
0951 **LOGADIUS** Soph.

0952 LUCIUS Med.
0953 LYCOMEDES Med.
0954 LYCUS Med.
0955 LYCUS Med.
0956 LYSIAS Med.
0957 MACHAERION Med.
0958 DEMETRIUS IXION Gramm.
0959 MAGNUS Med.
0960 MAGNUS ὁ ἀρχιατρός Med.
0961 MAGNUS Med.
0962 MAGNUS Med.
0963 MAGNUS ὁ κλινικός Med.
0964 Chrysantus GRATIANUS Med.
0965 MAGNUS Med.
0966 MANETHO Med.
0967 MANTIAS Med.
0968 MARCELLINUS II Med.
0969 MARCIANUS Med.
0970 MARCUS Med.
0971 OENIADES Lyr.
0972 MARCUS TELENTIUS Med.
0973 MARINUS Med.
0974 HERMAS Med.
0975 PHANIUS Med.
0976 MEGES Med.
0977 MELETUS Med.
0978 MELITO Med.
0979 Apius PHASCUS Med.
0980 Tiberius Claudius MENECRATES Med.
0981 STESICHORUS II Lyr.
0982 MENECRITUS Med.
0983 MENELAUS Med.
0984 MENEMACHUS Med.
0985 MENESTHEUS Med.
0986 MENIPPUS Med.
0987 PODANITES Med.
0988 SIMMIAS Med.
0989 MENOETIUS Med.
0990 PHILIPPUS <Med.>
0991 MINUCIANUS Med.
0992 MITHRIDATES VI Eupator <Med.>
0993 MNASEAS Med.
0994 MOSCHION ὁ διορθωτής Med.
0995 [NECHEPSO et PETOSIRIS] Astrol.
0996 NEILAMMON Med.
0997 NILEUS Med.
0998 Tiberius Claudius NERO Imperator <Med.>
0999 NICERATUS Med.
1000 SOCRATES Med.
1001 NICOLAUS Med.
1002 TIMOSTHENES Geogr.
1003 SOCRATION Med.
1004 THESSALUS Med. et Astrol.
1005 NICOSTRATUS Med.
1006 NONNUS Med.
1007 NYMPHODOTUS Med.
1008 OLYMPICUS Med.
1009 XENOCRATES Med.
1010 ORESTINUS Med.
1011 ORION Med.
1012 OTHO Med.
1013 PACCIUS ANTIOCHUS Med.
1014 PAMPHILUS Med.
1015 PAMPHILUS <Med.>
1016 <OSTANES Magus>

1017 PASIO Med.
1018 PATROCLUS Med.
1019 PAULUS Med.
1020 PAULINUS Med.
1021 MEROPIS
1022 OLYMPIUS Med.
1023 PERIGENES Med.
1024 PETINUS Med.
1025 PETRONAS Med.
1026 PETRONIUS Med.
1027 PETRUS Med.
1028 THEODORUS Med.
1030 PHILINUS Med.
1031 PHILIPPUS Med.
1032 BUPHANTUS Med.
1033 HERACLIDES Med.
1034 PHILOCLES Med.
1035 MARCINUS Med.
1036 PHILONIDES Med.
1037 PHILOTAS Med.
1038 PHYLOTIMUS Med.
1039 Claudius PHILOXENUS Med.
1040 MAXIMIANUS Med.
1041 POLYDEUCES Med.
1042 PLATO Med.
1043 PLATYSEMUS Med.
1044 MONOIMUS Gnost.
1045 POLLES Med.
1046 APELLES Gnost.
1047 AMERIAS Gramm.
1048 POLYIDUS Med.
1049 TELEPHANES Med.
1050 THEOPHILUS et NARCISSUS Scr. Eccl.
1051 POMPEIUS SABINUS Med.
1052 POSIDONIUS Phil.
1053 PRASION Med.
1054 PRIMION Med.
1055 PRISCIANUS Med.
1056 PROCLUS Med.
1057 PROËCHIUS Med.
1058 PROTEUS Med.
1059 PROXENUS Med.
1060 PTOLEMAEUS Med.
1061 PUBLIUS Med.
1062 PYRAMUS Med.
1063 PYTHIUS Med.
1064 QUADRATUS Med.
1065 QUINTUS Med.
1066 SABINUS Med.
1067 RIPALUS Med.
1068 RES GESTAE DIVI AUGUSTI
1069 SATYRUS Med.
1070 SERAPION Med.
1071 SOTION Biogr.
1072 SERGIUS Med.
1073 Clemens SERTORIUS Med.
1074 SEVERUS Med.
1075 SOLON Med.
1076 SOSANDRUS Med.
1077 SOSICRATES Med.
1079 PHILAGRIUS Med.
1080 STRATON Med.
1081 STRATON Med.
1082 SYNERUS Med.
1083 ISIGONUS Paradox.
1084 TELAMON Med.
1085 THARSEUS Med.
1086 ANONYMUS THEBANUS Med.

1087 CLEOPHON Trag.
1088 THEMISON Med.
1089 URBANUS Med.
1090 THEODORUS Med.
1091 THEODOSIUS Med.
1092 THEON Med.
1093 THEOPHILUS Med.
1094 THEODORIDES Trag.
1095 THEUDAS Med.
1096 EUARETUS Trag.
1097 THREPTUS Med.
1098 TIBERIUS Imperator <Med.>
1099 TIMOCLIANUS Med.
1100 TIMOCRATES Med.
1101 TIMOTHEUS Med.
1102 TITUS Imperator <Med.>
1103 TRYPHON ὁ ἀρχαῖος Med.
1104 TRYPHON Med.
1105 TIMAEUS Astrol.
1106 TURPILIANUS Med.
1107 Terentius VALENS Med.
1108 XENOPHON Med.
1109 ZENO Med.
1110 ZENO Med.
1111 ZENOPHILUS Med.
1112 ZEUXIS Major Med.
1113 ZEUXIS Med.
1114 ZOILUS Med.
1115 ARCHESTRATUS Trag.
1116 ZOPYRUS Med.
1117 ZOSIMUS Med.
1118 Pseudo-DIOSCORIDES Med.
1119 ANONYMUS NEAPOLITANUS Med.
1120 ANAXIMANDER Junior Hist.
1121 ANAXIMENIS MILESII EPISTULAE
1122 ANDRON Paradox.
1123 ANDRON Hist.
1124 ANDRONICUS RHODIUS Phil.
1125 ANDROTION Hist.
1126 ANUBION Poet. Astrol.
1127 ANONYMA DE MUSICA SCRIPTA BELLERMANNIANA
1128 ANONYMI COMMENTARIUS IN PLATONIS THEAETETUM
1129 ANONYMI DE BARBARISMO ET SOLOECISMO Gramm.
1130 ANONYMI VALENTINIANI Theol.
1131 ANONYMUS AD AVIRCIUM MARCELLUM CONTRA CATAPHRYGAS
1132 ANONYMA ALEXANDRI Phil.
1133 ANONYMUS DIODORI Phil.
1134 ANONYMUS IAMBLICHI Phil.
1135 ANONYMUS PHOTII Phil.
1136 ANONYMUS PRESBYTER Scr. Eccl.
1137 ANONYMUS PYTHAGOREUS Astrol.
1138 LYCON Phil.
1139 ANONYMI HISTORICI (FGrH)
1140 ANTICLIDES Hist.
1141 ANTIMACHUS Epic.
1142 ANTIGONUS Astrol.
1143 ANTIOCHUS Phil.
1144 ANTIOCHUS Astrol.
1145 ANTIOCHUS Hist.

1342 **EMPEDOCLES** Poet. Phil.
1343 **EPARCHIDES** Hist.
1344 **EPICA ADESPOTA (CA)**
1345 **EPICA INCERTA (CA)**
1346 **EPHRAEM** Scr. Eccl.
1347 **[EPIMENIDES]** Phil.
1348 **EPIPHANES** Gnost.
1349 **EPISTULA A MARTYRIBUS LUGDUNENSIBUS**
1350 **EPISTULA AD DIOGNETUM**
1351 **EPIGONI**
1352 **EPISTULA ECCLESIARUM APUD LUGDUNUM ET VIEN-NAM**
1353 **EPITAPHIUM ABERCII**
1354 **ERGIAS** Hist.
1355 **ERINNA** Lyr.
1356 **ESDRAS V/VI**
1357 **EUDEMUS** Phil.
1358 **EUDOXUS** Astron.
1359 **PANAETIUS** Phil.
1360 **<EURYPHAMUS>** Phil.
1361 **EUMEDES** Comic.
1362 **<EURYTUS>** Phil.
1363 **EURYTUS** Lyr.
1364 **EVANGELIUM AEGYPTIUM**
1365 **MELAMPUS** Scriptor De Divinatione
1366 **EVANGELIUM BARTHOLO-MAEI**
1367 **EURIPIDIS EPISTULAE**
1368 **EVANGELIUM EBIONITUM**
1369 **EVANGELIUM MARIAE**
1370 **EVANGELIUM NAASSENUM**
1371 **EVANGELIUM PETRI**
1372 **EVANGELIUM EVAE**
1373 **EVANGELIUM PHILIPPI**
1374 **EVANGELIUM SECUNDUM HEBRAEOS**
1375 **EVANGELIUM THOMAE**
1376 **EUDEMUS** Rhet.
1377 **FAVORINUS** Phil.
1378 **FRAGMENTA EVANGELIO-RUM INCERTORUM**
1379 **FRAGMENTUM ALCHEMI-CUM**
1380 **HERMAGORAS Minor** Rhet.
1381 **FRAGMENTUM SYNODICAE EPISTULAE CONCILII CAESA-RIENSIS**
1382 **FRAGMENTUM TELIAMBI-CUM**
1383 **GEMINUS** Astron.
1384 **PHILEMON III** Comic.
1385 **GLAUCUS** Hist.
1386 **HISTORIA ALEXANDRI MAGNI**
1387 **(H)AGIAS-DERCYLUS** Hist.
1388 **HARMODIUS** Hist.
1389 **HARPOCRATION** Gramm.
1390 **HECATAEUS** Hist.
1391 **HEGEMON** Epigr.
1392 **HEGESANDER** Hist.
1393 **HEGESIANAX** Epic. et Astron.
1394 **HEGESIAS** Hist.
1395 **HEGESINUS** Epic.
1396 **HEGESIPPUS** Epigr.
1397 **HEGESIPPUS** Hist.
1398 **HEGESIPPUS** Scr. Eccl.

1399 **PAMPHILUS** Trag.
1400 **HELIODORUS** Perieg.
1401 **HELLADIUS** Epigr.
1402 **HEPHAESTION** Gramm.
1403 **HERACLEON** Gnost.
1404 **APOLLONIUS** Gramm.
1405 **HERACLIDES Criticus** Perieg.
1406 **HERACLIDES** Hist.
1407 **HERACLIDES LEMBUS** Hist.
1408 **HERACLIDES** Gramm.
1409 **HERACLIDES PONTICUS** Phil.
1410 **HERACLIDES** Epigr.
1411 **HERACLITI EPHESII EPISTU-LAE**
1412 **Pseudo-HERACLITI EPISTU-LAE**
1413 **HERACLITUS** Paradox.
1414 **HERACLITUS** Phil.
1415 **HERACLITUS** Epigr.
1416 **(H)EREN(N)IUS PHILO** Hist. et Gramm.
1417 **HERMAGORAS** Rhet.
1418 **HERMAPION** Hist.
1419 **HERMAS** Scr. Eccl.
1420 **HERMIAS** Iamb.
1421 **HERMIPPUS** Gramm. et Hist.
1422 **HERMOCREON** Epigr.
1423 **HERMODORUS** Epigr.
1424 **HERMOGENES** Hist.
1425 **HERMONAX** Epic.
1426 **<HERODES ATTICUS>** Soph.
1427 **HERODORUS** Hist.
1428 **HESTIAEUS** Hist.
1429 **HIEROCLES** Phil.
1430 **HIERONYMUS** Phil.
1431 **HIPPARCHUS** Astron. et Geogr.
1432 **<HIPPARCHUS>** Phil.
1433 **HIPPARCHUS** <Epigr.>
1434 **HIPPIAS** Soph.
1435 **HIPPIAS** Hist.
1436 **<HIPPODAMUS>** Phil.
1437 **HIPPON** Phil.
1438 **HIPPYS** Hist.
1439 **HERMARCHUS** Phil.
1440 **HONESTUS** Epigr.
1441 **IAMBLICHUS** Scr. Erot.
1442 **IDOMENEUS** Hist.
1443 **IGNATIUS** Scr. Eccl.
1444 **ILIAS PARVA**
1445 **ILIU PERSIS**
1446 **ION** Eleg.
1447 **IRENAEUS** Scr. Eccl.
1448 **ISIDORUS** Gnost.
1449 **ISIDORUS** Epigr.
1450 **ISTER** Hist.
1451 **JOSEPHUS ET ASENETH**
1452 **JUBA II** <Hist.>
1453 **JUNCUS** Phil.
1454 **JUSTINUS** Gnost.
1455 **KERYGMA PETRI**
1456 **LACO** Epigr.
1457 **Julius LEONIDAS** Math. et Astrol.
1458 **LEONIDAS** Epigr.
1459 **LEPIDUS** Hist.
1460 **LESBONAX** Gramm.
1461 **LEUCIPPUS** Phil.
1462 **LIBER ELDAD ET MODAD**
1463 **LIBER ENOCH**
1464 **LIBER JUBILAEORUM**

1465 **[LINUS]** Epic.
1466 **LOLLIANUS** Scr. Erot.
1467 **LOLLIANUS** Soph.
1468 **LUCILLIUS** Epigr.
1469 **LYCEAS** Hist.
1470 **LYCUS** Hist.
1471 **LYRICA ADESPOTA (SLG)**
1472 **LYSISTRATUS** Epigr.
1473 **MACEDONIUS I** Epigr.
1474 **Quintus MAECIUS** Epigr.
1475 **MAIISTAS** Epic.
1476 **MAMERCUS** Eleg.
1477 **MANETHO** Hist.
1478 **Pseudo-MANETHO** Hist.
1479 **MARCI AURELII EPISTULA**
1480 **MARIA JUDAEA** Alchem.
1481 **MARSYAS Pellaeus et MARSYAS Philippeus** Hist.
1482 **CYRANIDES**
1483 **MARTYRIUM ET ASCENSIO ISAIAE**
1484 **MARTYRIUM POLYCARPI**
1485 **MARTYRIUM PTOLEMAEI ET LUCII**
1486 **MATRON** Parodius
1487 **MAXIMUS** Astrol.
1488 **MAXIMUS** Scr. Eccl.
1489 **MEGASTHENES** Hist.
1490 **<MEGILLUS>** Phil.
1491 **MELANTHIUS** Hist.
1492 **MELEAGER** Epigr.
1493 **MELINNO** Lyr.
1494 **MELISSUS** Phil.
1495 **MELITO** Apol.
1496 **MEMNON** Hist.
1497 **MENAECHMUS** Hist.
1498 **MENANDER** Hist.
1499 **MENECLES** Hist.
1500 **MENECRATES** Poet. Phil.
1501 **MENECRATES** Epigr.
1502 **MENECRATES** Epigr.
1503 **MENECRATES** Hist.
1504 **MENELAUS** Epic.
1505 **MENESTHENES** Hist.
1506 **MENODOTUS** Hist.
1507 **<METOPUS>** Phil.
1508 **METRODORUS** Phil.
1509 **<MILON>** <Phil.>
1510 **MIMI ANONYMI**
1511 **MIMNERMUS** Trag.
1512 **MINYAS**
1513 **MNASALCES** Epigr.
1514 **MNASEAS** Perieg.
1515 **MOERIS** Attic.
1516 **MOLPIS** Hist.
1517 **MOSCHION** Paradox.
1518 **Quintus MUCIUS SCAEVOLA** Epigr.
1519 **MUNDUS MUNATIUS** Epigr.
1520 **MUSICIUS** Epigr.
1521 **VITA ET SENTENTIAE SE-CUNDI**
1522 **MYRINUS** Epigr.
1523 **MYRON** Hist.
1524 **NAUMACHIUS** Epic.
1525 **NEANTHES** Hist.
1526 **NEOPTOLEMUS** Gramm.
1527 **NEPUALIUS** Phil.
1528 **NESTOR** Epic.

1727 **THEOTIMUS** Hist.
1728 **THESEUS** Hist.
1729 **THRASYMACHUS** Phil.
1730 **THYILLUS** Epigr.
1731 **THYMOCLES** Epigr.
1732 **TIMACHIDAS** Hist.
1733 **TIMAEUS** Hist.
1734 **TIMAEUS** Phil.
1735 **TIMON** Phil.
1736 **TIMONAX** Hist.
1737 **TITANOMACHIA**
1738 **TRAGICA ADESPOTA**
1739 **TRAJANUS Imperator**
1740 **TRYPHON** Epigr.
1741 **<TUDICIUS GALLUS>** Epigr.
1742 **TULLIUS GEMINUS** Epigr.
1743 **TULLIUS LAUREA** Epigr.
1744 **TYMNES** Epigr.
1745 **TULLIUS SABINUS** Gramm.
1746 **VALENTINUS** Gnost.
1747 **VITA ADAM ET EVAE**
1749 **VITAE HESIODI PARTICULA**
1750 **VITAE PROPHETARUM**
1751 **XANTHUS** Hist.
1752 **XENAGORAS** Hist. et Geogr.
1753 **XENION** Hist.
1754 **XENOPHONTIS EPISTULAE**
1755 **ZOSIMUS** Epigr.
1756 **DEMETRIUS** Gramm.
1757 **JULIUS** Epic.
1758 **HABRON** Gramm.
1759 **SENTENTIAE PYTHAGOREO-RUM**
1760 **Gaius SUETONIUS TRANQUIL-LUS** Hist. et Gramm.
1761 **SULPICIUS MAXIMUS** Epic.
1762 **THRASYLLUS** Astrol.
1763 **TRYPHON II** Gramm.
1764 **VETTIUS VALENS** Astrol.
1765 **VITA AESOPI**
1766 **TATIANUS** Apol.
1767 **ARISTARCHUS** Philol.
1768 **AQUILA** Int. Vet. Test.
1769 **SYMMACHUS** Int. Vet. Test.
1770 **THEODOTION** Int. Vet. Test.
1771 **MONTANUS et MONTANIS-TAE** Theol.
1772 **PARALEIPOMENA JEREMIOU**
1773 **METRODORUS** Phil.
1774 **LIBER ELCHESAI**
1775 **Pseudo-AGATHON** Epigr.
1776 **AGRAPHA**
1777 **AMBROSIUS Rusticus** Med.
1778 **ANDROSTHENES** Perieg.
1779 **ANONYMUS EPICUREUS** Phil.
1780 **ALCIMENES** Comic.
1781 **PHILIPPUS** Comic.
1782 **AUGEAS** Comic.
1783 **CALLICRATES** Comic.
1784 **<HERACLITUS>** Comic.
1785 **PARAMONUS** Comic.
1786 **SOGENES** Comic.
1787 **[MENIPPUS]** Comic.
1788 **PHORMIS** Comic.
1790 **PROTAGORAS** Astrol.
1791 **MENANDRI ET PHILISTIONIS SENTENTIAE**
1792 **BIOTTUS** Comic.
1793 **TIMOXENUS** Comic.

1794 **PHILOCLES** Comic.
1795 **CHAERION** Comic.
1796 **HERMINUS** Phil.
1797 **CHOLIAMBICA ADESPOTA (ALG)**
1798 **ARRIANUS** Astron.
1799 **EUCLIDES** Geom.
1800 **EUBOEUS** Parodius
1801 **PARODICA ANONYMA**
1802 **VERSUS HEROICI**
1803 **BRUTI EPISTULAE**
1804 **NINUS**
1805 **VITAE HOMERI**
1806 **CASSIUS** Med.
1807 **MAGO <Med.>**
1808 **SOLONIS LEGES**
1809 **Claudius DIDYMUS Junior** Gramm.
1810 **SELEUCUS** Gramm.
1811 **METRODORUS Major** Phil.
1812 **DEMARATUS** Hist.
1813 **ANONYMUS DE PLANTIS AE-GYPTIIS**
1814 **PTOLEMAIS** Phil.
1815 **SAPPHO et ALCAEUS** Lyr.
1816 **EPICA ADESPOTA (GDRK)**
1817 **FRAGMENTA ANONYMA (PsVTGr)**
1818 **ACESTODORUS** Hist.
1819 **Pseudo-DEMOSTHENES** Epigr.
1820 **SEUTHES** Astrol.
1821 **IAMBICA ADESPOTA (ALG)**
1822 **Julius CASSIANUS** Gnost.
1823 **MARCUS** Gnost.
1824 **UAPHRIS EPISTULA**
1825 **SALOMONIS EPISTULAE**
1826 **SURONIS EPISTULA**
1827 **SYRUS** Astrol.
1828 **PAMPHILA** Hist.
1829 **<ZOROASTER Magus>**
1830 **XENARCHUS** Phil.
1831 **HEGETOR** Med.
1832 **ACESANDER** Hist.
1833 **PRATINAS** Trag.
1834 **PYTHION** Med.
1835 **AGROETAS** Hist.
1836 **ANONYMI AULODIA**
1837 **NICIAS** Gramm.
1839 **POLYPHRASMON** Trag.
1840 **EURIPIDES II** Trag.
1841 **COMANUS** Gramm.
1842 **CORNELIUS** Scr. Eccl.
1843 **NICOMACHUS** Trag.
1844 **HERA[CLIDES]** Trag.
1845 **CALLISTRATUS** Trag.
1846 **SPINTHARUS** Trag.
1847 **EUDORUS** Hist.
1848 **MELETUS Junior** Trag.
1849 **DEMETRIUS** Trag.
1850 **CHARES** Gramm.
1858 **ORATIO MANASSIS**
1859 **LIBER JANNES ET MAMBRES**
1864 **ALEXANDER** Hist.
1865 **ANTIPATER** Epigr.
1866 **POSIDONIUS** Med.
1867 **CRITO** Hist.
1868 **DAMASTES** Hist.
1869 **POLUS** Rhet. et Hist.
1870 **PHILISTIDES** Hist.

1871 **BION** Hist.
1872 **GORGUS** Epigr.
1873 **SATYRUS "Zeta"** Hist.
1874 **Gaius Julius THEOPOMPUS** Myth.
1875 **ARISTODEMUS** Myth. et Hist.
1876 **XENOPHON** Hist.
1877 **SILENUS** Hist.
1878 **ACESTORIDES** Hist.
1879 **ANTIOCHUS** Hist.
1880 **PHIDALIUS** Hist.
1881 **DIONYSIUS** Hist.
1882 **ARISTOCLES** Myth.
1883 **ABARIS** Hist.
1884 **ANTIDAMAS** Hist.
1885 **ARISTODICUS** Hist.
1886 **POLYARCHUS** Hist.
1887 **CAUCALUS** Rhet.
1888 **MATRIS** Hist.
1889 **ONASUS** Hist.
1890 **MODERATUS** Phil.
1891 **ABAS** Hist.
1892 **THEODORUS** Hist.
1893 **SISYPHUS** Hist.
1894 **DARES** Hist.
1895 **PLESIMACHUS** Hist.
1896 **DOSITHEUS** Hist.
1897 **ELEUSIS** Hist.
1898 **ANTIPATER** Hist.
1899 **ARISTONICUS** Hist.
1900 **BOTRYAS** Hist.
1901 **DEMETRIUS** Hist.
1902 **<NICIAS>** Hist.
1903 **TELLIS** Hist.
1904 **THEODORUS** Hist.
1905 **EUHEMERUS Scriptor De Sacra Historia**
1906 **SIMONIDES** Epic.
1907 **CRATIPPUS** Hist.
1908 **DAIMACHUS** Hist.
1909 **DIONYSODORUS** Hist.
1910 **ANTIPATER** Hist.
1911 **DIYLLUS** Hist.
1912 **EUPHANTUS** Hist.
1913 **EUMELUS** Hist.
1914 **PSAON** Hist.
1915 **EUDOXUS** Hist.
1916 **MENODOTUS** Hist.
1917 **DEMETRIUS** Hist.
1918 **TIMAGENES** Hist.
1919 **BION** Rhet.
1920 **Gaius SULPICIUS GALBA** Hist.
1921 **JASON** Hist. et Gramm.
1922 **CHRYSERUS** Hist.
1923 **STESIMBROTUS** Hist.
1924 **THEMISTOGENES** Hist.
1925 **HEGEMON** Hist.
1926 **XENOPHON** Hist.
1927 **CEPHISODORUS** Hist.
1928 **THEODECTES** Hist.
1929 **ANTIPATER** Hist.
1930 **LAMACHUS** Hist.
1931 **STRATTIS** Hist.
1932 **BAETO** Hist.
1933 **NICANDER** Hist.
1934 **PHILONIDES** Hist.
1935 **ARCHELAUS** Hist.
1936 **EPHIPPUS** Hist.
1937 **NICOBULE** Hist.

2175 <AUTOCHARIS> Hist.
2176 THRASYLLUS Hist.
2177 Tiberius Claudius POLYBIUS Hist.
2179 PYTHEUS-SATYRUS Hist.
2180 JUDAS Hist.
2181 MOSES Alchem.
2182 STAPHYLUS Hist.
2183 JASON Hist.
2184 Tiberius CLAUDIUS Nero Germanicus Hist.
2185 DIONYSIUS Phil.
2186 LEO Hist.
2187 POSIDONIUS Hist.
2188 PHILIPPUS Hist.
2189 CALLINICUS Soph.
2190 [CLITONYMUS] Hist.
2191 GLAUCIPPUS Hist.
2192 [AGATHARCHIDES] Hist.
2193 [ARETADES] Hist.
2194 [ARISTIDES] Hist.
2195 [CHRYSERMUS] Hist.
2196 [DERCYLLUS] Hist.
2197 [DOROTHEUS] Hist.
2198 [DOSITHEUS] Hist.
2199 [CALLISTHENES] Hist.
2200 LIBANIUS Rhet. et Soph.
2201 [CTESIPHON] Hist.
2202 [MENYLLUS] Hist.
2203 [THEOPHILUS] Hist.
2204 AUTOCRATES Hist.
2205 AUTESION Hist.
2206 DIOCLES Hist.
2207 ATHANIDAS Hist.
2208 DEMETRIUS Hist.
2209 CHERSIPHRON-METAGENES Hist.
2210 ANAXICRATES Hist.
2211 TELESARCHUS Hist.
2212 LYCEAS Hist.
2213 [TIMOTHEUS] Hist.
2214 ARCHITIMUS Hist.
2215 AR(I)AETHUS Hist.
2216 ARISTIPPUS Hist.
2217 NICIAS Hist.
2218 CALLIPHON et DEMOCEDES Med. et Phil.
2219 AMELESAGORAS Hist.
2221 ANTIOCHUS-PHERECYDES Hist.
2222 CADMUS Junior Hist.
2223 ARISTON Hist.
2224 ASCLEPIADES Gramm.
2225 PARM(EN)ISCUS Phil.
2226 ICCUS Phil.
2227 PARON Phil.
2228 MENESTOR Phil.
2229 XUTHUS Phil.
2230 BOÏDAS Phil.
2231 THRASYALCES Phil.
2232 DAMON Mus.
2233 Pseudo-POLEMON
2234 OENOPIDES Phil.
2235 HIPPOCRATES Math.
2236 EUTROPIUS Hist.
2237 THEODORUS Math.
2238 SCOPAS (?) Hist.
2239 PYTHAGORISTAE (D-K) Phil.
2240 HICETAS Phil.

2241 XENOPHILUS Phil. et Mus.
2242 ECHECRATES Phil.
2243 APOCALYPSIS SEDRACH
2244 DAMON et PHINTIAS Phil.
2245 SIMUS Phil.
2246 LYCON Phil.
2247 PETRON Phil.
2248 ACTA XANTHIPPAE ET POLY-XENAE
2249 DRACO Hist.
2250 MELITO Hist.
2251 THEODORUS Hist.
2252 CALLISTRATUS Gramm.
2253 ANTIPHANES Junior Hist.
2254 AMMONIUS Hist.
2255 GORGIAS Hist.
2256 TIMOSTHENES Hist.
2257 DIONYSIUS Hist.
2258 SOTADES Phil.
2259 HABRON Hist.
2260 HIPPASUS Hist.
2261 ARISTOMENES Hist.
2262 LYSIMACHIDES Hist.
2263 CHARICLES Hist.
2264 TELEPHANES Hist.
2265 DIODORUS Perieg.
2266 PAXAMUS Hist.
2267 LYCUS Hist.
2268 TIMAGORAS Hist.
2269 ARISTODEMUS Hist. et Gramm.
2270 CALLIPPUS Hist.
2271 AMPHION Hist.
2272 PHOCUS Phil.
2273 DAMON Hist.
2274 HESYCHIUS Illustrius Hist.
2275 THEAGENES Phil.
2276 ZENIS Hist.
2277 HYPERMENES Hist.
2278 PHANODICUS Hist.
2279 NICOCHARES Hist.
2280 DINARCHUS Hist.
2281 DEMOTELES Hist.
2282 MELISSEUS Hist.
2283 APOLLONIUS Hist.
2284 ANAXANDRIDAS Hist.
2285 ALCETAS Hist.
2286 CERCOPS Phil.
2287 FRAGMENTUM STOICUM
2288 TEUPALUS Hist.
2289 ECHEPHYLIDAS Hist.
2290 ARISTARCHUS Hist.
2291 CRATYLUS Phil.
2292 ARISTODEMUS Hist.
2293 EUALCES Hist.
2294 ZENO Phil.
2295 APOLLODORUS Hist.
2296 ARISTOTELES Hist.
2297 PROXENUS Hist.
2298 LYSANIAS Hist.
2299 DEMODAMAS Hist.
2300 PROMATHIDAS Hist.
2301 TIMOGENES Hist. et Rhet.
2302 ARISTOCLES Hist.
2303 ARCHELAUS Phil.
2304 IDAEUS Phil.
2305 CLIDEMUS Phil.
2306 XENOMEDES Hist.
2307 ARTEMON Hist.
2308 DEMOGNETUS Hist.

2309 JASON Hist.
2310 POSIDIPPUS Hist.
2311 HEROPYTHUS Hist.
2312 ERXIAS Hist.
2313 ANTISTHENES Phil.
2314 DIOGENES Phil.
2315 DIODORUS Hist.
2316 DIOXIPPUS Hist.
2317 HERMIAS Phil.
2318 MACARIUS Hist.
2319 APOLLODORUS Phil.
2320 ECHEMENES Hist.
2321 LAOSTHENIDAS Hist.
2322 ANTENOR Hist.
2323 PETELLIDAS Hist.
2324 DINARCHUS Hist.
2325 MENECLES Hist.
2326 DEI(L)OCHUS Hist.
2327 POLYGNOSTUS Hist.
2328 DIOGENES Hist.
2329 PHERECYDES Hist.
2330 SCAMON Hist.
2331 MYRSILUS Hist.
2332 THEOLYTUS Hist.
2333 POSSIS Hist.
2334 NAUSIPHANES Phil.
2335 PRAXION Hist.
2336 HEREAS Hist.
2337 AESCHYLUS Hist.
2338 CADMUS Hist.
2339 MAEANDRIUS Hist.
2340 DIOTIMUS Hist.
2341 ARISTOCRITUS Hist.
2342 ARISTIDES Hist.
2343 EUDEMUS Hist.
2344 PHILTEAS Hist.
2345 AGL(A)OSTHENES Hist
2346 ANDRISCUS Hist.
2347 DEMEAS Hist.
2348 DIOGENES Hist.
2349 PYRANDER Hist.
2350 ANTIPATER Hist.
2351 ANTISTHENES Hist.
2352 ARISTION Hist.
2353 ARISTONYMUS Hist.
2354 DIONYSIUS Hist.
2355 XENIADES Phil.
2356 EUCRATES Hist.
2357 GORGON Hist.
2358 HAGELOCHUS Hist.
2359 HAGESTRATUS Hist.
2360 HIERON Hist.
2361 NICASYLUS Hist.
2362 ONOMASTUS Hist.
2363 TIMOCRITUS Hist.
2364 ZENO Hist.
2365 EUDEMUS Hist.
2366 PHAENNUS Hist.
2367 THEOGNIS Hist.
2368 AELURUS Hist.
2369 GORGOSTHENES Hist.
2370 HIEROBOLUS Hist.
2372 EUAGON Hist.
2373 OLYMPICHUS Hist.
2375 LEO Hist.
2376 XENOPHON Hist.
2377 AESCHRION Epic.
2378 AENEAS Hist.
2379 ATHENACON Hist.